Lecture Notes in Computer Science 4734

Commenced Publication in 1973
Founding and Former Series Editors:
Gerhard Goos, Juris Hartmanis, and Jan van Leeuwen

Joachim Biskup   Javier Lopez (Eds.)

Computer Security – ESORICS 2007

12th European Symposium on Research in Computer Security
Dresden, Germany, September 24-26, 2007
Proceedings

 Springer

Volume Editors

Joachim Biskup
University of Dortmund
Computer Science Department
August-Schmidt-Strasse 12, 44221 Dortmund, Germany
E-mail: joachim.biskup@cs.uni-dortmund.de

Javier Lopez
University of Malaga
Computer Science Department, E.T.S.I. Informatica
Campus Teatinos, 29071 Malaga, Spain
E-mail: jlm@lcc.uma.es

Library of Congress Control Number: 2007934540

CR Subject Classification (1998): E.3, D.4.6, C.2.0, H.2.0, K.6.5, K.4.4

LNCS Sublibrary: SL 4 – Security and Cryptology

ISSN	0302-9743
ISBN-10	3-540-74834-2 Springer Berlin Heidelberg New York
ISBN-13	978-3-540-74834-2 Springer Berlin Heidelberg New York

Springer is a part of Springer Science+Business Media

springer.com

© Springer-Verlag Berlin Heidelberg 2007
Printed in Germany

Typesetting: Camera-ready by author, data conversion by Scientific Publishing Services, Chennai, India
Printed on acid-free paper   SPIN: 12118670   06/3180   5 4 3 2 1 0

Foreword

These proceedings contain the papers selected for presentation at the 12th European Symposium on Research in Computer Security – ESORICS 2007 – held in Dresden, Germany, September 24–26, 2007.

ESORICS has become *the* European research event in computer security. The symposium started in 1990 and has been organized on alternate years in different European countries. It attracts an international audience from both the academic and industrial communities. From 2002 it has taken place yearly.

As solicited in the call for papers, the contributions present theory, mechanisms, applications, or practical experience on all traditional or emerging topics relevant for security in computing systems, approximately covering the following topics:

- security architecture and secure components (trusted computing modules, smartcards, personal computing devices, networks, information systems, applications, peer-to-peer connections, language-based security, ...)
- access control (authorization, privileges, delegation, revocation, credentials, authentication, accountability, safety analysis, ...)
- information control (data flows, information flows, inferences, covert channel analysis, ...)
- applied cryptography (protocol design, protocol verification, authentication protocols, identity management, key distribution, ...)
- tolerance and survivability (attack models, vulnerability analysis, intrusion detection, malware collection and analysis, ...)
- security management (requirements engineering, policy specification, trust evaluation, policy enforcement, ...)
- secure electronic commerce, administration, and government (digital rights management, intellectual property protection, privacy-enhancing technologies, e-voting, ...)
- formal methods in security (security models, security verification, ...)

The 164 papers submitted were each reviewed by three members of the program committee, and subsequently intensively – and partially controversially – discussed not only by the reviewers, but in principle by all committee members. In fact, more than 350 messages were posted on the discussion boards, containing additional evaluations, technical concerns, positive or negative opinions on the relevance, and many more aspects. Finally, 39 papers were included in the program and are presented in these proceedings.

We were very pleased that Michael K. Reiter accepted the invitation to talk about his view on how redundancy, diversity and modularity can be used to implement trustworthy services.

As in the two previous years, ESORICS 2007 was accompanied by four specialized security workshops whose results are independently documented:

- 1st International Workshop on Run Time Enforcement for Mobile and Distributed Systems (REM2007)
- Security Aspects of RFID Usage
- 3rd International Workshop on Security and Trust Management (STM 07)
- Signal Processing in the Encrypted Domain

We gratefully acknowledge the fact that many colleagues offered their time and energy to make ESORICS 2007 possible. In particular, we would like to thank all the members of the program committee and their additional reviewers for the careful evaluations and fair discussions. Additionally, we benefited greatly from the organizational and technical support from Ulrich Flegel, Jan-Hendrik Lochner, Marcel Preuß, and Sandra Wortmann from the University of Dortmund; Rodrigo Roman from the University of Malaga; and Stefan Berthold, Sebastian Clauß, Martina Gersonde, Silvia Labuschke, and Sandra Steinbrecher from Dresden University of Technology.

Finally, and most importantly, we sincerely thank all the authors who submitted their work, in particular those who presented their results during the symposium, and all the attendees for the stimulating discussions. We hope that readers will find these proceedings useful for their future work on computer security.

September 2007

Joachim Biskup
Javier Lopez
Andreas Pfitzmann

Organization

General Chair

Andreas Pfitzmann   Dresden University of Technology, Germany

Program Chair

Joachim Biskup   University of Dortmund, Germany

Program Vice-chair

Javier Lopez   University of Malaga, Spain

Workshop Chair

Sandra Steinbrecher   Dresden University of Technology, Germany

Local Organization

Stefan Berthold	Dresden University of Technology, Germany
Sebastian Clauß	Dresden University of Technology, Germany
Martina Gersonde	Dresden University of Technology, Germany
Silvia Labuschke	Dresden University of Technology, Germany

Program Committee

Anas Abou el Kalam	ENSIB, France
Ross Anderson	Cambridge University, UK
Vijay Atluri	Rutgers University, USA
Michael Backes	Saarland University, Germany
Joan Borrell	Autonomous University of Barcelona, Spain
Gilles Barthe	INRIA Sophia-Antipolis, France
David Basin	ETH Zurich, Switzerland
Elisa Bertino	Purdue University, USA
David Chadwick	University of Kent, UK
Bruno Crispo	Free University Amsterdam, Netherlands
Frederic Cuppens	ENST Bretane, France
Marc Dacier	Institut Eurécom, France

Sabrina De Capitani di Vimercati	University of Milan, Italy
Robert Deng	Singapore Management University, Singapore
Josep Domingo-Ferrer	Rovira i Virgili University, Spain
Dieter Gollmann	Hamburg University of Technology, Germany
Pieter Hartel	Twente University, Netherlands
Audun Josang	Queensland University of Technology, Australia
Christopher Kruegel	Vienna University of Technology, Austria
Michiharu Kudo	IBM Tokyo Research, Japan
Helmut Kurth	ATSEC, Germany
Miroslaw Kutylowski	Wroclaw University of Technology, Poland
Kwok-Yan Lam	Tsinghua University, China
Heiko Mantel	Darmstadt University of Technology, Germany
Fabio Martinelli	CNR Pisa, Italy
Fabio Massacci	University of Trento, Italy
Catherine Meadows	Naval Research, USA
Naftaly Minsky	Rutgers University, USA
David Naumann	Stevens Institute of Technology, USA
Flemming Nielson	Technical University of Denmark, Denmark
Martin Olivier	University of Pretoria, South Africa
Jose Onieva	University of Malaga, Spain
Bart Preneel	Catholic University Leuven/Louvain, Belgium
Jean-Jacques Quisquater	Catholic University Leuven/Louvain, Belgium
Peter Ryan	University of Newcastle upon Tyne, UK
Pierangela Samarati	University of Milan, Italy
Shiuhpyng Shieh	National Chiao Tung University, Taiwan
Vitaly Shmatikov	University of Texas, USA
Einar Snekkenes	Gjøvik University College, Norway
Michael Waidner	IBM Zurich Research, Switzerland
Duminda Wijesekera	George Mason University, USA
Marianne Winslett	University of Illinois, USA
Avishai Wool	Tel Aviv University, Israel
Jianying Zhou	I2R, Singapore

Additional Reviewers

Isaac Agudo, Srikanth Akkiraju, Jordi Aragones-Vilella, Joonsang Baek, Sruthi Bandhakavi, Anindya Banerjee, Ivan Barenys Garcia, Oscar Barenys Garcia, Joerg Bauer, Ohad Ben-Cohen, Gustavo Betarte, Abhilasha Bhargav-Spantzel, Przemyslaw Blaszkiewicz, Giulia Boato, Damiano Bolzoni, Justin Brickell, Richard Brinkman, Jeremy Bryans, Ileana Buhan, Roberto Cascella, Jordi Castellà-Roca, Jan Cederquist, Ling Cheung, Daniel Chong, Siu-Leung Chung, Michael Clarkson, Richard Clayton, Marijke Coetzee, Ricardo Corin, Cas Cremers, Nora Cuppens, Marcin Czenko, Vanesa Daza, Marnix Dekker, Claudia Diaz, Ehud Doron, Ernest Foo, Mohamed R. Fouad, Han Gao, Meng

Ge, Zbigniew Golebiewski, Stefan Gruner, Benjamin Grégoire, Satoshi Hada, Ragib Hasan, Manuel Hilty, Bart Jacobs, Romain Janvier, Engin Kirda, Marek Klonowski, Lukasz Krzywiecki, Przemyslaw Kubiak, Boris Köpf, Pascal Lafourcade, Yassine Lakhnech, Anna Lauks, Adam J. Lee, Benoît Libert, Matteo Maffei, Ajay Mahimkar, Antoni Martínez-Ballesté, Josep M. Mateo-Sanz, Guerric Meurice de Dormale, Kazuhiro Minami, Soumyadeb Mitra, Jose A. Montenegro, Andreas Moser, Makoto Murata, Srijith Nair, Sebastian Nanz, Gregory Neven Christoffer Rosenkilde Nielsen, Elisabeth Oswald, Panos Periorellis, Van Hau Pham, David Pichardie, Georgios Portokalidis, Christian W. Probst, Thomas Quillinan, Alexander Reinhard, Tamara Rezk, Ruben Rios, Wojciech Rutkowski, Ayda Saidane, Patrick Schaller, Francesc Sebe, Naishin Seki, Agusti Solanas, Christoph Sprenger, Robert Stroud, Henning Sudbrock, Hongwei Sun, Tamir Tassa, Olivier Thonnard, Laurent Théry, Terkel K. Tolstrup, Alberto Trombetta, Hein Venter, Eric Vetillard, Alexandre Viejo, Zhiguo Wan, Shuhong Wang, Yuji Watanabe, Rebecca N. Wright, Yongdong Wu, Fan Yang, Yanjiang Yang, Artsiom Yautsiukhin, Ting Yu, Filip Zagorski, Santiago Zanella Beguelin, Nicola Zannone, Marcin Zawada, Charles Zhang, Yu Zhang, Anna Zych

ESORICS Steering Committee

Michael Backes, Joachim Biskup, Frederic Cuppens, Marc Dacier, Sabrina De Capitani di Vimercati, Yves Deswarte, Simon Foley, Dieter Gollmann, Sokratis Katsikas, Helmut Kurth, Javier Lopez, Jean-Jacques Quisquater, Joachim Posegga, Peter Ryan (chair), Pierangela Samarati (vice-chair), Einar Snekkenes, Michael Waidner

Table of Contents

Security Management and Secure Electronic Activities

Formal Methods in Security I

Information Control and Access Control

Applied Cryptography II

Secure Electronic Activities

Formal Methods in Security III

Trustworthy Services and the Biological Analogy

Michael K. Reiter

University of North Carolina at Chapel Hill

Abstract. Biological systems survive through a combination of redundancy, diversity and modularity. It has been argued that these principles can also be applied to construct information services that survive a variety of hostile attacks, including even the compromise of computers that help implement the service. Despite nearly 30 years of research to advance these principles and to apply them to the construction of trustworthy services, each remains an active and fruitful topic of research. In this talk we will describe recent progress in achieving redundancy, diversity and modularity, and in using these to implement trustworthy services. This progress, we will argue, is paving the way to next-generation services that are significantly more resilient than today's. We will also discuss challenges that remain in achieving this goal.

J. Biskup and J. Lopez (Eds.): ESORICS 2007, LNCS 4734, p. 1, 2007.

Security of Multithreaded Programs by Compilation

Gilles Barthe[1], Tamara Rezk[2], Alejandro Russo[3], and Andrei Sabelfeld[3]

[1] INRIA Sophia Antipolis, France
[2] MSR-INRIA
[3] Dept. of Computer Science and Engineering, Chalmers University of Technology, Sweden

Abstract. Information security is a pressing challenge for mobile code technologies. In order to claim end-to-end security of mobile code, it is necessary to establish that the code neither intentionally nor accidentally propagates sensitive information to an adversary. Although mobile code is commonly multithreaded low-level code, the literature is lacking enforcement mechanisms that ensure information security for such programs. This paper offers a modular solution to the security of multithreaded programs. The modularity is three-fold: we give modular extensions of sequential semantics, sequential security typing, and sequential security-type preserving compilation that allow us enforcing security for multithreaded programs. Thanks to the modularity, there are no more restrictions on multithreaded source programs than on sequential ones, and yet we guarantee that their compilations are provably secure for a wide class of schedulers.

1 Introduction

Information security is a pressing challenge for mobile code technologies. Current security architectures provide no end-to-end security guarantees for mobile code: such code may either intentionally or accidentally propagate sensitive information to an adversary. However, recent progress in the area of language-based information flow security [22] indicates that insecure flows in mobile code can be prevented by program analysis.

While much of existing work focuses on source languages, recent work has developed security analyses for increasingly expressive bytecode and assembly languages [4, 10,16,3,5]. Given sensitivity annotations on inputs and outputs, these analyses provably guarantee noninterference [11], a property of programs that there are no insecure flows from sensitive inputs to public outputs.

It is, however, unsettling that information flow for multithreaded low-level programs has not been addressed so far. It is especially concerning because multithreaded bytecode is ubiquitous in mobile code scenarios. For example, multithreading is used for preventing screen lock-up in mobile applications [15]. In general, creating a new thread for long and/or potentially blocking computation, such as establishing a network connection, is a much recommended pattern [13].

This paper is the first to propose a framework for enforcing secure information flow for multithreaded low-level programs. We present an approach for deriving security-type systems that provably guarantee noninterference. On the code consumer side, these type systems can be used for checking the security of programs before running them.

J. Biskup and J. Lopez (Eds.): ESORICS 2007, LNCS 4734, pp. 2–18, 2007.

Our solution goes beyond guarantees offered by security-type checking to code consumers. To this end, we have developed a framework for security-type preserving compilation, which allows code producers to derive security types for low-level programs from security types for source programs. This makes our solution practical for the scenario of untrusted mobile code. Moreover, even if the code is trusted (and perhaps even immobile), compilers are often too complex to be a part of the trusted computing base. Security-type preserving compilation removes the need to trust the compiler, because the type annotations of compiled programs can be checked directly at bytecode level.

The single most attractive feature of our framework is that security is guaranteed by source type systems that are no more restrictive than ones for sequential programs. This might be counterintuitive: there are covert channels in the presence of threads, such as internal timing channels [28], that do not arise in a sequential setting. Indeed, special primitives for interacting with the scheduler have been designed (e.g., [18]) in order to control these channels. The pinnacle of our framework is that such primitives are automatically introduced in the compilation phase. This means that source-language programmers do not have to know about their existence and that there are no restrictions on dynamic thread creation at the source level. At the target level, the prevention of internal timing leaks does not introduce unexpected behaviors: the effect of interacting with the scheduler may only result in disallowing certain interleavings. Note that disallowing interleavings may, in general, affect the liveness properties of a program. Such a trade-off between between liveness and security is shared with other approaches (e.g., [26, 28, 24, 25, 18]).

For an example of an internal timing leak, consider a simple two-threaded source-level program, where hi is a sensitive (high) and lo is a public (low) variable:

$$\text{if } hi \ \{\texttt{sleep}(100)\}; lo := 1 \ \| \ \texttt{sleep}(50); lo := 0$$

If hi is originally non-zero, the last command to assign to lo is likely to be $lo := 1$. If hi is zero, the last command to assign to lo is likely to be $lo := 0$. Hence, this program is likely to leak information about hi into lo. In fact, all of hi can be leaked into lo via the internal timing channel, if the timing difference is magnified by a loop (see, e.g., [17]).

In order for the timing difference of the thread that branches on hi not to make a difference in the interleaving of the assignments to lo, we need to ensure that the scheduler treats the first thread as "hidden" from the second thread: the second thread should not be scheduled until the first thread reaches the junction point of the if. We will show that the compiler enforces such a discipline for the target code so that the compilation of such source programs as above is free of internal timing leaks.

Our work benefits from modularity, which is three-fold. First, the framework has the ability to modularly extend sequential semantics. This grants us with language-independence from the sequential part. Further, the framework allows modular extensions of sequential security type systems. Finally, security type preserving compilation is also a modular extension of the sequential counterpart.

To illustrate the applicability of the framework, we instantiate it with some scheduler examples. These examples clarify what is expected of a scheduler to prevent internal timing leaks. Also, we give an instantiation of the source language with a simple imperative language, as well as an instantiation of the target language with a simple assembly language that features an operand stack, conditions, and jumps. As we will discuss, these instantiations are for illustration only: we expect our results to apply to languages close to Java and Java bytecode, respectively.

Our approach pushes the feasibility of replacing trust assumptions by type checking for mobile-code security one step further. It is especially encouraging that we inherit the main benefit of recent results on enforcing secure information flow by security-type systems [3]: compatibility with bytecode verification, and no need to trust the compiler.

2 Syntax and Semantics of Multithreaded Programs

This section sets the scene by defining the syntax and semantics for multithreaded programs. We introduce the notion of secure schedulers that help dealing with covert channels in the presence of multithreading.

Syntax and program structure. Assume we have a set Thread of thread identifiers, a partially ordered set Level of security levels, a set LocState of local states and a set GMemory of global memories. The definition of programs is parameterized by a set of sequential instructions SeqIns. The set of all instructions extends SeqIns by a dynamic thread creation primitive start pc that spawns a new thread with a start instruction at program point pc.

Definition 1 (Program). *A program P consists of a set of program points $\mathcal{P}$, with a distinguished entry point 1 and a distinguished exit point* exit, *and an instruction map* insmap$_P : \mathcal{P} \setminus \{\text{exit}\} \rightarrow$ Ins, *where* Ins $=$ SeqIns $\cup \{$start $pc\}$ *with* $pc \in \mathcal{P} \setminus \{\text{exit}\}$. *We sometimes write $P[i]$ instead of* insmap$_P$ i.

Each program has an associated successor relation $\mapsto \subseteq \mathcal{P} \times \mathcal{P}$. The successor relation describes possible successor instructions in an execution. We assume that exit is the only program point without successors, and that any program point i s.t. $P[i] =$ start pc is not branching, and has a single successor, denoted by $i + 1$ (if it exists); in particular, we do not require that $i \mapsto pc$. As common, we let $\mapsto^*$ denote the reflexive and transitive closure of the relation $\mapsto$ (similar notation is used for other relations).

Definition 2 (Initial program points). *The set $\mathcal{P}_{init}$ of initial program points is defined as:* $\{i \in \mathcal{P} \mid \exists j \in \mathcal{P}, \ P[j] =$ start $i\} \cup \{1\}$.

We assume the attacker level $k \in$ Level partitions all elements of Level into *low* and *high* elements. Low elements are no more sensitive than k: an element ℓ is low if $\ell \leq k$. All other elements (including incomparable ones) are high. We assume that the set of high elements is not empty. This partition reduces the set Level to a two-element set $\{low, high\}$, where $low < high$, which we will adopt without loss of generality.

Programs come equipped with a *security environment* [5] that assigns a security level to each program point and is used to prevent *implicit flows* [9]. The security environment is also used by the scheduler to select the thread to execute.

Definition 3 (Security environment, low, high, and always high program points).

1. A security environment is a function $se : \mathcal{P} \rightarrow$ Level.

2. *A program point $i \in \mathcal{P}$ is* low, *written* $L(i)$, *if* $se(i) = low$; high, *written* $H(i)$, *if* $se(i) = high$; *and* always high, *written* $AH(i)$, *if* $se(j) = high$ *for all points j such that* $i \mapsto^* j$.

Semantics. The operational semantics for multithreaded programs is built from an operational semantics for sequential programs and a scheduling function that picks the thread to be executed among the currently active threads. The scheduling function takes as parameters the current state, the execution history, and the security environment.

Definition 4 (State).

1. *The set* SeqState *of sequential states is a product* LocState $\times$ GMemory *of the local state* LocState *and global memory* GMemory *sets.*
2. *The set* ConcState *of concurrent states is a product* (Thread $\rightharpoonup$ LocState) $\times$ GMemory *of the partial-function space* (Thread $\rightharpoonup$ LocState), *mapping thread identifiers to local states, and the set* GMemory *of global memories.*

It is convenient to use accessors to extract components from states: we use $s.\mathsf{lst}$ and $s.\mathsf{gmem}$ to denote the first and second components of a state s. Then, we use $s.\mathsf{act}$ to denote the set of active threads, i.e., $s.\mathsf{act} = \mathsf{Dom}(s.\mathsf{lst})$. We sometimes write $s(tid)$ instead of $s.\mathsf{lst}(tid)$ for $tid \in s.\mathsf{act}$. Furthermore, we assume given an accessor pc that extracts the program counter for a given thread from a local state.

We follow a concurrency model [18] that lets the scheduler distinguish between different types of threads. A thread is *low* (resp., *high*) if the security environment marks its program counter as low (resp., high). A high thread is *always high* if the program point corresponding to the program counter is always high. A high thread is *hidden* if it is high but not always high. (Intuitively, the thread is hidden in the sense that the scheduler will, independently from the hidden thread, pick the following low threads.) Formally, we have the following definitions:

$$s.\mathsf{lowT} = \{tid \in s.\mathsf{act} \mid L(s.\mathsf{pc}(tid))\}$$
$$s.\mathsf{highT} = \{tid \in s.\mathsf{act} \mid H(s.\mathsf{pc}(tid))\}$$
$$s.\mathsf{ahighT} = \{tid \in s.\mathsf{act} \mid AH(s.\mathsf{pc}(tid))\}$$
$$s.\mathsf{hidT} = \{tid \in s.\mathsf{act} \mid H(s.\mathsf{pc}(tid)) \wedge \neg AH(s.\mathsf{pc}(tid))\}$$

A scheduler treats different classes of threads differently. To see what guarantees are provided by the scheduler, it is helpful to foresee what discipline a type system would enforce for each kind of threads. From the point of view of the type system, a low thread becomes high while being inside of a branch of a conditional (or a body of a loop) with a high guard. Until reaching the respective junction point, the thread may not have any low side effects. In addition, until reaching the respective junction point, the high thread must be hidden by the scheduler: no low threads may be scheduled while the hidden thread is alive. This prevents the timing of the hidden thread from affecting the interleaving of low side effects in low threads. In addition, there are threads that are spawned inside of a branch of a conditional (or a body of a loop) with a high guard. These threads are always high: they may not have any low side effects. On the other hand, such threads do not have to be hidden in the same way: they can be interleaved with both low and high threads. Recall the example from Section 1. The intention is that the scheduler treats the first thread (which is high while it is inside the branch) as "hidden" from the second (low) thread: the second thread should not be scheduled until the first thread reaches the junction point of the `if`.

We proceed to defining computation history and secure schedulers, which operate on histories as parameters.

Definition 5 (History).

1. *A history is a list of pairs* (tid, ℓ) *where* $tid \in$ Thread *and* $\ell \in$ Level. *We denote the empty history by* ϵ^{hist}.
2. *Two histories* h *and* h' *are indistinguishable, written* $h \overset{\text{hist}}{\sim} h'$, *if* $h|_{low} = h'|_{low}$, *where* $h|_{low}$ *is obtained from* h *by projecting out pairs with the high level in the second component.*

We denote the set of histories by History. We now turn to the definition of a secure scheduler. The definition below is of a more algebraic nature than that of [18], but captures the same intuition, namely that a secure scheduler: i) always picks an active thread; ii) chooses a high thread whenever there is one hidden thread; and iii) only uses the names and levels of low and the low part of histories to pick a low thread.

Definition 6 (Secure scheduler). *A secure scheduler is a function* pickt : ConcState $\times$ History $\rightharpoonup$ Thread, *subject to the following constraints, where* $s, s' \in$ ConcState *and* $h, h' \in$ History:

1. *for every* s *such that* $s.\text{lowT} \cup s.\text{highT} \neq \emptyset$, pickt$(s, h)$ *is defined, and* pickt$(s, h) \in s.\text{act}$;
2. *if* $s.\text{hidT} \neq \emptyset$, *then* pickt$(s, h) \in s.\text{highT}$; *and*
3. *if* $h \overset{\text{hist}}{\sim} h'$ *and* $s.\text{lowT} = s'.\text{lowT}$, *then* $\langle$pickt$(s, h), \ell\rangle :: h \overset{\text{hist}}{\sim} \langle$pickt$(s', h'), \ell'\rangle ::$ h', *where* $\ell = se(s.\text{pc}(\text{pickt}(s, h)))$ *and* $\ell' = se(s'.\text{pc}(\text{pickt}(s', h')))$.

Example 1. Consider a round-robin policy: pickt$(s, h) = rr(AT, last(h))$, where $AT = s.\text{act}$, and the partial function $last(h)$ returns the identity of the most recently picked thread recorded in h (if it exists). Given a set of thread ids, an auxiliary function rr returns the next thread id to pick according to a round-robin policy. This scheduler is insecure because low threads can be scheduled even if a hidden thread is present, which violates req. 2 above.

Example 2. An example of a secure round-robin scheduler is defined below. The scheduler takes turns in picking high and low threads.

$$\text{pickt}(s, h) = \begin{cases} rr(AT_L, last_L(h)), & \begin{array}{l} \text{if } h = \epsilon^{\text{hist}} \text{ or} \\ h = (\text{tid}, L).h' \text{ and } AT_H = \emptyset \text{ and } AT_L \neq \emptyset \text{ or} \\ h = (\text{tid}, H).h' \text{ and } \text{hidT} = \emptyset \text{ and } AT_L \neq \emptyset \end{array} \\ rr(AT_H, last_H(h)), & \begin{array}{l} \text{if } \text{hidT} \neq \emptyset \text{ or} \\ h = (\text{tid}, H).h' \text{ and } AT_L = \emptyset \text{ and } AT_H \neq \emptyset \text{ or} \\ h = (\text{tid}, L).h' \text{ and } AT_H \neq \emptyset \end{array} \end{cases}$$

We assume that AT_L and AT_H are functions of s that extract the set of identifiers of low and high threads, respectively, and the partial function $last_\ell$ returns the identity of

$$\frac{\mathsf{pickt}(s,h) = ctid \quad s.\mathsf{pc}(ctid) = i \quad P[i] \in \mathsf{SeqIns}}{s, h \leadsto_{\mathrm{conc}} s.[\mathsf{lst}(ctid) := \sigma, \mathsf{gmem} := \mu], \langle ctid, se(i) \rangle :: h}$$

$$\frac{\mathsf{pickt}(s,h) = ctid \quad s.\mathsf{pc}(ctid) = i \quad P[i] \in \mathsf{SeqIns}}{s, h \leadsto_{\mathrm{conc}} s.[\mathsf{lst} := \mathsf{lst} \setminus ctid, \mathsf{gmem} := \mu], \langle ctid, se(i) \rangle :: h}$$

$$\frac{\mathsf{pickt}(s,h) = ctid \quad s.\mathsf{pc}(ctid) = i \quad P[i] = \mathsf{start}\, pc}{s, h \leadsto_{\mathrm{conc}} s.[\mathsf{lst}(ctid) := \sigma', \mathsf{lst}(ntid) := \lambda_{\mathrm{init}}(pc)], \langle ctid, se(i) \rangle :: h}$$

Fig. 1. Semantics of multithreaded programs

$$\frac{P[i] \in \mathsf{SeqIns} \quad i \vdash_{\mathsf{seq}} S \Rightarrow T}{se, i \vdash S \Rightarrow T} \qquad \frac{P[i] = \mathsf{start}\, pc \quad se(i) \leq se(pc)}{se, i \vdash S \Rightarrow S}$$

Fig. 2. Typing rules

the most recently picked thread at level ℓ recorded in h, if it exists. The scheduler may only pick active threads (cf. req. 1). In addition to the alternation between high and low threads, the scheduler may only pick a low thread if there are no hidden threads (cf. req. 2). The separation into high and low threads ensures that for low-equivalent histories, the observable choices of the scheduler are the same (cf. req. 3).

To define the execution of multithreaded programs, we assume given a (deterministic) sequential execution relation $\leadsto_{\mathsf{seq}} \subseteq \mathsf{SeqState} \times \mathsf{SeqState}$ that takes as input a current state and returns a new state, provided the current instruction is sequential.

We assume given a function $\lambda_{\mathrm{init}} : \mathcal{P} \to \mathsf{LocState}$ that takes a program point and produces an initial state with program pointer pointing to pc. We also assume given a family of functions fresht_ℓ that takes as input a set of thread identifiers and generates a new thread identifier at level ℓ. We assume that the ranges of fresht_ℓ and $\mathsf{fresht}_{\ell'}$ are disjoint whenever $\ell \neq \ell'$. We sometimes use fresht_ℓ as a function from states to Thread.

Definition 7 (Multithreaded execution). *One step execution* $\leadsto_{\mathrm{conc}} \subseteq (\mathsf{ConcState} \times \mathsf{History}) \times (\mathsf{ConcState} \times \mathsf{History})$ *is defined by the rules of Figure 1. We write* $s, h \leadsto_{\mathrm{conc}} s', h'$ *when executing* s *with history* h *leads to state* s' *and history* h'.

The first two rules of Figure 1 correspond to non-terminating and terminating sequential steps. In the case of termination, the current thread is removed from the domain of lst. The last rule describes dynamic thread creation caused by the instruction $\mathsf{start}\, pc$. A new thread receives a fresh name $ntid$ from $\mathsf{fresht}_{se(i)}$ where $se(i)$ records the security environment at the point of creation. This thread is added to the pool of threads under the name $ntid$. All rules update the history with the current thread id and the security environment of the current instruction. The evaluation semantics of programs can be derived from the small-step semantics in the usual way. We let *main* be the identity of the main thread.

Definition 8 (Evaluation semantics). *The evaluation relation* $\Downarrow_{\mathrm{conc}} \subseteq (\mathsf{ConcState} \times \mathsf{History}) \times \mathsf{GMemory}$ *is defined by the clause* $s, h \Downarrow_{\mathrm{conc}} \mu$ *iff* $\exists s', h'. \; s, h \leadsto_{\mathrm{conc}}^\star$

$s', h' \wedge s'.\text{act} = \emptyset \wedge s'.\text{gmem} = \mu$. We write $P, \mu \Downarrow_{\text{conc}} \mu'$ as a shorthand for $\langle f, \mu \rangle, \epsilon^{\text{hist}} \Downarrow_{\text{conc}} \mu'$, where f is the function $\{\langle main, \lambda_{\text{init}}(1) \rangle\}$.

3   Security Policy

Noninterference is defined relative to a notion of indistinguishability between global memories. For the purpose of this paper, it is not necessary to specify the definition of memory indistinguishability.

Definition 9 (Noninterfering program). *Let $\sim_g$ be an indistinguishability relation on global memories. A program P is* noninterfering *if for all memories $\mu_1, \mu_2, \mu'_1, \mu'_2$:*

$$\mu_1 \sim_g \mu_2 \text{ and } P, \mu_1 \Downarrow \mu'_1 \text{ and } P, \mu_2 \Downarrow \mu'_2 \text{ implies } \mu'_1 \sim_g \mu'_2$$

4   Type System

This section introduces a type system for multithreaded programs as an extension of a type system for noninterference for sequential programs. In Section 5, we show that the type system is sound for multithreaded programs, in that it enforces the noninterference property defined in the previous section. In Section 6, we instantiate the framework to a simple assembly language.

Assumptions on type system for sequential programs. We assume given a set LType of local types for typing local states, with a distinguished local type T_{init} to type initial states, and a partial order $\leq$ on local types. Typing judgments in the sequential type system are of the form $se, i \vdash_{\text{seq}} \text{S} \Rightarrow \text{T}$, where se is a security environment, i is a program point in program P, and S and T are local types.

Typing rules are used to establish a notion of typable program [1]; typable programs are assumed to satisfy several properties that are formulated precisely in Section 5.

Type system for multithreaded programs. The typing rules for the concurrent type system have the same form as those of the sequential type system and are given in Figure 2.

Definition 10 (Typable multithreaded program). *A concurrent program P is typable w.r.t. type $\mathcal{S} : \mathcal{P} \to$ LType and security environment se, written $se, \mathcal{S} \vdash P$, if*

1. *$\mathcal{S}_i = \text{T}_{\text{init}}$ for all initial program points i of P (initial program point of main threads or spawn threads); and*
2. *for all $i \in \mathcal{P}$ and $j \in \mathcal{P}: i \mapsto j$ implies that there exists $\text{S} \in$ LType such that $se, i \vdash \mathcal{S}_i \Rightarrow \text{S}$ and $\mathcal{S}_j \leq \text{S}$.*

5   Soundness

The purpose of this section is to prove, under sufficient hypotheses on the sequential type system and assuming that the scheduler is secure, that typable programs are noninterfering. Formally, we want to prove the following theorem:

---

[1] The notion of typable sequential program is a particular case of typable multithreaded program.

Theorem 1. *If the scheduler is secure and* $se, \mathcal{S} \vdash P$, *then* P *is noninterfering.*

Throughout this section, we assume that P is a typable program, i.e., $se, \mathcal{S} \vdash P$, and that the scheduler is secure. Moreover, we state some general hypotheses that are used in the soundness proofs. We revisit these hypotheses in Section 6 and show how they can be fulfilled.

State equivalence. In order to prove noninterference, we rely on a notion of state equivalence. The definition is modular, in that it is derived from an equivalence between global memories $\sim_g$ and a partial equivalence relation $\sim_l$ between local states. (Intuitively, partial equivalence relations on local and global memories represent the observational power of the adversary.) In comparison to [3], equivalence between local states (operand stacks and program counters for the JVM) is not indexed by local types, since these can be retrieved from the program counter and the global type of the program.

Definition 11 (State equivalence). *Two concurrent states* s *and* t *are:*

1. *equivalent w.r.t. local states, written* $s \overset{\mathsf{lmem}}{\sim} t$, *iff* $s.\mathsf{lowT} = t.\mathsf{lowT}$ *and for every* $tid \in s.\mathsf{lowT}$, *we have* $s(tid) \sim_l t(tid)$.
2. *equivalent w.r.t. global memories, written* $s \overset{\mathsf{gmem}}{\sim} t$, *iff* $s.\mathsf{gmem} \sim_g t.\mathsf{gmem}$.
3. *equivalent, written* $s \sim t$, *iff* $s \overset{\mathsf{gmem}}{\sim} t$ *and* $s \overset{\mathsf{lmem}}{\sim} t$.

In order to carry out the proofs, we also need a notion of program counter equivalence between two states.

Definition 12. *Two states* s *and* s' *are pc-equivalent, written,* $s \overset{\mathsf{pc}}{\approx} s'$ *iff* $s.\mathsf{lowT} = t.\mathsf{lowT}$ *and for every* $tid \in s.\mathsf{lowT}$, *we have* $s.\mathsf{pc}(tid) = t.\mathsf{pc}(tid)$.

Unwinding lemmas. In this section, we formulate unwinding hypotheses for sequential instructions and extend them to a concurrent setting. Two kinds of unwinding statements are considered: a *locally respects unwinding result*, which involves two executions and is used to deal with execution in low environments, and a *step consistent unwinding result*, which involves one execution and is used to deal with execution in high environments. From now on, we refer to local states and global memories as λ and μ, respectively.

Hypothesis 1 (Sequential locally respects unwinding). *Assume* $\lambda_1 \sim_l \lambda_2$ *and* $\mu_1 \sim_g \mu_2$ *and* $\lambda_1.\mathsf{pc} = \lambda_2.\mathsf{pc}$. *If* $\langle \lambda_1, \mu_1 \rangle \leadsto_{\mathsf{seq}} \langle \lambda_1', \mu_1' \rangle$ *and* $\langle \lambda_2, \mu_2 \rangle \leadsto_{\mathsf{seq}} \langle \lambda_2', \mu_2' \rangle$, *then* $\lambda_1' \sim_l \lambda_2'$ *and* $\mu_1' \sim_g \mu_2'$.

In addition, we also need a hypothesis on the indistinguishability of initial local states.

Hypothesis 2 (Equivalence of local initial states). *For every initial program point* i, *we have* $\lambda_{\mathrm{init}}(i) \sim_l \lambda_{\mathrm{init}}(i)$.

We now extend the unwinding statement to concurrent states; note that the hypothesis $s'.\mathsf{lowT} = t'.\mathsf{lowT}$ is required for the lemma to hold. This excludes the case of a thread becoming hidden in an execution and not another (i.e., a high while loop).

Lemma 1 (Concurrent locally respects unwinding). *Assume* $s \sim t$ *and* $h_s \overset{\text{hist}}{\sim} h_t$ *and* $\text{pickt}(s, h_s) = \text{pickt}(t, h_t) = \text{ctid}$ *and* $s.\text{pc}(\text{ctid}) = t.\text{pc}(\text{ctid})$. *If* $s, h_s \leadsto_{\text{conc}} s', h_{s'}$ *and* $t, h_t \leadsto_{\text{conc}} t', h_{t'}$, *and* $s'.\text{lowT} = t'.\text{lowT}$, *then* $s' \sim t'$ *and* $h_{s'} \overset{\text{hist}}{\sim} h_{t'}$.

The proof of this and other results can be found in the full version [7] of the paper.

We now turn to the second, so-called step consistent, unwinding lemma. The lemma relies on the hypothesis that the current local memory is high, i.e., invisible by the attacker. Formally, highness is captured by a predicate $High^{\text{lmem}}(\lambda)$ where λ is a local state.

Hypothesis 3 (Sequential step consistent unwinding). *Assume* $\lambda_1 \sim_l \lambda_2$ *and* $\mu_1 \sim_g \mu_2$. *Let* $\lambda_1.\text{pc} = i$. *If* $\langle \lambda_1, \mu_1 \rangle \leadsto_{\text{seq}} \langle \lambda_1', \mu_1' \rangle$ *and* $High^{\text{lmem}}(\lambda_1)$ *and* $H(i)$, *then* $\lambda_1' \sim_l \lambda_2$ *and* $\mu_1' \sim_g \mu_2$.

Lemma 2 (Concurrent step consistent unwinding). *Assume* $s \sim t$ *and* $h_s \overset{\text{hist}}{\sim} h_t$ *and* $\text{pickt}(s, h) = \text{ctid}$ *and* $s.\text{pc}(\text{ctid}) = i$ *and* $High^{\text{lmem}}(s(\text{ctid}))$ *and* $H(i)$. *If* $s, h_s \leadsto_{\text{conc}} s', h_{s'}$ *and* $s'.\text{lowT} = t.\text{lowT}$, *then* $s' \sim t$ *and* $h_{s'} \overset{\text{hist}}{\sim} h_t$.

The proofs of the unwinding lemmas are by a case analysis on the semantics of concurrent programs.

The next *function.* The soundness proof relies on the existence of a function next that satisfies several properties. Intuitively, next computes for any high program point its minimal observable successor, i.e., the first program point with a low security level reachable from it. If executing the instruction at program point i can result in a hidden thread (high if or high while), then $\text{next}(i)$ is the first program point such that $i \mapsto^{\star} \text{next}(i)$ and the thread becomes visible again.

Hypothesis 4 (Existence of next **function).** *There exists a function* $\text{next} : \mathcal{P} \rightharpoonup \mathcal{P}$ *such that the* next *properties (NeP) hold:*

NePd) $\text{Dom}(\text{next}) = \{ i \in \mathcal{P} | H(i) \wedge \exists j \in \mathcal{P}. \, i \mapsto^{\star} j \wedge \neg H(j) \}$
NeP1) $i, j \in \text{Dom}(\text{next}) \wedge i \mapsto j \Rightarrow \text{next}(i) = \text{next}(j)$
NeP2) $i \in \text{Dom}(\text{next}) \wedge j \notin \text{Dom}(\text{next}) \wedge i \mapsto j \Rightarrow \text{next}(i) = j$
NeP3) $j, k \in \text{Dom}(\text{next}) \wedge i \notin \text{Dom}(\text{next}) \wedge i \mapsto j \wedge i \mapsto k \wedge j \neq k \Rightarrow \text{next}(j) = \text{next}(k)$
NeP4) $j \in \text{Dom}(\text{next}) \wedge i, k \notin \text{Dom}(\text{next}) \wedge i \mapsto j \wedge i \mapsto k \wedge j \neq k \Rightarrow \text{next}(j) = k$

Intuitively, properties **NeP1**, **NeP2**, and **NeP3** ensure that the next of instructions within an outermost high conditional statement coincides with the junction point of the conditional; in addition, properties **NeP1**, **NeP2**, and **NeP4** ensure that the next of instructions within an outermost high loop coincides with the exit point of the loop.

In addition to the above assumptions, we also need another hypothesis that relates the domain of next to the operational semantics of programs. In essence, the hypothesis states that, under the assumptions of the concurrent locally respects unwinding lemma, either the executed instruction is a low instruction, in which case the program counter of the active thread remains equal after one step of execution, or that the executed instruction is a high instruction, in which case the active thread is hidden in one execution (high loop) or both (high conditional).

$$e ::= x \mid n \mid e \; op \; e \qquad c ::= x := e \mid c; c \mid \text{if } e \text{ then } c \text{ else } c \mid \text{while } e \text{ do } c \mid \text{fork}(c)$$

$$
\begin{aligned}
instr ::= \quad & \text{binop } op \quad && \text{binary operation on stack} \\
\mid \quad & \text{push } n \quad && \text{push value on top of stack} \\
\mid \quad & \text{load } x \quad && \text{load value of } x \text{ on stack} \\
\mid \quad & \text{store } x \quad && \text{store top of stack in variable } x \\
\mid \quad & \text{ifeq } j \quad && \text{conditional jump} \\
\mid \quad & \text{goto } j \quad && \text{unconditional jump} \\
\mid \quad & \text{start } j \quad && \text{creation of a thread}
\end{aligned}
$$

where $op \in \{+, -, \times, /\}$, $n \in \mathbb{Z}$, $x \in \mathcal{X}$, and $j \in \mathcal{P}$.

Fig. 3. Source and target language

Hypothesis 5 (Preservation of pc equality). *Assume $s \sim t$; $\text{pickt}(s, h_s) = \text{pickt}(t, h_t)$ $= ctid$; $s(ctid).\text{pc} = t(ctid).\text{pc}$; $s, h_s \leadsto_{\text{conc}} s', h_{s'}$; and $t, h_t \leadsto_{\text{conc}} t', h_{t'}$. Then, $s'(ctid).\text{pc} = t'(ctid).\text{pc}$; or $s'(ctid).\text{pc} \in \text{Dom}(\text{next})$; or $t'(ctid).\text{pc} \in \text{Dom}(\text{next})$.*

The final hypothesis is about visibility by the attacker:

Hypothesis 6 (High hypotheses).

1. *For every program point i, we have $High^{\text{lmem}}(\lambda_{\text{init}}(i))$.*
2. *If $\langle \lambda, \mu \rangle \leadsto_{\text{seq}} \langle \lambda', \mu' \rangle$ and $High^{\text{lmem}}(\lambda)$ and $H(\lambda.\text{pc})$ then $High^{\text{lmem}}(\lambda')$.*
3. *If $High^{\text{lmem}}(\lambda_1)$ and $High^{\text{lmem}}(\lambda_2)$ then $\lambda_1 \sim_l \lambda_2$.*

Theorem 1 follows from the hypotheses above. For the proof details, we refer to the full version of the paper [7].

6 Instantiation

In this section, we apply our main results to a simple assembly language with conditional jumps and dynamic thread creation. We present the assembly language with a semantics and a type system for noninterference but without considering concurrent primitives and plug these definitions into the framework for multithreading. Then, we present a compilation function from a simple while-language with dynamic thread creation into assembly code. The source and target languages are defined in Figure 3. The compilation function allows us to easily define control dependence regions and junction points in the target code. Function next is then defined using that information. Moreover, we prove that the obtained definition of next satisfies the properties required in Section 5. Finally, we conclude with a discussion about how a similar instantiation can be done for the JVM.

Sequential part of the language. The instantiation requires us to define the semantics and a type system to enforce noninterference for the sequential primitives in the language. On the semantics side, we assume that a local state is a pair $\langle os, pc \rangle$ where os is an operand stack, i.e., a stack of values, and pc is a program counter, whereas a global state μ is a map from variables to values. The operational semantics is standard and therefore we omit it. We also define $\lambda_{\text{init}}(pc)$ to be the local state $\langle \epsilon, pc \rangle$, where ϵ is the empty operand stack.

$$\frac{P[i] = \text{push } n}{se, i \vdash_{\text{seq}} st \Rightarrow se(i) :: st} \qquad \frac{P[i] = \text{binop } op}{se, i \vdash_{\text{seq}} k_1 :: k_2 :: st \Rightarrow (k_1 \sqcup k_2 \sqcup se(i)) :: st}$$

$$\frac{P[i] = \text{store } x \qquad se(i) \sqcup k \le \Gamma(x)}{se, i \vdash_{\text{seq}} k :: st \Rightarrow st} \qquad \frac{P[i] = \text{load } x}{se, i \vdash_{\text{seq}} st \Rightarrow (\Gamma(x) \sqcup se(i)) :: st}$$

$$\frac{P[i] = \text{goto } j}{se, i \vdash_{\text{seq}} st \Rightarrow st} \qquad \frac{P[i] = \text{ifeq } j \qquad \forall j' \in \text{reg}(i), \ k \le se(j')}{se, i \vdash_{\text{seq}} k :: st \Rightarrow \text{lift}_k(st)}$$

Fig. 4. Transfer rules

The enforcement mechanism consists of local types which are stacks of security levels, i.e., LType = Stack(Level); we let τ_{init} be the empty stack of security levels. Typing rules are summarized in Figure 4, where $\text{lift}_k(st)$ denotes the point-wise extension of $\lambda k'. \ k \sqcup k'$ to stacks of security levels, and reg : $\mathcal{P} \rightharpoonup \wp(\mathcal{P})$ denotes the region of branching points. We express the chosen security policy by assigning a security level $\Gamma(x)$ to each variable x.

Similarly to [4], the soundness of the transfer rules relies on some assumptions about control dependence regions in programs. Essentially, these regions represent an over-approximation of the range of branching points. This concept is formally introduced by the functions reg : $\mathcal{P} \rightharpoonup \wp(\mathcal{P})$ and jun : $\mathcal{P} \rightharpoonup \mathcal{P}$, which respectively compute the control dependence region and the junction point for a given instruction. Both functions need to satisfy some properties in order to guarantee noninterference in typable programs. These properties are known as SOAP properties [4]. In Section 6, we will show that these properties can be guaranteed by compilation.

In the full version [7] we instantiate definitions of local and global state equivalences to establish the soundness of the type system.

Concurrent extension. As shown in Definition 7, the concurrent semantics is obtained from the semantics for sequential commands together with a transition for the instruction `start`. Moreover, the sequential type system in Figure 4 is extended by the typing rules presented in Figure 2 to consider concurrent programs.

The proof of noninterference for concurrent programs relies on the existence of the function next. Similarly to the technique of [6], we name program points where control flow can branch or writes can occur. We add natural number labels to the source language as follows:

$$c ::= [x := e]^n \mid c; c \mid [\text{if } e \text{ then } c \text{ else } c]^n \mid [\text{while } e \text{ do } c]^n \mid [\text{fork}(c)]^n$$

This labeling allows us to define control dependence regions for the source code and use this information to derive control dependence regions for the assembly code. We introduce two functions, sregion and tregion, to deal with control dependence regions in the source and target code, respectively.

Definition 13 (function sregion). *For each branching command $[c]^n$, sregion(n) is defined as the set of labels that are inside of the command c except for those ones that are inside of* `fork` *commands.*

$$\mathcal{E}(x) = \text{load } x \quad \mathcal{E}(n) = \text{push } n \quad \mathcal{E}(e \ op \ e') = \mathcal{E}(e) :: \mathcal{E}(e') :: \text{binop } op$$

$$\mathcal{S}(x := e, \ T) = (\mathcal{E}(e) :: \underline{\text{store }} x, \ T)$$

$$\mathcal{S}(c_1; \ c_2, \ T) = let \ (lc_1, \ T_1) = \mathcal{S}(c_1, \ T); (lc_2, \ T_2) = \mathcal{S}(c_2, \ T_1);$$
$$in \ (lc_1 :: lc_2, \ T_2)$$

$$\mathcal{S}(\text{while } e \text{ do } c, \ T) = let \ le = \mathcal{E}(e); (lc, \ T') = \mathcal{S}(c, \ T);$$
$$in \ (\text{goto } (pc + \#lc + 1) :: lc :: le :: \underline{\text{ifeq }} (pc - \#lc - \#le),$$
$$T')$$

$$\mathcal{S}(\text{if } e \text{ then } c_1 \text{ else } c_2, \ T) = let \ le = \mathcal{E}(e); (lc_1, \ T_1) = \mathcal{S}(c_1, \ T); (lc_2, \ T_2) = \mathcal{S}(c_2, \ T_1);$$
$$in \ (le :: \underline{\text{ifeq }} (pc + \#lc_2 + 2) :: lc_2 :: \text{goto } (pc + \#lc_1 + 1) ::$$
$$lc_1, \ T_2)$$

$$\mathcal{S}(\text{fork(c)}, \ T) = let \ (lc, \ T') = \mathcal{S}(c, \ T); in \ (\underline{\text{start }} (\#T' + 2), \ T' :: lc :: \text{return})$$

$$\mathcal{C}(c) = let \ (lc, \ T) = \mathcal{S}(c, \ []); in \ \text{goto } (\#T + 2) :: T :: lc :: \text{return}$$

Fig. 5. Compilation function

As in [6], control dependence regions for low-level code are defined based on the function sregion and a compilation function. For a complete source program c, we define the compilation $\mathcal{C}(c)$ in Figure 5. We use symbol $\#$ to compute the length of lists. Symbol $::$ is used to insert one element to a list or to concatenate two existing lists. The current program point in a program is represented by pc. The function $\mathcal{C}(c)$ calls the auxiliary function $\mathcal{S}$ which returns a pair of programs. The first component of that pair stores the compiled code of the main program, while the second one stores the compilation code of spawned threads. We now define control dependence regions for assembly code and respective junction points.

Definition 14 (function tregion**).** *For a branching instruction $[c]^n$ in the source code, $tregion(n)$ is defined as the set of instructions obtained by compiling the commands $[c']^{n'}$, where $n' \in sregion(n)$. Moreover, if c is a while loop, then $n \in \text{tregion}(n)$. Otherwise, the goto instruction after the compilation of the else-branch also belongs to $\text{tregion}(n)$.*

Junction points are computed by the function jun. The domain of this function consist of every branching point in the program. We define jun as follows:

Definition 15 (junction points). *For every branching point $[c]^n$ in the source program, we define $\text{jun}(n) = max\{i | i \in \text{tregion}(n)\} + 1$.*

Having defined control dependence regions and junction points for low-level code, we proceed to defining next. Intuitively, next is only defined for instructions that belong to regions corresponding to the outermost branching points whose guards involved secrets. For every instruction i inside of an outermost branching point $[c]^n$, we define $\text{next}(i) = \text{jun}(n)$. Observe that this definition captures the intuition about next given in the beginning of Section 5. However, it is necessary to know, for a given program, what are the outermost branching points whose guards involved secrets. With this in mind, we extend one of the type systems given in [6] to identify such points. We add some rules

$$\frac{\vdash_\alpha c : E \qquad \vdash_\alpha c' : E}{\vdash_\alpha c ; c' : E} \qquad\qquad \frac{\vdash e : L \qquad \vdash_\alpha c : E}{\vdash_\alpha [\text{while } e \text{ do } c]_\alpha^n : E}$$

$$\frac{\vdash e : L \qquad \vdash_\alpha c : E \qquad \vdash_\alpha c' : E}{\vdash_\alpha [\text{if } e \text{ then } c \text{ else } c']_\alpha^n : E} \qquad\qquad \frac{\vdash e : H \qquad \vdash_\bullet c : E}{\vdash_\bullet [\text{while } e \text{ do } c]_\bullet^n : E}$$

$$\frac{\vdash e : H \qquad \vdash_\bullet c : E \qquad \vdash_\bullet c' : E}{\vdash_\bullet [\text{if } e \text{ then } c \text{ else } c']_\bullet^n : E} \qquad\qquad \frac{\vdash_\alpha c : E \qquad E = \text{lift}_\alpha(E, \text{labels}(c))}{\vdash_\alpha [\text{fork}(c)]_\alpha^n : E}$$

ASSIGN
$$\frac{\vdash e : k \qquad k \sqcup E(n) \le \Gamma(x)}{\vdash_\alpha [x := e]_\alpha^n : E}$$

TOP-H-WHILE
$$\frac{\vdash e : H \qquad \vdash_\bullet c : E \qquad E = \text{lift}_H(E, \text{sregion}(n))}{\vdash_\circ [\text{while } e \text{ do } c]_\bullet^n : E}$$

TOP-H-COND
$$\frac{\vdash e : H \qquad \vdash_\bullet c : E \qquad \vdash_\bullet c' : E \qquad E = \text{lift}_H(E, \text{sregion}(n))}{\vdash_\circ [\text{if } e \text{ then } c \text{ else } c']_\bullet^n : E}$$

Fig. 6. Intermediate typing rules for high-level language commands

for outermost branching points that involved secrets together with some extra notations to know when a command is inside of one of those points or not.

A source program c is typable, written $\vdash_\circ c : E$, if its command part is typable with respect to E according to the rules given in Figure 6. The typing judgment has the form $\vdash_\alpha [c]_{\alpha'}^n : E$, where E is a function from labels to security levels. Function E can be seen as a security environment for the source code which allows to easily define the security environment for the target code. If R is a set of points, then $\text{lift}_k(E, R)$ is the security environment E' such that $E'(n) = E(n)$ if $n \notin R$ and $E'(n) = k \sqcup E(n)$ for $n \in R$. For a given program c, $\text{labels}(c)$ returns all the label annotations in c. Variable α denotes if c is part of a branching instruction that branches on secrets ($\bullet$) or public data ($\circ$). Variable α' represents the level of the guards in branching instructions. The most interesting rules are $TOP - H - COND$ and $TOP - H - WHILE$. These rules can be only applied when the branching commands are the outermost ones and when they branch on secrets. Observe that such commands are the only ones that are typable considering $\alpha = \circ$ and $\alpha' = \bullet$. Moreover, the type system prevents *explicit* (via assignment) and *implicit* (via control) flows [9]. To this end, the type system enforces the same constraints as standard security type systems for sequential languages (e.g., [29]). Explicit flows are prevented by rule $ASSIGN$, while implicit flows are ruled out by demanding a security environment of level H inside of commands that branch on secrets. The type system guarantees information-flow security at the same time as it identifies the outermost commands that branch on secrets. Function next is defined as follows:

Definition 16 (function next). *For every branching point c in the source program such that $\vdash_\circ [c]_\bullet^n$, we have that $\forall k \in \text{tregion}(n).\text{next}(k) = \text{jun}(n)$.*

This definition satisfies the properties from Section 5, as shown by the following lemma.

Lemma 3. *Definition 16 satisfies properties **NePd** and **NeP1–4**.*

Notice that one does not need to trust the compiler in order to verify that properties **NePd** and **NeP1–4** are satisfied. Indeed, these properties are intended to be checked independently from the compiler by code consumers. We are now in condition to show the soundness of the instantiation.

Corollary 1 (Soundness of the instantiation). *Hypotheses 1–6 from Section 5 are satisfied by the instantiation, and therefore the derived type system guarantees noninterference for multithreaded assembly programs.*

Hypotheses 1–3 follow from the unwinding lemmas of [5]; Hypothesis 4 from Lemma 3, and Hypotheses 5 and 6 from the definitions of next and $High^{lmem}$, respectively.

Type preserving compilation. The compilation of sequential programs is type-preserving, as shown in previous work [6]. Our framework allows extending type-preservation to multithreading. Moreover, it enables us to obtain a key *non-restrictiveness* result: although the source-level type system is no more restrictive than a typical type system for a sequential language (e.g., [29]), the compilation of (possibly multithreaded) typable programs is guaranteed to be typable at low-level. Due to the lack of space, we only give an instantiation of this result to the source and target languages of this section:

Theorem 2. *For a given source-level program c, assume $nf(c)$ is obtained from c by replacing all occurrences of* fork(d) *by d. If command $nf(c)$ is typable under the Volpano-Smith-Irvine type system [29] then $se, S \vdash C(c)$ for some se and S.*

This theorem and Theorem 1 entail the following corollary:

Corollary 2. *If command $nf(c)$ is typable under the Volpano-Smith-Irvine type system [29] then $C(c)$ is secure.*

Java Virtual Machine. The modular proof technique developed in the previous section is applicable to a Java-like language. If the sequential type system is compatible with bytecode verification, then the concurrent type system is also compatible with it. This implies that Java bytecode verification can be extended to perform security type checking. Note that the definition of a secure scheduler is compatible with the JVM, where the scheduler is mostly left unspecified. Moreover, it is possible to, in effect, override an arbitrary scheduler from any particular implementation of JVM with a secure scheduler that keeps track of high and low threads as a part of an application's own state (cf. [27]).

However, some issues arise in the definition of a concurrent JVM: in particular, we cannot adapt the semantics and results of [3] directly, because the semantics of method calls is big-step. Instead, we must rely on a more standard semantics where states include stack frames, and prove unwinding lemmas for such a semantics; fortunately, the technical details in [4] took this route, and the same techniques can be used here.

Another point is that the semantics of the multithreaded JVM obtained by the method described in Section 2 only partially reflects the JVM specification. In particular, it ignores object locks, which are used to perform synchronization throughout program execution. Dealing with synchronization is a worthwhile topic for future work.

7 Related Work

Information flow type systems for low-level languages, including JVML, and their relation to information flow type systems for structured source languages, have been studied by several authors [4, 10, 16, 6, 3, 5]. Nevertheless, the present work provides, to the best of our knowledge, the first proof of noninterference for a concurrent low-level language, and the first proof of type-preserving compilation for languages with concurrency.

This work exploits recent results on interaction between the threads and the scheduler [18] in order to control internal timing leaks. Other approaches [26, 28, 24, 25] to handling internal timing rely on $protect(c)$ which, by definition, hides the internal timing of command c. It is not clear how to implement $protect()$ without modifying the scheduler (unless the scheduler is cooperative [19, 27]). It is possible to prevent internal timing leaks by spawning dedicated threads for computations that involve secrets and carefully synchronizing the resulting threads [17]. However, this implies high synchronization costs. Yet other approaches prevent internal timing leaks in code by disallowing any races on public data [30, 12]. However, they wind up rejecting such innocent programs as $lo := 0 \parallel lo := 1$ where lo is a public variable. Still other approaches prevent internal timing by disallowing low assignments after high branching [8, 2]. Less related work [1, 23, 20, 21, 14] considers external timing, where an attacker can use a stopwatch to measure computation time. This work considers a more powerful attacker, and, as a price paid for security, disallows loops branching on secrets. For further related work, we refer to an overview of language-based information-flow security [22].

8 Conclusions

We have presented a framework for controlling information flow in multithreaded low-level code. Thanks to its modularity and language-independence, we have been able to reuse several results for sequential languages. An appealing feature enjoyed by the framework is that security-type preserving compilation is no more restrictive for programs with dynamic thread creation than it is for sequential programs. Primitives for interacting with the scheduler are introduced by the compiler behind the scenes, and in such a way that internal timing leaks are prevented.

We have demonstrated an instantiation of the framework to a simple imperative language and have argued that our approach is amenable to extensions to object-oriented languages. The compatibility with bytecode verification makes our framework a promising candidate for establishing mobile-code security via type checking.

Acknowledgment . This work was funded in part by the Sixth Framework programme of the European Community under the MOBIUS project FP6-015905.

References

1. Agat, J.: Transforming out timing leaks. In: Proc. ACM Symp. on Principles of Programming Languages, pp. 40–53. ACM Press, New York (January 2000)
2. Matos, A.A.: Typing secure information flow: declassification and mobility. PhD thesis, Ecole Nationale Supérieure des Mines de Paris (2006)

3. Barthe, G., Pichardie, D., Rezk, T.: A certified lightweight non-interference java bytecode verifier. In: Niccola, R.D. (ed.) European Symposium on Programming. LNCS, Springer, Heidelberg (2007)
4. Barthe, G., Rezk, T.: Non-interference for a JVM-like language. In: Fähndrich, M. (ed.) Proceedings of TLDI'05, pp. 103–112. ACM Press, New York (2005)
5. Barthe, G., Rezk, T., Basu, A.: Security types preserving compilation. Journal of Computer Languages, Systems and Structures (2007)
6. Barthe, G., Rezk, T., Naumann, D.: Deriving an information flow checker and certifying compiler for java. In: S&P'06. SP '06: Proceedings of the 2006 IEEE Symposium on Security and Privacy, pp. 230–242. IEEE Computer Society, Los Alamitos (2006)
7. Barthe, G., Rezk, T., Russo, A., Sabelfeld, A.: Security of multithreaded programs by compilation. Technical report, Chalmers University of Technology (2007), located at http://www.cs.chalmers.se/~russo/esorics07full.pdf
8. Boudol, G., Castellani, I.: Noninterference for concurrent programs and thread systems. Theoretical Computer Science 281(1), 109–130 (2002)
9. Denning, D.E., Denning, P.J.: Certification of programs for secure information flow. Comm. of the ACM 20(7), 504–513 (1977)
10. Genaim, S., Spoto, F.: Information Flow Analysis for Java Bytecode. In: Cousot, R. (ed.) VMCAI 2005. LNCS, vol. 3385, pp. 346–362. Springer, Heidelberg (2005)
11. Goguen, J.A., Meseguer, J.: Security policies and security models. In: Proc. IEEE Symp. on Security and Privacy, pp. 11–20. IEEE Computer Society Press, Los Alamitos (April 1982)
12. Huisman, M., Worah, P., Sunesen, K.: A temporal logic characterisation of observational determinism. In: Proc. IEEE Computer Security Foundations Workshop, IEEE Computer Society Press, Los Alamitos (July 2006)
13. Knudsen, J.: Networking, user experience, and threads. Sun Technical Articles and Tips (2002),
    http://developers.sun.com/techtopics/mobility/midp/articles/threading/
14. Köpf, B., Mantel, H.: Eliminating implicit information leaks by transformational typing and unification. In: Dimitrakos, T., Martinelli, F., Ryan, P.Y.A., Schneider, S. (eds.) FAST 2005. LNCS, vol. 3866, pp. 47–62. Springer, Heidelberg (2006)
15. Mahmoud, Q.H.: Preventing screen lockups of blocking operations. Sun Technical Articles and Tips (2004),
    http://developers.sun.com/techtopics/mobility/midp/ttips/screenlock/
16. Medel, R., Compagnoni, A., Bonelli, E.: A typed assembly language for non-interference. In: Coppo, M., Lodi, E., Pinna, G.M. (eds.) ICTCS 2005. LNCS, vol. 3701, pp. 360–374. Springer, Heidelberg (2005)
17. Russo, A., Hughes, J., Naumann, D., Sabelfeld, A.: Closing internal timing channels by transformation. In: Asian Computing Science Conference (ASIAN'06). LNCS, Springer, Heidelberg (2007)
18. Russo, A., Sabelfeld, A.: Securing interaction between threads and the scheduler. In: Proc. IEEE Computer Security Foundations Workshop, pp. 177–189. IEEE Computer Society Press, Los Alamitos (July 2006)
19. Russo, A., Sabelfeld, A.: Security for multithreaded programs under cooperative scheduling. In: Virbitskaite, I., Voronkov, A. (eds.) PSI 2006. LNCS, vol. 4378, Springer, Heidelberg (2007)
20. Sabelfeld, A.: The impact of synchronisation on secure information flow in concurrent programs. In: Bjørner, D., Broy, M., Zamulin, A.V. (eds.) PSI 2001. LNCS, vol. 2244, pp. 225–239. Springer, Heidelberg (2001)

21. Sabelfeld, A., Mantel, H.: Static confidentiality enforcement for distributed programs. In: Hermenegildo, M.V., Puebla, G. (eds.) SAS 2002. LNCS, vol. 2477, pp. 376–394. Springer, Heidelberg (2002)
22. Sabelfeld, A., Myers, A.C.: Language-based information-flow security. IEEE J. Selected Areas in Communications 21(1), 5–19 (2003)
23. Sabelfeld, A., Sands, D.: Probabilistic noninterference for multi-threaded programs. In: Proc. IEEE Computer Security Foundations Workshop, pp. 200–214. IEEE Computer Society Press, Los Alamitos (July 2000)
24. Smith, G.: A new type system for secure information flow. In: Proc. IEEE Computer Security Foundations Workshop, pp. 115–125. IEEE Computer Society Press, Los Alamitos (June 2001)
25. Smith, G.: Probabilistic noninterference through weak probabilistic bisimulation. In: Proc. IEEE Computer Security Foundations Workshop, pp. 3–13. IEEE Computer Society Press, Los Alamitos (2003)
26. Smith, G., Volpano, D.: Secure information flow in a multi-threaded imperative language. In: Proc. ACM Symp. on Principles of Programming Languages, pp. 355–364. ACM Press, New York (January 1998)
27. Tsai, T.C., Russo, A., Hughes, J.: A library for secure multi-threaded information flow in Haskell. In: Proc. of the 20th IEEE Computer Security Foundations Symposium, July 2007, IEEE Computer Society Press, Los Alamitos (to appear)
28. Volpano, D., Smith, G.: Probabilistic noninterference in a concurrent language. J. Computer Security 7(2–3), 231–253 (1999)
29. Volpano, D., Smith, G., Irvine, C.: A sound type system for secure flow analysis. J. Computer Security 4(3), 167–187 (1996)
30. Zdancewic, S., Myers, A.C.: Observational determinism for concurrent program security. In: Proc. IEEE Computer Security Foundations Workshop, pp. 29–43. IEEE Computer Society Press, Los Alamitos (June 2003)

Efficient Proving for Practical Distributed Access-Control Systems*

Lujo Bauer[1], Scott Garriss[1], and Michael K. Reiter[2]

[1] Carnegie Mellon University
[2] University of North Carolina at Chapel Hill

Abstract. We present a new technique for generating a formal proof that an access request satisfies access-control policy, for use in logic-based access-control frameworks. Our approach is tailored to settings where credentials needed to complete a proof might need to be obtained from, or reactively created by, distant components in a distributed system. In such contexts, our approach substantially improves upon previous proposals in both computation and communication costs, and better guides users to create the most appropriate credentials in those cases where needed credentials do not yet exist. At the same time, our strategy offers strictly superior proving ability, in the sense that it finds a proof in every case that previous approaches would (and more). We detail our method and evaluate an implementation of it using both policies in active use in an access-control testbed at our institution and larger policies indicative of a widespread deployment.

1 Introduction

Much work has given credence to the notion that formal reasoning can be used to buttress the assurance one has in an access-control system. While early work in this vein *modeled* access-control systems using formal logics (e.g., [9,18]), recent work has imported logic into the system as a means to *implement* access control (e.g., [6]). In these systems, the resource monitor evaluating an access request requires a proof, in formal logic, that the access satisfies access-control policy. In such a proof, digitally signed credentials are used to instantiate formulas of the logic (e.g., "K_{Alice} **signed delegate** (Alice, Bob, resource)" or "K_{CA} **signed** K_{Alice} **speaksfor** K_{CA}.Alice"), and then inference rules are used to derive a proof that a required policy is satisfied (e.g., "Manager **says open**(resource)"). The resource monitor, then, need only validate that each request is accompanied by a valid proof of the required policy.

Because the resource monitor accepts *any* valid proof of the required policy, this framework offers potentially a high degree of flexibility in how proofs are constructed. This flexibility, however, is not without its costs. First, it is essential that the logic is sound and free from unintended consequences, giving rise to a rich literature in designing appropriate authorization logics (e.g., [9,19,16,14]). Second, and of primary concern in this paper, it must be possible to efficiently find proofs for accesses that should be allowed. Rather than devising a proving strategy customized to each application, we would prefer to develop a general proof-building strategy that is driven by the logic itself and that is effective in a wide range of applications.

---

* This work was supported in part by NSF grant 0433540, grant DAAD19-02-1-0389 from the Army Research Office, and the AFRL/IF Pollux project.

J. Biskup and J. Lopez (Eds.): ESORICS 2007, LNCS 4734, pp. 19–37, 2007.

In this paper we focus on systems where needed credentials are distributed among different components, if they exist at all, and may be created at distant components reactively and with human intervention. Such systems give rise to new requirements for credential-creation and proof-construction algorithms. To address these requirements, we combine a number of new and existing techniques into a proof-generation strategy that is qualitatively different from those proposed by previous works. In comparison to these works (notably [4]), we show that our strategy offers dramatic improvements in the efficiency of proof construction in practice, consequently making such systems significantly more useable. Moreover, our strategy will find proofs whenever previous algorithms would (and sometimes even when they would not). Our method builds from three key principles. First, our method strategically delays pursuing "expensive" subgoals until, through further progress in the proving process, it is clear that these subgoals would be helpful to prove. Second, our method precomputes delegation chains between principles in a way that can significantly optimize the proving process on the critical path of an access. Third, our method eliminates the need to hand-craft *tactics*, a fragile and time-intensive process, to efficiently guide the proof search. Instead, it utilizes a new, systematic approach to generating tactics from the inference rules of the logic.

The technique we report here is motivated by an ongoing deployment at our institution of a testbed environment where proof-based access control is used to control access to both physical resources (e.g., door access) and information resources (e.g., computer logins). The system has been deployed for over a year, guards access to about 35 resources spanning two floors of our office building, and is used daily by over 35 users. In this deployment, smartphones are used as the vehicle for constructing proofs and soliciting consent from users for the creation of new credentials, and the cellular network is the means by which these smartphones communicate to retrieve needed proofs of subgoals. In such an environment, both computation and communication have high latency, and so limiting use of these resources is essential to offering reasonable response times to users. And, for the sake of usability, it is essential that we involve users in the proof generation process (i.e., to create new credentials) infrequently and with as much guidance as possible. We have developed the technique we report here with these goals in mind, and our deployment suggests that it offers acceptable performance for the policies with which we have experimented and is a drastic improvement over previous approaches. All of the examples used in this paper are actual policies drawn from the deployment. We evaluate the scalability of our algorithm on larger, synthetically generated policies in Section 4.2 and show that the quantity of precomputed state remains reasonable and the performance advantage of our approach remains or increases as the policy grows. Our approach has applications beyond the particular setting in which we describe it; we briefly discuss one such application in Section 5.

The contributions of this paper are to: (1) identify the requirements of a proving algorithm in a distributed access-control system with dynamic credential creation (Section 2); (2) propose mechanisms for precomputing delegation chains (Section 3.2) and systematically generating tactics (Section 3.3); (3) describe a technique for utilizing these pre-computed results to find proofs in dramatically less time than previous approaches (Section 3.3); and (4) evaluate our technique on a collection of policies representative of those used in practice (Section 4.1) and those indicative of a larger

$\phi ::= s$ **signed** $\phi' \mid p$ **says** ϕ' (s ranges over strings and p over principals)

$\phi' ::= $ **open** $(s) \mid p$ **speaksfor** $p \mid$ **delegate**(p, p, s)

$$\frac{pubkey \text{ signed } F}{\text{key}(pubkey) \text{ says } F} \qquad (\text{SAYS-I})$$

$$\frac{A \text{ says } (B \text{ speaksfor } A) \quad B \text{ says } F}{A \text{ says } F} \qquad (\text{SPEAKSFOR-E})$$

$$\frac{A \text{ says } (A.S \text{ says } F)}{A.S \text{ says } F} \qquad (\text{SAYS-LN})$$

$$\frac{A \text{ says } (B \text{ speaksfor } A.S) \quad B \text{ says } F}{A.S \text{ says } F} \qquad (\text{SPEAKSFOR-E2})$$

$$\frac{A \text{ says } (\text{delegate}(A, B, U)) \quad B \text{ says } (\text{open}(U, N))}{A \text{ says } (\text{open}(U, N))} \qquad (\text{DELEGATE-E})$$

Fig. 1. A sample access-control logic [4]

deployment (Section 4.2). In Section 5, we discuss the use of our techniques in the context of additional logics, systems and applications. Proofs of our theorems, and discussion of related work elided due to space constraints, can be found in our accompanying technical report [5].

2 Goals and Contributions

As discussed in Section 1, we will describe new techniques for generating proofs in an authorization logic that an access request is consistent with access-control policy. It will be far easier to discuss our approach in the context of a concrete authorization logic, and for this purpose we utilize the same sample logic as we used in previous work [4], which is reproduced in Figure 2. However, our techniques are not specific to this logic, or even necessarily to a logic-based system; rather, they can be adapted to a wide range of authorization systems provided that they build upon a similar notion of delegation, as discussed in Section 5.

If pubkey is a particular public key, then **key**(pubkey) is the principal that corresponds to that key. If Alice is a principal, we write Alice.secretary to denote the principal whom Alice calls "secretary." The formulas of our logic describe principals' beliefs. If Alice believes that the formula F is true, we write Alice **says** F. To indicate that she believes a formula F is true, a principal signs it with her private key—the resulting sequence of bits will be represented by the formula pubkey **signed** F, which can be transformed into a belief (**key**(pubkey) **says** F) using the SAYS-I inference rule. To describe a resource that a client wants to access, we use the **open** constructor. A principal believes the formula **open**(*resource*) if she thinks that it is OK to access *resource*.[1] Delegation is described with the **speaksfor** and **delegate** predicates. The formula Alice **speaksfor** Bob indicates that Bob has delegated to Alice his authority to make access-control decisions about any resource. **delegate**(Bob, Alice, *resource*) transfers to Alice only the authority to access the resource called *resource*.

---

[1] **open** takes a nonce as a second parameter, which we omit here for simplicity.

2.1   Requirements

To motivate our requirements, we use as an example a simple policy in use on a daily basis in our system. This policy is chosen for illustrative purposes; the performance advantage of our technique actually widens as the policy becomes more complicated (see Section 4.2). All the resources in our example are owned by our academic department, and so to access a resource (resource) one must prove that the department has authorized the access (Dept **says open**(resource)).

Alice is the manager in charge of a machine room with three entrances: door1, door2, and door3. To place her in charge, the department has created credentials giving Alice access to each door, e.g., K_{Dept} **signed delegate**(Dept, Alice, door1). Alice's responsibilities include deciding who else may access the machine room. Instead of individually delegating access to each door, Alice has organized her security policy by (1) creating a group Alice.machine-room; (2) giving all members of that group access to each door (e.g., K_{Alice} **signed delegate**(Alice, Alice.machine-room, door1)); and, finally, (3) making individuals like Bob members of the group (K_{Alice} **signed** (Bob **speaksfor** Alice.machine-room)).

Suppose that Charlie, who currently does not have access to the machine room, wishes to open one of the machine-room doors. When his smartphone contacts the door, it is told to prove Dept **says open**(door1). The proof is likely to require credentials created by the department, by Alice, and perhaps also by Bob, who may be willing to redelegate the authority he received from Alice.

Previous approaches to distributed proof generation (notably [4] and [21]) did not attempt to address three requirements that are crucial in practice. Each requirement may appear to be a trivial extension of some previously studied proof-generation algorithm. However, straightforward implementation attempts suffer from problems that lead to greater inefficiency than can be tolerated in practice, as will be detailed below.

Credential creation. Charlie will not be able to access door1 unless Alice, Bob, or the department creates a credential to make that possible. The proof-generation algorithm should intelligently guide users to create the "right" credential, e.g., K_{Alice} **signed** (Charlie **speaksfor** Alice.machine-room), based on other credentials that already exist. This increases the computation required, as the prover must additionally investigate branches of reasoning that involve credentials that have not yet been created.

Exposing choice points. When it is possible to make progress on a proof in a number of ways (i.e., by creating different credentials or by asking different principals for help), the choice points should be exposed to the user instead of being followed automatically. Exposing the choice points to the user makes it possible both to generate proofs more efficiently by taking advantage of the user's knowledge (e.g., Charlie might know that Bob is likely to help but Alice isn't) and to avoid undesired proving paths (e.g., bothering Alice at 3AM with a request to create credentials, when she has requested she not be). This increase in overall efficiency comes at a cost of increased local computation, as the prover must investigate all possible choice points prior to asking the user.

Local proving. Previous work showed that proof generation in distributed environments was feasible under the assumption that each principal attempted to prove only the formulas pertaining to her own beliefs (e.g., Charlie would attempt to prove formulas like Charlie says F, but would immediately ask Bob for help if he had to prove Bob says G) [4]. In our example, if Charlie asks Alice for help, Alice is able to create sufficient credentials to prove Dept says open(door1), even though this proof involves reasoning about the department head's beliefs. Avoiding a request to the department head in this case improves the overall efficiency of proof generation, but in general requires Alice to try to prove all goals for which she would normally ask for help, again increasing the amount of local computation.

The increase in computation imposed by each requirement may seem reasonable, but when implemented as a straightforward extension of previous work, Alice's prover running on a Nokia N70 smartphone will take over 5 *minutes* to determine the set of possible ways in which she can help Charlie gain access. Using the technique described in this paper, Alice is able to find the most common options (see Section 3.3) in 2 seconds, and is able to find a provably complete set of options in well less than a minute.

2.2 Insights

We address the requirements outlined in Section 2.1 with a new distributed proving strategy that is both efficient in practice and that sacrifices no proving ability relative to prior approaches. The insights embodied in our new strategy are threefold and we describe them here with the help of the example from Section 2.1.

Minimizing expensive proof steps. In an effort to prove Dept says open(door1), suppose Charlie's prover directs a request for help to Alice. Alice's prover might decompose the goal Dept says open(door1) in various ways, some that would require the consent of the user Alice to create a new credential (e.g., Alice says Charlie speaksfor Alice.machine-room) and others that would involve making a remote query (e.g., to Dept, since this is Dept's belief). We have found that naively pursuing such options inline, i.e., when the prover first encounters them, is not reasonable in a practical implementation, as the former requires too much user interaction and the latter induces too much network communication and remote proving.

We employ a *delayed* proof procedure that vastly improves on these alternatives for the policies we have experimented with in practice. Roughly speaking, this procedure strategically bypasses formulas that are the most expensive to pursue, i.e., requiring either a remote query or the local user consenting to signing the formula directly. Each such formula is revisited only if subsequent steps in the proving process show that proving it would, in fact, be useful to completing the overall proof. In this way, the most expensive steps in the proof process are skipped until only those that would actually be useful are determined. These useful steps may be collected and presented to the user to aid in the decision-making process.

Precomputing delegation chains. A second insight is to locally precompute and cache delegation chains using two approaches: the well-studied *forward chaining* algorithm [22] and *path compression*, which we introduce here. Unlike backward chaining, which recursively decomposes goals into subgoals, these techniques work forward from a prover's available credentials (its *knowledge base*) to derive both facts and metalogical implications of the form "if we prove Charlie says F, then we can prove David says F". By computing these implications off the critical path, numerous lengthy branches can be avoided during backward chaining. While these algorithms can theoretically produce a knowledge base whose size is exponential in the number of credentials known, our evaluation indicates that in practice most credentials do not combine, and that the size of the knowledge base increases roughly linearly with the number of credentials (see Section 4.2). As we discuss in Section 3.3, the chief challenge in using precomputed results is to effectively integrate them in an exhaustive time-of-access proof search that involves hypothetical credentials.

If any credential should expire or be revoked, any knowledge derived from that credential will be removed from the knowledge base. Each element in the knowledge base is accompanied by an explicit derivation (i.e., a proof) of the element from credentials. Our implementation searches the knowledge base for any elements that are derived from expired or revoked credentials and removes them. Our technique is agnostic to the underlying revocation mechanism.

Systematic tactic generation. Another set of difficulties in constructing proofs is related to constructing the tactics that guide a backward-chaining prover in how it decomposes a goal into subgoals. One approach to constructing tactics is simply to use the inference rules of the logic as tactics. With a depth-limiter to ensure termination, this approach ensures that all possible proofs up to a certain size will be found, but is typically too inefficient for use on the critical path of an access because it may enumerate all possible proof shapes. A more efficient construction is to hand-craft a set of tactics by using multiple inference rules per tactic to create a more specific set of tactics [13]. The tactics tend to be designed to look for certain types of proofs at the expense of completeness. Additionally, the tactics are tedious to construct, and do not lend themselves to formal analysis. While faster than inference rules, the hand-crafted tactics can still be inefficient, and, more importantly, often suffer loss of proving ability when the policy grows larger or deviates from the ones that inspired the tactics.

A third insight of the approach we describe here is a new, *systematic* approach for generating tactics from inference rules. This contribution is enabled by the forward chaining and path compression algorithms mentioned above. In particular, since our prover can rely on the fact that all delegation chains have been precomputed, its tactics need not attempt to derive the delegation chains directly from credentials when generating a proof of access. This reduces the difficulty of designing tactics. In our approach, an inference rule having to do with delegation gives rise to two tactics: one whose chief purpose is to look up previously computed delegation chains, and another that identifies the manner in which previously computed delegation chains may be extended by the creation of further credentials. All other inference rules are used directly as tactics.

3   Proposed Approach

The prover operates over a *knowledge base* that consists of tactics, locally known credentials, and facts that can be derived from these credentials. The proving strategy we propose consists of three parts. First, we use the existing technique of forward chaining to extend the local knowledge base with all facts that it can derive from existing knowledge (Section 3.1). Second, a path-compression algorithm (which we introduce in Section 3.2) computes delegation chains that can be derived from the local knowledge base but that cannot be derived through forward chaining. Third, a backward-chaining prover uses our systematically generated tactics to take advantage of the knowledge generated by the first two steps to efficiently compute proofs of a particular goal (e.g., Dept says open(door1)) (Section 3.3).

The splitting of the proving process into distinct pieces is motivated by the observation that if Charlie is trying to access door1, he is interested in minimizing the time between the moment he indicates his intention to access door1 and the time he is able to enter. Any part of the proving process that takes place *before* Charlie attempts to access door1 is effectively invisible to him. By completely precomputing certain types of knowledge, the backward-chaining prover can avoid some costly branches of investigation, thus reducing the time the user spends waiting.

3.1 Forward Chaining

Forward chaining (FC) is a well-studied proof-search technique in which all known ground facts (true formulas that do not contain free variables) are exhaustively combined using inference rules until either a proof of the formula contained in the query is found, or the algorithm reaches a fixed point from which no further inferences can be made. We use a variant of the algorithm known as incremental forward chaining [22] in which state is preserved across queries, allowing the incremental addition of a single fact to the knowledge base. The property we desire from FC is *completeness*—that it finds a proof of every formula for which a proof can be found from the credentials in the knowledge base (KB). More formally:

Theorem 1. *After each credential $f \in KB$ has been incrementally added via* FC, *for any $p_1 \ldots p_n \in KB$, if $(p_1 \wedge \ldots \wedge p_n) \supset q$ then $q \in KB$.*

If forward chaining is invoked on a knowledge base for which there is no fixed point, the algorithm is not guaranteed to terminate. Because of this, forward chaining is frequently restricted to Datalog knowledge bases, for which it can be shown to be complete [22]. Our logic includes some functions that are not representable in Datalog, but we show that these functions are crafted to not affect completeness. For a proof of Theorem 1 and all other theorems in this paper, please see our technical report [5].

3.2 Path Compression

A *path* is a delegation chain between two principals A and B such that a proof of B says F implies that a proof of A says F can be found. Some paths are represented directly in the logic (e.g., B speaksfor A). Other paths, such as the path between A and C that results from the credentials K_A signed (B speaksfor A) and K_B signed (C speaksfor B), cannot be expressed directly—they are metalogical constructs, and cannot be computed by FC. More formally, we define a path as follows:

Definition 1. *A path $(A$ says F, B says $F)$ is a set of credentials $c_1, \ldots, c_n$ and a proof P of $(c_1, \ldots, c_n, A$ says $F) \supset B$ says F.*

For example, the credential K_{Alice} signed Bob speaksfor Alice will produce the path $(Bob$ says F, Alice says $F)$, where F is an unbound variable. Now, for any concrete

```
0    global set paths                                  /* All known delegation chains. */
1    global set incompletePaths                        /* All known incomplete chains. */

2    PC(credential f)
3        if (credToPath(f) = ⊥), return                /* If not a delegation, do nothing. */
4        (x, y) ← depends-on(f)                        /* If input is a third-person delegation,
5        if (((x, y) ≠ ⊥) ∧ ¬((x, y) ∈ paths))            add it to incompletePaths. */
6            incompletePaths ← incompletePaths ∪ (f, (x, y))
7        return

8        (p, q) ← credToPath(f)                        /* Convert input credential into
9        add-path((p, q))                                 a path. */

10       foreach (f', (x', y')) ∈ incompletePaths      /* Check if new paths make any
11           foreach (p'', q'') ∈ paths                    previously encountered third-
12               if((θ ← unify((x', y'), (p'', q''))) ≠ ⊥)   person credentials useful. */
13                   (p', q') ← credToPath(f')
14                   add-path((subst(θ, p'), subst(θ, q')))

15   add-path(chain (p, q))
16       local set newPaths = {}
17       paths ← union((p, q), paths)                  /* Add the new path to set
18       newPaths ← union((p, q), newPaths)               of paths. */

19       foreach (p', q') ∈ paths
20           if((θ ← unify(q, p')) ≠ ⊥)                /* Try to prepend new path to
21               c ← (subst(θ, p), subst(θ, q'))          all previous paths. */
22               paths ← union(c, paths)
23               newPaths ← union(c, paths)

24       foreach (p', q') ∈ paths
25           foreach (p'', q'') ∈ newPaths             /* Try to append all new paths
26               if((θ ← unify(q', p'')) ≠ ⊥)             to all previous paths. */
27                   c ← (subst(θ, p'), subst(θ, q''))
28                   paths ← union(c, paths)
```

Fig. 2. PC, an incremental path-compression algorithm

formula g, if Bob **says** g is true, we can conclude Alice **says** g. If Bob issues the credential K_{Bob} **signed delegate**(Bob, Charlie, resource), then we can construct the path (Charlie **says open**(resource), Bob **says open**(resource)). Since the conclusion of the second path unifies with the premise of the first, we can combine them to construct the path (Charlie **says open**(resource), Alice **says open**(resource)). Unlike the two credentials above, some delegation credentials represent a meaningful path only if another path already exists. For example, Alice could delegate authority to Bob on behalf of Charlie (e.g., K_{Alice} **signed delegate**(Charlie, Bob, resource)). This credential by itself is meaningless because Alice lacks the authority to speak on Charlie's behalf. We say that this credential *depends on* the existence of a path from Alice to Charlie, because this path would give Alice the authority to speak on Charlie's behalf. Consequently, we call such credentials *dependent*, and others *independent*.

Algorithm. Our path compression algorithm, shown in Figure 2, is divided into two subroutines: PC and add-path. The objective of PC is to determine if a given credential represents a meaningful path, and, if so, add it to the set of known paths by invoking add-path. add-path is responsible for constructing all other possible paths using this new path, and for adding all new paths to the knowledge base. The subroutine subst performs a free-variable substitution and unify returns the most general substitution (if one exists) that, when applied to both parameters, produces equivalent formulas.

PC ignores any credential that does not contain a delegation statement (Line 3 of Figure 2). If a new credential does not depend on another path, or depends on a path that exists, it will be passed to add-path (Line 9). If the credential depends on a path that does not exist, the credential is instead stored in *incompletePaths* for later use (Lines 5–7). Whenever a new path is added, PC must check if any of the credentials in *incompletePaths* are now meaningful (Lines 10–12), and, if so, covert them to paths and add the result to the knowledge base (Lines 13–14).

After adding the new path to the global set of paths (Line 17), add-path finds the already-computed paths that can be appended to the new path, appends them, and adds the resulting paths to the global set (Lines 19–23). Next, add-path finds the existing paths that can be prepended to the paths created in the first step, prepends them, and saves the resulting paths (Lines 24–28). To prevent cyclic paths from being saved, the union subroutine adds a path only if the path does not represent a cycle. That is, $\text{union}((p, q), S)$ returns S if $\text{unify}(p, q) \neq \perp$, and $S \cup \{(p, q)\}$ otherwise.

Completeness of PC. The property we desire of PC is that it constructs all possible paths that are derivable from the credentials it has been given as input. We state this formally below.

Theorem 2. *If* PC *has completed on* KB, *then for any* A, B *such that* $A \neq B$, *if for some* F (B **says** $F \supset A$ **says** F) *then* (B **says** F, A **says** F) $\in KB$.

For the proof of Theorem 2, please see our technical report [5]. Informally: We first show that add-path will combine all paths that can be combined—that is, for any paths (p, q) and (p', q') if q unifies with p' then the path (p, q') will be added. We then show that for all credentials that represent a path, add-path is immediately invoked for independent credentials (Line 9), and all credentials that depend on the existence of another path are passed to add-path whenever that path becomes known (Lines 10–14).

3.3 Backward Chaining

Backward-chaining provers are composed of tactics that describe how formulas might be proved and a backward-chaining engine that uses tactics to prove a particular formula. The backward-chaining part of our technique must perform two novel tasks. First, the backward-chaining engine needs to expose choice points to the user. At each such point the user can select, e.g., which of several local credentials to create, or which of several principals to ask for help. Second, we want to craft the tactics to take advantage of facts precomputed through forward chaining and path compression to achieve greater efficiency and better coverage of the proof space than previous approaches.

Delayed backward chaining. While trying to generate a proof, the prover may investigate subgoals for which user interaction is necessary, e.g., to create a new credential or to determine the appropriate remote party to ask for help. We call these subgoals *choice subgoals*, since they will not be investigated unless the user explicitly chooses to do so. The distributed theorem-proving approach of our previous work [4] attempted to pursue each choice subgoal as it was discovered, thus restricting user interaction to a series of yes or no questions. Our insight here is to pursue a choice subgoal only after all other choice subgoals have been identified, thus *delaying* the proving of all choice subgoals until input can be solicited from the user. This affords the user the opportunity to guide the prover by selecting the choice subgoal that is most appropriate to pursue first.

Converting the algorithm from previous work to the delayed strategy is straightforward. Briefly, the delayed algorithm operates by creating a placeholder proof whenever it encounters a choice subgoal. The algorithm then backtracks and attempts to find alternate solutions, returning if it discovers a proof that does not involve any choice subgoals. If no such proof is found, the algorithm will present the list of placeholder proofs to the user, who can decide which one is most appropriate to pursue first. As an optimization, heuristics may be employed to sort or prune this list. As another optimization, the prover could determine whether a choice subgoal is worth pursing by attempting to complete the remainder of the proof before interacting with the user. This algorithm will identify a choice subgoal for every remote request made by previous approaches, and will additionally identify a choice subgoal for every locally creatable credential such that the creation of the credential would allow the completion of the proof from local knowledge. For a more detailed description, please see our technical report [5].

Tactics. In constructing a set of tactics to be used by our backward-chaining engine, we have two goals: the tactics should make use of facts precomputed by FC and PC, and they should be generated systematically from the inference rules of the logic.

If a formula F can be proved from local credentials, and all locally known credentials have been incrementally added via FC, then, by Theorem 1, a proof of F already exists in the knowledge base. In this case, the backward-chaining component of our prover need only look in the knowledge base to find the proof. Tactics are thus used only when F is not provable from local knowledge, and in that case their role is to identify choice subgoals to present to the user.

Since the inference rules that describe delegation are the ones that indirectly give rise to the paths precomputed by PC, we need to treat those specially when generating tactics; all other inference rules are imported as tactics directly. We discuss here only delegation rules with two premises; for further discussion see Section 5.

Inference rules about delegation typically have two premises: one that describes a delegation, and another that allows the delegated permission to be exercised. Since tactics are applied only when the goal is not provable from local knowledge, one of the premises must contain a choice subgoal. For each delegation rule, we construct two tactics: (1) a *left* tactic for the case when the choice subgoal is in the delegation premise, and (2) a *right* tactic for the case when the choice subgoal is in the other premise.[2] We call tactics generated in this manner LR tactics.

---

[2] For completeness, if there are choice subgoals in both premises, one will be resolved and then the prover will be rerun (see [5] for details). In practice, we have yet to encounter a circumstance where a single round of proving was not sufficient.

$$\frac{A \text{ says } (B \text{ speaksfor } A) \quad B \text{ says } F}{A \text{ says } F} \qquad \text{(SPEAKSFOR-E)}$$

left tactic   prove(A **says** F) :- pathLookup(B **says** F, A **says** F),
                                     prove(B **says** F).

right tactic   prove(A **says** F) :- proveWithChoiceSubgoal(A **says** (B **speaksfor** A)),
                                     factLookup(B **says** F).

Fig. 3. Example construction of LR tactics from an inference rule

The insight behind the left tactic is that instead of looking for complete proofs of the delegation premise in the set of facts in the knowledge base, it looks for proofs among the paths precomputed by PC, thus following an arbitrarily long delegation chain in one step. The premise exercising the delegation is then proved normally, by recursively applying tactics to find any remaining choice subgoals. Conversely, the right tactic assumes that the delegation premise can be proved only with the use of a choice subgoal, and restricts the search to only those proofs. The right tactic may then look in the knowledge base for a proof of the right premise in an effort to determine if the choice subgoal is useful to pursue.

Figure 3 shows an inference rule and the two tactics we construct from that rule. All tactics are constructed as *prove* predicates, and so a recursive call to *prove* may apply tactics other than the two shown. The *factLookup* and *pathLookup* predicates inspect the knowledge base for facts produced by FC and paths produced by PC. The *proveWithChoiceSubgoal* acts like a standard *prove* predicate, but restricts the search to discard any proofs that do not involve a choice subgoal. We employ rudimentary cycle detection to prevent repeated application of the same right rule.

Optimizations to LR. The dominant computational cost of running a query using LR tactics is repeated applications of right tactics. Since a right tactic handles the case in which the choice subgoal represents a delegation, identifying the choice subgoal involves determining who is allowed to create delegations, and then determining on whose behalf that person wishes to delegate. This involves exhaustively searching through all paths twice. However, practical experience with our deployed system indicates that people rarely delegate on behalf of anyone other than themselves. This allows us to remove the second path application and trade completeness for speed in finding the most common proofs. If completeness is desired, the optimized set of tactics could be run first, and the complete version could be run afterwards. We refer to the optimized tactics as LR′. This type of optimization is made dramatically easier because of the systematic approach used to construct the LR tactics.

Alternative approaches to caching. Naive constructions of tactics perform a large amount of redundant computation both within a query and across queries. An apparent solution to this problem is to cache intermediate results as they are discovered to avoid future recomputation. As it turns out, this type of caching does not improve performance, and even worsens it in some situations. If attempting to prove a formula with an unbound variable, an exhaustive search requires that all bindings for that variable be investigated. Cached proofs will be used first, but as the cache is not necessarily all-inclusive, tactics must be applied as well. These tactics in turn will re-derive the proofs that are in cache. Another approach is to make caching part of the proving engine (e.g., Prolog) itself. Tabling algorithms [10] provide this and other useful properties, and have well-established implementations (e.g., http://xsb.sourceforge.net/). However, this approach precludes adding to cache proofs that are discovered via different proving techniques (e.g., FC, PC, or a remote prover using a different set of tactics).

Completeness of LR. Despite greater efficiency, LR tactics have strictly greater proving ability than the depth-limited inference rules. We state this formally below.

Theorem 3. *Given one prover whose tactics are depth-limited inference rules (IR), and a second prover that uses LR tactics along with FC and PC, if the prover using IR tactics finds a proof of goal F, the prover using LR tactics will also find a proof of F.*

For the proof of Theorem 3, please see our technical report [5]. Informally: We first show show that provers using LR and IR are locally equivalent—that is, if IR finds a complete proof from local knowledge then LR will do so as well and if IR identifies a choice subgoal then LR will identify the same choice subgoal. We show this by first noting that if IR finds a complete proof from local knowledge, then a prover using LR will have precomputed that same proof using FC. We show that LR and IR find the same choice subgoals by induction over the size of the proof explored by IR and noting that left tactics handle the case where the proof of the right premise of an inference rule contains a choice subgoal and that right tactics handle the case where the the left premise contains a choice subgoal. Having shown local equivalence, we can apply induction over the number of remote requests made to conclude that a prover using LR will find a proof of F if a prover using IR finds a proof of F.

4 Empirical Evaluation

Since the usability of the distributed access-control system as a whole depends on the timeliness with which it can generate a proof of access, the most important evaluation metric is the amount of time it takes either to construct a complete proof, or, if no complete proof can be found, to generate a list of choices to give to the user. We also consider the number of subgoals investigated by the prover and the size of the knowledge base produced by FC and PC. The number of subgoals investigated represents a coarse measure of efficiency that is independent of any particular Prolog implementation.

We compare the performance of five proving strategies: three that represent previous work and two (the combination of FC and PC with either LR or LR′) that represent the strategies introduced here. The strategies that represent previous work are backward chaining with depth-limited inference rules (IR), inference rules with basic cycle detection (IR-NC), and hand-crafted tactics (HC). HC evolved from IR during our early deployment as an effort to improve the efficiency of the proof-generation process. As such, HC represents our best effort to optimize a prover that uses only backward chaining to the policies used in our deployment, but at the cost of theoretical completeness.

We analyze two scenarios: the first represents the running example presented previously (which is drawn from our deployment), and the second represents the policy described by our previous work [4], which is indicative of a larger deployment. As explained in Section 4.2, these large policies are the most challenging for our strategy.

Our system is built using Java Mobile Edition (J2ME), and the prover is written in Prolog. We perform simulations on two devices: a Nokia N70 smartphone, which is the device used in our deployment, and a dual 2.8 Ghz Xeon workstation with 1 GB of memory. Our Prolog interpreter for the N70 is JIProlog (http://www.ugosweb.com/jiprolog/) due to its compatibility with J2ME. Simulations run on the workstation use SWI-Prolog (http://www.swi-prolog.org/).

4.1 Running Example

Scenario. As per our running example, Alice controls access to a machine room. We simulate a scenario in which Charlie wishes to enter the machine room for the first time. To do so, his prover will be asked to generate a proof of Dept **says** open(door1). His prover will immediately realize that Dept should be asked for help, but will continue to reason about this formula using local knowledge in the hope of finding a proof without making a request. Lacking sufficient authority, this local reasoning will fail, and Charlie will be presented with the option to ask Dept for help. Preferring not to bother the department head, Charlie will decide to ask his manager, Alice, directly.

Creating a complete proof in this scenario requires three steps: (1) Charlie's prover attempts to construct a proof, realizes that help is necessary, and asks Alice, (2) Alice's phone constructs a proof containing a delegation to Charlie, and (3) Charlie assembles Alice's response into a final proof. As Alice's phone holds the most complicated policy, step 2 dominates the total time required to find a proof.

0	K_{Dept} **signed** (**delegate**(Dept, Alice, door1))
1	K_{Dept} **signed** (**delegate**(Dept, Alice, door2))
2	K_{Dept} **signed** (**delegate**(Dept, Alice, door3))
3	K_{Alice} **signed delegate**(Alice, Alice.machine-room, door1)
4	K_{Alice} **signed delegate**(Alice, Alice.machine-room, door2)
5	K_{Alice} **signed delegate**(Alice, Alice.machine-room, door3)
6	K_{Alice} **signed** (Bob **speaksfor** Alice.machine-room)
7	K_{Alice} **signed** (David **speaksfor** Alice.machine-room)
8	K_{Alice} **signed** (Elizabeth **speaksfor** Alice.machine-room)
9	K_{Dept} **signed delegate**(Dept, Alice, office)
10	K_{Dept} **signed** (**delegate**(Dept, Dept.residents, lab-door))
11	K_{Dept} **signed** (Alice **speaksfor** Dept.residents)
12	$K_{Charlie}$ **signed open**(door1)

Fig. 4. Credentials on Alice's phone

13	K_{Dept} **signed** (**delegate**(Dept, Dept.residents, lab-door))
14	K_{Dept} **signed** (Charlie **speaksfor** Dept.residents)
15	$K_{Charlie}$ **signed open**(door1)

Fig. 5. Credentials on Charlie's phone

Policy. The policy for this scenario is expressed in the credentials known to Alice and Charlie, shown in Figures 4 and 5. The first six credentials of Figure 4 represent the delegation of access to the machine-room doors from the department to Alice, and her redelegation of these resources to the group Alice.machine-room. Credentials 6–8 indicate that the group Alice.machine-room already includes Bob, David, and Elizabeth. Notably, Alice has not yet created a credential that would give Charlie access to the machine room. We will analyze the policy as is, and with the addition of a credential that adds Charlie to the machine-room group. Credentials 9–11 deal with other resources that Alice can

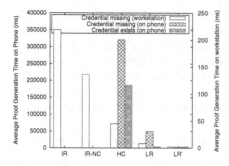
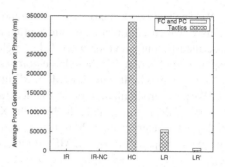

Fig. 6. Alice's prover generates complete proof or list of credentials that Alice can create

Fig. 7. Aggregate proving time: Charlie's before help request + Alice's + Charlie's after help request

access. The final credential is given to Alice when Charlie asks her for help: it indicates Charlie's desire to open door1.

Charlie's policy (Figure 5) is much simpler. He has access to a shared lab space through his membership in the group Dept.residents, to which the department has delegated access. He has no credentials pertaining to the machine room.

The only credential in Figures 4 and 5 that was created at the time of access is the one indicating Charlie's desire to access door1. This means that FC and PC have already been run on all other credentials.

Performance. Figure 6 describes the proving performance experienced by Alice when she attempts to help Charlie. Alice wishes to delegate authority to Charlie by giving him membership in the group Alice.machine-room. We show performance for the case where this credential does not yet exist, and the case where it does. In both cases, Alice's phone is unable to complete a proof with either IR or IR-NC as both crash due to lack of memory after a significant amount of computation. To demonstrate the relative performance of IR and IR-NC, Figure 6 includes (on a separate y-axis) results collected on a workstation. IR, IR-NC, and HC were run with a depth-limit of 7, chosen high enough to find all solutions on this policy.

In the scenario where Alice has not yet delegated authority to Charlie, HC is over six times slower than LR, and more than two orders of magnitude slower than LR'. If Alice has already added Charlie to the group, the difference in performance widens. Since FC finds all complete proofs, it finds the proof while processing the credentials supplied by Charlie, so the subsequent search by LR and LR' is a cache lookup. The result is that a proof is found by LR and LR' almost 60 times faster than HC. When run on the workstation, IR and IR-NC are substantially slower than even HC.

Figure 7 shows the total time required to generate a proof of access in the scenario where Alice must reactively create the delegation credential (IR and IR-NC are omitted as they crash). This consists of Charlie's initial attempt to generate a proof, Alice's proof generation that leads to the creation of a new credential, and Charlie assembling Alice's reply into a final proof. The graph also shows the division of computation between the incremental algorithms FC and PC and the backward search using tactics. In overall computation, HC is six times slower than LR and 60 times slower than LR'. This does not include the transit time between phones, or the time spent waiting for users to choose between different options.

Since computation time is dependent on the Prolog implementation, as a more general metric of efficiency we also measure the number of formulas investigated by each strategy. Figure 8 shows the total number of formulas investigated (including redundant computation) and the number of unique formulas investigated (note that each is measured on a separate y-axis). LR and LR′ not only investigate fewer unique formulas than previous approaches, but drastically reduce the amount of redundant computation.

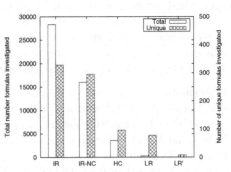

Fig. 8. Formulas investigated by Alice

4.2 Large Policies

Although our policy is a real one used in practice, in a widespread deployment it is likely that policies will become more complicated, with users having credentials for dozens of resources spanning multiple organizations. Our primary metric of evaluation is proof-generation time. Since backward chaining only considers branches, and hence credentials, that are relevant to the proof at hand, it will be least efficient when all credentials must be considered, e.g., when they are generated by members of same organization. As a secondary metric, we evaluate the size of the knowledge base, as this directly affects the memory requirements of the application as well as the speed of unification. Since credentials from the same organization are more likely to be combined to produce a new fact or path, the largest knowledge base will occur when all credentials pertain to the same organization. In this section, we evaluate a policy where all credentials pertain to the same organization as it represents the worst case for both metrics.

Policy. We evaluate our work with respect to the policy presented in our previous work [4]. This policy represents a university-wide deployment. In addition to its larger size, this policy has a more complex structure than the policy described in Section 4.1.

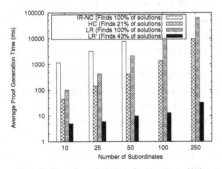

Fig. 9. Proof generation in larger policies

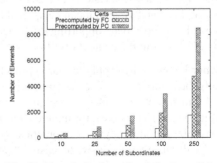

Fig. 10. Knowledge base size in larger policies

For example, the university maintains a certification authority (CA) that binds names to public keys, thus allowing authority to be delegated to a principal's name. Furthermore, many delegations are made to roles (e.g., Dept.Manager1), to which principals are assigned using additional credentials.

We simulate the performance of our approach on this policy from the standpoint of a principal who has access to a resource via a chain of three delegations (assembled from 10 credentials), and wants to extend this authority to a subordinate.

Performance. Figure 9 shows the proof-generation time of the different strategies for different numbers of subordinates on the workstation. For these policies, the depth limit used by IR, IR-NC, and HC must be 10 or greater. However, IR crashed at any depth limit higher than 7, and is therefore not included in these simulations. Simulations on this policy used a depth-limit of 10. IR-NC displays the worst performance on the first three policy sizes, and exhausts available memory and crashes for the two largest policies. HC appears to outperform LR, but, as the legend indicates, was unable to find 11 out of the 14 possible solutions, including several likely completions, the most notable of which is the desired completion Alice **says** (Charlie **speaksfor** Alice. machine-room). This completion is included in the subset of common solutions that LR′ is looking for. This subset constitutes 43% of the total solution space, and LR′ finds all solutions in this subset several orders of magnitude faster than any other strategy.

The size of the knowledge base for each policy is shown in Figure 10. The knowledge base consists of certificates and, under LR and LR′, facts and paths precomputed by FC and PC. We observe that many credentials from the same policy cannot be combined with each other, yielding a knowledge base whose size is approximately linear with respect to the number of credentials.

In summary, the two previous, theoretically complete approaches (IR and IR-NC) are unable to scale to the larger policies. HC, tailored to run on a particular policy, is unable to find a significant number of solutions when used on larger policies. LR is able to scale to larger policies while offering theoretical completeness guarantees. LR′, which is restricted to finding a common subset of solutions, finds all of those solutions dramatically faster than any other approach.

5   Generality of Our Approach

Although we described and evaluated our technique with respect to a particular access-control logic and system, it can be applied to others, as well. There are three aspects of generality to consider: supporting the logical constructs used by other logics, performing efficiently in the context of different systems, and enabling other applications.

Other logics. When applying our approach to other logics, we must consider individually the applicability of each component of our approach: FC, PC, and the generation of LR tactics. We consider our technique with respect to only monotonic authorization logics, i.e., logics where a formula remains provable when given more credentials. This constraint is commonly used in practical systems (cf., [8]).

As discussed previously, to ensure that the forward-chaining component of our prover terminates, the logic on which it is operating should be a subset of Datalog, or, if function symbols are allowed, their use must be constrained (as described in Section 3.1). This is sufficient to express most access-control logics, e.g., the logics of SD3 [17], Cassandra [7], and Binder [11], but is not sufficient to express higher-order logic, and, as such, we cannot fully express the access-control logic presented by Appel and Felten [2]. The general notion of delegation introduced in Definition 1 is conceptually very similar to that of the various logics that encode SPKI [1,19,16], the RT family of logics [20], Binder [11], Placeless Documents [3], and the domain-name service logic of SD3 [17], and so our technique should apply to these logics as well.

Our path-compression algorithm and our method for generating LR tactics assume that any delegation rule has exactly two premises. Several of the logics mentioned above (e.g., [17,11,3]) have rules involving three premises; however, initial investigation suggests that any multi-premise rule may be rewritten as a collection of two-premise rules.

Path compression requires a decidable algorithm for computing the intersection of two permissions. That is, when combining the paths (Alice says F, Bob says F) and (Bob says open(door1), Charlie says open(door1)), we need to determine the intersection of F and open(door1) for the resulting path. For our logic, computing the permission is trivial, since in the most complicated case we unify an uninstantiated formula F with a fully instantiated formula, e.g., open(door1). In some cases, a different algorithm may be appropriate: for SPKI, for example, the algorithm is a type of string intersection [12].

Other systems. Our strategies should be of most benefit in systems where (a) credentials can be created dynamically, (b) credentials are distributed among many parties, (c) long delegation chains exist, and (d) credentials are frequently reused. Delayed backward chaining pursues fewer expensive subgoals, thus improving performance in systems with properties (a) and (b). Long delegation chains (c) can be effectively compressed using either FC (if the result of the compression can be expressed directly in the logic) or PC (when the result cannot be expressed in the logic). FC and PC extend the knowledge base with the results of their computation, thus allowing efficient reuse of the results (d).

These four properties are not unique to our system, and so we expect our technique, or the insights it embodies, will be useful elsewhere. For example, Greenpass [15] allows users to dynamically create credentials. Properties (b) and (c) have been the focus of considerable previous work, notably SPKI [1,19,16], the DNS logic of SD3 [17], RT [20], and Cassandra [7]. Finally, we feel that (d) is common to the vast majority of access-control systems, as a statement of delegation is typically intended to be reused.

Other applications. There are situations beyond our smartphone-oriented setting when it is necessary to efficiently compute similar proofs and where the efficiency offered by our approach is welcome or necessary. For example, user studies conducted at our institution indicated that, independently of the technology used to implement an access-control system, users strongly desired an auditing and credential-creation tool that would allow them to better understand the indirect effects on policy of creating new credentials by giving them real-time feedback as they experimented with hypothetical credentials. If Alice wants to create a new credential K_{Alice} **signed delegate**(Alice, Alice.machine-room, door4), running this hypothetical credential through the path-compression algorithm could inform Alice that an effect of the new credential is that Bob now has access to door4 (i.e., that a path for door4 was created from Bob to Alice). Accomplishing an equivalent objective using IR or IR-NC would involve assuming that everyone is willing to access every resource, and attempting to prove access to every resource in the system—a very inefficient process.

6   Conclusion

In this paper we presented a new approach to generating proofs that accesses comply with access-control policy. Our strategy is targeted for environments in which credentials must be collected from distributed components, perhaps only after users of those components consent to their creation, and our design is informed by such a testbed we have deployed and actively use at our institution. Our technique embodies three contributions, namely: novel approaches for minimizing proof steps that involve remote queries or user interaction; methods for inferring delegation chains off the critical path of accesses that significantly optimize proving at the time of access; and a systematic approach to generating tactics that yield efficient backward chaining. We demonstrated analytically that the proving ability of this technique is strictly superior to previous work, and demonstrated empirically that it is efficient on policies drawn from our deployment and will scale effectively to larger policies. Our method will generalize to other security logics that exhibit the common properties detailed in Section 5.

References

[1] Abadi, M.: On SDSI's linked local name spaces. Journal of Computer Security 6(1-2), 3–21 (1998)
[2] Appel, A.W., Felten, E.W.: Proof-carrying authentication. In: Proceedings of the 6th ACM Conference on Computer and Communications Security, ACM Press, New York (1999)
[3] Balfanz, D., Dean, D., Spreitzer, M.: A security infrastructure for distributed Java applications. In: Proceedings of the 2000 IEEE Symposium on Security & Privacy, IEEE Computer Society Press, Los Alamitos (2000)
[4] Bauer, L., Garriss, S., Reiter, M.K.: Distributed proving in acess-control systems. In: Proceedings of the 2005 IEEE Symposium on Security & Privacy, IEEE Computer Society Press, Los Alamitos (2005)
[5] Bauer, L., Garriss, S., Reiter, M.K.: Efficient proving for practical distributed access-control systems. Technical Report CMU-CyLab-06-015R, Carnegie Mellon University (2007)
[6] Bauer, L., Schneider, M.A., Felten, E.W.: A general and flexible access-control system for the Web. In: Proceedings of the 11th USENIX Security Symposium (2002)
[7] Becker, M., Sewell, P.: Cassandra: Flexible trust management, applied to electronic health records. In: Proceedings of the 17th IEEE Computer Security Foundations Workshop, IEEE Computer Society Press, Los Alamitos (2004)
[8] Blaze, M., Feigenbaum, J., Strauss, M.: Compliance checking in the PolicyMaker trust-management system. In: Hirschfeld, R. (ed.) FC 1998. LNCS, vol. 1465, Springer, Heidelberg (1998)
[9] Burrows, M., Abadi, M., Needham, R.: A logic of authentication. ACM Transactions on Computer Systems 8(1), 18–36 (1990)

[10] Chen, W., Warren, D.S.: Tabled evaluation with delaying for general logic programs. Journal of the ACM 43(1), 20–74 (1996)

[11] DeTreville, J.: Binder, a logic-based security language. In: Proceedings of the 2002 IEEE Symposium on Security and Privacy, IEEE Computer Society Press, Los Alamitos (2002)

[12] Ellison, C.M., Frantz, B., Lampson, B., Rivest, R.L., Thomas, B.M., Ylonen, T.: SPKI Certificate Theory, RFC2693 (1999)

[13] Felty, A.: Implementing tactics and tacticals in a higher-order logic programming language. Journal of Automated Reasoning 11(1), 43–81 (1993)

[14] Garg, D., Pfenning, F.: Non-interference in constructive authorization logic. In: CSFW'06. Proceedings of the 19th Computer Security Foundations Workshop (2006)

[15] Goffee, N.C., Kim, S.H., Smith, S., Taylor, P., Zhao, M., Marchesini, J.: Greenpass: Decentralized, PKI-based authorization for wireless LANs. In: Proceedings of the 3rd Annual PKI Research and Development Workshop (2004)

[16] Halpern, J., van der Meyden, R.: A logic for SDSI's linked local name spaces. Journal of Computer Security 9, 47–74 (2001)

[17] Jim, T.: SD3: A trust management system with certified evaluation. In: Proceedings of the 2001 IEEE Symposium on Security & Privacy, IEEE Computer Society Press, Los Alamitos (2001)

[18] Lampson, B., Abadi, M., Burrows, M., Wobber, E.: Authentication in distributed systems: Theory and practice. ACM Transactions on Computer Systems 10(4), 265–310 (1992)

[19] Li, N., Mitchell, J.C.: Understanding SPKI/SDSI using first-order logic. International Journal of Information Security (2004)

[20] Li, N., Mitchell, J.C., Winsborough, W.H.: Design of a role-based trust management framework. In: Proceedings of the 2002 IEEE Symposium on Security & Privacy, IEEE Computer Society Press, Los Alamitos (2002)

[21] Minami, K., Kotz, D.: Secure context-sensitive authorization. Journal of Pervasive and Mobile Computing 1(1) (2005)

[22] Russell, S., Norvig, P.: Artificial Intelligence, A Modern Approach, 2nd edn. Prentice Hall, Englewood Cliffs (2003)

Maintaining High Performance Communication Under Least Privilege Using Dynamic Perimeter Control*

Paul Z. Kolano

NASA Advanced Supercomputing Division, NASA Ames Research Center
M/S 258-6, Moffett Field, CA 94035 U.S.A.
kolano@nas.nasa.gov

Abstract. From a security standpoint, it is preferable to implement least privilege network security policies in which only the bare minimum of TCP/UDP ports on internal hosts are accessible from outside the perimeter. Unfortunately, organizations with such policies can no longer communicate using common multiport protocols that require randomly chosen ports for auxiliary connections. This paper introduces a new approach for maintaining such communication under least privilege while achieving maximum performance. By dynamically modifying perimeter ACLs, inbound auxiliary connections are only allowed through the perimeter at exactly the times required. These modifications are made transparently to external users and with minimal changes to internal configuration. A prototype implementation of the **D**ynamic **P**erimeter **E**nfo**r**cement system, called Diaper, has been implemented and tested with several applications.

Keywords: Firewalls, grids, high performance networking, multiport protocols, network access control, security.

1 Introduction

A fundamental dictate of computer security is the *Principle of Least Privilege*, which states that "every program and every user of the system should operate using the least set of privileges necessary to complete the job" [28]. In networks, privilege traditionally corresponds to the set of TCP/UDP ports that are allowed to traverse a perimeter established by some form of *perimeter enforcer* such as a firewall or router/switch with access control lists (ACLs). A typical least privilege network policy might contain the rules (1) allow all outbound traffic to non-blacklisted hosts, (2) allow inbound traffic in direct response to established outbound traffic, (3) allow inbound traffic to a small set of well-known server control ports, and (4) deny all other traffic. In this policy, users on external hosts are limited to the least possible set of privileges necessary to provide some predetermined set of capabilities to them. Namely, they are only allowed to initiate connections to the control ports of designated network services, which are already bound, thus cannot be used for any other purpose. Internal users can generate arbitrary outbound traffic to non-blacklisted hosts and receive inbound responses to that traffic, but internal services they start are not directly accessible from beyond the perimeter.

---

* This work is supported by the NASA Advanced Supercomputing Division under Task Order NNA05AC20T (Contract GS-09F-00282) with Advanced Management Technology Inc.

J. Biskup and J. Lopez (Eds.): ESORICS 2007, LNCS 4734, pp. 38–54, 2007.

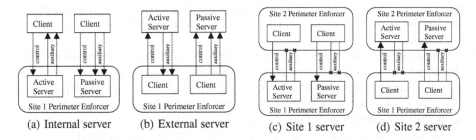

(a) Internal server   (b) External server   (c) Site 1 server   (d) Site 2 server

Fig. 1. Basic multiport service models   **Fig. 2.** Communication breakdown

While such a policy works well for single port protocols such as SSH and HTTP, it breaks down when utilizing multiport protocols. Figure 1 shows the basic multiport protocol models. Each model consists of a client and a server, one of which is inside and one of which is outside the perimeter created by the perimeter enforcer. To request a specific service provided by the server, the client connects to a statically determined *control port* on the server, after which it establishes a set of *auxiliary connections* over dynamically determined ports. Each server is designated as either *active* or *passive*. An active server is one that initiates the auxiliary connections to the client. A passive server is one that listens for the auxiliary connections from the client. While traditionally associated with the FTP protocol, which uses separate control and data channels, these same models are just as applicable to modern protocols for grids, high performance file transfer, voice over IP, multimedia over IP, and other applications.

By default, the least privilege policy above supports the internal active server and external passive server models. Since all inbound auxiliary connections are denied, it does not support the internal passive server or external active server models. Figure 2 shows the breakdown in multiport protocols when two sites both utilize a least privilege policy. As can be seen, it is impossible for the two sites to communicate since the models that are supported by one site are exactly the models not supported by the other.

The easiest solution for many organizations is to permanently open up the perimeter and allow inbound traffic to a subset of unprivileged ports, which can then be used for auxiliary connections. Since these ports are accessible from anywhere, however, it is easier for attackers to hijack or interfere with auxiliary connections. In addition, applications only listen on these ports at specific times related to control port traffic, thus these ports are usually not bound until that time and can be used for other purposes. These may range from running software still under development to running unauthorized services or authorized services with unauthorized versions and/or configurations to Trojans acting without a user's knowledge waiting for malicious connections. The ports associated with these uses are now directly accessible from outside the perimeter and are subject to attack and/or unauthorized utilization.

Several approaches try to resolve this problem without resorting to permanent perimeter openings such as protocol-aware firewalls, routers/switches with network login, specialized proxies, new low-level protocols, etc. These approaches suffer from various drawbacks including the need for changes to client/server software and/or practices, requiring special trust relationships with other entities, substantial degradation of network performance, and inability to handle arbitrary protocols and applications.

This paper presents a new approach for Dynamic Perimeter Enforcement called Diaper, which provides a general-purpose mechanism for maintaining least privilege network security policies while still supporting full utilization of multiport protocols. Diaper protects a site from unauthorized network flows by dynamically applying ACLs on the perimeter enforcer that temporarily allow specific paths through the perimeter at exactly the times required. The appropriate paths and times are derived by observing system calls from within the services that require them. Since Diaper operates at the system call level, it can guarantee that temporary openings cannot be utilized for other purposes since ports are already bound at the time they are allowed through the perimeter. Perimeter openings are only authorized for a single external host, thus making it more difficult to hijack or interfere with auxiliary connections. Diaper requires no changes to software or practices outside of the perimeter, only minimal changes inside, and can be deployed in configurations varying in size from a single host running a software firewall to an organization running multiple hardware perimeter enforcers. Finally, since Diaper utilizes the ACLs of network devices themselves, it does not degrade network performance allowing protocols to operate at the highest speeds possible.

This paper is organized as follows. Section 2 presents related work. Section 3 describes perimeter observation using system call interposition. Section 4 discusses how the perimeter is opened and closed. Section 5 describes implementation and performance. Finally, Section 6 presents conclusions and future work.

2   Related Work

There are a variety of efforts related to the problem addressed by this paper. Stateful firewalls such as Cisco's IOS Firewall [5] can interpret the control channels of specific protocols to determine when an auxiliary port needs to be opened between a given pair of hosts. Only unencrypted protocols can be supported, however, and such support is generally limited to a small set of standardized protocols. To increase support for new protocols, the NAI Labs Wrappers [7] allow system administrators and even users to add custom proxies into the firewall under the supervision of a system call wrapper that prevents subversion of perimeter policy due to bugs or malicious code. This approach does not help with encrypted control channels, however, and is unsuitable for high performance environments since it is deployed on software firewalls.

In general, even hardware stateful firewalls are unsuitable since they are significantly behind the performance curve of routers and switches. For example, the Juniper Netscreen-5400 is one of the few firewalls on the market with 10 gigabit interfaces [16], but only supports 5 Gb/s per interface. The Force10 P10 intrusion prevention appliance [8] operates at 10 Gb/s line-rate, but has no stateful capabilities. The first 10 Gb/s line-rate router, however, was available from Juniper six years earlier [17]. This performance lag is likely to continue as vendors move to 100 Gb/s and beyond.

Routers and switches often support another approach through network login mechanisms such as Cisco's Lock-and-Key [6], where initially all network traffic is denied until users authenticate themselves, after which a static set of ports is opened up from the originating host to internal resources. This approach supports maximum line-rates, but requires users to perform additional authentication and typically opens more ports than needed. Another built-in option is a virtual private network (VPN) [36], where an external host or network can be granted access to the internal network using an authenticated, encrypted connection. VPNs require either special trust relationships set up between organizations or additional steps performed by the user. In addition, the encryption used to guarantee privacy and integrity also degrades performance. For example, the Juniper Netscreen-5400, which is one of the fastest existing VPNs, is only capable of 2.5 Gb/s over each 10 gigabit interface [16].

SOCKS [21] is a protocol that allows clients to traverse firewalls through the use of a proxy server that relays packets from one side of the firewall to the other. SOCKS requires special software to communicate with SOCKS servers and external users must have knowledge of which sites require SOCKS and which do not, which SOCKS server is responsible for each host of a given site, and which set of authentication credentials must be used to access each SOCKS server. In addition, since the SOCKS server must relay every packet, but is not supported in high speed network devices, SOCKS is unsuitable for high performance environments.

Hole punching [9] is a network address translation (NAT) traversal technique where peers behind different NAT firewalls exchange contact information through a well-known rendezvous server and then use a specific series of outbound messages to open inbound paths through the firewall. Hole punching allows high performance communication, but requires special client software, knowledge of which sites utilize the technique and with which rendezvous servers, and a trust relationship with each server.

Many related projects are motivated by the use of grids across organization firewalls. The Globus grid middleware requires a large number of ports to be left open [38], which creates many difficulties behind restrictive firewalls [1]. Hillier proposes the use of a log reader to wait for a successfully authenticated Globus "ping", after which it parses the source host and adds an appropriate rule to the firewall to allow access to a statically-defined range of ports from that host [12]. Dyna-Fire [11] is a dynamic firewall service that allows a host to access specific ports after receiving an appropriate *port knocking* sequence (i.e. a pattern of connection attempts to closed ports). Both of these approaches are essentially network login mechanisms with the same disadvantages.

Condor is another grid middleware that requires many port openings [18]. Dynamic Port Forwarding (DPF) [31] allows services on private internal hosts to lease external IP address/port pairs from a NAT firewall, which are sent to external clients for use in direct connections. Firewall requests are not authenticated, however, and the internal host is opened up to all external hosts. Cooperative On-Demand Opening (CODO) [30] adds more restrictive openings and basic authentication to DPF, but only supports basic multiprocess applications and only when they are recompiled with the CODO library. Generic Connection Brokering (GCB) [31] uses an external proxy to relay packets between external clients and internal servers, with drawbacks similar to SOCKS.

Voice over IP (VoIP) and multimedia over IP (MoIP) also use multiport communication models, thus are difficult to deploy behind firewalls [29]. Many proposed solutions involve adding knowledge of related protocols such as the Session Initiation Protocol

(SIP) into the firewall itself [22]. In the Distributed Dynamic Firewall Architecture [27], control channels are observed by protocol-specific proxies, which direct filters to allow and deny traffic as needed. Fung et al. enhanced SOCKS with additional UDP handling to support the Real-Time Streaming Protocol (RTSP) [10]. These solutions are similar to stateful firewalls with similar drawbacks.

An alternative approach is to let applications themselves control firewall behavior as needed. The Firewall Control Protocol (FCP) [20] was proposed as a standard for firewall query and control by applications that was originally motivated by the difficulties of deploying SIP servers behind firewalls. This approach relies on the standardization of FCP and its acceptance and integration by firewall vendors, however, which is a long-term effort. Universal Plug and Play (UPnP) [23] defines a similar capability in its Internet Gateway Device (IGD) specification, which allows clients to control UPnP-enabled gateways to permit inbound network access when needed. The IGD specification does not define any access control mechanisms, however, thus is only suitable for home networks with minimal security requirements.

The multiport problem is an artifact of basic TCP/UDP design, which only allows a single stream of data per port. Several new protocols such as the Stream Control Transmission Protocol (SCTP) [32] have been proposed to enable multiplexing of many streams into one. These protocols are not widely supported, however, thus cannot be used with existing implementations of software and cannot take advantage of existing higher level protocol support in network devices.

3   Perimeter Observation

Diaper is based on the notion of a *pinhole*, which is a dynamic rule that allows TCP/UDP traffic to pass from a specific external host to a specific port on a specific internal host. The basic approach is to open a pinhole exactly when the external host needs to establish an inbound auxiliary connection and to close that pinhole exactly when the external host no longer needs the connection. By using this approach, sites with least privilege policies can still communicate, but users cannot hijack pinholes for their own purposes because the internal host will already be using the associated ports.

A single pinhole corresponds to a TCP/UDP ACL on a perimeter enforcer, which is defined by the 5-tuple of protocol, source IP address, source port, destination IP address, and destination port. Since pinholes only require basic ACLs, which can be done at line-rate on many network devices, the pinhole approach supports performance at the maximum capacity of the network itself. To successfully implement a pinhole approach, however, it is necessary to accurately determine three key pieces of information: which internal ports will be used for auxiliary connections, when these connections are needed, and which external host will initiate them.

3.1   Observer Location

This information may be observed at various locations in the network. The most appealing location is on the perimeter enforcer, which has access to all network traffic passing between client and server. In this case, all setup is self-contained on the device mediating network traffic. Unfortunately, at this location, every protocol must be handled differently, encrypted protocols cannot be supported at all, and hardware enforcers can only support the limited set of unencrypted protocols implemented by the vendor.

The least desirable observer locations are on the external host and in the external client/server. To open pinholes appropriately, users or software on external hosts must be given the authority to do so, which gives them the capability to change the internal site's network security policy, thus does not conform least privilege. In addition, the security mechanisms are no longer transparent since they require the installation of new software or modifications to the invocation of existing software as well as managing these changes across different sites that may require different configurations.

An observer on the internal host, but not in the internal client/server, requires no external changes and has access to information beyond that of a perimeter observer such as logs generated, kernel structures modified, etc. A log reader approach suffers from imprecision due to the lag between when an activity is performed and when it is logged. A kernel observer could provide the required information, but kernel development is difficult and error-prone and would affect every process on the internal host.

The final alternative is an observer in the internal client/server itself, which has access to detailed information about every aspect of program operation including variables, functions, system calls, etc. Modifying client/server source code is undesirable as different implementations use different programming languages, data structures, naming conventions, error conditions, etc. that must all be handled differently. In addition, these modifications must be kept up-to-date with the latest patches and revisions. Although services may have very different implementations, they are all built on top of the same set of standard system calls. Furthermore, with the advent of *system call interposition* [15], system calls can be changed dynamically on a per application basis without changes to existing code. A set of such system call modifications is known as an *interposition agent*. The application of this technique for the observation of perimeter information is described in the next section.

3.2 Diaper Interposition Agent

All TCP and UDP sessions share the same basic flow of Standard C Library system calls that occur between an initiator and a listener. In a TCP session, both parties create a socket using socket(). The listener binds its socket to a local address and port number using bind() and then indicates its willingness to receive connections on the socket using listen(). The initiator can then connect to the listening address using connect(). When the listener is ready to process inbound connections, it accepts one of the waiting connections using accept(). Finally, the two parties communicate using read() and write(), and at the completion of communication, they close their sockets using close(). UDP sessions are similar, but connectionless, thus after bind(), both parties can immediately send and receive datagrams using sendto() and recvfrom(). Equivalent system calls exist in the Windows Sockets API [24], but will not be discussed further.

In the models of Figure 1, clients and servers can be both initiators as well as listeners and have identical network system call behavior after the establishment of the control channel. Thus, the same Diaper interposition agent can be used to intercept the system calls of internal passive servers as well as internal clients used to connect to external active servers. The agent processes the control channel appropriately based on whether the wrapped application first connects outbound like a client or waits for inbound connections like a server. The combined functionality allows the agent to additionally handle mixed-mode applications, such as Iperf [13], that act as both a client and a server with auxiliary connections in both directions.

The main challenge in observing the required information by intercepting system calls is in grouping together separate unrelated system calls to obtain a complete picture of the information. At the point just after a bind(), it is known in both TCP and UDP sessions that a socket will be used to listen for external connections on a specific port number. This is also when it is safe to open a pinhole to that port since after bind(), a port can no longer be used by any other process on that host. The pinhole can be opened from this time up until just before accept() or recvfrom(), neither of which can succeed unless inbound traffic was already allowed to the port. Diaper opens a pinhole immediately after every bind() on an external interface, as shown in Figure 5, except the first bind() in the internal passive server case as that bind() is used to establish the control channel. The intercepted bind() does not return to the caller until the pinhole has been successfully opened or an error occurs.

To open a pinhole for an auxiliary connection requires knowledge of which external host will initiate a connection, which is not known until an accept() or recvfrom() completes on the same port. Thus, this information can only be obtained by associating the auxiliary connection with a previously established control channel connection for which the external host is already known. For clients, it is assumed that the control channel is established during the first outbound TCP/UDP connection from an unconnected state, thus the external address for subsequent auxiliary connections is obtained from the address in the last successful control channel connect() or sendto(). For servers, it is assumed that the first externally bound TCP/UDP port is the control port, thus the external address is obtained from each accept() or recvfrom() on this port.

The association of auxiliary ports with control ports must be handled differently depending on the concurrency model of the client/server. The three major concurrency models [25] are *multiprocess*, where each connection is managed by a separate process, *multithreaded*, where each connection is managed by a separate thread, and *multiplexed*, where all connections are managed by the same process/thread using non-blocking I/O. Association in the multiprocess model is straightforward as each control connection is managed by a different process that spawns its own auxiliary connection processes. In this case, the external address in auxiliary processes is the address of the host connected to the parent control socket. The multithreaded model is similar with each control connection managed by a different thread that spawns its own auxiliary connection threads. In this case, however, multiple threads may share the same memory space, thus care must be taken to store the control thread IP address in a thread-safe location. The other complication is the existence of multiple thread implementations. Diaper currently supports only POSIX threads. The basic flow of system calls in multiprocess and multithreaded servers is shown in Figure 3. The only difference is the use of pthread_create() instead of fork() and pthread_exit() instead of exit() in the multithreaded model.

The multiplexed model is significantly different. In a multiplexed client/server, poll() and/or select() system calls are used to determine which sockets have data waiting,

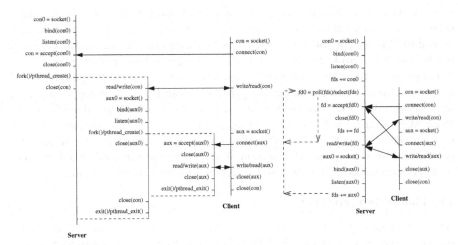

Fig. 3. Multiprocess/multithreaded concurrency   **Fig. 4.** Multiplexed concurrency

thus preventing the single thread of execution from blocking during accept() or read(). Since poll() and select() may return any number of sockets, a multiplexed client/server may handle any number of arbitrarily ordered control and auxiliary connections in a single round of implementation-dependent processing. Diaper manages this complexity by intercepting poll() and select() and artificially limiting the concurrency during each round to a single socket (with starvation prevention using a round robin approach). Since auxiliary connections will only be created when a need for them arises during control channel processing, the external address used to open an auxiliary pinhole can be obtained from the socket that is currently being processed. The basic flow of system calls in multiplexed servers is shown in Figure 4.

The final piece of information needed by the interposition agent is the point at which each auxiliary connection is no longer needed so that the associated pinhole can be closed. The basic approach is to examine each close() system call to determine if it is closing a socket associated with an open pinhole. Care must be taken to avoid closing pinholes prematurely due to duplication of sockets caused by accept() and fork(). A close() on a listening socket that has already been accepted (i.e. not the accepted socket) does not trigger a pinhole close nor does a close() on a listening socket that has not been accepted, but which has been preceded by a fork(). In the latter case, closing the pinhole becomes the responsibility of the child process. Pinholes are also closed in the same manner within exit() and _exit() system calls and within signal handlers.

4   Perimeter Control

Once all of the required information has been observed by the interposition agent and a pinhole request has been generated, that request must be carried out on the perimeter enforcer. The *perimeter controller* is defined to be the system that interacts with the perimeter enforcer to dynamically open and close pinholes upon request. In order to interact with the perimeter enforcer, the perimeter controller may need to be in special proximity to it. For a hardware device such as a switch or router, the controller may need to be on a host attached to the device's management port. For a software enforcer such as Iptables [14], the controller must usually be on the same host. Since network services will be hosted and invoked on potentially many different systems, pinhole requests generated by an interposition agent must be authenticated and sent to the perimeter controller host. After a request reaches the perimeter controller, it is authorized against a set of allowed perimeter changes. Finally, the request is executed by making the appropriate ACL changes on the perimeter enforcer. Figure 5 shows the components of the perimeter controller and the flow through a multiprocess internal passive server. Diaper was designed as a modular collection of servers with unique functions that can be combined or replaced individually with different implementations as desired.

4.1   Pinhole Authentication

When a pinhole request is generated by an interposition agent, it must be sent to the perimeter controller for execution. Before execution, the perimeter controller must verify that the request came from a legitimate source. The component on the perimeter controller that authenticates requests is called the *remote pinhole authentication server*. With the need to support the external active server model, remote authentication becomes subject to a number of complications. In this model, a client running inside the perimeter must request pinholes for auxiliary connections from the external active server. Clients are executed by normal users, but users must not be able to modify the perimeter policy directly. Instead, requests are carried out indirectly on their behalf by a component on the client host called the *local pinhole authentication server*.

Local Authentication. The local authentication server runs with administrator privileges and reads pinhole requests from interposition agents. After a request is received, the local authentication server authenticates to the remote authentication server on the user's behalf, after which the request is passed on for further processing. Users cannot read the remote authentication credentials, thus cannot make direct requests. The local authentication server must also guarantee that only authorized clients in system directories that need pinholes are able to request them and that those clients are not under the control of mechanisms such as LD_PRELOAD or ptrace().

To achieve these goals, authorized clients are wrapped with a simple setuid program. The owner of the wrapper may be any valid user recognized by the local authentication server and is designated as the *local delegate* for that particular client. The wrapper first opens a temporary file descriptor used to communicate with the local authentication server. It then clears unsafe environment variables such as LD_PRELOAD and LD_LIBRARY_PATH and preloads the interposition agent. Finally, the wrapper permanently drops all delegate privileges and executes the original command with the original arguments. The FD_CLOEXEC flag is immediately set on the file descriptor by the agent to prevent abuse by any local shell escapes, etc. that a client may implement. User-level mechanisms for dynamically modifying application behavior are disabled by the kernel since the wrapper is a setuid program.

When a client's interposition agent needs to make a pinhole request, it searches for an open file descriptor not owned by itself. The ability to write to this descriptor provides assurance that the client has been executed by the setuid wrapper. A second descriptor is

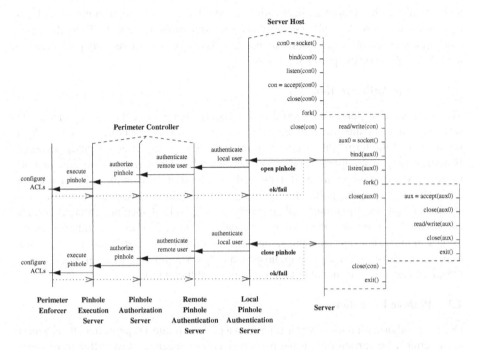

Fig. 5. Diaper event flow in multiprocess internal passive server

opened by the client itself based on a name provided by the local authentication server to obtain the invoking user's identity and prevent replay attacks.

Note that the internal passive server model works similarly, but since servers typically run with elevated privileges to service multiple users, a setuid wrapper is not required. Instead, the interposition agent running in the server intercepts the setuid(), seteuid(), and setreuid() system calls. At this point, before dropping privileges, the appropriate file descriptor is created, after which the same authentication scheme is used.

Remote Authentication. Remote authentication ensures that only legitimate users can access the perimeter controller in order to issue pinhole requests. The actual mechanism used to enforce this policy between the local and remote authentication servers can take any form. In the Diaper implementation, a stock SSH server is used with an extremely restrictive login shell called Mash [19] that does not allow remote delegates to do anything besides issue pinhole requests via a command created for that purpose. Each local authentication server defines a mapping from each of its local delegates to a *remote delegate* known to the remote authentication server for which it possesses authentication credentials. These credentials are then used to transmit locally authenticated requests to the remote authentication server for further processing.

An undesirable, but unavoidable risk of allowing non-interactive requests to the perimeter controller is the need for the remote delegate credentials to be unprotected beyond standard file system discretionary access controls. For instance, an SSH private key cannot be encrypted or else the local authentication server cannot use it to authenticate to the remote authentication server. Thus, a root compromise of a local authentication server host allows the attacker to issue pinhole requests. To mediate this risk, authenticated pinhole requests are first checked against a site security policy before being carried out on the perimeter enforcer.

4.2   Pinhole Authorization

The component responsible for validating authenticated pinhole requests against a site security policy is called the *pinhole authorization server*. A site policy is defined by a set of rules of the form "(allow|deny) <remote delegate> <end user> (tcp|udp) <source IP address range> <source port range> <destination IP address range> <destination port range>". A pinhole is permitted if it allowed by at least one rule in the policy and is not denied by any rule in the policy. Fairly restrictive policies can be imposed by employing service or host specific remote delegates. For example, host specific remote delegates can be used to minimize the damage of local authentication server compromises by using a remote delegate with the same name as each host "$host_i$" and a rule "allow $host_i$ * * * * $host_i$ *". In this setup, hosts can only open pinholes to themselves, thus a breach of one host does not affect the security of all the others.

4.3   Pinhole Execution

Once the authorization server determines that a pinhole request is permitted, that request must actually be carried out on the perimeter enforcer. Since many different requests may be received around the same time, access to the perimeter enforcer must be strictly controlled to avoid interference between requests. The required mutual exclusion and perimeter enforcer interaction is provided by the *pinhole execution server*. This server only accepts requests from root-level processes, such as the authorization server. Requests are processed in batches by a single process as will be described in Section 5.1.

Each pinhole request is translated into an ACL update command on the perimeter enforcer, which varies by the enforcer's type and vendor. Some products have APIs or SNMP-based mechanisms for manipulating the running configuration. Those without such support require scripting of the command-line interface. Diaper currently supports one software enforcer (Iptables) and four classes of hardware enforcers (Cisco IOS devices, Force10 FTOS devices, Foundry IronWare OS devices, and Juniper JunOS devices). Additional enforcer types can be added in a modular fashion.

The pinhole execution server also detects and cleans up stale pinholes, which are those that are no longer needed by any process, but which are still active on the perimeter enforcer. This can occur when a process receives a SIGKILL before it is able to clean up its own pinholes or after a crash of the pinhole execution server itself. A related condition is when the ACL state of the perimeter enforcer does not match that of the pinhole execution server as could potentially occur after a reboot of the perimeter enforcer or a manual update by an administrator. Both of these cases are handled by a periodic status check of the perimeter enforcer's ACLs. Stale pinholes are detected using ACL accounting functionality that counts how many packets have matched a given ACL. A pinhole is considered stale and will be closed if its packet count does not change between two consecutive status calls. Using this approach, Diaper's pinhole state is resilient even across failures and restarts of multiple components.

5   Implementation and Performance

A prototype of Diaper has been fully implemented. The local pinhole authentication server, pinhole authorization server, and pinhole execution server are written in Perl. The remote pinhole authentication server is a stock SSH server. The interposition agent is written in Bypass [33], which is a minimal syntactic wrapper around C/C++ code that isolates the user from differences in system call interfaces and implementations between Unix operating systems. Bypass supports layering of multiple agents, thus using the Diaper agent does not preclude using other agents for other purposes.

Diaper has been fully tested on Linux, but can run on any Unix operating system with a library preload mechanism. The agent is compiled into a shared library, which is loaded into applications by setting the appropriate preload environment variable (e.g. LD_PRELOAD, _RLD_LIST, etc.) before the application is executed. With the exception of POSIX thread support, all of the intercepted system calls are a core part of the Standard C Library, which is linked into almost every application on Unix operating systems, thus Diaper is likely to work correctly with the vast majority of dynamically linked multiport applications without modification. The same approach can also be used on Windows systems by utilizing an equivalent mechanism such as Fault Tolerant Interposition Agents [3]. The Diaper interposition agent is around 1000 lines of Bypass C++ code. The setuid wrapper is about 50 lines of C code.

The test network consisted of an internal host, an external host, and a perimeter controller, each on a 2.4 GHz Pentium 4 Linux box connected by 100 Mb/s Ethernet through three types of perimeter enforcer: Iptables, a Cisco 6500, and a Force10 E600. The least privilege policy of Section 1 was applied to each perimeter enforcer. Raw performance numbers were also gathered for a Foundry MLX-4 and a Juniper MX960.

5.1   Scalability

The main bottleneck in the Diaper architecture is the perimeter enforcer. While the various Diaper servers can be scaled using standard server load balancing techniques, the perimeter enforcer is a unique resource that must be involved in every interaction. The two main scalability measures of a perimeter enforcer are the maximum number of ACLs that can be in effect at any given time without appreciable performance degradation and the maximum rate at which ACLs can be updated.

Hardware enforcers typically have no performance degradation regardless of the number of ACLs in effect due to special Ternary Content Addressable Memory (TCAM) that can perform simultaneous line-rate lookups across the entire ACL space. TCAM is expensive, however, thus, depending on the vendor, is usually limited to somewhere between thousands and tens of thousands of ACL entries per interface. Software enforcers have access to large amounts of cheap memory, thus can theoretically support very large numbers of ACLs. Since standard memory is not optimized for large scale parallel lookups, however, performance degrades significantly as more and more ACLs are applied. Thus, the practical limit for these enforcers is usually between thousands and tens of thousands of ACLs total.

The other limiting factor is the maximum rate at which ACLs can be updated. Figures 6 and 7 show the time required to apply ACLs sequentially and in batches using Iptables,

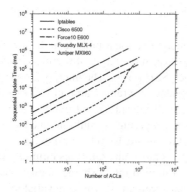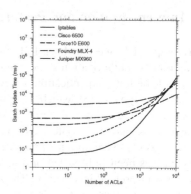

Fig. 6. Sequential update times   **Fig. 7.** Batch update times

a Cisco 6500, a Force10 E600, a Foundry MLX-4, and a Juniper MX960. As can be seen, significant performance gains can be achieved by batching ACL updates together. Figure 8 shows the update rates achieved with different batch sizes when no ACLs are initially in effect. The optimal batch size is approximately 200 for Iptables, 300 for the Cisco 6500, 1000 for the Force10 E600, 5000 for the Foundry MLX-4, and 4200 for the Juniper MX960, achieving effective rates of 10000, 1220, 445, 1070, and 446 updates per second, respectively. The pinhole execution server processes ACLs in batches of the optimal size when at least that many requests are queued, thereby maximizing the update rate. As shown in Figure 9, the maximum achievable rate can only be maintained up to a certain number of existing ACLs before factors such as exhaustion of the TCAM or kernel caches are encountered. The update performance of the Force10 E600 and the Foundry MLX-4 degrades far less dramatically than the others as the number of ACLs in effect increases. The Juniper MX960 has several orders of magnitude more ACL capacity than the others, but is hampered by a slow ACL compilation process. The Foundry MLX-4 has the best overall ACL performance with a high maximum update rate and almost no degradation as existing ACLs increase.

To determine the suitability of Diaper to a particular organization, the ACL characteristics of that organization's perimeter enforcer must be compared to its expected network traffic patterns. Namely, the expected average number of concurrent multiport protocol connections must be less than the ACL capacity of the perimeter enforcer and the initiation/termination rate of those protocols must be less than the maximum update rate achievable with a number of ACLs in effect equal to the average number of connections. To handle bursty traffic where the average number of connections is less than the ACL capacity of the perimeter enforcer, but the maximum number of connections is sometimes greater, the pinhole execution server keeps track of ACL usage and buffers requests until the load returns to normal. If the ACL characteristics of the primary perimeter enforcer are not adequate for the expected traffic, there are still many possible deployment options due to the flexibility of the Diaper architecture.

First, Diaper can be deployed on a per application basis, thus the protocol load may easily be shared with other approaches. For example, a network login capability can be used to offload portions of the traffic such as long running MoIP sessions while Diaper can dynamically control the remaining traffic. Second, Diaper is designed to control

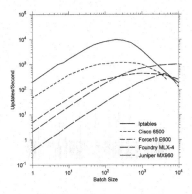

Fig. 8. Batch update rates

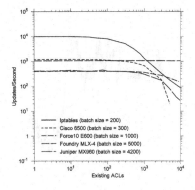

Fig. 9. Update rate degradation

both firewalls as well as core routers and switches with no modifications necessary beyond the perimeter. By deploying multiple perimeter controllers each in charge of a different network device, the natural segmentation of network traffic provided by internal switches and routers can be used to combine the ACL capacities of multiple devices. A similar approach can be used with a sequence of perimeter enforcers on the border. Finally, Diaper is lightweight enough to be deployed on every host in the network that runs its own software enforcer. In this case, the perimeter enforcer, perimeter controller, and internal host are all one and the same. The organization perimeter enforcer can statically allow some subset of traffic to pass through to the end hosts, which themselves can dynamically control which connections they will and will not allow.

As a sanity check for the scalability results, publicly available packet traces of FTP connections to Lawrence Berkeley National Laboratory [26] were analyzed to determine the requirements for a real organization. The traces represent over 22,000 FTP control connections and over 49,000 data connections consisting of more than 3,200,000 packets between 320 unique servers and 5832 unique clients over a 10 day period. Figure 10 shows the number of open FTP data connections over time, which represents the maximum number of perimeter enforcer ACLs required at any given time. Figure 11 shows the ACL updates per second required to open/close the corresponding pinholes. As can be seen, although the traces encompass one of the most prevalent multiport protocols and a fairly large number of hosts and connections, the ACL usage and update rate requirements are very modest and could easily be handled by any of the perimeter enforcers tested. Additional study is needed, however, to assess whether such requirements are typical of all organizations and multiport protocols.

5.2   High Performance File Transfer

Diaper was tested with a variety of high performance file transfer protocols that represent a wide cross-section of existing multiport protocol behavior including TCP and UDP control streams, TCP and UDP data streams, encrypted control streams, multiple data streams, and internal passive/external active server models with multiprocess, multiplexed, and multithreaded concurrency. The applications used for testing include BbFTP [2], BetaFTPD [4], Tsunami [34], UDT [35], Vsftpd (SSL mode) [37], and

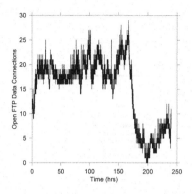

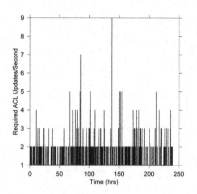

Fig. 10. Open data connections   **Fig. 11.** Required update rate

Wzdftpd [39]. None of the corresponding protocols besides unencrypted FTP (i.e. BetaFTPD and Wzdftpd) are supported by existing firewalls due to either their use of encryption on the control channel or their nonstandard research-oriented nature.

Table 1 shows the overhead in milliseconds introduced by Diaper while transferring a 100 MB file through three types of perimeter enforcer using each of the applications. The overhead was measured against the same transfers through statically authorized ports without the agent wrapper. In these tests, overhead was proportional to the number of ACL updates divided by the ACL update speed of the given perimeter enforcer plus a slight overhead of around 15 ms per update. No benefit was gained from batching in the multiple stream BbFTP case as it binds its auxiliary ports sequentially. Overall, Diaper operated correctly with a variety of protocols with minimal overhead.

Table 1. Diaper overhead (ms) during 100 MB file transfer

Application	Server Model	Control	Data	Concurrency	Iptables	Cisco 6500	Force10 E600
BbFTP (1 stream)	Internal Passive	TCP	TCP	Multiprocess	30.1	61.6	397
BbFTP (2 stream)	Internal Passive	TCP	TCP	Multiprocess	68.4	137	755
BbFTP (4 stream)	Internal Passive	TCP	TCP	Multiprocess	149	293	1570
BbFTP (8 stream)	Internal Passive	TCP	TCP	Multiprocess	400	682	3410
BetaFTPD	Internal Passive	TCP	TCP	Multiplexed	29.8	64.1	373
Tsunami	External Active	TCP	UDP	Multiprocess	29.9	68.3	406
UDT	External Active	UDP	UDP	Multiprocess	29.5	62.9	370
Vsftpd (SSL mode)	Internal Passive	TCP	TCP	Multiprocess	29.4	66.9	406
Wzdftpd	Internal Passive	TCP	TCP	Multithreaded	30.8	68.9	426

6   Conclusions and Future Work

This paper has described a new approach for enabling least privilege network security policies based on **D**ynamic **P**erimeter **E**nforcement called Diaper. Diaper observes the behavior of network services to identify the specific inbound perimeter access that is required at any given time and dynamically adjusts the ACLs of a perimeter enforcer to open and close the perimeter accordingly. It supports inbound access for both clients and servers and is completely transparent to external users. Internal services must be invoked slightly differently, but no source code modifications nor changes to user usage patterns are required. Through the use of the Diaper framework, each site can have the tightest perimeter policy possible and yet still communicate at the highest bandwidth with almost any multiport application.

There are a variety of directions for future research. The ACL characteristics of additional perimeter enforcers will be evaluated and corresponding support added to the pinhole execution server. Scalability analysis will be performed on additional multiport protocols when corresponding packet traces become available. Support for NAT environments and a Windows interposition agent will also be investigated. Alternatives to library preloading will be studied to enable support of static binaries. For deployment in real-world security settings, mechanisms for redundancy and resiliency must be added such as automatic fail-over based on factors including the health of the Diaper servers and the perimeter controller's connectivity to the perimeter enforcer. Finally, additional pinhole authorizations can be added including time-based permissions and dynamic permissions on the pinhole execution server that can, for example, limit the number of pinholes that any one user can have open at once.

References

1. Baker, M., Ong, H., Smith, G.: A Report on Experiences Operating the Globus Toolkit Through a Firewall. Sep. 2001.
2. BbFTP. http://doc.in2p3.fr/bbftp.
3. Benso, A., Chiusano, S., Prinetto, P.: A COTS Wrapping Toolkit for Fault Tolerant Applications Under Windows NT. 6th IEEE Intl. On-Line Testing Wkshp., Jul. 2000.
4. BetaFTPD. http://betaftpd.sourceforge.net.
5. Cisco Systems, Inc.: Cisco IOS Firewall Design Guide. Jan. 2006.
6. Cisco Systems, Inc.: Lock-and-Key: Dynamic Access Lists. Jan. 2005.
7. Epstein, J., Thomas, L., Monteith, E.: Using Operating System Wrappers to Increase the Resiliency of Commercial Firewalls. 16th Annual Computer Security Appl. Conf., Dec. 2000.
8. Force10 Networks, Inc.: Force10 Networks Introduces the Industry's First Line-Rate 10 Gigabit Intrusion Prevention System to Secure High Perf. Networks. Press release, Apr. 2006.
9. Ford, B., Srisuresh, P., Kegel, D.: Peer-to-Peer Communication Across Network Address Translators. USENIX Annual Tech. Conf., Apr. 2005.
10. Fung, K.P., Chang, R.K.C.: A Transport-Level Proxy for Secure Multimedia Streams. IEEE Internet Computing, vol. 4, num. 6, 2000.
11. Green, M.L., Gallo, S.M., Miller, R.: Grid-Enabled Virtual Organization Based Dynamic Firewall. 5th IEEE/ACM Intl. Wkshp. on Grid Computing, Nov. 2004.
12. Hillier, J.: A "Dynamic" Firewall. UK GRID Firewall Wkshp., Dec. 2002.
13. Iperf. http://dast.nlanr.net/Projects/Iperf.
14. Iptables. http://www.netfilter.org.
15. Jones, M.B.: Interposition Agents: Transparently Interposing User Code at the System Interface. 14th ACM Symp. on Operating System Principles, Dec. 1993.
16. Juniper Networks, Inc.: Juniper Networks Enhances and Extends High-End Security Portfolio. Press release, Aug. 2005.
17. Juniper Networks, Inc.: Juniper Networks Ships Full-Performance M160 Router with OC-192c/STM-64 Interfaces. Press release, Mar. 2000.

18. Kewley, J.: Using Condor Effectively in the Presence of Personal Firewalls. Oct. 2004.
19. Kolano, P.Z.: Mesh: Secure, Lightweight Grid Middleware Using Existing SSH Infrastructure. 12th ACM Symp. on Access Control Models and Technologies, Jun. 2007.
20. Kuthan, J.: Internet Telephony Traversal Across Decomposed Firewalls and NATs. 2nd IP Telephony Wkshp., Apr. 2001.
21. Leech, M., Ganis, M., Lee, Y., Kuris, R., Koblas, D., Jones, L.: SOCKS Protocol Version 5. IETF Request for Comments 1928, Mar. 1996.
22. Martin, C., Johnston, A.: SIP Through NAT Enabled Firewall Call Flows. IETF Internet Draft, Aug. 2001.
23. Microsoft Corporation: Understanding Universal Plug and Play. Jun. 2000.
24. Microsoft Corporation: Windows Sockets 2. Mar. 2005.
25. Pai, V.S., Druschel, P., Zwaenepoel, W.: Flash: An Efficient and Portable Web Server. USENIX Annual Tech. Conf., Jun. 1999.
26. Pang, R., Paxson, V.: A High-level Programming Environment for Packet Trace Anonymization and Transformation. 2003 ACM SIGCOMM Conf., Aug. 2003.
27. Roedig, U., Ackermann, R., Rensing, C., Steinmetz, R.: A Distributed Firewall for Multimedia Applications. Wkshp. "Sicherheit in Netzen und Medienstromen", Sep. 2000.
28. Saltzer, J.H., Schroeder, M.D.: The Protection of Information in Computer Systems. Proc. of the IEEE, vol. 63, num. 9, 1975.
29. Shore, M.: H.323 and Firewalls: Problem Statement and Solution Framework. IETF Internet Draft, Feb. 2000.
30. Son. S., Allcock, B., Livny, M.: CODO: Firewall Traversal by Cooperative On-Demand Opening. 14th IEEE Intl. Symp. on High Performance Distributed Computing, Jul. 2005.
31. Son, S., Livny, M.: Recovering Internet Symmetry in Distributed Computing. 3rd Intl. Symp. on Cluster Computing and the Grid, May 2003.
32. Stewart, R., Xie, Q. et al.: Stream Control Transmission Protocol. IETF Request for Comments 2960, Oct. 2000.
33. Thain, D., Livny, M.: Multiple Bypass: Interposition Agents for Distributed Computing. J. Cluster Computing, vol. 4, num. 1, 2001.
34. Tsunami. http://anml.iu.edu/projects.html.
35. UDT. http://sourceforge.net/projects/dataspace.
36. Venkateswaran, R.: Virtual Private Networks. IEEE Potentials, vol. 20, num. 1, 2001.
37. Vsftpd. http://vsftpd.beasts.org.
38. Welch, V.: Globus Toolkit Firewall Requirements. Oct. 2006.
39. Wzdftpd. http://www.wzdftpd.net.

Pragmatic XML Access Control Using Off-the-Shelf RDBMS

Bo Luo, Dongwon Lee, and Peng Liu*

The Pennsylvania State University
{bluo,dongwon,pxl20}@psu.edu

Abstract. As the XML model gets more popular, new needs arise to specify *access control* within XML model. Various XML access control models and enforcement methods have been proposed recently. However, by and large, these approaches either assume the support of security features from XML databases or use proprietary tools outside of databases. Since there are currently few commercial XML databases with such capabilities, the proposed approaches are not yet practical. Therefore, we explore the problem of "Is is possible to fully support XML access control in RDBMS?" We formalize XML and relational access control models using *deep set* operators. Then we show that the problem of XML AC atop RDBMS is amount to the problem of converting XML deep set operators into *equivalent* relational deep set operators. We show the conversion algebra and identify the properties to ensure the correct conversion. Finally, we present three practical implementations of XML access controls using off-the-shelf RDBMS and their performance results.

1 Introduction

The XML model [1] has emerged as the *de facto* standard for storing and exchanging information in the Internet Age. As more information is exchanged over the Web, the issues of security become increasingly important. Such issues span from data level security to network level security to high-level access controls. In this paper, our focus is on how to support *access control* for XML data. Many access control methods extending the XML model to incorporate security aspects have been proposed recently (e.g., [2,3,4,5]). To the lesser or greater extent, however, XML access control enforcement mechanisms proposed in the research community neglect the fact that the most XML data still resides in RDBMS. In the scenario of RDBMS-backed XML database systems (hereafter *XRDB*), XML documents are stored in RDBMS and query-answering is conducted through a conversion layer. In the scenario of XML publishing, relational data is compiled into XML format for distribution and exchange. For both scenarios, we enjoy the benefit of XML model while taking advantage of the maturity of the off-the-shelf RDBMS. In both scenarios, it is desirable to natively specify access controls on the XML side, but they need to be enforced on the

---

* Peng Liu was supported in part by NSF CCR-0233324.

J. Biskup and J. Lopez (Eds.): ESORICS 2007, LNCS 4734, pp. 55–71, 2007.

RDBMS. We believe that current XML access control enforcement mechanism research is in a sense re-inventing wheels without utilizing existing relational access control models or leveraging on security features that are readily available in relational products. In short, our goal in this paper is to answer the question: *When is it (not) possible to support XML access control using RDBMS? Why? How?*

Challenges. First, the major challenges of supporting XML access control in XRDB systems stem from the inherent discrepancy of XML and relational data models. Relational data model features a structure of two-dimensional table, while XML features a hierarchical data model. When XML data are shredded into relational data model, not all transformation algorithms can fully preserve structural properties of XML model [6]. The inherent incompatibility of two data models leads to the fundamental discrepancy between two access control models. Second, relational access control policies define authorized actions of "cells," where each cell is an impartible element and whose accessibility is explicitly expressed. However, XML nodes are hierarchically nested, and XML data model inherently takes "answer by subtree model" (e.g., querying for `//foo` yields the whole subtree rooting at node `<foo/>`). Therefore, for any XML node, an action could be: authorized/unauthorized to the whole subtree, or partially authorized. The later case does not occur in relational access control model. Finally, in XML model, we can control the access right of each individual node. In traditional relational model, the smallest granularity that we may control is a column via GRANT/REVOKE. Therefore, we need to employ more recent developments of RDBMS access controls (e.g., Oracle VPD) to enable cell level access control.

Key contributions. (1) To our best knowledge, this work is the first one to algebraically formalize XML access control in both native XML (XDB) and XRDB environment. (2) This work takes the first steps to define the *equivalent objects* and *equivalent operations* between native XML and XRDB systems. With this concept, we can migrate all the exciting features of native XML systems into XRDB by converting the atomic operations into equivalent relational counterparts. In this paper, we take the feature of fine-grained XML access control for a pilot study, and the results are encouraging. (3) This work shows for the first time that the "security" of XRDB can be achieved by finding the "equivalent" relational operators for three specific deep-set operators. This finding provides a viable way to build secure XRDB systems. (4) Finally, this work proposes several practical approaches to implement the viable way "discovered" by our theory.

2   Related Work

2.1   XML and Relational Access Control

Current access control research can be categorized into two groups: access control modeling and access control enforcement mechanisms.

On the model side, several XML access control models have been proposed. Starting with [7] for HTML documents; [8,3] describes XML access control with

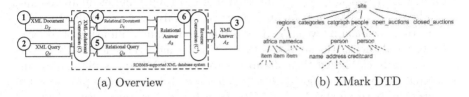

(a) Overview   (b) XMark DTD

Fig. 1. Overview architecture and an example XML schema

an authorization sheet to each document or DTD. [4] proposed and XML access control model to deal with authorization priorities and conflict resolution. [9] introduced provisional authorization and XACL. [10] formalizes the way of specifying *objects* in XML access control using XPath. Most of the proposals adopt either *role-based access control* (e.g. [12]) or *credential-based access control* (e.g. [13]). The major difference between them is the way they identify users. Credential-based access control is more flexible and powerful in this aspect. However, in the research of access control enforcement mechanisms, people tend to choose a relatively simple access control model to avoid distraction.

XML access control enforcement mechanisms in native XML environment have been intensively studied in recent years. They are categorized into four classes: (1) engine level mechanisms implement security check inside XML database engine; each XML node is tagged with a label [15,16,17] or an authorization list [18,19], and filtered during query processing. (2) view based approaches build security views that only contain access-granted data [20,21,22]. [1](3) pre-processing approaches check user queries and enforce access control rules before queries are evaluated, such as the static analysis approach [23,14], QFilter approach [24], access condition table approach [25], policy matching tree[26], secure query rewrite (SQR) approach [27], etc. (4) [28] considers access control of streaming XML data and apply security check at client side, using a filtering mechanism. More recently, [29,30] takes encryption issues into consideration, and [31,32] focus on protecting the privacy and security associated with XML tree structure.

Relational access control models can be classified into two categories: *multilevel security models* [33,34,35] and *discretionary security models (DAC)*. Most real world database systems implement a table/column level DAC similar to the one implemented in System R [36]. View-based approaches is the traditional method to enable row-level access control, while Oracle's VPD is the most recent development. Finally, some advanced access control models (e.g., [37,38]) are proposed in a more theoretical manner.

2.2   XML and Relational Conversion

As illustrated in Figure 1(a), in XRDB: XML data D_X are converted into D_R and stored in RDBMS; user issues XML query Q_X (XPath or XQuery) using

---

[1] When a view-based approach implements virtual views without materializing them, it is inherently a pre-processing approach.

published XML schema; Q_X is converted into Q_R (SQL) and evaluated against D_R; relational answer A_R is finally converted to XML (A_X) to return to user.

Toward conversion between XML and relational models, an array of research has addressed the particular issues lately. On the industry side, database vendors are busily extending their databases to adopt XML types. Shredding and non-shredding are two major pathes that followed by commercial products. Oracle provides both un-shredded (CLOB) and shredded storage options [40]. Microsoft supports XML shredding and publishing through mid-tier approach in SQL Server 2000, and adds CLOB storage in SQL Server 2005 [41]. IBM proposes the first native XML storage in DB2 9, but shredded XML storage (through schema decomposition) is still kept as an important feature [42,43]. On the research side, various proposals have been made recently, mainly either schema-based (e.g., [44,45,46]) or schema-oblivious (e.g., [47,48]) approaches.

In terms of access control, some commercial products apply existing column level access control of RDBMS on XML data stored in CLOB columns. None of these approaches supports or discusses fine-grained access control. Finally, to our best knowledge, the only work that is directly relevant to our proposal is [5]. [5] proposes an idea of using RDBMS to handle XML access controls, in a rather limited setting. In our vision paper [49], we addressed some issues and challenges of enforcing XML access control atop RDBMS. We provide the algebraic analysis and explore practical solutions in this paper.

Our framework is not tied to a particular conversion method. Throughout this paper, we use shared-inlining [45] and XRel [48] as the examples of schema-based and schema-oblivious conversion methods, respectively. Briefly, XRel decomposes XML documents into document, element, attribute, text, and path tables. In this approach, each node is stored as one record in the element table, and each distinct path is stored as one record in the pth table. As a simple example, we decompose an XMark ([50], Figure 1(b)) document using XRel and show part of element table in Figure 2 (b). As we can see, element 252 is a node of path 164 ("/site/people", as stored in the path table); which starts from offset 33996 (byte) and ends at 36229 in the original XML document.

3   Preliminaries

3.1   XML Access Control Policy

Access control models define the semantics and syntax of access control policies. Although they could be very complicated, the essential is to describe *subjects*, *objects*, *actions* and all the variations around it. Fortunately, there is no discrepancy in identifying *subjects* and defining *actions* in XML and relational environment, e.g., they both could adopt RBAC or CBAC to identify users. As we described in Section 1, shredding XML access control models into relational ones is a challenging task, because of the fundamental discrepancies of XML and Relational data models. Therefore, challenges reside in *object*-related components of access control models, while issues that only relate to *subjects* and *actions* are trivial. Thus, our subsequent discussion focuses more on *object* part.

In this paper, we adopt the model proposed in [3] as the basis; other models like [23,28,24,51] can be used as well with a reasonable change.

Definition 1 (XML Access Control Rule) . *An XML access control policy is specified by a set of* **access control rules**: $R_X = \{\textbf{subject}, \textbf{object}, \textbf{action}, \textbf{sign}\}$, *where subject is to whom an authorization is granted, object is a set of XML nodes (in XPath) to which the policy is applied, action is one of read, write, or update, and sign* $\in \{+, -\}$ *refers to access granted or denied, respectively.* □

In this model, access is prohibited by default. Negative rule takes precedence when it conflicts with positive rules. All access controls propagate to the entire subtree rooting at *object*, complying with the answer-by-tree XML semantics. If a rule applies to context node only, we add "/text()" to its *object* field.

3.2 XML to Relational Conversion

Remark 1. *A relational to XML conversion method contains: (1)* $C_D()$ *to convert XML to relational data, (2)* $C_Q()$ *to convert XML query (XQuery or XPath) to SQL, and (3)* C^{-1} *to convert relational answer back to XML.* □

That is, $Q_R = C_Q(Q_X)$, $D_R = C_D(D_X)$, and $A_X = C^{-1}(A_R)$. From this, the process of "evaluating XML query on XRDB" can be modeled as:

$$A_X = C^{-1}(A_R) = C^{-1}(Q_R\langle D_R\rangle) = C^{-1}(C_Q(Q_X)\langle C_D(D_X)\rangle) \qquad (1)$$

Remark 2 . *An X2R conversion algorithm is lossless iff: (1) (lossless node conversion)* $\forall$ *XML node* x_i, $C_D^{-1}(C_D(x_i)) = x_i$; *(2) (lossless node set decomposition)* $\forall$ *XML node set* $\{x_1, ..., x_n\}$, $C_D^{-1}(C_D(\{x_1, ...x_n\})) = C_D^{-1}(\{C_D(x_1), ...C_D(x_n)\}) = \{C_D^{-1}(C_D(x_1)), ...C_D^{-1}(C_D(x_n))\}$; *and (3) (exclusive conversion)* $C_D(x_1) = C_D(x_2)$ *only when* $x_1 = x_2$, *and* $C_D^{-1}(r_1) = C_D^{-1}(r_2)$ *only when* $r_1 = r_2$. □

Remark 3 . *An X2R conversion algorithm is correct iff:* $\forall$ *query* Q *and* $\forall$ *document* X, $Q\langle X\rangle = C^{-1}(Q_R\langle D_R\rangle) = C^{-1}(C_Q(Q_X)\langle C_D(X)\rangle)$. □

Definition 2 (Soundness) . *An X2R conversion algorithm A is* **sound** *iff it is lossless and correct.* □

In the remainder of the paper, we assume that the conversion algorithm being used is *sound*. We ignore the order of XML nodes when we compare the correctness, since this feature is not supported in most X2R conversion algorithms.

In the research community, most X2R conversion algorithms support a subset of XQuery/XPath (e.g., /, //, * and predicates). Our approach does not alter the query or data conversion algorithm. Therefore, for a particular X2R conversion method X, we support everything that X supports. For ease of understanding, we do not use predicates in the examples, however, we test queries with predicates in our experiments.

3.3 Deep Set Operators

In [52], we propose deep set operators for XML, as extensions of conventional set operators defined in XPath [53] and XQuery [54]. Here, we briefly revisit them, and later demonstrate how they are used to formalize XML access control.

Definition 3 (deep set operators). *The* deep-union *operator* $(\overset{D}{\cup})$ *takes node sequences* $\langle P \rangle$ *and* $\langle Q \rangle$ *as operands, and returns a sequence of nodes (1) who exist as a node or as a descendant in* **either** *operand sequences, and (2) whose parent does not satisfy (1). Formally,* $\langle P \rangle \overset{D}{\cup} \langle Q \rangle = \{n | (n \in \langle P_d \rangle \vee n \in \langle Q_d \rangle) \wedge (n :: parent() \notin \langle P_d \rangle \wedge n :: parent() \notin \langle Q_d \rangle)\}$ *where* $P_d = P/descendant - or - self()$. *The* deep-intersect *operator* $(\overset{D}{\cap})$ *takes node sequences* $\langle P \rangle$ *and* $\langle Q \rangle$ *as operands, returns a sequence of nodes (1) who exist as a node or as a descendant in* **both** *operand sequences, and (2) whose parent does not satisfy (1). Formally,* $\langle P \rangle \overset{D}{\cap} \langle Q \rangle = \{n | (n \in \langle P_d \rangle \wedge n \in \langle Q_d \rangle) \wedge (n :: parent() \notin \langle P_d \rangle \vee n :: parent() \notin \langle Q_d \rangle)\}$. *Finally, the* deep-except *operator* $(\overset{D}{-})$ *takes node sequences* $\langle P \rangle$ *and* $\langle Q \rangle$ *as operands, for each node* $\langle p_i \rangle$ *in* $\langle P \rangle$, *it remove* $\langle p_i \rangle \overset{D}{\cap}_X \langle Q \rangle$ *from the subtree of* $\langle p_i \rangle$ *and return the remaining.* $\qquad\square$

3.4 XML Access Control in XDB and XRDB

XML access control is to ensure that only *safe answer* (SA) is returned. As in [55,52], safe answer of Q includes all the XML nodes n such that: (1) $n \in \langle Q \rangle$, (2) the access of n is granted by positive rules, and (3) the access of n is *not* denied by negative rules. Therefore, the precise semantics of "safe answer," SA_X is:

$$SA_X = \langle Q_X \rangle \overset{D}{\cap}_X [(\langle R^+_{X_1} \rangle \overset{D}{\cup}_X ... \overset{D}{\cup}_X \langle R^+_{X_n} \rangle) \overset{D}{-}_X (\langle R^-_{X_1} \rangle \overset{D}{\cup}_X ... \overset{D}{\cup}_X \langle R^-_{X_m} \rangle)] \, (2)$$

Equation (1) models XML query evaluation in XRDB. Similarly, (2) models how only safe XML answers, SA_X, are returned. Combine them, we have:

Definition 4 (Secure XRDB). *An XRDB is secure iff* $\forall$ *ACR set* ACR_X *and* $\forall$ *query* Q_X, *it always returns the safe answer:* $A_X \equiv SA_X$. *Therefore,*

$$C^{-1}(\{C_Q(Q_X)\langle C_D(D_X)\rangle\}') \equiv \langle Q_X \rangle \overset{D}{\cap}_X [(\langle R^+_{X1} \rangle \overset{D}{\cup}_X ...) \overset{D}{-}_X (\langle R^-_{X1} \rangle \overset{D}{\cup}_X ...)] \, (3)$$
$$\square$$

Note that $\{C_Q(Q_X)\langle C_D(D_X)\rangle\}'$ indicates that access control mechanism intervenes in relational query processing. Our goal in this paper is to enforce XML access controls on RDBMS so that Equation 3 holds in *XRDB* setting. In this way, we need to convert *access control rules* R_X and *deep set operators* into their *equivalent* relational counterpart.

```
1. {user, /site/people/person, read, +}          SELECT e0.DOCID, e0.ELEMENTID, e0.PATHID, e0.ST, e0.ED
2. {user, /site/people/person/credicard, read, -} FROM document d, element e0, pth p0
                                                  WHERE p0.pathexp LIKE '#%/people'
                   (a)                            AND e0.pathid = p0.pathid AND d.docid = e0.docid
                                                                        (c)
```

DOCID	ELEMENTID	PATHID	ST	ED	
0	252	164	33996	36229	\<people\>
0	293	165	35592	35826	\<person\>
0	299	165	35832	36217	\<person\>
0	303	188	35989	36032	\<creditcard\>

```
                   (b)
```
```
SELECT e0.DOCID, e0.ELEMENTID, e0.PATHID, e0.ST, e0.ED
FROM document d, element e0, pth p0
WHERE p0.pathexp LIKE '#%/people#/person'
AND e0.pathid = p0.pathid AND d.docid = e0.docid
                   (d)
```

Fig. 2. Naive enforcement of "equivalent" relational ACR leads to wrong answer

4 XML Access Control in XRDB: The Theory

All entities of the 4-tuple XML access control model, except *object*, can be directly adopted to relational access control model. We apply an X2R algorithm $C(R_X.object)$ to get $R_R.object$. Therefore, we get "equivalent" relational ACR:

$$R_R = \{R_X.subject, C(R_X.object), R_X.action, R_X.sign\}$$

However, naive enforcement of the converted relational access control rules may lead to security leakage, as demonstrated in the following example:

Example 1. Consider two rules of Fig. 2(a) with XRDB(XRel) – an XRDB employing XRel [48] as the conversion algorithm. The "element" table is partly shown in Fig. 2(b). Rule 1 indicates that a user is allowed to access \<person\> nodes, i.e., nodes 293 and 299 (record 2 and 3 in Fig. 2 (b)), and rule 2 indicates that a user cannot access \<credicard\> nodes, i.e., node 303. Naive enforcement will grant access to the record 2, 3; and revoke the access to record 4.

Query "//people" is desired to yield an answer containing two \<person\> nodes, since they are the accessible descendants of the requested node. However, the converted SQL query (Fig. 2(c)) yields no answer since access to record 1 is prohibited by default. Moreover, for a query "//person", the converted SQL (Fig. 2(d)) returns both \<person\> nodes to the user (with the unauthorized \<creditcard\> node). This is so because both records of element 293 and 299 are accessible, while revoking access to element 303 does not affect its ancestor.□

4.1 Object and Operation Equivalency

To solve the problem illustrated in Example 1, we propose our framework of supporting access control in XRDB systems. First, we define object and operation equivalency between XML and relational.

Definition 5 (Object Equivalency). *When both $R = C(X)$ and $X = C^{-1}(R)$ hold for XML node set X and relation R, we consider X and R equivalent w.r.t. C/C^{-1}, and denote as $X \equiv R$.* □

Note that, when we talk about equivalency of X and R, we have to predefine the context, i.e., select the X2R conversion algorithm C/C^{-1}. For a XML node set X, $C(X)$ may be different under different X2R conversion algorithms.

Definition 6 (Operation Equivalency). *Suppose $X_1 \equiv R_1$ and $X_2 \equiv R_2$ w.r.t. C/C^{-1}. Then, an XML operation OP_X is equivalent to a relational operation OP_R (denoted as $OP_X \equiv OP_R$) w.r.t. C and C^{-1} if:*

$$C(X_1 \ OP_X \ X_2) = C(X_1) \ OP_R \ C(X_2) = R_1 \ OP_R \ R_2 \qquad \square$$

Note that XML operator takes node sets as operands while its equivalent relational counterpart may not take two generic relations as operands. Each operand is the equivalent objects of corresponding XML node set, which may be tables, columns, records, etc. Relational operations require operands to be domain compatible (e.g., intersect, union etc.). We loosen this requirement for OP_R.

With the concept of operation equivalency, we can migrate all the exciting features of XML into XRDB by converting the atomic operations into equivalent relational operation. Our secure XRDB problem is articulated as follows:

Lemma 1. *In XRDB(C), if we can find relational operators, $\overset{D}{\cup}_R$, $\overset{D}{\cap}_R$, and $\overset{D}{-}_R$, which are equivalent to XML deep set operators, $\overset{D}{\cup}_X$, $\overset{D}{\cap}_X$, and $\overset{D}{-}_X$, w.r.t. the X2R conversion algorithm C, we are able to enforce XML access control in XRDB(C) such that Equation (3) always holds.* ∎

Please refer to [56] for detailed proof. Now we need to find equivalent operations such that $\overset{D}{\cup}_R \equiv \overset{D}{\cup}_X$, $\overset{D}{\cap}_R \equiv \overset{D}{\cap}_X$ and $\overset{D}{-}_R \equiv \overset{D}{-}_X$. Again, equivalency is based on specific X2R conversion method, therefore, the existence and representation of relational deep set operators also depends on the particular X2R conversion. Hereafter, we analyze the role of each deep set operator in (2) and the existence of its equivalent relational counterpart under different X2R conversion algorithms.

4.2   On Equivalent Conversion of Deep Set Operators

Deep-union operator is used to integrate all the accessible nodes defined by individual positive rules (also, all the inaccessible nodes defined by negative rules). With the property $P \overset{D}{\cup} Q \subseteq P \cup Q$ [52], Remark 1 is rewritten into:

$$\langle P \rangle \overset{D}{\cup}_X \langle Q \rangle = \{n | (n \in \langle P \rangle \vee n \in \langle Q \rangle) \wedge (n \notin \langle P//* \rangle \wedge n \notin \langle Q//* \rangle)\} \quad (4)$$

Let $r = C(n)$. When C/C^{-1} is sound according to Definition 2, we have:

$$C(\langle P \rangle \overset{D}{\cup}_X \langle Q \rangle) = \{r | [r \in C(\langle P \rangle) \vee r \in C(\langle Q \rangle)] \wedge [r \notin C(\langle P//* \rangle) \wedge r \notin C(\langle Q//* \rangle)]\}$$

Here, since we are to find $\overset{D}{\cup}_R$ such that $C(\langle P \rangle) \overset{D}{\cup}_R C(\langle Q \rangle) = C(\langle P \rangle \overset{D}{\cup}_X \langle Q \rangle)$:

$$C(\langle P \rangle) \overset{D}{\cup}_R C(\langle Q \rangle) = \{r | [r \in C(\langle P \rangle) \vee r \in C(\langle Q \rangle)] \wedge [r \notin C(\langle P//* \rangle) \wedge r \notin C(\langle Q//* \rangle)]\}$$

The condition of $[r \in C(\langle P \rangle) \vee r \in C(\langle Q \rangle)]$ is essentially the regular union. It is composed by set containment and Boolean operations. In XRDB, set containment check is supported when the soundness requirement in Definition 2 is fulfilled, and Boolean operation is generally supported in RDBMS. $[r \notin C(\langle P//* \rangle)$

$\wedge\ r \notin C(\langle Q//*\rangle)]$ tends to support deep semantics. It requires XRDB to be able to identify if $r \in C(\langle P//*\rangle)$ for any given relational object r and set $C(\langle P\rangle)$.

Lemma 2. *To implement deep-union operator in XRDB(C), the X2R conversion algorithm C should: (1) fulfil the soundness requirement stated in Definition 2; and (2) for given node n and node set $\langle P\rangle$, it should be able to check the containment condition of: $C(n) \in C(\langle P//*\rangle)$, e.g., it should recognize if $C(n)$ is a descendant of any node $C(p_i)$;*   ∎

At present, all X2R conversion algorithms (we are aware of) fulfill Lemma 2.

Deep-intersect operator is used to calculate the exact overlapping of queried data and accessible data (i.e. $\langle Q\rangle$ and $\langle ACR\rangle$). It is defined as:

$$C(\langle P\rangle \overset{D}{\cap}_X \langle Q\rangle) = \{r|[r \in C(\langle P\rangle) \wedge\ r \in C(\langle Q\rangle)]\ \wedge [r \notin C(\langle P//*\rangle) \vee r \notin C(\langle Q//*\rangle)]\}$$
(5)

Compare with 4, they only differ in logical operators. Therefore, Lemma 2 could be directly extended to deep-intersect.

Example 2. In Example 1, a query "//people" yields <people> nodes, i.e. element 252, (record 1 in Fig. 2 (b)). Meanwhile, *object* field of access control rule 1, "/site/people/person", yields <person> nodes, i.e. element 293 and 299 (record 2 and 3 in Fig. 2 (b). In XRel, each XML node is marked with "*start*" and "*end*" offset. Node containment is checked through comparison of the offsets: for nodes p_1 and p_2, if $(p_1.start < p_2.start)$ and $(p_1.end > p_2.end)$, p_2 is an descendant of p_1. Here, we can tell that node 293 and 299 are descendants of node 292. Therefore, "//people $\overset{D}{\cap}_X$ //person" yields node 293 and 299. Comparing with Example 1, "//people ∩ //person" yields *Null*.   □

The operands of XML deep-union/intersect operators may contain different nodes. In RDBMS, where domain compatibility is strictly enforced, their relational equivalent counterpart might be domain incompatible (e.g. a row "intersect" a cell). This happens in schema-based X2R conversion (e.g. [44,45]), where different XML nodes could be converted to tables, rows, etc. To tackle this problem, we employ new RDBMS techniques, e.g. Oracle VPD, to enable fine-control of relational tables to create relational views with any group of cells.

Deep-except is used to remove inaccessible nodes from the answer. Recall that, in our XML access control model, all nodes are inaccessible by default. When a user is prohibited to access a node, there is no need to write a negative rule to revoke accessibility unless the node is covered by positive rules (ACR^+). Thus, negative rules are only used to specify exceptions to global permissions, i.e. "revoke" access granted by ACR^+. Deep except operator is used to enforce negative rules. Regarding whether deep except could be implemented in XRDB with X2R conversion algorithm, it depends upon the characteristics of specific negative rule. In particular, we distinguish two types of negative rules:

Definition 7 (Node elimination vs. Descendant elimination rules). *A negative rule in ACR restricts user from access a set of nodes $\{r_1^-,...r_n^-\}$. If* **none** *of the nodes is a descendant of the context node of a positive rule, i.e.:*

$$r_i^- \notin \langle R^+//* \rangle, \quad \forall r_i^- \in \{r_1^-,...r_n^-\}; \forall \langle R^+ \rangle \in \langle ACR^+ \rangle$$

then it is called a **node elimination (NE)** *negative rule. Else, if one of the nodes is a descendant of the context node of a positive rule, i.e.:*

$$r_i^- \in \langle R^+//* \rangle, \quad \exists r_i^- \in \{r_1^-,...r_n^-\}; \exists \langle R^+ \rangle \in \langle ACR^+ \rangle$$

it is called a **descendant elimination (DE)** *negative rule.* □

Intuitively, *"Node Elimination"* negative rule removes context node from $\langle ACR^+ \rangle$. For XML nodes covered by node elimination negative rules $\langle ACR_1^- \rangle$, deep-except operator directly removes them from $\langle ACR^+ \rangle$:

$$\langle ACR^+ \rangle \overset{D}{-}_X \langle ACR_1^- \rangle = \{n | n \in \langle ACR^+ \rangle \wedge n \notin \langle ACR_1^- \rangle\}$$

Essentially, this is the regular except semantics. In this way, in XRDB, we have,

$$C(\langle ACR^+ \rangle) \overset{D}{-}_R C(\langle ACR_1^- \rangle) = \{r | r \in C(\langle ACR^+ \rangle) \wedge r \notin C(\langle ACR_1^- \rangle)\}$$

To support deep except operator for node elimination negative rules only, the conditions described in Lemma 2 still apply.

On the other hand, *"Descendant Elimination"* negative rule removes descendants from context node of $\langle ACR^+ \rangle$. It takes more burden to process descendant elimination negative rules, where real "deep" semantics is required. That is,

$$\langle ACR^+ \rangle \overset{D}{-}_X \langle ACR_2^- \rangle = \{deepRemove(n, n \overset{D}{\cap}_X \langle ACR_2^- \rangle) | n \in \langle ACR^+ \rangle\}$$

where $deepRemove(p, \langle Q \rangle)$ takes a node and a set of its descendants as operands, removes the descendants from the subtree of the node and return the remaining. This function may not be directly converted to relational.

Lemma 3. *When deep-except operator takes node specified by descendant elimination negative rules as the second operand, it is implemented through deepRemove() operation. To implement deep-except operator that supports descendant elimination negative rules in XRDB(C), the X2R conversion algorithm X should: (1) fully satisfy Lemma 2; and (2) for any node n_1 and its descendant n_2, $C(n_2)$ should be part of $C(n_1)$; and in the reverse conversion of $n_1 = C^{-1}(C(n_1))$, node n_2 in the subtree is entirely converted from $C(n_2)$.* ∎

Example 3. For instance, in Example 1, Rule 2 is a descendant elimination negative rule since it revoke access towards descendants of node (<person>).

In XRDB(XRel) [48], descendants are converted to independent records that are stand alone from ancestors. As shown in Fig. 2(b), to reconstruct a <person> node, $C_{XRel}^{-1}()$ only takes record 2 to reconstruct a full node. The descendant

<creditcard> is included in the answer, but the record 4 is not touched by $C_{XRel}^{-1}()$. Therefore, XRel violates condition (2) of Lemma 3, so that we cannot directly implement deep-except operator to support descendant elimination rules. When user requests for "//person", we are not able to revoke access towards <creditcard> child from RDBMS side.

In Shared-Inlining [45] approach, <person> nodes are translated into a table, and <creditcard> nodes take a column. The relational schema is [57]:

```
Person(Id, ParentId, Person, Person_address, Person_address_city, ...
..., Person_address_zipcode, Person_creditcard, ......)
```

Here, the ancestor-descendant relationship is kept such that each row represents a "person" node, and each cell represents a child node. Therefore, to obtain //person$-_X^D$//creditcard, we just mask "person_creditcard" column in the table; and the reconstructed XML tree of "person" node will not have corresponding child, i.e., "creditcard" node is removed from the XML answer.   □

5   XML Access Control Enforcement in XRDB

Figures 3 shows a general framework for XML access control in XDB and XRDB. There are three categories of XML access control enforcement mechanisms: (1) view-based approach (① ④ in Fig. 3); (2) pre-processing approach (② ⑤ in Fig. 3); and (3) post-processing approach (③ ⑥ in Fig. 3). In this section, we articulate the algebra of these approaches using deep set operators.

5.1   View-Based Approach

When access control is first enforced on XML documents to create *views*, it is the traditional view-based approach. In this model, XML view V_X (or *safe document SD*) is constructed, and query is evaluated against the view

$$SA = Q\langle V_X \rangle = Q[(\langle R_{X1}^+ \rangle \overset{D}{\cup}_X ... \overset{D}{\cup}_X \langle R_n^+ \rangle) \overset{D}{-}_X (\langle R_1^- \rangle \overset{D}{\cup}_X ... \overset{D}{\cup}_X \langle R_m^- \rangle)]$$

Fig. 3. Access control enforcement approaches in XML DB and XRDB

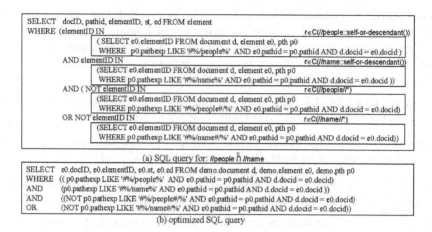

Fig. 4. Enforcing XML access control via external pre-processing

To convert this approach into XRDB, we can either convert XML view into relational view, as shown in ① of Figure 3; or construct relational view using converted relational ACR, ④ of Figure 3. They are formalized as:

$$SA = C^{-1}(Q_R\langle V_R\rangle) = C^{-1}(Q_R\langle C(V_X)\rangle) \tag{6}$$

$$\text{and} \qquad SA = C^{-1}(Q\langle V_R\rangle) = C^{-1}(Q\langle C(ACR_X)\langle D_R\rangle\rangle) \tag{7}$$

5.2 Pre-processing Approach

In preprocessing model, *safe query SQ* is constructed as:

$$SQ_X = Q_X \stackrel{D}{\cap}_X [(\ R_{X1}^+ \stackrel{D}{\cup}_X ... \stackrel{D}{\cup}_X\ R_{Xn}^+) \stackrel{D}{-}_X\ (R_{X1}^- \stackrel{D}{\cup}_X ... \stackrel{D}{\cup}_X R_{Xm}^-)]$$

Safe answer is yielded by evaluating safe query against the original document: $SA_X = SQ_X\langle D_X\rangle$. To extend this approach to XRDB, we have: (1) XML Query Rewriting: as shown in ② in Fig. 3, we convert the safe XML query into SQL, and answer it with regular XRDB; and (2) Relational Query Rewriting: as shown in ⑤ in Fig. 3, we convert original Q_X into SQL Q_R. and then we rewrite it into safe query SQ_R. They are formalized as

$$SA_X = C^{-1}(SQ_R\langle D_R\rangle) = C^{-1}(C(SQ_X)\langle D_R\rangle) \tag{8}$$

$$\text{and} \qquad SQ_R = Q_R \stackrel{D}{\cap}_R [(\ R_{R1}^+ \stackrel{D}{\cup}_R ... \stackrel{D}{\cup}_R\ R_{Rn}^+) \stackrel{D}{-}_X\ (R_{R1}^- \stackrel{D}{\cup}_X ... \stackrel{D}{\cup}_X R_{Rm}^-)] \tag{9}$$

Example 4. Let use revisit the previous examples: we manage XMark document in XRDB(XRel). Suppose we have access control rule ⟨user, //people, read, +⟩, and user submits query //name. Figure 4(a) shows the relational query for $C(//people) \stackrel{D}{\cap}_R C(//name)$, which is implemented according to the definition in Equation 5 (we marked up all the sub-queries). Moreover, this query could be further optimized, as shown in Figure 4(b). □

Another method is to use Oracle VPD. Oracle version 8.1.5 introduces a new security feature supporting non-view-based fine-grained access control, namely *Row Level Security* or *Virtual Private Database*. It allows users to control accessibility towards row/cell level. With VPD, we are able to tailor relational data into any shape we want. To utilize VPD for access control in XRDB, we first construct relational predicates from the converted relational access control rules ACR_R, then define a VPD policy to enforce the predicates on converted SQL queries. Moreover, cell level access control capability of VPD is of special importance to XRDB systems that use schema-based X2R conversion algorithm, such as Inlining. In those XRDB systems, XML nodes are converted to different types of relational objects: tables, rows and cells. In this way, $\langle ACR \rangle$ may not be conventional relations, e.g. it could be arbitrary combinations of columns, rows and/or individual cells.

5.3 Post-processing Based Approach

In native XML DB, access control through post-processing described as:

$$SA_X = ACR\langle A_X \rangle = ACR\langle Q_X \langle D_X \rangle \rangle$$

In XRDB, this approach could be conducted through: (1) XML answer filtering (③ in Fig. 3); or (2) relational answer filtering (⑥ in Fig. 3). (1) is similar to the postprocessing approach in [55], while (2) evaluates relational query Q_R to obtain unsafe relational answer, and process ACR_R against the answers:

$$SA_X = C^{-1}(SA_R) = C^{-1}(ACR_R\langle A_R \rangle) = C^{-1}(ACR_R\langle Q_R \langle D_R \rangle \rangle)$$

However, the post-processing filters require the intermediate answers ($\langle A_R \rangle$ or $\langle A_X \rangle$) to retain information of the original paths for ACR to operate on. As an example of this approach, [28] check streaming XML data against both query and ACR at the same time. Since it works in the streaming data environment, full paths are retained. However, in most X2R conversion algorithms, the intermediate answer A_R or A_X does not contain full path information. Therefore, postprocessing approaches are not suitable for all applications.

6 Experimental Validation

To show that the proposed theory and implementations are practical yet efficient, we show our preliminary experimental results.

An XML document with 8517 nodes are generated by XMark [50]. We use XRDB(XRel) [48], with Oracle 10g as underlying RDBMS. We design five roles, abbreviated as A (administrator), M, RU, S and U, respectively. We do not have any descendant elimination negative rules since XRDB(XRel) cannot directly handle it (Lemma 3. We generate four groups of synthetic XPath queries, each has a different setting of wildcards and predicates.

In the XRDB(XRel), we convert all rules into relational, and enforce them through views and VPD. For a comparison, we also enforce same rule sets on the same XML document in native XML environment. We enforce XML access

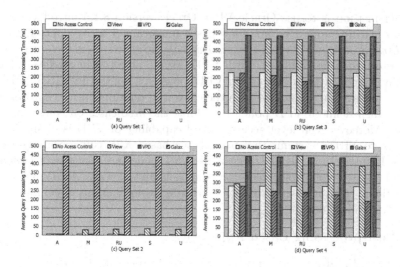

Fig. 5. Query processing time for four sets of queries

control rules using QFilter [24], and answer XML queries using Galax. In all the experiments, we use the *query processing time* as an evaluation metric. Figure 5 shows the results. Comparing both view-based and VPD-based approaches with the reference (no security enforcement), our approaches do not add much overhead for fine-grained access control. Meanwhile, the size of accessible data gets smaller with security enforcement. Therefore, querying on smaller set of records is even faster than that on no-security case.

7   Conclusion

In this paper, we propose a generic analysis to the access control problem in XRDB. We first analyze XML control models to propose a formal description of XML access control using deep set operators. Then we articulate the problem of XML access control in XRDB as essentially the problem of XML/Relational object and operation equivalency and conversion. We show that, equivalent counterparts of deep set operators in relational model are needed to fully implement XML access control in XRDB. We analyze the definition and semantics of each operator, and show how they can be converted to XRDB through two lemmas. Although detailed conversion implementation is connected with the specific X2R conversion algorithm used in XRDB, we propose an algebraic description of these operators. Moreover, we study possible implementations of XML access control in XRDB. We categorize them into three approaches, and formally describe the semantics of each approach using deep set operators. Finally, we show the validity of our approaches using experiment results.

References

1. Bray, T., Paoli, J., Sperberg-McQueen (Eds), C.M.: Extensible Markup Language (XML) 1.0 (2nd Ed.). W3C Recommendation (2000)
2. Godik, S., Moses (Eds), T.: eXtensible Access Control Markup Language (XACML) Version 1.0 (2003)
3. Damiani, E., De Capitani di Vimercati, S., Paraboschi, S., Samarati, P.: A Fine-Grained Access Control System for XML Documents. ACM TISSEC 5(2) (May 2002) 169–202
4. Bertino, E., Ferrari, E.: Secure and Selective Dissemination of XML Documents. ACM TISSEC 5(3) (August 2002) 290–331
5. Tan, K.L., Lee, M.L., Wang, Y.: Access Control of XML Documents in Relational Database Systems. In: IC, Las Vegas, NV (June 2001)
6. Barbosa, D., Freire, J., Mendelzon, A.O.: Designing Information-preserving Mapping Schemes for XML. In: VLDB, Trondheim, Norway (2005) 109–120
7. Samarati, P., Bertino, E., Jajodia, S.: "An Authorization Model for a Distributed Hypertext System". IEEE TKDE 8(4) (1996) 555–562
8. Damiani, E., Vimercati, S.D.C.D., Paraboschi, S., Samarati, P.: Design and Implementation of an Access Control Processor for XML Documents. Computer Networks 33(6) (2000) 59–75
9. Kudo, M., Hada, S.: XML Document Security Based on Provisional Authorization. In: ACM CCS. (2000)
10. Fundulaki, I., Marx, M.: Specifying access control policies for xml documents with xpath. In: ACM SACMAT. (2004) 61–69
11. Fernandez, E., Gudes, E., Song, H.: A Model of Evaluation and Administration of Security in Object-Oriented Databases. IEEE TKDE 6(2) (1994) 275–292
12. Wang, J., Osborn, S.L.: A role-based approach to access control for XML databases. In: ACM SACMAT. (2004) 70–77
13. Bertino, E., Castano, S., Ferrari, E.: Securing XML Documents with Author-X. IEEE Internet Computing 5(3) (2001) 21–31
14. Murata, M., Tozawa, A., Kudo, M., Hada, S.: XML access control using static analysis. ACM TISSEC 9(3) (2006) 292–324
15. Damiani, E., di Vimercati, S.D.C., Paraboschi, S., Samarati, P.: Securing XML Documents. In: EDBT. (2000) 121–135
16. Cho, S., Amer-Yahia, S., Lakshmanan, L.V., Srivastava, D.: Optimizing the Secure Evaluation of Twig Queries. In: VLDB, Hong Kong, China (August 2002)
17. Xiao, Y., Luo, B., Lee, D.: Security-Conscious XML Indexing. In: DASFAA, Bangkok, Thailand (2007)
18. Yu, T., Srivastava, D., Lakshmanan, L.V., Jagadish, H.V.: Compressed Accessibility Map: Efficient Access Control for XML. In: VLDB, Hong Kong, China (2002)
19. Jiang, M., Fu, A.W.C.: Integration and Efficient Lookup of Compressed XML Accessibility Maps. IEEE TKDE 17(7) (2005) 939–953
20. Stoica, A., Farkas, C.: Secure XML Views. In: DBSec. (2002) 133–146
21. Fan, W., Chan, C.Y., Garofalakis, M.: Secure XML querying with security views. In: SIGMOD. (2004) 587–598
22. Kuper, G., Massacci, F., Rassadko, N.: Generalized XML security views. In: SACMAT. (2005) 77–84
23. Murata, M., Tozawa, A., Kudo, M.: XML Access Control using Static Analysis. In: ACM CCS, Washington D.C. (2003)

24. Luo, B., Lee, D., Lee, W.C., Liu, P.: QFilter: Fine-Grained Run-Time XML Access Control via NFA-based Query Rewriting. In: ACM CIKM, Washington D.C., USA (November 2004)
25. Qi, N., Kudo, M.: Access-condition-table-driven access control for xml databases. In: ESORICS. (2004) 17–32
26. Qi, N., Kudo, M.: Xml access control with policy matching tree. In: ESORICS. (2005) 3–23
27. Mohan, S., Sengupta, A., Wu, Y.: Access control for XML: a dynamic query rewriting approach. In: CIKM. (2005) 251–252
28. Bouganim, L., Ngoc, F.D., Pucheral, P.: Client-Based Access Control Management for XML Documents. In: VLDB, Toronto, Canada (2004)
29. Bertino, E., Ferrari, E., Provenza, L.P.: Signature and Access Control Policies for XML Documents. In: ESORICS. (2003) 1–22
30. Carminati, B., Ferrari, E., Bertino, E.: Securing XML data in third-party distribution systems. In: CIKM. (2005) 99–106
31. Finance, B., Medjdoub, S., Pucheral, P.: The case for access control on XML relationships. In: CIKM. (2005) 107–114
32. Mohan, S., Wu, Y.: IPAC: an interactive approach to access control for semi-structured data. In: VLDB, VLDB Endowment (2006) 1147–1150
33. Jajodia, S., Sandhu, R.: Toward a Multilevel Secure Relational Data Model. In: SIGMOD. (May 1990)
34. Winslett, M., Smith, K., Qian, X.: Formal Query Languages for Secure Relational Databases. ACM TODS $19(4)$ (1994) 626–662
35. Sandhu, R., Chen, F.: The Multilevel Relational (MLR) Data Model. ACM TISSEC $1(1)$ (1998)
36. Griffiths, P.P., Wade, B.W.: An Authorization Mechanism for a Relational Database System. ACM TODS $1(3)$ (September 1976) 242–255
37. Jajodia, S., Samarati, P., Sapino, M.L., Subrahmanian, V.S.: Flexible Support for Multiple Access Control Policies. ACM TODS $26(2)$ (June 2001) 214–260
38. Jajodia, S., Samarati, P., Subrahmanian, V.S., Bertino, E.: A Unified Framework for Enforcing Multiple Access Control Policies. In: ACM SIGMOD. (May 1997) 474–485
39. Gabillon, A., Bruno, E.: Regulating access to XML documents. In: DBSec. (2002) 299–314
40. Murthy, R., Liu, Z.H., Krishnaprasad, M., Chandrasekar, S., Tran, A.T., Sedlar, E., Florescu, D., Kotsovolos, S., Agarwal, N., Arora, V., Krishnamurthy, V.: Towards an enterprise XML architecture. In: ACM SIGMOD. (2005) 953–957
41. Rys, M.: XML and relational database management systems: inside Microsoft SQL Server 2005. In: ACM SIGMOD. (2005) 958–962
42. Nicola, M., van der Linden, B.: Native XML support in DB2 universal database. In: VLDB. (2005) 1164–1174
43. Beyer, K., Ozcan, F., Saiprasad, S., der Linden, B.V.: DB2/XML: designing for evolution. In: ACM SIGMOD. (2005) 948–952
44. Deutsch, A., Fernandez, M.F., Suciu, D.: Storing Semistructured Data with STORED. In: ACM SIGMOD, Philadephia, PA (Jun. 1998)
45. Shanmugasundaram, J., Tufte, K., He, G., Zhang, C., DeWitt, D., Naughton, J.: Relational Databases for Querying XML Documents: Limitations and Opportunities. In: VLDB, Edinburgh, Scotland (September 1999)
46. Lee, D., Chu, W.W.: Constraints-preserving Transformation from XML Document Type Definition to Relational Schema. In: ER, Salt Lake City, UT (2000) 323–338

47. Florescu, D., Kossmann, D.: Storing and Querying XML Data Using an RDBMS. "IEEE Data Eng. Bulletin **22**(3) (Sep. 1999) 27–34

48. Yoshikawa, M., Amagasa, T., Shimura, T., Uemura, S.: XRel: A Path-Based Approach to Storage and Retrieval of XML Documents using Relational Databases. ACM TOIT **1**(2) (November 2001) 110–141

49. Lee, D., Lee, W.C., Liu, P.: Supporting XML Security Models using Relational Databases: A Vision. In: XSym, Berlin, Germany (September 2003)

50. Schmidt, A.R., Waas, F., Kersten, M.L., Florescu, D., Manolescu, I., Carey, M.J., Busse, R.: The XML Benchmark Project. Technical Report INS-R0103, CWI (April 2001)

51. Qi, N., Kudo, M., Myllymaki, J., Pirahesh, H.: A function-based access control model for xml databases. In: ACM CIKM. (2005) 115–122

52. Luo, B., Lee, D., Lee, W.C., Liu, P.: Deep Set Operators for XQuery. In: ACM SIGMOD Workshop on XIME-P, Baltimore, MD, USA. (2005)

53. Berglund, A., Boag, S., Chamberlin, D., Fernndez, M.F., Kay, M., Robie, J., Simeon, J.: XML Path Language (XPath) 2.0. W3C Working Draft (November 2003)

54. Boag, S., Chamberlin, D., Fernndez, M.F., Florescu, D., Robie, J., Simeon, J.: XQuery 1.0: An XML Query Language. W3C Working Draft (November 2003)

55. Luo, B., Lee, D., Lee, W.C., Liu, P.: A Flexible Framework for Architecting XML Access Control Enforcement Mechanisms. In: VLDB Workshop on SDM, Toronto, Canada (2004)

56. Luo, B., Lee, D., Liu, P.: Pragmatic XML access control using off-the-shelf RDBMS. Technical report, Penn State University (2007)

57. Lu et al., H.: What makes the differences: benchmarking XML database implementations. ACM TOIT **5**(1) (2005) 154–194

Conditional Privacy-Aware Role Based Access Control

Qun Ni[1], Dan Lin[1], Elisa Bertino[1], and Jorge Lobo[2]

[1] Department of Computer Science, Purdue University, W. Lafayette, IN 47907, USA
{ni,lindan,bertino}@cs.purdue.edu
[2] IBM Watson Research Center, Hawthorne, NY 10598, USA
jlobo@us.ibm.com

Abstract. Privacy is considered critical for all organizations needing to manage individual related information. As such, there is an increasing need for access control models which can adequately support the specification and enforcement of privacy policies. In this paper, we propose a model, referred to as Conditional Privacy-aware Role Based Access Control (P-RBAC), which supports expressive condition languages and flexible relations among permission assignments for more complex privacy policies. Efficient algorithms for detecting conflicts, redundancies, and indeterminism for a set of permission assignments are presented. In the paper we also extend Conditional P-RBAC to Universal P-RBAC by taking into account hierarchical relations among roles, data and purposes. In comparison with other approaches, such as P3P, EPAL, and XACML, our work has achieved both expressiveness and efficiency.

1 Introduction

Privacy is today a key issue in information technology (IT)[24] and has received increasing attention from consumers, stakeholders, and legislators. Legislative acts, such as the Health Insurance Portability and Accountability Act (HIPAA) [27] for healthcare and the Gramm Leach Bliley Act (GLBA)[28] for financial institutions, require enterprises to protect the privacy of their customers. To address privacy, enterprises have adopted various strategies to protect customer data and to communicate their privacy policies to customers, such as publishing privacy policies on websites [2] possibly based on P3P, or incorporating privacy seal programs (e.g. TRUSTe [25], ESRB, BBBOnline, CPAWebTrust). Those approaches however cannot truly safeguard consumers because they do not address how consumer personal data is actually handled after it is collected. Enterprises' actual practices might intentionally or unintentionally violate the privacy policies published at their websites. Privacy protection can only be achieved by enforcing privacy policies within an enterprise's online and offline data processing systems. Therefore enforceability of privacy policies is the key to a solution for privacy protection.

Conventional access models, such as Mandatory Access Control (MAC) and Discretionary Access Control (DAC), are not designed to enforce privacy policies

J. Biskup and J. Lopez (Eds.): ESORICS 2007, LNCS 4734, pp. 72–89, 2007.

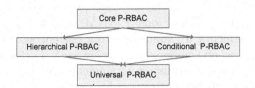

Fig. 1. A family of conceptual P-RBAC models

and barely meet the requirements of privacy protection [8]. However, existing access control technology can be used as a starting point for managing personal identifiable information in a trustworthy fashion [20]. A language used for privacy policies must be the same as or integrated with the language used for access control policies, because both types of policy usually control access to the same resources and should not conflict with one another [3]. Under this promise, we have proposed a family of Privacy-aware Role Based Access Control (P-RBAC) models (see Figure 1) [17] that naturally extend classical RBAC models [7,23] to support privacy policies. Due to the complexity and variety of privacy policies and privacy requirements from different organizations, we employ a "Divide and Conquer" methodology. That is, the models in our P-RBAC family are designed to meet different levels of requirements and handle different problems. The P-RBAC family includes four models: Core P-RBAC, Hierarchical P-RBAC, Conditional P-RBAC and Universal P-RBAC. Core P-RBAC is the basic model and is able to directly represent privacy-crucial information, such as purpose of data use and obligations. However, although Core P-RBAC can be used to describe commonly used public privacy policies and some acts, the limited expressiveness of its condition language makes it not suitable for representing internally enforceable privacy policies for large scale enterprises and/or complex applications. Specifically, Core P-RBAC has the following limitations. First, Core P-RBAC only supports equality constraints on context variables in finite domains. Second, conditions are restricted to conjunctions of atomic formulas. Third, it only supports one type of relation, that we refer to as AND, among different permission assignments. The type of relation adopted by a set of permission assignments is crucial in determining which obligations need to be executed and which conditions have to be meet when several permissions may apply to the same request[1].

In this paper, we address the aforementioned shortcomings by developing two advanced models, the Conditional P-RBAC and the Universal P-RBAC. Conditional P-RBAC supports more expressive condition languages and more flexible relations between permission assignments. Moreover, we extend the limited analysis operation in [17] to redundancy check, indeterministic obligation

---

[1] In standard policy languages, such as EPAL[10] and XACML[18], the relations between rules are not clearly defined. In order to handle possible interactions or conflicts between rules, EPAL and XACML adopt a simple approach: making only one rule applicable and simply ignoring all other rules. In contrast, relations between permission assignments in P-RBAC models are explicitly defined.

enforcement check, conflict check and coverage queries. Universal P-RBAC adds the concept of hierarchy to Conditional P-RBAC, and it is thus able to support more complex requirements. To summarize, our current work has the following five major differences when compared to existing work: 1) Domains, atomic conditions, and relations among permission assignments are carefully crafted to meet the most demanding needs from privacy polices while keeping the complexity of policy analysis tractable; 2) Special structures are proposed to process obligations appearing in multiple permission assignments that can simultaneously apply; 3) Indeterminism in obligation enforcement among policies is identified and a solution is proposed; and 4) Efficient algorithms for detecting conflicts, indeterminism and redundancies of a new permission assignment against *all* existing permission assignments[2] are presented.

2 A Summary of Core P-RBAC

Core P-RBAC [17] is the foundation of the P-RBAC family models. It includes seven sets of entities: Users(U), Roles(R), Data(D), Actions(A), Purposes(P), Obligations(O), and Conditions (C) expressed by a customized language, referred to as LC_0. A user in the Core P-RBAC model is a human being, and a role represents a job function or job title within the organization with some associated semantics regarding the authority and responsibility conferred on a member of the role. Data in P-RBAC means any information relating to an identified or identifiable individual. An action is an executable image of a program, which upon invocation executes some function for the user. The types of action and data objects that P-RBAC controls depend on the type of system in which they are deployed.

The motivations for i ntroducing Purposes, Conditions, and Obligations in Core P-RBAC originate from OECD Guidelines [19] on the Protection of Privacy and Transborder Flows of Personal Data, current privacy laws in the United States, and public privacy policies of some well-known organizations. The OECD guidelines are, to the best of our knowledge, the most well-known set of private information protection principles, on which many other guidelines, data-protection laws, and public privacy policies are based. Purposes which are bound to actions on data in Core P-RBAC directly reflect the OECD *Data Quality Principle*, *Purpose Specification Principle*, and *Use Limitation Principle*. Purposes are widely used for specifying privacy rules in legislative acts and actual public policies. Obligations, that is, actions to be performed after an action has been executed on data objects, are also part of many privacy policies. Conditions, that is, prerequisites to be met before any action can be executed, are frequent components of privacy policies too.

Core P-RBAC directly models the above notions. In Core P-RBAC, as in classical RBAC, permissions are assigned to roles and users obtain such permissions by being assigned to roles. The distinctive feature of Core P-RBAC

---

[2] The significance of comparing a new permission assignment against all pre-existing assignments simultaneously as opposed to pair-wisely is elaborated in Section 4.1.

lies in the complex structure of privacy permissions, which reflects the highly structured ways of expressing privacy rules to represent the essences of OECD principles and Privacy acts. Hence, aside from the data and the action to be performed on it, a privacy permission explicitly states the intended purpose of the action along with the conditions under which the permission can be granted and the obligations that are to be finally performed. Conditions are represented by conjunction of equality constraints over *context variables*, which record privacy-relevant requirements taken into account when enforcing privacy permissions. The following definition introduces Core P-RBAC. We refer the readers to [17] for additional details.

Definition 1. *The Core P-RBAC model is composed of the following components:*
- *A set U of users, a set R of roles, a set D of data, a set P of purposes, a set A of actions, a set O of obligations, and a condition language LC_0.*
- *The set of Privacy-sensitive Data Permission $PDP = \{(a, d, p, c, o)| \ a \in A, \ d \in D, \ p \in P, \ c$ is an expression of LC_0, $o \in \mathcal{P}(O)\}$, where $\mathcal{P}(O)$ denotes the powerset of O.*
- *User Assignment $UA \subseteq U \times R$, a many-to-many mapping user to role assignment relation.*
- *Privacy-sensitive Data Permission Assignment $PDPA \subseteq R \times PDP$, a many-to-many mapping privacy-sensitive data permission to role assignment relation.* □

For simplicity, we use (r, a, d, p, c, o) to denote a permission assignment in the rest of the paper.

3 Conditional P-RBAC

A major shortcoming of Core P-RBAC is the limited expressive power of its condition language LC_0. For example, LC_0 is not able to express conditions like ($DataUser=$"Alice") OR ($DataUser=$"Bob") because it only supports conjunction as logical operator. LC_0 cannot deal with conditions like (8am < $currentTime$ < 5pm) either because it only supports equality comparisons.

However, enhancing the expressiveness may result in a condition language which is not tractable. In particular, to determine whether a condition in a permission assignment can be satisfied is essentially the classic NP-complete satisfiability problem (SAT) where only a few classes of formulae are tractable. Therefore, for practical purposes, we divide our problem into two subcases, a tractable case and an intractable case, by carefully investigating commonly used conditions in privacy policies. Correspondingly, we define Conditional P-RBAC as characterized by a two-fold solution as follows.

- We define a more expressive condition language LC_1 and introduce the concept of *simple permission assignment set*, for which SAT is tractable.
- We define a fully expressive condition language LC_2 and introduce the concept of *advanced permission assignment set*, for which SAT is theoretically intractable but remains tractable in practice given a reasonable assumption.

3.1   Context Variable Domains and Atomic Conditions

Definition 2. *In both LC_1 and LC_2, conditions are expressed against context variables in the following domains with respective relational operators that have the standard semantics:*

- *Integer domain $\mathcal{I}$ with operators $<, \leq, =, \neq, >, \geq$.*
- *String domain $\mathcal{S}$ with operators $<, \leq, =, \neq, >, \geq$.*
- *Real domain $\mathcal{R}$ with operators $<, \leq, =, \neq, >, \geq$.*
- *Date domain $\mathcal{D}$ with operators $<, \leq, =, \neq, >, \geq$.*
- *Time domain $\mathcal{T}$ with operators $<, \leq, =, \neq, >, \geq$.*
- *A finite tree domain $\mathcal{H}$ with operators $<, \leq, =, \neq, >, \geq, \prec, \preceq, \succ, \succeq, \asymp, \not\asymp$.*
- *A finite partially ordered discrete domain $\mathcal{PO}$ with operators $<, \leq, =, \neq, >, \geq, \prec, \preceq, \succ, \succeq, \asymp, \not\asymp$.*
- *A finite unordered discrete domain $\mathcal{UD}$ with operators $=, \neq$.* □

These domains are commonly used in various kinds of policies including privacy policies. For example, X.500 directories and XML data are in the tree domain; some security labels and role hierarchies are in the partially ordered discrete domain; Boolean values and data subject's consent are in the unordered discrete domain. Most relational operators are easily understood and thus here we only explain some relational operators used in the tree domain and the partially ordered domain. Let x be a context variable in a tree domain T_x and let $v \in T_x$, $x < v$ denotes that x is a descendant of v, while $x \prec v$ means x is a direct descendent(child) of v. Similarly, the operator $>$ represents the ancestor relation while $\succ$ describes the direct ancestor (parent) relation. The operators $\asymp$ and $\not\asymp$ represent comparability and non-comparability tests between domain elements respectively.

Definition 3. *The atomic conditions of LC_1 and LC_2 are defined as follows:*
- *Let D_x be one of the domains introduced by Definition 2; let x_i and x_j be variables in D_x; let v be a constant in D_x; let $op_r \in \{=, \neq\}$; then $x_i\ op_r\ v$ is an atomic condition, referred to as **equality atomic condition**.*
- *Let D_x be one of the domains introduced by Definition 2 different from domain $\mathcal{UD}$; let x_i and x_j be variables in D_x; let v be a constant in D_x; let $op_r \in \{<, \leq, >, \geq\}$; then $x_i\ op_r\ v$ is an atomic condition, referred to as **order atomic condition**.*
- *Let D_x be domain $\mathcal{H}$ or domain $\mathcal{PO}$; let x_i and x_j be variables in D_x; let v be a constant in D_x; let $op_r \in \{\prec, \preceq, \succ, \succeq, \asymp, \not\asymp\}$; then $x_i\ op_r\ v$ is an atomic condition, referred to as **hierarchy atomic condition**.* □

Note that for all domains in Definition 2, except $\mathcal{UD}$, the order atomic condition is more expressive than the equality atomic condition because the equality operation is just a special case of order relation. One typical class of condition in policies are range condition such as $x \in (0, 13]$. Ranges can be easily represented by two order atomic conditions. We also do not define negation of atomic conditions in the totally ordered domain (i.e. integer, real, string, date, and time) as atomic conditions because it can be easily expressed by using corresponding negative relational operators. For example, a negation of atomic condition (*not* OwnerAge ≤ 13) can be represented as (OwnerAge > 13).

3.2   The Condition Language LC_1 and Simple Permission Assignment Sets

Given the definition of atomic conditions, we now define LC_1 conditions.

Definition 4. *The conditions of LC_1 are defined as follows:*
- *An atomic condition is a condition of LC_1.*
- *Let c_i and c_j be conditions of LC_1; then $c_i \wedge c_j$ [3] is a condition of LC_1.* □

When dealing with multiple permission assignments including conditions and obligations, it is fundamental to understand the semantics associated with the permission when multiple assignments can be applied. For this purpose, we introduce two possible relations AND and OR. An AND relation for a set of permission assignments indicates that an access request related to these permission assignments will be authorized only if all conditions in these permission assignments are satisfied and all obligations are fulfilled thereafter. Alternatively, an OR relation for a set of permission assignments indicates that an access request related to these permission assignments will be authorized if one of the conditions in these permission assignments is satisfied and only the corresponding obligations in that permission assignment are fulfilled thereafter (more details about AND and OR relation are presented in Section 4.1). To handle AND and OR relations, we introduce the concept of Simple Permission Assignment Sets (SPAS).

Definition 5.
- *An atomic simple permission assignment set is a set $\{PA_1, PA_2, ..., PA_k\}$, such that the relation among the permission assignments in the set is AND.*
- *Let $SPAS_1$, ..., $SPAS_n$ be atomic SPASs, then $\{SPAS_1, ..., SPAS_n\}$ is a non-atomic SPAS, if (i) the relation among atomic SPAS's is OR; and (ii)$SPAS_i \cap SPAS_j = \emptyset$, $i, j \in [1..n] \wedge i \neq j$.*
- *An atomic SPAS is a SPAS; a non-atomic SPAS is a SPAS.* □

Many permission can be expressed using SPAS. e.g., SPAS allows different groups or departments to define their own permission assignments in one or several permission sets. Also, SPAS helps to specify the relation OR between permission assignments. Organizational privacy policies can then be represented by a finite number of atomic SPASs. Consider the following example: "Marketing employee can only access customers' email address for promotion if the customers are not under 13 and allow them to do so. If they are under 13, they need to get their parents' consent". The corresponding SPAS is as follows.

Example 1. $SPAS \equiv \{SPAS_1, SPAS_2\}$; $SPAS_1 \equiv \{$(MarketingEmployee, Read, EmailAddress, Promotion, OwnerAge $> 13 \wedge$ OwnerConsent=Yes, $\emptyset)\}$; $SPAS_2 \equiv \{$(MarketingEmployee, Read, EmailAddress, Promotion, OwnerAge $\leq 13 \wedge$ ParentalConsent=Yes, $\emptyset)\}$. □

---

[3] To avoid ambiguities, Boolean operators $\wedge$ and $\vee$ will be used in predicate conditions, while AND and OR will be used to denote relations between permission assignments.

The rationale behind LC_1 and $SPAS$ is to provide good expressiveness while guaranteeing the efficient generation of disjunctive OR forms by permission assignment normalization. Disjunctive normal form and permission assignment normalization ensure the efficiency of our analysis algorithms. We will detail these concepts and analysis in Section 4.

3.3 The Condition Language LC_2 and Advanced Permission Assignment Sets

Some applications may require the ability to specify more complex conditions that need both Boolean operators $\wedge$ and $\vee$. For example, the condition $(OwnerAge \leq 13 \wedge ParentalConsent = Yes) \vee (OwnerAge > 13 \wedge OwnerConsent = Yes)$. We define the language LC_2 to cover these cases.

Definition 6. *The conditions of LC_2 are defined as follows:*
- *An atomic condition is a condition of LC_2.*
- *Let c_i and c_j be conditions of LC_2; then $c_i \wedge c_j$ and $c_i \vee c_j$ are conditions of LC_2.*   □

Along with LC_2, an Advanced Permission Assignment Set(APAS) is defined to support the representation of different relations among permission assignments.

Definition 7. *Let S be a set of all possible permission assignments.*
- *An atomic APAS is a tuple $N[rel, pas, \emptyset]$, where N is an identifier, $rel \in \{AND, OR\}$ and pas is a finite subset of S.*
- *Let $rel \in \{AND, OR\}$, pas is a finite subset of S, and apas be a set of APAS; then a $N[rel, pas, apas]$ is an APAS.*   □

Example 2. Let PA_1, PA_2, ..., PA_{14} be permission assignments. An example APAS is $APAS_1$ [AND, $\{PA_1, PA_2\}$, $\{APAS_2$ [AND, $\{PA_3, PA_4\}$, $\{APAS_3$ [OR, $\{PA_5, PA_6\}$, $\emptyset]$, $APAS_4$ [OR, $\{PA_7, PA_8\}$, $\emptyset]\}]$, $APAS_5$ [OR, $\{PA_9, PA_{10}\}$, $\{APAS_6$ [AND, $\{PA_{11}, PA_{12}\}$, $\emptyset]$, $APAS_7$ [OR, $\{PA_{13}, PA_{14}\}$, $\emptyset]\}]\}]$, which can be represented as a tree(see Figure 2).   □

The advantage of APAS is that it provides a natural and flexible way to help administrate different levels of permission assignments. Example 2 could represent a company with two departments D_1 and D_2. D_1 has teams T_1 and T_2, and D_2 has teams T_3 and T_4. We may allow a senior privacy officer to administrate the whole APAS tree, and departmental privacy officers to maintain $APAS_2$ and $APAS_5$ respectively. If necessary, a privacy officer can also be assigned to several APAS nodes in the tree.

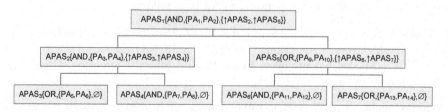

Fig. 2. An APAS tree

4   Consistency Checking in Conditional P-RBAC

In P-RBAC, when a new permission assignment is entered, the privacy officer needs to check how the new permission assignment interacts with existing ones. We refer to such task as **consistency checking** of permission assignments.

Definition 8. *A new permission assignment is consistent with pre-existing permission assignments if none of the following conditions hold:*

- *Redundancy. A permission assignment x is redundant with respect to a group of permission assignments $Y \equiv \{y_1, ..., y_n\} (n \geq 1)$ if the addition of x does not affect the behavior of the system governed by Y.*
- *Conflict. A permission assignment x conflicts with a group of permission assignments $Y \equiv \{y_1, ..., y_n\} (n \geq 1)$ if the addition of x results in that one action of the system governed by Y can be never carried out or there exists a conflict among new obligations.*
- *Indeterminism. A permission assignment x results in indetermination with respect to a group of permission assignments $Y \equiv \{y_1, ..., y_n\} (n \geq 1)$ if the addition of x results in that the enforcement of obligations governed by Y becomes nondeterministic.* □

Here the unchanged behavior in the definition of redundancy means given any data request, the system will make the same decision and execute the same set of obligations. Conflict happens if (i) the new condition created after the addition of x cannot be satisfied; or (ii) the new obligations introduced by x need to be added to a set of obligations of a permission assignment and the new obligations conflict with the set. Indeterminism arises because of the relations between conditions and obligations in privacy policies. For example, if there is a permission assignment $(MarketingEmployee, read, EmailAddress, promotion, ownerage \leq 13, notify(byPhone, optout))$, a new permission assignment$(MarketingEmployee, read, EmailAddress, promotion, ownerage \leq 19, notify(byEmail))$ that has OR relation with respect to the original permission assignment results in indeterministic obligation enforcement. For a kid who is ten, enforcement of $notify(byPhone, optout)$ or $notify(byEmail)$ is undetermined to system. Any policy language that supports both pre-conditions and post-actions may suffer from such a problem.

Based on the result of consistency checking, the privacy officer will accept or reject new permission assignments, resolve potential conflicts, or mark certain permission assignments as being inactive. Consistency checking can also include *coverage queries*. In some cases, the privacy officer may want to know if the permission assignments have been defined for a certain range of context variables. For example, a privacy officer may want to know if third parties can access purchase order information for research purposes between 19:00 and 22:00. In what follows, we present a normalization technique to carry out the above analysis in Conditional P-RBAC.

4.1 Permission Assignment Normalization

In Conditional P-RBAC, permission assignments are maintained as a SPAS or an APAS tree. Directly using such a set or tree structure to answer data requests or to detect whether there exists a conflict between a new permission assignment and the pre-existing permission assignments, may not be efficient because sometimes the entire set or the entire tree need to be traversed to find an answer. Therefore, it would be helpful to translate a SPAS (an APAS tree) into a form better suited for analysis; we call such a translation *permission assignment normalization*.

Observe that in a group of permission assignments, either in a SPAS or in an APAS, two permission assignments may interact with each other only when they share the same role, action, data and purpose. Otherwise, the permission assignments are incomparable[4]. Therefore, the goal of permission assignment normalization is to generate a new permission assignment set such that each combination of (role, action, data, purpose) only appears once in the set.

The benefit of the normalization for answering data access requests is obvious. Now the system can give an answer within constant time by using a hashing function $\mathcal{H}(r, a, d, p)$ to locate the permission assignment being queried. The same hashing function can be used to improve the efficiency of the consistency checking. It is worth noting that the normalization is extremely helpful in determining the relation between a new permission assignment and a group of permission assignments because a series of related permission assignments will become *one* permission assignment after the normalization. It is not sufficient to compare a new permission assignment against each existing permission assignment. For example, let D be a finite domain $\{a, b, c\}$ and x be a context variable on D, let P_1 and P_2 be two existing permission assignments with conditions $x \neq a$ and $x \neq b$ respectively, let P_3 be the new permission assignments with condition $x \neq c$, and we assume the other components of P_1, P_2 and P_3 are the same and they have an AND relation. Obviously P_3 does not conflict individually with P_1 or P_2, but conflicts with the integration of P_1 and P_2.

Definition 9. *Let S and S' be two permission assignment sets, we say the behavior of S' is equivalent to that of S if for any data access request, S' yields the same authorization decision and performs the same obligations as S.*   □

The normalization is challenging because we must guarantee that the behavior of a normalized permission assignment is equivalent to the original assignments. The difficulty lies in the analysis of conditions and obligations. In the following, we discuss the procedures for normalizing SPAS and APAS separately.

Permission Assignment Normalization on SPAS. To facilitate permission assignment normalization on SPAS, we first introduce the following structure.

Definition 10. *Let R be a set of roles, D be a set of data, P be a set of purposes, A be a set of actions, O be a set of obligations in Conditional P-RBAC;*

---

[4] The statement is not true if role hierarchies, data hierarchies and purpose hierarchies are considered. Such situation is discussed in Universal P-RBAC.

a condition-obligation structure is a set of tuples of the form (c, o) where c is a condition of LC_1 and $o \in \mathcal{P}(O)$; a normalized permission assignment is a 5-tuple (r, a, d, p, co) where $r \in R$, $a \in A$, $d \in D$, $p \in P$, and co is a condition-obligation structure.   □

The normalization algorithm for SPAS consists of two steps. First, for permission assignments with the same (role, action, data, purpose) in the same SPAS, we combine their conditions using the Boolean operator $\wedge$, and associate the new condition with the UNION of corresponding obligations. Second, we construct the condition-obligation structure for permission assignments with the same (role, action, data, purpose) in different SPASs. Given a normalized permission assignment (r, a, d, p, co) where $co = \{(c_i, o_i) \mid 0 < i < k\}$ and k is the number of atomic SPASs in the SPAS, if a single c_i is satisfied, the data access request is allowed and the corresponding obligations in o_i are performed later. The pseudo codes of the algorithms are shown in Figures 3 and 4. The time complexity of each algorithm is $O(n)$ assuming the number of permission assignments is n. We use Example 3 to illustrate ideas in the algorithms.

Algorithm CO-Normalization($NSPAS$)
Input: $NSPAS$ is a non-atomic SPAS with respect to the same (role, action, data, purpose)
1. $NPAL \leftarrow$ **nil**; // $NPAL$ is a normalized permission assignment list
2. $ConditionObligationStructure \leftarrow \emptyset$;
3. **for** each atomic $SPAS$ in the $NSPAS$
4. $(c, o) \leftarrow$ (**true**, $\emptyset$);
5.   **for** each permission assignment (r', a', d', p', c', o') in $SPAS$
6. $(c, o) \leftarrow (c \wedge c', o \cup o')$;
7. $ConditionObligationStructure \leftarrow ConditionObligationStructure \cup (c, o)$;
8. $NPAL \leftarrow$ List.CONS$((role, action, data, purpose, ConditionObligationStructure), NPAL)$;
9. **return** $NPAL$.

Fig. 3. CO-Normalization algorithm

Algorithm SPAS-Normalization($NSPAS$)
Input : $NSPAS$ is a non-atomic SPAS
1. $NPAL \leftarrow$ **nil**; // $NPAL$ is a normalized permission assignment list;
2. divide $NSPAS$ into $\{NSPAS_1, NSPAS_2, ..., NSPAS_n\}$,
    where $NSPAS_i$ consists of permission assignment with same (role, action, data, purpose);
3. **for** $i \leftarrow 1$ to n
4. $NPAL \leftarrow$ List.CONS(CO-Normalization($NSPAS_i$),$NPAL$);
5. **return** $NPAL$.

Fig. 4. SPAS-Normalization algorithm

Example 3. Consider a SPAS containing the following atomic SPASs:

$SPAS_1((r_{11}, a_{11}, d_{11}, p_{11}, c_{11}, o_{11}), (r_{12}, a_{12}, d_{12}, p_{12}, c_{12}, o_{12}), (r_{13}, a_{13}, d_{13}, p_{13}, c_{13}, o_{13})),$
$SPAS_2((r_{21}, a_{21}, d_{21}, p_{21}, c_{21}, o_{21}), (r_{22}, a_{22}, d_{22}, p_{22}, c_{22}, o_{22}), (r_{23}, a_{23}, d_{23}, p_{23}, c_{23}, o_{23})),$
$SPAS_3((r_{31}, a_{31}, d_{31}, p_{31}, c_{31}, o_{31}), (r_{32}, a_{32}, d_{32}, p_{32}, c_{32}, o_{32}), (r_{33}, a_{33}, d_{33}, p_{33}, c_{33}, o_{33})).$

We assume $(r_{11}, a_{11}, d_{11}, p_{11}) = (r_{21}, a_{21}, d_{21}, p_{21}) = (r_{22}, a_{22}, d_{22}, p_{22}) = (r_{31}, a_{31}, d_{31}, p_{31}) = (r_{32}, a_{32}, d_{32}, p_{32}) = (r_{33}, a_{33}, d_{33}, p_{33})$.

Suppose there is a data request DR concerning $(r_{11}, a_{11}, d_{11}, p_{11})$. Several possible cases exist according to the definition of SPAS:

- If DR satisfies c_{11}, the request will be authorized and obligations in o_{11} will be performed.
- If DR satisfies $c_{21} \wedge c_{22}$, then the request will be authorized and obligations in $o_{21} \cup o_{22}$ will be performed. The intuition of the union of obligations is as follows:
  - Since DR satisfies c_{21} in permission $(r_{21}, a_{21}, d_{21}, p_{21}, c_{21}, o_{21})$, obligations in o_{21} should be performed.
  - Since DR satisfies c_{22} in permission $(r_{22}, a_{22}, d_{22}, p_{22}, c_{22}, o_{22})$, obligations in o_{22} should be performed.
  - Duplicated obligations should be performed only once because generally several enforcements of a same obligation do not make sense.
- If DR satisfies $c_{31} \wedge c_{32} \wedge c_{33}$, then the request will be authorized and obligations in $o_{31} \cup o_{32} \cup o_{33}$ will be performed.
- Otherwise, the request will be denied.

Then, the normalized permission assignment set is :$(r', a', d', p', co'), (r_{12}, a_{12}, d_{12}, p_{12}, \{(c_{12}, o_{12})\}), (r_{13}, a_{13}, d_{13}, p_{13}, \{(c_{13}, o_{13})\}), (r_{23}, a_{23}, d_{23}, p_{23}, \{(c_{23}, o_{23})\})$, where $r' = r_{11}$, $a' = a_{11}$, $d' = d_{11}$, $p' = p_{11}$, and $co' = \{(c_{11}, o_{11}), (c_{21} \wedge c_{22}, o_{21} \cup o_{22}), (c_{31} \wedge c_{32} \wedge c_{33}, o_{31} \cup o_{32} \cup o_{32})\}$.   □

Based on the definition of condition-obligation structure, it is easy to prove the following lemma:

Lemma 1. *Algorithm CO-Normalization and SPAS-Normalization guarantee that the behavior of the normalized permission assignment set is equivalent to that of the original simple permission assignment set.*   □

Permission Assignment Normalization on APAS. The main difference between SPAS and APAS is the use of Boolean relation $\vee$ between conditions and the relation OR between permission assignments. However, we can still apply the same idea underlying the normalization of a SPAS to normalize an APAS tree because as in SPAS, permission assignments with different (role, action, data, purpose) in an APAS tree do not interfere with one another. The main challenge is again the processing of obligations. In order to solve the problem, we introduce a new concept, referred to as **condition-obligation binding**. The idea behind this concept is that the fact that the obligations must be fulfilled depends on the conditions satisfied by a data access request.

Definition 11. *Let c be a condition expressed according to LC_2, O be a set of obligations and $o \in \mathcal{P}(O)$. $[c, o]$ is a condition-obligation binding. If $[c_i, o_i]$ and $[c_j, o_j]$ are condition-obligation bindings, $[c_i, o_i] \wedge [c_j, o_j]$ and $[c_i, o_i] \vee [c_j, o_j]$ are condition-obligation bindings too. Further, $[c, o]$ is called a normal condition-obligation binding if c is a condition in LC_1 (i.e. a conjunction of atomic conditions).*   □

Lemma 2. *A condition-obligation binding supports the following transformations:*

- $[c_i \vee c_j, o] \Leftrightarrow [c_i, o] \vee [c_j, o]$.
- $[c_i \wedge (c_j \vee c_k), o] \Leftrightarrow [c_i \wedge c_j, o] \vee [c_i \wedge c_k, o]$.
- $[c_i, o_i] \wedge [c_j, o_j] \Leftrightarrow [c_i \wedge c_j, o_i \cup o_j]$. $\qquad\qquad\square$

The normalization algorithm for an APAS tree is as follows. First, we transform all permission assignments in the APAS tree into a new form $(r, a, d, p, [c, o])$. Second, we remove all relation operators and sub-trees by moving relation operators into condition-obligation bindings. For example, given $(r, a, d, p, [c_i, o_i])$ OR $(r, a, d, p, [c_j, o_j])$, we have $(r, a, d, p, [c_i, o_i] \vee [c_j, o_j])$. After this step, we obtain a set of permission assignments in the form of $(r, a, d, p, \sqcup_{i=1}^{n}[c_i, o_i])$ where $\sqcup \in \{\wedge, \vee\}$. Next, we convert $\sqcup_{i=1}^{n}[c_i, o_i]$ into $\vee_{j=1}^{m}[c_j, o_j]$, where $[c_j, o_j]$ is a normal condition-obligation binding, by using the transformations given in Definition 11. Finally, we transform $\vee_{j=1}^{m}[c_j, o_j]$ into a condition-obligation structure and generate a set of normalized permission assignments. The pseudo code is omitted due to space constraints. The following example illustrates the algorithm.

Example 4. Consider Example 2. Assuming that $APAS_1$ contains the following permission assignments: $PA_3 = (r_3, a_3, d_3, p_3, c_3, o_3)$, $PA_8 = (r_8, a_8, d_8, p_8, c_8, o_8)$ $PA_9 = (r_9, a_9, d_9, p_9, c_9, o_9)$, $PA_{13} = (r_{13}, a_{13}, d_{13}, p_{13}, c_{13}, o_{13})$ where $r_3 = r_8 = r_9 = r_{13}, a_3 = a_8 = a_9 = a_{13}, d_3 = d_8 = d_9 = d_{13}, p_3 = p_8 = p_9 = p_{13}$. The following steps are executed by the algorithm.

Step 1: Group permission assignments according to (role, action, data, purpose) and construct condition-obligation bindings, where we have:
$PA_3 = (r_3, a_3, d_3, p_3, [c_3, o_3])$, $PA_8 = (r_8, a_8, d_8, p_8, [c_8, o_8])$
$PA_9 = (r_9, a_9, d_9, p_9, [c_9, o_9])$, $PA_{13} = (r_{13}, a_{13}, d_{13}, p_{13}, [c_{13}, o_{13}])$

Step 2: Flatten the APAS tree by moving the relational operators into the permission assignments. We obtain $NPA' = (r_3, a_3, d_3, p_3, [c_3, o_3] \wedge [c_8, o_8] \wedge ([c_9, o_9] \vee [c_{13}, o_{13}]))$. We assume that c_3, c_8, c_9 and c_{13} are atomic conditions (a more general case of conditions is shown in our technical report).

Step 3: Transform the condition-obligation bindings in NPA' into a DNF as shown below.
$[c_3, o_3] \wedge [c_8, o_8] \wedge ([c_9, o_9] \vee [c_{13}, o_{13}]) \Rightarrow [c_3 \wedge c_8 \wedge c_9, o_3 \cup o_8 \cup o_9] \vee [c_3 \wedge c_8 \wedge c_{13}, o_3 \cup o_8 \cup o_{13}]$.

Step 4: Construct the condition-obligation structure and generate the normalized permission assignment: $NPA = (r_3, a_3, d_3, p_3, \{(c_3 \wedge c_8 \wedge c_9, o_3 \cup o_8 \cup o_9), (c_3 \wedge c_8 \wedge c_{13}, o_3 \cup o_8 \cup o_{13})\})$ $\qquad\square$

It is worth noting that the disjunctive normal form transformation for the condition-obligation bindings may be exponential to the number of atomic conditions. However, such situation rarely happens in practice due to the following observations. First, in real privacy policies, for each flattened permission assignment, the number of atomic conditions in the conditions is usually very small (e.g. ≤ 10). Second, the APAS-Normalization is linear with respect to the number of permission assignments, which has no direct relation with the total number of context variables. In other words, even if the total number of context variables were tens of thousands, the running time of our APAS-Normalization will still be linear in the total number of permission assignments.

4.2 Permission Assignment Maintenance

In conditional P-RBAC, we guarantee that there is no redundancy, indeterminism or conflict between a new permission and a pre-existing permission assignment set by taking the following steps when inserting a new permission assignment is issued.

1. Redundancy checking. If no error occurs, continue.
2. Conflict detection. If no error occurs, continue.
3. Indeterminism checking. If no error occurs, insert the new permission assignment.

Definition 12. *Let $NPAL$ be a normalized permission assignment set based on either a SPAS or an APAS set, PA' be a new permission assignment, NPA is the normalized permission assignment which have the same $(role, action, data, purpose)$ as PA', and NPA' is the normalized permission assignments of the addition of PA' in the pre-existing permission assignments.*

– *If either a condition of NPA' is not satisfiable or an obligation conflict is detected, we say PA' strongly conflicts with $NPAL$.*
– *Let $CO = \{(c_1, o_1), ..., (c_n, o_n)\}$ be a condition-obligation structure of NPA'. If a c_i, for $i \in [1, n]$, is not satisfiable, we say PA' weakly conflicts[5] with $NPAL$.*
– *If the context variable domain of NPA is the same as that of NPA' and the corresponding obligation sets are equivalent, we say PA' is redundant with respect to $NPAL$.*
– *Let $CO = \{(c_1, o_1), ..., (c_n, o_n)\}$ be a condition-obligation structure of NPA'. If there exist two tuple (c_i, o_i), $(c_j, o_j) \in CO$ such that $c_i \wedge c_j$ is satisfiable and $o_i \neq o_j$, we say PA' causes indeterminism of obligation enforcement in $NPAL$.* □

The coverage query can be very generic and depends on requirements and their implementations, therefore no formal definition is given here. The general case of coverage queries is that given some constraints on role, data, purpose, and context variables, the system checks whether they are satisfiable or unsatisfiable based on a permission assignment set.

Given the definition of redundancy, strong conflict, weak conflict, and indeterminism, our permission assignment normalization algorithms, and the domain elimination algorithms discussed in [1], the problems of redundancy checking, indeterminism checking, conflict detection and coverage queries are converted into a tractable satisfiability problem. We do not include more details due to space limitation.

---

[5] Weak conflict may indicate potential problems introduced by a new permission assignment because it causes some (c_i, o_i) to be totally useless.

5   Universal P-RBAC

Universal P-RBAC combines Hierarchical P-RBAC and Conditional P-RBAC, and inherits both their features. Such integration of Hierarchical P-RBAC and Conditional P-RBAC supports the specification of more complex relations between different permission assignments, which in turn raises several issues with respect to consistency check.

5.1   Hierachical P-RBAC

Hierarchical P-RBAC provides role hierarchies (RH), data hierarchies (DH) and purpose hierarchies (PH). Role hierarchies represent an important notion in RBAC [23,7], which reflect organization's lines of authority and responsibility. Mathematically, role hierarchies are partial orders. The purpose hierarchy is represented as a tree, where each purpose (except the root purpose) has exactly one parent purpose and there are no cycles. A parent node represents a more general purpose than its children nodes. Access for a parent purpose is allowed only when the access for all its children purpose is allowed. Like the purpose hierarchy, the data hierarchy is also a tree structure. Access to a parent data object is allowed only if access to all its children is allowed. Introducing the hierarchy concept compacts permission assignments (e.g., permission assignments with different purposes may be clustered providing all the child purposes are already covered), and also complicates consistency check.

5.2   Interactions Between Hierarchical P-RBAC and Conditional P-RBAC

As mentioned in previous section, inserting a new permission assignment requires checking redundancy, conflict and indeterminism. When there is no hierarchy (in the Conditional P-RBAC), those checks are carried out only on the permissions with the same (role, data, action, purpose) because each role (data, action or purpose) is independent of any of other roles. Once we introduce a hierarchy (in Universal P-RBAC), the situation becomes more complex. We now need to compare permission assignments of different roles (data, or purpose) since potential interactions may exist among these roles due to their hierarchical relations. To facilitate the discussion of such interactions, let us assume a new permission assignment to be $PA_n = (r_n, a_n, d_n, p_n, c_n, o_n)$.

The process of issuing PA_n includes two phases. The first phase checks if PA_n causes any redundancy, conflict or indeterminism problem against the existing permission assignment sets of role r_n, r_a and r_d, respectively, which is carried out in a temporary copy of existing permission assignment sets. If PA_n passes the check, the second phase will then update all influenced permission assignments.

In the first phase, there are four steps. First, we "virtually" [6] insert PA_n into current SPAS or APAS. Let NPA_n and NPA'_n be the normalized permission assignments containing (r_n, a_n, d_n, p_n) before and after the insertion

---

[6] The word "virtually" means the operation does not have any real effect on the system.

respectively. If a strong or weak conflict or indeterminism is detected during the construction of NPA'_n, or NPA'_n is redundant compared to NPA_n, the processing stops. Otherwise, we proceed to the second step which handles the effect of the data hierarchy. From here, our discussion is based on the normalized permission assignment set after the virtual insertion of PA_n. We compare NPA'_n = $\{(c_{n_1}, o_{n_1}), \cdots, (c_{n_i}, o_{n_i})\}$ with every such permission assignment NPA'_x = $(r_n, a_n, d_x, p_n, \{(c_{x_1}, o_{x_1}), \cdots, (c_{x_j}, o_{x_j})\})$, where d_x is a descendant or an ancestor of d_n, denoted as $d_x \preceq d_n$ and $d_x \succeq d_n$ respectively. If NPA'_n provides broader authorizations than its previous version NPA_n, we need to correspondingly increase the authorization on the data which is a descendant of d_n. The reason is that according to the definition of the data hierarchy, if a user can access data d_n under a certain condition, he should also be able to access data d_x ($d_x \preceq d_n$) under the same condition. The increase of the authorization is achieved by combining the condition-obligation bindings of NPA'_n and NPA'_x. Specifically, the new permission assignment for d_x is $NPA''_x = (r_n, a_n, d_x, p_n, \{(c_{x_1}, o_{x_1}), \cdots, (c_{x_j}, o_{x_j})\} \bigcup \{(c_{n_1}, o_{n_1}), \cdots, (c_{n_i}, o_{n_i})\})$. During the combination, we need to check if there exists indeterminism of obligation enforcement.

In the other case when NPA'_n is stricter than before, we need to check NPA'_x with $d_x \succeq d_n$. If the solution domain of c_x is covered by c_n, no more changes are needed according to the same reason above. Otherwise, it means that c_x defines some situations which cannot be satisfied by c_n. In other words, there are some permissions authorized by NPA'_x but not authorized by NPA'_n, which conflicts with the functionality of the data hierarchy. Therefore, we remove NPA'_x and dispatch its permission to its child nodes except d_n. For example, if d_y is a child node of d_x ($d_y \neq d_n$), it will receive a permission assignment $PA_y = (r_n, a_n, d_y, p_n, \{(c_{x_1}, o_{x_1}), \cdots, (c_{x_j}, o_{x_j})\})$. After that, we need to normalize the permission assignment sets again.

Next, we consider the purpose hierarchy. The processing is omitted because the purpose hierarchy has the same structure as the data hierarchy.

The final step in the first phase is to propagate the changes to the ancestor roles of r_n. The basic rule is to guarantee that parent roles have all the permissions of their child roles. The specific operation is as follows. If an updated permission assignment of r_n is different from its previous version, we need to replace the correspondingly inherited permission assignment for its parent roles with the new one and renormalize permissions for its parents. After the normalization, if the parent roles obtain different permissions, we repeat the procedure for the corresponding grandparent roles. Note that these changes may be propagated all the way to the top of the role hierarchy.

All the permission assignments modified in the first phase are made in a temporary copy of the original permission assignments because the process may stop at any time due to conflict, indeterminism, or redundancy problems. We finally update all these changes to the system in the second phase.

Our maintenance algorithm may look complicated. However, it is worth noting that the frequency of policy changes (i.e. permission insertion) is much less than that of data requests. By taking care of all possible issues during the insertion phase which needs to be executed only once, we are then able to reduce response time for each data request.

6   Related Work

In this section, we compare our proposal to three proposals that are most closely related, that is P3P[29], EPAL[10] and XACML [18]. P3P enables websites to express their privacy practices in a standard format that can be retrieved automatically and interpreted easily by agents. However, P3P is not able to describe complex conditions like the age constraint, and it is also not an enforceable policy language. EPAL [4] is proposed to encode enterprise's privacy-related data-handling policies and practices, which can be imported and enforced by a privacy-enforcement system. XACML [18] is a well known access control model based on XML. Its main goal is to provide an application independent policy language which enables the use of arbitrary attributes in different types of policies. Both EPAL and XACML aim at providing large flexibilities of writing policies, but leave the policy analysis task to policy analyzers. For example, they use a very simple strategy to handle conflicts among rules. That is, when multiple rules in one policy yield different decisions for a same request, EPAL and XACML will simply choose the decision from one rule according to the rule combining algorithm and ignore the effects of other rules. One of such strategies, i.e. first applicable rule, may cause problems as discussed in [5]. In addition, obligation processing is rather preliminary in both EPAL and XACML. Unlike existing approaches, our models achieve a balance between expressiveness and tractability, and also guarantee that the insertion of a new policy will not affect the consistency of existing policies.

Besides the policy languages, we are also aware of analysis tools for XACML policies, such as [9,14,26]. Most of them simplify the analysis and focus on core functions only. It is not clear if they can be easily extended to support analysis on the full functionality. Since they are orthogonal to our work, we do not present the details here. In the definition of domain and atomic conditions, we refer to work on constraint databases [12,15,21,22]. Compared to other works on obligations [6,11,16], our idea on condition-obligation binding and indeterminism is new.

7   Conclusion

In this paper, we proposed Conditional P-RBAC and Universal P-RBAC for specifying complex privacy policies. The key design criterion is to balance efficiency and expressiveness. The definition of domains and atomic conditions are carefully chosen to reflect the wide needs for enforceable privacy policies and to meet our efficiency goal, so does the design of condition languages and permission assignment sets. We have taken into account the effect of hierarchical relations among roles, data and purposes, which further enhance the expressiveness of our approach. As part of future work, we plan to introduce a sticky policy paradigm[13] into P-RBAC and develop a formal method to describe and manage obligations and to automatically detect possible conflicts between obligations and between obligations and actions.

Acknowledgement

The work reported in this paper has been partially supported by IBM under the OCR project "Privacy and Security Policy Management". Participants to this project are: Carnegie Mellon University, IBM T.J. Watson Research Center, Purdue University.

References

1. Agrawal, D., Giles, J., Lee, K.-W., Lobo, J.: Policy ratification. In: POLICY'05. Proceedings of the Sixth IEEE International Workshop on Policies for Distributed Systems and Networks, Stockholm Sweden, pp. 223–232. IEEE Computer Society, Los Alamitos (2005)
2. Amazon.com: Amazon privacy notice, available at http://www.amazon.com/exec/obidos/tg/browse/-/468496/102-8997954-0573735
3. Anderson, A.H.: A comparison of two privacy policy languages: Epal and xacml. In: SWS '06: Proceedings of the 3rd ACM workshop on Secure web services, pp. 53–60. ACM Press, New York (2006)
4. Ashley, P., Hada, S., Karjoth, G., Powers, C., Schunter, M.: Enterprise privacy authorization language (epal 1.2). W3C Member Submission 10 (November 2003), available at http://www.w3.org/Submission/EPAL/
5. Barth, A., Mitchell, J.C., Rosenstein, J.: Conflict and combination in privacy policy languages. In: WPES '04: Proceedings of the 2004 ACM workshop on Privacy in the electronic society, pp. 45–46. ACM Press, New York (2004)
6. Bettini, C., Jajodia, S., Wang, X., Wijesekera, D.: Obligation monitoring in policy management. In: POLICY'02. Proceedings of the 3rd International Workshop on Policies for Distributed Systems and Networks, Washington, DC, USA, p. 2. IEEE Computer Society, Los Alamitos (2002)
7. Ferraiolo, D.F., Sandhu, R., Gavrila, S., Kuhn, D.R., Chandramouli, R.: Proposed nist standard for role-based access control. ACM Trans. Inf. Syst. Secur. 4(3), 224–274 (2001)
8. Fischer-Hubner, S.: IT-security and privacy: design and use of privacy-enhancing security mechanisms. Springer, Heidelberg (2001)
9. Fisler, K., Krishnamurthi, S., Meyerovich, L.A., Tschantz, M.C.: Verification and change-impact analysis of access-control policies. In: Inverardi, P., Jazayeri, M. (eds.) ICSE 2005. LNCS, vol. 4309, pp. 196–205. Springer, Heidelberg (2006)
10. IBM Zurich Research Laboratory, Switzerland: The enterprise privacy authorization language (epal 1.1), available at http://www.zurich.ibm.com/security/enterprise-privacy/epal/
11. Irwin, K., Yu, T., Winsborough, W.H.: On the modeling and analysis of obligations. In: CCS '06: Proceedings of the 13th ACM conference on Computer and communications security, pp. 134–143. ACM Press, New York (2006)

12. Kanellakis, P.C., Kuper, G.M., Revesz, P.Z.: Constraint query languages (preliminary report). In: PODS '90: Proceedings of the ninth ACM SIGACT-SIGMOD-SIGART symposium on Principles of database systems, pp. 299–313. ACM Press, New York (1990)

13. Karjoth, G., Schunter, M., Waidner, M.: Platform for enterprise privacy practices: Privacy-enabled management of customer data. In: Dingledine, R., Syverson, P.F. (eds.) PET 2002. LNCS, vol. 2482, pp. 69–84. Springer, Heidelberg (2003)

14. Kolovski, V., Hendler, J., Parsia, B.: Formalizing xacml using defeasible description logics, available at `http://www.mindswap.org/~kolovski/xacml_tr.pdf`

15. Li, N., Mitchell, J.C.: Datalog with constraints: A foundation for trust management languages. In: Dahl, V., Wadler, P. (eds.) PADL 2003. LNCS, vol. 2562, pp. 58–73. Springer, Heidelberg (2002)

16. Mont, M.C., Beato, F.: On parametric obligation policies: Enabling privacy-aware information lifecycle management in enterprises. Tech. Report HPL-2007-7, Trusted Systems Laboratory, HP Laboratories Bristol, available at `http://www.hpl.hp.com/techreports/2007/HPL-2007-7.pdf`

17. Ni, Q., Trombetta, A., Bertino, E., Lobo, J.: Privacy aware role based access control. In: SACMAT '07. Proceedings of the 12th ACM symposium on Access control models and technologies. ACM Press, Sophia Antipolis, France (2007)

18. OASIS: extensible access control markup language (xacml) 2.0, available at `http://www.oasis-open.org/`

19. Organisation for Economic Co-operation and Development: Oecd guidelines on the protection of privacy and transborder flows of personal data of 1980, available at `http://www.oecd.org/`

20. Powers, C.S.: Privacy promises, access control, and privacy management. In: ISEC '02: Proceedings of the Third International Symposium on Electronic Commerce, Washington, DC, USA, p. 13. IEEE Computer Society, Los Alamitos (2002)

21. Revesz, P.Z.: Constraint databases: A survey. In: Thalheim, B. (ed.) Semantics in Databases. LNCS, vol. 1358, pp. 209–246. Springer, Heidelberg (1998)

22. Revesz, P.Z.: Safe datalog queries with linear constraints. In: Maher, M.J., Puget, J.-F. (eds.) CP 1998. LNCS, vol. 1520, pp. 355–369. Springer, Heidelberg (1998)

23. Sandhu, R.S., Coyne, E.J., Feinstein, H.L., Youman, C.E.: Role-based access control models. IEEE Computer 29(2), 38–47 (1996)

24. Smith, S.W., Spafford, E.H.: Grand challenges in information security: Process and output. IEEE Security and Privacy, 69–71 (January 2004)

25. TRUSTe.org: An independent, nonprofit enabling trust based on privacy for personal information on the internet, available at `http://www.truste.org/`

26. Tschantz, M.C., Krishnamurthi, S.: Towards reasonability properties for access-control policy languages with extended xacml analysis. Tech. Report CS-06-04, CS, Brown University, available at `http://www.cs.brown.edu/publications/techreports/reports/CS-06-04.html`

27. United State Department of Health: Health insurance portability and accountability act of 1996, available at `http://www.hhs.gov/ocr/hipaa/`

28. U.S. Senate Committee on Banking, Housing, and Urban Affairs: Information regarding the gramm-leach-bliley act of 1999, available at `http://banking.senate.gov/conf/`

29. W3C: Platform for privacy preferences (p3p) project, available at `http://www.w3.org/P3P`

Satisfiability and Resiliency in Workflow Systems

Qihua Wang and Ninghui Li

Center for Education and Research in Information Assurance and Security
and Department of Computer Science
Purdue University

Abstract. We propose the role-and-relation-based access control (R^2BAC) model for workflow systems. In R^2BAC, in addition to a user's role memberships, the user's relationships with other users help determine whether the user is allowed to perform a certain step in a workflow. For example, a constraint may require that two steps must not be performed by users who have a conflict of interest. We also study the workflow satisfiability problem, which asks whether a set of users can complete a workflow. We show that the problem is **NP**-complete for R^2BAC, and is **NP**-complete for any workflow model that supports certain simple types of constraints (e.g., constraints that state certain two steps must be performed by two different users). After that, we apply tools from parameterized complexity theory to better understand the complexities of this problem. We show that the problem is fixed-parameter tractable when the only relations used are $=$ and $\neq$, and is fixed-parameter intractable when user-defined binary relations can be used. Finally, we study the resiliency problem in workflow systems, which asks whether a workflow can be completed even if a number of users may be absent. We formally define three levels of resiliency in workflow systems, namely, static resiliency, decremental resiliency and dynamic resiliency, and study computational problems related to these notions of resiliency.

1 Introduction

Workflow systems are used in numerous domains, including production, purchase order processing, and various management tasks. Workflow authorization systems have gained popularity in the research community [1,3,5,10,12]. A workflow divides a task into a set of well-defined sub-tasks (called *steps* in the paper). Security policies in workflow systems are usually specified using authorization constraints. One may specify, for each step, which users are authorized to perform it. In addition, one may specify the constraints between users who perform different steps in the workflow. For example, one may require that two steps must be performed by different users for the purpose of separation of duty [4]. Oftentimes, constraints in workflow authorization systems need to refer to relationships among users. For example, the rationale under a separation of duty policy that requires 2 users to perform the task is that this deters and controls fraud, as the collusion of 2 users are required for a fraud to occur. However, when two users are close relatives, then collusion is much more likely. To achieve the objective of deterring and controlling fraud, the policy should require that two different steps in a workflow must be performed by users who are not in conflict of interest with each other. In different environments, the conflict-of-interest relation need to be defined differently.

J. Biskup and J. Lopez (Eds.): ESORICS 2007, LNCS 4734, pp. 90–105, 2007.

For instance, inside an organization's system, relationships such as close relatives (e.g., spouses and parent-child) can be maintained and users who are close relatives may be considered to be in conflict of interest. In a peer-review setting, conflict of interest may be based on past collaborations, common institutions, etc. For another example, one university may have a policy that a graduate student's study plan must be first approved by the student's advisor and then by the graduate officer in the student's department. To specify such a constraint, one needs to define and refer to the advisor-student binary relation.

In this paper, we introduce the role-and-relation-based access control (R^2BAC) model for workflow systems. The model is role-based in the sense that individual steps of a workflow are authorized for roles. The model is relation-based in the sense that user-defined binary relations can be used to specify constraints and an authorized user is prevented from performing a step unless the user satisfies these constraints. R^2BAC is a natural step beyond Role-Based Access Control (RBAC) [9], especially in the setting of workflows. As a role defines a set of users, which can be viewed as a unary relation among the set of all users, a binary relation is the natural next step.

One fundamental problem in any workflow authorization systems is the *workflow satisfiability problem* (WSP), which asks whether a workflow can be completed in a certain system configuration. We show that WSP is **NP**-complete in R^2BAC. Furthermore, we show that the intractability is inherent in any workflow authorization systems that support some simple kinds of constraints. In particular, we show that WSP is **NP**-hard in any workflow system that supports *either* constraints that require two steps must be performed by different users *or* constraints that require one step must be performed by a user who also performs at least one of several other steps. Such intractability results are somewhat surprising and discouraging, because the constraints involved are simple and natural. It is also unsatisfying as such results do not shed light on the computation cost one has to pay by introducing additional expressive features such as user-defined binary relations, since the complexity of WSP is **NP**-complete with or without them. Finally, the practical significance of such intractability results is unclear, as in real-world workflow systems, the number of steps should be small.

To address these issues, we apply tools from *parameterized complexity* [6] to WSP. Parameterized complexity is a measure of computational complexity of problems with multiple input parameters. Parameterized complexity enables us to perform finer-grained study on the computational complexity of WSP. We show that if only equality and inequality relations are used and the number of steps in the workflow is treated as a parameter, WSP is fixed-parameter tractable. More specifically, the problem can be solved in $O(f(k)n)$, where f is a function, k is the number of steps in the workflow, and n is the size of the problem. As the number of steps is relatively small in practice, this result shows that it is possible to solve WSP efficiently, when only equality and inequality relations are used. Also, we show that if user-defined relations are allowed, WSP is fixed-parameter intractable. More specifically, WSP is $W[1]$-hard and is in the complexity class $W[2]$; both of $W[1]$ and $W[2]$ are parameterized complexity classes within **NP**. This illustrates that while supporting user-defined binary relations increases the expressive power, it also introduces a computational cost. We note that a naive algorithm solving WSP in R^2BAC takes time $O(kn^{k+1})$, which may be acceptable when k is small. The complexity $O(kn^{k+1})$ is not considered fixed-parameter tractable because one cannot separate n and k in the complexity to the form of $f(k)n^{\alpha}$, where $f(k)$ is independent of n and α is a constant independent of k. We also note that it is also possible to develop algorithms with heuristic optimizations that can solve WSP efficiently for practical instances; the study of such algorithms is beyond the scope of this paper.

In many situations, it is not enough to ensure that a workflow can be completed in the current system configuration. In particular, when the workflow is designed to complete a critical task, it is necessary to make sure that the workflow can be completed even if certain users become absent in emergency situations. In other words, *resiliency* is important in workflow systems. The notion of resiliency policies in access control has been recently introduced [8]. Unlike traditional security policies about access control, which focus on ensuring that access is properly *restricted* so that users who should not have access do not get access, resiliency policies aim at ensuring that access is properly *enabled* so that the system is resilient to the absence of users. The goal of resiliency policies is to guarantee that even if a number of users become absent in certain emergent situation, the remaining users can still finish the crucial tasks. An example resiliency policy is as follows: Upon the absence of up to four users, there must still exist three mutually disjoint sets of users such that the users in each set together have all permissions to carry out a critical task. Such a policy would be needed when one needs to be able to send up to three teams of users to different sites to perform a certain task, perhaps in response to some emergent events.

A challenging problem with both theoretical and practical interest is resiliency in workflow systems. Resiliency in workflow systems differs from the resiliency policies proposed in [8] in two aspects. First, due to the existence of authorization constraints, even if a set of users together are authorized to perform all steps in a workflow, it is still possible that they cannot complete the task. Second, as a workflow consists of a sequence of steps and finishing all these steps may take a relatively long time, it is possible that certain users become absent at some point and come back later. In other words, the set of available users may change during the execution of a workflow. Therefore, more refined notions of resiliency for workflow systems are needed. In this paper, we introduce three levels of resiliency in workflow systems and study the complexity of checking resiliency.

The contributions of this paper are as follows:

- We propose the role-and-relation-based access control (R^2BAC) model for workflow systems. R^2BAC naturally extends RBAC to use binary relations to specify authorization constraints and capture many security requirements commonly encountered in workflows.
- We show that WSP in R^2BAC is **NP**-complete in general. We also show that WSP remains **NP**-hard for any workflow model that supports one of two simple kinds of constraints. Such results are inherent to features of workflow authorization systems and are independent from specific modeling approaches.
- We apply tools from the parameterized complexity theory to WSP and show that it is fixed-parameter tractable when only equality and inequality relations are allowed. However, when user-defined binary relations can be used, WSP becomes fixed-parameter intractable. This clearly illustrates the computational cost incurred by having user-defined binary relations and gives algorithmic insights and ideas about solving WSP in the fixed-parameter tractable (but **NP**-complete) case.

To the best of our knowledge, this paper is the first to use parameterized complexity in access control policy analysis. As a number of policy analysis problems in access control have been shown to be **NP**-complete, we believe that parameterized complexity theory can be fruitfully applied to these problems to shed insight on the causes of hardness in these problems as well as to give new algorithmic insights.

- We formally define three levels of resiliency in workflow systems. In *static resiliency*, up to t users are absent before the execution of an instance of a workflow. We show that checking whether a set of users is statically resilient for a workflow is **NP**-hard and is in $\mathbf{coNP^{NP}}$, a complexity class in the Polynomial Hierarchy. In *decremental resiliency*, users may become absent during the execution of an instance of a workflow, absent users will never come back for the same workflow instance, and at most t users may be absent in the end. *Dynamic resiliency* differs from decremental resiliency in that absent users may come back later and work on the same workflow instance, and at most t users may be absent at any given point of time. We show that checking whether a set of users is decremental resilient or dynamic resilient for a workflow is **PSPACE**-complete.

The remainder of the paper is organized as follows. We introduce the R^2BAC model in Section 2. After that, we study the workflow satisfiability problem in Section 3 and study parameterized complexity of the problem in Section 4. We then define and study resiliency problems in workflow systems in Section 5. We discuss related work in Section 6 and conclude in Section 7.

2 The Role-and-Relation-Based Access Control Model for Workflow Systems

In this section, we introduce the Role-and-Relation-Based Access Control (R^2BAC) model for workflow systems. We start with a motivating example.

Example 1. In an academic institution, submitting a grant proposal to an outside sponsor via the sponsor program services (SPS) is modeled as a workflow with five steps[1] (see Figure 1).

1. Preparation: A faculty member prepares a proposal and sends it to the business office of his or her department.
2. Budget: An account clerk prepares the budget, checks the proposal, and submits it to the SPS office.
3. Expert Review: A regulation expert in the SPS office reviews the proposal to check whether the proposal satisfies various regulations, e.g., those governing export control and human subject research.
4. Account Review: An account manager reviews the proposal and the budget.
5. Submission: An account manager submits the proposal to the outside sponsor.

---

[1] This is a simplified version of the process in the authors' institution, which also requires signatures of the department head and the dean's office.

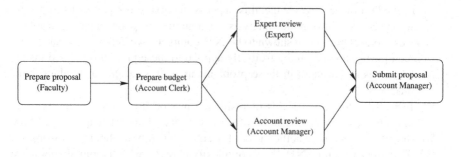

Fig. 1. A workflow for grant proposal submission to outside sponsor via the sponsor program services (SPS)

In the workflow, steps `expert review` and `account review` may be performed concurrently while all other steps must be carried out sequentially. The step `preparation` can be performed by any personnel who can serve as a primary investigator, while the step `budget` must be carried out by an account clerk. A regulation expert is authorized to review the proposal in the step `expert review`. The privilege to perform steps `account review` and `submission` is granted to account managers.

The workflow has the following constraints.

1. Steps `preparation`, `budget`, `expert review` and `account review` must be performed by four different users.
2. The account clerk who signs the proposal must be in the same department as the faculty member who prepares the proposal.
3. The persons who review the proposal must not have a conflict of interest with the one submitting the proposal.
4. The account manager who reviews the proposal is responsible to submit it to the outside sponsor.

In the above, Constraint 2 reflects certain procedural and duty requirements, while Constraint 1 enforces the principle of separation of duty. Constraint 3 follows the spirit of separation of duty and goes beyond that. Rather than simply requiring that the two steps must be performed by different people, the constraint requires that the people who perform the two steps must not have a conflict of interest. Constraint 4 enforces a binding-of-duty policy [5] by requiring two tasks be performed by the same user.

As security and practical requirements vary from tasks to tasks, the specification of constraints plays a crucial role in the expression of workflow. As demonstrated in Example 1, binary relations play an important role in expressing authorization constraints. Most existing workflow authorization models support only a few pre-defined binary relations, which limits the expressive power of these models. For example, the model proposed in [10] supports only six pre-defined binary relations $\{=, \neq, <, \leq, >, \geq\}$ between users and roles. Hence, there is no way to express relations like "in the same department" or "is a family member". The model in [5] supports user-defined relations. Our role-and-relation-based access control (R^2BAC) model for workflow systems extends the model in [5] by explicitly combining roles and relations and by supporting more sophisticated forms of constraints using these relations.

We now introduce formal definitions for R^2BAC. Note that $\mathcal{U}$, $\mathcal{R}$ and $\mathcal{B}$ are names of all possible users, roles and binary relations in the system, respectively.

Definition 1 (Configuration). A *configuration* is given by a tuple $\langle U, UR, B \rangle$, where $U \subseteq \mathcal{U}$ is a set of users, $UR \subseteq U \times \mathcal{R}$ is the user-role membership relation and $B = \{\rho_1, \cdots, \rho_m\} \subseteq \mathcal{B}$ is a set of binary relations such that $\rho_i \subseteq U \times U$ ($i \in [1, m]$). For convenience, we assume that when ρ is in B, $\bar{\rho}$ is also in B, where $(u_1, u_2) \in \bar{\rho}$ if and only if $(u_1, u_2) \notin \rho$. Also, $\bar{\bar{\rho}}$ is the same as ρ. Furthermore, we assume that B contains two predefined binary relations "=" and "$\neq$", which denote equality and inequality, respectively.

A configuration $\langle U, UR, B \rangle$ defines the environment in which a workflow is to be run. In particular, B should define all the binary relations that appear in any constraint in workflows to be run in the environment.

Definition 2 (Workflow and Constraints). A *workflow* is represented as a tuple $\langle S, \preceq, SA, C \rangle$, where S is a set of steps, $\preceq \subseteq S \times S$ defines a partial order among steps in S, $SA \subseteq \mathcal{R} \times S$, and C is a set of constraints, each of which takes one of the following forms:

1. $\langle \rho(s_1, s_2) \rangle$: the user who performs s_1 and the user who perform s_2 must satisfy the binary relation ρ.
2. $\langle \rho(\exists X, s) \rangle$: there exists a step $s' \in X$ such that $\langle \rho(s', s) \rangle$ holds, i.e., the user who performs s' and the user who performs s satisfy ρ.
3. $\langle \rho(s, \exists X) \rangle$: there exists a step $s' \in X$ such that $\langle \rho(s, s') \rangle$ holds.
4. $\langle \rho(\forall X, s) \rangle$: for each step $s' \in X$, $\langle \rho(s', s) \rangle$ must hold.
5. $\langle \rho(s, \forall X) \rangle$: for each step $s' \in X$, $\langle \rho(s, s') \rangle$ must hold.

Intuitively, in a workflow $\langle S, \preceq, SA, C \rangle$, that $s_i \preceq s_j$ ($i \neq j$) indicates that step s_i must be performed before step s_j. Steps s_i and s_j may be performed *concurrently*, if neither $s_i \preceq s_j$ nor $s_j \preceq s_i$. SA is called *role-step authorization* and $(r, s) \in SA$ indicates that members of role r is authorized to perform step s.

Example 2. Consider the workflow for submitting a grant proposal in Example 1. Let $s_{prepare}$, s_{budget}, s_{xp_review}, s_{ac_review} and s_{submit} denote the five steps in the workflow. The constraints of the workflow can be represented in tuple-based specification as follows.

1. $\langle \neq (s_{budget}, s_{prepare}) \rangle$, $\langle \neq (s_{xp\_review}, \forall\{s_{prepare}, s_{budget}\}) \rangle$,
   $\langle \neq (s_{ac\_review}, \forall\{s_{prepare}, s_{budget}, s_{xp\_review}\}) \rangle$
   These require that the first four steps in the workflow must be performed by four different users.
2. $\langle \rho_{same\_dept}(s_{budget}, s_{prepare}) \rangle$
   $(u_x, u_y) \in \rho_{same\_dept}$ when u_x and u_y are in the same department. The constraint requires that the person who signs the proposal must be in the same department as the person who prepares it.

3. $\langle \overline{p}_{conflict\_interest}(\forall\{s_{xp\_review}, s_{ac\_review}\}, s_{prepare})\rangle$

   $(u_x, u_y) \in p_{conflict\_interest}$ when u_x and u_y have a conflict of interest. The constraint requires that the person who reviews the proposal must not have a conflict of interest with the person who prepares it.

4. $\langle = (s_{submit}, s_{ac\_review})\rangle$

   The constraint requires that `account review` and `submission` must be performed by the same person.

Definition 3 (Plans and Partial Plans). A *plan* P for workflow $W = \langle S, \preceq, SA, C\rangle$ is a subset of $\mathcal{U} \times S$ such that, for every step $s_i \in S$, there is exactly one tuple (u_a, s_i) in P, where $u_a \in \mathcal{U}$. A *partial plan* PP for W is a subset of $\mathcal{U} \times S$ such that, for every step $s_i \in S$, there is at most one tuple (u_a, s_i) in PP, where $u_a \in \mathcal{U}$. And $(u_a, s_i) \in PP$ implies that, for every $s_j \preceq s_i$, there exists $u_b \in \mathcal{U}$ such that $(u_b, s_j) \in PP$.

Intuitively, a plan assigns exactly one user to every step in a workflow, while a partial plan does this for only a portion of the steps in the workflow. Furthermore, if a step is in a partial plan, then its prerequisite steps must also be in the partial plan.

Definition 4 (Valid Plan). Given a workflow $W = \langle S, \preceq, SA, C\rangle$, and a configuration $\Gamma = \langle U, UR, B\rangle$, we say that a user u is an *authorized user* of a step $s \in S$ under Γ if and only if there exists a role r such that $(u, r) \in UR$ and $(r, s) \in SA$. We say that a plan P *is valid for* W under Γ if and only if for every $(u, s) \in P$, u is an authorized user of s, and no constraint in C is violated. We say that W is *satisfiable* under Γ if and only if there exists a plan P that is valid for W under Γ.

Note that there can be multiple valid plans for a workflow W under a configuration. In fact, it is the existence of multiple valid plans that makes it possible for W to be completed even if a number of users are absent. In situations where the configuration changes during the execution of a workflow instance (e.g. users become absent), we will have to change our plan at runtime and thus constraints need to be checked at runtime as well. If a constraint c contains $\forall$, then it is checked whenever a step restricted by c is to be executed. Other kinds of constraints are checked before the last step restricted by the constraint is to be executed.

Definition 5 (Valid Partial Plan). Given a workflow $\langle S, \preceq, SA, C\rangle$ and a configuration $\langle U, UR, B\rangle$, let $s_1, \cdots, s_m$ be a sequence of steps such that $s_i \not\preceq s_j$ when $i > j$. A partial plan PP is *valid* with respect to the sequence $s_1, \cdots, s_i$ if it assigns one user to each step in $s_1, \cdots, s_i$ and no constraint that is checked before the execution of s_i is violated by PP.

3 The Workflow Satisfiability Problem

One fundamental problem in workflow authorization systems is the Workflow Satisfiability Problem (WSP), which checks whether a workflow W is satisfiable under a configuration Γ. Note that, given configuration $\langle U, UR, B\rangle$, checking whether W is satisfiable under Γ is equivalent to checking whether there is a valid plan for W under Γ. In this section, we study the computational complexity of WSP.

3.1   Computational Complexity of WSP for R^2BAC

Theorem 1. WSP is **NP**-complete in R^2BAC.

The proof of Theorem 1 consists of two parts. The first part is Lemma 1, which shows that WSP is in **NP** in R^2BAC. In the second part, Lemma 2 and Lemma 3 show that WSP is **NP**-hard in two restricted cases. Due to page limit, proofs to the following lemmas are given in our technical report [11].

Lemma 1. WSP is in **NP** in R^2BAC.

Intuitively, a nondeterministic Turing can guess a plan and check whether the plan is valid in polynomial time.

Lemma 2. WSP is **NP**-hard in R^2BAC, if the workflow uses constraints of the form $\langle \neq (s_1, s_2) \rangle$.

To prove the above lemma, we use a reduction from the **NP**-complete GRAPH K-COLORABILITY problem. In the reduction, vertices in a graph are mapped to steps in the workflow, while colors are mapped to users. In the GRAPH K-COLORABILITY problem, the number of vertices is normally much larger than the number of colors. Hence, the number of steps in the constructed workflow is much larger than the number of users, which is rarely the case in practice. Such a phenomenon indicates that classical complexity framework is inadequate to study the complexity of WSP in a real-word setting. This motivates us to apply the tool of parameterized complexity to perform finer-grained study of the complexity of WSP, which will be discussed in Section 4.

Lemma 3. WSP is **NP**-hard in R^2BAC, if the workflow uses constraints of the form $\langle = (s, \exists X) \rangle$.

The proof of this lemma uses a reduction from the **NP**-complete HITTING SET problem to WSP.

   Although WSP is intractable in general in R^2BAC, the problem is in **P** for certain special cases. Lemma 4 states a tractable case for WSP.

Lemma 4. WSP is in **P** in R^2BAC, if the workflow only has constraints in the forms of $\langle = (s_1, s_2) \rangle$, $\langle = (s, \forall X) \rangle$ or $\langle = (\forall X, s) \rangle$.

3.2   The Inherent Complexity of Workflow Systems

In Section 3.1, we show that WSP is **NP**-hard in R^2BAC in general. In this section, we stress that the intractability of WSP is inherent to certain fundamental features of workflow authorization systems and independent from modeling approaches. We say that a workflow system supports the feature of *user-step authorization* if it allows one to specify (either directly or indirectly) which users are allowed to perform which steps in the workflow. User-step authorization is probably the most fundamental feature and almost all workflow systems found in existing literatures support such feature. A *user-inequality constraint* states that certain two steps cannot be performed by the same user, i.e., $\langle \neq (s_1, s_2) \rangle$ in R^2BAC. An *existence-equality constraint* states that a certain step must be performed by a user who performs at least one step in a given set of steps, i.e., $\langle = (s, \exists X) \rangle$ in R^2BAC.

Theorem 2. Checking whether a set of users can complete a workflow is **NP**-hard for any workflow system that satisfies either (or both) of the followings:

– The system supports user-step authorization and user-inequality constraints.
– The system supports user-step authorization and existence-equality constraints.

The proof to Theorem 2 follows from the proofs of Lemmas 2 and 3. Please refer to [11] for details.

Note that user-inequality constraints are widely used in existing literatures to enforce separation of duty in workflow systems. Many workflow models [3,10,5] support such type of constraints. Existence-equality constraints are a natural way to enforce the general form of binding of duty policies, which require a step be performed by one of those users who have performed some prerequisite steps.

4   Beyond Intractability of WSP

In Section 3, we have shown that WSP is **NP**-complete in R^2BAC for the general case as well as the two special cases where only a simple form of constraints are used. Such results are, however, unsatisfying, as they do not shed light on the computation cost associated with introducing additional expressive features such as user-defined binary relations, since the complexity of WSP is **NP**-complete in all the three cases. Such a phenomenon indicates that classical computational complexity does not precisely capture the computational difficulty of different cases of WSP. Furthermore, the practical significance of such intractability results is unclear. The input to WSP consists of many aspects, such as the number of steps in the workflow, the number of constraints and the number of users in the configuration etc. In practice, some aspects of the input will not take a large value. For instance, even though the number of users may be large, the number of steps in the workflow is expected to be small. An interesting question arises is whether WSP can be solved efficiently given the restriction that the number of steps is small.

To address these issues, we apply tools from the theory of parameterized complexity [6] to WSP.

4.1   Why Parameterized Complexity?

Parameterized complexity is a measure of complexity of problems with multiple input parameters. The theory of parameterized complexity was developed in the 1990s by Rod Downey and Michael Fellows. It is motivated, among other things, by the observation that there exist hard problems that (most likely) require exponential runtime when complexity is measured in terms of the input size only, but that are computable in a time that is polynomial in the input size and exponential in a (small) parameter k. Hence, if k is fixed at a small value, such problems can still be considered 'tractable' despite their traditional classification as 'intractable'.

In classical complexity, a decision problem is specified by two items of information: (1) the input to the problem, and (2) the question to be answered. In parameterized complexity, there are three parts of a problem specification: (1) the input to the problem,

(2) the aspects of the input that constitute the parameter, and (3) the question to be answered. Normally, the parameter is selected because it is likely to be confined to a small range in practice. The parameter provides a systematic way of specifying restrictions of the input instances. Some **NP**-hard problems can be solved by algorithms that are exponential only in a fixed parameter while polynomial in the size of the input. Such an algorithm is called a *fixed-parameter tractable* algorithm. More specifically, an algorithm for solving a problem is a fixed-parameter tractable algorithm, if when given any input instance of the problem with parameter k, the algorithm takes time $O(f(k)n^\alpha)$, where n is the size of the input, k is the parameter, α is a constant (independent of k), and f is an arbitrary function.

If a problem has a fixed-parameter tractable algorithm, then we say that it is a fixed-parameter tractable problem and belongs to the class **FPT**. For example, the **NP**-complete VERTEX COVER asks, given a graph G and an integer k, whether there is a size-k set V' of vertices, such that every edge in G is adjacent to at least one vertex in V'. This problem is in **FPT** when taking k as the parameter, as there exists a simple algorithm with running time of $O(2^k n)$, where n is the size of G. Note that not all intractable problems are in **FPT**. For instance, the **NP**-complete DOMINATING SET problem is fixed-parameter intractable. Given a graph G and an integer k, DOMINATING SET asks whether there is a size-k set V' of vertices such that every vertex in G is either in V' or is connected to a vertex in V' by an edge. For DOMINATING SET, there is no significant alternative to trying all size-k subsets of vertices in G and there are $O(n^k)$ such subsets, where n is the number of vertices.

Finally, we would like to point out that a problem in **FPT** does not necessarily mean that it can be efficiently solved as long as the parameter is small. Note that $f(k)$ may be a function that grows very fast over k. For instance, an $O(k^{k^k} n)$ algorithm is not practical even if k is as small as 5, just as we cannot claim that a problem in **P** can be solved efficiently when the best algorithm takes time $O(n^{100})$. However, showing that a problem is in **FPT** has significant impact as experiences have shown that improvement on fixed-parameter tractable algorithms are oftentimes possible. For instance, when VERTEX COVER was first observed to be solvable in $O(f(k)n^3)$, $f(k)$ was such a function that the algorithm is utterly impractical even for $k = 1$. An $O(2^k n)$ algorithm was proposed later, and then an algorithm with running time $O(kn + (4/3)^k k^2)$ was revealed. Right now, VERTEX COVER is well-solved for input of any size, as long as the parameter value is $k \leq 60$. Parameterized complexity offers a fresh angle into designing algorithms for such problems.

In this paper, we only study which subcases of WSP are in **FPT** and which are not. Improvement on the fixed-parameter tractable algorithms for the **FPT** cases is beyond the scope of this paper.

4.2   Fixed Parameter Tractable Cases of WSP

As the number of steps in a workflow is likely to be small in practice, we select the number of steps as the parameter for WSP. We first show that a special case of WSP in which only the $\neq$ relation is allowed is in **FPT**. The proof gives a fixed-parameter tractable algorithm and illustrates the intuition why this problem is in **FPT**.

Lemma 5. WSP in R^2BAC is in **FPT**, if $\neq$ is the only binary relation used by constraints in the workflow. In particular, given a workflow W and a configuration Γ, WSP can be solved in time $O(k^{k+1}n)$, where k is the number of steps in W and n is the size of the entire input to the problem.

Proof. A constraint using binary relation $\neq$ requires a certain step to be performed by a user who does not perform certain other step(s). Since there are k steps in W, if step s is authorized to no less than k users in U, then we can always find an authorized user of s, who is not assigned to any other steps in W. In other words, we only need to consider those steps that are authorized to less than k users in U, and there are at most k such steps. We construct partial plans for these steps by trying all combinations of authorized users and there are no more than k^k such combinations. Verifying whether a plan is valid can be done in $O(kn)$, as there are $O(n)$ constraints and each constraints restricts at most k steps. Therefore, checking whether U can complete W can be done in time $O(k^{k+1}n)$.

Theorem 3. WSP is in **FPT** in R^2BAC, if $=$ and $\neq$ are the only binary relations used by constraints in the workflow.

This Theorem subsumes Lemma 5. Please refer to [11] for its proof.

4.3   WSP Is Fixed Parameterized Intractable in General

A natural question to ask is whether WSP is still in **FPT** when user-defined binary relations are allowed in the workflow. We show that the answer is "no". Similar to proving a problem is intractable in classical complexity framework, we prove that a problem is fixed-parameter intractable by reducing another fixed-parameter intractable problem to the target problem. To preserve fixed-parameter tractability, we need to use a kind of reduction different from the classical ones used in **NP**-completeness proofs. We say that L reduces to L' by a *fixed-parameter reduction* if given an instance $\langle x, k \rangle$ for L, one can compute an instance $\langle x' = g_1(\langle x, k \rangle), k' = g_2(k) \rangle$ in time $O(f(k)|x|^\alpha)$ such that $\langle x, k \rangle \in L$ if and only if $\langle x', k' \rangle \in L'$, where g_1 and g_2 are two functions and α is a constant. Note that many classical reductions are not fixed-parameter reduction as they do not carry enough structure, and lead to lose of control for the parameter.

Under parameterized complexity, each problem falls somewhere in the hierarchy: $\mathbf{P} \subseteq \mathbf{FPT} \subseteq W[1] \subseteq W[2] \subseteq \cdots \subseteq W[P] \subseteq \mathbf{NP}$. If a problem is $W[1]$-hard, then it is believed to be fixed-parameter intractable. To understand the classes $W[t]$, we can start by viewing a 3CNF formula as a (boolean) decision circuit, consisting of one input for each variable and structurally a large *and* gate taking inputs from a number of small *or* gates. (Some wires in the circuit may include a negation.) The *or* gates are small in that each of them takes 3 inputs, and the *and* gate is large in that it takes an unbounded number of inputs. The *weft* of a decision circuit is the maximum number of large gates on any path from the input variable to the output line. The *weighted satisfiability* problem for decision circuits asks whether a decision circuit has a weight k satisfying assignment (i.e., a satisfying assignment in which at most k variables are assigned true). The class $W[t]$ includes all problems that are fixed parameter reducible to the weighted satisfiability problem for decision circuits of weft t.

The following theorem states that WSP is fixed-parameter intractable in R^2BAC when user-defined binary relations are allowed in the workflow.

Theorem 4. WSP is $W[1]$-hard in R^2BAC if user-defined binary relations are used in constraints.

The proof to the above theorem is given in [11]. In the proof, we reduce the $W[1]$-complete INDEPENDENT SET problem to WSP.

We conclude from Theorem 3 and Theorem 4 that supporting user-defined binary relations introduces additional complexity to WSP in R^2BAC. Parameterized complexity reveals such a fact that is hidden by classical complexity framework and allows us to better understand the source of complexity of WSP in R^2BAC. We point out that a naive algorithm solving WSP for R^2BAC, which enumerates all possible plans and verifies each of them, takes time $O(kn^{k+1})$, which may be acceptable when k is small. We also note that it is possible to develop algorithms with heuristic optimizations that can solve WSP efficiently for practical instances; the study of such algorithms is beyond the scope of this paper.

Finally, we provide an upperbound for WSP in R^2BAC in the parameterized complexity framework. Please refer to [11] for the proof to Theorem 5.

Theorem 5. WSP in R^2BAC is in $W[2]$.

It remains open whether WSP is $W[1]$-complete or $W[2]$-complete.

5 Resiliency in Workflow Systems

We have studied the workflow satisfiability problem (WSP) in previous sections. In many situations, it is not enough to ensure that a workflow is satisfiable in the current system configuration. In particular, when the workflow is designed to complete a critical task, it is necessary to guarantee that even if certain users are absent unexpectedly, the workflow can still be completed. Resiliency is a property of those system configurations that can satisfy the workflow even with absence of some users.

In this section, we define and study resiliency in workflow systems. The workflow model we use is R^2BAC. Before giving formal definitions of resiliency in workflow systems, let us consider several possible scenarios.

1. The execution of instances of a workflow is done in a relatively short period of time, say within fifteen minutes. Although it is possible that certain users are absent before the execution of a workflow instance, it is unlikely that available users become absent during the execution of the workflow instance. In other words, the set of users who are available for a workflow instance is stable.
2. The execution of instances of a workflow takes a relatively long period of time, say within one day. Some users may not come to work on the day when a workflow instance is executed. Furthermore, some users may have to leave at some point (e.g. between the execution of two steps) before the workflow instance is completed and will not come back to work until the next day. In such a situation, the set of users available to the workflow instance becomes smaller and smaller over time. Such a scenario would also be possible in potentially hazardous situations such as battlefield and fire-fighting.

3. The execution of instances of a workflow takes a long period of time. For example, only a single step of the workflow is performed each day. Since the set of users who come to work may differ from day to day, the set of available users may differ from step to step.

We capture the above three scenarios by proposing three levels of resiliency in workflow systems. They are *static (level-1) resiliency*, *decremental (level-2) resiliency* and *dynamic (level-3) resiliency*. In static resiliency, a number of users are absent before the execution of a workflow instance, while remaining users will not be absent during the execution; in decremental resiliency, users may be absent before or during the execution of a workflow instance, and absent users will not become available again; in dynamic resiliency, users may be absent before or during the execution of a workflow instance and absent users may become available again. In all cases, we assume that the number of absent users at any point is bounded by a parameter t. We now give formal definitions of the three levels of resiliency.

Definition 6 (Static Resiliency). Given a workflow W and an integer $t \geq 0$, a configuration $\langle U, UR, B \rangle$ is *statically resilient* for W up to t absent users if and only if for every size-t subset U' of U, W is satisfiable under $\langle (U - U'), UR, B \rangle$.

Intuitively, a configuration is statically resilient for a workflow if the workflow is still satisfiable after removing t users from the configuration.

Definition 7 (Decremental Resiliency). Given a workflow $W = \langle S, \preceq, SA, C \rangle$ and an integer t, a configuration $\langle U, UR, B \rangle$ is *decrementally resilient* for W up to t absent users, if and only if Player 1 can always win the following two-person game when playing optimally.

Initialization: $PP \leftarrow \emptyset, U_0 \leftarrow U, S_0 \leftarrow S, t_0 \leftarrow t$ and $i \leftarrow 1$.

Round i of the Game:
1. Player 2 selects a set U'_{i-1} such that $|U'_{i-1}| \leq t_{i-1}$.
   $U_i \leftarrow (U_{i-1} - U'_{i-1})$ and $t_i \leftarrow (t_{i-1} - |U'_{i-1}|)$.
2. Player 1 selects a step $s_{a_i} \in S_{i-1}$ such that $\forall s_b (s_b \prec s_{a_i} \Rightarrow s_b \notin S_{i-1})$.
   Player 1 selects a user $u \in U_i$.
   $PP \leftarrow PP \cup \{(u, s_{a_i})\}$ and $S_i \leftarrow (S_{i-1} - \{s_{a_i}\})$.
   If PP is not a valid partial plan with respect to the sequence $s_{a_1}, \cdots, s_{a_i}$, then Player 1 loses.
3. If $S_i = \emptyset$, then Player 1 wins; otherwise, let $i \leftarrow (i+1)$ and the game goes on to the next round.

In each round, Player 2 may remove a certain number of users and then Player 1 has to pick a remaining step that is ready to be performed and assign an available user to it. The total number of users Player 2 may remove throughout the game is bounded by t. A configuration is decrementally resilient for a workflow if there is always a way to complete the workflow no matter when and which users are removed, as long as the total number of absent users is bounded by t.

Also, in Definition 7, we assume that Player 1 plays optimally, which implies that in each round, Player 1 has to consider not only the next step but also all future steps.

Definition 8 (Dynamic Resiliency). Given a workflow $W = \langle S, \preceq, SA, C \rangle$ and an integer t, a configuration $\langle U, UR, B \rangle$ is *dynamically resilient* for W up to t absent users, if and only if Player 1 can always win the following two-person game when playing optimally.

Initialization: $PP \leftarrow \emptyset$, $S_0 \leftarrow S$ and $i \leftarrow 1$.
Round i of the Game:
1. Player 2 selects a set U'_{i-1} of up to t users.
   $U_i \leftarrow (U - U'_{i-1})$.
2. Player 1 selects a step $s_{a_i} \in S_{i-1}$ such that $\forall s_b(s_b \prec s_{a_i} \Rightarrow s_b \notin S_{i-1})$.
   Player 1 selects a user $u \in U_i$.
   $PP \leftarrow PP \cup \{(u, s_{a_i})\}$ and $S_i \leftarrow (S_{i-1} - \{s_{a_i}\})$.
   If PP is not a valid partial plan with respect to the sequence $s_{a_1}, \cdots, s_{a_i}$, then
   Player 1 loses.
3. If $S_i = \emptyset$, then Player 1 wins; otherwise, let $i \leftarrow (i+1)$ and the game goes on
   to the next round.

Intuitively, Player 2 may temporarily remove up to t users from the configuration at the beginning of each round. Then, Player 1 has to select a remaining step that is ready to be performed and assign an available user to it. After that, the configuration is restored and the next round of the game starts.

By definition, dynamic (level-3) resiliency is stronger than decremental (level-2) resiliency, which is in turn stronger than static (level-1) resiliency.

5.1 Computational Complexities of Checking Resiliency

In this section, we study computational problems related to resiliency in workflow systems. Due to page limit, proofs are given in [11].

Theorem 6. Checking whether a configuration Γ is statically resilient for a workflow W up to t users, which is called the *Static Resiliency Checking Problem* (SRCP), is **NP**-hard and is in $\mathbf{coNP^{NP}}$.

It remains open whether SRCP is $\mathbf{coNP^{NP}}$-complete or not. Readers who are familiar with computational complexity theory will recognize that $\mathbf{coNP^{NP}}$ is a complexity class in the Polynomial Hierarchy. Because the Polynomial Hierarchy collapses when $\mathbf{P} = \mathbf{NP}$, showing that an **NP**-hard decision problem is in the Polynomial Hierarchy, although is not equivalent to showing that the problem is **NP**-complete, has the same consequence: the problem can be solved in polynomial time if and only if $\mathbf{P} = \mathbf{NP}$.

Theorem 7. Checking whether a configuration Γ is decremental resilient for a workflow W up to t users, which is called the *Decremental Resiliency Checking Problem* (CRCP), is **PSPACE**-complete.

Checking whether Γ is dynamically resilient for a W up to t users, which is called the *Dynamic Resiliency Checking Problem* (DRCP), is **PSPACE**-complete.

To prove the above theorem, we reduce the **PSPACE**-complete QUANTIFIED SATISFIABILITY problem to CRCP and DRCP. Intuitively, we use user-step assignments in workflow to simulate truth assignments for boolean variables.

6 Related Work

Bertino et al. [3] introduced a language to express workflow authorization constraints as clauses in a logic programming language. The language supports a number of pre-defined relations for constraint specification. Bertino et al. [3] also proposed searching algorithms to assign users to complete a workflow. This work does not support user-defined binary relations, nor does it formally study computational complexity of the workflow satisfiability problem. Tan et al. [10] studied the consistency of authorization constraints in workflow systems. The model in [10] supports six predefined binary relations: $\{=, \neq, <, \leq, >, \geq\}$, but not user-defined relations. Atluri and Huang [1] proposed a workflow authorization model that focuses on temporal authorization. This model does not support constraints about users performing different steps in a task. Atluri and Warner [2] proposed a model that supports conditional delegation in workflow systems. Delegation is a potential mechanism to achieve resiliency. In this paper, we consider resiliency without using delegation. We plan to extend our definitions on resiliency to take delegation into account and study how to use delegation to achieve resiliency in workflow systems. Furthermore, in [12], Warner and Atluri considered authorization constraints that span multiple instances of a workflow. Their model supports predefined relations with emphasis on inter-instance constraints. Inter-instance problems in workflow systems is an interesting research area. The models in [2,12] do not support user-defined relations. Finally, Kang et al. [7] investigated access control mechanisms for inter-organizational workflow. Their workflow model authorizes steps to roles and supports dynamic constraints. However, they do not explicitly point out how constraints are specified and what kinds of constraints are supported besides separation of duty. Their paper mainly focuses on infrastructure design and implementation.

The workflow authorization model proposed by Crampton [5] is probably the one that is most closely related to R^2BAC. The model in [5] supports user-defined binary relations; however, it does not support quantifiers in constraints, so that constraints of the form $\langle \rho(\exists X, s) \rangle$ cannot be expressed in that model. Crampton [5] also studied the workflow satisfiability problem and presented a polynomial time algorithm for their model. However, the algorithm is incorrect.[2] As we have pointed out in Theorem 2, the workflow satisfiability problem is **NP**-hard in general for any workflow model that supports user-inequality constraints. Since the model in [5] supports such type of constraints, a polynomial time algorithm for the satisfiability problem in their model could not exist.

None of the work mentioned above have given the computational complexity results of the Workflow Satisfiability Problem, whereas we give a clear characterization using parameterized complexity. Also, the resiliency problem in workflow has not been studied before in the literature.

The concept of resiliency policies in access control is first formally proposed by Li et al. [8]. To our knowledge, this paper is the first to define and study resiliency problems in workflow systems. There are major difference between resiliency in workflow systems and the resiliency policies proposed in [8], and we have discussed the differences in Section 1.

---

[2] We have verified the bug with the author of [5]. Please refer to [11] for more details.

7 Conclusion

We have proposed a role-and-relation-based model (R^2BAC) for workflow systems, and have shown that the workflow satisfiability problem in R^2BAC is **NP**-complete. We have also shown that the problem remains intractable for any workflow model that supports certain simple types of constraints such as user-inequality constraints and existence-equality constraints. We then apply tools from parameterized complexity to better understand the complexities of the problem. Furthermore, we have formally defined three levels of resiliency in workflow systems, namely, static resiliency, decremental resiliency and dynamic resiliency. We have also shown that checking whether a system configuration is statically resilient for a workflow is **NP**-hard and is in the Polynomial Hierarchy, and the same problems for decremental resiliency and dynamic resiliency are **PSPACE**-complete.

References

1. Atluri, V., Huang, W.: An authorization model for workflows. In: Martella, G., Kurth, H., Montolivo, E., Bertino, E. (eds.) ESORICS 96. LNCS, vol. 1146, pp. 44–64. Springer, Heidelberg (1996)
2. Atluri, V., Warner, J.: Supporting conditional delegation in secure workflow management systems. In: SACMAT '05: Proceedings of the tenth ACM symposium on Access control models and technologies, pp. 49–58. ACM Press, New York (2005)
3. Bertino, E., Ferrari, E., Atluri, V.: The specification and enforcement of authorization constraints in workflow management systems. ACM Transactions on Information and System Security 2(1), 65–104 (1999)
4. Clark, D.D., Wilson, D.R.: A comparision of commercial and military computer security policies. In: Proceedings of the 1987 IEEE Symposium on Security and Privacy, pp. 184–194. IEEE Computer Society Press, Los Alamitos (May 1987)
5. Crampton, J.: A reference monitor for workflow systems with constrained task execution. In: SACMAT 2005. Proceedings of the Tenth ACM Symposium on Access Control Models and Technologies, Stockholm, Sweden, pp. 38–47. ACM Press, New York (June 2005)
6. Downey, R., Fellows, M.: Parameterized Complexity. Springer, Heidelberg (1999)
7. Kang, M.H., Park, J.S., Froscher, J.N.: Access control mechanisms for inter-organizational workflow, pp. 66–74 (2001)
8. Li, N., Tripunitara, M.V., Wang, Q.: Resiliency policies in access control. In: CCS. Proc. ACM Conference on Computer and Communications Security, ACM Press, New York (November 2006)
9. Sandhu, R.S., Coyne, E.J., Feinstein, H.L., Youman, C.E.: Role-based access control models. IEEE Computer 29(2), 38–47 (1996)
10. Tan, K., Crampton, J., Gunter, C.: The consistency of task-based authorization constraints in workflow systems. In: CSFW. Proceedings of the 17th IEEE Computer Security Foundations Workshop, pp. 155–169. IEEE Computer Society Press, Los Alamitos (2004)
11. Wang, Q., Li, N.: Satisfiability and resiliency in workflow systems. Technical Report CERIAS-TR-2007-28, Center for Education and Research in Information Assurance and Security, Purdue University (2007)
12. Warner, J., Atluri, V.: Inter-instance authorization constraints for secure workflow management. In: SACMAT. Proc. ACM Symposium on Access Control Models and Technologies, pp. 190–199. ACM Press, New York (2006)

Completeness of the Authentication Tests*

Shaddin F. Doghmi, Joshua D. Guttman, and F. Javier Thayer

The MITRE Corporation
shaddin@stanford.edu, {guttman,jt}@mitre.org

Abstract. Protocol participants manipulate values, transforming the cryptographic contexts in which they occur. The rules of the protocol determine which transformations are permitted. We formalize these transformations, obtaining new versions of the two *authentication tests* from earlier strand space papers.

We prove that the new versions are *complete*, in this sense: any collection of behaviors that satisfies those two authentication tests, when combined with some feasible adversary behavior, yields a possible execution.

We illustrate the strengthened authentication tests with brief analyses of three protocols.

1 Introduction

Cryptographic protocols are designed to control the ways that protocol participants transform messages. The protocol determines when a critical value may be transmitted within new forms of message. If the critical value has so far occurred only within a particular set of cryptographic contexts, then a participant may be *authenticated* by the way she transforms it to occur in a new context. A protocol preserves *secrecy* by ensuring that no participant's transformation will remove it from a class of safe contexts.

Protocol analysis within a simple Dolev-Yao model [5] may be completely formalized in terms of this idea.

In this paper, we support this assertion, using two forms of the transformation principle. One form covers the case in which the critical value is a fresh, unguessable value such as a nonce or session key. The other covers the case in which the critical value is an encrypted message. Each is a strengthened *authentication test*, various versions of which have appeared in earlier papers [9,10,11,13]. We illustrate the different aspects of the strengthened authentication tests in reference to a protocol due to Perrig and Song [13], Yahalom's protocol [3], and a new protocol we call the ambassador's protocol. The authentication tests are sensitive only to the regular (non-adversary) protocol behavior and a set of values assumed uncompromised; they are insensitive to specific adversary behavior.

We work within the strand space model [10], so local behaviors of regular principals are represented by regular strands, and adversary behavior is represented by penetrator strands. Possible executions are represented by bundles. (See Definitions 2–5.)

---

* Supported by the National Security Agency and by MITRE-Sponsored Research.

J. Biskup and J. Lopez (Eds.): ESORICS 2007, LNCS 4734, pp. 106–121, 2007.

Our main result is *completeness* for the authentication tests, in the following sense. Suppose that a collection of regular strands has been chosen, as well as a collection X of values that we assume the adversary did not originally possess and will not guess. Then there exists a bundle $\mathcal{B}$ containing exactly the given strands, without the adversary using the values X, if and only if those strands and the values X satisfy the authentication tests (Prop 5).

An implementation called CPSA uses most aspects of the strengthened authentication tests. It searches for all the minimal, essentially different executions that a protocol allows, as described in [4]. We call these minimal, essentially different executions *shapes*. CPSA checks authentication and secrecy properties, since these are easily read off from the set of shapes. By the undecidability of these properties [6], there exist protocols for which the set of shapes is infinite; however, for many protocols the set of shapes is very small, and frequently only one or two.

Related work. There is a vast body of work on protocol analysis. Much, such as Cryptyc [7] and ProVerif [1], aim at sound but not complete methods. Others, for instance Athena [13], do a search involving both regular and adversary behaviors. We here propose a method that is complete in the sense we have mentioned, but considers adversary behavior only in the most limited way. In particular, the authentication tests consider only whether given values—generally, keys—are available to the adversary, but not what actions are needed to synthesize the values received by the regular participants.

Roadmap to this paper. In Section 2 we give the basic strand space definitions, adapted to our current needs. Section 3 summarizes three examples that together illustrate many aspects of protocol analysis. Section 4 defines the key idea of a message "occurring only within" certain contexts in another message; we also provide a number of examples that will be used later in the paper. Section 5 gives the authentication test principles, and illustrates how to use them to analyze our three examples. Section 6 considers the adversary in more detail, and gives the crucial lemma for completeness. Finally, Section 7 introduces the notion of skeleton and uses it to formalize completeness. Appendix A fills in the proof of the key lemma.

2 Terms, Strands, and Bundles

In this section, we give background definitions, which are somewhat more general than those in the extended version of [4].

2.1 Algebra of Terms

Terms (or messages) form a free algebra A, built from (typed) atoms and (untyped) indeterminates $g, h, \ldots$ via constructors.

The atoms may be partitioned into some types, e.g. *keys*, *nonces*, etc. We assume A contains infinitely many atoms of each type.

An inverse operator is defined on atomic keys. There may be additional functions on atoms, such as an injective *public key of* function mapping principals to keys, or an injective *long term shared key of* function mapping pairs of principals to keys. These functions are not constructors, and their results are atoms. For definiteness, we include here functions $\mathsf{pubk}(a), \mathsf{ltk}(a)$ mapping principals to (respectively) their public keys and to a symmetric key shared on a long-term basis with a fixed server S. $\mathsf{pubk}(a)^{-1}$ is a's private key, where $\mathsf{pubk}(a)^{-1} \neq \mathsf{pubk}(a)$. By contrast, $\mathsf{ltk}(a)^{-1} = \mathsf{ltk}(a)$.

Terms in A are freely built from atoms and indeterminates using *tagged concatenation* and *encryption*. The tags are chosen from a set of constants written in sans serif font (e.g. tag). The tagged concatenation using tag of t_0 and t_1 is written $\mathsf{tag}\,\hat{}\,t_0\,\hat{}\,t_1$. Tagged concatenation using the distinguished tag null of t_0 and t_1 is written $t_0\,\hat{}\,t_1$.

Encryption takes a term t and a term t' serving as a key, and yields a term as result written $\{\!|t|\!\}_{t'}$. Protocols generally use a term t' as a key only if it is of some special forms, such as an atomic key or a term produced by hashing (used as a symmetric key). We regard hashing as encryption with a public key the inverse of which is not known to any principal. We extend the inverse function to non-atomic keys by stipulating that if K is non-atomic, then $K^{-1} = K$. We write $\{\!|t|\!\}_K$ to cover both the case of atomic and non-atomic K.

We regard terms as abstract syntax trees, where atoms and indeterminates are the leaves. A concatenation $\mathsf{tag}\,\hat{}\,t_0\,\hat{}\,t_1$ has a root node labeled tag and the two immediate subtrees representing t_0, t_1. An encryption $\{\!|t_0|\!\}_{t_1}$ has a root labeled with t_1, and one immediate subtree representing t_0.

Replacements are essentially homomorphisms on the algebra A:

Definition 1 (Replacement, Application). *A* replacement is a function α mapping atoms and indeterminates to A, such that (1) for every atom a, $\alpha(a)$ is an atom of the same type as a, and (2) α is a homomorphism with respect to the operations on atoms, e.g., $\alpha(K^{-1}) = (\alpha(K))^{-1}$ and $\alpha(\mathsf{pubk}(a)) = \mathsf{pubk}(\alpha(a))$.

The *application* of α to t, written $t \cdot \alpha$, homomorphically extends α's action on atoms and indeterminates. More explicitly, if $t = a$ is an atom, then $a \cdot \alpha = \alpha(a)$; if $t = g$ is an indeterminate, then $g \cdot \alpha = \alpha(g)$ and:

$$(\mathsf{tag}\,\hat{}\,t_0\,\hat{}\,t_1) \cdot \alpha = \mathsf{tag}\,\hat{}\,(t_0 \cdot \alpha)\,\hat{}\,(t_1 \cdot \alpha)$$
$$(\{\!|t|\!\}_K) \cdot \alpha = \{\!|t \cdot \alpha|\!\}_{K \cdot \alpha}$$

We extend the homomorphism $\_ \cdot \alpha$ to larger objects such as pairing and sets; thus, $(x, y) \cdot \alpha = (x \cdot \alpha, y \cdot \alpha)$, and $S \cdot \alpha = \{x \cdot \alpha : x \in S\}$. If $x \notin \mathsf{A}$ is a simple value such as an integer or a symbol, then $x \cdot \alpha = x$.

2.2   Strands and Origination

Directed messages represent transmission and reception of messages, where the direction $+$ means transmission, and the direction $-$ means reception:

Definition 2 (Strand Spaces). *A* direction *is one of the symbols* $+, -$. *A* directed term *is a pair* (d, t) *with* $t \in \mathsf{A}$ *and* d *a direction, normally written* $+t, -t$. $(\pm\mathsf{A})^*$ *is the set of finite sequences of directed terms.*

A strand space *over* A *is a structure containing a set* Σ *and two mappings: a* trace mapping $\mathsf{tr} : \Sigma \to (\pm\mathsf{A})^*$ *and a* replacement application operator $(s, \alpha) \mapsto s \cdot \alpha$ *such that* $\mathsf{tr}(s \cdot \alpha) = (\mathsf{tr}(s)) \cdot \alpha$.

By a *strand*, we just mean any member of some strand space Σ.

Definition 3. *A* penetrator strand *has trace of one of the following forms:*

M_t: $\langle +t \rangle$ *where* $t \in text, principal, nonce$ K_K: $\langle +K \rangle$ *with atomic key* K

$\mathsf{C}_{g,h}$: $\langle -g, -h, +g\char`\^h \rangle$                       $\mathsf{S}_{g,h}$: $\langle -g\char`\^h, +g, +h \rangle$

$\mathsf{E}_{h,K}$: $\langle -K, -h, +\{\!|h|\!\}_K \rangle$ $\mathsf{D}_{h,K}$: $\langle -K^{-1}, -\{\!|h|\!\}_K, +h \rangle$.

If s *is a penetrator strand, then* $s \cdot \alpha$ *is a penetrator strand of the same kind.*

The *subterm* relation, written $\sqsubseteq$, is the least reflexive, transitive relation such that (1) $t_0 \sqsubseteq \mathsf{tag}\char`\^t_0\char`\^t_1$; (2) $t_1 \sqsubseteq \mathsf{tag}\char`\^t_0\char`\^t_1$; and (3) $t \sqsubseteq \{\!|t|\!\}_K$. Notice, however, $K \not\sqsubseteq \{\!|t|\!\}_K$ unless (anomalously) $K \sqsubseteq t$. The subterms of t are the terms represented by the subtrees of t's abstract syntax tree. We say that a key K is *used for encryption* in a term t if for some t_0, $\{\!|t_0|\!\}_K \sqsubseteq t$.

A *node* is a pair $n = (s, i)$ where $i \leq \mathsf{length}(\mathsf{tr}(s))$; $\mathsf{strand}(s, i) = s$; and the *direction* and *term* of n are those of $\mathsf{tr}(s)(i)$. We prefer to write $s \downarrow i$ for the node $n = (s, i)$. A term t *originates* at node n if n is positive, $t \sqsubseteq \mathsf{msg}(n)$, and $t \not\sqsubseteq \mathsf{msg}(m)$ whenever $m \Rightarrow^+ n$. Thus, t originates on n if t is part of a message transmitted on n, and t was neither sent nor received previously on this strand.

2.3   Protocols and Bundles

Definition 4 (Protocols). *A* candidate $\langle \Pi, \mathsf{strand\_non}, \mathsf{strand\_unique} \rangle$ *consists of: (1) a finite set* Π *of strands called the* roles *of the protocol; (2) a function* $\mathsf{strand\_non}$ *mapping each role* r *to a finite set of keys* $\mathsf{strand\_non}_r$, *the non-originating keys of* r; *and (3) a function* $\mathsf{strand\_unique}$ *mapping each role* r *to a finite set of atoms* $\mathsf{strand\_unique}_r$, *the uniquely originating atoms of* r.

A candidate $\langle \Pi, \mathsf{strand\_non}, \mathsf{strand\_unique} \rangle$ *is a* protocol *if (1)* $K \in \mathsf{strand\_non}_r$ *implies that* K *does not occur in any node of* r, *but either* K *or* K^{-1} *is used for encryption on some term of* $\mathsf{tr}(r)$; *and (2)* $a \in \mathsf{strand\_unique}_r$ *implies that* a *originates on* r.

The regular strands *of* $\langle \Pi, \mathsf{strand\_non}, \mathsf{strand\_unique} \rangle$ *form the set of instances of the roles,* $\Sigma_\Pi = \{r \cdot \alpha : r \in \Pi\}$.

The set $\mathcal{N}$ of all nodes forms a directed graph $\mathcal{G} = \langle \mathcal{N}, (\to \cup \Rightarrow) \rangle$ with edges $n_1 \to n_2$ for communication (with the same term, directed from positive to negative node) and $n_1 \Rightarrow n_2$ for succession on the same strand.

Definition 5 (Bundle). *A finite acyclic subgraph* $\mathcal{B} = \langle \mathcal{N}_\mathcal{B}, (\to_\mathcal{B} \cup \Rightarrow_\mathcal{B}) \rangle$ *of* $\mathcal{G}$ *is a* bundle *if (1) when* $n_2 \in \mathcal{N}_\mathcal{B}$ *is negative, there is exactly one* $n_1 \in \mathcal{N}_\mathcal{B}$ *with* $n_1 \to_\mathcal{B} n_2$; *and (2) if* $n_2 \in \mathcal{N}_\mathcal{B}$ *and* $n_1 \Rightarrow n_2$, *then* $n_1 \Rightarrow_\mathcal{B} n_2$.

When $\mathcal{B}$ is a bundle, $\preceq_\mathcal{B}$ is the reflexive, transitive closure of $(\to_\mathcal{B} \cup \Rightarrow_\mathcal{B})$.

$\mathcal{B}$ is a *bundle over* $\langle \Pi, \mathsf{strand\_non}, \mathsf{strand\_unique} \rangle$ if for every $s \downarrow i \in \mathcal{B}$, (1) either $s \in \Sigma_\Pi$ or s is a penetrator strand; (2) if $s = r \cdot \alpha$ and $a \in \mathsf{strand\_non}_r \cdot \alpha$, then a does not occur in $\mathcal{B}$; and (3) if $s = r \cdot \alpha$ and $a \in \mathsf{strand\_unique}_r \cdot \alpha$, then a originates at most once in $\mathcal{B}$.

We say that a strand s is *in* $\mathcal{B}$ if s has at least one node in $\mathcal{B}$. Henceforth, assume fixed some arbitrary protocol $\langle \Pi, \mathsf{strand\_non}, \mathsf{strand\_unique} \rangle$.

Proposition 1. *Let $\mathcal{B}$ be a bundle. $\preceq_{\mathcal{B}}$ is a well-founded partial order. Every non-empty set of nodes of $\mathcal{B}$ has $\preceq_{\mathcal{B}}$-minimal members. If $a \sqsubseteq \mathsf{msg}(n)$ for any $n \in \mathcal{B}$, then a originates at some $m \preceq_{\mathcal{B}} n$.*

If α is a replacement, and $\mathcal{B}$ is a bundle, then $\mathcal{B} \cdot \alpha$ is a bundle.

$\mathcal{B} \cdot \alpha$ is a bundle *over* the same protocol if the replacement α does not cause the origination assumptions to fail.

3   Some Example Protocols

We consider here three relevant protocol examples.

Example 1 (Perrig-Song). The PS protocol (Fig. 1) is due to Perrig and Song, or rather, invented by their automated protocol generator [13]. Here, A and B share a long-term symmetric key, and the purpose of the protocol is to provide mutual authentication using the key. If the nonces are chosen to be Diffie-Hellman values, i.e. $N_a = g^x, N_b = g^y$, then the participants can combine those values to obtain an authenticated shared secret g^{xy} at the end.

The authors mention a reflection attack if B's name is omitted from the second message.

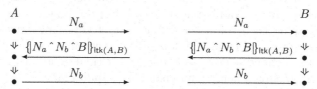

Fig. 1. PS symmetric key protocol

Example 2 (Yahalom). The Yahalom protocol [3] is also a symmetric key protocol, in this case using a key server to generate a session key whose reception by A is confirmed to B in the protocol (Fig. 2). This clever and compact protocol uses a surprising range of the tricks of protocol analysis.

Example 3 (The Ambassador's Protocol). A new protocol, which we call the ambassador's protocol, illustrates a rarely used aspect of the complete authentication tests. In this protocol (Fig. 3), a government G delivers a signed and encrypted authorization to its ambassador A. If negotiations are successful, then the ambassador performs the decryption and delivers the commitment to

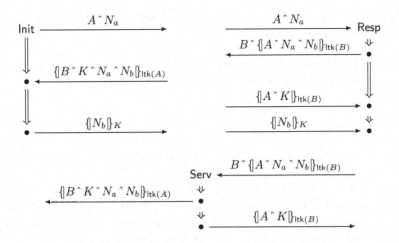

Fig. 2. Yahalom protocol (forwarding removed)

the foreign government F, which countersigns and returns the now reciprocal commitment to G. Typically, G would perform its first step with many potential messages m; after negotiations, the ambassador would select an appropriate session to complete. It is important that the commitments are encrypted so that A's portfolio of negotiating strategies is not disclosed to F. The fact that a particular commitment is decrypted tells G that the negotiations completed with this outcome.

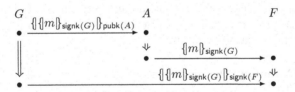

Fig. 3. The Ambassador's Protocol

4 "Occurs Only Within"

The most important idea for stating the strengthened authentication tests is of a term t_0 occurring only within specific forms in some other term.

Suppose that a set $S = \{\{t_0\}_{K_0}, \{t_1\}_{K_1}, \dots\}$ contains only encryptions. We say that a term t occurs only within S in t' if every path through the abstract syntax tree of t' that ends with t traverses a member of S.[1] The recursive formulation of Definition 6 is equivalent.

---

[1] In our terminology (Section 2), the K in $\{t\}_K$ is not an occurrence as a subterm, and no path in the syntax tree reaches it.

When $t \not\sqsubseteq t'$, then no path reaches it, so t occurs only within S in t' for every set of encryptions S, vacuously.

Definition 6 (Occurs only within/outside). *Let S be a set of encryptions. A term t_0 occurs only within S in t, if:*

1. $t_0 \not\sqsubseteq t$; or
2. $t \in S$; or
3. $t \neq t_0$, and either (3a) $t = \{\!|t_1|\!\}_K$ and t_0 occurs only within S in t_1, or else (3b) $t = \mathsf{tag}^\smallfrown t_1 {}^\smallfrown t_2$ and t_0 occurs only within S in each t_i ($i = 1, 2$).

It *occurs outside S in t* if t_0 does not occur only within S in t.

We say that t *has exited S passing from t_0 to t_1* if t occurs only within S in t_0 but t occurs outside S in t_1. Term t *exits S at a node n* if t occurs outside S in $\mathsf{msg}(n)$ but occurs only within S in every $\mathsf{msg}(m)$ for $m \prec n$.

If it occurs outside S, this means that $t_0 \sqsubseteq t$ and there is a non-empty path from the root to an occurrence of t_0 as a subterm of t that traverses no $t_1 \in S$. "Occurring only within" is similar to "being protected by a set of hat-terms" [2].

Example 4 (PS Occurrences). N_b occurs only within the singleton set

$$S_{ps} = \{\{\!|N_a {}^\smallfrown N_b|\!\}_{\mathsf{ltk}(A,B)}\}$$

in the term $\{\!|N_a {}^\smallfrown N_b|\!\}_{\mathsf{ltk}(A,B)}$. It has exited S_{ps} passing from $\{\!|N_a {}^\smallfrown N_b|\!\}_{\mathsf{ltk}(A,B)}$ to N_b. This provides the responder's guarantee.

$\{\!|N_a {}^\smallfrown N_b|\!\}_{\mathsf{ltk}(A,B)}$ occurs only within the null set $\emptyset$ in N_a, that is, it does not occur at all in N_a. However, this encryption occurs outside $\emptyset$ in $\{\!|N_a {}^\smallfrown N_b|\!\}_{\mathsf{ltk}(A,B)}$. This provides the initiator's guarantee.

Example 5 (Yahalom Occurrences). N_b exits $S_{Y,1} = \{\{\!|A {}^\smallfrown N_a {}^\smallfrown N_b|\!\}_{\mathsf{ltk}(B)}\}$ passing from $\{\!|A {}^\smallfrown N_a {}^\smallfrown N_b|\!\}_{\mathsf{ltk}(B)}$ to the server's output $\{\!|B {}^\smallfrown K {}^\smallfrown N_a {}^\smallfrown N_b|\!\}_{\mathsf{ltk}(A)}$. The nonce N_b exits the larger set

$$S_{Y,2} = \{\{\!|A {}^\smallfrown N_a {}^\smallfrown N_b|\!\}_{\mathsf{ltk}(B)}\} \cup \{\{\!|B {}^\smallfrown K'' {}^\smallfrown N_a {}^\smallfrown N_b|\!\}_{\mathsf{ltk}(A)} : K'' \text{ is a key}\}$$

when passing from $\{\!|A {}^\smallfrown N_a {}^\smallfrown N_b|\!\}_{\mathsf{ltk}(B)}$ to any term of the form $\{\!|N_b|\!\}_{K'}$. When $K' \neq K$, N_b has exited $S_{Y,2} \cup \{\{\!|N_b|\!\}_{K'}\}$ when passing from $\{\!|A {}^\smallfrown N_a {}^\smallfrown N_b|\!\}_{\mathsf{ltk}(B)}$ to $\{\!|N_b|\!\}_K$.

The correctness of the protocol, for the responder, relies on these three steps.

Example 6 (Ambassador's Protocol). The signed message $\{\!|m|\!\}_{\mathsf{signk}(G)}$ occurs outside the empty set $\emptyset$ in $\{\!|m|\!\}_{\mathsf{signk}(G)}$.

It has exited $S_a = \{\{\!|\{\!|m|\!\}_{\mathsf{signk}(G)}|\!\}_{\mathsf{pubk}(A)}\}$ passing from $\{\!|\{\!|m|\!\}_{\mathsf{signk}(G)}|\!\}_{\mathsf{pubk}(A)}$ to $\{\!|m|\!\}_{\mathsf{signk}(G)}$.

5   The Strengthened Authentication Tests

When a principal follows the rules of a protocol, it transforms the way that a critical value occurs in messages. A critical value that has hitherto occurred only within a limited set of forms is freed from them, and retransmitted in a new form. The outgoing and incoming authentication tests describe the possible executions of protocols using this idea. The outgoing test deals with the case where the critical value is a uniquely originating atom, and the incoming test deals with the case where it is an encryption.

5.1   The Outgoing Authentication Test

We say that t is *disclosed* in $\mathcal{B}$ iff $\mathsf{msg}(n) = t$ for some $n \in \mathcal{B}$. By the definitions of the penetrator strands for encryption and decryption (Definition 3), if the adversary uses K for encryption or decryption anywhere in $\mathcal{B}$, then K is disclosed in $\mathcal{B}$. If K^{-1} is not disclosed, it cannot decrypt any term encrypted with K.

We say that t is *disclosed before m* in $\mathcal{B}$, iff, for some $n \in \mathcal{B}$, $\mathsf{msg}(n) = t$ and $n \prec_{\mathcal{B}} m$. If a key is not disclosed before a negative node m, then the adversary cannot use that key to prepare the term received on m.

Proposition 2 (Outgoing Authentication Test). *Suppose an atom a originates uniquely at a regular node n_0 in bundle $\mathcal{B}$, and suppose for some $n_1 \in \mathcal{B}$, a has exited S passing from $\mathsf{msg}(n_0)$ to $\mathsf{msg}(n_1)$, where S is a set of encryptions.*

Then either (1) there exists some $\{\!| t |\!\}_K \in S$ such that K^{-1} is disclosed before n_1 in $\mathcal{B}$, or else (2) a exits from S at some positive regular $m_1 \preceq_{\mathcal{B}} n_1$. If in case (2) n_0 and m_1 lie on different strands, then for some negative $m_0 \in \mathcal{B}$ with $a \sqsubseteq \mathsf{msg}(m_0)$,

$$n_0 \prec_{\mathcal{B}} m_0 \Rightarrow^+ m_1 \preceq_{\mathcal{B}} n_1.$$

Proof. Suppose, contrary to case (1), that no K^{-1} for $\{\!| t |\!\}_K \in S$ is disclosed before n_1 in $\mathcal{B}$. Apply Prop. 1 to $T =$

$$\{m \colon m \preceq_{\mathcal{B}} n_1 \text{ and } a \text{ occurs outside } S \text{ in } \mathsf{msg}(m)\};$$

$n_1 \in T$, so T has $\preceq_{\mathcal{B}}$-minimal members m_1. Since keys K used in S have K^{-1} not disclosed before n_1, m_1 cannot lie on a decryption penetrator D-strand. By unique origination, a does not lie on a M-strand or K-strand. By the definitions of S and "occurs only within," m_1 does not lie on a S-, C-, or E-strand. Thus, m_1 lies on some $s \in \Sigma_\Pi$. If n_0 does not lie on s, then a does not originate on s, so $a \sqsubseteq \mathsf{msg}(m_0)$ for some negative m_0, with $m_0 \Rightarrow^+ m_1$. $\square$

In the outgoing test, we call $m_0 \Rightarrow^+ m_1$ an *outgoing transforming edge* for a, S. It transforms the occurrence of a, causing a to exit S. We call (n_0, n_1) an *outgoing test pair* for a, S when a originates uniquely at n_0 and a has exited S passing from $\mathsf{msg}(n_0)$ to $\mathsf{msg}(n_1)$. We also sometimes call m_1 an *outgoing transforming node* and n_1 an *outgoing test node*.

Example 7. In the Perrig-Song protocol, with responder role s_r, the nodes $(s_r \downarrow 2), (s_r \downarrow 3)$ form an outgoing test pair for N_b, S_{ps}, where S_{ps} is as given in Example 4.

The initiator role s_i has the only outgoing transforming edge for N_b, S_{ps}, lying on $s_i \downarrow 2 \Rightarrow s_i \downarrow 3$. Hence, if any bundle $\mathcal{B}$ has uncompromised long term key $\mathsf{ltk}(A, B)$, and $\mathcal{B}$ contains the three nodes of any responder strand, then $\mathcal{B}$ also contains the three nodes of an initiator strand with matching parameters.

This is the responder's authentication result.

Many protocols can be verified using only singleton sets like S_{ps}, and this was the part of the outgoing authentication test given in [10,8]. However, there are other protocols in which the same critical value is transformed more than once, and these protocols cannot be verified using only singleton sets S. For instance, in the Yahalom protocol, the responder's nonce N_b is transformed first by the key server and then again by the initiator. To verify the presence of the initiator,

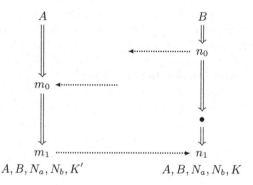

Fig. 4. Yahalom bundle containing responder

we use a set that includes the original form transmitted by the responder, and also all forms that could be produced from it by means of a server strand. To cause N_b to escape from this set $S_{Y,2}$, a server strand cannot suffice: we need an initiator strand.

Example 8 (Yahalom: Inferring Initiator). As in Example 5, letting

$$S_{Y,2} = \{\{\!|A \,\hat{}\, N_a \,\hat{}\, N_b|\!\}_{\mathsf{ltk}(B)}\} \cup \{\{\!|B \,\hat{}\, K'' \,\hat{}\, N_a \,\hat{}\, N_b|\!\}_{\mathsf{ltk}(A)}: K'' \text{ is a key } \},$$

by Prop. 2, if $\mathcal{B}$ contains a full Yahalom responder strand, then either one of the keys $\mathsf{ltk}(A), \mathsf{ltk}(B)$ is compromised, or else there is an initiator strand in $\mathcal{B}$ agreeing on A, B, N_a, N_b, although possibly not on the session key K' (Fig. 4). Another application of Prop. 2 allows us to interpolate a server run into the middle column of Fig. 4, as shown in Fig 5. We instantiate n_0, n_1 from the theorem by the nodes labeled n_0 and n_1' in Fig. 5. This application uses the singleton set $S_{Y,1}$ from Example 5.

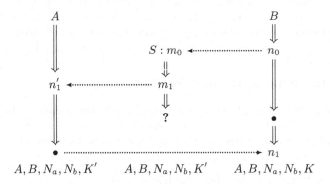

Fig. 5. Yahalom bundle containing responder and server

The outgoing authentication test is also the main theorem for establishing secrecy for session keys and other values that are transmitted in protocols. Long-term keys, which are typically used but never transmitted in any form in protocols, are typically secret only by assumption. However, the outgoing test allows us to infer that a session key—such as the one in the Yahalom protocol—will remain secret assuming that the participants' long-term keys are uncompromised.

Example 9 (Yahalom Session Key Secrecy). Suppose that $\mathcal{B}$ is a bundle in which $\mathsf{ltk}(A), \mathsf{ltk}(B)$ are uncompromised, in which K' originates uniquely on a server strand s_s with parameters A, B, N_a, N_b, K'. Then K' is uncompromised in $\mathcal{B}$. The reason is that otherwise, we may apply Prop. 2 to the set

$$S_{Y,3} = \{\{|B \,\hat{}\, K' \,\hat{}\, N_a \,\hat{}\, N_b|\}_{\mathsf{ltk}(A)}, \{|A \,\hat{}\, K'|\}_{\mathsf{ltk}(B)}\}.$$

There is no role of the protocol that, having received K' occurring only within $S_{Y,3}$, would retransmit it outside this form. Thus, given that the keys used in $S_{Y,3}$ are assumed uncompromised, we have refuted the assumption that K' could occur compromised in $\mathcal{B}$.

Thus, secrecy relies on the absence of an outgoing transforming edge. We also use the outgoing test negatively to prove that values that otherwise could be different are in fact equal.

Example 10 (Yahalom Session Key Agreement). In Fig. 5, we must in fact have $K' = K$. Otherwise, N_b has exited the set

$$S_{Y,4} = S_{Y,2} \cup \{\{|N_b|\}_{K''} : K'' \neq K\}$$

passing from n_0 to n_1. However, we have assumed that $\mathsf{ltk}(A), \mathsf{ltk}(B)$ are uncompromised, and we have now ascertained that K' is uncompromised also. Thus, there would have to be a outgoing transforming edge for $N_b, S_{Y,4}$, but the Yahalom protocol does not furnish any role that would do so.

Thus, we have illustrated that the outgoing authentication test is a highly versatile protocol analysis tool. It allows repeated use of a nonce for authentication; it helps prove secrecy for values that a protocol distributes; and it allows us to prove equality of values when certain messages cannot be transformed by the protocol.

5.2   The Incoming Authentication Test

The incoming test principle is similar, except that the critical value is an encryption $t = \{|t_0|\}_K$. In this case, the transforming edge may be a single node m_1 that emits t, rather than the pair we have in the outgoing case. The node m_1 is not always preceded by another node m_0 that has received t.

Proposition 3 (Incoming Authentication Test). *Let* $t = \{|t_0|\}_K$ *and let* S *be a set of encryptions. If* t *occurs outside* S *in any* $n_1 \in \mathcal{B}$, *then either (1)* K *is disclosed before* n_1 *in* $\mathcal{B}$, *or (2) for some* K_0 *with* $\{|t|\}_{K_0} \in S$, K_0^{-1} *is disclosed before* n_1 *in* $\mathcal{B}$, *or (3)* t *exits* S *at some positive regular* $m_1 \preceq_{\mathcal{B}} n_1$.

Proof Sketch. Apply Prop. 1 to the set $T = \{m : m \preceq_{\mathcal{B}} n_1 \text{ and } t \text{ occurs outside } S \text{ in } \mathsf{msg}(m)\}$. □

We call m_1 an *incoming transforming node* for t, S, and n_1 an *incoming test node* for t, S. In our experience with existing protocols, Prop. 3 is almost always used with $S = \emptyset$, i.e. t does not occur at all before m_1. However, one can invent protocols, like the ambassador's protocol, requiring non-empty S, and completeness requires the stronger form. We first illustrate the more usual case $S = \emptyset$.

Example 11 (PS Initiator's Guarantee). Suppose that, in a PS bundle $\mathcal{B}$, A has transmitted N_a and received $\{|N_a \hat{\ } N_b \hat{\ } B|\}_{\mathsf{ltk}(A,B)}$. Then $\mathcal{B}$ contains at least the first two nodes of a matching responder strand, unless $\mathsf{ltk}(A, B)$ is compromised in $\mathcal{B}$. To prove this, one applies Prop. 3 to $t = \{|N_a \hat{\ } N_b \hat{\ } B|\}_{\mathsf{ltk}(A,B)}$, $S = \emptyset$, and $n_1 =$ the initiator's second node.

One can also use the incoming test in a similar way in the Yahalom protocol (see Fig. 5) to show that the server strand's last node—marked **?** there—has occurred.

Example 12 (Ambassador's Protocol). Let $\mathcal{B}$ be a bundle for the Ambassador's Protocol, and suppose that G's first and second nodes are both contained in $\mathcal{B}$. Then the ambassador A has a full run with the same message m.

To prove this, we apply Prop. 3 with $S = \{\{|\{|m|\}_{\mathsf{signk}(G)}|\}_{\mathsf{pubk}(A)}\}$. The message $\{|m|\}_{\mathsf{signk}(G)}$ has exited from S passing from G's first to G's second node. Thus, either $\mathsf{privk}(A)$ is compromised, or A has extracted $\{|m|\}_{\mathsf{signk}(G)}$ from S.

6   Penetrator Webs and Test Nodes

We can see that Props. 2–3 have some sort of completeness by considering the powers of the adversary. In essence, if any negative regular node is neither an outgoing test node nor an incoming test node, then the adversary can derive the term on it. Thus, only test nodes in this sense can provide authentication guarantees about the presence of regular activity. The rest could be the adversary's work.

To make this precise, we define penetrator webs, which characterize what the adversary can do with fixed inputs from the regular participants.

Definition 7 (Penetrator web, derivable). *Let $G = \langle \mathcal{N}_G, (\rightarrow_G \cup \Rightarrow_G) \rangle$ be a finite acyclic subgraph of $\langle \mathcal{N}, (\rightarrow \cup \Rightarrow) \rangle$ such that $\mathcal{N}_G$ consists entirely of penetrator nodes. G is a penetrator web with support S_{spt} and result R if S_{spt} and R are sets of terms and moreover:*

1. *If $n_2 \in \mathcal{N}_G$ is negative, then either $\mathsf{msg}(n_2) \in S_{\text{spt}}$ or there is a unique n_1 such that $n_1 \rightarrow_G n_2$.*
2. *If $n_2 \in \mathcal{N}_G$ and $n_1 \Rightarrow n_2$ then $n_1 \Rightarrow_G n_2$.*
3. *For each $t \in R$, either $t \in S_{\text{spt}}$ or for some positive $n \in \mathcal{N}_G$, $\mathsf{msg}(n) = t$.*

If V is a set of atoms, then term t_1 is derivable from S_{spt} avoiding V if there is a web G with support $S_G \subseteq S_{\text{spt}}$ and $t_1 \in R_G$, where no atom in V originates on a penetrator strand in G.

If $n \in \mathcal{B}$ is a negative node, then $\mathcal{B}$ includes a penetrator web G with result $R_G = \{\mathsf{msg}(n)\}$. Its support $S_G = \{\mathsf{msg}(m) : m$ is positive regular and $m \prec_\mathcal{B} n\}$.

When S_{spt} is a set of terms, we say that t *has exited* S_{enc} *passing from* S_{spt} *to* t_1 if for each $t_0 \in S_{\text{spt}}$, t has exited S_{enc} passing from t_0 to t_1. Def. 6 says that this means that t occurs only within the encryptions in S_{enc} in every $t_0 \in S_{\text{spt}}$, and t occurs outside S_{enc} in t_1.

In the following proposition, the first condition says that when $t_1 \neq \mathsf{msg}(n_1)$ is an outgoing test node $n_1 \in \mathcal{B}$, then we do not need to add an outgoing transforming edge. The second condition says that when $t_1 \neq \mathsf{msg}(n_1)$ is an incoming test node $n_1 \in \mathcal{B}$, we do not need to add an incoming transforming node. The conclusion is that the term is then derivable.

Proposition 4. *Let V be a set of atoms; let S_{spt} be a finite set of terms; and let t_1 be a term such that, for any $a \in V$, if $a \sqsubseteq t_1$, then $a \sqsubseteq t_0$ for some $t_0 \in S_{\text{spt}}$. Suppose the following conditions hold:*

1. *for all $a \in V$ and all sets of encryptions S_{enc}, if a has exited S_{enc} passing from S_{spt} to t_1, then there is some $\{\!|t|\!\}_{K_0} \in S_{\text{enc}}$, such that K_0^{-1} is derivable from S_{spt} avoiding V; and*
2. *for all encryptions $\{\!|t|\!\}_K$, and all sets of encryptions S_{enc}, if $\{\!|t|\!\}_K$ has exited S_{enc} passing from S_{spt} to t_1, then either K is derivable from S_{spt} avoiding V, or else some K_0^{-1} with $K_0 \in \mathsf{used}(S_{\text{enc}})$ is derivable from S_{spt} avoiding V.*

Then term t_1 is derivable from S_{spt} avoiding V.

A proof is in Appendix A. One can easily determine whether t is derivable from S_{spt}, since penetrator webs *normalize* [10, Proposition 5] so that all their destructive steps precede their constructive steps (cf. [12]). Thus, there are only as many intermediate values as there are subterms of $S_{\text{spt}} \cup \{t\}$.

7   Completeness

In order to extract the completeness result from Proposition 4, it is convenient to introduce the notion of *skeleton,* following [4]. A skeleton is potentially the regular (non-penetrator) part of a bundle or of some portion of a bundle. We may regard a bundle as "put together" using a skeleton and one penetrator web for each negative regular node within it.

A skeleton consists of nodes annotated with additional information, indicating order relations among the nodes, uniquely originating atoms, and non-originating atoms. We say that an atom a *occurs* in a set nodes of nodes if for some $n \in$ nodes, $a \sqsubseteq \mathsf{msg}(n)$. A key K is *used* in nodes if for some $n \in$ nodes, $\{\!|t|\!\}_K \sqsubseteq \mathsf{msg}(n)$. We say that a key K is *mentioned in* nodes if K or K^{-1} either occurs or is used in nodes. For a non-key a, a is mentioned if it occurs.

Definition 8. *A four-tuple* $\mathbb{A} = (\mathsf{nodes}_\mathbb{A}, \preceq_\mathbb{A}, \mathsf{non}_\mathbb{A}, \mathsf{unique}_\mathbb{A})$ *is a skeleton if:*

1. $\mathsf{nodes}_\mathbb{A}$ is a finite set of regular nodes; $n_1 \in \mathsf{nodes}$ and $n_0 \Rightarrow^+ n_1$ implies $n_0 \in \mathsf{nodes}_\mathbb{A}$;
2. $\preceq_\mathbb{A}$ is a partial ordering on $\mathsf{nodes}_\mathbb{A}$ such that $n_0 \Rightarrow^+ n_1$ implies $n_0 \preceq_\mathbb{A} n_1$;
3. $\mathsf{non}_\mathbb{A}$ is a set of atomic keys, and for all $K \in \mathsf{non}_\mathbb{A}$, either K or K^{-1} is used in $\mathsf{nodes}_\mathbb{A}$, and for all $K \in \mathsf{non}_\mathbb{A}$, K does not occur in $\mathsf{nodes}_\mathbb{A}$;
4. $\mathsf{unique}_\mathbb{A}$ is a set of atoms, and for all $a \in \mathsf{unique}_\mathbb{A}$, a occurs in $\mathsf{nodes}_\mathbb{A}$, and $a \in \mathsf{unique}_\mathbb{A}$ implies a originates at no more than one node in $\mathsf{nodes}_\mathbb{A}$.

We think of a skeleton as describing a set of bundles; for our present purposes it is enough to consider the bundles into which a skeleton may be embedded:

Definition 9. *If* $\mathbb{A} = (\mathsf{nodes}_\mathbb{A}, \preceq_\mathbb{A}, \mathsf{non}_\mathbb{A}, \mathsf{unique}_\mathbb{A})$ *is a skeleton and* $\mathcal{B}$ *is a bundle, then* $\mathbb{A}$ *is* embedded in $\mathcal{B}$ *if:*

1. For all $n \in \mathsf{nodes}_\mathbb{A}$, $n \in \mathcal{B}$;
2. If $n_0 \preceq_\mathbb{A} n_1$, then $n_0 \preceq_\mathcal{B} n_1$;
3. For all $K \in \mathsf{non}_\mathbb{A}$, K originates nowhere in $\mathcal{B}$;
4. For all $a \in \mathsf{unique}_\mathbb{A}$, a originates uniquely in $\mathcal{B}$.

The embedding is *tight* if for all regular $n \in \mathcal{B}$, $n \in \mathsf{nodes}_\mathbb{A}$, and whenever $n_0, n_1 \in \mathsf{nodes}_\mathbb{A}$ and $n_0 \preceq_\mathcal{B} n_1$, then $n_0 \preceq_\mathbb{A} n_1$.

A message t is *potentially compromised before* n *in* $\mathbb{A}$ if, letting

$$V = \mathsf{non}_\mathbb{A} \cup (\mathsf{unique}_\mathbb{A} \cap \{a \colon a \text{ originates somewhere in } \mathbb{A}\}),$$

and

$$S_{\mathrm{spt}} = \{\mathsf{msg}(m) \colon m \preceq_\mathbb{A} n \text{ and } n \text{ is positive }\},$$

t is derivable from S_{spt} avoiding V. Evidently, $\mathbb{A}$ is tightly embedded in a bundle if, for every negative $n \in \mathbb{A}$, $\mathsf{msg}(n)$ is potentially compromised before n in $\mathbb{A}$.

We regard a skeleton $\mathbb{A}$ as satisfying the authentication test properties when "disclosed before n" is interpreted as meaning potentially compromised before n. That is:

Definition 10. $\mathbb{A}$ satisfies the outgoing authentication test if and only if the following is true for all $n_0, n_1 \in \mathbb{A}$, and for all atoms a and sets of encryptions S. If a has exited S passing from n_0 to n_1, then either (1) there exists some $\{\!|t|\!\}_K \in S$ such that K^{-1} is potentially compromised before n_1 in $\mathbb{A}$, or else (2) a exits from S at some positive regular $m_1 \preceq_\mathbb{A} n_1$.

$\mathbb{A}$ satisfies the incoming authentication test if and only if the following is true for all $n_1 \in \mathbb{A}$, and for all encryptions $t = \{\!|t_0|\!\}_K$ sets of encryptions S. If t occurs outside S in any $n_1 \in \mathbb{A}$, then either (1) K is potentially compromised before n_1 in $\mathbb{A}$, or (2) for some K_0 with $\{\!|t|\!\}_{K_0} \in S$, K_0^{-1} is potentially compromised before n_1 in $\mathbb{A}$, or (3) t exits S at some positive regular $m_1 \preceq_\mathbb{A} n_1$.

We say that $\mathbb{A}$ *respects origination* if $n \preceq_\mathbb{A} m$ whenever, for any $a \in \mathsf{unique}_\mathbb{A}$, a originates at $n \in \mathbb{A}$ and a is mentioned in $\mathsf{msg}(m)$.

Proposition 5 (Completeness of Authentication Tests). *Let $\mathbb{A}$ respect origination. $\mathbb{A}$ satisfies the outgoing and incoming authentication tests if and only if there exists a bundle $\mathcal{B}$ such that $\mathbb{A}$ is tightly embedded into $\mathcal{B}$.*

Proof Sketch. From right to left, use Props. 2–3. From left to right, we must show that for every negative $n \in \mathbb{A}$, $\mathsf{msg}(n)$ is potentially compromised before n in $\mathbb{A}$. To do so, for any given negative $n \in \mathbb{A}$, we apply Prop. 4 to:

1. $V = \mathsf{non}_\mathbb{A} \cup U$ where $U = \mathsf{unique}_\mathbb{A} \cap \{a : a \text{ originates in } \mathbb{A}\}$; and
2. $S_{\mathrm{spt}} = \{\mathsf{msg}(m) : m \preceq_\mathbb{A} n \wedge m \text{ positive }\}$.   □

8   Conclusion

We have presented two principles about how messages are transformed in cryptographic protocols. These two principles are complete in the sense that whenever they are satisfied in a skeleton, then that skeleton describes a possible execution of the protocol, modulo some choice of adversary behavior.

This result is part of the justification for the search method of CPSA, which is based on the authentication tests [4]. CPSA tries to complete partial executions, by which we mean skeletons that are not tightly embedded into any bundle. It uses the authentication tests to consider what ingredients may need to be added to obtain a minimal execution. By considering the ingredients suggested by the authentication tests, it finds all minimal, essentially different executions. Thus, this paper provides the core justification for the claim in [4] that the search finds all the possibilities.

References

1. Abadi, M., Blanchet, B.: Analyzing security protocols with secrecy types and logic programs. Journal of the ACM 52(1), 102–146 (2005)
2. Bozga, L., Lakhnech, Y., Perin, M.: Pattern-based abstraction for verifying secrecy in protocols. In: Garavel, H., Hatcliff, J. (eds.) ETAPS 2003 and TACAS 2003. LNCS, vol. 2619, Springer, Heidelberg (2003)

3. Burrows, M., Abadi, M., Needham, R.: A logic of authentication. In: Proceedings of the Royal Society. Series A, vol. 426(1871), pp. 233–271 (December 1989)
4. Doghmi, S.F., Guttman, J.D., Javier Thayer, F.: Searching for shapes in cryptographic protocols. In: TACAS 2003. LNCS, vol. 4424, pp. 523–538. Springer, Heidelberg (2007), extended version at URL: http://eprint.iacr.org/2006/435
5. Dolev, D., Yao, A.: On the security of public-key protocols. IEEE Transactions on Information Theory 29, 198–208 (1983)
6. Durgin, N., Lincoln, P., Mitchell, J., Scedrov, A.: Multiset rewriting and the complexity of bounded security protocols. Journal of Computer Security 12(2), 247–311 (2004) (Initial version appeared in Workshop on Formal Methods and Security Protocols (1999))
7. Gordon, A.D., Jeffrey, A.: Types and effects for asymmetric cryptographic protocols. Journal of Computer Security 12(3/4), 435–484 (2003)
8. Guttman, J.D.: Security goals: Packet trajectories and strand spaces. In: Focardi, R., Gorrieri, R. (eds.) Foundations of Security Analysis and Design. LNCS, vol. 2171, pp. 197–261. Springer, Heidelberg (2001)
9. Guttman, J.D., Javier Thayer, F.: Authentication tests. In: Proceedings, 2000 IEEE Symposium on Security and Privacy, IEEE Computer Society Press, Los Alamitos (May 2000)
10. Guttman, J.D., Javier Thayer, F.: Authentication tests and the structure of bundles. Theoretical Computer Science 283(2), 333–380 (2000)
11. Guttman, J.D., Javier Thayer, F., Carlson, J.A., Herzog, J.C., Ramsdell, J.D., Sniffen, B.T.: Trust management in strand spaces: A rely-guarantee method. In: Schmidt, D. (ed.) ESOP 2004. LNCS, vol. 2986, pp. 325–339. Springer, Heidelberg (2004)
12. Paulson, L.C.: The inductive approach to verifying cryptographic protocols. Journal of Computer Security (1998) (also Report 443, Cambridge University Computer Lab.)
13. Perrig, A., Song, D.X.: Looking for diamonds in the desert: Extending automatic protocol generation to three-party authentication and key agreement protocols. In: Proceedings of the 13th IEEE Computer Security Foundations Workshop, IEEE Computer Society Press, Los Alamitos (July 2000)

A   Proof of Proposition 4

Proposition. *Let V be a set of atoms; let S_{spt} be a finite set of terms; and let t_1 be a term such that, for any $a \in V$, if $a \sqsubseteq t_1$, then $a \sqsubseteq t_0$ for some $t_0 \in S_{\mathrm{spt}}$. Suppose the following conditions hold:*

1. *for all $a \in V$ and all sets of encryptions S_{enc}, if a has exited S_{enc} passing from S_{spt} to t_1, then there is some $\{\!|t|\!\}_{K_0} \in S_{\mathrm{enc}}$, such that $K_0{}^{-1}$ is derivable from S_{spt} avoiding V; and*
2. *for all encryptions $\{\!|t|\!\}_K$, and all sets of encryptions S_{enc}, if $\{\!|t|\!\}_K$ has exited S_{enc} passing from S_{spt} to t_1, then either K is derivable from S_{spt} avoiding V, or else some $K_0{}^{-1}$ with $K_0 \in \mathsf{used}(S_{\mathrm{enc}})$ is derivable from S_{spt} avoiding V.*

Then term t_1 is derivable from S_{spt} avoiding V.

Proof. The proof is by structural induction on the pair (S_{spt}, t_1), i.e. the ordering under which $(S_{\mathrm{spt}}, t_1) \leq (S'_{\mathrm{spt}}, t'_1)$ iff $t_1 \sqsubseteq t'_1$, and for all $t \in S_{\mathrm{spt}}$, there is some $t' \in S'$ such that $t \sqsubseteq t'$.

Case $t_1 = a$: If $a \notin V$, then the one-node web originating a satisfies the conditions. Otherwise, $S^a = \{t \in S_{\mathrm{spt}} : a \sqsubseteq t\}$ is non-empty. If $a \in S^a$, then the empty web suffices. If some concatenation $t_0 \char`^ t'_0 \in S^a$, then apply the induction hypothesis to $S^a \setminus \{t_0 \char`^ t'_0\} \cup \{t_0\} \cup \{t'_0\}$. This asserts the existence of a penetrator web G_a deriving a. Obtain the desired web by prepending a separation S-strand above any occurrences of t_0 and t'_0 in G_a.

Otherwise, S^a consists entirely of encryptions, and a has exited S^a passing from S_{spt} to a. By condition 1, there is some $\{\!|t|\!\}_{K_0} \in S^a$ with K_0^{-1} derivable from S_{spt} avoiding V, using some web $G_{K_0^{-1}}$. Thus, applying the induction hypothesis to $(S^a \setminus \{\{\!|t|\!\}_{K_0}\}) \cup \{t\}$, we obtain a web G. We may prepend $G_{K_0^{-1}}$ and a decryption D-strand before G to obtain the required web.

Case $t_1 = t'_1 \char`^ t''_1$: Apply the induction hypothesis to t'_1 and t''_1, and append a concatenation C-strand after the resulting webs.

Case $t_1 = \{\!|t'_1|\!\}_K$: Suppose K is derivable from S_{spt} avoiding V, using some web G_K. Apply the induction hypothesis to t'_1, obtaining a web G. Append an encryption E-strand after G_K and G to derive $\{\!|t'_1|\!\}_K$.

Otherwise, by condition 2, some K_0^{-1} with $\{\!|t_0|\!\}_{K_0} \in S_{\mathrm{enc}}$ is derivable from S_{spt} avoiding V, using a web $G_{K_0^{-1}}$. Apply the induction hypothesis to $(S_{\mathrm{spt}} \setminus \{\{\!|t_0|\!\}_{K_0}\}) \cup \{t_0\}$, obtaining a web G. Prepend $G_{K_0^{-1}}$ and a decryption D-strand before G. □

SILENTKNOCK: **Practical, Provably Undetectable Authentication**

Eugene Y. Vasserman[1], Nicholas Hopper[1], John Laxson[2], and James Tyra[1]

[1] Computer Science and Engineering, University of Minnesota, Minneapolis, MN 55455 USA
[2] Stanford University, Box 15255, Stanford, CA 94309 USA

Abstract. Port knocking is a technique first introduced in the blackhat and trade literature to prevent attackers from discovering and exploiting potentially vulnerable services on a network host, while allowing authenticated users to access these services. Despite being based on some sound principles and being a potentially useful tool, most work in this area suffers from a lack of a clear threat model or motivation. We introduce a formal security model for port knocking that addresses these issues, show how previous schemes fail to meet our definition, and give a provably secure scheme that uses steganographic embedding of pseudorandom message authentication codes. We also describe the design and analysis of SILENTKNOCK, an implementation of this protocol for the Linux 2.6 operating system, that is provably secure, under the assumption that AES and a modified version of MD4 are pseudorandom functions, and integrates seamlessly with any existing application, with no need to recompile. Experiments indicate that the overhead due to running SILENTKNOCK on a server is minimal – on the order of 150 μs per TCP connection initiation.

1 Introduction

A *port scan* is a kind of network attack (or attack precursor) in which an adversary attempts to connect to all, or some subset of, TCP and UDP ports at a given IP address. Port scans are useful to attackers because the results often indicate the operating system, architecture, and even a set of specific binaries that a host is running. This information can then be used to determine what software exploits should be used to attack the host, or what level of compromise might be likely.

Of course, if a server runs no vulnerable software, a port scan is not a serious threat, but software security is a sufficiently hard problem that this cannot be seen as an immediate solution. A popular method of protecting against such network attacks is the firewall, which simply blocks all connection attempts to "internal" network hosts from "external" ones. Since there are many reasons why it might be desirable for a given service to be externally accessible — for instance, users may access a network service from a priori unknown network addresses depending on their physical location — this solution is not always satisfactory.

One class of proposed solutions to this problem is "port knocking": a firewall is deployed to protect a server, and before allowing a client connection to a particular port, that client must transmit a special "knock" that authenticates it. This knock may be either common to all authorized users of the system, or may be unique to a given user.

J. Biskup and J. Lopez (Eds.): ESORICS 2007, LNCS 4734, pp. 122–138, 2007.

Any attempts to connect that are not associated with the correct knock will be dropped; thus to an unauthorized user it should appear as if no network services are running on the server. A variety of knocking methods have been proposed, such as a sequence of (dropped) connection attempts [1], inclusion of a cryptographic authenticator in the initial connection request packet [2], "funny-looking" DNS lookups [3], and IPsec tunneling [4].

Many previous proposals for port knocking schemes have been accused of offering "security through obscurity", since it is trivially easy to detect and steal knocks in non-cryptographic systems. But making the distinction between flawed *implementations* which are only secure if the details of the system are unknown, and the *concept* of port knocking (that *even given the details of a port knocking scheme*, one cannot tell if it is being employed), we argue that this *concept* is not fundamentally flawed. Since revealing the presence of a service can only help an adversary — for example, by revealing which of a list of hundreds of exploits is the most likely to succeed, thereby decreasing the cost of an attack — the notion of concealing services from unauthenticated users (in addition to regular network and software security measures) is a potentially useful one. Separating authentication from applications is also a sound choice, since it enforces least privilege and economy of mechanism, in addition to easing deployment.

Given that the goal of a port knocking scheme should be to conceal the set of services running on a network host, all existing implementations have a serious flaw. Under relatively weak attack models, these schemes fail to conceal that a port knocking service itself is running. Since this service mediates access to all the other services exported by a host, exposing information about the presence and type of port knocking service a host is running is highly undesirable: under fail-closed semantics, crashing the port knocking service denies access to all services on the host, while under fail-open semantics detecting and crashing the port knocking service allows an ordinary port-scan to succeed. Of course, on most currently deployed operating systems, exploiting a code injection attack in a port knocking service would lead to a total compromise of the host. Since the port knocking service is such a high-value target, we argue that *the presence of port knocking itself should not be detectable*.

In this paper, we develop a formal security model which captures this notion. A formal security model is critically important in order to be certain that a given protocol, even one that seems secure at a glance, is *actually* secure. Examples of such "apparently secure" protocols, developed without formally stated security goals, are numerous [5, 6, 7], and some of them have been in operation for years (and have even become industry standards), before attacks were found. Note that all those protocols were originally designed for security, and even used well-known cryptographic primitives, but the protocols were not secure.

Essentially, our notion states that even though a (computationally bounded) adversary may observe many authenticated sessions and arbitrarily inject, delete, and reorder messages between the client and server, he cannot distinguish a port knocking client and server from a pair using ordinary TCP/IP, plus some out-of-band authentication mechanism that prevents other clients from connecting. That is, our definition allows the adversary to observe authenticated sessions and necessarily allows the adversary to observe that *somehow* sessions are being authenticated, but insists that no *additional* information about the authenticating mechanism is leaked. This leaves many plausible explanations for the behavior, such as dynamic firewall rules[1].

We prove that a scheme which is secure in our model also resists forgery and provides replay attack protection against a global active adversary. We give a protocol for a generic networking scheme, which makes rudimentary use of provably secure steganography [8], and prove that this protocol satisfies our strong notion of security. Furthermore, we describe and analyze the security of SILENTKNOCK, an implementation of our generic protocol for the Linux 2.6 TCP/IP stack. SILENTKNOCK combines simple TCP steganography [9] with a very fast cryptographic message authentication code (MAC) [10] to provide efficient, provably secure port knocking that integrates seamlessly with existing applications (with no need to recompile) by hooking directly into the operating system kernel. SILENTKNOCK produces packets that are provably indistinguishable from TCP packets generated by the Linux 2.6 implementation of TCP, under the assumption that AES and a variant of MD4 are pseudorandom functions[2]. No applications need to be altered, no shared libraries need to be replaced, and no potentially-conflicting protocols emerge. SILENTKNOCK is lightweight, has minimal computational overhead, and is freely available for download [12].

Related work. The first published description of a port knocking scheme seems to be the work of Barham *et al.* [2], who describe a scheme whereby a pass-phrase is transmitted (in cleartext) to a firewall either through a series of SYN packets, in a single "knock" packet, or as an option in the SYN packet. Krzywinski [1] describes a similar scheme where a client opens a port by attempting connections to a secret sequence of port numbers[3]; a number of similar systems are described at [13]. Several authors [3, 14, 4] have proposed that knocks should be cryptographically protected to prevent replay attacks, but still fundamentally involve the use of extra packets or nonstandard TCP options that allow the detection of a knock (these systems provide authentication only, i.e. they make no attempt to hide the use of authentication mechanisms). deGraaf *et al.* [4] and Manzanares *et al.* [15] describe some other attacks and weaknesses of previous port knocking schemes, which our notion of security precludes — that is, any scheme that satisfies our security notion necessarily is also secure against the attacks mentioned in these papers.

There is an extensive literature on TCP/IP steganography and covert channels [9, 16, 17, 18, 19], although Murdoch and Lewis [9] show that many of these proposals are easily detected. We introduce a cryptographic formulation of security similar to that in [8], and our notion of a secure port knocking scheme can be seen as a simple instance of a covert computation [20] or the dining Freemasons problem [21]. We are, however, unaware of previous work relating steganographic computation and port knocking, or

---

[1] e.g. a service that is only available at preset times, or a software firewall that allows the user to approve connection requests.

[2] Linux 2.6 chooses TCP sequence numbers using 24 rounds of MD4 applied to the source and destination IP address, destination port, and 32 secret random bits, using a randomly generated, secret initial chaining value that changes every 5 minutes. See the functions `secure_tcp_sequence_number` and `half_md4_transform` at [11].

[3] The server will monitor connection attempts on all closed ports and opens a port if a specific sequence of connection attempts is detected.

any previous work implementing the schemes of [20, 21]. We note that our system, like those in [20, 21] differs from covert channels alone because we provide covert one-way *authentication*, handle synchronization issues, and formally reason about what it should mean to hide an authentication service.

2 Formal Definition of Port knocking

In this section we provide our formal model of a secure TCP port knocking scheme, and prove several relationships between our definition and formalized versions of earlier security properties. We begin by stating our formal model of the TCP protocol:

Definition 1. *A TCP implementation is a triple $\mathcal{P}$ of efficient, probabilistic programs* Client, Server, *and* Init. Client *has three arguments: a* state s, *a* command c, *and a* packet r; Client(s, c, r) *outputs a new* state s', *and a* packet p. *Similarly,* Server *takes as input* state s, command c *and* packet p *and outputs a* state s', *a* packet r, *and a* message m. Init *takes as input either* client *or* server *and outputs a* state s.

Standard TCP Client *commands* are of the form "connect to port 80 from port 1234," "send M from port 1234 to port 80," or "close the connection to port 80 from port 1234." Server *commands* are of the form "listen on port 80" or "close the connection from C:1234 to S:80." With a null command, Client simply outputs the next packet to be sent to the server and Server outputs a packet acknowledging the input packet and a message consisting of the data received in the last packet. Client and server *state* includes the TCP states of all connections, and buffered messages. Standard TCP *packets* p have two fields we will make use of. The *syn* flag, $p.syn$, is always set on the first packet sent on a new connection. Packets with this flag set are the standard way of "knocking" at a port to establish a connection. TCP/IP connections are uniquely identified by the tuple (client IP, client port, server IP, server port) which we refer to as $p.id$.

For a given *command sequence* $C \in (command \times command)^*$ we define the *standard interaction* of a TCP implementation $\mathcal{P}$ as the following process. First, we initialize $s_0 = $ Init(server), $q_0 = $ Init(client), and set (p_0, r_0) to null. Then for each pair $(\kappa_i, \sigma_i) \in C$, we let $(q_i, p_i) = $ Client$(q_{i-1}, \kappa_i, r_{i-1})$ and $(s_i, r_i, m_i) = $ Server$(s_{i-1}, \sigma_i, p_{i-1})$. We define the *output* of the standard interaction on C, $\mathcal{P}(C)$, to be the concatenation $m_1 || m_2 || \cdots || m_\ell$.

Definition 2. *A Port knocking protocol is a TCP implementation $\mathcal{H}$ in which both* Client *and* Server *take as additional input a secret key. We let $\mathcal{H}_K(C)$ denote the result of the standard interaction between* Client *and* Server *where the key input to both is K.*

We say that $\mathcal{H}$ *extends* TCP implementation $\mathcal{P}$ if for every command sequence C, there is an efficiently computable command sequence C' such that $\mathcal{H}_K(C')$ and $\mathcal{P}(C)$ are computationally indistinguishable, for uniformly chosen K. This requirement states that a port knocking protocol, in which the client and server share a secret key, should allow any communication that is allowed by the TCP implementation it extends. We note that a TCP implementation is trivially an (insecure) port knocking protocol with null keyspace: every TCP session is initiated when the client "knocks" at the server port he wishes to connect to.

Security Condition. The informal idea behind our definition and construction is that a port knocking scheme should hide not only a set of network services, but the very fact that port knocking is in use, to the extent possible; and this condition should hold even against an adversary who is allowed to make connection attempts to the server and see authenticated connections by the client. To that end, we define security of a port knocking scheme $\mathcal{H}$ in terms of an adversary's inability to distinguish between two experiments, corresponding to two different "worlds" in which he might find himself. In both experiments, the adversary is given black-box access to Client and Server subroutines (i.e., oracles) that output only packets and maintain state internally, so the attacker may issue commands and deliver packets to the client and server. We stress that these oracles are "black boxes" only insofar as the adversary cannot *a priori* infer which of the two possible sets of oracles he is interacting with; adversaries are assumed to know the implementation details of each of the two possible oracle pairs.

In the "hidden world", these subroutines implement the Client and Server routines from $\mathcal{H}$, with a shared secret key K. The adversary is allowed to interact arbitrarily with these subroutines, and in particular may make as many queries to both as he desires. This models what an adversary who is attacking a port knocking implementation will see. In what we call the "plausible world," the client and server subroutines are essentially those of the TCP implementation $\mathcal{P}$, *except* that they are slightly modified. The "plausible" client and server are modified to share a queue of packets Q. Whenever the client generates a packet p, Q is scanned for a packet q with $q.id = p.id$; if none is found, p is added to the end of Q. The server also maintains a list Open of ids. Whenever it is called with a packet p, the server checks to see if $p.id \in$ Open, and if it is, calls $\mathcal{P}$.Server on p; if p is at the front of Q, the server adds $p.id$ to Open, removes p from Q, and calls $\mathcal{P}$.Server on p; otherwise, the server does not respond to p. In essence, client and server share an out-of-band signaling mechanism such that only recent connections initiated by the client are processed by the server. Notice that the packets output by the "plausible world" client are identical to the packets output by $\mathcal{P}$, and if the adversary simply relays the packets between Client and Server, he will see a perfectly normal TCP session. However, if the adversary interacts only with the Server oracle, his connection attempts will be ignored, because his packets are not on the shared queue. Thus this "plausible world" formalizes the idea of revealing that there is authentication going on, but not revealing any additional information about the authentication.

We say that a port knocking scheme is secure if an adversary who can see many authenticated sessions and attempt to make many connections cannot tell if he is in the "hidden world" or the "plausible world", that is, he cannot tell from the results of his attack whether port knocking or some other plausible form of authentication is being employed. Formally, we define the experiments $\mathsf{Exp}^{hw}_{\mathcal{H},A}$ and $\mathsf{Exp}^{pw}_{\mathcal{P},A}$ as in figure 1, and we define the *port knocking advantage of A against $\mathcal{H}$ with respect to $\mathcal{P}$* to be

$$\mathsf{Adv}^{pk}_{A,\mathcal{H},\mathcal{P}}(k) = \Pr[\mathsf{Exp}^{hw}_{\mathcal{H},A}(1^k) = 1] - \Pr[\mathsf{Exp}^{pw}_{\mathcal{P},A}(1^k) = 1] .$$

We say that $\mathcal{H}$ is a (t, q_C, q_S, ϵ)-*secure port knocking scheme with respect to $\mathcal{P}$* if for every time-t adversary A that makes at most q_C Client queries and q_S Server queries, $\mathsf{Adv}^{pk}_{A,\mathcal{H},\mathcal{P}}(k) \leq \epsilon$. We call such an adversary a (t, q_S, q_C) adversary.

Oracle HClient*(c, r):	Oracle HServer*(c, p):	Experiment $\mathsf{Exp}^{\mathsf{hw}}_{\mathcal{H}, A}(1^k)$:
1. $(q', p) \leftarrow \mathcal{H}.\mathsf{Client}(\mathsf{K}, \mathsf{Q}, c, r)$	1. $(s', r, m) \leftarrow \mathcal{H}.\mathsf{Server}(\mathsf{K}, \mathsf{S}, c, p)$	1. $\mathsf{K} \leftarrow U_k$.
2. $\mathsf{Q} \leftarrow q'$.	2. $\mathsf{S} \leftarrow s'$.	2. $\mathsf{Q} \leftarrow \mathcal{H}.\mathsf{Init}(\texttt{client})$.
3. $\mathbf{return}(p)$	3. $\mathbf{return}(r)$	3. $\mathsf{S} \leftarrow \mathcal{H}.\mathsf{Init}(\texttt{server})$.
		4. $\mathbf{return}A^{\mathsf{HClient}^*, \mathsf{HServer}^*}(1^k)$

Oracle PClient*(c, r):	Oracle PServer*(c, p):	Experiment $\mathsf{Exp}^{\mathsf{pw}}_{\mathcal{P}, A}(1^k)$:
1. $(q', p) \leftarrow \mathcal{P}.\mathsf{Client}(\mathsf{Q}, c, r)$	1. $\mathbf{if}$ $(p.syn$ and $p = front(\mathsf{RecentQ}))$ $\mathbf{then}$	1. $\mathsf{RecentQ} \leftarrow ()$.
2. $\mathsf{Q} \leftarrow q'$.	2. remove p from $\mathsf{RecentQ}$.	2. $\mathsf{Open} \leftarrow \emptyset$.
3. $\mathbf{if}$ $p.syn$ $\mathbf{then}$	3. Add $p.id$ to Open.	3. $\mathsf{Q} \leftarrow \mathcal{P}.\mathsf{Init}(\texttt{client})$.
4. append p to $\mathsf{RecentQ}$.	4. $\mathbf{else\ if}$ $(p.id \notin \mathsf{Open})$ $\mathbf{then}$	4. $\mathsf{S} \leftarrow \mathcal{P}.\mathsf{Init}(\texttt{server})$.
5. $\mathbf{return}(p)$	5. $p \leftarrow \emptyset$.	5. $\mathbf{return}$ $A^{\mathsf{PClient}^*, \mathsf{PServer}^*}(1^k)$
	6. $(s', r, m) \leftarrow \mathcal{P}.\mathsf{Server}(\mathsf{S}, c, p)$.	
	7. $\mathsf{S} \leftarrow s'$.	
	8. $\mathbf{return}(r)$	

Fig. 1. Definition of hidden world (top row) and plausible world (bottom row) experiments

Related notions. Given a new notion of security, it is natural to ask whether it is the *right* notion. In the full version, we give some evidence for the strength of our notion, by considering several security conditions which have been implicitly or explicitly used as the security goals of earlier port knocking schemes, and showing that our security notion is stronger.

3   System Design

In this section we introduce SILENTKNOCK, our implementation of a secure port knocking scheme, and discuss how this implementation embodies the security model defined above. We first discuss several adaptations necessary for secure and reliable interaction with TCP/IP, such as replay attack protection, client/server synchronization, and indistinguishability. Next, we analyze a number of possible attacks on our implementation. Finally, we present results showing our system in action. A generic presentation of the scheme, along with security proof, appears in the appendix.

SILENTKNOCK is designed to be an application-agnostic transport-level authentication layer. It resists forgery and replay attacks while leaking no further information about the authentication method employed. We use kernel hooks to ensure that applications do not need to explicitly support our system in order to benefit from it. We use keyed MACs as secure authenticators to resist forgery attacks and a two-part counter to counteract replay attacks while ensuring that client and server counters stay synchronized even in the presence of moderate packet loss. We provide an implementation of a previously proposed operating system-specific steganographic embedding scheme for TCP/IP [9] and use it to embed authentication information into TCP headers.

Universal Compatibility. We provide ease-of-use (for end-users, system administrators, and programmers) by choosing an application-agnostic design. By using hooks directly into the operating system kernel, we avoid modifying any of the network kernel or library calls made by application software or requiring supports for SOCKS-type proxies. This allows any application to transparently use SILENTKNOCK (without application awareness or modification), provided that the network protocol used by the application has a steganographic embedding/extraction method supported by SILENT-KNOCK . We note that for certain protocols, such as TCP, with many implementations that may have subtle differences, each implementation may require a different steganographic embedding routine to preserve indistinguishability. Our goal is to seamlessly support as many transport protocol implementations as possible, although currently only TCP under Linux 2.6 is supported.

Design Choices. Our implementation is designed to run on the Linux operating system with a 2.6 kernel. We chose Linux 2.6 due to our familiarity with the system and the availability of the netfilter/libIPQ API [25], which allowed us to implement our system entirely in user space instead of modifying the operating system. We use Poly1305-AES [10] as our MAC function since it is optimized specifically for network packets and has very fast implementations available for most processor types. We implement Murdoch and Lewis' system for embedding steganographic information into TCP initial sequence numbers (ISNs) [9] and use the TCP timestamp option (enabled by default in Linux 2.6) to embed an additional byte of information into the timestamp, delaying packets when needed. For additional details on the adjustments necessary to make random ISNs consistent with the Linux 2.6 network stack, see [9].

3.1 Protocol

The SILENTKNOCK algorithm is outlined in Figure 2. A SILENTKNOCK client initiates a connection (composes a TCP SYN packet) to a SILENTKNOCK-enabled server and steganographically embeds an authentication token into the packet. The embedding algorithm and resulting packet header structure are described in Figures 3 and 4, respectively. The server receives a SYN packet and extracts the authenticator. If verification is successful, the server allows the connection to continue, otherwise the packet is dropped. The client and server share a key, as well as a counter which is incremented for every client connection attempt (we discuss counter synchronization later). The counter prevents replay attacks by ensuring that every SYN packet sent by the client is different from any packets sent previously, and is also used as the nonce required by our MAC function. The key, initial counter, and resynchronization interval are exchanged out of band, since negotiation is impossible in case of one-way communication.

MAC. Instead of an additional sequence of knocks, we use a keyed MAC for client authentication, applying it to the source and destination (IP, port) tuples as well as the counter, so every connection attempt is guaranteed to contain a unique MAC. We employ Poly1305-AES [10] for our MAC function since it is designed specifically to work on small bits of data such as network packets and is implemented in optimized assembly for a number of popular platforms. The connection counter serves as the nonce required by Poly1305-AES. Assuming that AES is a pseudorandom permutation, an adversary should not be able to compose a valid MAC, or even distinguish one from random bits, for the next SYN packet without knowing the key (even if we assume that all other factors are public information).

Steganography and Indistinguishability. We use the TCP sequence number and timestamp fields of the TCP SYN packet to embed our MAC information [9]. Unfortunately, we are not able to include the complete MAC, as our current implementation

---

1. $B \rightarrow A$: $MAC_{k,ctr_B}(m)$; *encoded in TCP/IP headers of SYN packet*
2. A: Set $ctr_A \leftarrow ctr_A + 1$
   for $i = 0$ to ft:
      if $(MAC_{k,ctr_A-1+i}(m) = MAC_{k,ctr_B}(m))$
         Set $ctr_A \leftarrow ctr_A + i + 1$; *resynchronize counter if client is ahead*
         $A \rightarrow B$: SYN-ACK
         goto 5
3. B: **if** (SYN-ACK received) **then**
         Set $ctr_B \leftarrow ctr_B + 1$, **goto** 5; *connection was successful*
4. B: **if** (SYN-ACK not received) **then**
         Set $ctr_B \leftarrow ctr_B + 1$; *assume server got SYN, but SYN-ACK was lost*
         goto 3
5. A, B: proceed with TCP connection
   if (FIN or RST received) **then**
      goto 1

Fig. 2. The pseudocode for SILENTKNOCK. A is the server, B is the client, ctr_P is a per-IP-address counter maintained by principal P, k is a value derived from B's IP address and a symmetric key shared between A and B, m is a TCP flow identifier, and ft is a failure-tolerance parameter.

only allows a total of 32 bits to be embedded (24 bits in the sequence number and 8 bits — the least significant byte — in the timestamp), assuming Linux sequence numbers[4] (see Figure 4). Since we must not allow distinguishability based on discrepancy between the observed packet dispatch time and the packet timestamp, we delay packet transmission, but only use the last timestamp byte to minimize delay times. Although 32 bits is a relatively short MAC, recall that even at this length, an adversary would still have to compose, on average, 2^{32} packets to break the authentication (requiring, for example, 6 weeks to transmit over a T1 link). We remark that standard methods to deal with online guessing attacks can also be applied here, such as account freezing or processing delays.

One issue that arises when using the TCP timestamp field (rather than just the ISN) to encode MAC data is the possibility of lost SYN packets. For instance, if a client generates a SYN packet but a SYN-ACK from the server does not arrive, the client must re-transmit the SYN packet. However, TCP requires that re-transmitted SYN packets have the same sequence number but different timestamp [26], so we can no longer encode stegotext in the timestamp: if the SYN packet was lost due to a malicious host, or if an adversary is observing all SYN packets, that adversary would detect that the least significant byte of the timestamp in the original and re-transmitted SYN packets are identical. The probability of this is only $1/256$, so the adversary could conclude that SILENTKNOCK was in use.

To solve this problem, we ensure that the last byte of the timestamp looks random to our adversary, even when we are trying to re-transmit the same MAC. We can use two existing properties of our system to help us, the first having originally caused this problem: the higher order bytes of the new timestamp must be different from the one in the original SYN packet[5]. Secondly, we do not transmit the entire MAC (only the

---

[4] OpenBSD has 30 bits of entropy available in the sequence number, while Linux 2.6 only has 24 bits.

[5] In reality, we only use the middle two bytes of the timestamp, since the upper byte is extremely unlikely to change, and the bottom byte will be replaced by stegotext.

P : **TCP SYN packet**
$P_{seq} = \{S_1, S_2, S_3, S_4\}$: **Sequence number of packet P (4 bytes)**
$P_{ts} = \{T_1, T_2, T_3, T_4\}$: **Timestamp of packet P (4 bytes)**
$m = (IP_B, source\ port, IP_A, destination\ port)$: **Authentication information**
$MAC_{K,ctr}(m) = \{M_1, M_2, \ldots, M_{16}\}$: **16 byte MAC**
$S_2 = M_1, S_3 = M_2, S_4 = M_3$
$T_4 = h_M(\{T_2||T_3\})$: **n-Universal hash function**

Fig. 3. The steganographic encoding protocol. Decoding is performed by reversing the operations in this protocol.

first 32 bits), so the adversary has no knowledge of the rest. We use these undisclosed MAC bytes to key an n-universal hash function (e.g. $h_a(x) = a_1 x^{n-1} + a_2 x^{n-2} + \cdots + a_{n-1} x + a_n$) [27], which is applied to the middle bytes of the (changed) timestamp to determine the last byte of the timestamp, ensuring that any n or fewer distinct timestamps have last bytes that are indistinguishable from random. [6]. Since the server computes the same MAC, the server can reverse this process and extract the stegotext. Therefore we preserve the integrity and indistinguishability of stegotext in our timestamp even for re-transmitted packets (note that a packet will again need to be delayed so transmission time is consistent with the new timestamp).

Counter management. To protect against replay attacks, we employ a per-user counter, incremented after every connection attempt. If a given user has never before accessed a SILENTKNOCK-protected server, the counter is initialized to 0 by both the client and the server. The counter poses additional challenges, such as what happens when the client and server counters become desynchronized. Desynchronization can occur in two ways: either the client's SYN packet never arrives at the server, leading to the client having a counter higher than the server's, or the server's SYN-ACK can be lost, meaning the client and server are actually in sync, but the client does not know this. A client would have a hard time attempting to resynchronize after a failed connection, since the client does not know whether the server received the SYN packet and verification failed, or whether the server received and verified the SYN packet but the SYN-ACK was lost, or whether the SYN never arrived at the server. We allow for automatic in-protocol resynchronization after a certain time period.

For this purpose, we enforce the equation $ctr_{server} \leq ctr_{client}$ by having the client always increment its counter when sending a SYN packet. The server, however, will only increment its counter upon successful MAC validation, to prevent malicious desynchronization by sending bogus packets to the server. In the naïve scheme of insisting the counter be exactly right, the server and client may never again get into sync once desynchronized, since the client will increment its counter on each connection attempt, but the server's counter remains the same.

To counteract permanent desynchronization, we adopt a two-part counter design. Using a 64-bit counter, the first 32 bits (called the RESYNC field) are initialized to 0 (at the

---

[6] By default, Linux 2.6 TCP only attempts to re-transmit a failed SYN packet five times, so 5-universal hashes are sufficient. If this number were to change, both the client and the server would need to modify their hash function (for n retransmissions, an m-universal hash function, where $m \geq n$ must be used).

Source Port			Destination Port	
Adjusted for internal consistency	Sequence number			*MAC bytes 1-3*
Acknowledgement Number				
Offset	Reserved	Flags	Window	
Checksum			Urgent Pointer	
Timestamp				*Encoded MAC byte 4*
Timestamp Echo Reply				

Fig. 4. The TCP SYN packet after steganographic embedding. The "internal consistency" adjustment in the sequence number is performed to keep the modified sequence number consistent with what Linux is expected to produce.

time of first connection) and are incremented once every configured unit of time (such as every hour, day, month, leap-year, etc.). The time period must be agreed upon by the client and the server as part of out-of-band setup. The latter 32 bits (called the CTR field) are always reset to 0 when RESYNC is incremented. Using this two-part counter, we allow resynchronization to occur automatically once the RESYNC increment time elapses. If there is substantial relative clock drift between the client and server, it is possible that client connections will fail (or even become desynchronized) when the client initiates a connection at a time when one entity has incremented RESYNC and reset CTR but the other has not. However this is extremely unlikely and would repair itself during the next RESYNC increment. Checking more than one consecutive value of the counter as part of the MAC would make desynchronization unlikely for most (transient) network-level failures, but would also degrade security linearly, since it allows multiple MACs to be valid at any given time. If multiple counters are checked, the server should save the counter that matches whichever MAC successfully verified, and increment that counter for use next time. This way, the server and client should be in sync for the next connection attempt. (The number of alternate CTR values checked by the server is specified by the ft parameter in Figure 2.)

3.2 System Architecture

The SILENTKNOCK system is composed of two separate programs - " sknockd" (running on the server), and " knockproxy" (running on the client). Connections are authenticated on a per-flow instead of per-source (IP address) basis. While knockproxy actively modifies packets as they leave and enter the client machine, sknockd (on the server side) does not do any packet modification. Combined with the very low verification overhead of our chosen MAC function, this should minimize the load on the server. We use the libIPQ API to register interest in packets with certain flags and (IP, port) tuples with the kernel, and those packets are rerouted by the netfilter system to user-space[7]. On both client and server side, we only send packets we are potentially interested in to user space, to avoid excess context switching between user-space and kernel-space. Both sknockd and knockproxy currently detect closed connections

---

[7] This re-routing happens after processing by the network stack for outgoing packets, but before processing for incoming packets.

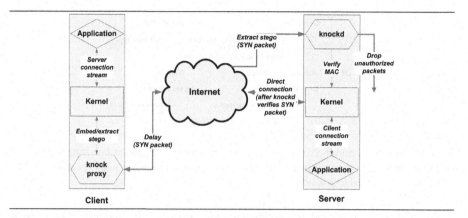

Fig. 5. The architecture of SILENTKNOCK. The client-side application initiates a connection to a server in the usual manner. The kernel composes a SYN packet, but knockproxy intercepts the packet before it is sent, and embeds a MAC into the ISN and timestamp fields. The server receives the packet, and sknockd examines it before passing it to the kernel. If sknockd successfully extracts and verifies the MAC, the packet is accepted by the kernel and passed to the application; otherwise it is dropped. Once the SYN packet is accepted, sknockd no longer examines other packets for that connection (except for terminating packets FIN and RST). knockproxy, however, is forced to rewrite every incoming and outgoing packet for the connection to prevent the client TCP stack from getting confused due to a sequence number mismatch.

by listening to FIN and RST packets, and timeout support (in case the FIN or RST packets are never received due to packet loss) will be added in the future.

Knock Daemon. sknockd, the server side of the SILENTKNOCK system, listens for connections on a port it reads from its configuration file (the port offering the protected service, i.e. SSH on port 22), and examines incoming SYN packets on those ports before the TCP/IP stack sees them. When a packet is received, sknockd checks the source IP address of the packet and retrieves the secret key as well as the counter for that IP address from its configuration file (per-user shared keys are also supported). Using the TCP steganographic algorithm, sknockd extracts stegotext from the packet, treats it as a MAC, and attempts to verify it. If verification succeeds the packet is accepted, and passed on to the TCP/IP stack, otherwise the packet is dropped. sknockd then increments the per-IP connection counter (CTR). This is the extent of sknockd's involvement with the connection — all other packets are processed directly by the network stack in the kernel, and are not seen by sknockd (except for detection of connection closing). Since the SYN packet is copied only once (from kernel to user space) and not modified (does not have to be copied back), and since our chosen MAC is very fast, the entire operation is very efficient. Furthermore, since only SYN packets are examined, the load on the server is minimized.

There is a small trick to preserving indistinguishability when we in fact are intercepting certain packets — we must prevent the adversary from being able to set the SYN flag on a packet that is part of an existing (previously authenticated) stream, because if sknockd drops that packet (due to incorrect MAC), the adversary will be able to conclude that SILENTKNOCK is in use. Therefore, when sknockd tells the netfilter to allow a certain connection (after verifying the MAC), we insert the AL-LOW rule into netfilter *before* the rule that forwards all SYN packets to sknockd. Thus, authenticated streams (having a known source (IP, port) tuple) are never again processed by sknockd, even if they (incorrectly) contain SYN packets, preserving default TCP stack behavior. This solution (inserting the ALLOW rule for a flow before the sknockd rule for SYNs) frees sknockd from storing any per-flow state outside of netfilter. The number of initial netfilter rules is linear in the number of SILENTKNOCK-protected services, and future rules scale linearly with the number of active connections to protected services. While the number of rules may become large with many active connections, this can not be avoided, and we must rely on the efficiency of the underlying packet filter implementation to scale gracefully under load. Memory requirements for per-user keys (and pre-computed MACs) are linear in the number of users configured, and per-IP counter storage is linear in the number of client IP addresses.

Knockproxy. knockproxy reads a configuration file to find out which servers support SILENTKNOCK, and for which services (listed by destination (IP, port) pairs). The configuration file also includes the key shared with the server, and the last value of the connection counter (if this is the first time connecting to that server, the counter is initialized to 0). knockproxy registers interest for all SYN packets going from localhost to that (IP, port) pair. When it receives such a SYN packet (generated by the local TCP/IP stack), it computes a MAC using the server shared key and steganographically encodes the information in the TCP initial sequence number and timestamp. It then registers interest for all incoming and outgoing packets for that (IP, port) tuple, increments the associated connection counter, and sends the packet over the wire[8]. Since we have modified the sequence number from what the local TCP stack expects it to be, we must modify it again in the return packets before the TCP stack sees them, otherwise we will confuse the stack and reset the connection. Likewise, we must continue to modify all future outgoing packets for that connection, otherwise the remote host will reset the connection when it detects a sequence number mismatch. Once the connection is closed, knockproxy de-registers interest in that tuple (connection closure is detected the same way for both sknockd and knockproxy). The number of initial netfilter rules is linear in the number of SILENTKNOCK-protected services that might be contacted, Future rules scale linearly in the number of active portknocked connections.

3.3 Timing Analysis

The indistinguishability of the SILENTKNOCK implementation relies on the adversary gaining no information through timing attacks — if sknockd takes an overly long time to process packets, a smart attacker with knowledge of traffic timing before SILENT-KNOCK was installed on a server would realize that some kind of additional processing is occurring (but not necessarily that SILENTKNOCK is in use). If the difference in timing is large enough, it makes for a good distinguisher for SILENTKNOCK in practice, even though timing information is not included in our formal model. On the other hand, if the timing difference is small (compared to timing noise between the adversary and the server — delays imposed by slower or overloaded routers, etc.) or the adversary

---

[8] The packet may be delayed, depending on the modification made to the timestamp field.

Table 1. Average time difference between receiving a SYN packet and emitting a SYN-ACK packet. The third experiment avoids the context switch incurred by user-space iptables manipulation, and gives a performance estimate for a sknockd kernel module.

Experiment	SSH only	sknockd	without commit
Average response time (μs)	242.86	389.33	295.44
St. Dev. (μs)	8.59	13.36	8.64
Slowdown factor	1	1.60	1.22

lacks precise knowledge of the timing characteristics of the server, this "side channel" will not lead to a good distinguisher in practice. Therefore, we have attempted to minimize this information leakage, and can minimize it further by implementing a number of optimizations, such as more aggressive pre-computation during idle time.

Results of our timings tests are shown in Table 1. We measure the time an SSH server running sknockd takes to process SYN packets and compare to an ordinary SSH server. We record the time between when the server receives a SYN packet (containing a valid MAC) and the time it sends a response (SYN-ACK) packet. The first column shows the baseline (standalone SSH server) time; the second column shows time with SSH and sknockd running together; the third column is similar to the second, except that sknockd has been modified to *not* make the iptables commit kernel call (iptc_commit), which inserts the iptables connection rule constructed by sknockd into the kernel packet filter table. We made this modification to simulate the amount of time the server would take to emit a SYN-ACK packet with sknockd running in kernel space, enabling direct manipulation of the packet filter table, without incurring the overhead of a user space to kernel context switch[9]. While servers running sknockd are always slower than servers running SSH alone, modifying sknockd to remove the iptables commit call reduces the time difference significantly.

Although information leakage (thought timing information) occurs in practice, the amount of information revealed is minor. Even using user-space sknockd, an adversary located a few hops away, and with perfect knowledge of the server timing distribution without sknockd, would need to witness several hundred accepted packets to gain a significant advantage in distinguishing sknockd from a dynamic firewall[10]; with the simulated kernel-space sknockd, the adversary is unlikely to detect the processing time difference unless he is located on the same LAN as the server. To further minimize this difference, we implemented AES pre-computation for Poly1305-AES nonces. At the moment we precompute only the initial counter value, but we can precompute and store values of the next several counters, allowing for verification to be performed without any online cryptographic computation.

While we do not test the client-side knockproxy for timing distinguishability, mainly due to time constraints, the use of knockproxy would be much more difficult to detect than sknockd. Since the processing of SYN packets occurs before

---

[9] We can currently account for at least 4 user-space/kernel context switches in sknockd.

[10] Due to the fact that 90% of Internet flows experience a standard deviation of 1ms or more in round-trip time [28], while the magnitude of timing difference even in the case of user space sknockd is only about 0.15 ms.

any observable event, and processing subsequent packets in a flow requires no manipulation of kernel data structures and no cryptographic computation, observable timing differences would be very small. If a remote adversary were to test for the presence of knockproxy, the largest observable effect would be in the re-transmit timeout, which may be altered by the packet delay imposed by timestamp modification. However, since retransmit clocks have granularity measured in seconds [26], and our timestamp modification has millisecond granularity, detection is unlikely.

4 Discussion

4.1 Limitations of SILENTKNOCK

Here we would like to note a number of limitations of our system. First, we only attempt to authenticate the start of a connection, but provides no guarantee that connections stay authentic. In other words, our system does not protect against connection hijacking (a well-known problem in TCP security) [29]. Furthermore, due to the limited bandwidth for authentication, SILENTKNOCK can only support symmetrically-keyed authentication. We believe it is up to the application to provide connection hijacking protection and relevant user authentication (e.g., SSH [6]).

Our solution relies on embedding stegotext in TCP/IP, and we are therefore limited in the size of the MAC field we can send. Currently, we only support 32 bits out of a 16-byte MAC. Furthermore, different operating systems have different TCP initial sequence number properties, and thus the amount of data that can be embedded in the SYN packet is highly dependent on the OS composing the packet. Thus, it is necessary that the server know the OS of the client in order to correctly extract the stegotext; alternatively, the server can attempt multiple extractions, but this will increase the cost of filtering and degrade security by a factor of the number of OSes supported.

Identities, Addresses, and NAT. In any distributed authentication system it is necessary to decide what the identities in a system correspond to. Three natural choices are to let identities correspond to network addresses, to physical hosts, or to human users. Our current implementation allows two options: identities (keys) may be associated either with IP addresses or users; each has different consequences for usability and security.

When identities are bound to IP addresses, we must assume that only a single client machine will be accessing a SILENTKNOCK-protected server from a given IP address, since a single counter is used for each identity. This assumption breaks down in the presence of NAT (network address translation) and similar devices. Therefore, in this scenario, we must limit our system to only one client per NAT. We stress, however, that unlike previous implementations, where NATs presented a security problem [15], adversaries sharing a NAT with a valid knockproxy client gain no advantage.

We also support associating identities with users by issuing a key to each user and checking the MAC on each SYN packet against each user's key. This can be done at essentially no extra computational cost due to the design of the Poly1305 MAC, which is computed by adding a keyed non-cryptographic hash of the message to the AES encryption of a nonce mod 2^{128}. Suppose we assign different AES keys (but a shared non-cryptographic hash) to different users, and precompute the AES encryption of different users' counters, for the next ft values. Then, given a packet p with embedded tag t, we can check whether $t = \mathrm{MAC}_{K,r}(p,n) = \mathrm{Poly}1305_r(p) + \mathrm{AES}_K(n) \mod 2^{32}$ for some user's key K and counter n as follows. We first compute $t - H(p) \mod 2^{32}$, and then we search for the resulting value in our table of precomputed encrypted nonces; if the value is found, we accept the packet and remove older encrypted counters for the same user. This search can be implemented in essentially constant time (with respect to the number of users) using a number of approaches, such as hash tables or tries. After accepting the packet, we insert the next precomputed nonce for the same user into the table. While this solves the NAT problem mentioned above, it causes security loss by a factor of the number of users (and thus the number of user keys) due to the requirement that we check the MAC against all user keys. Alternatively, once IPv6 is a viable alternative to IPv4, we may be able to use unique *target* IP addresses as part of the key, such that a server running sknockd has one IPv6 address per user.

Denial of Service. While we have implemented some measures to prevent distinguishing or denial of service attacks due to packet dropping, our scheme is vulnerable to a selective denial of service attack. An adversary who modifies *all* packets on a network by consistently rewriting sequence numbers or timestamps can cause MAC verification to fail at sknockd, while not impacting the status of most standard TCP traffic. We note that this attack is both expensive, in that it requires the attacker to touch every packet in — and maintain per-flow state for — all connections on a network, and may effect other protocols that authenticate the TCP header, such as IPsec [30] or TCP-MD5 [22]. Additionally, such selective denial of service is much easier for other port knocking or general IP service authentication schemes, as in those cases it is easy to identify knock sequences or authenticated packets and drop them, while maintaining no other state. Finally, if the server logs failed connection attempts, it will be easy to notice such attacks since, for instance, altering the timestamp will still give a 24-bit MAC match in the sequence number, which is unlikely.

4.2   Conclusion

Following our formal security model for port knocking, the SILENTKNOCK implementation provides a provably indistinguishable system with reasonable overhead, and an especially light load on the server. The system is currently usable by any Linux 2.6 application using TCP/IP as its network protocol, and is completely compatible with TCP/IP as described by relevant RFCs [26, 31]: it is possible for a client running knockproxy to connect to a server not running sknockd. Furthermore, since all "knocks" are destined for ports potentially providing services, the system is compatible with all currently-deployed firewalls, including host-based software firewalls.

We provide per-flow, *not* per-source (IP address) authentication, meaning that even if host A already has an active and authenticated connection to host B, a new connection from host A to host B (presumably using different outgoing port on host A's side) would need to be uniquely authenticated. Furthermore, all of the knock "sequences" we use are one-time (not replayable) since we employ a connection counter that is unique to every IP address, and thus every client.

4.3   Future Work

For future work, there are a number of implementation-level issues to address. The most pressing issue of these is porting `sknockd` to a kernel module, to eliminate the overhead of kernel/user space switching. Along with this conversion, we plan to implement several other optimizations, including more aggressive pre-computation. We expect that these modifications will further decrease overhead for `sknockd`.

Other possibilities for future work include the use of additional TCP/IP fields for steganographic embedding. For instance, under Linux 2.6, ephemeral TCP ports and IP IDs are assigned pseudorandomly per destination host, and change every five minutes. Thus, in an environment that requires a longer MAC, these fields could be utilized, gaining an additional 34 bits of authentication, at the expense of disallowing more than one connection to a given IP address and port per five minute period. Using the source port number and IP ID field, and limiting connections to once per five minute period would also allow extension of SILENTKNOCK to the UDP protocol, with 34 bits of authentication; unfortunately, the UDP header format does not include any other standard, variable elements, so 34 bits per five minutes seems to be an upper bound on the authentication strength for UDP.

Another important issue to address in the future is usability. Our current implementation is fairly configurable and relatively straightforward for computer scientists or system administrators to use. However, in order to be deployed widely, (say, as widely as VPNs), we will require a more friendly interface. A related issue that we have not addressed here is key management. It will be interesting to consider these issues in depth.

Acknowledgements. We thank Luis von Ahn, Yongdae Kim, David Molnar, Stephen Murdoch, and Hal Peterson for helpful discussions and comments regarding this paper. This work was supported by NSF grant CNS-0546162.

References

[1] Krzywinski, M.: Port knocking: Network authentication across closed ports. SysAdmin Magazine 12(6), 12–17 (2003)

[2] Barham, P., Hand, S., Isaacs, R., Jardetzky, P., Mortier, R., Roscoe, T.: Techniques for lightweight concealment and authentication in IP networks. Technical Report IRB-TR-02-009, Intel Research Berkeley (July 2002)

[3] Worth, D.: CÖK: Cryptographic one-time knocking. In: Black Hat USA (2004)

[4] deGraaf, R., Aycock, J., Jacobson, M.J.: Improved port knocking with strong authentication. In: Srikanthan, T., Xue, J., Chang, C.-H. (eds.) ACSAC 2005. LNCS, vol. 3740, pp. 451–462. Springer, Heidelberg (2005)

[5] Fluhrer, S., Mantin, I., Shamir, A.: Attacks on RC4 and WEP. RSA Laboratories, Cryptobytes 5(2) (2002)

[6] Bellare, M., Kohno, T., Namprempre, C.: Authenticated encryption in SSH: provably fixing the SSH binary packet protocol. In: Proc. CCS '02, pp. 1–11 (2002)

[7] Bleichenbacher, D.: Chosen ciphertext attacks against protocols based on the RSA encryption standard PKCS# 1. In: Krawczyk, H. (ed.) CRYPTO 1998. LNCS, vol. 1462, pp. 1–12. Springer, Heidelberg (1998)

[8] Hopper, N.J., Langford, J., Von Ahn, L.: Provably secure steganography. In: Yung, M. (ed.) CRYPTO 2002. LNCS, vol. 2442, pp. 77–92. Springer, Heidelberg (2002)

 [9] Murdoch, S.J., Lewis, S.: Embedding covert channels into TCP/IP. In: Barni, M., Herrera-Joancomartí, J., Katzenbeisser, S., Pérez-González, F. (eds.) IH 2005. LNCS, vol. 3727, pp. 247–261. Springer, Heidelberg (2005)
[10] Bernstein, D.J.: The Poly1305-AES message authentication code. In: Gilbert, H., Handschuh, H. (eds.) FSE 2005. LNCS, vol. 3557, Springer, Heidelberg (2005)
[11] Linux 2.6.17.13 kernel source. drivers/char/random.c
[12] Vasserman, E.Y., Hopper, N., Laxson, J., Tyra, J.: Silentknock (April 2007),
     http://www.cs.umn.edu/~eyv/knock/
[13] Krzywinski, M.: Port knocking, http://www.portknocking.org/
[14] Graham-Cumming, J.: Practical secure port knocking. Dr. Dobb's Journal (November 2004)
[15] Manzanares, A.I., Marquez, J.T., Estevez-Tapiador, J.M., Castro, J.C.H.: Attacks on port knocking authentication mechanism. In: Gervasi, O., Gavrilova, M., Kumar, V., Laganà, A., Lee, H.P., Mun, Y., Taniar, D., Tan, C.J.K. (eds.) ICCSA 2005. LNCS, vol. 3483, pp. 1292–1300. Springer, Heidelberg (2005)
[16] Ahsan, D.K.: Practical data hiding in TCP/IP. In: Proc. Workshop on Multimedia Security at ACM Multimedia, ACM Press, New York (2002)
[17] Rowland, C.H.: Covert channels in the TCP/IP protocol suite. First Monday 2(5) (1997)
[18] Conehead: Stego hasho. Phrack 9(55) (1999)
[19] MacDermid, T.: Stegtunnel,
     http://www.synacklabs.net/OOB/stegtunnel.html
[20] Ahn, L.v., Hopper, N., Langford, J.: Covert two-party computation. In: Proc. STOC '05, pp. 513–522 (2005)
[21] Bond, M., Danezis, G.: The dining freemasons: Security protocols for secret societies. In: Proc. 13th International Workshop on Security Protocols, Cambridge, England (April 2005)
[22] Heffernan, A.: Protection of BGP sessions via the TCP MD5 signature option (1998),
     http://www.ietf.org/rfc/rfc2385.txt
[23] Hoglund, G., Butler, J.: Rootkits: Subverting the Windows Kernel. Addison-Wesley Professional, Reading (2005)
[24] Ring, S., Cole, E.: Taking a lesson from stealthy rootkits. IEEE Security and Privacy 2(4), 38–45 (2004)
[25] Welte, H., Kadlecsik, J., Josefsson, M., McHardy, P., Kozakai, Y., Morris, J., Boucher, M., Russell, R.: The netfilter.org project, http://www.netfilter.org/
[26] Postel, J. (ed.): Transmission control protocol (1981),
     http://www.ietf.org/rfc/rfc0793.txt
[27] Carter, J.L., Wegman, M.N.: Universal classes of hash functions (extended abstract). In: Proc. STOC '77, pp. 106–112 (1977)
[28] Aikat, J., Kaur, J., Smith, F.D., Jeffay, K.: Variability in TCP round-trip times. In: Proc. IMC '03, pp. 279–284 (2003)
[29] Bellovin, S.M.: Security problems in the TCP/IP protocol suite. SIGCOMM Comput. Commun. Rev. 19(2), 32–48 (1989)
[30] Kent, S., Atkinson, R.: IP authentication header (November 1998),
     http://www.ietf.org/rfc/rfc2402.txt
[31] Jacobson, V., Braden, R., Borman, D.: TCP extensions for high performance (1992),
     http://www.ietf.org/rfc/rfc1323.txt
[32] Shoup, V.: On fast and provably secure message authentication based on universal hashing. In: Koblitz, N. (ed.) CRYPTO 1996. LNCS, vol. 1109, pp. 313–328. Springer, Heidelberg (1996)
[33] Boneh, D., Franklin, M.: Identity-based encryption from the weil pairing. SIAM J. Comput. 32(3), 586–615 (2003)

Generalized Key Delegation for Hierarchical Identity-Based Encryption

Michel Abdalla[1], Eike Kiltz[2], and Gregory Neven[1,3]

[1] Departement d'Informatique, École normale supérieure
Michel.Abdalla@ens.fr
http://www.di.ens.fr/~mabdalla
[2] Cryptology and Information Security Research Theme, CWI Amsterdam
kiltz@cwi.nl
http://kiltz.net
[3] Department of Electrical Engineering, Katholieke Universiteit Leuven
Gregory.Neven@esat.kuleuven.be
http://www.neven.org

Abstract. In this paper, we introduce a new primitive called identity-based encryption with wildcard key derivation (WKD-IBE, or "wicked IBE") that enhances the concept of hierarchical identity-based encryption (HIBE) by allowing more general key delegation patterns. A secret key is derived for a vector of identity strings, where entries can be left blank using a wildcard. This key can then be used to derive keys for any pattern that replaces wildcards with concrete identity strings. For example, one may want to allow the university's head system administrator to derive secret keys (and hence the ability to decrypt) for all departmental sysadmin email addresses sysadmin@*.univ.edu, where * is a wildcard that can be replaced with any string. We provide appropriate security notions and provably secure instantiations with different tradeoffs in terms of ciphertext size and efficiency. We also present a generic construction of identity-based broadcast encryption (IBBE) from any WKD-IBE scheme. One of our instantiation yields an IBBE scheme with constant ciphertext size.

1 Introduction

IDENTITY-BASED ENCRYPTION. Securely linking users to their public keys is a notorious obstacle in the adoption of public-key encryption schemes in practice. Most commonly, it is overcome by means of a public key infrastructure (PKI) where a trusted authority certifies, by means of a digital signature, the relation between users and their public keys. The high cost of setting up and maintaining such a PKI can be prohibitive for many organizations however. In 1984, Shamir [20] proposed identity-based encryption (IBE) as a cheaper alternative to traditional PKIs. Here, the public key of a user *is* his identity (e.g. his name or email address), while the corresponding private key is handed to him by a trusted key distribution center. It lasted until 2000 however for the first practical IBE schemes [18,7] to be proposed based on bilinear maps.

J. Biskup and J. Lopez (Eds.): ESORICS 2007, LNCS 4734, pp. 139–154, 2007.
© Springer-Verlag Berlin Heidelberg 2007

Hierarchical identity-based encryption (HIBE) schemes [14,12] are the hierarchical extension of IBEs where user identities are vectors of bit strings. The root entity generates private keys for users at the first level; users at level ℓ can derive keys for their children at level $\ell + 1$. This prevents the distribution center from becoming a bottleneck in the system, and at the same time reflects the hierarchical structure of many organizations and user identities, in particular email addresses. For example, the head of the computer science department of a university could be given the key for identity (edu,univ,cs) allowing him to derive keys for identities (edu,univ,cs,username) corresponding to email addresses username@cs.univ.edu.

WILDCARD KEY DERIVATION. Hierarchical key derivation is a useful feature, but has its limitations. For example, it would be reasonable to prevent end-users from further deriving keys for identities below them. This feature was referred to before as *limited delegation* by Boneh-Boyen-Goh [6], who show a tweak to their HIBE scheme offering exactly this functionality—albeit without a formal security notion or proof for their approach. In some circumstances, it could also be useful to be able to deviate from the hierarchical structure. For example, one may want to allow the university's head system administrator to derive keys for all departmental sysadmin email addresses sysadmin@*.univ.edu, where * is a wildcard that can be replaced with any string. As another example, it could be practical to provide a company like Google Inc. that registers its name at all top-level domains with a key for *@google.*.

These applications lead us to generalize the concept of HIBE schemes to *identity-based encryption with wildcard key derivation* (WKD-IBE), or more succinctly *wicked IBE*. After defining adequate security notions, we start looking for constructions. First observe that if a HIBE scheme allows a maximal hierarchy depth L to be fixed, then the limited-delegation property of [6] can be achieved generically by padding the identity vector with "dummy" strings at the unused lower levels. (But this may come at the cost of efficiency.) The more general functionality of wildcard key delegation cannot be achieved generically though. Nevertheless, we show that many of the existing HIBE schemes are amenable to a modification that enables wildcard key derivation, including the Gentry-Silverberg [12], Boneh-Boyen [5], Waters [21], and Boneh-Boyen-Goh [6] HIBE schemes. For the former three this may come as a bit of a surprise, because no limited-delegation tweaks were previously proposed for these schemes. We prove the security of the modified schemes under our new notions, thereby providing as a special case formal ground for the intuition of [6] regarding their limited-delegation tweak.

APPLICATION TO IDENTITY-BASED BROADCAST ENCRYPTION. Broadcast encryption [11] allows to encrypt a message to any subset $S \subseteq \{1, \dots, N\}$ of N users so that only users in S can decrypt the message. A trivial solution consists of concatenating encryptions of the message under the public key of each user in S separately, but this yields ciphertexts of size linear in $|S|$. The most efficient fully collusion-resistant (meaning where the adversary can corrupt all users outside of S) public-key broadcast encryption schemes are due to Boneh et al. [8], who present a first construction with constant-size ciphertexts and private keys but with $O(N)$-size public keys, and a second construction with $O(\sqrt{N})$-size ciphertexts and public keys.

Identity-based broadcast encryption (IBBE) is the natural extension of broadcast encryption to the identity-based setting. It is particularly appealing as a primitive because the total number of users in the system N is limited only by the size of the identity space. We propose a generic construction of an IBBE schemes from any WKD-IBE scheme. The construction inflates the private key size by a factor L being the maximal number of identities in a recipient set, but otherwise shares the same cost as the underlying wicked IBE.

Of all the instantiations of wicked IBE that we propose, the most attractive resulting IBBE scheme is that obtained from the scheme based on [6], because it achieves constant-size ciphertexts. However, it has the disadvantage of having private keys of size $O(L^2)$, where L is the maximum number of recipients in a ciphertext. The other concrete instantiations are less attractive because they have ciphertext size $O(L)$, just like the trivial scheme that concatenates individual ciphertexts. Unlike most other broadcast schemes however, they do have the remarkable feature that knowledge of the recipient set is not required in order to decrypt the message.

WILDCARD SIGNATURES. Just like the key derivation of an IBE scheme automatically gives rise to a signature scheme [7], a WKD-IBE scheme gives rise to a new primitive that we call a *wildcard signature scheme*. It allows a signer to issue a signature on a message containing wildcards, which anyone can replace with concrete values at a later point without invalidating the signature. Our constructions of wicked identity-based encryption yield a number of wildcard signature schemes with different tradeoffs.

RELATED WORK. Wicked identity-based encryption can be seen as the dual notion of identity-based encryption with wildcards [1] (WIBE). There, one can use wildcards in the recipient identity to which a ciphertext is encrypted, so that all users whose identity matches the recipient pattern can decrypt it. In fact, the notions of WKD-IBE and WIBE could be combined into a universal primitive that allows wildcards to be used in both the encryption and key derivation algorithms. Instantiations of this primitive can be obtained from all WKD-IBE schemes presented in this work, except for the one based on Gentry-Silverberg's HIBE [12].

Key-policy attribute-based encryption (KP-ABE) [13] associates to each decryption key an access structure consisting of a logical combination of attribute values using AND and OR gates. A ciphertext is encrypted under a set of descriptive attributes and can only be decrypted with a key whose access structure is satisfied by the set of attributes. As discussed in [13], HIBE schemes can be seen as a special case of KP-ABE schemes by mapping the identity vector (edu, univ, cs, sysadmin) to the access structure ($1\|$edu $\wedge$ $2\|$univ $\wedge$ $3\|$cs $\wedge$ $4\|$sysadmin). Likewise, wicked IBE can be seen as a special case of KP-ABE by letting the key for identity (edu, *, *, sysadmin) be given by the key for ($1\|$edu $\wedge$ $4\|$sysadmin). The wicked IBE scheme obtained through the first construction of [13] has the disadvantage of having public keys linear in the size of the attribute universe. The instantiation obtained from their second, large-universe construction is quite similar to the scheme that we derive from the Boneh-Boyen HIBE scheme [5]. None of the schemes derived from [13] achieve constant ciphertext size though, like our wicked IBE construction based on [6].

The use of HIBE schemes in the design of broadcast encryption schemes was first considered by Dodis and Fazio [10]. Chatterjee and Sarkar [9] gave a direct construction of an IBBE scheme that is closely related to the instantiation of our generic construction with the WKD-IBE scheme based on [6]. Our generic construction provides insight into the design of their scheme, but their construction contains some interesting efficiency-improving tweaks. The schemes are compared in more detail in Section 4.3.

In independent work, Shacham [19] formalizes the concept of *limited delegation* for HIBE schemes and proves this feature for the HIBE scheme of [6]. As we pointed out above, limited delegation for HIBEs can be seen as a special case of WKD-IBE where wildcards can only appear at the end of the identity vector. Our WKD-IBE scheme based on [6] can therefore be seen as a generalization of the result of [19].

2   Basic Definitions

In this section, we introduce some notation and computational problems that we will use throughout the rest of the paper. In doing so, we adopt the same notation and definition style used in [1].

NOTATION. Let $\mathbb{N} = \{0, 1, \ldots\}$ be the set of natural numbers. Let ε be the empty string. If $n \in \mathbb{N}$, then $\{0, 1\}^n$ denotes the set of n-bit strings, and $\{0, 1\}^*$ is the set of all bit strings. More generally, if S is a set, then S^n is the set of n-tuples of elements of S, $S^{\leq n}$ is the set of tuples of length at most n. If S is finite, then $x \xleftarrow{\$} S$ denotes the assignment to x of an element chosen uniformly at random from S. If A is an algorithm, then $y \leftarrow \mathsf{A}(x)$ denotes the assignment to y of the output of A on input x, and if A is randomized, then $y \xleftarrow{\$} \mathsf{A}(x)$ denotes that the output of an execution of $\mathsf{A}(x)$ with fresh coins is assigned to y.

THE DECISIONAL BILINEAR DIFFIE-HELLMAN ASSUMPTION [7]. Let $\mathbb{G}, \mathbb{G}_T$ be multiplicative groups of prime order p with an admissible map $\hat{e} : \mathbb{G} \times \mathbb{G} \to \mathbb{G}_T$. By admissible we mean that the map is bilinear, non-degenerate and efficiently computable. Bilinearity means that for all $a, b \in \mathbb{Z}_p$ and all $g \in \mathbb{G}$ we have $\hat{e}(g^a, g^b) = \hat{e}(g, g)^{ab}$. By non-degenerate we mean that $\hat{e}(g, g) = 1$ if and only if $g = 1$. Let $g \in \mathbb{G}$ be a generator. In such a setting, the bilinear decisional Diffie-Hellman (BDDH) problem is to determine, given g, $A = g^a$, $B = g^b$, $C = g^c$, and $Z = \hat{e}(g, g)^z$, whether $Z = \hat{e}(g, g)^{abc}$ for hidden values of a, b, c and z. More formally, let $\mathcal{A}$ be an adversary for the BDDH problem. Such an adversary has advantage ϵ in solving the BDDH problem if $\left| \Pr[\mathcal{A}(g, A, B, C, \hat{e}(g, g)^{abc}) = 1] - \Pr[\mathcal{A}(g, A, B, C, \hat{e}(g, g)^z) = 1] \right| \geq \epsilon$, where the probabilities are over the choice of a, b, c, z and over the random coins consumed by $\mathcal{A}$.

Definition 1. *The (t, ϵ)-BDDH assumption holds if no t-time adversary has at least ϵ advantage in the above game.*

We note that throughout this paper we will assume that the time t of an adversary includes its code size, in order to exclude trivial "lookup" adversaries.

THE BDHE ASSUMPTION. The ℓ-decisional bilinear Diffie-Hellman exponent (ℓ-BDHE) problem [6] in $\mathbb{G}$ is: given g, h and $g^{(\alpha^i)} \in \mathbb{G}$, for $i = 1, \ldots, \ell-1, \ell+1, \ldots, 2\ell$ as input, output $\hat{e}(g, h)^{(\alpha^\ell)} \in \mathbb{G}_T$. Boneh, Boyen and Goh, conjectured that the ℓ-BDHE is a hard problem, meaning with this that no polynomially bounded adversary $\mathcal{A}$ can solve it with more than negligible probability, over the random choices of $g, h \in \mathbb{G}$, the choice of $\alpha \in \mathbb{Z}_p$, and the random coin tosses of $\mathcal{A}$.

The decisional version of the problem can be defined in the usual manner. Let $\boldsymbol{y} = (g^\alpha, g^{(\alpha^2)}, \ldots, g^{(\alpha^{\ell-1})}, g^{(\alpha^{\ell+1})}, \ldots, g^{(\alpha^{2\ell})})$. An algorithm $\mathcal{B}$ that outputs a bit b, has advantage ϵ in solving the decisional ℓ-BDHE problem in $\mathbb{G}$ if $\left| \Pr\left[\mathcal{B}(g, h, \boldsymbol{y}, \hat{e}(g,h)^{(\alpha^\ell)}) = 1 \right] - \Pr\left[\mathcal{B}(g, h, \boldsymbol{y}, T) = 1 \right] \right| \geq \epsilon$, where the probabilities are taken over the random choices of $g, h \in \mathbb{G}$, the random choice of $\alpha \in \mathbb{Z}_p$, the random choice of $T \in \mathbb{G}_T$, and the internal coin tosses of $\mathcal{B}$.

Definition 2. *The decisional (t, ϵ, ℓ)-BDHE assumption holds in $\mathbb{G}$ if no t-time (probabilistic) algorithm has advantage at least ϵ in solving the decisional ℓ-BDHE problem in $\mathbb{G}$.*

3   Wicked Identity-Based Encryption

SYNTAX. A wicked identity-based encryption scheme (WKD-IBE) is a generalization of a HIBE scheme which allows for more general key delegation patterns. In a WKD-IBE scheme, secret keys are associated with patterns rather than identity vectors. A pattern P is a vector $(P_1, \ldots, P_\ell) \in (\{0,1\}^* \cup \{*\})^\ell$ of length $\ell \leq L$, where $*$ is a special wildcard symbol and L is the maximal depth of the WKD-IBE scheme. That is, each component of a pattern P is either a specific identity string or a wildcard. The main idea behind the WKD-IBE notion is that a user in possession of the secret key for a given pattern P can generate secret keys for any pattern P' that matches P. We say that a pattern $P' = (P'_1, \ldots, P'_{\ell'})$ matches P, denoted $P' \in_* P$, if and only if $\ell' \leq \ell$; $\forall\, i = 1 \ldots \ell'$, $P'_i = P_i$ or $P_i = *$; and $\forall\, i = \ell' + 1 \ldots \ell$, $P_i = *$.

More formally, a WKD-IBE scheme is a tuple of algorithms $\mathcal{WKD\text{-}IBE} = $ (Setup, KeyDer, Enc, Dec) providing the following functionality. The root authority generates a master key pair $(mpk, msk) \xleftarrow{\$} \mathsf{Setup}$. Via $sk_{P'} \xleftarrow{\$} \mathsf{KeyDer}(sk_P, P')$, a user possessing the secret key sk_P for a pattern $P = (P_1, \ldots, P_\ell)$ can derive a secret key for any pattern $P' \in_* P$. The secret key of the root identity is $msk = sk_{(*,\ldots,*)}$.

To create a ciphertext of message $m \in \{0,1\}^*$ intended for an identity $ID = (ID_1, \ldots, ID_\ell)$, the sender computes $C \xleftarrow{\$} \mathsf{Enc}(mpk, ID, m)$. Any user in possession of the secret key for a pattern P such that $ID \in_* P$ can decrypt the ciphertext using sk_P as $m \leftarrow \mathsf{Dec}(sk_P, C, ID)$. Correctness requires that for all key pairs

(mpk, msk) output by Setup, all messages $m \in \{0,1\}^*$, all $0 \leq \ell \leq L$, all patterns $P \in (\{0,1\}^* \cup \{*\})^\ell$, and all identities $ID \in (\{0,1\}^*)^{\ell'}$ such that $ID \in_* P$, Dec(KeyDer(msk, P), Enc(mpk, ID, m), ID) $= m$ with probability one.

SECURITY. We define the security of WKD-IBE schemes in a way that is very similar to the case of HIBE schemes, but where the adversary can query for the secret keys corresponding to arbitrary patterns, rather than specific identity vectors. Of course, the adversary is not allowed to query the key derivation oracle for any pattern matched by the challenge identity.

More specifically, security is defined through the following game with an adversary. In the first phase, the adversary is run on input of the master public key of a freshly generated key pair $(mpk, msk) \xleftarrow{\$} \mathsf{Setup}$. In a chosen-plaintext attack (IND-WKID-CPA), the adversary is given access to a key derivation oracle that on input a pattern $P \in (\{0,1\}^* \cup \{*\})^{\leq L}$ returns $sk_P \xleftarrow{\$} \mathsf{KeyDer}(msk, P)$.

At the end of the first phase, the adversary outputs two equal-length challenge messages $m_0^*, m_1^* \in \{0,1\}^*$ and a challenge identity $ID^* = (ID_1^*, \ldots, ID_{\ell*}^*)$ where $0 \leq \ell^* \leq L$. The adversary is given a challenge ciphertext $C^* \xleftarrow{\$} \mathsf{Enc}(mpk, ID^*, m_b^*)$ for a randomly chosen bit b, and is given access to the same oracles as during the first phase of the attack. The second phase ends when the adversary outputs a bit b'. The adversary is said to win the IND-WKID-CPA game if $b' = b$ and if it never queried the key derivation oracle for the key of any pattern P such that $ID^* \in_* P$. If $Succ$ is the event that the adversary wins the above game, then its advantage is defined as $\epsilon = 2 \cdot \Pr[Succ] - 1$.

Definition 3. *A WKD-IBE scheme is (t, q_K, ϵ) IND-WKID-CPA-secure if all t-time adversaries making at most q_K queries to the key derivation oracle have at most advantage ϵ in the IND-WKID-CPA game described above.*

SELECTIVE-IDENTITY SECURITY. As for the case of HIBEs, we also define the weaker selective-identity (sWKID) security notion IND-sWKID-CPA. The IND-sWKID-CPA definition is analogous to the IND-WKID-CPA one given above except that the adversary has to commit to the challenge identity at the beginning of the game, before the master public key is made available.

3.1   Constructions with Linear-Size Ciphertexts

A CONSTRUCTION FROM GENTRY-SILVERBERG'S HIBE SCHEME. In the following, we present a wicked IBE scheme based on the Gentry-Silverberg HIBE scheme [12]. The scheme uses L independent random oracles $H_i : \{0,1\}^* \to \mathbb{G}$ for $1 \leq i \leq L$. These can be derived from a single random oracle via standard techniques [4].

We provide some intuition into our construction by taking a closer look at the key derivation of (a slight variant of) the original Gentry-Silverberg HIBE scheme. For master secret key $\alpha \xleftarrow{\$} \mathbb{Z}_p$ and master public key $g_1 \leftarrow g^\alpha$, the decryption key of an identity (ID_0) at the top level is given by $sk_{(ID_0)} \leftarrow H_0(ID_0)^\alpha$. The key for a lower-level identity $(ID_0, \ldots, ID_\ell)$ is given by

$$sk_{(ID_0,\ldots,ID_\ell)} \leftarrow \left(H_0(ID_0)^\alpha \cdot \prod_{i=1}^{\ell} H_i(ID_i)^{r_i} , g^{r_1} , \ldots , g^{r_\ell} \right)$$

for random $r_1, \ldots, r_\ell \xleftarrow{\$} \mathbb{Z}_p$. One could "insert a wildcard" at level $1 \le j \le \ell$ by omitting the factor $H_j(ID_j)^{r_j}$ from the product in the first component and omitting the entry g^{r_j} in the vector; any value for ID_j can then be filled in later by choosing r_j, multiplying $H_j(ID_j)^{r_j}$ into the first component and inserting a new component g^{r_j}. Inserting a wildcard at the top level is not so easy though, as knowledge of the master key α is required to compute the factor $H_0(ID_0)^\alpha$. We therefore "disable" the top level by fixing it to identity $\perp$, or equivalently, by including $h_0 = H_0(\perp)$ in the public key. A similar fix can be used to prevent a user at level $\ell < L$ to further derive keys for users at levels $\ell + 1, \ldots, L$. Namely, the key is computed as if it were for the identity at level L with the components at levels $\ell + 1, \ldots, L$ fixed to $\perp$. Equivalently, one can include the elements $h_i = H_i(\perp)$ for $1 \le i \le L$ in the public key.

Before presenting the scheme, we first need to introduce some additional notation. If $P = (P_1, \ldots, P_\ell)$ is a pattern, then let $|P| = \ell$ be the length of P, let $\mathrm{W}(P)$ be the set containing all wildcard indices in P, i.e. the indices $1 \le i \le \ell$ such that $P_i = *$, and let $\overline{\mathrm{W}}(P)$ be the complementary set containing all non-wildcard indices. Clearly, $\mathrm{W}(P) \cap \overline{\mathrm{W}}(P) = \emptyset$ and $\mathrm{W}(P) \cup \overline{\mathrm{W}}(P) = \{1, \ldots, \ell\}$. We also extend the notations $P|_{\le i}$, $P|_{> i}$ and $P|_I$ that we introduced for identity vectors to patterns in the natural way. We are now ready to present the $\mathcal{GS\text{-}WKD\text{-}IBE}$ scheme in full details:

Setup. The root identity chooses random generators $g, h_0, \ldots, h_L \xleftarrow{\$} \mathbb{G}^*$. It chooses $\alpha \xleftarrow{\$} \mathbb{Z}_p$ and computes $g_1 \leftarrow g^\alpha$. It publishes $mpk \leftarrow (g, g_1, h_0, \ldots, h_L)$ as the master public key and keeps $msk \leftarrow h_0^\alpha$ secret.

Key Derivation. To compute a secret key for a pattern $P = (P_1, \ldots, P_\ell)$ directly from the master secret key, the root proceeds as follows. Let $I = \overline{\mathrm{W}}(P) \cup \{\ell + 1, \ldots, L\}$. For all $i \in I$ the root chooses $r_i \xleftarrow{\$} \mathbb{Z}_p$ and lets $b_i \leftarrow g^{r_i}$. It then computes $a \leftarrow msk \cdot \prod_{i \in \overline{\mathrm{W}}(P)} H_i(P_i)^{r_i} \cdot \prod_{i=\ell+1, \ldots, L} h_i^{r_i}$. The secret key for pattern P is $sk_P \leftarrow (a, (b_i)_{i \in I})$.

Anyone knowing this secret key can generate a key for a pattern $P' = (P'_1, \ldots, P'_{\ell'}) \in_* P$ as follows. Let $I' = \overline{\mathrm{W}}(P') \cup \{\ell' + 1, \ldots, L\}$. Note that $P' \in_* P$ implies that $I \subseteq I'$. For all $i \in I$, choose $r_i \xleftarrow{\$} \mathbb{Z}_p$ and compute $b'_i \leftarrow b_i \cdot g^{r_i}$; for all $i \in I' \setminus I$, choose $r_i \xleftarrow{\$} \mathbb{Z}_p$ and compute $b'_i \leftarrow g^{r_i}$. Finally, compute $a' \leftarrow a \cdot \prod_{i \in \overline{\mathrm{W}}(P')} H_i(P'_i)^{r_i} \cdot \prod_{i=\ell'+1}^{L} h_i^{r_i}$ and return the secret key $sk_{P'} \leftarrow (a', (b'_i)_{i \in I'})$.

Encryption. To encrypt a message $m \in \mathbb{G}_T$ to identity $ID = (ID_1, \ldots, ID_\ell)$ under $mpk = (g, g_1, h_0, \ldots, h_L)$, the sender chooses $t \xleftarrow{\$} \mathbb{Z}_p$, computes

$$C_0 \leftarrow g^t$$

$$C_i \leftarrow H_i(ID_i)^t \quad \text{for } i = 1, \ldots, \ell$$

$$C_i \leftarrow h_i^t \quad \text{for } i = \ell + 1, \ldots, L$$

$$C_{L+1} \leftarrow \hat{e}(g_1, h_0)^t \cdot m$$

and outputs the ciphertext $C = (C_0, \ldots, C_{L+1})$.

Decryption. A recipient knowing the secret key sk_P for a pattern $P = (P_1, \ldots, P_\ell)$ can decrypt a ciphertext $(C_0, \ldots, C_{L+1})$ intended to any identity $ID \in_* P$ as follows. Let $I = \overline{W}(P) \cup \{\ell + 1, \ldots, L\}$ and let $a_P = (a, (b_i)_{i \in I})$. The recipient recovers the plaintext as

$$m \leftarrow C_{L+1} \cdot \frac{\prod_{i \in I} \hat{e}(b_i, C_i)}{\hat{e}(C_0, a)}.$$

Note that the recipient need not even know the exact identity under which the message was encrypted.

The fact that decryption works can be seen as follows. Let $P = (P_1, \ldots, P_\ell)$ be a pattern, let $I = \overline{W}(P) \cup \{\ell + 1, \ldots, L\}$ and let $sk_P = (a, (b_i)_{i \in I})$ be a secret key for P. For all $i \in I$, let r_i be the discrete logarithm of b_i with respect to g, i.e. $b_i = g^{r_i}$. From the key derivation algorithm one can see that $a = h_0^\alpha \cdot \prod_{i \in \overline{W}(P)} H_i(ID_i)^{r_i} \cdot \prod_{i=\ell+1}^{L} h_i^{r_i}$. When $(C_0, \ldots, C_{L+1})$ is a ciphertext intended for $ID = (ID_1, \ldots, ID_{\ell'}) \in_* P$, we have that

$$\hat{e}(C_0, a) = \hat{e}\left(g^t, \ h_0^\alpha \cdot \prod_{i \in \overline{W}(P)} H_i(P_i)^{r_i} \cdot \prod_{i=\ell+1}^{L} h_i^{r_i}\right)$$

$$= \hat{e}(g^t, h_0^\alpha) \cdot \prod_{i \in \overline{W}(P)} \hat{e}\left(g^{r_i}, H_i(P_i)^t\right) \cdot \prod_{i=\ell+1}^{L} \hat{e}\left(g^{r_i}, h_i^t\right)$$

$$= \hat{e}(g_1, h_0)^t \cdot \prod_{i \in I} \hat{e}(b_i, C_i),$$

where the last equality holds because $P_i = ID_i$ for all $i \in \overline{W}(P)$ if $ID \in_* P$. Hence, the value of K at decryption is exactly the argument of H_2 at encryption, and the correct message is recovered.

The following theorem states the security of the above scheme in the selective-identity notion under the BDDH assumption in the random oracle model; the proof is given in the full version [2]. Security in the full-identity notion can be obtained at the cost of losing a factor $O(q_H^L)$ in the reduction.

Theorem 1. *Under the (t', ϵ') BDDH assumption, the $\mathcal{GS}$-$\mathcal{WKD}$-$\mathcal{IBE}$ scheme described above is (t, q_K, q_H, ϵ) IND-sWKID-CPA-secure in the random oracle model for $\epsilon \geq 2\epsilon'$ and $t \leq t' - (q_H + (q_K + 3)L)t_{\exp}$, where $t_{\exp}$ is the time required to perform an exponentiation in $\mathbb{G}$.*

CONSTRUCTIONS FROM BONEH-BOYEN'S AND WATERS' HIBE SCHEMES. The attentive reader will have noticed the resemblance of the above scheme with the HIBE schemes of Boneh-Boyen [5] and Waters [21]. Indeed, if identity strings are elements of $\mathbb{Z}_p^*$, then one can obtain a wicked IBE variant of [5] by setting $H_i(ID_i) = h_{i,0} h_{i,1}^{ID_i}$, where $h_{i,0}, h_{i,1}$ are random elements of $\mathbb{G}$ that are fixed in the master public key. This scheme can be proved IND-sWKID-CPA secure under the BDDH assumption in the standard (i.e., non-random oracle) model using a proof quite similar to the above analysis. Likewise, one can obtain a variant based on Waters' HIBE scheme when identities are n-bit strings by setting $H_i(ID_i = ID_{i,1} \ldots ID_{i,n}) = h_{i,0} \prod_{ID_{i,j}=1} h_{i,j}$. An analysis similar to the one in [21] can be used to prove this scheme IND-WKID-CPA secure under the BDDH assumption in the standard model at the cost of losing a factor $O((nq_K)^L)$ in the reduction.

3.2   Constructions with Constant-Size Ciphertexts

In this section, we describe efficient wicked IBE schemes with constant-size ciphertexts based on the Boneh-Boyen-Goh [6] and Waters [21] HIBE schemes. We build the wicked IBE scheme $\mathcal{BBG\text{-}WKD\text{-}IBE} = (\mathsf{Setup}, \mathsf{KeyDer}, \mathsf{Enc}, \mathsf{Dec})$ described as follows:

Setup. The trusted authority chooses random generators g from $\mathbb{G}$, a random $\alpha \in \mathbb{Z}_p$ and sets $g_1 \leftarrow g^\alpha$. Next, it picks random elements $g_2, g_3, h_1, \ldots, h_L$ from $\mathbb{G}$ and sets $g_4 \leftarrow g_2^\alpha$. The master public key is $mpk = (g, g_1, g_2, g_3, h_1, \ldots, h_L)$. The corresponding master secret key is $msk = g_4$.

Key Derivation. Let $P' = (P'_1, \ldots, P'_\ell) \in (\mathbb{Z}_p^* \cup \{*\})^{\leq L}$ be the pattern for which a secret key needs to be generated. To compute the secret key for P' from the master secret key, first a random $r \xleftarrow{\$} \mathbb{Z}_p$ is chosen, then the secret key $sk_{P'} = (a'_1, a'_2, b')$ for P' is constructed as

$$
a'_1 = g_4 \cdot \left(g_3 \prod_{i \in \overline{W}(P')} h_i^{P'_i} \right)^r \; ; \quad a'_2 = g^r \; ; \quad b' = (b_i = h_i^r)_{i \in W(P')} \; .
$$

In order to generate the secret key $sk_{P'}$ for pattern P' from the secret key $sk_P = (a_1, a_2, b)$ for pattern P such that $P' \in_* P$, ones simply chooses a random $r' \xleftarrow{\$} \mathbb{Z}_p$ and outputs $sk_{P'} = (a'_1, a'_2, b')$, where

$$
a'_1 = a_1 \cdot \left(g_3 \prod_{i \in \overline{W}(P')} h_i^{P'_i} \right)^{r'} \cdot \left(\prod_{i \in \overline{W}(P') \cap W(P)} b_i^{P'_i} \right)
$$

$$
a'_2 = a_2 \cdot g^{r'}
$$

$$
b' = \left(b'_i = b_i \cdot h_i^{r'} \right)_{i \in W(P')}
$$

Encryption. To encrypt a message $m \in \mathbb{G}_T$ for an identity $ID = (ID_1, \ldots, ID_\ell)$, the sender first chooses $t \xleftarrow{\$} \mathbb{Z}_p$ and outputs the ciphertext $C = (C_1, C_2, C_3) \in \mathbb{G} \times \mathbb{G} \times \mathbb{G}_T$, where

$$
C_1 = g^t \; ; \quad C_2 = \left(g_3 \prod_{i=1}^\ell h_i^{ID_i} \right)^t \; ; \quad C_3 = m \cdot \hat{e}(g_1, g_2)^t \; .
$$

Decryption. Let be the $C = (C_1, C_2, C_3)$ and $ID = (ID_1, \ldots, ID_\ell)$ be the identity to which the ciphertext was created. If the receiver is the root authority holding the master key msk, then he can recover the message by computing $C_3/\hat{e}(C_1, msk)$. Any other receiver holding a secret key for pattern P such that $ID \in_* P$ can decrypt the ciphertext as follows. Let $sk_P = (a_1, a_2, b)$ be the decryption key for the receiver. He can recover the message by computing

$$a'_1 \leftarrow a_1 \cdot \left(\prod_{i \in W(P)|_{\leq \ell}} b_i^{ID_i} \right) \quad \text{and} \quad m \leftarrow C_3 \cdot \frac{\hat{e}(a_2, C_2)}{\hat{e}(C_1, a'_1)}.$$

The fact that decryption works can be seen as follows. Since $ID \in_* P$, we have that $P_i = ID_i$ for all $i \in \overline{W}(P)|_{\leq \ell}$. Thus the quantity $\frac{\hat{e}(a_2, C_2)}{\hat{e}(C_1, a'_1)}$ becomes:

$$\frac{\hat{e}(a_2, C_2)}{\hat{e}(C_1, a_1 \prod_{i \in W(P)|_{\leq \ell}} b_i^{ID_i})} = \frac{\hat{e}(g^r, (g_3 \prod_{i=1}^{\ell} h_i^{ID_i})^r)}{\hat{e}(g^t, g_4 \cdot (g_3 \prod_{i \in \overline{W}(P)} h_i^{P_i})^r \cdot \prod_{i \in W(P)|_{\leq \ell}} b_i^{ID_i})}$$

$$= \frac{\hat{e}(g^r, (g_3 \prod_{i=1}^{\ell} h_i^{ID_i})^t)}{\hat{e}(g^t, g_4)\, \hat{e}(g^t, (g_3 \prod_{i=1}^{\ell} h_i^{ID_i})^r)} = \frac{1}{\hat{e}(g^t, g_4)} = \frac{1}{\hat{e}(g_1, g_2)^t}.$$

The following theorem states the security of the above scheme in the selective-identity notion under the ℓ-BDHE assumption in the standard model. The proof is given in the full version [2]. We remark that, interestingly, we can only prove security of the scheme based on the ℓ-BDHE assumption, whereas the weaker ℓ-BDHI assumption was sufficient for the security proof of the HIBE scheme [6].

Theorem 2. *Let $\mathcal{BBG}$-$\mathcal{WKD}$-$\mathcal{IBE}$ be the WKD-IBE scheme as described above. Under the decisional (t, ϵ, ℓ)-BDHE assumption, the $\mathcal{BBG}$-$\mathcal{WKD}$-$\mathcal{IBE}$ scheme of depth $L = \ell-1$ is $(t', q_K, 2\epsilon)$ IND-sWKID-CPA-secure where $t' = t - O(Lq_K') \cdot t_{exp}$ and t_{exp} is the time it takes to perform an exponentiation in $\mathbb{G}$.*

FULL SECURITY IN THE STANDARD MODEL. It is mentioned in [6] that using techniques from Waters [21] one can construct a variant of their HIBE scheme that achieves full security in the standard model. The same techniques can be also used to achieve full IND-WKID-CPA security in the standard model for the $\mathcal{BBG}$-$\mathcal{WKD}$-$\mathcal{IBE}$ scheme, at the cost of increasing the master public key size to $(n + 1)L + 3$ group elements, where n is the length of an identity string.

3.3   Full Security in the Random Oracle Model

As in the case of IBE and HIBE schemes [5,6], any WKD-IBE scheme $\mathcal{WKD}$-$\mathcal{IBE}$ that is IND-sWKID-CPA-secure can be transformed into a WKD-IBE scheme $\mathcal{WKD}$-$\mathcal{IBE}'$ that is IND-WKID-CPA-secure in the random oracle model, by replacing every pattern (or identity) at key derivation or encryption with the hash of that pattern, if that pattern is not a wildcard. That is, any given pattern $P = (P_1, \ldots, P_\ell)$ in $\mathcal{WKD}$-$\mathcal{IBE}$ is mapped onto a pattern $P' = (P'_1, \ldots, P'_\ell)$ in $\mathcal{WKD}$-$\mathcal{IBE}'$, where $P'_i = H_i(P_i)$ if $P_i \neq *$ or $P'_i = *$ otherwise, and H_i, $1 \leq i \leq L$ are independent random oracles mapping arbitrary bit strings into an appropriate range ID corresponding to the identity space of $\mathcal{WKD}$-$\mathcal{IBE}$. As in the cases of HIBE schemes, this transformation only works if the depth L is logarithmic in the security parameter due to the loss of a factor $O(q_{\mathrm{H}}^L)$ in the reduction. Moreover, $I\!D$ needs to be sufficiently large to make the probability of collisions in the output of the hash function negligible.

4   Application to Identity-Based Broadcast Encryption

4.1   Definitions

An identity-based broadcast encryption (IBBE) scheme is a tuple of algorithms $I\!B\!B\!E$ = (Setup, KeyDer, Enc, Dec) providing the following functionality. The trusted authority runs Setup to generate a master key pair (mpk, msk). It publishes the master public key mpk and keeps the master secret key msk private. When a user with identity ID wishes to become part of the system, the trusted authority generates a user decryption key $sk_{ID} \xleftarrow{\$} \mathsf{KeyDer}(msk, ID)$, and sends this key over a secure and authenticated channel to the user. To broadcast an encrypted message m to a set of users with identities $S = \{ID_1, \ldots, ID_k\}$ of cardinality $k \leq L$, the sender computes the ciphertext $C \xleftarrow{\$} \mathsf{Enc}(mpk, S, m)$, which can be decrypted by a user holding sk_{ID} for any $ID \in S$ as $m \leftarrow \mathsf{Dec}(sk_{ID}, C, S)$. Here the value L is an upper bound on the maximal number of distinct receivers for a broadcast encryption.

The security of an IBBE scheme is defined through the following game. In a first phase, the adversary is given as input the master public key mpk of a freshly generated key pair $(mpk, msk) \xleftarrow{\$} \mathsf{Setup}$. In a chosen-plaintext attack (IND-ID-CPA), the adversary is given access to a key derivation oracle that on input of an identity ID, returns the secret key $sk_{ID} \xleftarrow{\$} \mathsf{KeyDer}(msk, ID)$ corresponding to identity ID. At the end of the first phase, the adversary outputs two equal-length challenge messages $m_0^*, m_1^* \in \{0,1\}^*$ and a challenge set of identities $S^* = (ID_1^*, \ldots, ID_{k^*}^*)$, where $0 \leq k^* \leq L$. The game chooses a random bit $b \xleftarrow{\$} \{0,1\}^*$, generates a challenge ciphertext $C^* \xleftarrow{\$} \mathsf{Enc}(mpk, S^*, m_b^*)$ and gives C^* as input to the adversary for the second phase, during which it gets access to the same oracles as during the first phase. Assume that during the attack the adversary made key derivation queries for identities $ID_1, \ldots, ID_{q_K}$. The adversary wins the game if it outputs a bit $b' = b$ and $S^* \cap \{ID_1, \ldots, ID_{q_K}\} = \emptyset$.

Definition 4. *An IBBE scheme is $(t, q_{\mathrm{K}}, \epsilon)$-IND-ID-CPA-secure if all t-time adversaries making at most q_{K} queries to the key derivation oracle have at most advantage ϵ in winning the IND-ID-CPA game described above.*

SELECTIVE-IDENTITY SECURITY. As for the previous primitives, we further define the weaker (sID) security notion IND-sID-CPA. The IND-sID-CPA definition is analogous to the IND-ID-CPA one except that the adversary has to commit to the challenge set of identities $S^* = (ID_1^*, \ldots, ID_{k^*}^*)$ at the beginning of the game, before even seeing the public-key.

4.2   A Construction from Any Wicked IBE Scheme

First, observe that an IBBE scheme can be trivially constructed from any IBE scheme by concatenating ciphertext. Meaning, the IBBE encryption for the identity set $ID = \{ID_1, \ldots, ID_k\}$ is simply the concatenation of k separate ciphertexts, one for each identity ID_i in the set ID. This leads to IBBE ciphertext sizes that are a factor of k longer than the original IBE ciphertexts.

We now present a generic construction from any WKD-IBE scheme that, depending on the instantiation, can offer advantages over the trivial one. To any WKD-IBE scheme $\mathcal{WKD\text{-}IBE} = (\mathsf{Setup}, \mathsf{KeyDer}, \mathsf{Enc}, \mathsf{Dec})$, we associate an IBBE scheme $\mathcal{IBBE} = (\mathsf{Setup}, \mathsf{KeyDer'}, \mathsf{Enc'}, \mathsf{Dec'})$. For an identity $ID \in \{0,1\}^*$, define

$$P_i(ID) = (*, \ldots, *, \underbrace{ID}_{i\text{th position}}, *, \ldots, *)$$

as a pattern of length L that has ID at its ith position and the rest consists of wildcards.

Setup. Setup outputs whatever the WKD-IBE setup outputs.

Key Derivation. Let ID be the identity for which the user secret key sk_{ID} needs to be generated. The user secret key is defined as the set of L distinct WKD-IBE user secret keys

$$sk_{ID} = \{sk_{P_1(ID)}, \ldots, sk_{P_L(ID)}\},$$

where $sk_{P_i(ID)}$ can be computed by calling $\mathsf{KeyDer}(msk, P_i(ID))$.

Encryption. Let m be the message and let $S = \{ID_1, \ldots, ID_k\}$ be the set of broadcast recipients of cardinality $k \leq L$ that we assume to be ordered with respect to some unique standard ordering. The IBBE ciphertext is defined as the WKD-IBE encryption of message m and identity vector $ID = (ID_1, \ldots, ID_k)$.

Decryption. Let $sk_{ID} = \{sk_{P_1(ID)}, \ldots, sk_{P_L(ID)}\}$ be the user secret key of identity ID. Let $S = \{ID_1, \ldots, ID_k\}$ be the set of $k \leq L$ recipients to whom the ciphertext C was encrypted, and let index $1 \leq j \leq k$ be such that $ID = ID_j \in S$. It is clear that $(ID_1, \ldots, ID, \ldots, ID_k) \in_* P_j(ID)$, and therefore that the ciphertext can be decrypted as $m \leftarrow \mathsf{Dec}(sk_{P_j(ID)}, C, ID)$.

Theorem 3. *If $\mathcal{WKD\text{-}IBE}$ is a (t, q_K, ϵ) IND-sWKID-CPA-secure (resp. IND-WKID-CPA-secure) WKD-IBE scheme, then the IBBE scheme $\mathcal{IBBE}$ described above is (t, q_K, ϵ)-IND-sID-CPA-secure (resp. IND-ID-CPA-secure).*

The crucial observation is the following. Let $S^* = \{ID_1^*, \ldots, ID_{k^*}^*\}$ be the set of challenge broadcast receivers and let $ID_1, \ldots, ID_{q_K}$ be the identities an adversary attacking the IBBE scheme queries the user secret key for. The imposed requirement is that $S^* \cap \{ID_1, \ldots, ID_{q_K}\} = \emptyset$. For $1 \leq i \leq q_K$ and $1 \leq j \leq L$ consider the user secret keys for the patterns $P_j(ID_i) = (*, \ldots, *, ID_i, *, \ldots, *)$ (i.e., ID_i is at the jth position) that are established by the transformation when simulating the IBBE key derivation oracle. For a successful simulation we have to show that $ID^* = (ID_1^*, \ldots, ID_{k^*}^*) \notin_* P_j(ID_i)$. But this is the case since by $S^* \cap \{ID_1, \ldots, ID_{q_K}\} = \emptyset$ and we can guarantee that $ID_i \neq ID_l^*$ for all $1 \leq i \leq q_K$ and $1 \leq l \leq k$.

The above construction allows for the following trade off between ciphertext size and key size. If $L = L'A$, then one can obtain an IBBE scheme with ciphertext size of A times that of the WKD-IBE scheme, while having a key length that is only L' times that of the WKD-IBE scheme. The new scheme creates master public keys to allow for broadcast encryption to sets of maximal cardinality L'. To encrypt a message to a set of broadcast identities $S = \{ID_1, \dots, ID_k\}$ of cardinality $k \leq L$ split the set S into A smaller sets $S_1, \dots, S_A$, each of cardinality $L/A \leq L'$ and define the new broadcast ciphertext to be $(C_1, \dots, C_A)$, where C_i is the encryption of the message m to the set S_i.

4.3   Instantiations

Among all the instantiations of IBBE schemes based on WKD-IBE schemes, the most attractive one is that obtained from the WKD-IBE scheme based on [6] because it achieves constant-size ciphertexts. However, it has the disadvantage of having private keys of size $O(L^2)$. Instantiations with any of the other WKD-IBE schemes that we proposed are less attractive because they have ciphertext size $O(L)$, just like the trivial ciphertext-concatenation scheme. Unlike most other (public-key) broadcast schemes however, these instantiations do have the remarkable advantage that knowledge of the set of recipients is not required in order to decrypt the message.

Chatterjee and Sarkar [9] recently proposed a direct IBBE scheme that is closely related to our generic construction when instantiated with the WKD-IBE scheme based on [6]. Their scheme does not impose an a priori maximum on the number of recipients ℓ, but makes clever use of a non-cryptographic hash function to achieve an average ciphertext size $O(\ell/L)$ and private key size $O(L)$, where the "average" is taken over the recipients' identities. This means that when $\ell \leq L$, their scheme has constant ciphertext size on average. Worst-case however, their scheme has ciphertext size $O(\ell)$, which is worse than our construction.

5   Wicked and Wildcard Signatures

As observed by Naor [7], any IBE scheme automatically gives rise to a signature scheme by using as a signature on message m the decryption key for identity $ID = m$. Verification can be done by encrypting a random message to identity $ID = m$ and testing whether it decrypts correctly, but most concrete schemes have a more natural and efficient verification test. Likewise, one can construct an L-level hierarchical identity-based signature (HIBS) scheme from an $(L+1)$-level HIBE [12] by letting the signature on message m by identity $(ID_1, \dots, ID_\ell)$ be given by the decryption key for identity $(0\|ID_1, \dots, 0\|ID_\ell, 1\|m)$. The same technique can be used to construct *wicked identity-based signatures* (WKD-IBS), the signing analogue to wicked IBE. Here, a root authority derives secret signing keys for identity patterns with wildcards, from which anyone can further derive signing keys for matching patterns. An L-level WKD-IBS is constructed from an $(L + 1)$-level WKD-IBE by letting the signature on message m by identity $(ID_1, \ldots, ID_\ell)$ be given by the decryption key for identity $(0\|ID_1, \ldots, 0\|ID_\ell, 1\|m)$.

Alternatively, and perhaps more interestingly, one could also use the wildcard functionality as a homomorphism on the message being signed, rather than for the signers' identities. This yields a new primitive that we call *wildcard signatures*, that allow to sign message patterns instead of simple messages, possibly containing wildcards at certain positions. Given such a signature, anyone can compute a valid signature for any message created by replacing wildcards with concrete values. This could be used for example to implement signed fill-out forms, where each input field is represented by a wildcard in the message.

The construction from a WKD-IBE scheme is straightforward: the key pair is given by the master key pair of the WKD-IBE scheme. The signature on a message pattern P is given by the decryption key for P. Deriving a valid signature for a message pattern $P' \in_* P$ can be done by deriving a decryption key for P'. Verification is done by filling up the remaining wildcards with random messages to create a vector of messages M, encrypting a random message under identity M, and checking whether decryption using the signature as secret key returns the correct message. In fact, one can easily see that the schemes discussed here allow for more efficient deterministic verification algorithms.

Wildcard signatures can be seen as a special instance of homomorphic signatures [17,15,3,16]. Their relation to wicked IBE is particularly reminiscent of the relation between HIBS schemes and append-only signatures [16]. They can also be seen as the dual of redactable signatures [15] that allow anyone to erase parts of a signed message without invalidating the signature.

A fairly simple, generic construction from standard signatures also exists. Namely, for each wildcard in the message the signer generates a fresh key pair, and then signs the message together with all generated public keys. The overall signature also contains the public and secret keys corresponding to all wildcards. To replace a wildcard at position i with a concrete value, the i-th secret key is replaced with a signature on the new value under the i-th public key. The disadvantage of this generic construction is that signature length and verification time are both linear in the number of *original* wildcards in the message, even after these wildcards have been replaced with original values. The signature length and verification time of the scheme derived from the $\mathcal{BBG}$-$\mathcal{WKD}$-$\mathcal{IBE}$ scheme on the other hand is only linear in the number of wildcards that are still present in the message. Also, signatures generated by the generic construction are linkable in the sense that one can check whether a given signature was derived from a second one by filling in wildcards. The decryption keys of the $\mathcal{BBG}$-$\mathcal{WKD}$-$\mathcal{IBE}$ scheme, and therefore the signatures of the associated wildcard signature scheme, can be re-randomized to prevent this type of linkability.

Finally, one could even imagine *wicked wildcard signatures* that allow for wildcards in *both* the signers' identities and the messages being signed. Such schemes are easily constructed from a WKD-IBE scheme by using a different encoding for identity strings and messages, as was done in the construction of WKD-IBS schemes above.

Acknowledgements

The authors have been supported in part by the European Commission through the IST Program under Contract IST-2002-507932 ECRYPT. The second author was supported in part by research program Sentinels (http://www.sentinels.nl). Sentinels is being financed by Technology Foundation STW, the Netherlands Organization for Scientific Research (NWO), and the Dutch Ministry of Economic Affairs. The third author is a Postdoctoral Fellow of the Research Foundation – Flanders (FWO-Vlaanderen), and was supported in part by the European Commission through IST Program under Contract IST-2006-034238 SPEED, and in part by the IAP Program P6/26 BCRYPT of the Belgian State (Belgian Science Policy).

References

1. Abdalla, M., Catalano, D., Dent, A., Malone-Lee, J., Neven, G., Smart, N.: Identity-based encryption gone wild. In: Bugliesi, M., Preneel, B., Sassone, V., Wegener, I. (eds.) ICALP 2006. LNCS, vol. 4052, pp. 300–311. Springer, Heidelberg (2006)
2. Abdalla, M., Kiltz, E., Neven, G.: Generalized Key Delegation for Hierarchical Identity-Based Encryption. Cryptology ePrint Archive, Report 2007/221 (2007), http://eprint.iacr.org/
3. Bellare, M., Neven, G.: Transitive signatures: new schemes and proofs. IEEE Transactions on Information Theory 51(6), 2133–2151 (2005)
4. Bellare, M., Rogaway, P.: Random oracles are practical: A paradigm for designing efficient protocols. In: ACM CCS '93, pp. 62–73. ACM Press, New York (1993)
5. Boneh, D., Boyen, X.: Efficient selective-ID secure identity based encryption without random oracles. In: Cachin, C., Camenisch, J.L. (eds.) EUROCRYPT 2004. LNCS, vol. 3027, pp. 223–238. Springer, Heidelberg (2004)
6. Boneh, D., Boyen, X., Goh, E.-J.: Hierarchical identity based encryption with constant size ciphertext. In: Cramer, R.J.F. (ed.) EUROCRYPT 2005. LNCS, vol. 3494, pp. 440–456. Springer, Heidelberg (2005)
7. Boneh, D., Franklin, M.K.: Identity based encryption from the Weil pairing. SIAM Journal on Computing 32(3), 586–615 (2003)
8. Boneh, D., Gentry, C., Waters, B.: Collusion resistant broadcast encryption with short ciphertexts and private keys. In: Shoup, V. (ed.) CRYPTO 2005. LNCS, vol. 3621, pp. 258–275. Springer, Heidelberg (2005)
9. Chatterjee, S., Sarkar, P.: Multi-receiver identity-based key encapsulation with shortened ciphertext. In: Barua, R., Lange, T. (eds.) INDOCRYPT 2006. LNCS, vol. 4329, pp. 394–408. Springer, Heidelberg (2006)
10. Dodis, Y., Fazio, N.: Public key broadcast encryption for stateless receivers. In: Feigenbaum, J. (ed.) DRM 2002. LNCS, vol. 2696, pp. 61–80. Springer, Heidelberg (2003)
11. Fiat, A., Naor, M.: Broadcast encryption. In: Stinson, D.R. (ed.) CRYPTO 1993. LNCS, vol. 773, pp. 480–491. Springer, Heidelberg (1994)
12. Gentry, C., Silverberg, A.: Hierarchical ID-based cryptography. In: Zheng, Y. (ed.) ASIACRYPT 2002. LNCS, vol. 2501, pp. 548–566. Springer, Heidelberg (2002)

13. Goyal, V., Pandey, O., Sahai, A., Waters, B.: Attribute-based encryption for fine-grained access control of encrypted data. In: ACM CCS 06, pp. 89–98. ACM Press, New York (2006) (available as Cryptology ePrint Archive Report 2006/309)

14. Horwitz, J., Lynn, B.: Toward hierarchical identity-based encryption. In: Knudsen, L.R. (ed.) EUROCRYPT 2002. LNCS, vol. 2332, pp. 466–481. Springer, Heidelberg (2002)

15. Johnson, R., Molnar, D., Song, D.X., Wagner, D.: Homomorphic signature schemes. In: Preneel, B. (ed.) CT-RSA 2002. LNCS, vol. 2271, pp. 244–262. Springer, Heidelberg (2002)

16. Kiltz, E., Mityagin, A., Panjwani, S., Raghavan, B.: Append-only signatures. In: Caires, L., Italiano, G.F., Monteiro, L., Palamidessi, C., Yung, M. (eds.) ICALP 2005. LNCS, vol. 3580, pp. 434–445. Springer, Heidelberg (2005)

17. Rivest, R.: Two signature schemes. Slides from talk given at Cambridge University (October 2000)

18. Sakai, R., Ohgishi, K., Kasahara, M.: Cryptosystems based on pairing. In: SCIS 2000, Okinawa, Japan (January 2000)

19. Shacham, H.: The BBG HIBE has limited delegation. Cryptology ePrint Archive, Report 2007/201 (2007), http://eprint.iacr.org/

20. Shamir, A.: Identity-based cryptosystems and signature schemes. In: Blakely, G.R., Chaum, D. (eds.) CRYPTO 1984. LNCS, vol. 196, pp. 47–53. Springer, Heidelberg (1985)

21. Waters, B.R.: Efficient identity-based encryption without random oracles. In: Cramer, R.J.F. (ed.) EUROCRYPT 2005. LNCS, vol. 3494, pp. 114–127. Springer, Heidelberg (2005)

Change-Impact Analysis of Firewall Policies

Alex X. Liu

Department of Computer Science and Engineering
Michigan State University
East Lansing, MI 48824-1266, U.S.A
alexliu@cse.msu.edu

Abstract. Firewalls are the mainstay of enterprise security and the most widely adopted technology for protecting private networks. The quality of protection provided by a firewall directly depends on the quality of its policy (i.e., configuration). Due to the lack of tools for analyzing firewall policies, most firewalls on the Internet have been plagued with policy errors. A firewall policy error either creates security holes that will allow malicious traffic to sneak into a private network or blocks legitimate traffic and disrupts normal business processes, which in turn could lead to irreparable, if not tragic, consequences.

A major source of policy errors stem from policy changes. Firewall policies often need to be changed as networks evolve and new threats emerge. In this paper, we first present the theory and algorithms for firewall policy change-impact analysis. Our algorithms take as input a firewall policy and a proposed change, then output the accurate impact of the change. Thus, a firewall administrator can verify a proposed change before committing it.

1 Introduction

Serving as the first line of defense against malicious attacks and unauthorized traffic, firewalls are cornerstones of network security and have been widely deployed in businesses and institutions. A firewall is placed at the point of entry between a private network and the outside Internet such that all incoming and outgoing packets have to pass through it. The function of a firewall is to examine every incoming or outgoing packet and decide whether to accept or discard it. This function is specified by a sequence (i.e., an ordered list) of rules, which is called the "policy", *i.e.*, the configuration, of the firewall. Each rule in a firewall policy is of the form ⟨*predicate*⟩ → ⟨*decision*⟩. The ⟨*predicate*⟩ of a rule is a boolean expression over some packet fields such as source IP address, destination IP address, source port number, destination port number, and protocol type. The ⟨*decision*⟩ of a rule can be *accept*, *discard*, or a combination of these decisions with other options such as a logging option. The rules in a firewall policy often conflict. To resolve such conflicts, the decision for each packet is the decision of the first (i.e., highest priority) rule that the packet matches. Table 1 shows an example firewall.

J. Biskup and J. Lopez (Eds.): ESORICS 2007, LNCS 4734, pp. 155–170, 2007.

Table 1. An example firewall

Rule	Source IP	Destination IP	Source Port	Destination Port	Protocol	Action
r_1	*	192.168.0.1	*	25	TCP	accept
r_2	1.2.3.4	*	*	*	*	discard
r_3	*	*	*	*	*	accept

Although a firewall policy is a mere sequence of rules, correctly maintaining one is by no means easy. First, the rules in a firewall policy are logically entangled because of conflicts among rules and the resulting order sensitivity. Second, a firewall policy may consist of a large number of rules. A firewall on the Internet may consist of hundreds or even a few thousand rules in extreme cases. Last but not least, an enterprise firewall policy often consists of legacy rules that are written by different administrators, at different times, and for different reasons, which makes maintaining firewall policies even more difficult. Analyzing a large and complex sequence of logically related rules is certainly beyond human capability. Effective methods and tools for analyzing firewall policies, therefore, are crucial to the success of firewalls. However, firewall administrators are woefully under-assisted due to the lack of firewall policy analysis tools. Quantitative studies have shown that most firewalls on the Internet are plagued with policy errors [1]. A firewall policy error either creates security holes that will allow malicious traffic to sneak into a private network or blocks legitimate traffic and disrupts normal business processes, which in turn could lead to irreparable, if not tragic, consequences.

1.1 Motivations

Firewall policies are always subject to change due to a variety of reasons. Making policy changes is a major task of firewall administrators. For example, new network threats such as worms and viruses may emerge. To protect a private network from new attacks, firewall policies need to be changed accordingly. Modern organizations also continually transform their network infrastructure to maintain their competitive edge by adding new servers, installing new software and services, expanding connectivity, etc. In accordance with network changes, firewall policies need to be changed as well to provide necessary protection.

Unfortunately, making changes is a major source of firewall policy errors. Making correct firewall policy changes is remarkably difficult due to the interleaving nature of firewall rules. For example, when a firewall administrator inserts a new rule into a firewall policy, the meaning of the rules listed under this rule could be incorrectly changed without being noticed. Furthermore, firewall policy changes are made by human administrators, and it is common that human administrators make mistakes. It has been shown that administrator errors are the largest cause of failure for Internet services, and policy errors are the largest category of administrator errors [2].

Firewall policy errors can be dangerous and costly. On one hand, if a firewall policy error permits illegitimate communication, outside attackers may use these security holes to launch attacks. On the other hand, if a firewall policy error disallows legitimate communication, it may cause significant loss due to interrupted business. For example, if a firewall policy error prevents the communication between a web server and its supporting database server, all transactions that need such communication are disrupted.

1.2   The Problem

The fundamental problem in changing firewall policies is, how does a firewall administrator know that the change made to the firewall policies is correct? For example, suppose a firewall administrator wants to make a change to the firewall policy to allow a database server to talk to a web server. How does the administrator know that the change indeed enables this communication? Also, how does the administrator know that the change does not allow some other illegitimate traffic to flow as a side effect, given the subtle behavior of firewall rules? Such questions are exceptionally difficult to answer given the high complexity of firewall rules.

In this context, if there is a tool that takes a firewall configuration and a proposed change as input, then outputs the precise impact of the change, the errors caused by making policy changes would be greatly reduced. The impact of a change shows all the traffic that was formerly discarded, but is now accepted, and all the traffic that was formerly accepted, but is now discarded. The output impact must be human readable. With this tool on hand, a firewall administrator can examine the change-impact for unintended consequences.

1.3   Key Contributions

In this paper, we make the following three key contributions.

1. We develop a theory for firewall policy change-impact analysis. We identify four types of firewall policy changes: rule deletion, rule insertion, rule modification, and rule swap. For each type of change, we have a theorem that states the decisions of what packets will be changed due to the policy change. These theorems serve as the foundation for developing algorithms for computing firewall policy change-impact.
2. We present algorithms for firewall policy change-impact analysis. The input of our algorithms includes a firewall policy and a proposed change, and the output is the accurate impact of the change. Using our algorithms, an administrator can verify a proposed change before committing it.
3. We present a way to correlate the impact of a firewall policy change and the high level security requirements that the firewall needs to satisfy. We also present methods for making corrections if the impact of a change is not desirable.

Because the focus of this paper is on security policies, we simply use the term "firewall" to mean "firewall policy", "firewall rule set", or "firewall configuration" unless otherwise specified.

1.4   Road Map

The rest of this paper proceeds as follows. In Section 2, we show an example application of our firewall change-impact analysis tool. In Section 3, we present the theory foundation for firewall change-impact analysis. Based on these theorems, we develop algorithms for computing the impact of firewall changes in Section 4. In Section 5, we discuss some further issues for firewall change-impact analysis. In Section 6, we examine previous work and compare it with our approach. In Section 7, we give concluding remarks.

2   Example

In this section, we show an example application of our firewall policy change-impact analysis tool. Consider the example firewall in Table 1. We suppose that the private network behind this firewall has a mail server and a web server, whose IP addresses are 192.168.0.1 and 192.168.0.2 respectively. We further suppose that this firewall is required by its high level security policies to discard all packets from a malicious host whose IP address is 1.2.3.4.

Here we briefly explain the meaning of the three rules in Table 1. Rule r_1 means that all email packets to the email server are accepted. Note that for a packet, if its destination port number is 25 and its protocol type is TCP, then the packet is an email (SMTP) packet. Rule r_2 means that all packets from 1.2.3.4 are discarded. Rule r_3 means that all packets are accepted. Note that whenever a packet arrives at a firewall, the decision of the first rule that the packet matches is executed.

2.1   Rule Deletion

Suppose that the administrator of this firewall wants to delete rule r_1. Our change-impact analysis tool will output the following impact as shown in Table 2. The meaning of the impact is as follows: for the email packets from the malicious host 1.2.3.4 to the email server 192.168.0.1, before deleting rule r_1, the decision for such packets is *accept*; after deleting rule r_1, the decision for such packets is *discard*.

2.2   Rule Insertion

Suppose that the administrator of this firewall wants to insert the following rule above rule r_1:

Src IP	Dest. IP	Src Port	Dest. Port	Protocol	Action
*	192.168.0.2	*	80	TCP	accept

The meaning of this new rule is to accept all the HTTP packets to the web server 192.168.0.2. After the administrator gives this intended change and the original firewall in Table 1 to our change-impact analysis tool, the tool will output the following impact:

Table 2. Impact after deleting r_1 from the firewall in Table 1

Source IP	1.2.3.4
Destination IP:	192.168.0.1
Source Port:	*
Destination Port:	25
Protocol Type:	TCP
Decision before change:	accept
Decision after change:	discard

Table 3. Impact after inserting a rule above r_1 in the firewall in Table 1

Source IP	1.2.3.4
Destination IP:	192.168.0.2
Source Port:	*
Destination Port:	80
Protocol Type:	TCP
Decision before change:	discard
Decision after change:	accept

2.3 Rule Modification

Suppose that the administrator of this firewall wants to modify rule r_1 to be the following rule:

Src IP	Dest. IP	Src Port	Dest. Port	Protocol	Action
*	192.168.0.1	*	*	TCP	accept

The meaning of this modified rule is to accept all the TCP packets to the mail server 192.168.0.1. For this intended change, our change-impact analysis tool outputs the following impact:

2.4 Rule Swap

Suppose that the administrator of this firewall wants to swap rule r_1 and r_2. Similarly, for this intended change, our change-impact analysis tool outputs the same impact as shown in Table 2.

3 Change-Impact Analysis: Theorems

In this paper, we consider the following four types of changes that one can make to a firewall $\langle r_1, \cdots, r_n \rangle$. Recall that the predicate of the last rule in a firewall is always a tautology, which is for the purpose of ensuring the comprehensiveness property of the firewall. Therefore, we assume that one does not change the last rule. (Actually, given any firewall where the predicate of the last rule is not a

Table 4. Impact after modifying r_1 in the firewall in Table 1

Source IP	1.2.3.4
Destination IP:	192.168.0.1
Source Port:	*
Destination Port:	[1,24]
Protocol Type:	TCP
Decision before change:	discard
Decision after change:	accept
Source IP	1.2.3.4
Destination IP:	192.168.0.1
Source Port:	*
Destination Port:	[25, 65536]
Protocol Type:	TCP
Decision before change:	discard
Decision after change:	accept

tautology, we can modify the predicate of the last rule to be a tautology without changing the semantics of the firewall. Due to space limitation, we omit the proof.)

1. Deletion: delete rule r_i, where $1 \leq i \leq n-1$.
2. Insertion: insert a new rule r between r_i and r_{i+1}, where $1 \leq i \leq n-1$.
3. Modification: modify rule r_i to be r_i', where $1 \leq i \leq n-1$.
4. Swap: swap the two rules r_i and r_j, where $1 \leq i < j \leq n-1$.

Each rule in a firewall is associated with two sets of packets, a matching set and a resolving set [3]. More precisely, consider a firewall f that consists of n rules $\langle r_1, r_2, \cdots, r_n \rangle$. The matching set of a rule r_i, denoted $M(r_i)$, is the set of all packets that match r_i. The resolving set of a rule r_i, denoted $R(r_i, f)$, in firewall f is the set of all packets that match r_i, but do not match any r_j $(j < i)$ that is listed before r_i in f. The essence of the resolving set $R(r_i, f)$ of a rule r_i in firewall f is: for any packet p in $R(r_i, f)$, the decision of firewall f for packet p is the decision of rule r_i. Note that the matching set of a rule depends only on the rule itself, while the resolving set of a rule depends on both the rule itself and all the rules listed before it in a firewall.

3.1   Theory Foundation

The following four theorems lay the foundation for computing firewall change-impact. In this paper, we use $r.D$ to denote the decision of rule r, and $f(p)$ to denote the decision of the first (i.e., highest priority) rule that p matches in firewall f.

Theorem 1 (Rule Deletion Theorem). *Let f be a given firewall $\langle r_1, \cdots, r_n \rangle$. Suppose we delete rule r_i where $1 \leq i \leq n-1$. Let f' be the resulting firewall $\langle r_1, \cdots, r_{i-1}, r_{i+1}, \cdots, r_n \rangle$. We use g to denote the firewall $\langle r_{i+1}, \cdots, r_n \rangle$, which consists of the $n-i$ rules $r_{i+1}, \cdots, r_n$ after rule r_i in firewall f. For any packet p in Σ, consider the following two cases:*

1. if $p \in R(r_i, f)$, then $f(p) = r_i.D$ and $f'(p) = g(p)$, which means that f and f' may have different decisions for p;
2. if $p \in \Sigma - R(r_i, f)$, then $f(p) = f'(p)$, which means that f and f' have the same decision for p. $\square$

Theorem 2 (Rule Insertion Theorem). Let f be the given firewall $\langle r_1, \cdots, r_n \rangle$. Suppose we insert a new rule r between r_i and r_{i+1} where $1 \leq i \leq n-1$. Let f' be the resulting firewall $\langle r_1, \cdots, r_i, r, r_{i+1}, \cdots, r_n \rangle$. We use g to denote the firewall $\langle r_{i+1}, \cdots, r_n \rangle$, which consists of the $n-i$ rules $r_{i+1}, \cdots, r_n$ after rule r_i in firewall f. For any packet p in Σ, consider the following two cases:

1. if $p \in R(r, f')$, then $f(p) = g(p)$ and $f'(p) = r.D$, which means that f and f' may have different decisions for p;
2. if $p \in \Sigma - R(r, f')$, then $f(p) = f'(p)$, which means that f and f' have the same decision for p. $\square$

Theorem 3 (Rule Modification Theorem). Let f be the given firewall $\langle r_1, \cdots, r_n \rangle$. Suppose we modify rule r_i to be r_i' where $1 \leq i \leq n-1$. Let f' be the resulting firewall $\langle r_1, \cdots, r_{i-1}, r_i', r_{i+1}, \cdots, r_n \rangle$. We use g to denote the firewall $\langle r_{i+1}, \cdots, r_n \rangle$, which consists of the $n-i$ rules $r_{i+1}, \cdots, r_n$ after rule r_i in firewall f. For any packet p in Σ, consider the following four cases:

1. if $p \in R(r_i, f) \cap R(r_i', f')$, then $f(p) = r_i.D$ and $f'(p) = r_i'.D$;
2. if $p \in R(r_i, f) - R(r_i', f')$, then $f(p) = r_i.D$ and $f'(p) = g(p)$;
3. if $p \in R(r_i', f') - R(r_i, f)$, then $f(p) = g(p)$ and $f'(p) = r_i'.D$;
4. if $p \in \Sigma - R(r_i, f) \cup R(r_i', f')$, then $f(p) = f'(p)$, which means that f and f' have the same decision for p. $\square$

Theorem 4 (Rule Swap Theorem). Let f be the given firewall $\langle r_1, \cdots, r_n \rangle$. Suppose we swap the two rules r_i and r_j where $1 \leq i < j \leq n-1$. Let f' be the resulting firewall $\langle r_1, \cdots, r_{i-1}, r_j, r_{i+1}, \cdots, r_{j-1}, r_i, r_{j+1}, \cdots, r_n \rangle$. Let g be the firewall $\langle r_{i+1}, \cdots, r_n \rangle$, which consists of the $n-i$ rules after rule r_i in firewall f; and g' be the firewall $\langle r_{i+1}, \cdots, r_{j-1}, r_i, r_{j+1}, \cdots, r_n \rangle$, which consists of the $n-i$ rules after rule r_j in firewall f'. For any packet p in Σ, consider the following four cases:

1. if $p \in R(r_i, f) \cap R(r_j, f')$, then $f(p) = r_i.D$ and $f'(p) = r_j.D$;
2. if $p \in R(r_i, f) - R(r_j, f')$, then $f(p) = r_i.D$ and $f'(p) = g'(p)$;
3. if $p \in R(r_j, f') - R(r_i, f)$, then $f(p) = g(p)$ and $f'(p) = r_j.D$;
4. if $p \in \Sigma - R(r_i, f) \cup R(r_j, f')$, then $f(p) = f'(p)$. $\square$

4   Change-Impact Analysis: Algorithms

In this section, we present algorithms for computing the impact of firewall changes based on the theorems in Section 3. Given a firewall and a proposed change, our change-impact analysis algorithms output a set of so-called "impacts". An impact is of the form

$$\langle predicate \rangle \rightarrow \langle old\ decision \rangle\ vs.\ \langle new\ decision \rangle$$

The meaning of an impact is: the decision of the packets that satisfy the predicate is changed from ⟨*old decision*⟩ to ⟨*new decision*⟩. For ease of understanding, the predicates of all impacts computed for a change are non-overlapping.

4.1   Rule Deletion

Based on Theorem 1, to compute the impacts of deleting rule r_i, we first need to compute the resolving set $R(r_i, f)$. We represent the resolving set of a rule by a set of non-overlapping rules, the union of whose matching sets is exactly the resolving set. This set of non-overlapping rules is called an effective rule set of that rule [3]. More precisely, let r be a rule in a firewall f. A set of non-overlapping rules $\{e_1, e_2, \cdots, e_k\}$ is an *effective rule set* of r iff the following three conditions hold: (1) $R(r, f) = \bigcup_{i=1}^{k} M(e_i)$, (2) $M(r_i') \cap M(r_j') = \emptyset$ for $1 \leq i < j \leq k$, (3) every e_i has the same decision as r.

How to compute the effective rule set for a rule in a firewall has been discussed in our previous work on removing redundant rules in firewalls [3]. Interested readers can refer to [3] for more technical details. Here we show one example. Considering the example firewall in Figure 1. In this firewall, for simplicity, we assume each packet has only two fields, F_1 and F_2, and the domain of each field is [1,100]. The effective rule set of each rule is shown in Figure 2. Note that we use E_i to denote the effective rule set of rule r_i.

Next, we discuss how to compute the impact of rule deletion through an example. Consider the firewall in Figure 1. Suppose the change is to delete rule r_1, whose effective rule set E_1 is $\{F_1 \in [20, 50] \land F_2 \in [1, 70] \to accept\}$. According to Theorem 1, the question that we need to answer is: which packets that satisfy $F_1 \in [20, 50] \land F_2 \in [1, 70]$ are discarded by firewall ⟨r_2, r_3⟩?

To answer this question, we first convert firewall ⟨r_2, r_3⟩ to an equivalent non-overlapping firewall, as shown in Figure 3. (Two firewalls f_1 and f_2 are *equivalent* if and only if for any packet p, we have $f_1(p) = f_2(p)$. A *non-overlapping* firewall is a firewall whose rules are non-overlapping.)

Now the question is: which packets that satisfy $F_1 \in [20, 50] \land F_2 \in [1, 70]$ are discarded by the firewall in Figure 3? Given that this firewall is non-overlapping, we can answer this question by checking which discard rule in this firewall overlaps with the predicate $F_1 \in [20, 50] \land F_2 \in [1, 70]$. Obviously, the answer is rule r_1'. For the packets that satisfy both predicates $F_1 \in [20, 50] \land F_2 \in [1, 70]$ and $F_1 \in [1, 60] \land F_2 \in [40, 100]$, their decision by the original firewall is *accept*, but their decision by the modified firewall is *discard*. Therefore, the impact of deleting rule r_1 from the firewall in Figure 2 is as follows:

$$F_1 \in [20, 50] \land F_2 \in [40, 70] \to accept \; vs. \; discard$$

$$
\begin{aligned}
r_1 &: F_1 \in [20, 50] \; \land \; F_2 \in [1, \quad 70] \; \to \; accept \\
r_2 &: F_1 \in [1, \quad 60] \; \land \; F_2 \in [40, 100] \; \to \; discard \\
r_3 &: F_1 \in [1, \quad 100] \; \land \; F_2 \in [1, \quad 100] \; \to \; accept
\end{aligned}
$$

Fig. 1. A firewall example

$$E_1 : \{ \ F_1 \in [20, \ 50] \ \wedge \ F_2 \in [1, \ \ 70] \ \rightarrow accept$$
$$\}$$
$$E_2 : \{ F_1 \in [1, \ \ 19] \ \wedge \ F_2 \in [40, 100] \rightarrow discard$$
$$F_1 \in [51, \ 60] \ \wedge \ F_2 \in [40, 100] \rightarrow discard$$
$$F_1 \in [20, \ 50] \ \wedge \ F_2 \in [71, 100] \rightarrow discard$$
$$\}$$
$$E_3 : \{ F_1 \in [1, \ \ 19] \ \wedge \ F_2 \in [1, \ \ 39] \ \rightarrow discard$$
$$F_1 \in [51, \ 60] \ \wedge \ F_2 \in [1, \ \ 39] \ \rightarrow discard$$
$$F_1 \in [61, \ 100] \wedge \ F_2 \in [1, \ \ 100] \rightarrow discard$$
$$\}$$

Fig. 2. Effective rule sets

$$r_1' : \ F_1 \in [1, \ \ 60] \ \wedge \ F_2 \in [40, \ 100] \ \rightarrow discard$$
$$r_2' : \ F_1 \in [1, \ \ 60] \ \wedge \ F_2 \in [1, \ \ 39] \ \rightarrow accept$$
$$r_3' : \ F_1 \in [61, 100] \ \wedge \ F_2 \in [1, \ \ 100] \ \rightarrow accept$$

Fig. 3. A non-overlapping firewall

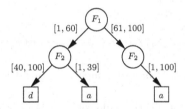

Fig. 4. A firewall decision diagram

For efficiency purposes, we represent a non-overlapping firewall using a firewall decision diagram [4]. For example, the non-overlapping firewall in Figure 3 can be represented using the firewall decision diagram in Figure 4.

The pseudocode of the algorithm for computing the impacts of rule deletion is shown in Figure 5. In this paper, we use $t.root$ to denote the root of a firewall decision diagram t, $I(e)$ to denote the label of an edge e, $F(v)$ to denote the label of a node v.

4.2 Rule Insertion

According to Theorem 2, computing the impacts of rule insertion is similar to that of rule deletion. Let f be the given firewall $\langle r_1, \cdots, r_n \rangle$. Suppose we insert a new rule r between r_i and r_{i+1} where $1 \le i \le n - 1$. Let f' be the resulting firewall $\langle r_1, \cdots, r_i, r, r_{i+1}, \cdots, r_n \rangle$. To compute the impacts of inserting rule r, we first compute the effective rule set of rule r in firewall f'. Second, we construct a firewall decision diagram for the firewall $\langle r_{i+1}, \cdots, r_n \rangle$. (Note that $\langle r_{i+1}, \cdots, r_n \rangle$ is a firewall because the last rule r_n can match any given packet.) Third, we traverse the firewall decision diagram to check which decision path

Computing Impacts of Rule Deletion
Input : A firewall $\langle r_1, \cdots, r_n \rangle$.
Output: Change-impacts of deleting rule r_i.
Steps:
1. Compute the effective rule set E_i of rule r_i;
   Let E_i be $\{e_1, \cdots, e_m\}$.
   Impacts $:= \emptyset$;
2. Construct a firewall decision diagram from
   $\langle r_{i+1}, \cdots, r_n \rangle$;
3. **for** $i := 1$ **to** m **do Compare**($t.root$, e_i);
   return E;

Compare(v, $(F_1 \in S_1) \wedge \cdots \wedge (F_d \in S_d) \to \langle dec \rangle)$)
1. **if** (v is a terminal node) and ($\langle dec \rangle \neq F(v)$)
   then/*Let $(F_1 \in S_1') \wedge \cdots \wedge (F_d \in S_d') \to F(v)$
       be the rule defined by the decision path
       containing node v;*/
   Impacts :=*Impacts*∪
   $\{(F_1 \in S_1 \cap S_1') \wedge \cdots \wedge (F_d \in S_d \cap S_d') \to \langle dec \rangle$ vs. $F(v)\}$;
2. **if** (v is a nonterminal node) **then**
   /*Let F_j be the label of v*/
   for each edge e in $E(v)$ **do**
      if $I(e) \cap S_j \neq \emptyset$ **then**
         Compare($e.t$, $(F_1 \in S_1) \wedge \cdots \wedge (F_d \in S_d) \to \langle dec \rangle)$)

Fig. 5. Computing impacts of rule deletion

conflicts with a rule in the effective rule set of r. For each conflict discovered, we output an impact. Due to space limitations, we omit the details of the algorithm for computing the impacts of rule insertion.

4.3 Rule Modification

Based on Theorem 3, to compute the impacts of modifying rule r_i in firewall f to be r_i', we first need to know how to compute $R(r_i, f) \cap R(r_i', f')$ and $R(r_i, f) - R(r_i', f')$, where f' denotes the firewall after modifying r_i. Next, we discuss how to compute them.

Given two resolving sets R_a and R_b, which are represented by the effective rule sets $\{e_1, \cdots, e_m\}$ and $\{\varepsilon_1, \cdots, \varepsilon_l\}$ respectively. Then we have $R_a \cap R_b = \cup_{i=1}^m \cup_{j=1}^l (M(e_i) \cap M(\varepsilon_j))$. Note that $M(e_i) \cap M(\varepsilon_j)$ can be computed as follows. Let rule e_i be $(F_1 \in S_1) \wedge \cdots \wedge (F_d \in S_d) \to \langle decision \rangle$ and rule ε_j be $(F_1 \in S_1') \wedge \cdots \wedge (F_d \in S_d') \to \langle decision \rangle$. Let rule r be $(F_1 \in S_1 \cap S_1') \wedge \cdots \wedge (F_d \in S_d \cap S_d') \to \langle decision \rangle$. Then we have $M(e_i) \cap M(\varepsilon_j) = M(r)$.

Given two resolving sets R_a and R_b, which are represented by the effective rule sets $\{e_1, \cdots, e_m\}$ and $\{\varepsilon_1, \cdots, \varepsilon_l\}$ respectively. Let r be the rule that any packet can match and f be the firewall $\langle \varepsilon_1, \cdots, \varepsilon_l, e_1, \cdots, e_m, r \rangle$. Then we have $R_a - R_b = \cup_{i=1}^m R(e_i, f)$. In other words, $R_a - R_b$ is the union of the effective rule set of every e_i in firewall $\langle \varepsilon_1, \cdots, \varepsilon_l, e_1, \cdots, e_m, r \rangle$.

Let f be the given firewall $\langle r_1, \cdots, r_n \rangle$. Suppose we modify rule r_i to be r_i' where $1 \leq i \leq n-1$. Let f' be the resulting firewall $\langle r_1, \cdots, r_{i-1}, r_i', r_{i+1}, \cdots, r_n \rangle$. The change-impacts of modifying rule r_i can be computed in the following steps:

1. Compute the effective rule set of rule r_i in firewall f, and that of rule r_i' in firewall f'.
2. If r_i and r_i' have the same decision, then skip this step. Otherwise, compute $R(r_i, f) \cap R(r_i', f')$. If $R(r_i, f) \cap R(r_i', f') \neq \emptyset$, then generate impacts accordingly. Note that the decision for any packet in $R(r_i, f) \cap R(r_i', f')$ is changed from the decision of r_i to that of r_i'.
3. Compute $R(r_i, f) - R(r_i', f')$ as follows. Let $\{e_1, \cdots, e_m\}$ and $\{\varepsilon_1, \cdots, \varepsilon_l\}$ be the effective rule sets of rule r_i in firewall f and rule r_i' in firewall f' respectively. Compute the effective rule sets of $e_1, \cdots, e_m$ in firewall $\langle \varepsilon_1, \cdots, \varepsilon_l, e_1, \cdots, e_m, r \rangle$ where r is a rule that any packet can match. Let U be the union of these effective rule sets. Then U represents $R(r_i, f) - R(r_i', f')$.
4. Construct a firewall decision diagram from firewall $\langle r_{i+1}, \cdots, r_n \rangle$.
5. Traverse the firewall decision diagram to check which decision path conflicts with a rule in U. Whenever a conflict is found, our tool outputs an impact.
6. Compute $R(r_i', f') - R(r_i, f)$ by computing the effective rule sets of $\varepsilon_1, \cdots, \varepsilon_l$ in firewall $\langle e_1, \cdots, e_m, \varepsilon_1, \cdots, \varepsilon_l, r \rangle$ where r is a rule that any packet can match. Let U' be the union of these effective rule sets. Then U' represents $R(r_i', f') - R(r_i, f)$.
7. Traverse the firewall decision diagram built from firewall $\langle r_{i+1}, \cdots, r_n \rangle$ to check which decision path conflicts with a rule in U'. Whenever a conflict is found, our tool outputs an impact.

4.4 Rule Swap

Based on Theorem 4, computing the impacts of swapping two rules is similar to that of rule modification. Due to space limitation, we omit the details of the algorithm for computing the impacts of rule swap.

5 Discussion

5.1 Prefix and Intervals

Real-life firewalls usually check five packet fields: source IP address, destination IP address, source port number, destination port number, and protocol type. Of these five fields, the first two fields are usually represented using prefix formats, and the last three fields are usually represented using integer intervals. Note that prefix formats and interval formats are interchangeable. For example, IP prefix 192.168.0.0/16 can be converted to the interval from 192.168.0.0 to 192.168.255.255, where an IP address can be regarded as a 32-bit integer. As another example, the interval [2, 8] can be converted to 3 prefixes: 001*, 01*, 1000.

To compute firewall change-impacts, we first convert the source and destination IP addresses from prefix formats to integer intervals. Note that every prefix can be converted to only one integer interval. Second, we run the algorithms described in Section 4 for computing firewall change-impacts. (Note that the impacts produced by our algorithms are in interval formats.) Third, for each impact computed, we convert the source and destination IP addresses from intervals to prefixes. Thus, the format of outputs are similar to that of original firewall rules, which are easy to understand for firewall administrators. (A w−bit integer interval can be converted to at most $2w - 2$ prefixes [5].)

5.2   High Level Impacts

Many companies or organizations have some "hard requirements" for their firewalls. A hard requirement can be interpreted as a set of non-overlapping firewall rules, which we call "hard rules". For example, assuming that the hard requirement for the firewall example in Table 1 is that the mail server 192.168.0.1 should be able to receive email packets from any host, this hard requirement can be interpreted as the following hard rule

Src IP	Dest. IP	Src Port	Dest. Port	Protocol	Action
*	192.168.0.1	*	25	TCP	accept

After firewall change-impacts are computed, we can compare each impact and the hard requirements of the firewall, and see which requirements are violated due to the change. For example, comparing the impact in Table 2 and the above hard rule, we see that this change violates the above hard rule, and henceforth the hard requirement. Correlating each impact computed with the hard requirements that the impact violates is helpful for firewall administrators to verify the correctness of each impact.

5.3   Making Corrections

After the impacts of a change are computed, the firewall administrator needs to verify that the impacts are indeed intended. If not all impacts are desirable, one approach for the firewall administrator is to revise the proposed change and compute impacts again; another approach for the firewall administrator is to commit desired impacts by correcting undesired impacts. Next, we show an example to illustrate the latter approach.

Consider the two impacts in Table 4. If the first impact is exactly what the administrator intends to do, and the second impact is not desired, we can keep the proposed change and add the following rule derived from the second (undesired) impact to the beginning of the modified firewall:

Src IP	Dest. IP	Src Port	Dest. Port	Protocol	Action
1.2.3.4	192.168.0.1	*	[25,65536]	TCP	discard

5.4   Complexity Analysis

Let n be the number of rules in a firewall, and d be the total number of distinct packet fields that are examined by a firewall. The complexity of our change-impact analysis algorithms is $O(n^d)$. Despite the high worst case complexities, our algorithms are practical for two reasons. First, d is bounded and is typically small. Real-life firewalls typically examine five packet fields: source IP address, destination IP address, source port number, destination port number, and protocol type. Second, the worst cases of our algorithms are extremely unlikely to happen in practice. To trigger the worst case, the rules in a firewall need to be exceedingly overlapping, which does not happen in real-life firewalls according to the statistics on real-life rule sets in [6].

6   Related Work

Numerous studies have been done on analyzing the change-impact of general programs in software engineering and programming language communities (e.g., [7,8]. However, little work has been done on analyzing the change-impact of firewall policies. Firewall policies and general programs are fundamentally different. While accurately and completely computing the impact of software changes is nearly impossible in general, the algorithms presented in this paper can compute the accurate and complete impact of firewall policy changes.

The closest to this work is our previous work on diverse firewall design [9]. In [9], an algorithm that can compute the semantic differences between two firewalls were presented. The algorithm in [9] can be used to compute change-impact of firewalls by comparing a firewall before changes and the firewall after changes. Comparing with the algorithm in [9], the change-impact analysis algorithms in this paper are much more efficient. Although the algorithm in [9] can handle the cases where a firewall administrator makes multiple changes at a time, in real life, a firewall administrator typically makes one change at a time.

Fisler and Krishnamurthi studied change-impact analysis of access control policies in their seminal paper [10]. They proposed a solution using multi-terminal binary decision diagrams to compute the impact of access control policy changes and verify whether an access control policy satisfies a given property. Their work is similar to ours in spirit, however, their solution cannot be applied to firewall policies because the access control policies studied in [10] are quite different from firewall policies. In [10], every attribute-value pair is encoded as one variable in the MTBDD. This is natural for the access control policies studied in [10], but is not feasible for firewall policies because of the explosive number (2^{88}) of attribute-value pairs.

Some interesting work has been done on firewall policy modelling and analysis. However, none of the previous work explored the change-impact analysis of firewall policies. A Lisp-like language was introduced in [11] for specifying a high-level packet filtering policy. In a similar vein, a UML-like language was presented in [12] for specifying global filtering policies. Detecting conflicts among firewall rules was studied in [13,14,15]. In [16,17,18,19,20], a few firewall analysis tools were presented. In [21], algorithms for detecting firewall policy anomalies in distributed environment were proposed. Some anomalies were defined and techniques for detecting anomalies were presented in [22,23].

There is previous work on firewall testing [25, 26, 27, 28, 29]. These testing techniques involve injecting packets into a firewall and checking whether the decisions of the firewall concerning the injected packets are correct. There are some tools currently available for network vulnerability testing, such as Satan and Nessus. These vulnerability testing tools scan a private network based on the current publicly known attacks, rather than the requirement specification of a firewall. Although these tools can possibly catch some of the errors that allow illegitimate access to the private network, they cannot find the errors that disable legitimate communication between the private network and the outside Internet.

7   Conclusions

Making changes to firewall policies is a major task that firewall administrators perform; yet, it is also a major source of firewall policies errors. To address this issue, in this paper, we propose a framework for conducting firewall policy change-impact analysis. Our contributions are three-fold. First, we lay the theory foundation for firewall change-impact analysis. Second, we present algorithms for computing firewall policy change-impacts. Third, we present methods for correlating the impact of a firewall policy change and the high level security requirements that the firewall needs to satisfy as well as methods for making corrections if the impact of a change is not desirable. Our algorithms can be practically used in the iterative process of firewall policy design and maintenance.

References

1. Wool, A.: A quantitative study of firewall configuration errors. IEEE Computer 37(6), 62–67 (2004)
2. Oppenheimer, D., Ganapathi, A., Patterson, D.A.: Why do internet services fail, and what can be done about it? In: Proceedings of the 4th USENIX Symposium on Internet Technologies and Systems (USITS-03) (March 2003)
3. Liu, A.X., Gouda, M.G.: Complete redundancy detection in firewalls. In: Jajodia, S., Wijesekera, D. (eds.) Data and Applications Security XIX. LNCS, vol. 3654, pp. 196–209. Springer, Heidelberg (2005)
4. Gouda, M.G., Liu, A.X.: Structured firewall design. Computer Networks Journal 51(4), 1106–1120 (2007)
5. Gupta, P., McKeown, N.: Algorithms for packet classification. IEEE Network 15(2), 24–32 (2001)
6. Gupta, P.: Algorithms for Routing Lookups and Packet Classification. PhD thesis, Stanford University (2000)
7. Horwitz, S.: Identifying the semantic and textual differences between two versions of a program. In: Proceedings of the ACM SIGPLAN Conference on Programming Language Design and Implementation, pp. 234–245. ACM Press, New York (1990)

8. Ren, X., Chesley, O.C., Ryder, B.G.: Using a concept lattice of decomposition slices for program understanding and impact analysis. IEEE Transactions on Software Engineering 32(9), 718–732 (2006)

9. Liu, A.X., Gouda, M.G.: Diverse firewall design. In: DSN-04. Proceedings of the International Conference on Dependable Systems and Networks, pp. 595–604 (June 2004)

10. Fisler, K., Krishnamurthi, S., Meyerovich, L., Tschantz, M.: Verification and change impact analysis of access-control policies. In: Inverardi, P., Jazayeri, M. (eds.) ICSE 2005. LNCS, vol. 4309, Springer, Heidelberg (2006)

11. Guttman, J.D.: Filtering postures: Local enforcement for global policies. In: Proceedings of IEEE Symposium on Security and Privacy, pp. 120–129. IEEE Computer Society Press, Los Alamitos (1997)

12. Bartal, Y., Mayer, A.J., Nissim, K., Wool, A.: Firmato: A novel firewall management toolkit. In: Proceeding of the IEEE Symposium on Security and Privacy, pp. 17–31. IEEE Computer Society Press, Los Alamitos (1999)

13. Hari, A., Suri, S., Parulkar, G.M.: Detecting and resolving packet filter conflicts. In: Proceedings of IEEE INFOCOM, pp. 1203–1212. IEEE Computer Society Press, Los Alamitos (2000)

14. Eppstein, D., Muthukrishnan, S.: Internet packet filter management and rectangle geometry. In: Symp. on Discrete Algorithms, pp. 827–835 (2001)

15. Baboescu, F., Varghese, G.: Fast and scalable conflict detection for packet classifiers. In: Proceedings of the 10th IEEE International Conference on Network Protocols, IEEE Computer Society Press, Los Alamitos (2002)

16. Mayer, A., Wool, A., Ziskind, E.: Fang: A firewall analysis engine. In: Proceedings of IEEE Symposium on Security and Privacy, pp. 177–187. IEEE Computer Society Press, Los Alamitos (2000)

17. Wool, A.: Architecting the lumeta firewall analyzer. In: Proceedings of the 10th USENIX Security Symposium, August 2001, pp. 85–97 (2001)

18. Hazelhurst, S., Attar, A., Sinnappan, R.: Algorithms for improving the dependability of firewall and filter rule lists. In: Proceedings of the Workshop on Dependability of IP Applications, Platforms and Networks (2000)

19. Eronen, P., Zitting, J.: An expert system for analyzing firewall rules. In: Proceedings of the 6th Nordic Workshop on Secure IT Systems (NordSec 2001), pp. 100–107 (2001)

20. Liu, A.X., Gouda, M.G., Ma, H.H., Ngu, A.H.: Firewall queries. In: Higashino, T. (ed.) OPODIS 2004. LNCS, vol. 3544, pp. 124–139. Springer, Heidelberg (2005)

21. Garca-Alfaro, J., Cuppens, F., Cuppens, N.: Analysis of policy anomalies on distributed network security setups. In: Gollmann, D., Meier, J., Sabelfeld, A. (eds.) ESORICS 2006. LNCS, vol. 4189, Springer, Heidelberg (2006)

22. Yuan, L., Chen, H., Mai, J., Chuah, C.N., Su, Z., Mohapatra, P.: Fireman: a toolkit for firewall modeling and analysis. In: IEEE Symposium on Security and Privacy, IEEE Computer Society Press, Los Alamitos (May 2006)

23. Al-Shaer, E., Hamed, H.: Discovery of policy anomalies in distributed firewalls. In: IEEE INFOCOM'04, pp. 2605–2616. IEEE Computer Society Press, Los Alamitos (March 2004)

24. CERT: Test the firewall system,
    http://www.cert.org/security-improvement/practices/p060.html

25. Hoffman, D., Prabhakar, D., Strooper, P.: Testing iptables. In: Proceedings of the 2003 conference of IBM Centre for Advanced Studies, pp. 80–91 (2003)

26. Jürjens, J., Wimmel, G.: Specification-based testing of firewalls. In: Bjørner, D., Broy, M., Zamulin, A.V. (eds.) PSI 2001. LNCS, vol. 2244, Springer, Heidelberg (2001)
27. Hoffman, D., Yoo, K.: Blowtorch: a framework for firewall test automation. In: Proceedings of the 20th IEEE/ACM international Conference on Automated software engineering, pp. 96–103. ACM Press, New York (2005)
28. Senn, D., Basin, D., Caronni, G.: Firewall conformance testing. In: Proceedings of the Testcom (Testing of Communicating Systems) (May 2005)
29. Lyu, M.R., Lau, L.K.Y.: Firewall security: Policies, testing and performance evaluation. In: COMPSAC 2000. Proceedings of the 24th International Conference on Computer Systems and Applications, pp. 116–121 (October 2000)

Fragmentation and Encryption to Enforce Privacy in Data Storage

Valentina Ciriani[1], Sabrina De Capitani di Vimercati[1],
Sara Foresti[1], Sushil Jajodia[2],
Stefano Paraboschi[3], and Pierangela Samarati[1]

[1] Università degli Studi di Milano, 26013 Crema, Italia
{ciriani,decapita,foresti,samarati}@dti.unimi.it
[2] George Mason University, Fairfax, VA 22030-4444
jajodia@gmu.edu
[3] Università degli Studi di Bergamo, 24044 Dalmine, Italia
parabosc@unibg.it

Abstract. Privacy requirements have an increasing impact on the realization of modern applications. Technical considerations and many significant commercial and legal regulations demand today that privacy guarantees be provided whenever sensitive information is stored, processed, or communicated to external parties. It is therefore crucial to design solutions able to respond to this demand with a clear integration strategy for existing applications and a consideration of the performance impact of the protection measures.

In this paper we address this problem and propose a solution to enforce privacy over data collections by combining data fragmentation with encryption. The idea behind our approach is to use encryption as an underlying (conveniently available) measure for making data unintelligible, while exploiting fragmentation as a way to break sensitive associations between information.

Keywords: Privacy, fragmentation, encryption.

1 Introduction

Information is today probably the most important and valued resource. Private and governmental organizations are increasingly gathering vast amounts of data, which are collected and maintained, and often include sensitive personally identifiable information. In such a scenario guaranteeing the privacy of the data, be them stored in the system or communicated to external parties, becomes a primary requirement.

Individuals, privacy advocates, and legislators are today putting more and more attention on the support of privacy over collected information. Regulations are increasingly being established responding to these demands, forcing organizations to provide privacy guarantees over sensitive information when storing, processing or sharing it with others. Most recent regulations (e.g., [2,14]) require

J. Biskup and J. Lopez (Eds.): ESORICS 2007, LNCS 4734, pp. 171–186, 2007.

that specific categories of data (e.g., data disclosing health and sex life, or data such as ZIP and date of birth that can be exploited to uniquely identify an individual) be either *encrypted* or *kept separate* from other personally identifiable information (to prevent their association with specific individuals). Information privacy guarantees may also derive from the need of preventing possible abuses of critical information. For instance, the "Payment Card Industry (PCI) Data Security Standard" [13] forces all the business organizations managing credit card information (e.g., VISA and MasterCard) to apply encryption measures when storing data. The standard also explicitly forbids the use of storage encryption as natively offered by operating systems, requiring that access to the encryption keys be separated from the operating system services managing user identities and privileges.

This demand for encryption is luckily coupled today with the fact that the realization of cryptographic functions presents increasingly lower costs in a computer architecture, where the factor limiting system performances is typically the capacity of the channels that transfer information within the system and among separate systems. Cryptography then becomes an inexpensive tool that supports the protection of privacy when storing or communicating information.

From a data access point of view, however, dealing with encrypted information represents a burden since encryption makes it not always possible to efficiently execute queries and evaluate conditions over the data. As a matter of fact a straightforward approach to guarantee privacy to a collection of data could consist in encrypting all the data. This technique is, for example, adopted in the database outsourced scenario [5,8], where a protective layer of encryption is wrapped around sensitive data, thus counteracting outside attacks as well as the curiosity from the server itself. The assumption underlying approaches applying such an encryption wrapper is that all the data are equally sensitive and therefore encryption is a price to be paid to protect them. This assumption is typically an overkill in many scenarious. As a matter of fact, in many situations data are not sensitive per se; what is sensitive is their association with other data. As a simple example, in a hospital the list of illnesses cured or the list of patients could be made publicly available, while the association of specific illnesses to individual patients is sensitive and must be protected. Hence, there is no need to encrypt both illnesses and patients if there are alternative ways to protect the association between them.

In this paper, we propose an approach that couples encryption together with data fragmentation. We apply encryption only when explicitly demanded by the privacy requirements. The combined use of encryption and data fragmentation has first been proposed in the context of data outsourcing [1]. In this proposal, privacy requirements are enforced by splitting information over two independent database servers (so to break associations of sensitive information) and by encrypting information whenever necessary. While presenting an interesting idea, the approach in [1] suffers from several limitations. The main limitation is that the privacy relies on the complete absence of communication among the two servers (which have to be completely unaware of each other). This assumption is clearly too strong and difficult to enforce in real environments. A collusion among the servers (or the users accessing them) easily breaches privacy. Also, the assumption of two servers limits the number of associations that can be solved by fragmenting data, often forcing the use of encryption.

In this paper, we propose an approach combining fragmentation and encryption that overcomes the above limitations. Our solution allows storing data on a single server and minimizes the amount of data represented only in encrypted format, therefore allowing for efficient query execution.

We frame our work in the context of relational databases. The reason for this choice is that relational databases are by far the most common solution for the management of the data subject of privacy regulations; also, they are characterized by a clear data model and simple query language that facilitate the design of a solution. We note, however, that our model could be easily adapted to the protection of data represented with other data models (e.g., records in files or XML documents).

Our work assumes that access to data is realized by an application that includes a compact trusted core, which is invoked every time there is the need to access sensitive information (i.e., applying decryption or reconstructing associations by linking fragments). By contrast, the DBMS needs not be trusted, since accessing single fragments or encrypted information does not expose to any privacy breach. This is a considerable advantage over previous proposals, developed, for example, in the data outsourcing scenario [5,8].

The contribution of this paper is threefold. First, we introduce confidentiality constraints as a simple, yet powerful, way to capture privacy requirements. Second, we provide a model formalizing the application of data fragmentation and encryption, which captures properties related to the correct representation of the data while minimizing encryption and fragmentation. Third, we propose a heuristic algorithm for the concrete identification of a fragmentation solution that satisfies the properties specified.

2   Confidentiality Constraints

We model, in a quite simple and powerful way, the privacy requirements through *confidentiality constraints*, which are sets of attributes, as follows.

Definition 1 (Confidentiality constraint). *Let $\mathcal{A}$ be a set of attributes, a confidentiality constraint is a subset $c \subseteq \mathcal{A}$.*

The semantics of a confidentiality constraint c is that the (joint) visibility of values of the attributes in c should be protected. When the constraint is a singleton set, then the semantics is that the individual attribute must be protected, that is, the list of the attribute values itself is confidential.

While simple, the definition above allows the expression of the different confidentiality requirements that may need to be expressed, such as the following.

- *The values assumed by some attributes are considered sensitive and therefore cannot be stored in the clear*. For instance, phone numbers or email addresses can be considered sensitive values (even if not associated with any identifying information).

- *The association between values of given attributes is sensitive and therefore should not be released.* For instance, while the list of (names of) patients in a hospital as well as the list of illnesses are by themselves not confidential, the association of patient's names with illnesses is considered sensitive.

Note that constraints specified on the association between attributes can derive from different requirements, as they can correspond to explicit protection of an association (as in the case of names and illnesses above) or to associations that could cause inference on other sensitive information. As an example of the latter, consider a hospital database and suppose that the names of patients are considered sensitive, and therefore cannot be stored in the clear, and that the association of DoB together with the ZIP code can work as a quasi-identifier [4,15] (i.e., DoB and ZIP can be used, possibly in association with external information, to help identifying patients and therefore infer, or reduce uncertainty about, their names). This inference channel can be simply blocked by specifying a constraint protecting the association of DoB with the ZIP code. As another example, consider the case where names are not considered sensitive but their association with Illness is. Suppose again that DoB together with the ZIP code can work as a quasi-identifier (then potentially leaking information on names). In this case, an association constraint will be specified protecting the association between DoB, ZIP code, and Illness, implying that the three attributes should never be accessible together in the clear.

In general, we are interested in enforcing a set of *well defined* confidentiality constraints, formally defined as follows.

Definition 2 (Well defined constraints). *A set of confidentiality constraints* $C = \{c_1,\ldots,c_m\}$ *is said to be* well defined *iff* $\forall c_i, c_j \in C, i \neq j, c_i \not\subseteq c_j$ *and* $c_j \not\subseteq c_i$.

According to this definition, a set of constraints C over A cannot contain a constraint that is a subset of another constraint. The rationale behind this property is that, whenever there are two constraints c_i, c_j and c_i is a subset of c_j (or vice versa), the satisfaction of constraint c_i implies the satisfaction of constraint c_j (see Sect. 3), and therefore c_j is redundant.

To model the problem of enforcing a set of well defined confidentiality constraints, we assume standard notations from the relational database model. Formally, let A be a set of attributes and D a set of domains. A relation schema R is a finite set of attributes $\{a_1,\ldots,a_n\} \subseteq A$ that are defined on a domain $D_i, i = 1,\ldots,n$. Notation $R(a_1,\ldots,a_n)$ represents a relation schema R over the set $\{a_1,\ldots,a_n\}$ of attributes. A tuple t over a set of attributes $\{a_1,\ldots,a_n\}$ is a function that associates with each attribute a_i a value $v \in D_i$. Notation $t[a]$ denotes value v associated with attribute a in t. A relation r over relation schema $R(a_1,\ldots,a_n)$ is a set of tuples over the set of attributes $\{a_1,\ldots,a_n\}$. In the following, when clear from the context, we will use R to denote either the relation schema R or the set of attributes in R.

MEDICALDATA

SSN	Name	DoB	ZIP	Illness	Physician
123-45-6789	A. Hellman	81/01/03	94142	hypertension	M. White
987-65-4321	B. Dooley	53/10/07	94141	obesity	D. Warren
246-89-1357	C. McKinley	52/02/12	94139	hypertension	M. White
135-79-2468	D. Ripley	81/01/03	94139	obesity	D. Warren

$c_0 = \{\text{SSN}\}$
$c_1 = \{\text{Name, DoB}\}$
$c_2 = \{\text{Name, ZIP}\}$
$c_3 = \{\text{Name, Illness}\}$
$c_4 = \{\text{Name, Physician}\}$
$c_5 = \{\text{DoB, ZIP, Illness}\}$
$c_6 = \{\text{DoB, ZIP, Physician}\}$

(a)   (b)

Fig. 1. An example of plaintext relation (a) and its well defined constraints (b)

For simplicity, and consistently with other proposals [1,15], we consider a single relation, r over a relation schema $R(a_1, \ldots, a_n)$, containing all the sensitive information that needs to be protected.

Example 1. Figure 1 illustrates an example of relation together with some confidentiality constraints on it. The reasons behind the constraints are as follows:

- the list of SSN of patients is considered sensitive (c_0);
- the association of patients' names with any other piece of stored information is considered sensitive ($c_1, \ldots, c_4$);
- DoB and ZIP together can be exploited to infer the name of patients (i.e., they can work as a quasi-identifier), consequently their association with other pieces of information is considered sensitive (c_5, c_6).

Note that also the association of patients' Name and SSN is sensitive and should be protected. However, such a constraint is not specified since it is redundant, given that SSN by itself has been declared sensitive (c_0). As a matter of fact, protecting SSN as an individual attribute implies automatic protection of its associations with any other attribute.

3   Fragmentation and Encryption for Constraint Satisfaction

Our approach to satisfy confidentiality constraints is based on the use of two techniques: encryption and fragmentation.

- *Encryption.* Consistently with how the constraints are specified, encryption applies at the attribute level, that is, it involves an attribute in its entirety. Encrypting an attribute means encrypting (tuple by tuple) all its values. To protect encrypted values from frequency attacks [16], we assume that a *salt*, which is a randomly chosen value, is applied on each encryption (similarly to the use of nonces in the protection of messages from replay attacks).
- *Fragmentation.* Fragmentation, like encryption, applies at the attribute level, that is, it involves an attribute in its entirety. Fragmenting means splitting sets of attributes so that they are not visible together, that is, the association among their values is not available without access to the encryption key.

It is straightforward to see that singleton constraints can be solved only by encryption. By contrast, an association constraint could be solved by either: *i)* encrypting any (one suffices) of the attributes involved in the constraint, so to prevent joint visibility, or *ii)* fragmenting the attributes involved in the constraint so that they are not visible together. In the following, we use the term *fragment* to denote any subset of a given set of attributes. A fragmentation is a set of fragments, as captured by the following definition.

Definition 3 (Fragmentation). *Let R be a relation schema, a fragmentation of R is a set of fragments $\mathcal{F}=\{F_1,\ldots,F_m\}$, where $F_i \subseteq R$, for $i = 1,\ldots,m$.*

At the physical level, a fragmentation translates to a combination of fragmentation and encryption. Each fragment F is mapped into a physical fragment containing all the attributes in F in the clear, while all the other attributes of R are encrypted. The reason for reporting all the original attributes (in either encrypted or clear form) in each of the physical fragments is to guarantee that any query can be executed by querying a single physical fragment. For the sake of simplicity and efficiency, we assume that all the attributes not appearing in the clear in a fragment are encrypted all together (encryption is applied on subtuples). Physical fragments are then defined as follows.

Definition 4 (Physical fragment). *Let R be a relation schema, and $\mathcal{F}=\{F_1, \ldots,F_m\}$ a fragmentation of R. For each $F_i=\{a_{i_1},\ldots,a_{i_n}\} \in \mathcal{F}$, the physical fragment of R over F_i is a relation schema $F_i^e(\underline{salt},enc,a_{i_1},\ldots,a_{i_n})$, where enc represents the encryption of all the attributes of R that do not belong to the fragment, combined before encryption in a binary XOR (symbol $\otimes$) with the salt.*

At the level of instance, given a fragment $F_i=\{a_{i_1},\ldots,a_{i_n}\}$, and a relation r over schema R, the physical fragment F_i^e of F_i is such that each plaintext tuple $t \in r$ is mapped into a tuple $t^e \in f_i^e$ where f_i^e is a relation over F_i^e and:

- $t^e[enc] = E_k(t[R - F_i] \otimes t^e[salt])$
- $t^e[a_{i_j}] = t[a_{i_j}]$, for $j = 1,\ldots,n$

The algorithm in Fig. 2 shows the construction and population of physical fragments. When the size of the attributes exceeds the size of an encryption block, we assume that encryption of the protected attributes uses a Cipher Block Chaining (CBC) mode [16], with the salt used as the Initialization Vector (IV); in the CBC mode, the clear text of the first block is actually encrypted after it has been combined in binary XOR with the IV.

Note that the salts, which we conveniently use as primary keys of physical fragments (ensuring no collision in their generation), need not be secret, because knowledge of the salts does not help in attacking the encrypted values as long as the encryption algorithm is secure and the key remains protected.

Given a relation r over schema R and a set of confidentiality constraints $\mathcal{C}$ on it, our goal is to produce a fragmentation that satisfies the constraints. However, we must also ensure that no constraint can be violated by recombining together two or more fragments. In other words, there cannot be attributes that can be

Algorithm 1 (Constraint resolution).

INPUT
A relation r over schema R
$C = \{c_1, \ldots, c_m\}$ /* well defined constraints */
OUTPUT
A set of physical fragments $\mathcal{F}^e_{=}\{F^e_1, \ldots, F^e_i\}$
A set of relations $\{f^e_1, \ldots, f^e_i\}$ over schemas $\{F^e_1, \ldots, F^e_i\}$

MAIN
$\mathcal{C}_\mathcal{F} := \{c \in \mathcal{C} : |c| > 1\}$ /* association constraints */
$\mathcal{A}_\mathcal{F} := \{a \in R: \{a\} \not\subseteq \mathcal{C}\}$
$\mathcal{F} := \mathbf{fragment}(\mathcal{A}_\mathcal{F}, \mathcal{C}_\mathcal{F})$
/* define physical fragments */
for each $F = \{a_{i_1}, \ldots, a_{i_l}\} \in \mathcal{F}$ **do**
 define relation F^e with schema:
   $F^e(\underline{salt}, enc, a_{i_1}, \ldots, a_{i_l})$
/* populate physical fragments instances */
 for each $t \in r$ **do**
   $t^e[salt] := \mathbf{generatesalt}(F, t)$
   $t^e[enc] := E_k(t[a_{j_1}\ldots a_{j_p}] \otimes t^e[salt])$ /* $\{a_{j_1}\ldots a_{j_p}\} = R - F$ */
   for each $a \in F$ **do** $t^e[a] := t[a]$
   insert t^e in f^e

Fig. 2. Algorithm that correctly fragments R

f^e_1			f^e_2				f^e_3			
salt	enc	Name	salt	enc	DoB	ZIP	salt	enc	Illness	Physician
s_1	α	A. Hellman	s_5	ε	81/01/03	94142	s_9	ι	hypertension	M. White
s_2	β	B. Dooley	s_6	ζ	53/10/07	94141	s_{10}	κ	obesity	D. Warren
s_3	γ	C. McKinley	s_7	η	52/02/12	94139	s_{11}	λ	hypertension	M. White
s_4	δ	D. Ripley	s_8	θ	81/01/03	94139	s_{12}	μ	obesity	D. Warren
(a)			(b)				(c)			

Fig. 3. An example of physical fragments for relation in Fig. 1(a)

exploited for linking. Since encryption is differentiated by the use of the salt, the only attributes that can be exploited for linking are the plaintext attributes. Consequently, ensuring that fragments are protected from linking translates into requiring that no attributes appear in clear form in more than one fragment.

The conditions above are formally captured by the following definition.

Definition 5 (Fragmentation correctness). *Let R be a relation schema, $\mathcal{F}$ be a fragmentation of R, and C a set of well defined constraints over R. $\mathcal{F}$ correctly enforces C iff the following conditions are satisfied:*

1. *$\forall F \in \mathcal{F}, \forall c \in C : c \not\subseteq F$ (each individual fragment satisfies the constraints);*
2. *$\forall F_i, F_j \in \mathcal{F}, i \neq j : F_i \cap F_j = \emptyset$ (fragments do not have attributes in common).*

Note that condition 1, requiring fragments not to be a superset of any constraint, implies that attributes appearing in singleton constraints do not appear in any fragment. As a matter of fact, as already noted, singleton constraints require the attributes on which they are defined to appear only in encrypted form. Figure 3 illustrates an example of fragmentation of the relation schema in Fig. 1(a) that correctly enforces the well defined constraints in Fig. 1(b).

Original query on R	Translation over fragment F_3^e

$Q_1 :=$ SELECT SSN, Name
    FROM   MedicalData
    WHERE Illness='obesity'
           AND
           Physician='D. Warren'
	$Q_1^3 :=$ SELECT salt, enc
	     FROM F_3^e
	     WHERE Illness='obesity'AND
	           Physician='D. Warren'
	
	$Q_1' :=$ SELECT SSN, Name
	     FROM $Decrypt(Q_1^3, Key)$

$Q_2 :=$ SELECT SSN, Name
    FROM   MedicalData
    WHERE Illness='obesity'
           AND
           Physician='D. Warren'
           AND
           ZIP='94139'
	$Q_2^3 :=$ SELECT salt, enc
	     FROM F_3^e
	     WHERE Illness='obesity'AND
	           Physician='D. Warren'
	
	$Q_2' :=$ SELECT SSN, Name
	     FROM $Decrypt(Q_2^3, Key)$
	     WHERE ZIP='94139'

Fig. 4. An example of query translation over a fragment

4   Executing Queries on Fragments

Fragmentation of a relation implies that only fragments (which are stored in place of the original relation to satisfy confidentiality constraints) will be available for queries. Note that, since every physical fragment of R contains all the attributes of R, either in encrypted or in clear form, no more than one fragment needs to be accessed to respond to a query. However, if the query executed over a fragment involves an attribute that is encrypted, an additional query may need to be executed (after decryption) by the application to evaluate the conditions on the attributes.

We consider generic *select-from-where* SQL queries that present relation R in the *from* clause, specify a conjunction of equality predicates in the *where* clause, and extract a subset of the R's attributes in the *select* clause.

Example 2. Consider the relation in Fig. 1(a) and its fragment F_3^e in Fig. 3(c).

– Consider a query Q_1 retrieving the Social Security Number and the name of the patients whose illness is *obesity* and whose physician is *D. Warren*. Figure 4 illustrates the translation of Q_1 to queries Q_1^3 executed by the DBMS on the fragment, and Q_1' executed by the application. Note that since both Illness and Physician are represented in the clear in F_3^e, the conditions in the *where* clause can be executed on the fragment itself, thus returning to the application only the tuples belonging to the final result.
– Consider a query Q_2 retrieving the Social Security Number and the name of the patients whose illness is *obesity*, whose physician is *D. Warren*, and whose ZIP is *94139*. Figure 4 illustrates the translation of Q_2 to queries Q_2^3 executed

by the DBMS on the fragment, and Q_2' executed by the application. Note that, since ZIP does not appear in the clear in the fragment, the condition on it needs to be evaluated by the application.

The cost of executing a query over a fragment depends on the number of plaintext attributes it contains and on their selectivity. A query optimizer can be used to select the fragment that allows the execution of more selective queries by the DBMS, thus decreasing the workload of the application and maximizing the efficiency of the execution.

5   Minimal Fragmentation

As the examples in Sect 4 have shown, the availability of plaintext attributes in a fragment permits an efficient execution of queries. Therefore, we aim at minimizing the number of attributes that are not represented in the clear in any fragment, because queries using those attributes will be generally processed inefficiently. In other words, we prefer fragmentation over encryption whenever possible and always solve association constraints via fragmentation.

The requirement on the availability of a plain representation for the maximum number of attributes can be captured by imposing that any attribute not involved in a singleton constraint must appear in the clear in at least one fragment. This requirement is represented formally by the definition of maximal visibility as follows.

Definition 6 (Maximal visibility). *Let R be a relation schema, and $\mathcal{C}$ be a set of well defined constraints. A fragmentation $\mathcal{F}$ of R maximizes visibility iff $\forall a \in R, \{a\} \notin \mathcal{C}: \exists F \in \mathcal{F}$ such that $a \in F$.*

Note that the combination of maximal visibility together with the second condition of Definition 5 imposes that each attribute that does not appear in a singleton constraint must appear in the clear in exactly one fragment.

Another important aspect to consider when fragmenting a relation to satisfy a set of constraints is to avoid excessive fragmentation. As a matter of fact, the availability of more attributes in the clear in a single fragment allows a more efficient execution of queries on the fragment.

Indeed, a straightforward approach for producing a fragmentation that satisfies the constraints while maximizing visibility is to define as many (singleton) fragments as the number of attributes not appearing in singleton constraints. Such a solution, unless demanded by the constraints, is however undesirable since it makes the evaluation of a query involving conditions on more than one attribute inefficient.

We are interested in finding a fragmentation that makes query execution efficient. A simple strategy to achieve this goal consists in finding a *minimum fragmentation* that is correct and maximizes visibility, while minimizing the number of fragments. This problem is *NP-hard* since it corresponds to the minimum hypergraph coloring problem [7]. It is also interesting to note that, assuming

$NP \neq ZPP$, there are no polynomial time approximation algorithms for coloring k-uniform hypergraphs with approximation ratio $O(n^{1-\epsilon})$ for any fixed $\epsilon > 0$ [10,17]. We propose therefore a definition of *minimality*, which can be exploited to find an efficient fragmentation through a heuristic (see Sect. 6).

To formally define minimality, we introduce the concept of fragment vector as follows.

Definition 7 (Fragment vector). *Let R be a relation schema, and $\mathcal{F} = \{F_1, \ldots, F_m\}$ be a fragmentation of R. The fragment vector $V_{\mathcal{F}}$ of $\mathcal{F}$ is a vector of fragments with an element $V_{\mathcal{F}}[a]$ for each $a \in \bigcup_{i=1}^{m} F_i$, where the value of $V_{\mathcal{F}}[a]$ is the unique fragment $F_j \in \mathcal{F}$ containing attribute a.*

Example 3. Let $\mathcal{F} = \{\{$Name$\}, \{$DoB,ZIP$\}, \{$Illness,Physician$\}\}$ be a fragmentation of the relation schema in Fig. 1(a). The fragment vector is the vector $V_{\mathcal{F}}$ such that:

- $V_{\mathcal{F}}[$Name$] = \{$Name$\}$;
- $V_{\mathcal{F}}[$DoB$] = V_{\mathcal{F}}[$ZIP$] = \{$DoB,ZIP$\}$;
- $V_{\mathcal{F}}[$Illness$] = V_{\mathcal{F}}[$Physician$] = \{$Illness,Physician$\}$.

Fragment vectors allow us to define a partial order between fragmentations as follows.

Definition 8 (Dominance). *Let R be a relation schema, and $\mathcal{F}$ and $\mathcal{F}'$ be two fragmentations of R maximizing visibility. Let $\mathcal{A}$ be the (equal) set of attributes in the two fragmentations. We say that $\mathcal{F}'$ dominates $\mathcal{F}$, denoted $\mathcal{F} \preceq \mathcal{F}'$, iff $V_{\mathcal{F}}[a] \subseteq V_{\mathcal{F}'}[a]$, for all $a \in \mathcal{A}$. Consequently, $\mathcal{F} \prec \mathcal{F}'$ iff $\mathcal{F} \preceq \mathcal{F}'$ and $\mathcal{F} \neq \mathcal{F}'$.*

Definition 8 states that solution $\mathcal{F}'$ dominates solution $\mathcal{F}$ if $\mathcal{F}'$ can be computed from $\mathcal{F}$ by merging two (or more) fragments composing $\mathcal{F}$.

Example 4. Let $\mathcal{F}_1 = \{\{$Name$\}, \{$DoB,ZIP$\}, \{$Illness,Physician$\}\}$ and $\mathcal{F}_2 = \{\{$Name$\}, \{$DoB$\}, \{$ZIP$\}, \{$Illness,Physician$\}\}$ be two fragmentations of the relation schema in Fig. 1(a). According to Definition 8, $\mathcal{F}_2 \prec \mathcal{F}_1$, since $\mathcal{F}_1$ can be obtained from $\mathcal{F}_2$ by merging fragments $\{$DoB$\}$ and $\{$ZIP$\}$.

We can formally define the *minimality* property as follows.

Definition 9 (Minimal fragmentation). *Let R be a relation schema, C be a set of well defined constraints, and $\mathcal{F}$ be a fragmentation of R. $\mathcal{F}$ is a minimal fragmentation iff all the following conditions are satisfied:*

1. *$\mathcal{F}$ correctly enforces C (Definition 5);*
2. *$\mathcal{F}$ maximizes visibility (Definition 6);*
3. *$\nexists \mathcal{F}'$ such that $\mathcal{F} \prec \mathcal{F}'$ and $\mathcal{F}'$ satisfies the two conditions above.*

According to this definition of minimality, a fragmentation $\mathcal{F}$ is *minimal* if and only if it is correct, it maximizes visibility, and all fragmentations that can be obtained from $\mathcal{F}$ by merging any two fragments in $\mathcal{F}$ violate at least one constraint.

Function 1 (Minimal fragmentation).

```
FRAGMENT(A_ToPlace, C_ToSolve)
F := ∅
for each a ∈ A_ToPlace do /* initialize arrays Con[] and N_con[] */
  Con[a] := {c ∈ C_ToSolve| a ∈ c}
  N_con[a] := |Con[a]|
repeat
  if C_ToSolve ≠ ∅ then
    let attr be an attribute with the maximum value of N_con[]
    for each c ∈ (Con[attr] ∩ C_ToSolve) do
      C_ToSolve := C_ToSolve − {c} /* adjust the constraints */
      for each a ∈ c do N_con[a] := N_con[a]−1 /* adjust array N_con[] */
  else /* since all the constrains are satisfied, choose any attribute in A_ToPlace */
    let attr be an attribute in A_ToPlace
  endif
  A_ToPlace := A_ToPlace − {attr}
  inserted := false /* try to insert attr in the existing fragments */
  for each F ∈ F do /* evaluate if F ∪ {attr} satisfies the constraints */
    satisfies := true
    for each c ∈ Con[attr] do
      if c ⊆ (F ∪ {attr}) then
        satisfies := false /* choose the next fragment */
        break
      endif
    if satisfies then
      F := F ∪ {attr} /* attr has been inserted in F */
      inserted := true
      break
    endif
  if NOT inserted then /* insert attr in a new fragment */
    add {attr} to F
  endif
until A_ToPlace = ∅
return(F)
```

Fig. 5. Function that finds a minimal fragmentation

Example 5. Consider fragmentations $\mathcal{F}_1$ and $\mathcal{F}_2$ of Example 4, and the set of constraints in Fig. 1(b). Since $\mathcal{F}_2 \prec \mathcal{F}_1$, $\mathcal{F}_2$ is not minimal. By contrast, $\mathcal{F}_1$ is minimal. As a matter of fact, $\mathcal{F}_1$ contains all attributes of relation schema MedicalData in Fig. 1(a), but SSN (maximize visibility); satisfies all constraints in Fig. 1(b) (correctness); no fragmentation obtained from it by merging any pair of fragments satisfies the constraints.

6   Computing a Minimal Fragmentation

Our heuristic method for computing a minimal fragmentation is based on the **fragment** function illustrated in Fig. 5. This function takes as input a set of attributes *A_ToPlace* to be fragmented, and a set of constraints *C_ToSolve*. It computes a minimal fragmentation $\mathcal{F}$ of *A_ToPlace* as follows.

First, the function initializes $\mathcal{F}$ to the empty set and creates two arrays *Con*[] and *N_con*[] that contain an element for each attribute a in *A_ToPlace*. Element *Con*[a] contains the set of constraints on a, and element *N_con*[a] is the number of non solved constraints involving a (note that, at the beginning, *N_con*[a] coincides with the cardinality of *Con*[a]). The function then executes a **repeat-until** cycle that, at each iteration, places an attribute *attr* into a fragment as follows. If there are constraints still to be solved (*C_ToSolve* $\neq \emptyset$) *attr* is selected as an attribute with the highest number of non-solved constraints. The reason for this choice is to bring all constraints to satisfaction in a few number of steps. Then, for each constraint *c* in *Con*[*attr*]∩*C_ToSolve*, the function removes *c* from *C_ToSolve* and, for each attribute *a* in *c*, decreases *N_con*[*a*] by one. Otherwise, that is, all constraints are solved (*C_ToSolve*= $\emptyset$), the function chooses *attr* by randomly extracting an attribute from *A_ToPlace* and removes it from *A_ToPlace*. Then, the function looks for a fragment *F* in $\mathcal{F}$ in which *attr* can be inserted without violating any constraint including *attr* that has already been solved (indeed, there is no need to check constraints that have not yet been solved). If such a fragment *F* is found, *attr* is inserted in *F*, otherwise a new fragment {*attr*} is added to $\mathcal{F}$. Note that the search for a fragment terminates as soon as a fragment is found (*inserted=true*). Also, the control on constraint satisfaction terminates as soon as a violation to constraints is found (*satisfies=false*).

Example 6. Figure 6 presents the execution, step by step, of function **fragment** applied to the example in Fig. 1. Here, for simplicity, we represent attributes with their initials. The left hand side of Fig. 6 illustrates the evolution of variables *attr*, $\mathcal{F}$, *C_ToSolve*, and *A_ToPlace*, while the right hand side graphically illustrates the same information through a matrix with a row for each attribute and a column for each constraint. If an attribute belongs to a non solved constraint c_i, the corresponding cell is set to ×; otherwise, if c_i is solved, the cell is set to ✓. At the beginning, $\mathcal{F}$ is empty, all constraints are not solved, and all attributes need to be placed. In the first iteration, function **fragment** chooses attribute *n*, since it is the attribute involved in the highest number of non solved constraints. The constraints in *Con*[*n*] become now solved, *N_con*[a_i] is updated accordingly, and fragment {*n*} is added to $\mathcal{F}$. Function **fragment** proceeds in analogous way by choosing attributes *d*, *z*, *i*, and *p*. The final solution is represented by the relations in Fig. 3.

The correctness and complexity of our approach are stated by the following theorems, whose complete proofs are omitted here for space constraints.

Theorem 1 (Correctness). *Function* **fragment** *terminates and finds a minimal fragmentation (Definition 9).*

Proof (sketch). The **repeat** loop terminates because *A_ToPlace* is finite, and in each iteration an attribute in *A_ToPlace* is extracted, and the loop is executed till *A_ToPlace* becomes empty. Moreover, all the inner **for** loops always consider a finite set of fragments and constraints. Each attribute *attr* in *A_ToPlace* is then inserted exactly in one existing fragment, if no constraint is violated; it is inserted in a new fragment, otherwise (maximal visibility and fragmentation correctness). Moreover, function **fragment** cannot generate two different fragments whose union does not violate any constraint (minimality). In fact, if merging the two

$\mathcal{F}=\emptyset$
$C\_ToSolve=\{c_1,c_2,c_3,c_4,c_5,c_6\}$
$A\_ToPlace=\{n,d,z,i,p\}$

	c_1	c_2	c_3	c_4	c_5	c_6	$N\_con[a_i]$
n	×	×	×	×			4
d	×				×	×	3
z		×			×	×	3
i		×		×			2
p				×		×	2
$ToSolve$	yes	yes	yes	yes	yes	yes	

$attr = n$
$Con[n]=\{c_1,c_2,c_3,c_4\}$

$\mathcal{F} = \{\{n\}\}$
$C\_ToSolve = \{c_5,c_6\}$
$A\_ToPlace = \{d,z,i,p\}$

	c_1	c_2	c_3	c_4	c_5	c_6	$N\_con[a_i]$
n	✓	✓	✓	✓			0
d	✓				×	×	2
z		✓			×	×	2
i			✓		×		1
p				✓		×	1
$ToSolve$	✓	✓	✓	✓	yes	yes	

$attr = d$
$Con[d]=\{c_1,c_5,c_6\}$

$\mathcal{F} = \{\{n\},\{d\}\}$
$C\_ToSolve = \emptyset$
$A\_ToPlace = \{z,i,p\}$

	c_1	c_2	c_3	c_4	c_5	c_6	$N\_con[a_i]$
n	✓	✓	✓	✓			0
d	✓				✓	✓	0
z		✓			✓	✓	0
i			✓		✓		0
p				✓		✓	0
$ToSolve$	✓	✓	✓	✓	✓	✓	

$attr = z$
$Con[z]=\{c_2,c_5,c_6\}$

$\mathcal{F} = \{\{n\},\{d,z\}\}$
$C\_ToSolve = \emptyset$
$A\_ToPlace = \{i,p\}$

	c_1	c_2	c_3	c_4	c_5	c_6	$N\_con[a_i]$
n	✓	✓	✓	✓			0
d	✓				✓	✓	0
z		✓			✓	✓	0
i			✓		✓		0
p				✓		✓	0
$ToSolve$	✓	✓	✓	✓	✓	✓	

$attr = i$
$Con[i]=\{c_3,c_5\}$

$\mathcal{F} = \{\{n\},\{d,z\},\{i\}\}$
$C\_ToSolve = \emptyset$
$A\_ToPlace = \{p\}$

	c_1	c_2	c_3	c_4	c_5	c_6	$N\_con[a_i]$
n	✓	✓	✓	✓			0
d	✓				✓	✓	0
z		✓			✓	✓	0
i			✓		✓		0
p				✓		✓	0
$ToSolve$	✓	✓	✓	✓	✓	✓	

$attr = p$
$Con[p]=\{c_4,c_6\}$

$\mathcal{F} = \{\{n\},\{d,z\},\{i,p\}\}$
$C\_ToSolve = \emptyset$
$A\_ToPlace = \emptyset$

	c_1	c_2	c_3	c_4	c_5	c_6	$N\_con[a_i]$
n	✓	✓	✓	✓			0
d	✓				✓	✓	0
z		✓			✓	✓	0
i			✓		✓		0
p				✓		✓	0
$ToSolve$	✓	✓	✓	✓	✓	✓	

Fig. 6. An example of function execution

fragments does not violate any constraint, the function would have inserted all the attributes in the first of the two fragments that was created.   ■

Theorem 2 (Complexity). *Given a set of constraints* $C=\{c_1,\ldots,c_m\}$ *and a set of attributes* $A=\{a_1,\ldots a_n\}$ *the complexity of function* **fragment***(A,C) is* $O(n^2m)$ *in time.*

Proof (sketch). To chose attribute *attr* from *A_ToPlace*, in the worst case the function **fragment** scans array *N_con[]*, and adjusts array *N_con[]* for each attribute involved in at least one constraint with *attr*. This operation costs $O(nm)$ for each attribute chosen. After the choosing phase, each attribute is inserted in a fragment. Note that the number of fragments is $O(n)$ in the worst case. To choose the right fragment that will contain *attr*, in the worst case the function tries to insert it in all the fragments $F \in \mathcal{F}$, and compares $F \cup \{attr\}$ with the constraints. Since the sum of the number of attributes in all the fragments is $O(n)$, then $O(n)$ attributes will be compared with the $O(m)$ constraints containing *attr*, giving, in the worst case, a $O(nm)$ complexity for each *attr*. Thus, the complexity of the second phase of function **fragment** is $O(n^2m)$.

Finally, the overall time complexity is therefore $O(n^2m)$.   ■

7   Related Work

A significant amount of research has recently been dedicated to the study of the outsourced data paradigm. Most of this research has assumed the data to be entirely encrypted, focusing on the design of techniques for the efficient execution of queries (Database As a Service paradigm). One of the first proposals towards the solution of this problem is presented in [8,9], where the authors propose storing additional indexing information together with the encrypted database. Such indexes can be used by the DBMS to select the data to be returned in response to a query. In [5] the authors propose a hash-based index technique for equality queries, together with a B+ tree technique applicable to range queries. In [18] the authors propose an indexing method which, exploiting B-trees, supports both equality and range queries, while reducing inference exposure thanks to an almost flat distribution of the frequencies of index values. In [3,5] the authors present different approaches for evaluating the inference exposure for encrypted data enriched with indexing information, showing that even a limited number of indexes can greatly facilitate the task for an attacker wishing to violate the confidentiality provided by encryption.

The first proposal suggesting the storage of plaintext data, while enforcing a series of privacy constraints, is presented in [1]. The main difference with the work proposed in this paper is that in [1] the authors suppose data to be stored on two remote servers, belonging to two different service providers, which never exchange information. This choice also forces to design a fragmentation schema with at most two separate fragments. The approach presented in our paper removes all these restrictions and appears more adequate to the requirements of real scenarios. Our approach may force the use of a greater amount of storage, but in typical environments this presents a smaller cost than that required for the management and execution of queries on remote database servers managed by fully independent third parties.

Our work may bring some resemblance with the work of classifying information while maximizing visibility [6]. However, while the two lines of work share the goal of ensuring protection and minimizing security measures enforcement, the consideration of fragmentation and encryption on the one side and security labeling on the other makes the problems considerably different.

The problem of fragmenting relational databases while maximizing query efficiency has been addressed by others in the literature and some approaches have been proposed [11,12]. However, these approaches are not applicable to our problem since they are only aimed at performance optimization and do not allow taking into consideration protection requirements.

8 Conclusions

We presented a model and a corresponding concrete approach for the definition and management of privacy requirements in data collection. Our work provides a direct response to the emerging demand by individuals as well as privacy regulators.

Besides being a technical contribution, we hope that our work can represent a step towards the effective enforcement, as well as the establishment, of privacy regulations. Technical limitations are in fact claimed as one of the main reasons why privacy cannot be achieved and, consequently, regulations not be put into enforcement. Research on the line of ours can then help in providing the building blocks for a more precise specification of privacy needs and regulations as well as their actual enforcement, together with the benefit of a clearer and more direct integration of privacy requirements within existing ICT infrastructures.

Acknowledgements

This work was supported in part by the European Union under contract IST-2002-507591, and by the Italian Ministry of Research, within programs FIRB, under project "RBNE05FKZ2", and PRIN 2006, under project "Basi di dati crittografate" (2006099978). The work of Sushil Jajodia was partially supported by the National Science Foundation under grants CT-0627493, IIS-0242237, and IIS-0430402.

References

1. Aggarwal, G., Bawa, M., Ganesan, P., Garcia-Molina, H., Kenthapadi, K., Motwani, R., Srivastava, U., Thomas, D., Xu, Y.: Two can keep a secret: a distributed architecture for secure database services. In: CIDR 2005. Proc. of the 2nd Conference on Innovative Data Systems Research, Asilomar, California, USA (January 2005)

2. California senate bill SB 1386 (September 2002)
3. Ceselli, A., Damiani, E., De Capitani di Vimercati, S., Jajodia, S., Paraboschi, S., Samarati, P.: Modeling and assessing inference exposure in encrypted databases. ACM Transactions on Information and System Security 8(1), 119–152 (2005)
4. Ciriani, V., De Capitani di Vimercati, S., Foresti, S., Samarati, P.: k-anonymity. In: Yu, T., Jajodia, S. (eds.) Security in Decentralized Data Management, Springer, Heidelberg (2007)
5. Damiani, E., De Capitani di Vimercati, S., Jajodia, S., Paraboschi, S., Samarati, P.: Balancing confidentiality and efficiency in untrusted relational DBMSs. In: CCS03. Proc. of the 10th ACM Conference on Computer and Communications Security, Washington DC, USA, October 2003, ACM Press, New York (2003)
6. Dawson, S., De Capitani di Vimercati, S., Lincoln, P., Samarati, P.: Maximizing sharing of protected information. Journal of Computer and System Sciences 64(3), 496–541 (2002)
7. Garey, M.R., Johnson, D.S.: Computers and intractability: a guide to the theory of NP-completeness. W.H. Freeman, New York (1979)
8. Hacigümüs, H., Iyer, B., Mehrotra, S.: Providing database as a service. In: ICDE'02. Proc. of the 18th International Conference on Data Engineering, San Jose, California, USA, IEEE Computer Society, Los Alamitos, California (February 2002)
9. Hacigümüs, H., Iyer, B., Mehrotra, S., Li, C.: Executing SQL over encrypted data in the database-service-provider model. In: Proc. of the 2002 ACM SIGMOD International Conference on Management of Data, Madison, Wisconsin, USA, ACM Press, New York (2002)
10. Krivelevich, M., Sudakov, B.: Approximate coloring of uniform hypergraphs. Journal of Algorithms 49(1), 2–12 (2003)
11. Navathe, S., Ceri, S., Wiederhold, G., Dou, J.: Vertical partitioning algorithms for database design. ACM Transaction on Database Systems 9(4), 680–710 (1984)
12. Navathe, S., Ra, M.: Vertical partitioning for database design: a graphical algorithm. In: Proc. of the 1989 ACM SIGMOD International Conference on Management of Data, Portland, Oregon, USA, ACM Press, New York (June 1989)
13. Payment card industry (PCI) data security standard (September 2006), https://www.pcisecuritystandards.org/pdfs/pci_dss_v1-1.pdf
14. Personal data protection code: Legislative Decree no. 196 (June 2003)
15. Samarati, P.: Protecting respondent's privacy in microdata release. IEEE Transactions on Knowledge and Data Engineering 13(6), 1010–1017 (2001)
16. Schneier, B.: Applied Cryptography: protocols, algorithms, and source code in C, 2nd edn. John Wiley & Sons, New York (1996)
17. Hofmeister, T., Lefmann, H.: Approximating Maximum Independent Sets in Uniform Hypergraphs. In: Brim, L., Gruska, J., Zlatuška, J. (eds.) MFCS 1998. LNCS, vol. 1450, Springer, Heidelberg (1998)
18. Wang, H., Lakshmanan, L.V.S.: Efficient secure query evaluation over encrypted XML databases. In: VLDB'06. Proc. of the 32nd International Conference on Very Large Data Bases, Seoul, Korea, ACM Press, New York (September 2006)

Information Confinement, Privacy, and Security in RFID Systems

Roberto Di Pietro[1] and Refik Molva[2]

[1] Dipartimento di Matematica
Università di Roma Tre
L.go S. Murialdo, 1 - 00146 Roma, Italy
dipietro@mat.uniroma3.it
[2] Institut Eurécom
2229, route des crêtes
Sophia-Antipolis, France
refik.molva@eurecom.fr

Abstract. This paper describes an identification and authentication protocol for RFID tags with two contributions aiming at enhancing the security and privacy of RFID based systems. First, we assume that some of the servers storing the information related to the tags can be compromised. In order to protect the tags from potentially malicious servers, we devise a technique that makes RFID identification server-dependent, providing a different unique secret key shared by each pair of tag and server. The proposed solution requires the tag to store only a single secret key, regardless of the number of servers, thus fitting the constraints on tag's memory. Second, we provide a probabilistic tag identification scheme that requires the server to perform simple bitwise operations, thus speeding up the identification process. The proposed tag identification protocol assures privacy, mutual authentication and resilience to both DoS and replay attacks. Finally, each of the two schemes described in this paper can be independently implemented to enhance the security of existing RFID protocols.

1 Introduction

Radio Frequency IDentification (RFID) is a technology for automated identification of objects and people. An RFID device, also known as *tag*, is a small microchip designed for wireless data transmission. It is generally attached to an antenna in a package that resembles an ordinary adhesive sticker. The applications of RFID ranges from cattle monitoring to e-passport [1].

The other components of an RFID system are readers and servers. A reader is a device querying tags for identification information, while all information about tags (ID, assigned keys, etc.) are maintained on servers. A server can be assigned multiple readers; in this case it only engages in communication with its constituent readers. It is generally assumed to have a single logical server that might resolve to multiple physically replicated servers. All communications between server and readers is assumed to be over private and authentic channels. Both readers and server do not suffer of constraints on power, processing, memory, and bandwidth.

J. Biskup and J. Lopez (Eds.): ESORICS 2007, LNCS 4734, pp. 187–202, 2007.

Furthermore, based on a widely agreed assumption, servers, readers and the link between them are assumed to be trusted in that only the tags and the communication channel between the tag and the readers are assumed to be potentially vulnerable to malicious attacks [1,2]. In this paper we relax this hypothesis by assuming a more general setting whereby tags, servers and readers can be subject to malicious attacks. In that context, we focus on the problem of tag identification by multiple servers that are either replicas of the same logical server or different servers governed by independent authorities like in the case of electronic passports. As a result of the relaxed security hypothesis, the new requirement in this setting is to cope with the compromise of servers. Apart from the obvious need to perform mutual authentication, as opposed to one-way authentication of the tag by the server, server compromise calls for new measures to prevent possible attacks originating from the leakage of secrets stored in the compromised server's authentication database. For instance, based on most existing tag authentication protocols, using the entries of a compromised server's authentication database, the attacker can fabricate duplicate tags (i.e. e-passports). The first contribution of this paper is an information confinement technique aiming at keeping the impact of server compromise limited. Thanks to this technique, the compromise of a server does not affect the authentication of any tag by other servers, be they replicas of the same logical server or different servers. A simple solution for confinement could consist of having each tag and server pair share a unique set of secrets. However, this solution would not be suitable with the memory constraints of RFID tags since with m servers, each RFID tag would have to store m pieces of information. The solution proposed in this paper requires the RFID tag to store a single secret key for all servers yet assuring the confinement property in case of server compromise.

Another challenging issue that affects the RFID systems is the responsiveness of the server during tag identification. It is usually the case that the server needs to search its DB of locally stored keys and to perform a cryptographic operation on each of these keys in order to identify the tag. In some scenarios the cost and the time required to identify a tag can be prohibitive due to the total number of tags that can potentially interact with the same server. Existing proposals for RFID identification try to reduce the complexity of the search operation performed by the server without requiring the tag to perform costly operations. Along the same lines, the second contribution of this paper is an efficient identification technique based on a probabilistic mechanism for the server to identify the tag that requires both the tag and the server to perform only bitwise operations. Through a three-way handshake protocol this identification technique also achieves mutual authentication, as well as resilience against DoS and replay attacks. Moreover, the proposed identification technique is shown to preserve the privacy of the tag. Finally, note that either of the two contributions can be independently incorporated into existing protocols.

The sequel of the paper is structured as follows: next section introduces the related work; Section 3 outlines the system assumptions and Section 4 presents a mutual authentication protocol incorporating the confinement and probabilistic identification techniques, while Section 5 is devoted to the security evaluation and overhead analysis of this protocol. Finally, in Section 6 we expose some concluding remarks.

2   Related Work

A standard approach to provide security in RFID protocols [3,4] consists of using a unique key for each tag such that only the verifier (server) knows all the keys. This approach suffers from an expensive time complexity on the server side. Indeed, because only symmetric cryptographic functions can be used, the server needs to explore its entire database in order to retrieve the identity of the tag it is interacting with. If n is the number of tags managed by the server, $O(n)$ cryptographic operations are required in order to identify one tag. The advantage of the server over an adversary is that the server knows in which subset of identifiers it needs to search while the adversary has to explore the full range of identifiers.

In [3] a proposal that requires just $\log_\delta n$ interactions between the server and a tag for the server to identify the tag is proposed. However, this approach requires $\log_\delta$ keys to be stored on each tag and in [5] it has been proved that this technique weakens the privacy when an adversary is able to tamper with at least one tag. Further, the more tags an adversary tampers with, the more privacy is exposed.

A general solution, also adopted in [2,4] is to employ hash chains to allow tag identification and mutual authentication between the tag and the server. However, note that the hash chain length corresponds to the lifetime of the tag, which must be therefore stated in advance, leading to a waste of memory on the server side. Moreover, as the same author of [2] recognizes, this solution is prone to DoS attack, in that an adversary can easily exhaust the hash chain via reading attempts.

In [5,6] the authors optimizes a technique originally proposed in [7]. This technique allows to trade-off between time and the memory required on the reader. In particular, the time T required to invert any given value in a set of N outputs of a one-way function $h(\circ)$ with the help of M units of memory is $T = N^2\gamma/M^2$, where γ is a factor (usually a small one: < 10) to account for success probability. However, note that the technique is still prone to DoS attack and requires more computations on the server side. Leveraging this idea, in [8] the authors propose a new RFID identification protocol —RIPP-FS— that enforces privacy and forward secrecy, as well as resilience to a specific DoS attack, where the goal of the adversary is to force the tag to overuse the hash chain that has a finite length originally set to last for the tag's expected lifetime.

Aforementioned solutions assume that servers are trusted and cannot be compromised. The first requirement raised by relaxing this hypothesis is for mutual authentication. An interesting solution to mutual authentication is exposed in [9]: the authors are inspired by the work in [10] to introduce the $HB+$ protocol, a novel, symmetric authentication protocol with a simple, low-cost implementation. The security of the HB+ protocol against active adversaries is proved and based on the hardness of the Learning Parity with Noise (LPN) problem. The protocol is based on r rounds, where r is the security parameter, and each round requires: the tag and the server to send a message of $|\ell|$ bits to each other, where $|\ell|$ is the key length; to perform two inner product over terms of $|\ell|$ bits. A further work [11] showed the vulnerability of the HB+ protocol against a man in the middle (MIM) attack. A fix to the MIM attack HB+ was subject to was proposed in [12], through the HB++ protocol. Furthermore, HB++ was proven in [13] to be subject to a particular attack in which the adversary could gain knowledge of the private key of the tag, hence jeopardizing the authentication mechanism.

3 System Assumptions/Model

The components of the system are: tags, readers and key distribution centers (KDCs). KDCs represent the authorities ruling over a set of tags. Each KDC generates a unique key k_i for every tag tag_i that is under its jurisdiction and securely stores it in the tag. The KDC also provides each reader $reader_j$ that is authorized to identify a tag tag_i that is under its jurisdiction with a derived tag identification key $k_{i,j}$ along with the identifier ID_i of the tag. Each tag can thus be identified by one or several readers based on the derived tag identification keys distributed by the KDC. Each reader keeps in a secure key database (KDB) the set of derived tag identification keys and identifiers of the tags it is authorized to identify. It should be noted that in this model a reader can be associated with more than one KDC or be able to identify tags issued by several authorities.

Each tag has the capability to run a pseudo random number generator (PRNG) and a secure hash function $h(\circ)$, as assumed in literature [2,3,5]. The KDC assigns a unique key k_i to tag_i. The derived tag identification key $k_{i,j}$ will be generated by the KDC during the initialization of $reader_j$'s KDB, based on the expression $k_{i,j} = h(k_i||reader_j||k_i)$, where $"||"$ denotes concatenation. In the following we will assume the KDB to host n entries and $KDB[g]$ to return the key $k_{g,j}$.

4 The Protocol

This section presents first the protocol through which the confinement and probabilistic identification techniques are implemented. Further details are then provided on the mutual authentication and the lookup process that is the underpinning of the probabilistic identification technique.

4.1 Overview of the Solution

Our proposal for tag identification and mutual authentication is based on a simple three-way handshake, as depicted in Figure 1. In the first flow, the reader sends a challenge and its identity to the tag. The tag replies with a response message computed based on its secret key, the identity of the reader, the challenge and a set of locally generated pseudo random numbers. The reader retrieves the identity of the tag through a lookup in its local database. If the lookup succeeds, the reader has authenticated the tag. The last flow of the protocol allows the tag to authenticate the reader. The main idea of our solution for information confinement is a reader-dependent identification mechanism that allows each reader (or the server to which the reader is connected to) to identify and authenticate a tag based on some long-term secret ($k_{i,j}$) that is different on each server whereas each tag keeps a unique secret identification key (k_i) for all readers. During the identification process each tag generates a temporary reader-dependent secret based on the identifier ID_j of the reader it is communicating with and its unique secret identification key k_i, computing $k_{i,j} = h(k_i||ID_j||k_i)$. The advantages of the reader-dependent mechanism are twofold:

- confinement of exposure: compromise of the long term secrets at a reader does not threaten the integrity of the identification by other readers.

– selective reader access or non-transferable tag identification capability: the set of readers authorized to perform tag identification can be controlled based on each reader's identity. Since the long-term identification secret for a tag is tightly bound with each reader's id, the identification capability cannot be transferred among readers with different identities and the set of tags each reader is authorized to identify can be determined based on the set-up of long-term identification keys.

Another innovative feature of our proposal is the efficiency of the lookup process. Based on the response message transmitted by the tag, the reader searches the matching entry of its database (if any) by iterative elimination of the entries that cannot match with the entry it is looking for. The response message includes a series of verification values $(\alpha_1, \ldots, \alpha_q)$ computed under the key $k_{i,j}$ associated with the tag and the reader. Each verification value allows the reader to eliminate about one half of the *active* entries in the KDB — where an active entry is an entry that has not been eliminated yet. By subsequently eliminating active entries at each step, the reader achieves the identification of the tag. Unlike other solutions whereby each step of the lookup process requires encryption or hashing, the lookup process we provide is efficient in that it requires $O(n \log n)$ bit-wise operations (where n is the number of tags) and only uses simple comparison of memory cells.

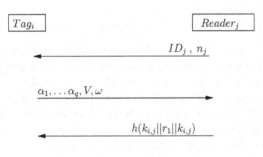

Fig. 1. The proposed protocol

4.2 Lookup Process

The lookup process allows the reader to identify the tag based on the following messages sent by the tag in the second flow of the protocol: $< \alpha_1, \ldots, \alpha_q, V, w >$, where $\omega = h(k_{i,j}||n_j||r_1||k_{i,j})$, V is a bit vector of length q and, for $p \in [1 \ldots q]$, it holds:

$$\alpha_p = k_{i,j} \oplus r_p \qquad (1)$$

$$V[p] = DPM(r_p) \qquad (2)$$

where the value r_p is the result of the invocation of the PRNG. Note that the bit length of r_p and $k_{i,j}$ is the same, that is $|k_{i,j}| = |r_p| = \ell$, and $r_p[i]$ denotes the ith bit of the bit vector r_p. In the following we assume, without losing of generality, that ℓ is a multiple of 3. The function $DPM : \{0,1\}^\ell \to \{0,1\}$ is defined as follows:

$$DPM(r_p) = P(M(S_1), \ldots, M(S_{\ell/3}))$$

where each S_i accounts for a triplet of bits of r_p as follows:

$$S_i = < r_p[3i - 2], r_p[3i - 1], r_p[3i] >, i = 1, \ldots, \ell/3$$

the function $M : \{0, 1\}^3 \to \{0, 1\}$ is the simple *majority* function, indicating whether its input has more 1s than 0s or viceversa:

$$M(b_1, b_2, b_3) = (b_1 \wedge b_2) \vee (b_1 \wedge b_3) \vee (b_2 \wedge b_3)$$

and $P : \{0, 1\}^{\ell/3} \to \{0, 1\}$ is the standard parity function; that is, given $T \in \{0, 1\}^{\ell/3}$, it holds:

$$P(T) = \bigoplus_{i=1}^{\ell/3} T[i].$$

For each value α_p ($p \in [1, \ldots q]$) transmitted by the tag, the reader will perform a check for each of its active entries. Let us focus on the gth entry of the KDB and assume it is active; the following check will be performed:

1. compute $r' = KDB[g] \oplus \alpha_p$;
2. check if $DPM(r') = V[p]$.

If the check fails, the gth entry is discarded and the next entry of the KDB, if any, is examined. However, if the check succeeds, the current entry of KDB cannot be discarded. Indeed, if $KDB[g]$ is the actual entry associated with the tag, that is, if $KDB[g] = k_{i,j}$, the check will succeed by construction. On the other hand, if the check fails, the current entry definitely cannot be the one associated with the tag. Finally, note that for each α_p on the average one half of the active entries are eliminated. A thorough analysis of the lookup process can be found in Section 4.4.

4.3 Mutual Authentication and Session Freshness

Assume that the look up process completes, returning a single entry of the KDB to the reader ($KDB[i]$). On one hand, as shown by the analysis of the lookup process in the next section, for an appropriate choice of the value q this will happen with high probability if the tag is a legitimate one, i.e. belonging to the set of tags recorded in the KDB. On the other hand, if the tag it is not a legitimate one, with high probability no entry will be returned. Hence, when the lookup procedure returns a single entry, we will assume in this subsection that the returned entry identifies the tag. Once the reader has identified the tag —let $k_{i,j}$ be the key in the KDB returned by the identification protocol —, the reader first recovers r_1 ($r_1 = \alpha_1 \oplus k_{i,j}$) and then proceeds to authenticate the tag and to verify the freshness of the session just computing $z = h(k_{i,j}||n_j||r_1||k_{i,j})$ and verifying whether $z = \omega$. If the latter match succeeds, the reader has successfully authenticated the tag and verified the freshness of the session.

In the following we show how the tag authenticates the reader. We start by observing that once the reader has successfully identified the tag, the reader can easily retrieve

---

Global variables: n ; q ; KDB
Input   : $< \alpha_1, \ldots, \alpha_q, V, w >$
Output   : The active entries of the KDB.

1.1 **for** $i=1$ **to** n **do**
1.2 | $Active[u] = True$
1.3 **end**
1.4 $count = 0; a = 0$
1.5 **while** $a < q$ **do**
1.6 | $u = 0$
1.7 | **while** $u < n$ **do**
1.8 | | **if** $Active[u]$ **then**
1.9 | | | $r' = \alpha_a \oplus KDB[u]$
1.10 | | | **if** DPM$(r') \neq V[a]$ **then**
1.11 | | | | $Active[u] = False$
1.12 | | | | $count + +$
1.13 | | | **end**
1.14 | | **end**
1.15 | | $u + +$
1.16 | **end**
1.17 | $a + +$
1.18 **end**
1.19 **if** $count = n$ **then**
1.20 | fail
1.21 **else**
1.22 | **return** $KDB[j]$ *s.t.* $Active[j] = True$
1.23 **end**

Algorithm 1. Lookup

each of the q values r_p ($p \in [1, \ldots, q]$) generated by the tag. Indeed, from Equation 1, r_p can be computed by the reader as: $r_p = \alpha_p \oplus KDB[i]$. Hence, the reader authenticates itself to the tag and assures the freshness of the session by sending to the tag the value $h(k_{i,j}||r_1||k_{i,j})$. If this value matches with the one locally stored on the tag - computed by the tag when r_1 was generated - then the tag authenticates the reader and it is also assured about the freshness of the session.

4.4 Analysis

Server compromise: in case $reader_j$ is compromised the attacker can only access $k_{i,j}$, $i = 1..n$. Under the assumption that the hash function is one-way, it is impossible to derive k_i from $k_{i,j}$; hence the attacker cannot impersonate any of the n tags within any run of the protocol with any other reader. Further, note that the reader cannot impersonate any reader other than $reader_j$ either.

Identification protocol: in the sequel we show that the lookup protocol completes and we prove its correctness.

Protocol termination: from Table 1 it can be verified that the protocol terminates after a finite number of iterations in the two inner loops; further, its completion takes at most $O(nq)$ steps, where each step consists of simple xor operations and a comparison. In the following it is shown that $q = O(\log n)$, yielding an overall complexity of $O(n \log n)$ bitwise comparisons.

Protocol correctness: the following lemma show that the proposed protocol will never reject a valid tag, while it could accept a bogus tag or return the wrong entry of the KDB for a valid tag, with a probability ϵ, where ϵ can be decided at design phase.

Lemma 1. *For each valid input to the the Lookup Process provided by a valid tag tag_i, $Active[i]$ will take on value $True$ on all iterations of the Lookup Process.*

Proof. By construction, the key $k_{i,j}$ corresponding to a valid input will never fail any of the tests in the inner loop starting at line 1.7 of Algorithm 1; hence, $Active[i]$ will never be assigned with the value $False$.   □

Lemma 2. *A randomly chosen input will be accepted by the Lookup Process with probability less than ϵ, where ϵ is chosen at design phase.*

Proof. Let $I = < \alpha_1, \ldots, \alpha_q, V, w >$ be a randomly chosen input for the Lookup Process. Let $X_i[u]$ be the random variable that takes on the value 1 if the value α_i will not set an entry of the Active vector to $False$ in Algorithm 1 — that is if $V[i] = P(M(\alpha_i \oplus k_{u,j}))$— and 0 otherwise. In order for I to be considered a valid input with respect to a single entry ($KDB[u]$) of the KDB, all q tests have to succeed. This happens with probability: $Pr[E_u] = Pr[X_1[u] = 1 \wedge X_2[u] = 1 \wedge \ldots \wedge X_q[u] = 1]$. Since the X_i are i.i.d, we have that $Pr[E_u] = Pr[X_1[u] = 1]^q$ where, as it will be shown in Lemma 3:

$$Pr[X_1[u] = 1] = \frac{1}{2}.$$

Since there are n entries in the KDB, the probability that at least one of them survives after q steps is $Pr[E_1 \vee \ldots \vee E_n] \leq nPr[E_1] < n(1/2)^q = (1/2)^{-q+\log n}$. Now let r be the highest integer such that $\epsilon \leq 2^{-r}$. If we set $q = r + \log n$, the lemma holds.   □

In Figure 2 we report an experiment to support the previous result. We implemented a simulator for Algorithm 1. We generated a KDB of 65,536 entries, and tested the number of active entries that were left in the KDB for an increasing size of the value q, that is the number of α_i sent by the tag to the reader. In particular, we varied q in the range $[(\log n)/2, \ldots, 10 + \log n]$, that is in the range $[8, \ldots, 26]$, using an incremental step of 1. On the x-axis we report the value q, while on the y-axis the number of active entries left in the KDB. To amortize statistical fluctuation, for each value of q, we performed 256 identification attempts, and we reported on the y-axis the number of active entries left in the KDB, averaged over these 256 protocol runs. As it can be seen from Figure 2, the number of active entries left in the KDB that result from the simulation is in accordance with the theoretical result of Lemma 2.

Theorem 1. *On a valid input I generated by a legitimate tag (tag_i) the Lookup Process will return only the entry $KDB[i]$ with probability at least $1 - \epsilon$, where ϵ is chosen at design phase.*

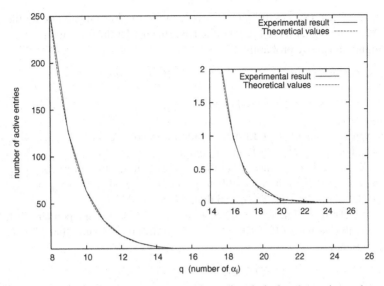

Fig. 2. Reader false acceptance rate: comparison of analytical and experimental results

Proof. This theorem can be reworded as: on a valid input, when the Lookup Process ends, the probability that only one entry of the *Active* vector is still set to *True* and that this entry is the one matching the input is $1 - \epsilon$. The proof of this theorem follows from Lemma 1 and Lemma2. Based on Lemma 1 the probability that the entry of the *Active* vector matching the input is set to *True* after the last iteration of the Lookup Process is 1. The probability that at least one more entry has the value *True* when the Lookup Process ends is the same as the probability that a randomly chosen input is accepted, that is less than ϵ by Lemma 2.

5   Security Analysis and Overhead

Due to space limitations, a formal proof of the security properties as well as a thorough comparison with [9] will appear in the extended version of this paper. Nevertheless, in the sequel of this paper we will provide an intuition on the soundness of the security properties.

5.1   Key Secrecy and Privacy

A run of the identification protocols sends q times over the communication channel between the tag and the reader the key of the tag, each time xored with a random value (r_p). Hence, so far the security and privacy provided is that of the One Time Pad (OTP), that is perfect security and privacy. However, it should be noted that the protocol leaks one bit of information for each of the values r_i; this bit is conveyed in $V[i]$.

Key secrecy. To provide an intuition of how the secrecy of the proposed scheme is affected by the leakage of $V[i] = DPM(r_i)$, let us compute what is the probability that a random values $r' \in \{0,1\}^{\ell}$ verifies $DPM(r') = DPM(r_i)$. Indeed, for an adversary to mount a successful attack, it is required to discriminate among the set of possible keys; the bigger the set of possible keys, the harder the task, and the bigger this set, the higher the above probability.

Lemma 3. *Given a value $p \in \{0,1\}$, for $r' \in_R \{0,1\}^\ell$ it holds that:*

$$Pr[DPM(r') = p] = \frac{1}{2}$$

Proof. Given a vector of d i.i.d binary random variable $X =< X_1, \ldots, X_d >$ and $p \in \{0,1\}$, there exist 2^{d-1} different assignment of values to $< X_1, \ldots, X_d >$ such that $\oplus_{j=1}^{d} X_j = p$. For instance, note that in our identification protocol, for a given S_i (e.g. $S_i =< 1,1,1 >$), it is possible to generate three other S_{i_j} ($S_{i_1} =< 1,1,0 >$, $S_{i_2} < 1,0,1 >$, $S_{i_2} =< 0,1,1 >$) such that: $M(S_i) = M(S_{i_j})$.

Let $X_i = M(S_i)$ and note that the S_i ($i = 1, \ldots, \ell/3$) are independent. It follows that it is possible to have $(4^{\ell/3})(2^{\ell/3-1}) = 2^{\ell-1}$ different r'_i such that $DPM(r_i) = DPM(r'_i)$. Hence,

$$Pr[DPM(r') = p] = \frac{2^{\ell-1}}{2^\ell} = \frac{1}{2}$$

.   □

Privacy. To study the impact of one bit leakage on privacy, we consider a hypothetical protocol based on the original identification protocol defined in Section 4.2 with a slight modification that consists of the substitution of the $DPM(\circ)$ function by the parity function. Thus in the hypothetical protocol, $V[i] = P(r_i) = D\hat{P}M(r_i)$. It can be shown that the modified version of the protocol is similar to the original one with respect to the number of messages required to identify the appropriate key in the KDB, that is $O(\log n)$ messages. Moreover, as for the confidentiality of the key, it easily follows from Lemma 3 that the leakage of the parity bit just halves the key space. However, when it comes to privacy, the hypothetical protocol is basically flawed.

Indeed, assume the attacker can observe two different runs of the identification protocol: $< \alpha_{1,1}, \ldots, \alpha_{1,q}, V_1, \omega_1 >$ and $< \alpha_{2,1}, \ldots, \alpha_{2,q}, V_2, \omega_2 >$. Its task is to distinguish, with a non negligible probability, if the two flows intercepted were originated by the same tag or not.

Note that for two random bit vectors r_1, r_2, it can be shown that $D\hat{P}M(r_1 \oplus r_2) = D\hat{P}M(r_1) \oplus D\hat{P}M(r_2)$ — that is, the parity computed over the xor of vectors r_1, r_2 is equal to xoring the result of the parity computed over each single vector; this introduces an imbalance in the probability distribution that could be leveraged by an adversary tampering with privacy. In particular, let δ be the event "$D\hat{P}M(\alpha_{1,i} \oplus \alpha_{2,i}) = V_1[i] \oplus V_2[i]$". We can express $Pr[k_1 \neq k_2|\delta]$ as $Pr[k_1 \neq k_2|\delta] = 1/2 - |adv|$. In a perfect privacy preserving solution, we would have $|adv| = 0$. When trading off privacy with identification capabilities, as it is the case when leaking one bit of information, we would like to have $|adv|$ as small as possible, and possibly such that $\lim_{\ell \to \infty} |adv| = 0$; the faster the convergence to zero, the less is the advantage gained by the adversary. However, in this modified protocol, we have that $adv = 1/6$, as formalized with the following lemma:

Lemma 4. *Given the event $\delta = $"$D\hat{P}M(\alpha_{1,i} \oplus \alpha_{2,i}) = V_1[i] \oplus V_2[i]$". Then $Pr[k_1 \neq k_2|\delta] = 1/2 - 1/6$.*

Proof.

$$Pr[k_1 \neq k_2|\delta] = 1 - Pr[k_1 = k_2|\delta] = 1 - Pr[(k_1 = k_2) \wedge \delta]/Pr[\delta] =$$

$$1 - \frac{Pr[\delta|(k_1 = k_2)]Pr[k_1 = k_2]}{Pr[\delta]} =$$

$$1 - \frac{Pr[\delta|(k_1 = k_2)]Pr[k_1 = k_2]}{Pr[\delta|k_1 = k_2]Pr[k_1 = k_2] + Pr[\delta|k_1 \neq k_2]Pr[k_1 \neq k_2]}.$$

Now, as noticed above, we have that: $Pr[\delta|(k_1 = k_2)] = 1$ and $Pr[\delta|(k_1 \neq k_2)] = 1/2$. Plugging these equalities in the above equation, we obtain:

$$Pr[k_1 \neq k_2|\delta] = 1 - \frac{1 \times 1/2}{(1 \times 1/2) + 1/2 \times 1/2} = 1 - \frac{2}{3} = \frac{1}{2} - \frac{1}{6}$$

$\square$

We believe that capitalizing on the imbalance of the distribution probability a thorough attack targeting the privacy of the hypothetical protocol could be mounted. However, this is out the scope of the paper; the discussion so far was meant to give the reader the intuition behind the main rationale for the privacy evaluation of the original protocol. In particular, the main threat against privacy can be expressed as the *advantage* —*adv*— that was given to the adversary when computing: $Pr[\delta|k_1 = k_2] = Pr[DPM(\alpha_{1,i} \oplus \alpha_{2,i}) = V_1[i] \oplus V_2[i]|k_1 = k_2] = \frac{1}{2} + |adv|$. Turning to the original protocol proposed in this paper, we notice that the following theorem holds.

Theorem 2. *Let δ be the event* "$DPM(\alpha_{1,i} \oplus \alpha_{2,i}) = V_1[i] \oplus V_2[i]$". *Then* $Pr[k_1 \neq k_2|\delta] = \frac{1}{2} - \frac{\epsilon}{2(2+\epsilon)}$, *where* $\epsilon = \left(\frac{1}{2}\right)^{\frac{2}{3}\ell}$.

Proof. Following the demonstration flow of Lemma 4 we can rewrite $Pr[k_1 \neq k_2|\delta]$ as:

$$Pr[k_1 \neq k_2|\delta] = 1 - \frac{Pr[\delta|(k_1 = k_2)]Pr[k_1 = k_2]}{Pr[\delta|k_1 = k_2]Pr[k_1 = k_2] + Pr[\delta|k_1 \neq k_2]Pr[k_1 \neq k_2]}.$$

It can be proved (see **conditioned** in Appendix) that $Pr[\delta|k_1 = k_2] = 1/2 + (1/2)^{\frac{2}{3}\ell+1}$. Hence:

$$Pr[k_1 \neq k_2|\delta] = 1 - \frac{(1/2 + (1/2)^{\frac{2}{3}\ell+1})(1/2)}{(1/2 + (1/2)^{\ell+1})(1/2) + (1/2)(1/2)} =$$

$$1 - \frac{1/2 + (1/2)^{\frac{2}{3}\ell+1}}{1/2 + (1/2)^{\frac{2}{3}\ell+1} + 1/2} = \frac{1/2}{1 + (1/2)^{\frac{2}{3}\ell+1}} = \frac{1}{2 + (1/2)^{\frac{2}{3}\ell}} = \frac{1}{2} - \frac{\epsilon}{2(2+\epsilon)},$$

where $\epsilon = \left(\frac{1}{2}\right)^{\frac{2}{3}\ell}$.

$\square$

Therefore, using the attack that originally targeted the hypothetical protocol, the advantage of the attacker on our protocol decreases exponentially fast with the length of the key. In particular, this also provides a method for determining the appropriate key length. Indeed, by setting the maximum advantage for the adversary to $2^{-\tau}$, a key length that provides to the adversary an advantage less than $2^{-\tau}$ is given by $\ell = \lceil (3/2)(\tau-2) \rceil$. The previous equation was based on the following consideration: $\frac{\tau}{2(2+\tau)} \leq \frac{\tau}{4}$. As an illustration, to provide the adversary with an advantage less than 2^{-80}, the key length could be set to $\ell = \lceil (3/2)(\tau - 2) \rceil = \lceil (3/2)(80 - 2) \rceil = 117$.

5.2 Mutual Authentication

By Lemma 2 a bogus reply message generated by an attacker can be accepted with probability less than ϵ only. Further, such a scenario can be made practically impossible by setting appropriate values for q in order to keep ϵ below a negligible value. Besides, even a successful attempt that achieves acceptance of the random input by the Lookup Process cannot compromise authentication, since the attacker would not be able to complete the remainder of the protocol flows without the knowledge of the legitimate tag's secret key. The choice of the particular expression $h(k_{i,j}||n_j||r_1||k_{i,j})$ combining the key and the nonces as part of the authentication scheme is justified in [14].

As for reply attacks, the freshness of a session is granted by binding the messages exchanged to the random values generated by both the tag (r_1), and the reader (n_j), as in Figure 1.

5.3 DoS Resilience

Opposed to other approaches [2,5,6], our protocol is stateless in that there is no need to store any state information such as timestamps or counter values beyond the execution of each protocol instance. The only piece of information that the tag has to persistently keep in memory is the key k_i. Hence, even if a tag is triggered t consecutive times by an attacker attempting to impersonate a legitimate reader, if the next reading is performed by a legitimate reader, the tag will be correctly identified since the state has not been modified. Statelessness thus bestows our protocol with an inherent countermeasure against denial of service attacks.

Furthermore, as a side advantage of statelessness, our protocol allows a tag to be read a practically unbounded number of times by a legitimate reader.

5.4 Overhead

The main computational overhead on the tag is due to the generation of the q values r_p. These values could be computed via a PRNG. Similarly to what proposed in [2], in practice it can be resolved as an iterated keyed hash (e.g., HMAC) computed on some cheap, weak pseudo random source (for instance circuitry noise) and keyed on $k_{i,j}$. The solutions in [15,16], matching the tight hardware constraints of RFID, could be adopted to serve as hash function. Further, the tag requires to compute $q\ell$ "and" ($\wedge$), $q\ell$ "or" ($\vee$) —due to the recurrent invocation of the function $M(\circ)$— and $q\ell/3$ more "xor" ($\oplus$) due to the invocation of the function $P(\circ)$. Note that the sum of the cost of all these "xor", "or" and "and" operations can be considered negligible.

As for the communications overhead, the tag is required to send q messages of $|\ell|$ bits (α_p), plus q bits (the bit vector V), and the result of the hash function, that can be considered of 160 bits. We focus on the main source of overhead, that is the q messages.

From Lemma 2, a practical value for q could be $2 \log n$; in this way the reader lookup protocol will return, when triggered by a legitimate query, more than one entry only with probability $1/n$ on the average. As discussed before note that, in case the lookup protocol returns a bogus entry, the authentication protocol will reject that entry. Note that a new round of the protocol could be invoked in case of such a failure. What is more important, in case of a protocol re-run due to the fact that in the KDB there are too many active entries left, is that the new values α_i can be matched against the active entries left in the KDB. In other words, the computations performed by the reader in the previous run will be leveraged to pursue identification.

The main computational overhead sustained by the reader is the tag identification; this operation requires in the worst case no more than just $O(n \log n)$ bitwise operations and $O(n \log n)$ bit comparison. As for the number of messages, the reader just sends three values for a total of $(h + m + n_o)$ bits where h is the size in bit of the output of the hash function, m is the number of bits required to identify a reader, and n_o is the size in bit of the nonce.

Last, one should note one caveat: the proposed protocol is particularly sensitive to the value n, as shown in Lemma 2, where n is the total number of tags the system is composed of. Hence, the protocol requires to devise at design time an upper bound n' on the number of tags. We believe this is not a critical limitation, since this upper bound will impact on the protocol requiring just $c \log n'$ messages, where c is a small constant as seen before and computing the logarithm over n' will attenuate the overhead of considering an upper bound. Furthermore, the value n' does not affect the storage requirements of the reader since the reader is only required to store the keys of the n tags that are actually deployed.

5.5 Protocol Comparison

A concise comparison of the properties provided by our protocol with regard to a few reference protocols is given in Table 1. Note that our protocol is the only one that fulfils all the properties. Due to page limitation, a detailed discussion enriched with few more properties will be provided in the extended version of this paper.

Table 1. Comparison of our proposal with some protocols in Section 2

Protocol	Properties			
	Privacy	Mutual auth.	DoS resilience	reply attack res.
Our [this paper]	Yes	Yes	Yes	Yes
OSK/OA [5]	Yes	Yes	No	Yes
CR/MW [3]	weak	Yes	Yes	Yes
Ya-Trap[2]	Yes	No	No	Yes

6 Concluding Remarks

As a first contribution of this paper we have relaxed the assumption that servers cannot be compromised and have provided a solution that limits the impact of server compromise. In particular, thanks to the confinement technique we provide, the compromise of a server has no impact on other servers, such as rekeying or update of critical data, or on the privacy of tags since the secret database of each server is made server-dependent. Second, we have proposed a probabilistic mechanism that preserves privacy and allows mutual authentication between server and tag. This mechanism is also resilient to DoS and replay attacks. Further, it only requires $O(n \log n)$ bitwise operations and comparisons on the data base of keys stored in a server, hence speeding up the search process. Moreover, the tag just requires to store a single key and the capability to run a PRNG and a hash function. Finally, the information confinement technique and the tag identification protocol could be independently incorporated into existing solutions.

Current work is aimed at devising a possibly general formal framework to evaluate the security and privacy of the proposed solution.

References

1. Juels, A.: Rfid security and privacy: A research survey. IEEE Journal on Selected Areas in Communications 24(2), 381–394 (2006)
2. Tsudik, G.: Ya-trap: Yet another trivial rfid authentication protocol. In: IEEE PerCom Workshops, pp. 640–643. IEEE Computer Society Press, Los Alamitos (2006)
3. Molnar, D., Wagner, D.: Privacy and security in library rfid: issues, practices, and architectures. In: CCS '04: Proceedings of the 11th ACM conference on Computer and communications security, pp. 210–219. ACM Press, New York (2004)
4. Rhee, K., Kwak, J., Kim, S., Won, D.: Challenge-response based RFID authentication protocol for distributed database environment. In: Hutter, D., Ullmann, M. (eds.) SPC 2005. LNCS, vol. 3450, pp. 70–84. Springer, Heidelberg (2005)
5. Avoine, G., Dysli, E., Oechslin, P.: Reducing time complexity in RFID systems. In: Preneel, B., Tavares, S. (eds.) SAC 2005. LNCS, vol. 3897, pp. 291–306. Springer, Heidelberg (2006)
6. Avoine, G., Oechslin, P.: A scalable and provably secure hash based RFID protocol. In: International Workshop on Pervasive Computing and Communication Security – PerSec 2005, Kauai Island, Hawaii, USA, March 2005, pp. 110–114. IEEE, IEEE Computer Society Press, Los Alamitos (2005)
7. Hellman, M.: A cryptanalytic time-memory tradeoff. IEEE Transactions on Information Theory 26, 401–406 (1980)
8. Conti, M., Di Pietro, R., Mancini, L.V., Spognardi, A.: RIPP-FS: an rfid identification, privacy preserving protocol with forward secrecy. In: Proceedings of the 3rd IEEE International Workshop on Pervasive Computing and Communication Security, IEEE Press, Los Alamitos (to appear, 2007)
9. Juels, A., Weis, S.: Authenticating pervasive devices with human protocols. In: Shoup, V. (ed.) CRYPTO 2005. LNCS, vol. 3621, pp. 293–308. Springer, Heidelberg (2005)
10. Hopper, N.J., Blum, M.: Secure human identification protocols. In: Boyd, C. (ed.) ASIACRYPT 2001. LNCS, vol. 2248, pp. 52–66. Springer, Heidelberg (2001)
11. Gilbert, H., Robshaw, M., Sibert, H.: An active attack against HB+ - a provably secure lightweight authentication protocol. Cryptology ePrint Archive, Report 2005/237 (2005)
12. Bringer, J., Chabanne, H., Emmanuelle, D.: HB^{++}: a lightweight authentication protocol secure against some attacks. In: IEEE International Conference on Pervasive Services, Workshop on Security, Privacy and Trust in Pervasive and Ubiquitous Computing – SecPerU 2006, Lyon, France, June 2006, IEEE, IEEE Computer Society Press, IEEE International Conference on Pervasive Services (2006)

13. Piramuthu, S.: HB and related lightweight authentication protocols for secure RFID tag/reader authentication. In: Collaborative Electronic Commerce Technology and Research – CollECTeR 2006, Basel, Switzerland (June 2006)
14. Menezes, A.J., van Oorschot, P.C., Vanstone, S.A.: Chapter 9 - Hash Functions and Data Integrity. In: Handbook of applied cryptography, CRC Press, Boca Raton, USA (1996)
15. Feldhofer, M., Wolkerstorfer, J., Rijmen, V.: Aes implementation on a grain of sand. IEE Proceedings - Information Security 152(1), 13–20 (2005)
16. Pramstaller, N., Rechberger, C., Rijmen, V.: A compact fpga implementation of the hash function whirlpool. In: FPGA '06: Proceedings of the 2006 ACM/SIGDA 14th international symposium on Field programmable gate arrays, pp. 159–166. ACM Press, New York (2006)
17. Matsui, M.: Linear cryptanalysis method for des cipher. In: Helleseth, T. (ed.) EUROCRYPT 1993. LNCS, vol. 765, pp. 386–397. Springer, Heidelberg (1994)

Appendix

conditioned. In the sequel, we want to evaluate the *advantage* —*adv*— that is given to the adversary in Equation 3:

$$Pr[DPM(\alpha_1 \oplus \alpha_2) = V[1] \oplus V[2]|k_1 = k_2] = \tfrac{1}{2} + \left(\tfrac{1}{2}\right)^{-\frac{\ell}{3}+1} \prod_{i=1}^{\ell/3} \tfrac{1}{8} \qquad (3)$$
$$= \tfrac{1}{2} + \left(\tfrac{1}{2}\right)^{\frac{2}{3}\ell+1}$$

Note that the lower $|adv|$, the harder would be for the adversary to perform an educated guess in distinguishing between the two tags.

$$Pr[DPM(\alpha_{1,i} \oplus \alpha_{2,i}) = V_1[i] \oplus V_2[i]|k_1 = k_2] =$$
$$Pr[DPM(r_{1,i} \oplus r_{2,i}) = V_1[i] \oplus V_2[i]] =$$
$$Pr[M(S_{1,1} \oplus S_{2,1}) \oplus \ldots \oplus M(S_{1,\ell/3} \oplus S_{2,\ell/3}) =$$
$$M(S_{1,1}) \oplus \ldots \oplus M(S_{1,\ell/3}) \oplus M(S_{2,1}) \oplus \ldots \oplus M(S_{2,\ell/3})] =$$
$$Pr[(M(S_{1,1} \oplus S_{2,1}) \oplus M(S_{1,1}) \oplus M(S_{2,1})) \oplus \ldots \oplus$$
$$(M(S_{1,\ell/3} \oplus S_{2,\ell/3}) \oplus M(S_{1,\ell/3}) \oplus M(S_{2,\ell/3})) = 0]$$

Now, let $Z_i = (M(S_{1,i} \oplus S_{2,i}) \oplus M(S_{1,i}) \oplus M(S_{2,i})$. We can rewrite Equation 3 as:

$$Pr[DPM(\alpha_1 \oplus \alpha_2) = V[1] \oplus V[2]|k_1 = k_2] = Pr[Z_1 \oplus \ldots \oplus Z_{\ell/3} = 0].$$

Note that the Z_i are independent, hence we can apply the piling-up-lemma [17], obtaining:

$$Pr[DPM(\alpha_1 \oplus \alpha_2) = V[1] \oplus V[2]|k_1 = k_2] =$$
$$Pr[Z_1 \oplus \ldots \oplus Z_{\ell/3} = 0] = \frac{1}{2} + 2^{\frac{\ell}{3}-1} \prod_{i=1}^{\ell/3} \left(Pr[Z_i = 0] - \frac{1}{2} \right)$$

It can be shown (see **Prob.** here below) that $Pr[Z_i = 0] = 10/16$, hence we have that:

$$Pr[DPM(\alpha_1 \oplus \alpha_2) = V[1] \oplus V[2] | k_1 = k_2] = \frac{1}{2} + \left(\frac{1}{2}\right)^{\frac{\ell}{3}-1} \prod_{i=1}^{\ell/3} \frac{1}{8}$$

$$= \frac{1}{2} + \left(\frac{1}{2}\right)^{\frac{2}{3}\ell+1}$$

Prob. Let $Z_i = (M(S_{1,i} \oplus S_{2,i}) \oplus M(S_{1,i}) \oplus M(S_{2,i}))$. We have that:

$$Pr[Z_i = 0] = Pr[(M(S_{1,i} \oplus S_{2,i}) \oplus M(S_{1,i}) \oplus M(S_{2,i}) = 0] =$$
$$Pr[M(S_{1,i} \oplus S_{2,i}) = 0 \wedge M(S_{1,i}) = 0 \wedge M(S_{2,i}) = 0]+$$
$$Pr[M(S_{1,i} \oplus S_{2,i}) = 0 \wedge M(S_{1,i}) = 1 \wedge M(S_{2,i}) = 1]+$$
$$Pr[M(S_{1,i} \oplus S_{2,i}) = 1 \wedge M(S_{1,i}) = 0 \wedge M(S_{2,i}) = 1]+$$
$$Pr[M(S_{1,i} \oplus S_{2,i}) = 1 \wedge M(S_{1,i}) = 1 \wedge M(S_{2,i}) = 0] =$$
$$\frac{10}{64} + \frac{10}{64} + \frac{10}{64} + \frac{10}{64} = \frac{5}{8}.$$

Indeed, let:

$[M(S_{1,i} \oplus S_{2,i}) = 0 \wedge M(S_{1,i}) = 0 \wedge M(S_{2,i}) = 0] = $ C1;
$[M(S_{1,i} \oplus S_{2,i}) = 0 \wedge M(S_{1,i}) = 1 \wedge M(S_{2,i}) = 1] = $ C2;
$[M(S_{1,i} \oplus S_{2,i}) = 1 \wedge M(S_{1,i}) = 0 \wedge M(S_{2,i}) = 1] = $ C3;
$[M(S_{1,i} \oplus S_{2,i}) = 1 \wedge M(S_{1,i}) = 1 \wedge M(S_{2,i}) = 0] = $ C4,

it is possible to build the truth table for the above variables that confirm our numerical results (the truth table is omitted due to space limitation).

A Logic for State-Modifying Authorization Policies

Moritz Y. Becker[1] and Sebastian Nanz[2]

[1] Microsoft Research, Cambridge, CB3 0FB, UK
moritzb@microsoft.com
[2] Technical University of Denmark, 2800 Kgs. Lyngby, Denmark
nanz@imm.dtu.dk

Abstract. We present a logic for specifying policies where access requests can have effects on the authorization state. The logic is semantically defined by a mapping to Transaction Logic. Using this approach, updates to the state are factored out of the resource guard, thus enhancing maintainability and facilitating more expressive policies that take the history of access requests into account. We also present a sound and complete proof system for reasoning about sequences of access requests. This gives rise to a goal-oriented algorithm for finding minimal sequences that lead to a specified target authorization state.

1 Introduction

Trust management [1] has become a leading approach for controlling the access to security critical services in distributed environments. One of the reasons for this success is the flexibility and expressiveness provided by their associated authorisation query languages for policy specification. As depicted in Figure 1, these languages allow the authorization policy to be factored out of the hardcoded resource guard and written explicitly as a list of declarative rules. When a principal requests access, the resource guard issues an authorization query to the policy evaluator. Access is granted only if the policy evaluator succeeds in proving that the request complies with the local policy and the authorization state. The latter is a database containing relevant environmental facts including knowledge obtained from (submitted or fetched) credentials.

This approach hugely increases the maintainability of complex systems, as modifying the declarative policy rules is much simpler than rewriting and recompiling pieces of procedural code hidden in the resource guard. However, often the resource guard will not only allow or deny access, but also update the authorization state after a successful request. In a role-based policy, for instance, the fact that a user has activated some role is inserted into the authorization state after a successful role activation request. Similarly, the fact may be removed from the state if the role is deactivated. There are many policies that depend on past interactions; relevant events must therefore be stored in the authorization state. Consider for example the following scenario, where a company policy specifies that payments are only executed if they are initiated and authorized

J. Biskup and J. Lopez (Eds.): ESORICS 2007, LNCS 4734, pp. 203–218, 2007.

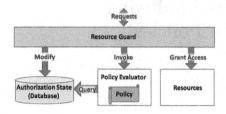

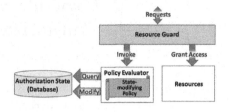

Fig. 1. Model of a policy-based authorization system

Fig. 2. Factoring out the state manipulations

by two different managers. The resource guard could then contain the following two procedures to implement this policy:

```
procedure initPay(X:Principal, P:Payment) {
  if query(isMgr(X)) and not(query(hasBeenInit(P))) then {
     insertFact(hasBeenInit(P));
     insertFact(hasInitPay(X, P))
   }
}
procedure authPay(X:Principal, P:Payment) {
  if query(isMgr(X)) and query(hasBeenInit(P)) and
     not(query(hasInitPay(X, P))) then
     insertFact(hasBeenAuth(P))
```

If user A attempts to initiate a payment P, the resource guard executes the procedure initPay(A, P), which issues queries to the policy evaluator to check whether A is a manager and that the payment has not already been initiated. If successful, the facts hasBeenInit(P) and hasInitPay(A, P) are inserted into the authorization state. A request of user B to authorize the same payment P is authorized if B can be proved to be a manager and that the payment has been initiated by someone else.

This example highlights a deficiency in current authorization languages: they cannot express updates of the authorization state, as required for many role-based, separation-of-duties and other history-dependent policies. Instead, updates have to be hard-coded into the resource guard, which leads to maintainability problems. Moreover, as the state changes happen outside the policy and are written in a Turing-complete language, rigorous analysis is difficult.

In this paper, we address this problem by introducing *SMP*, a logic for specifying policies with state-modifying user requests. State changes are thus factored out of the resource guard, as in Figure 2. For example, in our approach the above scenario could be modelled by the following two policy rules:

$$\mathsf{initPay}(X, P) \leftarrow \mathsf{isMgr}(X) \land \neg\mathsf{hasBeenInit}(P) \otimes$$
$$+\mathsf{hasBeenInit}(P) \otimes +\mathsf{hasInitPay}(X, P)$$
$$\mathsf{authPay}(X, P) \leftarrow \mathsf{isMgr}(X) \land \mathsf{hasBeenInit}(P) \land \neg\mathsf{hasInitPay}(X, P) \otimes$$
$$+\mathsf{hasBeenAuth}(P)$$

Intuitively, $+P$ specifies an insertion of a fact P into the authorization state, and the connective $\otimes$ expresses a serial execution of state changes.

The complexity of state-modifying policies calls for analysis tools that support policy authors in debugging policies. We present a proof system that describes all possible sequences of access requests which yield a certain outcome. This proof system is proved sound and correct with respect to the logic, and we describe a sound and complete algorithm for finding minimal sequences in the propositional case.

The remainder of this paper is structured as follows. In §2 we introduce *SMP* and motivate its syntax and semantics. In §3 we present a proof system for reasoning about sequences of access requests, and describe the related algorithm. In §4 we present a larger case study for using state-modifying authorization policies. We conclude in §5 with a discussion on related works. A technical report [2] contains full proofs.

2   A Logic for State-Modifying Policies

This section introduces the syntax and semantics of *SMP*. This logic is based on Datalog, but extends it with statements for state modification, henceforth called *effects*, and a simple form of negation. We assume a denumerable set of variables $\mathcal{X}$ and a first-order signature with constants $\mathcal{C}$ and disjoint sets of predicate symbols, *extensional* ($\mathcal{Q}_{ext}$) and *intensional* ($\mathcal{Q}_{int}$) ones, as in standard Datalog. In addition, we have a third set of so-called *command* predicate symbols $\mathcal{Q}_{cmd}$, intended to represent access requests. As usual, (extensional, intensional and command) *atoms* are formed by applying predicate symbols to ordered lists of constants or variables. A *literal* is either an atom P or a negated atom $\neg P$.

The extensional predicates are defined by an *extensional database* (EDB), a set of ground extensional atoms (*facts*). The validity of an extensional literal can thus be checked simply by inspecting the database. In the context of an authorization system, the database contains environmental facts that are relevant for authorization, e.g. hasInitPay(Alan, P123) or isUser(Alan). As we shall see later, facts may be inserted or removed from the database as the result of evaluating an access request. The database thus constitutes the transient state of an authorization system; hence we also call it the *authorization state*.

Definition 2.1. An *authorization state* **B** is a finite set of *facts*.

Intensional predicate symbols are defined by *rules*. A rule consists of an intensional atom P_{int} (the *head*) and a conditional *body*, a (possibly empty) conjunction of extensional or intensional literals: $P_{int} \leftarrow L_1 \wedge \ldots \wedge L_m$. For example, the intensional predicate symbol isMgr may be defined by a rule specifying that X is a manager if X is a user and if someone has registered X as a manager:

isMgr$(X) \leftarrow$ isUser$(X) \wedge$ hasRegisteredAsMgr(Y, X)

Negation is restricted to extensional atoms: $\neg P_{ext}$ holds if P_{ext} is not in the current authorization state. This is the simplest form of negation that is sufficient for our purposes.

Table 1. Syntax of *SMP*

Term	$t ::= X \mid a$	where $X \in \mathcal{X}, a \in \mathcal{C}$
Atom	$P_\tau ::= p(t_1, \ldots, t_k)$	where $p \in \mathcal{Q}_\tau, \tau \in \{ext, int, cmd\}$
Literal	$L ::= P_{int} \mid P_{ext} \mid \neg P_{ext}$	
Effect	$K ::= +P_{ext} \mid -P_{ext}$	
Rule	$Rl ::= P_{int} \leftarrow L_1 \wedge \ldots \wedge L_m$	where $m \geq 0$
	$\mid P_{cmd} \leftarrow L_1 \wedge \ldots \wedge L_m \otimes K_1 \otimes \ldots \otimes K_n$ where $m, n \geq 0$	

Access requests, or *commands*, are defined by *command rules*, i.e. rules with a command atom as head. In addition to the body, a command rule contains a (possibly empty) sequence of *effects* on the authorization state which are executed if all conditions in the body have been satisfied. An effect is either an insertion $(+P_{ext})$ of a fact P_{ext} into the authorization state or a removal $(-P_{ext})$. Effects are sequentially composed by the operator $\otimes$ from Transaction Logic. A command rule is thus of the form $P_{cmd} \leftarrow L_1 \wedge \ldots \wedge L_m \otimes K_1 \otimes \ldots \otimes K_n$. We sometimes write $\vec{L}$ to abbreviate $L_1 \wedge \ldots \wedge L_m$, and $\tilde{K}$ for $K_1 \otimes \ldots \otimes K_n$. Table 1 shows the complete *SMP* syntax.

Definition 2.2 (Well-formed Policy). A *policy* is a finite set of rules. A rule is *well-formed* if all variables of its effects also occur in the head; furthermore, if effects $+P_1$ and $-P_2$ occur in the same rule, then P_1 and P_2 are non-unifiable. A policy $\mathcal{P}$ is *well-formed* iff all rules in $\mathcal{P}$ are well-formed, and furthermore, whenever two ground instances of rules in $\mathcal{P}$ have the same head, their effects are identical.

The well-formedness conditions ensure that every ground command uniquely determines a sequence of ground effects, and furthermore, that the order of the sequence is irrelevant. As command literals cannot occur inside a body, effects can only occur at the top level: they are effectively decoupled from recursion. Recursive effects would not only be harder to compute and to comprehend, but worse, they would be non-deterministic.

Example 2.3. *We would like to write a policy for an online movie store. Informally, we would like to express that users can buy a movie online, and are then allowed to play it twice. This is expressed by the following transaction policy:*

$$\text{buy}(X, M) \quad \leftarrow +\text{bought}(X, M)$$
$$\text{play1}(X, M) \leftarrow \text{bought}(X, M) \wedge \neg \text{played1}(X, M) \otimes +\text{played1}(X, M)$$
$$\text{play2}(X, M) \leftarrow \text{played1}(X, M) \wedge \neg \text{played2}(X, M) \otimes +\text{played2}(X, M)$$

The semantics of *SMP* is formalized by modelling it as a fragment of Transaction Logic [3]. Transaction Logic is a general framework that incorporates database updates and transactions into first order logic. A Herbrand-style model theory of Transaction Logic is presented in detail in [3]. Based on this semantics, we define an entailment relation $\tilde{\mathbf{B}} \vDash_\mathcal{P} \phi$ between a sequence of authorization states

Table 2. *SMP* semantics

(pos)	$\mathbf{B} \vDash_{\mathcal{P}} P_{ext}$	iff $P \in \mathbf{B}$
(neg)	$\mathbf{B} \vDash_{\mathcal{P}} \neg P_{ext}$	iff $P \notin \mathbf{B}$
(and)	$\tilde{\mathbf{B}} \vDash_{\mathcal{P}} \phi \wedge \psi$	iff $\tilde{\mathbf{B}} \vDash_{\mathcal{P}} \phi$ and $\tilde{\mathbf{B}} \vDash_{\mathcal{P}} \psi$
(seq)	$\mathbf{B}_1, ..., \mathbf{B}_k \vDash_{\mathcal{P}} \phi \otimes \psi$	iff $\mathbf{B}_1, ..., \mathbf{B}_i \vDash_{\mathcal{P}} \phi$ and $\mathbf{B}_i, ..., \mathbf{B}_k \vDash_{\mathcal{P}} \psi$ for some $i \in \{1, ..., k\}$
(plus)	$\mathbf{B}_1, \mathbf{B}_2 \vDash_{\mathcal{P}} +P$	iff $\mathbf{B}_2 = \mathbf{B}_1 \cup \{P\}$
(min)	$\mathbf{B}_1, \mathbf{B}_2 \vDash_{\mathcal{P}} -P$	iff $\mathbf{B}_2 = \mathbf{B}_1 \setminus \{P\}$
(impl)	$\tilde{\mathbf{B}} \vDash_{\mathcal{P}} Q$	iff $Q \leftarrow \phi$ is a ground instantiation of a rule in $\mathcal{P}$ and $\tilde{\mathbf{B}} \vDash_{\mathcal{P}} \phi$
	where Q is not extensional	

$\tilde{\mathbf{B}}$ and a formula ϕ, in the context of a well-formed policy $\mathcal{P}$. This relation is presented in Table 2.

Intuitively, $\mathbf{B}_0, \ldots, \mathbf{B}_n \vDash_{\mathcal{P}} \phi$ means that the goal ϕ can be derived in the context of policy $\mathcal{P}$, starting from an initial authorization state $\mathbf{B}_0$. The evaluation of ϕ leads (via the intermediate states) to a final state $\mathbf{B}_n$. Rule (pos) and (neg) state that extensional literals are checked by inspecting the authorization state. This involves no effects, so the initial and final state are both identical. Rule (and) states that a database sequence $\tilde{\mathbf{B}}$ entails the conjunction of two formulae ϕ and ψ iff each of them is independently entailed by the same $\tilde{\mathbf{B}}$. In contrast, a serial composition $\phi \otimes \psi$ is entailed by $\mathbf{B}_1, ..., \mathbf{B}_k$ iff ϕ can be derived starting from $\mathbf{B}_1$ and ending in some intermediate state $\mathbf{B}_i$, and ψ can be derived starting from $\mathbf{B}_i$ and ending in $\mathbf{B}_k$. Rules (plus) and (min) straightforwardly describe the insertion and deletion of facts. Finally, rule (impl) defines the derivation for non-extensional literals.

3   Reasoning About User Requests

The increased complexity of state-modifying policies calls for proof techniques and tools to support the policy writer in establishing the correctness of a policy. For instance, in Example 2.3 a policy writer might like to determine the answers to the questions "Is there a command sequence that enables a user to play a movie without purchase?" and "Can a movie be played at least twice after purchase?". In this section, we develop a sound and complete proof system which determines the command sequences which yield a certain target authorization state, and also motivates an algorithm for deriving a finite abstraction of all such possible sequences.

3.1   State Constraints

In analyzing state-modifying policies, we are usually not interested in whether a specific authorization state is reachable. Rather, we wish to reason about the reachability of a family of target states that all satisfy some constraint; for example, all states containing some ground instantiation of the atom $\mathsf{played1}(X, M)$ but not the corresponding instantiation of $\mathsf{bought}(X, M)$. This would capture all states in which a movie has been played without purchase.

The following definition allows us to specify classes of authorization states by stating which atoms it must or must not contain.

Definition 3.1 (State Constraints). A *state constraint* D is a set of extensional literals. The notation D^+ (and D^-, respectively) is used to refer to the set of atoms derived from the positive (negative) literals in D. A state $\mathbf{B}$ *satisfies* a ground state constraint D iff $D^+ \subseteq \mathbf{B}$ and $D^- \cap \mathbf{B} = \emptyset$. A state constraint D is *consistent* iff $D^+ \cap D^- = \emptyset$.

For example, the state $\mathbf{B_0} = \{p(0), q(1), r(2)\}$ satisfies the state constraint $D = \{p(0), q(1), \neg r(1)\}$ because $D^+ = \{p(0), q(1)\} \subseteq \mathbf{B_0}$ and $D^- = \{r(1)\} \cap \mathbf{B_0} = \emptyset$. In this way D characterizes a family of states, namely the set of states that satisfy D. The state constraint $E = \{p(0), q(1), \neg p(0)\}$ is not consistent because $E^+ \cap E^- = \{p(0)\} \neq \emptyset$.

Example 3.2. *Continuing Example 2.3, a policy writer might be interested in establishing that there is no command sequence which leads to a state satisfying the constraint* $\{\neg \mathsf{bought}(X, M), \mathsf{played1}(X, M)\}$; *we will establish later that there exists no such sequence. On the other hand, we will be able to determine that the command sequence* $\mathsf{buy}(X, M) \otimes \mathsf{play1}(X, M)$ *leads from an arbitrary state to a state satisfying* $\{\mathsf{bought}(X, M), \mathsf{played1}(X, M)\}$.

Composing state constraints allows us to specify their transformation when a command is performed on them.

Definition 3.3 (Composition Operator). The operator $\circ$ defines a notion of composition for state constraints E and D:

$$(E \circ D)^+ = (D^+ \cup E^+) \setminus E^- \qquad (E \circ D)^- = (D^- \cup E^-) \setminus E^+$$

Intuitively, E can be interpreted as a set of effects, where positive literals in E are interpreted as insertions into D, and negative ones as removals. Then $E \circ D$ can be interpreted as the result of applying the effects in E to D. More precisely: it is the strongest constraint that is satisfied by states obtained by applying E to states satisfying D. For example, let $D = \{p(0), q(1), \neg r(1)\}$ as before and $E = \{\neg p(0), r(1), s(2)\}$ then $E \circ D = \{q(1), r(1), s(2), \neg p(0)\}$. This will enable us later to formulate the strongest postcondition when applying some command Q with effect E to a state constraint D.

Recall that the well-formedness conditions of policies ensure that every ground command atom is uniquely associated with a sequence of its effects. We can now define a mapping *eff* that maps a ground command atom to a state constraint that is equivalent to its effects:

Definition 3.4 (Specification of *eff*). Let Q be a ground command atom, and let $\tilde{K}$ be the (possibly empty) sequence of ground effects uniquely determined by it (in the context of a well-formed policy). Then $\mathit{eff}(Q)$ is defined as the state constraint

$$\mathit{eff}(Q) = \{P \ : \ +P \in \tilde{K}\} \cup \{\neg P \ : \ -P \in \tilde{K}\}$$

3.2 Preconditions and Effects

We wish to relate command sequences of the form $\tilde{S} = Q_1 \otimes \ldots \otimes Q_k$ to state constraints D that represent initial authorization states from which $\tilde{S}$ can successfully execute, and to state constraints D' that represent authorization states after executing the sequence. In other words, for all authorization states $\mathbf{B}$ and $\mathbf{B}'$ such that $\mathbf{B}$ satisfies D and $\mathbf{B}'$ satisfies D', $\mathbf{B}, \ldots, \mathbf{B}' \vDash_{\mathcal{P}} \tilde{S}$ should hold. We start by considering the case $k = 1$, where the command sequence consists of just one single command. The proof system developed in §3.3 then deals with command sequences of arbitrary lengths and captures exactly the above relationship between D, $\tilde{S}$ and D'.

In order to decide from which initial states a command successfully executes, we need to compute its *preconditions* as a state constraint. To determine the target states, we need to find its *effects*. For example, suppose a command predicate q is defined by a single policy rule (where p, r and s are all extensional):

$$q(X, Y) \leftarrow \neg p(X) \wedge r(Z) \otimes +p(X) \otimes -s(Y),$$

Then in order for the command $q(0, 1)$ to execute, the starting authorization state must satisfy the state constraint $\{\neg p(0), r(Z)\}$ containing the preconditions of the command. Likewise, due to the effects of the command, the end state contains $p(0)$ but cannot contain $s(1)$. Moreover, the atom $r(Z)$ is left untouched by the command, hence the end state satisfies $\{r(Z), p(0), \neg s(1)\}$.

The effects are easily obtained using the function *eff* defined in Definition 3.4 that reinterprets the sequence of effects as a state constraint (insertions $+P$ corresponds to positive literals P, and removals $-P$ to negative literals $\neg P$).

In the following, we define a function *pre* which yields the information about the (extensional) preconditions of a ground atom P. In the case where P is entirely defined by rules whose body literals are all extensional, it is easy to determine the preconditions. For instance, in the rule for $\mathsf{play1}(X, M)$ of Example 2.3 both bought and $\mathsf{played1}$ are extensional predicate symbols. Furthermore, $\mathsf{play1}$ is defined by only one single rule. Therefore the preconditions for executing $\mathsf{play1}(X, M)$ are given by a set containing only one state constraint:

$$pre(\mathsf{play1}(X, M)) = \{\{\mathsf{bought}(X, M), \neg\mathsf{played1}(X, M)\}\}$$

In general however, command predicates may be defined by multiple rules, and the body literals of those rules may be intensional, as in the following example.

Example 3.5. *We modify Example 2.3 by removing the* $\mathsf{buy}(X, M)$ *rule, and adding the following two rules (where* bought *is now an intensional predicate):*

$$\mathsf{bought}(X, M) \leftarrow \mathsf{bank}(Y), \mathsf{cardPayment}(X, Y, M)$$
$$\mathsf{bought}(X, M) \leftarrow \mathsf{freeTrial}(X)$$

These rules express that customer X has bought a movie M if he either paid for it using his credit card issued by a bank Y, or has signed up for a free trial offer *of the movie store. In this case,* pre(play1(X, M)) *is a set containing the two preconditions under which the command* play1 *can execute:*

$$F_1 = \{\text{bank}(Y), \text{cardPayment}(X, Y, M), \neg\text{played1}(X, M)\}$$
$$F_2 = \{\text{freeTrial}(X), \neg\text{played1}(X, M)\}$$

To specify *pre* formally, note that the bodies of the rules defining P determine its preconditions; in particular, the effects have no influence. We therefore introduce the following operation on policies that erases the effects:

Definition 3.6. Let $\mathcal{P}$ be a well-formed policy, and

$$Rl \equiv P_{cmd} \leftarrow L_1 \wedge \ldots \wedge L_m \otimes E_1 \otimes \ldots \otimes E_n$$

be one of its rules. Then $Rl^\star$ denotes the pure Datalog rule $P_{cmd} \leftarrow L_1 \wedge \ldots \wedge L_m$, where all effects have been removed. We write $\mathcal{P}^\star$ to denote the policy obtained from $\mathcal{P}$ by applying the $\star$-operation to all its rules.

We are now ready to specify *pre*:

Definition 3.7 (Specification of *pre*). The function *pre* is a mapping between ground atoms and sets of state constraints. It is defined by the following axiom which holds for any state **B** and ground atom P:

$$\exists\, F, \theta\ :\ F \in \text{pre}(P) \wedge \mathbf{B} \text{ satisfies } F\theta \quad \text{iff} \quad \mathbf{B} \vDash_{\mathcal{P}^\star} P$$

Read in the "only if"-direction, the axiom states that every authorization state satisfying a ground instantiation of a state constraint in $\text{pre}(P)$ indeed suffices as a precondition of P. In the "if"-direction, the axiom states that every extensional ground precondition is subsumed by some state constraint in $\text{pre}(P)$.

Note that literals in preconditions can also contain free variables, such as Y in the first rule of Example 3.5. These variables are instantiated by some substitution θ.

The function *pre* can be computed using *abduction* [4], a dual to *deduction*, where explanatory facts, e.g. F_1 in the example, are inferred from a desired result, e.g. bought(X, M), using some general (effect-free) logic program, $\mathcal{P}^\star$. Abduction algorithms for logic programs are documented in [5].

3.3   Proof System

Based on the notion of state constraints and the functions *pre* and *eff* defined above, we now present a Hoare-style proof system in which we can reason about pre- and postconditions of general command sequences. The proof system allows the inference of triples of the form $\{D_1\}\, \tilde{S}\, \{D_2\}$. Intuitively, this holds if $\tilde{S}$ can be executed from any authorization state satisfying D_1, and terminates in a state satisfying D_2. The empty command ε trivially transforms any ground and consistent state constraint G into itself, according to rule (eps). The rule (cmd) relates commands to their preconditions and postconditions based on *pre* and *eff*, but also incorporates precondition strengthening and postcondition

Table 3. Proof system

$$(\text{eps}) \frac{G \text{ is ground and consistent}}{\{G\}\,\varepsilon\,\{G\}} \qquad (\text{seq}) \frac{\{G_1\}\,\tilde{S}\,\{H\} \qquad \{H\}\,P\,\{G_2\}}{\{G_1\}\,\tilde{S} \otimes P\,\{G_2\}}$$

$$(\text{cmd}) \frac{\begin{array}{cc} G_1 \supseteq F\theta & F \in \text{pre}(P) & \text{eff}(P) \circ G_1 \supseteq G_2 \\ G_1 \text{ is ground and consistent} & P \text{ is ground} \end{array}}{\{G_1\}\,P\,\{G_2\}}$$

weakening: a command P transforms G_1 into G_2 if the following holds: there exists a substitution θ such that the free variables in a precondition $F \in \text{pre}(P)$ can be resolved with $G_1 \supseteq F\theta$, i.e. $F\theta$ is a weakest precondition for the execution of P and G_1 is strong enough to satisfy this preconditon; furthermore, G_2 has to be contained in $\text{eff}(P) \circ G_1$, i.e. G_2 is weaker than the *strongest postcondition* obtained by computing $\text{eff}(P) \circ G_1$. Finally, rule (seq) states that a sequence $\tilde{S}$ and a command P can be executed sequentially, if the postcondition of $\tilde{S}$ is strong enough to serve as a precondition for P.

The correctness of the proof system is ensured by the following soundness and completeness results, which relate it back to *SMP* semantics.

Theorem 3.8 (Soundness). *For all state constraints G, G', command sequences $\tilde{S} \neq \varepsilon$ and authorization states $\mathbf{B}_1$ the following holds. If $\{G\}\,\tilde{S}\,\{G'\}$ and $\mathbf{B}_1$ satisfies G, then there exists a sequence of authorization states $\mathbf{B}_1, ..., \mathbf{B}_n$ (for some $n \geq 1$) such that $\mathbf{B}_1, \dots, \mathbf{B}_n \vDash_{\mathcal{P}} \tilde{S}$ and $\mathbf{B}_n$ satisfies G'.*

Theorem 3.9 (Completeness). *For all sequences of authorization states $\mathbf{B}_1, ..., \mathbf{B}_n$ (where $n \geq 1$), command sequences $\tilde{S}$ and state constraints G' the following holds. If $\mathbf{B}_1, ..., \mathbf{B}_n \vDash_{\mathcal{P}} \tilde{S}$ and $\mathbf{B}_n$ satisfies G', then there exists G such that $\{G\}\,\tilde{S}\,\{G'\}$ and $\mathbf{B}_1$ satisfies G.*

3.4 Tabling Algorithm

The proof system gives rise to an algorithm for computing an abstraction of the set of all sequences which, given an authorization state $\mathbf{B}_0$ to start with, lead to states that are guaranteed to satisfy a target state constraint D. The only inputs to the algorithm are $\mathbf{B}_0$, D, and a well-formed program $\mathcal{P}$. We present this algorithm for the propositional case, i.e. the policy and the state constraints are variable-free. A prototype implementation of the algorithm has been used to confirm the results from the examples presented in this section.

The algorithm uses a goal-oriented search that attempts to construct sequences backwards. To ensure completeness and termination, and to prune the search trees, intermediate results are cached in a table and are reused. The technique of tabling, or memoing [6,7,8,9], has also been considered for policy evaluation [10,11]. Our algorithm works on *nodes* that represent both answers and unsolved goals which arise during the computation.

Table 4. Tabling algorithm

(root) $(\{\langle D_2\rangle\} \uplus \mathcal{N}, Ans, Wait) \to_{\mathcal{P}} (\mathcal{N} \cup \mathcal{N}_1 \cup \mathcal{N}_2, Ans, Wait)$
$\quad$ if $\quad \mathcal{N}_1 = \{\text{goal}\langle D_1; Q; D_2\rangle : Q$ is some command in $\mathcal{P}$, and $E \overset{\text{def}}{=} \mathit{eff}(Q)$
$\qquad\qquad\qquad E \cap D_2 \neq \emptyset$
$\qquad\qquad\qquad F \in \mathrm{pre}(Q)$
$\qquad\qquad\qquad D_1 \overset{\text{def}}{=} (D_2 \setminus E) \cup F$ is consistent
$\qquad\qquad\qquad D_2^+ \cap E^- = \emptyset$ and $D_2^- \cap E^+ = \emptyset\}$
$\qquad \mathcal{N}_2 = \{\text{ans}\langle D_2; \varepsilon; D_2\rangle \;\; : \mathbf{B}_0$ satisfies $D_2\}$

(ans) $(\{\text{ans}\langle D_1; \tilde{T}; D_2\rangle\} \uplus \mathcal{N}, Ans, Wait) \to_{\mathcal{P}} (\mathcal{N} \cup \mathcal{N}', Ans', Wait)$
$\quad$ if $\quad \nexists\, m \in Ans(D_2) \;:\; \text{ans}\langle D_1; \tilde{T}; D_2\rangle \preceq m$
$\qquad\quad \mathcal{N}' = \bigcup_{n' \in Wait(D_2)} \mathrm{merge}(\text{ans}\langle D_1; \tilde{T}; D_2\rangle, n')$
$\qquad\quad Ans' = Ans[D_2 \mapsto Ans(D_2) \cup \{\text{ans}\langle D_1; \tilde{T}; D_2\rangle\}]$

(goal_1) $(\{\text{goal}\langle D_1; Q; D_2\rangle\} \uplus \mathcal{N}, Ans, Wait) \to_{\mathcal{P}} (\mathcal{N} \cup \mathcal{N}', Ans, Wait')$
$\quad$ if $\quad D_1 \in \mathrm{dom}(Ans)$
$\qquad\quad \mathcal{N}' = \bigcup_{n' \in Ans(D_1)} \mathrm{merge}(n', \text{goal}\langle D_1; Q; D_2\rangle)$
$\qquad\quad Wait' = Wait[D_1 \mapsto Wait(D_1) \cup \{\text{goal}\langle D_1; Q; D_2\rangle\}]$

(goal_2) $(\{\text{goal}\langle D_1; Q; D_2\rangle\} \uplus \mathcal{N}, Ans, Wait) \to_{\mathcal{P}} (\mathcal{N} \cup \{\langle D_1\rangle\}, Ans', Wait')$
$\quad$ if $\quad D_1 \notin \mathrm{dom}(Ans)$
$\qquad\quad Ans' = Ans[D_1 \mapsto \emptyset]$
$\qquad\quad Wait' = Wait[D_1 \mapsto \{\text{goal}\langle D_1; Q; D_2\rangle\}]$

Definition 3.10 (Nodes). A *root node* is of the form $\langle D\rangle$ where D is a state constraint. An *answer node* is denoted $\text{ans}\langle D_1; \tilde{T}; D_2\rangle$, where $\tilde{T}$ is a sequence and D_1 and D_2 are state constraints, called the *pre-* and *postcondition* of $\tilde{T}$, respectively. The same terms apply to a *goal node* $\text{goal}\langle D_1; \tilde{T}; D_2\rangle$.

Intuitively, if $\langle D_2\rangle$ occurs in the node set the algorithm is working on, we are looking for command sequences which have D_2 as final state. Tables Ans and $Wait$ are defined to map state constraints into sets of answer and goal nodes, respectively. If $\text{ans}\langle D_1; \tilde{T}; D_2\rangle \in Ans(D_2)$, then $\tilde{T}$ is an answer to D_2, i.e. $\mathbf{B}_0$ satisfies D_1, and $\{D_1\}\,\tilde{T}\,\{D_2\}$. If $\text{goal}\langle D_1; \tilde{T}; D_2\rangle \in Wait(D_1)$, then $\tilde{T}$ is not yet an answer to D_2, but it is waiting for new answers to D_1 which can be resolved with the goal to give a new answer to D_2.

We present the algorithm as a state transition system in Table 4. A state is given by the current node set, the answer table, and the waiting table together.

Definition 3.11 (State). A *state* is a triple $(\mathcal{N}, Ans, Wait)$ where $\mathcal{N}$ is a set of nodes, Ans is an answer table, and $Wait$ is a wait table. For every consistent state constraint D, a state $(\{D\}, [D \mapsto \emptyset], [D \mapsto \emptyset])$ is an *initial state*. A state $\mathcal{S}$ is a *final state* iff there is no state $\mathcal{S}'$ such that $\mathcal{S} \to_{\mathcal{P}} \mathcal{S}'$.

When a new root $\langle D_2\rangle$ is spawned, it is processed by transition (root). If $\mathbf{B}_0$ satisfies D_2, then a single answer node $\text{ans}\langle D_2; \varepsilon; D_2\rangle$ is produced (set $\mathcal{N}_2$), corresponding to rule (eps) of the proof system. Set $\mathcal{N}_1$ contains goal nodes, which are produced according to the following scheme which corresponds to rule (cmd): for all commands Q, it is tested whether they can contribute at least one effect which occurs in D_2, by checking $E \cap D_2 \neq \emptyset$. Then for all preconditions $F \in pre(Q)$, a constraint D_1 is computed, which is obtained by removing all effects of Q from D_2 and adding the precondition F, thus reasoning *backwards* to a state, starting from which Q can execute and yield D_2. The constraint D_1 has to be consistent, and so must be the union $D_2 \cup E$, which is ensured by two further side conditions.

Before explaining the remaining rules, we need two further definitions. The first one deals with deriving new answers from given answers and corresponding goals.

Definition 3.12 (Merge). An answer node $n_1 \equiv \mathsf{ans}\langle D_1; \tilde{T}; D_2 \rangle$ and a goal node $n_2 \equiv \mathsf{goal}\langle E_1; Q; E_2 \rangle$ can be *merged* iff $D_2 = E_1$ and D_1, D_2, E_1, E_2 are all consistent. The resulting node is $n \equiv \mathsf{ans}\langle D_1; \tilde{T} \otimes Q; E_2 \rangle$, and we write $n = \mathsf{merge}(n_1, n_2)$.

In general, given an initial state $\mathbf{B}_0$ and a target state constraint D, there are infinitely many correct command sequences that lead from $\mathbf{B}_0$ to D. However, most of these answers are redundant in the sense that there is a shorter one consisting of the same atoms, or there is one with the same length but involves a smaller number of different commands. It turns out that, even if the complete set of answers is infinite, the set of "minimal" answers is finite. The presented algorithm always terminates and is complete with respect to this finite set of answers. All other answers are then *subsumed* by one of the computed answers.

The following definition defines the subsumption relation between answers. In this definition, let *atoms* be a function such that $atoms(Q_1 \otimes \cdots \otimes Q_k) = \{Q_1, ..., Q_k\}$ and $atoms(\varepsilon) = \emptyset$.

Definition 3.13 (Subsumption for Answers). Let $n \equiv \mathsf{ans}\langle D_1; \tilde{S}; D_2 \rangle$ and $m \equiv \mathsf{ans}\langle E_1; \tilde{T}; E_2 \rangle$. Then, n is said to be *subsumed by* m, written $n \preceq m$, iff

$$D_1 \supseteq E_1 \wedge D_2 = E_2 \wedge |\tilde{S}| \geq |\tilde{T}| \wedge atoms(\tilde{S}) \supseteq atoms(\tilde{T})$$

The idea is that node n is subsumed by m if m is a "better" answer: that is, n's precondition is at least as strong as m's, its postcondition is equal to m's, and its command sequence is at least as long as m's and involves the same (or more) atoms.

Answer nodes are processed by rule (ans). The rule executes if the answer node in question is not subsumed by another one already in $Ans(D_2)$. Then the node is added to the answer table, and it is merged with all waiting goals in $Wait(D_2)$. Goal nodes are processed by either (goal$_1$) or (goal$_2$), according to whether or not their precondition D_1 has been spawned before. If not, (goal$_2$) ensures that $\langle D_1 \rangle$ is spawned and that the answer and waiting tables are properly initialized for this new goal. Otherwise, (goal$_1$) prescribes that the goal node is merged with all answer nodes that might be already available for D_1, and that the waiting table is updated. The companion technical report [2] has a worked example demonstrating the functionality of the algorithm.

The correctness of the algorithm is stated in the following soundness and completeness theorems:

Theorem 3.14 (Soundness). *If* $(\mathcal{N}, \mathrm{Ans}, \mathrm{Wait})$ *is reachable from some initial state, then the following holds for all* $D_2 \in \mathrm{dom}(\mathrm{Ans})$: *if* $\mathrm{ans}\langle D_1; \tilde{T}; D_2 \rangle \in \mathrm{Ans}(D_2)$ *and* D_1 *is consistent, then* $\{D_1\}\,\tilde{T}\,\{D_2\}$ *and* $\mathbf{B}_0$ *satisfies* D_1.

Intuitively, the soundness theorem states that every answer produced by the algorithm is indeed a correct answer with respect to the proof system. By soundness of the proof system, the algorithm is then also sound with respect to the *SMP* semantics.

Theorem 3.15 (Completeness). *If* $(\mathcal{N}, \mathrm{Ans}, \mathrm{Wait})$ *is a final state reachable from some initial state, the following implication holds for all* $D_2 \in \mathrm{dom}(\mathrm{Ans})$: *if* $\{G_1\}\,\tilde{S}\,\{G_2\}$, $G_2 \supseteq D_2$, *and* $\mathbf{B}_0$ *satisfies* G_1 *then there exists* $\mathrm{ans}\langle D_1; \tilde{T}; D_2 \rangle \in \mathrm{Ans}(D_2)$ *such that* $\mathbf{B}_0$ *satisfies* D_1, $|\tilde{S}| \geq |\tilde{T}|$, *and* $\mathrm{atoms}(\tilde{S}) \supseteq \mathrm{atoms}(\tilde{T})$.

The completeness theorem states that if a sequence is a correct answer with respect to the proof system, then the algorithm produces an answer that is at least as good, in the sense that it may be shorter or involve a smaller number of different commands.

Finally, the following theorem proves that the algorithm always terminates.

Theorem 3.16 (Termination). *All transition paths starting from an initial state are of finite length.*

4   Case Study

This section presents a larger, non-trivial example policy from the area of electronic health care, based on [12]. The policy defines roles such as patient, clinician, or administrator. Users may be members of several roles, and may activate such roles within a session, in order to utilize the privileges associated with the roles. In the following example, a user may activate the patient role with the command activate. The command succeeds if the user is a member of that role (expressed by the predicate member), and as a result, a corresponding hasActivated fact is inserted into the authorization state. Patients can deactivate their own role if this fact is in the state. The deactivation entails the removal of the fact from the state.

$\mathrm{activate}(X, \mathtt{Patient}) \leftarrow \mathrm{member}(X, \mathtt{Patient}) \otimes +\mathrm{hasActivated}(X, \mathtt{Patient})$
$\mathrm{deactivate}(X, \mathtt{Patient}) \leftarrow \mathrm{hasActivated}(X, \mathtt{Patient}) \otimes -\mathrm{hasActivated}(X, \mathtt{Patient})$

For some groups of roles, the policy specifies a separation-of-duties constraint: users may be active in at most one of the roles at the same time. In the rule below, the clinician role may only be activated if the user is not already active in the administrator role. We also have a symmetric rule for administrators where "Clinician" and "Admin" are permuted. The deactivation rules for clinicians and administrators are similar to the one for patients above.

$\mathrm{activate}(X, \mathtt{Clinician}) \leftarrow \mathrm{member}(X, \mathtt{Clinician}) \wedge \neg\mathrm{hasActivated}(X, \mathtt{Admin}) \otimes$
$+\mathrm{hasActivated}(X, \mathtt{Clinician})$

In the examples above, role membership is a prerequisite for role activation. The following two clauses let administrators update the role membership assignment, using the commands register and unregister.

$$\text{register}(X, U, R) \leftarrow \text{hasActivated}(X, \text{Admin}) \otimes +\text{member}(U, R)$$
$$\text{unregister}(X, U, R) \leftarrow \text{hasActivated}(X, \text{Admin}) \wedge \text{registered}(U, R) \otimes$$
$$-\text{member}(U, R) \otimes -\text{hasActivated}(U, R)$$

Permission assignments typically do not manipulate the authorization state, but often specify conditions that depend on the state. The following clause is an example of a deny-override policy: it allows a clinician X to read data from a patient P's health record if X has a so-called legitimate relationship with the patient, and if the patient has not explicitly concealed the record from X.

$$\text{permitted}(X, \text{Read}, P) \leftarrow \text{hasActivated}(X, \text{Clinician}) \wedge \text{legitRelationship}(X, P) \wedge$$
$$\neg\text{denied}(P, X)$$

The command readEHR is executed when a user X attempts to read a patient P's electronic health record (EHR). The read access is stored in the authorization state for auditing purposes.

$$\text{readEHR}(X, P) \leftarrow \text{permitted}(X, \text{Read}, P) \otimes +\text{hasReadEHR}(X, P)$$

Patients can conceal data from a clinician using the command denyAccess, and remove the concealment with removeDenyAccess. The two corresponding clauses insert (or remove) a denied fact from the authorization state.

$$\text{denyAccess}(P, X) \leftarrow \text{hasActivated}(P, \text{Patient}) \otimes +\text{denied}(P, X)$$
$$\text{removeDenyAccess}(P, X) \leftarrow \text{hasActivated}(P, \text{Patient}) \wedge \text{denied}(P, X) \otimes$$
$$-\text{denied}(P, X)$$

Access to patient data is conditioned on a *legitimate relationship* between the requester and the patient. The following clause specifies that a legitimate relationship exists between a clinician X and a patient P if the patient has explicitly consented to treatment:

$$\text{legitRelationship}(X, P) \leftarrow \text{hasConsented}(P, X, \text{Treatment})$$

The following clauses manage the updates for hasConsented facts. Consent is here modelled as a two-step process: a clinician can request consent to treatment, and only then can the patient give consent.

$$\text{giveConsent}(P, X, \text{Treatment}) \leftarrow \text{hasActivated}(P, \text{Patient}) \wedge$$
$$\text{hasRequestedConsent}(X, P) \otimes$$
$$+\text{hasConsented}(P, X, \text{Treatment})$$
$$\text{requestConsent}(X, P, \text{Treatment}) \leftarrow \text{hasActivated}(X, \text{Clinician}) \otimes$$
$$+\text{hasRequestedConsent}(X, P, \text{Treatment})$$

Finally, patients can withdraw their consent to treatment. Similarly, clinicians can cancel the treatment. The command cancelTreatment removes both the consent request and the (possibly non-existing) patient consent fact from the authorization state.

$$\text{withdrawConsent}(P, X, \text{Treatment}) \leftarrow \text{hasActivated}(P, \text{Patient}) \wedge$$
$$\text{hasConsented}(P, X, \text{Treatment}) \otimes$$
$$-\text{hasConsented}(P, X, \text{Treatment})$$

$$\text{cancelTreatment}(X, P) \leftarrow \text{hasActivated}(X, \text{Clinician}) \otimes$$
$$-\text{hasRequestedConsent}(X, P, \text{Treatment}) \otimes$$
$$-\text{hasConsented}(P, X, \text{Treatment})$$

Suppose we start in an authorization state in which we know that Alice (A) is a member of the administrator role and has not activated the clinician role. Furthermore, Bob (B) has not explicitly concealed his data from Alice. We can then infer a command sequence that terminates in a state where Alice has read Bob's EHR:

{member(A, Admin), ¬hasActivated(A, Clinician), ¬denied(B, A)}
    activate(A, Admin) ⊗ register(A, A, Clinician) ⊗ register(A, B, Patient)⊗
    activate(B, Patient) ⊗ deactivate(A, Admin) ⊗ activate(A, Clinician)⊗
    requestConsent(A, B, Treatment) ⊗ giveConsent(B, A, Treatment) ⊗ readEHR(A, B)
{hasReadEHR(A, B)}

5 Discussion

Related work. Cassandra [10] is an authorization language that defines the actions of activating a role and deactivating a role, along with a transition system that updates the authorization state by inserting and removing corresponding "hasActivated" facts. Users can thus write state-dependent and implicitly state-manipulating policies, but this rather ad-hoc approach is inflexible and not very user-friendly. In a similar spirit, dynFAF [13] keeps track of the history of user requests by dynamically adding facts (with a time-stamp parameter) to the logic program. In dynFAF, facts are never removed; instead, permissions are signed, and permission revocation is modelled by adding a fact with a negative permission. In [14], a sub-language of Timed Default Concurrent Constraint Programming is used to specify dynamic policies. Their language, being almost a full-fledged procedural programming language, can express state changes triggered by both user requests as well as environmental changes. This high expressiveness comes at a price: policies are generally harder to analyze, and evaluation may not terminate.

Some languages such as Ponder [15] or XACML [16] support *obligation policies*. An obligation is a task to be executed after evaluating and enforcing an access request. Obligations are typically used for post-processing jobs such as auditing or for sending out notifications, but in principle an obligation could also be a call to an external function that updates the state. While this approach would move the effects from the hard-coded resource guard into the policy, it does not provide a precise semantics for the state changes.

Some work has been done on analyzing security properties in dynamic role-based systems, in the context of the role-based authorization language RT [17,18] and Administrative RBAC (ARBAC) [19], where members of administrative roles can modify the role membership and privilege assignments [20]. Security properties in the context of SPKI/SDSI certificates are analyzed in [21] by model checking pushdown automata. [22] presents a Datalog-based logical framework for representing and reasoning about access control policies. Neither of the two papers deals with policies updating the authorization state.

Changes to the policy itself can obviously affect the set of actions that are permitted or denied. Margrave [23] is a tool that can compute the consequences of changes to an XACML policy. Pucella and Weissman [24] consider systems in which policies (not just the facts) can change between state transitions. They introduce a modal logic that can capture the dynamic nature of such systems and prove its decidability in the propositional case. In [25], policies written in Datalog can refer to facts in the authorization state, as in our model. Events (such as access requests) can change the authorization state, and the changes are specified as a state machine whose transition labels are guarded by the policy. Security properties can then be analyzed by model checking formulas in first-order temporal logic.

6   Conclusion

In this paper, we have introduced *SMP*, a logic that not only expresses authorization conditions but can also specify effects of access requests on the authorization state. The effects are specified explicitly in the language (as opposed to e.g. a state machine). The logic can be seen as a mild non-monotonic extension of Datalog and has a formal semantics based on Transaction Logic. Existing authorization languages, especially Datalog-based ones, can thus be easily extended to support effects. Examples of *SMP*'s applicability have been shown in a case study on a policy for electronic health records. We have also presented an inference system for reasoning about sequences of user actions, and a sound and complete goal-oriented algorithm for computing minimal sequences (or proving their non-existence) in the propositional case.

References

1. Blaze, M., Feigenbaum, J., Keromytis, A.D.: The role of trust management in distributed systems security. In: Vitek, J. (ed.) Secure Internet Programming. LNCS, vol. 1603, pp. 185–210. Springer, Heidelberg (1999)
2. Becker, M.Y., Nanz, S.: A logic for state-modifying authorization policies. Technical Report MSR-TR-2007-32, Microsoft Research (2007)
3. Bonner, A.J., Kifer, M.: An overview of transaction logic. Theoretical Computer Science 133(2), 205–265 (1994)
4. Shanahan, M.: Prediction is deduction but explanation is abduction. In: International Joint Conference on Artificial Intelligence, pp. 1055–1060 (1989)

5. Kakas, A.C., Kowalski, R.A., Toni, F.: Abductive logic programming. Journal of Logic and Computation 2(6), 719–770 (1992)
6. Tamaki, H., Sato, T.: OLD resolution with tabulation. In: Third international conference on logic programming, pp. 84–98 (1986)
7. Dietrich, S.W.: Extension tables: Memo relations in logic programming. In: Symposium on Logic Programming, pp. 264–272 (1987)
8. Chen, W., Warren, D.S.: Tabled evaluation with delaying for general logic programs. Journal of the ACM 43(1), 20–74 (1996)
9. Toman, D.: Memoing evaluation for constraint extensions of Datalog. Constraints 2(3/4), 337–359 (1997)
10. Becker, M.Y., Sewell, P.: Cassandra: Flexible trust management, applied to electronic health records. In: 17th IEEE Computer Security Foundations Workshop (CSFW), pp. 139–154. IEEE Computer Society Press, Los Alamitos (2004)
11. Becker, M.Y., Fournet, C., Gordon, A.D.: Design and semantics of a decentralized authorization language. In: Computer Security Foundations Symposium (2007)
12. Becker, M.Y.: Information governance in NHS's NPfIT: A case for policy specification. International Journal of Medical Informatics 76(5-6) (2007)
13. Chen, S., Wijesekera, D., Jajodia, S.: Incorporating dynamic constraints in the flexible authorization framework. In: Samarati, P., Ryan, P.Y.A., Gollmann, D., Molva, R. (eds.) ESORICS 2004. LNCS, vol. 3193, pp. 1–16. Springer, Heidelberg (2004)
14. Jagadeesan, R., Marrero, W., Pitcher, C., Saraswat, V.: Timed constraint programming: a declarative approach to usage control. In: International Conference on Principles and Practice of Declarative Programming, pp. 164–175 (2005)
15. Damianou, N., Dulay, N., Lupu, E., Sloman, M.: The Ponder policy specification language. In: International Workshop on Policies for Distributed Systems and Networks, pp. 18–38 (2001)
16. OASIS: eXtensible Access Control Markup Language (XACML) Version 2.0 core specification (2005)
17. Li, N., Tripunitara, M.V.: Security analysis in role-based access control. In: Symposium on Access Control Models and Technologies, pp. 126–135 (2004)
18. Li, N., Mitchell, J.C., Winsborough, W.H.: Beyond proof-of-compliance: security analysis in trust management. Journal of the ACM 52(3), 474–514 (2005)
19. Sasturkar, A., Yang, P., Stoller, S.D., Ramakrishnan, C.R.: Policy analysis for administrative role based access control. In: Workshop on Computer Security Foundations, pp. 124–138 (2006)
20. Sandhu, R., Bhamidipati, V., Coyne, E., Canta, S., Youman, C.: The ARBAC97 model for role-based administration of roles: Preliminary description and outline. In: 2nd ACM Workshop on Role-Based Access Control, pp. 41–54. ACM Press, New York (1997)
21. Jha, S., Reps, T.: Analysis of SPKI/SDSI certificates using model checking. In: Computer Security Foundations Workshop (2002)
22. Bertino, E., Catania, B., Ferrari, E., Perlasca, P.: A logical framework for reasoning about access control models. ACM Trans. Inf. Syst. Secur. 6(1), 71–127 (2003)
23. Fisler, K., Krishnamurthi, S., Meyerovich, L.A., Tschantz, M.C.: Verification and change-impact analysis of access-control policies. In: Inverardi, P., Jazayeri, M. (eds.) ICSE 2005. LNCS, vol. 4309, pp. 196–205. Springer, Heidelberg (2006)
24. Pucella, R., Weissman, V.: Reasoning about dynamic policies. In: Foundations of Software Science and Computation Structures, pp. 453–467 (2004)
25. Dougherty, D.J., Fisler, K., Krishnamurthi, S.: Specifying and reasoning about dynamic access-control policies. In: Furbach, U., Shankar, N. (eds.) IJCAR 2006. LNCS (LNAI), vol. 4130, pp. 632–646. Springer, Heidelberg (2006)

Inductive Proofs of Computational Secrecy*

Arnab Roy[1], Anupam Datta[2], Ante Derek[1], and John C. Mitchell[1]

[1] Stanford University, Stanford, CA
{arnab,aderek,mitchell}@cs.stanford.edu
[2] Carnegie Mellon University, Pittsburgh, PA
danupam@cmu.edu

Abstract. Secrecy properties of network protocols assert that no probabilistic polynomial-time distinguisher can win a suitable game presented
by a challenger. Because such properties are not determined by trace-
by-trace behavior of the protocol, we establish a trace-based protocol
condition, suitable for inductive proofs, that guarantees a generic reduction from protocol attacks to attacks on underlying primitives. We use
this condition to present a compositional inductive proof system for secrecy, and illustrate the system by giving a modular, formal proof of
computational authentication and secrecy properties of Kerberos V5.

1 Introduction

Present-day Internet users and networked enterprises rely on key management
and related protocols that use cryptographic primitives. In spite of the staggering
financial value of, say, the total number of credit card numbers transmitted by
SSL/TLS in a day, we do not have correctness proofs that respect cryptographic
notions of security for many of these relatively simple distributed programs. In
light of this challenge, there have been many efforts to develop and use methods for proving security properties of network protocols. Historically, most efforts
used an abstract *symbolic model,* also referred to as the *Dolev-Yao* model [26,20].
More recently, in part to draw stronger conclusions from existing methods and
proofs, several groups of researchers have taken steps to connect the symbolic
model to probabilistic polynomial-time *computational models* accepted in cryptographic studies, *e.g.* [2,6,8,13,27,17,18,32].

A fundamental problem in reasoning about secrecy, such as computational
indistinguishability of a key from a randomly chosen value, is that such secrecy
properties are not trace properties – indistinguishability over a set of possible
runs is *not* defined by summing the probability of indistinguishability on each
run. As a result, it does not appear feasible to prove computational secrecy
properties by induction on the steps of a protocol. A central contribution of this
paper is a form of trace-based property, called *secretive,* suitable for inductive

* This work was partially supported by the NSF Science and Technology Center
TRUST and U.S. Army Research Office contract on Perpetually Available and Secure Information Systems (DAAD19-02-1-0389) to CMU's CyLab. The first author
was additionally supported by a Siebel Fellowship.

J. Biskup and J. Lopez (Eds.): ESORICS 2007, LNCS 4734, pp. 219–234, 2007.

and compositional proofs, together with a form of standard cryptographic reduction argument which shows that any attack on a secretive protocol yields an attack on cryptographic primitives used in the protocol. We give the cryptographic reduction in a precise form, by inductively defining the operational behavior of a simulator that simulates the protocol to the protocol adversary. An essential problem in defining the simulator, which interacts with a game providing access to the cryptographic primitives, is that the simulator has two candidate secrets, but must present a view of the protocol that is consistent with either candidate being the actual protocol secret.

After proving that secretive protocols yield black-box reductions, we present one inductive method for showing that a protocol is secretive, based on Computational Protocol Composition Logic (CPCL) [17,18]. In the process, we generalize a previous induction rule, so that only one core induction principle is needed in the logic. In contrast to proof systems for symbolic secrecy [28,31], the induction is over actions of honest parties and not the structure of terms. We also extend previous composition theorems [16,21] to the present setting, and illustrate the power of the resulting system by giving modular formal proofs of authentication and secrecy properties of Kerberos V5 and Kerberos V5 with PKINIT. We are also able to prove properties of a variant of the Needham-Schroeder-Lowe protocol that are beyond the standard rank function method [22,19].

Our approach may be compared with equivalence-based methods [6,27,14,5], used in [3] to derive some computational properties of Kerberos V5 from a symbolic proof. In equivalence-based methods, the behavior of a symbolic abstraction under symbolic attack must have the same observable behavior as a computational execution under computational (probabilistic polynomial-time) attack. In contrast, our approach only requires an implication between symbolic reasoning and computational execution. While we believe that both approaches have merit, the two are distinguished by (i) the need to additionally prove the absence of a "commitment problem" in [3], which appears to be a fundamental issue in equivalence-based security [15], and (ii) the open problem expressed in [3] of developing compositional methods in that framework. Symbolic abstractions for primitives like Diffie-Hellman key exchange are also problematic for equivalence-based approaches [4,7], but amenable to treatment in PCL. In contrast to other symbolic or computationally sound methods, PCL reasoning proceeds only over action sequences of the protocol program, yet the conclusions are sound for protocol execution in the presence of attack. This formalizes and justifies a direct reasoning method that is commonly used informally among researchers, yet is otherwise not rigorously connected to reduction arguments.

Section 2 describes the protocol process calculus and computational execution model. A trace-based definition of "secretive protocols" and relevant computational notions are explained in section 3. The proof system, and soundness and composition theorems are presented in section 4, and applied in the proofs for Kerberos in section 5. Conclusions appear in section 6. Many of the proofs and technical details in this paper are omitted due to space constraints—interested readers can find them in the full version of this paper [29].

2   Syntax and Semantics

We begin by reviewing a protocol notation, protocol logic, and a security model for key exchange developed in earlier work [16,17,18].

Modeling Protocols. Protocols are expressed in a process calculus by defining a set of *roles*, such as "Client", or "Server", each given by a sequence of actions such as sending or receiving a message, generating a new nonce, or decrypting or encrypting a message (see [16]). In a run of a protocol, a principal may execute one or more instances of each role, each execution constituting a *thread* identified by a pair $(\hat{X}, \eta)$, where $\hat{X}$ is a principal and η is a unique session identifier.

We illustrate the protocol process calculus using Kerberos V5 [25], which will be the running example in this paper. Our formulation is based on the A level formalization of Kerberos V5 in [12]. Kerberos provides mutual authentication and establishes keys between clients and application servers, using a sequence of two-message interactions with trusted parties called the Kerberos Authentication Server (KAS) and the Ticket Granting Server (TGS).

Kerberos has four roles, **Client**, **KAS**, **TGS** and **Server**. The pre-shared long-term keys between the client and KAS, the KAS and TGS, and the TGS and application server, will be written as $k_{X,Y}^{type}$ where X and Y are the principals sharing the key. The *type* appearing in the superscript indicates the relationship between X and Y: $c \to k$ indicates that X is acting as a client and Y is acting as a KAS, $t \to k$ for TGS and KAS and $s \to t$ for application server and TGS.

$$
\begin{array}{ll}
\textbf{Client} = (C, \hat{K}, \hat{T}, \hat{S}, t)\,[& \textbf{KAS} = (K)\,[\\[4pt]
\quad \textbf{new } n_1; & \quad \textbf{receive } \hat{C}.\hat{T}.n_1; \\[4pt]
\quad \textbf{send } \hat{C}.\hat{T}.n_1; & \quad \textbf{new } AKey; \\[4pt]
& \quad tgt := \textbf{symenc } AKey.\hat{C}, k_{T,K}^{t \to k}; \\[4pt]
\quad \textbf{receive } \hat{C}.tgt.enc_{kc}; & \quad enc_{kc} := \textbf{symenc } AKey.n_1.\hat{T}, k_{C,K}^{c \to k}; \\[4pt]
\quad text_{kc} := \textbf{symdec } enc_{kc}, k_{C,K}^{c \to k}; & \quad \textbf{send } \hat{C}.tgt.enc_{kc}; \\[4pt]
\quad \textbf{match } text_{kc} \textbf{ as } AKey.n_1.\hat{T}; & \quad]_K
\end{array}
$$

In the first stage, the client (C) generates a nonce (represented by **new** n_1) and sends it to the KAS (K) along with the identities of the TGS (T) and itself. The KAS generates a new nonce ($AKey$ - Authentication Key) to be used as a session key between the client and the TGS. It then sends this key along with some other fields to the client encrypted (represented by the **symenc** actions) under two different keys - one it shares with the client ($k_{C,K}^{c \to k}$) and one it shares with the TGS ($k_{T,K}^{t \to k}$). The encryption with $k_{T,K}^{t \to k}$ is called the ticket granting ticket (tgt). The client extracts $AKey$ by decrypting the component encrypted with $k_{C,K}^{c \to k}$ and recovering its parts using the **match** action which deconstructs $text_{kc}$ and associates the parts of this plaintext with $AKey$, n_1, and $\hat{T}$. The ellipses ($\dots$) indicates further client steps for interacting with KAS, TGS, and the application server that are omitted due to space constraints (see [31] for a full description).

Table 1. Syntax of the logic

Action Predicates:
a ::= Send(X, t) | Receive(X, t) | SymEnc(X, t, k) | SymDec(X, t, k) | New(X, n)
Formulas:
φ ::= a | t = t | Start(X) | Honest($\hat{X}$) | Possess(X, t) | Indist(X, t) |
     GoodKeyAgainst(X, t) | $\varphi \wedge \varphi$ | $\varphi \vee \varphi$ | $\exists V.\varphi$ | $\forall V.\varphi$ | $\neg\varphi$ | $\varphi \supset \varphi$ | $\varphi \Rightarrow \varphi$
Modal formulas:
Ψ ::= φ [Actions]$_X$ φ

In the second stage, the client gets a new session key ($SKey$ - Service Key) and a service ticket (st) to converse with the application server S which takes place in the third stage. The control flow of Kerberos exhibits a staged architecture where once one stage has been completed successfully, the subsequent stages can be performed multiple times or aborted and started over for handling errors.

Execution Model. We use a standard two-phase protocol execution model as in [11]. In the initialization phase, we assign roles to each principal, identify a subset that is honest, and provide encryption keys and random coins as needed. In the execution phase, the adversary executes the protocol by interacting with honest principals. We assume the adversary has complete control over the network, as in [11]. The length of keys and the running time of the protocol are polynomially bounded in the security parameter.

A *trace* is a record of all actions executed by honest principals and the attacker during protocol execution. Since honest principals execute roles defined by a symbolic process calculus, our traces contain symbolic descriptions of the actions of honest parties and a mapping of symbolic variables to bitstrings values. The attacker may produce and send arbitrary bitstrings, but the trace only records the send-receive actions of the attacker, and not its internal actions. Our traces also include the random bits (used by the honest parties, the adversary and the distinguisher), as well as a few other elements used in defining semantics of formulas over traces [17]. In section 3, which presents semantic arguments independent of the protocol logic, we omit these additional fields and refer to a trace as $\langle e, \lambda \rangle$, where e is a symbolic description of the trace and λ maps terms in e to bitstrings.

For technical reasons, we assume that honest parties conform to certain type conventions. These restrictions may be imposed by prefixing the values of each type (nonces, ids, constant strings, pairs, encryptions with key k, etc.) with a tag such as 'constant' or 'encrypted with key k' that are respected by honest parties executing protocol roles. The adversary may freely modify or spoof tags or produce arbitrary untagged bitrings.

Syntax of Computational PCL. The formulas of the logic are given in Table 1. Protocol proofs usually use modal formulas of the form $\psi[P]_X\varphi$. The informal reading of the modal formula is that if X starts from a state in which ψ holds, and executes the program P, then in the resulting state the security property φ

is guaranteed to hold irrespective of the actions of an attacker and other honest principals. Many protocol properties are naturally expressible in this form. Most formulas have the same intuitive meaning as in the symbolic model [16].

For every protocol action, there is a corresponding action predicate which asserts that the action has occurred in the run. For example, $\mathsf{Send}(X, t)$ holds in a run where the thread X has sent the term t. $\mathsf{Honest}(\hat{X})$ means that the principal $\hat{X}$ is acting honestly, *i.e.*, the actions of every thread of $\hat{X}$ precisely follows some role of the protocol. $\mathsf{Start}(X)$ means that the thread X did not execute any actions in the past. $\mathsf{Indist}(X, t)$ means that agent X cannot tell the bitstring representation of the term t from another bitstring chosen at random from the same distribution. The logical connectives have standard interpretations, except that conditional implication ($\Rightarrow$), related to a form of conditional probability, appears essential for reasoning about cryptographic reductions (see [17] for further discussion).

Semantics of Computational PCL. Intuitively, a protocol Q satisfies a formula φ, written $Q \models \varphi$ if for all adversaries and sufficiently large security parameters, the *probability* that φ "holds" is asymptotically close to 1 (in the security parameter). Intuitively, the meaning of a formula φ on a set T of computational traces is usually a subset $T' \subseteq T$ that respects φ in some specific way. For example, an action predicate such as Send selects a set of traces in which a send occurs. More precisely, the semantics $\llbracket \varphi \rrbracket (T, D, \epsilon)$ of a formula φ is inductively defined on the set T of traces, with distinguisher D and tolerance ϵ. The distinguisher and tolerance are only used in the semantics of Indist and $\mathsf{GoodKeyAgainst}$, where they determine whether the distinguisher has more than a negligible chance of distinguishing the given value from random or winning an IND-CCA game, respectively. The precise inductive semantics for formulas is given in [17].

The semantics of the predicate $\mathsf{GoodKeyAgainst}(X, k)$ is defined using a standard cryptographic-style game condition. It captures the intuition that a key output by a secure key exchange protocol should be suitable for use in some application protocol of interest (e.g. as a key for an IND-CCA secure encryption scheme) [18]. Formally, $\llbracket \mathsf{GoodKeyAgainst}(X, k) \rrbracket (T, D, \epsilon)$ is the complete set of traces T if the distinguisher D, who is given X's view of the run has an advantage less than ϵ in winning the IND-CCA game [9] against a challenger using the bitstring corresponding to term k as the key, and $\emptyset$ otherwise. Here the probability is taken by choosing a uniformly random trace $t \in T$ (which includes the randomness of all parties, the attacker and the distinguisher). The same approach can be used to define other game conditions.

A *trace property* is a formula φ such that for any set of protocol traces T, $\llbracket \varphi \rrbracket (T) = \bigcup_{t \in T} \llbracket \varphi \rrbracket (\{t\})$. The distinguisher and tolerance are omitted since they are not used in defining semantics for such predicates. Thus all action formulas, such as $\mathsf{Send}(X, m)$, are trace properties whereas aggregrate properties such as $\mathsf{Indist}(X, k)$ and $\mathsf{GoodKeyAgainst}\ (X, k)$ are not.

3   Secretive Protocols

In this section, we define a trace property of protocols and show that this property implies computational secrecy and integrity. The computational secrecy properties include key indistinguishability and key usability for IND-CCA secure encryption. These results are established first for the simple case when secrets are protected by pre-shared "level-0" keys (Theorem 1), then generalized (Theorems 2-3) under the condition that each key is protected by predecessor keys in an acyclic graph[1]. The proofs use standard cryptographic reductions.

Let s and $\mathcal{K}$ be the symbolic representations of a nonce and a set of keys associated with a specific thread in a trace $\langle e, \lambda \rangle$. Define $\Lambda(\mathcal{K})$ to be the set of bitstrings corresponding to the keys in $\mathcal{K}$, i.e., $\{\lambda(k) \mid k \in \mathcal{K}\}$.

Definition 1 (Secretive Trace). *A trace $\langle e, \lambda \rangle$ is a secretive trace with respect to s and $\mathcal{K}$ if the following properties hold for every thread belonging to honest principals:*

- *a thread which generates a new nonce r in e, with $\lambda(r) = \lambda(s)$, ensures that r is encrypted with a key k with bitstring representation $\lambda(k) \in \Lambda(\mathcal{K})$ in any message sent out.*
- *whenever a thread decrypts a message with a key k with $\lambda(k) \in \Lambda(\mathcal{K})$, which was produced by encryption with key k by an honest party, and parses the decryption, it ensures that the results are encrypted with some key k' with $\lambda(k') \in \Lambda(\mathcal{K})$ in any message sent out.*

To lift this definition of secretive traces to secretive protocols we need a way to identify the symbol s and the set of symbols $\mathcal{K}$ in each protocol execution trace. We do this by assuming functions $\bar{s}$ and $\bar{\mathcal{K}}$ that map a trace to symbols in the trace corresponding to s and the set of keys in $\mathcal{K}$ respectively. In applications, these mappings will be given by the semantics of logical formulas.

Definition 2 (Secretive Protocol). *Given the mappings $\bar{s}$ and $\bar{\mathcal{K}}$, a protocol $\mathcal{Q}$ is a secretive protocol with respect to s and $\mathcal{K}$ if for all probabilistic poly-time adversaries $\mathcal{A}$ and for all sufficiently large security parameters η, the probability that a trace t, generated by the interaction of $\mathcal{A}$ with principals following roles of $\mathcal{Q}$, is a secretive trace with respect to $\bar{s}(t)$ and $\bar{\mathcal{K}}(t)$ is overwhelmingly close to 1, the probability being taken over all adversary and protocol randomness.*

In proving properties of secretive protocols, we focus on the subset of protocol traces that are secretive. Adversary advantages retain the same asymptotic behavior over this set because non-secretive traces are a negligible fraction of all traces.

The general structure of the proofs of the secrecy theorems is by reduction of the appropriate protocol secrecy game to a multi-party IND-CCA game: given protocol adversary $\mathcal{A}$, we construct an adversary $\mathcal{A}'$ against a multi-party IND-CCA challenger which provides $|\mathcal{K}|$-party Left-or-Right encryption oracles $\mathcal{E}_{k_i}(LoR(\cdot, \cdot, b))$ parameterized by a challenge bit b and decryption oracles $\mathcal{D}_{k_i}(\cdot)$

---

[1] Some of the results here were presented in the informal WITS'07 [30] workshop.

for all $k_i \in \mathcal{K}$ (Following [9], $LoR(m_0, m_1, b)$ is a function which returns m_b). We use multi-party security definitions due to Bellare, Boldyreva and Micali [9] applied to symmetric encryption schemes. [2]

The strategy of $\mathcal{A}'$ is to provide a simulation of the *secretive protocol* to $\mathcal{A}$ by using these oracles such that the capability of $\mathcal{A}$ to break the indistinguishability or key usability of the nonce can be leveraged in some way to guess the challenge bit b of the multi-party IND-CCA challenger. To this end, $\mathcal{A}'$ employs a *bilateral simulator* $\mathcal{S}$ which randomly chooses two bit-strings s_0, s_1 as alternate representations of the putative secret s and then simulates execution of the protocol to the protocol adversary $\mathcal{A}$ for both the representations.

As with the execution of the actual protocol, $\mathcal{S}$ receives messages and scheduling information from $\mathcal{A}$ and acts according to the roles of the given protocol. The difference from a normal protocol execution is that in computing bitstring representations of terms that involve s, $\mathcal{S}$ does so for both representations of s. We will show that for secretive protocols the representation of s that $\mathcal{A}$ sees is determined by the challenge bit b of the CCA challenger. The operational semantics of the bilateral simulator is formally described in the full version of [30]. We explain the form of the definition using an example.

$$\frac{\triangleright\, \mathsf{m}' \quad \triangleright\, \mathsf{m}'' \quad \mathsf{m} := \mathsf{pair}\ \mathsf{m}', \mathsf{m}'';}{\triangleright\, \mathsf{m},\ lv(\mathsf{m}) = pair(lv(\mathsf{m}'), lv(\mathsf{m}'')),\ rv(\mathsf{m}) = pair(rv(\mathsf{m}'), rv(\mathsf{m}''))}$$

The notation $\triangleright\, \mathsf{m}$ means that the symbol m has been computationally evaluated according to the semantics. The premise of the rule requires that the symbols m and m' have already been evaluated and we are considering the action $\mathsf{m} :=$ $\mathsf{pair}\ \mathsf{m}', \mathsf{m}''$ in some thread. The functions lv and rv map a symbol to its bitstring values corresponding to the representations s_0 and s_1 of s respectively. The function $pair$ is the actual computational implementation of pairing. The conclusion of the rule states that $lv(\mathsf{m})$ is evaluated by pairing the bit-strings $lv(\mathsf{m}')$ and $lv(\mathsf{m}'')$ and similarly for $rv(\mathsf{m})$. In simulating the protocol to the protocol adversary, the simulator executes each action of the currently scheduled thread following this definition.

Suppose m is a term explicitly constructed from s. As $\mathcal{S}$ is simulating a *secretive protocol*, this term is to be encrypted with a key k in $\mathcal{K}$ to construct a message to be sent out to $\mathcal{A}$. So, $\mathcal{S}$ asks the encryption oracle of the $|\mathcal{K}|$-IND-CCA challenger to encrypt $(lv(m), rv(m))$ with k. In addition, this pair of bitstrings is recorded and the result of the query is logged in the set qdb_k. If a message construction involves decryption with a key in $\mathcal{K}$, $\mathcal{S}$ first checks whether the term to be decrypted was produced by an encryption oracle by accessing the log qdb_k—if not, then the decryption oracle is invoked; if yes, then $\mathcal{S}$ uses the corresponding encryption query as the decryption. In the second case the encryption query must have been of the form (m_0, m_1). Following the definition of *secretive protocol*, terms constructed from this decryption will be re-encrypted with a key in $\mathcal{K}$ before sending out. Thus we note here that all such replies will be consistent to $\mathcal{A}$ with respect to any choice of b. The situation

---

[2] In [9], IND-CCA2 security and multi-party IND-CCA security are shown to be asymptotically equivalent.

becomes trickier when encryption or decryption of a term is required with s as the key. In this case $\mathcal{S}$ encrypts or decrypts with s_0. We therefore always have $lv(m) = rv(m)$ for any message m being sent out.

One subtle issue arises when we consider term deconstructors such as unpairings, decryptions, and pattern matching actions: we need to ensure that the success of such actions are independent of the challenge bit b The type information carried by terms (mentioned in Section 2) ensures this consistency in an overwhelming number of traces. The proofs proceed by induction over the operational semantics of the simulator.

Theorem 1 (CCA security - level 1). *Assume that a probabilistic poly-time adversary interacts with a secretive protocol with respect to nonce s and a set of level-0 keys $\mathcal{K}$.*

- Key indistinguishability: *If s is not used as a key by the honest principals, the adversary has negligible advantage at distinguishing s from random after the interaction provided the encryption scheme is IND-CCA secure.*
- Key usability: *If the honest principals use s as a key, the adversary has negligible advantage at winning an IND-CCA game against a symmetric encryption challenger using the key s after the interaction provided the encryption scheme is IND-CCA secure.*

A *level-0* key for a protocol execution is an encryption key which is only used as a key but never as a payload. We now extend Theorem 1 to directed key hierarchies to reason about key distribution protocols such as Kerberos.

Let $\mathcal{K}$ be the symbolic representations of nonces and keys associated with a specific thread in a trace $\langle e, \lambda \rangle$. The *key graph* of $\mathcal{K}$ in a protocol is a directed graph with keys in $\mathcal{K}$ as vertices. There is an edge from key k_1 to k_2 if the protocol is secretive with respect to k_2 and a key set which includes k_1. Consider a directed acyclic key graph. Keys at the root are *level 0* keys. The *level* of any other key is one more than the maximum level among its immediate predecessors. For a set of keys $\mathcal{K}$ from a directed acyclic key graph, we define its *closure* $\mathcal{C}(\mathcal{K})$ to be the union of sets of keys at the root which are predecessors of each key in $\mathcal{K}$.

Theorem 2 (CCA security - Key DAGs). *Assume that a probabilistic poly-time adversary interacts with a secretive protocol with respect to nonce s and a set of keys $\mathcal{K}$ in a DAG (Directed Acyclic Graph) of finite and statically bounded level.*

- Key indistinguishability: *If s is not used as a key by the honest principals, the adversary has negligible advantage at distinguishing s from random after the interaction provided the encryption scheme is IND-CCA secure.*
- Key usability: *If the honest principals use s as a key, the adversary has negligible advantage at winning an IND-CCA game against a symmetric encryption challenger using the key s after the interaction provided the encryption scheme is IND-CCA secure.*

The following theorem establishes the integrity of encryptions done with nonces protected by key hierarchies. The security definition INT-CTXT for ciphertext integrity is due to [10] and also referred to as *existential unforgeability* of cipher-texts in [23].

Theorem 3 (CTXT integrity). *Assume that a probabilistic poly-time adversary interacts with a secretive protocol with respect to nonce s and a set of keys $\mathcal{K}$ in a DAG of finite, statically bounded levels. During the protocol run, if an honest principal decrypts a ciphertext with key s successfully, then with overwhelming probability the ciphertext was produced by an honest principal by encryption with s provided the encryption scheme is IND-CCA and INT-CTXT secure.*

4   Proof System

In this section, we present a general induction rule, axiomatize the informal definition of a *secretive protocol* given in Section 3 and formulate axioms stating that *secretive protocols* guarantee certain computational properties. The soundness proofs of these axioms are based on the theorems in Section 3.

4.1   Establishing Secretive Protocols

We introduce the predicate $\mathsf{Good}(X, m, s, \mathcal{K})$ to assert that the thread X constructed the term m in accordance with the rules allowing a *secretive protocol* with respect to nonce s and set of keys $\mathcal{K}$ to send out m. More formally, $[\![\mathsf{Good}(X, m, s, \mathcal{K})]\!](T, D, \epsilon)$ is the collection of all traces $t \in T$ where thread X constructs the term m in a 'good' way. Received messages, data of atomic type different from nonce or key, nonces different from s are all 'good' terms. Constructions that are 'good' consist of pairing or unpairing good terms, encrypting good terms, encrypting any term with a key in $\mathcal{K}$ and decrypting good terms with keys not in $\mathcal{K}$. The following axioms formalize reasoning about the Good predicate by induction on actions in protocol roles.

G0 $\mathsf{Good}(X, a, s, \mathcal{K})$, if a is of an atomic type different from nonce

G1 $\mathsf{New}(Y, n) \wedge n \neq s \supset \mathsf{Good}(X, n, s, \mathcal{K})$

G2 [receive $m;$]$_X$ $\mathsf{Good}(X, m, s, \mathcal{K})$

G3 $\mathsf{Good}(X, m, s, \mathcal{K})$ [a]$_X$ $\mathsf{Good}(X, m, s, \mathcal{K})$, for all actions a

G4 $\mathsf{Good}(X, m, s, \mathcal{K})$ [match m as $m';$]$_X$ $\mathsf{Good}(X, m', s, \mathcal{K})$

G5 $\mathsf{Good}(X, m_0, s, \mathcal{K}) \wedge \mathsf{Good}(X, m_1, s, \mathcal{K})$ [$m :=$ pair $m_0, m_1;$]$_X$ $\mathsf{Good}(X, m, s, \mathcal{K})$

G6 $\mathsf{Good}(X, m, s, \mathcal{K})$ [$m' :=$ symenc $m, k;$]$_X$ $\mathsf{Good}(X, m', s, \mathcal{K})$

G7 $k \in \mathcal{K}$ [$m' :=$ symenc $m, k;$]$_X$ $\mathsf{Good}(X, m', s, \mathcal{K})$

G8 $\mathsf{Good}(X, m, s, \mathcal{K}) \wedge k \notin \mathcal{K}$ [$m' :=$ symdec $m, k;$]$_X$ $\mathsf{Good}(X, m', s, \mathcal{K})$

In the following lemma, the additional field σ in the trace definition refers to an environment that maps free variables in a formula to bitstrings. The proof is by induction on the construction of 'good' terms.

Lemma 1. *If* $\mathsf{Good}(X, m, s, \mathcal{K})$ *holds for a trace* $\langle e, \lambda, \cdots, \sigma \rangle$, *then any bilateral simulator with parameters* $s, \mathcal{K}$, *executing symbolic actions e produces identical bitstring representations for m on both sides of the simulation, i.e., we will have* $\triangleright\, m$ *and* $lv(m) = rv(m)$.

The formula $\mathsf{SendGood}(X, s, \mathcal{K})$ asserts that all messages that thread X sends out are good and $\mathsf{Secretive}(s, \mathcal{K})$ asserts that all honest threads only send out good messages. Formally,

$$\mathsf{SendGood}(X, s, \mathcal{K}) \equiv \forall m.\, (\mathsf{Send}(X, m) \supset \mathsf{Good}(X, m, s, \mathcal{K}))$$
$$\mathsf{Secretive}(s, \mathcal{K}) \equiv \forall X.\, (\mathsf{Honest}(\hat{X}) \supset \mathsf{SendGood}(X, s, \mathcal{K}))$$

The axioms **SG0 − 2** are based on the definition of SendGood:

SG0 $\mathsf{Start}(X)\,[\,]_X\,\mathsf{SendGood}(X, s, \mathcal{K})$

SG1 $\mathsf{SendGood}(X, s, \mathcal{K})\,[\mathsf{a}]_X\,\mathsf{SendGood}(X, s, \mathcal{K})$, where a is not a send.

SG2 $\mathsf{SendGood}(X, s, \mathcal{K})\,[\mathbf{send}\ m;]_X\,\mathsf{Good}(X, m, s, \mathcal{K}) \supset \mathsf{SendGood}(X, s, \mathcal{K})$

SG1 is obviously valid for nonce generation, message receipt, encryption and pairing actions. Soundness for unpairing and decryption requires consistency of deconstructions in the bilateral simulation, e.g. unpairing should succeed on one side iff it succeeds on the other. Soundness of **SG2** follows from the operational semantics of the simulator on a send action and Lemma 1.

The **IND**$_{GOOD}$ rule which follows states that if all honest threads executing some basic sequence in the protocol locally construct good messages to be sent out, given that they earlier also did so, then we can conclude $\mathsf{Secretive}(s, \mathcal{K})$.

$$\mathbf{IND}_{GOOD} \quad \forall \rho \in \mathcal{Q}.\forall P \in BS(\rho).$$
$$\frac{\mathsf{SendGood}(X, s, \mathcal{K})\,[P]_X\,\varPhi \supset \mathsf{SendGood}(X, s, \mathcal{K})}{\mathcal{Q} \vdash \varPhi \supset \mathsf{Secretive}(s, \mathcal{K})} \ (*)$$

$(*)$: $[P]_X$ does not capture free variables in $\varPhi$, $\mathcal{K}$, s, and $\varPhi$ is a prefix closed trace formula.

A set of basic sequences (BS) of a role is any partition of the sequence of actions in a role such that if any element sequence has a **receive** then it is only at its beginning. The formula $\varPhi$ has to be *prefix closed* which means that it is a formula such that if it is true at some point in a trace, it is also true at all earlier points. This rule is an instance of a more general induction rule **IND** which is obtained by replacing $\mathsf{SendGood}(X, s, \mathcal{K})$ by a general trace formula $\varPsi(X)$ and requiring that $\mathsf{Start}(X)\,[\,]_X\,\varPhi \supset \varPsi(X)$. The instance of the latter formula, the base case of the induction, is trivially satisfied when $\varPsi(X)$ is $\mathsf{SendGood}(X, s, \mathcal{K})$ because of axiom **SG0**.

4.2 Relating Secretive Protocols to Good Keys

The remaining axioms relate the concept of a secretive protocol, which is trace-based, to complexity theoretic notions of security. As defined in section 3, a level-0 key is only used as a key. Note that this is a syntactic property and is evident from inspection of the protocol roles. Typically, a long-term key shared by two principals is level-0. A nonce is established to be a level-1 key when the protocol is proved to be a *secretive protocol* with respect to the nonce and a set of level-0 keys. This concept is extended further to define level-2 keys.

The formula $\mathsf{InInitSet}(X, s, \mathcal{K})$ asserts X is either the generator of nonce s or a possessor of some key in the closure $\mathcal{C}(\mathcal{K})$. $\mathsf{GoodInit}(s, \mathcal{K})$ asserts that all such threads belong to honest principals. Formally,

$$\mathsf{InInitSet}(X, s, \mathcal{K}) \equiv \exists k \in \mathcal{C}(\mathcal{K}). \; \mathsf{Possess}(X, k) \vee \mathsf{New}(X, s)$$

$$\mathsf{GoodInit}(s, \mathcal{K}) \equiv \forall X. \; (\mathsf{InInitSet}(X, s, \mathcal{K}) \supset \mathsf{Honest}(\hat{X}))$$

Our objective is to state that secrets established by *secretive protocols*, where possibly the secrets are also used as keys, are good keys against everybody except the set of people who either generated the secret or are in possession of a key protecting the secret. The formula $\mathsf{GoodKeyFor}$ expresses this property. For level-0 keys that we want to claim are possessed only by honest principals we use the formula $\mathsf{GoodKey}$.

$$\mathsf{GoodKeyFor}(s, \mathcal{K}) \equiv \forall X. \; (\mathsf{GoodKeyAgainst}(X, s) \vee \mathsf{InInitSet}(X, s, \mathcal{K}))$$

$$\mathsf{GoodKey}(k) \equiv \forall X. \; (\mathsf{Possess}(X, k) \supset \mathsf{Honest}(\hat{X}))$$

For protocols employing an IND-CCA secure encryption scheme, the soundness of the following axiom follows from theorems 1 and 2:

GK $\mathsf{Secretive}(s, \mathcal{K}) \wedge \mathsf{GoodInit}(s, \mathcal{K}) \Rightarrow \mathsf{GoodKeyFor}(s, \mathcal{K})$

If the encryption scheme is both IND-CCA and INT-CTXT secure then, the soundness of the following axioms follow from Theorem 3:

CTX0 $\mathsf{GoodKey}(k) \wedge \mathsf{SymDec}(Z, E_{sym}[k](m), k) \Rightarrow \exists X. \; \mathsf{SymEnc}(X, m, k)$,
  for level-0 key k.

CTXL $\mathsf{Secretive}(s, \mathcal{K}) \wedge \mathsf{GoodInit}(s, \mathcal{K}) \wedge \mathsf{SymDec}(Z, E_{sym}[s](m), s)$
  $\Rightarrow \exists X. \; \mathsf{SymEnc}(X, m, s)$

The **soundness theorem** is proved by showing that every axiom is a valid formula and that all proof rules preserve validity. Proofs for selected axioms are given in the full version of the paper [29].

Theorem 4 (Soundness). $\forall \mathcal{Q}, \varphi. \; \textit{if } \mathcal{Q} \vdash \varphi \; \textit{then} \; \mathcal{Q} \vDash \varphi$

Compositional Reasoning. We develop composition theorems that allow *secretive*-ness proofs of compound protocols to be built up from proofs of their parts. We consider three kinds of composition operations on protocols—*parallel, sequential,* and *staged*—based on our previous work [16,21]. However, adapting that approach for reasoning about secrecy requires new insights. One central concept in these compositional proof methods is the notion of an *invariant*. An invariant for a protocol is a logical formula that characterizes the environment in which it retains its security properties. While in previous work [16] the "honesty rule" **HON** is used for establishing invariants, reasoning about *secretive*-ness requires a more general form of induction, captured in this paper by the **IND** rule. Also, in proving that a protocol step does not violate *secretive*-ness, we need to employ derivations from earlier steps executed by the principal. In the technical presentation, this history information shows up as preconditions in the secrecy induction of the sequential and staged composition theorems. The statement of the theorems is similar to the theorems proved for the symbolic model in earlier work [31], but the proofs use the computational semantics. In particular we need a staged composition operation that extends sequential composition by allowing self loops and arbitrary backward arcs in this chain. This control flow structure is common in practice, e.g., Kerberos [25], IEEE 802.11i [1], and IKEv2 [24], with backward arcs usually corresponding to error handling or rekeying.

5   Analysis of Kerberos

Table 2 lists the security properties of Kerberos that we prove. The security objectives are of two types: authentication and secrecy. The authentication objectives take the form that a message of a certain format was indeed sent by some thread of the expected principal. The secrecy objectives take the form that a putative secret is a good key for certain principals. For example, $AUTH_{kas}^{client}$ states that when C finishes executing the **Client** role, some thread of $\hat{K}$ indeed sent the expected message; SEC_{akey}^{client} states that the authorization key is good after execution of the **Client** role by C; the other security properties are analogous. We abbreviate the honesty assumptions by defining $\mathsf{Hon}(\hat{X_1}, \hat{X_2}, \cdots, \hat{X_n}) \equiv \mathsf{Honest}(\hat{X_1}) \wedge \mathsf{Honest}(\hat{X_2}) \wedge \cdots \mathsf{Honest}(\hat{X_n})$. The formal proofs are omitted from this paper but present in the full version [29].

The overall proof structure demonstrates an interleaving of authentication and secrecy properties, reflecting the intuition behind the protocol design. We start with proving some authentication properties based on the presumed secrecy of long-term shared symmetric keys. As intended in the design, these authentication guarantees enable us to prove the secrecy of data protected by the long-term keys. This general theme recurs further down the protocol stages. Part of the data is used in subsequent stages as an encryption key. The secrecy of this transmitted encryption key lets us establish authentication in the second stage of the protocol. The transmitted key is also used to protect key exchange in this stage - the secrecy of which depends on the authentication established in the stage.

Theorem 5 (KAS Authentication). *On execution of the **Client** role by a principal, it is guaranteed with asymptotically overwhelming probability that the intended KAS indeed sent the expected response assuming that both the client and the KAS are honest. A similar result holds for a principal executing the **TGS** role. Formally, $KERBEROS \vdash AUTH_{kas}^{client}, AUTH_{kas}^{tgs}$.*

Authentication is achieved by the virtue of ciphertext integrity offered by the symmetric encryption scheme. At a high level, we reason that a ciphertext could have been produced only by one of the possessors of the corresponding key.

Theorem 6 (Authentication Key Secrecy). *On execution of the **Client** role by a principal, the Authentication Key is guaranteed to be good, in the sense of IND-CCA security, assuming that the client, the KAS and the TGS are all honest. Similar results hold for principals executing the **KAS** and **TGS** roles. Formally, $KERBEROS \vdash SEC_{akey}^{client}, SEC_{akey}^{kas}, SEC_{akey}^{tgs}$.*

Table 2. Kerberos Security Properties

$$SEC_{akey} : \mathsf{Hon}(\hat{C}, \hat{K}, \hat{T}) \supset (\mathsf{GoodKeyAgainst}(X, AKey) \vee \hat{X} \in \{\hat{C}, \hat{K}, \hat{T}\})$$

$$SEC_{skey} : \mathsf{Hon}(\hat{C}, \hat{K}, \hat{T}, \hat{S}) \supset (\mathsf{GoodKeyAgainst}(X, SKey) \vee \hat{X} \in \{\hat{C}, \hat{K}, \hat{T}, \hat{S}\})$$

$$AUTH_{kas} : \exists \eta.\ \mathsf{Send}((\hat{K}, \eta), \hat{C}.E_{sym}[k_{T,K}^{t \to k}](AKey.\hat{C}).E_{sym}[k_{C,K}^{c \to k}](AKey.n_1.\hat{T}))$$

$$AUTH_{tgs} : \exists \eta.\ \mathsf{Send}((\hat{T}, \eta), \hat{C}.E_{sym}[k_{S,T}^{s \to t}](SKey.\hat{C}).E_{sym}[AKey](SKey.n_2.\hat{S}))$$

$SEC_{akey}^{client} : [\textbf{Client}]_C\ SEC_{akey}$	$AUTH_{kas}^{client} : [\textbf{Client}]_C\ \mathsf{Hon}(\hat{C}, \hat{K}) \supset AUTH_{kas}$
$SEC_{akey}^{kas} : [\textbf{KAS}]_K\ SEC_{akey}$	$AUTH_{kas}^{tgs} : [\textbf{TGS}]_T\ \mathsf{Hon}(\hat{T}, \hat{K}) \supset \exists n_1.\ AUTH_{kas}$
$SEC_{akey}^{tgs} : [\textbf{TGS}]_T\ SEC_{akey}$	
	$AUTH_{tgs}^{client} : [\textbf{Client}]_C\ \mathsf{Hon}(\hat{C}, \hat{K}, \hat{T}) \supset AUTH_{tgs}$
$SEC_{skey}^{client} : [\textbf{Client}]_C\ SEC_{skey}$	$AUTH_{tgs}^{server} : [\textbf{Server}]_S\ \mathsf{Hon}(\hat{S}, \hat{T})$
$SEC_{skey}^{tgs} : [\textbf{TGS}]_T\ SEC_{skey}$	$\supset \exists n_2, AKey.\ AUTH_{tgs}$

Proof Sketch. Observe that in the first stage, the KAS sends out $AKey$ encrypted under two different keys - $k_{C,K}^{c \to k}$ and $k_{T,K}^{t \to k}$, and the client uses $AKey$ as an encryption key. As a first approximation we conjecture that in the entire protocol execution, $AKey$ is either protected by encryption with either of the keys in $\mathcal{K} = \{k_{C,K}^{c \to k}, k_{T,K}^{t \to k}\}$ or else used as an encryption key in messages sent to the network by honest principals. This seems like a claim to be established by induction. As a base case, we establish that the generator of $AKey$ (some thread of the KAS) satisfies the conjecture. The induction case is: whenever an honest principal decrypts a ciphertext with one of the keys in $\mathcal{K}$, it ensures that new terms generated from the decryption are re-encrypted with some key in $\mathcal{K}$ in any message sent out. The results (of the appropriate type) from such a decryption are however, allowed to be used as encryption keys, which as you can note is the case in the first stage of the client.

When we are reasoning from the point of view of the KAS (as in SEC_{akey}^{kas}), we already know the initial condition - that the KAS sent out $AKey$ encrypted under only these keys. However, when arguing from the point of view of the client and the TGS (as in SEC_{akey}^{client} and SEC_{akey}^{tgs}), we need to have some authentication conditions established first. These conditions are generally of the form that the KAS indeed behaved in the expected manner. Reasoning from this premise, we prove that our initial conjecture is correct.

In the formal proof, we show that Kerberos is a *secretive protocol* with respect to the nonce $AKey$ and the set of keys $\mathcal{K}$. The induction idea is captured, in its simplest form, by the proof rule IND_{GOOD}. However, as Kerberos has a staged structure we use the staged composition theorem which builds upon the rule IND_{GOOD}. The core of the proof is the *secrecy induction* which is an induction over all the basic sequences of all the protocol roles. The authentication condition Φ is easily derived from the KAS Authentication theorem (theorem 5). The staged composition theorem allows us to facilitate the secrecy induction by obtaining inferences from the information flow induced by the staged structure of Kerberos in a simple and effective way. The secrecy induction is modular as the individual basic sequences are small in themselves. Goodness of $AKey$ now follows from theorem 1 (CCA security - level 1), which is formally expressed by axiom **GK**.

Theorem 7 (TGS Authentication). *On execution of the* **Client** *role by a principal, it is guaranteed with asymptotically overwhelming probability that the intended TGS indeed sent the expected response assuming that the client, the KAS and the TGS are all honest. A similar result holds for a principal executing the* **Server** *role. Formally,* $KERBEROS \vdash AUTH_{tgs}^{client}, AUTH_{tgs}^{server}$.

Theorem 8 (Service Key Secrecy). *On execution of the* **Client** *role by a principal, the Service Key is guaranteed to be good, in the sense of IND-CCA security, assuming that the client, the KAS, the TGS and the application server are all honest. A similar result holds for a principal executing the* **TGS** *role. Formally,* $KERBEROS \vdash SEC_{skey}^{client}, SEC_{skey}^{tgs}$.

The proof of $AUTH_{tgs}^{server}$ is similar to the proof of theorem 5. The proof of $AUTH_{tgs}^{client}$ depends on the 'goodkey'-ness of $AKey$ established by theorem 6. For theorem 8, the idea is that the Service Key $SKey$ is protected by level-0 key $k_{S,T}^{s \rightarrow t}$ and level-1 key $AKey$. The proof of 'Secretive'-ness proceeds along the same line as for theorem 6 and uses derivations from theorem 7. Then we invoke axiom **GK** to establish $KERBEROS \vdash SEC_{skey}^{client}, SEC_{skey}^{tgs}$.

Kerberos with PKINIT. In the first stage of Kerberos with PKINIT [33], the KAS establishes the authorization key encrypted with a symmetric key which in turn is sent to the client encrypted with its public key. Since the protocol uses both public and symmetric keys at level 0, we formulate a definition of a joint public-symmetric key game. We then extend the proof system and prove all the syntactically analogous properties of the PKINIT version.

6   Conclusion

Computational secrecy properties, such as indistinguishability and suitability of a key ("GoodKey"), are not trace-based properties, making it awkward to reason inductively or compositionally about them. We therefore formulate the *secretive* trace-based property and prove that any secretive protocol can be used to construct a generic reduction from protocol attacks to attacks on underlying primitives. This allows computational secrecy to be established by direct inductive reasoning about a relatively natural and intuitive trace-based property.

A second contribution of the paper is a proof system for secrecy, in a formal logic based on inductive reasoning about protocol actions carried out by honest parties (only). We illustrate the power of this system by giving a modular, formal proof of computational authentication and secrecy properties of the Kerberos V5 protocol, thus addressing an open problem posed in [3]. Other proofs have been carried out, such as for a protocol that poses a challenge for the rank function method [19], but are omitted due to space constraints.

References

1. IEEE P802.11i/D10.0: Medium Access Control (MAC) security enhancements, amendment 6 to IEEE Standard for local and metropolitan area networks part 11: Wireless Medium Access Control (MAC) and Physical Layer (PHY) specifications (April 2004)
2. Abadi, M., Rogaway, P.: Reconciling two views of cryptography (the computational soundness of formal encryption). Journal of Cryptology 15(2), 103–127 (2002)
3. Backes, M., Cervesato, I., Jaggard, A.D., Scedrov, A., Tsay, J.-K.: Cryptographically sound security proofs for basic and public-key kerberos. In: Proceedings of 11th European Symposium on Research in Computer Security (to appear)
4. Backes, M., Pfitzmann, B.: Limits of the cryptographic realization of XOR. In: di Vimercati, S.d.C., Syverson, P.F., Gollmann, D. (eds.) ESORICS 2005. LNCS, vol. 3679, Springer, Heidelberg (2005)
5. Backes, M., Pfitzmann, B.: Relating symbolic and cryptographic secrecy. In: Proc. IEEE Symposium on Security and Privacy, pp. 171–182. IEEE, Los Alamitos (2005)
6. Backes, M., Pfitzmann, B., Waidner, M.: A universally composable cryptographic library. Cryptology ePrint Archive, Report 2003/015 (2003)
7. Backes, M., Pfitzmann, B., Waidner, M.: Limits of the reactive simulatability/uc of dolev-yao models with hashes. In: Gollmann, D., Meier, J., Sabelfeld, A. (eds.) ESORICS 2006. LNCS, vol. 4189, Springer, Heidelberg (2006)
8. Baudet, M., Cortier, V., Kremer, S.: Computationally Sound Implementations of Equational Theories against Passive Adversaries. In: Caires, L., Italiano, G.F., Monteiro, L., Palamidessi, C., Yung, M. (eds.) ICALP 2005. LNCS, vol. 3580, Springer, Heidelberg (2005)
9. Bellare, M., Boldyreva, A., Micali, S.: Public-key encryption in a multi-user setting: Security proofs and improvements. In: Preneel, B. (ed.) EUROCRYPT 2000. LNCS, vol. 1807, pp. 259–274. Springer, Heidelberg (2000)
10. Bellare, M., Namprempre, C.: Authenticated encryption: Relations among notions and analysis of the generic composition paradigm. In: Okamoto, T. (ed.) ASIACRYPT 2000. LNCS, vol. 1976, pp. 531–545. Springer, Heidelberg (2000)
11. Bellare, M., Rogaway, P.: Entity authentication and key distribution. In: Stinson, D.R. (ed.) CRYPTO 1993. LNCS, vol. 773, pp. 232–249. Springer, Heidelberg (1994)
12. Butler, F., Cervesato, I., Jaggard, A.D., Scedrov, A.: Verifying confidentiality and authentication in kerberos 5. In: Futatsugi, K., Mizoguchi, F., Yonezaki, N. (eds.) ISSS 2003. LNCS, vol. 3233, pp. 1–24. Springer, Heidelberg (2004)
13. Canetti, R., Herzog, J.: Universally composable symbolic analysis of mutual authentication and key-exchange protocols. In: Halevi, S., Rabin, T. (eds.) TCC 2006. LNCS, vol. 3876, pp. 380–403. Springer, Heidelberg (2006)
14. Cortier, V., Warinschi, B.: Computationally sound, automated proofs for security protocols. In: Sagiv, M. (ed.) ESOP 2005. LNCS, vol. 3444, pp. 157–171. Springer, Heidelberg (2005)
15. Datta, A., Derek, A., Mitchell, J., Ramanathan, A., Scedrov, A.: Games and the impossibility of realizable ideal functionality. In: Halevi, S., Rabin, T. (eds.) TCC 2006. LNCS, vol. 3876, Springer, Heidelberg (2006)
16. Datta, A., Derek, A., Mitchell, J.C., Pavlovic, D.: A derivation system and compositional logic for security protocols. Journal of Computer Security (2005)
17. Datta, A., Derek, A., Mitchell, J.C., Shmatikov, V., Turuani, M.: Probabilistic polynomial-time semantics for a protocol security logic. In: Caires, L., Italiano, G.F., Monteiro, L., Palamidessi, C., Yung, M. (eds.) ICALP 2005. LNCS, vol. 3580, pp. 16–29. Springer, Heidelberg (2005)

18. Datta, A., Derek, A., Mitchell, J.C., Warinschi, B.: Computationally sound compositional logic for key exchange protocols. In: Proceedings of 19th IEEE Computer Security Foundations Workshop, pp. 321–334. IEEE, Los Alamitos (2006)

19. Delicata, R., Schneider, S.A.: Towards the rank function verification of protocols that use temporary secrets. In: WITS '04. Proceedings of the Workshop on Issues in the Theory of Security (2004)

20. Fábrega, F.J.T., Herzog, J.C., Guttman, J.D.: Strand spaces: Why is a security protocol correct? In: Proceedings of the 1998 IEEE Symposium on Security and Privacy, Oakland, CA, May 1998, pp. 160–171. IEEE Computer Society Press, Los Alamitos (1998)

21. He, C., Sundararajan, M., Datta, A., Derek, A., Mitchell, J.C.: A modular correctness proof of IEEE 802.11i and TLS. In: CCS '05: Proceedings of the 12th ACM conference on Computer and communications security, ACM Press, New York (2005)

22. Heather, J.: Strand spaces and rank functions: More than distant cousins. In: Proceedings of CSFW, p. 104 (2002)

23. Katz, J., Yung, M.: Unforgeable encryption and chosen ciphertext secure modes of operation. In: Schneier, B. (ed.) FSE 2000. LNCS, vol. 1978, pp. 284–299. Springer, Heidelberg (2001)

24. Kauffman, C.: Internet key exchange (IKEv2) protocol. IETF Internet draft (1994)

25. Kohl, J., Neuman, B.: The Kerberos network authentication service (version 5). IETF RFC 1510 (September 1993)

26. Meadows, C.: A model of computation for the NRL protocol analyzer. In: Proceedings of 7th IEEE Computer Security Foundations Workshop, pp. 84–89. IEEE, Los Alamitos (1994)

27. Micciancio, D., Warinschi, B.: Soundness of formal encryption in the presence of active adversaries. In: Naor, M. (ed.) TCC 2004. LNCS, vol. 2951, Springer, Heidelberg (2004)

28. Pavlovic, D., Meadows, C.: Deriving secrecy properties in key establishment protocols. In: Gollmann, D., Meier, J., Sabelfeld, A. (eds.) ESORICS 2006. LNCS, vol. 4189, Springer, Heidelberg (2006)

29. Roy, A., Datta, A., Derek, A., Mitchell, J.C.: Inductive proofs of computational secrecy (2007), http://www.stanford.edu/~arnab/rddm-InductiveProofs.pdf

30. Roy, A., Datta, A., Derek, A., Mitchell, J.C.: Inductive trace properties for computational security. In: ACM SIGPLAN and IFIP WG 1.7. 7th Workshop on Issues in the Theory of Security, ACM Press, New York (2007)

31. Roy, A., Datta, A., Derek, A., Mitchell, J.C., Seifert, J.-P.: Secrecy analysis in protocol composition logic. In: Proceedings of 11th Annual Asian Computing Science Conference (2006)

32. Warinschi, B.: A computational analysis of the Needham-Schroeder(-Lowe) protocol. In: Proceedings of 16th Computer Science Foundation Workshop, pp. 248–262. ACM Press, New York (2003)

33. Zhu, L., Tung, B.: Public key cryptography for initial authentication in kerberos. Internet Draft (2006)

What, Indeed, Is Intransitive Noninterference?
(Extended Abstract)*

Ron van der Meyden

School of Computer Science and Engineering,
University of New South Wales
meyden@cse.unsw.edu.au

Abstract. This paper argues that Haigh and Young's definition of non-interference for intransitive security policies admits information flows that are not in accordance with the intuitions it seeks to formalise. Several alternative definitions are discussed, which are shown to be equivalent to the classical definition of noninterference with respect to transitive policies. Rushby's unwinding conditions for intransitive noninterference are shown to be sound and complete for one of these definitions, TA-security. Access control systems compatible with a policy are shown to be TA-secure, and it is also shown that TA-security implies that the system can be interpreted as an access control system.

1 Introduction

In this paper, we present a new argument against Haigh and Young's [HY87, Rus92] definition of intransitive noninterference, showing that it is too weak for the intuitions it seeks to capture. We present an example that shows that it allows information to flow to an agent, that could not have come from the agents from which it is permitted to acquire information.

This leads us to consider alternative definitions. We show that there is in fact a spectrum of different definitions of noninterference for possibly intransitive policies, including two new notions TA-security and TO-security that we introduce, which are based on intuitions about the transmission of information about actions and observations, respectively. We then study these new definitions from the point of view of proof techniques and an application that have been held in the literature to be of significance for intransitive noninterference. We begin with a discussion of "unwinding conditions," which provide a proof technique for noninterference, but can be taken as a definition of security in its own right. Rushby proved that the classical unwinding conditions of Goguen and Meseguer provide a complete proof technique for noninterference in the transitive case. He proposes a weakening of these conditions for intransitive policies (correcting an earlier proposal by Haigh and Young [HY87]). He establishes soundness of the

---

* Thanks to the Courant Institute, New York University, for hosting a sabbatical visit during which this research was conducted. Work of the author supported by an Australian Research Council Discovery grant.

J. Biskup and J. Lopez (Eds.): ESORICS 2007, LNCS 4734, pp. 235–250, 2007.

weakened unwinding conditions, but not completeness. We give an explanation of this: Rushby's conditions are not complete for the Haigh and Young definition of noninterference. Instead, they are sound and complete for the stronger notion of TA-security. There is a somewhat surprising subtlety in this statement: for completeness, the weakened unwinding conditions must be applied to the appropriate bisimilar system, but the existence of the weak unwindings is not preserved under bisimulation.

We also follow Rushby in considering the behaviour of the definitions on access control systems, the class of applications originally motivating the literature on noninterference. Rushby showed that access control systems satisfying a condition of structural consistency with a policy satisfy Haigh and Young's definition of intransitive noninterference. We argue that Rushby's definition of access control systems can be weakened, and that access control systems consistent with a policy satisfy the stronger notion of TA-security as well as Haigh and Young's definition of security. Moreover, we also show that TA-security implies that there is a way to interpret the system as an access control system in the weakened sense. This shows that TA-security is in some sense equivalent to the existence of an access control implementation of the system.

These results provide strong evidence that TA-security, rather than Haigh and Young's definition, best fits the original objectives for the notion of intransitive noninterference. Nevertheless, the stronger notion of TO-security may well be equally significant for practical purposes. As evidence of this, we prove that access control systems structurally consistent with a policy also satisfy the stronger notion of TO-security, provided we work with an appropriate notion of observation for such systems.

2   Intransitive Noninterference

The notion of *noninterference* was first proposed by Goguen and Meseguer [GM82]. Early work on this area was motivated by multi-level secure systems, and dealt with deterministic systems and partially ordered (hence transitive) information flow policies. A significant body of work has developed since then, with a particular focus on generalization to the case of nondeterministic systems [Sut86, WJ90, McC88, FG01, Rya01] and intransitive policies [Rus92, RG99, Ohe04]. We focus in this paper on intransitive policies in the deterministic case.

Several different types of semantic models have been used in the literature on noninterference. (See [MZ06] for a comparison and a discussion of their relationships.) We work here with the state-observed machine model used by Rushby [Rus92], but similar results would be obtained for other models. This model consists of deterministic machines of the form $\langle S, s_0, A, \text{step}, \text{obs}, \text{dom} \rangle$, where S is a set of states, $s_0 \in S$ is the *initial state*, A is a set of actions, $\text{dom} : A \to D$ associates each action to an element of the set D of security domains, $\text{step} : S \times A \to S$ is a deterministic transition function, and $\text{obs} : S \times D \to O$ maps states to an observation in some set O, for each security domain. We may also refer to security domains more succinctly as "agents". We write $s \cdot \alpha$ for the state reached by performing the sequence of actions $\alpha \in Actions^*$ from state s, defined inductively by $s \cdot \epsilon = s$, and $s \cdot \alpha a = \mathtt{step}(s \cdot \alpha, a)$ for $\alpha \in A^*$ and $a \in A$. Here ϵ denotes the empty sequence.

Noninterference policies, as they are now usually presented, are relations $\rightarrowtail \, \subseteq D \times D$, with $u \rightarrowtail v$ intuitively meaning that "actions of domain u are permitted to interfere with domain v", or "information is permitted to flow from domain u to domain v". Since, intuitively, a domain should be allowed to interfere with, or have information about, itself, this relation is assumed to be reflexive. In early work on noninterference, it is also assumed to be transitive.

Noninterference is given a formal semantics in the transitive case using a definition based on a "purge" function. Given a policy $\rightarrowtail$, we define the function $\mathtt{purge} : A^* \times D \rightarrow A^*$ by taking $\mathtt{purge}(\alpha, u)$ to be the subsequence of all actions a in α with $\mathtt{dom}(a) \rightarrowtail u$. (For clarity, we may use subscripting of agent arguments of functions, writing e.g., $\mathtt{purge}(\alpha, u)$ as $\mathtt{purge}_u(\alpha)$.) The system M is said to be *secure with respect to the transitive policy* $\rightarrowtail$ when for all $\alpha \in A^*$ and domains $u \in D$, we have $\mathtt{obs}_u(s_0 \cdot \alpha) = \mathtt{obs}_u(s_0 \cdot \mathtt{purge}_u(\alpha))$. That is, each agent's observations are as if only interfering actions had been performed. An equivalent formulation (which we state more generally for policies that are not necessarily transitive, in anticipation of later discussion) is the following:

Definition 1. *A system M is P-secure with respect to a policy $\rightarrowtail$ if for all sequences $\alpha, \alpha' \in A^*$ such that $\mathtt{purge}_u(\alpha) = \mathtt{purge}_u(\alpha')$, we have $\mathtt{obs}_u(s_0 \cdot \alpha) = \mathtt{obs}_u(s_0 \cdot \alpha')$.*

This can be understood as saying that agent u's observation depends only on the sequence of interfering actions that have been performed.

Haigh and Young [HY87] generalised the definition of the purge function to intransitive policies as follows. Intuitively, the intransitive purge of a sequence of actions with respect to a domain u is the largest subsequence of actions that could form part of a causal chain of effects (permitted by the policy) ending with an effect on domain u. More formally, the definition makes use of a function $\mathtt{sources} : A^* \times D \Rightarrow \mathcal{P}(D)$ defined inductively by $\mathtt{sources}(\epsilon, u) = \{u\}$ and

$$\mathtt{sources}(a\alpha, u) = \mathtt{sources}(\alpha, u) \cup \{\mathtt{dom}(a) \mid \exists v \in \mathtt{sources}(\alpha, u)(\mathtt{dom}(a) \rightarrowtail v)\}$$

for $a \in A$ and $\alpha \in A^*$. Intuitively, $\mathtt{sources}(\alpha, u)$ is the set of domains v such that there exists a sequence of permitted interferences from v to u within α. The *intransitive purge* function $\mathtt{ipurge} : A^* \times D \rightarrow A^*$ is then defined inductively by $\mathtt{ipurge}(\epsilon, u) = \epsilon$ and

$$\mathtt{ipurge}(a\alpha, u) = \begin{cases} a \cdot \mathtt{ipurge}(\alpha, u) & \text{if } \mathtt{dom}(a) \in \mathtt{sources}(a\alpha, u) \\ \mathtt{ipurge}(\alpha, u) & \text{otherwise} \end{cases}$$

for $a \in A$ and $\alpha \in A^*$. An alternative, equivalent formulation that we will find useful is the following: given a set $X \subseteq D$, define $\mathtt{ipurge}_X(\alpha)$ inductively by $\mathtt{ipurge}_X(\epsilon) = \epsilon$ and

$$\mathtt{ipurge}_X(\alpha a) = \begin{cases} \mathtt{ipurge}_{X \cup \{\mathtt{dom}(a)\}}(\alpha) \cdot a & \text{if } \mathtt{dom}(a) \rightarrowtail u \in X \\ \mathtt{ipurge}_X(\alpha) & \text{otherwise} \end{cases}$$

Then $\mathtt{ipurge}_u(\alpha)$ is identical to $\mathtt{ipurge}_{\{u\}}(\alpha)$. The intransitive purge function is then used in place of the purge function in Haigh and Young's definition:

Definition 2. *A system M is IP-secure with respect to a (possibly intransitive) policy $\rightarrowtail$ if for all sequences $\alpha \in A^*$, and $u \in D$, we have $\mathtt{obs}_u(s_0 \cdot \alpha) = \mathtt{obs}_u(s_0 \cdot \mathtt{ipurge}_u(\alpha))$.*

Since the function $\mathtt{ipurge}_u$ on A^* is idempotent, this definition, like the definition for the transitive case, can be formulated as: M is IP-secure with respect to a policy $\rightarrowtail$ if for all $u \in D$ and all sequences $\alpha, \alpha' \in A^*$ with $\mathtt{ipurge}_u(\alpha) = \mathtt{ipurge}_u(\alpha')$, we have $\mathtt{obs}_u(s_0 \cdot \alpha) = \mathtt{obs}_u(s_0 \cdot \alpha')$. It can be seen that $\mathtt{ipurge}_u(\alpha) = \mathtt{purge}_u(\alpha)$ when $\rightarrowtail$ is transitive, so IP-security is in fact a generalisation of the definition of security for transitive policies.

Roscoe and Goldsmith [RG99] (henceforth, RG) have argued that the Haigh and Young definition is incorrect. However, RG's arguments have not been universally accepted as compelling (see, e.g., [Ohe04]).

Nevertheless, we believe that a case can be made that IP-security is too weak, but on different grounds. Note that the intransitive purge $\mathtt{ipurge}_u(\alpha)$ preserves not just certain actions from the sequence α, but also their *order*. We claim that this allows u to "know" this order in situations where an intuitive reading of the policy would suggest that it ought not to know this order.

The notion of knowledge can be made precise using the the following notion of *view*. The definition uses an absorbtive concatenation function $\circ$, defined over a set X by, for $s \in X^*$ and $x \in X$, by $s \circ x = s$ if x is equal to the final element of s (if any), and $s \circ x = s \cdot x$ (ordinary concatenation) otherwise. Define the view of domain u with respect to a sequence $\alpha \in A^*$ using the function $\mathtt{view}_u : A^* \rightarrow (A \cup O)^*$ (where O is the set of observations in the system) defined by

$$\mathtt{view}_u(\epsilon) = \mathtt{obs}_u(s_0), \text{ and}$$
$$\mathtt{view}_u(\alpha a) = (\mathtt{view}_u(\alpha) \cdot b) \circ \mathtt{obs}_u(s_0 \cdot \alpha),$$

where $b = a$ if $\mathtt{dom}(a) = u$ and $b = \epsilon$ otherwise. That is, $\mathtt{view}_u(\alpha)$ is the sequence of all observations and actions of domain u in the run generated by α, compressed by the elimination of stuttering observations. Intuitively, $\mathtt{view}_u(\alpha)$ is the complete record of information available to agent u in the run generated by the sequence of actions α. The reason we apply the absorbtive concatenation is to capture that the system is asynchronous, with agents not having access to a global clock. Thus, two periods of different length during which a particular observation obtains are not distinguishable to the agent.

We may then say that agent u *knows* a fact ϕ about a sequence α if ϕ is true of all sequences α' such that $\mathtt{view}_u(\alpha) = \mathtt{view}_u(\alpha')$. Similarly, ϕ is *distributed knowledge* to a group G of agents in a sequence α if ϕ is true of all sequences α' such that $\mathtt{view}_u(\alpha) = \mathtt{view}_u(\alpha')$ for all $u \in G$. These are essentially the definitions of knowledge and distributed knowledge used in the literature on reasoning about knowledge [FHMV95], for an agent with *asynchronous perfect recall* . Intuitively, a fact is *distributed knowledge* to the set of agents G if it could be deduced after combining all the information that these agents have.

We may now present our example illustrating a weakness of IP-security. The essence of the example is that IP-security is consistent with an agent acquiring information that is not distributed knowledge to the agents from which it permitted (by an intransitive policy) to acquire information.

Example 1. Consider the intransitive policy $\rightarrowtail$ given by $H_1 \rightarrowtail D_1$, $H_2 \rightarrowtail D_2$, $D_1 \rightarrowtail L$ and $D_2 \rightarrowtail L$. Intuitively, H_1, H_2 are two High security domains, D_1, D_2 are two downgraders, and L is an aggregator of downgraded information. For this policy, channel control, one of the motivations for intransitive noninterference, would require that any information about L_1 and L_2 available to L must have reached L via the downgraders D_1 and D_2. We may capture this intuition more formally by expecting that if M is a system that is secure with respect to this policy, if a fact about H_1, H_2 is known to L, then it should be distributed knowledge to D_1, D_2. We show that if security is interpreted as $IP - security$, then this expectation can be false.

Define the system M with actions $A = \{h_1, h_2, d_1, d_2, l\}$ with domains $H_1, H_2,$ $D_1, D_2,$ and L, respectively. The set of states of M is the set of all strings in A^*. The transition function is defined by concatenation, i.e. for a state $\alpha \in A^*$ and an action $a \in A$, $\texttt{step}(\alpha, a) = \alpha a$. The observation functions are defined using the ipurge function associated to the above policy: $\texttt{obs}_u(\alpha) = [\texttt{ipurge}(\alpha, u)]$. (Here we put brackets around the sequence of actions when it is interpreted as an observation, to distinguish such occurrences from the actions themselves as they occur in a view.)

It is plain that M is IP-secure. For, if $\texttt{ipurge}(\alpha, u) = \texttt{ipurge}(\alpha', u)$ then $\texttt{obs}_u(s_0 \cdot \alpha) = [\texttt{ipurge}(\alpha, u)] = [\texttt{ipurge}(\alpha', u)] = \texttt{obs}_u(s_0 \cdot \alpha')$.

Consider the sequences of actions $\alpha_1 = h_1 h_2 d_1 d_2$ and $\alpha_2 = h_2 h_1 d_1 d_2$. Note that these differ in the order of the events h_1, h_2. Let ϕ state that there is an occurrence of h_1 before an occurrence of h_2.

Then we have $\texttt{obs}_L(\alpha_1) = [\texttt{ipurge}(\alpha_1, L)] = [h_1 h_2 d_1 d_2]$. It follows that in α_1, agent L knows ϕ. We demonstrate that α_2 is a witness showing ϕ is not distributed knowledge to $\{D_1, D_2\}$ in α_1. Plainly α_2 does not satisfy ϕ so we need to show $\texttt{view}_u(\alpha_1) = \texttt{view}_u(\alpha_2)$ for $u \in \{D_1, D_2\}$. For this, note

$\texttt{view}_{D_1}(\alpha_1)$
$= \texttt{obs}_{D_1}(\epsilon) \circ \texttt{obs}_{D_1}(h_1) \circ \texttt{obs}_{D_1}(h_1 h_2) \circ d_1 \circ \texttt{obs}_{D_1}(h_1 h_2 d_1) \circ \texttt{obs}_{D_1}(h_1 h_2 d_1 d_2)$
$= [\epsilon] \circ [h_1] \circ [h_1] \circ d_1 \circ [h_1 d_1] \circ [h_1 d_1]$
$= [\epsilon] \circ [\epsilon] \circ [h_1] \circ d_1 \circ [h_1 d_1] \circ [h_1 d_1]$
$= \texttt{obs}_{D_1}(\epsilon) \circ \texttt{obs}_{D_1}(h_2) \circ \texttt{obs}_{D_1}(h_2 h_1) \circ d_1 \circ \texttt{obs}_{D_1}(h_2 h_1 d_1) \circ \texttt{obs}_{D_1}(h_2 h_1 d_1 d_2)$
$= \texttt{view}_{D_1}(\alpha_2)$

The case for $u = D_2$ is symmetric. Thus, L has acquired information that cannot have come from the two sources D_1 and D_2 that are supposed to be, according to the policy, its only sources of information. $\qquad\square$

Our example has a rather different character to those of RG. We believe that it more convincingly demonstrates that IP-security allows information flows that contradict the intuitive meaning of the policy, at the level of abstraction at which the notion of noninterference is intended to operate (rather than the much more detailed level of abstraction to which RG tried to apply it.) We bolster the case for this claim in what follows, by showing that some alternative definitions are better behaved.

3   Alternative Definitions

As a response to Example 1, we consider several alternative definitions of security for intransitive policies.

To begin, let us consider why it was felt to be necessary to modify the definition of P-security for the intransitive case. For this, note that the system of Example 1 is not P-secure. For example, if we take $\alpha = h_1 d_1$ and $\alpha' = d_1$ then $\text{purge}_L(\alpha) = d_1 = \text{purge}_L(\alpha')$ but $\text{obs}_L(s_0 \cdot \alpha) = [\alpha] \neq [\alpha'] = \text{obs}_L(s_0 \cdot \alpha')$. However, this particular instance does not seem like it should be a counterexample to the security of the system. Intuitively, the fact that L observations differ on $s_0 \cdot \alpha$ and $s_0 \cdot \alpha'$ is justifiable, on the grounds that the action d_1 "downgrades" to L the fact that action h_1 has been performed. Thus, whereas IP-security is too weak, P-security seems to be too strong, since it does not permit an agent to forward information that it has acquired.

We are lead to propose two other definitions of security.[1] Both are based on a concrete model of the maximal amount of information that an agent may have after some sequence of actions has been performed, and state that an agent's observation may not give it more than this maximal amount of information. The definitions differ in the modelling of the maximal information, and take the view that an agent increases its information either by performing an action or by receiving information transmitted by another agent.

In the first model of the maximal information, what is transmitted when an agent performs an action is information about the actions performed by other agents. The following definition expresses this in a weaker way than the ipurge function.

Given sets X and A, let the set $T(X, A)$ be the smallest set containing X and such that if $x, y \in T(X, A)$ and $z \in A$ then $(x, y, z) \in T(X, A)$. Intuitively, the elements of $T(X, A)$ are are binary trees with leaves labelled from X and interior nodes labelled from A.

Given a policy $\rightarrowtail$, define, for each agent $u \in D$, the function $\text{ta}_u : A^* \to T(\{\epsilon\}, A)$ inductively by $\text{ta}_u(\epsilon) = \epsilon$, and, for $\alpha \in A^*$ and $a \in A$,

1. if $\text{dom}(a) \not\rightarrowtail u$, then $\text{ta}_u(\alpha a) = \text{ta}_u(\alpha)$,
2. if $\text{dom}(a) \rightarrowtail u$, then $\text{ta}_u(\alpha a) = (\text{ta}_u(\alpha), \text{ta}_{\text{dom}(a)}(\alpha), a)$.

Intuitively, $\text{ta}_u(\alpha)$ captures the maximal information that agent u may, consistently with the policy $\rightarrowtail$, have about the past actions of other agents. (The nomenclature is intended to be suggestive of *transmission* of information about

---

[1] The question of how exactly our definitions relate to RG's definitions is subtle and will be treated elsewhere.

actions.) Initially, an agent has information about what actions have been performed. The recursive clause describes how the maximal information $\mathbf{ta}_u(\alpha)$ permitted to u after the performance of α changes when the next action a is performed. If a may not interfere with u, then there is no change, otherwise, u's maximal permitted information is increased by adding the maximal information permitted to $\mathbf{dom}(a)$ at the time a is performed (represented by $\mathbf{ta}_{\mathbf{dom}(a)}(\alpha)$), as well the fact that a has been performed. Thus, this definition captures the intuition that an agent may only transmit information that it is permitted to have, and then only to agents with which it is permitted to interfere.

Definition 3. *A system M is TA-secure with respect to a policy $\rightarrowtail$ if for all agents u and all $\alpha, \alpha' \in A^*$ such that $\mathbf{ta}_u(\alpha) = \mathbf{ta}_u(\alpha')$, we have $\mathbf{obs}_u(s_0 \cdot \alpha) = \mathbf{obs}_u(s_0 \cdot \alpha')$.*

Intuitively, this says that each agent's observations provide the agent with no more than the maximal amount of information that may have been transmitted to it, as expressed by the functions $\mathbf{ta}$.

Example 2. Note that the system of Example 1 is not TA-secure. For,

$$
\begin{aligned}
\mathbf{ta}_L(h_1 h_2 d_1 d_2) &= (\mathbf{ta}_L(h_1 h_2 d_1), \mathbf{ta}_{D_2}(h_1 h_2 d_1), d_2) \\
&= ((\mathbf{ta}_L(h_1 h_2), \mathbf{ta}_{D_1}(h_1 h_2), d_1), \mathbf{ta}_{D_2}(h_1 h_2), d_2) \\
&= ((\mathbf{ta}_L(h_1), \mathbf{ta}_{D_1}(h_1), d_1), (\mathbf{ta}_{D_2}(h_1), \mathbf{ta}_{H_2}(h_1), h_2), d_2) \\
&= ((\epsilon, (\epsilon, \epsilon, h_1), d_1), (\epsilon, \epsilon, h_2), d_2)
\end{aligned}
$$

and

$$
\begin{aligned}
\mathbf{ta}_L(h_2 h_1 d_1 d_2) &= (\mathbf{ta}_L(h_2 h_1 d_1), \mathbf{ta}_{D_2}(h_2 h_1 d_1), d_2) \\
&= ((\mathbf{ta}_L(h_2 h_1), \mathbf{ta}_{D_1}(h_2 h_1), d_1), \mathbf{ta}_{D_2}(h_2 h_1), d_2) \\
&= ((\mathbf{ta}_L(h_1), (\mathbf{ta}_{D_1}(h_2), \mathbf{ta}_{H_1}(h_2), h_1), d_1), \mathbf{ta}_{D_2}(h_2), d_2) \\
&= ((\epsilon, (\epsilon, \epsilon, h_1), d_1), (\epsilon, \epsilon, h_2), d_2).
\end{aligned}
$$

So $\mathbf{ta}_L(h_1 h_2 d_1 d_2) = \mathbf{ta}_L(h_2 h_1 d_1 d_2)$, but $\mathbf{obs}_L(h_1 h_2 d_1 d_2) = [h_1 h_2 d_1 d_2]$ $\neq [h_2 h_1 d_1 d_2] = \mathbf{obs}_L(h_2 h_1 d_1 d_2)$. This illustrates that TA-security is in accordance with our intuitions about Example 1. □

The definition of TA-security has one aspect that might plausibly be questioned: it classifies as secure situations in which an agent transmits information to another that it has not actually observed. Whether one considers this to be a violation of security depends on one's attitude to forwarding of unobserved information. IP-security considers this acceptable, as does TA-security. However, it is possible to construct a definition that would consider this as insecure, by changing the definition of the function $\mathbf{ta}$.

Given a policy $\rightarrowtail$, for each domain $u \in D$, define the function $\mathbf{to}_u : A^* \rightarrow \mathcal{T}((A \cup O)^*, A)$ by $\mathbf{to}_u(\epsilon) = \mathbf{obs}_u(s_0)$ and

$$
\mathbf{to}_u(\alpha a) = \begin{cases} \mathbf{to}_u(\alpha) & \text{when } \mathbf{dom}(a) \not\rightarrowtail u, \\ (\mathbf{to}_u(\alpha), \mathbf{view}_{\mathbf{dom}(a)}(\alpha), a) & \text{otherwise.} \end{cases}
$$

Intuitively, this definition takes the model of the maximal information that an action a may transmit after the sequence α to be the fact that a has occurred, together with the information that $\mathrm{dom}(a)$ *actually* has, as represented by its view $\mathrm{view}_{\mathrm{dom}(a)}(\alpha)$. By contrast, TA-security uses in place of this the maximal information that $\mathrm{dom}(a)$ *may* have. (The nomenclature is intended to be suggestive of *transmission* of information about *observations*.) We may now base the definition of security on the function to rather than ta.

Definition 4. *The system M is TO-secure with respect to $\rightarrowtail$ if for all domains $u \in D$ and all $\alpha, \alpha' \in A^*$ with $\mathrm{to}_u(\alpha) = \mathrm{to}_u(\alpha')$, we have $\mathrm{obs}_u(s_0 \cdot \alpha) = \mathrm{obs}_u(s_0 \cdot \alpha')$.*

It is possible to give a flatter representation of the information in $\mathrm{to}_u(\alpha)$ that clarifies the relationship of this definition to P-security. Define the *possibly transmitted view* of domain u for a sequence of actions α to be the largest prefix $\mathrm{tview}_u(\alpha)$ of $\mathrm{view}_u(\alpha)$ than ends in an action a with $\mathrm{dom}(a) = u$. Then we have the following result, which intuitively says that u's observations depend only on (1) the parts of the views of other agents which are permitted to pass information to u, that they have actually acted to transmit, and (2) u's knowledge of the ordering of its own actions and the actions of these other agents.

Proposition 1. *M is TO-secure with respect to a policy $\rightarrowtail$ iff for all sequences $\alpha, \alpha' \in A^*$, and domains $u \in D$, if $\mathrm{purge}_u(\alpha) = \mathrm{purge}_u(\alpha')$ and $\mathrm{tview}_v(\alpha) = \mathrm{tview}_v(\alpha')$ for all domains $v \neq u$ such that $v \rightarrowtail u$, then $\mathrm{obs}_u(s_0 \cdot \alpha) = \mathrm{obs}_u(s_0 \cdot \alpha')$.*

The following result describes how these definitions are related. Like IP-security, the notions P-security, TO-security and TA-security are generalizations of the classical notion of noninterference in the transitive case.

Theorem 1. *With respect to a given policy $\rightarrowtail$,*

1. *if M is P-secure then M is TO-secure,*
2. *if M is TO-secure then M is TA-secure,*
3. *if M is TA-secure then M is IP-secure, and*
4. *if $\rightarrowtail$ is transitive then M is P-secure iff M is TO-secure iff M is TA-secure iff M is IP-secure.*

4   Unwinding Relations

In this section we relate our alternative definitions of security for intransitive policies to "unwinding conditions" that have been discussed in the literature as a way to prove noninterference [GM84]. We show that Rushby's proposed unwinding conditions for intransitive noninterference are most closely related to the notion of TA-security (where they provide a sound and complete proof method), although they are also sufficient for TO-security in a special case. We also show the somewhat suprising fact that Rushby's unwinding conditions are not preserved under bisimulation.

We begin by recalling Rushby's results on unwinding for intransitive nonintereference. Suppose we have for each domain u an equivalence relation $\sim_u$ on the states of M. Rushby discusses the following "unwinding" conditions on such equivalence relations.

OC: If $s \sim_u t$ then $\mathrm{obs}_u(s) = \mathrm{obs}_u(t)$.   (Output Consistency)

SC: If $s \sim_u t$ then $s \cdot a \sim_u t \cdot a$.   (Step Consistency)

LR: If $\mathrm{dom}(a) \not\rightarrowtail u$ then $s \sim_u s \cdot a$.   (Left Respect)

If these conditions are satisfied and $\rightarrowtail$ is a transitive policy, then M is P-secure [GM84]. Conversely, consider the particular equivalence relations $\approx_u$ on states, defined by $s \approx_u t$ if for all strings α in A^* we have $\mathrm{obs}_u(s \cdot \alpha) = \mathrm{obs}_u(t \cdot \alpha)$. Rushby uses these equivalence relations to show completeness of the unwinding conditions for transitive noninterference:

Proposition 2. *([Rus92] Theorem 6) Suppose M is P-secure with respect to the transitive policy $\rightarrowtail$. Then the relations $\approx_u$ satisfy OC, SC and LR.*

For intransitive noninterference he introduces the following condition:

WSC: If $s \sim_u t$ and $s \sim_{dom(a)} t$ then $s \cdot a \sim_u t \cdot a$. (Weak Step Consistency)

Define a *weak unwinding* on a system M with respect to a policy $\rightarrowtail$ to be a family of relations $\sim_u$, for $u \in D$, satisfying OC,WSC and LR. It will be convenient to have the following alternate characterization of this notion. Given a system M and a policy $\rightarrowtail$, let $\{\approx_u^{\mathrm{uw}}\}_{u \in D}$ be the smallest family of equivalence relations (under the pointwise containment order) satisfying WSC and LR.

Proposition 3. *There exists a weak unwinding for M with respect to $\rightarrowtail$ iff the relations $\approx_u^{\mathrm{uw}}$ satisfy OC.*

Rushby shows the following:

Proposition 4. *([Rus92], Theorem 7) Suppose that the relations $\{\sim_u\}_{u \in D}$ on a system M satisfy OC,WSC and LR. Then M is IP-secure for $\rightarrowtail$.*

However, he does not establish completeness of these unwinding conditions for IP-security. The following result yields an explanation of this fact.

Theorem 2. *Suppose that there exists a weak unwinding for M with respect to $\rightarrowtail$. Then M is TA-secure with respect to $\rightarrowtail$.*

Since, by Example 2, TA-security is stronger than IP-security, this result implies that the existence of equivalence relations $\sim_u$ satisfying conditions OC, WSC and LR is *not* a necessary condition for IP-security, since if this were the case, then every IP-secure system would be TA-secure.

This raises the question of whether the existence of weak unwindings is equivalent to TA-security instead. We now show that this question can be answered in the positive, provided it is formulated appropriately. The existence of weak unwindings turns out to have a somewhat surprising dependency on the structure of the system.

Given a system $M = \langle S, s_0, \text{step}, \text{obs}, \text{dom} \rangle$ with actions A, define the "un-folded" system $\text{uf}(M) = \langle S', s_0', \text{step}', \text{obs}', \text{dom} \rangle$ with actions A having the same domains as in M, by $S' = A^*$, $s_0' = \epsilon$, $\text{step}'(\alpha, a) = \alpha a$, and $\text{obs}_u'(\alpha) = \text{obs}_u(s_0 \cdot \alpha)$, where $s_0 \cdot \alpha$ is computed in M. Intuitively, this construction unfolds the graph of M into an infinite tree. Then we have the following.

Theorem 3. *M is TA-secure with respect to $\rightarrowtail$ iff there exists a weak unwinding on $\text{uf}(M)$ with respect to $\rightarrowtail$.*

It is reasonable to give a definition of security on M by reference to $\text{uf}(M)$ since these systems are bisimilar under the obvious notion of bisimulation on the state-observed system model. Bisimilarity of two systems is usually taken to imply their equivalence on all properties of interest. One might therefore expect from Theorem 3 that TA-security implies the existence of a weak unwinding on the system M as well as on $\text{uf}(M)$. It is the case that unwindings on M can be lifted to unwindings on $\text{uf}(M)$.

Proposition 5. *If there exists a weak unwinding for $\rightarrowtail$ on M then there exists a weak unwinding for $\rightarrowtail$ on $\text{uf}(M)$*

However, what we need, given Theorem 3, to deduce the existence of an unwind-ing on M from TA-security is the converse of this result. The following example shows that the converse does not hold. The reader may obtain some intuition for this example by noting that whereas weak unwinding seems to be sensitive to information about past actions, bisimulation cares only about the future. The essence of the example is that not enough past information is encoded in the states of the system M itself.

Example 3. Consider the system and policy depicted in Figure 1. There are actions a, b, c of domains $\text{A}, \text{B}, \text{C}$ respectively, and s_0 is the initial state. For all domains u other than D, we assume that the observation obs_u is the same on all states. TA-security therefore depends only on the behaviour of the system with respect to domain D, where there are two possible observations o, o' as indicated. We show that there does not exist a weak unwinding for $\rightarrowtail$ on M, but there does exist one on $\text{uf}(M)$.

For the former, we consider the relation family $\approx_u^{\text{uw}}$ on M. Note that since $\text{B} \not\rightarrowtail \text{D}$ and $s_0 \cdot b = s_1$ we have by LR that $s_0 \approx_\text{D}^{\text{uw}} s_1$. Similarly, since $\text{C} \not\rightarrowtail \text{A}$ we have $s_0 \approx_\text{A}^{\text{uw}} s_1$. Hence, by WSC, for the action a, we get $s_0 \approx_\text{D}^{\text{uw}} s_2$. Since

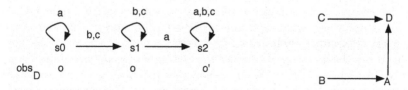

Fig. 1. An example showing TA-security does not imply existence of a weak unwinding

$obs_D(s_0) = o$ and $obs_D(s_2) = o'$, we have that $\approx_D^{uw}$ does not satisfy OC. Since $\approx_u^{uw}$ is the smallest family satisfying WSC and LR, there can exist no weak unwinding for $\rightarrowtail$ on M.

For the unwinding on $uf(M)$, consider $\approx_u^{uw} = \sim_u^{ta}$. Since this family of equivalence relations satisfies WSC and LR, it suffices to consider the property OC, where we need consider only the domain D, as already noted. Here, the only possible failure of OC is for states α, α' where $ta_D(\alpha) = ta_D(\alpha')$, $s_0 \cdot \alpha \in \{s_0, s_1\}$ and $s_0 \cdot \alpha' = s_2$. Now $s_0 \cdot \alpha' = s_2$ implies that α' contains either a b and a later a, or a c and a later a. View $ta_D(\alpha')$ as a tree with nodes of the form (x, y, e) representing a vertex labelled e with subtrees corresponding to x and y. Then this tree contains a path from a leaf to the root containing either b and later a, or c and later a. The same then applies to the identical tree for $ta_D(\alpha)$, which implies that α contains either a b and later a or a c and later a. But this means that $s_0 \cdot \alpha = s_2$, a contradiction. Hence the family $\approx_u^{uw}$ satisfies OC. □

Since $uf(M)$ and M are bisimilar, this example shows that bisimulation does not preserve existence of a weak unwinding. It is therefore necessary to either abandon the presumption that security properties are preserved under bisimulation, or adopt the stance that existence of a weak unwinding (on the system as presented) is not a sensible notion of security. We prefer the latter, but note that this does not hinder the utility of weak unwinding as a proof technique.

Further evidence of the utility of weak unwinding is the following result, which shows that it can also be used as a proof technique for TO-security. Define the relations $\approx_u^{obs}$ on states of a system M by $s \approx_u^{obs} t$ if $obs_u(s) = obs_u(t)$. Then we have the following sufficient condition for TO-security:

Proposition 6. *Suppose the relation family $\approx_u^{obs}$ is a weak unwinding on M with respect to $\rightarrowtail$. Then M is TO-secure with respect to $\rightarrowtail$.*

5   Access Control Systems

As a particular application of the unwinding conditions, Rushby [Rus92] discusses a notion of access control system that he formulates in order to give semantic content to the Bell-La Padula model [BP76] (which has been criticised for lacking semantics). He shows that every access control system satisfying a compatibility condition with respect to a noninterference policy is IP-secure. In this section, we formulate a weaker variant of Rushby's definitions, and show that it implies the stronger notion of TA-security. We also show that our weaker variant implies the even stronger notion of TO-security, provided we work with a specific, but intuitive, definition of observation in access control systems.

Moreover, we also show a converse to the result that access control systems are TA-secure, viz., that every system satisfying TA-security can be interpreted as an access control system. This proves the *equivalence* in some sense of access control and TA-security. We believe that these results, together with the example of Section 3 and the results of the previous section, provide strong evidence that

TA-security, rather than IP-security, is the notion that best realises the original objectives of the notion of intransitive noninterference.

According to Rushby, a *system with structured state* is a machine $\langle S, s_0, A, \text{step}, \text{obs}, \text{dom} \rangle$ together with

1. a set N of *names*,
2. a set V of *values*, and functions
3. $\text{contents} : S \times N \rightarrow V$, with $\text{contents}(s, n)$ interpreted as the value of object n in state s,
4. $\text{observe} : D \rightarrow \mathcal{P}(N)$, with $\text{observe}(u)$ interpreted as the set of objects that domain u can observe, and
5. $\text{alter} : D \rightarrow \mathcal{P}(N)$, with $\text{alter}(u)$ interpreted as the set of objects whose values domain u is permitted to alter.

For a system with structured state, when $u \in D$ and s is a state, write $\text{oc}_u(s)$ for the function mapping $\text{observe}(u)$ to values, defined by $\text{oc}_u(s)(n) = \text{contents}(s, n)$ for $n \in \text{observe}(u)$. Intuitively, $\text{oc}_u(s)$ captures all the content of the state s that is observable to u. Using this, we may define a binary relation $\sim_u^{\text{oc}}$ of *observable content equivalence* on S for each domain $u \in D$, by $s \sim_u^{\text{oc}} t$ if $\text{oc}_u(s) = \text{oc}_u(t)$.

In order to capture the conditions under which the machine operates in accordance with the intuitive interpretations of this extra structure, Rushby defines the following three *Reference Monitor Assumptions.*

RM1. If $s \sim_u^{\text{oc}} t$ then $\text{obs}_u(s) = \text{obs}_u(t)$.

RM2. If $s \sim_{dom(a)}^{\text{oc}} t$ and either $\text{contents}(s \cdot a, n) \neq \text{contents}(s, n)$ or $\text{contents}(t \cdot a, n) \neq \text{contents}(t, n)$ then $\text{contents}(s \cdot a, n) = \text{contents}(t \cdot a, n)$

RM3. If $\text{contents}(s \cdot a, n) \neq \text{contents}(s, n)$ then $n \in \text{alter}(dom(a))$.

The first of these says that an agent's observation depends only on the values of the objects observable to the agent. The third says that if an action can change the value of an object, then the agent of that action is in fact permitted to alter that object. The condition RM2 is more subtle. The following provides a possibly more perspicuous formulation of this condition:

Proposition 7. *RM2 is equivalent to the following: For all states s, either*

1. *for all $t \sim_{dom(a)}^{\text{oc}} s$, we have $\text{contents}(t \cdot a, n) = \text{contents}(t, n)$, or*
2. *for all $t \sim_{dom(a)}^{\text{oc}} s$, we have $\text{contents}(s \cdot a, n) = \text{contents}(t \cdot a, n)$*

That is, with the choice depending only on information observable to $dom(a)$, the effect of the action is either to make no change to n or to assign a new value to n that depends only on information observable to $dom(a)$.

In addition to the reference monitor assumptions, Rushby considers the condition:

AOI. If $\text{alter}(u) \cap \text{observe}(v) \neq \emptyset$ then $u \rightarrowtail v$.

Intuitively, this says that the ability to write to a value that an agent can observe counts as a way to interfere with that agent. Rushby shows the following:

Proposition 8. *([Rus92], Theorems 2,8) Suppose M is a system with structured state that satisfies RM1-RM3 and AOI. Then the family of relations $\sim^{oc}_u$ on M is a weak unwinding with respect to $\rightarrowtail$. Hence M is IP-secure for $\rightarrowtail$.*

By the results of the previous section, Rushby's result in fact yields the stronger conclusion that access control systems consistent with a policy are TA-secure. We can further strengthen this result by weakening the precondition.

Note that the condition RM2 says that the next value of n produced on performing an action a depends only on the values of names observable to $\mathrm{dom}(a)$. If n is not observable to $\mathrm{dom}(a)$, this may be too strong. Consider, for example, the situation where n represents a block of memory, and the action a writes to a single location within this block. Here the successor value depends on the value written (which will typically depend on the values of names observable to $\mathrm{dom}(a)$), but also on the previous value of n. Similarly, if the name n is an object in an object-oriented system, and the effect of the action is to call a method of this object, then the successor value will depend of the input parameters of the call (which will depend on values of names observable to $\mathrm{dom}(a)$), but also on the value of n. Thus, the condition RM2 can plausibly be weakened to the following.

[RM2′] For all actions a, states s, t and names $n \in \mathtt{alter}(dom(a))$, if $s \sim^{oc}_{\mathrm{dom}(a)} t$ and $\mathtt{contents}(s, n) = \mathtt{contents}(t, n)$ we have $\mathtt{contents}(s{\cdot}a, n) = \mathtt{contents}(t \cdot a, n)$.

That is, for $n \in \mathtt{alter}(dom(a))$, the value $\mathtt{contents}(s \cdot a, n)$ is a function of both $\mathtt{contents}(s, n)$ and $\mathrm{oc}_{\mathrm{dom}(a)}(s)$. Using Proposition 7 it can be seen that RM2 implies RM2′. The converse does not hold.

We now weaken Rushby's notion of access control system by replacing RM2 by RM2′. We define a system with structured states to be a *weak access control system* if it satisfies conditions RM1,RM2′, and RM3.

We also introduce a related notion on systems without structured states, that expresses that the system behaves as if it were an access control system. Say that a system M with states S *admits a weak access control implementation consistent with* $\rightarrowtail$ if there exists a set of names N, a set of values V and functions $\mathtt{observe} : D \times S \rightarrow \mathcal{P}(N)$, $\mathtt{alter} : D \times S \rightarrow \mathcal{P}(N)$ and $\mathtt{contents} : N \times S \rightarrow V$, with respect to which M is a weak access control system satisfying the condition AOI.

The following shows that weak access control systems compatible with a policy satisfy Rushby's unwinding conditions for intransitive noninterference:

Proposition 9. *Suppose M is a weak access control system consistent with $\rightarrowtail$. Then the family of relations $\sim^{oc}_u$ is a weak unwinding on M with respect to $\rightarrowtail$.*

We may also show a converse to this result, which leads to the conclusion that unwinding and weak access control systems are essentially equivalent.

Proposition 10. *Suppose that there exists a weak unwinding on M with respect to $\rightarrowtail$. Then M admits a weak access control interpretation consistent with $\rightarrowtail$.*

Combining these results with those of the previous section, we see that there is a close correspondence between TA-security, weak access control interpretations, and weak unwindings.

Corollary 1. *The following are equivalent*

1. *M is TA-secure with respect to $\rightarrowtail$,*
2. *$\mathrm{uf}(M)$ admits a weak access control interpretation consistent with $\rightarrowtail$,*
3. *there exists a weak unwinding on $\mathrm{uf}(M)$ with respect to $\rightarrowtail$.*

From Theorem 2 and Proposition 9, we also obtain the following.

Corollary 2. *If M is a weak access control system consistent with $\rightarrowtail$ then M is TA-secure for $\rightarrowtail$.*

This conclusion is a more general result than Proposition 8, in which we have both weakened the antecedent and strengthened the consequent. The following example shows that we cannot further strengthen the conclusion to TO-security.

Example 4. Consider the system for the policy $A \rightarrowtail B \rightarrowtail C$ with structured states for the set of names n_{AB}, n_{BC}, taking boolean values. Intuitively, these variables represent channels between the agents, so that $n_{AB} \in \mathrm{alter}(A) \cap \mathrm{observe}(B)$ and $n_{BC} \in \mathrm{alter}(B) \cap \mathrm{observe}(C)$. Plainly this is consistent with AOI. We represent states as tuples $s = (n_{AB}, n_{BC})$ with the obvious interpretation for contents. The initial state of the system is $(0,0)$. Domain A has actions a with semantics $n_{AB} := 1$ and B has action b with semantics $n_{BC} := n_{AB}$. The observation functions are defined on the state $s = (n_{AB}, n_{BC})$ by $\mathrm{obs}_A(s) = \mathrm{obs}_B(s) = \bot$ and $\mathrm{obs}_C(s) = n_{BC}$. It can be verified that this system satisfies RM1, RM2′, RM3. However, it does not satisfy TO-security. To see this, consider the sequences $\alpha = b$ and $\alpha' = ab$. Here we have $\mathrm{purge}_C(\alpha) = b = \mathrm{purge}_C(\alpha')$, and $\mathrm{tview}_B(\alpha) = \bot b = \mathrm{tview}_B(\alpha')$ but $\mathrm{obs}_C(s_0 \cdot \alpha) = 0 \neq 1 = \mathrm{obs}_C(s_0 \cdot \alpha')$. □

Notice that in this example, not all of the names observable to a domain have their contents visible in the observation of the domain. Say that a system with structured states is *fully observable* if in all states s we have $\mathrm{obs}_u(s) = \mathrm{oc}_u(s)$. Note that this means that the relations $\sim_u^{oc}$ and $\approx_u^{obs}$ coincide. We now obtain the following from Propositions 6 and 9. This shows that, modulo the reasonable assumption of full observability, we can derive a result similar to Corollary 2, but with the yet stronger conclusion of TO-security.

Corollary 3. *If M is a fully observable weak access control system consistent with $\rightarrowtail$ then M is TO-secure with respect to $\rightarrowtail$.*

A similar result does not hold with P-security in place of TO-security.

6   Conclusion

Our results have left open a number of technical questions. We have shown that weak unwindings provide a complete proof technique for TA-security, but have not provided a complete technique for TO-security. The reason for this is that there is inherently no tractable set of conditions on the states of the system that characterizes TO-security. We will treat this topic in a followup paper [Mey07] which deals with the complexity of the notions of security discussed in this paper. Another area requiring investigation is the generalization of our definitions to nondeterministic systems and systems that are not input-enabled, as has been studied for IP-security by von Oheimb [Ohe04]. More generally, one could consider extensions to the richer semantic framework of process algebra.

Both the fact, as argued by RG, that the notion of (intransitive) noninterference on its own falls short of expressing the correctness properties of downgraders that they sought to capture, and the fact, as we have shown, that there are several plausible notions of noninterference for intransitive policies, suggests that the notion of noninterference policy expressed by a relation $\rightarrowtail$ on domains lacks expressiveness that will be required in applications. We believe further work on richer formats for the expression of causality and information flow policies is warranted. The approach we have followed in this paper, of comparing an agent's actual information to an intuitive concrete operational model of the maximal information that an agent is permitted to have and transmit, could well be useful in this enterprise.

The specific case of downgrading policies has received some recent attention. Chong and Myers [CM04] have proposed a flexible language that attaches downgrading conditions to data items. Mantel and Sands [MS04] have proposed to introduce a programming annotation for downgrading, enabling the programmer to explicitly mark regions of code that are permitted to violate a transitive policy. They apply a definition based on IP-security. Bossi et al [BPR04] develop a theory of downgrading grounded in bisimulation-based notions of unwinding. Sabelfeld and Sands [SS05] lay out some general principles and direction for research in this area. It would be of interest to reconsider these contributions in the light of our results in this paper.

References

[BP76]   Bell, D.E., La Padula, L.J.: Secure computer system: unified exposition and multics interpretation. Technical Report ESD-TR-75-306, Mitre Corporation, Bedford, MA (March 1976)

[BPR04]   Bossi, A., Piazza, C., Rossi, S.: Modelling downgrading in information flow security. In: Proc. IEEE Computer Security Foundations Workshop, pp. 187–201. IEEE Computer Society Press, Los Alamitos (2004)

[CM04]   Chong, S., Myers, A.C.: Security policies for downgrading. In: 11th ACM Conf. on Computer and Communications Security (CCS), ACM Press, New York (October 2004)

[FG01]   Focardi, R., Gorrieri, R.: Classification of security properties (Part I: information flow). In: Focardi, R., Gorrieri, R. (eds.) Foundations of Security Analysis and Design. LNCS, vol. 2171, pp. 331–396. Springer, Heidelberg (2001)

[FHMV95] Fagin, R., Halpern, J.Y., Moses, Y., Vardi, M.Y.: Reasoning About Knowledge. MIT Press, Cambridge (1995)

[GM82]   Goguen, J.A., Meseguer, J.: Security policies and security models. In: Proc. IEEE Symp. on Security and Privacy, Oakland, pp. 11–20. IEEE Computer Society Press, Los Alamitos (1982)

[GM84]   Goguen, J.A., Meseguer, J.: Unwinding and inference control. In: IEEE Symp. on Security and Privacy, IEEE Computer Society Press, Los Alamitos (1984)

[HY87]   Haigh, J.T., Young, W.D.: Extending the noninterference version of MLS for SAT. IEEE Trans. on Software Engineering SE-13(2), 141–150 (1987)

[MB94]   Moses, Y., Bloom, B.: Knowledge, timed precedence and clocks (preliminary report). In: Proc. ACM Symp. on Principles of Distributed Computing, pp. 294–303. ACM Press, New York (1994)

[McC88]   McCullough, D.: Noninterference and the composability of security properties. In: Proc. IEEE Symp. on Security and Privacy, pp. 177–186. IEEE Computer Society Press, Los Alamitos (1988)

[Mey07]   van der Meyden, R.: The complexity of notions of intransitive noninterference (unpublished manuscript, 2007)

[MS04]   Mantel, H., Sands, D.: Controlled declassification based on intransitive noninterference. In: Chin, W.-N. (ed.) APLAS 2004. LNCS, vol. 3302, pp. 129–145. Springer, Heidelberg (2004)

[MZ06]   van der Meyden, R., Zhang, C.: A comparison of semantic models for noninterference. In: Proc. Workshop on Formal Aspects of Security and Trust, Hamilton, Ontario, Canada, August 2006. LNCS, Springer, Heidelberg (to appear), extended version at http://www.cse.unsw.edu.au/~meyden/research/publications.html

[Ohe04]   von Oheimb, D.: Information flow control revisited: Noninfluence = Noninterference + Nonleakage. In: Samarati, P., Ryan, P.Y.A., Gollmann, D., Molva, R. (eds.) ESORICS 2004. LNCS, vol. 3193, pp. 225–243. Springer, Heidelberg (2004)

[RG99]   Roscoe, A.W., Goldsmith, M.H.: What is intransitive noninterference? In: IEEE Computer Security Foundations Workshop, pp. 228–238. IEEE Computer Society Press, Los Alamitos (1999)

[Rus92]   Rushby, J.: Noninterference, transitivity, and channel-control security policies. Technical Report CSL-92-02, SRI International (December 1992)

[Rya01]   Ryan, P.Y.: Mathematical models of computer security. In: Focardi, R., Gorrieri, R. (eds.) Foundations of Security Analysis and Design. LNCS, vol. 2171, pp. 1–62. Springer, Heidelberg (2001)

[SS05]   Sabelfeld, A., Sands, D.: Dimensions and principles of declassification. In: Proceedings of the 18th IEEE Computer Security Foundations Workshop, pp. 255–269. IEEE Computer Society Press, Los Alamitos (2005)

[Sut86]   Sutherland, D.: A model of information. In: Proc. 9th National Computer Security Conf., pp. 175–183 (1986)

[WJ90]   Wittbold, J.T., Johnson, D.M.: Information flow in nondeterministic systems. In: IEEE Symposium on Security and Privacy, pp. 144–161. IEEE Computer Society Press, Los Alamitos (1990)

Traceability and Integrity of Execution in Distributed Workflow Management Systems *

Frederic Montagut[1] and Refik Molva[2]

[1] SAP Labs France, 805 Avenue du Docteur Maurice Donat,
Font de l'Orme, 06250 Mougins, France
[2] Institut Eurecom, 2229 Route des Cretes, 06904 Sophia-Antipolis, France
frederic.montagut@sap.com, refik.molva@eurecom.fr

Abstract. The execution of business processes in the decentralized setting raises security requirements due to the lack of a dedicated infrastructure in charge of management and control tasks. Basic security features including compliance of the overall sequence of workflow operations with the pre-defined workflow execution plan or traceability become critical issues that are yet to be addressed. In this paper, we suggest new security mechanisms capitalizing on onion encryption and group encryption techniques in order to assure the integrity of the distributed execution of workflows and to manage traceability with respect to sensitive workflow instances. We carry out an in depth analysis of the security properties offered by these mechanisms. Our solution can easily be integrated into distributed workflow management systems as its design is strongly coupled with the runtime specification of decentralized workflows.

Keywords: Integrity of execution, Traceability, Decentralized workflows.

1 Introduction

State of the art business processes may require a decentralized support of execution [1],[2],[3] because of their dynamicity or unusual execution environments. The flexibility of a distributed workflow enactment system on the other hand comes at the expense of security due to the lack a dedicated infrastructure to perform the management and control tasks during the execution of a business process. As a result, basic security features such as integrity of workflow execution assuring the compliance of the overall sequence of operations with the pre-defined workflow execution plan are no longer guaranteed. In addition, tracing back the identity of the business partners involved in a workflow instance becomes an issue without a trusted centralized coordination mechanism selecting workflow participants. As opposed to centralized workflow management systems, the distributed execution of workflows indeed raises new security requirements due to the lack of a dedicated coordinator. Yet, existing decentralized workflow management systems do not incorporate the appropriate mechanisms to meet the new security requirements in addition to the ones identified in the centralized setting. Even though some recent research efforts in the field of distributed workflow security have indeed

---

* This work has been partially sponsored by EU IST Directorate General as a part of FP6 IST project R4eGov and by SAP Labs France S.A.S.

J. Biskup and J. Lopez (Eds.): ESORICS 2007, LNCS 4734, pp. 251–266, 2007.

been focusing on issues related to the management of rights in business partner assignment or detecting conflicts of interest [4],[5],[6], basic security issues related to the security of the overall workflow execution such as integrity and evidence of execution have not yet been addressed. We already tackled some of these problems in a previous work [7] yet the solution we proposed did not take into account the management of security policies and business partners' trustworthiness.

In this paper, we present new mechanisms supporting the secure execution of workflows in the decentralized setting. These mechanisms capitalize on onion encryption techniques [8] and security policy models in order to assure the integrity of the distributed execution of workflows, to prevent business partners from being involved in a workflow instance forged by a malicious peer and to provide business partners' identity traceability for sensitive workflow instances. The suggested mechanisms can easily be integrated into the runtime specification of decentralized workflow management systems as illustrated in this paper using the pervasive workflow model specified in [3]. The remainder of the paper is organized as follows. Section 2 and 3 outline the pervasive workflow model and the associated security requirements, respectively. In section 4 our solution is specified while in section 5 the runtime specification of the secure distributed workflow execution is presented. Section 6 presents the security analysis of the proposed mechanisms. Finally section 7 discusses related work and section 8 presents the conclusion.

2   Workflow Model

The workflow management system used to support our approach was designed in [3]. This model supports the execution of business processes in environments without infrastructure and features a distributed architecture characterized by two objectives:

- fully decentralized: the workflow management task is carried out by a set of devices in order to cope with the lack of dedicated infrastructure
- dynamic assignment of business partners to workflow tasks: the actors can be discovered at runtime

Having designed an abstract representation of the workflow whereby business partners are not yet assigned to tasks, a partner launches the execution and executes a first set of tasks. Then the initiator searches for a partner able to perform the next set of tasks. Once the discovery phase is complete, a workflow message including all data is sent by the workflow initiator to the newly discovered partner and the workflow execution further proceeds with the execution of the next set of tasks and a new discovery procedure. The

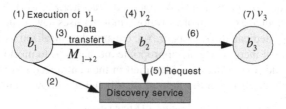

Fig. 1. Pervasive workflow runtime

sequence composed of the discovery procedure, the transfer of data and the execution of a set of tasks is iterated till the final set of tasks. In this decentralized setting, the data transmitted amongst partners include all workflow data. We note W the abstract representation of a distributed workflow defined by $W = \{(v_i)_{i \in [1,n]}, \delta\}$ where v_i denotes a vertex which is a set of workflow tasks that are performed by a business partner from the receipt of workflow data till the transfer of data to the next partner and δ is the set of execution dependencies between those vertices. We note $(M_{i \to j_p})_{p \in [1,z_i]}$ the set of workflow messages issued by b_i to the z_i partners assigned to the vertices $(v_{j_p})_{p \in [1,z_i]}$ executed right after the completion of v_i. The instance of W wherein business partners have been assigned to vertices is denoted $W_b = \{W_{iid}, (b_i)_{i \in [1,n]}\}$ where W_{iid} is a string called workflow instance identifier. This model is depicted in figure 1. In this paper, we only focus on a subset of execution dependencies or workflow patterns namely, SEQUENCE, AND-SPLIT, AND-JOIN, OR-SPLIT and OR-JOIN.

3 Security Requirements

3.1 Authorization

The main security requirement for a workflow management system is to ensure that only authorized business partners are assigned to workflow tasks during an instance. In the decentralized setting, the assignment of workflow tasks is managed by partners themselves relying on a service discovery mechanism. In this case, the business partner assignment procedure enforces a matchmaking procedure whereby business partners' security credentials are matched against security requirements for tasks.

3.2 Execution Proofs and Traceability

A decentralized workflow management system does not offer any guarantee regarding the compliance of actual execution of workflow tasks with the pre-defined execution plan. Without any trusted coordinator to refer to, the business partner b_i assigned to the vertex v_i needs to be able to verify that the vertices scheduled to be executed beforehand were actually executed according to the workflow plan. This is a crucial requirement to prevent any malicious peer from forging a workflow instance.

In our workflow execution model, candidate business partners are selected at runtime based on their compliance with a security policy. Partners' involvement in a business process can thus remain anonymous as their identity is not assessed in the partner selection process. In some critical business scenarios however, disclosing partners' identity may be required so that in case of dispute or conflict on the outcome of a sensitive task the stakeholders can be identified. In this case, the revocation of business partners' anonymity should only be feasible for some authorized party in charge of arbitrating conflicts, preserving the anonymity of identity traces is thus necessary.

3.3 Workflow Data Protection

In the case of decentralized workflow execution, the set of workflow data denoted $D = (d_k)_{k \in [1,j]}$ is transferred from one business partner to another. This raises major requirements for workflow data security in terms of integrity, confidentiality and access control as follows:

- data confidentiality: for each vertex v_i, the business partner b_i assigned to v_i should only be authorized to read a subset D_i^r of D
- data integrity: for each vertex v_i, the business partner b_i assigned to v_i should only be authorized to modify a subset D_i^w of D_i^r
- access control: the subsets D_i^r and D_i^w associated with each vertex v_i should be determined based on the security policy of the workflow

4 The Solution

4.1 Key Management

Two types of key pairs are introduced in our approach. Each vertex v_i is first associated with a policy pol_i defining the set of credentials a candidate partner needs to satisfy in order to be assigned to v_i. The policy pol_i is mapped to a key pair (PK_{pol_i}, SK_{pol_i}) where SK_{pol_i} is the policy private key and PK_{pol_i} the policy public key. Thus satisfying the policy pol_i means knowing the private key SK_{pol_i}, the inverse may however not be true depending on the policy private key distribution scheme as explained later on in section 6. The policy private key SK_{pol_i} can indeed be distributed by different means amongst which we distinguish three main types:

- Key sharing: a policy pol_i is associated with a single private policy key that is shared amongst principals satisfying pol_i. A simple key server KS_{pol_i} associated with pol_i can be used to distribute the policy private key SK_{pol_i} based on the compliance of business partners with pol_i. In this case, the partners satisfying pol_i share the same policy private key.
- Policy-based cryptography: a policy pol_i is expressed in a conjunctive-disjunctive form specifying the combinations of credentials a principal is required to satisfy to be compliant with the policy. A cryptographic scheme [9] is used to map credentials to keys denoted credential keys that can be combined to encrypt, decrypt and sign messages based on a given policy. Some trusted authorities are in charge of distributing credential keys to requesters when the latter satisfies some assertions (e.g. (jobtittle=director)∧(company=xcorp)). This scheme provides direct mapping between a policy and some key material and thus eases policy management as opposed to key sharing. No anonymity-preserving traceability solution is however offered as principals satisfying a given assertion may possess the same credential key.
- Group cryptography: a policy pol_i is mapped to a group structure in which a group manager distributes different private policy keys to group members satisfying pol_i.

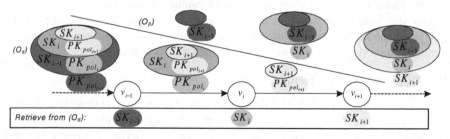

Fig. 2. Key management

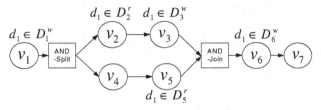

Fig. 3. Workflow example

A single encryption key is used to communicate with group members who however use their personal private key to decrypt and sign messages. This mechanism offers an identity traceability feature as only the group manager can retrieve the identity of a group member using a signature issued by the latter [10]. We note GM_{pol_i} the group manager of the group whose members satisfy pol_i. The management of policy key pair is as complex as for the key server solution since a group structure is required for each specified policy.

Second, we introduce vertex key pairs $(PK_i, SK_i)_{i \in [1,n]}$ to protect the access to workflow data. We suggest a key distribution scheme wherein a business partner b_i whose identity is *a priori* unknown retrieves the vertex private key SK_i upon his assignment to the vertex v_i. Onion encryption techniques with policy public keys PK_{pol_i} are used to distribute vertex private keys. Furthermore, execution proofs have to be issued along with the workflow execution in order to ensure the compliance of the execution with the pre-defined plan. To that effect, we also leverage onion encryption techniques in order to build an onion structure with vertex private keys to assure the integrity of the workflow execution. The suggested key distribution scheme (O_d) and the execution proof mechanism (O_p) are depicted in figure 2 and specified later on in the paper.

In the sequel of the paper, $\mathcal{M}$ denotes the message space, $\mathcal{C}$ the ciphertext space and $\mathcal{K}$ the key space. The encryption of a message $m \in \mathcal{M}$ with a key $K \in \mathcal{K}$ is noted $\{m\}_K$ and h_1, h_2 denote one-way hash functions.

4.2   Data Protection

The role of a business partner b_i assigned to a vertex v_i consists in processing the workflow data that are granted read-only and read-write access during the execution of v_i. We define a specific structure depicted in figure 4 called data block to protect workflow data accordingly. Each data block consists of two fields: the actual data d_k and a signature $sign_a(d_k) = \{h_1(d_k)\}_{SK_a}$. We note $B_k^a = (d_k, sign_a(d_k))$ the data block including the data segment d_k that has last been modified during the execution of v_a. The data block B_k^a is also associated with a set of signatures denoted H_k^a that is computed by b_a assigned to v_a. $H_k^a = \left\{\{h_1(\{B_k^a\}_{PK_l})\}_{SK_a} | l \in R_k^a\right\}$ where R_k^a is the set defined as follows. $R_k^a = \{l \in [1, n] | (d_k \in D_l^r)$ and $(v_l$ is executed after $v_a)$ and $(v_l$ is not executed after $v_{p(a,l,k)})\}$ where $v_{p(a,l,k)}$ denotes the first vertex executed after v_a such that $d_k \in D_{p(a,l,k)}^w$ and that is located on the same branch of the workflow as v_a and v_l. For instance, consider the example of figure 3 whereby d_1 is in D_1^w, D_2^r, D_3^w, D_5^r and D_6^w, $v_{(1,2,1)} = v_3$, $R_1^1 = \{2, 3, 5, 6\}$ and $R_1^3 = \{6\}$.

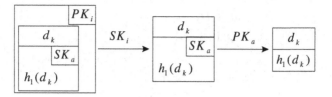

Fig. 4. Access to workflow data

When the business partner b_i receives the data block B_k^a encrypted with PK_i (i.e. he is granted read access on d_k), he decrypts the structure using SK_i in order to get access to d_k and $sign_a(d_k)$. b_i is then able to verify the integrity of d_k using PK_a, i.e. that d_k was last modified after the execution of v_a. Further, if b_i is granted write access on d_k, he can update the value of d_k and compute $sign_i(d_k)$ yielding a new data block B_k^i and a new set H_k^i. If on the contrary b_i receives B_k^a encrypted with PK_m (in this case v_m is executed after v_i), b_i can verify the integrity of $\{B_k^a\}_{PK_m}$ by matching $h_1(\{B_k^a\}_{PK_m})$ against the value contained in H_k^a.

The integrity and confidentiality of data access thus relies on the fact that the private key SK_i is made available to b_i only prior to the execution of v_i. The corresponding distribution mechanism is presented in the next section.

4.3 Vertex Private Key Distribution Mechanism

The objective of the vertex private key distribution mechanism is to ensure that only the business partner b_i assigned to v_i at runtime and whose identity is *a priori* unknown can access the vertex private key SK_i. To that effect, the workflow structure in terms of execution patterns is mapped with an onion structure O_d so that at each step of the execution a layer of O_d is peeled off using SK_{pol_i} and SK_i is revealed. The complete building process is specified in [7], the main results on the distribution of vertex private keys with respect to various workflow patterns are thus only reminded in this section.

Definition 1. *Let X a set. An onion O is a multilayered structure composed of a set of n subsets of X $(l_k)_{k\in[1,n]}$, such that $\forall k \in [1,n]$ $l_k \subseteq l_{k+1}$. The elements of $(l_k)_{k\in[1,n]}$ are called layers of O, in particular, l_1 and l_n are the lowest and upper layers of O, respectively. We note $l_p(O)$ the layer p of an onion O.*

Definition 2. *Let $A = (a_k)_{k\in[1,j]}$ and $B = (b_k)_{k\in[1,l]}$ two onion structures, A is said to be wrapped by B, when $\exists k \in [1,l]$ such that $a_j \subseteq b_k$.*

SEQUENCE workflow pattern. An onion structure assuring the distribution of vertex private keys is sequentially peeled off by partners. Considering a sequence of n vertices $(v_i)_{i\in[1,n]}$ b_1 assigned to v_1 initiates the workflow with the onion structure O.

$$O : \begin{cases} l_1 = \{SK_n\} \\ l_i = \{\{l_{i-1}\}_{PK_{pol_{n-i+2}}}, SK_{n-i+1}\} \text{ for } i \in [2,n] \\ l_{n+1} = \{\{l_n\}_{PK_{pol_1}}\} \end{cases}$$

For $i \in [2, n-1]$ the partner b_i assigned to v_i receives $\{l_{n-i+1}(O)\}_{PK_{pol_i}}$, reads $l_{n-i+1}(O)$ using SK_{pol_i} to retrieve SK_i and sends $\{l_{n-i}(O)\}_{PK_{pol_{i+1}}}$ to b_{i+1}.

AND-SPLIT workflow pattern. n business partners are concurrently contacted by a single partner, n different onions are therefore concurrently sent.

AND-JOIN workflow pattern. Since there is a single workflow initiator, the AND-JOIN pattern is preceded in the workflow by an AND-SPLIT pattern. When $n - 1$ branches merge into a vertex v_a, v_a is executed if and only if $n - 1$ messages are received. The vertex private key SK_a is thus divided into $n - 1$ parts contained in $n - 1$ onions to be received by v_a. Besides, in order to avoid redundancy, the onion structure associated with the sequel of the workflow execution right after v_a is only included in one of the onions received by v_a.

OR-SPLIT workflow pattern. This is an exclusive choice, a single onion is sent depending on the result of the OR-SPLIT condition. The onions associated with the branches that can be executed are thus wrapped beforehand.

OR-JOIN workflow pattern. Since there is a single workflow initiator, the OR-JOIN is preceded in the workflow by an OR-SPLIT pattern. A single branch is executed depending on the choice made at the previous OR-SPLIT in the workflow, thus a single onion is sent to the vertex into which the branches merge.

Complete key distribution scheme. The onion O_d enabling the vertex private keys distribution during the execution of the workflow depicted in figure 3 is defined as follows.

$$O_d = \{\{SK_1, \{SK_2, \{SK_3, \{SK_{6_1}, \overbrace{\{SK_7\}_{PK_{pol_7}}}^{\text{Sequel after} v_6}\}_{PK_{pol_6}}\}_{PK_{pol_3}}\}_{PK_{pol_2}},$$

$$\underbrace{\{SK_4, \{SK_5, \{SK_{6_2}\}_{PK_{pol_6}}\}_{PK_{pol_5}}\}_{PK_{pol_4}}}_{\text{First AND-SPLIT branch}}\}_{PK_{pol_1}}\}$$

Second AND-SPLIT branch

The onions associated with the two branches forming the AND-SPLIT pattern are wrapped by the layer corresponding to v_1. Only the first AND-SPLIT branch includes the sequel of the workflow after v_6.

4.4 Execution Proofs and Traceability

Along with the workflow execution, an onion structure O_{p_i} is built at each execution step i with vertex private keys in order to allow business partners to verify the integrity of the workflow execution and optionally to gather anonymity-preserving traces when traceability is required during the execution of a workflow. Based on the properties we introduced in section 4.1, group cryptography is the only mechanism that meets the needs of the policy private key distribution when identity traceability is needed. In that case, we define for a workflow instance, the workflow arbitrator W_{ar} who is a trusted third party able to disclose business partners' identity in case of dispute. The workflow arbitrator is contacted to revoke the anonymity of some business partners only in case of dispute, this is an optimistic mechanism.

The onion structure O_p is initialized by the business partner b_1 assigned to v_1 who computes $O_{p_1} = \{\{h_1(P_W)\}_{SK_{pol_1}}\}$ where P_W is called workflow policy and is defined as follows.

Definition 3. *The workflow specification S_W denotes the set $S_W = \{W, (J_i^r, J_i^w, pol_i)_{i \in [1,n]}, h_1\}$ where $J_i^r = \{k \in [1,j] | d_k \in D_i^r\}$ and $J_i^w = \{k \in [1,j] | d_k \in D_i^w\}$ (J_i^r and J_i^w basically specify for each vertex the set of data that are granted read-only and read-write access, respectively). S_W is defined at workflow design phase.*

The workflow policy P_W denotes the set $P_W = S_W \cup \{W_{iid}, W_{ar}, h_2\} \cup \{PK_i | i \in [1,n]\}$. P_W is a public parameter computed by the workflow initiator b_1 and that is available to the business partners involved in the execution of W.

The onion structure O_p is initialized this way so that it cannot be replayed as it is defined for a specific instance of a workflow specification. If traceability is required during the execution of some business processes, the signatures of business partners with policy private keys are collected during the building process of O_p so that anonymity can be later on revoked in case of dispute. Group encryption is used in this case to distribute policy private key and b_1 is in charge of contacting a trusted third party, sending it $(h_1(P_W), P_W)$ to play the role of workflow arbitrator for the instance.

At the step i of the workflow execution, b_i receives $O_{p_{i-1}}$ and encrypts its upper layer with SK_i to build an onion O_{p_i} which he sends to b_{i+1} upon completion of v_i. If traceability is required, b_i encrypts $\{O_{p_{i-1}}, \{h_1(P_W)\}_{SK_{pol_i}}\}$ with SK_i instead. Considering a set $(v_i)_{[1,n]}$ of vertices executed in sequence and assuming that traceability is needed we get:

$$O_{p_1} = \{\{h_1(P_W)\}_{SK_{pol_1}}\}$$
$$O_{p_2} = \{\{O_{p_1}, \{h_1(P_W)\}_{SK_{pol_2}}\}_{SK_2}\}$$
$$O_{p_i} = \{\{O_{p_{i-1}}, \{h_1(P_W)\}_{SK_{pol_i}}\}_{SK_i}\} \text{ for } i \in [3,n]$$

The building process of O_{p_i} is based on workflow execution patterns ; yet since it is built at runtime contrary to the onion O_d, this is straightforward. First, there is no specific rule for OR-SPLIT and OR-JOIN patterns. Second, when encountering an AND-SPLIT pattern, the same structure O_{p_i} is concurrently sent while in case of an AND-JOIN, the $n - 1$ onions received by a partner b_n are wrapped by a single structure: $O_{p_n} = \{\{O_{p_1}, O_{p_2}, .., O_{p_{n-1}}, \{h_1(P_W)\}_{SK_{pol_n}}\}_{SK_n}\}$. Considering the example depicted in figure 3 and assuming traceability is not required, at the end of the workflow execution the onion O_p is defined as follows.

$$O_p = \{\{\underbrace{\{\{\{\{h_1(P_W)\}_{SK_{pol_1}}\}_{SK_2}\}_{SK_3}}_{\text{First AND-SPLIT branch}}, \underbrace{\{\{\{h_1(P_W)\}_{SK_{pol_1}}\}_{SK_4}\}_{SK_5}\}_{SK_6}\}_{SK_7}}_{\text{Second AND-SPLIT branch}}$$

$\{h_1(P_W)\}_{SK_{pol_1}}$ is sent by b_1 assigned to v_1 to both b_2 and b_4 assigned to v_2 and v_4, respectively. The onion structure associated with the two branches forming the AND-SPLIT pattern thus includes $\{h_1(P_W)\}_{SK_{pol_1}}$ twice.

In order to verify that the workflow execution is compliant with the pre-defined plan when he starts the execution of the vertex v_i, the business partner b_i assigned to v_i just peels off the layers of $O_{p_{i-1}}$ using the vertex public keys of the vertices previously executed based on S_W. Doing so he retrieves the value $\{h_1(P_W)\}_{SK_{pol_1}}$ that should be equal to the one he can compute given P_W, if the workflow execution has been so far executed according to the plan. In case traceability is required by the execution, b_i also verifies the signatures of the business partners assigned to the vertices $(v_{j_p})_{p \in [1,k_i]}$ executed right before him i.e. b_i decrypts $\{h_1(P_W)\}_{SK_{pol_p}}$ for all $p \in [1, k_i]$. If b_i

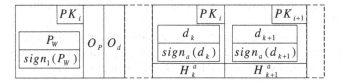

Fig. 5. Workflow message structure

detects that a signature is missing he contacts W_{ar} to declare the workflow instance inconsistent. In fact, business partners are in charge of contacting the workflow arbitrator when a signature is not valid and those who do not declare corrupted signatures are held responsible in place of partners whose signature is missing. In case of conflict on the outcome of some workflow tasks, the onion O_p is sent to the workflow arbitrator who is able to retrieve the signatures with policy private key of the stakeholders using P_W and with the help of some group managers the corresponding identities.

4.5 Vertex Key Pair Generation

Vertex key pairs have to be defined for a single instance of a workflow specification in order to avoid replay attacks. To that effect, we propose to capitalize on ID-based encryption techniques [11] in the specification of the set $(PK_i, SK_i)_{i \in [1,n]}$. For all $i \in [1, n]$ (PK_i, SK_i) is defined by:

$$\begin{cases} PK_i = h_1(W_{iid} \oplus S_W \oplus v_i) \\ SK_i = s \times h_2(PK_i) \end{cases}$$

where $s \in \mathbb{Z}_q^*$ for a prime q. s is called master key and is held by the vertex private key generator [11] who is in our case the workflow initiator. The signature scheme proposed in [12] can be used to compute the ID-based signatures required by the mechanisms we proposed. The public parameters such as the system public key (usually called P_{pub}) should be included in P_W. This vertex key pair specification has a double advantage. First vertex key pairs cannot be reused during any other workflow instance and second vertex public keys can be directly retrieved from W and W_{iid} when verifying the integrity of workflow data or peeling off the onion O_p.

4.6 Communication Protocol

In order to support a coherent execution of the mechanisms presented so far, workflow messages exchanged between business partners consist of the set of information that is depicted in figure 5.

Workflow data $(d_k)_{k \in [1,j]}$ are all transported between business partners and satisfy the data block specification. A single message may include several copies of the same data block structure that are encrypted with different vertex public keys based on the execution plan. This can be the case with AND-SPLIT patterns. Besides, workflow data can be stored in two different ways depending on the requirements for the execution. Either we keep the iterations of data resulting from each modification in workflow messages till the end of the execution or we simply replace data content upon completion of a vertex. The bandwidth requirements are higher in the first case since the size of messages increases as the workflow execution proceeds further.

P_W is required to retrieve vertex and policy public keys and specifies the workflow execution plan.

The two onion structures O_d and O_p are also included in the message.

Upon receipt of the message depicted in figure 5 a business partner b_i assigned to v_i retrieves first the vertex private key from O_d. He then checks that P_W is genuine i.e. that it was initialized by the business partner initiator of the workflow assigned to v_1. He is later on able to verify the compliance of the workflow execution with the plan using O_p and finally he can process workflow data.

5 Secure Execution of Decentralized Workflows

In this section we specify how the mechanisms presented so far are combined to support the secure execution of a workflow in the decentralized setting. After an overview of the execution steps, the secure workflow execution is described in terms of the workflow initiation and runtime specifications.

5.1 Execution Process Overview

Integrating security mechanisms to enforce the security requirements of the decentralized workflow execution requires a process strongly coupled with both workflow design and runtime specifications. At the workflow design phase, the workflow specification S_W is defined in order to specify for each vertex the sets of data that are accessible in read and write access and the credentials required by potential business partners to be assigned to workflow vertices. At workflow initiation phase, the workflow policy P_W is specified and the onion O_d is built. The workflow initiator builds then the first set of workflow messages to be sent to the next partners involved. This message generation process consists of the initialization of the data blocks and that of the onion O_p.

At runtime, a business partner b_i chosen to execute a vertex v_i receives a set of workflow messages. Those messages are processed to retrieve SK_i from the onion O_d and to access workflow data. Once the vertex execution is complete b_i builds a set of workflow messages to be dispatched to the next partners involved in the execution. In this message building process, the data and the onion O_p are updated.

The set of functional operations composing the workflow initiation and runtime specifications is precisely specified later on in this section. In the following N_k^i denotes the set defined by $N_k^i = \{l \in [1, n] | d_k \in D_l^r$ and v_l is executed right after $v_i\}$. Consider the example of figure 3: d_1 is accessed during the execution of the vertices v_1, v_2 and v_5 thus $N_1^1 = \{2, 5\}$.

5.2 Workflow Initiation

The workflow is initiated by the business partner b_1 assigned to the vertex v_1 who issues the first set of workflow messages $(M_{1 \to j_p})_{p \in [1, z_1]}$. The workflow initiation consists of the following steps.

1. Workflow policy specification: generate $(PK_i, SK_i)_{i \in [1,n]}$ and assign W_{ar}
2. Initialization of the onion O_d
3. Data block initialization: compute $\forall k \in [1, j]$ $sign_1(d_k)$

4. Data block encryption: $\forall k \in [1,j]$ determine N_k^1 and compute $\forall k \in [1,j], \forall l \in N_k^1$ $\{B_k^1\}_{PK_l}$

5. Data block hash sets: $\forall k \in [1,j]$ determine R_k^1 and compute $\forall k \in [1,j], \forall l \in R_k^1$ $\{h_1(\{B_k^1\}_{PK_l})\}_{SK_1}$

6. Initialization of the onion O_p: compute O_{p1}

7. Message generation based on W and $(N_k^1)_{k \in [1,j]}$

The steps one and two are presented in sections 4.5 and 4.3, respectively. The workflow messages are generated with respect to the specification defined in figure 5 and sent to the next business partners involved. This includes the initialization of the onion O_p and that of data blocks which are encrypted with appropriate vertex public keys.

5.3   Workflow Message Processing

A business partner b_i being assigned to a vertex v_i proceeds as follows upon receipt of the set of workflow messages $(M_{j_p \to i})_{p \in [1,k_i]}$ sent by the k_i business partners assigned to the vertices $(v_{j_p})_{p \in [1,k_i]}$ executed right before v_i.

1. Retrieve SK_i from O_d

2. Data block decryption with SK_i based on J_i^r

3. Execution proof verification: peel off the onion O_p

4. Data integrity check based on W and P_W

5. Vertex execution

6. Data block update: compute $\forall k \in J_i^w \; sign_i(d_k)$ and update d_k content

7. Data block encryption: $\forall k \in J_i^r$ determine N_k^i and compute $\forall k \in J_i^r, \forall l \in N_k^i$ $\{B_k^i\}_{PK_l}$

8. Data block hash sets: $\forall k \in J_i^w$ determine R_k^i and compute $\forall k \in J_i^w, \forall l \in R_k^i$ $\{h_1(\{B_k^i\}_{PK_l})\}_{SK_i}$

9. Onion O_p update: compute O_{p_i}

10. Message generation based on W and $(N_k^i)_{k \in [1,j]}$

After having retrieved SK_1 from O_d, b_i verifies the integrity of workflow data and that the execution of the workflow up to his vertex is consistent with the onion O_p. Workflow data are then processed during the execution of v_i and data blocks are updated and encrypted upon completion. Finally b_i computes O_{p_i} and issues the set of workflow messages $(M_{i \to j_p})_{p \in [1,z_i]}$ to the intended business partners.

6   Security Analysis

The parameters that are relevant to the security properties offered by the mechanisms presented in this paper are mainly twofold. First, there are several alternatives with respect to the management of the key pair (PK_{pol_i}, SK_{pol_i}), including simple key distribution based on the policy compliance, group key management or policy-based cryptography, on which the security properties verified by our solution depend. In fact, the main difference between the three policy private key distribution schemes we identified comes from the number of business partners sharing the same policy private key. As a matter of fact, the more partners share a given private key the easier it is for some unauthorized peer to get this private key and get access to protected data. Besides, the trustworthiness of business partners can not be controlled, especially when it comes to sharing workflow data with unauthorized peers once the vertex private key has been retrieved. In this context, the mechanisms presented in this paper verify some properties that do not depend on the underpinning policy private key distribution scheme while some other do. In the security evaluation of our solution, we make two assumptions:

- Security of policy keys: the public key encryption scheme used in the specification of the policy key pair (PK_{pol_i}, SK_{pol_i}) is semantically secure against a chosen ciphertext attack and the associated signature scheme achieves signature unforgeability
- Security of vertex keys: the public key encryption scheme used in the specification of the vertex key pair (PK_i, SK_i) is semantically secure against a chosen ciphertext attack and the associated signature scheme achieves signature unforgeability

6.1 Inherent Security Properties

Proposition 1. *Integrity of execution. Vertex private keys are retrieved by business partners knowing policy private keys associated with the policies specified in the workflow. Assuming that business partners do not share vertex private keys, the integrity of the distributed workflow execution is assured i.e. workflow data are accessed and modified based on the pre-defined plan specified by means of the sets J_i^r and J_i^w.*

Proof. This property is ensured by the onion O_d which assures distribution of the vertex keys used for accessing workflow data based on the workflow execution plan.

Assuming that a workflow initiator builds O_d based on the methodology specified in 4.3 and under the policy key security assumption, we claim that it is not feasible for an adversary $\mathcal{A}$ to extract the vertex private key SK_i from O_d if $\mathcal{A}$ does not know the set of policy private keys $(SK_{pol_{i_k}})_{k \in [1,l]}$ associated with the set of vertices $(v_{i_k})_{k \in [1,l]}$ executed prior to v_i in W. This is true as the structure of O_d is mapped to W.

Proposition 2. *Resilience to instance forging. Upon receipt of a workflow message, a business partner is sure that a set of business partners knowing policy private keys associated with the policies specified in the workflow have been assigned to the vertices executed so far provided that he trusts the business partners satisfying the policy pol_1.*

Proof. This property is enforced by the onion O_p whose building process is based on the workflow structure and vertex private keys. As stated in the previous claim, vertex private keys can only be retrieved by business partners knowing some policy private keys. We also claim that an adversary that does not verify a policy can not forge a workflow instance, i.e. that the adversary can not produce a workflow message pertaining to a valid workflow instance.

Assuming that a workflow initiator builds O_p based on the methodology specified in 4.4 and under the policy key security assumption, we claim that the onion structure O_p is unforgeable. The unforgeability property relies on two further properties:

1. a genuine onion structure O_p built during a previous instance of a workflow can not be replayed ;
2. an onion structure O_p can not be built by an adversary that is not trusted by business partners.

The first property is enforced by the fact that an onion structure O_p properly built is bound to a specific workflow policy P_W and thus can not be reused during an attempt to execute a malicious workflow instance. The second property is straightforward under the policy key security assumption as the policy-based signature scheme achieves signature unforgeability. Thus an adversary can not produce a valid onion $O_{p_1} = \{\{h_1(P_W)\}_{SK_{pol_1}}\}$.

Proposition 3. *Data Integrity. Assuming that business partners do not share vertex private keys they retrieve from the onion O_d, our solution achieves the following data integrity properties:*

- *Data truncation and insertion resilience: any business partner can detect the deletion or the insertion of a piece of data in a workflow message*
- *Data content integrity: any business partner can detect the integrity violation of a data block content in a workflow message*

Proof. The first property is ensured as the set of workflow data blocks that should be present in a workflow message is specified in P_W, the workflow message formatting has thus to be compliant with the workflow specification. The second property is assured by the fact that an adversary can not modify a given data block without providing a valid signature on this data block. This property relies on the unforgeability of the signature scheme used in the data block and hash set specifications.

These three security properties are sufficient to enable a coherent and secure execution of distributed workflows provided that business partners are trustworthy and do not share their policy or vertex private keys. The latter assumption is in fact hard to assess when sensitive information are manipulated during the workflow. We therefore introduced the traceability mechanism to meet the requirements of sensitive workflow executions.

6.2   Revocation of a Business Partner Anonymity

The main flaw of the basic security mechanisms we outlined is that the involvement of business partners in a workflow can remain anonymous thus preventing the detection of potential malicious peers who somehow got access to some policy private keys. To overcome this limitation when required, traceability with group cryptography has to be used during the execution of a business process. In this case the anonymity revocation mechanism provided with group cryptography can be seen as a penalty for business partners thus preventing potential malicious behaviors such as vertex private key sharing with unauthorized peers. Besides, policy private keys distributed by a group manager are intended for individual use which makes key leakage highly unlikely.

The following claims hold when the policy private key distribution scheme is based on group encryption techniques and traceability is required in the execution of workflows. As corollary of this assumption, we assume that vertex private keys are not shared with unauthorized peers, proposition 3 is thus verified.

Proposition 4. *Integrity of execution. The integrity of the distributed workflow execution is ensured or the workflow instance is declared inconsistent by the selected workflow arbitrator. Integrity of the distributed workflow execution consists in this case in performing the following tasks:*

- *workflow data are accessed and modified based on the pre-defined plan specified by means of the sets J_i^r and J_i^w ;*
- *signatures with policy private key are stored by the business partners involved in the workflow execution.*

Proof. Anonymity revocation is here a means to force business partners to behave properly during the execution of a workflow. If any malicious business partner is involved, he will not store his signature and we claim that the workflow instance will no longer be a valid one. The mechanism we proposed for anonymity revocation is as we mentioned optimistic and four scenarios can actually occur:

- A business partner detects that a signature is missing during the course of the workflow execution
- Each business partner stored his signature
- A set of business partners did not store their signature while some other partners did not declare the missing signatures to the workflow arbitrator
- A set of business partners assigned to vertices contiguously executed till the end of the workflow did not store their signature

In the first case, the workflow instance will be declared inconsistent by the workflow arbitrator. In the second case, trustworthy business partners have been involved in the workflow and their identity can be easily traced back by the workflow arbitrator. In the third case which is in fact highly unlikely to occur, the business partners who have not declared the missing signatures become responsible in place of the business partners who cheated. In the last case, nobody can be held responsible as apparently a group of untrustworthy business partners was involved in a fraud attempt and the workflow instance is declared inconsistent.

6.3 Discussion

As mentioned in the security analysis, group cryptography associated with anonymity revocation provides a full-fledged solution that meets the requirements of sensitive workflow instances. The other policy private key distribution schemes can be in fact used when the workflow execution is not sensitive or the partners satisfying the policies required by the workflow are deemed trustworthy. Our solution can still be optimized to avoid the replication of workflow messages. A business partner may indeed send the same workflow message several times to different partners satisfying the same security policy resulting in concurrent executions of a given workflow instance. Multiple instances can be detected by the workflow arbitrator when traceability is required or a solution based on a stateful service discovery mechanism can be also envisioned to solve this problem.

7   Related Work

Security of cross-organizational workflows in both centralized and decentralized settings has been an active research field over the past years mainly focusing on access control, separation of duty and conflict of interests [13],[14],[6] issues. However, in the decentralized setting issues related to the integrity of workflow execution and workflow instance forging, which are tackled in our paper have been left aside. In [5],[4] mechanisms are proposed for the management of conflicts of interest [15] during the distributed execution of workflows. These pieces of work specify solutions in the design of access control policies to prevent business partners from accessing data that are not part of their classes of interest. These approaches do not address the issue of policy enforcement with respect to integrity of execution in fully decentralized workflow management systems. Nonetheless, the access control policy models suggested in [5],[4] can be used to augment our work especially in the specification of the sets J_i^r and J_i^w at workflow design time.

Onion encryption techniques have been introduced in [8] and are widely used to enforce anonymity in network routing protocols [16] or mobile agents [17]. In our approach, we map onion structures with workflow execution patterns in order to build proofs of execution and enforce access control on workflow data. As a result, more complex business scenarios are supported by our solution than usual onion routing solutions. Furthermore, combined with policy encryption techniques, our solution provides a secure runtime environment for the execution of fully decentralized workflows supporting runtime assignment of business partners, a feature which had not been tackled so far.

Finally, our approach is suitable for any business scenarios in which business roles can be mapped to security policies that can be associated with key pairs. It can thus be easily integrated into existing security policy models such as chinese wall [15] security model.

8   Conclusion

We presented mechanisms towards meeting the security requirements raised by the execution of workflows in the decentralized setting. Our solution, capitalizing on onion encryption techniques and security policy models, protects the access to workflow data with respect to the pre-defined workflow execution plan and provides proofs of execution to business partners. In addition, those mechanisms combined with group cryptography provide business partners' identity traceability for sensitive workflow instances and can easily be integrated into the runtime specification of decentralized workflows. Our future work will focus on the integration of these security mechanisms into a transactional framework that we developed for the pervasive workflow model.

References

1. Barbara, D., Mehrotra, S., Rusinkiewicz, M.: Incas: Managing dynamic workflows in distributed environments. Journal of Database Management 7(1) (1996)
2. Cichocki, A., Rusinkiewicz, M.: Providing transactional properties for migrating workflows. Mob. Netw. Appl. 9(5), 473–480 (2004)

3. Montagut, F., Molva, R.: Enabling pervasive execution of workflows. In: Proceedings of the 1st IEEE International Conference on Collaborative Computing: Networking, Applications and Worksharing, CollaborateCom, IEEE Computer Society Press, Los Alamitos (2005)
4. Atluri, V., Chun, S.A., Mazzoleni, P.: A chinese wall security model for decentralized workflow systems. In: CCS '01: Proceedings of the 8th ACM conference on Computer and Communications Security, pp. 48–57. ACM Press, New York (2001)
5. Chou, S.C., Liu, A.F., Wu, C.J.: Preventing information leakage within workflows that execute among competing organizations. J. Syst. Softw. 75(1-2), 109–123 (2005)
6. Kang, M.H., Park, J.S., Froscher, J.N.: Access control mechanisms for inter-organizational workflow. In: SACMAT '01: Proceedings of the sixth ACM symposium on Access control models and technologies, pp. 66–74. ACM Press, New York (2001)
7. Montagut, F., Molva, R.: Enforcing integrity of execution in distributed workflow management systems. In: SCC 2007. 2007 International Conference on Services Computing, Salt Lake City, USA, July 9-13, 2007 (2007)
8. Syverson, P.F., Goldschlag, D.M., Reed, M.G.: Anonymous connections and onion routing. In: IEEE Symposium on Security and Privacy, USA, pp. 44–54. IEEE Computer Society Press, Los Alamitos (1997)
9. Bagga, W., Molva, R.: Policy-based cryptography and applications. In: Patrick, A.S., Yung, M. (eds.) FC 2005. LNCS, vol. 3570, Springer, Heidelberg (2005)
10. Ateniese, G., Camenisch, J., Joye, M., Tsudik, G.: A practical and provably secure coalition-resistant group signature scheme. In: Bellare, M. (ed.) CRYPTO 2000. LNCS, vol. 1880, pp. 255–271. Springer, Heidelberg (2000)
11. Boneh, D., Franklin, M.K.: Identity-based encryption from the weil pairing. In: Kilian, J. (ed.) CRYPTO 2001. LNCS, vol. 2139, pp. 213–229. Springer, Heidelberg (2001)
12. Paterson, K.: Id-based signatures from pairings on elliptic curves. Electronics Letters 38(18), 1025–1026 (2002)
13. Bertino, E., Ferrari, E., Atluri, V.: The specification and enforcement of authorization constraints in workflow management systems. ACM Trans. Inf. Syst. Secur. 2(1), 65–104 (1999)
14. Hung, P.C.K., Karlapalem, K.: A secure workflow model. In: ACSW Frontiers '03. Proceedings of the Australasian information security workshop conference on ACSW frontiers, pp. 33–41 (2003)
15. Brewer, D.F.C., Nash, M.J.: The chinese wall security policy. In: IEEE Symposium on Security and Privacy, pp. 206–214. IEEE Computer Society Press, Los Alamitos (1989)
16. Kong, J., Hong, X.: Anodr: anonymous on demand routing with untraceable routes for mobile ad-hoc networks. In: MobiHoc '03: Proceedings of the 4th ACM international symposium on Mobile ad hoc networking & computing, pp. 291–302. ACM Press, New York (2003)
17. Korba, L., Song, R., Yee, G.: Anonymous communications for mobile agents. In: Karmouch, A., Magedanz, T., Delgado, J. (eds.) MATA 2002. LNCS, vol. 2521, pp. 171–181. Springer, Heidelberg (2002)
18. Nanda, M.G., Karnik, N.: Synchronization analysis for decentralizing composite web services. In: Matsui, M., Zuccherato, R.J. (eds.) SAC 2003. LNCS, vol. 3006, pp. 407–414. Springer, Heidelberg (2004)
19. Tripathi, A.R., Ahmed, T., Kumar, R.: Specification of secure distributed collaboration systems. In: ISADS '03. Proceedings of the The Sixth International Symposium on Autonomous Decentralized Systems, p. 149 (2003)

Dynamic Information Flow Control Architecture for Web Applications

Sachiko Yoshihama[1], Takeo Yoshizawa[1], Yuji Watanabe[1], Michiharu Kudoh[1], and Kazuko Oyanagi[2]

[1] IBM Tokyo Research Laboratory, Yamato, Kanagawa, Japan
{sachikoy,ytakeo,muew,kudo}@jp.ibm.com
[2] Institute of Information Security, Yokohama, Kanagawa, Japan
oyanagi@iisec.ac.jp

Abstract. In typical Web applications, the access control at the database management system is not effective due to the dependency on application behavior. That is, once the information is retrieved, a careless application can easily leak the information to undesirable parties. In addition, database accounts are often shared for multiple Web users in order to allow connection pooling. We propose DIFCA-J (Dynamic Information Flow Control Architecture for Java), to keep track of and control fine-grained information propagation through execution of the program. DIFCA-J allows controlling the information flow at run-time, without needing to modify the source code of the target application or the Java VMs.

1 Introduction

In a typical three-tier Web application server (Figure 1), sensitive information, such as user's personal information or credit card numbers, is stored in a database. Access to the database is controlled at the database management system, and limited to only authorized users. However, such control is not sufficient to protect sensitive information.

First, after the application retrieves sensitive information from the database, it is up to the application code how to handle such information. An erroneous application may carelessly release such information to an undesirable destination. Furthermore, a single database table may contain data that belong to different classification levels. Some database systems support fine granular access control, but again, once the data is retrieved from the database, protection of the data depends on the application behavior.

Second, many of today's Web applications use a single database account for processing requests from multiple Web users, in order to effectively reuse database connections through connection pooling to optimize performance. The access control at the database is not effective when the same database account is used for all users. For example, a credit card number for a user A may be presented to user B due to a bug in the application, because the single database account cannot distinguish between users.

J. Biskup and J. Lopez (Eds.): ESORICS 2007, LNCS 4734, pp. 267–282, 2007.

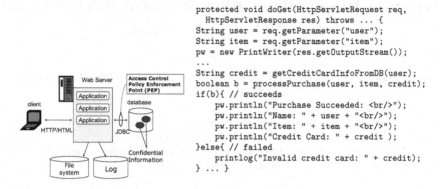

```
protected void doGet(HttpServletRequest req,
    HttpServletResponse res) throws ... {
String user = req.getParameter("user");
String item = req.getParameter("item");
pw = new PrintWriter(res.getOutputStream());
...
String credit = getCreditCardInfoFromDB(user);
boolean b = processPurchase(user, item, credit);
if(b){ // succeeds
    pw.println("Purchase Succeeded: <br/>");
    pw.println("Name: " + user + "<br/>");
    pw.println("Item: " + item + "<br/>");
    pw.println("Credit Card: " + credit );
}else{ // failed
    printlog("Invalid credit card: " + credit);
} ... }
```

Fig. 1. Three-tier Web App. Example **Fig. 2.** Problematic Servlet Code Example

Figure 2 shows a sample application in which a program bug can cause undesirable information flows. This is a simple example of an on-line shop servlet, which receives a user name and the item name from an HTTP request, and processes purchase request using the user's credit card number stored in the database. The `processPurchase` method checks the validity of the credit card number, and stops process by returning false when any problem is detected (e.g., the credit card is expired). We assume that the information received from the user via an HTTP request is not confidential, while credit card numbers in the database are confidential. (We assume that a proper user authentication takes place in advance, and the communication channel is protected by SSL or TLS, and thus the information in the HTTP request can be trusted.)

When looking at this program from the aspect of the confidentiality of the credit card number, it has two problems.

1. When the `processPurchase` method succeeds, the application sends back the credit card number to the user via an HTTP response. Although the credit card number belongs to the user, it should not be sent to the user unless necessary since the number may be peeped at over the user's shoulder, or leaked from the browser cache.
2. When the `processPurchase` method fails, the application outputs the user's credit card number into a log file. Confidential information should not be output into log files unless necessary.

We propose a system which prevents such undesirable information flow. That is, in the above example, the system detects undesirable information flow and stops processing when a credit card number is being output. In addition, when data is properly sanitized (e.g., when a credit card number is masked), the data should be "declassified" to indicate that it is no longer confidential.

In order to achieve fine-grained information flow control, language-based information flow control is receiving attention [1]. Much of the past research focuses on static analysis of information flow in a program using the type system or data flow analysis. However, we consider the practical use of such technologies to be difficult, because 1) It is difficult to analyze complicated data structures and control flows in multi-threaded object-oriented languages, 2) When a programing language is extended to include security functionality, existing software resources, such as libraries and development tools cannot be reused without adaptations, and 3) static analysis cannot take the dynamically generated code into account.

A dynamic information flow control approach has been proposed by Haldar, Chandra and Franz [2] [3] [4] to take advantage of the rich state information from a running application. They use a bytecode rewriting technique to modify the application bytecode to insert extra code for tracking the information flow of an application. Their approach tracks information propagation through method invocations and field access. We propose a Dynamic Information Flow Control Architecture for Java (DIFCA-J), inspired by the Haldar et al. approach. DIFCA-J inherits characteristics of being able to support dynamic conditions of running applications, not requiring any sourcecode from the target software, and being independent of Java VM implementations. In addition, in our system: 1) information flow is tracked and controlled at the granularity of primitive data types through most of the JVM instructions including logical and arithmetic computations, the operand stack and local variables operations, method invocation, and exceptions. 2) it effectively labels data for input or output from or to external environments, especially data exchanged with databases, and 3) it supports fine-grained application-level policies, including declassification policies. A more comparison with Haldar's approach is discussed in Section 6.

We implemented DIFCA-J on top of Apache Tomcat, and integrated Application Privacy Monitoring for JDBC (APM4JDBC) to enforce security policies in database (See Section 4).

The rest of the paper is organized as follows. Section 2 gives an overview of DIFCA-J and its basic concepts. Section 3 shows the architecture of DIFCA-J, and its detailed method for information flow control in execution of Java bytecode instructions. Section 4 describes integration of the databases for fine- grained information flow control between the database and the application server. Section 5 describes the current prototype implementation. Section 6 reviews related work, and Section 7 concludes the paper and covers our future research agenda.

2   Overview of DIFCA-J

We propose a Dynamic Information Flow Control Architecture for Java (DIFCA-J) to control the information flow of Java applications.

DIFCA-J allows administrators to define security labels for external resources (such as files, network and databases) as well as the information-flow policies between labels. During the execution of applications, DIFCA-J keeps track of propagation of security labels for the data, and detects any output that violates the policies.

The run-time functionality is inserted into the application bytecode as inline reference monitors (IRM) [5], using the bytecode rewriting technique. When the application is executed, the inserted IRM code communicates with the Access

Control Module (ACM), to notify it of the state of the running application. The ACM is implemented as a Java class, and a unique instance is created and associated with each thread. An ACM has an internal structure similar to a Java Virtual Machine (JVM). However, instead of holding data, an ACM holds security labels that are associated with data in the JVM. The ACM propagates security labels of data by synchronizing itself with the code execution of the JVM.

The ACM takes two sets of policies: the labeling policies, and the information-flow policies. Since the instrumented bytecode is independent of the policies, the policies can be late-bound to the application at run-time.

Labeling Policies. In DIFCA-J, any input or output to external resources is identified by Java APIs associated with the operation, that is represented in a form of pseudo-URI such as "java:*class_name.method_name*". Some resources require finer granular control for labels than APIs; e.g., the labels of files and network resources need to be identified by their locations, rather than by APIs. Therefore, such location are represented in the form of a URL.

In addition, a resource is either structured or unstructured, with regard to the labeling of its information. Examples of unstrucutred data are plain text files, where each file includes information with the same confidentiality. A database system is an example of a structured resource. Each datum in a database needs a more dedicated labeling policy, since each table may include columns with different classifications, and the classification may depend on the context of the query. DIFCA-J leverages Application Privacy Monitoring for JDBC (APM4JDBC) [6] to allow dynamic labeling of the database query results.

Information Flow Policies. DIFCA-J is policy agnostic and thus can flexibly adopt different types of policies, such as Biba [7], Bell-LaPadula [8], or the lattice model [9].

For the sake of simplicity, in the following example we use a simple Bell-LaPadula-type policy which has only two labels HIGH and LOW; i.e., information with the label HIGH cannot flow into LOW, while information with the label LOW can flow into HIGH. Labels are propagated when information flow occurs from explicitly labeled data.

Label Composition. When a value is derived from the composition of two values with different labels, the label of the resulting value becomes the composition of the two labels of the original values. Here, the composed label should be the Least Upper Bound (LUB) of the two labels; i.e., the lowest label which satisfy both of the two labels. For example, when $a + b = c$ where a is HIGH and b is LOW, the label of c needs to be HIGH. This is because when an attacker learns the values of both b and c, he can easily infer the value of a.

3   DIFCA-J Architecture

Figure 3 shows the architecture of DIFCA-J. IRMWriter takes the bytecode of an application as input, and inserts inline reference monitor (IRM) code into it.

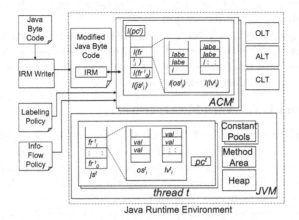

Fig. 3. DIFCA-J Architecture

This instrumentation process may happen either before application deployment, or on-the-fly when the code is loaded by a class loader.

A JVM has a JVM stack js^t for each thread t, which is a stack of frames, where each frame (fr_i^t, where i denotes the position on js^t) holds an operand stack os_i^t and a list of local variables lv_i^t for the method m_i^t that is being executed. When a new method m_{i+1}^t is called, a new frame fr_{i+1}^t is created and pushed onto js^t. Likewise, an ACM has a stack structure $l(js_t)$ corresponding to the JVM stack for each thread. Each $l(js_t)$ is a stack of frames-for-labels $l(fr_i^t)$. Instead of holding data operated upon by a method, each $l(fr_i^t)$ holds the labels of local variables $l(lv_i^t)$ and the operand stack $l(os_i^t)$ associated with the data.

As each bytecode instruction is executed in the application, the IRM code synchronizes the state of the ACM with the state of JVM so that the labels in $l(js^t)$ represents the security label of the data in js^t being operated upon in the application.

In a JVM, object instances and static field data are stored in the heap area. The ACM has three tables for holding the labels for the objects in the heap: the object label table (OLT) for the labels of objects and the fields of the objects, the array label table (ALT) for the labels of array elements, and the class label table (CLT) for the static fields of the classes.

A JVM also has a method area and a constant area for holding the bytecode of methods as well as the constant data of Java classes and interfaces. We regard these areas as non-confidential, and associate them with the special label NONE by default (i.e., $LUB(\text{NONE}, l) = l$ for any given label l, and either HIGH or LOW can flow to destination with the label NONE).

3.1 Information Flow in Java Bytecode

Programs written in the Java language are compiled into Java bytecode, a standard pseudo-machine language that is executed on a JVM [12]. Since we attempt to support applications with no source code, we target the Java bytecode to track the information flow of an application.

The JVM Specification [12] defines about 200 instructions, but in many cases a single semantic operation is defined in multiple instructions for different data types. Similarly, most instructions that concern local variables have variants that include frequently used local variable indices

3.2 Stack and Local Variable Operations

When information is exchanged between the operand stack os_i^t and the local variable table lv_i^t, e.g., by a LOAD or STORE instruction, the ACM propagates the label between $l(os_i^t)$ and $l(lv_i^t)$. When two values are combined to create a new value, e.g., as a result of a binary operation, the ACM obtains the composition of the two labels and associates it with the new value.

When a constant value is loaded onto os_i^t, the NONE label is associated with the value (unless the load operation was affected by an implicit flow as discussed later in Section 3.5).

For example, Figure 4(a) is a simple Java program which adds the variable b and the constant 1 and assign the result into the variable a. Figure 4(b) shows the bytecode representation of the same program.

The ACM follows the operations of the JVM. For example, the ACM first loads the labels of b from $l(lv_i^t)$ to $l(os_i^t)$ at the LOAD operation and then the label of 1 (NONE) to $l(os_i^t)$. When the ADD operation is executed, ACM obtains the composition of the two labels on $l(os_i^t)$, in this case $newlabel = LUB(l(os_i^t[j-1]), l(os_i^t)[j])$, where j denotes the highest position of $l(os_i^t)$ as of the time the operation is performed. Then the resulting $newlabel$ is pushed onto $l(os_i^t)$. Finally, the $newlabel$ is propagated to $l(lv_i^t)$ to be associated with the variable a at the ISTORE_1 operation.

3.3 Object and Field Access

Each object can be associated with a security label, but each field of an object may have different labels than the object itself. Therefore, our approach is designed to handle them separately.

A JVM stores objects into the heap area, and accesses to the fields are done through the GETFIELD and PUTFIELD instructions. The ACM stores the labels of the objects and their fields in the Object Label Table (OLT). The labels are propagated between OLT and os_i^t at each GETFIELD or PUTFIELD instruction. Similarly, the labels of static fields and the labels of array elements are managed in the Class Label Table (CLT) and the Array Label Table (ALT), respectively.

3.4 Method Invocation

When a method is invoked, information is propagated between the caller method and the callee method through method arguments and the return value.

When a method foo() invokes the method bar(), the method arguments are the output and the return value is the input, from the view point of foo(). In contrast, for bar(), the method arguments are the input and the return value is the output. Therefore, DIFCA-J allows defining the labeling policy of input and output for foo() and bar() separately. When an explicit policy is defined for an input to a method, then a security label is associated with the input data. When an explicit labeling policy is defined for the method output, then the label of the output data is compared with the label of the method, and execution is stopped when any violation of the information flow policy is detected. For example, when some data with label HIGH is being specified as an argument for a method with the output label LOW, that invocation causes an information-flow violation.

It should be noted that both the caller foo() and the callee bar() are not necessarily instrumented with IRM. The IRM Writer can only instrument the application code, and the standard Java libraries and the middleware (e.g., Web server) must not be modified. If the standard libraries are also IRM-enabled, the IRM code would recursively call the IRM code and the code could not be executed properly. Therefore, when foo() invokes bar(), there are four possibilities with regards to their IRM enablement: 1) both of foo() and bar() are IRM enabled, 2) only foo() is IRM enabled, 3) only bar() is IRM enabled, or 4) neither foo() nor bar() is IRM enabled.

In case 1), the label of the arguments is explicitly propagated by IRM by copying the labels from caller method's $l(os_i^t)$ to the callee method's $l(lv_{i+1}^t)$, while the arguments are copied from the os_i^t to lv_{i+1}^t. When returning from the method by the RETURN instruction, the label of the return value is popped from $l(os_{i+1}^t)$ and pushed to $l(os_i^t)$.

In case 2), since only m_i^t is IRM-enabled, the INVOKE instruction is IRM-enabled, but the RETURN instruction that is executed from m_{i+1}^t is not IRM-enabled. Therefore, the caller method m_i^t infers the label of the return value from the composition of the labels of the input arguments and the target object itself.

In case 3), since the caller method is not IRM-enabled, the callee does not receive the label of the input values unless an explicit policy is specified and thus the label NONE is associated with the input argument by default.

3.5 Implicit Flow

Even when no explicit flow occurs from HIGH to LOW, the HIGH information can be infered from the LOW information when the HIGH information affects the control flow of the program. For example, in the example code in Figure 5(a), the value of x can be inferred from the value of y after the if statement, since the value of y differs by the value of x. Such information flow is called an implicit flow [29].

In order to detect such an implicit flow, DIFCA-J associates a security label with the program counter to show any implicit flow caused by the execution of the code. Let pc^t be the program counter of the thread t and $l(pc^t)$ be the label associated with pc^t. In the above example, when the value of x causes a conditional branch in Line 3, $l(pc^t)$ is raised to HIGH. Then when the value is assigned to y, the label HIGH is propagated to the label of y.

Figure 5(b) shows the Java bytecode that is compiled from the Java source code in Figure 5(a). In Line 6 in the bytecode, IF_ICMPNE evaluates the value on

```
                                                            0: ICONST_1
                                                            1: ISTORE_1 // x
                        0: ICONST_1                         2: ICONST_0
                        1: ISTORE_1                         3: ISTORE_2 // y
                        2: ICONST_2                         4: ILOAD_1
                        3: ISTORE_2                         5: ICONST_1
                        4: ILOAD_2          1: x = 1; // HIGH    6: IF_ICMPNE #11
1: int a = 1;           5: ICONST_1         2: y = 0; // LOW     9: ICONST_1
2: int b = 2;           6: IADD             3: if(x == 1){      10: ISTORE_2 // y=1
3: a = b + 1;           7: ISTORE_1         4:   y = 1;         11: ...
                                            5: }
```

(a) Java Program   (b) Bytecode   (a) Java Program   (b) Bytecode

Fig. 4. Code Example for Addition   **Fig. 5.** Code Example for Branch

the os_i^t to branch conditionally. Lines 9 and 10 are the code that are executed conditionally depending on the two values that are on os_i^t (i.e., x and the constant 1). All of the values that are affected by these conditions need to be associated with the security label of the composition of the original value and the program counter. In the above example, when IF_ICMPNE is executed, $l(pc^t)$ becomes the composition of the label of x and the constant 1 (i.e., HIGH), and then in Line 9, the value propagated by the ISTORE instruction will be $LUB(l(os_i^t[j]), l(pc^t))$, which is the composition of the label of the value on the operand stack $l(os_i^t)$ and the label $l(pc^t)$.

Similarly, all of the IRM operations described before, need to compose $l(pc^t)$ in addition to the label of the operands. For example, when a constant value is loaded onto OS, the label $l = LUB(\text{NONE}, l(pc^t))$ is actually pushed onto $l(os_i^t)$. When multiple conditional branches are nesting, $l(pc^t)$ evolves to reflect the context; i.e., each time the pc^t reaches a new branch, $l(pc^t)$ is updated to be $LUB(l(pc^t), l(c))$ where $l(c)$ denotes the label of the branch condition. $l(pc^t)$ is reset at the join point of each conditional statement.

Strictly speaking, the implicit flow occurs whether or not the body of the if statement is executed; that is, one can infer that the value x is not 1 when the value of y is 0. It should be noted that a purely dynamic approach, can propagate the label only when the assignment is done, when there is no knowledge of other possible execution paths [25][26].

3.6 Exceptions

An exception in a Java program is caused by either 1) the JVM (e.g, division by zero), 2) a throw statement in the library code, or 3) a throw statement in the application code. In DIFCA-J, exceptions explicitly thrown by applications will be assigned the security label that is determined from the label of the data that is set in the exception as well as $l(pc^t)$ of the code that throws the exception. When an exception is not caught, the frames are popped in the JVM stack. In order to synchronize the stack depth, the IRM inserts default exception handlers to capture the exception, to synchronize the state of the ACM, and to throw the exception immediately.

When an exception is directly thrown by the JVM, the IRM's ability to detect the label of the exception object is limited. For example, when division by zero is reported by java.lang.ArithmeticException, it can be inferred that the dividision operand was 0. However, since this exception is caused by the JVM itself, it is difficult for the IRM to reflect the label of the operand to the label of the exception.

3.7 Multi-threading

The types of information flowing between threads in a multi-thread program can be classified into 4 types: 1) Initialization parameters of the child thread objects that are set by the parent thread, 2) Pairs of threads communicatiing through shared global objects (e.g., singleton objects), 3) Information exchanged via external resources such as files, databases, or system properties, or 4) Covert communication channels that make use of Java's multi-thread capabilities, such as thread synchronization and interruption.

In DIFCA-J, information flowing through 1) and 2) is captured since the labels of the objects in the heap area are managed by the global tables OLT, CLT, and ALT. Information exchanges through external resources can be captured as long as all of the resources are labeled properly.

3.8 Declassification

Declassification is an important issue for the practical use of an information flow control system to mitigate the label creeping problem [29]. For example, in a system that implements the Bell-LaPadula model with two labels HIGH and LOW, all processes that can read from both of HIGH and LOW information must not have a write permission to the LOW information. Therefore, as information propagates, information that originally had the LOW label tends to be associated with the HIGH label. Since each process is regarded as a black-box for the operating system level information flow control, it is difficult to avoid the label-creeping problem.

Even in a language-level information flow control system, the labels of data tend to become more strict as the program is executed. In particular, this trend is significant when the label of the program counter is composed into the labels of the variables to capture the implicit flows.

However in reality, not all information produced from confidential information is confidential. For example, credit card numbers are usually regarded as confidential, but it is a common practice to mask the credit card number except for the last 4 digits to make it public information that can be printed on the bill, e.g., "****-****-****-1234". Another example is a password. The password itself is confidential but its hash value or a boolean result of authentication, both derived from the password, are public information.

DIFCA-J supports declassification through a API-level declassification policy specification. For example, if there is an API method String mask(String creditcard) that masks a credit number except for the last 4 digits, the labeling policy can be defined to force the return value of this method to LOW, and thus allows declassification without modifying the code.

4 Labeling on Database Queries

JDBC (Java DataBase Connectivity) is a standard API for accessing databases from Java applications. The standard API encapsulates the complexity of each database management system and its driver, and allows Java applications to utilize databases without concerns about the implementation- specific differences. A typical Java application connects to a database using JDBC, "logs-in" with a user account registered with the database, and issues queries using SQL.

When the database management system employs an access control mechanism, the access permission is linked to the given database user ID. However, many of today's Web applications use a single database account for processing requests from multiple Web users, in order to effectively reuse database connections through connection pooling to optimize performance. Therefore, the access control at the database access point is ignored.

Application Privacy Monitoring for JDBC (APM4JDBC) [6] is a generic framework for a JDBC to intercept JDBC API calls and to insert customized behavior for each activation of the JDBC. Such behavior includes application-level access control for database queries as well as for recording database accesses for auditing purposes.

Figure 6 shows the architecture of APM4JDBC. Any query context (such as a web user account that is different from the database user account) can be corrected by the Context Handler, so that such information can be later utilized by the plug-in access controllers to filter and modify the SQL queries and responses.

DIFCA-J uses the APM4JDBC framework to collect the contexts of the database queries, and labels the retrieved data based on the policies and the contexts of the queries. For example, DIFCA-J allows putting different security labels for each column on the queried data (e.g., associate the HIGH label with the credit card number in our example scenario introduced in Section 1). Similarly, DIFCA-J allows controlling data output into the database (e.g., make sure that application will not write a value with the HIGH label into a database column which should only hold the LOW values). In addition, we can extend the labeling system to a richer model, such as the lattice model, and associate different labels for each user's transactions, and prevent contamination of information belonging to different users.

5 Prototype Implementation

DIFCA-J was prototyped on top of the Apache Tomcat Web container with JVM 1.5. The IRM Writer was implemented with Apache Byte Code Engineering Library (BCEL) [14], an open source toolkit for analyzing and modifying arbitrary Java bytecode. We modified the Web Application class loader in Tomcat to instrument only the bytecode of application classes when they are being loaded. The ACM is implemented as a singleton Java object.

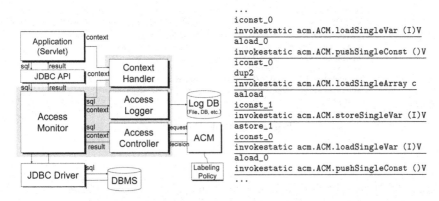

Fig. 6. APM4JDBC   **Fig. 7.** IRM Enabled Bytecode

Figure 7 shows an example of IRM-enabled bytecode after instrumentation. Lines with underlines are inserted IRM code that calls the ACM by invoking the methods of the ACM.

Limitations of the current prototype are that it does not support exceptions, and some policies (i.e., information flow policy and the database policies) are hard wired in Java code.

5.1 Policy Definition

The sample information flow policy is defined in a Java class which provides label comparison and composition as methods. The sample labeling policy (Fig. 8) defines the label LOW for the HTTP requests and responses, and to the printlog() method. The policy on the mask() method defines the declassification policy on the masked credit card numbers.

DIFCA-J requires labeling policy only on API that concern input and output of data. Therefore, the administrator's burden of policy definition is smaller than security enhanced language such as Jif [10]. E.g., only 4 entries of labeling policy is required in example application in Section 1; other methods that does not concern with input and output of data will just propagate the label.

When no explicit policy is defined, DIFCA-J infers that a label of the value returned from a standard library method is the composition of the labels of the target object and the arguments. When this inference rule fails, explicit labeling policies need to be defined for such API. However, it is possible to pre-define a set of policies for each standard library and deploy with DIFCA-J, in order to mitigate administrator's burden to define them by themselves.

The policy on the database, which associates the label HIGH with credit card numbers, is hard-coded in a Java class in the current prototype. But it is obvious that we can extend the system to allow more flexible policy definition. Since the example policy adopts the simplest two-level labels, no context information was used for labeling the database query results. However, the architecture is policy agnostic and we can easily extend the policy to accommodate finer-grained

```
<Policy>
 <InputRule><Label>LOW</Label><Type>argument</Type>
   <URI>java:foo.shop.Purchase.doGet</URI></InputRule>
 <InputRule> <Label>LOW</Label><Type>return</Type>
   <URI>java:foo.shop.Purchase.mask</URI></InputRule>
 <OutputRule><Label>LOW</Label><Type>argument</Type>
   <URI>java:foo.shop.Purchase.printlog</URI></OutputRule>
 </Policy>
```

Fig. 8. Example Policy

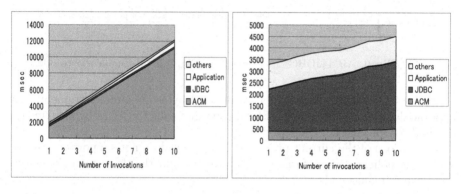

(a) Arithmetic Operations Web App.   (b) JDBC Web App.

Fig. 9. Performance Evaluation

policies in more flexible way; e.g., the credit card numbers that belong to different users are associated with different labels that corresponds to the user identities.

5.2   Performance Evaluation

We measured performance overhead of DIFCA-J in two types of Web applications, 1) only arithmetic operations without JDBC (Fig. 9(a)), and 2) sample application in Section 1 which uses JDBC iFig. 9(b)j. We ran each application for 10 times, and measured accumulated time consumption of each Java package using a profiler. The Web server (Apache Tomcat) and the MySQL database were set up on the same computer. In 1), the pure overhead by ACM over the original application class is about 18-24 times. In 2), JDBC connection and query consumes more than 90% of the entire execution time (even if excluding the connection establishment which occurs only once), and thus the overhead by ACM stays around 10%. But the pure overhead is about 13-18 times. IRMWriter instruments the bytecode only once when the application is loaded, and thus most of the overhead is resulted from ACM. Note that the pure overhead means the execution time comparison between the original application class itself and ACM, and the overhead in the turn-around-time of the Web application as a whole is smaller, especially when JDBC is involved. After instrumentation, each class file increases its size about 2-2.8 times.

In conclusion, although performance overhead caused by ACM is not small, we think that it is still acceptable in typical Web applications which uses JDBC.

6   Related Work

A number of prior research [7][8][9] have studied policy models to guarantee secure information flow. There are also technologies to implement the models. For example, the multi-level security (MLS) system implements the Bell-LaPadula [8] model, providing strong isolation from the hardware and the networks.

When the information flow control is implemented at the granularity of a system or a process, it is inevitable that securely designed information flow policies cause the label creeping problem [29], since the classification of information becomes more strict thorough propagation, making it increasingly difficult for the information to be shared effectively. Language-based information flow control is getting attention in order to allow for fine-grained information flow control. This section briefly reviews prior research work. The language-based information flow control can be classified into static approaches and dynamic approaches. More thorough survey of static approachs is found in [1].

Static Approaches. Kobayashi and Shirane [15] defined a small subset of Java bytecode and statically analyzes information flow within it. Barthe et al. [16][27][17] proved noninterference for a subset of Java bytecode and proved that the program written in a security-enhanced language can be compiled into bytecode without weakening the security properties. No implementation was reported. Genaim and Spoto [18] studied the information flow analysis of a more complete set of Java bytecode, and implemented their proposed method. Yu and Isam proposes Typed Assembly Language for Confidentiality (TALc) [28] for information flow analysis and proved its noninterference.

Jif [10][19][20] is an extension of the Java language, which allows defining security labels as types of program constructs. Programs written in Jif are compiled into ordinary Java bytecode, and thus have no dependencies on the run-time environment. However, existing applications need to be converted to Jif programs. Recently, Boniface et al. implemented an e-mail application in Jif [21] and evaluated its usefulness in realistic applications. Li and Zhancewic [22] addressed the information flow problem in Web applications with the security-enhanced scripting language. Static approaches for the declassification problem are found in [23] [13].

Dynamic Approaches. A dynamic approach is potentially more precise than the static approach since t can exploit the detailed conditions of the running programs. It also allows security policies to be defined dynamically.

Beres and Dalton [11] modified the operating system, to track information flow in the execution of machine language. A similar approach is applicable to Java, but it requires modification of the Java VM, and the resulting implementation is dependent on the JVM.

Erlingsson et al. [5] proposed inserting Inline Reference Monitors (IRMs) into Java bytecode to implement access control that is equivalent to the Java2 security architecture [24]. Haldar, Chandra, and Franz [2] [3] [4] proposed information flow control for Java using a bytecode rewriting technique. Their initial focus included "taint" propagation for values input into web applications, but can be easily extended to support richer labeling systems. According to Franz [4], they support label propagation at the granularity of Java objects and fields. The dynamic mechanism tracks information propagation at the time of method invocations and field access. They also employ static analysis for detecting implicit flows. The literature does not say if that their approach supports information propagation through all JVM instructions that involve operand stacks and local variables.

DIFCA-J was influenced by [2] [3] [4], but the major difference is the granularity of the label propagation. DIFCA-J supports information propagation through most of the JVM instructions, including arithmetic operations, array elements, multi-threading, and exceptions, and a policy based declassification mechanism. We also integrated APM4JDBC to effectively label database query results and to control input and output to the database through JDBC.

The problem of implicit flow in dynamic approach is addressed in [25][26] based on combination of dynamic and static analysis. Shroff [26] also addresses the problem by analyzing dependencies of data through monitoring multiple executions of the program. Since our work aims at detecting undesirable information flow by programming errors without modifying the application source code, it is not the focus of this paper to detect all implicit flows. However, we believe that the technique presented in this paper can be extended to collect information about the data dependencies and to detect indirect implicit flows.

7   Conclusions and Future Work

This paper proposes DIFCA-J, which enforces the language-based information flow control policies for Java applications. We use a bytecode rewriting technique to insert inline reference monitors (IRMs), and thus 1) the IRMs can utilize the detailed conditions of the running applications, 2) it does not require source code of the target application, and 3) the system is independent of JVM implementations. DIFCA-J tracks the propagation of information in the program through most of the JVM instructions, and controls the input and output to the external environment based on the given information flow policies. DIFCA-J also intercepts the JDBC queries to effectively label the query results, and control input to and output from the database.

However, the current proposal still leaves gaps for future research. First, the purely dynamic approach can discover only information flows that are actually executed, and especially cannot detect all of the implicit flows. Second, the current approach requires a bytecode-level IRM to be inserted for every bytecode instruction of the original code, and causes significant performance overhead. Third, since OLT stores object references with associated security labels, it prevents target objects from garbage collected, and causes memory overhead at run-time. Fourth, terminating the transaction due to the information flow violation may cause problems in database consistency. It is inherently difficult to handle such exceptions without modifying the applications. Some of the problems may be acceptable when using DIFCA-J for the pre-deployment test, but care needs to be taken to define the test cases with good coverage.

Usability and policy specification is another challenge that needs to be addressed. DIFCA-J does not require the source code of the target applications, but the policy writer still needs to understand the structure of the program and the semantics of the methods. Especially when a declassification policy is defined for a method, such a definition may easily introduce human error, unless the semantics of the method are well defined and the consequences of the declassification are well understood. This is a future topic for allowing easy and safe policy definitions without needing knowledge of the source code.

Acknowledgement

The authors wish to thank anonymous reviewers as well as our colleagues at the IBM Tokyo Research Laboratory and Institute of Information Security for their feedback and insights on earlier versions of this paper. This study was partly sponsored by the Ministry of Economy, Trade and Industry, Japan (METI) under a contract for the New-Generation Information Security R&D Program.

References

1. Sabelfeld, A., Myers, A.C.: Language-Based Information Flow Security. IEEE Journal on Selected Areas in Communications 21(1) (2003)
2. Haldar, V., Chandra, D., Franz, M.: Dynamic Taint Propagation for Java. In: Srikanthan, T., Xue, J., Chang, C.-H. (eds.) ACSAC 2005. LNCS, vol. 3740, Springer, Heidelberg (2005)
3. Haldar, V., Chandra, D., Franz, M.: Practical, Dynamic Information Flow for Virtual Machines. In: PLID (2005)
4. Franz, M.: Moving Trust Out of Application Programs: A Software Architecture Based on Multi-Level Security Virtual Machines (TR. 06-10), UC Irvine (2006)
5. Erlingsson, U., Schneider, F.B.: IRM Enforcement of Java Stack Inspection. In: IEEE Sympo. on S&P, IEEE Computer Society Press, Los Alamitos (2000)
6. Application Privacy Monitoring for JDBC (APM4JDBC): IBM AlphaWorks
7. Biba, K.: Integrity Considerations for Secure Computer Systems (MTR-3153). Technical report, MITRE (1975)
8. Bell, D.E., LaPadula, L.J.: Secure Computer System: Unified Exposition and Multics Interpretation (MTR-2997 Rev. 1). Technical report, MITRE (1976)
9. Denning, D.E.: The lattice model of secure information flow. Communications of the ACM 19(5), 236–243 (1976)
10. Myers, A.C.: JFlow: Practical Mostly-Static Information Flow Control. In: POPL (1999)
11. Beres, Y., Dalton, C.: Dynamic Label Binding at Run-time. In: New Security Paradigms Workshop (NSPW) (2003)

12. Lindholm, T., Yellin, F.: The Java Virtual Machine Specification. Addison-Wesley, Reading (1999)
13. Li, P., Zdancewic, S.: Downgrading policies and relaxed noninterference. In: POPL'05. Symposium on Principles of Programming Languages (2005)
14. Apache Byte Code Engineering Library (BCEL), http://jakarta.apache.org/bcel/
15. Kobayashi, N., Shirane, K.: Type-based Information Flow Analysis for Low-Level Languages. In: APLAS 2002 (2002)
16. Barthe, G., Basu, A., Rezk, T.: Security Types Preserving Compilation. In: Steffen, B., Levi, G. (eds.) VMCAI 2004. LNCS, vol. 2937, Springer, Heidelberg (2004)
17. Barthe, G., Naumann, D.A., Rezk, T.: Deriving an Information Flow Checker and Certifying Compiler for Java. In: IEEE Sympo. on S&P, IEEE Computer Society Press, Los Alamitos (2006)
18. Genaim, S., Spoto, F.: Information Flow Analysis for Java Bytecode. In: Cousot, R. (ed.) VMCAI 2005. LNCS, vol. 3385, Springer, Heidelberg (2005)
19. Zdancewic, S., et al.: Untrusted Hosts and Confidentiality: Secure Program Partitioning. In: SOSP. Symposium on Operating Systems Principles (2001)
20. Zheng, L., Chong, S., Myers, A.C., Zdancewic, S.: Using replication and partitioning to build secure distributed systems. In: IEEE Sympo. on S&P, IEEE Computer Society Press, Los Alamitos (2003)
21. Hicks, B., et al.: From Languages to Systems: Understanding Practical Application Development in Security-typed Languages. In: Jesshope, C., Egan, C. (eds.) ACSAC 2006. LNCS, vol. 4186, Springer, Heidelberg (2006)
22. Li, P., Zdancewic, S.: Practical Information-flow Control in Web-based Information Systems. In: CSFW (2005)
23. Myers, A.C., Sabelfeld, A.: Enforcing Robust Declassification. In: CSFW (2004)
24. Gong, L., et al.: Going Beyond the Sandbox: An Overview of the New Security Architecture in the Java Development Kit 1.2, USITS (1997)
25. Guernic, G.L., et al.: Automata-based Confidentiality Monitoring. In: ASIAN'06. Annual Asian Computing Science Conference (2006)
26. Shroff, P., Smith, S.F., Thober, M.: Dynamic Dependency Monitoring to Secure Information Flow. In: IEEE Computer Security Foundations Symposium, IEEE Computer Society Press, Los Alamitos (2007)
27. Barthe, G., Rezk, T.: Non-interference for a JVM-like language. In: TLDI (2005)
28. Yu, D., Islam, N.: A Typed Assembly Language for Confidentiality. In: Sestoft, P. (ed.) ESOP 2006 and ETAPS 2006. LNCS, vol. 3924, Springer, Heidelberg (2006)
29. Denning, D.E.: Cryptography and Data Security. Addison-Wesley, Reading (1982)

Cloak: A Ten-Fold Way for Reliable Covert Communications

Xiapu Luo, Edmond W.W. Chan, and Rocky K.C. Chang

Department of Computing
The Hong Kong Polytechnic University
{csxluo,cswwchan,csrchang}@comp.polyu.edu.hk

Abstract. In this paper, we propose *Cloak*—a new class of reliable timing channels—which is fundamentally different from other timing channels in several aspects. First, Cloak encodes a message by a unique distribution of N packets over X TCP flows. The combinatorial nature of the encoding methods increases the channel capacity largely with (N, X). Second, Cloak offers ten different encoding and decoding methods, each of which has a unique tradeoff among several important considerations, such as channel capacity and the need for packet marking. Third, the packet transmissions modulated by Cloak could be carefully crafted to mimic the normal TCP flows in a typical TCP-based application session. Although Cloak's basic idea is simple, we show in this paper how we tackle a number of challenging issues systematically. Our experiment results collected from PlanetLab nodes and a test bed suggest that Cloak is feasible under various network conditions and different round-trip delays.

Keywords: covert channel analysis, network security, attack models.

1 Introduction

In this paper, we consider data hiding techniques using network protocols as the cover. The communication channel under the cover is often referred to as a *network covert channel*. Network covert channels could pose a serious threat to the Internet security, because of their "proven" ability of stealthily exfiltrating stolen information (a hardware was built in [1]), coordinating an Internet-wide DDoS attacks [2] and Internet worm attack [3], coordinating a physical attack plan (a book was written about this possibility [4]), and other subversive operations. On the other *good* hand, they are useful for enhancing Internet privacy [5,6], watermarking encrypted flows in stepping stones [7], and tracking VoIP calls [8].

Similar to the classic covert channels in trusted computer systems, network covert channels could be classified into *storage channels* and *timing channels* [9,10]. In a storage channel, the encoder and decoder communicate covertly through "attributes of shared resources" [11], which could be any fields in a packet that can be "written" by the encoder and "read" by the decoder. The

J. Biskup and J. Lopez (Eds.): ESORICS 2007, LNCS 4734, pp. 283–298, 2007.

covert messages are encoded directly into these fields. Most existing network covert channels fall into this category. In a timing channel, the encoder and decoder communicate "through a temporal or ordering relationship of accesses to a shared resource" [11] which could be the timing of packet arrivals that can be modulated by the encoder and observed by the decoder. For example, an IP packet arrival within a time interval represents bit 1 and the absence of it represents bit 0 in an IP timing channel [12].

Existing network covert channels, however, suffer from low data rates in the presence of dynamic network conditions and *active network intermediaries* (ANI) (e.g., protocol scrubbers [13], traffic normalizer [14], and active wardens [15]). For example, the message encoding based on inter-packet delay is very sensitive to delay jitter, and packet losses affect the integrity of both timing and storage channels. On the other hand, storage channels do not suffer from these problems. Instead, their encoded messages could be altered by an ANI which modifies the replaceable header fields in the packets that pass through them.

In this paper, we propose *Cloak*—a new class of timing channels which is designed to be reliable under adverse network conditions. That is, Cloak's decoding accuracy is 100% even in the presence of packet losses, delay jitters, packet reordering, and packet duplications. The key elements responsible for this reliability property are using TCP data traffic as a cover (i.e., exploiting TCP's reliable transmission mechanism) and employing a fixed number of TCP packets (N) for encoding/decoding a message to avoid the inherent synchronization errors plaguing many network timing channels.

Another important deviation from other timing channels is that Cloak encodes a message with a unique distribution of N packets over X TCP flows, where $N, X > 1$. Due to the combinatorial nature of the encoding method, Cloak's channel capacity increases quickly with (N, X). Besides, Cloak offers ten different encoding and decoding methods. Each method tradeoffs among several conflicting design goals. Although Cloak uses multiple flows for the message encoding, the packet distribution over the flows can be carefully crafted to match with the normal TCP behavior in an application session. To our best knowledge, Cloak is the *first* network covert channel that exploits Enumerative Combinatorics [16] to convey hidden messages. Moreover, this original idea is generally enough for designing new covert channels and applying to other steganography problems.

The road map for the rest of this paper is as follows. Section 2 briefly discusses the previously proposed network timing channels. Section 3 presents the basic idea of message encoding in Cloak which is based on the well-known Twelvefold Way in the field of Enumerative Combinatorics. Section 4 details how we have resolved a number of difficult design issues for deploying Cloak in the Internet. Section 5 reports the test-bed and PlanetLab measurement results to evaluate Cloak's data rate under various network conditions and parameter settings. Section 6 summarizes this paper with a few venues of enhancing this work.

2   Related Work

Despite that information theorists have analyzed the capacity of covert timing channels for a long time, only recently have several practical timing channels emerged. On the network layer and above, there are so far two practical approaches to manipulating the packet timing: *ordered channels* and *inter-packet delay channels*. In the class of ordered channels, Kundur and Ahsan [17] propose to re-sort the original order of a flow of IPSec packets and use the out-of-orderliness to imbed messages. Chakinala et al. [18] further extend the approach to TCP packets and formalize various models for these ordered channels.

The class of inter-packet delay channels, on the other hand, embeds messages in the delay period between selected packets. Cabuk et al. [12] propose an IP timing channel, where an IP packet arrival during a timing interval is decoded as 1 and the absence of it is decoded as 0. Shah et al. recently [1] propose JitterBug, another timing channel to encode binary bits. Unlike the IP timing channel, JitterBug encodes binary bits into the packet inter-arrival times, and it does not need to inject new packets. Moreover, they have presented a convincing threat of leaking keyboard typed secrets, such as passwords, through the timing channel and have built a hardware to demonstrate its feasibility. Berk et al. [19] have considered using inter-packet delay of ICMP packets to encode one or multiple bits. For example, bit 1 is encoded by a longer inter-packet delay, whereas bit 0 is encoded by a smaller inter-packet delay.

3   The Basic Idea

3.1   Encoding Based on Packet-Flow Distributions

The covert messages in Cloak are encoded by a class of combinatorial objects—each covert message is encoded with a unique distribution of N TCP packets over X TCP flows. The encoder and decoder agree on the values of N and X beforehand. Furthermore, the encoder will transmit the next message *only* after receiving the ACKs for the message just sent. On the other side of the channel, the decoder starts decoding as soon as collecting N TCP packets from the encoder. Moreover, the encoder and decoder do not have to explicitly exchange the "codebook"; as will show in section 4.1, the encoding and decoding can be performed using unranking and ranking functions.

It is worthwhile to point out here that Cloak is reliable in the same sense of reliability in TCP even when the messages experience adverse network conditions. First of all, Cloak's decoding accuracy is not affected by delay jitters, because the encoding is not based on the actual time. Second, since the encoder sends a covert message one at a time, it can detect whether the decoder has successfully received the last message based on the ACKs for the N TCP packets. Upon detecting an unsuccessful reception, the encoder could "partially" resend the message. The decoder, on the other hand, will decode only after receiving N in-sequenced TCP packets from the encoder. Therefore, if Cloak is implemented using the normal TCP stack, no additional reliability mechanism is needed to guarantee Cloak's reliability.

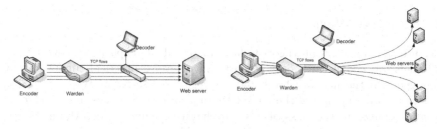

(a) The five TCP flows connect to the same Web server.

(b) The five TCP flows connect to different Web servers.

Fig. 1. Two covert communication scenarios between Cloak encoder and decoder

In Figure 1, we depict two different scenarios for the Cloak encoder and decoder to communicate. In both cases, we assume a warden on the encoder's network who guards against any network covert channels initiated from inside. The warden could be active or passive. In the first scenario (Figure 1(a)), the encoder establishes a "normal" HTTP session with a remote server which consists of five TCP flows. The encoder encodes the messages into the TCP flows; the decoder eavesdrops at any point of the path and decodes the messages. Moreover, the warden could not detect Cloak simply based on the presence of multiple TCP flows to the same server, because it is not uncommon to have multiple TCP flows in an HTTP session. Moreover, multi-thread upload or download (i.e., sending commands) also has similar traffic patterns.

In the second scenario (Figure 1(b)), the encoder establishes normal HTTP sessions with multiple servers which are dispersed at different locations. Therefore, the decoder should be located on the common routing path for all the servers. Although this approach restricts the decoder location, it can diffuse the relationship among the TCP flows. A simple approach for relaxing this restriction is to use distributed information collection, for example, through a botnet. Each bot will observe partial information and then sends it to the commander.

3.2 The Twelvefold Way

Besides the encoding algorithm just described, Cloak could admit other encoding methods. In fact, Cloak offers ten different encoding methods which are based on the well-known *Twelvefold Way* [16] in the field of Enumerative Combinatorics. The Twelvefold Way refers to twelve basic counting problems that count all the possible ways of putting N balls into X urns, and their results. Let the set of balls be $\mathbb{N}$ ($|\mathbb{N}| = N$) and the set of urns be $\mathbb{X}$ ($|\mathbb{X}| = X$). Each problem can be based on whether the balls and urns are distinguishable or not (e.g., by their colors), and three possible kinds of ball distributions over the urns: (1) no restriction, (2) at most one ball per urn, and (3) at least one ball per urn. These three cases can be equivalently represented by an arbitrary function $\mathbf{f}_A : \mathbb{N} \to \mathbb{X}$, an injective function $\mathbf{f}_I : \mathbb{N} \to \mathbb{X}$, and a surjective function $\mathbf{f}_S : \mathbb{N} \to \mathbb{X}$, respectively.

The correspondence between balls and urns, and packets and flows is obvious. Table 1 summarizes the Twelvefold Way using flows (urns) and packets (balls)

[16]. Each of the twelve results answers the corresponding counting problem (i.e., the total number of unique packet-flow distributions). Cases (11) and (12) obviously cannot be used in Cloak, therefore the ten encoding methods. In the rest of this paper, we refer the ten cases to as $\text{Cloak}^c(N, X)$, $c \in [1, 10]$. Due to the space limitation, we refer to [20] for the proofs of the results in Table 1.

Table 1. The Twelvefold Way and their relation to the ten (items 1-10) encoding methods in Cloak

Elements of $\mathbb{N}$ (TCP packets)	Elements of $\mathbb{X}$ (TCP flows)	f_A (no restriction)	f_I (at most 1 packet in a flow)	f_S (at least 1 packet in a flow)
Distinguishable	Distinguishable	X^N (1)	$N!C_X^N$ (2)	$X!S(N, X)$ (3)
Indistinguishable	Distinguishable	C_{N+X-1}^{X-1} (4)	C_X^N (5)	C_{N-1}^{X-1} (6)
Distinguishable	Indistinguishable	$\sum_{i=1}^{X} S(N, i)$ (7)	$\begin{cases} 1 \text{ if } N \le X \\ 0 \text{ if } N > X \end{cases}$ (11)	$S(N, X)$ (8)
Indistinguishable	Indistinguishable	$\sum_{i=1}^{X} P(N, i)$ (9)	$\begin{cases} 1 \text{ if } N \le X \\ 0 \text{ if } N > X \end{cases}$ (12)	$P(N, X)$ (10)

where
- $C_X^N = \frac{X!}{N!(X-N)!}$ and $S(N, X) = \frac{1}{X!} \sum_{j=1}^{X} (-1)^{X-j} C_X^j j^N$.
- $P(N, X)$ is the number of partitions of N into X parts.

According to Table 1, some encoding methods require distinguishable packets and/or distinguishable flows. The correspondence between the ball and urn distinguishability, and the flow and packet distinguishability is somewhat tricky. First of all, all TCP flows and packets are of course distinguishable. However, the original counting problems assume that the colors of the urns and balls do not change, but this is not the case for Cloak. For instance, the "marking information" in the flows and packets could be altered by an ANI. Therefore, the TCP flows (or packets) are considered distinguishable only if both encoder and decoder are able to identify the same flow (or packet).

3.3   The Ten-Fold Way in Cloak

In this section, we discuss the differences among the ten encoding methods and explain why we need all of them. The first important difference among them is their channel capacity. By modeling a Cloak channel as a classical information channel, we can obtain the capacity of a $\text{Cloak}^c(N, X)$ channel in bits/symbol based on the mutual information [21]. Since Cloak is reliable and there is only one set of covert messages, the channel capacity can be increased only by increasing the size of the covert message set. By denoting the Twelvefold Way result for $\text{Cloak}^c(N, X)$ by $T^c(N, X)$, a higher value of $T^c(N, X)$ therefore gives a higher channel capacity. Furthermore, each unique packet-flow distribution can encode an L-bit word, where $1 \le L \le \lfloor \log_2 T^c(N, X) \rfloor$.

In the following, we explain the relationships between the channel capacity and the flow and packet distinguishability. First, making the flows distinguishable increases the channel capacity (e.g., $T^1(N, X) > T^7(N, X)$). Similarly, making the packets distinguishable also increases the channel capacity (e.g., $T^1(N, X) > T^4(N, X)$). Finally, for each row in Table 1, the channel capacity for $\mathbf{f}_A$ is the largest, e.g., $T^1(N, X) > T^3(N, X)$, and $T^7(N, X) > T^8(N, X)$. Based on the channel capacity, we define *data rate* in bits/second as $\frac{C}{T_s}$, where T_s is the time for transmitting a message. The minimal time for transmitting a message in Cloak (i.e., the N packets in X flows) is one round-trip time (RTT) between the encoder and decoder. To achieve a reasonable channel capacity, we therefore consider $X > 1$ and $N > 1$ in the rest of this paper.

Besides the channel capacity, the ten encoding methods differ also in three other important aspects. The first one concerns the channels that require distinguishable packets (i.e., $c = 1, 3, 7, 8$). For these channels, the encoder usually adds "markers" to the TCP packets in order to make them distinguishable. The additional markers, however, could be "modified" when the packets traverse an active warden, which could result in decoding errors. In other words, there is a tradeoff between achieving a higher channel capacity by making the packets distinguishable and the decoding accuracy. Similar problems occur also to the channels with flow distinguishability. We have discussed how to make packet or flow distinguishable in the full paper [20].

The second one is connected to a head-of-line blocking (HoLB) problem. To explain the issue, consider $c = 1, 2$. the difference between them is that the second method caps the number of packets distributed to a flow to one. Therefore, in terms of the packet distribution, the flows for $c = 2$ differ at most by one packet, but that for $c = 1$ is N (i.e., all the packets are distributed to a single flow). The latter case may require several RTTs to complete the transmission of a message; thus, this HoLB problem, as we shall see later, could reduce the actual data rate significantly. The last issue is that some flows for the methods under $\mathbf{f}_A$ and $\mathbf{f}_I$ may become idle for a prolonged period of time, which may cause the remote servers to close the connection. However, those methods under $\mathbf{f}_S$ mitigate this problem by insisting each flow to carry at least one packet for each message.

4   Design Issues

In this section, we discuss a number of design elements that are central to a practical deployment of Cloak in the Internet and to Cloak's performance.

4.1   Message Encoding and Decoding

As mentioned in the last section, the encoder and decoder do not need to exchange a codebook explicitly. Instead, they use two special functions for encoding and decoding: Rank() and Unrank(). Each $\text{Cloak}^c(N, X)$ channel has its own function pair. The function Rank() takes in a flow-packet distribution and returns its *rank* that is the index of the flow-packet distribution in the decreasing lexicographically ordered array of all possible distributions, staring from 0. Unrank() does the opposite—taking in a rank and returning the corresponding flow-packet distribution.

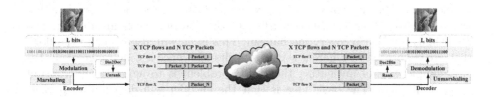

Fig. 2. The encoding and decoding processes in Cloak

Figure 2 depicts the encoding and decoding processes in Cloak. The encoder and decoder are assumed to have agreed on (c, N, X) beforehand. They could also dynamically change (c, N, X) by exploiting the random beacons widely available in the Internet. The messages are encoded based on L-bit words, where $1 \leq L \leq \lfloor \log_2 T^c(N, X) \rfloor$. There are three major steps involved in sending a covert message. Each L-bit word is first converted to the nonnegative decimal value (through the `Bin2Dec()` function) that serves as the rank for the corresponding packet-flow distribution. Then, `Unrank()` is invoked to compute the distribution. Finally, the encoder marshals the packet-flow code into the actual TCP flows and data packets. After sending the N packets over the X flows, the encoder has to receive the ACKs for the N packets before sending the next N packets. In the case of packet losses, Cloak may rely on TCP to recover them.

The three-step process above is exactly reversed for receiving a covert message. In the first step, the decoder unmarshalls the packet-flow distribution from the flows and packets received from the encoder. That is, the decoder collects exactly N TCP packets from the X flows before moving to the next step. Moreover, since the number of flows can be distinguished based on the order of the TCP three-way handshaking performed, the decoder can count the number of data packets in each flow. Similar as before, any TCP packet loss, duplication, or reordering can be taken care of by TCP. As soon as N packets are collected, the decoder feeds the distribution into `Rank()` which yields the corresponding rank. As a last step, the rank is converted back to the L-bit word (through the function `Dec2Bin()`). We refer the detailed ranking and unranking algorithms to the full paper [20].

4.2 A Head-of-Line Blocking Problem

In this section, we discuss a head-of-line blocking (HoLB) problem that we have encountered when conducting Internet experiments. The HoLB problem degrades the data rates of all encoding methods, except for $c = 2, 5$. To explain the problem, we consider an extreme scenario where most of the N packets are distributed to a single flow, while other flows receive at most one packet. Therefore, the total transmission time for the message is governed by the time required to transmit the packets in the most busy flow which prevents the encoder from transmitting the next message. Furthermore, since the TCP congestion window usually starts with one or two packets, it will take the busy flow's sender several RTTs to complete the transmissions, thus leading to a low data rate. The problem may become worse if there are packet losses in the most busy flow that will retransmit those packets according to the timeout mechanism or the fast retransmission/fast recovery mechanism. This issue will also occur to the flows that are connected to different servers which experience a wide range of RTTs.

A simple way of mitigating the HoLB problem is to aggressively transmit every N packets. The basic idea is that the encoder will dispatch all packets belonging to kth message after receiving ACK packets that acknowledge the data packets for the $(k-1)$th message or a timer with period T_E expires. If the encoder does not receive all the expected ACK packets before T_E, it will retransmit unacknowledged packets and reset the timer. T_E is usually set to the estimated RTT that is computed through the exponential weighted moving average (EWMA) of RTT samples, an approach similar to the one used in normal TCP. However, the downside is that the resulting traffic pattern will be different from normal TCP behavior. This has prompted us to design a new codeword scheme to be discussed next.

A D-limited codeword scheme. The D-limited codeword scheme essentially caps the maximum number of packets assigned to a flow to D; that is, it enforces $\max\{n_i\} \leq D$, where $D \geq 1$ is a constant. The choice of D should be chosen such that it is less than the encoder's TCP send window size in terms of packets. In this way, all the packets can be sent out in one RTT; otherwise, multiple RTTs would be needed for transmitting a message.

We use $c = 10$ (indistinguishable packets and flows) to illustrate how this codeword scheme works. We first define the following two quantities:

1. Let $\Upsilon(N)$ be the total number of ways to distribute N packets into TCP flows such that each flow is given *at most* D packets.
2. Let $\Gamma(N, D)$ be the total number of ways to distribute N packets into D flows such that each flow is assigned at least one packet. Note that $\Gamma(N, D) = P(N, D)$ if both packets and flows are indistinguishable (i.e., $c = 10$).

Theorem 1. *If both packets and flows are indistinguishable, $\Upsilon(N) = \sum_{i=1}^{D} P(N, i)$.*

Corollary 1. *To generate D-limited codewords from $P(N, D)$, we need at most $N + 1 - D$ flows to convey a message.*

Theorem 1 computes how much information this D-limited codeword scheme could transmit. Corollary 1, on the other hand, shows that if the upper bound on the number of flows is X, then $N \leq X + D - 1$. Their proofs are given in [20]. We now use Proposition 1 and Corollary 1 directly to construct D-limited codewords for $c = 10$:

1. **Encoding.** To transmit a message (a binary string), the encoder first calculates its decimal value and then uses Cloak[10]'s unranking algorithm to get the corresponding packet-flow distribution, denoted by ζ. After that, the encoder computes ζ's conjugate [16], denoted by ζ', and transmits packets according to ζ'.

2. **Decoding.** Upon receiving a packet-flow distribution ζ', the decoder first computes its conjugate ζ and then uses $\text{Cloak}^{10}(N, X)$'s ranking algorithm to decode the message.

To construct D-limited codewords for other encoding methods, we could adopt our general framework for designing new ranking and unranking algorithms [20]. That is, when the encoder receives ζ' from Cloak^9 or Cloak^{10}, it could expand ζ' by considering distinguishable packets or flows. For example, if only flows are distinguishable, we could permute the locations of flows that have different n_i and then increase the capacity in a way similar to $\lambda!$ or C_X^N. If only packets are distinguishable, we could consider how to partition them into different flows and therefore to increase the capacity in a way similar to $S(N, X)!$. If both flows and packets are distinguishable, we could permute the locations of packets that belong to different flows. The only requirement is not to change the value of n_i.

5 Experimental Results

In this section we discuss how Cloak's data rate is affected by the RTT, router hop distance, geographical locations, and various adverse network conditions. Besides, we evaluate the effect of the HoLB problem on Cloak, and its performance with the D-limited codeword scheme. We also compare Cloak's performance with other timing channels: IP timing channel (IPTime) [12] and JitterBug [1], wherever we find appropriate. We have conducted experiments in the real Internet environment using the PlanetLab platform, and our test-bed which permits controlled experiments configured with various network conditions. Here we present experiment results obtained from the Planetlab platform and leave the results from the test bed to [20].

We measure the data rate of the timing channels in terms of their *goodput* defined as:

$$G = (1 - p_e)\frac{M \times L}{T_d}, \tag{1}$$

where T_d is the total time required for delivering M L-bit covert messages, and p_e is the channel's bit error rate (BER). The BER is computed based on the *Levenshtein distance* which is given by the number of insertions, deletions, and substitutions needed to convert a source message into a decoded message. Since Cloak is reliable, its p_e is 0.

5.1 Implementation

We have implemented Cloak's encoder and decoder as a TCP client and a TCP listener, respectively, including the ten Rank() and Unrank() functions. We have implemented Bin2Dec(), Dec2Bin(), Rank(), and Unrank() as offline functions. That is, the encoder pre-computes all the packet-flow combinations, and the decoder starts decoding only after capturing all N packets from X flows.

Cloak. For the Cloak's encoder, we have implemented two types of transmission functions based on the TCP socket (Cloak(STREAM)) and the raw socket (Cloak(RAW)). In Cloak(STREAM), the system's TCP stack guarantees the transmission reliability, and its traffic pattern resembles normal TCP flows'. However, it may take several RTTs to complete a single codeword transmission, thus limiting its data rate. Cloak(RAW), on the other hand, applies the aggressive transmission mechanism discussed in section 4.2 to improve its data rate. We have also implemented a separate capturing thread in the encoder to monitor the ACK arrivals, in order to determine if the other side has received all the N packets. We have implemented the Cloak's decoder with `libpcap` v0.9.5 library to sniff TCP packets. Moreover, we use a snaplen of 96 bytes to reduce the overhead during the packet capturing operation. We did not observe any packet drops throughout the experiments.

IPTime and JitterBug. We have implemented both IPTime's and Jitter-Bug's encoding and decoding schemes as plug-in modules in the Cloak encoder and decoder, respectively. We employ UDP socket (i.e., `SOCK_DGRAM`), because the packet transmission in these two timing channels do not require reliability. During the encoding process, the plug-ins invoke the modulation function in the Cloak encoder to let the codeword bypass `Bin2Dec()` and `Unrank()`, and to marshal the binary stream directly into a flow of modulated UDP packets. Moreover, the encoder generates the modulated sequences complying with the specifications of IPTime and JitterBug. Both the IPTime's encoder and JitterBug's encoder use a fixed timing interval (or timing window) of w. The JitterBug's encoder, in addition, has a default tolerance parameter of $\varepsilon = w/4$. The corresponding plug-ins in the decoder perform the reverse procedures for decoding. Moreover, we did not implement any framing and error correction mechanism for Cloak, IPTime, and JitterBug.

5.2   The Setup of PlanetLab Experiment Platforms

We locate the encoders in nine geographically diverse PlanetLab nodes, and the decoders and a Web server in a campus network. The encoders send packets to the Web server, and the decoder eavesdrops the packets and decodes them. We have obtained a total of 17,545 RTT samples between the decoder and each PlanetLab node during the experiment period. Table 2 shows the nine Planet-Lab nodes with the router hop counts from the encoder to them and the RTT statistics with a 95% confidence interval. Note that the average RTTs range between 0.0652 seconds and 0.3418 seconds. Moreover, the RTT measurements for JP, KR, and CA have higher variations than the others.

5.3   PlanetLab Experiments

Experiment design. To observe the page limitation, we report experiment results only for Cloak[1](N, X). To study the effect of N, we fix X to 20 to give a large enough number of flows, and $N = \{5, 9, 10, 11, 15, 20, 30, 40, 50\}$ which covers a reasonable range of channel capacity. Similarly, to study the effect of X, we fix N to 20 and consider $X = \{4, 6, 8, 10, 12, 14\}$.

Table 2. Measured path characteristics between each PlanetLab site and the decoder machine

Locations	Hops	RTT		
		Means	Std. Dev.	95% Conf. Intervals
Shenyang, China (CN)	13	.0652	.0060	.0651/.0653
Tokyo, Japan (JP)	16	.0992	.0244	.0988/.0996
California, U.S. (CA)	14	.1767	.0230	.1763/.1770
Kansas, U.S. (KS)	16	.2176	.0056	.2175/.2177
Rhode Island, U.S. (RI)	13	.2267	.0074	.2266/.2268
Gwangju, Korea (KR)	18	.2343	.0356	.2338/.2348
Ghent, Belgium (BE)	16	.3075	.0048	.3074/.3075
London, UK (UK)	19	.3124	.0061	.3123/.3124
Lisbon, Portugal (PT)	17	.3418	.0171	.3415/.3420

To study the adverse effects of the HoLB problem, we have generated two sets of codewords (datasets 1 and 2) for each N in Cloak[1]$(N, 20)$. Each dataset consists of 100 L-bit ($M = 100$ and $L = \lfloor \log_2 X^N \rfloor$) codewords. Moreover, we assign each packet in dataset 2 to the 20 flows with equal probability; however, we intentionally assign more packets in dataset 1 to flow 1. We measure the *degree of HoLB* of a codeword by $H = \max_{0 \leq i < X} n_i$. Figure 3(a) plots the values of $\overline{H}$, the mean values of H for different values of N. As shown, the rate of increase in $\overline{H}$ for dataset 1 is about 10 times higher than that for dataset 2 when N is beyond 10. Moreover, we have generated other sets of codewords (datasets 3 and 4) for each X in Cloak[1]$(20, X)$. The codewords for datasets 3 and 4 are generated the same ways as for datasets 1 and 2, respectively. Figure 4(a) shows that the values of $\overline{H}$ for the two datasets diverge as X increases.

Experiment results. Figures 3(b), 3(c), 4(b), and 4(c) plot the average goodputs for the nine PlanetLab nodes with the four datasets of codewords. We compute the average goodput for each (N,X) tuple by performing 30 measurements. For each N or X, the nine nodes in the figures are sorted in the ascending order of their measured mean RTTs given in Table 2. We first report the results for datasets 2 and 4 (Figure 3(c) and Figure 4(c)) for which the packets are assigned uniformly to the 20 flows. Among all the nodes, CN achieves a maximum channel goodput of around 450 bit/s in Figure 3(c). Both figures also show that the average goodput $\overline{G}$ for the two smallest RTTs (nodes CN and JP) are the highest. However, the goodputs do not necessarily decrease with the RTTs. That is, although the goodputs are inversely proportional to the RTTs, there are other factors, such as packet losses, that could disturb the goodputs. Moreover, the increase seems to be more drastic for the case of increasing X. For example, the JP node's goodput is increased by more than four times as X increases from 4 to 12. On the other hand, the rates of increases for other nodes with longer RTTs are smaller. That is, a large RTT will reduce the gain obtained from the increase in the channel capacity.

Next, we evaluate the effects of the biased packet distributions on the average goodput. We first compare the results for datasets 1 and 2 (Figure 3(b)

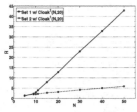 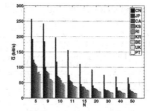 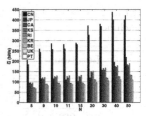

(a) The values of $\overline{H}$ for datasets 1 and 2 as a function of N.

(b) The average goodput for the PlanetLab nodes with dataset 1.

(c) The average goodput for the PlanetLab nodes with dataset 2.

Fig. 3. The results for the PlanetLab nodes: the average goodput verses N for Cloak[1]$(N, 20)$ with datasets 1 and 2

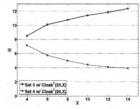 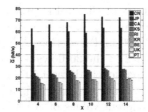 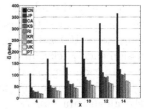

(a) The values of $\overline{H}$ for datasets 3 and 4 as a function of X.

(b) The average goodput for the PlanetLab nodes with dataset 3.

(c) The average goodput for the PlanetLab nodes with dataset 4.

Fig. 4. The results for the PlanetLab nodes: the average goodput verses X for Cloak[1]$(20, X)$ with datasets 3 and 4

and Figure 3(c)). The comparison reveals that they show opposite trends as N increases: the goodput decreases with N in Figure 3(b). It is important to point out that the scales of the two figures are actually different. Therefore, the goodputs in Figure 3(c) are all greater than the respective cases in Figure 3(b), except for $N = 5$. Since $\overline{H}$ increases with N as shown in Figure 3(a), it will take flow 1 a longer time to complete its packet transmission as N increases. For the comparison of datasets 3 and 4 (Figure 4(b) and Figure 4(c)), the goodputs in Figure 4(c) are all greater than the respective cases in Figure 4(b). However, unlike the previous cases, the goodputs in Figure 4(b) slightly improve as X increases, but the goodputs stop growing as X reaches 10. An increase in X in fact alleviates the HoLB problem, because flow 1 will become less busy; as a result, it is not surprising to see some improvement in the goodputs as X increases.

Evaluation of the D-limited codewords. To measure the performance of the D-limited codewords, we have selected five (JP, CA, KS, KR, and BE) out of the nine PlanetLab nodes to measure the average goodput of Cloak. Similar to the last section, we have generated a set of 100 L-bit binary codewords for each (N, X) tuple for Cloak[1](N, X), where $X = 6$ and $N = \{12, 16, 20\}$. We

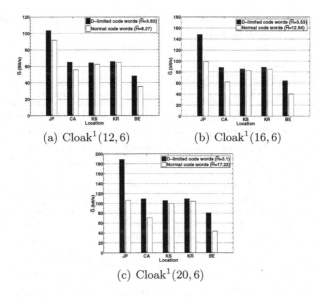

(a) Cloak[1](12,6)   (b) Cloak[1](16,6)

(c) Cloak[1](20,6)

Fig. 5. Comparing the average goodput for the normal codewords and the 6-limited codewords

use Cloak(STREAM) to encode them into two distinct sets of codewords: one generated by the D-limited codewords scheme with $D = 6$ and the other by the normal codewords. The average goodput is again based on 30 measurements.

Figure 5 compares the average goodputs of the two codewords for the five nodes. The figures show that the D-limited codeword always gives a higher goodput than the normal scheme for all nodes and for all three (N, X) tuples. Each figure also gives the average degrees of HoLB for the two codewords. The average degrees for the D-limited codewords are quite stable in all three cases, whereas the degree for the normal codewords is the highest in Figure 5(c), followed by Figure 5(b) and then by Figure 5(a). As a result, the percent of improvement of using the D-limited codewords also follows the same decreasing order for nodes JP, CA, and BE in Figures 5(a)-5(c). In particular, we have noticed a maximum gain of 77% from the JP node with Cloak[1](20,6). On the other hand, the nodes KS and KR attain much less gains; for example, the gain is only 1.6% for the KR node with Cloak[1](12,6). By examining the traffic traces, we have found that the packet loss rates at these two nodes are much lower than the others. Therefore, the normal scheme has already achieved a very high goodput; the additional benefit of adopting the D-limited scheme becomes marginal. We have also evaluated the performance of the aggressive transmission scheme and found that it could significantly increase Cloak's goodput [20].

Comparing Cloak, JitterBug, and IPTime. We have also conducted experiments on JitterBug and IPTime in the five PlanetLab nodes. In this set of experiments, we have generated another 100 packet-flow codewords using the normal Cloak[1](20,4) encoder with $\overline{H} = 5.86$. Each node uses both Cloak(RAW)

Table 3. The average goodput and average BER for Cloak, IPTime, and JitterBug obtained from five PlanetLab nodes

	95% confidence intervals of average goodput (average BER)		
	Cloak(RAW)	Cloak(STREAM)	JitterBug(RTT)
JP	203.86/216.28 (0)	55.17/58.57 (0)	13.01/13.04 (.0155)
CA	85.66/88.49 (0)	68.75/71.75 (0)	7.33/7.35 (.0265)
KS	90.77/91.00 (0)	66.57/69.26 (0)	6.13/6.14 (.0018)
KR	106.52/107.90 (0)	68.68/71.51 (0)	5.67/5.68 (.0012)
BE	63.88/64.20 (0)	44.69/45.61 (0)	4.36/4.36 (.0011)
	JitterBug(1.5RTT)	IPTime(RTT)	IPTime(1.5RTT)
JP	8.77/8.78 (.0164)	9.48/9.50 (.0363)	6.49/6.51 (.0209)
CA	4.76/4.81 (.0521)	5.43/5.47 (.0282)	3.68/3.69 (.0158)
KS	4.10/4.10 (.0010)	4.50/4.51 (.0112)	3.02/3.02 (.0088)
KR	3.81/3.81 (.0010)	4.17/4.18 (.0126)	2.80/2.81 (.0081)
BE	2.91/2.91 (.0007)	3.21/3.21 (.0076)	2.14/2.15 (.0066)

and Cloak(STREAM) to transmit the codewords. We set Cloak(RAW)'s T_E to the measured mean RTTs. For the JitterBug and IPTime experiments, the encoder marshals each respective binary codeword directly into a flow of modulated UDP packets with $w = \{RTT, 1.5RTT\}$. Both the average goodput and average BER are computed based on 30 samples.

We summarize the experiment results in Table 3. In each cell, the two leftmost values correspond to the lower limit of and the upper limit of the 95% confidence intervals for the same average goodput, and the rightmost value inside the parentheses corresponds to the measured average BER. We first point out that it is difficult to conduct a fair comparison among the three channels, because, for example, Cloak uses multiple flows whereas the other two use only one. Therefore, the comparison is based on how their goodputs are affected by the RTTs. Recall that the five nodes are sorted in an ascending order of their mean RTTs. For both Cloak channels, we do not find any general relationship between their goodputs and the RTTs, except that the lowest goodputs for both cases are given by the highest RTT (i.e., BE). On the other hand, the goodputs for JitterBug and IPTime show downward trends as the RTT increases. The magnitude of the goodput degradation is rather significant, which is between three to four times when comparing the goodputs for JP and BE. Their average BERs also show similar downward trends except for a couple points.

6   Conclusions and Future Work

In this paper, we propose Cloak, a new class of timing channels. The major design choices responsible for Cloak's attractive properties are the use of TCP as the cloaking medium, and the exploitation of Enumerative Combinatorics to encode a message into multiple TCP flows and a fixed number of TCP packets. The former provides the needed reliability for free, whereas the latter facilitates the use of the Twelvefold Way to increase the channel data rate and avoid decoding problems inherent in other network timing channels. We have implemented the Cloak encoder and decoder, and evaluated its goodput under controlled environment and in the wild. Moreover, we have in fact designed and evaluated a two-step detection algorithm for Cloak which, due to the space limit, could not be accommodated in this paper. Interested readers may refer to [20] for the algorithm and evaluation.

In a broader sense, our contribution in this work is to provide a new framework for designing more effective network covert channels. The ten encoding methods represent some of the design points in this framework. Based on this perspective, we should not rule out that there are other design points that possess other attractive properties. Therefore, one of the future work directions is to explore novel covert channel design with an even higher data rate than Cloak, for example. The other direction is on the detection aspect. Although the detection problem seems notoriously difficult, an active detection method is a promising approach. Another approach is to design more intelligent intermediaries that could reduce the channel data rate significantly.

Acknowledgment

The work described in this paper was partially supported by a grant from the Research Grant Council of the Hong Kong Special Administrative Region, China (Project No. PolyU 5080/02E) and a grant from the Cisco University Research Program Fund at Community Foundation Silicon Valley. The authors would like to thank the reviewers for their useful comments.

References

1. Shah, G., Molina, A., Blaze, M.: Keyboards and covert channels. In: Proc. USENIX Security (2006)
2. Singh, A., Nordstro, O., Lu, C., Santos, A.: Malicious ICMP tunneling: Defense against the vulnerability. In: Safavi-Naini, R., Seberry, J. (eds.) ACISP 2003. LNCS, vol. 2727, Springer, Heidelberg (2003)
3. Schechter, S., Smith, M.: Access for sale: A new class of worm. In: Proc. ACM Workshop on Rapid Malcode (WORM), ACM Press, New York (2003)
4. Rogers, R., Devost, M.: Hacking a Terror Network: The Silence Threat of Covert Channels. Syngress (2005)
5. Borders, K., Prakash, A.: Web Tap: Detecting covert Web traffic. In: Proc. ACM CCS, ACM Press, New York (2004)
6. Feamster, N., Balazinska, M., Harfst, G., Balakrishnan, H., Karger, D.: Infranet: Circumventing censorship and surveillance. In: Proc. USENIX Security (2002)
7. Wang, X., Reeves, D.: Robust correlation of encrypted attack traffic through stepping stones by watermarking the interpacket timing. In: Proc. ACM CCS, ACM Press, New York (2003)

8. Wang, X., Chen, S., Jajodia, S.: Tracking anonymous peer-to-peer VoIP calls on the Internet. In: Proc. ACM CCS, ACM Press, New York (2005)
9. Gligor, V.: A guide to understanding covert channel analysis of trusted systems (light pink book). Technical Report NCSC-TG-030, National Computer Security Center (1993)
10. DoD US: Department of defense trusted computer system evaluation criteria (orange book). Technical Report DoD 5200.28-STD, National Computer Security Center (1985)
11. Bishop, M.: Introduction to Computer Security. Addison-Wesley, Reading (2005)
12. Cabuk, S., Brodley, C., Shields, C.: IP covert timing channels: Design and detection. In: Proc. ACM CCS, ACM Press, New York (2004)
13. Watson, D., Smart, M., Malan, G., Jahanian, F.: Protocol scrubbing: Network security through transparent flow modification. In: IEEE/ACM Trans. Networking (2004)
14. Handley, M., Kreibich, C., Paxson, V.: Network intrusion detection: Evasion, traffic normalization, and end-to-end protocol semantics. In: Proc. USENIX Security Symp (2001)
15. Fisk, G., Fisk, M., Papadopoulos, C., Neil, J.: Eliminating steganography in Internet traffic with active wardens. In: Proc. Information Hiding Workshop (2002)
16. Stanley, R.: Enumerative Combinatorics. Cambridge University Press, Cambridge (1997)
17. Ahsan, K., Kundur, D.: Practical data hiding in TCP/IP. In: Proc. Workshop on Multimedia Security (2002)
18. Chakinala, R., Kumarasubramanian, A., Manokaran, R., Noubir, G., Rangan, C., Sundaram, R.: Steganographic communication in ordered channels. In: Proc. Information Hiding Workshop (2006)
19. Berk, V., Giani, A., Cybenko, G.: Detection of covert channel encoding in network packet delays. Technical Report TR2005536, Department of Computer Science, Dartmouth College (2005)
20. Luo, X., Chan, E., Chang, R.: Cloak: A ten-fold way for reliable covert communications (full version) (2007),
http://www.comp.polyu.edu.hk/~csrchang/CloakFull07.pdf
21. Yeung, R.: A First Course in Information Theory. Kluwer Academic, Dordrecht (2002)

Efficient Password-Based Authenticated Key Exchange Without Public Information*

Jun Shao[1], Zhenfu Cao[1,**], Licheng Wang[1], and Rongxing Lu[2]

[1] Department of Computer Science and Engineering
Shanghai Jiao Tong University
chn.junshao@gmail.com, zfcao@cs.sjtu.edu.cn, wanglc@sjtu.edu.cn
[2] Department of Electrical and Computer Engineering
University of Waterloo
rxlu.cn@gmail.com

Abstract. Since the first password-based authenticated key exchange (PAKE) was proposed, it has enjoyed a considerable amount of interest from the cryptographic research community. To our best knowledge, most of proposed PAKEs based on Diffie-Hellman key exchange need some public information, such as generators of a finite cyclic group. However, in a client-server environment, not all servers use the same public information, which demands clients authenticate those public information before beginning PAKE. It is cumbersome for users. What's worse, it may bring some secure problems with PAKE, such as substitution attack. To remove these problems, in this paper, we present an efficient password-based authenticated key exchange protocol *without* any public information. We also provide a formal security analysis in the non-concurrent setting, including basic security, mutual authentication, and forward secrecy, by using the random oracle model.

1 Introduction

With the rapid-developing of the Internet, people prefer to communicate with each other through the common but insecure channel, rather than traditional methods, such as ordinary mail. It demands a protocol that can provide mutual authentication and generation of a cryptographically-strong (high entropy) shared key for two communicating entities. Password-based authenticated key exchange (PAKE) is a such kind of protocol. In a PAKE, it allows two communicating entities to share a fresh authenticated session key by using a pre-shared human-memorable password. To date, there are two methods to construct a PAKE: the hybrid (i.e., password and public-key) method and the password-only method. In the former method, the two communicating entities share a password and the one additionally knows the public key of the other (see [17,12]), which demands a secure public-key infrastructure (PKI), thereby arising of issues of user registration,

---

* Supported by National 863 Project of China, No.2006AA01Z424, National Natural Science Foundation of China, No.60673079 and No.60572155, Research Fund for the Doctoral Program of Higher Education, No.20060248008.
** Corresponding author.

J. Biskup and J. Lopez (Eds.): ESORICS 2007, LNCS 4734, pp. 299–310, 2007.

key management, and key revocation. In contrast, in the latter method, the need of a secure PKI can be eliminated, which can make the protocol be more efficient and practical. Note that the pre-shared human-memorable password is low entropy, however, the fresh authenticated session key is high entropy. It seems paradoxical to get a high entropy key by only using a low entropy key. In other words, the latter method seems impossible. However, in 1992, Bellovin and Merritt [3] proposed the first such kind of protocol, named as *Encrypted Key Exchange*, by using a combination of symmetric and asymmetric cryptographic techniques. In their paper, they proposed two protocols, one is based on RSA [21], and the other is based on ElGamal public key encryption [9].

Due to its simplicity and convenience, password-only authenticated key exchange protocol has received much interest from the cryptographic research community, and most of proposed protocols are based on Bellovin and Merritt's work [4,20]. However, these protocols have not been proven secure. Until the results in [5,6], the security proof of PAKE was not treated rigorously. Following these results, a number of provable protocols and improvements have been put forth, in random oracle model [5,19,2,25,1], in ideal cipher model [6,2], and in standard model [10,15,14,16,11]. Most of provable PAKEs based on Diffie-Hellman key exchange need public information [15,14,2,1], such as generators of a finite cyclic group. However, in a client-server environment, not all servers choose the same public information, which would bring some security problems. For example, we use the protocol in [15], which *"do require that no one know the discrete logarithms of any of the generators with respect to any other"* [15]. If an adversary changes the generators (g_1, g_2, h, c, d) to (g_1', g_2', h', c', d'), which he knows the discrete logarithms. As a consequence, a client's password will be revealed after an execution of PAKE with the adversary. And then the adversary can impersonate the client. A natural method to resist this attack (named substitution attack) is to authenticate the public information before beginning PAKE, however, it is cumbersome to clients, and adds complexity to password-only PAKE. The other method is to remove the public information. To our best knowledge, there is no provable PAKE without public information, based on Diffie-Hellman key exchange. In this paper, we propose a such kind of PAKE, which is very efficient (it requires only four and five modular exponentiation computations on client's side and server's side, respectively). Furthermore, we give a formal security analysis in the non-concurrent setting, including basic secure, mutual authentication, and forward secrecy, by using the random oracle model.

1.1 Motivation

In this paper, we focus on the PAKE without public information. But what's the benefit we can get from this kind of PAKE? Firstly, we discuss the disadvantages of the PAKE with public information.

As mentioned above, to resist substitution attack, users must get valid public information. Although users can do it, there still exist some problems, which are described as follows.

- On the one hand, compared with the password, the public information is more complex and larger. For different servers, the public information is different, hence it is a heavy burden for users who store the public information.
- On the other hand, if users will not store the public information, they must get the public information before performing the protocol every time. To our best knowledge, there are two following methods to get the public information.
  - from a public board;
  - from a particular party trusted by communicating parties.

For the former one, the public board should be maintained by a particular trusted party, whom has to be trusted by all users and all servers, and the data the party maintains will be larger and larger with the number of servers increasing. Furthermore, on the one hand, if the public information for some server changes, which will raise the problems similar to the certificate management problem. On the other hand, if the party is corrupted by some adversary, the adversary can impersonate all users and all servers, such as in the protocols of [15,14].

For the latter method, before performing the PAKE with public information, the user must communicate with the particular trusted party, which will increase user's communication and computation burden. Furthermore, in the PAKE with public information, it requires that the party and server are connectable at the same time. If user cannot communicate with the party, the PAKE cannot be performed.

Now, we can say that the benefit from the PAKE without public information is to remove the above disadvantages.

1.2 Differences from Previous Work

In fact, the method proposed in this paper is very similar with that in [18,7], while not the same. On the one hand, in [18], the author proposed a PAKE named Open Key Exchange (OKE), where the server and the client only needs to share the password, while the author focuses on the PAKE based on the RSA problem, not the one based on Diffie-Hellman key exchange. On the other hand, it seems that our proposal belongs to the generic construction in [7], which extends the OKE construction by using *trapdoor hard-to-invert group isomorphisms*. However, in the generic construction, the PAKE needs *six* rounds[1], while our proposal just needs *four* rounds. Furthermore, although the concrete construction based on Diffie-Hellman key exchange in [7] needs the same rounds[2] as our proposal does, the shared information between the client and the server is different from our proposal. The concrete construction requires that the shared information is not only the password, but also the generator of a finite cyclic group, while in our proposal, the shared information is only the password.

---

[1] We add one round for the client authenticates the server's session key.

[2] We add one round for the client authenticates the server's session key.

In this paper, we aim to propose a provable PAKE based on Diffie-Hellman key exchange, where the client and the server only share the password. Our proposal can be considered as a natural extension of [18,7].

1.3   Organization

The rest of this paper is organized as follows. In Section 2, we first review the issues related to the security of password-based authenticated key exchange protocol. Then, we propose our protocol and its security analysis in Section 3 and Section 4, respectively. In what follows, we do comparisons our proposal with other PAKEs, and give some discussions on PAKE without public information in Section 5 and Section 6, respectively. Finally, we draw our conclusions in Section 7.

2   Preliminaries

In a password-only authenticated key exchange protocol, there are two entities, say *client* and *server* (denoted by C and S), both holding a secret password drawn from a small password space $\mathcal{P}$. Based on the password, client and server can authenticate each other and generate a fresh session key which is only known to the two of them. There is an active adversary, who controls all communications between client and server, and aims to defeat the goal of the protocol. The adversary can guess a value for the password and use this value in an attempt to impersonate a player, either *on-line* or *off-line*. For the former attack, it can be easily detected by the server after several failed attempts, and the server can halt the account for a while, while the latter one is not the same case due to its independence of the server. Thus, the fundamental security goal of a password-only authenticated key exchange protocol is to be secure against the latter attack. Our formal model of security for password-only authenticated key exchange protocols is based on the "oracle-based" model of Bellare, Pointcheval, and Rogaway [6]. In the following, we recall their definition of their model. For further details, we refer the reader to [6].

Notes, Initialization. Let I be the set of protocol entities, and C and S be two elements of I, but not fixed. Before running of the protocol, each pair of entities, $C, S \in I$, share a password *pwd*, randomly selected from the password space $\mathcal{P}$. The public information of the protocol, such as a set of cryptographic functions, are also specified. However, in our proposal, there does not exist any public information.

Execution of the Protocol. In a challenge-response protocol, entities' behave in response to received message is determined by the protocol. For each entity, she can execute the protocol multiple times with different entities, which is modeled as an unlimited number of *instances*[3]. We denote the i-th instance of entity C as Π_C^i. Since the adversary is assumed to control all communications among entities, she can interact with entities, which is modeled via access to oracles. The oracle types are as follows:

---

[3] The security analysis of our proposal is not in a concurrent setting.

$Send(C^i, M)$: This sends message M to instance C^i. The instance executes and responses as specified by the protocol. This oracle models the active attack.

$Execute(C^i, S^j)$: This executes the protocol between instances C^i and S^j honestly and outputs the transcript. This oracle models the passive attack.

$Reveal(I^i)$: This outputs the session key sk_I^i of I^i. This oracle models the misuse of session key.

$Test(I^i)$: This oracle can be used only once per challenge. The instance I^i generates a random bit b and sends its session key sk_I^i to the adversary if $b = 1$, or a random session key if $b = 0$.

We say that two instances C^i and S^j are *partners* if they both have accepted and hold the same messages sent and received by C^i (or S^j). An instance is said to be *fresh* if the instance has accepted and neither it nor its partner is queried to a Reveal oracle.

The notion of semantic security intuitively says that an adversary cannot effectively distinguish between a correct session key and a random session key. This is formally defined via a game, which is described as follows: it initialized by fixing a password pwd, randomly chosen from password space $\mathcal{P}$, let the adversary $\mathcal{A}$ ask a polynomial number of queries to the oracles as described above. During the game, the adversary queries a single Test oracle on a fresh instance. At the end of game, the adversary $\mathcal{A}$ outputs its guess b' on the bit b selected in the Test oracle. We define the advantage of $\mathcal{A}$ to be

$$\mathrm{Adv}_{\mathcal{A}}^{PAKE} = |\Pr|b = b'| - 1/2|.$$

Semantic security means that any efficient adversary's $\mathrm{Adv}_{\mathcal{A}}^{PAKE}$ is no more than $Q(k)/N + \epsilon(k)$, where k is the security parameter, $Q(k)$ is the maximum times of online attacks, N is the size of dictionary, and $\epsilon(\cdot)$ is a negligible function.

Computational Diffie-Hellman Assumption. Let $\mathbb{G} = \langle g \rangle$ be a finite cyclic group of order a k-bit prime number q. Computational Diffie-Hellman assumption means that there is no probabilistic polynomial time adversary can solve the following problem in $\mathbb{G}$ with non-negligible probability:

On input a tuple (g, g^x, g^y), where $x, y \in Z_q^*$, computing the value g^{xy}.

In the following, we denote ϵ_{cdh} as the probability that the adversary solves the above problem.

Decisional Diffie-Hellman Assumption. Let $\mathbb{G} = \langle g \rangle$ be a finite cyclic group of order a k-bit prime number q. Decisional Diffie-Hellman assumption means that there is no probabilistic polynomial time adversary can solve the following problem in $\mathbb{G}$ with non-negligible probability:

On input a quadruple (g, g^x, g^y, g^z), where $x, y, z \in Z_q^*$, outputs the decision whether $g^{xy} = g^z$.

In the following, we denote ϵ_{ddh} as the probability that the adversary solves the above problem.

```
                 client and server only share a password pwd.

          client                                          server

𝔾, q, g
r_C ∈_R Z_q*
R_C ← g^{r_C}
Flow_1 ← (𝔾, q, g, R_C, client)       Flow_1
                                  ──────────→
                                             Check q ∈ {k-bit prime},
                                                            g^q =? 1
                                                        (R_C)^q =? 1
                                                    Reject if not, else
                                                          r_S ∈_R Z_q*
                                                           R_S ← g^{r_S}
                                                 R_S* ← (R_C)^{pwd} R_S
                                                         R' ← (R_C)^{r_S}
                                  Flow_2     Flow_2 ← (R_S*, server)
                                  ←──────────
Check (R_S*)^q =? 1
Reject if not, else
R'_S ← R_S*(R_C)^{-pwd}
R ← (R'_S)^{r_C}
H_0, H_1, H_2 ∈_R 𝓕_H
v_C ← client||server||R_C||R'_S||R
α ← H_1(v_C)
Flow_3 ← (H_0, H_1, H_2, α)            Flow_3
                                  ──────────→
                                    Check whether H_0, H_1, H_2 ∈ 𝓕_H,
                                      v_S ← client||server||R_C||R_S||R'
                                                         α =? H_1(v_S)
                                                    Reject if not, else
                                                        sk_S ← H_0(v_S)
                                                          β ← H_2(v_S)
                                  Flow_4          Flow_4 ← β
                                  ←──────────
Check β =? H_2(v_C)
if not, sk_C ←⊥
else, sk_C ← H_0(v_C)
```

Fig. 1. Password-based authenticated key exchange without public information

3   Our Proposal

A high-level description of the protocol is given in Figure 1. Our protocol is in a finite cyclic group $\mathbb{G} = \langle g \rangle$ with a k-bit prime order q, where $\mathbb{G}$ is chosen by client C. $\mathcal{F}_H$ is denoted as the family of universal one-way hash function: $\{0,1\}^* \to \{0,1\}^{k'}$.

As shown on Figure 1, the protocol runs between a client C and a server S, who initially share a low-entropy secret string pwd, the password, uniformly drawn from the dictionary $\mathcal{P}$, without knowing other public parameters, such as the generator g of the underlying finite cyclic group $\mathbb{G}$, where k and k' are security parameters. Note that all computations are in $\mathbb{G}$.

The protocol consists of the following four flows.

1. The client first chooses a random finite cyclic group $\mathbb{G} = \langle g \rangle$ of order a k-bit prime number q, and selects a random number $r_C \in Z_q^*$, and computes the value $R_C \leftarrow g^{r_C}$, then it sends

$$(\mathbb{G}, q, g, R_C, client)$$

to the server as $Flow_1$.

2. After receiving $Flow_1$, the server first checks whether q is k-bit prime, g and R_C are two members of G with order q ($g^q \overset{?}{=} 1$ and $R_C^q \overset{?}{=} 1$). If not, reject $Flow_1$ and abort; otherwise, choose a random number $r_S \in Z_q^*$, and compute

$$R_S \leftarrow g^{r_s}, \ R_S^* \leftarrow (R_C)^{pwd} R_S, \ \text{and} \ R' \leftarrow (R_C)^{r_S},$$

then it sends $(R_S^*, server)$ to the client as $Flow_2$.

3. Upon receiving $Flow_2$, the client first checks whether R_S^* is a member of $\mathbb{G}$ with order q ($(R_S^*)^q \overset{?}{=} 1$), if not, reject $Flow_2$ and abort; otherwise, choose randomly three hash functions H_0, H_1, H_2 from $\mathcal{F}_H$, and compute

$$R_S' \leftarrow R_S^*(R_C)^{-pwd}, \ R \leftarrow (R_S')^{r_C}, \ \text{and} \ \alpha \leftarrow H_1(client||server||R_C||R_S'||R),$$

and send (H_0, H_1, H_2, α) to the client as $Flow_3$.

4. On receiving $Flow_3$, the server first checks whether H_0, H_1, H_2 are chosen from $\mathcal{F}_H$, and $\alpha \overset{?}{=} H_1(client||server||R_C||R_S||R')$. If not, reject $Flow_3$ and abort; otherwise, compute

$$sk_S \leftarrow H_0(client||server||R_C||R_S||R'), \ \beta \leftarrow H_3(client||server||R_C||R_S||R')$$

which the server sends to the client as $Flow_4$.

5. If $\beta \overset{?}{=} H_3(client||server||R_C||R_S'||R)$ holds on the client side, the client computes $sk_C \leftarrow H_0(client||server||R_C||R_S'||R)$, which means that they have successfully exchanged the session key.

Mutual Authentication. The server authenticates the client by $Flow_3$, and the client authenticates the server by $Flow_4$.

4 Security of Our Protocol

In this section, we deal with the semantic security goal in the non-concurrent setting, including the basic security of the protocol, mutual authentication goal, and forward-secrecy.

4.1 Basic Security

Theorem 1. *Let P be the protocol in Figure 1, where passwords are chosen from a dictionary $\mathcal{P}$ of size N, and let k and k' be the security parameters. Let $\mathcal{A}$ be an adversary which asks q_{ex} queries to* **Execute** *oracle, q_s queries to* **Send** *oracle, and q_h queries to the* **hash** *oracles. Then, in the non-concurrent setting:*

$$Adv_{\mathcal{A}}^{PAKE} < (q_{ex} + q_h + q_s)\epsilon_{ddh} + \frac{q_s}{2^{k'-1}} + \frac{2q_s}{N}$$

Proof Idea. We give our proof using similar techniques as described in [2,1]. We define a series of hybrid experiments, starting with the real attack and ending in an experiment in which the adversary's advantage is $1/2$, and for which we can bound the difference in the adversary's advantage between any two consecutive experiments. From these experiments, we can see that the **Execute**, **Send**, and **Reveal** oracle cannot help the adversary. Due to the lack of space, we give the proof in the full version [23].

4.2 Mutual Authentication

The following theorem shows that our protocol ensures mutual authentication, that is, a server/client instance will never accept a non-corresponding/non-expected client/server instance with non-negligible probability. We denote that AuthC/AuthS is the probability that a server/client instance accepts a non-corresponding/non-expected client/server instance.

Theorem 2. *Let us consider our protocol, where $\mathcal{P}$ is a finite dictionary of size N equipped with the uniform distribution. Let $\mathcal{A}$ be an an adversary against the security of our protocol, with less than q_s* **Send** *queries, q_{ex}* **Execution** *queries, and q_h* **hash** *queries. Then in the non-concurrent setting, we have*

$$\mathtt{AuthC} < (q_{ex} + q_s)\epsilon_{ddh} + \frac{q_s}{2^{k'-1}} + \frac{q_s}{N},$$

$$\mathtt{AuthS} < (q_{ex} + q_s)\epsilon_{ddh} + \frac{q_s}{2^{k'-1}} + \frac{2q_s}{N}.$$

Due to the lack of space, we give the proof in the full version [23].

4.3 Forward Secrecy

In this section, in order to deal with forward secrecy, we introduce a new kind of query named the **Corrupt**-query [2]:

Corrupt(I): This query models the adversary $\mathcal{A}$ have succeeded at getting the password pwd of the entity I. However, $\mathcal{A}$ does not get internal data of I.

Now, we say an instance is a `fresh` instance if before the `Corrupt`-query has been asked, the instance has accepted and neither it nor its partner is queried to a `Reveal` Oracle.

Forward-secrecy ensures that the adversary can not get any information about the session keys established before the password pwd is revealed. We use the same game in Section 2 to define forward-secrecy, and denote the advantage of $\mathcal{A}$ to be

$$Adv_{\mathcal{A}}^{PAKE-FS} = |Pr|b = b'| - 1/2|.$$

Forward-secrecy means that any efficient adversary's $Adv_{\mathcal{A}}^{PAKE-FS}$ is negligible.

Theorem 3. *Let us consider our protocol, where $\mathcal{P}$ is a finite dictionary of size N equipped with the uniform distribution. Let $\mathcal{A}$ be an an adversary against the security of our protocol, with less than q_s **Send** queries, q_{ex} **Execution** queries, and q_h **hash** queries. Then in the non-concurrent setting, we have*

$$Adv_{\mathcal{A}}^{PAKE-FS} < (q_{ex} + q_h + q_s)\epsilon_{ddh} + \frac{q_s}{2^{k'-1}} + \frac{2q_s}{N}.$$

Due to the lack of space, we give the proof in the full version [23].

5 Comparison

In this section, we will compare our proposal with the scheme in [13] (named IEEE) and the scheme in [1] (named AP05). From our viewpoint, the hash functions are not the public information, but the common sense, like the operator "+" in algebra. Since in our proposal, no matter which special finite cyclic group $\mathbb{G} = \langle g \rangle$ is, we can always use the hash function $SHA - 1$ only. For example, set $H_0 : SHA - 1(client||server||R_C||R_S||R||0)$, $H_1 : SHA-1(client||server||R_C||R_S||R||1)$, and $H_2 : SHA - 1(client||server||R_C||R_S||R||2)$.

Table 1. Comparison of PAKEs between with and without public information

		Our proposal	IEEE	AP05
public information		None	$\mathbb{G}, g, q, (\mathcal{E}_k, \mathcal{D}_k)$	$\mathbb{G}, g, q, M, N$
the total number of round		4	3	2
Authentication		Mutual	Unilateral	None
Computation Costs	Client's side	$4T_e{}^a + 1T_m{}^b$	$2T_e$	$3T_e + 2T_m$
	Server's side	$5T_e + 1T_m$	$2T_e$	$3T_e + 2T_m$
Communication Costs^c	Client's side	6	2	1
	Server's side	3	2	1

^{a} Time for a modular exponentiation computation
^{b} Time for a modular multiplication computation
^{c} Since the schemes all work in a finite cyclic group $\mathbb{G} = \langle g \rangle$ of order a k-bit prime number q, hence, we just consider the total number of data unit.

From Table 1, compared with IEEE and AP05, our proposal is a little bit inefficient than these two protocols.

- Its computational overhead is five more modular exponentiation computations than that in IEEE, and three more modular exponentiation computations than that in AP05. Since in our proposal, the server has to check the validity of $Flow_1$, and the client has to check the validity of $Flow_2$, but IEEE and AP05 do not need to do this.
- Its communication costs on client's side are more than that in IEEE and AP05. Since in our proposal, the client's terminal does need transmit the parameters. If we want to reduce the length of transmitting data, we can use the cyclic finite group on the elliptic curve.
- Since our proposal provides full functions including mutual authentication, while IEEE and AP05 do not. Hence, the total number of round in our proposal is more than that in IEEE and AP05.

6   Discussion

The Parameters Can Be Reused. Now, let us think more about our new kind of PAKE. We can find that there is no need for the client's terminal to generate new parameters each time. Since every server can perform the same as the proposed scheme suggests, hence, it allows the client to choose its own parameters once and re-use them for several different servers. In fact, if the client has a device with the parameters, then the same parameters can be used every time. We think it is very flexible and pretty attractive to users.

Generating And Testing The Parameters. In our proposal, the client's terminal should generate $\mathbb{G}, q, g$, and the server's terminal should verify these parameters. For the client's terminal, since the user can reuse the parameters, the time for generating the parameters is not a problem in our proposal. For the server's terminal, checking whether an element g in a cyclic finite group is a generator with a prime order q is fast, which just needs a exponentiation computation in the underlying cyclic finite group ($g^q \overset{?}{=} 1$). On the other hand, there exist fast algorithms to test primality [24,22]. As a result, the time for testing the parameters is not a problem in our proposal, neither.

Is There Existing PAKE Without Public Information? The answer is "Yes". Most PAKEs based on RSA [3,19,25] can be considered as the PAKE without public information, since the public key of RSA (n, e) is chosen by the client, and the client sends them to the server. However, our proposal is the first provable-secure PAKE without public information, only sharing password, based on Diffie-Hellman key exchange.

Can All PAKEs Be Changed Into The PAKE Without Public Information? The answer is also "Yes". If the protocol just needs one generator of the underlying finite cyclic group, it can be changed into the PAKE without public information by the method in our proposal. If the protocol needs more than one generators, it should need more communication and computation to compute the generators, such as performing a standard Diffie-Hellman key exchange [8] to get a generator.

7 Conclusion

In this paper, to remove the disadvantages raised by getting valid public information, we have proposed an efficient password-based authenticated exchange protocol without public information. Furthermore, we gave its security proof in the non-concurrent setting, including basic security, mutual authentication, and forward secrecy, by using the random oracle model.

Compared with the PAKEs with public information, our proposal is a little bit inefficient in terms of computational complexity. However, since the parameters can be reused in our proposal, it is very flexible and attractive to users.

References

1. Abdalla, M., Pointcheval, D.: Simple Password-based Encrypted Key Exchange Protocols. In: Menezes, A.J. (ed.) CT-RSA 2005. LNCS, vol. 3376, pp. 191–208. Springer, Heidelberg (2005)
2. Bresson, E., Chevassut, O., Pointcheval, D.: Security Proofs for an Efficient Password-Based Key Exchange. In: Proc. of the 10th ACM Conference on Computer and Communication Security, pp. 241–250. ACM Press, New York (2003)
3. Bellovin, S.M., Merritt, M.: Encrypted key exchange: Password-based protocols secure against dictionary attacks. In: Proc. of the IEEE Symposium on Research in Secruity and Privacy, pp. 72–84. IEEE Computer Society Press, Los Alamitos (1992)
4. Bellovin, S.M., Merritt, M.: Augmented encrypted key exchange: A passowrd-based protocol secure against dictionary attacks and password file compromise. In: ACM CCS 1993, pp. 244–250. ACM Press, New York (1993)
5. Boyko, V., MacKenzie, P., Patel, S.: Provably secure password authenticated key exchange using Diffie-Hellman. In: Preneel, B. (ed.) EUROCRYPT 2000. LNCS, vol. 1807, pp. 156–171. Springer, Heidelberg (2000)
6. Bellare, M., Pointcheval, D., Rogaway, P.: Authenticated key exchange secure against dictionary attack. In: Preneel, B. (ed.) EUROCRYPT 2000. LNCS, vol. 1807, pp. 139–155. Springer, Heidelberg (2000)
7. Catalano, D., Pointcheval, D., Pornin, T.: IPAKE: Isomorphisms for Password-based Authenticated Key Exchange. In: Franklin, M. (ed.) CRYPTO 2004. LNCS, vol. 3152, pp. 477–493. Springer, Heidelberg (2004)
8. Diffie, W., Hellman, M.: New Directions in Cryptography. IEEE Trans. Info. Theory 22(6), 644–654 (1976)
9. ElGamal, T.: A Public Key Cryptosystem and a Signature Scheme Based on Discrete Logarithms. IEEE Transactions on Information Theory IT-31(4), 469–472 (1985)

10. Goldreich, O., Lindell, Y.: Session-key generation using human passwords only. In: Kilian, J. (ed.) CRYPTO 2001. LNCS, vol. 2139, pp. 408–432. Springer, Heidelberg (2001)

11. Gennaro, R., Lindell, Y.: A framework for password-based authenticated key exchange. In: Biham, E. (ed.) EUROCRPYT 2003. LNCS, vol. 2656, pp. 524–542. Springer, Heidelberg (2003)

12. Halevi, S., Krawczyk, H.: Public-Key Cryptography and Password Protocols. ACM Trans. on Info. and Sys. Security 2(3), 230–268 (1999)

13. IEEE Standard 1363-2000: Standard Specifications for Public Key Cryptography. IEEE (August 2000), available from http://grouper.ieee.org/groups/1363

14. Kobara, K., Imai, H.: Pretty-simple password-authenticated key-exchange under standard assumptions. IEICE Trans. E85-A(10), 2229–2237 (2002)

15. Katz, J., Ostrovsky, R., Yung, M.: Efficient Password-Authenticated Key Exchange Using Human-Memorable Passwords. In: Pfitzmann, B. (ed.) EUROCRYPT 2001. LNCS, vol. 2045, pp. 475–494. Springer, Heidelberg (2001)

16. Katz, J., Ostrovsky, R., Yung, M.: Forward Screcy in Password-only Key Exchange Protocols. In: Cimato, S., Galdi, C., Persiano, G. (eds.) SCN 2002. LNCS, vol. 2576, pp. 29–44. Springer, Heidelberg (2003)

17. Lomas, T.M.A., Gong, L., Saltzer, J.H., Needham, R.M.: Reducing Risks from Poorly-Chosen Keys. ACM Operating Systems Review 23(5), 14–18 (1989)

18. Lucks, S.: Open Key Exchange: How to Defeat Dictionary Attacks Without Encrypting Public Keys. In: Christianson, B., Lomas, M. (eds.) Security Protocols. LNCS, vol. 1361, pp. 79–90. Springer, Heidelberg (1998)

19. MacKenzie, P., Patel, S., Swaminathan, R.: Password-authenticated key exchange based on RSA. In: Okamoto, T. (ed.) ASIACRYPT 2000. LNCS, vol. 1976, pp. 599–613. Springer, Heidelberg (2000)

20. Jablon, D.P.: Strong password-only authenticated key exchange. SIGCOMM Computer Communications Review 26(5), 5–26 (1996)

21. Rivest, R., Shamir, A., Adleman, L.: A Method for Obtaining Digital Signatures and Public Key Cryptosystems. Communications of the ACM 21(2), 120–126 (1978)

22. Solovay, R., Strassen, V.: A fast Monte-Carlo test for primality. SIAM Journal of Computing 6(1) (1977)

23. Shao, J., Cao, Z., Wang, L., Lu, R.: Efficient Password-based Authenticated Key Exchange without Public Information. Cryptology ePrint Archieve: Report (2007)

24. Weisstein, E. W.: Primality Testing Is Easy, http://mathworld.wolfram.com/news/2002-08-07/primetest/

25. Zhang, M.: New Approaches to Password Authenticated Key Exchange Based on RSA. In: Lee, P.J. (ed.) ASIACRYPT 2004. LNCS, vol. 3329, pp. 230–244. Springer, Heidelberg (2004)

Improved Anonymous Timed-Release Encryption

Konstantinos Chalkias, Dimitrios Hristu-Varsakelis, and George Stephanides

Computational Systems and Software Engineering Laboratory,
Department of Applied Informatics,
University of Macedonia,
Thessaloniki, Greece
chalkias@java.uom.gr, {dcv,steph}@uom.gr

Abstract. We revisit the problem of "sending information into the future" by proposing an anonymous, non-interactive, server-based Timed-Release Encryption (TRE) protocol. We improve upon recent approaches by Blake and Chan, Hwang et al., and Cathalo et al., by reducing the number of bilinear pairings that users must compute, and by enabling additional pre-computations. Our solution compares favorably with existing schemes in terms of computational efficiency, communication cost and memory requirements, and is secure in the random oracle model.

Keywords: timed-release encryption, bilinear pairings, pre-computations, multiple receivers.

1 Introduction

Timed-Release Encryption (TRE) is a special field of cryptography that studies the problem of "sending information into the future", i.e., encrypting a message so that it cannot be decrypted by anyone, including the designated recipients, until a future time chosen by the sender. This problem was originally posed in [22] and then explored further in [27].

There are numerous applications in distributed computing and networks that require TRE, such as sealed-bid auctions in which one seeks to provide assurance that bids cannot be opened by anyone (including the auction board) before the end of the bidding period [27], payment schedules, and key escrow. Other examples include the release of important documents (e.g., memoirs, wills, press articles) [27]; e-voting which requires delayed opening of votes [26]; internet programming contests, where participating teams cannot access the challenge problem before the beginning of the contest [3]; delayed verification of signed documents, such as lottery [29] and check cashing, contract signing [14], and verification of online card game results [13].

Solutions to the TRE problem follow one of two basic techniques. The first is based on so-called time-lock puzzles [24,27,1], [8,18,19], where the receiver must perform non-stop, non-parallelizable computation in order to recover a message. Although this approach does not involve a trusted third party, it puts immense computational overhead on the receiver, it makes encryption dependent on the receiver's CPU speed, and does not guarantee that the message will be retrieved at a precise moment in the future. To sidestep these problems, a second approach developed, based on the use of trusted

J. Biskup and J. Lopez (Eds.): ESORICS 2007, LNCS 4734, pp. 311–326, 2007.

time-servers. The server-based approach relieves the receiver from performing non-stop computation, and can specify the decryption time with precision. The trade-off is the required interaction between the (trusted) server and the users. To ensure security, scalability and anonymity, a time-server should have as little interaction as possible with the users. Ideally, this server should not be involved in the encryption or decryption process, and should only provide a common time reference by periodically releasing unforgeable, time-embedded information, which will be used to decrypt timed-release ciphertexts. The vast majority of the early attempts at TRE did not satisfy this last requirement.

In the early nineties, [22] proposed a system where the server is a trusted escrow agent, storing messages and releasing them to the designated recipients at specified times. That approach did not provide anonymity, and the server knew the content of the message and its release time. Another approach, combining symmetric and asymmetric encryption, was proposed by [27]; it required active interaction between senders and server, and thus guaranteed anonymity only for receivers. To provide sender anonymity, [16] proposed a solution in which interaction was needed between the server and the receiver only. In that scheme, the receiver's anonymity is compromised because server and receiver must engage in a conditional oblivious transfer protocol.

Recently, there have been attempts to use bilinear pairing-based schemes for TRE. The work in [7] mentioned TRE as one of the possible applications of Identity Based Encryption (IBE), and [25] implemented that idea. Although IBE is certificate-less, their scheme was not scalable, because the server must generate and transmit to each receiver a unique secret key, corresponding to a specific time instant. Other TRE approaches allow the recovery of past time-specific trapdoors from a current trapdoor. Among them are the protocol in [6] which uses the tree-like structure of [9] backwards, and [13] which uses a hash chain for the construction of the trapdoors. In both cases, the root of the tree-like structure and the hash chain, respectively, correspond to the "last" time instant for which a trapdoor can be produced, which implies an upper bound on the lifetime of their systems.

The first attempt at scalable, server-passive, user-anonymous TRE was due to Blake and Chan [3], as recently as three years ago. The breakthrough of that pairing-based approach is that the server does not interact with either the sender or the receiver; its sole responsibility is to provide a common time reference by releasing time-specific *universal* (i.e., receiver-independent) trapdoors. In fact, the server need not even be aware of the existence of a sender or receiver; hence, user anonymity and message privacy are guaranteed. That work has formed the basis for the majority of modern TRE schemes [26]. Hwang, Yum and Lee [20] proposed a user-anonymous TRE scheme that had similarities with that of Blake and Chan but could also provide a pre-open capability, meaning that the sender can decide to allow "early" decryption by issuing to the receiver a secondary trapdoor (different from the one to be given later by the time server). Another efficient anonymous TRE scheme that can take advantage of pre-computations[1] — and forms the point of departure for this work — was proposed by Cathalo, Libert and Quisquater [10].

---

[1] By pre-computation we mean that some of the calculations necessary to run a protocol can be performed off-line, prior to specifying a message or a receiver.

The contribution of this paper is to combine the desirable properties of existing TRE schemes in order to create a new, efficient, server-passive, provably-secure, pairing-based, user-Anonymous TRE protocol (termed AnTRE). A key advantage of our protocol is its simple public key format which enables pairing pre-computations and leads to significant computational savings. Recently-proposed TRE schemes either use a more complex public key format [3,10], thus requiring pairing-based verification of users' public keys, or lack support for pre-computations [3,20]. In terms of computational efficiency, our protocol is more than twice as fast as the best existing approaches when sending to *unknown* receivers, while also comparing favorably when sending the same information to multiple (more than two) receivers. Moreover, under our approach, the amount of data (public keys and pre-computed values) to be stored in the sender's machine is very small compared to that of other schemes [10]. In our scheme, as in [3], the time-server does not need to store any of the required trapdoors, since it can generate them on demand, using its own private key. Moreover, the time-server has a passive role and its sole responsibility is to periodically publish time-specific trapdoors, avoiding any interaction at all with either the sender or the receiver, thus providing user-anonymity.

The remainder of this paper is organized as follows. In Section 2 we define our model for anonymous TRE. In Section 3 we describe the proposed protocol and its security properties. Section 4 compares our protocol with three of the best-known TRE approaches in terms of computational efficiency and memory usage.

2   TRE Model

2.1   Modeling a User-Anonymous TRE Scheme

There are two types of entities involved in a general TRE scheme: a trusted time-server that periodically issues authenticated time-specific trapdoora, and users that act either as senders or as receivers. In this work, we assume that ciphertexts always contain information about their release-time. We will let $T \in \{0,1\}^\tau$, $\tau \in \mathbb{N}$ denote time. For instance, T could indicate the τ-bit string representation of a specific time instant (e.g. T = "10:00AM, October 10, 2007 GMT from the Denver Atomic Clock used in Global Positioning System (GPS)"). Based on these assumptions, an anonymous TRE scheme (AnTRE) consists of a quintuple of polynomial-time algorithms:

AnTRE.Setup: *It is run by the time-server; it takes as input a security parameter 1^k, and returns system parameters params that include the server's public key, s_{pub}, for which the corresponding private key, s_{pr}, is securely stored, to be used in the generation of all time-specific trapdoors.*

AnTRE.ReleaseT *is run by the time-server; given the server's private key s_{pr}, and a time $T \in \{0,1\}^\tau$, it returns a verifiable time trapdoor s_T.*

AnTRE.KeyGen: *This is a key generation algorithm run by a user. Its inputs are a security parameter 1^k and the system parameters params; it returns a private/public key pair (u_{pr}, u_{pub}).*

AnTRE.Enc *is run by the sender of a message m. It takes as inputs the system parameters params, the message m, the release time $T \in \{0,1\}^{\tau}$, and the public keys of both receiver and time server (u_{pub} and s_{pub} respectively), and returns a ciphertext C that the recipient must be unable to decrypt before being given the trapdoor that is to be published by the server at a later time.*

AnTRE.Dec: *This is a decryption algorithm that takes as inputs a ciphertext (C,T), the system parameters params, a private key u_{pr}, and a time-specific trapdoor s_T, and returns a plaintext m or an error message.*

2.2   Adversarial Models

We distinguish between two kinds of adversaries. One is a so-called *outside* attacker that models a "curious" time-server (i.e., one that knows the time-specific trapdoor for any time) trying to decrypt a ciphertext he may have intercepted. This attacker is challenged on a random user's public key for which he is equipped with a decryption oracle. A second adversary is an *inside* attacker that models a malicious, "impatient" receiver, trying to decrypt a ciphertext before its designated release time. In that case, the adversary has knowledge of the receiver's private key, but does not have any information about the time-server's private key and the specific trapdoor that will be published at the appointed time. We assume that an inside attacker can freely choose the public key on which he is challenged in a "find-then-guess" game, to be made precise shortly. The adversary can also access a release-time oracle returning trapdoors for any time period, except the one for which the challenge ciphertext is computed. Furthermore, in a chosen-ciphertext scenario, he is given access to an oracle decrypting other ciphertexts than the challenge. In the AnTRE model, this adversary is called chosen-time period and ciphertext attacker (CTCA).

Definition 1 ([10]). *Let $\mathcal{A}$ be an outside adversary. An AnTRE scheme is said to be secure against chosen-ciphertext attacks (IND-CCA secure) if no polynomially bounded adversary $\mathcal{A}$ has a non-negligible advantage in the following game:*

1. A challenger, CH, takes a security parameter 1^k and runs AnTRE.Setup(1^k) and AnTRE.KeyGen to obtain a list of public parameters, params, and a key pair (u_{pr}, u_{pub}). The public key u_{pub}, params, and the server's private key, s_{pr}, are given to $\mathcal{A}$, while the private key, u_{pr}, is kept secret.

2. $\mathcal{A}$ has access to a decryption oracle, AnTRE.Decrypt(.), which given a ciphertext (C, T) and the time-specific trapdoor s_T (always computable by anyone who knows s_{pr}), returns the decryption of C using the private key u_{pr}. At some point, $\mathcal{A}$ outputs two equal-length messages m_0, m_1 and a challenge time-period T^*. He gets a ciphertext $(C^*, T^*) = AnTRE.Encrypt(m_b, u_{pub}, params, T^*)$, for $b \xleftarrow{R} \{0,1\}$, computed under the public key u_{pub}.

3. $\mathcal{A}$ issues a new sequence of queries but is prohibited from asking for the decryption of the challenge for the time period T^*. He eventually outputs a bit b', and wins if $b' = b$. His advantage is $Adv_{AnTRE,\mathcal{A}}^{IND-CCA}(\mathcal{A}) := |Pr[b' = b] - 1/2|$.

Definition 2 ([10]). *Let $\mathcal{A}$ be an inside adversary. An AnTRE scheme is said to be secure against chosen-time period and ciphertext attacks (IND-CTCA secure) if no polynomially bounded adversary, $\mathcal{A}$, has a non-negligible advantage in the following game:*

1. The challenger, CH, takes the security parameter 1^k and runs AnTRE.Setup(1^k) to return the resulting public parameters params to $\mathcal{A}$. The server's public key, s_{pub}, is given to $\mathcal{A}$, while the corresponding private key, s_{pr}, is kept secret.

2. $\mathcal{A}$ has access to a release-time oracle AnTRE.ReleaseT(.) returning trapdoors s_T for any time T. $\mathcal{A}$ is also given access to a decryption oracle, AnTRE.Dec(.), which given a ciphertext C and a receiver's public key, u_{pub}, provided by $\mathcal{A}$, computes the decryption of C using s_T, but without knowing the corresponding user's private key u_{pr}. At some moment, $\mathcal{A}$ outputs messages m_0, m_1, an arbitrary public key u^*_{pub}, and a time instant T^* that has not been submitted to the AnTRE.ReleaseT oracle. He receives the challenge (C^*, T^*) =AnTRE.Enc(m_b, u^*_{pub}, params, T^*), for a hidden bit $b \xleftarrow{R} \{0,1\}$.

3. $\mathcal{A}$ issues a new sequence of release-time queries for any time instant T^* and decryption queries for any ciphertext but the challenge (C^*, T^*), for the public key u^*_{pub}. He eventually outputs a bit b' and wins if $b' = b$. His advantage is $Adv^{IND-CTCA}_{AnTRE,\mathcal{A}}(\mathcal{A}) := |Pr[b' = b] - 1/2|$.

3 Proposed Protocol

In order to construct time-specific trapdoors, we will use the short signature scheme from [4] and [30]. This scheme was initially used in the selective-ID secure IBE in [5] which was proven to be secure without random oracles. In our case, the proposed TRE protocol detailed below is based on the anonymous TRE protocol in [10], the first to make use of such signature schemes for TRE purposes. Its security proofs hold in the random oracle model [2]. In the following, we describe the proposed protocol, named AnTRE. We will sometimes refer to AnTRE as the "full" version of our protocol, in order to distinguish it from its simpler, "basic" counterpart which is used in the security proofs and is included in Appendix A.

3.1 Preliminaries

For the purposes of this work, we will require an abelian, additive finite group $\mathbb{G}_1$, of prime order q, and an abelian multiplicative group, $\mathbb{G}_2$, of the same order. For example, $\mathbb{G}_1$ may be the group of points on an elliptic curve. We will let P denote the generator of $\mathbb{G}_1$. Also, H_1, H_2, H_3, H_4 will be four secure hash functions, with $H_1 : \{0,1\}^\tau \mapsto \mathbb{Z}_q^*$, $H_2 : \{0,1\}^n \mapsto \{0,1\}^k$, $H_3 : \mathbb{G}_2 \mapsto \mathbb{Z}_q^*$, $H_4 : \mathbb{G}_1 \mapsto \{0,1\}^{n+k_0}$, where $n, k_0 \in \mathbb{N}$. Finally, $e : \mathbb{G}_1 \times \mathbb{G}_1 \mapsto \mathbb{G}_2$ will be a bilinear pairing, defined below.

Definition 3. *Let $\mathbb{G}_1$ be an additive cyclic group of prime order q generated by P, and $\mathbb{G}_2$ be a multiplicative cyclic group of the same order. A map $\hat{e} : \mathbb{G}_1 \times \mathbb{G}_1 \mapsto \mathbb{G}_2$ is called a bilinear pairing if it satisfies the following properties:*

– *Bilinearity:* $\hat{e}(aV, bQ) = \hat{e}(bV, aQ) = \hat{e}(abV, Q) = \hat{e}(V, abQ) = \hat{e}(V, Q)^{ab}$ *for all* $V, Q \in \mathbb{G}_1$ *and* $a, b \in \mathbb{Z}_q^*$.
– *Non-degeneracy: there exist* $V, Q \in \mathbb{G}_1$ *such that* $\hat{e}(V, Q) \neq 1$.
– *Efficiency: there exists an efficient algorithm to compute the bilinear map.*

Admissible bilinear pairings can be constructed via the Weil and Tate pairings [21]. For a detailed description of pairings and conditions under which they can be applied to elliptic curve cryptography, see [21,28].

3.2 Full Version of AnTRE

To send a message m that will be decrypted at (or after) a pre-defined time instant T, the following protocol is to be executed (see also [12] for tabular form):

AnTRE.Setup: given security parameters k and k_0, where k_0 is polynomial in k, the setup algorithm:
1. Outputs a k-bit prime number q, two groups $\mathbb{G}_1$, $\mathbb{G}_2$ of order q, an admissible bilinear map $\hat{e} : \mathbb{G}_1 \times \mathbb{G}_1 \mapsto \mathbb{G}_2$ and an arbitrary generator $P \in \mathbb{G}_1$.
2. Chooses the cryptographic hash functions $H_1 : \{0,1\}^\tau \mapsto \mathbb{Z}_q^*$, $H_2 : \{0,1\}^{n+k_0+\tau} \mapsto \{0,1\}^{2k}$, $H_3 : \mathbb{G}_2 \mapsto \mathbb{Z}_q^*$, $H_4 : \mathbb{G}_1 \mapsto \{0,1\}^{n+k_0+2k}$ for some $n, \tau \in \mathbb{N}$. These functions will be treated as random oracles when it comes to security considerations.
3. Generates the time-server's private key, $s \xleftarrow{R} \mathbb{Z}_q^*$, and the corresponding public key, $S = sP \in \mathbb{G}_1^*$.
4. Chooses the message space $M = \{0,1\}^n$ and the ciphertext space $C = \mathbb{G}_1 \times \mathbb{G}_1 \times \{0,1\}^{n+k_0+2k+\tau}$.
The public parameters are $params := \{k, k_0, q, \mathbb{G}_1, \mathbb{G}_2, P, S, \hat{e}, H_1, H_2, H_3, H_4, n, M, C\}$.

AnTRE.ReleaseT: given a time instant $T \in \{0,1\}^\tau$, its hash value $t = H_1(T)$, and the server's private key s, it returns the time-specific trapdoor $s_T = (s+t)^{-1}P \in \mathbb{G}_1^*$.

AnTRE.KeyGen: given *params*, it chooses a private key $b \in \mathbb{Z}_q^*$ and produces receiver's public key $B = bP \in \mathbb{G}_1^*$.

AnTRE.Enc: to encrypt $m \in \{0,1\}^n$ using the time information $T \in \{0,1\}^\tau$ and the receiver's public key B, the sender executes the following:
1. Choose $x \xleftarrow{R} \{0,1\}^{k_0}$, compute $t = H_1(T) \in \mathbb{Z}_q^*$ and $h = H_2(m||x||T) \in \{0,1\}^{2k}$ and get $r_1, r_2 \in \mathbb{Z}_q^*$, where $r_1||r_2 = \bar{h}$, where $\bar{h}$ denotes the $2k$-bit integer value of h.
2. Compute $c_1 = r_1 S + r_1 tP \in \mathbb{G}_1^*$ and $c_2 = r_2 P \in \mathbb{G}_1^*$.
3. Compute $d = H_3(\hat{e}(P,P)^{r_1}) \in \mathbb{Z}_q^*$.
4. Compute $K = H_4(dr_2 B) \in \{0,1\}^{n+k_0+2k}$ and then $c_3 = (m||x||h) \oplus K \in \{0,1\}^{n+k_0+2k}$. The ciphertext is $C := \langle c_1, c_2, c_3, T \rangle$.

AnTRE.Dec: given $C := \langle c_1, c_2, c_3, T \rangle$, the trapdoor s_T and his private key b, the recipient computes $d = H_3(\hat{e}(c_1, s_T)) \in \mathbb{G}_1$, and the session key $K = H_4(dbc_2) \in \{0,1\}^{n+k_0+2k}$. He is then able to retrieve the message as $m||x||h = K \oplus c_3$. To verify the message, he checks whether $H_2(m||x||T) = h$.

The following two theorems (proofs are included in Appendix B) concern the security properties of AnTRE. In particular, the proposed protocol is secure against IND-CTCA and IND-CCA attackers.

Theorem 1. *Assume that a polynomial-time IND-CTCA attacker has a non-negligible advantage $\varepsilon(k)$ against AnTRE when making q_{H_i} queries to random oracles H_i $\forall i \in \{1,2,3,4\}$ and q_T time server queries. Then the q-BDHI[2] problem can be solved (in polynomial time) with non-negligible probability.*

Theorem 2. *Assume that a polynomial-time IND-CCA attacker has a non-negligible advantage $\varepsilon(k)$ against AnTRE when making q_{H_i} queries to random oracles H_i $\forall i \in \{1,2,3,4\}$. Then the CDH [3] problem can be solved (in polynomial time) with non-negligible probability.*

4   Comparisons

In this section, we compare AnTRE with three of the best-known existing approaches to non-interactive server-based anonymous TRE: the BC-TRE scheme proposed by Blake and Chan [3], HYL-TRE proposed by Hwang, Yum and Lee [20,15], and CLQ-TRE [4] proposed by Cathalo, Libert and Quisquater [10].

4.1   Computational Efficiency

Because some of the protocols mentioned previously allow for pre-computations under certain circumstances, we distinguish between three cases of anonymous TRE: i) message transmission to *unknown* receivers, ii) transmission to *known* receivers (in which case there is no need to verify their public keys), and iii) messages sent to multiple recipients with the same release-time.

For the purposes of calculating the computing time needed to run each protocol, we will let Pa denote the pairing operation, Sm scalar multiplication in $\mathbb{G}_1$, PSm parallel scalar multiplication of the form $aP + bQ$ in $\mathbb{G}_1$, Ex exponentiation in $\mathbb{G}_2$, Mtp map-to-point hashing, and Inv inversion in $\mathbb{Z}_q$. To make a fair comparison, the cost of each operation will be related to that of an elliptic curve scalar multiplication (M). Table 1 summarizes the benchmarking results using the *MIRACL* open-source library [23], considering an order-q subgroup of a supersingular elliptic curve E over F_p, where p is a 512 bit prime and q is a 160 bit prime. Pairing values belong to a finite field of 1024 bits.

If we assume that $\hat{e}(P,P)$ is computed in advance and included among the public parameters, then the encryption phase of AnTRE requires the following operations: 1 PSm to compute c_1, 1 Sm for c_2, 1 Ex for d, and 1 Sm to compute K. That is, no pairing computations are necessary at execution time, and the total cost of the encryption phase

---

[2] The q-Bilinear Diffie-Hellman Inversion Problem (q-BDHI) is: given $(Q, aQ, a^2Q, ..., a^qQ) \in \mathbb{G}_1^{q+1}$, compute $\hat{e}(Q,Q)^{a^{-1}} \in \mathbb{G}_2$.

[3] The Computational Diffie-Hellman Problem (CDH) is: given $Q \in \mathbb{G}_1$, aQ, bQ for some $a,b \in \mathbb{Z}_q^*$, compute $abQ \in \mathbb{G}_1$.

[4] We note that [10] uses multiplicative notation for the groups $\mathbb{G}_1$ and $\mathbb{G}_2$.

Table 1. Cost of basic operations in relation to that of an elliptic curve scalar multiplication

Operation	Notation	Cost
Bilinear Pairing	Pa	$9M$
Parallel Scalar Multiplication in $\mathbb{G}_1$	PSm	$1.2M$
Scalar Multiplication in $\mathbb{G}_1$	Sm	$1M$
Exponentiation in $\mathbb{G}_2$	Ex	$1M$
Map-To-Point	Mtp	$0.7M$
Inversion in $\mathbb{Z}_q$	Inv	$0.4M$

is equivalent to $4.2M$. In the decryption phase, the recipient must perform 1 Pa operation to calculate the point value d, and 1 Sm to produce K, thus the total decryption cost is approximately $10M$. Tables 2 and 3 summarize the comparisons of computational cost for the cases of *unknown* and *known* receivers, respectively.

Table 2. Computational cost comparison of BC-TRE, HYL-TRE, CLQ-TRE, and proposed AnTRE protocol (sending to *unknown* receivers)

Protocol	Encryption		Decryption		Total
BC-TRE	$3Pa + 2Sm + 1Mtp$	$= 29.7M$	$1Pa + 1Ex$	$= 10M$	$39.7M$
HYL-TRE	$1Pa + 1PSm + 2Sm + 1Mtp$	$= 12.9M$	$2Pa + 1Sm$	$= 19M$	$31.9M$
CLQ-TRE	$2Pa + 1PSm + 1Ex$	$= 20.2M$	$1Pa + 1PSm + 1Ex$	$= 11.2M$	$31.4M$
Proposed	$1PSm + 2Sm + 1Ex$	$= 4.2M$	$1Pa + 1Ex$	$= 10M$	$14.2M$

Table 3. Computational cost comparison of BC-TRE, HYL-TRE, CLQ-TRE, and proposed AnTRE protocol (sending to *known* receivers)

Protocol	Encryption		Decryption		Total
BC-TRE	$1Pa + 2Sm + 1Mtp$	$= 11.7M$	$1Pa + 1Ex$	$= 10M$	$21.7M$
HYL-TRE	$1Pa + 1PSm + 2Sm + 1Mtp$	$= 12.9M$	$2Pa + 1Sm$	$= 19M$	$31.9M$
CLQ-TRE	$1PSm + 1Ex$	$= 2.2M$	$1Pa + 1PSm + 1Ex$	$= 11.2M$	$13.4M$
Proposed	$1PSm + 2Sm + 1Ex$	$= 4.2M$	$1Pa + 1Ex$	$= 10M$	$14.2M$

Remarks: We note that neither BC-TRE nor HYL-TRE support pairing pre-computations, because the sender must compute a pairing that depends on the release time. Moreover, these two protocols require a special hash function, *map-to-point*, which is needed for mapping strings onto cyclic groups, and which is much less efficient than plain hash functions [30,10,23]. Furthermore, unlike BC-TRE and CLQ-TRE, AnTRE retains the same efficiency whether or not the receivers are *known* entities. It is also worth mentioning that BC-TRE and CLQ-TRE use a slightly different public key format, with users' public key consisting of two points in $\mathbb{G}_1$ instead of one (as in conventional cryptographic schemes).

This means that on the first use of any public key (for transmitting to an *unknown* receiver) the sender must verify the validity of this two-point public key, to ensure that the recipient will be able to decrypt the message. Such verification is not needed in our proposed protocol or in HYL-TRE.[5]

Transmitting to multiple receivers. AnTRE is practical for encrypting a message to multiple receivers with the same release-time (e.g., in an Internet programming contest). In our approach, the value of d (in AnTRE.Dec) can be calculated by anyone who knows the time-specific trapdoor s_T. Also, the session key, K, depends on d, c_2 (sent in the clear), and the recipient's private key, u_{pr}. Thus, if one wishes to use AnTRE to send a message to multiple receivers, he is able to use the same random values r_1 and r_2 for all of them. In that case, the computed session key K (and thus c_3 as well) will differ from receiver to receiver; the corresponding ciphertexts will be of the form $C < c_1, c_2, c_{3.1}...c_{3.N}, T >$. Finally, because c_1, c_2 and d are computed only once, the total encryption cost per receiver will be $\frac{3.2M}{N} + 1M$, where N is the number of receivers. Compared to CLQ-TRE [10] suitably modified for multiple receivers (it costs approximately $2.2M$ for *known* receivers), our approach is more efficient, even in the special case of *known* receivers, if the number of designated recipients is greater than two. Although BC-TRE and HYL-TRE can be modified for improved efficiency when sending to multiple receivers, neither of them can avoid the pairing computation during the encryption process (to the best of our knowledge), and thus they appear to be less efficient compared to AnTRE and CLQ-TRE.

4.2 Communication Cost

In order to compare the communication complexity of the four TRE schemes, we must take into account the bit-length of both the transmitted public keys and the ciphertext. As we have mentioned in Section 4.1, in BC-TRE and CLQ-TRE the users' public keys consist of two elliptic curve points, i.e., $u_{pub} \in \mathbb{G}_1 \times \mathbb{G}_1$, while in the proposed AnTRE and HYL-TRE protocols $u_{pub} \in \mathbb{G}_1$. Consequently, if the recipient is an *unknown* entity, the cost to download the recipient's public key from a public database for BC-TRE and CLQ-TRE is twice that of the proposed AnTRE and HYL-TRE schemes.

The ciphertext space (including transmission of time information) of each scheme is:

- IND-CCA secure BC-TRE:[6] $C_{BC-TRE} = \mathbb{G}_1 \times \{0,1\}^{n+k_0+\tau}$.
- HYL-TRE: $C_{HYL-TRE} = \mathbb{G}_1 \times \mathbb{G}_1 \times \mathbb{G}_2 \times \{0,1\}^{n+k_0+\tau}$.
- CLQ-TRE: $C_{CLQ-TRE} = \mathbb{G}_1 \times \{0,1\}^{n+k_0+\tau}$.
- Proposed AnTRE: $C_{AnTRE} = \mathbb{G}_1 \times \mathbb{G}_1 \times \{0,1\}^{n+k_0+2k+\tau}$.

---

[5] When comparing the cost of implementations of the above approaches, we did not include the cost of a group membership test for the public keys. We note, however, that the schemes [3,10] use two points in their public keys (ours uses only one) and would thus require some additional checking

[6] As the basic BC-TRE has not been proven to be secure against IND-CCA attacks, it could be modified using the technique in [17].

BC-TRE and CLQ-TRE have a smaller ciphertext space than AnTRE (about 1 elliptic curve point less), while the ciphertext space of HYL-TRE is the largest because of the pairing value (e.g., 1024 bits) that must be transmitted.

4.3 Storage Requirements

In settings where TRE needs to be executed in low-end, limited-memory computing systems (e.g., smartcards and other handheld computing devices), the memory/storage requirements of the protocol(s) to be used must be taken into account. As noted in Section 4.1, the user's public key space for AnTRE and HYL-TRE is a single elliptic curve point $u_{pub} \in \mathbb{G}_1$, while for the other two protocols it consists of two points, i.e., $u_{pub} \in \mathbb{G}_1 \times \mathbb{G}_1$. As a result, BC-TRE and CLQ-TRE require twice the memory to store the public keys for *known* receivers. Moreover, CLQ-TRE and AnTRE are the only two of the protocols considered here that enable pre-computations at a minor cost of storing $\hat{e}(P,P) \in \mathbb{G}_2$, leading to increased efficiency.[7]

5   Conclusions

We have presented a new, server-based cryptographic scheme for anonymous timed-release encryption, and proved that is IND-CCA and IND-CTCA secure in the random oracle model. Our protocol requires no interaction between users and the server, whose sole responsibility is to publish time-specific trapdoors that correspond to specific time instants. We compared our approach with three of the best-known existing TRE schemes; the main advantage of the proposed protocol is its low computational cost and memory storage requirements. Other properties of the proposed scheme include scalability and practicality when sending a message to multiple receivers.

References

1. Bellare, M., Goldwasser, S.: Encapsulated Key Escrow. MIT Laboratory for Computer Science Technical Report 688 (1996)
2. Bellare, M., Rogaway, P.: Random Oracles Are Practical: A Paradigm for Designing Efficient Protocols. In: 1st ACM Conf. on Computer and Communications Security, pp. 62–73. ACM Press, New York (1993)
3. Blake, I.F., Chan, A.C.-F.: Scalable, Server-Passive, User-Anonymous Timed Release Cryptography. In: 25th IEEE Intl. Conf. on Distributed Computing Systems, pp. 504–513. IEEE Computer Society Press, Los Alamitos (2005)
4. Boneh, D., Boyen, X.: Short Signatures Without Random Oracles. In: Cachin, C., Camenisch, J.L. (eds.) EUROCRYPT 2004. LNCS, vol. 3027, pp. 56–73. Springer, Heidelberg (2004)
5. Boneh, D., Boyen, X.: Efficient Selective-ID Secure Identity Based Encryption Without Random Oracles. In: Cachin, C., Camenisch, J.L. (eds.) EUROCRYPT 2004. LNCS, vol. 3027, pp. 223–238. Springer, Heidelberg (2004)

---

[7] We did not include here the memory cost during real-time execution (volatile memory) because it depends on the implementation of the basic elliptic curve operations.

6. Boneh, D., Boyen, X., Goh, E.-J.: Hierarchical Identity Based Encryption with Constant Size Ciphertext (2005), available at http://eprint.iacr.org/2005/015
7. Boneh, D., Franklin, M.: Identity Based Encryption From the Weil Pairing. In: Kilian, J. (ed.) CRYPTO 2001. LNCS, vol. 2139, pp. 213–229. Springer, Heidelberg (2001)
8. Boneh, D., Naor, M.: Timed Commitments and Applications. In: Bellare, M. (ed.) CRYPTO 2000. LNCS, vol. 1880, pp. 236–254. Springer, Heidelberg (2000)
9. Canetti, R., Halevi, S., Katz, J.: A Forward Secure Public Key Encryption Scheme. In: Biham, E. (ed.) Advances in Cryptology – EUROCRPYT 2003. LNCS, vol. 2656, pp. 254–271. Springer, Heidelberg (2003)
10. Cathalo, J., Libert, B., Quisquater, J.-J.: Efficient and Non-interactive Timed-Release Encryption. In: Qing, S., Mao, W., Lopez, J., Wang, G. (eds.) ICICS 2005. LNCS, vol. 3783, pp. 291–303. Springer, Heidelberg (2005)
11. Cathalo, J., Libert, B., Quisquater, J.-J.: Unpublished Extended version of [10], personal communication
12. Chalkias, K., Hristu-Varsakelis, D., Stephanides, G.: A Protocol for Improved Timed-Release Encryption. Technical Report, Computational Systems and Software Engineering Laboratory, Department of Applied Informatics, University of Macedonia (2007), available at: http://csse.uom.gr/eprints/58/01/AnTRE-full.pdf
13. Chalkias, K., Stephanides, G.: Timed Release Cryptography from Bilinear Pairings Using Hash Chains. In: Leitold, H., Markatos, E. (eds.) CMS 2006. LNCS, vol. 4237, pp. 130–140. Springer, Heidelberg (2006)
14. Damgard, I.: Practical and probably secure release of a secret and exchange of signatures. In: Helleseth, T. (ed.) EUROCRYPT 1993. LNCS, vol. 765, pp. 200–217. Springer, Heidelberg (1994)
15. Dent, A.W., Tang, Q.: Revisiting the Security Model for Timed-Release Public-Key Encryption with Pre-Open Capability (2006), available at http://eprint.iacr.org/2006/306.pdf
16. Crescenzo, G.D., Ostrovsky, R., Rajagopalan, S.: Conditional Oblivious Transfer and Timed-Release Encryption. In: Stern, J. (ed.) EUROCRYPT 1999. LNCS, vol. 1592, pp. 74–89. Springer, Heidelberg (1999)
17. Fujisaki, E., Okamoto, T.: How to Enhance the Security of Public-Key Encryption at Minimum Cost. In: Imai, H., Zheng, Y. (eds.) PKC 1999. LNCS, vol. 1560, pp. 53–68. Springer, Heidelberg (1999)
18. Garay, J., Jakobsson, M.: Timed Release of Standard Digital Signatures. In: Blaze, M. (ed.) FC 2002. LNCS, vol. 2357, pp. 168–182. Springer, Heidelberg (2003)
19. Garay, J., Pomerance, C.: Timed Fair Exchange of Standard Signatures. In: Wright, R.N. (ed.) FC 2003. LNCS, vol. 2742, pp. 190–207. Springer, Heidelberg (2003)
20. Hwang, Y.H., Yum, D.H., Lee, P.J.: Timed-Release Encryption with Pre-open Capability and its Application to Certified E-mail System. In: Zhou, J., Lopez, J., Deng, R.H., Bao, F. (eds.) ISC 2005. LNCS, vol. 3650, pp. 344–358. Springer, Heidelberg (2005)
21. Joux, A.: The Weil and Tate Pairings as Building Blocks for Public Key Cryptosystems (Survey). In: Fieker, C., Kohel, D.R. (eds.) Algorithmic Number Theory. LNCS, vol. 2369, pp. 20–32. Springer, Heidelberg (2002)
22. May, T.: Timed-Release Crypto, manuscript (1993), available at http://www.hks.net.cpunks/cpunks-0/1560.html
23. Ltd, S.S.: Miracl - Multiprecision Integer and Rational Arithmetic C/C++ Library (See: http://indigo.ie/mscott/)
24. Mao, W.: Timed Release Cryptography. In: Vaudenay, S., Youssef, A.M. (eds.) SAC 2001. LNCS, vol. 2259, pp. 342–357. Springer, Heidelberg (2001)

25. Mont, M.C., Harrison, K., Sadler, M.: The HP time vault service: Innovating the way confidential information is disclosed at the right time. In: 12th Intl. World Wide Web Conf., pp. 160–169. ACM Press, New York (2003)
26. Osipkov, I., Kim, Y., Cheon, J.-H.: Timed-Release Public Key Based Authenticated Encryption (2004), available at http://eprint.iacr.org/2004/231
27. Rivest, R.L., Shamir, A., Wagner, D.A.: Time-Lock Puzzles and Timed-Release Crypto. MIT Laboratory for Computer Science Technical Report 684 (1996)
28. Stogbauer, M.: Efficient Algorithms for Pairing-Based Cryptosystems. Diploma Thesis: Darmstadt University of Technology, Dept. of Mathematics (2004)
29. Syverson, P.F.: Weakly Secret Bit Commitment: Applications to Lotteries and Fair Exchange. In: 11th IEEE Computer Security Foundations Workshop, pp. 2–13. IEEE Computer Society Press, Los Alamitos (1998)
30. Zhang, F., Safavi-Naini, R., Susilo, W.: An Efficient Signature Scheme from Bilinear Pairings and Its Applications. In: Bao, F., Deng, R., Zhou, J. (eds.) PKC 2004. LNCS, vol. 2947, pp. 277–290. Springer, Heidelberg (2004)

A   Basic Version of the Protocol

A "basic" version of AnTRE, termed BasicAnTRE, will be useful when discussing the security of our protocol (Appendix B). The ReleaseT and KeyGen algorithms of BasicAnTRE are identical to those of AnTRE (Sec. 3.2). The Setup, Encryption and Decryption primitives are as follows:

AnTRE.Setup: given security parameters k and k_0, where k_0 is polynomial in k, the setup algorithm:

1. Outputs a k-bit prime number q, two groups $\mathbb{G}_1$, $\mathbb{G}_2$ of order q, an admissible bilinear map $e : \mathbb{G}_1 \times \mathbb{G}_1 \mapsto \mathbb{G}_2$ and an arbitrary generator $P \in \mathbb{G}_1$.

2. Chooses the following cryptographic hash functions: $H_1 : \{0,1\}^\tau \mapsto \mathbb{Z}_q^*, H_2 : \{0,1\}^n \mapsto \{0,1\}^{k_0}, H_3 : \mathbb{G}_2 \mapsto \mathbb{Z}_q^*, H_4 : \mathbb{G}_1 \mapsto \{0,1\}^{n+k_0}$ for some $n \in \mathbb{N}$. These functions will be treated as random oracles when it comes to security considerations.

3. Generates the time-server's private key $s \xleftarrow{R} \mathbb{Z}_q^*$ and the corresponding public key $S = sP \in \mathbb{G}_1^*$.

4. Chooses the message space to be $M = \{0,1\}^n$ and the ciphertext space is $C = \mathbb{G}_1 \times \mathbb{G}_1 \times \{0,1\}^{n+k_0}$.

The public parameters are $params := \{k, k_0, q, \mathbb{G}_1, \mathbb{G}_2, P, S, \hat{e}, H_1, H_2, H_3, H_4, n, M, C\}$.

AnTRE.Enc: to encrypt $m \in \{0,1\}^n$ using the time information $T \in \{0,1\}^\tau$ and the receiver's public key B, the sender executes the following:

1. Choose random $r_1, r_2 \in \mathbb{Z}_q^*$, compute $t = H_1(T) \in \mathbb{Z}_q^*$.
2. Compute $h = H_2(m)$.
3. Compute $c_1 = r_1 S + r_1 t P \in \mathbb{G}_1^*$ and $c_2 = r_2 P \in \mathbb{G}_1^*$.
4. Compute $d = H_3(\hat{e}(P,P)^{r_1}) \in \mathbb{Z}_q^*$.
5. Compute $K = H_4(dr_2 B) \in \{0,1\}^{n+k_0}$ and then $c_3 = (m\|h) \oplus K \in \{0,1\}^{n+k_0}$.

The ciphertext is $C := \langle c_1, c_2, c_3, T \rangle$.

AnTRE.Dec: given $C := \langle c_1, c_2, c_3, T \rangle$, the trapdoor s_T and his private key b, the recipient computes $d = H_3(\hat{e}(c_1, s_T)) \in \mathbb{G}_1$ and the session key $K = H_4(dr_2 B) \in \{0,1\}^{n+k_0}$.

Then, he is able to retrieve the message as $m\|h = K \oplus c_3$. To verify the message, he checks whether $H_2(m) = h$.

B   Security Proofs for AnTRE

Our proofs are in the random oracle model, and follow those of Theorems 2 and 3 of [11] (an extended version of [10]). We will first consider the security of BasicAnTRE, described in Appendix A. As in [10], AnTRE results from a variant of the first Fujisaki-Okamoto transform [17] applied to BasicAnTRE, by hashing the message m, a random number x, and a time T, and using the resulting bits in order to encrypt. This conversion is slightly different from the one in [17] because the hash function H_2 takes as an additional input the time T. Including T among the inputs is necessary (the encryption algorithm of BasicAnTRE is parameterized by T) and enables a knowledge extractor to simulate the behavior of a decryption oracle with the same probability as the plaintext extractor in the security proof of the Fujisaki-Okamoto conversion [17]. Our security proofs apply the modified version of Theorem 3 from [17], established in [11].

B.1   Proof of Theorem 1 - Security Against "Impatient" Recipients

We first show that BasicAnTRE is secure against chosen time and plaintext attacks (IND-CTPA)[8] [10], using a slightly modified form of the security proof in [11,10] (similar to [4], [5]). Assuming an IND-CTPA attacker $\mathcal{A}$ which succeeds against BasicAnTRE with non-negligible probability, $\varepsilon(k)$, we will construct an algorithm $\mathcal{B}$ which takes as inputs $< P, \alpha P, \alpha^2 P, \alpha^3 P, ..., \alpha^q P >$, for some interger q, and computes $\hat{e}(P,P)^{\alpha^{-1}}$ with non-negligible probability.

Let q_T be the number of queries made by $\mathcal{A}$ to the time server. Without loss of generality, we will assume that $q_T = q_{H_1} - 1 = q - 1$ (if $q_T < q_{H_1} - 1$, then $\mathcal{B}$ can issue dummy queries to the time-server broadcast oracle for itself). Initially, $\mathcal{B}$ chooses $\ell \xleftarrow{R} \{1,...,q\}$ and $a,b \xleftarrow{R} \mathbb{Z}_q^*$ and sets $I_\ell = ab \in \mathbb{Z}_p^*$. Then, he chooses $I_i \xleftarrow{R} \mathbb{Z}_q^*$ and computes $w_i = \frac{I_\ell - I_i}{a} \; \forall \, i \in \{1,...,q\}\backslash\{\ell\}$.

Next, $\mathcal{B}$ uses its input to compute a generator $Q \in \mathbb{G}_1$ and a server public key $s_{pub} = xQ$ for some $x \in \mathbb{Z}_q^*$, such that $\mathcal{B}$ can know all of the q_T pairs $(I_i, (I_i + x)^{-1}Q)$, $i \neq \ell$, as in [4]. He does this in the following manner. $\mathcal{B}$ expands the polynomial $f(z) = \prod_{i=0, i\neq\ell}^q (z + w_i) = \sum_{j=0}^{q-1} c_j z^j$, to find c_j's. Then, $Q, U \in \mathbb{G}_1$ are obtained as

$$Q = \prod_{j=0}^{q-1}(\alpha^j P)c_j = f(\alpha)P \in \mathbb{G}_1, \quad U = \prod_{j=1}^{q}(\alpha^j P)c_{j-1} = \alpha f(\alpha)P = \alpha Q.$$

Similarly to [4], the q_T pairs $(w_i, Q_i = (w_i + \alpha)^{-1}Q)$ can then be obtained from expanding $f_i(z) = \frac{f(z)}{z + w_i} = \sum_{j=0}^{q-2} d_j z^j$ and computing

$$Q_i = \prod_{j=0}^{q-2}(\alpha^j P)d_j = f_i(\alpha)P = \frac{f(\alpha)}{a + w_i}P = (\alpha + w_i)^{-1}Q, \; \forall \, i \in \{1,...,q\}\backslash\{\ell\}.$$

---

[8] This type of adversary is defined similarly to IND-CTCA, but without access to a decryption oracle .

Now, $\mathcal{B}$ chooses the time-server's public key to be $s_{pub} = -aU - I_\ell Q = (-a)\alpha Q - abQ = -a(\alpha+b)Q$. Thus, the server's private key (which is unknown to $\mathcal{B}$), is $x = -a(\alpha+b) = -a\alpha - I_\ell \in \mathbb{Z}_q^*$, and for all $i \in \{1,...,q\}\setminus\{\ell\}$ we have:

$$(I_i, -a^{-1}Q_i) = (I_i, (I_i - a\alpha - I_\ell)^{-1}Q)$$

and

$$(I_i, (I_i+x)^{-1}Q) = (I_i, (I_i - a\alpha - I_\ell)^{-1}Q),$$

thus

$$(I_i, -a^{-1}Q_i) = (I_i, (I_i+x)^{-1}Q).$$

$\mathcal{B}$ now has knowledge of all q_T pairs $(I_i, (I_i+x)^{-1}Q)$ because he can compute I_i, Q, Q_i from $(P, \alpha P, \alpha^2 P, \alpha^3 P, ...\alpha^q P)$ as described above. Armed with this information, he will be able to provide correctly formed values each time $\mathcal{A}$ queries H_1 for a given time, or requests the trapdoor value for the same time. To proceed, $\mathcal{B}$ starts $\mathcal{A}$ on input $s_{pub} = (-aU - I_\ell Q)$ and initializes a counter, $v = 0$. During the game we assume that: i) all H_1 queries are distinct, and ii) $\mathcal{A}$ produces her challenge request at T^*, for which he asks the hash value $H_1(T^*)$. $\mathcal{B}$ answers queries to random oracles as follows:

- H_1: $\mathcal{B}$ answers I_v and increments $v = 1, 2, ...$
- For $i = 2, 3, 4$ (H_i): On input γ_λ, $\lambda = 1, 2, ..., q_{H_i}$, $\mathcal{B}$ selects a random $\eta_{i,\lambda}$ and stores $(\gamma_\lambda, \eta_{2,\lambda})$ into a list L_i. Each incoming query input is matched against those already on the corresponding list; if the same query has been asked again, $\mathcal{B}$ returns the same value as before.
- Queries to time-server: On input $T_v, v = 1, 2, ...$, if $v = \ell$, $\mathcal{B}$ stops and reports "failure"; otherwise returns the trapdoor value for T_v, $-a^{-1}Q_v = (I_n+x)Q$, to $\mathcal{A}$.

After the find stage, $\mathcal{A}$ outputs $< m_0, m_1, T^* >$ and a valid public key u_{pub} to be challenged on. If $T^* \neq T_\ell$ ($\mathcal{B}$ did not guess correctly which T_i the attack will occur on), then $\mathcal{B}$ stops and reports "failure". Otherwise, he selects $\sigma \xleftarrow{R} \in \mathbb{Z}_q^*$ and a random string c_3^* to return the challenge $C^* :< c_1^*, c_2^*, c_3^* >$, with $c_1^* = -a\sigma Q, c_2^* = r_2 Q$. To elucidate $\mathcal{B}$'s choice of c_1^*, recall that $\mathcal{B}$ should send something of the form $c_1^* = r_1(t + x)Q$, $c_2^* = r_2 Q$, with $t = I_\ell$ (corresponding to $H_1(T^*)$) and $x = -a\alpha - I_\ell$ (unknown server's private key). In the simulation set up by $\mathcal{B}$, it would be $c_1^* = r_1(I_\ell - a\alpha - I_\ell)Q = r_1(-a\alpha)Q$, for r_1 random. Now, assume that $r_1 = \frac{\sigma}{\alpha}$, so that $\sigma = r_1\alpha$. Then, sending $c_1^* = -a\sigma Q$ to $\mathcal{A}$, for random σ, would be precisely the same as if we had used $r_1 = \frac{\sigma}{\alpha}$ to encrypt. Realizing that c_3^* is not properly formatted, would require $\mathcal{A}$ to query $H_4(d\beta c_2)$ with non-negligible probability (if not, one could construct an algorithm for inverting the *XOR* function with non-negligible probability). Whether or not the private key β is known to $\mathcal{A}$, it can be easily shown that computing the "correct" input to H_4 (which is $d\beta r_2 Q$) with non-negligible probability, implies that $\mathcal{A}$ must query H_3 on input $\hat{e}(Q, Q)^{r_1}$ with non-negligible probability to compute d, the latter being the output of a random oracle. $\mathcal{B}$ has the opportunity to detect that event and use $\hat{e}(Q, Q)^{r_1}$ to compute $\hat{e}(Q, Q)^{a^{-1}}$.

If $\mathcal{A}$ is successful in guessing the hidden bit with non-negligible probability, then using standard arguments it can be shown that $\mathcal{A}$ is very likely to query H_3 on $\hat{e}(Q, Q)^{r_1}$ at some time of the game, if the latter mimics perfectly the real attack environment. To produce its output, $\mathcal{B}$ selects a random γ from its L_3 list, so that with probability $\varepsilon(k)\frac{1}{q_{H_3}}$, γ is $\hat{e}(Q,Q)^{r_1}$. Then, $\gamma = \hat{e}(Q,Q)^{r_1} = \hat{e}(P,P)^{\frac{\sigma f^2(\alpha)}{\alpha}}$. If we let $f^2(z) = \sum_{j=0}^{2q-2}\phi_j z^j$ so that $f^2(\alpha)/\alpha = \phi_0/\alpha + \sum_{j=1}^{2q-2}\phi_j\alpha^{j-1}$, then we can solve for $\hat{e}(P,P)^{a^{-1}}$ from γ, as:

$$\hat{e}(P,P)^{a^{-1}} = \left(\gamma^{\sigma^{-1}}\prod_{j=1}^{2q-2}\hat{e}(P,P)^{(\alpha^{j-1})(-\phi_j)}\right)^{\phi_0^{-1}},$$

where the ϕ_j can be computed from the known coefficients of $f(z)$, and the $\hat{e}(P,P)$, ..., $\hat{e}(P,P)^{2q-3}$ are computed from $\mathcal{B}$'s inputs $< P, \alpha P, \alpha^2 P, \alpha^3 P, ..., \alpha^q P >$. This contradicts the assumption that the q-BDHI problem is hard. We conclude that BasicAnTRE is IND-CTPA secure. Now, the IND-CTPA security of BasicAnTRE implies IND-CTCA security of AnTRE using a Lemma very similar to Lemma 2 of [11] (itself derived from Theorem 3 of [17]) with minor modifications. The proof (omitted here because of space limitations) can be found in a fuller version of this paper [12].

Lemma 1. *In the random oracle model, an IND-CTCA attacker $\mathcal{A}$ having non-negligible advantage ε against AnTRE when making q_D decryption queries and q_{H_i} queries to oracles $H_i, (i = 1, ..., 4)$, implies an IND-CTPA attacker $\mathcal{B}$ with non-negligible advantage against BasicAnTRE.*

We note that the proof [12] of the last lemma addresses the single-receiver case. If a message is sent to $N > 1$ receivers, then the corresponding ciphertexts differ only in their c_3 parts, and a malicious receiver may attempt to read his message early by obtaining multiple $c_{3,i}$ values, $i = 1, ..., N$, for the same message m and time T. Doing so can be shown to be computationally difficult [12]. The complete argument is omitted because of space limitations.

B.2 Proof of Theorem 2 - Security Against "Curious" Servers

We first show that BasicAnTRE is secure against chosen plaintext attacks (IND-CPA)[9] [10]. Assume that there exists a polynomial-time IND-CPA attacker $\mathcal{A}$ which has a non-negligible advantage, $\varepsilon(k)$, against BasicAnTRE, asking n_i queries to random oracles $h_i, i = 1, ..., 4$. We will show that there exists an algorithm, $\mathcal{B}$, which solves the CDH problem with non-negligible probability, in polynomial time, using $\mathcal{A}$ as a subroutine. The algorithm $\mathcal{B}$ will accept as inputs P, aP and bP, and will compute abP, for $a, b \in \mathbb{Z}_q^*$. Our scheme follows the proof of Theorem 3 in Cathalo et. al [10], where $\mathcal{B}$ uses part of the challenge ciphertext, c_1, c_2 to elicit $\mathcal{A}$ to make a random oracle query with the desired input, in this case a known multiple of abP.

$\mathcal{B}$ operates by assigning any valid key pair $(s, S = sP)$, to the time server, and starts $\mathcal{A}$ with inputs P, bP (public key against which $\mathcal{A}$ is to be tested), and the server's secret key, s. $\mathcal{B}$ answers $\mathcal{A}$'s queries to $H_1, ..., H_4$, as follows. For each $H_i, i = 1, ..., 4$, $\mathcal{B}$ answers each query at random; each time, $\mathcal{B}$ records the input and the reply it gave on a list, L_i, so that if an oracle is queried again on the same input, $\mathcal{B}$ will return the same number.

---

[9] This type of adversary is defined similarly to IND-CCA, but without access to a decryption oracle.

After finishing its queries, $\mathcal{A}$ outputs m_0, m_1, T^*. At that point, $\mathcal{B}$ creates a challenge ciphertext to return to $\mathcal{A}$ as follows. He chooses r_1 at random and a message m also at random. He checks whether H_1 has previously been queried on T^*, in which case he sets t to its prior response, found in the list L_1. If the opposite is true, then $\mathcal{B}$ assigns t to be a random number, which he records in L_1. $\mathcal{B}$ then sets $c_1 = r_1 S + r_1 t P$, and $c_2 = aP$. To produce c_3, $\mathcal{B}$ first checks whether the value $\hat{e}(c_1, (s+t)^{-1}P) = \hat{e}(P,P)^{r_1}$ has been presented by $\mathcal{A}$ as a query to H_3. If so, $\mathcal{B}$ finds its previous reply from the list L_3 and sets d to that number, otherwise he sets d to a random number which it records on L_3, as specified previously. Finally, $\mathcal{B}$ chooses K at random, sets $c_3 = (m||H_2(m)) \oplus K$ and then sends the challenge (c_1, c_2, c_3, T^*) to $\mathcal{A}$.

From $\mathcal{A}$'s point of view, the challenge appears to be properly formated. To recognize that c_3 is not an encryption of either m_0 or m_1, $\mathcal{A}$ would have to request $H_4(dbc_2)$, for $d = H_3(\hat{e}(c_1, s_T))$, known to $\mathcal{B}$; doing so would enable $\mathcal{B}$ to obtain the solution to the CDH problem by computing $d^{-1}dbc_2 = abP$. On the other hand, because the simulation set up by $\mathcal{B}$ mimics a genuine attack environment perfectly, one can show using standard arguments that if $\mathcal{A}$ succeeds in guessing the hidden bit b, it is very likely to query oracle H_4 on input dr_2bP (e.g., if that were not the case, $\mathcal{A}$ could be used to produce an algorithm that inverts the XOR operation with non-negligible probability), and in particular, the probability of $\mathcal{A}$ doing so is some $\varepsilon'(k)$, non-negligible. In that case, $\mathcal{B}$ has the chance to detect $\mathcal{A}$'s query and compute the CDH solution. Thus, when $\mathcal{A}$ halts, $\mathcal{B}$ ignores her result, and selects at random an entry from his list L_4. For the number, g, that was his reply to the corresponding query, he computes and outputs $d^{-1}g$, having correctly guessed at the value of abP with probability $\varepsilon'(k)/n_4$, where n_4 is a polynomial bound on the number of H_4 queries made by $\mathcal{A}$ during her attack. This contradicts the assumed hardness of the CDH problem. We conclude that BasicAnTRE is IND-CPA secure.

The IND-CCA security of AnTRE follows from the IND-CPA security of BasicAnTRE, via a result whose proof is very similar to that of Lemma 1 and is omitted.

Lemma 2. *In the random oracle model, an IND-CCA attacker $\mathcal{A}$ having non-negligible advantage ε against AnTRE when making q_D decryption queries and q_{H_i} queries to oracles $H_i, (i = 1..4)$, implies an IND-CPA attacker $\mathcal{B}$ with non-negligible advantage against BasicAnTRE.*

As in the case of Lemma 1, the proof of Lemma 2 must account for the fact that if a message is sent to $N > 1$ receivers, then a malicious server might then have access to multiple $c_{3,i}$ values, $i = 1, ..., N$, for the same message m and time T, from which he could attempt to read the message. An argument for why this is computationally difficult is given in [12].

Encryption Techniques for Secure Database Outsourcing

Sergei Evdokimov and Oliver Günther

Humboldt-Universität zu Berlin
Spandauer str. 1, 10178 Berlin, Germany
{evdokim,guenther}@wiwi.hu-berlin.de

Abstract. While the idea of database outsourcing is becoming increasingly popular, the associated security risks still prevent many potential users from deploying it. In particular, the need to give full access to one's data to a third party, the database service provider, remains a major obstacle. A seemingly obvious solution is to encrypt the data in such a way that the service provider retains the ability to perform relational operations on the encrypted database. In this paper we present a model and an encryption scheme that solves this problem at least partially. Our approach represents the provably secure solution to the database outsourcing problem that allows operations exact select, Cartesian product, and projection, and that guarantees the probability of erroneous answers to be negligible. Our scheme is simple and practical, and it allows effective searches on encrypted tables: For a table consisting of n tuples the scheme performs search in $O(n)$ steps.

1   Introduction

In this paper we consider the problem in which one party (Alice) owns a database and wants to outsource it to a second party (Bob), even though the trust of Alice in Bob is limited. Alice wants to be sure that the data she outsources is exposed neither to another party nor to Bob. Legal options, such as contracts, are available, but their effectiveness is often limited [1].

If, for example, the database is acquired by other company, it may be unclear whether the new owner is bound by the contract [2]. As Amazon says it: "In the unlikely event that Amazon.com Inc., or substantially all of its assets are acquired, customer information will of course be one of the transferred assets". If the data were encrypted, this problem could not arise.

Ideally, Alice would like to have the data encrypted and only give the ciphertext to Bob, the database service provider. But if Bob is not trusted, he cannot participate in the encryption/decryption process. Usually Bob does not just store the data, but also processes non-trivial queries sent by Alice and therefore should be able to process these queries without decrypting the stored data. About 30 years ago, Rivest et al. [3] described a possible approach for solving such a problem they called *privacy homomorphism*. They proposed a scheme to

J. Biskup and J. Lopez (Eds.): ESORICS 2007, LNCS 4734, pp. 327–342, 2007.

encrypt data in such a way that certain operations can be performed on the ciphertext without decrypting it.

In this paper we present *privacy homomorphism* for the relational operations exact select, projection and Cartesian product. Additionally the scheme allows insert, exact delete, exact update and union with duplicates. Exact select, exact delete and exact update are variants of select, delete and update operations with condition predicates (WHERE-part of the corresponding SQL queries) restricted to a combination of equalities connected by AND or OR. The result of a union with duplicates is the union of two relations without duplicate tuples being removed.

Our approach displays the following key characteristics

- Our scheme is *provably secure* and can sustain a chosen-plaintext and a posteriori chosen-ciphertext attacks.
- Our scheme reveals *nothing but the number of tuples that share a queried value* while performing an exact select .
- Our scheme allows to *efficiently* perform the supported operations on an encrypted database. The scheme does not affect the time needed to perform projection, Cartesian product and insert operations. Checking whether a tuple satisfies an equality condition of an exact select requires $O(1)$ operations; therefore exact update, exact delete and exact select require $O(n)$ operations, where n is the number of tuples in the queried relation.
- Our scheme also avoids a problem of many previous solutions, such as the outsourcing approach of Hacıgümüş et al. [4] or the search algorithms on encrypted data of Goh [5] and Song et al. [6]. All those solutions may return erroneous tuples that do not satisfy the select condition. This requires Alice each time to perform postfiltering of the received result set, which reduces the performance and complicates the development process of a client software. This especially becomes an issue when Alice uses a mobile device for accessing the encrypted database. The only scheme that allows to perform search on encrypted data and does not require postfiltering is described in [7]. This scheme, however, can hardly be applied to databases since a search on encrypted data is restricted to the search with predefined keywords, which constitutes a severe limitation. The scheme we are proposing also may include erroneous tuples in the result set of an exact select operation but the probability of such an error is negligible.

2 Relevant Definitions Notions of Security

In this section we briefly introduce some cryptographic primitives and definitions used in the paper. We use the standard cryptography definitions; see, e.g., [8],[9].

By $\{0,1\}^n$ we define the set of all binary strings of length n. By $k \xleftarrow{R} \mathcal{K}$ we say that k is randomly and uniformly chosen from set $\mathcal{K}$.

Definition 1 (pseudo-random function). *A mapping $F : \mathcal{K} \times \mathcal{X} \mapsto \mathcal{Y}$, where $\mathcal{K} = \{0,1\}^n$, is a* pseudo-random function *if for every PPT oracle algorithm A, every positive polynomial $p(n)$, and all sufficiently large n, the advantage*

$AdvA < 1/p(n)$. *The advantage is defined as*

$$\mathrm{Adv} A = |Pr[A^{F_k} = 1] - Pr[A^{\phi} = 1]|,$$

where ϕ is a function chosen randomly and uniformly from the set of all functions that map $\mathcal{X}$ to $\mathcal{Y}$.

A function that after a certain point decreases faster than one over any polynomial is called *negligible*. Thus, it also can be said that the advantage is negligible.

Consider now set of plaintexts $\mathcal{X} = \{0,1\}^m$, set of ciphertexts $\mathcal{Y} = \{0,1\}^l$ and set of keys $\mathcal{K} = \{0,1\}^n$.

Definition 2 (symmetric encryption scheme). *An encryption scheme is a triple $(\mathcal{K}, E, D)$, where $E : \mathcal{K} \times \mathcal{X} \mapsto \mathcal{Y}$ is a PPT algorithm (encryption algorithm) that maps a key $k \in \mathcal{K}$ and a plaintext $x \in \mathcal{X}$ into a corresponding ciphertext $c \in \mathcal{Y}$ and $D : \mathcal{K} \times \mathcal{Y} \mapsto \mathcal{X}$ is a polynomial-time algorithm (decryption algorithm) that maps a key k and a ciphertext c into a corresponding plaintext x. It must hold that $D_k(E_k(x)) = x$. Keys are chosen randomly and uniformly from the key space $\mathcal{K}$. The bit length n of the keys is called security parameter of the scheme.*

The security of an encryption scheme is defined as follows:

Definition 3 (indistinguishability of encryptions). *An encryption scheme $(\mathcal{K}, E, D)$ is* indistinguishably secure *if for every $x, y \in \mathcal{X}$, every PPT algorithm A, every positive polynomial p, and all sufficiently large n, the advantage $\mathrm{Adv} A_{xy} < 1/p(n)$. The advantage is defined as*

$$\mathrm{Adv} A_{xy} = |\mathrm{Pr}\left[A(E_k(x)) = 1\right] - \mathrm{Pr}\left[A(E_k(y)) = 1\right]|.$$

In our paper we will also use a construct called *pseudo-random permutation*, an indistinguishably secure encryption scheme that is a bijection and for which $\mathcal{X} = \mathcal{Y}$.

Definition 3 guarantees security only if a key is used once. In order to securely encrypt several messages, a new key should be generated for each new encryption. But often it should be possible to securely encrypt several messages using the same key. Encryption schemes that allow this are called indistinguishably secure for multiple messages:

Definition 4 (indistinguishability of encryptions for multiple messages). *An encryption scheme $(\mathcal{K}, E, D)$ is* indistinguishably secure for *multiple messages if for every $\bar{x} = (x_1, \ldots, x_t), \bar{y} = (y_1, \ldots, y_t)$, every PPT algorithm A, every positive polynomial p, and all sufficiently large n, the advantage $\mathrm{Adv} A_{\bar{x}\bar{y}} < 1/p(n)$. The advantage is defined as*

$$\mathrm{Adv} A_{\bar{x}\bar{y}} = |\mathrm{Pr}\left[A(\bar{E}_k(\bar{x})) = 1\right] - \mathrm{Pr}\left[A(\bar{E}_k(\bar{y})) = 1\right]|.$$

$\bar{E}_k(\bar{x})$ denotes the sequence of ciphertexts that are produced by encrypting each x_i with encryption algorithm E_k: $\bar{E}_k(\bar{x}) = (E_k(x_1), \ldots, E_k(x_t))$.

The indistinguishability definitions provided so far guarantee the protection only from a "passive" adversary. But in real applications the adversary can also be "active" and additionally cause the sender to encrypt a message of her choice (chosen-plaintext attack) or even cause the receiver to decrypt the ciphertext of her choice (chosen-ciphertext attack). Formally this is described as the ability of the adversary to query the encryption (decryption) oracle in case of a chosen-plaintext (chosen-ciphertext) attack.

Definition 5 (indistinguishability under chosen-plaintext attack (IND-CPA)). *An encryption scheme* $(\mathcal{K}, E, D)$ *is* indistinguishably secure under a chosen-plaintext attack *if for every* $x, y \in \mathcal{X}$, *every PPT algorithm* A^{E_k} *with access to encryption oracle* E_k, *every positive polynomial* p, *and all sufficiently large* n, *advantage* $\mathrm{Adv} A_{xy}^{E_k} < 1/p(n)$. *The advantage is defined as*

$$\mathrm{Adv} A_{xy}^{E_k} = |\Pr[A^{E_k}(E_k(x)) = 1] - \Pr[A^{E_k}(E_k(y)) = 1]|.$$

According to [9], Definition 4 and Definition 5 are equivalent: If an encryption scheme is indistinguishably secure for multiple messages then the scheme is also IND-CPA secure.

A chosen-ciphertext attack can be represented as the following game:

1. The challenger generates key k: $k \xleftarrow{R} \mathcal{K}$.
2. The adversary asks the decryption oracle for the plaintexts corresponding to the ciphertexts of her choice.
3. The challenger generates two plaintext strings and gives the adversary the encryption of one of them.
4. The adversary may additionally ask the oracle for the decryption of some ciphertexts except for the decryption of the received challenge.
5. The adversary tries to guess which of the two strings he was given and halts.

The described attack is called *posteriori chosen-ciphertext attack* (IND-CCA2). When step 4 is omitted, the attack is called *a-priori chosen-ciphertext attack* (IND-CCA). It is clear that security against IND-CCA2 attack guarantees security against IND-CCA attack. Further in the paper, when speaking about chosen-ciphertext indistinguishability we will suggest IND-CCA2.

Definition 6 (posteriori chosen-ciphertext attack indistinguishability (IND-CCA2)). *An encryption scheme* $(\mathcal{K}, E, D)$ *is* indistinguishable with respect to posteriori chosen-ciphertext attack *if for every* $x, y \in \mathcal{X}$, *every PPT algorithm* A^{D_k} *with access to decryption oracle* D_k, *every positive polynomial* p, *and all sufficiently large* n, *the advantage* $\mathrm{Adv} A_{xy}^{D_k} < 1/p(n)$. *The advantage is defined as*

$$\mathrm{Adv} A_{xy}^{D_k} = |\Pr[A^{D_k}(E_k(x)) = 1] - \Pr[A^{D_k}(E_k(y)) = 1]|.$$

Usually, in scenarios where a chosen-ciphertext attack is possible, a chosen-plaintext attack is possible too. Therefore, when speaking about chosen-ciphertext attacks we will also assume the possibility of a chosen-plaintext attack. Also, when speaking about indistinguishable security, we will imply indistinguishable security for multiple messages or IND-CPA security.

3 Related Work and Security Analysis of Existing Approaches

As mentioned, the idea of a privacy homomorphism was first described by Rivest et al. [3]. There it was also mentioned that one of the most promising applications of privacy homomorphisms could be encryption of databases. If the privacy homomorphism preserved some of the relational operations, then it would be possible to process encrypted relations without decrypting them.

In 2001 Hacıgümüş et al. [4] described an encryption scheme that allowed to perform all relational operations on an encrypted database and made the statistical attack on the scheme less obvious as in the example described above. According to the scheme, the domain of each attribute is partitioned into intervals, and each attribute value is mapped to the interval that contains it. Then the intervals are deterministically encrypted and attached to the secure encryptions of the tuples. Thus, some information about the attribute values is preserved and can be used for the query processing. For example, an exact select operation will return the tuples with the attribute values contained in the interval that is stated as the argument of the select operation. This requires Alice (the user) to perform postfiltering in order to remove the tuples that have the attribute values that belong to the queried interval and are not equal to the argument of the original select operation.

It is easy to show that the proposed approach does not comply with Definition 4. Consider two tables:

ID	salary
171	4900
481	1200

Table 1

ID	salary
171	4900
481	4900

Table 2

According to the scheme, the salaries in the first table are likely to be mapped to different intervals. The salaries in the second table will be mapped to the same interval. Since the intervals are encrypted deterministically, the ciphertexts that correspond to the intervals of the "salary" attribute of the first table will be different and the analogous intervals' encryptions for the second table will be identical. Hence, algorithm A can determine to which table corresponds the received ciphertext: If the ciphertexts that correspond to the "salary" intervals are different, A outputs 0; otherwise 1. Clearly, the advantage for such an algorithm is non-negligible.

In modern cryptography, the weakest requirement for an encryption scheme to have any practical applications is IND-CPA security. In case of IND-CCA2 security, it may seem that the assumption of an adversary's ability to decrypt ciphertexts of her choice is very unlikely to be satisfied. However, the successful chosen-ciphertext attack on the widely used internet security protocol SSL discovered by Bleichenbacher [10] demonstrates the relevancy of IND-CCA2 security.

The encryption scheme that allows to perform exact selects on encrypted relations and is IND-CPA and IND-CCA2 secure is described in [11]. The scheme is based on encryption techniques that allow to perform searches on encrypted data [5],[6]. It uses the similarity between searching for text documents that contain a defined keyword and exact select operation for databases. The idea behind the scheme is to bijectively map tuples of the relation to text documents by treating each attribute value as a sequence of characters or "word", encrypt the resulting documents with the scheme that supports searches on encrypted data, and, instead of issuing exact selects, issue the corresponding search operations. E.g, Table 1 from the example above can be mapped to the following set of documents:

$$\boxed{\begin{array}{l} 171\#ID4900SL \\ 1200SL481\#ID \end{array}}$$

In this example each attribute value is mapped to the word consisting of 6 symbols where '#' is the padding symbol and "ID" and "SL" are identifiers that help to map the words back to the values of the corresponding attributes (ID and salary). The mapping of the tuples to the documents define the way exact selects are converted to the search operations: E.g., in order to process the exact select SELECT * FROM Table1 WHERE salary=4900 Bob performs the search for documents that contain word "4900SL".

Disadvantages of the proposed method include the necessity of postfiltering of an exact select results (since the schemes [5], [6] allow with high probability the inclusion of erroneous tuples in the result of a search operation) and the infeasibility of projection and Cartesian product, due to the impossibility to concatenate and split encrypted tuples.

In [12] Yang et al. proposed the encryption scheme similar to the one we discuss in this paper. In their work they introduce own security model and base the security analysis of the scheme on the different notion of security. However, though the approach they take for building the encryption scheme is correct, the analytical part of the paper contains several serious flaws. So, as it can be easily illustrated by a counterexample, the definition of security on which the authors base their reasoning in fact does not require a database to be encrypted at all. Additionally, the authors mistakenly suppose that their scheme does not include erroneous tuples in the resulting set of a processed query. For the more detailed analysis of this work refer to Appendix A.

4   Secure Database Encryption

In this section we show how to construct an encryption scheme that can serve as a privacy homomorphism for a well-defined subset of relational operations. First we show how to perform encryption and decryption of a database, then we provide the proof of IND-CPA security of the scheme. Algorithms for the relational operators follow in Section 5.

4.1   Construction

We build our scheme as the combination of *cryptographic primitives*. The term cryptographic primitive describes an elementary cryptographic algorithm that

Table 1. Corresponding attributes and data types

Attribute of R	Attribute of R^E	Type of Attribute
ID	f4FR32	int
Name	aSC3f7	string[100]
...		
Address	sF3nD4	String[200]

satisfies certain security requirements and is used as a building block for encryption schemes.

Our encryption scheme uses the following cryptographic primitives:

- $(\mathcal{K}, E, D)$, $\mathcal{K} = \{0,1\}^m$, $\mathcal{X} = \{0,1\}^m$, $E : \mathcal{K} \times \mathcal{X} \mapsto \mathcal{Y}$ is a symmetric encryption schema that is IND-CPA secure and key space and space of plaintexts are identical.
- $(\mathcal{K}^0, E^0, D^0)$, $E^0 : \mathcal{K}^0 \times \mathcal{X} \mapsto \mathcal{Y}^0$ is a symmetric encryption schema that is IND-CPA secure.
- $P : \mathcal{K}' \times \mathcal{X} \mapsto \mathcal{X}$, $\mathcal{X} = \{0,1\}^m$ is a pseudo-random permutation. Since $\mathcal{K} = \mathcal{X}$ we can also write $P : \mathcal{K}' \times \mathcal{X} \mapsto \mathcal{K}$

Key generation. Alice generates the encryption key $\hat{k}$ that is a triple (k_0, k_1, k_2), where $k_0 \overset{R}{\leftarrow} \mathcal{K}_0$, $k_1 \overset{R}{\leftarrow} \mathcal{K}'$, $k_2 \overset{R}{\leftarrow} \mathcal{K}'$: k^0 is the key for encryption scheme $(\mathcal{K}^0, E^0, D^0)$, k_1, k_2 are the keys for pseudo-random permutation P (k_1, k_2 are chosen independently).

Encryption. Suppose that Alice wants to encrypt a relational database that consists of several relations. The idea behind the scheme is to augment encryptions of every attribute value with an additional piece of information, viz., a search tag that will allow Bob to execute search on the ciphertexts without getting any information about the corresponding plaintext values.

Each relation is encrypted separately, so we describe the encryption algorithm for an arbitrary attribute value of a relation $R(a_1 : D_1, \ldots, a_l : D_l)$. Without loss of generality we suppose that $D_i \cap D_j = \emptyset, i \neq j$.[1] The encryption algorithm maps the relation R to an encrypted relation R^E that has the same number of attributes but the domains of the attributes are changed to binary strings. Since the information about the domains will be not available after encryption, Alice is responsible for saving this information and performing correct type conversions during the decryption process (this will be discussed later in more detail).

Before starting the encryption, Alice generates key $\hat{k}$ and then performs tuple-by-tuple encryption of relation R, separately encrypting each attribute value. Let $x \in D_i$ be a plaintext value of attribute a_i. The encryption algorithm treats plaintext x as a binary value and encrypts it by performing the following steps:

1. Plaintext x is encrypted with encryption function E^0 and key k_0: $c = E_{k_0}^0(x)$.

---

[1] If not, then elements of each domain D_i can be appended with bits that uniquely identify attribute a_i within the table.

2. Pseudo-random permutation P generates key k_s: $k_s = P_{k_1}(x)$. Key k_s will be used for generating the search tag.
3. Plaintext x is deterministically encrypted by pseudo-random permutation P with key k_2: $s = P_{k_2}(x)$
4. Using ciphertext s and key k_s the search tag is generated: $t = E_{k_s}(s)$.
5. The output of the algorithm is the pair (t, c).

With $\hat{E}$ denoting the encryption algorithm, whole procedure can be described as

$$\hat{E}_{\hat{k}}(x) := (E_{P_{k_1}(x)}(P_{k_2}(x)), E_{k_0}^0(x)), \tag{1}$$

where $\hat{k} = (k_0, k_1, k_2)$.

After the encryption procedure was applied to each attribute value of tuple $< a_1 : x_1, \ldots, a_l : x_l >$, the resulting ciphertexts form a new tuple $< a_1^E : (t_1, c_1), \ldots, a_l^E : (t_l, c_l) >$ that belongs to relation R^E. In order to hide the structure of the database, the names of the attributes should be changed ($a_i \neq a_i^E$). To correctly decrypt the encrypted relation, Alice should store the information about the correspondences between the attributes of relation R and the attributes of the relation R^E. Also, as mentioned earlier, the encryption changes the domains of the attributes to a raw binary data. The information about the domains of original attributes should also be maintained by Alice (Table 1).

In order to use the described encryption scheme for encrypting values of different attributes, the domains of relation R^E should be of the same length. That means that, before being encrypted, the values should be padded up to the length of the domain that has the longest binary representation. Note that it is very unlikely that an attribute containing very long values will be used by an exact select (e.g., attributes that contain full address, long text, multimedia data etc.). Such attributes should either be split into several shorter attributes or encrypted with a conventional secure encryption scheme if no select queries are expected for them.

Decryption. The decryption is performed by decrypting the attribute values of every tuple of relation R^E and filling relation R with the corresponding plaintexts tuples taking into account the information from Table 1. The decryption of ciphertext (t, c) is performed straightforwardly:

$$\hat{D}_{\hat{k}}(t, c) := D_{k_0}(c) = x, \tag{2}$$

where $\hat{k} = (k_0, k_1, k_2)$.

Using the information stored in Table 1 the plaintext is converted to the appropriate type and saved as the value of the corresponding attribute.

The final scheme is defined as $(\hat{\mathcal{K}}, \hat{E}, \hat{D})$, where $\hat{E}$ is defined according to (1), $\hat{D}$ is defined according (2) and $\hat{\mathcal{K}} = (\mathcal{K}^0 \times \mathcal{K}' \times \mathcal{K}')$.

4.2 Proofs of Security

Theorem 1. *Encryption scheme $(\hat{\mathcal{K}}, \hat{E}, \hat{D})$ is IND-CPA secure.*

A proof of the theorem is presented in the full version of the paper.

Even though the encryption scheme $(\hat{\mathcal{K}}, \hat{E}, \hat{D})$ provides IND-CPA security, the scheme is vulnerable to IND-CCA2 attack. Even if we strengthen the security of cryptographic primitives and require IND-CCA2 security for encryption schemes $(\mathcal{K}, E, D)$ and $(\mathcal{K}^0, E^0, D^0)$ the resulting scheme $(\hat{\mathcal{K}}, \hat{E}, \hat{D})$ will still be vulnerable to a posteriori chosen-ciphertext attack that can allow an adversary to recover the plaintext from a given ciphertext.

Theorem 2. *Encryption scheme* $(\hat{\mathcal{K}}, \hat{E}, \hat{D})$ *is not IND-CCA2 secure.*

Proof sketch. For our scheme, where $\hat{E}_{\hat{k}}(x) = (t, c)$, the distinguishing algorithm proceeds as follows:

1. The algorithm queries the encryption oracle for x and gets ciphertext (t', c').
2. The algorithm queries the decryption oracle for (t', c). This query is allowed and returns some α (note that if the algorithm is input x, then $\alpha = x$).
3. If $\alpha = x$ the algorithm outputs 1; otherwise 0.

Clearly, the advantage of the algorithm is non-negligible.   □

The scheme can be easily modified to be IND-CCA2 secure. There exist standard techniques that make an IND-CPA secure encryption scheme secure against CCA2 attack. The underlying idea is to make it infeasible for an adversary having access to a decryption oracle to forge a legitimate ciphertext. One of the possibilities is to augment the ciphertext with a tag containing "Message Authentication Code" (MAC). A ciphertext is considered legitimate if in a pair (c, MAC), MAC is the valid authentication code of c. The simplest way for generating MAC for a ciphertext is to input the ciphertext into a pseudo-random function and use the output as the authentication code.

We define the IND-CCA2 secure version of encryption scheme $(\hat{\mathcal{K}}, \hat{E}, \hat{D})$ as $(\hat{\mathcal{K}}', \hat{E}', \hat{D}')$ and construct it as follows:

Let $F : \mathcal{K}^F \times \mathcal{Y} \times \mathcal{Y}^0 \mapsto \mathcal{Y} \times \mathcal{Y}^0$ or $F_{k_F}(t, c) = a$, $k_F \in \mathcal{K}^F$, $t \in \mathcal{Y}$, $c \in \mathcal{Y}^0$, $a \in \mathcal{Y} \times \mathcal{Y}^0$.

Key generation. $\hat{k}' \xleftarrow{R} \hat{\mathcal{K}}'$, where $\hat{\mathcal{K}}' = \hat{\mathcal{K}} \times \mathcal{K}^F = \mathcal{K} \times \mathcal{K}^p \times \mathcal{K}^p \times \mathcal{K}^F$.

Encryption. $\hat{E}'_{\hat{k}'}(x) = (\hat{E}_{\hat{k}}(x), F_{k_F}(\hat{E}_{\hat{k}}(x))) = (t, c, F_{k_F}(c, t)) = (t, c, a)$, where $\hat{k}' = (\hat{k}, k_f) = (k, k_1, k_2, k_F)$.

Decryption. $\hat{D}'_{\hat{k}'}(t, c, a) = \hat{D}_{\hat{k}}(t, c) = D_k(c)$ if $F_{k_F}(t, c) = a$ otherwise the ciphertext is not legitimate and is thus rejected.

According to [9], the encryption scheme $(\hat{\mathcal{K}}', \hat{E}', \hat{D}')$ is IND-CCA2 secure.

Since the only difference between schemes $(\hat{\mathcal{K}}, \hat{E}, \hat{D})$ and $(\hat{\mathcal{K}}', \hat{E}', \hat{D}')$ is the authentication tag that is simply attached to the ciphertext, all the operations that are feasible under scheme $(\hat{\mathcal{K}}, \hat{E}, \hat{D})$ will remain feasible under scheme $(\hat{\mathcal{K}}', \hat{E}', \hat{D}')$. Note that unlike scheme $(\hat{\mathcal{K}}, \hat{E}, \hat{D})$ that does not require search tag for decryption, in order to perform decryption of ciphertext (t, c, a), the scheme $(\hat{\mathcal{K}}', \hat{E}', \hat{D}')$ needs all the members of the triple in order to check the legitimacy of the ciphertext. That means that if a database is encrypted with scheme

$(\hat{\mathcal{K}}', \hat{E}', \hat{D}')$, the complete triples (t, c, a) should be sent to Alice, thus tripling the amount of transferred data compared to the case when the scheme $(\hat{\mathcal{K}}, \hat{E}, \hat{D})$ is used.

5   Operations on Encrypted Relational Databases

In this section we discuss the relational operations that are feasible under the proposed scheme and security implications that arise when some of operations are performed.

5.1   Allowed Operations

The encryption schema described above allows to perform the following subset of relational operations on encrypted relations: exact select, projection, Cartesian product and equijoin. Also the scheme allows to perform union with duplicates, exact update, exact delete and insert.

Exact Select. The proposed encryption scheme allows to perform exact selects (SELECT...FROM...WHERE <attribute_name>=<value>) on the encrypted relation without decrypting it. Exact selects with more than one selection attribute connected by AND or OR are discussed at the end of this section.

Suppose, that exact select $\sigma_{a_i.x_q}$ should be performed on relation R that is encrypted and stored as R^E. Then the following actions should be performed:

1. Alice transforms the query $\sigma_{a_i.x_q}$ into the following triple

$$(q, k_q, a_i^E) = (P_{k_2}(x_q), P_{k_1}(x_q), a_i^E), \tag{3}$$

   where a_i^E is the name of the attribute of relation R^E that corresponds to attribute a_i. The corresponding attributes are taken from the structure analogous to Table 1.

2. Tuple by tuple, Bob checks every value (t, c) of attribute a_i^E for the following equality:

$$D_{k_q}(t) = q. \tag{4}$$

   The tuples that satisfy the equality are marked.

3. After all the tuples of the relation R^E are checked, Bob sends the marked tuples to Alice. The search tags of the attribute values are not needed for the decryption and can thus be discarded. That would reduce the amounts of the data transferred to Alice by about half.

4. Using key k_0, Alice decrypts the received ciphertexts.

Recall that, when encrypting plaintext x, the encryption algorithm $\hat{E}$ generates a key $k_s = P_{k_1}(x)$ and a ciphertext $s = E_{k_s}(P_{k_2}(x))$. If the ciphertext (t, c), whose search tag was checked at step 2, is the encryption of x_q, then $k_s = k_q$, $s = q$, and equality (4) holds true due to

$$D_{k_q}(t) = D_{k_q}(E_{k_s}(s)) = D_{k_q}(E_{k_s}(P_{k_2}(x_q))) = P_{k_2}(x_q) = q.$$

Therefore, all the tuples that have encryption of x_q as the value of attribute a_i^E will be marked and included in the result set.

Note that the triple provided by Alice does not contain any plaintext values. That allows Bob to perform search for $a_i.x_q$ without $a_i.x_q$ itself being revealed.

However, we cannot call this scheme privacy homomorphism in a strict sense, since the set of marked tuples may contain tuples that do not belong to the actual solution. This can happen due to following collision:

$$D_{P_{k_1}(x_q)}(E_{P_{k_1}(x)}(P_{k_2}(x))) = P_{k_2}(x_q), \tag{5}$$

where $x_q \neq x$, $\hat{k} = (k_0, k_1, k_2)$.

In general the probabilities of such collisions vary depending on encryption scheme $(\mathcal{K}, E, D)$. A good candidate to minimize this probability is the IND-CPA secure one-time pad based encryption scheme constructed as follows:

- Key generation: $k \xleftarrow{R} \mathcal{K}$.
- Encryption: $E_k(x) := (r, f_k(r) \oplus x)$, where $f : \mathcal{K} \times \mathcal{X} \mapsto \mathcal{X}$ is a pseudo-random function, $r \xleftarrow{R} \mathcal{X}$.
- Decryption: $D_k(r, c) := f_k(r) \oplus c$.

The scheme is simple, efficient and, according to [9], IND-CPA secure.

In order to use this scheme as $(\mathcal{K}, E, D)$ we require $k, r, x \in \{0, 1\}^m$ and $f : \{0, 1\}^m \times \{0, 1\}^m \mapsto \{0, 1\}^m$. Using this implementation of $(\mathcal{K}, E, D)$ we can rewrite (5) as

$$f_{P_{k_1}(x_q)}(r) \oplus f_{P_{k_1}(x)}(r) \oplus P_{k_2}(x) = P_{k_2}(x_q) \Leftrightarrow f_{P_{k_1}(x_q)}(r) \oplus f_{P_{k_1}(x)}(r)$$
$$= P_{k_2}(x_q) \oplus P_{k_2}(x).$$

Consider the ideal case where instead of pseudo-random functions $f_{P_{k_1}(x_q)}, f_{P_{k_1}(x)}$ random functions ϕ, ψ are used. Then

$$\Pr[\phi(r) \oplus \psi(r) = P_{k_2}(x_q) \oplus P_{k_2}(x), x \neq x_q, r \xleftarrow{R} \mathcal{X}] = \frac{1}{2^m}.$$

The probability that the collision (5) will not occur is the probability of the inverse event or

$$\Pr[\phi(r) \oplus \psi(r) \neq P_{k_2}(x_q) \oplus P_{k_2}(x), x \neq x_q, r \xleftarrow{R} \mathcal{X}] = 1 - 2^{-m}.$$

In order to estimate the probability that there will be no collisions when equality (4) is checked for a set of different values $\{x_1, \ldots, x_{t(m)}\}$, where $x_i \neq x_q$, $x_i \neq x_j$, $i \neq j$ and t is a positive polynomial, we note that in the ideal case, for each x_i the random function ϕ_i is chosen independently and thus the events that correspond to the collisions for each x_i are also independent. Therefore the probability that, when performing an exact select σ_{x_q} on values $\{x_1, \ldots, x_{t(m)}\}$, no collisions occur is

$$(1 - \Pr[\phi(r) \oplus \psi(r) = P_{k_2}(x_q) \oplus P_{k_2}(x), x \neq x_q, r \xleftarrow{R} \mathcal{X}])^{t(m)} = (1 - 2^{-m})^{t(m)}.$$

Analogously, to each new query there corresponds a randomly chosen function ψ_i. The probability of event $\Re$ that corresponds to the absence of collisions when querying $t(m)$ values with $s(t)$ different queries is

$$\Pr(\Re) = (1 - \Pr[\phi(r) \oplus \psi(r) = P_{k_2}(x_q) \oplus P_{k_2}(x), x \neq x_q,\, r \overset{R}{\leftarrow} \mathcal{X}])^{t(m)s(m)}$$
$$= (1 - 2^{-m})^{t(m)s(n)}.$$

The lower bound of probability $\Pr(\Re)$ can be estimated as

$$\Pr(\Re) = \left(1 - \frac{1}{2^m}\right)^{t(m)s(m)} > \left(1 - \frac{t(m)s(m)}{2^m}\right) = \left(1 - \frac{p(m)}{2^m}\right) \qquad (6)$$
$$> \left(1 - \frac{1}{p(m)}\right)$$

for sufficiently large m and positive polynomial p. The probability that there will be at least one collision is $1 - \Pr(\Re) < 1/p(m)$, which is negligible.

This estimation was performed for the case in which functions ψ, ϕ are chosen randomly and uniformly. If instead we use pseudo-random functions $f_{P_{k_1}(x_q)}, f_{P_{k_1}(x)}$, it can be easily shown that the pair $(f_{P_{k_1}(x_q)}, f_{P_{k_1}(x)})$ is indistinguishable from the pair (ψ, ϕ). Suppose that there exist a set of values and a set of queries, such that probability $1 - \Pr(\Re)$ is non-negligible. Then using these sets we can build an algorithm that distinguishes between (ψ, ϕ) and $(f_{P_{k_1}(x_q)}, f_{P_{k_1}(x)})$ with non-negligible probability. Due to the polynomial sizes of the sets the algorithm works in polynomial time. That contradicts the indistinguishability of (ψ, ϕ) and $(f_{P_{k_1}(x_q)}, f_{P_{k_1}(x)})$. Therefore, when the pseudo-random functions are used the probability of the collision is also negligible.

In order to process an exact select $\sigma_{a_i.x}$ for a relation consisting of u tuples, Bob should only check whether equality (4) holds true for the value of attribute a_i of every tuple. Every check requires $O(1)$ operations and therefore processing of the query for the whole relation will be done in $O(u)$ operations.

Projection. Since the attributes of the relation are encrypted separately, in order to perform projection $\pi_{a_i,\ldots a_j}(a_1, \ldots a_l)$, Alice simply provides the name of the corresponding encrypted attributes and Bob performs $\pi_{a_i^E,\ldots a_j^E}(a_1^E, \ldots a_l^E)$ on the encrypted relation.

Cartesian product. Cartesian product of two encrypted relations is carried out just as with unencrypted relations - by returning all combinations of tuples of the encrypted relations. Again, this is possible because the attributes are encrypted separately and, as a result, ciphertexts can be concatenated.

Equijoin. The encryption scheme allows to perform equijoin as a combination of of Cartesian product and exact select. The feasibility of equijoin makes it possible to preserve the foreign key associations between the relations.

Union with duplicates. The union of two encrypted relations is performed by simply including the tuples of both relations in the resulting one. Note that duplicate removal is not possible because Bob has no means to determine on his own whether two ciphertexts correspond to identical or different tuples.

Exact update. Exact update is feasible due to the feasibility of exact select and separate encryption of the attribute values: Exact select allows to specify the tuples that should be updated and separate encryption allows to replace the encrypted attribute values of the tuples with the new ones. For example, consider the following update query: `UPDATE table1 SET salary = 3500 WHERE name = "John Smith"`. Alice transforms the query into tuple $(c, a_c^E, s, k_s, a_i^E)$ and sends it to Bob. The last three values allow to run the exact select query for getting the tuples to be updated. The first two values are the encryption of the new attribute value (3500) and the attribute name of the encrypted relation that corresponds to the one that should be updated (salary).

Exact delete. In order to run exact delete, Alice sends to Bob a triple (s, k_s, a_i^E) so that Bob can find the tuples to be deleted and then remove them from the encrypted relation.

Insert. To insert a tuple, Alice encrypts it and sends it to Bob, who simply appends it to the corresponding relation.

Logical operations. It is also possible to run operations with conditions consisting of several equalities connected by AND or OR. In case of a pair of equalities connected by a logical operation α, Alice sends a pair of triples connected by α to Bob: $(s_i, k^{s_i}, a_i^E)\,\alpha\,(s_j, k^{s_j}, a_j^E)$, where $\alpha \in \{\text{AND}, \text{OR}\}$. If $\alpha = \text{AND}$, Bob marks the tuple when (4) holds true for both triples. If $\alpha = \text{OR}$, Bob marks the tuple when (4) holds true for one of the triples (conditions built of more than two equalities connected by AND or OR can be treated in an analogous manner).

When there is a negation of the equality condition (NOT operation), Bob marks those tuples for which (4) does not hold.

5.2   Security Analysis

It is important to understand that when an encryption scheme is a privacy homomorphism the indistinguishability alone may not guarantee the security of the encrypted data. In some cases in order to perform an operation on the encrypted data Alice has to provide Bob with additional input that is dependent on the encryption key or the data itself. To see how this can become a problem, consider a database privacy homomorphism that encrypts a table and queries with an indistinguishably secure encryption scheme using two independently generated keys - one for the table and another for the queries. In order to provide Bob with the ability to run queries issued by Alice the encrypted table is appended with the key used for encrypting the queries and each query is appended with the key used for encrypting the table. When Alice issues a query she encrypts the corresponding SQL statement with the appropriate key and sends it to Bob. Bob, in turn, by using the key he got with the encrypted table and the key that he has received with the query decrypts the table and the query, runs the query and send the result to Alice. As a result, on the one hand we have a database privacy homomorphism that securely encrypts the table and the queries and supports all possible relational operations. But on the other hand that homomorphism gives no security at all after an operation was performed.

Therefore, for a privacy homomorphism it is always necessary to estimate the amounts of information disclosed when performing operations feasible under this homomorphism. Concerning our case, all the feasible operations except for exact select and those that are based on it (exact delete, exact update) do not provide Bob with any data that depends on the keys or on the encrypted table. As for exact select, we can show that when such queries are processed nothing except for the frequencies of queried attribute values is revealed to Bob. Intuitively, that means that when given an encrypted table and a sequence of queries Bob cannot get significantly more information about the table than when he is given the encrypted table, knows queried attributes and knows which tuples each query returns.

To express this formally, consider a database privacy homomorphism $(\mathcal{K}, E, D)$ that allows exact selects. Let m_i be a message to which Alice maps exact select q_i and which is then given to Bob so that he could process this query, and let $R_{E_k(T)}(m_i)$ be a set of references pointing to the tuples of encrypted table $E_k(T)$ that constitute a resulting set of query m_i.

Definition 7. *An exact select for database privacy homomorphism $(\mathcal{K}, E, D)$ reveals nothing except for the frequencies of queried attribute values if for every PPT algorithm A there exist a PPT algorithm A' such that for every table T, every polynomial p', every sequence of exact selects $q_1, \ldots, q_t$, $t \le p'(n)$, every polynomially-bounded function f, every polynomial p and all sufficiently large n*

$$\Pr\left[A(m_1, \ldots, m_t, E_k(T)) = f(T)\right]$$
$$< \Pr\left[A'(R_{E_k(T)}(m_1), \ldots, R_{E_k(T)}(m_t), E_k(T)) = f(T)\right] + \frac{1}{p(n)}$$

And for our database privacy homomorphism $(\hat{\mathcal{K}}, \hat{E}, \hat{D})$ we can formulate the following theorem

Theorem 3. *Database privacy homomorphism $(\hat{\mathcal{K}}, \hat{E}, \hat{D})$ reveals nothing except for the frequencies of queried attribute values.*

A proof of the theorem is presented in the full version of the paper.

6   Conclusion

In this paper we presented an encryption scheme that allows the secure outsourcing of a substantial subset of relational database operators: exact select, Cartesian product, projection, exact update, exact insert and exact delete. Our approach represents the first solution to the database outsourcing problem that is provably secure and supports such an extensive set of relational operators.

We conclusively proved the security of our scheme and showed how to reduce the probability of having erroneous tuples in the answer to an exact select query to a negligible level. Moreover, we presented some thoughts on how to perform indexing and hashing in the context of encrypted database outsourcing. The development of efficient and secure hashing and indexing schemes for encrypted database outsourcing remains an important topic for future research.

References

1. Boyens, C., Günther, O.: Trust Is not Enough: Privacy and Security in ASP and Web Service Environments. In: Manolopoulos, Y., Návrat, P. (eds.) ADBIS 2002. LNCS, vol. 2435, Springer, Heidelberg (2002)
2. Oracle: Oracle Buys PeopleSoft,
   http://www.oracle.com/corporate/press/2004_dec/acquisition.html
3. Rivest, R.L., Adleman, L., Dertouzos, M.L.: On Data Banks and Privacy Homomorphisms. In: DeMillo, R., Dobkin, D., Jones, A., Lipton, R. (eds.) Foundations of Secure Computation, Academic Press, London (1978)
4. Hacıgümüş, H., Iyer, B., Li, C., Mehrotra, S.: Executing SQL over Encrypted Data in the Database-Service-Provider Model. In: Proceedings of the 28th SIGMOD Conference on the Management of Data, ACM Press, New York (2002)
5. Goh, E.J.: Secure Indexes. Cryptology ePrint Archive: Report 2003/216, http://eprint.iacr.org/2003/216/
6. Song, D.X., Wagner, D., Perrig, A.: Practical Techniques for Searches on Encrypted Data. In: IEEE Symposium on Security and Privacy, IEEE Computer Society Press, Los Alamitos (2000)
7. Boneh, D., Crescenzo, G., Ostrovsky, R., Persiano, G.: Public-key Encryption with Keyword Search. In: Cachin, C., Camenisch, J.L. (eds.) EUROCRYPT 2004. LNCS, vol. 3027, Springer, Heidelberg (2004)
8. Goldreich, O.: Foundations of Cryptography, vol. Basic Tools. Cambridge University Press, Cambridge (2001)
9. Goldreich, O.: Foundations of Cryptography, vol. Basic Applications. Cambridge University Press, Cambridge (2004)
10. Bleichenbacher, D.: Chosen Ciphertext Attacks Against Protocols Based on The RSA Encryption Standard PKCS#1. In: Advances in Cryptology (1998)
11. Evdokimov, S., Fischmann, M., Günther, O.: Provable security for outsourcing database operations. In: ICDE '06: Proceedings of the 22nd International Conference on Data Engineering, IEEE Computer Society, Los Alamitos (2006)
12. Yang, Z., Zhong, S., Wright, R.N.: Privacy-Preserving Queries on Encrypted Data. In: Gollmann, D., Meier, J., Sabelfeld, A. (eds.) ESORICS 2006. LNCS, vol. 4189, Springer, Heidelberg (2006)
13. Krawczyk, H., Bellare, M., Canetti, R.: HMAC: Keyed-Hashing for Message Authentication (1997)

A   Comments on the Encryption Scheme Presented in [12]

Yang et al. propose their own security model for privacy-preserving query protocols. First, they introduce the notion of the *minimum information revelation* of exact select query q issued to table T, which is the set of coordinates of the cells satisfying the condition of the query. Denoting the minimum information reve- lation by $R_T(q)$ they present their version of the definition of the query protocol revealing nothing but $R_T(q)$:

Definition 8. *A one-round query protocol reveals nothing beyond the minimum information revelation if for any polynomial* poly() *and all sufficiently large n, there exists a PPT algorithm S (called a simulator) such that for any $t < \text{poly}(k)$, any polynomial-size circuit family $\{A_n\}$, any polynomial $p()$, and any exact select queries $q_1, \ldots, q_t$ for the advantage defined as*

$$\text{Adv}A = |\Pr[A_n(q_1, \ldots, q_t, m_1, \ldots, m_t), E_k(T)) = 1]$$
$$- \Pr[A_n(q_1, \ldots, q_t, S(R_{E_k(T)}(E'_{k'}(q_1)), \ldots, R_{E_k(T)}(E'_{E_{k'}(T)}(q_t)), E_k(T)))) = 1]|$$

it holds that $\text{Adv}A < 1/p(n)$.

However, this definition contains one serious flaw: It does not impose any require- ments on the security of the encryption scheme that is used to encrypt table T. As an example, consider a protocol that performs no encryption at all and op- erates with plaintext tables and queries. In such protocol for any table T (query q_i) $E_k(T) = T$ ($m_i = q_i$) it is trivially to build simulator S that by observing $E_k(T)$ and $R_{E_k(T)}(m_1), \ldots, R_{E_k(T)}(m_t)$ reconstructs queries $q_1, \ldots, q_t$ and re- turns them with $E_k(T)$ as the output. Clearly, with such simulator $\text{Adv}A = 0$ – thus, the protocol which gives no security at all satisfies the proposed definition.

The encryption scheme and the querying algorithm proposed by Yang et al. exploits the approach similar to the one we proposed in Section 4. But by proving that the described query protocol satisfies Definition 8 Yang et al. claim that the protocol reveals only number of tuples sharing the queried value and the queried attribute. As we have just shown, this definition, actually, says nothing about the strength of the encryption and the level of security provided by the protocol.

Also, without any formal argumentation Yang et al. claim that their protocol returns those, and only those tuples that satisfy an issued exact select query. However, by applying the same reasoning as we did in Section 5.1 one can easily see that the protocol may allow erroneous tuples to be included in the resulting set.

It is worth to mention that the described issues as well address the query protocol with enhanced security, which Yang et al. construct to minimize the amount of information leaked when the table is being queried.

Click Passwords Under Investigation

Krzysztof Gołofit

Warsaw University of Technology, Faculty of Electronics and Information Technology
Nowowiejska 15/19, 00-665 Warsaw, Poland
Warsaw University, Faculty of Psychology, Stawki 5/7, 00-183 Warsaw, Poland
K.Golofit@elka.pw.edu.pl

Abstract. The paper explores one of the graphical authentication techniques as the possible solution to the most important problems of traditional passwords. The aim of this work is to bring together the technical (cryptological) and non-technical (psychological) awareness into the research on passwords (click passwords in this case). Security issues of any authentication mechanism (relying on knowledge) should not be considered without analysis of the human factor – since the users' human nature was identified as a source of major weaknesses of conventional authentication. The paper deals with techniques which reduce password space and make passwords guesses feasible. Four types of pictures areas (of graphical interfaces) were investigated in order to bring to light common vulnerabilities – three of them were identified as types, which the graphical keypads should avoid. Statistics exposing strong tendentiousness in click passwords selection were presented as well. Furthermore, the paper presents a discussion on several issues of title authentication with regard to traditional passwords and other graphical techniques.

Keywords: Click Passwords, PassPoints, Passlogix, graphical authentication, keypad, human factor, dictionary attacks, picture passwords.

1 Introduction

According to recent reports, there are many vulnerabilities typical for alphanumerical passwords. Statistics from actual systems and many researches show that the users are, as usual 'the weakest link in the security chain'. One of the major problems is the difficulty of remembering passwords, the other, ignoring security requirements. Users tend to create either too short passwords or passwords that though long enough are easy to guess. There is an informal rule stating that passwords which are easy to remember, are mostly also easy to break. According to Bruce Schneier [1], passwords' length distribution based on 34,000 users (Fig.1) shows that 65% of passwords have only up to 8 characters and almost 95% up to 10 characters. Other research [2] shows that only 17% of the inquired IT professionals use complex passwords (including letters, numbers and symbols) and 72% stated that they almost never or never change their access codes. Moreover, 52% of professional users tend to share their passwords and 65% of them have only one or two passwords to access the majority of services. A study of information contained within the passwords [3] shows that 66% of users' passwords are

J. Biskup and J. Lopez (Eds.): ESORICS 2007, LNCS 4734, pp. 343–358, 2007.

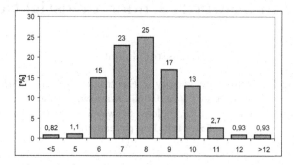

Fig. 1. Passwords' length distribution of 34,000 users (according to [1])

designed making use of personal characteristics thereof, where 32% contained names of people, places or things (three quarters of respondents used those for some passwords). Moreover, the common constructions involve full information in the passwords − 75%, partial − 13.5%, or combination − 7.5%. Almost all respondents reuse passwords − particularly 4.45 passwords are used in 8.18 systems. Once again, the adage that 'system fails when users pick the passwords for their own' finds many confirmations. On the other hand, strong passwords imposed on users bring no solution as well − because people cannot and/or would not remember strong passwords and will write them down instead. According to [4] and [5] we can say: there will be either about 80% remembered weak passwords (created by users) or strong passwords (generated by the system) in 80% written down.

Many alternative authentication solutions have been invented and developed to address the proper security level − in order to avoid weaknesses connected with knowledge-based methods. One group of techniques (involving a physical factor in the authentication process − called 'something you have') focuses on utilizing all kinds of tokens, one-time passwords, magnetic stripes and proximity cards, iButtons, cryptographic cards, etc. The other kind of research makes use of methods (called 'something you are') based on biometric information like fingerprints, voiceprints, the patterns of blood vessels on the eye retina, the topography of the eye iris, the geometry of the hand, facial patterns, DNA codes or even thoughts (cerebral waves). However, all of the aforementioned solutions have two significant disadvantages. First, they may become unacceptably expensive when a large number of users are involved. Second, access to the system is strongly dependent on the suitable interfaces − which makes such methods comparatively less universal (in the context of mobility) and in some cases, impossible to use. Additionally, biometrics is extremely vulnerable to a replay attack because the personal information cannot be changed.

In the past few years we have been observing a growing interest in graphical authentication techniques as an alternative to the alphanumerical passwords. There are significant advantages, which directly address well-known vulnerabilities of the traditional authentication mechanisms. Regardless of their application (in either weak or strong authentication), graphical methods might provide higher level of security and/or lower implementation costs. On the contrary, as long as the discipline is still new, there is no knowledge about most possibilities of attacks – therefore weaknesses and drawbacks should be subject to thorough and careful investigation. This paper deals with the method called *Click Passwords* (*PassPoints, Passlogix* as well).

2   Related Work

By graphical authentication we mean those of knowledge-based methods, which include graphical aspect(s) in the authentication process. There are a few distinct grounds, which aroused the interest in graphical techniques. On one hand, graphical authentication methods are particularly useful for mobile devices or systems that have no keyboards [6]. On the other hand, there are methods resistant to *shoulder-surfing* attacks – enabling to log in 'in the crowd' (or in the places monitored by video cameras) [7], [8]; there are also obvious advantages coming from resistance to *malware* (malicious software) like *key-loggers* or *mouse-trackers* [9]. Notwithstanding, the leading inclination is still to construct authentication system, which will prevent from choosing trivial passwords and which will allow to remember passwords with the cryptographically proper length.

Click passwords. There are three techniques, known as *Passlogix* [10], *Pass-Points* [11] (Fig.2) and *Click passwords* [12] based essentially on the same idea – users create passwords by choosing several arbitrary points in the picture. The login process requires performing the right sequence of clicked points with an assumed tolerance. One of the main problems is the need for picture's area's decomposition (arbitrary chosen polygons – groups of pixels), because of two simultaneous facts. First, there is a tolerance to inaccuracy of chosen points (screen pixels), second, we are not allowed to keep the coordinates of password points (only hash function results). As a consequence, a few schemes of picture decomposition were invented (some illustrated on Fig.3).

Fig. 2. Examples od graphical interfaces of *Passlogix*, [10] and *PassPoints*, [11]

The main goal of the click password systems (according to [12]) is to improve security (to maximize the password space). The password space through a proper chosen picture and through proper pixels assignments (to polygons) can reach very impressive values — even hundreds of thousands of points in the password base — from the technical point of view. On the contrary, there appears human tendentiousness that can significantly decrease the final space of choices — these issues are inspected farther in this paper. Nevertheless, we still lack (statistically) convincing evidence that click passwords can be easier to remember than the text based (assuming the same security level).

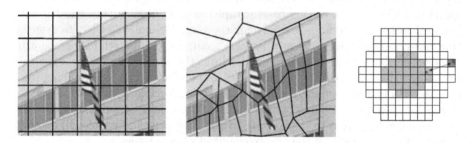

Fig. 3. Picture decomposition methods: regular grid (left), optimized *Voronoi tiling* (middle) and classification based on distance from arbitrary chosen points (right), [12]

Picture passwords. There is a group of methods where users choose and memorize a sequence of graphical elements (pictures) selected from a matrix of elements. With the name *picture passwords* we will usually identify interfaces consisting of large groups of elements (e.g. few dozens or a hundred) — although there are methods called *graphical PINs* that are usually used for small mobile devices (with few or several elements in the password base — Fig.4). Among picture passwords techniques there is a scheme called *Déjà Vu* — designed with non-describable abstract images [13], schemes based on images denoted 'Face' and 'Story' [14], thumbnail photos (quite similar to regular polygons of click passwords) [6] and others [15]. The general principle of those methods is essentially the same — the differences can be found in the graphical material, matrices

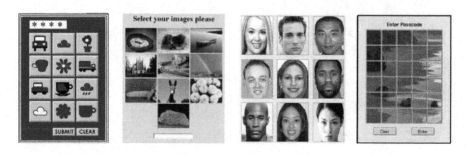

Fig. 4. Examples of *graphical PINs* (sources: [16], [17], [14], [6], respectively)

size (number of elements) and purpose. Those methods are particularly interesting (according to other research [9]) because of technical possibility of preventing users from choosing trivial passwords. On top of this, there is an approach to make the authentication process resistant to 'key logging' as well as to 'mouse tracking' software or hardware. Moreover, by choosing proper set of pictures, there was also proved (in [9]) the *picture password superiority*.

To get a basic idea of the scope of graphical authentication techniques there are a few more methods worth mentioning. A technique called *Draw-a-secret* (*DAS*) where the sequence of tap regions constitutes the password [18]. There are methods based on drawing the signature using mouse or light pen [19]. There are passwords (words) created as a response to automatically generated inkblots [20] (quite close to Rorschach's inkblots). There are other original techniques like *Pass-Go* − inspired by and based on the scheme of old Chinese game [21]. There is *RAF* (*Recall a Formation*) scheme with two-dimensional picture passwords and *Mouse Motion* technique with intuitional mouse movements [15].

There is no psychological research, which can directly justify the superiority of graphical authentication. Although there is a phenomenon called *picture superiority effect* (term introduced by Nelson et al. in 1976, [22]) stating that pictures are much more likely to be remembered than words. However, in the experiments both pictures and words characterize the same concepts, e.g. word 'sun' vs. 'a drawing of the sun' − there is no knowledge about sequences of various pictures, various picture points or alphanumerical characters. There exists the *dual-coding theory* (introduced by Paivio, [23], [24]) saying that both visual and verbal information are processed differently and along distinct channels. Concrete concepts presented as pictures are encoded into both systems; however, abstract concepts are recorded only verbally. On the basis that separate information representations are processed in each channel there exists a part of Pavio's theory called *coding redundancy hypothesis*. It states that "memory increases directly with the number of alternative memory codes available for an item". It can be an argument in favor of click passwords when the users both name and picture their passwords − but also we do not know how single characters or their sequences will be coded.

Moreover, there are series of interesting researches, which can help to understand how to create efficient methods based on graphical materials. For example, study of what kind of information will be remembered over relatively long periods of time [25]; how people remember nonsensical material and what are the conditions to improve memory for pictures [26]; what is the role of prior knowledge in recognition [27]; what is the influence on memory when words and pictures are or are not recognized [28]; how we recognize pictures with or without additional details [29]; what is the influence of symmetry in the remembered material [30] and how can we manipulate with the colour (versus b&w), high versus low information, semantic versus sensory processing [31]. These (and many more that were omitted) can be only a clue to understand which factors should be taken into consideration when constructing the authentication mechanism, but none of them answers the question about strong and/or weak points of click passwords.

Nevertheless it shows how useful for the graphical authentication *mnemonics* (widespread nowadays) can be found.

3   Origins of Click Passwords Cryptanalysis

While the discipline is still in its infancy, there is no wide range of practical implementations and we have no direct observations on security of click passwords. We do not know much about possible attacks on the graphical authentication systems. There are a few hypotheses (below) that can result in disclosure of vulnerabilities of the picture material. An attempt has been made to identify universal weaknesses of the keypad images use in the authentication process. This knowledge can also result in proper design of the graphical interface by avoiding indicate regions. The hypotheses appear to be (entirely or partially) obvious, but as long as there are no appropriate results, we cannot refer to those as to vulnerabilities. Apart from effects affirmations, we would like to know about strength of those relations and on that ground conclude how dangerous potential attacks can be.

H1. First hypothesis is based on the belief that people would not choose points in the area where there are no footholds (spots) that can be clicked. Although we can imagine a scenario such that someone measures the distance from some objects and selects the password points in the *flat* area, even though the time and effort necessary to memorize such points make those choices quite unreliable. Thus, the first hypothesis states that there will be significant difference in choices between the regular and the *flat* area (first & fourth area on Fig.5).

Fig. 5. Four types of examined areas (1: *flat*, 2: *irregular*, 3: *structural*, 4: *commonplace*) and below the same areas after high frequency filtering (edge detection)

H2. In the second case we deliver spots (footholds) that can be easily pointed in the picture. But there are two things making the memorizing difficult. First, there is no order (regular structure) – the points are chaotically spread. Second, the elements do not differ in particular way (easy to remember) from each other.

The suitable material for such research can be provided for instance by 'breaking waves of the sea' or 'leaves on the lawn' (as the second area on the Fig.5). High frequency filtering shows that there are many points to be clicked, but it is hard to believe that there is an efficient way to remember thus chosen points. Therefore, like in H1, we do not expect that points in the second area (on Fig.5) will be frequently chosen by the participants.

H3. The last of the examined areas is a *structural* region (third on Fig.5), for which there are three criteria. First, there should be footholds that can be easily pointed in the picture. Second, the elements must not have particular differences. And third, there should be a quite straightforward opportunity to memorize chosen points (as for example the number of row and column of such arrangement). In this area we expect to observe two effects (as H3 and H4). The first one determines H3 − just like before, there will be less interest in this area, compared with the regular one.

H4. According to H3 and the third *structural* area of Fig.5, when someone decides to make the password based on this region, the choices will be weak from the cryptographical point of view. The tendency (expected by H4) should be seen as a graphical arrangement of the password points − far from random one. Similar effect was observed in [9] (research on picture passwords), where participants selected row, column or diagonal of the picture passwords' elements (the more sophisticated ideas in passwords picking were based on e.g. moves of the chess knight).

We need one more clarification − what is the fourth area type in the Fig.5 − called *commonplace*. Commonplaces are the regions, which are the references areas for H1−H3 hypotheses in every keypad image. It is almost impossible to define 'what the areas are', but it is quite simple to define 'what the areas are not'. They are none of the previous areas (1−3 on the Fig. 5) − they can consist of those regions (as a matter of fact they have to), but only in small fragments (not in general).

Method. One of the main requirements when exploring human tendencies is to test a large number of subjects. In the described research the verification of the memorized passwords was given up. On one hand there was no control over malicious behaviour of the participants, but on the other hand, there was the possibility to put more subjects to the test. It had been certainly assured that the participants were convinced that in one week there would be a second part of the experiment (remembering and reproducing passwords).

Subjects. There were 301 experiment participants − students at the Warsaw University of Technology (Faculty of Electronics and Information Technology) in general from third up to 10th semester of studies. Table 1 presents more accurate characteristics of participants groups.

Apparatus. Keypad I (*palace*) and Keypad II (*street*) were created with regard to the four hypotheses (H1−H4). First observations (of groups I and II − almost 80 participants) did not result in passwords placed in the third (*structural*) area

Table 1. Characteristic of the experiment participants with regard to keypad types

Groups:	I	II	III	IV	V	VI	Overall:
Number of Subjects:	46	32	36	69	60	58	301
Females / Males:	0/46	3/29	1/35	3/66	3/57	4/54	14/287
Semester of study:	3	6-10	5	4	4	6	3-10
Keypad I (palace):	26	7	3	24	19	20	99
Keypad II (street):	20	25	6	23	25	19	118
Keypad III (tower):	–	–	27	22	16	19	84
Rejected:	0	0	1	0	3	1	5

(there were too little choices). There was no chance to confirm the H4 hypothesis. To address the problem of lack of choices the third keypad was created (Keypad III − *tower*) where the *structural* area can be found nearly solely (on the sky) with the *commonplace* regions reduced to minimum (existing only as the edges of the office building). The boundaries and the percentage share of areas were plotted on every keypad illustration.
− Keypad I − *palace* (size 200mm x 120mm) − Fig. 6; area types: 1, 2, 4.
− Keypad II − *street* (size 200mm x 120mm) − Fig. 8; area types: 1, 3, 4.
− Keypad III − *tower* (size 120mm x 160mm) − Fig. 10; area types: 1, 3, (4).

Procedure. Instructions attached to the keypads asked the participants to choose and remember passwords consisting of seven picture points and the subjects were informed that the picture points should be remembered in the right order. There was no time restriction.

Results. All results (raw and processed) were presented graphically and numerically. The left charts of the Figures 7, 9, 10_b present hundreds of users' real choices (679, 812 and 581 − respectively) − but the same points (or points located in the direct neighbourhood thereof) aren't visible. More informative with regard to near placed choices are two-dimensional histograms (Figures 7, 9, 10_b on the right) − consisting of the 4mm x 4mm cells. The darker cell, the more choices were counted in favor thereof. Statistics for the area types (raw and based on the percentage share of areas in the image), statistics for the participants' choices (real and based on the percentage share of clicks according to the areas) and the densities of choices depending on the area types, were collected in Tables 2, 3, 4 (on the left) − respectively to the keypads.

The major results with regard to the H1 − H3 hypotheses are located in the last columns (Density) of aforementioned tables, where the number of choices were standardized for the sizes of areas. Thus, the outcomes indicate the mean numbers of choices per one square centimetre. The every keypad results show that each of the three area types (with density from 0.13 up to 0.69 choices in 1 cm^2) was chosen by participants definitely more rarely than the regular regions (with density from 5.19 up to 5.56 choices in 1 cm^2). It makes the *commonplace* about ten times more attractive a region. In consequence the strength of hypotheses relations were:

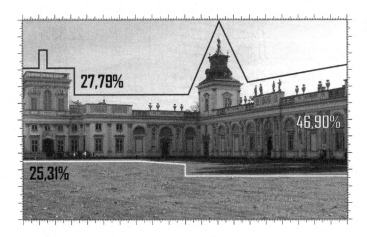

Fig. 6. Keypad I (*palace*); percentage share of areas: *flat, commonplace, irregular*. [32]

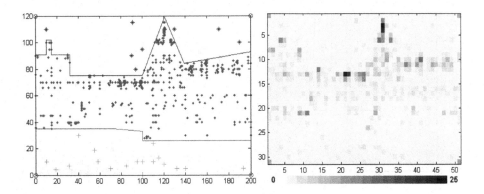

Fig. 7. Users' choices (left) and 51x31 '*heat map*' histogram (right) of the Keypad I

Table 2. Statistics of users' choices based on the Keypad I (*palace*)

Type of area:	Area [cm²]	Area [%]	Choices [−]	Choices [%]	Density [c-s/cm²]
1: flat	66.70	27.79	9	1.33	0.135
2: irregular	60.73	25.31	19	2.80	0.313
4: commonplace	112.57	46.90	626	92.19	5.561
0: keypad corners	0	0	25	3.68	∞

Histogram (heat map) area				
1 %	3 %	5 %	10%	20%
Percent of users' choices				
[%]	[%]	[%]	[%]	[%]
29.0	53.9	67.0	83.5	100

H1 − 41.2x, 7.5x and 42,7x (respectively to the Keypads I, II, III);
H2 − 17,8x (in the Keypad II);
H3 − 11,5x and 9,1x (respectively to the Keypads II and III).
H4 − unfortunately there were only nine passwords among 83 and only 4 of

Fig. 8. Keypad II (*street*); percentage share of areas: *flat, structural, commonplace.* [33]

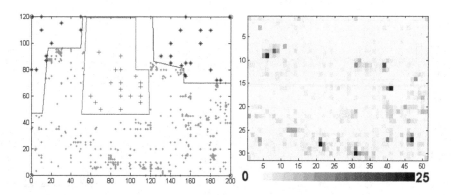

Fig. 9. Users' choices (left) and 51x31 *'heat map'* histogram (right) of the Keypad II

Table 3. Statistics of users' choices based on Keypad II (*street*)

Type of area:	Area [cm^2]	Area [%]	Choices [–]	Choices [%]	Density [c-s/cm^2]
1: flat	53.72	22.38	37	4.56	0.689
3: structural	42.08	17.53	19	2.34	0.451
4: commonplace	144.2	60.01	749	92.24	5.194
0: keypad corners	0	0	7	0.86	∞

Histogram (heat map) area				
1 %	3 %	5 %	10%	20%
Percent of users' choices				
[%]	[%]	[%]	[%]	[%]
32.9	53.3	64.7	81.3	100

them inside the '*structural*' area (what makes about 11% and 5% of all choices respectively) that could confirm the H4 hypothesis (those passwords are illustrated on Fig.10 — top-right). Like before the subjects avoided the *structural* area (which was selected nine times more rarely than the reference region).

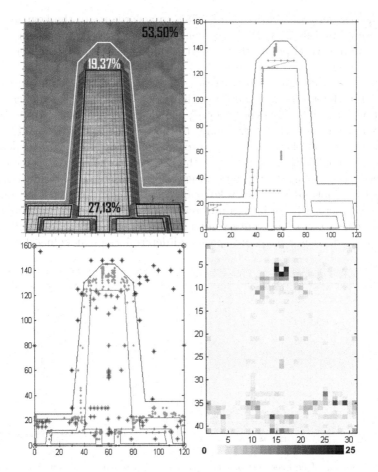

Fig. 10. Keypad III (*tower*) and the percentage share of areas: *flat*, *structural* and *block edges* (top-left); examples of passwords according to H4 (top-right); all users' choices (bottom-left) and 31x41 '*heat map*' histogram (bottom-right). [33]

Table 4. Statistics of users' choices based on Keypad III (*tower*)

Type of area:	Area [cm²]	Area [%]	Choices [−]	Choices [%]	Density [c-s/cm²]
1: flat	102.7	53.5	30	5.16	0.292
3: structural	52.1	27.1	71	12.2	1.363
4: block edges	37.2	19.4	464	79.9	12.478
0: keypad corners	0	0	16	2.75	∞

Histogram (heat map) area				
1 %	3 %	5 %	10%	20%
Percent of users' choices				
[%]	[%]	[%]	[%]	[%]
32.9	59.4	72.6	88.8	100

Nevertheless there are also further observations – unintended but interesting findings reported in this paper. As the first of unforeseen results appeared the next type of users' choices – the corners of the keypads. The percentage shares of all choices were 3.7%, 0.86% and 2.75% in accordance to the keypads' order (as presented in Tab. 2, 3, 4). The socond was farther tendentiousness.

There were several points (hot spots) within every keypad that were chosen especially often. A decent illustration of this effect are the 'heat maps' (Figures 7, 9, 10_b – on the right) and statistics based on the 4mm x 4mm histograms presented in the Tables 2, 3 and 4 (on the right). Those tables demonstrate the general percentage of all keypad choices included in 1%, 3%, 5%, 10% and 20% of histograms areas - what corresponds to the right chart on Figure 11.

Two graphs (Fig.11) were presented to exemplify how strong the tendentiousness of the people's choices can be – the number of choices and percentage of all choices with regard to the percentage of keypads areas were illustrated. It can easily be noticed that every keypad includes more than 50% of all clicks (choices) in merely 3% of histogram areas. Moreover particularly different keypads are characterized by quite similar curves – such strong tendentiousness dramatically decreases password space and determines great vulnerability.

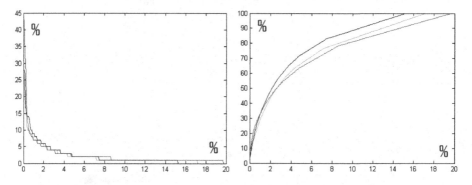

Fig. 11. Number of choices per one cell 4x4mm - decreasing ordered (left) and percentage of all choices (right), both with reference to the top 20% of histograms areas

4   Discussion of *Pros* and *Cons*

All presented results are only a small part of group of issues that should be taken into consideration before the practical use of click passwords (and related methods). This section is a compilation of conclusions of presented and so far not mentioned issues – regarding to the traditional alphanumerical passwords and picture passwords as well.

Advantages of Click Passwords

1. There are possibilities of significant enlargement of the password space of click passwords. In the traditional passwords, the base does not exceed one hundred (b^n – password space, b – base, n – password length,). Picture passwords offer the password base up to ten times larger. Technically, the click passwords space can be much greater than in the picture passwords

(hundreds of thousands) − but including strong tendentiousness in passwords selection, we do not know about real security strength of click passwords (that seems to be at picture passwords level).

2. Theoretically, there are possibilities of personalizing the passwords (what in most cases prevents from dictionary attacks) via individual interface pictures (using various images). However, there is a threat based upon tendentiousness of choices − for this reason every image should be tested at least in semi-large group of people.

3. There is a possibility to make the authentication process resistant to 'key logging' − which is obvious (due to not using the keyboard).

4. Sharing passwords with other users is much more difficult as well as noting passwords down or giving them away as a result of social engineering attack. While traditional passwords can be easily written down or spelled out, giving a click password out is very troublesome. This feature of click passwords is much better than in the picture passwords.

5. The password '*incrementation effect*' consisting in periodic, recurrent and obvious changes made to the passwords (e.g. a password change from "*11ES-oRiCS06*" to "*12ESoRiCS07*)" can be neutralized. It is because there are no sequences or numbers when the keypad image was properly chosen (e.g. avoiding *structural* areas). And even when user changes only one point of the password − it is still hard to guess which one and where is the new one. What is more, there is always a way to force users to significantly change their passwords by exchange the keypad picture.

6. Likewise, rule "one system − one password" can be ensured by different keypad images in the systems where unique password codes are required.

7. There is a possibility for undemanding and inexpensive implementation (compared to biometric or cryptographic hardware).

Disadvantages of Click Passwords

1. Deterministic methods of picture decomposition will always result in some percentage of irritated or frustrated users. Even dealing with the best decomposition, there is always a probability (and statistically, certainty) that someone chooses password point in a polygon's border − and in half of the tries will fail the authentication process. As a matter of fact there is a usual trade-off between mentioned probability and the passwords space.

2. There is no technical possibility to prevent users from choosing trivial passwords (as distinct from picture passwords). The most important effort is to choose the proper keypad image. But only statistical analysis based on large (enough) group of people can confirm the right choice of the picture.

3. There is no possibility to make the authentication process resistant to 'mouse tracking' (as distinct from picture passwords). Every linear transformation of the keypad image can be easily cracked. Non-linear transformations require several more authentications but also can give the password (or its approximation) away.

4. More time needed to enter the password. Although we can expect shortening of the passwords (in comparison to alphanumerical passwords), we should

not expect better time performance in entering click passwords (even after the users have learnt the order of points).

5. Graphical interface is required – which means that the graphical authentication methods will be less universal (in terms of mobility) and troublesome in implementation (in comparison to traditional passwords).

6. There is no resistance to *shoulder-surfing* attacks – there is a better chance to observe the password entered on the screen than the alphanumerical password typed with traditional keyboard. (There are some picture passwords techniques dealing with *shoulder-surfing* attacks though).

7. There are many people who dislike: changes, giving up their habits, technical novelties, graphical interfaces (i.e. unix or linux users) and "compulsion to better life" (as in "we know what is better for you").

8. As for today, the discipline is still new and there may be many attacks, of which we cannot be aware at the present time.

5 Conclusions

In the paper four hypotheses were investigated in order to reveal universal weaknesses of the click password interfaces – three of them were proved right. The results determined three types of areas that will significantly decrease the password space. Additionally there was (unintentionally) distinguished strong tendentiousness of chosen passwords. Every of three keypad images indicates several common points that were chosen much more likely by the participants. It was shown that only 3% of the keypad image area includes more than 50% of all users' choices. On one hand, the possibilities of attacks on the authentication mechanism based on click passwords were exposed; on the other hand, the same results are useful as a way to improve security of this kind of authentication mechanisms.

A variety of technical and non-technical issues and conclusions, regarding click passwords, picture passwords and traditional passwords, was discussed in the paper. In order to understand peoples choices better and identify the potential causes of tendentiousness in click passwords selection, the eye tracking system will be further investigated.

References

1. Schneier, B.: Real-World Passwords. Crypto-Gram Newsletter (December 15, 2006)
2. Magalhaes, S.T., Revett, K., Santos, H.D.: Generation of Authentication Strings From Graphic Keys. International Journal of Computer Science and Network Security 6(3B), 240–246 (2006)
3. Brown, A.S., Bracken, E., Zoccoli, S., Douglas, K.: Generating and remembering passwords. Applied Cognitive Psychology 18, 641–651 (2004)
4. Carstens, D.S., McCauley-Bell, P., Malone, L.C., DeMara, R.F.: Evaluation of the Human Impact of Password Authentication Practices on Information Security. Informing Science Journal 7, 67–85 (2004)
5. Zviran, M., Haga, W.J.: User authentication by cognitive passwords: an empirical assessment. JCIT 5, 137–144 (1990)

6. Jansen, W., Gavrila, S., Korolev, V., Ayers, R., Swanstrom, R.: Picture Password: A Visual Login Technique for Mobile Devices. National Institute of Standards and Technology, NISTIR 7030

7. Zhi, L., Qibin, S., Yong, L., Giusto, D.D.: An Association-Based Graphical Password Design Resistant To Shoulder-Surfing Attack. In: ICME. IEEE International Conference on Multimedia and Expo, IEEE Computer Society Press, Los Alamitos (2005)

8. Weinshall, D., Kirkpatrick, S.: Passwords You'll Never Forget, but Can't Recall. In: CHI. Proceedings of Conference on Human Factors in Computing Systems, Vienna, Austria, pp. 1399–1402 (2004)

9. Goofit, K.: Picture Passwords Superiority and Picture Passwords Dictionary Attacks (article seems to appear on SIS'07)

10. Paulson, L.D.: Taking a graphical approach to the password. Computer 35 (2002)

11. Wiedenbeck, S., Waters, J., Birget, J.C., Brodskiy, A., Memon, N.: Authentication using graphical passwords: Basic results. In: HCII 2005. Human-Computer Interaction International, Las Vegas (July 25-27, 2005)

12. Kirovski, D., Nebojsa, J., Roberts, P.: Click Passwords. Security and Privacy in Dynamic Env. 201, 351–363 (2006)

13. Dhamija, R., Perrig, A., Déjà Vu, A.: A User Study Using Images for Authentication. In: Proceedings of the 9th USENIX Security Symposium (2000)

14. Davis, D., Monrose, F., Reiter, M.K.: On User Choice in Graphical Password Schemes. In: Proceedings of the 13th USENIX Security Symposium, pp. 151–164 (August 2004)

15. Suo, X.: A Design and Analysis of Graphical Password. M.Sc. thesis, Georgia State University (2006)

16. Tricerion: The Usability of Picture Passwords (April 2007), http://www.tricerion.com/

17. Angeli, A., Coventry, L., Johnson, G.I., Coutts, M.: Usability and user authentication: Pictorial passwords vs. PIN. In: McCabe, P.T. (ed.) Contemporary Ergonomics, pp. 253–258. Taylor & Francis, London (2003)

18. Jermyn, I., Mayer, A., Monrose, F., Reiter, M., Rubin, A.: The design and analysis of graphical passwords. In: USENIX (1998)

19. Syukri, A.F., Okamoto, E., Mambo, M.A: User Identification System Using Signature Written with Mouse. In: Boyd, C., Dawson, E. (eds.) ACISP 1998. LNCS, vol. 1438, pp. 403–441. Springer, Heidelberg (1998)

20. Stubblefield, A., Simon, D.R.: Inkblot Authentication. Microsoft Technical Report MSR-TR-2004-85 (2004)

21. Tao, H.: Pass-Go, a New Graphical Password Scheme. Master thesis, Univeristy of Ottawa, Ontario, Canada (June 2006)

22. Nelson, D.L., Reed, U.S., Walling, J.R.: Picture superiority effect. Journal of Experimental Psychology: Human Learning & Memory 2, 523–528 (1976)

23. Paivio, A.: Imagery and verbal processes. Holt, Rinehart & Winston, New York (1971)

24. Paivio, A.: Mental representations: A dual-coding approach. Oxford University Press, New York (1986)

25. Mandler, J., Ritchey, G.: Long-term memory for pictures. Journal of Experimental Psychology: Human Learning and Memory, 386–396 (1977)

26. Bower, G.H., Karlin, M.B., Dueck, A.: Comprehension and Memory For Pictures. Memory and Cognition 3, 216–220 (1975)

27. Long, D.L., Prat, C.S.: Memory for Star Trek: The Role of Prior Knowledge Recognition Revisited. Journal of Experimental Psychology: Learning, Memory, and Cognition 28(6), 1073–1082 (2002)
28. Kroll, J.F., Potter, M.C.: Recognizing words, Pictures, and Concepts - A Comparison of Lexical, Object, and Reality Decisions. Journal Of Verbal Learning And Verbal Behavior 23, 39–66 (1984)
29. Pezdek, K., Maki, R., Valencia-Laver, D., Whetstone, T., Stoeckert, J., Dougherty, T.: Picture Memory: Recognizing Added and Deleted Details. Journal of experimental psychology. Learning, memory, and cognition 14(3), 468–476 (1988)
30. Attneave, F.: Symmetry, Information and Memory Patterns. American Journal of Psychology 68, 209–222 (1955)
31. Childers, T.L., Houston, M.J.: Conditions for a Picture-Superiority Effect on Consumer Memory. Journal of Consumer Research 11, 643–654 (1984)
32. Jakub600, Wilanów: Graphical material (processed and published with author's consent) All rights reserved, http://www.obiektywni.pl
33. CorelDRAW: Clipart and Photos. Graphical material used for research comes from CorelDRAW distribution (license for ISE PW). All rights reserved

Graphical Password Authentication
Using Cued Click Points *

Sonia Chiasson[1,2], P.C. van Oorschot[1], and Robert Biddle[2]

[1] School of Computer Science, Carleton University, Ottawa, Canada
[2] Human-Oriented Technology Lab, Carleton University, Ottawa, Canada
{chiasson,paulv}@scs.carleton.ca, robert_biddle@carleton.ca

Abstract. We propose and examine the usability and security of Cued Click Points (CCP), a cued-recall graphical password technique. Users click on one point per image for a sequence of images. The next image is based on the previous click-point. We present the results of an initial user study which revealed positive results. Performance was very good in terms of speed, accuracy, and number of errors. Users preferred CCP to PassPoints (Wiedenbeck et al., 2005), saying that selecting and remembering only one point per image was easier, and that seeing each image triggered their memory of where the corresponding point was located. We also suggest that CCP provides greater security than PassPoints because the number of images increases the workload for attackers.

Keywords: Graphical Passwords, Computer Security, Authentication, Usable Security, User Study.

1 Introduction

Various graphical password schemes [14] have been proposed as alternatives to text-based passwords. Research and experience have shown that text-based passwords are fraught with both usability and security problems that make them less than desirable solutions [21]. Psychology studies have revealed that the human brain is better at recognizing and recalling images than text [8]; graphical passwords are intended to capitalize on this human characteristic in hopes that by reducing the memory burden on users, coupled with a larger full password space offered by images, more secure passwords can be produced and users will not resort to unsafe practices in order to cope.

In this paper, we propose a new click-based graphical password scheme called Cued Click Points (CCP). It can be viewed as a combination of PassPoints [19,20], Passfaces [9], and Story [5]. A password consists of one click-point per image for a sequence of images. The next image displayed is based on the previous click-point so users receive immediate implicit feedback as to whether they are on the correct path when logging in. CCP offers both improved usability and security.

We conducted an in-lab user study with 24 participants and a total of 257 trials. Users had high success rates, could quickly create and re-enter their

---

* version: June 29, 2007.

J. Biskup and J. Lopez (Eds.): ESORICS 2007, LNCS 4734, pp. 359–374, 2007.

passwords, and were very accurate when entering their click-points. Participants rated the system positively and indicated that they preferred CCP to a PassPoints-style system. They also said that they appreciated the immediate implicit feedback telling them whether their latest click-point was correctly entered.

A preliminary security analysis of this new scheme is also presented. Hotspots (i.e., areas of the image that users are more likely to select) are a concern in click-based passwords [6,16], so CCP uses a large set of images that will be difficult for attackers to obtain. For our proposed system, hotspot analysis requires proportionally more effort by attackers, as each image must be collected and analyzed individually. CCP appears to allow greater security than PassPoints; the workload for attackers of CCP can be arbitrarily increased by augmenting the number of images in the system. As with most graphical passwords, CCP is not intended for environments where shoulder-surfing is a serious threat.

Section 2 provides background information on related techniques. Cued Click Points (CCP) is described in Section 3, the user study and its results are available in Sections 4 and 5 respectively, and an initial security analysis is given in Section 6. Section 7 provides an interpretation and discussion of the results including possible enhancements, while conclusions and future work appear in Section 8.

2   Background and Related Work

Graphical password schemes can be grouped into three general categories based on the type of cognitive activity required to remember the password: recognition, recall, and cued recall [5,12]. Recognition is the easiest for human memory whereas pure recall is most difficult since the information must be accessed from memory with no triggers. Cued recall falls somewhere between these two as it offers a cue which should establish context and trigger the stored memory [12].

Among existing graphical passwords, CCP most closely resembles aspects of Passfaces [9], Story [5], and PassPoints [19,20]. Therefore these graphical password schemes are presented in more detail. Conceptually, CCP is a blend of the three; in terms of implementation, it is most similar to PassPoints. It also avoids the complex user training requirements found in a number of graphical password proposals, such as that of Weinshall [18].

Passfaces [9] is a graphical password scheme based primarily on recognizing human faces. During password creation, users select a number of images from a larger set. To log in, users must identify one of their pre-selected images from amongst several decoys. Users must correctly respond to a number of these challenges for each login. Davis et al. [5] implemented their own version called Faces and conducted a long-term user study. Results showed that users could accurately remember their images but that user-chosen passwords were predictable to the point of being insecure.

Davis et al. [5] proposed an alternative scheme, Story, that used everyday images instead of faces and required that users select their images in the correct order. Users were encouraged to create a story as a memory aid. It fared somewhat worse than Faces for memorability [5], but user choices were much less predictable.

The idea of click-based graphical passwords originated with Blonder [2] who proposed a scheme where a password consisted of a series of clicks on predefined regions of an image. Later, Wiedenbeck et al. [19,20] proposed PassPoints, wherein passwords could be composed of several (e.g., 5) points anywhere on an image. They also proposed a "robust discretization" scheme [1], with three overlapping grids, allowing for login attempts that were approximately correct to be accepted and converting the entered password into a cryptographic verification key.

Wiedenbeck et al. [19,20] examined the usability of PassPoints in three separate in-lab user studies to compare text passwords to PassPoints, test whether the choice of image impacted usability, and determine the minimum size of the tolerance square. The overall conclusion was that PassPoints was a usable authentication scheme.

We recently conducted two user studies [3] on a PassPoints-style system. Our initial lab study revisited the original usability claims, explored usability of such passwords on a wider range of images (17 images), and gathered information about users' password choices. Next, we conducted a large-scale field study that examined click-based graphical passwords in practice.

Intuitively, it seems obvious that some areas of an image are more attractive to users as click-points [13]. If this phenomenon is too strong, the likelihood that attackers can guess a password significantly increases. If attackers learn which images are being used, they can select a set of likely hotspots through image processing tools or by observing a small set of users on the target image and then building an attack dictionary based on those points [6,16]. For further discussion, see Section 6.

3   Cued Click Points

Cued Click Points (CCP) is a proposed alternative to PassPoints. In CCP, users click one point on each of $c = 5$ images rather than on five points on one image. It offers cued-recall and introduces visual cues that instantly alert valid users if they have made a mistake when entering their latest click-point (at which point they can cancel their attempt and retry from the beginning). It also makes attacks based on hotspot analysis more challenging, as we discuss later. As shown in Figure 1, each click results in showing a next-image, in effect leading users down a "path" as they click on their sequence of points. A wrong click leads down an incorrect path, *with an explicit indication of authentication failure only after the final click*. Users can choose their images only to the extent that their click-point dictates the next image. If they dislike the resulting images, they could create a new password involving different click-points to get different images.

We envision that CCP fits into an authentication model where a user has a client device (which displays the images) to access an online server (which authenticates the user). We assume that the images are stored server-side with client communication through SSL/TLS. For further discussion, see Section 6.

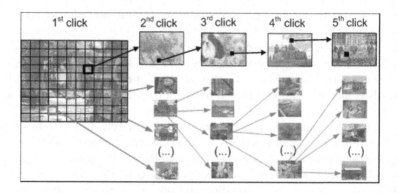

Fig. 1. CCP passwords can be regarded as a choice-dependent path of images

For implementation, CCP initially functions like PassPoints. During password creation, a discretization method (e.g., see [1]) is used to determine a click-point's tolerance square and corresponding grid. For each click-point in a subsequent login attempt, this grid is retrieved and used to determine whether the click-point falls within tolerance of the original point. With CCP, we further need to determine which next-image to display.

Similar to the PassPoints studies, our example system had images of size 451x331 pixels and tolerance squares of 19x19 pixels. If we used robust discretization [1], we would have 3 overlapping candidate grids each containing approximately 400 squares and in the simplest design, 1200 tolerance squares per image (although only 400 are used in a given grid). We use a function $f(username, currentImage, currentToleranceSquare)$ that uniquely maps each tolerance square to a next-image. This suggests a minimum set of 1200 images required at each stage. One argument against using fewer images, and having multiple tolerance squares map to the same next-image, is that this could potentially result in misleading implicit feedback in (albeit rare) situations where users click on an incorrect point yet still see the correct next-image.

Each of the 1200 next-images would have 1200 tolerance squares and thus require 1200 next-images of their own. The number of images would quickly become quite large. So we propose re-using the image set across stages. By re-using images, there is a slight chance that users see duplicate images. During the 5 stages in password creation, the image indices $i_1, ..., i_5$ for the images in the password sequence are each in the range $1 \leq i_j \leq 1200$. When computing the next-image index, if any is a repeat (i.e., the next i_j is equal to i_k for some $k < j$), then the next-image selection function f is deterministically perturbed to select a distinct image.

A user's initial image is selected by the system based on some user characteristic (as an argument to f above; we used *username*). The sequence is re-generated on-the-fly from the function each time a user enters the password. If a user enters an incorrect click-point, then the sequence of images from that point onwards will be incorrect and thus the login attempt will fail. For an attacker who does not know the correct sequence of images, this cue will not be helpful.

We expect that hotspots [6,16] will appear as in PassPoints, but since the number of images is significantly increased, analysis will require more effort which increases proportionally with the configurable number of images in the system. For example, if attackers identify thirty likely click-points on the first image, they then need to analyze the thirty corresponding second images (once they determine both the indices of these images and get access to the images themselves), and so on, growing exponentially.

A major usability improvement over PassPoints is the fact that legitimate users get immediate feedback about an error when trying to log in. When they see an incorrect image, they know that the latest click-point was incorrect and can immediately cancel this attempt and try again from the beginning. The visual cue does not explicitly reveal "right" or "wrong" but is evident using knowledge only the legitimate user should possess. As with text passwords, PassPoints can only safely provide feedback at the end and cannot reveal the cause of error. Providing explicit feedback in PassPoints before the final click-point could allow PassPoints attackers to mount an online attack to prune potential password subspaces, whereas CCP's visual cues should not help attackers in this way. Another usability improvement is that being cued to recall one point on each of five images appears easier than remembering an ordered sequence of five points on one image.

4   User Study

We conducted an in-lab user study of CCP with 24 participants. The methodology was reviewed and approved by the university's research ethics committee. The participants (12 females and 12 males) were university students with diverse backgrounds. None were specifically studying computer security but all were regular web users. They ranged in age from 17 to 26 years. Two had participated in our previous in-lab study [3], testing a PassPoints-style system.

All participants completed an individual one-hour session in our usability lab. They first read and signed the consent form and were given an introduction to the tasks they would be completing during the session. This introduction included showing them an example image with superimposed squares, demonstrating how accurate they needed to be when re-entering their points. The tolerance squares used in this study were 19x19 pixels. We also explained that the next image in the sequence depended on where they clicked on the current image. They were told that if they suddenly saw an image they did not recognize during the Confirm or Login phases, then they were likely on the wrong path. Participants completed two practice trials followed by at most 12 real trials. In total, 257 real CCP trials were completed.

A trial consisted of the following steps. The phases indicated in steps 1, 2, and 5 represent the password phases used in later analysis.

1. Create phase: Create a password by clicking on one point in each of five system-selected images presented in sequence.

2. Confirm phase: Confirm this password by re-entering it correctly. Users incorrectly confirming their password could retry the confirmation or return to Step 1. A new password started with the same initial image, but generally included different images thereafter, depending on the click-points.

3. Two questions: Answer two 10-point Likert-scale questions on the computer about their current password's ease of creation and predicted memorability. Likert-scale questions ask respondents to indicate their level of agreement with the given statement on a scale ranging from strongly agree to strongly disagree.

4. MRT: Complete a Mental Rotations Test (MRT) puzzle [10]. This paper-based task was used to distract users for a minimum of 30 seconds by giving them a visual task to complete in order to clear their working memory.

5. Login phase: Log in with their current password. If users noticed an error during login, they could cancel their login attempt and try again. Alternatively, if they did not know their password, they could create a new password, effectively returning to Step 1 of the trial with the same initial image as a starting point. If users felt too frustrated with the particular images to try again, they could skip this trial and move on to the next trial.

Participants completed as many trials as they wished in the one-hour session, to a maximum of 14 (2 practice + 12 real trials). At the midpoint, participants took a break and completed a demographics questionnaire. The last ten minutes of the session were devoted to completing a Likert-scale and open-ended questionnaire about their perceptions and opinions of these graphical passwords. For each participant, data from the two practice trials were discarded, so all results reported in this paper are based on data from the subsequent trials.

When time remained in the one-hour session, participants were given one further task: to complete a trial with our PassPoints-style system, where they selected five points on one image. The experimenter was careful to identify the second system as "the other system we are looking at" rather than the "old" system, to not bias participants into thinking that they should rate CCP more favourably. Users were then asked which version they preferred.

A prototype application was developed in J#. A set of 330 images was compiled from personal collections as well as from websites providing free-for-use images. The prototype system did not hash the passwords or use a discretization method as would a real system, but simply stored the exact pixel coordinates so that the users' choice of click-points and their accuracy on re-entry could be examined. The system also implemented an improvised image selection process to reduce the size of the required image set since with several unique trials per participant, we would have needed several thousand images to implement the proposed scheme. The first time a user clicked on a point, a new image was associated with that point. If a user clicked within the tolerance region of that point again, either for re-entering or for resetting a password, the same image was shown. Once associated with a click-point, an image was not re-used for any other click-point during the entire session. Only areas where the user clicked had images associated with them, therefore reducing the total number of images required while still behaving in a manner consistent with the actual proposed scheme from the user's perspective.

Consistent with published PassPoints results, the images were 451x331 pixels in size and were displayed on a 19-inch screen with its resolution set to 1024x768 pixels. We used tolerance squares of size 19x19 (PassPoints studies report a 20x20 pixel tolerance).

Three methods were used to collect data in this study: system logs, question-naires, and observations. The system recorded the exact pixel coordinates of each click-point on every image visited by participants for every Create, Confirm, or Login attempt, along with the time of each event.

A post-test questionnaire was used to gather information about users' perceptions and opinions. A second questionnaire was used to collect demographic data to help frame the results of the study. Users were also asked two online questions immediately after successfully confirming their password to get an immediate reaction of how easy it was to create the password and how difficult they expect it would be to remember their password in a week.

Finally, an observer sat with each participant throughout the session, noting any difficulties or unexpected behaviour as well as comments made by the participants. While participants were not instructed to use a talk-aloud protocol, they were not discouraged from speaking if they had comments as they worked. Because comments may have slowed down completion times, any questions by the observer were asked between trials where they would not affect the timings.

5   Collected Results

Restarts. Participants used the reset button as soon as they saw an incorrect image and realized they were on the wrong path. This effectively cancelled the current attempt and returned them to the first image where they could start entering their password again. A few times, participants restarted even when they saw the correct image because they had forgotten the image. Failed login attempts (where users pressed the login button and were explicitly told that their password was incorrect) occurred only when users clicked on the wrong point for the last image since they did not receive any implicit feedback for that click-point. Because these were so few, failed login attempts are included in the restart counts. Participants said that confirming the password helped them to remember it. Once they had successfully confirmed the password, logging on even after the distraction task was relatively easy. This fact is reflected in Table 1 which shows that the vast majority of restarts occurred during the Confirm phase.

Four participants completed all their trials without any restarts, i.e., they made no errors during the entire session. In total, 201 of 257 trials (79%) were

Table 1. Total number of restarts, success rates, and completion times per phase

	Create	Confirm	Login
Total Number of Restarts	7	101	14
Success Rates	251/257 (98%)	213/257 (83%)	246/257 (96%)
Mean Time (SD)(in seconds)	24.7 (16.4)	10.9 (13.1)	7.4 (5.5)
Median Time (in seconds)	19.1	7.4	6.0

completed without restarts in any phase. The success rates were high for all phases, as shown in Table 1. Success rates were calculated as the number of trials completed without errors or restarts over the total number of trials.

Accuracy. Participants were extremely accurate in re-entering their passwords. As a measure of accuracy, all individual click-points in the Confirm and Login phases were evaluated. This totalled 1569 click-points for the Confirm phase and 1325 click-points for the Login phase. For each point, the accuracy was computed as the maximum of $|x_{original} - x_{current}|$ and $|y_{original} - y_{current}|$. All click-points were considered in the analysis, even those that were unsuccessful. A few times, participants reached an incorrect image and still proceeded to click on a point. These were included in the 51+ category since the point was obviously forgotten. As indicated in Figure 2, 86% of points were within 4 pixels of the original click-point for the Confirm phase compared to 92% for the Login phase. Falling within 4 pixels of the original point means that these click-points would have been accepted within a tolerance square of 9x9 pixels.

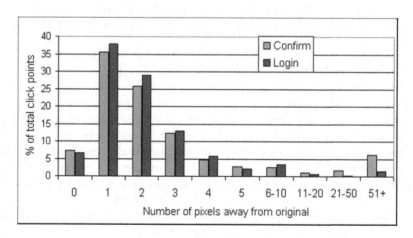

Fig. 2. Accuracy for each phase

Times for password entry. As expected, participants took longest to create their password and then were progressively quicker in entering it during the Confirm and Login phases. The reported times encompass from the first click in a phase until the last click, including any restarts. The mean and median times reflected in Table 1 are slightly elevated because some participants paused to comment as they were entering their password, which slowed their performance. Despite this fact, login times are well below 10 seconds and the total time to create and confirm a CCP password is approximately half a minute, which we expect would be quite acceptable in many applications or environments.

Questionnaires. Participants completed two sets of Likert-scale questions. Ten-point Likert scales were used, where 1 indicted strong disagreement and 10 equalled strong agreement with the given statement. First they answered two online questions immediately after successfully confirming each of their passwords. They gave both "ease of creating a password" and "ease of remembering their password in a week" median scores of 5 (means of 4.6). Secondly, they completed a post-test questionnaire at the end of the one-hour session. In Table 2, we report on a subset of the questions, corresponding to the questions reported in our study of a PassPoints-style system [3]. Some of the questions were inverted to avoid bias; as a result the scores for the statements marked with (*) were reversed before calculating the means and medians. A higher score always indicates a more positive result for CCP.

Table 2. Questionnaire responses. Scores are out of 10. * indicates scale was reversed.

Questions	Mean	Median
I could easily create a graphical password	8.2	8.5
* Someone who knows me would be better at guessing my graphical password than a stranger	4.4	5
Logging on using a graphical password was easy	7.5	7
Graphical passwords are easy to remember	7.2	6.5
* I prefer text passwords to graphical passwords	3.6	5
* Text passwords are more secure than graphical passwords	4.4	5
I think that other people would choose different points than me for a graphical password	8.0	8
With practice, I could quickly enter my graphical password	8.3	9

All post-test questionnaire questions had median values of neutral or higher, with several questions showing high levels of satisfaction. Participants showed some concern over the perceived security of graphical passwords and indicated a preference for text-based passwords. Looking at the two online questions shows that users initially felt that it was somewhat difficult to select passwords. Interestingly, by the time they responded to the post-test questionnaire, they felt much better about password creation. They also showed some hesitation about whether they would be able to remember their password in a week. This may have been exacerbated by the fact that they were creating multiple passwords in a row and did not feel that they would be able to remember all of them. Additionally, in [3] we show that long-term memorability of click-based passwords did not appear to be an issue.

Preference between CCP and PassPoints. When time permitted, participants were introduced to a PassPoints-style system and asked which they preferred. Ten participants attempted a trial with the PassPoints-style system. An additional two people had participated in our earlier study [3]. Of these 12 people, 9 strongly preferred CCP, one preferred PassPoints, and two felt that PassPoints was easier but that CCP was more secure.

User choice. Users were told in the preamble to the session to pretend that their passwords were protecting bank information and as such they should choose points that were memorable to them but difficult for others to guess. Users took these instructions seriously and many commented on how they were avoiding certain areas because they would be too easy to guess or because they felt that others would select the same points.

Users developed strategies for selecting their points. Some tried to pick geometric patterns that applied across images such as selecting items in a row along the bottom of the images, but most talked about picking things that have meaning to them such as their initial from a sign or a familiar toy. One participant made up elaborate stories about each of the click-points. Users indicated that they preferred to click on things that were small and "clickable", such as centers of letters or circles.

Participants felt strongly about the suitability of some images, with strongest reactions to images they disliked. They preferred images that were not too cluttered, that contained a variety of distinct items, that had small well-defined areas, and that featured contrasting colors. The most disliked images were those that were uniform and repetitive, such as a circuit board or field of flowers, that were highly cluttered, or that had few items with well-defined borders.

6   Preliminary Security Analysis

Any proposed authentication scheme needs to be evaluated in terms of possible threats. We begin by clarifying our target scenario for CCP and the particular assumptions made about the system.

We recommend that CCP be implemented and deployed in systems where offline attacks are not possible, and where any attack will be made against an online system that can limit the number of guesses made per account in a given time period (this limit should include restarts as well). This follows related comments by Davis et al. [5] regarding Faces and Story, even though we expect the security of CCP to be substantially stronger than those schemes. We further assume that all communication between the client and server will be made securely through SSL, maintaining secrecy of selected click-points and corresponding images, therefore avoiding simple attacks based on network sniffing.

We suggest that the image mappings (the mapping of tolerance squares to next-images based on f) be done on a per-user basis as a function of the username, as a form of salting to complicate the construction of general attack dictionaries. We also suggest that the image set across all users is a superset containing a very large number of images and that users are assigned a subset of these images for their image-maps.

General attacks against such a system, where attackers try to break into any account [11], are slowed due to the precautions mentioned above. We assume that the function f would eventually become known to attackers. Hotspot analysis might be used to increase the efficiency of an attack dictionary but images would need to be collected and such a dictionary would need to be generated on a per-user basis. Online attacks against specific users are more worrisome and require further examination. Even for online systems where the account is locked after t failed login attempts, non-trivial security is still necessary to guard against system-wide attacks over W accounts since an attacker gets $t * W$ guesses per time window [11]. Several scenarios are discussed below.

Shoulder-surfing and other information capture from users. Most graphical passwords are vulnerable to shoulder-surfing attacks [15]. With today's small cameras and camera phones, it is easy to video-capture a user's screen or keyboard as they are logging in. CCP is also susceptible to such attacks and indeed in its present form the change in images may be easier to see from further away than mouse pointer movements in PassPoints. With knowledge of which images to look for in systems allowing sufficient numbers of online guesses, attackers could try a brute-force attack of clicking on points until the correct next image appears and use this in a divide-and-conquer password recovery.

If the username, the image sequence, and the click-points are observed through shoulder-surfing then an attacker has all of the information needed to break in to the account, as is the case with PassPoints and most other password systems. Having a compromised computer is also a threat because malware may capture the login information and relay that information elsewhere. Whereas a keylogger suffices for text passwords, for graphical passwords software is needed to capture the images and the cursor positions.

When only some of the information is known, it can be used to narrow the search for a correct guess. With PassPoints, knowing the username is enough to retrieve the user's sole image. Hotspot analysis [6,16] can then be conducted on that particular image. With CCP, the username and an online guess reveal only the first image so hotspot analysis of this image gives only limited information to an attacker.

Knowing some images and their position in a user's sequence allows pruning of an attack dictionary. The more images are known, the smaller the attack dictionary and the easier the attacker's job. Thus CCP is not suitable in environments where shoulder-surfing is a realistic threat, or environments where user images can otherwise be recorded (e.g., by insiders, malicious software on the client machine, etc.).

Hotspots and dictionary attacks. In cases where attackers are not in a position to capture information from the user, they are limited to what they can deduce through image analysis.

Hotspots are specific areas in the image that have a higher probability of being selected by users as part of their passwords. If attackers can accurately predict the hotspots in an image, then a dictionary of passwords containing combinations of these hotspots can be built. Hotspots are known to be problematic for PassPoints [6,16]; further analysis is needed to determine whether precautions such as carefully selecting images can minimize this threat.

Our example system had 400 tolerance squares per grid for a given image. Because the chosen grid is stored during password creation, the correct grid is always retrieved by the system during login so the fact that there are several grids (and 1200 images) does not come into play. This means that for each image, there is a 1/400 chance of clicking within the correct tolerance square. However, due to hotspots some of these have a much higher probability of being correct than others. Knowing the hotspots would allow an attacker to modify an attack dictionary to test passwords with higher probability first. For example, re-examining the data from our larger PassPoints-style study [3] we found that, as a general result across 17 images used, the 30 largest hotspots on an image cover approximately 50% of user-chosen click-points. Assuming that attackers are first able to extract the necessary images and perform hotspot analysis, there is approximately a 3% ($.5^5$) chance that a password is contained in a dictionary of 2^{25} entries built entirely from hotspots.

A key advantage of CCP over PassPoints is that attackers need to analyze hotspots on a large set of images rather than only one image since they do not know the sequence of images used for a given password. Secondly, using different subsets of images for different users means that an attacker must somehow gather information about the specific subset assigned to the current user.

Further testing is required to gather a larger sample of click-points per image for CCP, but preliminary analysis provides evidence that users are no more likely to select a popular hotspot as their click-point in CCP than with PassPoints. When presented with the same images, users selected similar points in both our CCP and PassPoints-style [3] user studies.

7   Further Discussion

From a usability point of view, CCP appears quite successful. Participants were satisfied, their performance was good in terms of success rates and accuracy, and they felt that using this type of password was getting easier as they progressed through the session. The median time required to create (19.1 seconds) and confirm a password (7.4 seconds) is acceptable and login times (6.0 seconds) are reasonable as well. Success rates were high, with 96% of logins being successful.

Users appreciated the implicit feedback. As soon as they saw an unfamiliar image, they knew they were on the wrong path and restarted. They liked being able to narrow down exactly which click was erroneous. They also felt that seeing each image triggered the memory of where they had clicked.

Participants were surprisingly accurate in their targeting of click-points. During the Login phase, 92% of click-points fell within a 9x9 pixel square of the original click-points. In agreement with our earlier studies with a PassPoints-style system [3], the accuracy findings for CCP provide further evidence that tolerance squares as small as of 9x9 pixels may be acceptable terms of usability. Our previous studies [3] also showed that varying screen resolutions did not appear to impact performance so we predict that the same will apply to CCP.

We can also compare results of CCP with our own PassPoints-style user studies [3]. When comparing only the lab studies, participants performed similarly well in terms of login accuracy and success rates. The median login click-time for our PassPoints-style system was 7.0 seconds while for CCP it was 6.0 seconds but CCP's time also included "think-time" as each image appeared (as opposed to PassPoints where the majority of "think-time" occurred before the first click and as such is not included in these click-time results). Of those participants who tried both systems, a strong preference for CCP was evident. The most common reasons were because seeing each image triggered their memory of their click-point, there was no need to remember the order of the click-points, and they received implicit feedback about the correctness of their latest click. This comparison is somewhat biased since users had much more practice with one system than the other, but these responses do correspond to what would intuitively be expected.

7.1   Potential Improvements

With any password-based authentication scheme, a primary goal is to maximize the effective password space (i.e., that subset of the full password space actually used in practice) in order to make it more resistant to attack. A few alternatives exist to increase the effective password space for CCP.

Adding more click-points. As with PassPoints, one way to increase the password space is to increase the number of click-points contained in a password. This comes at the cost of increasing the memory burden on users. Although we have no empirical evidence to support this hypothesis, it seems that the negative impact would be less with CCP than with PassPoints since a one-to-one mapping between images and click-points in CCP would appear to be easier for users to manage. Therefore moving to 6 click-points may be a reasonable strategy for CCP. Alternatively it is possible to enforce a minimum number of clicks (images) but allow users to decide for themselves how many clicks their password contains, similar to minimum password lengths for text-based passwords. In this case, the system would continue to show the next image in the sequence but the user would determine at which point to stop clicking and press the login button. Granted, most users would probably pick the minimum length, but a user concerned about security could build a longer password. If k bits of security are assumed per image used, then for a password using c images, the security would be $c * k$.

Adjusting the image and tolerance sizes. A simple way of enlarging the password space is to use larger images or reduce the tolerance. Both have the effect of adding squares to the grids. Tolerance cannot be reduced past a certain threshold because it becomes impossible for users to enter their passwords. Results of this and our earlier study [3] however indicate that it may be possible to reduce tolerance more than was originally believed [19] (at least on full-sized monitors) since users were very accurate in targeting their click-points. For example, with images of size 451x331 as used in these studies, there are approximately 400 19x19 pixel grid squares, giving $2^{8.6}$ squares per image. If we reduced the tolerance squares to 9x9 pixels, this would increase to $2^{10.9}$ squares per image. With CCP, we can multiply by 5 for the number of images in the password sequence, increasing from 2^{43} to $2^{54.5}$ choices. Enlargement of the image is restricted by the size of the screen used. Increasing the size of the image may also make it more susceptible to shoulder-surfing. Zooming, which has been suggested elsewhere, including by Wiedenbeck et al. [20] for PassPoints, often has usability problems of its own, and thus we hesitate to propose it here.

Using a larger set of images. At minimum, the size of CCP's total image set should match the number of squares in a tolerance grid (i.e., 400 in our example system). This strategy would imply that the set of images in the system is re-used across users and at each stage in the password for each user.

In this case, if users make a mistake during login, there is a small chance that they accidentally see an image belonging somewhere else in their password sequence. They may realize the mistake immediately or subsequently when an unknown next-image appears. The possibility of such collisions can be reduced or eliminated if the number of images is increased to reduce the overlap between password stages. However, depending on implementation details, this could imply that the entire sequence could be deduced from knowing only the last image in a password as discussed below.

As suggested earlier, it is possible to have a larger set of images in the system and to use a subset for each user. Additionally, the subset for each user may also hold extra images so that not every image is re-used at each stage. This can reduce the possibility of collisions during incorrect login. It also increases the amount of work required by attackers to identify images and determine hotspots as this work increases proportionally with the number of images used in the system. If attackers are using a brute-force attack where a dictionary is built from all possible combinations of images and click-points, then this also forces a larger dictionary of size $totalImages * totalGridSquares * totalClicks$. In comparison, with PassPoints only one image needs to be analyzed per user and this image is accessible by simply knowing the username.

If attackers know the image-mapping function f and the set of images used, then having more images has no effect on the password space beyond requiring more processing time to determine hotspots. However, even if attackers know f, collecting the set of images still poses a challenge because they must either have insider access to the system or they must discover the images one at a time by selecting different click-points during login attempts on the particular account. This can prove time-consuming since the number of unsuccessful login attempts allowed on a particular account can be restricted (e.g., see [17]). When both f and the image set are known, the password space is determined by the number of paths through the image-map tree (generated by f), based on the number of squares in the tolerance grid, not the number of images available. If a dictionary was built containing all paths through the tree, the number of entries would be the same (2^{43} for grids containing 400 squares and 5 clicks) regardless of the number of images used (although the entries would be different).

In cases where attackers know f and the set of images used, as well as one or more images in the password (gathered through shoulder-surfing or malware installed on the client machine), then having a very large set of images for a given user actually reduces the attacker's search space (although the amount of work required for hotspot analysis is still increased). Since not all images will be used within each image-map, attackers can use this information to eliminate branches of the image-map tree that do not contain the known image at the correct stage. At the extreme case where there are no duplicate images, then knowing the last image of a sequence would identify a unique path through the tree and reveal the password. Conversely, when all images are re-used at each stage then no branches can be eliminated and knowing the last image will not result in a unique path.

Another alternative for increasing the number of images available is to use larger images but crop them differently for each user. This would complicate hotspot analysis for attackers because the coordinates of hotspots determined for one account could not be applied directly to other accounts.

8   Conclusions and Future Work

The proposed Cued Click Points scheme shows promise as a usable and memorable authentication mechanism. By taking advantage of users' ability to recognize images and the memory trigger associated with seeing a new image, CCP has advantages over PassPoints in terms of usability. Being cued as each image is shown and having to remember only one click-point per image appears easier than having to remember an ordered series of clicks on one image. In our small comparison group, users strongly preferred CCP.

We believe that CCP offers a more secure alternative to PassPoints. CCP increases the workload for attackers by forcing them to first acquire image sets for each user, and then conduct hotspot analysis on each of these images. Furthermore, the system's flexibility to increase the overall number of images in the system allows us to arbitrarily increase this workload.

Future work should include a thorough assessment of the viability of CCP as an authentication mechanism, including a long term study of how these passwords work in practice and whether longer CCP passwords would be usable. The security of CCP also deserves closer examination, and should address how attackers might exploit the emergence of hotspots.

Acknowledgements. We thank the participants of our lab study and the reviewers for their valuable feedback. The first and third authors are supported in part by the "Legal and Policy Approaches to Identity Theft" project funded by ORNEC. The second author acknowledges NSERC for funding his Discovery Grant and his Canada Research Chair in Network and Software Security.

References

1. Birget, J.C., Hong, D., Memon, N.: Graphical Passwords Based on Robust Discretization. IEEE Trans. Info. Forensics and Security 1(3) (September 2006)
2. Blonder, G.E.: Graphical Passwords. United States Patent 5,559,961 (1996)
3. Chiasson, S., Biddle, R.R., van Oorschot, P.C.: A Second Look at the Usability of Click-based Graphical Passwords. ACM SOUPS (2007)
4. Cranor, L.F., Garfinkel, S.: Security and Usability. O'Reilly Media (2005)
5. Davis, D., Monrose, F., Reiter, M.K.: On User Choice in Graphical Password Schemes. In: 13th USENIX Security Symposium (2004)
6. Dirik, A.E., Menon, N., Birget, J.C.: Modeling user choice in the PassPoints graphical password scheme. ACM SOUPS (2007)
7. Jermyn, I., Mayer, A., Monrose, F., Reiter, M.K., Rubin, A.D.: The Design and Analysis of Graphical Passwords. In: 8th USENIX Security Symposium (1999)
8. Nelson, D.L., Reed, U.S., Walling, J.R.: Picture Superiority Effect. Journal of Experimental Psychology: Human Learning and Memory 3, 485–497 (1977)
9. Passfaces (last accessed: December 1, 2006), http://www.realuser.com
10. Peters, M.: Revised Vandenberg & Kuse Mental Rotations Tests: forms MRT-A to MRT-D. Technical Report, Department of Psychology, University of Guelph (1995)
11. Pinkas, B., Sander, T.: Securing Passwords Against Dictionary Attacks. ACM CCS (2002)
12. Renaud, K.: Evaluating Authentication Mechanisms. In: [4], ch. 6
13. Renaud, K., De Angeli, A.: My password is here! An investigation into visio-spatial authentication mechanisms. Interacting with Computers 16, 1017–1041 (2004)
14. Suo, X., Zhu, Y., Owen, G.S.: Graphical Passwords: A Survey. In: Annual Computer Security Applications Conference (2005)
15. Tari, F., Ozok, A.A., Holden, S.H.: A Comparison of Perceived and Real Shoulder-surfing Risks between Alphanumeric and Graphical Passwords. ACM SOUPS (2006)
16. Thorpe, J., van Oorschot, P.C.: Human-Seeded Attacks and Exploiting Hot-Spots in Graphical Passwords. In: 16th USENIX Security Symposium (2007)
17. van Oorschot, P.C., Stubblebine, S.: On Countering Online Dictionary Attacks with Login Histories and Humans-in-the-Loop. ACM Trans. Information and System Security 9(3), 235–258 (2006)
18. Weinshall, D.: Cognitive Authentication Schemes Safe Against Spyware (Short Paper). In: IEEE Symposium on Security and Privacy (2006)
19. Wiedenbeck, S., Birget, J.C., Brodskiy, A., Memon, N.: Authentication Using Graphical Passwords: Effects of Tolerance and Image Choice. ACM SOUPS (2005)
20. Wiedenbeck, S., Waters, J., Birget, J.C., Brodskiy, A., Memon, N.: PassPoints: Design and longitudinal evaluation of a graphical password system. International Journal of Human-Computer Studies 63, 102–127 (2005)
21. Yan, J., Blackwell, A., Anderson, R., Grant, A.: Password Memorability and Security: Empirical Results. IEEE Security & Privacy Magazine 2(5) (2004)

Obligations and Their Interaction with Programs

Daniel J. Dougherty[1], Kathi Fisler[1], and Shriram Krishnamurthi[2]

[1] Department of Computer Science, WPI
{dd,kfisler}@cs.wpi.edu
[2] Computer Science Department, Brown University
sk@cs.brown.edu

Abstract. Obligations are pervasive in modern systems, often linked to access control decisions. We present a very general model of obligations as objects with state, and discuss its interaction with a program's execution. We describe several analyses that the model enables, both static (for verification) and dynamic (for monitoring). This includes a systematic approach to approximating obligations for enforcement. We also discuss some extensions that would enable practical policy notations. Finally, we evaluate the robustness of our model against standard definitions from jurisprudence.

1 Introduction

Modern society recognizes a strong linkage between rights and responsibilities, or between privileges and corresponding obligations. This connection between rights and obligations carries over to computer systems also: when a system is given the right to perform a certain action, there is often a corresponding obligation on the system's subsequent behavior. For instance, when a system is permitted to access a particular resource, such as a file descriptor, the obligation may vary from having to return that resource, not over-use that resource, or not share that resource. In fact, in computer systems, the mere *attempt* to obtain a right may incur an obligation: for instance, when a password-guarded access is denied, the system may be obliged to log the denial.

This connection between rights and obligations ought to be reflected in our descriptions of access-control policies. A popular modern access control language such as XACML [1] (and similarly, EPAL [2]) repeatedly associates obligations with decisions and provides a syntactic element for specifying them, but then says,

> There are no standard definitions for these actions in version 2.0 of XACML. (<Obligations>) elements are returned to the PEP [policy enforcement point] for enforcement.

and provides little further information on the structure or interpretation of obligations.

This paper contributes in three respects: by providing a rich model of obligations; by linking these to program actions; and by defining how to perform verification and monitoring of the resulting systems. Our model is unique in several ways: obligations are stateful entities, reflecting the fact that they can change over time; obligations are linked to program actions while still permitting separate expression of policy from program; and the model is abstract enough to encompass a tremendous variety of obligations,

J. Biskup and J. Lopez (Eds.): ESORICS 2007, LNCS 4734, pp. 375–389, 2007.

which we demonstrate by employing the taxonomy of a standard American legal reference, Black's Law Dictionary [3].

2 Motivating Examples

Obligations impose many kinds of constraints. Some of these constraints are positive (that a person repay a loan; once a file is read, subsequent messages must be encrypted), while others are negative (that companies not sell email addresses to third parties; once a file is read, no messages can be sent). Some require a single action in bounded time (return a library book within 3 weeks), while others require repeated behaviors (renew a subscription annually). Some carry penalties for violation (interest on late payments), while others bear no repercussion (failing to acknowledge a closed bug report). The following examples are representative of the constraints in realistic systems:

Example 1 (*File check-out and return*). A code versioning tool restricts which developers may check out critical files. Furthermore, at most one developer can have write permission for a critical file at any time. When a developer is given access to a file, she is obligated to eventually check the file back in.

Example 2 (*Logging following access denial*). When a user attempts to access a document for which he lacks the required credentials, every subsequent attempt to access documents by that user must be logged.

Example 3 (*Delegation in a bug tracker*). In a bug-tracking system for a software company, users submit bug reports online. An employee scans each report and delegates responsibility for handling the bug to an appropriate developer. As developers work on bugs, they in turn may delegate the handling to other developers. Each developer is obligated to eventually close every bug report they are assigned to that is not awaiting additional input from some user.

Example 4 (*Incremental payment*). An online store allows customers to accumulate balances in their accounts and pay them off incrementally. Purchasing an item obligates the buyer to pay the seller the purchase price.

A viable model of obligations should capture and support reasoning about all of these examples, yet no prior model does. Example 1 is generally supported, but rarely the others. Example 2 arises on a denied, rather than permitted action. Examples 3 and 4 require obligations to have state. Section 7 provides more detail in evaluating related work using these criteria.

3 Foundational Model

Obligations arise in response to user or program actions. In our model we will assume that actions triggering obligations are governed by access-control policies, though this assumption can be relaxed with only minimal changes to our formalism. We treat obligations as constraints on future behavior, and do not address provisions (constraints on current or past behaviors) except insofar as these are used in access control. We describe our model of systems and obligations abstractly, to accommodate a wide variety of concrete implementations.

We represent program executions by infinite sequences π of state/action pairs, or *paths*:

$$\pi = (s_0, a_0), (s_1, a_1), \ldots$$

Let $\Pi_{States,Actions}$ denote the set of paths over *States* and *Actions*; we will suppress the subscript on Π when *States* and *Actions* are clear from context. In the abstract model, the precise nature of the sets *States* of states and *Actions* of actions is irrelevant; in particular we are not assuming a finite-state framework. In order to represent the fact that obligations are conferred upon, and by, different *agents* in a system, we assume that each action is associated with an agent, or with several agents acting concurrently.

A *system* S is a set of paths. If $\rho \in S$ we say that ρ is a *run* of S. In the usual way we can model terminating runs by incorporating a halting state which transitions only to itself.

3.1 Policies

Obligations arise most frequently as an aspect of a rich notion of access control: "permissions with strings attached," in Minsky and Lockman's phrase [4]. Our conception of pure access control is standard: in a given state a policy evaluates a request to perform an action and returns a decision (possible decisions generally include Permit and Deny). We make no assumptions about the language in which policy rules are expressed.

Since our interest in this paper is in access-control policies enriched with a notion of obligations, henceforth the term *policy* will refer the following notion.

Definition 1. A *policy* for a system S is a tuple $(Decs, Obls, P, \gamma)$, where

- *Decs* is a set of access decisions,
- *Obls* is a set of *obligations*,
- $P : States \times Actions \rightarrow Decs \times 2^{Obls}$, and
- $\gamma : Obls \rightarrow 2^{\Pi}$.

P determines the access control decision and defines the obligations that arise at each state-action pair. If Ω is an obligation, $\gamma(\Omega)$ is the set of paths which satisfy Ω; we say that this set of paths is the *obligation condition* for Ω. For brevity we will often simply use P to refer to the policy. A system together with a policy determine a *policy-informed program* [5]. This definition does not stipulate how the program handles denials, but is flexible enough to permit the pruning of such paths from the obligation condition.

Consider Example 1 from Section 2. Assume the system maintains information about availability and credentials in relations *Available(f)* and *MayEdit(d,f)*, where f and d denote files and developers, respectively. Let states of the system be sets of facts (closed atomic formulas) over these relations. Assume the system recognizes actions *RequestEdit(d,f)* and *CheckIn(d,f)* to denote that developers want to check out and return files, respectively. The following policy elements formally capture this scenario:

- *Obls* contains one obligation $O_{d,f}$ for each developer d and file f.
- $P(s, RequestEdit(d,f)) = \langle \text{Permit}, \{O_{d,f}\} \rangle$ if *Available(f)* and *MayEdit(d,f)* are both true in s, otherwise $P(s, RequestEdit(d,f)) = \langle \text{Deny}, \emptyset \rangle$.
- $\gamma(O_{d,f}) = $ the set of all paths that contain (at some stage) action *CheckIn(d,f)*.

As obligations specify behavior that a system may or may not respect, we introduce terminology for various relationships between systems and the obligations arising from policies.

Definition 2. If $\pi = (s_0, a_0), (s_1, a_1), \ldots$ is a path and P is a policy, we say that obligation Ω is *created* at stage $i > 0$ of π if $\Omega \in P(s_{i-1}, a_{i-1})$; in this case π *satisfies* Ω if the path $(s_i, a_i), (s_{i+1}, a_{i+1}), \ldots$ is in $\gamma(\Omega)$. The path π *obeys the policy* P if it satisfies each obligation created at each stage of the path. A system obeys a policy P if each of its runs obeys P.

These definitions treat obligations as constraints on entire paths. As such it does not, in general, make sense to speak about them being true or false at a specific state of a computation. But we do note that sometimes it makes intuitive sense to speak of an obligation being discharged at a certain time (e.g., making a log entry) or being violated at a certain time (e.g., publishing a file in violation of a privacy policy). This can be captured formally as follows.

Definition 3. Let S be a system, let $\rho = (s_0, a_0), (s_1, a_1), \ldots$ be a run of S, and let Ω be an obligation created at stage i of ρ. The obligation Ω is *discharged* at a stage $n \geq i$ of π if every run of S with prefix $(s_0, a_0), \ldots, (s_n, a_n)$ satisfies Ω. The obligation Ω is *violated* at stage $n \geq i$ of ρ if no run of S with prefix $(s_0, a_0), \ldots, (s_n, a_n)$ satisfies Ω.

According to the standard taxonomy of system properties defined in Alpern and Schneider [6] an obligation is violable if and only if its condition is a *safety condition*; it is easy to see that an obligation is dischargeable if and only if the negation of its condition is a safety condition; following Manna and Pnueli [7] we refer to these as *guarantee conditions*. (What Manna and Pnueli term an "obligation", however, is merely a boolean combination of safety and guarantee conditions.)

It is often useful to be able to *monitor* a system for policy compliance, especially when dealing with black-box components or those running on untrusted platforms. It is precisely the safety obligations that, in principle, can be the target of runtime monitoring. In Section 5 we consider the problems of detecting whether an obligation is a safety or guarantee obligation, and if not, how to compute an appropriate "best approximation."

3.2   Aren't Obligations Just Fairness Properties?

Our view of obligations as constraining future execution behaviors (paths) of a system suggests a theoretical connection between obligations and the notion of fairness. We cannot, however, reduce obligations to fairness for a few reasons. For one, fairness is a static and global property of a system's execution (usually of the environment), whereas obligations arise dynamically based on actions. This marks obligations as a special class of progress properties. More subtly, fairness is treated as an *assumption* (which may be verified) so that, for instance, a verifier excludes unfair paths; in contrast, while obligations *should* be met, systems expect them to be violated and seek compensation. Video rental stores, for example, oblige customers to return videos by a deadline, but a priori specify late fees because they expect some customers to violate the obligation (and benefit financially from their doing so!).

3.3 Path Specifications

In fact, our formal model has avoided fixing any particular language for paths at all. Instead, it allows any specification of paths for describing conditions; standard languages for paths, such as automata and temporal logic, seem natural concrete choices. If we do choose to use temporal logic, the set of obligations that arise in practice suggest that a minimal set of operators for capturing conditions should include those of LTL, including both the strong and weak variants of the until operator, as well as the unless operator (the dual of until). Example 1 of Section 2 is naturally specified using the "eventually" operator of LTL, while Example 2 clearly requires the "globally" operator.

The application at hand may require that actions of particular agents lead to obligations being fulfilled. See Example 3. LTL is not rich enough to capture the nuances of having several agents, but temporal logics such as ATL* [8] do offer such capabilities. Situations such as Example 4 require something more than propositional temporal logics; this will be explored in detail in the next section.

Finally, many obligations involve bounded time, or intervals of time. Examples include requiring someone to pay by a particular time, or to reverify contact information on an annual basis. While LTL can express such constraints using the next-state operator, such specifications are often clumsy. Other logics [9] provide more nuanced handling of time constraints; the choice of language for describing time is closely tied to to the choice of program model.

The main point of this discussion is to highlight the range of path specification languages that may be useful in devising a concrete language for obligations. We strongly believe that a useful theoretical treatment of obligations should be independent of, or at least parameterized over, the program models and path specifications that arise in particular applications.

4 Obligations Have State

Many interesting notions of obligation go beyond requiring that a single action be taken (or forbidden). This leads us to confront some subtle issues concerning modeling the interaction of policies and programs. Consider Example 4. Suppose A buys an item from B for 10 dollars. Describing the obligation condition as a payment action for 10 dollars isn't right, because debt can be paid in installments. Therefore, tracking the obligation may require maintaining state. In addition to enabling obligations to track state, we should also permit policy authors to use a different vocabulary than that of the program's internal data structures (for instance, the obligation may be in terms of what is owed, while the program only tracks what has been paid).

To make this precise we now settle on some notation for describing program states and the structure of individual obligations. First we tackle the problem of distinct vocabularies. By a *signature* Σ we mean a graded set of relation symbols and constants; we let Facts$_\Sigma$ denote the set of all closed atomic formulas over such a signature. We assume that states of a system are Herbrand structures over signatures; so states are subsets of the set Facts$_{\Sigma_S}$ of all facts over signature Σ_S. Other recent works have employed similar models of software as transition systems over relational facts [10,11].

The policy author works over a different relational signature Σ_O of the terms that capture the state of an obligation. States in policy-informed programs are comprised of facts over $\Sigma_S \cup \Sigma_O$; let $States^{Ob}$ denote the set of all such states.

We can now model the *state* associated with each obligation as follows.

Definition 4. An *obligation state* over Σ_O for a system over $States$ and $Actions$ is a tuple containing at least two fields: (1) a representation of a set of paths in $\Pi_{States^{Ob},Actions}$ (capturing the condition) and (2) a subset of $Facts_O$. The set of all such states is denoted *ObStates*.

The "at least" in this definition allows a particular policy language to store additional information with an obligation. Section 6 gives examples of such extensions that arise in practice.

When a policy author defines Σ_O in order to express obligations, she also needs to specify how the obligation state evolves based on system states and actions. This is given in the form of a function.

Definition 5. An *update function* for Σ_O, $States$ and $Actions$ is a function U of type $States \times Actions \times Facts_O \rightarrow Facts_O$. U^{Ob} denotes this function lifted to $States \times Actions \times ObStates \rightarrow ObStates$ by applying U to each element of $Facts_O$ in an $ObStates$.

Consider Example 4 again. Let $Pay(A,B,n)$ be a program action denoting A paying n dollars to B, and $Owes(A,B,x)$ denote the internal state of the obligation that records the current debt. The update function is the natural one: most actions leave the balance unaltered, but an action $Pay(A,B,y)$ transforms the state of the debt to $Owes(A,B,(x-y))$.

Example 3 regarding delegation also highlights the importance of state in obligations. The state of the obligation associated with a bug would include a field for the agent currently responsible for the obligation. This field can be written by the update function in response to a system action corresponding to delegation of responsibility for the bug. Section 6 discusses why creating separate obligations on each delegation is not necessarily an appropriate alternative to capturing state.

Having refined what it means to be an obligation, we must now refine what it means for a path to satisfy an obligation (thereby refining Definition 2). We first define a function U^* that maps paths over $(States \times Actions)$ to paths over $(States^{Ob} \times Actions)$ as follows.

Definition 6. Let U be an update function, and let β_0 be a subset of $Facts_O$. When π is a path over $(States \times Actions)$, the path $U^*(\pi, \beta_0)$ is the path whose actions are the same as that of π and whose states are given by

$$s_0^* = (s_0, \beta_0)$$
$$s_{n+1}^* = (s_{n+1}, U(s_n, a_n))$$

Definition 7. Let Ω be an obligation with condition ϕ and initial set of Σ_O facts β_0. Then Ω is satisfied in a path π over Σ_S if and only if $U^*(\pi, \beta_0)$ satisfies ϕ.

5   Static Analysis and Monitoring of Obligations

We now discuss two styles of analyses, one static and the other dynamic.

5.1 Automata-Theoretic Static Analyses

Having provided a basic model of obligations, we now turn to some analyses we might want to perform.

1. Does a certain run of the system satisfy a given obligation Ω?
2. Does there exist a run of the system in which Ω is satisfied?
3. At a particular state in a run, has obligation Ω been discharged or violated?
4. Does a given model of a policy-informed program satisfy all of its obligations? (This is useful as different models of the same system and its environment may satisfy different obligations.)
5. For a given system condition ϕ, is ϕ satisfied by all runs of the system that satisfy their obligations?
6. When does one obligation imply another in the context of the given system? Are two given obligations contradictory? Does one obligations policy entail another in an absolute sense? Does one obligations policy entail another in the context of the given system?

In this section we assume a finite-state representation of programs and policies. In particular we assume that for a given policy P the set *Obls* of obligations is finite. We further assume that the obligations in question do not involve different agents in any essential way. The generalization of the automata-based techniques [12] of this section to the multi-agent setting is a topic of future work.

In this setting the essential strategy for answering questions such as those above is to capture obligations by automata. In this section we show in Corollary 9 that for each obligation Ω we can construct a Büchi automaton $\mathcal{A}_\Omega$ that accepts precisely those paths that satisfy Ω. In Theorem 10 we show how to combine such automata for the individual obligations to build a Büchi automaton $\mathcal{A}_P$ that accepts precisely those paths that satisfy (all of the obligations in) policy P.

Now suppose that the set of runs of the system S is given by a Büchi automaton $\mathcal{A}_S$. If we then take the cross product of $\mathcal{A}_S$ with $\mathcal{A}_\Omega$ then the resulting automaton accepts precisely the system runs that satisfy Ω. Questions such as 1, 2, and 3 can then be answered using standard algorithms over Büchi automata. If we instead take the cross product of $\mathcal{A}_S$ with $\mathcal{A}_P$ we can address questions such as 4 and 5. Questions such as 6 are equivalent to questions of language containment for Büchi automata, for which algorithms are well-known [13].

The rest of this section develops these ideas formally.

Definitions. A Büchi automaton is a tuple $\mathcal{A} = (\Sigma, Q, Q_0, \Delta, F)$ where Q is a finite set of states, $Q_0 \subseteq Q$ is a set of initial *states*, Σ is a input alphabet, $\Delta \subseteq Q \times \Sigma \times Q$ is a *transition relation*, and $F \subseteq Q$ is the set of *fair states*. A *run* of $\mathcal{A}$ on an infinite word $\alpha \in \Sigma^\omega$ is an infinite sequence r of states from Q such that $r(0) \in Q_0$ and $(r(i), \alpha(i), r(i+1)) \in \Delta$ for all $i \geq 0$. Such a run is *accepting* if $r(i) \in F$ for infinitely many i. The word α is accepted by $\mathcal{A}$ if there is an accepting run of $\mathcal{A}$ on α.

Let Φ_O abbreviate $|\text{Facts}_O|$, the number of facts over the signature Σ_O.

Proposition 8. *Let $\mathcal{A}$ be a Büchi automaton over $2^{\text{Facts}_S \cup \text{Facts}_O}$; let β_0 be a set of Σ_O facts. Then there is a Büchi automaton $\mathcal{A}_*$ over 2^{Facts_S} such that for every path π over (States $\times$ Actions)*

$$\mathcal{A}_* \text{ accepts } \pi \text{ if and only if } \mathcal{A} \text{ accepts } U^*(\pi, \beta_0)$$

The size of $\mathcal{A}_*$ is $|\mathcal{A}| \cdot 2^{\Phi_O}$.

Proof. This is an instance of a general construction, which will be easier to outline in a more abstract setting.

Let Σ_A and Σ_B be alphabets, and suppose $u : \Sigma_A \to \Sigma_B$. Then from any ω-sequence $\alpha = a_0, a_1, \ldots$ over Σ_A and initial element b_0 from Σ_B we can build an ω-sequence $u^*(\alpha, b_0)$ over $\Sigma_A \times \Sigma_B$: $(a_0, b_0), (a_1, b_1) \ldots$ where each b_{i+1} is $u(a_i)$.

It will suffice to show in this setting that given a Büchi automaton $\mathcal{A}$ over $\Sigma_A \times \Sigma_B$ we can build a Büchi automaton $\mathcal{A}_*$ over Σ_A such that for every sequence such as α above,

$$\mathcal{A}_* \text{ accepts } \alpha \text{ if and only if } \mathcal{A} \text{ accepts } u^*(\alpha, b_0)$$

since we may take Σ_A to be 2^{Facts_S}, Σ_B to be 2^{Facts_O} (note that $2^{\text{Facts}_S \cup \text{Facts}_O}$ is naturally isomorphic to $2^{\text{Facts}_S} \times 2^{\text{Facts}_O}$), b_0 to be β_0 and u to be U^*.

Let $\mathcal{A}$ be $((\Sigma_A \times \Sigma_B), Q, Q_0, \Delta, F)$. Define $\mathcal{A}_*$ to be $(\Sigma_A, (Q \times \Sigma_B), (Q_0 \times \{\beta_0\}), \Delta_*, (F \times \Sigma_B))$ where Δ_* is defined by

$$\Delta_*((s, b), a) = (\Delta(s, (a, b)), u(a))$$

To see that this works, consider a sequence α and let r be any run of $\mathcal{A}_*$ on α, $r = (s_0, b_0), (s_1, b_1), \ldots$. First note that each b_{i+1} is precisely $u(a_i)$. It is then easy to see that the sequence $s_0, s_1, \ldots$ obtained by taking the first component of each pair in r is a run of $\mathcal{A}$ on $u^*(\alpha, b_0)$, and furthermore all such $\mathcal{A}$-runs can be obtained in this way. This establishes the desired relation between $\mathcal{A}_*$ and $\mathcal{A}$.

Corollary 9. *Let Ω be an obligation for system S whose condition is expressed as a temporal logic formula of size $|\Omega|$. We can build a Büchi automaton $\mathcal{A}_\Omega$ accepting precisely those paths $\pi \in 2^\Pi$ that satisfy Ω. The size of $\mathcal{A}_\Omega$ is bounded by $2^{|\Omega| + \Phi_O}$.*

Proof. Let $\mathcal{A}$ be a Büchi automaton over $2^{\text{Facts}_S \cup \text{Facts}_O}$ corresponding to the obligation condition for Ω, and let β_0 be the initial Facts_O facts for Ω. As is well-known, the size of $\mathcal{A}$ is bounded by $2^{|\Omega|}$. The automaton $\mathcal{A}_*$ constructed as in Proposition 8 is of size $2^{|\Omega|} \cdot 2^{\Phi_O} = 2^{|\Omega| + \Phi_O}$ and accepts those paths π such that $\mathcal{A}$ accepts $U^*(\pi, \beta_0)$. By Definition 7 these are the paths that satisfy the condition for Ω, so we may take $\mathcal{A}_\Omega$ to be $\mathcal{A}_*$.

Note that the factor of 2^{Φ_O} above is a generous bound: the actual set of Σ_O facts arising in the states of $\mathcal{A}_*$ is the set of facts which can arise in a sequence of U-updates to the initial Σ_O facts in the obligation Ω.

It is not surprising that a given obligation can be represented as an automaton. Each of the infinitely many paths through a system, though, induces its own sequence of obligations to be fulfilled. Hence, it is perhaps surprising that these obligation automata can be combined into a single finite-state automaton for the whole system.

Theorem 10. *Let P be a policy for system S. We can build a Büchi automaton $\mathcal{A}_P$ accepting precisely those paths $\pi \in 2^\Pi$ that satisfy P.*

Proof. Given $\mathcal{A}_\Omega$, define the automaton $\mathcal{A}'_\Omega$ which, intuitively, "sleeps" until a system transition is taken that creates the obligation Ω. Formally, we construct $\mathcal{A}'_\Omega$ by starting with $\mathcal{A}_\Omega$ and adding a new state q_0 to $\mathcal{A}_\Omega$, which will serve as the sole initial state. The transition relation Δ' is the extension of the transition function Δ of $\mathcal{A}_\Omega$ defined as follows.

For each pair (s, a):

- Add $\{(q_0, (s, a), q_0)\}$ to Δ';
- if obligation Ω arises due to action a out of s, that is, if $\Omega \in P(s, a)$, then add $\{(q_0, (s, a), r) \mid r$ was an initial state of $\mathcal{A}_\Omega\}$ to Δ'.

The automaton $\mathcal{A}_P$ is the product $\prod\{\mathcal{A}'_\Omega \mid \Omega \in Obls\}$.

5.2 Dynamic Monitoring of Safety and Guarantee Obligations

We have seen that a violable obligation is one whose condition is a safety condition, and a dischargeable obligation is one whose condition is a guarantee condition. Under the natural topology on the set $\Pi_{States, Actions}$ of all paths of a system the safety conditions are precisely the closed sets and the liveness conditions are precisely the open sets [6].

The previous notions generalize immediately to the set of runs of a system S: we simply take the subspace topology. In this way we may define the notion of S-*safety condition* and S-*guarantee* condition. A set of paths might define a safety condition (for example) relative to a system even if it fails to be a safety condition in the absolute sense. This yields the appropriate notions of safety and guarantee relevant to obligations being discharged or to be violated in a system. In general, obligations that forbid some action are S-safety conditions, while obligations that demand some action eventually are S-guarantee conditions. Any obligation with a deadline is both S-safety and S-guarantee. Some obligations are neither: the canonical examples are LTL "until" conditions.

Suppose that S is finite-branching, that is, for every state s there are only finitely many pairs of the form (s, a) that can arise in the system. By an easy application of Kőnig's Lemma, if P is both an S-safety and an S-guarantee and S is finite-branching then Ω has a "deadline". That is, there is a single i such that for every run ρ of S, Ω is either discharged or violated before stage i.

Approximating Obligations for Monitoring. When a policy cannot be monitored precisely (such as one that is neither safety nor guarantee) and must be approximated, it is valuable to construct a "best" approximation.

Definition 11. Let P be any condition. The S-*safety closure* $\widehat{P}$ of P is the intersection of all S-safety conditions containing P. The S-*interior* P^o of P is the union of all S-guarantee conditions contained in P.

The S-safety closure of a condition is a safety condition: it is closed just because closed sets are closed under intersection. Clearly $\widehat{P}$ is the smallest S-safety condition containing P. Of course, when P is a S-safety condition, $\widehat{P} = P$. Similarly, the S-interior P^o of a condition is the largest S-guarantee condition contained in P.

Given an arbitrary $\mathcal{P}$, the monitoring system can monitor the S-safety condition $\widehat{\mathcal{P}}$. If a run fails $\widehat{\mathcal{P}}$ it certainly fails $\mathcal{P}$ and, by definition, $\widehat{\mathcal{P}}$ is the smallest condition which can be used to soundly check $\mathcal{P}$-failure. By an analogous argument we may view $\mathcal{P}^o$ as the best dischargeable approximation to $\mathcal{P}$: if a run satisfies $\mathcal{P}^o$ then it is guaranteed to satisfy $\mathcal{P}$, and $\mathcal{P}^o$ is the largest S-guarantee condition with this property.

Computing the Approximations. Alpern and Schneider [14] characterized the Büchi automata that accept safety properties. It is easy to see from their analysis how to construct, from a given automaton $\mathcal{A}$, an automaton accepting the closure of the language of $\mathcal{A}$. So to generate an automaton characterizing the S-safety closure of an obligation Ω, construct $\mathcal{A}_\Omega$ as in Section 5.1 and compute its closure. Complementation yields an algorithm for S-guarantee approximation.

6   Evaluation: Modeling Black's

The American legal community has a well-developed taxonomy of obligations in their standard reference, Black's Law Dictionary [3, pages 1104-5]. It is therefore useful to consider how many of Black's obligation types can be captured in the framework we have defined.

Black's describes 30 distinct types of obligations (plus several synonyms and one, correal, that combines other types). Two of these (moral and natural) discuss concepts that lie outside the scope of computing systems. Four (contractual, conventional, obediential, and statutory) capture the source or rationale for introducing an obligation. Some models of programs and their environments could include sufficient information to capture these variations, while others do not. We therefore do not consider these in our analysis, but the data structure for obligations in our model could hold the information needed to distinguish these forms given sufficient program models. The rest fall into 21 classes that have different implications for a model of obligations, including how they arise and evolve. Figure 1 describes these classes and their implications for modeling.

The model that we have presented supports all but two of the Black's classes once obligation states are taken to be arbitrary data structures. Divisible obligations are not supported, as we assume a single obligation condition. Substitute obligations could be encoded, but are not supported naturally. Natural support would require the update function to be able to change the condition, which is beyond the scope of the current model (due to the type of the update function). While defining such an update function is easy, defining the semantics of satisfying obligations in this context is harder. Assume that conditions were expressed as temporal logic formulas; our definition of satisfaction requires each condition to hold from the state at which it was created. If the condition could change before being satisfied, the formula would have to be rewritten to capture a statement roughly corresponding to "the specified formula holds unless the conditions occur to change the condition". One could encode a substitute obligation by writing such a condition formula at the outset, but an explicit specification through the update function would be clearer, and we believe preferable.

The Black's classes illustrate that the structure of obligations is both subtle and important. Consider an obligation of the form "do A; otherwise do B and C". This

Category	Description	Requires
absolute	condition must be discharged as originally stated, with no modification	update function cannot modify agents or condition
accessory	incidental to another obligation	link obligations in data structure
alternative	obliged may satisfy one of several conditions	data structure with multiple conditions or disjunction in condition formulas
bifactoral, joint, community, solidary	multiple obligated or obligating agents party to a single condition	data structure with multiple obligated or obligating agents
conditional	arises from an event that might not occur	conditions in creation rules
conjunctive	multiple conditions required which may be enforced separately	data structure with multiple conditions; conjunction in formulas insufficient as sub-obligations have separate identity
current	currently enforceable but not past due	recognize when obligation is created
determinate	condition refers to objects by identity	object identity in condition language
divisible	can be divided into parts (without the consent of the parties)	ability to change condition and to associate different subconditions with different obligated agents
heritable	successor of obligated may become liable	ability to update agents
indeterminate	condition refers to objects by attribute	object attributes in condition language
perfect	legally enforceable and binding	"strong" interpretation of condition, capturable in formulas
personal	obligated must personally fulfill obligation	notion of which agents act to fulfill obligations (e.g., as expressed in ATL*)
primary	arises from essential purpose of an action	nothing
primitive	must be satisfied before some others	capture ordering on obligations and refer to order during analysis
pure	enforceable and past due	detecting when obligations are created, satisfied, discharged and violated
secondary	incident to a primary obligation or compensates for other unsatisfied obligation	link obligations in data structure; creation policy checks other obligations' status
several	different conditions required for different agents (obligated or obligating)	data structure groups obligations
simple	arises unconditionally	creation rules without conditions
single	no penalty for non-fulfillment	"weak" interpretation of condition, capturable in formulas
substitute	replaces another, extinguished, obligation	ability to delete obligations and to tie creation to status of other obligations

Fig. 1. Classes of obligations in Black's and their implications for a comprehensive model

is a default obligation with a conjunctive obligation in its secondary clause. Because of such conditions, we cannot rely on just the conjunction of top-level obligations to capture all the desired obligation structure. Identity is critical for understanding divisible obligations: the Black's description is ambiguous on whether the component obligations should have separate identities, but whether they do has implications for formal analysis of obligations. In either case, it is clear that our model needs to have a way to refer to an obligation as an identifiable entity, even as its condition potentially evolves. This justifies our model containing both a set of obligations (effectively naming individual obligations) and a separate association of obligation states with obligations.

7   Related Work

Deontic logic [15] is a formal system concerned with reasoning about obligations. Indeed, deontic logic has frequently been used to analyze the structure of normative reasoning in the law. Standard deontic logic is a modal logic, with a unary modality **ob**, so if ϕ is a formula then (**ob** ϕ) is a formula. Formulas are interpreted over Kripke structures, where states represent possible worlds. Permission is precisely the dual of obligation in this logic, so it is natural that several authors ([16,17,18] and others) have approached the interaction between authorization and obligations in computing systems from this perspective. The approach we pursue here is crucially different from the modal logic approach. Since we view obligations as expressing constraints on computations, it does not make sense to ask whether an obligation "holds" at a state.

Minsky and Lockman recognized the essential association of obligations with permissions some time ago [4]. Their informal syntax and semantics supports a rich taxonomy of obligations (including deadlines and both positive and negative obligations), but does not handle state. Mont's [19] rich taxonomy of privacy obligations for enterprises provides more detailed implementation requirements and state contents for obligations than ours, but lacks formal semantics and our theoretical treatment of analysis. Mont's model supports some features, such as compensatory actions and additional requirements on future actions, that are not cleanly expressible in our policy notations.

Irwin, Yu, and Winsborough [20] propose a formal model of obligations inspired by the idea that an obligation is a contract between a system and a subject. They define a notion of secure system state based the concept of *accountability* for violation of an obligation, and explore the complexity of checking accountability properties. Though there are many similarities between their approach and ours, we have a somewhat more general system model and a richer semantics of obligations.

Several works focus mainly on specifying, rather than analyzing, obligations. Park and Sandhu [21] view obligations as current or past conditions constraining access requests (resembling provisions [22]). Constraints on future behavior are limited to a predicate that must hold so long as the system retains access to an object. Our model divorces obligations from the lifetime of permissions, and can also associate them with denied requests. Sloman [23] distinguishes authorization (actions that may occur) from obligation (actions that must or must not occur). The Ponder policy language [24] views obligations as actions that must be executed when certain events occur, but these conditions do not support temporal operators. Kudo and Hada [25] fix a set of primitive obligations (such as logging) that happen when access is granted, but also fail to support temporal operators.

Some models support analysis of obligations policies outside the context of program models. Abrahams, et al.'s [26] model allows for obligations to not be satisfied, and can associate obligations with denials. Temporal constructs on obligations are implicit and limited to eventuality (for positive obligations) and globally (for negative obligations). Schaad and Moffett [27,28,29] explore interactions between agents in the context of obligations, addressing delegation, review and supervision, and revocation. They represent and analyze obligations using Alloy [30] but do not present a general formal semantics for them. Bettini, et al. [22] model access-control policies with both provisions and obligations. Their model, like ours, links obligations to policy rules and defines them using a separate signature of terms. It includes actions to be executed when an obligation is satisfied or fulfilled. They focus on a semantics for when obligations apply, but assume that atomic obligations are interpreted by a server, which they do not model. Backes, et al. [31] extend EPAL with a model of obligations and containment between them, and also assume a server for atomic obligations. This assumption makes monitoring possible at the expense of less expressive obligations (Section 5.2). Neither work accounts for the stateful nature of obligations, which this paper shows is extremely valuable for modeling numerous scenarios (and complicates the definition of obligations).

Work that explores obligations in the context of program models tends to focus on the impact of programs on obligations, whereas our more general model supports reasoning about the impact of obligations on programs. These works also fail to capture obligations with state. Hilty, Basin and Pretschner [32] explore the role of obligations for data providers, focusing on privacy and intellectual property management. They specify obligations using Distributed Temporal Logic (DTL) [33], which supports a rich notion of agents. They discuss a variety of strategies for enforcing non-monitorable obligations by weakening them; we have outlined a systematic approach for approximating obligations motivated by enforcement. May, et al. [34] model privacy policies with obligations using an extension of the classical access-control matrix. Their work explores the interactions of policies and programs, but not the implications of this interaction on the structure of obligations (as in our Section 4). Barth, et al. [35] model privacy policies as rules conditioned on both past and future behaviors and programs as sequences of events that transmit information. Unlike us, they assume agents cannot violate obligations.

8   Conclusion and Future Work

This paper has presented a model of obligations and their interaction with an ambient system. Obligations are viewed as a means for expressing constraints on the future behavior of a system, have state, and can fail to be fulfilled. The combination of these assumptions, the generality of our model, and our model of system-policy interaction distinguish our work from other treatments of obligations. The paper has demonstrated several useful analyses including a systematic means for approximating obligations for monitoring.

Although the paper has demonstrated that this model of obligations is quite rich, it cannot support some kinds of obligations that arise in practice, such as divisible and substitute obligations (see Section 6), and obligations that require new behavior (such as additional authentication checks) on every subsequent execution of a particular action [19]. The latter reflects a fundamental assumption in our model that the policy does not add, remove, or alter behaviors of the system. Relaxing this assumption is an important topic for future work.

Next, because obligations may not be fulfilled, it is natural to speak of compensatory actions (akin to those used in database transactions). While these can be encoded in the obligation conditions in our model, they enjoy no distinguished status and thus cannot be reasoned about directly. It could be useful to ask, for example, whether a system that fails some property in the presence of unfulfilled obligations will satisfy the property under a specific set of compensations, or to try to synthesize information about the compensations that could cover all unfulfilled obligations.

Further, the ability to decide various questions about obligations using automata theory points the way to a *logic of obligations*. This would offer a contrast to attempts to apply deontic logic to obligations.

Finally, we would like to support richer notions of agents and analyses that account for them. Section 3.3 raised the question of whether a particular agent could fulfill its obligations. It would also be interesting to try synthesizing minimal models of agents that guarantee satisfaction of their obligations. Both questions require closer attention to agent-aware logics like ATL* for specifying conditions and their corresponding models of system behavior.

Acknowledgments. We thank Dan Ignatoff and Felix Geller for their assistance on this project, and the anonymous reviewers for their helpful comments. This work is partially funded by NSF grant CNS-0627310. We commemorate the passing of Cupcake during the authoring of this paper.

References

1. Moses, T.: eXtensible Access Control Markup Language (XACML) version 1.0. Technical report, OASIS (February 2003)
2. Ashley, P., Hada, S., Karjoth, G., Powers, C., Schunter, M.: Enterprise privacy authorization language (EPAL 1.2), http://www.w3.org/Submission/EPAL/
3. Garner, B.A. (ed.): Black's Law Dictionary, 8th edn. Thomson-West Publishers (2004)
4. Minsky, N.H., Lockman, A.: Ensuring integrity by adding obligations to privileges. In: International Conference on Software Engineering, pp. 92–102 (1985)
5. Dougherty, D.J., Fisler, K., Krishnamurthi, S.: Specifying and reasoning about dynamic access-control policies. In: International Joint Conference on Automated Reasoning, pp. 632–646 (August 2006)
6. Alpern, B., Schneider, F.B.: Defining liveness. Information Processing Letters 21, 181–185 (1985)
7. Manna, Z., Pnueli, A.: The Temporal Logic of Reactive and Concurrent Systems. Springer, Heidelberg (1992)
8. Alur, R., Henzinger, T.A., Kupferman, O.: Alternating-time temporal logic. Journal of the ACM 49(5), 672–713 (2002)
9. Alur, R., Henzinger, T.A.: Logics and Models of Real-Time: A Survey. In: Real Time: Theory in Practice, pp. 74–106 (1991)

10. Deutsch, A., Sui, L., Vianu, V.: Specification and verification of data-driven web services. In: Principles of Database Systems, pp. 71–82 (2004)
11. Yahav, E., Reps, T., Sagiv, M., Wilhelm, R.: Verifying temporal heap properties specified via evolution logic. In: Degano, P. (ed.) ESOP 2003 and ETAPS 2003. LNCS, vol. 2618, pp. 204–222. Springer, Heidelberg (2003)
12. Vardi, M.Y.: Verification of concurrent programs: The automata-theoretic framework. Annals of Pure and Applied Logic 51(1-2), 79–98 (1991)
13. Clarke, E., Grumberg, O., Peled, D.: Model Checking. MIT Press, Cambridge (2000)
14. Alpern, B., Schneider, F.B.: Recognizing safety and liveness. Distributed Computing 2(3), 117–126 (1987)
15. von Wright, G.H.: Deontic logic. Mind 60, 1–15 (1951)
16. Bartha, P.: Conditional obligation, deontic paradoxes, and the logic of agency. Annals of Mathematics and Artificial Intelligence 9(1-2), 1–23 (1993)
17. Jamroga, W., van der Hoek, W., Wooldridge, M.: On obligations and abilities. In: Deontic Logic in Computer Science, pp. 165–181 (2004)
18. Kooi, B.P., Tamminga, A.M.: Conflicting obligations in multi-agent deontic logic. In: Deontic Logic in Computer Science, pp. 175–186 (2006)
19. Mont, M.C.: A system to handle privacy obligations in enterprises. Technical Report HPL-2005-180, HP Laboratories Bristol (October 2005)
20. Irwin, K., Yu, T., Winsborough, W.H.: On the modeling and analysis of obligations. In: Computer and Communications Security, pp. 134–143 (2006)
21. Park, J., Sandhu, R.: The UCON$_{ABC}$ usage control model. ACM Transactions on Information and System Security 7(1), 128–174 (2004)
22. Bettini, C., Jajodia, S., Wang, X., Wijesekera, D.: Obligation monitoring in policy management. In: Policies for Distributed Systems and Networks, pp. 2–12 (2002)
23. Sloman, M.: Policy driven management for distributed systems. Journal of Network and Systems Management 2(4) (1994)
24. Damianou, N., Dulay, N., Lupu, E., Sloman, M.: The Ponder specification language. In: Policies for Distributed Systems and Networks (2001)
25. Kudo, M., Hada, S.: XML document security based on provisional authorization. In: Computer and Communications Security, pp. 87–96 (2000)
26. Abrahams, A., Eyers, D., Bacon, J.: An asynchronous rule-based approach for business process automation using obligations. In: Rule-Based Programming, pp. 93–104 (2002)
27. Schaad, A., Moffett, J.D.: Delegation of obligations. In: Policies for Distributed Systems and Networks, pp. 25–35 (2002)
28. Schaad, A.: An extended analysis of delegating obligations. In: Data and Applications Security, pp. 49–64 (2004)
29. Schaad, A.: Revocation of obligation and authorisation policy objects. In: Data and Applications Security, pp. 28–39 (2005)
30. Jackson, D.: Alloy: a lightweight object modelling notation. ACM Transactions on Software Engineering and Methodology 11(2), 256–290 (2002)
31. Backes, M., Pfitzmann, B., Schunter, M.: A toolkit for managing enterprise privacy policies. In: European Symposium on Research in Computer Security, pp. 101–119 (2003)
32. Hilty, M., Basin, D.A., Pretschner, A.: On obligations. In: European Symposium on Research in Computer Security, pp. 98–117 (2005)
33. Ehrich, H.D., Caleiro, C.: Specifying communication in distributed information systems. Acta Informatica 36(8), 591–616 (2000)
34. May, M.J., Gunter, C.A., Lee, I.: Privacy APIs: Access control techniques to analyze and verify legal privacy policies. In: Computer Security Foundations Workshop (2006)
35. Barth, A., Datta, A., Mitchell, J.C., Nissenbaum, H.: Privacy and contextual integrity: Framework and applications. In: Symposium on Security and Privacy (2006)

On the Privacy of Concealed Data Aggregation*

Aldar C.-F. Chan[1]** and Claude Castelluccia[2]

[1] School of Computing, National University of Singapore
aldar@comp.nus.edu.sg
[2] INRIA Rhône-Alpes, France
Claude.Castelluccia@inria.fr

Abstract. A formal treatment to the privacy of concealed data aggregation (CDA) is given. While there exist a handful of constructions, rigorous security models and analyses for CDA are still lacking. Standard security notions for public key encryption schemes, including semantic security and indistinguishability against chosen ciphertext attacks, are refined to cover the multi-sender nature and aggregation functionality of CDA in the security model. A generic CDA construction based on public key homomorphic encryption is given, along with a proof of its security in the proposed model. The security of two existing schemes is also analyzed in the proposed model.

1 Introduction

Concealed data aggregation (CDA) in which multiple source nodes send encrypted data to a sink along a concast tree with ciphertext aggregation performed en route is an active research problem, particularly in sensor networks [1,3,10,26]. Privacy and message authentication are the two main security goals of CDA. This work focuses on the security model for privacy of CDA.

The privacy goal is two-fold. First, the privacy of the data has to be guaranteed end-to-end, that is, only the sink could learn about the final aggregation result and only a negligible amount of information about the final aggregate should be leaked out to any eavesdropper or node along the path. Each node should only have knowledge about its data, but no information about the data of other nodes. Second, to reduce communication overhead, the data from different source nodes have to be efficiently combined by intermediate nodes (i.e. aggregation) along the path. Nevertheless, these intermediate nodes should not learn any information about the final aggregate in an ideal scheme. It appears that these two goals are in conflict. As a result, deliberate study on the security definitions and rigorous analyses on CDA schemes are necessary. While there are a handful of CDA constructions [1,3,10,26] achieving various levels of privacy-efficiency

---

* The work described in this paper is based on results of IST FP6 STREP UbiSec&Sens. UbiSec&Sens receives research funding from the European Commission's Sixth Framework Programme. Apart from this, the European Commission has no responsibility for the content of this paper. The information in this document is provided as is and no guarantee or warranty is given that the information is fit for any particular purpose. The user thereof uses the information at its sole risk and liability.
** Part of this work was done while Aldar C-F. Chan was at INRIA.

J. Biskup and J. Lopez (Eds.): ESORICS 2007, LNCS 4734, pp. 390–405, 2007.

tradeoff, a rigorous treatment to the security definitions, notions and analyses of CDA is still lacking. This work aims to fill the gap.

While there has been a solid foundation in cryptography for both private-key [23,17,16] and public-key [13,20,5,12] encryption, a refinement to the standard security models is needed to cover the salient features in the CDA scenario: First, a CDA scheme can be based on private key or public key cryptography. That is, the encryption function of a CDA scheme could be public or private. Second, CDA is a many-to-one (multi-sender single-receiver) cryptosystem while cryptosystems in the literature are either one-to-one [16,13] or one-to-many [24,8]. Third, CDA includes the aggregation functionality on encrypted data whose adversary model needs a new definition. In this paper, we extend the standard security notions of semantic security and indistinguishability against chosen-ciphertext attacks to the CDA setting and analyze existing schemes [3,26].

1.1 Related Work

Westhoff et. al gave the first CDA construction in [26,10] based on the Domingo-Ferrer private key homomorphic encryption [6] and coined the term CDA. The scheme allows additive aggregation. Castelluccia et. al [3] constructed a stream cipher like CDA scheme for additive aggregation. In [1], Westhoff et. al. gave a private aggregation scheme for comparing encrypted data; however, the security of the proposed scheme is not reasonably high. It is fair to say that, despite the existence of these CDA constructions, a rigorous security model and analysis for CDA are still missing in the literature.

1.2 Our Contributions

The main contribution of this paper is the formalization of CDA. We extend the standard security notions of encryption schemes to cover the CDA scenario. Our security model covers both private-key and public-key based CDA constructions and takes into account the possibility of insider attacks due to compromised source nodes, as compared to [26,10] which do not explicitly consider the threat of compromised nodes. It also includes the case in which the global randomness for encryption is prescribed beforehand or chosen by the sink and broadcast to the source nodes [3].

We also give a generic CDA construction based on any public key homomorphic encryption scheme. Provided that the underlying homomorphic encryption scheme is semantically secure, the CDA construction achieves semantic security against any coalition with up to $n - 1$ compromised nodes where n is the total number of nodes in the system.[1]

Based on the CDA security model proposed in this paper, we analyze two existing schemes, namely, WGA [26] and CMT [3]. We show that WGA is only secure when there is no compromised node. Whereas, if the underlying pseudorandom function family (used for key generation) is (computationally) indistinguishable from a truly random

---

[1] In a general scenario, not all of the n nodes need to report in a given slot; only a subset of the n nodes contribute to the final aggregate. Without loss of generality, we assume all the n nodes contribute in the aggregation in the following discussion.

function, CMT can be proven to be semantically secure even when there are $n - 1$ compromised nodes. For the pseudorandom function assumption to be held, it appears that a larger modulus size is needed as compared to that used in the original scheme. As an alternative, a hash variant of CMT which does not require a revision on the modulus size is given. Security preserves in the hashed variant if, given a uniformly distributed input, the hash function output follows a uniform distribution.

The rest of the paper is organized as follows. We give a brief introduction to the notations used in this paper in the next section. The definition of CDA and related security notions are presented in Sections 3 and 4 respectively. In Section 5, a generic CDA construction is given. The security of two existing schemes is analyzed in Section 6. We conclude the paper in Section 7.

2   Notations

We follow the notations for algorithms and probabilistic experiments that originate in [14]. A detailed exposition can be found there. We denote by $z \leftarrow A(x, y, \ldots)$ the experiment of running probabilistic algorithm A on inputs $x, y \ldots$, generating output z. We denote by $\{A(x, y, \ldots)\}$ the probability distribution induced by the output of A. The notations $x \leftarrow \mathcal{D}$ and $x \in_R \mathcal{D}$ are equivalent and mean randomly picking a sample x from the probability distribution $\mathcal{D}$; if no probability function is specified for $\mathcal{D}$, we assume x is uniformly picked from the sample space. We denote by $\mathbb{N}$ the set of non-negative integers. As usual, PPT denote probabilistic polynomial time. An empty set is always denoted by ϕ.

3   Definitions

A typical CDA scheme includes a sink R and a set U of n source nodes (which are usually sensor nodes) where $U = \{s_i : 1 \leq i \leq n\}$. Denote the set of source identities by ID; in the simplest case, $ID = [1, n]$. In the following discussion, $hdr \subseteq ID$ is a header indicating the source nodes contributing to an encrypted aggregate. Given a security parameter λ, a CDA scheme consists of the following polynomial time algorithms.

Key Generation (KG). Let $\mathsf{KG}(1^\lambda, n) \to (dk, ek_1, ek_2, \ldots, ek_n)$ be a probabilistic algorithm. Then, ek_i (with $1 \leq i \leq n$) is the encryption key assigned to source node s_i and dk is the corresponding decryption key given to the sink R.

Encryption (E). $\mathsf{E}_{ek_i}(m_i) \to (hdr_i, c_i)$ is a probabilistic encryption algorithm taking a plaintext m_i and an encryption key ek_i as input to generate a ciphertext c_i and a header $hdr_i \subset ID$. Here hdr_i indicates the identity of the source node performing the encryption; if the identity is i, then $hdr_i = \{i\}$.

 We sometimes denote the encryption function by $\mathsf{E}_{ek_i}(m_i; r)$ to explicitly show by a string r the random coins used in the encryption process.

Decryption (D). Given an encrypted aggregate c and its header $hdr \subseteq ID$ (which indicates the source nodes included in the aggregation), $\mathsf{D}_{dk}(hdr, c) \to m/\perp$ is a deterministic algorithm which takes the decryption key dk, hdr and c as inputs and returns the plaintext aggregate m or possibly $\perp$ if c is an invalid ciphertext.

Aggregation (Agg). With a specified aggregation function f, the aggregation algorithm $\mathsf{Agg}_f(hdr_i, hdr_j, c_i, c_j) \rightarrow (hdr_l, c_l)$ aggregates two encrypted aggregates c_i and c_j with headers hdr_i and hdr_j respectively (where $hdr_i \cap hdr_j = \phi$) to create a combined aggregate c_l and a new header $hdr_l = hdr_i \cup hdr_j$. Suppose c_i and c_j are the ciphertexts for plaintext aggregates m_i and m_j respectively. The output c_l is the ciphertext for the aggregate $f(m_i, m_j)$, namely, $\mathsf{D}_{dk}(hdr_l, c_l) \rightarrow f(m_i, m_j)$. *Note that the aggregation algorithm does not need the decryption key dk or any of the encryption keys ek_i as input; it is a public algorithm.*

Depending on constructions, the aggregation function f could be any associative function, for instance, f could be the sum, multiplicative product, max, etc.. Leveraging on the associativity property, we abuse the notation in this paper: we denote the composition of multiple copies of f simply by $f(m_1, m_2, \ldots, m_i)$ irrespective of the order of aggregation and call it the f-aggregate on $m_1, m_2, \ldots, m_i$; to be precise, it should be written as $f(f(f(m_1, m_2), \ldots), m_i)$ with a certain aggregation order.

It is intentional to include the description of the header hdr in the above definition so as to make the CDA security model as general as possible (to cover schemes requiring headers in their operations). Nonetheless, generating headers or including headers as input to algorithms should not be treated as a requirement in the actual construction or implementation of CDA algorithms. For constructions which do not need headers (such as the generic construction given in Section 5), all hdr's can simply be treated as the empty set ϕ in the security model and the discussions in this paper still apply.

Typical CDA Operation. The operation of CDA runs as follows. In the initialization stage, the sink R runs KG to generate a set of encryption keys $\{ek_i : 1 \leq i \leq n\}$ and the corresponding decryption key dk and distributes each one of the encryption keys to the corresponding source, say, ek_i to s_i. Depending on constructions, the encryption keys ek_i could be private or public, but the decryption key dk has to be private in all cases.

At a certain instant, the sink selects a subset $S \subseteq U$ of the n sources to report their data. Each $s_i \in S$ uses its encryption key ek_i to encrypt its data represented by the plaintext m_i, giving a ciphertext c_i. We do not pose restrictions on whether global or local random coins should be used for encryption. If each source generates its random coins individually, the random coins are said to be local; if the random coins are chosen by the sink and broadcast to all source nodes, they are global. Global random coins are usually public. When global random coins are used, we do not pose restriction on the reuse of randomness despite that, in practice, each global random coin is treated as nonce, that is, used once only. The generic construction given in Section 5 uses local random coins whereas the CMT scheme [3] uses a global nonce.

Usually, the source nodes form a concast tree over which the encrypted data are sent. In order to save communication cost, aggregation is done en route to the sink whenever possible. When a node s_i in the tree receives x ciphertexts, say $(hrd_{i_1}, c_{i_1}), \ldots, (hdr_{i_x}, c_{i_x})$, from its children nodes[2] (with identities $i_1, \ldots, i_x \in S$), it aggregates these ciphertexts along with its own ciphertext (hdr_i, c_i) by running Agg_f

---

[2] It is possible that some of these ciphertexts are already the encryption of aggregated data rather than the encryption of a single plaintext.

successively. The concast tree structure ensures that any pair of these headers have an empty intersection. Suppose $c_{i_1}, \ldots, c_{i_x}$ are the ciphertexts for the plaintext aggregates $m_{i_1}, \ldots, m_{i_x}$. The resulting ciphertext is: (hdr_l, c_l) where $hdr_l = hdr_{i_1} \cup \ldots \cup hdr_{i_x} \cup hdr_i$ and c_l is the encryption of the aggregate $f(m_{i_1}, \ldots, m_{i_x}, m_i)$.

Eventually, a number of encrypted aggregates will arrive at the sink which combines them through running Agg_f to obtain a single encrypted aggregate c_{sink} and then applies the decryption algorithm to c_{sink} to get back the plaintext aggregate $f(\ldots, m_i, \ldots)$ with $s_i \in S$. We require the CDA be *correct* in the sense that when the encryption and decryption are performed with matched keys and correct headers and all the aggregations are run properly, the decryption should give back an f-aggregate of all the data applied to the encryption.

4 Security Notions

Two types of oracle queries (adversary interaction with the system) are allowed in the security model, namely, the encryption oracle $\mathcal{O}_E$ and the decryption oracle $\mathcal{O}_D$. Their details are as follows:

Encryption Oracle $\mathcal{O}_E(i, m)$. For fixed encryption and decryption keys, on input an encryption query $\langle i, m \rangle$, the encryption oracle retrieves s_i's encryption key ek_i and runs the encryption algorithm on m and replies with the ciphertext $\mathsf{E}_{ek_i}(m; r)$ and its header hdr. In case global random coins are used, the random coins r are part of the query input to $\mathcal{O}_E$.

Decryption Oracle $\mathcal{O}_D(hdr, c)$. For fixed encryption and decryption keys, on input a decryption query $\langle hdr, c \rangle$ (where $hdr \subseteq ID$), the decryption oracle retrieves the decryption key dk and runs the decryption algorithm D and sends the result $\mathsf{D}_{dk}(hdr, c)$ as the reply.

The encryption oracle is needed in the security model since the encryption algorithm in some CDA could use private keys, for examples [3,26]. In case the encryption algorithm does not use any secret information, an adversary can freely generate the ciphertext on any message of his choice without relying on the encryption oracle.

4.1 Security Against Chosen Ciphertext Attacks (CCA)

To define security (more precisely, indistinguishability) against adaptive chosen ciphertext attacks (IND-CCA2), we use the following game played between a challenger and an adversary, assuming there is a set U of n source nodes. If no PPT adversary, even in collusion with at most t compromised node (with $t < n$), can win the game with non-negligible advantage (as defined below), we say the CDA scheme is t-secure.[3]

Definition 1. *A CDA scheme is t-secure (indistinguishable) against adaptive chosen ciphertext attacks if the advantage of winning the following game is negligible in the security parameter λ for all PPT adversaries.*

---

[3] The adversary is allowed to freely choose parameters n and t.

Collusion Choice. The adversary chooses to corrupt t source nodes. Denote the set of these t corrupted nodes and the set of their identities by S' and I' respectively.

Setup. The challenger runs KG to generate a decryption key dk and n encryption keys $\{ek_i : 1 \leq i \leq n\}$, and gives the subset of t encryption keys $\{ek_j : s_j \in S'\}$ to the adversary but keeps the decryption key dk and the other $n - t$ encryption keys $\{ek_j : s_j \in U \backslash S'\}$.

Query 1. The adversary can issue to the challenger two types of queries:[4]
  - Encryption Query $\langle i_j, m_j \rangle$. The challenger responds with $\mathsf{E}_{e_{i_j}}(m_j)$.
  - Decryption Query $\langle hdr_j, c_j \rangle$. The challenger responds with $\mathsf{D}_{dk}(hdr_j, c_j)$.

Challenge. Once the adversary decides that the first query phase is over, it selects a subset S of d source nodes (whose identities are in the set I) such that $|S \backslash S'| > 0$, and outputs two different sets of plaintexts $M_0 = \{m_{0k} : k \in I\}$ and $M_1 = \{m_{1k} : k \in I\}$ to be challenged. The only constraint is that the two resulting plaintext aggregates x_0 and x_1 are not equal where $x_0 = f(\ldots, m_{0k}, \ldots)$ and $x_1 = f(\ldots, m_{1k}, \ldots)$.

    The challenger flips a coin $b \in \{0, 1\}$ to select between x_0 and x_1. The challenger then encrypts[5] each $m_{bk} \in M_b$ with ek_k and aggregates the resulting ciphertexts in the set $\{\mathsf{E}_{ek_k}(m_{bk}) : k \in I\}$ to form the ciphertext C of the aggregate, that is, $\mathsf{D}_{dk}(I, C) = x_b$, and gives (I, C) as a challenge to the adversary.

Query 2. The adversary is allowed to make more queries (both encryption and decryption) as previously done in Query 1 phase but no decryption query can be made on the challenged ciphertext C. Nevertheless, the adversary can still make a decryption query on a header corresponding to the set S except that the ciphertext has to be chosen different from the challenged ciphertext C.

Guess. Finally, the adversary outputs a guess $b' \in \{0, 1\}$ for b.

Result. The adversary wins the game if $b' = b$. The advantage of the adversary is defined as: $Adv_{\mathcal{A}} = \left| Pr[b' = b] - \frac{1}{2} \right|$.

Note that in CDA what the adversary is interested in is the information about the final aggregate. Consequently, in the above game, the adversary is asked to distinguish between the ciphertexts of two *different* aggregates x_0 and x_1 as the challenge, rather than to distinguish two different sets of plaintexts M_0 and M_1. By picking elements for M_0 and M_1, the adversary is essentially free to choose x_0 and x_1. Allowing the adversary to choose the two sets M_0, M_1 is to give him more flexibility in launching attacks. When an adversary cannot distinguish between the ciphertexts of two different aggregates (of his choice) with probability of success non-negligibly greater than $1/2$, this means, in essence, he can learn no information about an aggregate from its ciphertext.

---

[4] In case global random coins are used, the adversary is allowed to choose and submit his choices of random coins for both encryption and decryption queries. Depending on whether the encryption keys are kept secret, the encryption queries may or may not be needed.

[5] In case global random coins are used for encryption, the challenger chooses and passes them to the adversary. If a *nonce* is used, the global random coins should be chosen different from those used in the Query 1 phase and no query on them should be allowed in the Query 2 phase.

4.2 Semantic Security

Semantic security, which is equivalent to indistinguishability against chosen plaintext attacks (IND-CPA), is defined by the same game as in the definition of security against chosen ciphertext attacks in Section 4.1 except that no query to the decryption oracle $\mathcal{O}_D$ is allowed. Similar to the definition in Section 4.1, a CDA scheme is said to be t-secure when it can still achieve semantic security against a PPT adversary corrupting at most t compromised nodes.

For a CDA scheme to be useful, it should at least achieve semantic security. In the notion of semantic security, the main resource for an adversary is the encryption oracle $\mathcal{O}_E$. In some schemes like [26,3], the adversary may not know the encryption keys, meaning he might not have access to the encryption oracle in the real environment. Nevertheless, in sensor networks, he is able to obtain the encryption of any plaintext of his choice by manipulating the sensing environment and recording the sensed value using his own sensors. Hence, chosen plaintext attacks are still a real threat to CDA.

4.3 One-Wayness

One-wayness is the weakest possible security notion for encryption. A CDA scheme is t-secure in one-wayness if no PPT attacker, corrupting at most t nodes, should be able, with non-negligible probability of success, to recover the plaintext aggregate matching a given ciphertext. To define one-wayness more formally, we can use the same game in Section 4.1 except that no query is allowed and the adversary can make no choice in the challenge phase but is given a ciphertext of a certain aggregate x (encrypted using at least one encryption key not held by the adversary) and asked to recover x.

5   A Generic CDA Construction

In this section, a generic construction of semantically secure CDA (using local random coins) is given based on any semantically secure public-key homomorphic encryption. The result is not surprising but could be useful. Note that an asymmetric key homomorphic encryption is used in this construction, compared to the symmetric key encryption used in the WGA construction [26]. An asymmetric key encryption is necessary in order to guard against possible insider attacks from compromised nodes.

5.1 Public Key Homomorphic Encryption

A public key homomorphic encryption scheme is a 4-tuple (KG, E, D, A). The key generation algorithm KG receives the security parameter 1^λ as input and outputs a pair of public and private keys (pk, sk). E and D are the encryption and decryption algorithms. Given a plaintext x and random coins r, the ciphertext is $E_{pk}(x; r)$ and $D_{sk}(E_{pk}(x; r)) = x$. The homomorphic property allows one to operate on the ciphertexts using the poly-time algorithm A without first decrypting them; more specifically, for any x, y, r_x, r_y, A can generate from $E_{pk}(x; r_x)$ and $E_{pk}(y; r_y)$ a new ciphertext of the form $E_{pk}(x \otimes y; s)$ for some s. The operator $\otimes$ could be addition, multiplication or others depending on specific schemes; for instance, it is multiplication for RSA [22] or ElGamal [7] and addition for Paillier [21].

As observed in previous work in the literature, due to the homomorphic property, achieving IND-CCA2 security could be impossible for homomorphic encryption. The notion of security against CCA1 attacks is not often considered in practical constructions. Hence, semantic security or the equivalent notion of IND-CPA security appears to be the de facto security notion for homomorphic encryption schemes. In brief, the IND-CPA notion can be described by the following game: in the Setup phase, the challenger runs $KG(1^\lambda)$ to generate a pair of public and private keys, gives the public key to the adversary but keeps the private key. The adversary can freely encrypt any message of his choice using the public key. The adversary chooses two different messages m_0, m_1 and gives them to the challenger which flips a coin $b \in \{0, 1\}$ and gives $E_{pk}(m_b; r)$ to the adversary. The adversary has to output a guess b' for b and his advantage of winning the game is defined as $\left| Pr[b' = b] - \frac{1}{2} \right|$. If the advantage of winning the above game is negligible in the security parameter λ for all PPT adversaries, then the scheme is IND-CPA secure.

5.2 Concealed Data Aggregation from Public Key Homomorphic Encryption

Assume there are n source nodes in total. Suppose there exists a semantically secure public-key homomorphic encryption scheme $(KG^{HE}, E^{HE}, D^{HE}, A^{HE})$ with homomorphism on operator $\otimes$. We can construct a semantically secure CDA scheme, tolerating up to $n - 1$ compromised nodes, with aggregation function of the form: $f(m_i, m_j) = m_i \otimes m_j$. The construction is as follows: (The headers are included in the following description for completeness; they are not needed in the construction. In fact, all these hdr_i's are the empty set ϕ.)

Key Generation (KG). Run $KG^{HE}(1^\lambda)$ to generate (pk, sk). Set the CDA decryption key $dk = sk$ and each one of the CDA encryption keys to be pk, that is, $ek_i = pk, \forall i \in [1, n]$.

Encryption (E). Given a plaintext data m_i, toss the random coins r_i needed for E^{HE} and output $c_i = E_{pk}^{HE}(m_i; r_i)$. Set the header $hdr_i = \phi$. Output (hdr_i, c_i).

Decryption (D). Given an encrypted aggregate c and its header hdr, run D^{HE} using the private key sk to decrypt c and output $x = D_{sk}^{HE}(c)$ as the plaintext aggregate.

Aggregation (Agg). Given two CDA ciphertexts (hdr_i, c_i) and (hdr_j, c_j), the aggregation can be done using the homomorphic property of the encryption scheme. Generate $c_l = A^{HE}(c_i, c_j)$ and $hdr_l = hdr_i \cup hdr_j$. Output (hdr_l, c_l).

Correctness. Without loss of generality, we consider the case with only two plaintext messages m_i and m_j and ignore the header part as it is always equal to ϕ. The corresponding ciphertexts for m_i and m_j are $c_i = E_{pk}^{HE}(m_i; r_i)$ and $c_j = E_{pk}^{HE}(m_j; r_j)$ for some random coins r_i, r_j. If the aggregation is done using Agg as described above, the aggregation result c_l should be equal to $E_{pk}^{HE}(m_i \otimes m_j; s)$ for some s. In essence, this value is $E_{pk}^{HE}(f(m_i, m_j), s)$. With the correctness property of the homomorphic encryption scheme, $D_{sk}^{HE}(c_l)$ should give back $m_i \otimes m_j$ which is the aggregate $f(m_i, m_j)$.

The security of the CDA construction is best described by the following theorem.

Theorem 1. *For a total of n source nodes, the above CDA construction is semantically secure against any collusion of at most $n - 1$ compromised nodes, assuming that the underlying homomorphic encryption scheme is semantically secure. The advantage for any PPT adversary in breaking the semantic security of the CDA construction is bounded above by the advantage achievable (by all PPT adversaries) in breaking the semantic security of the underlying homomorphic encryption scheme.*

Proof. It is trivial that security against $n - 1$ compromised nodes implies security against $t < n - 1$ compromised nodes, and the advantages are related by a constant factor with respect to λ. Hence, we consider the case with $n - 1$ compromised nodes.

We prove by contradiction. Assume the underlying homomorphic encryption is semantically secure, that is, all PPT algorithms have negligible advantage to break the semantic security of the scheme. Suppose there exists a PPT adversary $\mathcal{A}$ which, in coalition with $n - 1$ nodes, can break the semantic security property of the CDA construction with non-negligible advantage. We show how to use $\mathcal{A}$ to construct another algorithm $\mathcal{A}'$ to break the semantic security of the homomorphic encryption as follows:

Algorithm $\mathcal{A}'$

Setup. Receive the public key pk from the challenger and pass it to the n source nodes. Allow the adversary $\mathcal{A}$ to choose any $n - 1$ nodes to corrupt.

Query. Since no private key is needed for encryption, no $\mathcal{O}_E$ query is necessary.

Challenge. In the challenge phase, receive from $\mathcal{A}$ two sets of plaintext messages $M_0 = \{m_{01}, m_{02}, \ldots, m_{0n}\}$ and $M_1 = \{m_{11}, m_{12}, \ldots, m_{1n}\}$. Since $\mathcal{A}$ has corrupted $n - 1$ nodes, $|M_0|$ and $|M_1|$ have to be equal to n. Compute $x_0 = f(m_{01}, m_{02}, \ldots, m_{0n})$ and $x_1 = f(m_{11}, m_{12}, \ldots, m_{1n})$ and output x_0, x_1 to the challenger for a challenged ciphertext c. (Note that the constraint posed on the challenge in Definition 1 in Section 4.1 assures that $x_0 \neq x_1$.)

Guess. Let the challenged ciphertext $c = E_{pk}^{HE}(x_b; r)$ for some unknown random coins r where $b \in \{0, 1\}$ is unknown. Pass c as the challenge for $\mathcal{A}$. When $\mathcal{A}$ outputs b', output b' as a guess for b to the challenger.

In the above simulation, the challenge c is generated by first aggregating the plaintext and then encrypting the plaintext aggregate with some random coins r. In a real attack, each $m_{bi} \in M_b$ is encrypted with some random coins r_i and the resulting ciphertexts are then aggregated to generate c, which in essence is the ciphertext for the plaintext aggregate encrypted with some random coins s whose relationship with r_i's is unknown. If these r_i's are independently picked at random, then the resulting randomness s would have the same distribution as a randomly picked r. Hence, the distributions of the challenge c generated by the two processes are indistinguishable. In other words, the view of the adversary $\mathcal{A}$ in the above simulation is essentially the same as that in a real attack.

Let $Adv_{\mathcal{A}}^{\text{CDA-IND-CPA}}(\lambda)$ be the advantage of the adversary $\mathcal{A}$ in breaking the semantic security of the CDA construction. The advantage $Adv_{\mathcal{A}'}^{\text{HE-IND-CPA}}(\lambda)$ of $\mathcal{A}'$ in breaking the semantic security of the underlying homomorphic encryption is then:

$$Adv_{\mathcal{A}'}^{\text{HE-IND-CPA}}(\lambda) = Adv_{\mathcal{A}}^{\text{CDA-IND-CPA}}(\lambda).$$

If $Adv_{\mathcal{A}}^{\text{CDA-IND-CPA}}(\lambda)$ is non-negligible, so is $Adv_{\mathcal{A}'}^{\text{HE-IND-CPA}}(\lambda)$ (a contradiction). $\quad\square$

6 Security Analysis of Existing Schemes

In this section, we analyze two practical schemes in the literature in the proposed security model, and propose modifications to one of them in Section 6.3.

6.1 WGA [26]

WGA uses Domingo-Ferrer's symmetric-key homomorphic encryption as a building block. Each source node uses the same encryption key ek and the sink's decryption key $dk = ek$. When there is no compromised node, if the underlying symmetric-key homomorphic encryption is semantically secure, then WGA achieves semantic security. The analysis is straightforward. Suppose there is an adversary $\mathcal{A}$ which can break the semantic security of WGA. It is trivial that $\mathcal{A}$ can be used as a subroutine of another algorithm $\mathcal{A}'$ to break the semantic security of the underlying encryption. Besides, any encryption oracle query from $\mathcal{A}$ can be answered easily by $\mathcal{A}'$ using the query result from the challenger of the underlying encryption scheme; in other words, the view to $\mathcal{A}$ in this simulation is indistinguishable from that in the real attack.

However, as few as one node is compromised, the adversary knows the decryption key and can gain the knowledge of all future aggregates by just passive eavesdropping, that is, not even one-wayness can be achieved if there exists compromised nodes.

6.2 CMT [3]

CMT can be considered as a practical modification of the Vernam cipher or one-time pad [25] to allow plaintext addition to be done in the ciphertext domain. Basically, there are two modifications. First, the exclusive-OR operation is replaced by an addition operation. By choosing a proper modulus, multiplicative aggregation is also possible in CMT.[6] Second, instead of uniformly picking a key at random from the key space, the key is generated by a certain deterministic algorithm (with an unknown seed) such as a pseudorandom function [11]. As a result, the information-theoretic security (which requires the key be at least as long as the plaintext) in the Vernam cipher is replaced with a security guarantee in the computational-complexity theoretic setting in CMT.

The operation of the CMT scheme is as follows: (The description could be slightly different from the original scheme [3] as the procedures to generate the encryption keys from a pseudorandom function are filled in.) Let p be a large enough integer used as the modulus. Assume the key length is λ bits. Then p could be 2^λ. Besides, global random coins are used in CMT, that is, the sink chooses and broadcasts a public nonce to all nodes.

In the following description, let $F = \{F_\lambda\}_{\lambda \in \mathbb{N}}$ be a pseudorandom function family where $F_\lambda = \{f_s : \{0,1\}^\lambda \to \{0,1\}^\lambda\}_{s \in \{0,1\}^\lambda}$ is a collection of functions indexed by a key $s \in \{0,1\}^\lambda$. For details on pseudorandom functions, [11] has a comprehensive description. Loosely speaking, given a function f_s from a pseudorandom function ensemble with unknown key s, any PPT distinguishing procedure allowed to get the values of $f_s(\cdot)$ at (polynomially many) arguments of its choice should not be able to

---

[6] CMT can achieve either additive or multiplicative aggregation but not both at the same time.

tell (with non-negligible advantage in λ) whether the answer of a new query (with the argument not queried before) is supplied by f_s or randomly picked from $\{0,1\}^\lambda$.

Key Generation (KG). Randomly pick $K \in \{0,1\}^\lambda$ and set it as the decryption key dk. For each $i \in [1, n]$, $ek_i = f_K(i)$ is the encryption key for source node s_i with identity i.

Encryption (E). Given an encryption key ek_i, a plaintext data m_i and a broadcast nonce r from the sink, output $c_i = (m_i + f_{ek_i}(r)) \bmod p$. Set the header $hdr_i = \{i\}$. Output (hdr_i, c_i). *Note: each r has to be used once only.*

Decryption (D). Given the ciphertext (hdr, c) of an aggregate and a nonce r used in the encryption, generate $ek_i = f_K(i), \forall i \in hdr$. Output the plaintext aggregate $x = (c - \sum_{i \in hdr} f_{ek_i}(r)) \bmod p$.

Aggregation (Agg). Given two CDA ciphertexts (hdr_i, c_i) and (hdr_j, c_j), compute $c_l = (c_i + c_j) \bmod p$ and $hdr_l = hdr_i \cup hdr_j$ and output (hdr_l, c_l).

How good the CMT scheme achieves IND-CPA security relies on how good the underlying key generation function is as a pseudorandom function. As a consequence, the required modulus size is determined mainly by the parameters of the conjectured pseudorandom function family used, rather than the size of the largest plaintext aggregate. There are various constructions of pseudorandom functions [18,19,15,2], each of which is based on a different computational assumption and requires different computational resources; it is therefore difficult to evaluate the efficiency of the CMT scheme without seeing the actual implementation. The security of the CMT can be summarized by the following theorem.

Theorem 2. *The CMT scheme is semantically secure against any collusion with at most $n - 1$ compromised nodes, assuming $F_\lambda = \{f_s : \{0,1\}^\lambda \to \{0,1\}^\lambda\}_{s \in \{0,1\}^\lambda}$ is a pseudorandom function.*

Proof. Without loss of generality, we prove the security of a modified version of CMT in which each encryption key is uniformly picked from $\{0,1\}^\lambda$, compared with keys generated by a pseudorandom function in the actual CMT scheme. We then provide a justification why the inference applies to the actual CMT implementation.

Indistinguishability Property of a Pseudorandom Function. Assume f is taken from a pseudorandom function. Then for a fixed input argument x and and an unknown, randomly picked key K, the following two distributions are computationally indistinguishable provided that polynomially many (say q) evaluations of $f_K(\cdot)$ have been queried:

$$\{y = f_K(x) : y\}, \{y \leftarrow \{0,1\}^\lambda : y\}.$$

That is, the output $f_K(x)$ is computationally indistinguishable from a randomly picked number from $\{0,1\}^\lambda$ to any PPT distinguisher who has knowledge of the input argument x and a set of polynomially many 2-tuples $(x_i, f_K(x_i))$ where $x_i \neq x$. More formally, for any PPT distinguisher $\mathcal{D}$,

$$|Pr[y = f_K(x) : \mathcal{D}(x, y) = 1] - Pr[y \leftarrow \{0,1\}^\lambda : \mathcal{D}(x, y) = 1]| < \varepsilon(\lambda)$$

where $\varepsilon(\lambda)$ is a negligible function in λ.

Suppose there exists a PPT adversary D which can break the semantic security of CMT with non-negligible advantage Adv_D^{CMT}. We show in the following how D can be used to construct an algorithm D' which can distinguish the above distributions with non-negligible advantage. Assume the key K in question is unknown to D'.

Algorithm D'

Setup. Allow the adversary D to choose any $n-1$ sources to corrupt. Randomly pick $n-1$ encryption keys $ek_i \in_R \{0,1\}^\lambda$ and pass them to the adversary. Assume node n is uncorrupted. The encryption key for node n is taken to be K, the key of the pseudorandom function D' is being challenged with. That is, K is unknown to D'.

Query. Upon receiving an encryption query $\langle i_j, m_j \rangle$ with nonce r_j, return $c_j = (f_{ek_{i_j}}(r_j) + m_j) \bmod p$ if $i_j \neq n$. Otherwise, pass r_j to query the pseudorandom function to get back $f_K(r_j)$ and reply with $c_j = (f_K(r_j) + m_j) \bmod p$.

Challenge. In the challenge phase, receive from D two sets of plaintext messages $M_0 = \{m_{01}, m_{02}, \ldots, m_{0n}\}$ and $M_1 = \{m_{11}, m_{12}, \ldots, m_{1n}\}$.

Randomly pick a number w and output it to the pseudorandom function challenger to ask for a challenge. Note w is the nonce used for CDA encryption in the challenge for D. The pseudorandom function challenger flips a coin $b \in \{0,1\}$ and returns t_b, which is $f_K(w)$ when $b = 0$ and randomly picked from $\{0,1\}^\lambda$ when $b = 1$. These two cases corresponds to the two distributions discussed above.

Randomly flip a coin $d \in \{0,1\}$, and return the challenge ciphertext c_d to D where $c_d = \sum_{i=1}^n m_{di} + \sum_{i=1}^{n-1} f_{ek_i}(w) + t_b$.

Guess. D returns its guess b'. Return b'' which is 0 when $b' = d$ and 1 otherwise.

Obviously, if D is PPT, then D' is also PPT. Denoting the expression $\sum_{i=1}^n m_{di} + \sum_{i=1}^{n-1} f_{ek_i}(w)$ by X_d, the challenge passed to D can be expressed as $c_d = X_d + t_b$. When $b = 0$, $t_b = f_K(w)$; when $b = 1$, t_b is a randomly picked number from $\{0,1\}^\lambda$. In the following discussion, we denote the output of D on input c_d by $D(c_d)$. The probability of success for D' to distinguish between $f_K(w)$ and a random number is:

$$
\begin{aligned}
Pr_{D'}^{PRF}[Success] &= Pr[b'' = b] \\
&= \tfrac{1}{2}\{Pr[b'' = 0 | b = 0] + Pr[b'' = 1 | b = 1]\} \\
&= \tfrac{1}{4}\{Pr[b'' = 0 | b = 0, d = 0] + Pr[b'' = 0 | b = 0, d = 1] \\
&\quad + Pr[b'' = 1 | b = 1, d = 0] + Pr[b'' = 1 | b = 1, d = 1]\} \\
&= \tfrac{1}{4}\{Pr[D(t_0 + X_0) = 0] + Pr[D(t_0 + X_1) = 1] \\
&\quad + Pr[D(t_1 + X_0) = 1] + Pr[D(t_1 + X_1) = 0]\} \\
&= \tfrac{1}{4}\{Pr[D(t_0 + X_0) = 0] + Pr[D(t_0 + X_1) = 1] \\
&\quad + 1 + Pr[D(t_1 + X_0) = 1] - Pr[D(t_1 + X_1) = 1]\} \\
&= \tfrac{1}{4}\{2Pr_D^{CMT}[Success] + 1 \\
&\quad + (Pr[D(t_1 + X_0) = 1] - Pr[D(t_1 + X_1) = 1])\}.
\end{aligned}
$$

Note that $t_0 + X_0$ and $t_0 + X_1$ are valid CMT ciphertexts for the two challenges plaintext sets M_0 and M_1 respectively. In the last step, we make use of the fact that the probability of success for D to break the semantic security of CMT is given by:

$$
Pr_D^{CMT}[Success] = \frac{1}{2} Pr[D(t_0 + X_0) = 0] + \frac{1}{2} Pr[D(t_0 + X_1) = 1].
$$

Rearranging terms, we have

$$
\begin{aligned}
&4Pr_{D'}^{PRF}[Success] && = 2Pr_D^{CMT}[Success] + 1 \\
&+Pr[D(t_1 + X_1) = 1] - Pr[D(t_1 + X_0) = 1] && \\
&4(Pr_{D'}^{PRF}[Success] - \tfrac{1}{2}) && = 2(Pr_D^{CMT}[Success] - \tfrac{1}{2}). \\
&+Pr[D(t_1 + X_1) = 1] - Pr[D(t_1 + X_0) = 1] &&
\end{aligned}
$$

Taking absolute value on both sides and substitute $Adv_{D'}^{PRF} = |Pr_{D'}^{PRF}[Success] - \tfrac{1}{2}|$ and $Adv_D^{CMT} = |Pr_D^{CMT}[Success] - \tfrac{1}{2}|$, we have

$$
2Adv_{D'}^{PRF} + \frac{1}{2}|Pr[D(t_1 + X_1) = 1] - Pr[D(t_1 + X_0) = 1]| \geq Adv_D^{CMT}.
$$

Since t_1 is a randomly picked number, $\{t_1 + X_0\}$ and $\{t_1 + X_1\}$ are identically distributed. That is, for any PPT algorithm D, $Pr[D(t_1+X_0) = 1] = Pr[D(t_1+X_1) = 1]$. Hence,

$$
2Adv_{D'}^{PRF}(\lambda) \geq Adv_D^{CMT}(\lambda).
$$

Note also that:

$$
\left| Pr[y = f_K(x) : D'(x, y) = 1] - Pr[y \leftarrow \{0,1\}^\lambda : D'(x, y) = 1] \right| = 2Adv_{D'}^{PRF}(\lambda).^7
$$

If Adv_D^{CMT} is non-negligible in λ, then so is $Adv_{D'}^{PRF}$. As a result, if D can break the semantic security of CMT with non-negligible advantage, D' could distinguish between the output of pseudorandom function f and a random number. Equivalently, $|Pr[y = f_K(x) : D'(x, y) = 1] - Pr[y \leftarrow \{0,1\}^\lambda : D'(x, y) = 1]|$ is non-negligible (a contradiction to the indistinguishability property of a pseudorandom function).

The above security argument applies to the actual CMT implementation since the view of the adversary D in the above simulation is in essence the same as that in the actual CMT scheme. For each one of the $n-1$ corrupted node, the encryption key is $f_{K'}(i)$ ($1 \leq i \leq n - 1$) for some randomly picked master key K'. By the property of pseudorandom function, $f_{K'}(i)$ is indistinguishable from a randomly picked key (as used in the above simulation game) for all PPT distinguisher algorithms. For the uncorrupted node, its output for encryption is now $f_{f_{K'}(n)}(x)$ instead of $f_K(x)$ (with randomly picked K) as used in the above simulation game. It can be shown by a contrapositive argument that, for fixed n and given x, the two distributions are computationally indistinguishable, that is,

$$
\{K' \leftarrow \{0,1\}^\lambda : (x, f_{f_{K'}(n)}(x))\} \stackrel{c}{\equiv} \{K \leftarrow \{0,1\}^\lambda : (x, f_K(x))\}.
$$

The argument is as follows: Assume f is a pseudorandom function. That is, $A = \{K' \leftarrow \{0,1\}^\lambda : f_{K'}(n)\}$ is indistinguishable from $B = \{K \leftarrow \{0,1\}^\lambda : K\}$ for

---

[7] The derivation is as follows.

$$
\begin{aligned}
&\left| Pr[y = f_K(x) : D'(x, y) = 1] - Pr[y \leftarrow \{0,1\}^\lambda : D'(x, y) = 1] \right| \\
&= \left| 1 - Pr[y = f_K(x) : D'(x, y) = 0] - Pr[y \leftarrow \{0,1\}^\lambda : D'(x, y) = 1] \right| \\
&= \left| 1 - 2Pr_{D'}^{PRF}[Success] \right| \\
&= 2 \cdot \left| Pr_{D'}^{PRF}[Success] - \tfrac{1}{2} \right| \\
&= 2 \cdot Adv_{D'}^{PRF}(\lambda)
\end{aligned}
$$

all PPT distinguishers. If there exists a PPT distinguisher D which can distinguish between $X = \{K' \leftarrow \{0,1\}^\lambda : (x, f_{f_{K'}(n)}(x))\}$ and $Y = \{K \leftarrow \{0,1\}^\lambda : (x, f_K(x))\}$, we can use D to distinguish between A and B. The idea is when we receive a challenge s which could be from A or B, we send x and $f_s(x)$ as a challenge for D. If s belongs to A, $(x, f_s(x))$ belongs to X, and if s belongs to B, $(x, f_s(x))$ belongs to Y. We could thus distinguish X from Y (a contradiction).   □

6.3   A Hashed Variant of CMT

As discussed in the previous section, when pseudorandom functions are used to generate encryption keys for CMT, the modulus size has to be revised and the advantage of short ciphertext in CMT is lost. In order to maintain the same ciphertext size, the output of the pseudorandom function can be hashed down by some good hash function $h : \{0,1\}^\lambda \to \{0,1\}^l$ where λ is the security parameter for the pseudorandom function and l is the size of the maximum plaintext aggregate. Instead of using the output of the pseudorandom function directly for encryption, its hashed value is input to the encryption algorithm. For a given plaintext m_i, a nonce r and an encryption key e_i, the ciphertext of the hashed CMT is: $c_i = (m_i + h(f_{e_i}(r))) \bmod p'$ where $|p'| = l$. The decryption algorithm is modified accordingly to hash the output of the pseudorandom function and then subtract the hash values from the ciphertext.

Requirement on the Hash Function. In order to preserve semantic security for the hashed CMT scheme, the hash function $h : \{0,1\}^\lambda \to \{0,1\}^l$ needs to satisfy the following property: $\{t \leftarrow \{0,1\}^\lambda : h(t)\}$ has a uniform distribution over $\{0,1\}^l$.

We can actually view h as a length-compressing function which matches the output length of a pseudorandom function with the size of the modulus in use. While the idealized hash function in the random oracle model is sufficient to fulfill the above mentioned requirement, it is probably more than necessary.

Note that for an ideal pseudorandom function family, h might simply be implemented by truncating the pseudorandom function output to fit the modulus size. However, to take into account of the imperfectness of the conjectured pseudorandom function families used in practice, it could be preferable if the pseudorandom function output is divided into small segments which are then combined by taking exclusive OR. Of course, the output size of the pseudorandom function has to be a multiple of the modulus size to implement this approach.

Security of the Hashed CMT. Only a few modifications to the security proof in Section 6.2 are needed in order to prove the security of the hashed variant.

First, in the algorithm D', all cipertexts are now generated using the hashed values of the pseudorandom function outputs or replies from the challenger of D'. With such changes, we now denote the expression $\sum_{i=1}^n m_{di} + \sum_{i=1}^{n-1} h(f_{ek_i}(w))$ by X_d. Of course, the modulus size would be l instead of λ.

Second, the challenge passed to D would be: $c_d = X_d + h(t_b)$. Then the derivation for the advantage expressions is essentially the same as that for CMT.

Third, the security proof of CMT relies on the fact that $\{t_1 \leftarrow \{0,1\}^\lambda : t_1 + X_0\}$ and $\{t_1 \leftarrow \{0,1\}^\lambda : t_1 + X_1\}$ are identical distribution. On the contrary, to prove the security of hashed CMT, we need the following distributions to be identical:

$$\{t_1 \leftarrow \{0,1\}^\lambda : h(t_1) + X_0\}, \{t_1 \leftarrow \{0,1\}^\lambda : h(t_1) + X_1\}.$$

If h fulfills the requirement mentioned above, then $\{t_1 \leftarrow \{0,1\}^\lambda : h(t_1)\}$ is the uniform distribution over $\{0,1\}^l$. Consequently, the above two distributions are identical. This thus conclude the proof that hashed CMT is semantically secure.

The modification of the hash variant of CMT shares similarities with the hashed Diffie-Hellman scheme to get rid of the group encoding problem [4,9] in the algebraic group used. While the hash function has to be modeled as a random oracle in order to prove the security of the hashed Diffie-Hellman scheme, the security proof of CMT applies to the hash variant of CMT without relying on the random oracle model. The main reason for the difference is: in the security proof for the hashed Diffie-Hellman scheme, the random oracle is used for answering queries to the decryption oracle, while in hashed CMT, no decryption oracle access is allowed in the security model as we only prove hashed CMT achieves semantic security.

7   Conclusions

In this paper, we give a rigorous treatment to the CDA problem. More specifically, we extend standard privacy notions to cover the CDA scenario which is a multiple-sender cryptosystem and supports aggregation. We also give a generic CDA construction based on any semantically secure public key encryption scheme and prove that it achieves semantic security. Besides, we analyze the security of two existing constructions, namely WGA and CMT, in the proposed model. We also propose a hashed variant of CMT to achieve security and efficiency simultaneously. As future work, we will study security model for aggregate authenticity; however, secure versions of the natural extension of MAC [2] (supporting message aggregation) may not exist. The reason is that if such a MAC scheme exists, it can be used to construct, from any semantically secure CDA, an IND-CCA2 secure CDA (which may not be achievable).

References

1. Acharya, M., Girao, J., Westhoff, D.: Secure comparison of encrypted data in wireless sensor networks. In: The Proceedings of WiOpt 2005 (April 2005)
2. Bellare, M., Canetti, R., Krawczyk, H.: Keying hash functions for message authentication. In: Koblitz, N. (ed.) CRYPTO 1996. LNCS, vol. 1109, pp. 1–15. Springer, Heidelberg (1996)
3. Castelluccia, C., Mykletun, E., Tsudik, G.: Efficient aggregation of encrypted data in wireless sensor networks. In: The Proceedings of MobiQuitous'05, pp. 1–9 (July 2005)
4. Chevallier-Mames, B., Paillier, P., Pointcheval, D.: Encoding-free ElGamal encryption without random oracles. In: Yung, M., Dodis, Y., Kiayias, A., Malkin, T.G. (eds.) PKC 2006. LNCS, vol. 3958, pp. 24–26. Springer, Heidelberg (2006)
5. Dolev, D., Dwork, C., Naor, M.: Nonmalleable cryptography. SIAM Journal on Computing 30(2), 391–437 (2000)
6. Domingo-Ferrer, J.: A provably secure additive and multiplicative privacy homomorphism. In: Chan, A.H., Gligor, V.D. (eds.) ISC 2002. LNCS, vol. 2433, pp. 471–483. Springer, Heidelberg (2002)

7. ElGamal, T.: A public key cryptosystem and a signature scheme based on discrete logarithms. IEEE Transactions on Information Theory IT-30(4), 469–472 (1985)
8. Fiat, A., Naor, M.: Broadcast encryption. In: Stinson, D.R. (ed.) CRYPTO 1993. LNCS, vol. 773, pp. 480–491. Springer, Heidelberg (1994)
9. Gennaro, R., Krawczyk, H., Rabin, T.: Secure hashed Diffie-Hellman over non-DDH groups. In: Cachin, C., Camenisch, J.L. (eds.) EUROCRYPT 2004. LNCS, vol. 3027, pp. 361–381. Springer, Heidelberg (2004)
10. Girao, J., Westhoff, D., Schneider, M.: CDA: Concealed data aggregation in wireless sensor networks. In: ICC'05. The Proceedings of IEEE International Conference on Communication, IEEE Computer Society Press, Los Alamitos (May 2005)
11. Goldreich, O.: Foundations of Cryptography: Part 1. Cambridge University Press, Cambridge (2001)
12. Goldreich, O.: Foundations of Cryptography: Part 2. Cambridge University Press, Cambridge (2004)
13. Goldwasser, S., Micali, S.: Probabilistic encryption. Journal of Computer and System Sciences 28(2), 270–299 (1984)
14. Goldwasser, S., Micali, S., Rivest, R.: A secure signature scheme secure against adaptive chosen-message attacks. SIAM Journal on Computing 17(2), 281–308 (1988)
15. Iwata, T., Kurosawa, K.: OMAC: One-key CBC MAC. In: Johansson, T. (ed.) FSE 2003. LNCS, vol. 2887, pp. 129–153. Springer, Heidelberg (2003)
16. Katz, J., Yung, M.: Characterization of security notions for probabilistic private-key encryption. Journal of Cryptology 19(1), 67–95 (2006)
17. Luby, M.: Pseudorandomness and Cryptographic Applications. Princeton University Press, Princeton, NJ, USA (1996)
18. Naor, M., Reingold, O.: Number-theoretic constructions of efficient pseudo-random functions. In: FOCS'97. The Proceedings of IEEE Symposium on Foundations on Computer Science, pp. 458–467. IEEE Computer Society Press, Los Alamitos (1997)
19. Naor, M., Reingold, O., Rosen, A.: Pseudorandom functions and factoring. SIAM Journal on Computing 31(5), 1383–1404 (2002)
20. Naor, M., Yung, M.: Public-key cryptosystems provably secure against chosen-ciphertext attacks. In: STOC 1990. ACM Symposium on Theory of Computing, pp. 427–437. ACM Press, New York (1990)
21. Paillier, P.: Public-key cryptosystems based on composite degree residuosity classes. In: Stern, J. (ed.) EUROCRYPT 1999. LNCS, vol. 1592, pp. 223–238. Springer, Heidelberg (1999)
22. Rivest, R., Shamir, A., Adleman, L.: A method for obtaining digital signatures and public-key cryptosystems. Communications of ACM 21(2), 120–126 (1978)
23. Shannon, C.E.: Communication theory of secrecy systems. Bell Systems Technical Journal 28, 656–715 (1949)
24. Shoup, V., Gennaro, R.: Securing threshold cryptosystems against chosen ciphertext attack. Journal of Cryptology 15(2), 75–96 (2002)
25. Vernam, G.S.: Cipher printing telegraph systems for secret wire and radio telegraphic communications. Journal of the American Institute of Electrical Engineers 45, 105–115 (1926) (See also US patent #1,310,719)
26. Westhoff, D., Girao, J., Acharya, M.: Concealed data aggregation for reverse multicast traffic in sensor networks: Encryption, key distribution, and routing adaption. IEEE Transactions on Mobile Computing 5(10), 1417–1431 (2006)

Synthesizing Secure Protocols*

Véronique Cortier[1], Bogdan Warinschi[2], and Eugen Zălinescu[1]

[1] Loria UMR 7503 & CNRS & INRIA Lorraine, Project Cassis
{Veronique.Cortier,Eugen.Zalinescu}@loria.fr
[2] Computer Science Department, University of Bristol
bogdan@cs.bris.ac.uk

Abstract. We propose a general transformation that maps a cryptographic protocol that is secure in an extremely weak sense (essentially in a model where no adversary is present) into a protocol that is secure against a fully active adversary which interacts with an *unbounded* number of protocol sessions, and has absolute control over the network. The transformation works for arbitrary protocols with any number of participants, written with usual cryptographic primitives. Our transformation provably preserves a large class of security properties that contains secrecy and authenticity.

An important byproduct contribution of this paper is a modular protocol development paradigm where designers focus their effort on an extremely simple execution setting – security in more complex settings being ensured by our generic transformation. Conceptually, the transformation is very simple, and has a clean, well motivated design. Each message is tied to the session for which it is intended via digital signatures and on-the-fly generated session identifiers, and prevents replay attacks by encrypting the messages under the recipient's public key.

1 Introduction

Cryptographic protocols are small programs designed to ensure secure communications over an untrusted network. Their security is of crucial importance due to their widespread use in critical systems and in day-to-day life. Unfortunately, designing and analyzing such protocols is a notoriously difficult and error-prone task, largely due to the potentially unbounded behavior of malicious agents.

In this paper we contribute to a popular technique that has been developed to cope with this problem. Under the paradigm that we study, one can start with the design of a simple version of a system intended to work in restricted environments (*i.e.* with restricted adversaries) and then obtain, via a generic transformation, a more robust system intended to work in arbitrary environments.

---

* The work described in this paper has been supported in part by the European Commission through the IST Programme under Contract IST-2002-507932 ECRYPT, and by the French ACI Satin and the French ACI Jeunes Chercheurs JC9005. The information in this document reflects only the author's views, is provided as is and no guarantee or warranty is given that the information is fit for any particular purpose. The user thereof uses the information at its sole risk and liability.

J. Biskup and J. Lopez (Eds.): ESORICS 2007, LNCS 4734, pp. 406–421, 2007.

More specifically, we introduce one such transformation that takes as input a protocol that is secure (in a sense that we discuss below) in a *single* execution of the protocol, with *no adversary* present (not even a passive eavesdropper). The output of the transformation is a protocol that withstands a realistic adversary with absolute control of the communication between an unbounded number of protocol sessions. The details of our transformation are useful to understand how security is transfered from the simple to the more complex setting.

Our transformation. At a high level, the transformation works by first dynamically generating a unique session identifier for the session, bounding messages to sessions by signing their concatenation with the identifier of the session for which they are intended, and finally, hiding the message from the adversary using encryption under the public key of the recipient. More specifically, the transformation is as follows. Consider a protocol with k participants $A_1, \ldots, A_k$ and n exchanges of messages.

$$A_{i_1} \to A_{j_1} : \ m_1$$
$$\vdots$$
$$A_{i_n} \to A_{j_n} : \ m_n$$

The transformed protocol starts with a preliminary phase, where each participant A_i broadcasts a fresh nonce N_i to all others participants. The concatenation of the nonces with the identities of the participants forms a session identifier sessionID $= \langle A_1, A_2, \ldots, A_k, N_1, N_2, \ldots, N_k \rangle$. Note that the adversary may interfere with this preliminary phase and may, for instance, intercept and replace some of the nonces. Such a behavior would however be detected in the next phase. The remainder of the protocol works roughly as the original one except that each message is sent together with a signature on the message concatenated with the session identifier, and the whole construct is encrypted under the recipient's public key:

$$A_{i_1} \to A_{j_1} : \ \{\!\!\{m_1, [\![m_1, p_1, \mathsf{sessionID}]\!]_{\mathsf{sk}(A_{i_1})}\}\!\!\}_{\mathsf{pk}(A_{j_1})}$$
$$\vdots$$
$$A_{i_n} \to A_{j_n} : \ \{\!\!\{m_n, [\![m_n, p_n, \mathsf{sessionID}]\!]_{\mathsf{sk}(A_{i_n})}\}\!\!\}_{\mathsf{pk}(A_{j_n})}$$

where the p_i's are the current control points in the participant's programs. We write $[\![m]\!]_{\mathsf{sk}(A)}$ for the message m tied with its signature with the signing key of A and $\{\!\!\{m\}\!\!\}_{\mathsf{pk}(A)}$ for the encryption of m under the public encryption key of A.

Security preservation. Intuitively, our transformation ensures that an active adversary cannot tamper with the messages sent during an execution of the (transformed) protocol between honest participants. The transformation also ensures that the adversary cannot learn these messages. In turn, these properties imply that many security statements that hold about a single execution of the protocol, in the absence of an adversary, are inherited by the transformed protocol, even if executed in the presence of an active adversary. Clearly, the transformation does not preserve all imaginable security properties (for example, any anonymity that the original protocol might enjoy is lost due to the use of public key encryption). We identify a class of logic formulas which if satisfied in single executions of the original protocol are also satisfied by the transformed protocol in the presence of active adversaries. The class that we consider is interesting in that it includes standard formulations for secrecy and authentication (for example injective agreement and several other weaker variants [14]).

Simple protocol design. Our transformation enables more modular and manageable protocol development. One can start by building a protocol with the desirable properties built-in, and bearing in mind that no adversary is actually present. Then, the final protocol is obtained using the transformation that we propose. We remark that designers can easily deal with the case of single session and it is usually the more involved setting (multi-party, many-session) that causes the real problems. Our transformation can be applied to any kind of protocols, with any number of participants (although, the number of participants in each session should not be too large for efficiency).

Simple protocol verification. In standard protocol design, the potentially unbounded behavior of malicious agents makes verification of protocols an extremely difficult task. Even apparently simple security properties like secrecy are undecidable in general [9]. One obvious approach to enable verifiability is to consider restrictions to smaller protocol classes. For example, it can be shown that for finite number of parallel sessions secrecy preservation is co-NP-complete [17]. Most automatic tools are based on this assumption, which is often sufficient to discover new attacks but does not allow in general to prove security properties. It is also possible to ensure verifiability of protocols even for unbounded number of sessions by restricting the form of messages, and/or the ability to generate new nonces, e.g. [9,3,4], but only a few such results do not make this unreasonably strong assumption [15,16].

For the class of protocols obtained via our transformation, security verification is significantly trivialised. Indeed, for a *single, honest* execution, security is in fact closer to correctness, and should be easily carried out automatically.

Related work. The kind of modular design paradigm that we propose is rather pervasive in cryptographic design. For example, Goldreich, Micali, and Wigderson show how to compile arbitrary protocols secure against participants that honestly follow the protocol (but may try to learn information they are not entitled to) into protocols secure against participants that may arbitrarily deviate from the protocol [10]. Bellare, Canetti, and Krawczyk have shown how to transform a protocol that is secure when the communication between parties is authenticated into one that remains secure when this assumption is not met [2]. All of the above transformations have a different goal, apply to protocols that need to satisfy stronger requirements than ours, and are also different in their design.

Our work is inspired by a recent compiler introduced by Katz and Yung [12] which transforms any group key exchange protocol secure against a passive adversary into one secure against an active adversary. Their transformation is, in some sense, simpler since they do not require that the messages in the transformed protocol are encrypted. However, their transformation is also weaker since although it requires that the protocol be secure against passive adversaries, these adversaries still can corrupt parties adaptively (even after the execution has finished). Furthermore, while their transformation is sufficient for the case of group key exchange, it fails to guarantee the transfer of more general security properties. The reason for the failure is that an adversary can obtain a message (e.g. a ciphertext) from a session with only honest participants, and get information about the message (e.g. the underlying plaintext) by replaying it in some other sessions for which he can produce the necessary digital signatures.

Our transformation might be viewed as a way of transforming protocols into fail-stop protocols, introduced by Gong and Syverson [11], where any interference of an attacker is immediately observed and causes the execution to stop. But for fail-stop protocols, it is still necessary to consider the security issues related to the presence of passive adversaries. Here we achieve more since we obtain directly secure protocols. Moreover, a major difference is that we provide formal proof of the security of the resulting protocols while the approach of [11] is rather a methodology for prudent engineering. In particular, there are no proved guarantees on the security of the resulting protocols.

Datta, Derek, Mitchell, and Pavlovic [8] propose a methodology for modular development of protocols where security properties are *added* to a protocol through generic transformations. In contrast, our transformation starts from protocols where the security property is built-in. Abadi, Gonthier, and Fournet give a compiler for programs written in a language with abstractions for secure channels into an implementation that uses cryptography [1] and is similar to ours in the sense that it aims to eliminate cryptographic security analysis in involved settings. However the overall goal is different.

2   Protocols

In this section we give a language for specifying protocols and define their execution in the presence of passive and active adversaries. For simplicity of presentation, we use a model that does not directly capture probabilistic primitives. Nevertheless, our theorems and proofs easily extend to a model that models randomness explicitly (e.g. through the use of labels as in [6]).

2.1   Syntax

We consider protocols specified in a language similar to the one of [6] allowing parties to exchange messages built from identities and randomly generated nonces using asymmetric and symmetric encryption and digital signatures.

Consider the algebraic signature Σ with the following sorts. A sort ID for agent identities, sorts SigKey, VerKey, AsymEKey, AsymDKey, SymKey containing keys for signing, verifying, public-key encryption, public-key decryption, and symmetric encryption algorithms. The algebraic signature also contains sorts Nonce, Ciphertext, Signature, and Pair for nonces, ciphertexts, signatures, and pairs, respectively. The sort Term is a supersort containing, besides all other sorts enumerated above, a sort Int for integers having $\mathbb{Z}$ as the support set. There are eight operations: the four operations $\mathsf{ek, dk, sk, vk}$ are defined on the sort ID and return the asymmetric encryption key, asymmetric decryption key, signing key, and verification key associated to the input identity. The other operations that we consider are pairing, public and symmetric key encryption, and signing. Their ranges and domains are as follows.

- $\langle \_,\_ \rangle$: $\mathsf{Term} \times \mathsf{Term} \to \mathsf{Pair}$
- $\{\![\_]\!\}_\_$: $\mathsf{AsymEKey} \times \mathsf{Term} \to \mathsf{Ciphertext}$
- $\{\![\_]\!\}_\_$: $\mathsf{SymKey} \times \mathsf{Term} \to \mathsf{Ciphertext}$
- $[\![\_]\!]_\_$: $\mathsf{SigKey} \times \mathsf{Term} \to \mathsf{Signature}$

Let $\mathsf{X.a, X.n, X.k, X.c, X.s, X.t}$ be sets of variables of sort agent, nonce, (symmetric) key, ciphertext, signature and term respectively, and $\mathsf{X} = \mathsf{X.a} \cup \mathsf{X.n} \cup \mathsf{X.k} \cup \mathsf{X.c} \cup \mathsf{X.s} \cup \mathsf{X.t}$. Protocols are specified using the terms in $T_\Sigma(\mathsf{X})$ of the free algebra generated by X over the signature Σ. We suppose that pairing is left associative and write $\langle m_1, m_2, \ldots, m_l \rangle$ for $\langle \langle \langle m_1, m_2 \rangle, m_3 \rangle \ldots, m_l \rangle$. When unambiguous, we may omit the brackets.

Throughout the paper we fix a constant $k \in \mathbb{N}$ that represents the number of protocol participants and we write $[k]$ for the set $\{1, 2, \ldots, k\}$. Furthermore, without loss of generality, we fix the set of agent variables to be $\mathsf{X.a} = \{A_1, A_2, \ldots, A_k\}$, and partition the set of nonce (and key) variables, according to the party that generates them. Formally:

$$\mathsf{X.n} = \cup_{A \in \mathsf{X.a}} \mathsf{X_n}(A) \text{ where } \mathsf{X_n}(A) = \{N_A^j \mid j \in \mathbb{N}\}$$
$$\mathsf{X.k} = \cup_{A \in \mathsf{X.a}} \mathsf{X_k}(A) \text{ where } \mathsf{X_k}(A) = \{K_A^j \mid j \in \mathbb{N}\}$$

This partition avoids to have to specify later which of the nonces (symmetric keys) are generated by the party executing the protocol, or are expected to be received from other parties.

Roles and protocols. The messages that are sent by participants are specified using terms in $T_\Sigma(\mathsf{X})$. The individual behavior of each protocol participant is defined by a *role* describing a sequence of message reception/transmission which we call *steps* or *rules*. A k-party protocol consists of k such roles together with an association that maps each step of a role that expects some message m to the step of the role where the message m is produced. Notice that this association essentially defines how the execution of a protocol should proceed in the absence of an adversary.

Definition 1 (Roles and protocols). *The set of* roles *is defined by* $\mathsf{Roles} = ((\{\mathsf{init}\} \cup T_\Sigma(\mathsf{X})) \times (T_\Sigma(\mathsf{X}) \cup \{\mathsf{stop}\}))^*$. *A k-party protocol is a pair* $\Pi = (\mathcal{R}, \mathcal{S})$ *where* $\mathcal{R}$ *is a mapping* $\mathcal{R} : [k] \to \mathsf{Roles}$ *that maps* $i \in [k]$ *to the role executed by the i'th protocol participant and* $\mathcal{S} : [k] \times \mathbb{Z} \hookrightarrow [k] \times \mathbb{Z}$ *is a partial mapping that returns for each role/control-point pair (r, p), the role/control-point pair* $(r', p') = \mathcal{S}(r, p)$ *which emits the message to be processed by role r at step p.*

We assume that a protocol specification is such that the r'th role of the protocol $\mathcal{R}(r) = ((\mathsf{rcv}_r^1, \mathsf{snt}_r^1), (\mathsf{rcv}_r^2, \mathsf{snt}_r^2), \ldots)$, is executed by player A_r. Informally, the above definition says that at step p, A_r expects to receive a message of the form specified by rcv_r^p and returns the message snt_r^p. It is important to notice that the terms rcv_r^p and snt_r^p are not actual messages but specify how the message that is received and the message that is output should look like. The messages init and stop are used to initiate and signal successful termination of role executions. We note that for technical reasons we sometimes use negative control points (with negatively indexed role rules).

Example 1. The Needham-Schroeder-Lowe protocol [13]

$$A \rightarrow B : \ \{\!|N_a, A|\!\}_{\mathsf{ek}(B)}$$
$$B \rightarrow A : \ \{\!|N_a, N_b, B|\!\}_{\mathsf{ek}(A)}$$
$$A \rightarrow B : \ \{\!|N_b|\!\}_{\mathsf{ek}(B)}$$

is specified as follows: there are two roles $\mathcal{R}(1)$ and $\mathcal{R}(2)$ corresponding to the sender's role and the receiver's role.

$\mathcal{R}(1) : \Big(\mathsf{init},\ \{\!|N_{A_1}^1, A_1|\!\}_{\mathsf{ek}(A_2)}\Big)$ $\qquad\qquad\qquad$ $\mathcal{S}(1,1) = (0,0)$
$\qquad\quad\ \Big(\{\!|N_{A_1}^1, N_{A_2}^1, A_2|\!\}_{\mathsf{ek}(A_1)},\ \{\!|N_{A_2}^1|\!\}_{\mathsf{ek}(A_2)}\Big)$ $\qquad$ $\mathcal{S}(1,2) = (2,1)$
$\mathcal{R}(2) : \Big(\{\!|N_{A_1}^1, A_1|\!\}_{\mathsf{ek}(A_2)},\ \{\!|N_{A_1}^1, N_{A_2}^1, A_2|\!\}_{\mathsf{ek}(A_1)}\Big)$ $\quad$ $\mathcal{S}(2,1) = (1,1)$
$\qquad\quad\ \Big(\{\!|N_{A_2}^1|\!\}_{\mathsf{ek}(A_2)},\ \mathsf{stop}\Big)$ $\qquad\qquad\qquad\qquad\qquad$ $\mathcal{S}(2,2) = (1,2)$

Executable protocols. Clearly, not all protocols written using the syntax above are meaningful. We only consider the class of *executable protocols*, *i.e.* protocols for which each role can be implemented in an executable program, using only the local knowledge of the corresponding agent. This requires in particular that any sent message (corresponding to some snt_r^p) is always deducible from the previously received messages (corresponding to $\mathsf{rcv}_r^1, \ldots, \mathsf{rcv}_r^p$). Also we demand that $\mathcal{S}$ is consistent. In particular, this means that for a fixed role r, $\mathcal{S}(r, p)$ is defined on exactly $|\mathcal{R}(r)|$ consecutive integers, where $|S|$ denotes the cardinality of the set S.

2.2 Formal Execution Model

We start with the description of the execution model of the protocol in the presence of an active attacker. The model that we consider is rather standard. The parties in the system execute a (potentially unbounded) number of protocol sessions with each other. The communication is under the complete control of the adversary who can intercept, drop, or modify the messages on the network.

The messages transmitted between parties are terms of the algebra T^f freely generated over the signature Σ by an arbitrary fixed set of identities $\mathsf{T}_{\mathsf{ID}}^f$ together with the sets for types SymKey and Nonce defined by:

$$\mathsf{T}_{\mathsf{SymKey}}^f = \{\mathsf{k}^{a,j,s} \mid a \in \mathsf{T}_{\mathsf{ID}}^f, j \in \mathbb{N}, s \in \mathbb{N}\} \cup \{\mathsf{k}^j \mid j \in \mathbb{N}\}$$
$$\mathsf{T}_{\mathsf{Nonce}}^f = \{\mathsf{n}^{a,j,s} \mid a \in \mathsf{T}_{\mathsf{ID}}^f, j \in \mathbb{N}, s \in \mathbb{N}\} \cup \{\mathsf{n}^j \mid j \in \mathbb{N}\}$$

Informally, one should think of the constant $\mathsf{k}^{a,j,s}$ (respectively $\mathsf{n}^{a,j,s}$) as the j'th key (respectively nonce) generated by party a in session s. Constants k^j and n^j represent keys and nonces produced by the adversary.

To each protocol we associate the set of its valid execution traces. First we clarify what execution traces are and then present the association.

A *global state* of an execution is given by a triple (SId, f, H). Here, SId is the set of role session ids currently executed by protocol participants, f is a global assignment function that keeps track of the local state of each existing session and H is the set of messages that have been sent on the network so far.

More precisely, each role session has an associated unique session identifier $s \in \mathbb{N}$. However, by language abuse (and overloading the notion), we say that a *session id* is a tuple of the form $(s, r, (a_1, a_2, \ldots, a_k))$, where s is the unique identifier for the session, r is the index of the role that is executed in the session and $a_1, a_2, \ldots, a_k \in \mathsf{T}_{\mathsf{ID}}^f$ are the identities of the parties that are involved in the session. We write SID for the set $(\mathbb{N} \times \mathbb{N} \times (\mathsf{T}_{\mathsf{ID}}^f)^k)$ of all session ids.

Mathematically, the global assignment f is a function $f : \mathsf{SId} \rightarrow ([\mathsf{X} \hookrightarrow \mathsf{T}^f] \times \mathbb{N} \times \mathbb{Z})$, where $\mathsf{SId} \subseteq \mathsf{SID}$ represents the session ids initialized in the execution. For each such session id $\mathsf{sid} \in \mathsf{SId}$, $f(\mathsf{sid}) = (\sigma, r, p)$ returns its local state. Here, r is the same role index as in sid, the function σ is a substitution, that is a partial instantiation of the variables of the role $\mathcal{R}(r)$ and $p \in \mathbb{Z}$ is the control point of the program. We sometimes write $X\sigma$ for $\sigma(X)$. We denote by GA the set $[\mathsf{SID} \hookrightarrow ([\mathsf{X} \hookrightarrow \mathsf{T}^f] \times \mathbb{N} \times \mathbb{Z})]$ of all possible global assignments.

Finally, the messages that may be sent on the network can be essentially any element of T^f, so we write Msgs for the set 2^{T^f} (where 2^S is the power set of S).

An *execution trace* is a sequence

$$(S_0, f_0, H_0) \xrightarrow{\alpha_1} (S_1, f_1, H_1) \xrightarrow{\alpha_2} \ldots \xrightarrow{\alpha_n} (S_n, f_n, H_n)$$

such that for each $0 \leq i \leq n$, $(S_i, f_i, H_i) \in (2^{\mathsf{SID}} \times \mathsf{GA} \times \mathsf{Msgs})$ and α_i is one of the *actions* **corrupt**, **new**, and **send** with appropriate parameters that we clarify below. This corresponds to the intuition that transitions between two global states are caused by actions of the adversary who can corrupt users, initiate new sessions of the protocol between users that he chooses, and send messages to existing sessions.

For a k-party protocol Π, the transitions between global states are as follows:

- The adversary corrupts agents: $(\mathsf{SId}, f, H) \xrightarrow{\textbf{corrupt}(a_1, \ldots, a_l)} (\mathsf{SId}, f, H')$ where $a_1, \ldots, a_l \in \mathsf{T}_{\mathsf{ID}}^f$ and $H' = \cup_{1 \leq j \leq l} \mathbf{kn}(a_j) \cup H$. Here, $\mathbf{kn}(a_j)$ denotes the knowledge of a_j: if A is a variable, or a constant of sort agent, we define its knowledge by $\mathbf{kn}(A) = \{\mathsf{dk}(A), \mathsf{sk}(A)\}$ *i.e.* an agent knows its secret decryption and signing key. The adversary corrupts parties by outputting a set of identities. In return, the adversary receives the secret keys corresponding to the identities. In this paper we are only concerned with the case of static corruption so this transition only occurs at the beginning of an execution trace.

- The adversary initiates new sessions: $(\mathsf{SId}, f, H) \xrightarrow{\textbf{new}(r, a_1, \ldots, a_k)} (\mathsf{SId}', f', H)$ where $1 \leq r \leq k$, $a_1, \ldots, a_k \in \mathsf{T}_{\mathsf{ID}}^f$, and f' and SId' are defined as follows. Let $s = |\mathsf{SId}| + 1$, be the session identifier of the new session. Then $\mathsf{SId}' = \mathsf{SId} \cup \{(s, r, (a_1, \ldots, a_k))\}$ and the function f' is defined by:

$$\frac{}{S \vdash m} \; m \in S \qquad \frac{}{S \vdash a, \mathsf{ek}(a), \mathsf{vk}(a), \mathsf{k}^j, \mathsf{n}^j} \; j \in \mathbb{N} \qquad \text{Initial knowledge}$$

$$\frac{S \vdash m_1 \quad S \vdash m_2}{S \vdash \langle m_1, m_2 \rangle} \qquad \frac{S \vdash \langle m_1, m_2 \rangle}{S \vdash m_i} \; i \in \{1, 2\} \qquad \text{Pairing and unpairing}$$

$$\frac{S \vdash k \quad S \vdash m}{S \vdash \{\!|m|\!\}_k} \qquad \frac{S \vdash \{\!|m|\!\}_k \quad S \vdash k}{S \vdash m} \qquad \text{Sym. encryption/decryption}$$

$$\frac{S \vdash m}{S \vdash \{\!|m|\!\}_{\mathsf{ek}(a)}} \qquad \frac{S \vdash \{\!|m|\!\}_{\mathsf{ek}(a)} \quad S \vdash \mathsf{dk}(a)}{S \vdash m} \qquad \text{Asym. encryption/decryption}$$

$$\frac{S \vdash \mathsf{sk}(a) \quad S \vdash m}{S \vdash [\![m]\!]_{\mathsf{sk}(a)}} \qquad \frac{S \vdash [\![m]\!]_{\mathsf{sk}(a)}}{S \vdash m} \qquad \text{Signature}$$

Fig. 1. Deduction rules for the formal adversary. In the above, $a \in \mathsf{T}^f_{\mathsf{ID}}$

- $f'(\mathsf{sid}) = f(\mathsf{sid})$ for every $\mathsf{sid} \in \mathsf{Sld}$.
- $f'(s, r, (a_1, \ldots, a_k)) = (\sigma, r, p_0)$ where p_0 is the initial control point of role r and σ is a partial function $\sigma : \mathsf{X} \hookrightarrow \mathsf{T}^f$ defined by $\sigma(A_j) = a_j$ for $1 \le j \le k$, $\sigma(N^j_{A_r}) = \mathsf{n}^{a_r, j, s}$ for $j \in \mathbb{N}$ and $\sigma(K^j_{A_r}) = \mathsf{k}^{a_r, j, s}$ for $j \in \mathbb{N}$. We recall that the principal that executes role $\mathcal{R}(r)$ is represented by variable A_r thus, in that role, every variable of the form $X^j_{A_r}$ represents a nonce or a symmetric key generated by A_r.

- The adversary sends messages to sessions: $(\mathsf{Sld}, f, H) \xrightarrow{\mathsf{send}(\mathsf{sid}, m)} (\mathsf{Sld}, f', H')$ where $\mathsf{sid} \in \mathsf{Sld}$ and $m \in \mathsf{T}^f$. H' and f' are defined as follows. We define $f'(\mathsf{sid}') = f(\mathsf{sid}')$ for every $\mathsf{sid}' \in \mathsf{Sld} \setminus \{\mathsf{sid}\}$. Let $f(\mathsf{sid}) = (\sigma, r, p)$ for some σ, r and p, and let $\mathcal{R}(r) = ((\mathsf{rcv}^1_r, \mathsf{snt}^1_r), \ldots, (\mathsf{rcv}^{k_r}_r, \mathsf{snt}^{k_r}_r))$ be the role executed in this session. There are two cases:

  - Either there exists a substitution σ' such that $m = \mathsf{rcv}^p_r \sigma'$ and σ' extends σ, that is, $X\sigma' = X\sigma$ whenever σ is defined on X. Then $f'(\mathsf{sid}) = (\sigma', r, p + 1)$ and $H' = H \cup \{\mathsf{snt}^p_r \sigma'\}$. We say that m is *accepted*.
  - Or we let $f'(\mathsf{sid}) = f(\mathsf{sid})$ and $H' = H$ (the state remains unchanged).

As usual, we are only interested in *valid* execution traces – those traces where the adversary only sends messages that he can compute out of his knowledge and the messages it had seen on the network. The adversary can derive new information using the relation $\vdash$. Intuitively, $S \vdash m$ means that the adversary is able to compute the message m from the set of messages S; the adversarial abilities are captured by the definition in Figure 1. The only rule that is perhaps less standard is the last one. It essentially states that out of a signature an adversary could compute the message that is signed, which is theoretically possible for any secure digital signature scheme.

The set of valid execution traces is described by the following definition.

Definition 2 (Valid execution traces). *An execution trace* $(\mathsf{Sld}_0, f_0, H_0) \to \dots \to (\mathsf{Sld}_n, f_n, H_n)$ *is valid if*

- $H_0 = \mathsf{Sld}_0 = \emptyset$, $(\mathsf{Sld}_0, f_0, H_0) \to (\mathsf{Sld}_1, f_1, H_1)$ *for one of the three transitions described above and for every* $1 \leq i \leq n$, $(\mathsf{Sld}_i, f_i, H_i) \to (\mathsf{Sld}_{i+1}, f_{i+1}, H_{i+1})$ *for one of the last two transitions described above;*
- *moreover, the messages sent by the adversary can be computed using* $\vdash$, *i.e. whenever* $(\mathsf{Sld}_i, f_i, H_i) \xrightarrow{\mathsf{send}(\mathsf{sid},m)} (\mathsf{Sld}_{i+1}, f_{i+1}, H_{i+1})$ *then* $H_i \vdash m$.

Given a protocol Π, *we write* $\mathsf{Exec}(\Pi)$ *for the set of valid execution traces of* Π.

Example 2. Playing with the Needham-Schroeder-Lowe protocol described in Example 1, an adversary can corrupt an agent a_3, start a new session for the second role with players a_1, a_2 and send the message $\{\!|n(a_3,1,1), a_1|\!\}_{ek(a_2)}$ to the player of the second role. The corresponding valid trace execution is:

$$(\emptyset, f_1, \emptyset) \xrightarrow{\mathbf{corrupt}(a_3)} (\emptyset, f_1, \mathbf{kn}(a_3)) \xrightarrow{\mathbf{new}(2,a_1,a_2)} (\{\mathsf{sid}_1\}, f_2, \mathbf{kn}(a_3))$$
$$\xrightarrow{\mathbf{send}(\mathsf{sid}_1, \{\!|n_3, a_1|\!\}_{ek(a_2)})} (\{\mathsf{sid}_1\}, f_3, \mathbf{kn}(a_3) \cup \{\{\!|n_3, n_2, a_2|\!\}_{ek(a_1)}\}),$$

where $\mathsf{sid}_1 = (1, 2, (a_1, a_2))$, $n_2 = \mathsf{n}(a_2,1,1)$, $n_3 = \mathsf{n}(a_3,1,1)$, and f_2, f_3 are defined as follows: $f_2(\mathsf{sid}_1) = (\sigma_1, 2, 1)$, $f_3(\mathsf{sid}_1) = (\sigma_2, 2, 2)$ where $\sigma_1(A_1) = a_1$, $\sigma_1(A_2) = a_2$, $\sigma_1(N_{A_2}^1) = n_2$, and σ_2 extends σ_1 by $\sigma_2(N_{A_1}^1) = n_3$.

Given an arbitrary trace $\mathsf{tr} = (\mathsf{Sld}_0, f_0, H_0) \xrightarrow{\alpha_1} \dots \xrightarrow{\alpha_n} (\mathsf{Sld}_n, f_n, H_n)$ with $n \in \mathbb{N}$, we define the set of *corrupted agents* of a trace tr by $\mathsf{CA}(\mathsf{tr}) = \{a_1, \dots, a_l\}$ if $\alpha_1 = \mathbf{corrupt}(a_1, \dots, a_l)$ and $\mathsf{CA}(\mathsf{tr}) = \emptyset$ otherwise. The set $\mathsf{Sld}^h(\mathsf{tr})$ of honest session identifiers is the set of session identifiers that correspond to sessions between non-corrupt agents:

$$\mathsf{Sld}^h(\mathsf{tr}) = \{\mathsf{sid} \in \mathsf{Sld}_n \mid \mathsf{sid} = (s, r, (a_1, \dots, a_k)), \mathsf{CA}(\mathsf{tr}) \cap \{a_1, \dots, a_k\} = \emptyset\}.$$

Also, for a trace tr we denote by $\mathsf{I}(\mathsf{tr})$ the set of indexes i of the transitions and global states of tr. For example the above trace has $\mathsf{I}(\mathsf{tr}) = \{0, 1, \dots, n\}$. If sid is a session id then we denote by $\mathsf{Ag}(\mathsf{sid})$ the set of agents involved in this session, that is $\mathsf{Ag}(\mathsf{sid}) = \{a_1, \dots, a_k\}$ when $\mathsf{sid} = (\cdot, \cdot, (a_1, \dots, a_k))$.

3   Security Properties

We use a simple logic introduced in [5] to express security properties for protocols specified in the language given in the previous section. We recall this logic, define its semantics and provide several examples of security properties that can be expressed within.

3.1   A Logic for Security Properties

The formulas of logic capture trace properties and, in particular, they allow quantification over the local states of agents. We define the set of local states

$$[\![\mathsf{NC}(\mathsf{tr}, a)]\!] = \begin{cases} 1 & \text{if } a \text{ does not appear in a corrupt action,} \\ & i.e. \text{ if } e_1 \xrightarrow{\mathbf{corrupt}(a_1,\ldots,a_l)} e_2, \text{ intr} = (e_1, e_2, \ldots, e_n), \\ & \text{we have } a \neq a_i, \forall 1 \leq i \leq l, \\ 0 & \text{otherwise} \end{cases}$$

$$[\![\forall \mathcal{LS}_{r,p}(\mathsf{tr}).\varsigma\ \phi(\mathsf{tr})]\!] = \begin{cases} 1 & \text{if } \forall (\sigma, r, p) \in \mathcal{LS}_{r,p}(\mathsf{tr}), \text{ we have } [\![\phi(\mathsf{tr})[\%]]\!] = 1, \\ 0 & \text{otherwise.} \end{cases}$$

$$[\![\exists \mathcal{LS}_{r,p}(\mathsf{tr}).\varsigma\ \phi(\mathsf{tr})]\!] = \begin{cases} 1 & \text{if } \exists (\sigma, r, p) \in \mathcal{LS}_{r,p}(\mathsf{tr}), \text{ s.t. } [\![\phi(\mathsf{tr})[\%]]\!] = 1, \\ 0 & \text{otherwise.} \end{cases}$$

$$[\![\exists! \mathcal{LS}_{r,p}(\mathsf{tr}).\varsigma\ \phi(\mathsf{tr})]\!] = \begin{cases} 1 & \text{if } \exists! \, \mathsf{sid} \in \mathsf{Sld}(\mathsf{tr}), \exists i \in \mathsf{I}(\mathsf{tr}) \text{ s.t.} \\ & f_i(\mathsf{sid}) = (\sigma, r, p) \text{ and } [\![\phi(\mathsf{tr})[\%]]\!] = 1, \\ 0 & \text{otherwise.} \end{cases}$$

Fig. 2. Interpretation of formulas in $\mathcal{L}$

of a trace $\mathsf{tr} = (\mathsf{Sld}_i, f_i, H_i)_{1 \leq i \leq n}$ for role r at step p by $\mathcal{LS}_{r,p}(\mathsf{tr}) \triangleq \{(\sigma, r, p) \mid \exists i \in [n], \exists \mathsf{sid} \in \mathsf{Sld}_i, \text{ s.t. } f_i(\mathsf{sid}) = (\sigma, r, p)\}$. Note that the cardinality of this set equals the number of agents that are playing role r and that have reached control point p.

We assume an infinite set XSub of meta-variables for substitutions. The logic contains tests between terms where variables are substituted by variable substitutions. More formally, let $\mathsf{T}_{\mathsf{Sub}}$ be the algebra defined by:

$$\mathsf{T}_{\mathsf{Sub}} ::= \varsigma(X) \mid g(\mathsf{T}_{\mathsf{Sub}}) \mid h(\mathsf{T}_{\mathsf{Sub}}, \mathsf{T}_{\mathsf{Sub}})$$

where $\varsigma \in \mathsf{XSub}$, $X \in \mathsf{X}$, and $g, h \in \Sigma$ of arity 1 and 2 respectively.

Besides standard propositional connectors, the logic has a predicate to specify honest agents, equality and inequality tests between terms, and existential and universal quantifiers over the local states of agents.

Definition 3. *The formulas of the logic $\mathcal{L}$ are defined by induction as follows:*

$$\phi(\mathsf{tr}) ::= \mathsf{NC}(\mathsf{tr}, \varsigma(A)) \mid t_1 = t_2 \mid \neg\phi(\mathsf{tr}) \mid \phi(\mathsf{tr}) \wedge \phi(\mathsf{tr}) \mid \phi(\mathsf{tr}) \vee \phi(\mathsf{tr})$$
$$\mid \forall \mathcal{LS}_{r,p}(\mathsf{tr}).\varsigma\ \phi(\mathsf{tr}) \mid \exists \mathcal{LS}_{r,p}(\mathsf{tr}).\varsigma\ \phi(\mathsf{tr}) \mid \exists! \mathcal{LS}_{r,p}(\mathsf{tr}).\varsigma\ \phi(\mathsf{tr})$$

where tr *is a parameter of the formula,* $A \in \mathsf{X}.a$, $\varsigma \in \mathsf{XSub}$, $t_1, t_2 \in \mathsf{T}_{\mathsf{Sub}}$ *and* $r, p \in \mathbb{N}$. *As usual, we may use* $\phi_1 \Rightarrow \phi_2$ *as a shortcut for* $\neg\phi_1 \vee \phi_2$.

Here the predicate $\mathsf{NC}(\mathsf{tr}, \varsigma(A))$ is used to specify non corrupted agents. The quantifications $\forall \mathcal{LS}_{r,p}(\mathsf{tr}).\varsigma$ and $\exists \mathcal{LS}_{r,p}(\mathsf{tr}).\varsigma$ are over local states of agent r at step p in trace tr, and they bound the variable substitution ς. The semantics of our logic is defined for *closed* formula as follows: standard propositional connectors and negation are interpreted as usual. Equality is syntactic equality. The interpretation of quantifiers and the predicate NC is shown in Figure 2.

A *security property* ϕ should be seen in this paper as an abstraction of the form $\phi \triangleq \lambda\mathsf{tr}.\phi(\mathsf{tr})$, where the tr parameter is used only to define the semantics of such formulas. By abuse of notation we therefore ignore this parameter and write $\phi \in \mathcal{L}$ for a security property. Informally, a protocol Π satisfies ϕ if $\phi(\text{tr})$ is true for all traces of Π. Formally:

Definition 4 (Satisfiability). *Let Π be a protocol and $\phi \in \mathcal{L}$ be a security property. We say that Π satisfies the security property ϕ, and write $\Pi \models \phi$ if for any trace $\text{tr} \in \text{Exec}(\Pi)$, $[\![\phi(\text{tr})]\!] = 1$.*

3.2 Examples of Security Properties

In this section we show how to specify secrecy and several variants of authentication, including those from Lowe's hierarchy [14], in the given security logic.

A secrecy property. Let Π be a k-party executable protocol. To specify our secrecy property we use a standard encoding. Namely, we add a role to the protocol, $\mathcal{R}(k+1) = (Y, \text{stop})$, where Y is a new variable of sort Term. It can be seen as some sort of witness as it does nothing but waits for receiving a piece of public data.

Informally, the definition of the secrecy property ϕ_s states that, for any local state of an agent playing role r in which a nonce (or a key) X was created in an honest session, a witness (i.e. an agent playing role $k + 1$) cannot gain any knowledge on X. Formally, the property is specified by the following formula:

$$\phi_s(\text{tr}) = \forall \mathcal{LS}_{r,1}(\text{tr}).\varsigma \left(\bigwedge_{l \in [k]} NC(\text{tr}, \varsigma(A_l)) \Rightarrow \forall \mathcal{LS}_{k+1,2}(\text{tr}).\varsigma' \left(\varsigma(X) \neq \varsigma'(Y) \right) \right)$$

Intuitively, the formula states that for all local states of an agent executing role r (in session ς) and being at his initial control point (i.e. 1), if only honest agents are playing in ς then for all local states of an agent executing role $k + 1$ (in session ς') and being at his final control point (i.e. 2), the value of the secret (i.e. X) in ς is different from the value of the received message (i.e. Y) in ς'.

As a side remark, notice that it is possible to also model the secrecy of a data X received during an honest session: we would simply specify the control point p (instead of 1) at which the date is received by the role r. Moreover, in both cases (that is, X created or received) the formula is always true for honest, single session traces. It will follow that our transformation preserves secrecy of all nonces or keys used in sessions that involve only honest parties.

Authentication properties. We show how to use the logic defined above to specify the injective agreement [14] between two parties A and B. Informally, this property states that whenever an A completes a run of the protocol, apparently with B, then there is unique run of B apparently with A such that two agents agree on the values of some fixed variables, provided that A and B are honest. As usual nothing is guaranteed in sessions involving corrupted agents.

Let p_1 be the length of A's role and p_2 be the control point at which B should have received all data items from A. Then, the above intuition is captured by the following formula:

$$\phi_a(\mathsf{tr}) \triangleq \forall \mathcal{LS}_{1,p_1}(\mathsf{tr}).\varsigma \left(\mathsf{NC}(\mathsf{tr}, A\varsigma) \wedge \mathsf{NC}(\mathsf{tr}, B\varsigma) \Rightarrow \right.$$

$$\left. \exists! \mathcal{LS}_{2,p_2}(\mathsf{tr}).\varsigma' \left((A\varsigma = A\varsigma') \wedge (B\varsigma = B\varsigma') \wedge \bigwedge_{1 \leq i \leq n}(X_i\varsigma = X_i\varsigma') \right) \right)$$

Intuitively, the formula states that for all local states of an agent having finished executing the first role (in session ς), if the two agents (executing the two roles in ς) are honest in ς then there exists an unique local state of an agent having finished executing the second role (in session ς') and such that the agents agree on their identitites and on the values of the variables that are common to the two roles.

It is easy to modify this formula in order to obtain formulas corresponding to the other variants of authentication from Lowe's hierarchy.

4   Transformation of Protocols

The core idea of the transformation is to have parties agree on some common, dynamically generated, session identifier s, and then transmit the encryption of a message m of the original protocol accompanied by a signature on $m\|s$.

The modification of the source protocol is performed in two steps. We first introduce an initialization phase, where each agent generates a fresh nonce which is distributed to all other participants. The idea is that the concatenation of all these nonces and all the identities involved in the session plays the role of a unique session identifier. To avoid underspecification of the resulting protocol we fix a particular way in which the nonces are distributed. First, each agent generates a fresh nonce and then sends the nonces he received so far together with his nonce to the next agent. That is, in Alice-Bob notation, $A_i \rightarrow A_{i+1} : N_{A_1}, \dots, N_{A_i}$, for all i in the sequence $1, \dots, k-1$. Then, once the last agent received all nonces, each agent forwards the concatenation of all nonces to its predecesor. That is, $A_i \rightarrow A_{i-1} : N_{A_1}, \dots, N_{A_k}$, for all i in the sequence $k, \dots, 2$. In this way, at the end of this first phase all agents know each other's nonces.

We remark that the precise order in which participants send these nonces does not really matter, and we do not require that these nonces be authenticated in some way. In principle an active adversary is allowed to forward, block or modify the messages sent during the initialization phase, but behaviours that deviate from the intended execution of the protocol are detected in the next phase.

In the second phase of the transformed protocol, the execution proceeds as prescribed by Π with the difference that to each message m that needs to be sent, the sending parties also attaches a signature $[\![m, p, \mathsf{nonces}]\!]_{\mathsf{sk'}(a)}$ and encrypts the whole construct with the intended receiver public key. p is the current control point and nonces is the concatenation of the nonces received during the first phase with the identities of the participants involved in the protocol.

Intuitively, the adversary cannot impersonate users in honest sessions (since in this case it would need to produce digital signatures on their behalf), and cannot learn secrets by replaying messages from one session to another (since messages are encrypted, and any blindly replayed message would be rejected due to un-matching session identifiers). The control-point p plays within a session the same role as nonces between sessions: messages not matching the correct control point are rejected.

To avoid confusion and unintended interactions between the signatures and the encryptions produced by the compiler and those used in the normal execution of the protocol, the former use fresh signatures and public keys. Formally, we extend the signature Σ with four new function symbols sk', vk', ek' and dk' which have exactly the same functionality (that is the same sort and similar deduction rules) with sk, vk, ek and dk respectively.

This formalizes the assumption that in the transformed version of Π each agent a has associated two pairs of verification/signing keys $((\mathsf{vk}(a), \mathsf{sk}(a))$ and $(\mathsf{vk}'(a), \mathsf{sk}'(a)))$ and two pairs of encryption/decryption keys $((\mathsf{ek}(a), \mathsf{dk}(a))$ and $(\mathsf{ek}'(a), \mathsf{dk}'(a)))$ and that these new pairs of keys were correctly distributed previously to any execution of the protocol. We assume that source protocols are constructed over Σ only.

Definition 5 (Transformed protocol). *Let $\Pi = (\mathcal{R}, \mathcal{S})$ be a k-party executable protocol such that the nonce variables $N^0_{A_k}$ do not appear in $\mathcal{R}$ (which can be ensured by renaming the nonce variables of Π) and all the initial control points are set to 1 (which can be ensured by rewriting the function $\mathcal{S}$).*

The transformed protocol $\widetilde{\Pi} = (\widetilde{\mathcal{R}}, \widetilde{\mathcal{S}})$ is defined as follows: $\widetilde{\mathcal{R}}(r) = \mathcal{R}^{\mathsf{init}}(r) \cdot \mathcal{R}'(r)$ and $\widetilde{\mathcal{S}} = \mathcal{S}^{\mathsf{init}} \cup \mathcal{S}$ where $\cdot$ denotes the concatenation of sequences and $\mathcal{R}^{\mathsf{init}}$, $\mathcal{R}'$ and $\mathcal{S}^{\mathsf{init}}$ are defined as follows:

$$\mathcal{R}^{\mathsf{init}}(r) = \big((\mathsf{nonces}_{r-1}, \mathsf{nonces}_r), (\mathsf{nonces}_k, \mathsf{nonces}_k)\big), \quad \forall 1 \leq r < k,$$
$$\mathcal{S}^{\mathsf{init}}(r, -1) = (r-1, -1), \quad \mathcal{S}^{\mathsf{init}}(r, 0) = (r+1, 0), \quad \forall 1 \leq r < k,$$
$$\mathcal{R}^{\mathsf{init}}(k) = \big((\mathsf{nonces}_{k-1}, \mathsf{nonces}_k)\big) \qquad \mathcal{S}^{\mathsf{init}}(k, 0) = (k-1, -1)$$

with $\mathsf{nonces}_0 = \mathsf{init}$ and $\mathsf{nonces}_j = \langle N^0_{A_1}, N^0_{A_2}, \ldots, N^0_{A_j} \rangle$ for $1 \leq j \leq k$.

Let $\mathcal{R}(r) = \big((\mathsf{rcv}^p_r, \mathsf{snt}^p_r)\big)_{p \in [k_r]}$. Then $\mathcal{R}'(r) = \big((\widetilde{\mathsf{rcv}}^p_r, \widetilde{\mathsf{snt}}^p_r)\big)_{p \in [k_r]}$ such that if $\mathsf{rcv}^p_r = \mathsf{init}$ then $\widetilde{\mathsf{rcv}}^p_r = \mathsf{fake}$, if $\mathsf{snt}^p_r = \mathsf{stop}$ then $\widetilde{\mathsf{snt}}^p_r = \mathsf{stop}$ and otherwise

$$\widetilde{\mathsf{rcv}}^p_r = \{\mathsf{rcv}^p_r, [\![\mathsf{rcv}^p_r, p', \mathsf{nonces}]\!]_{\mathsf{sk}'(A_{r'})}\}_{\mathsf{ek}'(A_r)},$$
$$\widetilde{\mathsf{snt}}^p_r = \{\mathsf{snt}^p_r, [\![\mathsf{snt}^p_r, p, \mathsf{nonces}]\!]_{\mathsf{sk}'(A_r)}\}_{\mathsf{ek}'(A_{r''})}$$

where $(r', p') = \mathcal{S}(r, p)$, $(r, p) = \mathcal{S}(r'', p'')$ and $\mathsf{nonces} = \langle A_1, \ldots, A_k, \mathsf{nonces}_k \rangle$.

The initial control point is now set to -1 (or 0 for A_k) since actions have been added for the initialization stage. The special message fake is used to model for example the situation where an agent waits for more than one message in order to reply or when an agent sends more than one reply.

5   Main Result

We identify a class of executions, which we call honest, single session executions which, intuitively, correspond to traces where just one session is executed, session in which all parties are honest and there is no adversary. Our only hypothesis will be that the initial protocol has to be secure in this very weak setting.

Definition 6 (Honest, single session trace). *Let $\Pi = (\mathcal{R}, \mathcal{S})$ be a k-party protocol and* $\mathrm{tr} = (\mathsf{Sld}_0, f_0, H_0) \xrightarrow{\alpha_1} \ldots \xrightarrow{\alpha_n} (\mathsf{Sld}_n, f_n, H_n)$ *be a valid trace of Π. The trace* tr *is an* honest, single session trace *if there are k agent identities $a_1, \ldots, a_k$ such that*

- *for $1 \le i \le k$, $\alpha_i = \mathbf{new}(i, a_1, \ldots, a_k)$,*
- *for $k+1 \le i \le n$, $\alpha_i = \mathbf{send}(\mathrm{sid}, m)$, $m = \mathsf{rcv}_r^p \sigma$ where $f_i(\mathrm{sid}) = (\sigma, r, p+1)$, and there exists $j < i$ such that $f_j(\mathrm{sid}') = (\sigma', r', p')$, $\mathcal{S}(r, p) = (r', p')$, and $m = \mathsf{snt}_{r'}^{p'} \sigma'$ for some sid'.*

Let $\mathsf{Exec}^{p,1}(\Pi)$ *be the set of honest, single session traces of Π.*

Definition 7 (Passive, single session satisfiability). *Let Π be a protocol and $\phi \in \mathcal{L}$ be a security property. We say that Π satisfies the security property ϕ for passive adversaries and a single session, and write $\Pi \models^{p,1} \phi$ if for any trace* $\mathrm{tr} \in \mathsf{Exec}^{p,1}(\Pi)$, $[\![\phi(\mathrm{tr})]\!] = 1$.

Transferable security properties. We identify a fragment $\mathcal{L}'$ of the logic $\mathcal{L}$ defined in Section 3 whose formulas specify the properties that can be transferred from the honest, single session case to the full active adversary case.

Definition 8. *The set $\mathcal{L}'$ consists of those formulas $\phi(\mathrm{tr})$ with*

$$\phi(\mathrm{tr}) = \forall \mathcal{LS}_{r,p}(\mathrm{tr}).\varsigma \left(\bigwedge_{l \in [k]} \mathsf{NC}(\mathrm{tr}, \varsigma(A_l)) \Rightarrow \bigwedge_{i \in I} \left(\mathcal{Q}_i \, \mathcal{LS}_{r_i, p_i}(\mathrm{tr}).\varsigma_i \bigwedge_{j \in J_i} \tau_j^i(u_j^i, v_j^i) \right) \right)$$

where $\mathcal{Q}_i \in \{\forall, \exists, \exists!\}$, and for all $i \in I$, for all $j \in J_i$, if $\mathcal{Q}_i = \forall$ then $\tau_j^i \in \{\neq\}$ and if $\mathcal{Q}_i \in \{\exists, \exists!\}$ then $\tau_j^i \in \{=, \neq\}$; moreover, for each $i \in I$, if $\mathcal{Q}_i = \forall$ (respectively $\mathcal{Q}_i = \exists!$) then for all (there is) $j \in J_i$ we have that (such that $\tau_j^i \in \{=\}$ and) there exists at least a subterm $\varsigma(X)$ in u_j^i or v_j^i with X a nonce or key variable.

As usual, we require security properties to hold in sessions between honest agents. This means that no guarantee is provided in a session where a corrupted agent is involved. But this does not prevent honest agents from contacting corrupted agents in parallel sessions. Properties that can be expressed in our fragment $\mathcal{L}'$ are correspondence relations between (data in) particular local states of agents in different sessions. It is a non-trivial class since e.g. the logical formulas given in Section 3 for expressing secrecy and authentication are captured by the above definition.

Transference result. The main result of this paper is the following transference theorem. It informally states that the formulas of $\mathcal{L}'$ that are satisfied in single, honest executions of a protocol are also satisfied by executions of the transformed protocol in the presence of a fully active adversary.

Theorem 1. *Let Π be a protocol and $\widetilde{\Pi}$ the corresponding transformed protocol. Let $\phi \in \mathcal{L}'$ be a security property. Then $\Pi \models^{p,1} \phi \Rightarrow \widetilde{\Pi} \models \phi$.*

The main intuition behind the proof is that any execution in the presence of an active adversary is closely mirrored by some *honest* execution (i.e. an execution with no adversarial interference plus some additional useless sessions). We define honest executions next.

Honest executions. Recall that we demand that protocols come with an intended execution order, in which the designer specifies the source of each message in an execution. Roughly, in an honest execution trace one can partition the set of session ids in sets of at most k role sessions (each corresponding to a different role of the protocol) such that messages are exchanged only within partitions, and the message transmission within each partition follows the intended execution specification. Since we cannot prevent an intruder to create new messages and sign them with corrupted signing keys, clearly the property can hold only for session identifiers corresponding to honest participants. The above ideas are captured by the following definition.

Definition 9 (Honest execution traces). *Let Π be an executable protocol. An execution trace* $\mathsf{tr} = (\mathsf{SId}_0, f_0, H_0) \xrightarrow{\alpha_1} \ldots \xrightarrow{\alpha_n} (\mathsf{SId}_n, f_n, H_n)$ *is honest if it is valid and there is a partition* PrtSId *of the honest role session identifiers* $\mathsf{SId}^h(\mathsf{tr})$ *such that:*

1. *for all $S \in \mathsf{PrtSId}$, for all $\mathsf{sid}, \mathsf{sid}' \in S$ with $\mathsf{sid} \neq \mathsf{sid}'$ and $\mathsf{sid} = (s, r, (a_1, \ldots, a_k))$ and $\mathsf{sid}' = (s', r', (a'_1, \ldots a'_k))$, we have $r \neq r'$, and $a_j = a'_j$ for all $1 \leq j \leq k$; that is, in any protocol session each of the participants execute different roles[1] and the agents agree on their communication partners;*

2. *whenever $(\mathsf{SId}_{i-1}, f_{i-1}, H_{i-1}) \xrightarrow{\mathbf{send}(\mathsf{sid}, m)} (\mathsf{SId}_i, f_i, H_i)$ with $\mathsf{sid} \in \mathsf{SId}^h(\mathsf{tr})$, m accepted, $m \neq \mathsf{fake}$ and $m = \mathsf{rcv}_r^p \sigma$, $p \geq 1$, we have that there are $\mathsf{sid}' \in [\mathsf{sid}]$ and $i' < i$ such that $m = \mathsf{snt}_{r'}^{p'} \sigma'$ and $\mathcal{S}(r, p) = (r', p')$ where $f_i(\mathsf{sid}) = (\sigma, r, p+1)$, $f_{i'}(\mathsf{sid}') = (\sigma', r', p')$, and $[\mathsf{sid}]$ is the partition to which sid belongs to.*

Notice that the above definition considers partial executions in which not all roles finish their execution, and where not all roles in a protocol session need to be initialized. The following lemma states that for any transformed protocol, an active intruder cannot interfere with the execution of honest sessions.

Lemma 1. *Let Π be a protocol and $\widetilde{\Pi}$ the corresponding transformed protocol. In $\widetilde{\Pi}$, any valid execution trace is an honest execution trace.*

Then it remains to show that any property expressed in $\mathcal{L}'$ that holds for one honest, single session trace also holds for any honest execution trace of the transformed protocol. It relies in particular on the fact that due to encryption, fresh values of honest sessions cannot occur in dishonest sessions. Moreover, honest execution traces actually correspond to the honest, single session trace of the initial protocol. More details and full proofs are available in [7].

---

[1] Consequently, each partition consists of at most k role sessions.

References

1. Abadi, M., Fournet, C., Gonthier, G.: Secure implementation of channel abstractions. Inf. Comput. 174(1), 37–83 (2002)
2. Bellare, M., Canetti, R., Krawczyk, H.: A modular approach to the design and analysis of authentication and key exchange protocols (extended abstract). In: STOC '98. Proceedings of the thirtieth annual ACM symposium on Theory of computing, pp. 419–428. ACM Press, New York (1998)
3. Blanchet, B., Podelski, A.: Verification of cryptographic protocols: Tagging enforces termination. In: Gordon, A.D. (ed.) ETAPS 2003 and FOSSACS 2003. LNCS, vol. 2620, Springer, Heidelberg (2003)
4. Comon-Lundh, H., Cortier, V.: New decidability results for fragments of first-order logic and application to cryptographic protocols. In: Nieuwenhuis, R. (ed.) RTA 2003. LNCS, vol. 2706, pp. 148–164. Springer, Heidelberg (2003)
5. Cortier, V., Hördegen, H., Warinschi, B.: Explicit Randomness is not Necessary when Modeling Probabilistic Encryption. In: ICS 2006. Workshop on Information and Computer Security, Timisoara, Romania (September 2006)
6. Cortier, V., Warinschi, B.: Computationally Sound, Automated Proofs for Security Protocols. In: Sagiv, M. (ed.) ESOP 2005. LNCS, vol. 3444, pp. 157–171. Springer, Heidelberg (2005)
7. Cortier, V., Warinschi, B., Zălinescu, E.: Synthesizing secure protocols. Inria research report, INRIA (April 2007), available at http://www.loria.fr/čortier/Papiers/compiler.pdf
8. Datta, A., Derek, A., Mitchell, J.C., Pavlovic, D.: A derivation system and compositional logic for security protocols. J. Comput. Secur. 13(3), 423–482 (2005)
9. Durgin, N., Lincoln, P., Mitchell, J., Scedrov, A.: Undecidability of bounded security protocols. In: Proc. of the Workshop on Formal Methods and Security Protocols (1999)
10. Goldreich, O., Micali, S., Wigderson, A.: How to play any mental game. In: STOC '87. Proceedings of the nineteenth annual ACM conference on Theory of computing, pp. 218–229. ACM Press, New York (1987)
11. Gong, L., Syverson, P.: Fail-stop protocols: An approach to designing secure protocols. In: DCCA-5. Proceedings of the 5th International Working Conference on Dependable Computing for Critical Applications, pp. 44–55 (1995)
12. Katz, J., Yung, M.: Scalable protocols for authenticated group key exchange. In: Boneh, D. (ed.) CRYPTO 2003. LNCS, vol. 2729, pp. 110–125. Springer, Heidelberg (2003)
13. Lowe, G.: Breaking and fixing the Needham-Schroeder public-key protocol using FDR. In: Margaria, T., Steffen, B. (eds.) TACAS 1996. LNCS, vol. 1055, pp. 147–166. Springer, Heidelberg (1996)
14. Lowe, G.: A hierarchy of authentication specifications. In: CSFW 1997, Rockport, Massachusetts, USA, IEEE Computer Society Press, Los Alamitos (1997)
15. Lowe, G.: Towards a completeness result for model checking of security protocols. In: CSFW 1998, IEEE Computer Society Press, Los Alamitos (1998)
16. Ramanujam, R., Suresh, S.P.: A decidable subclass of unbounded security protocols. In: WITS'03. Proc. IFIP Workshop on Issues in the Theory of Security, Warsaw (Poland), pp. 11–20 (2003)
17. Rusinowitch, M., Turuani, M.: Protocol insecurity with finite number of sessions is NP-complete. In: CSFW 2001, pp. 174–190. IEEE Computer Society Press, Los Alamitos (2001)

A Cryptographic Model for Branching Time Security Properties – The Case of Contract Signing Protocols[*]

Véronique Cortier[1], Ralf Küsters[2], and Bogdan Warinschi[3]

[1] CNRS, Loria
veronique.cortier@loria.fr
[2] ETH Zurich
ralf.kuesters@inf.ethz.ch
[3] University of Bristol
bogdan@cs.bris.ac.uk

Abstract. Some cryptographic tasks, such as contract signing and other related tasks, need to ensure complex, branching time security properties. When defining such properties one needs to deal with subtle problems regarding the scheduling of non-deterministic decisions, the delivery of messages sent on resilient (non-adversarially controlled) channels, fair executions (executions where no party, both honest and dishonest, is unreasonably precluded to perform its actions), and defining strategies of adversaries against all possible non-deterministic choices of parties and arbitrary delivery of messages via resilient channels. These problems are typically not addressed in cryptographic models and these models therefore do not suffice to formalize branching time properties, such as those required of contract signing protocols.

In this paper, we develop a cryptographic model that deals with all of the above problems. One central feature of our model is a general definition of fair scheduling which not only formalizes fair scheduling of resilient channels but also fair scheduling of actions of honest and dishonest principals. Based on this model and the notion of fair scheduling, we provide a definition of a prominent branching time property of contract signing protocols, namely balance, and give the first *cryptographic* proof that the Asokan-Shoup-Waidner two-party contract signing protocol is balanced.

---

[*] The first and third author were partly supported by ACI Jeunes Chercheurs JC9005 and ARA SSIA Formacrypt. The second author was supported by the SNF under Grant 200021-116596/1. The work described in this paper has been supported in part by the European Commission through the IST Programme under Contract IST-2002-507932 ECRYPT. The information in this document reflects only the author's views, is provided as is and no guarantee or warranty is given that the information is fit for any particular purpose. The user thereof uses the information at its sole risk and liability.

J. Biskup and J. Lopez (Eds.): ESORICS 2007, LNCS 4734, pp. 422–437, 2007.

1   Introduction

Cryptographic tasks, such as contract signing [1,15,8] and other related tasks, need to ensure complex, branching time properties, i.e., properties of the overall structure of the set of all possible executions of a protocol (as opposed to properties of single execution traces). Examples of such properties are balance [11] and abuse-freeness [15]. Defining such properties requires to cope with several challenges that are typically not addressed in cryptographic models. The main challenges include: modeling non-deterministic behavior of honest parties, resilient (non-adversarially controlled) channels, fair executions in which no party, honest or *dishonest*, can unreasonably be precluded to perform its actions, and strategies of adversaries to achieve certain goals against all possible behaviors of resilient channels and honest parties; the existence or absence of such strategies is a branching time property of a protocol, not a property of a single execution trace. Providing a computational model that deals with all such challenges and applying it to branching time properties of contract signing protocols is the main purpose of this paper.

We illustrate the above points via the balance property for (two-party) optimistic contract signing protocols as first defined by Chadha et al. [11] in a symbolic (Dolev-Yao based) model. These protocols can be used by two parties, A and B, to obtain each other's signature on a previously agreed contractual text with the help of a trusted third party (TTP), which, however, is only contacted in case of a problem. If and when the TTP is contacted depends on *non-deterministic decisions* of the parties. For example, A may decide to send an abort request to the TTP in case she doesn't want to wait any longer for a message from B, or suspects that B is dishonest. Contract signing protocols typically assume that A and B communicate with the TTP over *resilient (non-adversarially controlled) channels*: without such channels an adversary could block all messages from/to the TTP. Now, balance for an honest party A and a dishonest party B, as defined by Chadha et al., requires that in a protocol run it is not possible to reach a state where B has both i) a *strategy* to obtain a signed contract from A (no matter how A, the TTP, and the resilient channels behave) and ii) a (possibly different) *strategy* to prevent A from obtaining a signed contract from B (no matter how A, the TTP, and the resilient channels behave). Since, when following one of these strategies, the adversary, i.e., B, has to achieve his goal—obtaining a signed contract or preventing A from obtaining a signed contract—against the behavior of other entities that he cannot control or foresee (non-deterministic choices of A and delivery of messages on resilient channels), in a computational model it is necessary to determine the behavior of these entities by a *scheduler* which is *independent* of the adversary, and in fact, may work against the adversary. Moreover, for the balance property to make sense, the scheduler should not stop the run of a system if one of the entities in the system (A, the TTP, the resilient channels, the adversary) "can still take an action". In other words, the scheduling should be *fair* for all entities (both honest and dishonest). For example, if at some point A could still contact the TTP, then the scheduler should not stop the run of the system at this point but should eventually schedule A: contacting the TTP might enable A to get the contract. Stopping the system before scheduling A would be unfair and unrealistic since no one stops A from contacting the TTP in a real protocol run. Note that a scheduler is just an imaginary entity that is only needed to *model* how things are potentially scheduled in a real protocol run. Conversely, if B (the adversary) wants to send a message to the TTP, the scheduler should not stop the run of the system but eventually schedule B: sending a message to the TTP might enable B to obtain a signed contract which he otherwise might not be able to get. Again, stopping the system before scheduling B would be unfair and unrealistic since no one stops B from contacting the TTP in a real protocol run. Note that B is an arbitrary adversary (machine), and hence, a general notion of fair scheduling is needed to capture whether "B can still take an action" (e.g., send a message).

Clearly, standard cryptographic models, in which only one adversary is considered controlling the complete communication network, and honest principals can not make non-deterministic choices are insufficient for dealing with the class of protocols and properties considered here. Some cryptographic models take some (not all) of the above aspects into account, but with a different focus and in a way not suitable for the classes of protocols and properties we consider (see the related work).

CONTRIBUTION OF THIS PAPER. In this paper, we propose a computational model that deals with the challenges mentioned above and allows to specify complex, branching time properties.

More precisely, our model is based on a general computational model for systems of interactive Turing machines (ITMs). The model is presented in Section 3. Based on this model, we define a security-specific model (see Section 4) where we use ITMs to capture the behavior of the honest principals, the adversary, the network and resilient channels, and the scheduler. The purpose of the scheduler is to resolve non-deterministic behavior of honest principals, to schedule the resilient channels, and to trigger the adversary. As explained above, modeling the scheduler as an entity independent of the adversary is important. The adversary and the scheduler are each equipped with what we call a *view oracle* which can be invoked by these entities to obtain a *view* on the history of the run of the protocol so far, and hence, to adapt their actions accordingly; typically, the adversary and the scheduler have different view oracles, and hence, different views on the history. The view of the adversary typically includes all messages on the network channels and only messages on those resilient channels which are not required to be read-protected. Conversely, the scheduler might have complete information about the resilient channels. The exact definition of the views (view oracles) depends on the security properties considered and can be adapted depending on the strength of the security guarantee desired. The ITMs that we use cannot be exhausted and can respond to an unbounded number of requests, as for example needed when modeling the TTP in contract signing protocols. Also, this, for example, ensures that the scheduler cannot exhaust the adversary or honest parties, which otherwise would lead to unrealistic runs (recall that the scheduler is only an imaginary entity that is used to model reality).

As mentioned, fair scheduling is an important ingredient in the definition of many security properties, and it is non-trivial to define in computational, resource-bounded settings. We provide a general definition of when a scheduler is fair for a system of ITMs (see Section 5). We emphasize that our definition is independent of the specific structure of the system or the specific ITMs used in the system. This is important as we need to capture fair scheduling also for arbitrary dishonest parties, i.e., adversary machines. Intuitively, we call a scheduler fair for a system if it does not stop the run of the system at a point where at least one of the other machines in the system, e.g., honest parties, the adversary, resilient channels, "can still take an action", e.g., an honest principal could (non-deterministically) decide to start an abort protocol, a resilient channel could deliver a message, or the adversary is ready to send a message to an honest principal. We formalize that a machine "can still take an action" in a general way as follows: We say that a machine can take an action if the machine can be activated by the scheduler with some input so that at the end of the activation the machine has changed its local configuration, and hence, performed some action. (We note that according to our definition of ITMs, if an ITM outputs a message, then it changes its local configuration.) The above definition in particular applies to adversary machines and also to honest parties and resilient channels. For example, if at some point A in a contract signing protocol could either wait for a message from B or contact the TTP to run the abort protocol and the scheduler schedules A to run the abort protocol with TTP, then A changes its local configuration, e.g., goes from state q_{wait} to state q_{abort}. While there does not exist a fair scheduler for every system, we identify sufficient, reasonable conditions for a system to have a fair scheduler. The way fair scheduling is defined here appears to be new and is of interest independent of its application to branching time properties (see also the related work).

Based on our computational model and the notion of fair schedulers, we provide a definition for balance of (contract signing) protocols (see Section 6). In this definition, we need to quantify (universally and existentially) over two different schedulers. The first scheduler may be unfair and may collude with the adversary in order to reach a certain point in the protocol run. The second one has to be fair, but tries to prevent the adversary from achieving his goal. As a proof of concept, we apply our definition to the ASW two-party optimistic contract-signing protocol [1], which is presented in Section 2, and show it to be balanced when implemented with primitives that satisfy standard security assumptions (see Section 6.2). Our proof of balance of this protocol is the first computational proof of this (now rigorously defined) property for a contract signing protocol.

We point the reader to the long version of our paper [13] for further details.

RELATED WORK. Rigorous models, security definitions as well as analysis methods and tools for branching time properties of contract signing protocols have been proposed in [11,22,21,25,22,5,12,19,20]. However, all these works are based on the symbolic (Dolev-Yao) model and do not consider the more involved computational case.

Backes et al. [7] (see also [6]) proposed a definition of fair scheduling in a computational model. While they only consider fair scheduling of channels (which is insufficient for branching time properties), our definition is concerned with fair scheduling of arbitrary machines. Other works that use some kind of fairness in specific settings are [3] and [16]. None of the mentioned works, [7,6,3,16], studies branching time properties or properties of contract signing protocols.

Asokan, Shoup, and Waidner [2] propose a fair contract signing protocol and present a computational model to study fairness of their protocol. However, the model and the notion of fair scheduling that they use is tailored to their specific setting and does not apply to branching time properties.

Canetti et al. [10] study a computational model based on probabilistic I/O automata (PIOAs) in which non-deterministic behavior of principals can be modeled. However, they focus on simulation-based security and do not study fairness issues or branching time properties.

2   A Running Example: The ASW Protocol

In this section, we provide an informal description of the ASW protocol [1]. This protocol is our running example which we use throughout the paper to provide intuition for the models and the notions that we introduce. A more formal description in terms of the model that we propose in this paper can be found in [13].

CRYPTOGRAPHIC PRIMITIVES. The ASW protocol uses concatenation, signatures and hashing. We denote the concatenation of bit strings $m_1, \ldots, m_n$ by $\langle m_1, \ldots, m_n \rangle$, and sometimes by $m_1, \ldots, m_n$. We assume that every m_i can uniquely be recovered from the concatenation. Verification and signing keys of principal P are denoted by v_P and s_P, respectively. The signature of m generated using s_P is denoted by $\mathsf{sig}_{v_P}(m)$. We require for the associated signature verification algorithm $\mathsf{sigver}(\cdot, \cdot, \cdot)$ that $\mathsf{sigver}(m, s, v_P) = \mathsf{true}$ if s is a signature on m generated using s_P, and that $\mathsf{sigver}(m, s, v_P) = \mathsf{false}$ otherwise. We write $\mathsf{sig}[m, v_P]$ for $\langle m, \mathsf{sig}_{v_P}(m) \rangle$, and write $h(m)$ for the hash of message m.

PROTOCOL DESCRIPTION. The ASW protocol enables two principals A (the originator) and B (the responder) to obtain each other's signature on a previously agreed contractual text text (a fixed bit string) with the help of a trusted third party (TTP) T, which however is only invoked in case of problems. In other words, the ASW protocol is an optimistic two-party contract-signing protocol.

There are two kinds of valid contracts: the standard contract, which is of the form $\langle \mathsf{sig}[m_A, v_A], N_A, \mathsf{sig}[m_B, v_B], N_B \rangle$, and the replacement contract, which is of the form $\mathsf{sig}[\langle \mathsf{sig}[m_A, v_A], \mathsf{sig}[m_B, v_B] \rangle, v_T]$, where N_A and N_B are nonces, generated by A and B, respectively, $m_A = \langle v_A, v_B, v_T, \mathsf{text}, h(N_A) \rangle$ and $m_B = \langle \mathsf{sig}[m_A, v_A], h(N_B) \rangle$.

The ASW protocol consists of three subprotocols: the exchange, abort, and resolve protocol. These subprotocols are explained next.

Exchange protocol. First A sends the message $\mathsf{sig}[m_A, v_A]$ indicating A's interest to sign the contract. By sending this message, A "commits" to signing the contract. Then, similarly, B indicates his interest to sign the contract, by replying with $\mathsf{sig}[m_B, v_B]$. Finally, first A and then B reveal N_A and N_B, respectively.

Abort protocol. If, after A has sent her first message, B does not respond, A may contact T to abort, i.e., A runs the abort protocol with T. Note that A may wait as long as she wants before contacting T (non-deterministic action). In the abort protocol, A first sends $a_A = \mathsf{sig}[\langle \mathsf{aborted}, \mathsf{sig}[m_A, v_A]\rangle, v_A]$. If T has not received a resolve request before (see below), then T sends back to A the *abort token* $a_T = \mathsf{sig}[\langle \mathsf{aborted}, a_A\rangle, v_T]$. Otherwise (if T received a resolve request, which in particular involves the messages $\mathsf{sig}[m_A, v_A]$ and $\mathsf{sig}[m_B, v_B]$ from above), it sends the *replacement contract* $r_T = \mathsf{sig}[r, v_T]$ to A, where $r = \langle \mathsf{sig}[m_A, v_A], \mathsf{sig}[m_B, v_B]\rangle$.

Resolve protocol. If, after A has sent the nonce N_A, B does not respond, A may contact T to resolve, i.e., A runs the resolve protocol with T. Again, A may wait for as long as she wants before contacting T (non-deterministic action). In the resolve protocol, A sends the message r to T. If T has not sent out an abort token before, then T returns the replacement contract r_T, and otherwise T returns the abort token a_T. Analogously, if, after B has sent the nonce N_B, A does not respond, B may contact T to resolve, i.e., B runs the resolve protocol with T similarly to the case for A.

We note that the communication with T (for both A and B) is carried out over resilient channels. More specifically, these channels are authenticated, so the adversary can read their content but he is not entitled to modify, delete, or delay messages sent over these channels.

3   The General Computational Model

Our general computational model is defined in terms of systems of interactive Turing machines (ITMs) and is related to the models in [4,9,14,17]. However, our exposition follows more closely that of [24].

ITMs. An *(inexhaustible) interactive Turing machine (ITM, for short)* M is a probabilistic Turing machine with the following tapes: a *security parameter tape* for storing the security parameter, a *random tape* for storing random coins, zero or more *input* and *output tapes*, and *work tapes*. The input and output tapes have names; different tapes have different names. These determine how ITMs are connected in a system of ITMs. If an ITM sends a message on an output tape named c, then only an ITM with an input tape named c can receive this message. An ITM M may use oracles, called *the oracles associated with the ITM*. If the oracles $\mathcal{O}_1, \ldots, \mathcal{O}_n$ are associated with M we sometimes write $M(\mathcal{O}_1, \ldots, \mathcal{O}_n)$ instead of M to emphasize this fact. The runtime of an ITM is polynomially bounded per activation (in the security parameter, the current input, and the size of the current configuration). This allows the ITM to "scan" the complete incoming message and its complete current configuration. Hence, an ITM can not be exhausted (therefore the name *inexhaustible* interactive Turing machine).

SYSTEMS OF ITMS. A *system* $\mathcal{S}$ of ITMs is a parallel composition $M_1 \parallel \cdots \parallel M_n$ of ITMs M_i, $i = 1, \ldots, n$. These machines communicate over input and output tapes; at every time only one ITM is active and all other ITMs wait for new input. A machine is activated when it receives input on one of its input tapes. If a machine does not activate another machine (by outputting a message), the so-called *master ITM* is triggered. We require w.l.o.g. that if a machine outputs a message, then its local configuration changes. Given $\mathcal{S} = M_1 \parallel \cdots \parallel M_n$, we write $\mathcal{S}(1^\eta, r_1, \ldots, r_n)$ for the system obtained from $\mathcal{S}$ by writing a security parameter η on the security parameter tapes and random coins $r_i \in \{0,1\}^*$ on the random tapes of the M_i. A run of $\mathcal{S}(1^\eta, r_1, \ldots, r_n)$ is defined to be a sequence of global configurations q where a *global configuration* q is a tuple $(q_1, \ldots, q_n)$ of the configurations q_i of the single machines M_i, for every $i = 1, \ldots, n$.

In general, a run of a system does not necessarily terminate. For example, if in $\mathcal{S} = M_1 \parallel M_2$ the ITMs M_1 and M_2 are connected via enriching input tapes, then they can send message back and forth between each other forever.

We say that a system $\mathcal{S}$ is a *polynomial-time system* if there exists a probabilistic Turing machine which simulates runs of $\mathcal{S}$ and whose runtime is polynomially bounded in the security parameter with overwhelming probability. For polynomial-time systems, we denote by $\mathcal{S}(\eta)$ the random variable that returns runs of $\mathcal{S}$ with security parameter η where the coins for the ITMs in $\mathcal{S}$ are chosen uniformly at random. We write $\mathcal{S}(\eta) \rightsquigarrow q$ to say that the final global configuration in a run returned by $\mathcal{S}(\eta)$ is q. If q' is a global configuration for $\mathcal{S}(\eta)$, we write $\mathcal{S}_{q'}(\eta)$ to denote the distribution of runs obtained when the initial configuration of the ITMs in $\mathcal{S}$ are defined according to q' (with possibly random coins added on random tapes if needed). In case q' is drawn from a family $D = \{D_\eta\}_\eta$ of distributions, we write $\mathcal{S}_D(\eta)$ for the random variable that returns a run according to the following experiment: $q' \xleftarrow{R} D_\eta$, output $\mathcal{S}_{q'}(\eta)$. We define $\mathcal{S}_{q'}(\eta) \rightsquigarrow q$ and $\mathcal{S}_D(\eta) \rightsquigarrow q$ analogously to $\mathcal{S}(\eta) \rightsquigarrow q$. Here, and in the rest of the paper we only consider families of distributions D that are polynomially samplable, i.e., that are the output of a probabilistic polynomial-time Turing machine.

Given a system $\mathcal{S}$, we call an ITM $\mathcal{E}$ an *environment* for $\mathcal{S}$ if i) the runtime of $\mathcal{E}$ is polynomial in the security parameter alone (and independent of the length of the input that $\mathcal{E}$ receives) and ii) $\mathcal{E}$ is I/O-compatible with $\mathcal{S}$, i.e., $\mathcal{E}$ only writes to external input tapes of $\mathcal{S}$ and $\mathcal{E}$ only reads from external output tapes of $\mathcal{S}$. Adopting terminology from [18], we call $\mathcal{S}$ *reactively polynomial* if $\mathcal{S} \parallel \mathcal{E}$ is a polynomial-time system for every environment $\mathcal{E}$ of $\mathcal{S}$ where $\mathcal{E}$ does not have an associated oracle.

4   The Security-Specific Model

Based on the general computational model introduced above, we define below the security-specific model. In this model, we consider specific systems of ITMs, called protocol systems. These systems consist of protocol machines, which determine the actions of honest principals, an adversary machine, a scheduler, and buffers for network and resilient channels. The adversary does not have complete control over the communication. Specifically, while we let the adversary control the network, he does not control resilient channels, i.e., the adversary can not modify, delete, or delay messages sent on this channel. (We often allow the adversary to read messages sent on resilient channels, though.) The purpose of the scheduler is to schedule messages sent over resilient channels, i.e., the scheduler decides when and which messages written on the resilient channel are delivered. Also, the scheduler resolves non-deterministic choices made by honest principals, e.g., whether to wait for a message of another party or to abort the protocol. Furthermore, the scheduler determines when the adversary is activated. In particular, the adversary is not necessarily scheduled as soon as an honest principal outputs a message. Instead some message sent on a resilient channel or an honest principal that needs to make a non-deterministic decision might be scheduled first (by the scheduler). However, if the adversary sends a message to an honest principal this principal is activated right away. Allowing the scheduler to first schedule other entities (honest principals or resilient channels) would significantly weaken the power of the adversary.

PROTOCOLS. A *protocol* Π is defined by a tuple $(\mathcal{H}, \mathcal{D}, \{\mathbf{H}_i\}_{i \in \mathcal{H}})$ where $\mathcal{H}$ and $\mathcal{D}$ are finite disjoint sets of names of *honest* and *dishonest principals*, respectively, and $\{\mathbf{H}_i\}_{i \in \mathcal{H}}$ is a family of ITMs, called protocol machines (see below), which specify honest principals; dishonest principals will be simulated by the adversary. We define $\mathcal{P} = \mathcal{H} \cup \mathcal{D}$ to be the set of all principals. We note that $\mathbf{H}_i$ may specify the actions of principal i in one session of a specific protocol, e.g., it specifies one session of the initiator of the ASW protocol, or multiple sessions of i in possibly different roles.

PROTOCOL SYSTEMS. A system induced by Π consists of the protocol machines of Π, an adversary machine $\mathbf{A}$, a scheduler machine $\mathbf{S}$, and buffer machines for the network and resilient channels. More precisely, a *(protocol) system $\mathcal{S}$ for Π* is of the form

$$\mathcal{S} = (\|_{i \in \mathcal{H}} \mathbf{H}_i) \ \| \ (\|_{i \in \mathcal{H}, j \in \mathcal{P}} \mathbf{Net}_j^i) \| \ (\|_{i \in \mathcal{H}, j \in \mathcal{P}} \mathbf{RC}_j^i) \ \| \ \mathbf{A} \ \| \ \mathbf{S}$$

where $\mathbf{H}_i$, $i \in \mathcal{H}$, is a protocol machine of Π modeling an honest principal, $\mathbf{Net}_j^i$, $i \in \mathcal{H}$, $j \in \mathcal{P}$ is a network buffer (machine) on which i sends messages over the network intended for j, $\mathbf{RC}_j^i$, $i \in \mathcal{H}$, $j \in \mathcal{P}$ is a resilient channel buffer (machine) on which i sends messages intended for j, $\mathbf{A}$ is the adversary (machine), and $\mathbf{S}$ the scheduler (machine). We call $\mathcal{S}$ the *system induced by Π, $\mathbf{A}$, and $\mathbf{S}$* and denote it by $\mathcal{S}(\Pi, \mathbf{A}, \mathbf{S})$. We refer to the system $\mathcal{S}$ with $\mathbf{A}$ and $\mathbf{S}$ removed by $\mathcal{S}(\Pi)$. Analogously, we refer to the system $\mathcal{S}$ with $\mathbf{S}$ removed by $\mathcal{S}(\Pi, \mathbf{A})$. We now explain informally how the machines of $\mathcal{S}(\Pi, \mathbf{A}, \mathbf{S})$ work and how they are connected via tapes (see [13] for details).

A network buffer machine $\mathbf{Net}_j^i$ receives messages from $\mathbf{H}_i$ and stores them. The adversary has typically access to these messages.

A resilient channel buffer machine $\mathbf{RC}_j^i$ stores messages and interacts with $\mathbf{H}_i$ just as $\mathbf{Net}_j^i$. In addition, $\mathbf{RC}_j^i$ is scheduled by the scheduler who determines which messages are delivered. The adversary may or may not have access to $\mathbf{RC}_j^i$. This depends on whether or not $\mathbf{RC}_j^i$ should be read-protected.

A protocol machine $\mathbf{H}_i$ may send messages to the network buffers $\mathbf{Net}_j^i$ and the resilient channel buffers $\mathbf{RC}_j^i$ for every $j \in \mathcal{P}$ as explained above. If $\mathbf{H}_i$ does not produce output, the scheduler $\mathbf{S}$ is activated. A protocol machine $\mathbf{H}_i$ can be activated by messages from the network (the adversary), the resilient channels (these messages are guaranteed to be authentic), and the scheduler. Messages from the scheduler are meant to resolve non-deterministic choices made by $\mathbf{H}_i$ (these messages are assumed to come from a fixed, finite set of messages).

The adversary machine $\mathbf{A}$ is associated with an oracle, called the *view oracle*, which can be invoked by $\mathbf{A}$ to obtain a *view* on the history of the run of the overall system so far. The view usually does not contain full information about the history. It is typically restricted to the content of the network buffers so far and the content of (some) of the resilient channel buffers, depending on whether these channels are supposed to be read-protected. In addition to invoking the view oracle, $\mathbf{A}$ can send messages to honest principals either via network (unauthenticated) or resilient channel connections (authenticated). A message sent by the adversary on one of these channels is delivered directly. The adversary machine $\mathbf{A}$ can only be activated by the scheduler. We only allow adversary machines for which the system $\mathcal{S}(\Pi, \mathbf{A})$ is reactively polynomial.

The scheduler $\mathbf{S}$ is also associated with a *view oracle* which provides $\mathbf{S}$ with a *view* on the history of the run of the overall system so far. Typically this view will be different from the view of the adversary and depending on the security property may contain full information about the history, no information at all, or something in between. As explained above, the purpose of $\mathbf{S}$ is to resolve non-deterministic choices of honest principals ($\mathbf{H}_i$), to schedule messages on resilient channels, and to determine when the adversary $\mathbf{A}$ is triggered. For this purpose, $\mathbf{S}$ sends appropriate messages to these machines.

5 Fair Schedulers

Intuitively, we define a scheduler to be fair if it does not stop the run of a system when at least one of the (other) machines in the system can still take an action, e.g., an honest principal could start an abort protocol, a resilient channel could deliver a message, or the adversary is ready to output a message to an honest principal. As already explained in the introduction, fair scheduling is important in the definition of many security properties, such as fairness and balance for contract signing protocols.

The problem of defining fair schedulers is to make precise what it means that a machine "can still take an action". Notice that we need a general definition that works for arbitrary machines (honest principal machines, resilient channel machines, *and adversary machines*) not only for specific machines, such as specific buffers as in [7,6].

Roughly speaking, we say that a machine "can still take an action" if the machine can be activated by the scheduler with some input so that at the end of the activation the machine has changed its local configuration, i.e., scheduling the machine causes it to make some progress or to perform some action. (Recall from Section 3 that if an ITM sends out a message, then it changes its local configuration.) For example, if an adversary machine wants to send a message to an honest principal, then when it is triggered by the scheduler it would send the message and change its local configuration. Hence, a fair scheduler has to eventually trigger the adversary as the adversary "can still take an action" in the above sense. Similarly, a fair scheduler has to eventually trigger a protocol machine that does not receive a message from the network but has the option of contacting the TTP, as contacting the TTP causes the protocol machine to change its local configuration.

We note that a scheduler does not necessarily know when a machine, including the adversary, "can still take an action" in the sense just explained. Hence, it might schedule such a machine even though this machine does not want to take an action. However, a machine can always read the message received from the scheduler (possibly even query the view oracle in case of the adversary) and, in case it does not want to take an action, it can return to its old local configuration. Note that here we use that ITMs cannot be exhausted. In case of exhaustible ITMs unrealistic runs would occur.

The above discussion motivates the following definition of fair schedulers. Roughly speaking, the definition below says that if the run of a system stops, then even if in the system the old scheduler is replaced by a new one (even one with full information on the history of the run), the new scheduler cannot continue the run of the system (at least not with non-negligible probability) such that one of the ITMs in the system changes its local configuration. In other words, a fair scheduler may only stop the run of a system if no ITM in the system (other than the scheduler itself) can or wants to take a further action, i.e., no other scheduler can cause an ITM to change its local configuration. We state this definition for general systems rather than only for protocol systems (Section 4). In this definition, we use what we call a full-information oracle. Called at some point in a run of a system, a *full-information oracle* returns the whole history of the run so far for all machines involved including the random coins used so far by the ITMs. We state the definition for the case that the initial global configuration comes from a family $D = \{D_\eta\}_\eta$ of distributions. This is useful for modeling, for example, an initialization phase.

Definition 1. *Let Q be a reactively polynomial system which does not contain a master ITM. An ITM S is a fair scheduler for Q and a family $D = \{D_\eta\}_\eta$ of distributions on (initial) global configurations if it is an environment for Q and if for every environment S' for Q which has access to a full-information oracle the probability that the following experiment returns 1 is negligible in the security parameter η:*
$Exp(\eta, S, S')$:

Run Q with S, i.e.: $S_D(\eta) \rightsquigarrow q'$ with $S = Q \,\|\, S$

Continue the run with $\boldsymbol{S'}$ instead of $\boldsymbol{S}$, i.e.: $\mathcal{S}'_{q''}(\eta) \rightsquigarrow q'''$ with $\mathcal{S}' = Q \parallel \boldsymbol{S'}$ and q'' is obtained from q' by replacing the configuration of $\boldsymbol{S}$ by the initial configuration of $\boldsymbol{S'}$ and writing the history of the run so far on one of the work tapes of $\boldsymbol{S'}$.

If there exists an ITM M in Q such that the local configuration of M in q' is different from the corresponding local configuration in q''', then output 1, and otherwise, output 0.

Applied to protocol systems (Section 4), a fair scheduler may only stop if i) the resilient channel buffers are empty, ii) triggering a protocol machine with any message (among the finite set of possible once, e.g., `abort`) does not change the local configuration of this machine, and iii) triggering the adversary machine with the message `schedule` does not change the local configuration of this machine (which means that the adversary does not want to take a step anymore).

Since ITMs cannot be exhausted they might change their local configuration whenever they are invoked. Hence, a fair scheduler would never be allowed to stop. Thus, we observe:

Observation 1 *There are systems for which no fair scheduler exists.*

SYSTEMS WITH FAIR SCHEDULERS. We now identify some reasonable restrictions on protocols and adversaries as to ensure the existence of a fair scheduler. Due to space limitations, we only provide informal definitions. First, we put a restriction on the adversary.

Definition 2. *(informal) An adversary machine for a protocol Π, view oracles $\mathcal{O}_{adv}$, $\mathcal{O}_{sch}$, and a family of distributions $D = \{D_\eta\}_\eta$ on (initial) global configurations D is fairness-enabling if the number of configuration changes of the adversary in every run of the system $\mathcal{S} = \mathcal{S}(\Pi, \boldsymbol{A}(\mathcal{O}_{adv}), \boldsymbol{S}(\mathcal{O}_{sch}))$ (and hence, the number of actions, such as sending messages, the adversary can perform) can be bounded by a polynomial which is independent of the scheduler $\boldsymbol{S}(\mathcal{O}_{sch})$.*

The immediate analog to the definition above for protocol machines would be too restrictive since the number of configuration changes of a protocol machine might depend on the number of interactions with the adversary, and hence, depends on the adversary. For example, if a TTP is modeled in such a way that it reacts to all requests (which could come from the adversary), then the number of configuration changes of the TTP depends on the adversary. This motivates the following definition.

Definition 3. *(informal) Given oracles $\mathcal{O}_{adv}$ and $\mathcal{O}_{sch}$, and a family of distributions $D = \{D_\eta\}_\eta$ on (initial) global configurations, a protocol Π is fairness-enabling if the number of configuration changes of protocol machines in Π in every run of the system $\mathcal{S} = \mathcal{S}(\Pi, \boldsymbol{A}(\mathcal{O}_{adv}), \boldsymbol{S}(\mathcal{O}_{sch}))$ can be bounded by a polynomial which may depend on $\boldsymbol{A}(\mathcal{O}_{adv})$ but not on $\boldsymbol{S}(\mathcal{O}_{sch})$.*

The following theorem states that for every fairness-enabling protocol and every fairness-enabling adversary, there exists a fair scheduler (even without access to a view oracle). Hence, for systems built from fairness-enabling protocols and adversaries, fair scheduling is possible. In the rest of the paper, we concentrate on such systems, which seem to capture all realistic cases. In order to state and prove the theorem, we first need to be more precise about the view oracle of adversaries.

A view oracle is called an *adversary view oracle* if it is a deterministic polynomial-time algorithm which when invoked in a run of a protocol system gets as input the history of the run so far, except for the history of the scheduler, i.e., the history of the configurations (including the random coins used so far) of all machines in the system, except for the history of the configurations of the scheduler. We require that if the configurations of the ITMs, other than the scheduler, in a run of the protocol system have not changed from one point in the run to the next step in the run, then the adversary view oracle returns the same view as before. Note that even if the adversary view oracle obtains as input the full history of the system (excluding the scheduler) it typically will only return a restricted view on that history to the adversary.

Theorem 2. *For every fairness-enabling protocol Π, view oracle $\mathcal{O}_{sch}$, adversary view oracle $\mathcal{O}_{adv}$, polynomially samplable family of distributions $D = \{D_\eta\}_\eta$ on (initial) global configurations, and fairness-enabling adversaries $A = A(\mathcal{O}_{adv})$, there exists a scheduler S (even one without access to a view oracle) that is fair for $S(\Pi, A)$ and D.*

6   Balanced Protocols and Results for the ASW Protocol

In this section, we define the notion of balance and show that the ASW protocol is balanced. The definition makes use of the previously introduced concept of fair scheduling.

6.1   Definition of Balance

The notion of balance for (two-party) contract-signing protocols was first introduced by Chadha et al. [11] in the symbolic (Dolev-Yao) setting. In a nutshell, their definition says that a protocol is balanced for an honest signer, say A, if no "unbalanced" state can be reached in a run of the contract-signing protocol where a run involves A, the Dolev-Yao intruder playing the role of the dishonest signer B, the TTP, the network and resilient channels. A state is *unbalanced* (for A) if in this state B has both i) a strategy to obtain a signature on the contract from A and ii) a (possibly different) strategy to prevent A from obtaining a signature on the contract from B. In other words, B can unilaterally determine the outcome of the protocol, which puts him in an advantageous position, for example, when making a deal with another party. In the first phase—*reaching* an (unbalanced) state— the non-deterministic choices made by honest principals and the way messages on resilient channels are scheduled might help B to reach the (unbalanced) state. However, in the second phase, B needs to have the mentioned strategies to achieve the two goals—obtaining a valid contract and preventing A from obtaining a valid contract—, and these strategies have to work no matter what non-deterministic choices the honest principals make and no matter how messages on resilient channels are scheduled.

Now, we introduce a computational analogue of the notion that we sketched above. We measure the success probability of an adversary that tries to undermine the balancedness of the protocol via an experiment which works in two phases (see below for a formal definition): In the first phase, the protocol runs along with the adversary **A** and a scheduler **S** which may resolve non-deterministic choices of honest principals and schedule messages on resilient channels and the adversary in a way that helps **A**. At the end of this phase, a state (global configuration), say q, is reached. Now, one of the two goals (having the contract or preventing the other party from getting one) is picked (by some function **challenge**) and the adversary is asked to reach the chosen goal, starting from q but now running with a different scheduler which will try to resolve non-deterministic choices of honest principals and schedule resilient channels and the adversary in a way that is disadvantageous for **A**. Intuitively, for balanced protocols, from any state q that is reached, at least for one of the two goals the probability that the adversary can reach this goal should be low.

In the following definition, we require that the scheduler used in the second phase of the experiment is fair in order to ensure that protocol runs are in fact completed both by honest parties *and* the adversary. This is crucial for two reasons: On the one hand, the adversary might otherwise be prevented from taking further actions, but these actions may be necessary for the adversary to achieve the required goal. Hence, the scheduling would be unfair for the adversary. And in fact, it would be unrealistic since in real protocol runs no one stops the adversary from taking further actions. On the other hand, honest principals might otherwise be prevented from taking counter-measures to the misbehavior of the adversary. Hence, the scheduling would be unfair (and again unrealistic) for the honest parties. Note that achieving fair scheduling for both honest parties and the adversary is guaranteed by our definition of fair scheduling (Section 5). However, a notion only based on fair message delivery [7,6] would be insufficient.

In order to ensure that, in the second phase, fair scheduling is possible, we split the adversary in two parts, **A** (for the first phase) and **A**′ (for the second phase) and require that **A**′ is fairness-enabling. The scheduler used in the first phase is not required to be fair (in particular it can stop at arbitrary points), and adversary **A** is not assumed to be fairness-enabling.

The definition of balance is parameterized by two deterministic polynomial-time algorithms, goal_1 and goal_2, the *goal functions*, which given a global configuration return 1 (goal reached) or 0 (failed to reach the goal), e.g., goal_1 might formalize "A does not have a signed contract from B" and goal_2 might formalize "B has a signed contract from A" (see Section 6.2). Parameterizing the definition of balance by the goal functions seems unavoidable since, for example, what a signed contract is and what it means for a party to have a signed contract are details that may differ from one protocol to another (see, e.g., [1] and [15]). We call a deterministic polynomial-time algorithm which given a global configuration returns 1 (requiring the adversary to achieve goal_1) or 2 (requiring the adversary to achieve goal_2) a *challenge function*.

Definition 4. *Let Π be a protocol and goal_1 and goal_2 be deterministic poly-nomial-time algorithms as above. Let $\mathcal{O}_{sch}$ and $\mathcal{O}'_{sch}$ be view oracles, and $\mathcal{O}_{adv}$ and $\mathcal{O}'_{adv}$ be adversary view oracles. Then, Π is called* balanced *w.r.t. goal_1, goal_2, $\mathcal{O}_{adv}$, $\mathcal{O}'_{adv}$, $\mathcal{O}_{sch}$, and $\mathcal{O}'_{sch}$ if for all adversary machines $A = A(\mathcal{O}_{adv})$ and $A' = A'(\mathcal{O}'_{adv})$ for Π, and all (not necessarily fair) schedulers $S = S(\mathcal{O}_{sch})$ for Π, there exists a challenge function* challenge *such that if A' is fairness-enabling for Π, $\mathcal{O}'_{sch}$, $\mathcal{O}_{adv}$, and a family $D = \{D_\eta\}_\eta$ of distributions on (initial) global configurations defined below, then there exists a scheduler $S' = S'(\mathcal{O}'_{sch})$ fair for $S(\Pi, A')$ and D such that the probability that the following experiment returns 1 is negligible in the security parameter η.*

$Exp(\eta, \Pi, A, A', S, S', \text{goal}_1, \text{goal}_2, \text{challenge})$:

$S(\eta) \rightsquigarrow q$ where $S = S(\Pi, A, S)$.

$i = \text{challenge}(q)$.

$S'_{q'}(\eta) \rightsquigarrow q''$ where $S' = S(\Pi, A', S')$, the initial configuration of A' is obtained by writing i and the current configuration of A on the work tape of A', and q' is obtained from q by replacing the configuration of S by the initial configuration of S' and the configuration of A by the initial configuration of A'.

Return $\text{goal}_i(q'')$.

The distribution D_η is defined to be the distribution of q' in the above experiment. (Note that $D = \{D_\eta\}$ is polynomially samplable.)

We emphasize that the above experiment can be simulated in polynomial time. This is a crucial fact when trying to show that a protocol is balanced via a proof by reduction. Note that while one could provide challenge and S' with more information, giving them less information only makes the balance property stronger. We also point out that in typical applications of the above definition the protocol Π will be fairness-enabling w.r.t. $\mathcal{O}'_{sch}$, $\mathcal{O}'_{adv}$, and D, and hence, fair scheduling is possible in the second phase of the experiment.

6.2   The ASW Protocol Is Balanced

We prove that the ASW protocol is balanced for i) the case that an honest initiator A runs an instance of the protocol with a dishonest responder B (modeled as the adversary) and an honest TTP T, and ii) the case that an honest responder B runs an instance of the protocol with a dishonest initiator A (modeled as the adversary) and an honest TTP T. More formally, we need to specify the protocols, oracles, and functions used as parameters in the balance definition.

Let $\Pi^{\text{ASW-A}}$ denote the protocol with honest parties A, T, and W, and dishonest party B where A acts as an initiator, T as a TTP, and W as a "watch dog". Formal specifications of A and T in terms of ITMs can be found in [13]. We note that A writes Contract on some of her work tapes if according to the specification of the protocol she has a valid contract (standard or replacement) with B and T on the contractual text. The watch dog W is used to check whether the adversary (dishonest B) has a valid contract. The protocol $\Pi^{\text{ASW-B}}$ is defined similarly, except that now A is dishonest and B is honest. The formal specification of the responder B as ITM can be found in [13]. It is not hard to check that $\Pi^{\text{ASW-A}}$ and $\Pi^{\text{ASW-B}}$ are fairness-enabling w.r.t. the distribution used in Definition 4 and that $\mathcal{S}(\Pi^{\text{ASW-A}})$ and $\mathcal{S}(\Pi^{\text{ASW-A}})$ are reactively polynomial.

We define the view oracles $\mathcal{O}_{adv}^{\text{ASW}}$ and $\mathcal{O}_{adv'}^{\text{ASW}}$ for the adversary to be adversary view oracles (Section 5) which return the history of all network and resilient channel buffers in the system (but no other machines). In particular, resilient channel buffers are not required to be read protected.

To get strong security guarantees, we allow the scheduler in the first phase of the definition of the balance property to see what the adversary sees plus the history of the configurations of the adversary (including the random coins used by the adversary); $\mathcal{O}_{sch}^{\text{ASW}}$ is defined accordingly. Conversely, we make the scheduler in the second phase weak by defining $\mathcal{O}_{sch'}^{\text{ASW}}$ in such a way that it does not provide any information about the history. For a global configuration q let $\text{goal}_1(q) = 1$ iff the honest party (A in $\Pi^{\text{ASW-A}}$ and B in $\Pi^{\text{ASW-B}}$) does not have a contract, i.e., Contract is not written on one of its work tapes. Let $\text{goal}_2(q) = 1$ iff the adversary has a valid contract, i.e., Contract is written on a work tape of the watch dog.

We are now ready to state the theorem on balance of the ASW protocol. The theorem holds for instances of the protocol implemented with primitives that satisfy standard cryptographic assumptions (see [13] for precise definitions).

Theorem 3. *If the signature scheme is existentially unforgeable under chosen message attacks and the hash function is preimage resistant, then $\Pi^{\text{ASW-A}}$ and $\Pi^{\text{ASW-B}}$ are balanced w.r.t.* goal_1, goal_2, $\mathcal{O}_{adv}^{\text{ASW}}$, $\mathcal{O}_{adv'}^{\text{ASW}}$, $\mathcal{O}_{sch}^{\text{ASW}}$, *and* $\mathcal{O}_{sch'}^{\text{ASW}}$.

The theorem should extend to the case that a party runs multiple copies of the protocol provided that different instances of the protocol use unique session identifiers (see [13]).

References

1. Asokan, N., Shoup, V., Waidner, M.: Asynchronous protocols for optimistic fair exchange. In: S&P 1998, pp. 86–99. IEEE Computer Society Press, Los Alamitos (1998)
2. Asokan, N., Shoup, V., Waidner, M.: Optimistic fair exchange of digital signatures. IEEE Journal on Selected Areas in Communications 18(4), 593–610 (2000)
3. Backes, M., Pfitzmann, B.: Computational probabilistic non-interference. In: Gollmann, D., Karjoth, G., Waidner, M. (eds.) ESORICS 2002. LNCS, vol. 2502, pp. 1–23. Springer, Heidelberg (2002)
4. Backes, M., Pfitzmann, B., Waidner, M.: Secure Asynchronous Reactive Systems. Technical Report 082, Cryptology ePrint Archive (2004)
5. Backes, M., Datta, A., Derek, A., Mitchell, J.C., Turuani, M.: Compositional analysis of contract signing protocols. In: CSFW 2005, Washington, DC, USA, pp. 94–110. IEEE Computer Society Press, Los Alamitos (2005)
6. Backes, M., Hofheinz, D., Müller-Quade, J., Unruh, D.: On fairness in simulatability-based cryptographic systems. In: FMSE 2005, Preprint on IACR ePrint 2005/294, pp. 13–22 (September 2005)
7. Backes, M., Pfitzmann, B., Steiner, M., Waidner, M.: Polynomial fairness and liveness. In: CSFW 2002, pp. 160–169. IEEE Computer Society Press, Los Alamitos (2002)

8. Baum-Waidner, B., Waidner, M.: Round-optimal and abuse free optimistic multi-party contract signing. In: Welzl, E., Montanari, U., Rolim, J.D.P. (eds.) ICALP 2000. LNCS, vol. 1853, pp. 524–535. Springer, Heidelberg (2000)
9. Canetti, R.: Universally Composable Security: A New Paradigm for Cryptographic Protocols. Technical report, Cryptology ePrint Archive (December 2005), online available at http://eprint.iacr.org/2000/067.ps
10. Canetti, R., Cheung, L., Kaynar, D., Liskov, M., Lynch, N., Pereira, O., Segala, R.: Time-bounded Task-PIOAs: A Framework for Analyzing Security Protocols. In: Dolev, S. (ed.) DISC 2006. LNCS, vol. 4167, pp. 238–253. Springer, Heidelberg (2006)
11. Chadha, R., Kanovich, M.I., Scedrov, A.: Inductive methods and contract-signing protocols. In: Samarati, P. (ed.) CCS 2001, pp. 176–185. ACM Press, New York (2001)
12. Chadha, R., Mitchell, J.C., Scedrov, A., Shmatikov, V.: Contract Signing, Optimism, and Advantage. In: Amadio, R.M., Lugiez, D. (eds.) CONCUR 2003. LNCS, vol. 2761, pp. 361–377. Springer, Heidelberg (2003)
13. Cortier, V., Küsters, R., Warinschi, B.: A Cryptographic Model For Branching Time Security Properties — the Case of Contract Signing Protocols. Technical Report 251, Cryptology ePrint Archive (2007)
14. Datta, A., Küsters, R., Mitchell, J.C., Ramanathan, A.: On the Relationships Between Notions of Simulation-Based Security. In: Kilian, J. (ed.) TCC 2005. LNCS, vol. 3378, pp. 476–494. Springer, Heidelberg (2005)
15. Garay, J.A., Jakobsson, M., MacKenzie, P.: Abuse-free optimistic contract signing. In: Wiener, M.J. (ed.) CRYPTO 1999. LNCS, vol. 1666, pp. 449–466. Springer, Heidelberg (1999)
16. Hofheinz, D., Müller-Quade, J.: A synchronous model for multi-party computation and the incompleteness of oblivious transfer. In: FCS 2004 (2004)
17. Hofheinz, D., Müller-Quade, J., Unruh, D.: Polynomial Runtime in Simulatability Definitions. In: CSFW 2005, pp. 156–169. IEEE Computer Society Press, Los Alamitos (2005)
18. Hofheinz, D., Müller-Quade, J., Unruh, D.: A simple model of polynomial time UC. In: The ECRYPT Workshop on Models for Cryptographic Protocols – MCP'06 (2006)
19. Kähler, D., Küsters, R.: Constraint Solving for Contract-Signing Protocols. In: Abadi, M., de Alfaro, L. (eds.) CONCUR 2005. LNCS, vol. 3653, pp. 233–247. Springer, Heidelberg (2005)
20. Kähler, D., Küsters, R., Wilke, T.: Deciding Properties of Contract-Signing Protocols. In: Diekert, V., Durand, B. (eds.) STACS 2005. LNCS, vol. 3404, pp. 158–169. Springer, Heidelberg (2005)
21. Kähler, D., Küsters, R., Wilke, T.: A Dolev-Yao-based Definition of Abuse-free Protocols. In: Bugliesi, M., Preneel, B., Sassone, V., Wegener, I. (eds.) ICALP 2006. LNCS, vol. 4052, pp. 95–106. Springer, Heidelberg (2006)
22. Kremer, S., Raskin, J.-F.: Game analysis of abuse-free contract signing. In: CSFW 2002, pp. 206–220. IEEE Computer Society Press, Los Alamitos (2002)
23. Kremer, S., Raskin, J.-F.: A game-based verification of non-repudiation and fair exchange protocols. In: Larsen, K.G., Nielsen, M. (eds.) CONCUR 2001. LNCS, vol. 2154, pp. 551–565. Springer, Heidelberg (2001)
24. Küsters, R.: Simulation-Based Security with Inexhaustible Interactive Turing Machines. In: CSFW 2006, pp. 309–320. IEEE Computer Society Press, Los Alamitos (2006)
25. Shmatikov, V., Mitchell, J.C.: Finite-state analysis of two contract signing protocols. TCS 283(2), 419–450 (2002)

Security Evaluation of Scenarios Based on the TCG's TPM Specification[*]

Sigrid Gürgens[1], Carsten Rudolph[1], Dirk Scheuermann[1], Marion Atts[2], and Rainer Plaga[2]

[1] Fraunhofer – Institute for Secure Information Technology SIT
Rheinstrasse 75, 64295 Darmstadt, Germany
{guergens,rudolphc,scheuermann}@sit.fraunhofer.de
[2] Federal Office for Information Security (BSI), Godesberger Allee 185-189,
53175 Bonn, Germany
{rainer.plaga,marion.atts}@bsi.bund.de

Abstract. The Trusted Platform Module TPM is a basic but nevertheless very complex security component that can provide the foundations and the root of security for a variety of applications. In contrast to the TPM, other basic security mechanisms like cryptographic algorithms or security protocols have frequently been subject to thorough security analysis and formal verification. This paper presents a first methodic security analysis of a large part of the TPM specification. A formal automata model based on asynchronous product automata APA and a finite state verification tool SHVT are used to emulate a TPM within an executable model. On this basis four different generic scenarios were analysed with respect to security and practicability: secure boot, secure storage, remote attestation and data migration. A variety of security problems and inconsistencies was found. Subsequently, the TPM specification was adapted to overcome the problems identified. In this paper, the analysis of the remote attestation scenario and some of the problems found are explained in more detail.

1 Introduction

The Trusted Platform Module TPM as specified by the Trusted Computing Group TCG [3] provides basic security mechanisms like protected storage areas, computation of cryptographic functions and attestation of integrity measurement. The TPM specification is highly complex and it is diffcult to verify that secure architectures can be based on it. Consequently, (and rather unsurprisingly), errors, inaccurate descriptions and inconsistencies were found in previous versions of the specification. However, as the TPM is supposed to be a trust and security anchor it is necessary that the specification defines a secure TPM. Previous work on analysing the security of the TPM has so far only covered small

[*] This work was initialized and funded by the German BSI (Federal Office for Information Security).

J. Biskup and J. Lopez (Eds.): ESORICS 2007, LNCS 4734, pp. 438–453, 2007.
© Springer-Verlag Berlin Heidelberg 2007

details. The goal of the work presented in this paper was to provide a first systematic, scenario-based security analysis covering large parts of the specification. A variety of problems was found and documented. All of them were discussed within the TCG (in particular with the TPM and Infrastructure working groups) and resulted in changes, amendments and corrections to revision 94 and newer versions of the TPM specifications.

In the first step of the project, TPM-based protocols were developed for four generic scenarios, namely secure boot, secure storage, remote attestation and data migration. The particular sequences of TPM commands were documented in detail and simulated using the SH Verification Tool [8,5]. Subsequently, attack scenarios were developed for all scenarios and the previously developed protocols were analysed with respect to these attack scenarios. Finally, the study was completed by analysing several generic attack scenarios and general, scenario-independent issues concerning TPM commands and data structures. The chosen analysis approach was a combination of formal, tool-supported analysis and thorough review by security experts. The scenarios use the different TPM authorisation protocols (e.g. object independent OIAP and object specific OSAP) and allowed to consider the interplay of the different TPM commands and security mechanisms for the security analysis.

In the following sections we give a short overview of the TPM and the automata model for the analysis. Because it is impossible for space reasons to elaborate on our results of all four generic scenarios we chose a concrete "remote attestion" scenario as an illustrative example to demonstrate the analysis approach and to explain some of the problems that were found.

Finally, the mitigation strategies and changes to the TPM specification that resulted from the problems are explained.

2   A Short Introduction to TPM Technology

A TPM [3] usually is implemented as a chip integrated into the hardware of a platform (such as a PC, a laptop, a PDA, a mobile phone). A TPM owns shielded locations (i.e. no other instance but the TPM itself can access the storage inside the TPM) and protected functionality (the functions computed inside the TPM can not be tampered with). The TPM can be accessed directly via TPM commands or via higher layer application interfaces (the Trusted Software Stack, TSS).

The TPM offers two main basic mechanisms: it can be used to provide evidence of the current state of the platform it is integrated in and applications that are running on the platform, and it can protect data on the platform (such as cryptographic keys). For realizing these mechanisms the TPM contains a crypto co-processor, a hash and an HMAC algorithm, a key generator, etc.

In order to prove a certain platform configuration, all parts that are engaged in the boot process of the platform (BIOS, master boot record, etc.) are measured (e.g. integrity check hash values for software) by a so-called root of trust for measurement (RTM) on the platform, and the final result of the accumulated hash values is stored inside the TPM in a so-called Platform Configuration Register (PCR). An entity that wants to verify that the platform is in a certain configuration requires the TPM to sign the content of the PCR using a so-called Attestation Identity Key (AIK), a key particularly generated for this purpose. The verifier checks the signature and compares the PCR values to some reference values. Equality of the values proves that the platform is in the desired state. Finally, in order to verify the trustworthiness of an AIK's signature, the AIK has to be accompanied by a certificate issued by a trusted Certification Authority, a so-called Privacy CA (P-CA). Note that an AIK does **not** prove the identity of the TPM owner.

Keys generated and used by the TPM have different properties: Some (so-called non-migratable keys) can not be used outside the TPM that generated them, some (like AIKs) can only be used for specific functions. Particularly interesting is that keys can be tied to PCR values (by specifying PCR number and value in the key's public data). This has the effect that such a key will only be used by the TPM if the platform configuration (or some application) is in a certain state (i.e. if the PCR the key is tied to contains a specific value). In order to prove the properties of a particular key, for example to prove that a certain key is tied to specific PCR values, the TPM can be used to generate a certificate for this key by signing the key properties using an AIK.

TPM keys have a defined structure whose one part contains public information like the key's public part or binding to specific PCR values. The sensitive part of the key contains information like the key's private part and authorization data. It is encrypted by the key's parent key, whose sensitive information is again encrypted by its parent, thus constituting a key hierarchy whose root is the so-called Storage Root Key (SRK).

In order for any key to be used by a TPM (e.g. for decryption), the key's usage authorization value has to be presented to the TPM. This together with the fact that the TPM specification requires a TPM to prevent dictionary attacks provides the property that only entities knowing the key's authorization value can use the key.

Non-migratable keys are especially useful for preventing unauthorized access to some data stored on the platform. Binding such a key to specific PCR values and using it to encrypt data to be protected achieves two objectives: The data can not be decrypted on any other platform (because the key is non-migratable), and the data can only be decrypted when the specified PCR contains the specified value (i.e. when the platform is in a specific secure configuration and is not manipulated).

3   Description of a Concrete "Remote Attestation" Scenario

The following concrete scenario is used throughout the rest of paper for explanation of the security analysis that was originally carried out on more generic scenarios. The example scenario reflects a typical corporate IT environment where the use of TPMs can actually improve security processes. We consider two employees Bob and Alice. Bob's PC is equipped with a Trusted Platform Module TPM protecting information on the PC and measuring the PC's configuration. Alice's PC may or may not be equipped with a TPM. The TPMs of the company are owned by the company's IT administration (ITadmin), i.e. the process of "taking ownership" of the TPM was executed by the IT administration and the TPM's Owner Authorisation value is only known to ITadmin. Bob and ITadmin are having local (physical) and remote access to Bob's PC.

The main goal of using the TPM in this is to give Alice the ability to bind data to a particular configuration of Bob's PC. This way Alice shall be assured that her security requirements are satisfied by Bob's PC although it is not under Alice's control. These requirements concern data Alice wants to make available to Bob, in particular Alice has the following requirements:

- The data shall only be available on a platform determined by herself (i.e. on Bob's PC). Therefore, initially during the attestation a particular identity key (actually providing pseudonymity) associated with a particular platform (i.e. with TPM) is fixed and the data shall not be available on any other platform.
- Furthermore, Alice requires that the data shall only be readable by Bob, i.e. that no other actor (neither on Bob's PC nor on any other platform) shall be able to read the data without Bob's or Alice's consent.

This results in the security requirement that the data shall be confidential for Alice and Bob, i.e. nobody else shall ever get to know the data, in particular it shall not be known by ITadmin.

We use the following assumptions:

1. Alice trusts the Privacy CA used for attestation and trusts a TPM certified by P-CA in that it acts according to the specification.
2. Processes on a specifically configured platform PF (i.e. Bob's PC) and Alice's own PC do not make available any data to other processes, platforms, platform users or devices.
3. Alice trusts Bob not to deliberately or accidently make the data available to others.
4. Bob does not make available any key usage authorization data he knows to other TPM users or to ITadmin.

To prohibit that the data leaves Bob's PC it is configured in a specific way known to Alice. The main mechanism to provide platform configuration information is by using the TPM_Quote command and sending the result, i.e. current PCR information signed with a certified identity key AIK. This process is one of the basic TPM mechanisms. More details on TPM_Quote can be found in part 3 of the TPM specification [2]. One practical example of secure boot with description of the attestation can be found in the work of Sailer et al. [11]. Additionally, in order to enforce the security policies, Alice needs to ensure that the configuration is still the same when data is decrypted by the TPM. This

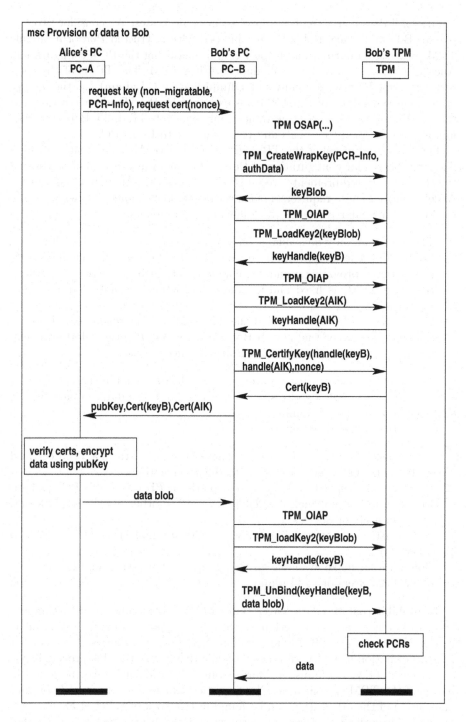

Fig. 1. MSC visualising a sequence of TPM commands

can be achieved by binding a key to particular PCR values that allow the TPM to use it only after having checked that platform and system state meet certain conditions, and to use this key for encryption of the data.

This can be achieved as follows:

- Alice requires Bob to provide a TPM generated key (more precisely, the public part of such a key) that is non-migratable and bound to certain PCR values reflecting the correct state of Bob's PC. Additionally Alice requires a certificate for this key in order to be able to verify the key's properties.
- Alice uses this key to encrypt the data she wants to make available to Bob.
- For decrypting the data, Bob loads the key into his TPM, the TPM returns a key handle and then Bob can reference the key through the key handle and use the TPM for decryption. Only if his PC is in the state acceptable to Alice the TPM will actually decrypt the data.

The message sequence (MSC) chart in Figure 1 shows a more detailed description of the command sequences.

4 Security Evaluation Using Asynchronous Product Automata (APA)

In this section we introduce the Fraunhofer SIT approach for security evaluation. We model the entities of a system using asynchronous product automata (APA). APA are a universal and very flexible operational description concept for cooperating systems [9]. It "naturally" emerges from formal language theory [8]. APA are supported by the SH-verification tool (SHVT) that provides components for the complete cycle from formal specification to exhaustive analysis and verification [9].

Asynchronous product automata (APA) and the SHVT have been successfully used in the past to model and analyse the security of cryptographic protocols (see for example [6] or [5]). This section gives an introduction in the previous work on cryptographic protocols that provides the foundations for the security validation of TPM based scenarios.

4.1 Specification of Cryptographic Protocols Using APA

An APA can be seen as a family of elementary automata. The set of all possible states of the whole APA is structured as a product set; each state is divided into state components. In the following the set of all possible states is called state set. The state sets of elementary automata consist of components of the state set of the APA. Different elementary automata are "glued" by shared components of their state sets. Elementary automata can "communicate" by changing the content of shared state components.

Figure 2 shows a graphical representation of an APA for a system that contains Bob's PC and TPM and the TPM owner ITadmin. The boxes are elementary automata and the ellipses represent their state components.

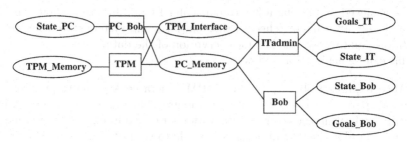

Fig. 2. APA model with Bob's PC and TPM and ITadmin

The neighbourhood relation N (graphically represented by an arc) indicates which state components are included in the state of an elementary automaton and may be changed by a state transition of this automaton. For example, automaton TPM may change TPM_Interface but cannot read or change the state of State_IT.

Each protocol participant P is modelled by an appropriate number of elementary automata that perform the agent's actions, accompanied by an adequate number of state components. What is appropriate depends on the environment and the attack model that shall be modelled. In order to reduce the state space it is often convenient to use one elementary automaton per agent. In the model shown in Figure 2, each agent (i.e. the TPM, Bob, Bob's PC and ITadmin) owns a state component for storing keys and other data specifying its current state. The state component Goals is used to add predicates describing goals the agents shall reach with the protocol (see Section 4.2).

The figure shows the structure of the APA. Communication of the automata is achieved by adding to and removing data from shared state components. By providing PC_Bob and ITadmin with access to TPM_Interface and PC_Memory (modelling storage space on Bob's PC) we model the fact that both agents have access to the TPM and to Bob's PC. Also, TPM has access to these shared components.

The full specification of the APA includes the state sets (the data types), the transition relations of the elementary automata and the initial state, which we will explain in the following paragraphs.

State sets, messages and cryptography. The basic message sets, symbolic functions, messages, state component sets etc. depend on the scenario to be analysed. For what is needed to analyse classical protocols like Needham-Schroeder (symmetric and public key) [7], Otway-Rees [10] etc., we refer the reader to [5]. For protocols using other cryptographic primitives and needing other attack models, the definitions can be adapted easily. Examples of more complex protocols that have been analysed include fair non-repudiation protocols [6]. In the following we will concentrate on the details concerning the analysis of TPM scenarios.

State sets of components. For the definition of the domains of the state components as well as for the definition of the set of messages, we use as basicsets a set of natural numbers, a set of agents' names, a set of random numbers and nonces, a set of constants. We use key names and flags to model various different key types, and a set of security predicates on global states. For TPM analysis, we additionally use a set containing all TPM structures (see [1] for their specification).

The union of all sets of agents, constants, etc., represents the set of *atomic messages*, based on which we construct a set $\mathcal{M}$ of messages by concatenation and application of symbolic functions.

Symbolic functions. We use a system of formal cryptographic primitives. This allows to specify a system in a very realistic way because all variables of the protocol are considered. A good system of axioms is necessary to represent a cryptographic model as real as possible. Each of these symbolic functions models one specific kind of cryptographic system. An HMAC for example (HMACs are used to protect TPM commands and answers) is defined by $HMAC(key1, data1) = HMAC(key2, data2)$ implying $key1 = key2$ and $data1 = data2$. All these properties together define for each $m \in \mathcal{M}$ a unique shortest normal form (up to commutativity). The set $\mathcal{Messages}$ is the set of all these normal forms of elements $m \in \mathcal{M}$.

Now elements of $\mathcal{Messages}$ constitute the content of the state components except the agents' Goals component which contains predicates on global states. For the formal definition of state sets and further symbolic functions we refer the reader to [5].

State transition relations and initial state. To specify the agents' actions we use so-called *state transition patterns* describing state transitions of the corresponding elementary automaton. As an example of a state transition pattern, Table 1 shows the specification of a state transition where the TPM receives the command TPM_OSAP. We use internal state components *new_nonce* and *new_handle* to model the generation of nonces and session handles by the TPM.

The lines above $\overset{\text{TPM}}{\rightarrow}$ indicate the necessary conditions for automaton TPM to transform a state transition, the lines behind specify the changes of the state. $\hookrightarrow$ and $\hookleftarrow$ denote that some data is added to and removed from a state component, respectively. TPM does not perform any other changes within this state transition. The syntax and semantics of state transition patterns for APA is explained in more detail in [4].

Finally, the initial state has to be specified. It contains in particular all data stored in TPM_Memory when taking ownership. We do not go into further detail here.

The above specification can now be executed in the SH Verification Tool. Thus, the correctness of the specification can be verified and the behaviour visualised. The following section explains how this specification is extended to include malicious behaviour in order to evaluate the security of the TPM command sequence.

Table 1. TPM receives command TPM_OSAP

(TPM_OSAP)	Pattern name
$(X, entityType, entityValue, entity, nonceOddOSAP,$ $nonces, nonceEven, nonceEvenOSAP, sharedSecret,$ $authSecret, authHandle)$	Variables used in the pattern
$(entityValue, entity) \in TPM\_Memory,$	TPM checks that entity the OSAP shall authorize is loaded
$\overset{TPM}{\to}$	state transition is performed by TPM
$(X, TPM, ('TPM\_OSAP', entityType, entityValue,$ $nonceOddOSAP)) \hookleftarrow TPM\_Interface,$	OSAP command is removed from TPM_Interface
$authSecret := get\_authData(entityType, entity),$	entity auth value is assigned to authSecret
$nonces \hookleftarrow new\_nonce,$ $authHandle \hookleftarrow new\_handle,$	Nonce (handle) list is removed from $new\_nonce(new\_handle)$ and assigned to $nonces$ $(authHandle)$
$nonceEven := head(nonces),$ $nonceEvenOSAP := head(tail(nonces)),$	$nonceEven/nonceEvenOSAP$ are assigned a new nonce
$tail(tail(nonces)) \hookrightarrow new\_nonce,$ $tail(authHandle) \hookrightarrow new\_handle,$	Rest of the nonces (handles) are returned to new_nonce (new_handle)
$sharedSecret := hmac(authSecret,$ $(nonceEvenOSAP, nonceOddOSAP)),$	$sharedSecret$ is assigned the OSAP secret
$(TPM\_OSAP, head(authHandle), nonceEven,$ $nonceEvenOSAP, sharedSecret) \hookrightarrow TPM\_Memory,$	TPM stores session secret and nonces in TPM_Memory
$(TPM, X, (head(authHandle), nonceEven,$ $nonceEvenOSAP)) \hookrightarrow TPM\_Interface$	TPM returns authHandle and nonces to caller

4.2 Security Goals and Malicious Behaviour

Security goals. In our model, the state components Goals are used to specify security goals. Whenever an agent P performs a state transition after which a specific security goal shall hold from the agent's view, a predicate representing the goal is added to the respective Goals component. Note that the content of Goals has no influence on the system behaviour, i.e. on the occurrence of state transitions.

A system is secure (within the scope of our model) if a predicate is true whenever it is element of a Goals component. In the SH Verfication Tool, a generic break condition continuously evaluates all predicates in Goals during the computation of the reachability graph. The computation is stopped as soon as an attack is found, i.e. one of the predicates is not satisfied in the current state.

For the analysis of the scenario introduced in Section 3, it is, for example, necessary to consider confidentiality. The **confidentiality** of a message m in state s can directly be decided by looking at the content of state components. As long as the dishonest agent (or agents) does not own the cleartext of m, this message can be considered confidential. In order to express that agent P considers message m to be confidential, the predicate $(P, conf, m)$ is added to *Goals*.

Introducing dishonest behaviour. In order to perform a security evaluation, our model includes the explicit specification of dishonest behaviour, i.e. behaviour that contradicts the protocol specification. For each type of dishonest behaviour, the APA includes one elementary automaton with the respective state components and state transition relations for specifying the concrete actions. The behaviour of the attack APA depends on the attack model we want to use. As will be explained in Section 5, various different scenarios have to be considered, e.g. whether or not the attacker has access to the TPM of the agent to be attacked. Our APA model can capture any combination of these scenarios.

The elementary automaton of a dishonest agent is specified according to the attack model to be considered. This usually includes the ability of the automaton to read all tuples from state components it has access to, to extract any parts from the tuples, add them to its knowledge and use this to construct new tuples and to add these to state components it has access to. It also includes the ability to apply symbolic functions to messages it knows and to decrypt ciphertext it knows provided it knows the necessary key as well. For the particular TPM attack model the elementary automaton of a malicious agent knows all TPM command structures and can generate TPM commands and other messages by concatenation of data it knows.

5   TPM Evaluation

5.1   General Considerations

In this section we discuss the various attack possibilities that have to be considered for scenario based on TPM functionality. They are concerned with the question of who knows key authorization data as well as with questions related to particular TPM commands.

The specific intentions of an attacker may be different: First of all, an attacker may be interested in getting access to certain secret data, i.e. in breaking data confidentiality, e.g. authorization data necessary to execute certain TPM commands. Another attacker's strategy may consist of breaking data integrity. In this case, he does not directly want to get access to certain secret data but just wants to forge certain data protected by the TPM or the contents of a TPM command causing the TPM to perform another action than the one intended by the honest actor. Furthermore, an attacker may just want to be able to use the TPM for certain actions he is not authorized to perform, independently of any specific confidential data.

Before using a key, the TPM requires authorization data for this key. The derivation and quality of this authorization data is not specified by the standard.

Therefore, one has to assume that an attacker can get hold of one or more authorization data. Thus independently of a specific scenario the consequences of combinations of the following cases have to be considered:

1. An attacker E knows TPM owner authorization.
2. An attacker E knows SRK authorization.
3. An attacker E knows the authorization data of the key to be used.
4. An attacker E knows the authorization data of the key to be used plus authorization data for all keys in the above key hierarchy.
5. An attacker E does not know any key authorization data.
6. An attacker E owns/does not own another TPM2.
7. An attacker E has access to the TPM.
8. An attacker E has no access to the TPM, but to PF.

Knowing authorization data. An attacker knowing the TPM owner authorization may execute certain TPM commands explicitly reserved for the owner. This includes the possibility of changing the owner authorization data and the authorization data for the SRK. By doing this, the use of all TPM keys is blocked for other users and the TPM owner. This is particularly relevant if an application is using the TPM and key usage authorization fails. Knowing the SRK authorization alone enables an attacker to load a large amount of keys since the SRK is typically used as a parent key for many other keys. However, it is not sufficient to change the SRK authorization data.

If an attacker only knows the authorization data of a key other than the SRK he can use the key with the TPM (e.g. for decryption of data) provided that the key is already loaded to the TPM. For being able to also load a key, he additionally needs to know the authorization data of all keys in the above key hierarchy up to a key already loaded (or the SRK). Knowing a key's and its parent's authorization data and being able to load the parent enables an attacker to change the key's authorization data, again with the effect that the key can not be used by anybody else. Attacks based on the knowledge of key authorization data are highly relevant for breaking data confidentiality.

Attacks without knowledge of authorization data. An attacker not knowing any authorization data will not be able to directly access any confidential data or to directly execute any specific TPM functions. He may just be able to forge data or manipulate communication between an honest actor and the TPM where no authorization data are needed (like changing PCR values). In case the attacker knows the public part of a TPM storage key and has access to the platform, he can generate data or key blobs using this key and substitute other data or key blobs that have this key as parent. Even if the attacker does not know any public TPM key but has access to the platform, he can substitute blobs by appropriate data he knows from earlier activities. This is highly relevant for breaking the data integrity of key or data blobs.

Attacks with additional TPM. Owning another TPM2 enables an attacker to perform other specific malicious actions: By placing his TPM2 in a state as desired by the honest actor he can give the actor the impression that the target

TPM is in the desired state although it is not. In general, this attack strategy may be followed independent of having access to TPM, and it is especially interesting in combination with manipulation of the platform. Such attacks are especially relevant for the scenarios of Secure Boot and Attestation where the control of the platform state plays an important role.

5.2   Evaluation of the Scenario

For the analysis of the example scenario we assume that Bob and Alice have determined a unique AIK to use for attestation. In our attack model we consider the case where ITadmin acts dishonestly and tries to get hold of the data intended for Bob. We concentrate on the situation where ITadmin does not use a further TPM. Other attack models are possible, the attacker may be some outside entity having or not having access to Bob's PC and TPM and owning or not owning another TPM. The corresponding APA model is shown in Figure 3.

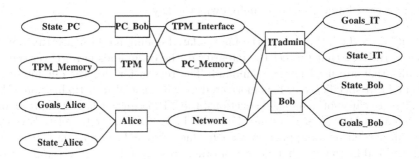

Fig. 3. APA attack model: ITadmin attacks Bob

Manipulation of TPM key handles. The aim of ITadmin is to be able to decrypt the data intended for Bob. Recall that Bob needs to transfer the public part of his key *keyB* to Alice which is used by Alice to encrypt the data. According to the MSC shown in Section 3, Bob first creates *keyB*, then loads it, and then lets the TPM generate a certificate for this key, using the AIK both Bob and Alice agreed on. We assume that ITadmin does not own this AIK, i.e. does not know its authorization data. This allows the following to happen:

- Bob (i.e. Bob's PC) loads *keyB* and receives the key handle.
- Bob loads his AIK and receives its key handle.
- Bob sends TPM_CertifyKey command including the following parameters:
  - key handles of AIK and of *keyB*,
  - Alice's nonce,
  - HMAC based on the usage authorization data of the AIK, according to the TPM specification Part 3 [2] not covering the key handles,
  - HMAC based on the usage authorization data of his own key *keyB*, also not covering the key handles.
- ITadmin blocks this command.

- ITadmin then loads its own key *keyIT*, receiving a key handle for this key.
- Then ITadmin removes the HMAC authorizing *keyB* and the key handle for *keyB* from the TPM_CertifyKey command and adds the key handle for its own key *keyIT* and a new HMAC authorizing this key.
- Now the TPM generates a certificate not for *keyB* but for *keyIT*, using Bob's AIK, and returns this certificate, accompanied by an HMAC based on the AIK authorization data and a second HMAC based on the authorization data of *keyIT*.
- ITadmin blocks this message again, thus Bob's PC will never receive any reply (it would not accept the certificate anyway since it expects the second HMAC to be based on the authorization data of Bob's own key *keyB* which ITadmin can not generate).
- ITadmin can now send the public part of *keyIT* to Alice, accompanied by a certificate generated with an AIK not owned by ITadmin.
- Alice accepts this key since it has the required properties and since Alice has no way of knowing who actually owns the key.

Why does the TPM accept the manipulated command TPM_CertifyKey? In general HMACs that protect the integrity of the commands never cover the key handles that are used in the command. The reason for this lies outside of the actual TPM specification. It is motivated by what is called virtualization of key handles: Because of memory restrictions, the TPM can not handle more than a certain amount of keys at a time. Thus the TPM might have to delete keys that are still needed by an application. Each time a key is loaded again it usually is assigned a different key handle. So in order to release higher level applications from the task of having to re-load keys and to handle different key handles, these applications just use one virtual key identifier. The process of re-loading keys and managing the relation between this one identifier and the changing key handles is kept by lower layer software, for example by the TPM Software Stack (TSS), that provides an API to the application on one hand and communicates with the TPM on the other hand. Nevertheless, applications shall be able to construct and check HMACs for TPM commands. As this cannot be done with the virtual key handle, key handles are not included.

Since the key handles of TPM_CertifyKey are not covered by the HMACs, exchanging the key handle for *keyB* and the corresponding HMAC does not invalidate the HMAC corresponding to the AIK. Hence both HMACs are valid and the TPM processes the command. In Section 6 we will explain how this attack can be avoided.

Integrity of key blobs. As explained in Section 2, keys generated by the TPM have a certain structure. The public part contains information like the key being or not being migratable, like PCR values the key may be bound to, it contains the actual public key part, etc. The sensitive part is encrypted using the key's parent and contains the private key part, the key authorization data, etc. However, this structure does not allow to identify the key other than by its public key part. Hence the integrity of a key can not be protected by TPM functionality, i.e. if no additional measures are taken the exchange of one key by another key that has the same parent will not be noticed.

We assume now that between the creation of Bob's key and its loading into the TPM some time passes, i.e. that meanwhile the key is stored in PC_Memory. We assume further that ITadmin knows the parent key of $keyB$ (e.g. because it is the SRK). Thus ITadmin can generate its own key blob for some key $keyIT$ using the parent key of $keyB$. It can now substitute the key blob of $keyB$ stored in PC_Memory by its own, unnoticed by Bob (and Bob's PC). Now the following command sequence can happen:

- Bob (i.e. Bob's PC) loads ITadmin's destination key $keyIT$ instead of his own and receives the key handle.
- Bob loads his AIK.
- Bob sends TPM_CertifyKey command including the key handles of his AIK and of $keyIT$, Alice's nonce, an HMAC based on the usage authorization data of the AIK, again not covering the key handles, and an HMAC based on the usage authorization data of his own key $keyB$, also not covering the key handles.
- ITadmin blocks this command, removes the HMAC authorizing $keyB$ and adds a new HMAC authorizing its own key $keyIT$.
- The rest of the process is as described above: TPM generates a certificate for $keyIT$, using Bob's AIK, and returns this certificate.
- ITadmin blocks this message again and then can send $keyIT$ to Alice, accompanied by a certificate generated with an AIK not owned by ITadmin.

In both cases described above ITadmin and not Bob will receive the data intended for Bob. The case where ITadmin has a further TPM3 for his own platform PF3 available does not make any difference in this attack scenario.

6   Risk Mitigation in the Further Evolution of the TPM Specification

As explained in the introduction, the security problems introduced here are the result of work conducted for the German Federal Office for Information Security (BSI). We introduced the results of our work into the TPM working group of the TCG (the ones explained in this paper and others as well). In consequence newer revisions of the TPM specification include remarks that point out the encountered problems and and give hints as to how they can be avoided.

In order to avoid the possibility to manipulate the TPM_CertifyKey command a so-called *transport session* can be established that encrypts command and response data. To do this, before starting the command sequence shown in Figure 1, the TPM user that wants the TPM to generate a certificate for a key has to do the following (for example directly before sending the TPM_CertifyKey command, see Figure 1).

- start an OIAP session with TPM_OIAP and load a key she owns with TPM_LoadKey

- use the public part of this key to encrypt a symmetric key to be used within the transport session (inside or outside of the TPM),
- set the TPM_TRANSPORT_ENCRYPT flag within TPM_TRANSPORT_ATTRIBUTES which is contained in TPM_TRANSPORT_PUBLIC, one of the parameters of the TPM command,
- send TPM_EstablishTransport to the TPM containing TPM_TRANSPORT_PUBLIC and the encrypted session key.

The TPM generates a transport session handle, decrypts the session key and stores both for later use (note that for transport sessions as well as for OIAP and OSAP sessions, a so-called rolling nonce procedure is used, we omit the technical details here). It then returns the transport handle (among other information).

Now instead of sending TPM_CertifyKey in clear, the command has to be wrapped with the established session key and included as *wrappedCmd* parameter in TPM_ExecuteTransport, refering to the transport session using the respective handle. The TPM decrypts the command, processes it as usual and returns the wrapped response. Note that wrapping the command means that encryption is performed only on the command data, i.e. key handles and HMACs etc. are kept in cleartext. Hence this does not yet prohibit to manipulate TPM_CertifyKey. However, if the command parameter TPM_NONCE that can be used to ensure the freshness of the certificate indeed contains a nonce which is additionally not known to a possible attacker, she can exchange the key handle but can not produce the respective HMAC since this has to cover the nonce as well. So confidentiality of the nonce is an important precondition for prohibiting manipulation of TPM_CertifyKey using a transport session.

Preserving the integrity of key blobs is more difficult and depends on the actual context the key shall be used in. In our scenario where the key is not used by the TPM but only certified, one possibility to verify the key's integrity is to load the key and then use it, for example for verifying a signature generated with this key. In cases where the key shall actually be used by the TPM different key usage authorization data will reveal that the wrong key blob has been loaded.

7   Conclusions

The Trusted Platform Module TPM, used accurately, provides the means to considerably enhance the security of platforms and systems. Yet it is highly complex and hence the specification is difficult to understand. Previous work on the security evaluation of TPM functionality has covered only small details. In this paper we presented some results of a first systematic security evaluation covering large parts of the specification. Our work revealed certain problems that can lead to security flaws and resulted in later revisions of the specification containing remarks that address these problems. Work by the TPM working group of the TCG on the specification is still in progress, our future work will address security evaluations of next generation TPM specifications.

Acknowledgement

We thank the members of the TPM working group of the TCG, in particular David Grawrock and Ken Goldman, for fruitful discussions and their kind support regarding our collaboration. We further thank Thomas Caspers for helpful suggestions.

References

1. TCG Trusted Computing Group: TPM Main Part 2 TPM Structures Specification Version 1.2 Level 2 Revision 103 (2007), www.trustedcomputing.org
2. TCG Trusted Computing Group: TPM Main Part 3 Commands Specification Version 1.2 Level 2 Revision 103 (March 2007), www.trustedcomputing.org
3. Trusted Computing Group: TCG TPM Specification 1.2 (2006), http://www.trustedcomputing.org
4. Gürgens, S., Ochsenschläger, P., Rudolph, C.: Authenticity and Provability – a Formal Framework. GMD Report 150, GMD – Forschungszentrum Informationstechnik GmbH (2001)
5. Gürgens, S., Ochsenschläger, P., Rudolph, C.: Role based specification and security analysis of cryptographic protocols using asynchronous product automata. In: Hameurlain, A., Cicchetti, R., Traunmüller, R. (eds.) DEXA 2002. LNCS, vol. 2453, Springer, Heidelberg (2002)
6. Gürgens, S., Rudolph, C.: Security Analysis of (Un-) Fair Non-repudiation Protocols. Formal aspects of computing (2004)
7. Needham, R., Schroeder, M.: Using encryption for authentication in large networks of computers. Communications of the ACM 21, 993–999 (1978)
8. Ochsenschläger, P., Repp, J., Rieke, R.: Abstraction and composition – a verification method for co-operating systems. Journal of Experimental and Theoretical Artificial Intelligence 12, 447–459 (2000)
9. Ochsenschläger, P., Repp, J., Rieke, R., Nitsche, U.: The SH-Verification Tool – Abstraction-Based Verification of Co-operating Systems. Formal Aspects of Computing, The Int. Journal of Formal Methods 11, 1–24 (1999)
10. Otway, D., Rees, O.: Efficient and timely mutual authentication. Operating Systems Reviews 21, 8–10 (1987)
11. Sailer, R., Zhang, X., Jaeger, T., van Doorn, L.: Design and implementation of a TCG-based integrity measurement architecture. In: Proceedings of the 13th USENIX Security Symposium. USENIX Association (2004)

Analyzing Side Channel Leakage of Masked Implementations with Stochastic Methods*

Kerstin Lemke-Rust and Christof Paar

Horst Görtz Institute for IT Security
Ruhr University Bochum
44780 Bochum, Germany
{lemke,cpaar}@crypto.rub.de

Abstract. Side channel cryptanalysis is a collective term for implementation attacks aiming at recovering secret or private keys from a cryptographic module by observing its physical leakage at run-time. Stochastic methods have already been introduced for first order differential side channel analysis. This contribution provides a compendium for the use of stochastic methods on masked implementations, i.e., on implementations that use internal random numbers in order to effectively prevent first order side channel attacks. Practical evidence is given that stochastic methods are also well suited for analyzing masked implementations, especially, as they are capable of combining several chosen components of different internal states for a multivariate side channel analysis.

Keywords: Side Channel Cryptanalysis, Stochastic Methods, Boolean Masking, Multivariate Side Channel Analysis, Higher-Order Side Channel Analysis.

1 Introduction

Traditionally, cryptanalysis employs mathematical tools to evaluate the security claims by cryptographers. However, once cryptographic schemes are implemented in integrated circuits such as smartcards, the resulting cryptographic implementation can no longer be solely seen as a mathematical object. Moreover and much more impressively, recent research results in the last decade have demonstrated that implementation attacks are a serious threat to cryptographic modules.

In reality, information flow also occurs on measurable physical channels such as the execution time, the power consumption, and the electromagnetic emanation of a cryptographic implementation. These channels are known as *side channels* in literature and may leak information on internal states of a cryptographic implementation at run-time. An adversary is said to be successful if side channel cryptanalysis yields to a critical entropy loss of a secret or private key used in a cryptographic implementation.

---

* Supported by the European Commission through the IST Contract IST-2002-507932 ECRYPT, the European Network of Excellence in Cryptology.

J. Biskup and J. Lopez (Eds.): ESORICS 2007, LNCS 4734, pp. 454–468, 2007.

This contribution deals with the usage of instantaneous physical observables in the immediate vicinity of the cryptographic device, e.g., power consumption or electromagnetic radiation [9,6]. The underlying working hypothesis for side channel cryptanalysis assumes that measurable observables depend on the internal state of a cryptographic algorithm whereby this dependency is specific for each implementation. This dependency can be predicted, e.g., by assuming a standard leakage model such as the Hamming weight or Hamming distance of internal states [2] at key recovery. More powerful attacks, however, aim at learning the exploitable side channel leakage prior to key recovery.

Such advanced attacks have been proposed by [4,15]. They consist of two stages, a so-called *profiling stage* and a *key recovery stage*. Both stages use the same implementation, but usually differ in assumptions on the available knowledge. In the context of this contribution it is assumed that plaintext (or ciphertext), keys and masking values are known at the profiling stage. At key recovery only plaintext (or ciphertext) is assumed to be known to the adversary. Both approaches [4,15] have in common that key recovery applies the maximum likelihood principle based on multivariate Gaussian probability densities that have been estimated during profiling. Reference [4] introduces template attacks that acquire empirical probability densities for each key dependency. For use with block ciphers, stochastic methods [15] approximate the probability density by considering selected basis functions of internal states for profiling, thus offering a significant reduction of required efforts. Additionally, by testing suitable basis functions a developer can gain insights in the nature of the side channel leakage. Reference [7] provides a performance analysis for templates and stochastic methods. It concludes that T-Test based templates are usually the method of choice, however, stochastic methods are of importance in case the adversary is limited at profiling. Limitations at profiling may be caused by a low number of measurements or by a high number of subkey dependencies for a given cipher.

In response to Differential Side Channel Analysis (DSCA) developers of cryptographic implementations may include randomization techniques such as secret splitting or masking schemes, e.g., [3,5]. These randomization techniques shall prevent from predicting any relevant bit in any cycle of the implementation. As result, statistical tests using physical observables at *one* instant, i.e., first order side channel analysis, cannot be assumed to be successfully applied in key recovery. However, as already indicated in [9] high-order differential analysis can combine multiple instants from within a measurement trace. Previous work on second-order DSCA [11,17] constructs a new leakage signal by multiplying (or subtracting) the observables at related time instants before statistics is applied. This reduction generally loses information if compared to a multivariate analysis. By assuming that the leakage signals follow the n-bit Hamming weight model [8] provided a derivation on the height of the expected second-order DPA signals and [14] uses predicted probability density functions to improve second-order power analysis. Further practical results for second- and higher-order DPA acting on the Hamming weight assumption are given by [13,16]. Moreover, Template-enhanced DPA attacks were introduced in [1] to defeat masking under the assumption that the adversary has access to an implementation with a biased random number generator during profiling. Reference [12] evaluates different types of template attacks attacks on masked implementations and concludes that a template based DPA attack leads to the best results.

This contribution elaborates stochastic methods for analyzing masked implementations and provides experimental case studies for a boolean masking scheme in Section 3.

2   Stochastic Methods on a Masked Implementation

2.1   Introduction to the Stochastic Model

The stochastic model [15] for non-masked implementations assumes that the adversary measures physical observables at time t in order to guess a subkey $k \in \{0,1\}^s$. The letter $x \in \{0,1\}^d$ denotes a known part of the data, i.e., plaintext or ciphertext, respectively. A physical observable $I_t(x,k)$ at time t is seen as a random variable

$$I_t(x,k) = h_t(x,k) + R_t . \tag{1}$$

The first summand $h_t(x,k)$ quantifies the deterministic part of the measurement as far it depends on x and k. The term R_t denotes a random variable that does not depend on x and k. R_t includes all kinds of noise as there are intrinsic and external noise, noise of the measurement apparatus and algorithmic noise that stems from deterministic contributions that do not depend on x and k. The random variable $I_t(x,k)$ is interpreted as 'displaced' noise R_t with mean displacement $h_t(x,k)$. Without loss of generality one may assume that $\mathbb{E}(R_t) = 0$ since otherwise one could replace $h_t(x,k)$ and R_t by $h_t(x,k) + \mathbb{E}(R_t)$ and $R_t - \mathbb{E}(R_t)$, respectively. It follows $\mathbb{E}(I_t(x,k)) = h_t(x,k)$. In this contribution, random variables are denoted with capital letters while their realizations, i.e. measured quantities, are denoted with the respective small letters.

Stochastic methods profile the real physical leakage by approximation within a suitable chosen vector subspace that is spanned by basis functions of one or several intermediate results of the cryptographic implementation. For practical purposes, it is important to note that the subkey space is chosen to be sufficiently small as at key recovery all subkey hypotheses have to be tested.

Example 1. For an unmasked implementation of AES, one may use the intermediate result $x_0 := S(x \oplus k)$, i.e. the 8-bit output of the AES S-box S given 8-bit data x and an 8-bit subkey k. A suitable vector subspace is spanned by the constant function 1 and the single bits of x_0. See [15] for more details.

In the stochastic model profiling aims to determine a function $h_t^*(\cdot,\cdot)$ that is 'close' to the unknown function $h_t(\cdot,\cdot)$. For simplicity, attention is restricted to the set of functions $\mathcal{F}_{u;t}$, that is a real vector subspace spanned by u known functions $g_{tl} \colon \{0,1\}^d \times \{0,1\}^s \to \mathbb{R}$ for each instant t:

$$\mathcal{F}_{u;t} := \{h' \colon \{0,1\}^d \times \{0,1\}^s \to \mathbb{R} \mid \sum_{l=0}^{u-1} \beta_l g_{tl} \text{ with } \beta_l \in \mathbb{R}\} \tag{2}$$

One may assume that the functions g_{tl} are linearly independent so that $\mathcal{F}_{u;t}$ is isomorphic to $\mathbb{R}^u$.

2.2 The Stochastic Model for Masked Implementations

As already outlined in [15] the stochastic model of Section 2.1 can be generalized to the presence of masking. This generalized model assumes that the adversary measures physical observables at time t that additionally depend on a mask $y \in \{0,1\}^v$. A physical observable $I_t(x, y, k)$ at time t is seen as a random variable

$$I_t(x, y, k) = h_t(x, y, k) + R_t \tag{3}$$

The first summand $h_t(x, y, k)$ quantifies the deterministic part of the measurement as far it depends on x, y, and k. The term R_t denotes a random variable that does not depend on x, y, and k and fulfills $\mathbb{E}(R_t) = 0$.

For the approximation at masked implementation, a real vector subspace $\mathcal{F}_{u;t}$ is used that is spanned by u known functions $g_{tl} : \{0,1\}^d \times \{0,1\}^v \times \{0,1\}^s \to \mathbb{R}$ for each instant t:

$$\mathcal{F}_{u;t} := \{h' : \{0,1\}^d \times \{0,1\}^v \times \{0,1\}^s \to \mathbb{R} \mid \sum_{l=0}^{u-1} \beta_l g_{tl} \text{ with } \beta_l \in \mathbb{R}\} \tag{4}$$

The detailed algorithms for profiling masked implementations are provided in SubSect. 2.3. SubSect. 2.4 presents decision strategies for key recovery.

2.3 Profiling

Under the assumption that the adversary has access to the random numbers used for masking profiling works similar to [15]. In the context of this explanation, we assume that the adversary uses a known static key k for all N measurement vectors that are assumed to be available at the profiling stage. Alternatively, it is possible to use known variable keys instead that are loaded randomly for each measurement.

Profiling is split into up to three tasks:

1. Estimation of the deterministic part $h_t(x, y, k)$,
2. Selection of (relevant) instants for a multivariate characterization, and
3. Estimation of the multivariate noise.

This contribution considers the two main methods of the stochastic model [15]: the *minimum principle* and the *maximum likelihood principle*. Both differ in certain parts of the profiling and key recovery phase. While it is sufficient for the minimum principle to profile the deterministic side channel leakage and to select relevant instants, the maximum likelihood principle additionally requires an estimation of the multivariate noise. Table 1 summarizes the differences.

Table 1. Tasks for the minimum principle and the maximum likelihood principle. Note that the number of measurements N is split into two disjoint subsets N_1 and N_2 with $N_1 + N_2 = N$ for the maximum likelihood principle.

Method	Minimum Principle	Maximum Likelihood Principle
Estimation of the deterministic part	yes (N samples)	yes (N_1 samples)
Selection of instants	yes (N samples)	yes (N_1 samples)
Estimation of the noise	no	yes (N_2 samples)

Estimation of the deterministic part: For the following explanations a $p \times N$ matrix $\mathbf{I}$ is introduced that is defined by the N measurement vectors $\boldsymbol{i}_i \in \mathbb{R}^p$ with $1 \leq i \leq N$:

$$\mathbf{I} = \begin{pmatrix} i_{11}(x_1, y_1, k) & i_{12}(x_1, y_1, k) & \dots & i_{ip}(x_1, y_1, k) \\ i_{21}(x_2, y_2, k) & i_{22}(x_2, y_2, k) & \dots & i_{2p}(x_2, y_2, k) \\ \cdot & \cdot & & \cdot \\ \cdot & \cdot & & \cdot \\ \cdot & \cdot & & \cdot \\ i_{N1}(x_N, y_N, k) & i_{N2}(x_N, y_N, k) & \dots & i_{Np}(x_N, y_N, k) \end{pmatrix} \quad (5)$$

The i-th row vector is the original i-th measurement vector. For each row vector there is an associated plaintext (or ciphertext) $x_i \in \{0,1\}^d$ and an associated mask $y_i \in \{0,1\}^v$. The j-th column vector of matrix $\mathbf{I}$ is $\boldsymbol{i}_j{}^{col} := (i_{1j}, i_{2j}, \dots, i_{Nj})^T$ and includes all measurement values for the same instant j. In the following, the notation $i_{ij}(x_i, y_i, k)$ is used instead of $i_t(x_i, y_i, k)$. Profiling of the deterministic part is done separately for each instant, i.e., for profiling purposes the column vector $\boldsymbol{i}_j{}^{col}$ is the starting point.

For each sampled instant $j \in \{1, \dots, p\}$, the adversary chooses u_j functions g_{jl} with $0 < l \leq u_j$ that span the vector subspace $\mathcal{F}_{u_j;j}$. In the presence of masking the vector subspace is reasonably spanned by two (or more) intermediate results that occur during computation. This yields a joint probability density of the side channel leakage at two (or more) intermediate results.

Example 2. One choice for profiling is to choose the n-bit intermediate results y and $x \oplus y \oplus k$ in case of a boolean masking scheme (see Section 3 for details). One may define a $2n + 1$ dimensional vector subspace that is spanned by the constant function 1 and the single bits of y and $x \oplus y \oplus k$.

The fitting problem to be solved is to find real valued coefficients $\boldsymbol{\beta}_j := (\beta_{j0}, \dots, \beta_{j,u_j-1})^T$ such that the measurement quantities $i_{ij}(x_i, y_i, k)$ and controlled quantities $g_{j0}(x_i, y_i, k), \dots, g_{j,u_j-1}(x_i, y_i, k)$ are linked by

$$i_{ij}(x_i, y_i, k) = \beta_{j0} + \sum_{l=1}^{u_j-1} \beta_{jl} g_{jl}(x_i, y_i, k) \ \forall i \in \{1, \dots, N\}$$

in $\mathcal{F}_{u_j;j}$. This then yields an approximation on the deterministic part of the side channel for the instantiation of the stochastic variable I_j at sampled instant

j given the controlled variables $g_{j0}(x, y, k), \ldots, g_{j,u_j-1}(x, y, k)$ with $g_{j0}(x, y, k)$ being the constant function 1. The coefficient β_{j0} gives the expectation value of the non-data dependent signal part. The coefficients β_{jl} with $l \neq 0$ are the data dependent signal portions, thereby indicating the points in time where exploitable side channel leakages occurs.

The coefficients $\boldsymbol{\beta}_j$ are approximated with least squares estimates. The $N \times u_j$ design matrix for this problem is

$$
\mathbf{M} = \begin{pmatrix}
1 & g_{j1}(x_1, y_1, k) & g_{j2}(x_1, y_1, k) & \cdots & g_{j,u_j-1}(x_1, y_1, k) \\
1 & g_{j1}(x_2, y_2, k) & g_{j2}(x_2, y_2, k) & \cdots & g_{j,u_j-1}(x_2, y_2, k) \\
\cdot & \cdot & & & \cdot \\
\cdot & \cdot & & & \cdot \\
\cdot & \cdot & & & \cdot \\
1 & g_{j1}(x_N, y_N, k) & g_{j2}(x_N, y_N, k) & \cdots & g_{j,u_j-1}(x_N, y_N, k)
\end{pmatrix}. \tag{6}
$$

The solution to the general linear least square problem is then given by

$$
\boldsymbol{\beta}_j^* = \left(\mathbf{M}^T \mathbf{M}\right)^{-1} \mathbf{M}^T i_j{}^{col} \tag{7}
$$

provided that $\mathbf{M}^T \mathbf{M}$ is regular. As result, for each sampled instant $j \in \{1, \ldots, p\}$ the deterministic part is estimated by

$$
\widetilde{h}_j^*(x, y, k) = \sum_{l=0}^{u_j-1} \beta_{jl}^* g_{jl}(x, y, k) . \tag{8}
$$

Selection of (relevant) instants: It is highly desirable to sort out instants that do not contribute to the deterministic leakage in order to reduce noise as well as the dimension of the characterization problem for the maximum likelihood approach. Instant selection algorithms aim to find the points of interest j with significant contributing coefficients β_{jl}^* for $l > 0$. An appropriate method for selecting contributing instants is based on the T-Test and can be found in [7]. Previous algorithms based on the squared Euclidean norm $\|b\|^2 := \|(\beta_{j1}^*, \beta_{j2}^*, \ldots, \beta_{j,u_j-1}^*)\|^2 = \sum_{i=1}^{u_j-1} \beta_{ji}^{*\,2}$ of contributing coefficients are given in [15].

Estimation of the multivariate noise: For the maximum likelihood principle one needs to determine a multivariate density. Therefore, it is assumed that the random vector $\boldsymbol{R_t}$ is jointly normally distributed with covariance matrix $\mathbf{C} = (c_{uv})_{1 \leq u, v \leq m}$, i.e. $c_{uv} := \mathbb{E}(R_{t_u} R_{t_v}) - \mathbb{E}(R_{t_u})\mathbb{E}(R_{t_v})$. For this task the adversary uses a complementary set that consists of $N_2 = N - N_1$ measurement curves to estimate the distribution of the m-dimensional random vector $\boldsymbol{R_t} = \boldsymbol{I_t}(X, Y, k) - \boldsymbol{h_t}(X, Y, k)$. Herein, the vector $\boldsymbol{t}$ stands for $(t_1, \ldots, t_m)$, i.e., the m selected instants. $\boldsymbol{R_t}$ and $\boldsymbol{I_t}$ denote the random vector $(R_{t_1}, \ldots, R_{t_m})$ and $(I_{t_1}, \ldots, I_{t_m})$, respectively. For the estimation of the covariance matrix $\mathbf{C}$, the adversary computes the N_2 vectors $\boldsymbol{z}_i := \boldsymbol{i_t}(x_i, y_i, k) - \widetilde{\boldsymbol{h}}_t^*(x_i, y_i, k)$.

If the covariance matrix $\mathbf{C}$ is regular the random vector $\boldsymbol{R_t}$ is estimated to have the m-dimensional density $\widetilde{f}_{\mathbf{C}}$ with

$$\widetilde{f}_{\mathbf{C}} \colon \mathbb{R}^m \to \mathbb{R} \qquad \widetilde{f}_{\mathbf{C}}(\boldsymbol{z}) = \frac{1}{\sqrt{(2\pi)^m \det \mathbf{C}}} \exp\left(-\frac{1}{2}\boldsymbol{z}^T \mathbf{C}^{-1} \boldsymbol{z}\right). \qquad (9)$$

2.4 Key Recovery

Key recovery targets the same implementation that is now loaded with an unknown key k° and uses internally generated random numbers for masking. For the analysis, N_3 measurements are assumed to be available. In the key recovery phase, however, knowledge of the masks $y_1, \ldots, y_{N_3}$ cannot be assumed. Note that the measured quantities $i_t(x_i, y_i, k^\circ)$ depend on two unknown values, the ever-changing value y_i and the fixed value k°.

From a logical point of view masking reduces the adversary's information. At a non-masked implementation the adversary is able to predict any intermediate result if the guessed subkey k is equal to k° [15]. Therefore the adversary is able to estimate on $\widetilde{\boldsymbol{h}}_t^*(x_i, k)$ and to obtain a probability measure to indeed observe each subkey k. At a masked implementation the actual intermediate result has to be treated as an unknown number in the most general case. Instead of *one* intermediate result and therefore *one* estimated density a masked intermediate result can attain *all* outcomes $\widetilde{\boldsymbol{h}}_t^*(x_i, 0, k)$ up to $\widetilde{\boldsymbol{h}}_t^*(x_i, 2^v - 1, k)$. The best adversarial strategy is to use *all* possible outcomes weighted with the probability for each random number $y' \in \{0,1\}^v$. If these random numbers are unbiased and independent then $\mathbb{P}(y_i = y') = 2^{-v}$ for all $i \leq N_3$ and $y' \in \{0,1\}^v$.

Minimum Principle: The adversary evaluates

$$\alpha_{MP}(x_1, \ldots, x_{N_3}; k) := \frac{1}{N_3} \sum_{i=1}^{N_3} \min_{y' \in \{0,1\}^v} \|i_t(x_i, y_i, k^\circ) - \widetilde{\boldsymbol{h}}_t^*(x_i, y', k)\|^2 \qquad (10)$$

and decides for the subkey $k' \in \{0,1\}^s$ that minimizes $\alpha_{MP}(x_1, \ldots, x_{N_3}; k)$:

$$k' = \arg \min_{k \in \{0,1\}^s} \alpha_{MP}(x_1, \ldots, x_{N_3}; k). \qquad (11)$$

Equations (10) and (11) are referred to as the minimum principle in the presence of masking. Small values of the squared Euclidean norm $\|i_t(x_i, y_i, k^\circ) - \widetilde{\boldsymbol{h}}_t^*(x_i, y', k)\|^2$ indicate small deviations of the side channel leakage from the deterministic part and therefore enhance the probability for indeed observing the event of $y' = y_i$ and $k = k^\circ$. Accordingly, the guess of a subkey k is probably not correct if high values of the term $\|i_t(x_i, y_i, k^\circ) - \widetilde{\boldsymbol{h}}_t^*(x_i, y', k)\|^2$ are attained for all possible masks.

Maximum Likelihood Principle: The adversary hence decides for the subkey

$$k' = \arg \max_{k \in \{0,1\}^s} \alpha_{MLP}(x_1, \ldots, x_{N_3}; k) \qquad (12)$$

that maximizes the term

$$\alpha_{MLP}(x_1, \ldots, x_{N_3}; k) := \prod_{i=1}^{N_3} \sum_{y' \in \{0,1\}^v} \mathbb{P}(y_i = y') \widetilde{f}_{\mathbf{C}} \left(\mathbf{i}_t(x_i, y_i, k^\circ) - \widetilde{\mathbf{h}}_t^*(x_i, y', k) \right)$$

(13)

among all $k \in \{0,1\}^s$. The mixture of densities on the right-hand side of (13) also depends on the unknown random numbers $y_1, \ldots, y_{N_3}$.

Maximizing the term $\alpha_{MLP}(x_1, \ldots, x_{N_3}; k)$ in (13) is equivalent to maximizing $\ln(\alpha_{MLP}(x_1, \ldots, x_{N_3}; k))$. By setting $\mathbf{z}_{i,y',k} = \mathbf{i}_t(x_i, y_i, k^\circ) - \widetilde{\mathbf{h}}_t^*(x_i, y', k)$ in the multivariate Gaussian density and neglecting constant factors of the Gaussian distribution in equation (9), $\ln(\alpha_{MLP}) := \ln(\alpha_{MLP}(x_1, \ldots, x_{N_3}; k))$ results in

$$\ln(\alpha_{MLP}) := \sum_{i=1}^{N_3} \ln \left(\sum_{y' \in \{0,1\}^v} \mathbb{P}(y_i = y') \cdot \exp\left(-\frac{1}{2} \cdot \mathbf{z}_{i,y',k}^T \mathbf{C}^{-1} \mathbf{z}_{i,y',k} \right) \right).$$

(14)

For high values of N_3, using the term in (14) is the practical method of choice for guessing the subkey

$$k' = \arg \max_{k \in \{0,1\}^s} \ln(\alpha_{MLP}(x_1, \ldots, x_{N_3}; k)).$$ (15)

3   Experimental Analysis of a Masked Implementation

Parameters with an impact on efficiency in side channel cryptanalysis include (i) the quantity of inherent leakage (chip dependent), (ii) the quality of the laboratory equipment (lab dependent), and (iii) the algorithms' ability to extract information (method dependent). Among them, this experimental analysis deals with the method dependent part. Experiments have been carried out with a standard microcontroller that is commercially available and does not incorporate any hardware side channel countermeasures. These experiments are used for a proof of concept of our proposed algorithms. The absolute success rates given here are specific for our implementation. Moreover, improvements of the laboratory equipment used may be conceivable and the analysis of physically secured integrated circuits may require significantly enhanced efforts. For a fair comparison of different methods in the presence of masking, e.g., with the different types of template attacks in [12] it is absolutely necessary to use the same set of measurement vectors. The concrete physical leakage function of the cryptographic implementation has presumably also an impact on efficiency, i.e., some previously proposed methods may work nicely only if the physical leakage corresponds to the Hamming weight.

This section focuses on an application of the most general case for higher order analysis in the presence of masking, i.e., an implementation of boolean masking is considered that is typically the first step of, e.g., a masked AES or DES implementation. At a masked cryptographic implementation it is further necessary to switch the mask at non-linear or arithmetic operations which is not

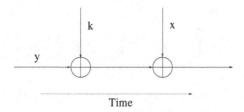

Fig. 1. Process of boolean masking

considered as part of this experimental analysis. Then the situation is even more favorable because of additional leakage signals, e.g., caused by S-Box processing or the use of a restricted form of masking.

The implementation done on an 8-bit microprocessor AT90S8515 proceeds as shown in Fig. 1. Note that there are different implementation choices of masking. Alternatively, it can be assumed that $x \oplus y$ is computed first before adding the key k, as, e.g., done in [11]. The motivation for the choice of this implementation in Fig. 1 is based on the fact that neither $x \oplus k$ nor $x \oplus y$ should be observable at a single point in time. Leakage on y, k, x, $y \oplus k$ and $y \oplus k \oplus x$, however, remains observable at single instants.

The physical channel used is the power consumption of the 8-bit microprocessor AT90S8515. By using the estimation of the deterministic part it was assured that first order differential analysis is prevented by verifying that leakage of the intermediate results $k \oplus x$ and $y \oplus x$ at single instants is negligible if any.

3.1 Profiling Phase

Concretely, four measurement series were recorded with $N = 10,000$ measurements each using different fixed keys. Further, one additional measurement series includes $N = 20,000$ measurements with varying keys drawn randomly from a uniform distribution. All these series were used for profiling purposes.

For profiling a 'white-box' model is assumed, i.e., x, k, and y are known. Profiling applies the stochastic model at the two intermediate results $y \in \{0,1\}^8$ and $(y \oplus k \oplus x) \in \{0,1\}^8$. More concretely, the vector subspace is spanned by the constant function 1, the bits of y, and the bits of $x \oplus y \oplus k$ yielding an 17 dimensional vector subspace. In a first try, the deterministic part $h_j^*(x, y, k)$ was approximated by

$$\widetilde{h}_j^*(x, y, k) = \beta_{j0}^* \cdot 1 + \sum_{l=1}^{8} \beta_{jl}^* \cdot g_l(y) + \sum_{l=9}^{16} \beta_{jl}^* \cdot g_{l-8}(x \oplus y \oplus k) . \quad (16)$$

Herein, the function $g_l : \{0,1\}^8 \to \{0,1\}$ outputs the l-th bit of an 8-bit data item with a bit ordering from the most significant bit ($l = 1$) to the least significant bit ($l = 8$). The coefficients β_{jl}^* are determined by solving (7). As result, it turned out that leakage signals of y and $x \oplus y \oplus k$ are well separated in time. Therefore, it is appropriate to reduce the number of dimensions during profiling which helps

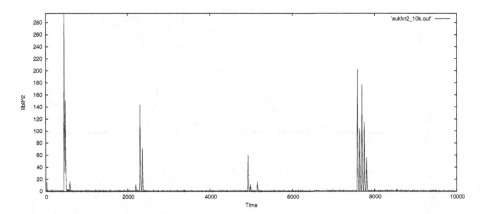

Fig. 2. Squared Euclidean norm $\|b\|^2 = \|(\beta^*_{j1}, \beta^*_{j2}, ..., \beta^*_{j16})\|^2$ of the bit depending coefficients as result of profiling according to equation (17) by using the measurement series with varying key data. Note that this computation includes two sets of basis functions in subsequent, but separated time frames. High values for $\|b\|^2$ indicate instants with significant deterministic side channel leakage.

in suppressing noise in the estimation process. For the refined application of (7), the chosen vector subspace depends on the time instant j, i.e., y is profiled if $0 < j \le 2500$ and $x \oplus y \oplus k$ is profiled if $2500 < j \le 10000$:

$$\tilde{h}^*_j(x, y, k) = \begin{cases} \beta^*_{j0} \cdot 1 + \sum_{l=1}^{8} \beta^*_{jl} \cdot g_l(y) & \text{if } 0 < j \le 2500 \\ \beta^*_{j0} \cdot 1 + \sum_{l=9}^{16} \beta^*_{jl} \cdot g_{l-8}(x \oplus y \oplus k) & \text{if } 2500 < j \le 10000 \end{cases} \quad (17)$$

Accordingly, the coefficients β^*_{jl} are set to zero if not profiled in the given time frame:

$$\beta^*_{jl} := \begin{cases} 0 & \text{if } (9 \le l \le 16) \text{ and } (0 < j \le 2500) \\ 0 & \text{if } (1 \le l \le 8) \text{ and } (2500 < j \le 10000) \end{cases}$$

Fig. 2 shows the squared Euclidean norm of the data dependent coefficients β^*_{jl} with $l > 0$ as result of solving (7) given the vector subspaces of (17).

Profiling by using the vector subspace given in (17) was also applied to four measurement series with different fixed keys. By comparing experimental profiling results it turned out that the estimated coefficients β^*_{jl} differ significantly for different measurement series at a few instants (see Fig. 3). There are even leakage contributions that are completely suppressed in the series with varying keys, thus indicating that there is key dependent leakage which averages to zero if considering profiling based on varying keys. The selection of relevant instants for the series with varying keys yielded ten instants. For the series with fixed keys two additional signals were found and included in the set of selected instants.

According to Table 1, all N measurements were used for estimating β^*_{jl} for the minimum principle. Profiling for the maximum likelihood principle uses the setting $N_1 = N_2 = N/2$, i.e., half of the measurements were used for estimating

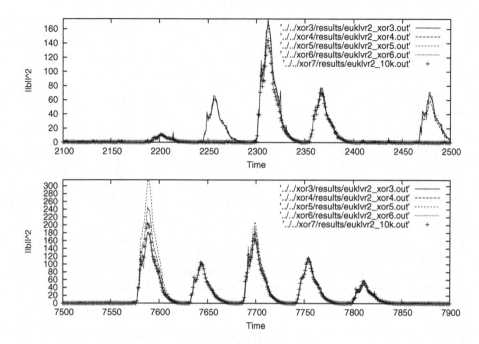

Fig. 3. Squared Euclidean norm $\|b\|^2 = \|(\beta_{j1}^*, \beta_{j2}^*, ..., \beta_{j16}^*)\|^2$ of the bit depending coefficients after profiling for different series. In these time frames, e.g., in the upper plot around offset 2260 and 2480, profiling results with fixed keys give a signal part that is wiped out if profiling is done with varying keys. The lower plot shows resulting differences in the estimation for fixed keys. For each series, 10, 000 single measurements were used.

β_{jl}^*. For the maximum likelihood principle, based on the selected instants, the covariance matrix for the multivariate Gaussian density was then computed as described in SubSect. 2.3.

3.2   Key Recovery Phase

At key recovery, the adversary generally only knows x and aims at retrieving the fixed key k°. Key recovery was done at a series with fixed keys provided that the series assigned for profiling was different. As far as key recovery according to the maximum likelihood principle is concerned equations (14) and (15) were used.

Maximum Likelihood Principle: Results for 'varying key' profiling are based on a ten-dimensional covariance matrix and are summarized in Table 2.

Note that in case of misses of the correct key value often a closely related key value differing only at one bit is obtained instead, especially at high values of N_3. Such an observation is reasonable, as differential side channel analysis on a boolean operation yields to related key hypotheses [10]. Results for 'fixed key' profiling can be found in Table 3 by using a twelve-dimensional covariance

Table 2. Success Rate (SR) that the correct key value is the best candidate as result of (14) by using N_3 randomly chosen measurements (100 repetitions). Profiling was done with variable keys with $N_1 = N_2 = 10000$.

N_3	SR Series no. 1	SR Series no. 2	SR Series no. 3	SR Series no. 4
10	8 %	9 %	5 %	6 %
20	20 %	24 %	14 %	13 %
30	26 %	33 %	22 %	24 %
50	53 %	53 %	36 %	34 %
100	82 %	78 %	55 %	62 %
200	92 %	95 %	79 %	82 %
400	98 %	99 %	93 %	96 %

Table 3. Profiling with fixed key for series no 2, no. 3, and no. 4 with $N_1 = N_2 = 5000$ and key recovery on series no 1. Success Rate (SR) that the correct key value is the best candidate as result of (14) by using N_3 randomly chosen measurements (100 repetitions).

N_3	SR Profiling Series no. 2	SR Profiling Series no. 3	SR Profiling Series no. 4
10	0 %	4 %	4 %
20	5 %	11 %	12 %
30	11 %	25 %	17 %
50	6 %	21 %	32 %
100	24 %	53 %	53 %
200	42 %	78 %	76 %
400	50 %	96 %	86 %

matrix. Table 3 applies three different probability densities (obtained from series no. 2, 3, and 4) to series no. 1 yielding results of various quality. This is a clear indicator for a lack of symmetry at some instants. If comparing Table 2 with Table 3 the average success rate for key recovery is 69 % for 'varying key' profiling while it is 43 % for 'fixed key' profiling at $N_3 = 100$. Trial classifications on the profiling series themselves, however, yield success rates of 97 % at $N_3 = 100$. These results lead to two conclusions. First, it is indicated that profiling for all subkeys will clearly increase success rates and second, the use of a measurement series with varying keys is advantageous if profiling for all subkeys is not feasible, e.g., because of limitations at the profiling stage.

Maximum Likelihood Principle with Known Masking Values: Here, we consider an artificial case that key recovery can be done with known masking values, i.e., masking is completely ineffective. This might be a realistic case if the random number generator used for generating masking values is predictable, e.g., as result of physical modification or of special insights in the construction. The procedure for key recovery was modified in such a way that y is known and is equivalent to a first order side channel analysis. Results are presented in Table 4. For example, for $N_3 = 10$ the success rate to obtain the correct key value is 62.0 %. Among the key misses, a total amount of 25.5 % aggregates

Table 4. Summarizing the results of key recovery with knowledge of masking values. Success Rate (SR) that the correct key value is the best candidate (1000 repetitions) on series no. 1.

N_3	SR (Known masking values)
2	8.8 %
3	17.2 %
5	31.3 %
7	46.0 %
10	62.0 %
20	89.1 %
30	97.3 %
50	99.5 %

Table 5. Summarizing the results of the application of the minimum principle. Profiling was done on the series with varying keys and it was $N = 20,000$. Success Rate (SR) that the correct key value is the best candidate (100 repetitions) on series no. 1.

N_3	SR (Minimum Principle)
10	5 %
20	11 %
30	12 %
50	14 %
100	42 %
200	65 %
400	89 %

at eight related key values differing only by one bit from the correct key value. The security gain of masking in terms of N_3 can be quantified if comparing to Table 2, series no. 1. If considering success rates of about 90 %, N_3 is enlarged by roughly a factor of ten.

Minimum Principle: For the application of the minimum principle, the series with varying keys was used for profiling and the choice of time instants was identical to the application of the maximum likelihood principle. The results give evidence that the minimum principle works in practice. Success rates of 42 % if $N_3 = 100$ and of 89 % if $N_3 = 400$ were obtained by using series no. 1 (see Table 5). These results can be compared with the column for series no. 1 in Table 2 and reveal a noticeable efficiency loss if compared to the maximum likelihood principle.

4   Conclusion

This contribution provides a compendium for the application of stochastic methods on masked implementations. Stochastic methods do not require any assumption of the physical leakage model, instead they provide an approximation of the side channel leakage in any given vector subspace as result of the profiling stage. Because of that, stochastic methods are indeed a practical alternative for analyzing masked cryptographic implementations and may be important for a developer of a masked cryptographic implementation in order to figure out remaining side channel leakage.

References

1. Agrawal, D., Rao, J.R., Rohatgi, P., Schramm, K.: Templates as Master Keys. In: Rao, J.R., Sunar, B. (eds.) CHES 2005. LNCS, vol. 3659, pp. 15–29. Springer, Heidelberg (2005)
2. Brier, E., Clavier, C., Olivier, F.: Correlation Power Analysis with a Leakage Model. In: Joye, M., Quisquater, J.-J. (eds.) CHES 2004. LNCS, vol. 3156, pp. 16–29. Springer, Heidelberg (2004)
3. Chari, S., Jutla, C.S., Rao, J.R., Rohatgi, P.: Towards Sound Approaches to Counteract Power-Analysis Attacks. In: Wiener, M.J. (ed.) CRYPTO 1999. LNCS, vol. 1666, pp. 398–412. Springer, Heidelberg (1999)
4. Chari, S., Rao, J.R., Rohatgi, P.: Template Attacks. In: Kaliski Jr., B.S., Koç, Ç.K., Paar, C. (eds.) CHES 2002. LNCS, vol. 2523, pp. 13–28. Springer, Heidelberg (2003)
5. Coron, J.-S., Goubin, L.: On Boolean and Arithmetic Masking against Differential Power Analysis. In: Paar, C., Koç, Ç.K. (eds.) CHES 2000. LNCS, vol. 1965, pp. 231–237. Springer, Heidelberg (2000)
6. Gandolfi, K., Mourtel, C., Olivier, F.: Electromagnetic Analysis: Concrete Results. In: Koç, Ç.K., Naccache, D., Paar, C. (eds.) CHES 2001. LNCS, vol. 2162, pp. 251–261. Springer, Heidelberg (2001)
7. Gierlichs, B., Lemke-Rust, K., Paar, C.: Templates vs. Stochastic Methods. In: Goubin, L., Matsui, M. (eds.) CHES 2006. LNCS, vol. 4249, pp. 15–29. Springer, Heidelberg (2006)
8. Joye, M., Paillier, P., Schoenmakers, B.: On Second-Order Differential Power Analysis. In: Rao, J.R., Sunar, B. (eds.) CHES 2005. LNCS, vol. 3659, pp. 293–308. Springer, Heidelberg (2005)
9. Kocher, P.C., Jaffe, J., Jun, B.: Differential Power Analysis. In: Wiener, M.J. (ed.) CRYPTO 1999. LNCS, vol. 1666, pp. 388–397. Springer, Heidelberg (1999)
10. Lemke, K., Schramm, K., Paar, C.: DPA on n-Bit Sized Boolean and Arithmetic Operations and Its Application to IDEA, RC6, and the HMAC-Construction. In: Joye, M., Quisquater, J.-J. (eds.) CHES 2004. LNCS, vol. 3156, pp. 205–219. Springer, Heidelberg (2004)
11. Messerges, T.S.: Using Second-Order Power Analysis to Attack DPA Resistant Software. In: Paar, C., Koç, Ç.K. (eds.) CHES 2000. LNCS, vol. 1965, pp. 238–251. Springer, Heidelberg (2000)
12. Oswald, E., Mangard, S.: Template Attacks on Masking – Resistance is Futile. In: Abe, M. (ed.) CT-RSA 2007. LNCS, vol. 4377, pp. 243–256. Springer, Heidelberg (2006)
13. Oswald, E., Mangard, S., Herbst, C., Tillich, S.: Practical Second-Order DPA Attacks for Masked Smart Card Implementations of Block Ciphers. In: Pointcheval, D. (ed.) CT-RSA 2006. LNCS, vol. 3860, pp. 192–207. Springer, Heidelberg (2006)
14. Peeters, E., Standaert, F.-X., Donckers, N., Quisquater, J.-J.: Improved Higher-Order Side-Channel Attacks with FPGA Experiments. In: Rao, J.R., Sunar, B. (eds.) CHES 2005. LNCS, vol. 3659, pp. 309–323. Springer, Heidelberg (2005)

15. Schindler, W., Lemke, K., Paar, C.: A Stochastic Model for Differential Side Channel Cryptanalysis. In: Rao, J.R., Sunar, B. (eds.) CHES 2005. LNCS, vol. 3659, pp. 30–46. Springer, Heidelberg (2005)
16. Schramm, K., Paar, C.: Higher Order Masking of the AES. In: Pointcheval, D. (ed.) CT-RSA 2006. LNCS, vol. 3860, pp. 208–225. Springer, Heidelberg (2006)
17. Waddle, J., Wagner, D.: Towards Efficient Second-Order Power Analysis. In: Joye, M., Quisquater, J.-J. (eds.) CHES 2004. LNCS, vol. 3156, pp. 1–15. Springer, Heidelberg (2004)

Insider Attacks Enabling Data Broadcasting on Crypto-Enforced Unicast Links

André Adelsbach[1,*] and Ulrich Greveler[2]

[1] Telindus S.A
Security, Audit and Governance Services (SAGS)
2, rue des Mines, L-4244 Esch/Alzette, Luxembourg
andre.adelsbach@telindus.lu
[2] Fachhochschule Münster
Fachbereich Elektrotechnik und Informatik
Stegerwaldstr. 39, 48565 Steinfurt, Germany
greveler@fh-muenster.de

Abstract. Most wireless communication techniques rely on broadcast media on the physical layer, i.e., the actual signal can be received by any party in a certain coverage area. Furthermore, there are cable-based networks, such as HFC (hybrid fiber/coaxial) networks that use a shared transmission medium (coaxial cable) to bridge the last mile.

A common means to perform *secure unicast (point-to-point)* communication over such wireless or shared transmission media is by applying cryptographic protocols on higher layers of the protocol stack. As of today, a common assumption in the design and analysis of such communication protocols is that both end-points (user and carrier) behave correctly according to the cryptographic protocol, because they want to preserve security against outsiders who might be sniffing private communication of legitimate users. However, under certain conditions users may not be interested in protecting their unicast communication against outsiders. Instead, users may try to extend their communication power/resources by means of *insider attacks* against the communication protocol.

Such insider attacks pose new threats to providers of communication services and have, to the best of our knowledge, been neglected so far. In this paper we will discuss insider attacks against several communication systems that can break the unicast communication enforced by cryptographic means by the carrier of the communication infrastructure.

1   Introduction

Most wireless communication techniques rely on broadcast media on the physical layer, i.e., the actual signal can be received by any party in a certain coverage area. Furthermore, there are cable-based networks, such as HFC (hybrid

---

* The information in this paper is provided as is, and no guarantee or warranty is given or implied that the information is fit for any particular purpose. The user thereof uses the information at its sole risk and liability. The views expressed herein are solely the author's and should not be attributed to his employer or their clients.

J. Biskup and J. Lopez (Eds.): ESORICS 2007, LNCS 4734, pp. 469–484, 2007.
© Springer-Verlag Berlin Heidelberg 2007

fiber/coaxial) networks that use a shared transmission medium (coaxial cable) to bridge the last mile.

A common means to perform secure unicast (point-to-point) communication over such wireless or shared transmission media is by applying cryptographic protocols on higher layers: both communication end-points (user and carrier) set up a session key, which is then used to build secure (private and authentic) unicast communication by means of encryption and message authentication. As of today, a common assumption in the design and analysis of such communication protocols is that both end-points (user and carrier) behave correctly according to the cryptographic protocol, because they want to preserve security against outsiders.

However, if carriers have more power/resources in terms of bandwidth or coverage, users may not be interested in protecting their unicast communication against outsiders. Instead, users may try to extend their communication power/resources by means of *insider attacks* against the communication protocol. Such insider attacks pose new threats to these protocols and have, to the best of our knowledge, been neglected so far.

In this paper we present insider attacks, which can break the unicast communication enforced by the carrier of the communication infrastructure. We define a corresponding abstract communication model and sketch concrete instantiations that are deployed in practice: satellite ISPs, WIMAX ISPs and cable (DOCSIS) ISPs. We illustrate the effects of insider attacks mainly in terms of satellite ISPs, because here the effects of insider attacks are most striking: the user normally has a terrestrial link to the carrier and no means to broadcast data at all, while the carrier can broadcast its signals over huge footprints, covering millions of square kilometers. Our strongest insider attack may allow any end-user to make clear-text satellite broadcasts via the ISP's satellite, even if the downlink (data sent from the satellite to earth) is properly encrypted by the satellite ISP, thereby breaking the unicast communication structure enforced by the satellite ISP.

1.1   Outline

In Section 2 we introduce the general communication and attacker model and discuss state-of-the-art instantiations of this abstract communication model. Special emphasis is on satellite ISPs, as we consider them the most interesting scenario for insider attacks. In Section 3 we discuss several possible insider attacks against communication protocols that allow an insider attacker to broadcast messages via the ISP, although the ISP applies encryption. Section 4 we consider state-of-the-art communication systems and show that they are susceptible to our attacks. We conclude in Section 5.

2   Communication Models

Before going into the details of our analysis, we introduce the abstract communication model assumed in the remainder of this paper.

2.1   Abstract Communication Model

The abstract communication model is as follows (cf. Figure 1): the *carrier* of the communication infrastructure (also referred to as *ISP*), has a direct connection to the Internet and offers Internet connectivity to its *users*. We consider one of these legitimate users to be the *insider attacker*. The carrier/ISP communicates to its users via a physical broadcast medium or shared medium. As such, the communication (signals) from the carrier to its users can be received by any *outsider* in range of the broadcasted signals or having access to the shared medium. However, outsiders do not have access to the broadcasted message as it is normally encrypted with a key shared between user and carrier to preserve confidentiality against outsiders. Communication from the users to the carrier may be either via broadcast/shared-medium (visible to outsiders) or via a private communication link (not visible to outsiders).

Goal of the insider attacker is to make the carrier broadcast any message he likes, such that it can be received by outsiders.

Below we review wireless- and shared-medium-based ISPs and communication technologies that are state-of-the-art instantiations of this abstract communication model and, as such, susceptible to the attacks considered in our contribution. *Throughout the paper we assume that the insider attacker has read-access to its key-material, which in practice might require hardware tampering if the protocol is implemented completely in hardware.*

More specifically, we will review three types of ISPs: Satellite ISPs, WIMAX ISPs and Cable ISPs. As satellite-based ISPs have the biggest asymmetry in terms of coverage, we consider them the most attractive target for insider attacks as discussed below. Therefore, we will mainly focus on satellite-based ISPs to illustrate these attacks. However, it is important to note that our attacks also apply to other wireless/shared-medium communication protocols.

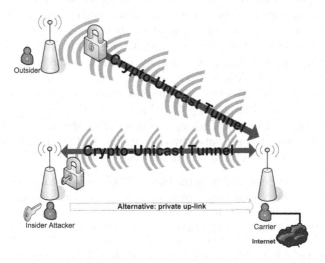

Fig. 1. Abstract Communication and Attacker Model

2.2   Satellite ISPs

A satellite is a specialised *wireless* transmitter placed in terrestrial orbit for television broadcast, radio communications and data services, such as Internet access. Especially in low-infrastructure areas with limited physical/terrestrial networks, satellites provide high-speed access to the Internet. Some of the existing digital communication satellites transmit TV signals together with data communication so a user can use her dish and digital receiver for TV reception as well as one-way Internet access. Satellite-based Internet access comes in two flavours:

- One-Way with PSTN/ISDN up-link (asymmetric): In this lower cost option the satellite handles only the data downstream with outbound data travelling via modem/ISDN offering high download bandwidth[1] and a rather small terrestrial up-link bandwidth (up to $2 \cdot 64$ KBit/s).
- Two-Way with DVB-RCS up-link (symmetric): The more expensive two-way access requires a satellite terminal, e.g., a VSAT (Very Small Aperture Terminal), at the user's side and yields higher bandwidth for up-links (up to 2 MBit/s). Other types of return channels are under consideration, but are not broadly available yet (examples are *Return Channel Cable* and *Return Channel Terrestrial*).

Independent of the flavour (one-way or two-way), users and provider of satellite-based data services have highly asymmetric capabilities, both in terms of bandwidth (45 MBit/s downlink vs. 2MBit/s up-link) and in terms of coverage: the user normally has a terrestrial link to the carrier and no means to broadcast data at all.[2] The carrier, on the other hand, can broadcast its signals from the *exposed orbital satellite position* all over a huge footprint, covering millions of square kilometers and hundreds of millions receiver.

Below we consider the operation of an (asymmetric) one-way satellite ISP, because it is still more relevant. To illustrate how one-way satellite-based ISPs operate, consider the setting where a user fetches a file from a web server. A user establishes a small bandwidth dial-up Internet connection, e.g., using an ISDN line to some ISP (which is not necessarily the same as the satellite ISP). In order to initiate a download a request is sent through the dial-up line to an ISP proxy server (Fig. 2, Step 1), which relays the request to the desired destination (Fig. 2, Step 2). The reply coming from the server (e.g., a HTML page) (Fig. 2, Step 3) is re-routed by the satellite ISP so that it will not come back to the user's PC through the dial-up line. Instead it will be encapsulated

---

[1] The current bandwidth (applying the Digital Video Broadcasting (DVB) standards [5]) offers a maximum data transfer rate of 45 MBit/s on one transponder frequency being shared among several users for the downstream. However the provider often limits the downstream bandwidth per user to a certain value, e.g., 1024 KBit/s.

[2] Even if the user had a VSAT being able to send data, this would not allow broadcasts with a comparable coverage, both because the transmitting power is significantly lower and, even more importantly, the dish is located on earth, allowing only to broadcast to a limited area (line of sight).

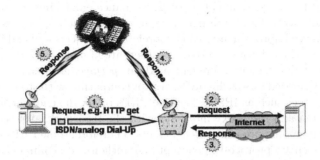

Fig. 2. How a satellite Internet connection works

together with the user's specific IP address into a signal based on the DVB standard and the ISP ground station relays it to the satellite (Figure 2, Step 4). The satellite broadcasts it and the user, having a satellite dish, a usual DVB card and a dedicated proxy software, decodes the response on his PC. The proxy software completes the TCP communication transparently for the application or operating system (Fig. 2, Step 5).

Due to the broadcast character of satellite signals, the signal dedicated for this user can be received by anyone in the footprint of the satellite.

2.2.1 Performance vs. Security

Satellite communication links differ in several characteristics from terrestrial channels used for Internet communication [3]: Firstly, satellite communication links have a relative large latency, due to the large altitude of satellites.[3]

This large latency also results in a long feedback loop between sending a TCP packet and receiving the corresponding acknowledgement. Another important characteristic is that satellite channels have a higher bit-error rate than wired terrestrial networks.

As these characteristics would result in a significant performance degradation of the TCP protocol[4], performance enhancing techniques have to be applied by the satellite ISP in order to achieve a satisfactory performance. Important examples for performance enhancing techniques are

- local TCP acknowledgements by the ISP's proxy (to speed up TCP slow start),
- local negative acknowledgements to improve error recovery,
- local TCP retransmissions from the satellite ISP to the client if a packet was lost on the satellite link (improve error recovery),

For details, we refer the interested reader to [2,3,4].

---

[3] According to [2] many satellites are located at the Geostationary Orbit with an altitude of approx. 36.000 km. This results in a propagation delay of at least 279 ms for one hop (station-to-satellite-to-ground).

[4] As delayed feedbacks and transmission errors are interpreted as signals of network congestion, TCP would automatically reduce the transmission rate. For more details see [3].

Satellite ISPs use a combination of performance enhancing techniques along this line to improve the overall performance of their Internet access. Moreover, application layer improvements, such as prefetching objects embedded in HTML documents that have been requested by a user, are in place. Unfortunately, these performance enhancements, implemented in *performance enhancing proxies (PEPs)* and operated by satellite ISPs, are not compatible with standard low-level security measures such as IPSEC because PEPs break the end-to-end semantics of a connection and the proxy interferes with the transport layer security measures, e.g., by sending pre-acknowledgements. Therefore, some PEPs also include proprietary security protocols to encrypt and authenticate communication.

2.3   WIMAX ISPs

The first WIMAX standard, known as 802.16-2001, incorporated a pre-existing standard, DOCSIS (Data Over Cable Service Inferface Specification). However, due to the different threat models of wired and wireless communication, security of the original 802.16-2001 standard failed to provide adequate protection. Johnston and Walker [7] discuss several security weaknesses of the original standard, some of which are:

- use of 56-Bit DES encryption in CBC-mode (cipher block chaining)
- lack of mutual authentication: base station does not have to authenticate itself
- no formally defined and weak authorization security association, paving the way for replay attacks

This security level had been considered sufficient, because 802.16 had originally been designed to be a *line-of-sight* point-to-multipoint communication system. As new features, such as mobility and non-line/near-line of sight (NOLS) were to be included in the standard, these security weaknesses became increasingly pressing and have been addressed by improving the 802.16 security mechanisms in the new version of the standard IEEE 802.16-2004.

The security sublayer consists of two main components: first, the *PKM (Privacy and Key Manangement) protocol*, providing network access control (authentication based on public key cryptography and X.509 certificates) and secure key distribution from the base station (BS) to the subscriber station (SS). Second, the *encapsulation protocol*, defining a set of supported cryptographic suites and rules for applying these suites to encrypt (and authenticate) MAC PDU payload. Besides DES CBC packet data encryption, 802.16-2004 defines AES encryption in CCM (Counter Mode with Cipher Block Chaining MAC) mode as an additional packet data encryption algorithm.

3   Insider Attacks and Countermeasures

3.1   A General Definition

Classically, *insider attackers* are able to use a given computer system with a level of authority granted to them and violate their organization's security policy [11].

The insider attack is often considered as the primary human threat to computer systems since users that operate inside an organization have specific motives and legitimate access to systems that are detached from public networks. The commonly held views that most attacks come from the inside is a myth, though [10].

In the following we consider a different class of insider attacks, where the insider does not compromise a *system* from the inside of an organization but rather misuses a communication protocol for his own purposes, actively attacking security mechanisms established by the carrier.

3.2   What Is the Motivation for Attackers?

There are several answers to this questions: first, attackers may want to break the unicast communication to get improved broadcast capabilities, which they do not have otherwise. This motive applies mainly to Satellite ISPs or Cable ISPs.

Second, even if the capabilities of users and carriers are more or less equal, an insider attacker may try to make the carrier broadcast illegal content, rather than broadcasting the content himself. This motive applies to all use-cases, including Satellite ISPs, WIMAX ISPs and Cable ISPs.

3.3   Why Is This a Problem for Carriers?

Again, there are several answers to this question. First, breaking the unicast structure may destroy the carrier's business model, because they may want to sell broadcasts at a significantly higher price than unicast communication. Loosing the ability to enforce unicast communication may destroy such business models.

The second reason is the carrier's potential liability for clear-text data broadcasts triggered by users. Even if the carrier disclaimed liability of such "unauthorized" broadcasts, these broadcasts may still significantly harm the carrier's reputation. Furthermore, doing broadcasts normally requires permissions by government, e.g. the FCC (Federal Communications Commission) in the U.S. By breaking the unicast communication insider attackers can misuse the carrier's infrastructure to perform their own broadcasts without such permission. By operating such susceptible infrastructure, carriers may be held liable as well.

Moreover, according to "Data Retention" legislation carriers of telecommunication infrastructures are (or will be required)[5] to retain, amongst others, data necessary to trace and identify the *destination* of a communication. Given the perfect receiver anonymity provided by broadcasts, carriers can not even collect this data.

---

[5] In Europe the so called "Data Retention Directive", issued on 15th of March 2006, will harmonise the data retention obligations of providers of publicly available electronic communications services or of public communications networks. This directive has to be adopted by national legislation in EU countries until September 15th 2007. In the U.S., according to the "Electronic Communication Transactional Records Act 18 USC s 2703(f)", ISPs have to retain records for 90 days upon request of a government entity.

Finally, the ability to perform data broadcasts, having the same coverage as the carrier itself, may be used to attack other services, operated by the same carrier. Consider, as an example the satellite-based broadcast of Pay-TV. There are well-known attacks, referred to as *card-sharing attacks*, where a legitimate Pay-TV customer that paid for the TV broadcast, sends the required decryption keys to its peers. Today, the latter is mostly done via unicast Internet communication, which does not scale to large groups. However, as we will see below, insider attackers may misuse Satellite ISPs to broadcast Pay-TV keys using the same satellite infrastructure that distributes the encrypted Pay-TV content. This may significantly harm the business model of the Pay-TV provider and, indirectly, the business model of the carrier operating the satellite.

3.4   Insider Attacks on Crypto-Enforced Unicast-Communication

Crypto-based communication protocols distinguish two phases in general:

1. first, the *key-agreement phase*, where a common session key is set up between user and carrier and,
2. second, the actual *encrypted transmission phase*, where the session key is used to encrypt messages before transmission over the broadcast/shared-medium.

Insider attacks may address both phases and we will consider them separately in the following sub-sections.

3.5   Leaking the Key

Leaking the encryption key is always a straightforward option for an insider and there are several ways to leak the key material to outsiders. Besides sending the key material to the outsiders directly, it is also possible to distribute the session-key in a more advanced way.

- **Send the key to the outsiders via direct communication:** This is a straightforward way, but requires the insider attacker to communicate to each outsider individually. For large groups of outsiders, this seems to be infeasible. Furthermore, if the overall goal of the insider attacker is to preserve the anonymity of the outsiders (receivers of its communication), he must not communicate with the outsiders directly.
- **Publish the key in a newsgroup or electronic message board:** This is a straightforward way to publish the secret key, while preserving the anonymity of outsiders. However, it requires each outsider to access the published key.
- **Build a covert channel to broadcast the key via the broadcast/ shared-medium:** Here, the insider attacker may for example build a covert timing channel by sending/requesting (encrypted) data packets via the broadcast/shared-channel and encoding the key by following a certain timing pattern. Outsiders may observe the timing-pattern of these (encrypted) packets and reconstruct the key, allowing them to decrypt the packets afterwards.

Although this approach seems viable, it certainly involves a certain over-head to communicate the key. On the other hand, it preserves the perfect receiver anonymity offered by broadcast channels and allows receivers (out-siders) to stay completeley passive and, thus, untraceable.

These methods are most efficient, if the communication protocol uses long-term secrets and there are no session-keys or session-keys are distributed via the broadcast/shared-medium. In this case it is sufficient to distribute the long-term secrets once. This applies to the following types of key-agreement:

- **point-to-point key update using symmetric encryption.** a long-term symmetric key is used to distribute all further short-lived (session) keys. Here, the insider attacker can leak the long-term key once, such that all further (session) key updates leak to outsiders if the key-update is done via the broadcast/shared-channel.
- **Key-predistribution schemes** are always vulnerable if the leakage of pre-distributed keys is sufficient for the outsiders to derive the short-lived keys. This is for instance the case for Blom's symmetric key pre-distribution sys-tem, the Otway-Rees protocol or the Needham-Schroeder public-key protocol.

Countermeasures. Since the intentional leakage of an agreed two-party session key to a third party by one of the parties cannot ultimately be prevented, coun-termeasures can only *complicate* the insider attacker's task, either by forcing the insider to communicate directly to the group of outsiders or increasing the data-rate necessary to distribute the key, or *deter* the insider from publishing his key. We consider the following countermeasures:

- **Use private channel for key agreement.** The party intending to compli-cate the insider attack (the carrier in our setting) can use non-broadcast/non-shared channels (e.g., the dial-up connection in case of one-way satellite ISPs) for key agreement purposes. Regarding satellite ISPs the dial-up connection should be favored for key-exchange. Therefore, outsiders can not benefit from knowing long-term keys if the session key is updated via a non-broadcast channel. Instead, the insider attacker has to distribute each key-update sep-arately, as described above, or attack the actual key-agreement protocol (see below).
- **Increasing the rate of key-updates** also increases the rate in which the insider attacker has to send the updated keys to the outsiders. As the rate of key-updates increases, insider attacks become less attractive.
- **Include sensitive data** that the insider attacker probably does not want to disclose to the group of outsiders. If, as an example, the insider attacker is forced to include information, such as credit card numbers, account balances, date-of-birth or authentication credentials into his keys, he needs to disclose all this information to other parties that he might not trust in extensively. The need to disclose confidential data does then discourage insider attackers.

3.6   Insider Attacks on Key-Agreement

Besides leaking keys to outsiders, the insider attacker may try to attack the key-exchange protocol itself in order to always yield a *fixed key* that is known a-priori to the outsiders - so there is no need to communicate it to the outsiders. However, as two-party key establishment is inevitably insecure when the secret key is revealed by one of the parties after running the key-agreement protocol, two-party key-agreement protocols often do not address insider attacks.

Nevertheless, the setting has been considered before and Menezes et al. ([9], Chap. 12) refer to it as *key control*: "*In some protocols (key transport), one party chooses a key value. In others (key agreement), the key is derived from joint information, and it may be desirable that neither party be able to control or predict the value of the key*". Obviously, the inside attacker favors the setting where he (or the eavedroppers) can predict the value of a key.

Certain widely-used key agreement protocols have not been designed to prevent insider attackers and, therefore, should not be used in the communication models considered in this paper.

– **Shamir's no-key protocol.** Shamir's no-key protocol is a key transport protocol that does not require any shared or public keys and provides protection from passive attackers.[6]

The protocol works as follows: the first party A selects the secret key K, chooses a random value a (co-prime to $p - 1$) and sends K^a mod p to the second party B. When B receives K^a mod p he chooses a random value b and sends $(K^a)^b$ mod p to A. Finally, A sends K^b mod $p = (K^{ab})^{a^{-1}}$ mod p to B, who can decrypt $K = (K^b)^{b^{-1}}$ mod p.

If the insider attacker starts the protocol he can always select a fixed key K, e.g., $x12345678$, known a-priori to the outsiders. Otherwise, if the carrier acts as A, initiates the protocol and selects a good key K, the insider attacker B can choose a fixed value $b = 1$, such that outsiders can intercept $K^b = K^1$ in the last step of the protocol. In the latter case the insider attack works only if the key-exchange is done via the broadcast or shared medium (e.g., WIMAX-, Cable- or symmetric Satellite ISPs).

– **Diffie-Hellman key agreement.** Let p be an appropriate prime and let g be a generator of $\mathbb{Z}_p^*$. The basic Diffie-Hellman key agreement works as follows: first, A chooses a random secret a and sends g^a mod p to B. Then B chooses a random secret b and sends g^b mod p to A. Now A computes $K = (g^b)^a = g^{ab}$ and B computes $K = (g^a)^b = g^{ab}$.

Here, the insider attacker A can always select a fixed "random" secret a, known a-priori to outsider outsiders. This allows outsiders to compute the agreed fresh key $K = (g^b)^a$ mod p for every random secret b chosen by party B. Furthermore, the insider attacker may choose secrets a of small order or

---

[6] As the parties do not share any shared or public keys, the protocol is not secure against active attackers as messages cannot be authenticated, which paves the way for man-in-the-middle attackers.

even $a = 0$. The former restricts the order of the overall key K (cf. Menezes et al [9]) and the latter always yields the degenerate key $K = g^0 = 1$.

The latter attack even works if the key-agreement is not performed via the broadcast/shared-medium, but e.g., via the dial-up connection in the one-way Satellite-ISP setting.

Note, that there exist checks to detect this kind of attack. The point is that these checks are not necessary to protect communication against outsiders, but they are mandatory to prevent insider attacks.

3.7 Insider Attacks on Encrypted Transmission

As discussed above, one possibility to break the crypto-enforced unicast communication is to *give the outsiders access to the encryption key*, either by distributing the encryption key or by attacking the key-agreement protocol in order to yield keys that are a-priori known to outsiders.

In addition to these attacks it is also possible to attack the actual *encrypted transmission phase*. The basic idea is *to make the carrier broadcast the desired messages as its **ciphertexts***. To achieve this the insider attacker may request specially crafted messages from the carrier, which, upon *encryption* by the carrier, result in the attacker's desired message. The carrier will then broadcast the attacker's messages as part of the encrypted payload. In this way, the insider attacker can make the carrier broadcast any message he likes. In the following we will consider this attack in more details.

Let m be a message, let E be the encryption function used by the carrier and let k be the (symmetric) encryption key. The "attack" depends on the following observation: for many encryption algorithms E it is straightforward to compute a function E^{-1}, such that

$$E(k, E^{-1}(k, m)) = m$$

holds for any key k and any message m.

Assuming that the carrier uses an encryption algorithm E having this property, our idea is as follows: the insider attacker, wanting the carrier to broadcast m, computes $d = E^{-1}(k, m)$ and requests a download of d (e.g., from its own server) via the carrier. The carrier fetches d from the insider attacker's server. Before sending it back to the attacker via the broadcast/shared-medium, the carrier encrypts d, which results in the desired *cipher-text* m, which the carrier finally sends over the broadcast/shared-medium. The overall attack is illustrated in Figure 3 in terms of asymmetric Satellite ISPs.

Below we consider some well-known, commonly used encryption algorithms and show that they are susceptible to this insider attack.

1. **Block Ciphers in Electronic Codebook mode (ECB):** In ECB mode of operation the message is divided into blocks that are encrypted individually by applying the block cipher to each block. For block ciphers there is an encryption function E and a decryption function D, such that the following holds: $m = E(k, d)$ and $d = D(k, m)$. Therefore, in this case, $E^{-1}()$ is

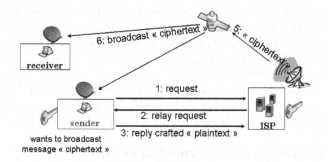

Fig. 3. Attack on encrypted transmission

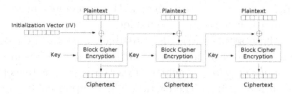

Cipher Block Chaining (CBC) mode encryption

Fig. 4. CBC Mode of Operation (Source [8])

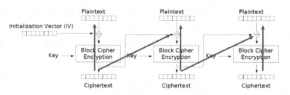

Cipher Block Chaining (CBC) mode encryption

Fig. 5. E^{-1} for CBC Mode of Operation

identical to the decryption algorithm D, i.e., if an insider attacker wants the carrier to broadcast a certain "ciphertext" m, he simply has to request a crafted message $d = D(k, m)$ via the carrier.

2. **Stream Ciphers:** If the carrier applies a stream cipher, XORing the message with a pseudo-random key stream $PRNG(k)$ generated from k, the user may simply XOR the message m with the same pseudo-random key stream to get the desired crafted message $d = m \oplus PRNG(k)$.

   Practical examples of such stream ciphers are RC4 and block ciphers operated in Output Feedback (OFB) or Counter Mode (CTR).[7]

---

[7] Basically, CTR mode computes the key stream by encrypting a nonce and a counter using the encryption key. As the nonce in CTR stays fixed throughout a connection and the counter value is increased deterministically, the attacker can predict the whole key stream once he knows the nonce.

3. **Further Block Cipher Modes of Operation:** Cipher-block chaining (CBC) mode of operation is illustrated in Figure 4 and the computation of E^{-1} is straightforward, as illustrated in Figure 5.

Remark: Note, that the IV required in block cipher modes of operation is also known to the insider attacker. It is either a part of the key, i.e., known before applying the attack, or sent to the insider attacker when starting the transmission. In the latter case, the insider can start its attack (crafting suitable packets) after he received the IV at the beginning of the transmission.

Remark: Note, that the insider attacker can even make the carrier broadcast messages that are specifically encrypted, such that only certain outsiders can read the message. For others (carrier or police), such messages look completely unsuspicious.

3.7.1   Countermeasures

Hardware implementations. A straightforward countermeasure is to fully implement the communication protocol, including both key-agreement and transmission phase, in hardware. A pure hardware implementation makes it harder for the *average attacker* to manipulate the key-agreement protocol to enforce weak keys or to get direct access to the session key and mount the corresponding attacks on the encrypted transmission. Even if the hardware implementation could be attacked by patching the hardware, this attack would not scale as good as purely software-based attacks and, therefore, one may consider it kind of a countermeasure for low profile attackers.

Randomising Encryption. Let m be the message stream that has been requested by the user and that has to be forwarded to the user via the broadcast/shared-medium.

One possible countermeasure is to let the carrier add a random prefix x of fixed size to each message m before encrypting and forwarding it. By randomizing the encryption the insider attacker cannot craft messages that would lead to the desired ciphertext. On the other hand, this countermeasure is only effective for encryption schemes where a random prefix to the plaintext affects the whole ciphertext and it reduces the throughput of the down-link. Furthermore, it seems to be necessary that the carrier starts the encrypted transmission of $x||m$ only after m has been completeley received from the Internet, because otherwise the insider attacker could still adapt the tail of message m accordingly after he received the prefix x.

Fresh random message keys. Another possible solution is to let the carrier choose a fresh random message-key r for each message m and let the carrier send $E_r(m)||E_k(r)$. Here, again it is important that the insider attacker does not get to know r before message m has been completely received by the carrier. Otherwise, the insider attacker may again craft m, such that encryption with r yields at least partly to the desired ciphertext. This countermeasure seems to be effective, but again reduces the throughput and introduces computational overhead for the ISP due to extensive generation of message-keys. Furthermore, it may increase the latency, because the user cannot access a prefix of m before $E_k(r)$ has been received. We consider further analysis of these countermeasures as interesting future work.

4   Case Studies

4.1   DOCSIS and WIMAX

The WIMAX key management protocol (PKM) allows key transport from carrier to user. Similarly, the BPI+ (Baseline Privacy Interface (Plus)) of the DOCSIS standard involves a key transport protocol (BPKM - Baseline Privacy Key Management). As such, these protocols are not susceptible to insider attacks against the key-agreement phase, where the insider attacker enforces weak, a-priori known keys to be used. However, an insider attacker may still extract its key and distribute it to the outsiders.

DOCSIS 1.1 packet data encryption specifies 56-Bit DES encryption in CBC mode and according to DOCSIS 3.0 the CMTS (carrier) has to support 56-Bit DES and 128-Bit AES, both in CBC mode. As such, Cable ISPs are susceptible to the insider attack against encryption as illustrated above.

WIMAX (802.16-2004) specifies 56-Bit DES in CBC mode as being mandatory to implement, whereas AES in CCM mode is not mandatory. Both CBC and CCM, which uses Counter Mode (CTR) for encryption, are susceptible to the insider attacks discussed above.

4.2   Satellite ISPs

Satellite ISPs offer the best gain for insider attackers, because users and satellite ISPs have completely different capabilities: the satellite ISPs sends its data through a satellite, being in an exposed orbit position, thereby being able to broadcast its signal over a huge area. Contrary, the user can only send its data through a terestrial uplink (point-to-point) or satellite up-link.

Although satellite signals offer no confidentiality due to their broadcast character, several satellite ISPs provide optional or no encryption at all [1], but solely rely on MAC-filters in DVB-cards or software drivers, which blind out transmissions of other users. However, similar to standard network adapters, DVB-cards can be put in a promiscuous mode, allowing anyone to receive the complete data downstream of a satellite. Given such weak non-cryptographic security measures, it is very easy to break the "enforced" unicast communication to achieve satellite broadcasts in practice.

There are PEPs that offer encryption, but their internals are not publicly specified. This makes it harder to analyse, which security mechanisms are actually implemented and whether these are susceptible to any of the attacks discussed above.

An analysis of software PEPs performed at Ruhr-University of Bochum [6] showed that it is quite straightforward to locate and extract the session key in the PEP software during runtime. Furthermore, the analysis (and searching the web) revealed that these PEPs use Diffie-Hellman key exchange (which might be susceptible as discussed above) and Blowfish encryption, which might be susceptible, if used in a susceptible mode of operation (see above).

5 Conclusion

We considered insider attacks against crypto-enforced unicast communication via wireless or shared communication media. Here the goal of an insider attacker is to break the unicast-communication that is enforced by cryptographic means.

We argued that it is important for carriers of such communication infrastructures, e.g., satellite ISPs or WIMAX ISPs to enforce unicast communication by means of strong cryptography. Current practice of some satellite ISPs that do leave users the choice to deactivate encryption or do not offer encryption at all, paves the way to misuse the carrier's broadcast capabilities, e.g., to broadcast copyrighted or illegal content over whole continents.

Even if the carrier encrypts its communication via the broadcast-/shared-medium we showed that it is not sufficient to focus on the classical outsider attacks when choosing key-agreement and encryption protocols. In addition to these classical attacks, it is crucial to consider insider attacks, as discussed in this paper. We showed that state-of-the-art communication systems such as WIMAX, DOCSIS or satellite ISPs are susceptible to these attacks, allowing insiders to break the crypto-enforced unicast communication and make the carrier broadcast arbitrary data. The effect is most striking in the case of satellite ISPs, where an insider attacker can make the carrier broadcast any message to the whole footprint of the satellite.

Acknowledgements

We like to thank Stephan Groß and Sandra Steinbrecher for interesting discussions regarding wireless communication protocols. Moreover, we thank Michael Steiner and Ahmad-Reza Sadeghi for providing their comments on insider attacks. Finally, many thanks go to the anonymous reviewers who provided detailed, insightful and critical commentary on this paper.

References

1. Adelsbach, A., Greveler, U.: Satellite Communication without Privacy – Attacker's Paradise. In: Federrath, H. (ed.) Sicherheit, GI. LNI, vol. 62 (2005)
2. Allman, M., Dawkins, S., Glover, D., Griner, J., Tran, D., Henderson, T., Heidemann, J., Touch, J., Kruse, H., Ostermann, S., Scott, K., Semke, J.: Ongoing TCP Research Related to Satellites. Internet Request for Comment RFC 2760, Internet Engineering Task Force (February 2000)
3. Allman, M., Glover, D., Sanchez, L.: Enhancing TCP Over Satellite Channels using Standard Mechanisms. Internet Request for Comment RFC 2488, Internet Engineering Task Force (January 1999)

4. Border, J., Kojo, M., Griner, J., Montenegro, G., Shelby, Z.: Performance Enhancing Proxies Intended to Mitigate Link-Related Degradations. Internet Request for Comment RFC 3135, Internet Engineering Task Force (June 2001)
5. DVB Project: Dvb project homepage, http://www.dvb.org
6. Haskes, T., Kopperschläger, J.: Analysis of a satellite isp client (unpublished bachelor theses November 2005)
7. Johnston, D., Walker, J.: Overview of ieee 802.16 security. IEEE Security & Privacy 2(3), 40–48 (2004)
8. Lunkwill: CBC illustration. Wikipedia (2004),
   http://en.wikipedia.org/wiki/Image:Cbc_encryption.png
9. Menezes, A.J., van Oorschot, P.C., Vanstone, S.A.: Handbook of Applied Cryptography. CRC Press series on discrete mathematics and its applications. CRC Press, Boca Raton, USA (1997)
10. Eugene Schultz, E.: A framework for understanding and predicting insider attacks. Computers and Security 21(6), 526–531 (2002)
11. Tuglular, T., Spafford, E.H.: A framework for characterization of insider computer misuse. Purdue University (unpublished paper, 1997)

Towards Modeling Trust Based Decisions: A Game Theoretic Approach

Vidyaraman Sankaranarayanan, Madhusudhanan Chandrasekaran ,
and Shambhu Upadhyaya

University at Buffalo, Buffalo NY 14260, USA
Phone.: 716-645-3180, Fax.: 716-645-3464
{vs28,mc79,shambhu}@cse.buffalo.edu

Abstract. Current trust models enable decision support at an implicit level by means of thresholds or constraint satisfiability. Decision support is mostly included only for a single binary action, and does not explicitly consider the purpose of a transaction. In this paper, we present a game theoretic model that is specifically tuned for decision support on a whole host of actions, based on specified thresholds of risk. As opposed to traditional representations on the real number line between 0 and +1, Trust in our model is represented as an index into a set of actions ordered according to the agent's preference. A base scenario of *zero trust* is defined by the equilibrium point of a game described in normal form with a certain payoff structure. We then present the *blind trust* model, where an entity attempts to initiate a trust relationship with another entity for a one-time transaction, without any prior knowledge or recommendations. We extend this to the *incentive trust* model where entities can offer incentives to be trusted in a multi-period transaction. For a specified risk threshold, both models are analyzed by using the base scenario of *zero trust* as a reference. Lastly, we present some issues involved in the translation of our models to practical scenarios, and suggest a rich set of extensions of the generalized game theoretic approach to model decision support for existing trust frameworks.

Keywords: Decision Support, Game Theory, Incentives, Risk, Trust.

1 Introduction

The three dominant characteristics of trust are *vulnerability*, *risk* and *expectation* (or *uncertainty*). All trust models encompass these characteristics and present definitions, representations, evaluations and operations on the notion of trust (see [1,2,3,4,5] and the references therein). Decision support for trust models and frameworks must involve an accurate estimation of the uncertainty of other agent's actions. The level to which an agent is willing to tolerate the loss due to the uncertainty is the risk threshold. Most trust models/frameworks enable decision support based on threshold values or constraint satisfiability (e.g., *automated trust negotiations* first initiated by Winsborough et al. [6] and later extended in [7,8,9]) or some aggregation metric of recommendations (e.g., Fuzzy

J. Biskup and J. Lopez (Eds.): ESORICS 2007, LNCS 4734, pp. 485–500, 2007.

metrics [10]) based on past history, like recommender systems (RS) [11]. In most of the previous works that present generic trust models, the decision making criteria, i.e., the translation from trust to action, is left to the agent, and rightly so, because such translations are usually context dependent. Decision support is not explicitly embedded into the trust model; rather the agent is expected to make decisions for a single action based on thresholds or constraints, depending on the model. Such threshold or constraint specification is for a single binary action and is not applicable when the agent has a multitude of action choices. The traditional trust values of 0 to +1 are not particularly conducive towards the direct translation of trust to a multitude of actions; an additional mapping function is required for decision support.

In this paper, we present a model of trust based decisions using a game theoretic approach. In our model, agents have a multitude of action choices and interact with other agents with some (possibly zero) trust. The trust of an agent (on other agents) is represented as an index into the action set of the agent. Thus, the very value of trust enables decision support, even at the level of the abstract model. In other words, the trust value describes the action to be initiated in an interaction. We extend the work of other trust models by going beyond defining trust notions; taking our intuition from *automated trust negotiations* [6], our model assumes that every trust interaction has a purpose, and thus, *both* (and in general *all*) interacting agents must have something to gain at the end of an interaction. With this purpose in mind, we first present a base scenario/game where interacting agents do not trust each other, and thus play at their equilibrium point in game theoretic terms. We then present the basic *blind trust* model, which is a one-time transaction between two agents. Here, an agent is assumed to trust another agent for reasons outside the scope of the model; no assumptions on the application domain are made, neither are reasons for trusting an agent provided. At this point, we define the notion of a *desired action* (in game theoretic terms) that formalizes the expectation of a trusting agent. We then define two types of risk in the *blind trust* model and evaluate the number of rounds of sequential game play a trusting agent (or truster) may expect to play for a given risk tolerance. Next we consider the purpose of a trust interaction and present the *incentive trust* model, where agents can provide an incentive to other agents in order to adhere to a minimal trust level that is established or agreed upon in advance. The *incentive trust* model also provides an advantage to a newly entering agent in the transaction who has no history; instead of starting from a default low trust value, the agent may quickly build up its reputation by offering incentives. In both these models, we use the base scenario as a reference point for determining the loss of an agent when trust is misplaced or violated. This loss is used to derive metrics for estimating the risk faced by an agent. Finally, we present a rich set of models and frameworks to which the general game theoretic approach may be extended. To the best of our knowledge, such explicit decision support and analysis in trust models through a game theoretic approach has not been done so far.

In this paper, we do not explicitly define the notions of trust (and distrust), (atomic) purpose of the trust relationship, etc. These notions have been well defined in previous works [4,1,5] (also see [3,2] and the references therein for a listing of previous works and models); indeed, the core notion of trust could stem from any of the prior works that not only define fundamental concepts well, but also provide means for evaluating and performing other operations (like comparison) on trust through the history of past transactions. Unlike previous approaches, the purpose of this work is to provide a game theoretic model of trust based decisions. This work represents a natural progression of existing trust models to provide explicit decision support for agents with a multitude of action choices. By proper mechanism design [12,13], game theoretic models can also subsume other models to provide a well analyzed decision support theory.

1.1 Summary of Contributions

The contributions of this paper are in the theoretical realm of trust and are summarized as follows.

1. We present a game theoretic model for enabling trust based decision support by defining trust as an index into the action set of a trusting agent.
2. A *blind trust* model is presented, where agents engage in repeated games; two types of risk are defined and the number of rounds an agent may expect to play is analyzed for a given risk threshold.
3. An *incentive trust* model, where all interacting agents stand to gain at the end of the transaction is presented.
    (a) Sufficient conditions are derived for both the agent offering the incentive and the trusting agent/truster in order for the interaction to be successful.
    (b) This model offers a mechanism for a new agent to start an interaction with a high level of trust instead of the default low value by offering incentives.
4. We present directions for the translation of the game theoretic models for practical applications and suggest potentially rich areas of future works.

The rest of this paper is organized as follows. Section 2 describes the related work; Section 3 presents a brief background and intuitive description of the game theoretic approach of our model. Section 4 presents the base scenario of *zero trust*, the *blind trust* and *incentive trust* models. Section 5 presents some of the issues involved in applying the game theoretic models to practical applications. Concluding remarks and directions for future works are presented in Section 6.

2   Related Work

The work in this paper primarily focuses on enabling decision support for agents operating on the notion of trust. By its very definition [1,2,3,4,5], trust implies a certain amount of risk due to uncertainty in the interacting agents decision criteria. Trust and risk have both been used to decide or optimize the effective payoff [14] or lower the expected loss [15]. Their relationship towards decision support has been investigated in [16]. An important factor of reciprocity in terms of trust has been experimentally investigated in [17].

Game theoretic descriptions and analysis of trust have been investigated by [18]; some games that cannot be represented in a normal form have been investigated experimentally [19]. Decision support based on trust has been investigated for electronic transactions [20], trust negotiations [7,8,21,9,6], etc. In fact, almost all trust models incorporate some decision criteria at least implicitly; however most of them are binary or threshold based, in that an action may be initiated if a certain constraint is satisfied or the trust value is above a certain threshold. In this work, we explicitly consider the purpose of any trust transaction and assume that all interacting entities gain at the end of the transaction. Our work is similar to game theoretic modeling of an auction marketplace, where agents choose actions with optimal payoffs. The work by Lam et al. [14] discusses trade in open marketplaces using trust and risk, and is the closest to the work in this paper. Our work substantially builds on the work of previous trust models by providing a model for trust based decision support, particularly in situations where an agent has a multitude of actions to choose from; agents can not only decide which action to take based on their trust value, but also evaluate the number of rounds of interaction (game) they can engage for a given threshold of risk.

3   Background and Overview

In order to make this paper self sufficient, we first give a brief descriptive background of a 2-player game and its corresponding Nash Equilibrium. We then present an overview of our notion of trust in a 2-player game. A 2-player play game is defined as a game between the players denoted as P_1 and P_2. Each player is required to operate simultaneously over an action space. On the completion of an action, both players receive a payoff or a reward depending on the actions chosen by themselves and the other player. Games where the players have opposing goals are called non-cooperative games. The goal of each player is to maximize his or her own payoff. Towards this goal, each player develops a strategy over his/her actions spaces, thereby ensuring the best payoff in the game. Assuming that both players know each others action space and their corresponding payoffs, their strategy will be to choose the *best response* action for the other player's best strategy. Furthermore, assuming both players are perfectly rational, i.e., they both can efficiently compute each others best strategy recursively, their final action will be one from which each can hope to gain nothing by deviating unilaterally. Intuitively, such a 'final' action results in 'equilibrium' for both players; in order to maximize their payoffs, each player only need to play that particular action, regardless of how many times the game is played. Such an action profile is called a Nash Equilibrium.

In the interest of keeping the overview concise and intuitive, a number of details have been omitted; e.g., not all games have a single action strategy that results in equilibrium; there is usually a probability distribution on the action space that also results in equilibrium (such an action profile is called a mixed strategy, while the previous single action equilibrium is called a pure strategy). The reader is referred to [22,23] for a more detailed exposition on game theory.

We now describe the incorporation of trust into a standard 2-player non-zero sum game. In any game in the equilibrium situation, players have no incentive to deviate from their chosen actions. We formulate our model as follows. Consider the players (P_1, P_2) whose equilibrium actions are (a_1, b_1) with a payoff of (50, 50). If P_1 were to choose some other action a_2, then in a typical game, there exists a *best response* action b_2 for player P_2 such that the effective payoff is (40,100), i.e., P_2's payoff would be larger than the equilibrium payoff *and* P_1's payoff would be smaller (maybe negative too, but we assume positive payoffs). Now assume that there exists an action b_3, called *the desired response*, for player P_2 such that the payoff is (60, 70), i.e., both players stand to gain from the equilibrium payoff, but player P_2 stands to gain lesser that the optimum *best response* for action a_2 (which happens to be action b_2). Thus, player P_1 is said to trust player P_2, if on playing a_2, there is an expectation that P_2 would respond with b_3 instead of b_2, thereby leading to a profit on both sides, but *not necessarily the maximum allowable* for player P_2. Now imagine a continuum of such actions a_k, a_{k+1}, etc., for P_1 such that P_2 can respond with actions b_k, b_{k+1}, etc., such that their payoffs are increasingly better than the equilibrium payoff, but P_2's payoff is lesser that the best response actions $b_{best-response}$ to a_k, a_{k+1}, etc. Then P_1's trust in P_2 is the index k into his action profile. If the action profiles are suitably ordered, an increasing index value indicates an increasing level of trust.

The intuition behind our model is simple: an act of trust implies, amongst other things, (a) a potential *vulnerability* on the part of the trusting agent, (b) a threshold of *risk* the trusting agent is willing to tolerate and (c) an uncertainty (or *expectation*) on the response of the other agent: i.e., the three dominant characteristics, *vulnerability*, *risk* and *expectation/uncertainty* have to be embedded into the model. The *vulnerability* on the part of the trusting agent is expressed by its deviation from the equilibrium play. The extent to which the trusting agent is willing to expose itself to the vulnerability is the *risk*. The responding agent may initiate the *best response* (and hence violate the trust placed in him) or initiate the *desired response*; thus, there is an *uncertainty* on the response type. The equilibrium point/action profile forms the *Base Scenario*, where the players do not trust each other.

3.1   *Blind Trust* and *Incentive Trust* Models

The *blind trust* model presents the scenario where an agent trusts another agent with no assurances or guarantees. In this model, the vulnerability faced by an agent when trusting another agent is expressed in terms of the possible loss of payoff for one round. Then, given the risk an agent is willing to take (the maximum vulnerability), we analyze the number of rounds of the game the player may expect to play before getting back to the equilibrium play. Thus far, the trust of a single player is unconditional; we now introduce the *incentive trust* model where users can trade a predefined amount of their payoffs before the initiation of single round of the game. We now consider the interactions between players and their decision criteria when there is an expectation of a return at a later point in time, i.e., there is a *purpose* to the entire transaction and all involved entities expect to gain something at the end of the transaction. Many trust relationships fall under this category. Consider a customer who interacts with a service provider; the customer may pay a premium for a service that he expects at a later time. Thus, the customer can be said to trust the service provider to keep his end of the contract. Such a scenario is also applicable in the security field, in *Automated Trust Negotiation* mechanisms and protocols. Trust Negotiation was first introduced by Winsborough [6] as a means for agents to negotiate their trust with other agents in a heterogeneous environment. A commonly quoted example is the interaction between a potential customer Alice and a service provider Bob. The simplified scenario is as follows: a customer Alice wishes to make a purchase from Bob, a service provider, but is initially unwilling to provide any means of authentication (Drivers License, Credit Card Number, etc.). Bob provides Alice with a certificate from the Better Business Bureau (BBB) stating that he is indeed a service provider with a certain standing. The BBB certificate is verified by Alice and it 'helps' her to make a trust decision about Bob; she provides her Resellers License/Credit Card number to Bob to make a purchase. Bob verifies her license/CC number and completes the transaction. This example is illustrative of the general trust transaction: (a) there is a purpose to the transaction and (b) both (and in general all) agents stand to gain at the end of the transaction. We analyze these scenarios and present decision making criteria for specified risk thresholds.

3.2   A Note on Mechanism Design

Finally, we conclude with a note on the concept of mechanism design [12,13] in game theory. Loosely speaking, mechanism design can be viewed as a technique for designing a game so that *rational* and *selfish* agents do not have an incentive to deviate from the desired behavior of the game designer. Proper mechanism design maps the desired behavior of agents to the equilibrium play so that no agent can gain by deviating from the equilibrium point. From a purely game theoretic viewpoint, assuming agents are selfish and rational, the equilibrium play is desirable. However, in our model, we stipulate a deviation from the equilibrium play, towards a play that leads to a greater, but not necessarily maximum payoff, in order to embed the notion of *vulnerability* of an agent. Thus, there is no stipulation for an agent to adhere to a specific action set; if there were one, we would not be able to embed the notion of *vulnerability* and *uncertainty*; indeed, a stipulation of any kind would imply determinism, which runs contrary to free will or choice of an agent. However, there are game theoretic constructs like satisficing game theory [24,25], amongst others, that can model users (as opposed to automated agents). We mention such games in Section 6 on extensions of this model; they are not considered in this paper. Herein, we shall use the terms agent, user or player interchangeably; they imply the same entity unless specifically mentioned otherwise.

4   Trust Based Decision (TBD) Model

4.1   Base Scenario: *Zero Trust*

We now fix the base scenario, which is a 2-player game with a Nash Equilibrium. Our notations closely follow standard game theoretic expositions as in [26]; although our models consider only 2 players, the notations are kept generic. The trust game G_τ is defined by:

$$G_\tau = \{N, (A_i)_{i \in N}, (u_i)_{i \in N}\} \tag{1}$$

where N is the set of players, A_i is the action space of player i and u_i is the payoff function for player i, defined as $u_i: \mathbf{A} \to \mathbb{R}$, where $\mathbf{A} = \times_{i \in N} A_i$ and $\mathbb{R}$ is the set of real numbers. We assume that N and A_i are finite sets. Player i has at his disposal the actions $a_i \in A_i$. We denote the action spaces of all other players other than i as $A_{-i} = \times_{j \in N \setminus \{i\}} A_j$ and a single element as $a_{-i} \in A_{-i}$. The repeated rounds of the game G_τ are referred to as the *supergame*, which consists of a finite sequence of the game G_τ, where the players choose the actions $a_i(t) \in A_i$ at time instant t. For a sequence of k plays, we denote the history of player i by $H_i(k) = \{a_i(1), a_i(2), \ldots, a_i(k)\} \forall a_i(.) \in A_i$ and each element of $H_i(k)$ by $h_i(k)$. The payoff of player i at the end of any round is given by $u_i(a_i, a_{-i})$. The best response action of player i is defined as $b_i(a_{-i}) = \{a_i \in A_i : u_i(a_i, a_{-i}) \geq u_i(a_i^*, a_{-i}) \forall a_i^* \in A_i\}$, i.e., given the plays of all the opponents a_{-i}, the action $b_i(a_{-i})$ ensures the best payoff for player i. Hereafter, $b_i(a_{-i})$ is denoted simply as b_i. We assume that the game's payoff structure allows for (at least) a single equilibrium point, at which the action profile of the players is (b_i, b_{-i}). Thus the single round payoff of the player i is given by $u_i(b_i, b_{-i})$. Intuitively, the cumulative payoff of a sequence of k plays is $k.u_i(b_i, b_{-i})$. However, for the game G_τ, similar to [26], we define the cumulative payoff to be a discounted one, where the weights of the payoffs of older sequences are progressively lesser.

Definition 1. *The discounted cumulative payoff in the game G_τ, of player i over a sequence of k play's, discounted by a factor of $\delta \in (0, 1)$, is defined as:*

$$C_i(\delta, k) = (1 - \delta) \sum_{m=1}^{k} \delta^{k-m} u_i(a_i(m), a_{-i}(m)) \tag{2}$$

Unless otherwise specified, we shall denote $C_i(\delta, k)$ as $C_i(\delta)$. This formulation places greater relevance to the most recent play (the kth play) and progressively decreases the payoff of the past plays. From a trust game viewpoint, this is intuitive; the closer δ is to 1, the greater the relevance to the most recent play (due to the factor δ^{k-m}). Note that $\delta \in (0, 1)$ and does not ever assume the value of 0 or 1. However, if we set $\delta = 0, C_i(\delta) = 1$; this can be interpreted as setting no relevance at all to any of the plays, and hence the payoff incurred at any stage is a constant: in the context of the model, setting no relevance to the plays makes no sense and hence such a setting is invalid.[1] In the base scenario,

---

[1]   We thank an anonymous reviewer for bringing out this point.

the action taken by the players are the best responses to the action spaces of other players; hence the cumulative payoff of player i is obtained when $a_i(.) = b_i$ and $a_{-i}(.) = b_{-i}$ in Eq. 2. We denote this best response cumulative payoff as $C_i^*(\delta)$. The two values of per round payoff, $u_i(b_i, b_{-i})$ and cumulative discounted payoff $C_i^*(\delta)$ are used to refer to the *Base Scenario* with no trust.

4.2 Blind Trust

In this model, player i wants to initiate a trust relationship with the remaining players. His goal is now to obtain the *desired response* from the remaining players as opposed to the *best response* b_{-i} played by the remaining players in the *Base Scenario*.

Definition 2. *For an action $a_i \in A_i$, the desired response $d_i(a_i)$ of player i is defined as an action from the set A_{-i} that increases the payoff of all players from the equilibrium payoff, but does not provide the maximum possible payoff to all the players other than possibly player i.*

$$d_i(a_i) = \{a_{-i} \in A_{-i} : u_i(a_i, a_{-i}) \geq u_i(b_i, b_{-i}),$$
$$u_{-i}(a_i, b_{-i}) \geq u_{-i}(a_i, a_{-i}) \geq u_i(b_i, b_{-i})\} \tag{3}$$

The desired response of player i is also denoted simply as d_i, where the action a_i is understood to have been initiated. Note that $d_i(a_i) \in A_{-i}$ and is not necessarily unique. Depending on the application domain, there may exist multiple $d_i(a_i)$; however, their existence does not affect our model from a decision theoretic viewpoint.

Definition 3. *The index value τ of actions $a_i^\tau \in A_i$ in a strictly increasing ordering given by $u_i(a_i^1, d_i) \leq u_i(a_i^2, d_i) \leq \cdots \leq u_i(a_i^\tau, d_i) \leq \cdots \leq u_i(a_i^T, d_i)$ is defined as the trust that player i places on the remaining players.*

Note that the desired action d_i for a_i^τ is *not* (necessarily) the same for all index values. In situations where the context is clear, the symbol τ is used to represent the trust of player i; in more generic terms, $\tau(i \rightarrow -i)$ represents the cumulative trust of player i on the remaining players, while $\tau(i \rightarrow j)$ represents the trust of player i on player j. In the interest of keeping the formulation generic and extensible, the notations of i and $-i$ have been used; herein, we shall restrict ourselves to N $= 2$, i.e., there are two players in the game G_τ; thus $i \in \{1,2\}$ ($-i$ denotes the 'other' player). In the formulations that follow, replacing $i = 1$ and $-i = 2$ represents the model for the two player scenario. The trust value $\tau \in \{1, T\}$, where T is the maximum index. As a technical device, we may also include a zero value in τ where the index value of zero is associated with the best response action (and hence no trust).

In the basic *blind trust* scenario, player i assigns a trust value $\tau = 1$, and waits for the response from player $-i$. From the game theoretic viewpoint, this game is a turn based game, where player $-i$ knows the action taken by player i before his turn to play. We call this model a *blind trust* model since there is no prior communication between the two players for a contractual agreement on the action set, etc. Player i blindly trusts player $-i$ and hopes for a reciprocation. At this point, player $-i$ may reciprocate by initiating the desired response d_i or the best response b_{-i}. The initiation of the desired response indicates the beginning of a trust relationship.

From this basic *blind trust* Model, we wish to address several questions. First, given that an agent (player i) wishes to initiate a trust relationship, what is the vulnerability faced by player i? Secondly, assume that player i initiates a *blind trust* relationship in the hopes of a future collaboration. Initially, player $-i$ may simply act in a 'rational'[2] manner and initiate the best response action, but may eventually reconsider or 'understand' that player i wishes to initiate a trust relationship. The reasons for the establishment and evolution of the trust relationship are contextual and application/domain dependent, and are hence outside the scope of this paper. However, the relevant question is: given the amount of risk (maximum vulnerability) that player i is willing to tolerate, what is the number of rounds of play that player i may expect to play? Towards answering this question, we first define two types of risk and then evaluate the expected number of rounds.

Instantaneous Per-Round and Cumulative Risk: The risk faced by a player i are categorized into two types: the *instantaneous per-round risk* and the *cumulative k-stage risk*.

Definition 4. *The instantaneous per-round risk ρ_i of player i when initiating action a_i^τ with a trust τ on player $-i$ is defined as the ratio of the difference between the equilibrium payoff $u_i(b_i, b_{-i})$ and the best response $u_i(a_i^\tau, b_i)$ to the equilibrium payoff.*

$$\rho_i(\tau) = (1 - \frac{u_i(a_i^\tau, b_{-i})}{u_i(b_i, b_{-i})}) \qquad (4)$$

Note that, by the very definition of best response actions, $u_i(a_i^\tau, b_{-i}) \leq u_i(b_i, b_{-i})$ (otherwise, $a_i^\tau = b_i$). Thus, $\rho_i(\tau)$ is the risk faced by the player i when trusting player $-i$ with a value of τ. Intuitively, the *simplified cumulative k-stage risk* is $k.\rho_i(\tau)$, assuming that the player $-i$ plays the best response for all the k sequences of the game.

Recall that we have defined a cumulative discounted payoff for the game G_τ in definition 1, Eq. 2, i.e., the payoff of the kth round is discounted by a factor $(1 - \delta)$. Towards this, a discounted cumulative k-stage risk is defined, similar to definition 4. We first derive the discounted cumulative k-stage equilibrium payoff and best response payoff. The *discounted cumulative k-stage equilibrium payoff* of player i can be derived by substituting $a_i(m) = b_i$ and $a_{-i}(m) = b_{-i}$ $\forall m = \{1, 2, \ldots, k\}$ in Eq. 2.

$$C_i^{eq}(\delta) = (1 - \delta) \sum_{m=1}^{k} \delta^{k-m} u_i(b_i, b_{-i}) = u_i(b_i, b_{-i})(1 - \delta^k) \qquad (5)$$

---

[2] 'Rational' in the game theoretic sense, not in the context of the application domain.

Note that the discounted equilibrium payoff is in fact the same as the equilibrium payoff for any single round if $\delta \to 0$, in which case, it is almost *independent* of the number of rounds over which the game is played. Similarly, the *discounted cumulative k-stage best response payoff* of player i can be derived by substituting $a_i(m) = a_i^\tau$ and $a_{-i}(m) = b_{-i} \; \forall \; m = \{1,2,\ldots,k\}$ in Eq. 2.

$$C_i^{best}(\delta) = (1 - \delta) \sum_{m=1}^{k} \delta^{k-m} u_i(a_i^\tau, b_{-i}) = u_i(a_i^\tau, b_{-i})(1 - \delta^k) \qquad (6)$$

Definition 5. *The discounted cumulative k-stage risk $\sigma_i(\tau, k)$ of player i over a sequence of k plays of the game G_τ for the histories $H_i(k)$ and $H_{-i}(k)$ is defined as the ratio of the difference between the equilibrium payoff $C_i^{eq}(\delta)$ and the best response payoff $C_i^{best}(\delta)$ to the equilibrium payoff.*

$$\sigma_i(\tau, k) = \frac{C_i^{eq}(\delta) - C_i^{best}(\delta)}{C_i^{eq}(\delta)} = \rho_i(\tau) \qquad (7)$$

Usually, the cumulative risk is evaluated until player $-i$ plays the desired action $d_i(a_i^\tau)$.

Expected Number of Plays: Consider the situation when player i wishes to initiate a trust relationship and initiates the action a_i^τ instead of b_i. Assume that the maximum amount of risk the player i is willing to undertake is r_i. We now evaluate the number of rounds that player i may expect to play.

Consider the *simplified cumulative k-stage risk*, $k.\rho_i(\tau)$. In this case, the maximum number of rounds player i can afford to play is $k_{max} = \frac{\rho_i(\tau)}{r_i}$. Now assume that at any round of the k stages, the probability that player $-i$ switches from b_{-i} to d_i is p. This probability is available to the player i through some context specific mechanism, also called a *belief* in game theoretic literature. The probability that player $-i$ switches from b_{-i} to d_i at the kth round is $p(1 - p)^{k-1}$. Thus the number of rounds player i may expect to play is $\sum_{m=1}^{k_{max}} mp(1 - p)^{m-1}$. Thus, considering the *simplified cumulative k-stage risk*, the number of rounds player i may expect to play is:

$$E[k] = \frac{1 - (k_{max} + 1)(1 - p)^{k_{max}} + k_{max}(1 - p)^{k_{max}+1}}{p} \qquad (8)$$

where $k_{max} = \frac{\rho_i(\tau)}{r_i}$. Now, lets consider the *discounted cumulative k-stage risk* $\sigma_i(\tau, k)$, which is equal to $\rho_i(\tau)$. It can be observed trivially, that if the risks are discounted for past rounds of the game, then player i may continue to play the game infinitely if $r_i > \rho_i(\tau)$, just one round if $r_i = \rho_i(\tau)$ and may not play at all if $r_i < \rho_i(\tau)$; i.e., the expected number of rounds is 1. Thus, for the discounted case, the specification of the player's *absolute risk* is not useful to determine the maximum number of rounds. Instead, we define the *discounted loss* (in payoff) for the player i for k rounds as:

$$L_i(k) = C_i^{eq}(\delta) - C_i^{best}(\delta) = (u_i(b_i, b_{-i}) - u_i(a_i^\tau, b_{-i}))(1 - \delta^k) \qquad (9)$$

Let the loss that player i is willing to sustain in the trust initiative be l_i. Thus, the maximum number of rounds is given by:

$$L_i(k_{max}) = l_i \Rightarrow k_{max} = \frac{\log(1 - \frac{l_i}{u_i(b_i, b_{-i}) - u_i(a_i^\tau, b_{-i})})}{\log \delta} \tag{10}$$

Note that the loss l_i is not the absolute loss, but is the (maximum) an agent is willing to sustain relative to the best response action b_{-i}; hence $l_i < (u_i(b_i, b_{-i}) - u_i(a_i^\tau, b_{-i}))$. Note also that k_{max} is inversely proportional to $\log \delta$, i.e., a players maximum number of rounds depends on the extent to which he is willing to discount past payoffs (or equivalently, losses). The expected number of rounds, assuming that the probability that player $-i$ switches from b_{-i} to d_i is p, is given by:

$$E[k] = \frac{1 - (k_{max} + 1)(1 - p)^{k_{max}} + k_{max}(1 - p)^{k_{max}+1}}{p} \tag{11}$$

where k_{max} is given by Eq. 10.

Compensatory Update Strategy: Once the player $-i$ responds with d_i, player i may update the value of τ. Given that we are dealing with payoff values, we may use an update strategy that assigns τ based on the payoff values. Our previous work [27] describes a *Compensatory Trust Model* (CTM), where the trust value may be updated as part of a compensation given to player $-i$ based on his forgone payoff. We briefly describe the intuition behind the update strategy based on the CTM. When player $-i$ initiates the desired action d_i at a particular round, denote his loss of payoff as $l_{-i} = (u_{-i}(a_i^\tau, b_{-i}) - u_{-i}(a_i^\tau, d_i))$, and the gain in payoff of player i as $g_i = (u_i(a_i^\tau, d_i) - u_i(a_i^\tau, b_{-i}))$. To 'share' the loss and gain equally, player i would have to transfer a payoff of $l_{-i} + \frac{1}{2}(g_i - l_{-i})$ to player $-i$. This transfer may be made figuratively by updating the trust value proportionally, for some $\delta \in (0,1)$, $\tau = \delta(l_{-i} + \frac{1}{2}(g_i - l_{-i}))$, i.e., the trust update is proportional to the discount δ of the payoffs. This is the 'compensation' that player i pays to player $-i$; hence the name *Compensatory Update Strategy*. This scheme can be extended to include the risk faced by player i or the loss of payoff in a k-stage game. As mentioned before, we do not present new trust assignment and update methodologies; apart from the CTM update described above, any update mechanism may be used to assign and update trust.

4.3   Incentive Trust

The *incentive trust* model considers the purpose of a trust transaction and models the scenario where agents may provide incentives to be trusted. Consider the game G_τ with the players i and $-i$. The basic philosophy behind the trust transaction, unlike the *blind trust* model, is the expectation of a return in trust or value/payoff by a player. Towards this, we recast the game play described in [28] to fit into our model. The *incentive trust* model is a game played over three time periods. The play of the *incentive trust* model is described as follows:

Initial Setup: Player $-i$ wants player i to (a) trust him with a level of $\tau(i \rightarrow -i)$, hereafter denoted as τ and (b) initiate the action a_i^τ. Towards this, player $-i$ states p_{-i}, his *stated* probability that he will respond with the action d_i, the desired action instead of b_{-i}, the best response action. q_{-i} is the *true* probability that player $-i$ will respond with the action d_i, the desired action instead of b_{-i}, the best response action. In a similar vein, let p_i be the *stated* probability (while q_i is the real probability) that player i will initiate action a_i^τ. Both p_{-i} and p_i are public knowledge.

Time Period 1: Player $-i$ transfers a payoff of $f(p_{-i})$ as a support/proof of his commitment to respond with the desired action d_i, where $f(.)$ is a function whose specification is to be determined.

Time Period 2: Player i, on receiving the support of $f(p_{-i})$ initiates the action a_i^τ.

Time Period 3: Player $-i$, in turn, initiates the desired action d_i.

The expected payoff of player i, $w(p_{-i})$ can be split into the following components:

1. Player i gets a payoff of $f(p_{-i})$ in time period 1.
2. Player i gets a payoff of *only* $(1 - p_{-i})q_i u_i(a_i^\tau, b_{-i})$ if player $-i$ cheats and responds with the best response b_{-i} instead of the desired response.
3. Player i gets a payoff of $q_i p_{-i} u_i(a_i^\tau, d_i)$ if he acts with action a_i^τ and player $-i$ responds with the desired action.

Thus, the expected payoff of player i is given as:

$$w(p_{-i}) = f(p_{-i}) + q_i\{(1 - p_{-i})u_i(a_i^\tau, b_{-i}) + p_{-i}u_i(a_i^\tau, d_i)\} \qquad (12)$$

Similarly, the expected payoff of player $-i$, $z(p_i)$ can be split into the following components:

1. If Player i initiates an action of a_i^τ,
   (a) Player $-i$ gets a payoff of $p_i(1 - q_{-i})u_{-i}(a_i^\tau, b_{-i})$ if he responds with the best action b_{-i}.
   (b) Player $-i$ gets a payoff of $p_i q_{-i} u_{-i}(a_i^\tau, d_i)$ if he responds with the desired action d_i.
2. If Player i does not initiate an action of a_i^τ, then player $-i$ loses a payoff of $(1 - p_i)f(p_{-i})$.

Thus, the expected payoff of player $-i$ is given as:

$$z(p_i) = p_i(1 - q_{-i})u_{-i}(a_i^\tau, b_{-i}) + p_i q_{-i} u_{-i}(a_i^\tau, d_i) - (1 - p_i)f(p_{-i}) \qquad (13)$$

Analysis: Consider the entire transaction and the purpose of the model: from the viewpoint of player i, we would like to obtain an optimal guarantee $f(p_{-i})$ from player $-i$. Player $-i$, on the other hand, would like to ensure he at least has a non-zero payoff from the entire transaction. Since Player i has the first position advantage, given p_{-i}, he can fix the value of $f(p_{-i})$ that he receives from player $-i$. The optimal value $f_{opt}(p_{-i})$ is thus given by the first-order condition $w'(p_{-i}) = 0$.

$$f_{opt}(p_{-i}) = p_{-i}q_i\{u_i(a_i^\tau, b_{-i}) - u_i(a_i^\tau, d_i)\} + c \tag{14}$$

where c is a constant such that $c \geq 0$. If $f(p_{-i})$ satisfies Eq. 14, then player i can expect a payoff of $w(p_{-i}) = q_i u_i(a_i^\tau, b_{-i}) + c$, independent of p_{-i}. From the viewpoint of player $-i$, the condition to be satisfied is $z(p_i) \geq 0$. Thus, we derive the condition for q_{-i}, taking into account the value of $f(p_{-i})$ given in Eq. 14.

$$q_{-i} \geq \frac{p_i u_{-i}(a_i^\tau, b_{-i}) + (1 - p_i)c}{p_i(u_{-i}(a_i^\tau, b_{-i}) - u_{-i}(a_i^\tau, d_i)) + (1 - p_i)p_{-i}(u_i(a_i^\tau, b_{-i}) - u_i(a_i^\tau, d_i))} \tag{15}$$

Note that q_{-i} is not only dependent on p_i, but also on p_{-i}, on account of its dependence on $f(p_{-i})$. Since player $-i$ is the initiator in this model, it is his responsibility to ensure a high enough value of q_{-i} in order to 'break even' in the transaction.

5 From Theory to Practice: Some Issues

The translation of game theoretic models to practical application scenarios is not without its problems [29]. Although the *blind trust* and *incentive trust* models capture the purpose of a trust transaction at an intuitive level, there are some issues that should be addressed before its translation to practical scenarios. We illustrate some of these issues and suggest directions for practical usage.

1. We have assumed that each user's payoff is transferable to the other user; e.g., in the *incentive trust* model player $-i$ initially transfers an amount of $f(p_{-i})$. Games where players can transfer their payoffs to others can be modeled by a class of games called Transferable Utility (TU) games, which also permit coalitions among groups of players. In practical scenarios, transferable payoffs have to be defined either in terms of monetary values or resources/services/QoS-guarantees, etc., depending on the application domain.

2. We have not defined the semantics of the game which would indicate the relevance of the equilibrium (or no trust) plays. The semantics of the game must be defined for the particular application domain where the model is applied to.

3. The most difficult part is the cohesion of the semantics of the game with the *zero trust* interaction. In practical scenarios, *zero trust* usually implies a lack of interaction and thus, no game plays at all. Bridging the game semantics so that game plays occur in all scenarios is a challenging task; in particular, the process of mechanism design must accurately map to the scenarios so that the evaluation of iterated plays is relevant to the situation under consideration. Of particular interest here is to model games which also specify distrust.

4. The specification or formulation of the utility functions is the first step towards enabling decision support based on trust. Depending on the application domain, utility functions may be formulated in functional form or, if feasible, can be specified in discrete form for each action in the action set. The works [30,31] provide methodologies for the construction of utility functions depending on the history of an agent's utility realization.

5. One of the pitfalls of game theoretic analysis is the existence of recursive reasoning about the other agent's knowledge [32]. The manifestation of this pitfall is best illustrated with the *incentive trust* model. For example, player i decides $f(p_{-i})$ based on the value of p_{-i}, the stated probability of player $-i$ that he will play the desired action d_i instead of the best response b_{-i}. Although, there is a constant $c \geq 0$ involved in Eq. 12 which gives player i a leeway in choosing $f(p_{-i})$, it may be argued that player $-i$ can quote a low value of p_{-i} and hence, the value of c must be chosen by player i, depending, amongst other factors, on player i's belief in the value of p_{-i}. Such an analysis path usually leads to recursive reasoning and as illustrated by experimental evidence [32,33,34], is not advisable in modeling what essentially is a subjective concept, beyond maybe two or three levels. Obviously, if $p_{-i} < \frac{1}{2}$, player i would not even consider entering into the transaction; neither would player $-i$ enter the transaction if $f(p_{-i})$ is too high.

6   Conclusion and Future Work

The purpose of most trust models and frameworks is to provide some form of decision support for an agent or user. Previous works in trust models have focused on defining the notion of trust and evaluating it based on parametric representations, recommendations, etc. They provide decision support at an implicit level, either through threshold based schemes or constraint satisfiability. This paper provides a game theoretic approach to model trust based decisions. The model takes a holistic view of a trust interaction by considering the ultimate purpose of the transaction which may be spread over multiple periods. The very definition of trust as an index into the agent's action set provides decision support. Research in this direction has a potential to provide quantitative decision support for trust frameworks with a multitude of actions choices. Future work on this model comprise of two distinct paths: *extensions* and *practical applications*. Trust decisions that are taken based on the recommendations of other players can be incorporated into the model by means of an information structure. Furthermore, the generic game G_τ assumes the existence of at least one equilibrium point; the model can be improved by defining games with predefined payoff structures [35] that imply the existence of a pure equilibrium point. Lastly, trust negotiations that are made by people instead of automated agents have properties different from automated agents. Satisficing game theory provides a mathematical basis for user preferences/negotiations [24], which also account for the interests of users in the welfare of other users.

References

1. Levien, R.: Advogato Trust Metric. Phd thesis, UC Berkeley (2003)
2. Kemal, B., Bruno, C., Andrew, S.T.: How to incorporate revocation status information into the trust metrics for public-key certification. In: ACM Symposium on Applied Computing, TRECK Track, ACM Press, New York (2005)
3. Josang, A., Ismail, R., Boyd, C.: A survey of trust and reputation systems for online service provision. Decision Support Systems 43(2), 618–644 (2007)
4. Ji, M., Orgun, M.A.: Trust management and trust theory revision. IEEE Transactions on Systems, Man and Cybernetics, Part A 36(3), 451–460 (2006)
5. Ray, I., Chakraborty, S.: A vector model of trust for developing trustworthy systems. In: Samarati, P., Ryan, P.Y.A., Gollmann, D., Molva, R. (eds.) ESORICS 2004. LNCS, vol. 3193, pp. 260–275. Springer, Heidelberg (2004)
6. Winsborough, W., Seamons, K., Jones, V.: Automated trust negotiation. Technical report, North Carolina State University at Raleigh (2000)
7. Winsborough, W.H., Li, N.: Towards practical automated trust negotiation. In: Policy 2002. Proceedings of the Third International Workshop on Policies for Distributed Systems and Networks, pp. 92–103. IEEE Computer Society Press, Los Alamitos (June 2002)
8. Yu, T., Winslett, M.: Policy migration for sensitive credentials in trust negotiation. In: WPES '03. Proceedings of the 2003 ACM workshop on Privacy in the electronic society, pp. 9–20. ACM Press, New York (2003)
9. Yu, T., Winslett, M., Seamons, K.E.: Interoperable strategies in automated trust negotiation. In: CCS '01. Proceedings of the 8th ACM conference on Computer and Communications Security, pp. 146–155. ACM Press, New York (2001)
10. Aringhieri, R., Damiani, E., Vimercati, S.D.C.D., Paraboschi, S., Samarati, P.: Fuzzy techniques for trust and reputation management in anonymous peer-to-peer systems. Journal of the American Society for Information Science and Technology 57(4), 528–537 (2006)
11. Avesani, P., Massa, P., Tiella, R.: A trust-enhanced recommender system application: Moleskiing. In: SAC 2005, pp. 1589–1593. ACM Press, New York (2005)
12. Asselin, F., Jaumard, B., Nongaillard, A.: A technique for large automated mechanism design problems. In: IAT '06. Proceedings of the IEEE/WIC/ACM international conference on Intelligent Agent Technology, Washington, DC, USA, pp. 467–473. IEEE Computer Society, Los Alamitos (2006)
13. Dash, R., Ramchurn, S., Jennings, N.: Trust-based mechanism design. In: Proceedings of the Third International Joint Conference on Autonomous Agents and MultiAgent Systems, pp. 748–755. ACM Press, New York (2004)
14. Lam, Y.H., Zhang, Z., Ong, K.L.: Trading in open marketplace using trust and risk. In: IAT '05. Proceedings of the IEEE/WIC/ACM International Conference on Intelligent Agent Technology, Washington, DC, USA, pp. 471–474. IEEE Computer Society, Los Alamitos (2005)
15. Cvrcek, D., Moody, K.: Combining trust and risk to reduce the cost of attacks. In: Herrmann, P., Issarny, V., Shiu, S.C.K. (eds.) iTrust 2005. LNCS, vol. 3477, pp. 372–383. Springer, Heidelberg (2005)
16. Josang, A., Presti, S.: Analysing the relationship between risk and trust. In: Proceedings of the Second International Conference on Trust Management, Oxford (2004)
17. Cox, J.C.: How to identify trust and reciprocity. Games and Economic Behavior 46(2), 260–281 (2004)

18. Baras, J.S., Jiang, T.: Cooperative games, phase transitions on graphs and distributed trust in manet. In: 43rd IEEE Conference on Decision and Control, vol. 1, pp. 93–98. IEEE Computer Society Press, Los Alamitos (2004)
19. Wu, D.J., Kimbrough, S.O., Fang, Z.: Artificial agents play the 'mad mex trust game': a computational approach. In: HICSS. Proceedings of the 35th Annual Hawaii International Conference on System Sciences, Hawaii, pp. 389–398 (2002)
20. Josang, A.: Trust-based decision making for electronic transactions. In: Fourth Nordic Workshop on Secure IT Systems (NORDSEC'99), Stockholm, Sweden, Stockholm University Report 99-005 (1999)
21. Chen, W., Clarke, L., Kurose, J.F., Towsley, D.F.: Optimizing cost-sensitive trust-negotiation protocols. In: INFOCOM, pp. 1431–1442 (2005)
22. Davis, M.: Game Theory: A nontechnical introduction. Dover, Mineola, NY (1983)
23. Luce, R.D., Raiffa, H.: Games and Decisions. Dover, Mineola, NY (1989)
24. Archibald, J.K., Hill, J.C., Johnson, F.R., Stirling, W.C.: Satisficing negotiations. IEEE Transactions on Systems, Man, and Cybernetics, Part C 36(1), 4–18 (2006)
25. Candale, T., Sen, S.: Effect of referrals on convergence to satisficing distributions. In: AAMAS '05. Proceedings of the fourth international joint conference on Autonomous agents and multiagent systems, pp. 347–354. ACM Press, New York (2005)
26. Carmona, G.: A strong anti-folk theorem. International Journal of Game Theory 34(1), 131–151 (2006)
27. Vidyaraman, S., Upadhyaya, S.: A trust assignment model based on alternate actions payoff. In: Stølen, K., Winsborough, W.H., Martinelli, F., Massacci, F. (eds.) iTrust 2006. LNCS, vol. 3986, pp. 339–353. Springer, Heidelberg (2006)
28. Huberman, B.A., Wu, F., Zhang, L.: Ensuring trust in one time exchanges: solving the qos problem. NETNOMICS 7(1), 27–37 (2005)
29. Mahajan, R., Rodrig, M., Wetherall, D., Zahorjan, J.: Experiences applying game theory to system design. In: PINS '04. Proceedings of the ACM SIGCOMM workshop on Practice and theory of incentives in networked systems, pp. 183–190. ACM Press, New York (2004)
30. Restificar, A., Haddawy, P.: Constructing utility models from observed negotiation actions. In: Proceedings of the Eighteenth Joint International Conference on Artificial Intelligence, pp. 1404–1405 (2003)
31. Afriat, S.: The construction of utility functions from expenditure data. Cowles Foundation Discussion Papers 177, Cowles Foundation, Yale University (1964)
32. Colman, A.M.: Depth of strategic reasoning in games. Trends in Cognitive Sciences 7(1), 2–4 (2003)
33. Hedden, T., Zhang, J.: What do you think i think you think?: Strategic reasoning in matrix games. Cognition 85(1), 1–36 (2002)
34. Stahl, D.O., Wilson, P.W.: Experimental evidence on players' models of other players. Journal of Economic Behavior & Organization 25(3), 309–327 (1994)
35. Monderer, D., Shapley, L.S.: Potential games. Games and Economic Behavior 14(1), 124–143 (1996)

Extending the Common Services of eduGAIN with a Credential Conversion Service

Gabriel López[1], Óscar Cánovas[2], Diego R. Lopez[3], and Antonio F. Gómez-Skarmeta[1]

[1] Department of Information Engineering and Communications
gabilm@um.es, skatmeta@dif.um.es
[2] Department of Computer Engineering
University of Murcia, Spain
ocanovas@um.es
[3] Red.es - RedIRIS
diego.lopez@rediris.es

Abstract. We are experiencing the emergence of federated approaches to resource sharing. In these approaches, trust links are established among different autonomous organizations in order to grant users in any of them access to shared resources with a single identity, stated by the organization the user belongs to. However, some of those federations are working using different schemas for representing user attributes, both from a semantic and a syntax point of view. This fact makes difficult the interoperability of heterogeneous federations based on different authorization systems. The work presented in this paper benefits from an existing proposal for building confederations, eduGAIN, to address that issue. As we will see, it will be necessary a way to establish the relationships between attributes and technologies from different federations and to define how those relationships can be published and managed. We present the required conversion policy, the entities in charge of the conversion process, and the communication protocols for conversion requests and for publishing the policies.

1 Introduction

In recent years, a significant number of federated approaches to resource sharing have raised in large organizations. In these approaches, trust links are established among those different autonomous organizations in order to grant access to shared resources according to the user's identity, stated by the organization the user belongs to. Important examples of these approaches are the establishment of academic federations worldwide, such as eduroam [21] or MAMS [3]. In those scenarios where users are moving among the different organizations, it is important to take into account what kind of credentials are exchanged among those domains and how these credentials will be managed by each organization.

It is worth noting that one of the main objectives of federations is to create collections of resources and users from geographically distributed organizations. Although those distributed organizations can make use of independent authorization systems for local purposes, all of them must be unified to provide a common authorization service

J. Biskup and J. Lopez (Eds.): ESORICS 2007, LNCS 4734, pp. 501–514, 2007.
© Springer-Verlag Berlin Heidelberg 2007

at federation level. To address the drawbacks related to the use of different authorization technologies, we must define a service for converting identities, names, attributes, resources, actions, policies, and formats between administrative domains.

During this paper, we are going to consider two federations based on different authentication and authorization technologies. For example, we can think in a Shibboleth-based federation [20], such as MAMS [3] or Haka [2], and an eduroam-based federation, which is based on RADIUS technology [19]. Many other examples can be found using technologies or solutions such as PAPI [14], PERMIS[5], etc. These federations need to establish a trust relationship for resource sharing.

As we show in this paper, the trust fabric among those organizations can be defined by means of eduGAIN [15], which provides with the required entities, protocols and technologies that can get in touch those federations. eduGAIN provides an easy way to locate the authentication and authorization services. For example, Alice, a U.S. researcher belonging to the Shibboleth-based federation, from now on *Home Institution (HI)*, wants to access to the wireless network in an eduroam-enabled institution, from now on *Remote Institution (RI)*, during a conference that takes place in an European university. In this case, RI will probably access to the authentication and authorization services located in HI, the former in order to obtain an authentication statement defining Alice as a valid user, the latter to obtain Alice attributes in HI, i.e. role, entitlement, etc. All this information is required in RI in order to take the right access control decision.

While eduGAIN provides a protocol for exchanging credentials between federations, even for solving the WAYF (Where Are You From?) problem of locating the authentication and authorization points for each federation, there is still an open issue: the way heterogeneous credentials from federations, based on different technologies or languages, should be managed. Following the previous example, roles for Alice might be expressed in HI by means of a SAML *AttributeStatement* sentence [9], which contains attribute *eduPersonEntitlement* with value *urn:mace:ri.edu:researchgrant:55523981*, that is, Alice works in RI with research grant number 55523981. However, this kind of information might be represented in the RI federation, also by means of SAML statements, but using attribute *urn:mace:terena.org:schac:personalPosition* with value *urn:mace:terena.org:schac:personalPosition:es:hi.edu:research*. Furthermore, another practical example could be found when the HI is based on the PERMIS system, where a X.509 Attribute Certificate [10], containing a *permisRole* attribute, should be translated into the previous SAML sentence.

It is needed, therefore, a way to establish the relationships between attributes and technologies from different federations and to define how those relationships can be published and managed by those institutions. The first issue requires a conversion policy able to define whether attribute A from HI, in a specific format, is equivalent to attribute B in RI, in a different one. The second issue implies the definition of entities in charge of the conversion process, where those entities would be located (inside/outside federations, etc.), and the communication protocols for conversion requests and for publishing conversion policies.

The rest of this paper is structured as follows. Section 2 provides an overview of the eduGAIN infrastructure. Section 3 introduces the *Credential Conversion Service*, which defines a generic conversion process for authorization credentials. Section 4 defines how the conversion service can be integrated in the eduGAIN infrastructure, defining the architectural components, how the required information is published, and the communication profile. Section 5 describes an example of conversion policies by means of the XACML specification [7]. Section 6 gives an overview of the different existing schemas for user attributes and, finally, section 7 presents our main remarks.

2   eduGAIN

The main aim of eduGAIN [15] is to build an interoperable Authentication and Authorization Infrastructure (AAI) to interconnect different existing federations. In this way, eduGAIN is responsible for finding the federation where a roaming user belongs to, translates the messages between the federation internal protocols and eduGAIN and vice versa, and establishes the trust fabric among the participating institutions.

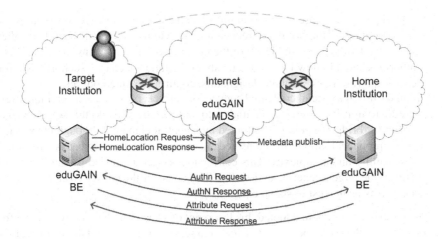

Fig. 1. eduGAIN infrastructure

The main goal is achieved defining a set of common services, where it is included the MetaData Service (MDS), and a confederation-aware element, called Bridging Element (BE), responsible for connecting the different federations to eduGAIN. As Figure 1 shows, metadata related to federations are published by means of the MDS. These metadata include information for locating the authentication and authorization points of the federation. Then, the appropriate authentication and authorization requests are routed by the remote BE toward the user's home institution. This scheme is also valid in order to communicate different institutions belonging to the same federation, as [13] describes for Universal Single Sign On purposes.

The specific way the authentication and authorization processes are carried out in eduGAIN are defined by different profiles. Currently, a profile compatible with Shibboleth, called *Web SSO*, and another one that does not require human intervention, called *Automated Client*, are defined. Moreover, additional profiles are being developed, as for instance a DAMe [1] profile based on NAS-SAML [17].

3   A Generic Credential Conversion Service

The proposal presented in this paper is based on a previous work defining a generic Credential Conversion Service (CCS) [6], which describes a bridge between heterogeneous authorization systems. In order to define how a target institution could manage credentials coming from a source institution (source credentials), and to translate them into an internal representation (target credentials), we can consider several alternatives from an authorization management point of view:

1. Policy Enforcement Points (PEP) and Policy Decision Points (PDP) of the target institution must be able to understand every kind of source credentials. In this way, no conversion is needed. However, depending on the number of PEPs, PDPs, end users, resources, or actions, this option can present several problems derived from scalability and complexity, as bridging policies must be made widely available and applications must be developed with full support for several authorization proposals.
2. Authorities of the source institution must be able to generate whatever kind of assertion containing the privileges related to their end users, which might be further interpreted by the PEPs and PDPs of the target institution. This involves that these authorities should know lots of details about the target scenario, such as URIs for actions and resources, attribute designators, confirmation methods, etc.
3. To make use of a special credential conversion service, provided at a common level, in order to translate source credentials into target credentials. In this way, the conversion (or bridging) policy is enforced by a central element (although the service can be replicated among different nodes), minimizing the drawbacks associated to scalability and complexity. This conversion service is trusted by the PEPs and PDPs of the target scenario, an therefore they consider the converted credentials as trustworthy as the rest of statements.

The generic CCS system adopted this last point of view (which is really suitable for eduGAIN since there is a specific set of common services) and defined the set of profiles and statements that will be needed in order to deploy such a service. Specifically, it is composed by two different profiles (pull and push based) governing how to exchange and to embed SAML assertions, and by several architectural entities involved in the conversion process. In order to be adapted to eduGAIN, the proposal has been slightly modified using the pull profile, as we will see in next sections.

It is worth mentioning the SAML statements that were designed for CCS purposes, as they will be used here for eduGAIN. Those extensions are two new SAML elements defined in the CCS namespace: *ccs:WrappedStatement* is used to encapsulate the credentials; and *ccs:ConversionQuery* is the representation format of a conversion request sent to the CCS.

WrappedStatements are formed by the following components:

- *StatementType* defines the type of credential being wrapped. Following the SAML rules, it is defined as a URI. The prefix is `urn:ccs:names:credential`, and some defined values are `x509`, `x590ac`, `saml`, `sdsi`, `spki`. The prefix `urn:ccs:names` is experimental and, once *eCCS* consolidated, it would be added to the eduGain namespace `urn:geant:edugain`.

- *Encoding* specifies the encoding used to express the credential. Usually, every certification standard has its own encoding formats, such as DER encoding for X.509 certificates, canonical s-expressions for SPKI certificates, or XML for SAML assertions. It is also defined as a URI (prefix urn:ccs:names:encoding).
- *WrappedData*. This field contains one or more credentials of type *StatementType*, which are formatted using *Encoding* method. As several credentials can be related to a specific target scenario, the number of occurrences of this field is unbounded.

On the other hand, *ConversionQuery* extends *saml:SubjectQuery* and also includes the following components:

- *Recipient* is a new attribute defining the entity that will receive the resulting SAML assertions. Following the SAML rules, it is defined as a URI that makes reference to some well known architectural entity. The recipient is an optional element, and if it is not specified the CCS will send the SAML assertions to the default entity specified in the conversion policy.
- The *samlp:RespondWith* element contained in every SAML request should be used to specify the type of SAML assertion that will be generated in response to the conversion query.
- An element to include the *WrappedStatements*.

4   A Credential Conversion Service for eduGAIN

Once we have presented both eduGAIN and the generic CCS, this section defines a new *Credential Conversion Service* for eduGAIN *(eCCS)*.

Two main issues need to be addressed by this service: first, to use an inter-federation credential representation, able to represent the set of credentials defined by each federation in a common language; second, to define where this *eCCS* will be located, the interaction with the rest of components and the kind of information to be exchanged.

Regarding the first issue, it is required to define a common credential representation, from now on *eduGAIN Common Credentials (eCC)*, which will be managed by the eduGAIN infrastructure. HI will need to define the relationship between the internal credentials and *eCC*. In the same way, RI has to publish how its internal credentials can be translated into *eCC*. For example, in academic federations, a good choice for *eCC* is the set of attributes defined in the DAMe project [1], which is based on both the SCHAC [18] and eduPerson [12] proposals, and tries to homogenize an inter-federation set of attributes. Following the previous example, HI's attributes will be based on the *eduPerson* schema. Therefore, *eduPersonEntitlement*, for example, will be translated into the eCC attribute *urn:mace:terena.org:schac:personalPosition*.

Regarding the second issue, the first step is to make *eCCS* available. Here we can find two approaches: the first one is where *eCCS* is a centralized service belonging to the common eduGAIN services; the second one is where it is a distributed service belonging to each federation. The former is more transparent for federation institutions whereas the latter provides more flexibility and functionality to those institutions. This work describes the first one as the generic case which provides the more wide vision of the problem. The second one would be a specific case where for example, the publication of conversion policies is not necessary. In eduGAIN those common services are located in the *Common eduGAIN Services* component.

The second step is to define how each federation will publish the relationship between its internal credentials and *eCC*. It is an in advance step before the real interaction between federations occurs, and it is described in section 4.2.

Following the generic approach, once all this information has been published in the *MDS*, the system operates as follows. A user coming from HI tries to gain access to a protected Resource located in RI. The user will be authenticated (following the eduroam hierarchy, for example), and the Resource will use the eduGAIN infrastructure (BE in remote institution, RBE) in order to locate where the user attributes can be retrieved from and, if necessary, how they could be converted to the *eCC* format. Then, a check is performed in order to determine whether the source credentials have to be converted. In that case, the MDS will return the location of a BE in the home institution (HBE) where credentials in source format can be obtained from. It is worth noting that HI can define one single BE to obtain both attributes in source and non-source format, or to define different BEs. Consequently, the RBE, after obtaining the source credentials, will make use of the new *eCCS* module in order to convert them to the needed schema.

The *eCCS* operates as follows. It will receive the conversion request and will make a double conversion process: first, translating the source credentials into the *eCC* format; second translating the *eCC* credentials into the target format. The whole process is described in next sections.

4.1 Proposed Architecture

Figure 2 shows how the new module named *eCCS* has been added to the *Common eduGAIN Services*, and the relationship with the rest of components.

- *Resource*: Protected resource belonging to a federation which requires valid authentication and attribute credentials in order to grant access to end users.
- *Policy Decision Point, PDP*: This component checks the *Resource Access Policy* related to the protected resource. Authorization decisions are based on user attributes.
- *Attribute Authority (AA)*: Also known as the Identity Provider. This component uses an *Attribute Release Policy* in order to decide which user attributes can be released under specific circumstances.
- *Bridging Elements (BE)*: BEs (located in home and remote institutions) establish trust links among authentication and authorization components and user applications. In this case, we extend this component in order to integrate the conversion process. The main aim of a RBE in this scenario is to locate the user attributes and to issue *Credential Conversion Requests* to the corresponding *eCCS*. This module will receive an Attribute Response including the user's credentials in a valid internal representation (target format).
- *eduGAIN Credential Conversion Service*: The *eCCS* entity is responsible for the credential conversion process. Conversion requests received from an institution must include the following elements: the source credentials to be converted and the identifiers of the home and target institutions. With this information, the *eCCS*

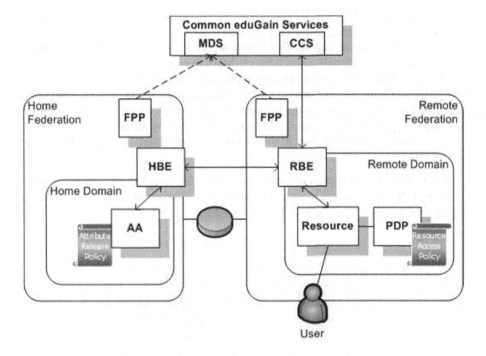

Fig. 2. CCS for eduGAIN architecture

will carry out the double conversion process previously described. If the conversion process is successful, the *eCCS* will respond with an Attribute Response message.

– *Federation Peering Points (FPPs)*: FPPs are the components responsible for publishing the relationship between the source format and the common credential format, that is, the conversion policy. That publication has to be done prior to any interaction between federations. It is important to note that if the *eCCS* were a distributed service it would be connected to the FPP in order to define the metadata environment for this federation, and the publication process would not be necessary.

Finally, it is worth noting that this centralized approach can be distributed among the different federations using the same basic components. The CCS element could be part of the FPPs, and therefore performing the conversion in a distributed way. However, we still need a policy to express the conversion process and an interface to exchange the conversion messages between the CCS and the BE. As we will see, the design provided in this paper is also suitable for this approach as it addresses the same functionality.

4.2   Publication of Metadata Related to the eCCS

In the general case, in order to allow foreign institutions to make use of the user credentials defined in a federation, each institution/federation has to publish the following information:

- A conversion policy which defines how the credentials used in the institution can be translated into the common representation (*eCC*).
- Expected credential format. This format represents the internal credential format of an institution. It will be used by the MDS to process the received information requests. MDS will compare the expected credential format published by the home institution with the one specified in the information request. If both formats are different, MDS will return the location of a BE able to return the user credentials in a wrapped statement, which will be later translated by the *eCCS*.
- The Bridging Element which will return user credentials in source format (by means of wrapped statements).

The FPP of each institution will make use of the *MetaDataPublish* message, defined by eduGAIN, and extended in order to convey such information. eduGAIN MetaData follows the format defined in SAML v2.0 [8].

```
<md:EntityDescriptor entityID="https://hi.edu/AttributeService"
    xmlns:xsi="http://www.w3.org/2001/XMLSchema-instance"
    xmlns:md="urn:oasis:names:tc:SAML:2.0:metadata"
    xmlns:xacml="urn:oasis:names:tc:xacml:2.0:policy:schema:os"
    xsi:schemaLocation="urn:oasis:names:tc:SAML:2.0:metadata schemas/saml-schema-metadata-2.0.xsd">
    <md:AttributeAuthorityDescriptor xsi:type="md:AttributeAuthorityDescriptorType"
                        protocolSupportEnumeration="urn:oasis:names:tc:SAML:2.0:protocol">
            <md:AttributeService Location="https://hi.edu/saml/BEService/SourceFormat"
                        Binding="urn:oasis:names:tc:SAML:2.0:bindings:SOAP">
            </md:AttributeService>
            <md:AttributeService Location="https://hi.edu/saml/BEService/WrappedFormat"
                        Binding="urn:oasis:names:tc:SAML:2.0:bindings:SOAP">
            </md:AttributService>
            <md:AttributeProfile>urn:oid:1.3.6.1.4.1.5923.1.1.2 (eduPerson)</md:AttributeProfile>
            <md:Extensions><xacml:PolicySet>XACML conversion policy</xacml:PolicySet></md:Extensions>
    </md:AttributeAuthorityDescriptor>
    <md:Organization>
            <md:OrganizationName xml:lang="en">Home Institution</md:OrganizationName>
            <md:OrganizationDisplayName xml:lang="en">Home Institution</md:OrganizationDisplayName>
            <md:OrganizationURL xml:lang="en">www.hi.edu</md:OrganizationURL>
    </md:Organization>
</md:EntityDescriptor>
```

Fig. 3. Credential conversion publication

Figure 3 describes the example of a publication message used by an institution, in this case HI (*md:Organization*). HI publishes two *AttributeServices*, the first one (*SourceFormat*) will return the user attributes in source format, which is not the case of this work. On the other hand, the second service (*WrappedFormat*) is in charge of returning the attributes as described in section 3. Each service describes its location and the protocol binding required to access the service, in this case, the SOAP protocol.

The *AttributeAuthorityDescriptor* also specifies the kind of attribute schema used in the HI. In this case, following the previous example, HI is based on the *eduPerson* scheme. Finally, HI has to publish the conversion policy, which is based on XACML and described in section 5.

It is important to note that this publication process is not necessary when the *eCCS* service is distributed among federations. The next section describes the interaction among components and how the conversion process is carried out.

4.3   CCS Profile for eduGAIN

This section describes a conversion profile for the eduGAIN architecture. It shows the communication between components and the kind of information exchanged.

In this profile, due to RI defines the access control rules based on the user authentication and authorization processes (the former by means of the authentication credentials and the latter by means of attribute credentials), it needs to obtain the user attributes before taking the right decision. As already mentioned, source and target credential formats are different, so RI will need to use the eCCS in order to translate the user credentials into a suitable representation.

Following the previous example, HI will be based on Shibboleth, where user attributes follow the eduPerson specification, and they will be represented by means of SAML assertions. RI will be based on the eduroam infrastructure, where the DAMe project has defined a the set of attributes mainly based on SCHAC, and they are also represented by means of SAML. For the sake of simplicity, we will suppose the *eCC* is also based on SCHAC.

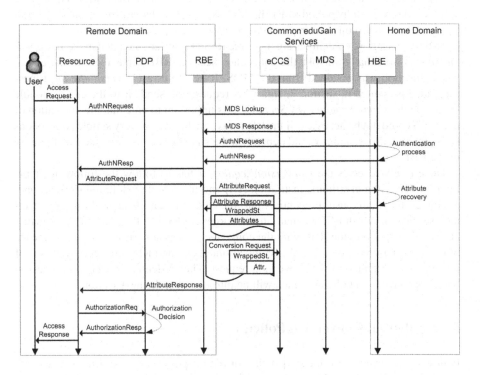

Fig. 4. CCS profile for eduGAIN

First, user authentication must be performed. In our example, the user could present either a login/password pair or a X.509 identity certificate credentials, which could be authenticated by means of a direct trust relationship among institutions or the use of a pre-established certification hierarchy. During the process of discovering HI's information, RBE will receive the attribute solicitation point (HBE). It is important to note that, inside the *Home Lookup* message, RBE has to include the expected kind of credentials (schema). If MDS discovers those credentials are different to the ones provided by HI, it will return the location of the HBE which will return the user credentials as wrapped statements. The communication protocol between BEs and MDS is based on the REST [11] protocol, and it is widely described in [16].

Once the user is authenticated, user attributes must be obtained. RBE is aware of users who do not belong to HI, for example, by means of information included in their authentication credentials, so their attributes have to be recovered from their home domain. Then, RBE queries the HBE in order to obtain the user attributes.

The query contains an *AttributeRequest* message defined by eduGAIN, which includes the user's subject and the kind of attributes expected by Resource and, optionally, a resource identification. The binding used in the inter-federation communication will depend on the particular scenario. A common solution is to use SOAP/HTTP.

HBE receives the *AttributeRequest* message and, through the internal Attribute Authority located in HI, it recovers the user attributes. Following the example previously described, those attributes, which are based on eduPerson, need to be wrapped in some way in order to be transported to RI. In this case, the *AttributeResponse* message sent by the HBE is based on the *WrappedStatement* sentence presented in section 3.

RBE detects those credentials are in source format (they are included in the *WrappedStatement*), so it has to invoke the conversion service. RBE sends them to the *eCCS*, whose location was obtained from the MDS. It generates a *ConversionRequest* message, also presented in section 3, signs this request and sends it to the *eCCS* module located in the *Common eduGAIN Services*. It is important to note that the invocation of the *eCCS* could not be necessary if the RBE was able to manage very simple conversions between credentials, and it would depend on the specific scenario and the functionality of the RBE.

Once *eCCS* receives the *ConversionRequest*, it has to follow the following steps: First, to detect the user home institution (HI) and the remote institution (RI); second, to convert the source user credentials into the *eCC* type and format; third, to convert the user credentials in *eCC* format into the target credentials type and format; finally, *eCCS* will respond to the RBE with the converted credentials. HI is detected by means of the information contained in the wrapped statement, and RI is detected by means of information contained in the conversion request. The credential conversion process is based on conversion policies, which will be introduced in the next section.

5   Credential Conversion Policies

Following the design described in [6], the conversion policies will be structured according to a common schema. Depending on the type of conversion (from a source format to the common format or vice versa) the information contained in the policies will change. These are the main fields:

- *Subject*: Two subjects specifying the source and destination domains. One of them must make reference to the eduGAIN common credentials (*eCC*), depending on the direction of the specific conversion rules.

- *Resource*: The resource elements represent the attributes issued by the source domain that need to be translated into target attributes.
- *Action*: This policy contains only the *convert* action.
- *Obligation*: Every permitted conversion will involve an obligation, which specifies how to translate the credentials.

```
<PolicySet PolicySetId="ConversionPolicy">                <Policy PolicyId="urn:ccs:shibtocommon1 ">
  <Target>                                                   <Target/>
    <Actions>                                                <Rule RuleId="Rule1" Effect="Permit">
      <Action>                                                 <Target>
        <ActionMatch MatchId="...:string-equal">                 <Resources>
          <AttributeValue DataType="...#string"> convert            <Resource>
          </AttributeValue>                                          <ResourceMatch MatchId="...:string-equal">
          <ActionAttributeDesignator AttributeId="..:action"           <AttributeValue DataType="...#string">
              DataType="...#string"/>                                    1.3.6.1.4.1.5923.1.1.1.7 (eduPersonEntitlement)
        </ActionMatch>                                                 </AttributeValue>
      </Action>                                                        <ResourceAttributeDesignator AttributeId="...:resource-id"
    </Actions>                                                             DataType="...#string"/>
  </Target>                                                          </ResourceMatch>
  <PolicySet PolicySetId="ToCommon">                                 <ResourceMatch MatchId="...:string-equal">
    <Target>                                                           <AttributeValue DataType="...#string">
      <Subjects>                                                         urn:mace:ri.edu:researchgrant:55523981
        <Subject>                                                      </AttributeValue>
          <SubjectMatch MatchId="...:string-equal">                    <ResourceAttributeDesignator AttributeId="...:value"
            <AttributeValue DataType="...#string">                         DataType="...#string"/>
              o=ShibDomain,c=C                                       </ResourceMatch>
            </AttributeValue>                                       </Resource>
          <SubjectAttributeDesignator                             </Resources>
            AttributeId="...:Federation"                         </Target>
            DataType="...#string"/>                            </Rule>
          </SubjectMatch>                                      <Obligations>
        </Subject>                                               <Obligation ObligationId="urn:ccs:Obligation1" FulfillOn="Permit">
        <Subject>                                                  <AttributeAssignment DataType="...#string"
          <SubjectMatch MatchId="...:string-equal">                   AttributeId="urn:mace:terena.org:schac:personalPosition ">
            <AttributeValue DataType="...#string">                    urn:mace:terena.org:schac:personalPosition:es:hi.edu:research
              CommonDomain                                         </AttributeAssignment>
            </AttributeValue>                                     </Obligation>
          <SubjectAttributeDesignator                           </Obligations>
            AttributeId="...:eduGAIN"                          </Policy>
            DataType="...#string"/>                          </PolicySet>
          </SubjectMatch>                                  </PolicySet>
        </Subject>
      </Subjects>
    </Target>
```

Fig. 5. Conversion Policy example

Figure 5 shows a simple Conversion Policy to translate Shibboleth attributes into *eCC* credentials (SCHAC-based). For example, *ToCommon* defines an attribute that can be translated from the domain *o=ShibDomain,c=C* to the common domain. There is only an allowed action, *convert*. The involved domains are specified using the *Subject* element, and for each attribute of the source domain it is necessary to define a conversion policy. This specific policy defines the *Rule* element specifying the attribute to be translated (type and value), and an *Obligation* element specifying the target *eCC* attribute. For example, the policy described in figure 5 defines that the *ShibDomain* attribute type *eduPersonEntitlement* and value *urn:mace:ri.edu:researchgrant:55523981* must be translated into the *eCC* pair attribute type *schac:personalPosition*, with value *urn:mace:terena.org:schac:personalPosition:es:hi.edu:research*.

It is worth noting that the addition of home domains involves additional *PolicySet* elements, and more attributes per domain requires more *Policy* elements.

Regarding to scalability, the use of XACML do not necessarily involves that the size of the conversion policy might run into megabits. In fact, the number of attributes to be considered for authorization purposes is usually low, and the set of values that can be assigned to those attributes is also reduced. Moreover, the conversion rules will be applicable in most cases for large sets of users without requiring the modification of the policy, taken profit of the XACML structure.

6 Related Work

This work is mainly influenced by the different existing schemas for user attributes, and therefore a general analysis of those schemas would be worthy.

Attributes are most commonly of a descriptive nature and associate a characteristic with an entity. User attributes provide information about users that can be used in addition to or instead of the user's unique identity to make authorization decisions. Such attributes are used in combination with access policy to offer rights to specific resources.

As we show in this paper, user information is transmitted between different domains for authorization purposes. There is a set of the user information that is relevant to the specific protected resource and the environment. The selection of the user attributes will be realistic, and in this case will be mainly based on educational attributes.

There has been a lot of effort done by several research groups which are also aligned with the technologies (Shibboleth, eduGAIN) used in this proposal. Shibboleth relies on the eduPerson [12] schema, a schema for higher educational user attributes defined by Internet2 and EDUCAUSE initiative. eduGAIN, on the other hand, has focused its user attributes interest on the so called Schema for Academia. SCHAC [18] has been defined by TERENA initiative with the aim of carrying out some work in the area of attributes coordination.

Thanks to the definition of the eduPerson and SCHAC, higher educational institutional directories are provided with a common list of attributes and definitions, also very helpful for inter-institutional data exchange. Additionally, eduPerson and SCHAC are not independent each other. SCHAC, which has been developed after eduPerson had been released, covers the eduPerson schema as a subset of its defined attributes. SCHAC covers from specific defined attributes to other general already defined attribute schemas. This relationship benefits inter-institutional interoperability between SCHAC and eduPerson compliant institutions.

As we have previously commented, the DAMe project mainly focuses on a roaming environment where user attributes are used to provide access control to the network. eduGAIN and DAMe contributors have considered as a basic set of attributes, which are basically a subset of SCHAC attributes, and that we called eduGAIN Common Credentials (eCC).

7 Conclusions and Future Work

The proposal presented in this paper has been designed to provide an interoperability service for confederations of heterogeneous federations. We provide the elements, policies and communication profiles needed to address this challenge, using eduGAIN as the most suitable starting point. Our work is mainly focused on the educational environment, but it can be considered appropriate for any other scenario since it does not depend on the specific semantic behind the attributes or resources.

As a statement of direction, a suitable scenario where this approach would very useful is the Grid computing. The integration of *eCCS* with technologies such as VOMS [4] will allow the relationship of Grid federations based on the different technologies in an easy and scalable way.

Acknowledgements

This work has been partially funded by Daidalos FP6-IP-506997 and DAMe.

References

1. DAMe Project, http://dame.inf.um.es
2. Haka, http://www.csc.fi/english/institutions/haka
3. Meta-Access Management System (MAMS),
   http://www.melcoe.mq.edu.au/projects/MAMS/
4. Alfieri, R., Cecchini, R., Ciaschini, V., dell'Agnello, L., Gianoli, A., Spataro, F., Bonnassieux, F., Broadfoot, P., Lowe, G., Cornwall, G., Jensen, J., Kelsey, D., Frohner, A., Groep, D.L., de Cerff, W.S., Steenbakkers, M., Venekamp, G., Kouril, D., McNab, A., Mulmo, O., Silander, M., Hahkala, J., Lorentey, K.: Managing dynamic user communities in a grid of autonomous resources. In: Proceedings of Conference for Computing in High Energy and Nuclear Physics (March 2003)
5. Chadwick, D.W., Otenko, A., Ball, E.: Role-Based Access Control With x.509 Attribute Certificates. IEEE Internet Computing 7(2), 62–69 (2003)
6. Cánovas, O., Lopez, G., Gómez-Skarmeta, A.F.: A Credential Conversion Service for SAML-based scenarios. In: Katsikas, S.K., Gritzalis, S., Lopez, J. (eds.) EuroPKI 2004. LNCS, vol. 3093, pp. 297–305. Springer, Heidelberg (2004)
7. Anderson, A., et al.: EXtensible Access Control Markup Language (XACML) Version 1.0. OASIS Standard (February 2003)
8. Cantor, S., et al.: Metadata for the OASIS Security Assertion Markup Language (SAML) V2.0 (March 2005)
9. Eve, M., Prateek, M., Rob, P.: Assertions and Protocols for the OASIS Security Assertion Markup Language (SAML)v1.1. OASIS Standard (September 2003)
10. Farrel, S., Housley, R.: An Internet Attribute Certificate Profile for Authorization. Request for Comments (RFC) 3281 (April 2002)
11. Fielding, R.T., Taylor, R.N.: Principled design of the modern web architecture. ACM Transactions on Internet Technology (TOIT) 2(2), 62–69 (2003)
12. Directory Working Group Internet2 Middleware Architecture Committee for Education: EduPerson Specification (200312) (December 2003), http://www.educause.edu/eduperson/
13. Kerver, B., Stanica, M., Rauschenbach, J., Wierenga, K.: Deliverable DJ5.3.1: Documentation on GÉANT2 Universal Single Sign-On (uSSO) Requirements, GN2 JRA5. Geant 2 (February 2007)
14. López, D.: PAPI: simple and ubiquitous access to Internet information servers. In: Proceedings of 4TH International JISC/CNI Conference (June 2002)
15. López, D.R., Macias, J., Molina, M., Rauschenbach, J., Solberg, A., Stanica, M.: Deliverable DJ5.2.3.1: Best Practice Guide - AAI Cookbook, 1st edn. GN2 JRA5. Geant 2 (September 2006)

16. López, D.R., Solberg, A., Stanica, M.: eduGAIN Profiles and Implementation Guidelines, GN2 JRA5. Geant 2 (December 2006)
17. López, G., Cánovas, O., Gómez, A.F., Jimenez, J.D., Marín, R.: A Network Access Control Approach based on the AAA Architecture and Authorzation Attributes. Journal of Network and Computer Applications JNCA 30(3), 900–919 (to be published, 2007)
18. TF-EMC2 SCHAC project: SCHAC Schema for Academia Attribute Definitions For Individual Data Version 1.2.0 (May 2006)
19. Rigney, C., Rubens, A., Simpson, W., Willens, S.: Remote Authentication Dial In User Service (RADIUS). Internet Research Task Force, Request for Comments (RFC) 2865 (June 2000)
20. Scavo, T., Cantor, S.: Shibboleth Architecture. Technical Overview, Working Draft 02 (June 2005)
21. Wierenga, K., Florio, L.: Eduroam: past, present and future. In: TERENA Networking Conference (2005)

Incorporating Temporal Capabilities in Existing Key Management Schemes

Mikhail J. Atallah[1], Marina Blanton[2], and Keith B. Frikken[3]

[1] Department of Computer Science, Purdue University
mja@cs.purdue.edu
[2] Department of Computer Science and Engineering, University of Notre Dame
mblanton@cse.nd.edu
[3] Department of Computer Science and Systems Analysis, Miami University
frikkekb@muohio.edu

Abstract. The problem of key management in access hierarchies studies ways to assign keys to users and classes such that each user, after receiving her secret key(s), is able to *independently* compute access keys for (and thus obtain access to) the appropriate resources defined by the hierarchical structure. If user privileges additionally are time-based, the key(s) a user receives should permit access to the resources only at the appropriate times. This paper presents a new, provably secure, and efficient solution that can be used to add time-based capabilities to existing hierarchical schemes. It achieves the following performance bounds: (i) to be able to obtain access to an arbitrary contiguous set of time intervals, a user is required to store at most 3 keys; (ii) the keys for a user can be computed by the system in constant time; (iii) key derivation by the user within the authorized time intervals involves a small constant number of inexpensive cryptographic operations; and (iv) if the total number of time intervals in the system is n, then the server needs to maintain public storage larger than n by only a small asymptotic factor, e.g., $O(\log^* n \log \log n)$ with a small constant.

1 Introduction

This work addresses the problem of key management in access control systems, with the emphasis on time-based access control policies. Consider a system where all users are divided into a set of disjoint classes, and a user is granted access to a specific access class for a period of time specified by its beginning and end. In such systems, it is common for the access classes to be organized in a hierarchy, and a user obtains access to the resources at her own class and the resources associated with all descendant classes in the hierarchy. When a user joins the system and is granted access to a certain class for a specific duration of time, she is given a key (or a set of keys) which allows her to *independently* derive access keys for all resources she is entitled to have access during her time interval. For hierarchically organized user classes this means that the key allows the user to access objects at her access class and all descendant classes in the hierarchy during the time interval specified. Note that the time interval is user-specific and might be different for each user in the system.

There is a wide range of applications that follow this model and which would benefit from automatic enforcement of access policies through efficient key management.

J. Biskup and J. Lopez (Eds.): ESORICS 2007, LNCS 4734, pp. 515–530, 2007.

Such applications include (among others) role-based access control (RBAC) models, subscription-based services, content distribution, and cryptographic directories or file systems. In all of these examples we use the current time to enforce time-based policies. Additionally, instead of being based on the current time, access control policies can be based on the time in the past and permit access to historical data. For example, a user might buy access to data such as historical transactions, prices, legal records, etc. for a specified time interval in the past, e.g., the year of 1920. These different notions of time can be combined, e.g., a user buys access to 1920 data and is entitled to access it for two weeks starting from today.

If we let the lifetime of a system be partitioned into n short time intervals, the existence of time-based access control policies requires the access keys to be changed during each time interval. In this work, we concentrate on applications where the system is setup to support a large number of such time intervals. For example, access key to a video stream might change at least once a day (thus, permitting users to subscribe on any given day). If the system is setup for a few years, this results in n being in thousands. Likewise, if the application of interest is access to historical data, say, for the last century, the number of time intervals will tend to be even higher. Thus, a small number of keys per user and efficient access with large n's is the goal of this work.

The notion of security for time-based hierarchical key assignment (KA) schemes was formalized only recently by Ateniese et al. [5]. Thus, in the current paper we use their security definitions and provide a new efficient solution to the problem of key management in systems with time-based access control policies. The approach we propose is provably secure and relies only on the security of pseudo-random functions (PRFs). In addition, our solution does not impose any requirements or constraints on the mechanisms used to enforce policies in systems where access control is not time-based (e.g., for a hierarchy of user classes). This means that our solution can be built on top of an existing scheme to make it capable of handling time. In the rest of this paper, we refer to a scheme without the support for temporal access control as a *time-invariant* scheme, and we refer to a scheme that supports temporal access control policies as *time-based*.

Existing efficient time-invariant key management schemes for user hierarchies are based on the notion of key derivation: a user receives a single key, and all other access keys a user might need to possess according to her privileges can be derived from that key. In the most general formulation of the problem, inheritance of privileges is modeled through the use of a directed graph, where a node corresponds to a class and a parent node can derive the keys of its descendants. In this paper we follow the same model, but, unlike previous work, apply key derivation techniques to time.

In a setup with n time intervals, the server is likely to maintain information linear in n. By building a novel data structure, we only slightly increase the storage space at the server beyond the necessary $O(n)$ and at the same time are able to achieve other attractive characteristics. In more detail, our solution enjoys the following properties:

- To be able to obtain access to an arbitrary contiguous set of time intervals, a user is required to store at most 3 keys.
- The above-mentioned keys to be given to a user can be computed in constant time from that user's authorized set of contiguous time intervals.

- Key derivation within the authorized time intervals involves a small constant number of cryptographic operations and thus is independent of the number of time intervals in the systems or the number of time intervals in the user's access rights.
- If the total number of time intervals in the system is n, then the increase of the public storage space at the server due to our solution is only by a small asymptotic factor, e.g., $O(\log^* n \log \log n)$ with a small constant.
- All operations are very efficient, and no expensive public-key cryptography is used.

We provide several solutions with slightly different characteristics, where the difference is due to the building blocks used in our construction. These solutions are summarized in Table 3. An extension of our techniques also allows to support access rights that can be stated as periodic expressions.

While the results given above correspond to a time-based key assignment scheme with a single resource or user class, we can use them to construct a time-based key assignment scheme for a user hierarchy. We show that our construction favorably compares to existing schemes and provides an efficient solution to the problem (the comparison is given at the end of the paper in Section 7). Additionally, our scheme is balanced in the sense that all resource consumption such as the client's private storage, computation to derive keys, and the server public storage are minimized with tradeoffs being possible. This allows the scheme to work even with very weak clients and not to burden the server with excessive storage. Furthermore, our scheme is provably secure under standard complexity assumptions.

In the rest of the paper, we first review related literature in Section 2. In Section 3 we define the model and give some preliminaries. Section 4 gives a preliminary data structure, which we use in Section 5 to build our improved scheme. Thus, the core of our solution lies in Section 5 along with its analysis. In Section 6 we show how to use the scheme to build a time-based key assignment scheme for a user hierarchy. Finally, Section 7 compares our solution with other existing schemes and concludes. Several extensions of our scheme and security proofs can be found in [4].

2 Related Work

The literature on time-invariant key assignment (KA) schemes in a user hierarchy is extensive, and its survey is beyond the scope of this paper. For an overview of such publications, see, e.g., [2] and [11].

While the list of publications on time-invariant KA schemes is very large, the number of publications that consider time-based policies and provide schemes for them is rather modest. The time-based setting and the first scheme was introduced by Tzeng [17]. The scheme, however, was later shown to be insecure against collusion of multiple users [22]. Subsequent work of Huang and Chang [12], Chien [10], and Yeh [20] was also shown to be insecure against collusion (in [16], [21,14], and [5], respectively).

Among very recent publications, Wang and Laih [19] present a time-based hierarchical KA scheme. While their scheme is shown to be collusion-resilient, the notion of security, however, is not formalized and no clear adversarial model is given in that work. Tzeng [18] also describes a time-based hierarchical key assignment scheme, which is used as a part of an anonymous subscription system. The scheme is proven to resist collusion attacks; however, no formal model of adversarial behavior is provided. The work of Ateniese et al. [5] is the first result that provides a formal framework for time-based hierarchical KA schemes and gives provably secure solutions, both secure against key recovery and with pseudo-random keys. Concurrently with and independently from this work, time-based solutions have been developed by De Santis et al. [15]. Section 7 compares all solutions.

There is extensive literature on broadcast encryption and multicast security, which might be considered applicable here. There are, however, crucial differences in the models, which prevent us from using solutions from those domains. First, broadcast encryption and multicast security schemes permit access to a single resource instead of a hierarchy and cannot be composed in an obvious way to solve our problem. More importantly, they assume that each client obtains key updates for each time interval, which is impossible in our model: no private channels between the server and a client after the initial issuance of the user keys is assumed, the client is allowed to remain off-line, and can access the resources at her own discretion. The only exception from the above online requirement that we are aware of is the work of Briscoe on multicast key management [9]. That solution builds a binary tree from the time intervals, thus achieving $O(\log n)$ secret keys and $O(\log n)$ key derivation time.

Finally, the access control literature has a large body of work on temporal access control models (see, e.g., [7,8]). These models, however, concentrate on policy specification and not on key assignment and derivation mechanisms.

3 Problem Description and Preliminaries

3.1 The Model

While the motivation for this work comes from the need to support access control policies with temporal constraints in user hierarchies, the problem does not need to be limited to this particular setting. That is, an efficient solution to the key management problem in temporal access control can find use in other domains. Therefore, we provide a very general formulation of the problem, without any assumptions on the environment in which it is used. Of course, access control in user hierarchies remains the most immediate and important application of our techniques. Thus, in Section 6 we will show how our solution can be used to realize temporal access control for user hierarchies.

Now let us assume that we are given a resource, and the owner of this resource would like to control user access to that resource using time-based policies. For that purpose, the lifetime of the system is partitioned into short time intervals (normally, of a length of a day or shorter), and the access key for that resource changes every time interval. Let n denote the number of time intervals in the system, $T = \{t_1, \ldots, t_n\}$ denote the intervals, and $K = \{k_{t_1}, \ldots, k_{t_n}\}$ denote the corresponding access keys.

Now assume that a user $\mathcal{U}$ is authorized to access that resource during a contiguous set of time intervals $T_{\mathcal{U}} \subseteq T$, where $T_{\mathcal{U}} = \{t_{start}, \ldots, t_{end}\}$. Following the notation of [5], we use the *interval-set* over T, denoted by $\mathcal{P}$, which is the set of all non-empty contiguous subsequences of T, i.e., $T_{\mathcal{U}} \in \mathcal{P}$ for any $T_{\mathcal{U}}$. With such access rights, $\mathcal{U}$ should receive or should be able to compute the keys $K_{T_{\mathcal{U}}} \subseteq K$, where for each $t \in T_{\mathcal{U}}$ the key $k_t \in K_{T_{\mathcal{U}}}$. We denote the private information that $\mathcal{U}$ receives by $S_{T_{\mathcal{U}}}$.

Obviously, storing $|T_\mathcal{U}|$ keys at the user end is not always practical, and significantly more efficient solutions are possible. Then a *time-based key assignment scheme* assigns keys to the time intervals and users, so that time-based access control is enforced in a correct and efficient manner. Such key generation is assumed to be performed by a central authority CA, but once a user is issued the keys, there is no interaction with other entities. More formally, we define a time-based KA scheme as follows:

Definition 1. *Let T be a set of distinct time intervals and $\mathcal{P}$ be the interval-set over T. A time-based key assignment scheme consists of algorithms* (Gen, Assign, Derive) *s.t.:*

Gen *is a probabilistic algorithm, which, on input a security parameter 1^κ and the set of time intervals T, outputs (i) a key k_t for any $t \in T$; (ii) secret information Sec associated with the system; and (iii) public information Pub. Let $(K, \text{Sec}, \text{Pub})$ denote the output of this algorithm, where K is the set of all keys.*

Assign *is a deterministic algorithm, which, on input a time sequence $T_\mathcal{U} \in \mathcal{P}$ and secret information Sec, outputs private information $S_{T_\mathcal{U}}$ for $T_\mathcal{U}$.*

Derive *is a deterministic algorithm, which, on input a time sequence $T_\mathcal{U}$, time interval $t \in T_\mathcal{U}$, private information $S_{T_\mathcal{U}}$, and public information Pub, outputs the key k_t for time interval t. The correctness requirement is such that, for each time sequence $T_\mathcal{U} \in \mathcal{P}$, each time interval $t \in T_\mathcal{U}$, each private information $S_{T_\mathcal{U}}$, each key $k_t \in K$, and each public information Pub that $\text{Gen}(1^\kappa, T)$ and $\text{Assign}(T_\mathcal{U}, \text{Sec})$ can output, $\Pr[\text{Derive}(T_\mathcal{U}, t, S_{T_\mathcal{U}}, \text{Pub}) = k_t] = 1$.*

Note that in many cases the Assign algorithm can be a part of the Gen algorithm, i.e., private values $S_{T_\mathcal{U}}$ for every $T_\mathcal{U} \in \mathcal{P}$ are generated at the system initialization time. We, however, separate these algorithms to account for cases where retrieving $S_{T_\mathcal{U}}$ from Sec is not straightforward (which is the case in our scheme). In such cases, merging these two algorithms together will needlessly complicate Gen.

Also note that since a user accesses the server's public storage for key derivation purposes, there is no need for additional time synchronization mechanisms between the user and the server: the current time interval can be stored as a part of the public information the server maintains.

We distinguish between two different notions of security for a time-based KA scheme: security against *key recovery* and security with respect to *key indistinguishability* (i.e., schemes with pseudo-random keys). A time-based KA scheme can also be secure against static or adaptive adversaries. In [5], however, it was shown that the security of a time-based hierarchical KA scheme against a static adversary is polynomial-time equivalent to the security of that scheme against an adaptive adversary for both security goals (key recovery and key indistinguishability). While in the current discussion we are not concerned with hierarchical schemes, our setting can be considered to be a special case of a hierarchy with a single class. Thus, in this work we only provide definitions of a time-based KA scheme secure against a static adversary; and a proof of security under such definitions will imply security against an adaptive adversary.

In our definition of a scheme secure against static adversary, let adversary $\mathcal{A}_{st}$ attack the security of the scheme at time $t \in T$. $\mathcal{A}_{st}$ is allowed to corrupt all users with no access to k_t and, when finished, is asked to guess k_t. We consider a scheme to be secure only if $\mathcal{A}_{st}$ has at most negligible probability in outputting the correct key.

In addition to the security requirements, an efficient KA scheme is evaluated by the following criteria: (i) The size of the private data a user must store; (ii) The time it takes the system to assign a user its keys; (iii) The amount of computation necessary for a user to generate an access key for the target time interval; and (iv) The amount of information the service provider must maintain for public access.

3.2 Key Derivation

Our approach relies heavily on the notion of key derivation. In our solution, we use the same key derivation techniques that were used in [1]. The crucial difference, however, is that in [1] key derivation was used between user classes (to provide a time-invariant scheme for a user hierarchy), while in this work we use key derivation for the data structures that we build. This is possible because the techniques of [1] work for an arbitrary directed acyclic graph (DAG), and we review them next.

Assume that we are given a DAG denoted by $G = (V, E)$, where V is the set of nodes and E is the set of edges. Let $Anc(v, G)$ denote the set of ancestors of node v in G including v itself, and let $Desc(v, G)$ denote the set of descendants of v in G including v itself. Let $F^\kappa : \{0, 1\}^\kappa \times \{0, 1\}^* \to \{0, 1\}^\kappa$, for a security parameter κ, be a family of pseudo-random functions (PRFs) that, on input of a κ-bit key and a string, outputs a κ-bit string that is indistinguishable from a random string (note that a PRF can be implemented very efficiently as HMAC [6] or CBC MAC). For brevity, instead of $F^\kappa(k, x)$, we may write $F_k(x)$. Also, when the graph G is clear from the context, we may omit it in the ancestry functions and use $Anc(v)$ and $Desc(v)$.

To be able to derive keys, we need two algorithms:

- Set is an algorithm for assigning keys to the graph which takes as input a security parameter 1^κ and a DAG $G = (V, E)$ and outputs (i) an access key k_v for each $v \in V$, (ii) secret information S_v for each $v \in V$, and (iii) public information Pub.
- Derive is an algorithm for deriving keys which takes as input nodes $v, w \in V$, secret information S_v for v, and public information Pub. It outputs the access key k_w for w, if $w \in Desc(v, G)$.

The derivation method we use is from [1], and is sufficient to achieve security against key recovery:

- Set($1^\kappa, G$): For each node $v \in V$, select a random secret key $k_v \in \{0, 1\}^\kappa$ and set $S_v = k_v$. For each node $v \in V$, select a unique public label $\ell_v \in \{0, 1\}^\kappa$ and store it in Pub. For each edge $(v, w) \in E$, compute public information $y_{v,w} = k_w \oplus F_{k_v}(\ell_w)$, where $\oplus$ denotes bitwise XOR, and store it in Pub.
- Derive(v, w, S_v, Pub): Let $(v, w) \in E$. Given $S_v = k_v$ and Pub, derivation of k_w can be performed as $k_w = F_{k_v}(\ell_w) \oplus y_{v,w}$, where ℓ_w and $y_{v,w}$ are publicly available in Pub. More generally, if there is a directed path between nodes v and u in G, u's key can be derived from v's key by considering each edge on the path.

3.3 Shortcut Techniques

Our constructions use the so-called shortcut edges: a *shortcut edge* is an edge that is not in the original graph G but is in the transitive closure of G. Such edges are added to

Table 1. Performance of shortcut schemes for one-dimensional graphs

Scheme	Private storage	Key derivation	Public storage
2HS [2]	1	2 op.	$O(n \log n)$
3HS [1]	1	3 op.	$O(n \log \log n)$
4HS [2]	1	4 op.	$O(n \log^* n)$
$\log^*$HS [2]	1	$O(\log^* n)$ op.	$O(n)$

G for performance reasons. Note that addition of shortcut edges does not affect partial order relationship between the nodes, i.e., we may add a shortcut edge (v, w) to the graph only if there is already a directed path from node v to w in the original graph.

In this work we rely on efficient shortcut techniques from prior literature for a graph of dimension 1 (i.e., a total order), reviewed in [4]. Here we only summarize the performance of existing schemes, any of which can be used as a building block in our constructions. Consider a directed graph of dimension 1 consisting of n vertices. The performance of known solutions for such graphs is given in Table 1. In the table, we denote by sHS a solution where the distance between any two nodes (i.e., the diameter of the graph) is at most s, i.e., a so-called s-Hop Scheme.

Throughout this work we may use $\mathcal{S}1(n)$ to denote any shortcut scheme for graphs of dimension 1 applied to a total order of size n. We also use $space(\mathcal{S}1(n))$ and $time(\mathcal{S}1(n))$ to denote its public storage and key derivation complexity, respectively.

4   Building Basic Data Structure

As was mentioned above, all of our constructions are based on the notion of key derivation in a graph. Throughout the rest of the paper, when we say that there is a directed edge from v to w in G, it implies that v is capable of deriving w's key using its own key. This means that, for the data structures that we build (all of which are DAGs), there will be a public and secret information associated with each node, and there will be public information corresponding to each edge.

Our preliminary data structure is rather simple and consists of two main steps: building a grid of size $n \times n$ (where n is the number of time intervals in the system) and applying one-dimensional shortcut techniques to parts of the grid. A more detailed description follows.

1. Build half of a grid of dimension $n \times n$ with the time intervals $t_1, \ldots, t_n$ being on its diagonal (see Figure 1). In the grid, we denote by $v_{1,1}$ the root node; node $v_{i,j}$ is located at the row i and column j (i.e., $v_{2,1}$ is "below" $v_{1,1}$ and $v_{1,2}$ is "on the left" of $v_{1,1}$). There is a directed edge from each $v_{i,j}$ to $v_{i+1,j}$, and from each $v_{i,j}$ to $v_{i,j+1}$. The time interval t_i corresponds to the node $v_{i,n-i}$.

   From this data structure it should be clear that, given a key for $v_{i,j}$, all keys for time intervals $t_i, \ldots, t_{n-j+1}$ can be derived from it (in the worst-case $O(n)$ time).

2. Next, we apply a one-dimensional shortcut scheme $\mathcal{S}1$ to each row and column of the grid (see Figure 2). More precisely, we add shortcuts to the data structure to be able to derive $v_{i,x}$'s key from $v_{i,y}$'s key for any $x > y$ (and similarly $v_{x,j}$'s key

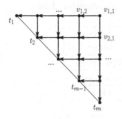

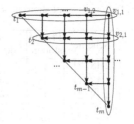

Fig. 1. Building a grid for the ba-   **Fig. 2.** Adding shortcuts to the grid
sic scheme

Table 2. Performance of the basic (and preliminary) scheme

Underlying scheme	Private storage	Key derivation	Public storage
2HS	1	≤ 4 op.	$O(n^2 \log n)$
3HS	1	≤ 6 op.	$O(n^2 \log \log n)$
4HS	1	≤ 8 op.	$O(n^2 \log^* n)$
$\log^*$HS	1	$O(\log^* n)$ op.	$O(n^2)$

from $v_{y,j}$'s key for any $x > y$) in a small number of steps instead of previous $O(n)$ time. This is done at the expense of $O(space(\mathcal{S}1(n)))$ additional shortcuts per row or column and therefore $O(n \cdot space(\mathcal{S}1(n)))$ total shortcuts.

Having this, now a user entitled to have access during time intervals $T_{\mathcal{U}} = \{t_x, \ldots, t_y\} \in \mathcal{P}$ can receive a single key corresponding to node $v_{x,n-y+1}$. Key derivation of the key corresponding to the current time interval $t_i \in T_{\mathcal{U}}$ now consists of at most $2 \cdot time(\mathcal{S}1(n))$ steps: at most $time(\mathcal{S}1(n))$ steps are needed to derive $v_{i,n-y+1}$'s key from that of $v_{x,n-y+1}$, and then at most $time(\mathcal{S}1(n))$ steps are needed to derive $v_{i,n-i+1}$'s key (which corresponds to t_i) from that of $v_{i,n-y+1}$.

Table 2 summarizes the performance of the basic scheme, when used with various one-dimensional schemes.

5   An Improved Scheme

This section describes a solution that achieves significantly better performance than the previous scheme. We first present a new data structure and then fill other parts in to provide a full-fledged time-based KA scheme.

At a high level, to build a new data structure, we partition all time intervals in the system into coarse "chunks" ($\sqrt{n}$ chunks of $\sqrt{n}$ time intervals each) and apply the basic scheme to the chunks. If access is to be granted to a large time interval that spans across boundaries of these chunks, we can use this level of granularity to assign keys. If, on the other hand, the interval to which the user should obtain access is contained within a chunk, we recursively apply this procedure to the time intervals within each chunk to support time-based access control of finer granularity. If a time interval spans across different chunks, but contains partial chunks at the beginning and at the end of the user's sequence of time intervals, then we utilize the coarse chunk's keys along with two new types of keys that are introduced later.

5.1 Reducing Storage Space

This section describes the tree data structure we build; how it is used is covered in the next sections. For the purposes of presentation of this work, we let $n = 2^{2^q}$ for some integer q. This allows us to avoid using rounding notation $\lfloor x \rfloor$ and $\lceil x \rceil$ throughout the algorithms and results in a cleaner presentation (note that this assumption is purely to make the presentation cleaner, and the solution will work without this assumption). Our procedure for building the data structure takes as inputs a node v and the set $T = \{t_1, \ldots, t_n\}$, and then recursively builds a tree for the set rooted at v. Due to the recursive nature of this function, we use $\hat{T}$ to denote the working set of the current function invocation and $|\hat{T}|$ to denote the size of $\hat{T}$. Then the data structure is constructed as described below:

Algorithm DataStructBuild$(v, \hat{T})$:

1. If $|\hat{T}| = 2$ (i.e., $q = 0$), then return. Otherwise, continue with the steps below.

2. Partition $\hat{T}$ into $\sqrt{|\hat{T}|}$ sets of $\sqrt{|\hat{T}|}$ contiguous time intervals each, call these $\hat{T}_1, \ldots, \hat{T}_{\sqrt{|\hat{T}|}}$. That is, if $\hat{T} = \{t_1, \ldots, t_{|\hat{T}|}\}$, then $\hat{T}_i = \{t_{i\sqrt{|\hat{T}|}+1}, \ldots, t_{i\sqrt{|\hat{T}|}+\sqrt{|\hat{T}|}}\}$.
   Create a node v_i for each $\hat{T}_i$, and make v_i a child of v.

3. Generate a problem $Coarse(\hat{T})$, derived from $\hat{T}$ by treating each $\hat{T}_i$ as a black box (i.e., "merging" the constituents of $\hat{T}_i$ into a single item). Note that the size of set $Coarse(\hat{T})$ is $\sqrt{|\hat{T}|}$.

4. Store at node v an instance of the basic scheme for $Coarse(\hat{T})$, denoted $D(v)$. $D(v)$ supports performance of: 1 key, $O(time(\mathcal{S}1(|\hat{T}|)))$ key derivation, and $O(space(\mathcal{S}1(|\hat{T}|)))$ space; but $D(v)$ can only process an interval if it is the union of a contiguous subset of $Coarse(\hat{T})$ (i.e., it cannot handle intervals whose endpoints are inside the $\hat{T}_i$'s, as it cannot "see" inside a $\hat{T}_i$).

5. Also store at node v two solutions of one-dimensional problems on $\hat{T}$: One is for intervals all of which start at the right boundary of $\hat{T}$ and end inside $\hat{T}$ (we call this the *right-anchored* problem and denote the one-dimensional structure for it by $R(v)$); another is for intervals all of which start at the left boundary of $\hat{T}$ and end inside $\hat{T}$ (we call this the *left-anchored* problem and denote the one-dimensional structure for it by $L(v)$). Note that having $R(v)$ and $L(v)$ enables the handling of an interval that lies within $\hat{T}$ and also has its left or right endpoint at a boundary of $\hat{T}$, with performance of: 1 key, $O(time(\mathcal{S}1(|\hat{T}|)))$ steps per key derivation, and $O(space(\mathcal{S}1(|\hat{T}|)))$ space.

6. Recursively apply the scheme to each child of $\hat{T}$; that is, call DataStructBuild$(v_i, \hat{T}_i)$ in turn for each $i = 1, 2, \ldots, \sqrt{|\hat{T}|}$.

Figure 3 gives an illustration of how the data structure is built. The total space of the data structure satisfies the recurrence $S(n) \leq \sqrt{n}S(\sqrt{n}) + c_1 \cdot space(\mathcal{S}1(n))$ if $n > 2$ and $S(2) = c_2$, where c_1 and c_2 are constants. Thus, $S(n) = O(space(\mathcal{S}1(n)) \log \log n)$.

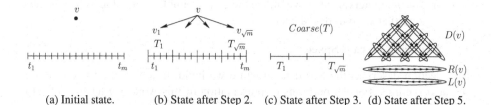

(a) Initial state.   (b) State after Step 2.   (c) State after Step 3.   (d) State after Step 5.

Fig. 3. Construction of the data structure for the improved scheme (first level of recursion)

5.2   Key Assignment

We now turn our attention to which keys are given to a user with access to an arbitrary $T_{\mathcal{U}} \in \mathcal{P}$. In what follows, v is a node of the above tree data structure, $\hat{T}$ is the set of time intervals associated with v, and I is a sequence of time intervals for which the keys must be given. The recursive procedure below, when invoked on any $T_{\mathcal{U}}$ and our data structure, returns a set of (at most 3) keys associated with $T_{\mathcal{U}}$.

Algorithm AssignKeys($I, v, \hat{T}$):
1. If v is a leaf, then return a key for each of the (at most two) time intervals in I. Otherwise, continue with the next step.
2. Let $v_1, \ldots, v_{\sqrt{|\hat{T}|}}$ be the children of v, and let $\hat{T}_1, \ldots, \hat{T}_{\sqrt{|\hat{T}|}}$ be the respective sets of times associated with these children. We distinguish two cases:
   (a) I overlaps with only one set $\hat{T}_i$. Then we return the keys from the recursive call AssignKeys($I, v_i, \hat{T}_i$).
   (b) I overlaps with all of $\hat{T}_k, \hat{T}_{k+1}, \ldots, \hat{T}_{k+\ell}$, where $\ell \geq 1$. These $\ell + 1$ intervals are handled in 3 different ways: Those completely contained in I are collectively processed using the $D(v)$ structure, resulting in one key. If $\hat{T}_k$ overlaps with I, but is not contained in I, then it is right-anchored and is processed using $R(v_k)$, resulting in one key. If $\hat{T}_{k+\ell}$ overlaps with I, but is not contained in I, then it is left-anchored and is processed using $L(v_{k+\ell})$, resulting in one key. Those (at most) 3 keys are returned.

One can also lower the time complexity of the above algorithm to $O(time(\mathcal{S}1(n)))$ (e.g., it can be constant). We show how to achieve this in [4].

All keys given to users must be labeled with the level at which they were retrieved in the data structure, i.e., the distance from the root node. This is necessary for achieving constant-time computation of access keys, which will be explained in the next section. To make key derivation simpler, we also label user keys with their type; namely: D, R, or L. In addition, if a user receives more than a single key for her time sequence $T_{\mathcal{U}}$, each key is labeled with a range of time intervals to which it permits access.

To summarize, we assume that a key given to a user will be labeled with four values $(lev, type, t_a, t_b)$, where $0 \leq lev \leq \log \log n$, $type \in \{R, L, D\}$, and $t_a, t_b \in T$ such that $t_a < t_b$. For example, if a user with access rights to $T_{\mathcal{U}} = \{t_{start}, \ldots, t_{end}\}$ is given private information consisting of three keys $S_{T_{\mathcal{U}}} = \{k_1, k_2, k_3\}$, then k_1 could be labeled with (l, R, t_{start}, t_a), k_2 with $(l-1, D, t_{a+1}, t_b)$, and k_3 with (l, L, t_{b+1}, t_{end}).

5.3   Content Distribution

At time $t \in T$, the service provider wants to make certain content (possibly very voluminous) available to the users with access rights at time interval t. To do so, the content is encrypted with the access key k_t using a symmetric encryption scheme and is made available to all users in the encrypted form (by placing it in a public location, broadcasting it to the users, or by other means). In our scheme the server also needs to ensure that the keys that users derive for t allow them to derive k_t. There are $O(\log \log n)$ such keys for t in the data structure access to which should allow access to k_t. Since the data structure has $(\log \log n + 1)$ levels, such keys are:

- Keys from $R(v)$, for some v in the data structure, one from each level.
- Keys from $L(v)$, similarly, for a single v per level.
- Keys corresponding to $D(v)$, one from each level l, $0 \leq l \leq \log \log n - 1$.

We refer to these keys as *enabling keys*. The server places in the public domain information that permits derivation of k_t from any of the enabling keys above. Additionally, the server labels the public derivation information associated with each of the enabling keys with the level and the type (i.e., R, L, or D) of the corresponding enabling key. This is needed to permit fast constant-time derivation of the access key.

5.4   Key Derivation

A user $\mathcal{U}$ with access to the sequence of time intervals $T_{\mathcal{U}} = \{t_{start}, \ldots, t_{end}\} \in \mathcal{P}$ receives private information $S_{T_{\mathcal{U}}}$ consisting of 1, 2, or 3 keys that permit her to derive enabling keys for each $t \in T_{\mathcal{U}}$. In the most general (and common) case, such private information consists of 3 keys – denoted by k_1, k_2, and k_3 – labeled as (l, R, t_{start}, t_a), $(l - 1, D, t_{a+1}, t_b)$, and (l, L, t_{b+1}, t_{end}), respectively, for some l, a, and b. Let us assume, without loss of generality, that if the number of keys is less than 3, then the missing keys are set to empty strings with k_1 remaining of type R, key k_2 of type D, and key k_3 of type L. Then to obtain the enabling key for a time interval $t_i \in T_{\mathcal{U}}$, $\mathcal{U}$ executes a derivation algorithm which we sketch here:

Algorithm DeriveKey$(T_{\mathcal{U}}, t_i, S_{T_{\mathcal{U}}}, \mathsf{Pub})$:
1. Parse $S_{T_{\mathcal{U}}}$ as $k_1(l, R, t_{start}, t_a)$, $k_2(l - 1, D, t_{a+1}, t_b)$, $k_3(l, L, t_{b+1}, t_{end})$.
2. If $t_i \in \{t_{start}, \ldots, t_a\}$, find the node v at level l such that $R(v)$ permits access to t_i (note that such node v can be computed in constant time using index i of the time interval t_i). Use k_1 and the public information about the edges in Pub to derive the key corresponding to t_i and return that enabling key.
3. Similarly, if $t_i \in \{t_{b+1}, \ldots, t_{end}\}$, locate the node v at level l s.t. $L(v)$ permits access to t_i. Use k_3 and Pub to derive an enabling key for t_i and return that key.
4. Finally, if $t_i \in \{t_{a+1}, t_b\}$, locate v at level $l - 1$ such that $D(v)$ permits access to t_i; use k_2 and Pub to derive an enabling key for t_i and return it.

Key derivation complexity in all of the above cases is $O(time(\mathcal{S}1(n)))$.

5.5   Putting Everything Together

In this section we summarize our construction and show its performance. All proofs corresponding to our security theorems can be found in [4]. Figure 4 gives a complete

---

Algorithm Gen($1^\kappa, T$):

1. Create a root node $root$ for the data structure and run DataStuctBuild($root, T$). Let $G = (V, E)$ denote the tree structure returned.
2. For each $v \in V$, randomly choose a secret key $k_w \in \{0, 1\}^\kappa$ and a unique public label $\ell_w \in \{0, 1\}^\kappa$ associated with each node w in $D(v)$, $R(v)$, and $L(v)$.
3. For each $v \in V$, construct public information for each edge in $D(v)$, $R(v)$, and $L(v)$ using the key derivation method, e.g., for an edge (w, u), its public value is $y_{w,u} \in \{0, 1\}^\kappa$.
4. For each $t \in T$, randomly choose a secret key $k_t \in \{0, 1\}^\kappa$ and a unique public label $\ell_t \in \{0, 1\}^\kappa$.
5. For each $t \in T$, let $V_t \subset V$ denote the set of nodes in G access to which implies access to t. Then for each V_t, for each $v \in V_t$:
   (a) find in $D(v)$ the node corresponding to the time interval t; call it w.
   (b) create an edge from w to t by computing public information using enabling key k_w, t's secret key k_t, public label ℓ_t, and the key derivation method. Mark such an edge with the level of v and type D.
   (c) repeat (a) and (b) for $R(v)$ and $L(v)$, using types R and L, respectively.
6. Let K consist of the secret keys k_t for each $t \in T$ and Sec consist of the remaining secret keys k_w. Also let Pub consist of G, all public labels (of the form ℓ_w and ℓ_t), and public information about all edges generated above.

Algorithm Assign($T_\mathcal{U}$, Sec):

1. Execute AssignKeys($T_\mathcal{U}, root, T$), where $root$ is the root node of G.
2. Set $S_{T_\mathcal{U}}$ to the keys computed and return $S_{T_\mathcal{U}}$.

Algorithm Derive($T_\mathcal{U}, t, S_{T_\mathcal{U}}$, Pub):

1. If $t \notin T_\mathcal{U}$, return a special rejection symbol $\perp$.
2. Execute DeriveKey($T_\mathcal{U}, t, S_{T_\mathcal{U}}$, Pub) to compute an enabling key for t; call it k_t'.
3. Use k_t' along with its (level-type) label and Pub to derive key k_t.

Fig. 4. Proposed time-based key assignment scheme

description of our time-based KA scheme. In addition to the algorithms given in previous sections, we specify how they are used. Table 3 summarizes performance of our solution. The security of our solution comes from the way key derivation is performed in a DAG and is not due to the details of the data structures built.

Theorem 1. *Assuming the security of the family of PRFs F^κ, the time-based key assignment scheme given in Figure 4 is both complete and sound with respect to key recovery in the presence of a static adversary.*

To achieve a stronger notion of key indistinguishability, our solution will require a slightly different key derivation method. Intuitively, we decouple the keys used in the public information from the actual access keys, so that now it is not feasible to test access keys using the public information. The separation is performed using an additional invocation of a PRF, where the keys to be used in Pub are computed as $F(0||k)$ and the access keys are computed as $F(1||k)$. This key derivation method is described in [1] (full version only).

Then in our scheme of Figure 4, we use this enhanced key derivation method in Step 3 of the Gen algorithm (i.e., in data structures $D(v)$, $R(v)$, and $L(v)$). This means

Table 3. Performance of the improved scheme

Underlying scheme	Private storage	Key derivation	Public storage
2HS	≤ 3	≤ 5 op.	$O(n \log n \log \log n)$
3HS	≤ 3	≤ 7 op.	$O(n(\log \log n)^2)$
4HS	≤ 3	≤ 9 op.	$O(n \log^* n \log \log n)$
$\log^*$HS	≤ 3	$O(\log^* n)$ op.	$O(n \log \log n)$

that now someone with access to a certain key in, for instance, $R(v)$ and who guesses an unauthorized key correctly, cannot use the public information for that data structure to test the key. This change implies the corresponding change in the Derive algorithm.

So far we devised a solution to support access rights that span across a contiguous sequence of intervals. It is also possible to support periodic access rights that span across a contiguous set of time periods but the time intervals themselves might be discontinuous within a period. If we treat time as a single dimension and the solution presented in this work as a solution to one-dimensional problem, it is possible to extend our approach to higher dimensions. An extension to dimension 2, which is useful in the geo-spatial context, is presented in [3]. This two-dimensional solution can be used to conveniently address the problem of periodic access rights with a small number of keys per user: we use one dimension to specify periods in user access rights and the other dimension to specify individual time slots within a period. We omit further details here.

Full version [4] gives extensions to this solution. In particular, we show how to extend the lifetime of the system beyond the original n time intervals and how to generalize the scheme to further decrease the public space using a key-space tradeoff.

6   Temporal Access Control for a User Hierarchy

In systems with hierarchically organized access classes, such a hierarchy is normally modeled as a directed acyclic access graph which we denote by G_U. In such a graph, each node corresponds to an access class and the edges form a partial order relationship between the classes. An edge from node v to node w means that the parent node v inherits privileges of the node w (while the converse is not true). This implies that a user with access to a specific class obtains access to the resources at that class and the resources at all of the descendant classes in the hierarchy. With this setup, it is possible to assign each class a single secret key and let users obtain keys of their descendant classes through a key derivation process. Similar to a general graph, in an access graph G_U a directed path from node v to w means that w's keys are derivable from v's key.

Now if we equip the model with time-based policies, in addition to computing keys of descendant classes, a user should be able to compute keys based on time. That is, a user $\mathcal{U}$ entitled to access class $v \in V_U$ during a sequence of time intervals $T_{\mathcal{U}} \in \mathcal{P}$ obtains private information that permits her to compute keys $k_{v,t}$ for her access class v and each $t \in T_{\mathcal{U}}$ (time-based key derivation). In addition, the private information allows $\mathcal{U}$ to compute, for each $t \in T_{\mathcal{U}}$, keys $k_{w,t}$ for each descendant access class w in the user hierarchy (class-based key derivation). Thus, key derivation now consists of two

Table 4. Comparison of time-based hierarchical KA schemes

Scheme	Public information	Private information	Key derivation	Operation type	Complexity assumption
Encryption-based [5]	$O(|V_U|^2|T|^3)$	1	1	decryption	one-way functions
Pairing-based [5]	$O(|V_U|^2)$	$O(|T|)$	1	pairing evaluation	Bilinear Diffie-Hellman
Binary tree	$O(|E_U||T|)$	$O(\log|T|)$	$O(\log|T|+diam(G_U))$	PRF	one-way functions
ISPIT+(3,1)-CSBT +EBC [15]	$O(|E_U||T| + |V_U||T|\cdot \log|T|(\log\log|T|)^2)$	≤ 3	$O(diam(G_U))$	decryption	IND-P1-CO encryption [13]
Our 4HS-based	$O(|E_U||T| + |V_U||T|\cdot \log^* n \log\log|T|)$	≤ 3	$O(diam(G_U))$	PRF	one-way functions
ISPIT+(3,1)-CSBT +EBC [15]	$O(|E_U||T| + |V_U||T|\cdot \log|T| \log\log|T|)$	≤ 3	$O(\log^*|T|+diam(G_U))$	decryption	IND-P1-CO encryption [13]
Our log*HS-based	$O(|E_U||T| + |V_U||T|\cdot \log\log|T|)$	≤ 3	$O(\log^*|T|+diam(G_U))$	PRF	one-way functions

dimensions, which can potentially be performed using drastically different techniques. We give details on how to extend out current scheme to this hierarchically-temporal based model in the full version [4].

7   Comparison with Existing Solutions

Table 4 compares performance of our scheme with other existing solutions; only security against recovery was considered. In the table, $diam(G_U)$ denotes the diameter of the graph (i.e., maximum distance between nodes) that bounds the number of operations necessary to derive a descendant class's key in the user hierarchy G_U. Also, $|E_U|$ denotes the number of edges in G_U. The table does not list private storage at the server since it is equivalent for all solutions. Before proceeding with comparing existing results, we briefly explain what these parameters mean.

In the great majority of cases, the depth of user hierarchies is a small constant, resulting in small constant $diam(G_U)$. In cases where the depth of the original graph G_U is fairly large and it is unacceptable to have the user perform $diam(G_U)$ operations, the graph can be modified to significantly reduce $diam(G_U)$. This is done by inserting shortcut edges at random (if $diam(G_U) = O(V_U)$) or using the techniques of [1] and [2] that reduce $diam(G_U)$ to a small constant at the expense of small increase in the public storage associated with the hierarchy[1]. Thus, in this case $diam(G_U)$ is also a small constant, and parameter $|E_U|$ will need to be replaced with a slightly larger value.

We also would like to mention that the schemes [19,18] are not listed in the table due to the difference in the expressive power. These solutions allow a user to obtain access to an arbitrary subsequence of time intervals, but require significantly slower key derivation of $O(|V_U| \cdot |T|)$ modular exponentiations.

---

[1] The techniques of [1] and [2] may fail on hierarchies of high dimensions, but we believe that such cases are very rare for the applications we consider in this work.

Considering that small private user storage and fast key derivation, followed by reasonable server storage are the main evaluation criteria, we can analyze the solutions as follows. The Pairing-based scheme of [5] will have the slowest key derivation time among all of the schemes listed, as it uses pairing evaluation rather than fast encryption or PRF operations. Additionally, the number of secret keys a user has to maintain is large. Compared to the Encryption-based scheme of [5], our key derivation time is higher by a constant factor, private storage is similar (i.e., three keys instead of one), but the amount of public information the server must maintain in our scheme is much lower than in that scheme.

While the simple binary-tree approach has asymptotically higher performance, for small values of $|T|$ it will be preferred due to its simplicity. However, for the applications we envision, other solutions exhibit better performance. Thus, our recommendation is to use the simplest approach suitable for a particular setup.

The work of De Santis et al. [15] lists solutions with different performance parameters, and we include only selected two here. We chose two schemes that require a user to store 3 private keys (like in our solutions) and where time-based key derivation involves $O(1)$ and $O(\log^* n)$ decryptions, respectively. This allows us to directly compare the schemes of [15] with our schemes. As can be seen from the table, the solutions exhibit very similar performance with CSBT-based constructions having an additional factor of $\log |T|$ in the public storage space. Moreover, they do not discuss key assignment, but it does not look like their key assignment can be done in constant time, whereas our scheme allows constant time key assignment.

To summarize, our solution offers very attractive characteristics and superior performance compared to other existing solutions: each user in the system receives a small (≤ 3) number of keys, constant-time key assignment to a user, (off-line) computation of any access key involves a small number of very efficient operations, and the public storage required by our solution is only slightly higher than the number of access keys that the system must maintain.

Acknowledgments

The authors would like to thank Michael Rabinovich for his excellent suggestion of using the geo-spatial key assignment scheme to address temporal key assignment for periodic expressions. Mikhail Atallah is supported in part by Grants IIS-0325345 and CNS-0627488 from the National Science Foundation, and by sponsors of the Center for Education and Research in Information Assurance and Security. Marina Blanton was supported by Intel Ph.D. fellowship, work was performed while at Purdue University.

References

1. Atallah, M., Blanton, M., Fazio, N., Frikken, K.: Dynamic and efficient key management for access hierarchies. In: ACM Conference on Computer and Communications Security (CCS'05) (preliminary version), Full version is available as Technical Report TR 2006-09, CERIAS, Purdue University (2006)
2. Atallah, M., Blanton, M., Frikken, K.: Key management for non-tree access hierarchies. In: ACM Symposium on Access Control Models and Technologies (SACMAT'06), pp. 11–18 (2006) (Full version is available as Technical Report TR 2007-30, CERIAS, Purdue University)

3. Atallah, M., Blanton, M., Frikken, K.: Efficient techniques for realizing geo-spatial access control. In: ASIACCS'07. ACM Symposium on Information, Computer and Communications Security, pp. 82–92. ACM Press, New York (2007)
4. Atallah, M., Blanton, M., Frikken, K.: Incorporating temporal capabilities in existing key management schemes. Full version, available as Cryptology ePrint Archive Report 2007/245 (2007), http://eprint.iacr.org/2007/245
5. Ateniese, G., De Santis, A., Ferrara, A., Masucci, B.: Provably-secure time-bound hierarchical key assignment schemes. In: CCS'06. ACM Conference on Computer and Communications Security, ACM Press, New York (2006)
6. Bellare, M., Canetti, R., Krawczyk, H.: Keying hash functions for message authentication. In: Koblitz, N. (ed.) CRYPTO 1996. LNCS, vol. 1109, Springer, Heidelberg (1996)
7. Bertino, E., Bettini, C., Ferrari, E., Samarati, P.: An access control model supporting periodicity constraints and temporal reasoning. ACM Transactions on Database Systems (TODS) 23(3), 231–285 (1998)
8. Bertino, E., Bonatti, P., Ferrari, E.: TRBAC: A temporal role-based access control model. In: SACMAT'00. ACM Symposium on Access Control Models and Technologies, pp. 21–30. ACM Press, New York (2000)
9. Briscoe, B.: MARKS: Zero side effect multicast key management using arbitrarily revealed key sequences. In: Rizzo, L., Fdida, S. (eds.) Networked Group Communication. LNCS, vol. 1736, pp. 301–320. Springer, Heidelberg (1999)
10. Chien, H.: Efficient time-bound hierarchical key assignment scheme. IEEE Transactions of Knowledge and Data Engineering (TKDE) 16(10), 1301–1304 (2004)
11. Crampton, J., Martin, K., Wild, P.: On key assignment for hierarchical access control. In: CSFW'06. IEEE Computer Security Foundations Workshop, IEEE Computer Society Press, Los Alamitos (2006)
12. Huang, H., Chang, C.: A new cryptographic key assignment scheme with time-constraint access control in a hierarchy. Computer Standards & Interfaces 26, 159–166 (2004)
13. Katz, J., Yung, M.: Characterization of security notions for probabilistic private-key encryption. Journal of Cryptology 19, 67–95 (2006)
14. De Santis, A., Ferrara, A., Masucci, B.: Enforcing the security of a time-bound hierarchical key assignment scheme. Information Sciences 176(12), 1684–1694 (2006)
15. De Santis, A., Ferrara, A., Masucci, B.: New constructions for provably-secure time-bound hierarchical key assignment schemes. In: SACMAT'07. ACM Symposium on Access Control Models and Technologies, ACM Press, New York (2007)
16. Tang, Q., Mitchell, C.: Comments on a cryptographic key assignment scheme for access control in a hierarchy. Computer Standards & Interfaces 27, 323–326 (2005)
17. Tzeng, W.: A time-bound cryptographic key assignment scheme for access control in a hierarchy. IEEE Transactions on Knowledge and Data Engineering (TKDE) 14(1), 182–188 (2002)
18. Tzeng, W.: A secure system for data access based on anonymous authentication and time-dependent hierarchical keys. In: ASIACCS'06. ACM Symposium on Information, Computer and Communications Security, pp. 223–230. ACM Press, New York (2006)
19. Wang, S.-Y., Laih, C.-S.: Merging: an efficient solution for a time-bound hierarchical key assignment scheme. IEEE Transactions on Dependable and Secure Computing 3(1), 91–100 (2006)
20. Yeh, J.: An RSA-based time-bound hierarchical key assignment scheme for electronic article subscription. In: CIKM'05. ACM International Conference on Information and Knowledge Management, pp. 285–286. ACM Press, New York (2005)
21. Yi, X.: Security of Chien's efficient time-bound hierarchical key assignment scheme. IEEE Transactions of Knowledge and Data Engineering (TKDE) 17(9), 1298–1299 (2005)
22. Yi, X., Ye, Y.: Security of Tzeng's time-bound key assignment scheme for access control in a hierarchy. IEEE Transactions on Knowledge and Data Engineering (TKDE) 15(4), 1054–1055 (2003)

A Policy Language for Distributed Usage Control

M. Hilty[1], A. Pretschner[1], D. Basin[1], C. Schaefer[2], and T. Walter[2]

[1] Information Security, ETH Zurich, Switzerland
{hiltym,pretscha,basin}@inf.ethz.ch
[2] DoCoMo Euro-Labs, Munich, Germany
{schaefer,walter}@docomolab-euro.com

Abstract. We present the Obligation Specification Language (OSL), a policy language for distributed usage control. OSL supports the formalization of a wide range of usage control requirements. We also present translations between OSL and two rights expression languages (RELs) from the DRM area. These translations make it possible to use DRM mechanisms to enforce OSL policies. Furthermore, the translations enhance the interoperability of DRM mechanisms and allow us to apply OSL-specific monitoring and analysis tools to the RELs.

1 Introduction

Many kinds of digitally stored and processed data should only be used in restricted ways. Personal data, for example, is collected during activities such as online shopping, using loyalty cards, interaction with public administrations, and using mobile phones. To protect the privacy of the data subjects, there exist laws and regulations governing the use of personal data. Private businesses also have a keen interest in protecting their trade secrets, which turns out to be difficult, for example, when different corporations collaborate in virtual enterprises. Similarly, the creators of music, video, or other artistic works want their intellectual property rights to be respected when others use their creations.

Usage control [23,25] is an extension of access control that covers not only who may access which data, but also how the data may or may not be used afterwards. We study usage control in the context of distributed systems with different actors who take the roles of data providers (who distribute data) and data consumers (who request and receive data). When a data provider gives a data item to a data consumer, certain conditions apply. *Provisions* are those conditions that refer to the past and are concerned with whether the data item may be released in the first place. Other conditions govern the future usage of the data, so-called *obligations* [4]. Examples of obligations include "do not distribute document D to anyone outside of the organization," "play movie M at most 5 times," and "notify the author whenever document D is modified." In this paper, we focus exclusively on obligations because provisions have been thoroughly studied in the area of access control.

J. Biskup and J. Lopez (Eds.): ESORICS 2007, LNCS 4734, pp. 531–546, 2007.

There are two strategies for enforcing obligations [15]. A *control mechanism* is a consumer-side component that makes sure that obligations cannot be violated. Existing control mechanisms have been developed in the DRM area. An *observation mechanism* consists of a consumer-side signaling mechanism and a provider-side monitor. When the monitor detects the violation of an obligation, it can trigger a compensating action such as a penalty [14].

Problem Statement. We address three related problems. The first is the lack of a general-purpose policy language for usage control that provides adequate support for the common structures encountered in usage control requirements. While there exist specification languages both in the area of privacy (e.g., EPAL [2] and P3P [30]) and DRM (e.g., ODRL [28] and XrML [31]), these languages are special-purpose and only cover requirements that are encountered in their respective areas. The second is that policy languages usually lack a semantics that can be used for specifying or configuring enforcement mechanisms or for checking the adherence to policies. Conversely, for many mechanisms, it is not always clear what sort of policies they can enforce. The third problem is that the different specification languages and enforcement mechanisms in usage control (particularly DRM) are often not interoperable.

Contributions. We present the Obligation Specification Language (OSL), a language for expressing requirements from many application areas of usage control. This includes constraints on the duration of a usage and the kinds of permission-like statements that are often used in digital rights management. We also define a formal semantics for OSL. Together with other results [14,15]—which include a model of enforcement mechanisms, analysis techniques for reasoning about policies and mechanisms, and an approach to monitoring whether obligations expressed in OSL are adhered to—this language builds a framework that provides tools for specifying, reasoning about, and enforcing usage control requirements.

We also show how to define translations between OSL and a REL, which we have implemented for subsets of the two most widely used rights expression languages, namely XrML and ODRL. This yields a formal semantics for these RELs and has additional benefits. First, defining the translation from a REL to OSL makes it possible to use the analysis and monitoring techniques mentioned above for the REL. Second, RELs are often used to configure DRM mechanisms. By being translating OSL into a REL, we can employ the mechanisms that use this REL to enforce OSL policies. We have implemented a proof of concept Microsoft's RMS [20], which uses XrML. Third, once the translations between OSL and several RELs are defined, we can use OSL as an intermediate language to translate between the different RELs. This is a step towards increasing the interoperability of DRM mechanisms.

Structure. We analyze usage control requirements in §2 and present the syntax and semantics of OSL in §3. In §4, we show how to translate between OSL and a REL. Related work is surveyed in §5 and in §6, we conclude with an outlook on future work. An extended version of this paper is available as a technical report [15].

2   Usage Control Requirements

We have performed a requirements study in usage control based on interviews with public administrations, data protection officers, health care providers, military organizations, and numerous commercial organizations [13]. We have also carried out a detailed study on usage control requirements in mobile communication [16]. We present the distilled results of our requirements analysis with respect to obligations. Afterwards, we discuss the two modalities that play a central role in describing usage control requirements.

2.1   Obligations

Obligational formulae are conditions on the usage of data, e.g., "delete document D within 30 days" or "do not give D to anybody else." Examples for data usage are the processing, rendering, execution, management, or distribution of such data. An obligational formula becomes an *obligation* once a data consumer has received the data and committed to the conditions. We refer to this process of data reception and commitment as the *activation* of an obligational formula. An obligation has thus the form "if (activation) then (obligational formula)." In OSL, we specify obligational formulae but refer to them as obligations for the sake of simplicity. Similarly, we also talk about the activation of an obligation.

Obligations can take two different forms. *Usage restrictions* prohibit certain usages under given circumstances, and *action requirements* express mandatory actions that must be executed either unconditionally (i.e., not in direct connection with a usage) or after a specified usage has been performed.

Conditions specify circumstances under which usage restrictions or action requirements apply. They are divided into time conditions, cardinality conditions, event-defined conditions, purpose conditions, and environment conditions. Usage restrictions are statements of a form equivalent to "if *condition* then not *usage*." Examples are "document D must not be printed after more than 20 days" and "movie M may only be played once." Action requirements are statements of a form equivalent to "if *condition* then *action*." Examples are "delete data D 30 days after reception" and "notify the data owner after each usage of data D." Note that action requirements and usage restrictions may look similar. For example, "notify the data owner before each usage of data D" is a usage restriction because it prohibits using D if the notification has not been not sent before. We briefly discuss each type of condition below. In the examples given, the respective conditions are typeset in *italics*.

TIME CONDITIONS include, for example, "file F must be deleted *within 7 days*", "F must *never* be distributed", or "movie stream M must *not* be viewed *for more than a total of 5 hours*." We have not encountered examples like "action A must *eventually* be executed" where no time limit is given for the execution of an action. Instead, one sets a time limit like "action A must be executed *within 2 years*." CARDINALITY CONDITIONS refer to the number of occurrences of given events. Examples include "movie M may *only* be played *once*" or "view trailer D *at most twice* before the movie M is paid." EVENT-DEFINED CONDITIONS define situations in terms of the occurrence of events. An example of an event-defined condition is "*if the data provider revokes document D*, the document must not be used anymore," or "document D must not be further distributed *until the author officially releases D*." PURPOSE CONDITIONS refer to the purpose of use. For example, objects that are labelled "for *personal use only*" must not be used in a business context. ENVIRONMENT CONDITIONS relate to the internal and external environment of the data consumer. This includes the adherence to technical or organizational standards (e.g., Common Criteria or the Sarbanes-Oxley Act) as well as aspects of the physical environment such as the data consumer's geographical location. An example is "document D may only be opened *within Europe*."

Conditions can be combined to describe complex circumstances. For example, the obligation "movie M may be viewed at most 3 times and only within 30 days" combines a time condition and a cardinality condition. Moreover, usage restrictions and action requirements can be combined to form complex policy statements. For example, the following obligational formula combines an action requirement with a time condition and a usage restriction with a purpose condition: "document D needs to be deleted within 7 days and must not be shown in public."

2.2   Modalities

There are different ways of specifying policies. One approach, which is often employed in informal regulations (e.g., privacy regulations) and system specifications, is to explicitly define *requirements* on the system execution. This approach uses a "must" modality in the sense that every requirement must be satisfied. In contrast, a REL specifies exclusive *rights* to execute given actions under specific conditions. Such rights specify what may happen with data and therefore use a "may" modality. An exclusive right to perform a usage implies that all other usages are forbidden, but the prohibited usages are not specified explicitly.

Many usage control requirements are not equally easy to express in both modalities. In the DRM area, where typically only a few usages are allowed, rights are often easier to specify. This is particularly the case if the set of prohibited usages is large or even unbounded (e.g., if usages are parameterized). In the privacy area, where the laws and regulations often express explicit prohibitions, it is rather the other way around. Furthermore, the requirements document for ODRL version 2.0 [21] states that expressing prohibitions can also be desirable in the DRM area. As a consequence, we support both modalities in OSL. The "must" modality is inherited from temporal logic, and the "may" modality has been included via dedicated permission operators.

3   The Obligation Specification Language (OSL)

We introduce the syntax and semantics of OSL. We formalize both in Z, a formal language based on typed set theory and first-order logic with equality. We have chosen Z because of its rich notation, which we explain as it is encountered. We have also given a more user-friendly syntax to OSL [15], which we do not present in this paper due to space restrictions. The current version of OSL supports all usage control requirements identified above, except environment conditions.

3.1 Events and Traces

The semantics of our language is defined over traces with discrete time steps. At each time step, a set of events can occur. An event corresponds to the execution of an action and we use these two terms interchangeably. We formalize different aspects of events and traces.

Event Classes and Parameters. Each *Event* has a name and parameters, specifying additional details about the event. For example, a usage event can indicate on which data item it is performed or by which device. Parameters are represented using a partial function ($\nrightarrow$) from parameter names to parameter values. We often describe parameters by their function graph. An example of an event in this syntax is $(play, \{(object, m)\})$, where *play* is the event name and the parameter with name *object* has value m (i.e., the object m is played).

Each event belongs to an event *class*. Possible event classes include *usage* and *other*, the latter standing for all non-usage events, e.g., payments or notifications. This distinction enables us to prohibit all usages on a data item while still allowing other events such as payments. The definition of events in Z is shown below. *EventName*, *ParamName*, and *ParamValue* define basic types for event names, parameter names, and parameter values, respectively. In Z, basic types are defined by listing their names in square brackets.

$$[EventName, ParamName, ParamValue] \quad Params : ParamName \nrightarrow ParamValue$$
$$EventClass == \{usage, other\} \quad\quad\quad Event == EventName \times Params$$
$$getclass : EventName \rightarrow EventClass$$

Indexed Events. An important usage control requirement is the restriction of the accumulated usage time. To cater for usages that last a specified time, we introduce *indexed events*. We assume that at each step of a trace, there is an indexed event for each usage that is currently executed. The start of the usage is represented by an indexed event with the index *start*, and all following indexed events have the index *ongoing*. For example, if the time step is 1 minute and a user plays a movie m for 3 minutes, the resulting indexed events occurring in the trace are $((play, \{(object, m)\}), start)$, $((play, \{(object, m)\}), ongoing)$, and $((play, \{(object, m)\}), ongoing)$. In OSL, we can explicitly refer to the start of an event or to all parts of it (cf. §3.2). *IndEvent* defines indexed events and *Trace* defines traces. The formalization of the above assumption is omitted due to space limitations but can be found in the technical report [15].

$$IndEvent == Event \times \{start, ongoing\} \quad Trace : \mathbb{N} \rightarrow \mathbb{P}\, IndEvent$$

Event Declarations. So far, we have not defined what events can occur in a concrete system. To this end, we introduce event declarations. An event declaration contains the event name, the event class, and a partial function that defines the name and possible values of each parameter. Note that such an event declaration is purely syntactic and says nothing about the meaning of an event, i.e., which event in a real system it describes. The specification of dedicated ontologies is outside the scope of this paper.

$$EventDecl == EventName \times EventClass \times (ParamName \nrightarrow \mathbb{P}\, ParamValue)$$

3.2 Syntax

An OSL policy consists of a set of event declarations and a set of obligational formulae. Each obligational formula consists of the data consumer's name and a logical expression. *SubID* is the set of possible names of data consumers.

$$OSLPolicy == \mathbb{P}\, EventDecl \times \mathbb{P}\, OblFormula$$
$$OblFormula == SubID \times \Phi$$

Φ defines the syntax of the logical expressions contained in obligational formulae. $E_{fst}(e)$ refers to the start of an event e and $E_{all}(e)$ to ongoing events as well (cf. §3.1). Z allows EBNF-style definitions as used below.

$$\Phi ::= \underline{true} \mid \underline{false} \mid E_{fst}\langle\!\langle Event \rangle\!\rangle \mid E_{all}\langle\!\langle Event \rangle\!\rangle \mid \underline{not}\langle\!\langle \Phi \rangle\!\rangle \mid \underline{and}\langle\!\langle \Phi \times \Phi \rangle\!\rangle \mid \underline{or}\langle\!\langle \Phi \times \Phi \rangle\!\rangle \mid$$
$$\underline{implies}\langle\!\langle \Phi \times \Phi \rangle\!\rangle \mid \underline{until}\langle\!\langle \Phi \times \Phi \rangle\!\rangle \mid \underline{always}\langle\!\langle \Phi \rangle\!\rangle \mid \underline{after}\langle\!\langle \mathbb{N} \times \Phi \rangle\!\rangle \mid \underline{within}\langle\!\langle \mathbb{N} \times \Phi \rangle\!\rangle \mid$$
$$\underline{during}\langle\!\langle \mathbb{N} \times \Phi \rangle\!\rangle \mid \underline{repmax}\langle\!\langle \mathbb{N} \times \Phi \rangle\!\rangle \mid \underline{repuntil}\langle\!\langle \mathbb{N} \times \Phi \times \Phi \rangle\!\rangle \mid$$
$$\underline{permitonlyevname}\langle\!\langle \mathbb{P}\, EventName \times Params \rangle\!\rangle \mid$$
$$\underline{permitonlyparam}\langle\!\langle \mathbb{P}\, ParamValue \times ParamName \times EventName \times Params \rangle\!\rangle$$

We define an additional restriction on the policy syntax (omitted here): we demand that all events that are mentioned in a policy are compliant with the event declaration, i.e., they may only contain parameters that are declared and corresponding values. Fewer parameters are allowed in a policy, because of the implicit universal quantification over unspecified parameters (cf. §3.4).

3.3 Informal Semantics

We first informally describe the semantics of OSL's operators. They are classified into propositional operators, temporal operators, cardinality operators, and permit operators. An example for a complete OSL policy is given in Section 4.2.

Propositional Operators. The operators $\underline{not}$, $\underline{and}$, $\underline{or}$, and $\underline{implies}$ have the same semantics as their propositional counterparts $\neg$, $\wedge$, $\vee$, and $\Rightarrow$.

Temporal Operators. The $\underline{until}$ operator corresponds to the *weak until* operator from LTL [24]. We use the weak version of the until operator because it is better suited for expressing usage control requirements (cf. §2.1). We generalize the *next* operator of LTL to $\underline{after}$, which takes a natural number n as input and refers to the time after n time steps. With $\underline{after}$, we can express concepts like $\underline{during}$ (something must hold constantly during a given time interval) and $\underline{within}$ (something must hold at least once during a given time interval).

Cardinality Operators. Cardinality operators restrict the number of occurrences of a specific event or the accumulated duration of an event. The $\underline{repuntil}$

operator limits the maximum number of times an event may occur until another event occurs. For example,

$$repuntil(3, E_{fst}(play, \{(object, m)\}),$$
$$E_{fst}((pay, \{(currency, USD), (amount, 10), (recipient, r)\}))))$$

states that the movie m must not be played more than 3 times until a payment of \$10 is made to r. With _repuntil_, we can also define _repmax_, which is syntactic sugar for defining the maximum number of times an event may occur in the unlimited future. For example,

$$repmax(5, E_{all}(play, \{(object, s)\}))$$

requires that the movie stream s must not be played for more than 5 time steps. This example shows that by using E_{all} instead of E_{fst}, the cardinality operators can be used to limit accumulated usage time. In the semantics definition below, we restrict the cardinality operators to arguments of these two forms. The reason for this restriction is that we allow multiple similar events to occur within one time step. For example, the movie m may be played on two devices simultaneously, which counts twice in the _repuntil_ example above.

Permit Operators. In OSL, we support both the "must" and the "may" modalities. The former is given by OSL's LTL-like semantics, and the latter is supported by two designated operators: these operators allow one to specify that out of a given set of usages events, only selected usage events are allowed. The operator _permitonlyevname_ defines the names of the usage events that are exclusively allowed with a set of given parameters. For example, the expression

$$permitonlyevname(\{play, print\}, \{(object, oid)\})$$

states that the only usages permitted on the object oid are $play$ and $print$. It does not say anything about non-usage events or events with different parameters (e.g., if a usage is applied to a different data object). Similarly, _permitonlyparam_ only allows certain values for a given parameter of an event. It prohibits all other values for this parameter. For example, the expression

$$permitonlyparam(\{s_1, s_2\}, recipient, send, \{(object, doc)\})$$

specifies that out of all $send$ events with doc as the "object" parameter, only those where the "recipient" parameter has the value s_1 or s_2 are allowed. In other words, doc may only be sent to s_1 or s_2. The first argument of _permitonlyparam_ is the set of allowed parameter values, the second argument is the name of the parameter whose values should be restricted, and the third and fourth argument define an underspecified event.

3.4   Formal Semantics

When specifying events in obligations, we implicitly quantify over unmentioned parameters. For example, if an obligation prohibits event $(play, \{(object, objB)\})$, then the event $(play, \{(object, objB), (device, dev123)\})$ is prohibited as well. To specify this, we define the relation *refinesEv*, which checks whether one event e_2 refines another event e_1. This is the case iff both have the same event name and all parameters of e_1 have the same value in e_2. e_2 can also have additional parameters. With the help of *refinesEv*, we can also define the satisfaction relation for event expressions, $\models_e$. This defines whether an indexed event corresponds to an expression of the form $E_{fst}(e)$ or $E_{all}(e)$, where e is an event. The semantics of a logical expression $\varphi : \Phi$ is defined by the binary relation $\models_f$.

The relations *refinesEv*, $\models_e$, and $\models_f$ are defined in Figure 1. We specify them using an *axiomatic definition* in Z: the upper part of an axiomatic definition contains the signature and in the lower part, the properties of the functions and relations are specified. In Z, relations are declared with $\leftrightarrow$. We also use the following Z notation: $e_1.2$ refers to the second component of e_1, $\#$ denotes the size of a set, and dom refers to the domain of a function.

A policy is satisfied by a trace iff all obligations specified in the policy are satisfied by the trace. The definition of obligation satisfaction builds on the above semantics but requires a system model that includes activations of obligations (cf. §2.1). Such a system model is presented in [15].

4   Language Translations

In this section, we present translations between OSL and the most widely used rights expression languages, ODRL and XrML. We use the term *license* for policies expressed in a REL. We start by explaining our reasons for translating between OSL and rights expression languages, show how to define such translations, and highlight several key issues using the example of the translations between OSL and a subset of ODRL. We have published the formal specification of these translations in a technical report [15]. We have also implemented these translations in software, both for the ODRL subset mentioned above and for a comparable subset of XrML.

4.1   Purpose

There are several reasons for defining the translations between OSL and different RELs. The first reason is the need for enforcing OSL policies. Current enforcement mechanisms are almost exclusively from the DRM area and use licenses or rights objects written in a REL. Thus, the ability to translate OSL policies into rights objects makes it possible to re-use such mechanisms to enforce OSL policies. As OSL is not limited to DRM, this opens the door to automatically enforcing non-DRM policies (e.g., privacy policies) with DRM mechanisms. By defining translations from privacy policy languages into OSL (which is future work), we will be able to close the gap between the areas of privacy and DRM, which are seen as antipodes by many people.

The second reason for providing translation schemes is that the translation from a REL to OSL gives a formal semantic to the REL. While the formal semantics for some parts of ODRL and XrML have been defined in earlier work, the translations that we present immediately provide a formal semantics to parts

$\underline{\quad refinesEv \quad} : Event \leftrightarrow Event$

$\forall e_1, e_2 : Event \bullet e_2 \, refinesEv \, e_1 \Leftrightarrow e_1.1 = e_2.1 \wedge e_1.2 \subseteq e_2.2$

$\underline{\quad \models_e \quad} : IndEvent \leftrightarrow \Phi$

$\forall ie : IndEvent; \; \varphi : \Phi \bullet ie \models_e \varphi \Leftrightarrow$
$\quad \exists e : Event \bullet ie.1 \, refinesEv \, e$
$\qquad \wedge ((\varphi = E_{fst}(e) \wedge ie.2 = start) \vee \varphi = E_{all}(e))$

$\underline{\quad \models_f \quad} : (Trace \times \mathbb{N}) \leftrightarrow \Phi$

$\forall t : Trace; \; n : \mathbb{N}; \; \varphi : \Phi \bullet (t, n) \models_f \varphi \Leftrightarrow$
$\quad \varphi = \underline{true}$
$\quad \vee \, \exists e : Event; \; ie : IndEvent \bullet (\varphi = E_{fst}(e) \vee \varphi = E_{all}(e)) \wedge ie \in t(n) \wedge ie \models_e \varphi$
$\quad \vee \, \exists \psi : \Phi \bullet \varphi = \underline{not}(\psi) \wedge \neg ((t, n) \models_f \psi)$
$\quad \vee \, \exists \psi, \chi : \Phi \bullet \varphi = \underline{or}(\psi, \chi) \wedge ((t, n) \models_f \psi \vee (t, n) \models_f \chi)$
$\quad \vee \, \exists \psi, \chi : \Phi \bullet \varphi = \underline{until}(\psi, \chi)$
$\qquad \wedge (\exists u : \mathbb{N} \mid n \leq u \bullet ((t, u) \models_f \chi \wedge (\forall v : \mathbb{N} \mid n \leq v < u \bullet (t, v) \models_f \psi))$
$\qquad\quad \vee (\forall v : \mathbb{N} \mid n \leq v \bullet (t, v) \models_f \psi))$
$\quad \vee \, \exists i : \mathbb{N}; \; \psi : \Phi \bullet \varphi = \underline{after}(i, \psi) \wedge (t, n + i) \models_f \psi$
$\quad \vee \, \exists l : \mathbb{N}; \; \psi, \chi : \Phi; \; e : Event \bullet$
$\qquad \varphi = \underline{repuntil}(l, \psi, \chi) \wedge (\psi = E_{fst}(e) \vee \psi = E_{all}(e))$
$\qquad \wedge ((\exists u : \mathbb{N} \mid n \leq u \bullet (t, u) \models_f \chi \wedge (\forall v : \mathbb{N} \mid n \leq v < u \bullet \neg((t, v) \models_f \chi))$
$$\wedge (\sum_{j=0}^{u} \#\{ie : IndEvent \mid ie \in t(n + j) \wedge ie \models_e \psi\}) \leq l)$$
$$\vee (\sum_{j=0}^{\infty} \#\{ie : IndEvent \mid ie \in t(n + j) \wedge ie \models_e \psi\}) \leq l)$$
$\quad \vee \, \exists ex : \mathbb{P} \, EventName; \; ps : Params \bullet \varphi = \underline{permitonlyevname}(ex, ps)$
$\qquad \wedge \forall en : EventName \mid getclass(en) = usage \wedge en \notin ex \bullet$
$\qquad\quad (t, n) \models_f \underline{always}(\underline{not}(E_{all}((en, ps))))$
$\quad \vee \, \exists ex : \mathbb{P} \, ParamValue; \; pn : ParamName; \; en : EventName; \; ps : Params \bullet$
$\qquad \varphi = \underline{permitonlyparam}(ex, pn, en, ps) \wedge pn \notin \mathsf{dom} \, ps$
$\qquad \wedge \forall pv : ParamValue \mid pv \notin ex \bullet$
$\qquad\quad (t, n) \models_f \underline{always}(\underline{not}(E_{all}((en, ps \cup \{(pn, pv)\}))))$
$\quad \vee \, \exists \psi, \chi : \Phi \bullet \varphi = \underline{and}(\psi, \chi) \wedge (t, n) \models_f \underline{not}(\underline{or}(\underline{not}(\psi), \underline{not}(\chi)))$
$\quad \vee \, \exists \psi, \chi : \Phi \bullet \varphi = \underline{implies}(\psi, \chi) \wedge (t, n) \models_f \underline{or}(\underline{not}(\psi), \chi)$
$\quad \vee \, \exists \psi : \Phi \bullet \varphi = \underline{always}(\psi) \wedge (t, n) \models_f \underline{until}(\psi, \underline{false})$
$$\quad \vee \, \exists i : \mathbb{N}; \; \psi : \Phi \bullet \varphi = \underline{within}(i, \psi) \wedge (t, n) \models_f \bigvee_{i=0}^{n-1} \underline{after}(i, \varphi)$$
$$\quad \vee \, \exists i : \mathbb{N}; \; \psi : \Phi \bullet \varphi = \underline{during}(i, \psi) \wedge (t, n) \models_f \bigwedge_{i=0}^{n-1} \underline{after}(i, \varphi)$$
$\quad \vee \, \exists l : \mathbb{N}; \; \psi : \Phi \bullet \varphi = \underline{repmax}(l, \psi) \wedge (t, n) \models_f \underline{repuntil}(l, \psi, \underline{false})$

Fig. 1. Semantics of OSL

of ODRL, including parts for which this has not yet been done (cf. §5). It is important to note that the formal semantics of OSL makes it possible to perform logical analysis on policies [15] and to check for adherence to obligations at runtime [14]. So we gain both (1) the possibility to use control mechanisms from the DRM area to enforce OSL policies as described above and (2) the possibility to analyze DRM licenses and to use our observation mechanisms to enforce them.

Finally, there is a need for more interoperability among DRM technologies in order to increase user acceptance. One problem in this area is that different mechanisms use different languages for describing their licenses [18,10]. There are two possible solutions to this problem. One solution is to standardize a language for describing licenses and use it for all developed mechanisms. However, such a solution is currently not on the horizon. The other solution is to translate between the different RELs. Some attempts have been made to directly translate between RELs (e.g., [8]). In contrast, by defining translations from OSL to the different RELs and vice versa, we enable the use of OSL as an intermediate language for translating between different RELs. This approach scales up well and is not only limited to XrML and ODRL, but also other RELs like PDRL [1] or Octopus [19]. However, we have not yet defined the translations for more languages; this remains as future work.

4.2 Specification and Implementation

We have implemented the translations between OSL and a subset of ODRL as well as between OSL and a subset of XrML. The XrML subset used is comparable to the ODRL subset, which is described below. As the translations for ODRL and XrML are similar, we focus here on ODRL and use this example to point out the strengths and weaknesses of our approach. More details about translating ODRL into OSL are published in a technical report [15].

A Brief Introduction to ODRL. ODRL [28] is an XML-based language for describing the terms and conditions of using intellectual property in digital form. We give a short, incomplete overview of ODRL. ODRL subjects are intellectual property *rights holders* and *end users*. Data objects are called *assets*. ODRL expresses *offers*, which are proposals from rights holders for specific rights on their assets, and *agreements*, which result when two parties commit to a set of rights on an asset. Agreements in ODRL can be compared to obligations, while offers are outside of the scope of this paper.

A *permission* is the right to perform certain *activities* with an asset and can be accompanied by *constraints* and *requirements*. Examples of activities are *play*, *print*, *display*, and *execute*. In our model, these activities correspond to usages. Constraints express conditions that the end user must satisfy to be allowed to perform the corresponding activity, and requirements specify additional actions that the end user must execute, such as payments. An example for an ODRL license is provided at the end of this section.

The ODRLc Subset of ODRL. We have defined the translations for a subset of ODRL to keep the definition of the translation reasonably sized and because

ODRL contains concepts that are not within the scope of OSL. The subset we consider, ODRLc ("ODRL compact"), is very close to the REL used by the Open Mobile Alliance (OMA) [22] and therefore of practical relevance. We have introduced a few structural simplifications with regard to the OMA REL that do not limit the expressiveness of the language. Also, we have not included those elements of the OMA REL that are not part of ODRL. However, we also support a few ODRL concepts that are not included in the OMA REL. For example, we have included a reduced set of payment requirements in ODRLc to illustrate that such requirements can easily be expressed in OSL. We also support device constraints, which restrict the set of devices that are allowed to perform a usage. A more detailed description of ODRLc can be found in [15].

Translating ODRLc into OSL. The translation from ODRLc to OSL is defined for all ODRLc licenses because OSL is strictly more expressive than ODRLc. Since both OSL policies and ODRL licenses are tree structured, we define the translation top-down on the ODRLc tree. Because an ODRL license specifies rights, we use a _permitonlyevname_ expression to prohibit all usages not explicitly permitted in the license. In ODRL, all specified constraints and requirements must be simultaneously satisfied and therefore form a logical conjunction. In OSL, we create a separate obligation for each of them. Since all obligations inside an OSL policy are implicitly conjoined, the conjunction of the constraints and requirements naturally follows.

Translating OSL into ODRLc. Because OSL is strictly more expressive than ODRLc as mentioned above, only a subset of OSL can be translated to ODRLc. Identifying this subset is the difficult part of defining the translation. We take a pragmatic approach to this by employing pattern matching over syntax. For example, all formulae of the form $(sid, \underline{repmax}(n, E_{fst}(ue)))$, where sid is a subject ID, $n \in \mathbb{N}$, and ue is a usage event, are translated into a <count> constraint in ODRL, which expresses a cardinality condition. The problem is that $(subjA, \underline{and}(\underline{repmax}(n, E_{fst}((backup, \{(object, mov)\}))), \underline{true}))$ is semantically a cardinality condition as well, but not a syntactic instance of the above pattern. Because syntactic pattern matching requires obligations to be in an implicitly defined canonical form, the translation for this obligation is therefore undefined.

   This limitation on the translation could be lifted by extending it to semantically equivalent representations. This would, however, involve computationally expensive deductive reasoning. In particular, since LTL can be completely embedded into OSL and checking the semantic equivalence of two LTL formulae is PSPACE-complete [29], checking the semantic equivalence of two OSL formulae is PSPACE-hard.

Example. We now show an example of a translation from ODRLc to OSL. The corresponding ODRLc license is shown below. This license states that _Alice_ may play the movie _mov_ for at most 5 hours, and only on player _pl_. Furthermore, _Alice_ may create at most one backup of the movie. No usage other than _play_ and _backup_ is allowed.

```
<o-ex:rights>
  <o-ex:agreement>
    <o-ex:asset>
      <o-ex:context><o-dd:uid>mov</o-dd:uid></o-ex:context>
    </o-ex:asset>
    <o-ex:permission>
      <o-dd:play>
        <o-ex:constraint><o-dd:accumulated>P5h</o-dd:accumulated></o-ex:constraint>
        <o-ex:constraint><o-dd:hardware>
          <o-ex:context><o-dd:uid>pl</o-dd:uid></o-ex:context>
        </o-dd:hardware></o-ex:constraint>
        <o-ex:constraint><o-dd:individual>Alice</o-dd:individual></o-ex:constraint>
      </o-dd:play>
      <o-dd:backup>
        <o-ex:constraint><o-dd:count>1</o-dd:count></o-ex:constraint>
        <o-ex:constraint><o-dd:individual>Alice</o-dd:individual></o-ex:constraint>
      </o-dd:backup>
    </o-ex:permission>
  </o-ex:agreement>
</o-ex:rights>
```

This ODRL license is translated into the OSL policy shown below. The first obligation prohibits all usages except *play* and *backup*. The second one corresponds to the <accumulated> constraint on the *play* action, the third one to the <hardware> constraint on the *play* action, and the fourth obligation to the <count> constraint on the *backup* action. In the OSL policy shown below, we assume that the time step in a trace is set to 1 hour.

$$
\begin{aligned}
(\{ \\
&(play, usage, \{(object, ObjID), (device, DevID)\}), \\
&(backup, usage, \{(object, ObjID), (device, DevID)\}), \\
\}, \{ \\
&(Alice, \underline{permitonlyevname}(\{play, backup\}, \{(object, mov)\})), \\
&(Alice, \underline{repmax}(5, E_{all}((play, \{(object, mov)\})))), \\
&(Alice, \underline{permitonlyparam}(\{pl\}, device, play, \{(object, mov)\})), \\
&(Alice, \underline{repmax}(1, E_{fst}((backup, \{(object, mov)\})))) \\
\})
\end{aligned}
$$

Summary of the Results. While the translation from ODRLc to OSL is total, the translation in the other direction is only partial. This is partly because OSL is more expressive than ODRLc and partly because the translation is defined by syntactic pattern matching. Using deductive reasoning to compute semantic equivalence classes would allow us to extend the translation, but this is computationally expensive. The same issues also apply to the translations that we have implemented for XrML.

The translation from ODRLc to OSL yields a formal semantics for a significant subset of ODRL. Within the limitations mentioned above, the translations from OSL to ODRL and XrML enable us to issue licenses for existing DRM mechanisms based on OSL policies. We have implemented both translations in Java. On the basis of the OSL-XrML translator, we have implemented a proof of concept that automatically creates licenses for Microsoft's RMS [20] from OSL policies.

The translations between OSL and ODRL/XrML can be composed to translate between ODRL and XrML, using OSL as an intermediate language. We have done this using the above mentioned implementations. Of course, this only works for requirements that can be expressed in both RELs. For the subsets we have defined for ODRL and XrML, this is not a problem because they are similar in their expressivity. But generally, this issue must be taken into account.

There is one more additional point worth noting: XrML contains so-called *stateful conditions* that use an external piece of data to store the effect of previous usages on the license. For example, cardinality conditions may be specified with the help of an external counter that has to be checked each time a usage is attempted. This approach mixes the specification of a requirement (how many times a usage may be performed in total) with the implementation of its enforcement (where the counter is located and when it must be decremented). Because OSL is a pure specification language, we have excluded state references from the XrML subset we use in the translations and only specify the initial values instead.

5   Related Work

Some specification languages for usage control requirements have been developed in the area of privacy protection. P3P [30] is a language for stating the privacy practices of websites. It is tailored to this domain and not extensible. EPAL [2] is a more flexible language for privacy policies that adds the purpose of use to the access decision. It also allows for obligations, but does not treat them in detail. We have already mentioned XrML [31] and ODRL [28] as the most prominent policy languages in DRM.

There have been previous attempts to give a formal semantics to ODRL and XrML. Pucella and Weissman [27] give a formal semantics to a subset of ODRL by a translation into many-sorted first-order logic. They treat temporal aspects rather rudimentarily and the duration of events is not considered. Furthermore, their semantics is not suited for monitoring the adherence to policies at runtime. Holzer et al. [17] present a semantics based on automata. They present automata for different conditions but do not define how they compose for multiple rights and conditions. For example, the automaton presented on the lower half of page 7 cannot cope with events other than *display*. García et al. [9] formalize ODRL policies using the OWL-based framework IPROnto [7], which is an ontology for DRM. Like other approaches, this formalization cannot, in its current state, be used for checking the adherence to complex policies at runtime and does not consider the duration of usage. We are only aware of one formal semantics that has been defined for XrML. Halpern and Weissman [12] have chosen an approach similar to the one for ODRL mentioned above [27], with similar strengths and weaknesses.

Gunter et al. [11] present a semantics for DRM licenses that is based on sequences of events, but they do not apply this semantics to any existing REL. Chong et al. [5] present LicenseScript, a language for expressing DRM licenses. The main difference between LicenseScript and OSL is that OSL is a language for specifying policies (i.e., we describe which executions are allowed), whereas

LicenseScript can express complicated licenses (e.g., involving cardinalities) only by including instructions that concern the enforcement of the licenses (i.e., decreasing counters). Therefore, licenses expressed in LicenseScript do not explicitly tell the data consumer what is allowed and what is not allowed. Pucella and Weissman [26] present a logic for reasoning about digital rights based on temporal logic. The main focus of their work is to define whether a set of policies permits or obligates certain actions. Only one action is permitted per time step and neither temporal conditions nor cardinality conditions can be expressed conveniently. Barth et al. [3] have developed a privacy policy language that is based on LTL and has data subjects as a central concept. Their language is only concerned with the distribution of data.

UCON [23,32] extends access control with the concepts of decision continuity and attribute mutability. In UCON, an access can last for some duration with multiple related and subsequent actions, for example, performing calculations on data on a server. Access decisions can be made before or during the access (decision continuity) and subject or object attributes can change during an access (attribute mutability). While in OSL, we specify what the data consumer is allowed to do (for example, playing a movie for at most 20 minutes), UCON can be used to specify how a mechanism counts the elapsed time and compares it to the maximal allowed value. In this regard, UCON is complementary to our approach because it can be used for implementing mechanisms on different devices. What UCON cannot cover, however, are action requirements. For example, UCON-based mechanisms cannot enforce that a piece of data is deleted after 30 days, independently of whether it is used during that time. Also, we can use OSL to specify that the above movie may be played for maximal 20 minutes even if different players are involved, which cannot be expressed in UCON.

Cooper and Montague [6] discuss differences between ODRL and XrML and suggest that the usage of profiles that reduce a language to the part that can be translated into the other language is a good way to proceed. Other interoperability-related work is surveyed in §4.1.

6   Conclusions

We have presented OSL, a rich language that can specify policies from many different application areas. We have determined the usage control requirements that OSL supports in dedicated requirements studies. The semantics of OSL is based on temporal logic, which enables the use of different analysis methods and runtime monitoring techniques, as has been shown in related work [14,15]. The translations that we have presented allow us to enforce, in part, policies specified in OSL using existing enforcement mechanisms from the DRM area. Our goal is to be able to flexibly employ different mechanisms for enforcing OSL policies, depending on which mechanism is applicable to a given requirement. The proof of concept that we have implemented for RMS is just a first step in this direction. The formal semantics we get for the RELs goes beyond what has been previously defined for XrML and ODRL and we have also provided a step towards more interoperability in DRM.

We conclude by discussing current limitations of OSL and suggest directions for future work. From the types of conditions we have identified in our requirements study, OSL cannot fully cover environment conditions. Some environment conditions can be expressed with the help of event parameters but others would require the introduction of subject attributes into our model, which is future work. The fact that OSL uses abstract events instead of concrete system events comes at a cost: the need to define the semantics of these events. One problem here is that the mapping from abstract events like "play" or "display" to concrete events of a system is usually done by the mechanism vendors and is not transparent. This complicates the selection of suitable mechanisms for a given requirement. The definition of dedicated ontologies for events is an area for future work. It is not entirely clear how to assign a semantics to events and, while it seems desirable to have device-independent policies, the device-specific semantics cannot be ignored. Additional areas for future work are addressing rights propagation, defining a translation based on semantic equivalence classes of OSL policies, defining translation schemes for additional RELs, and the implementation of these translations. Last but not least, the ideas presented in this paper should be evaluated in case studies.

References

1. Adobe: Portable Document Rights Language (PDRL) Specification (2005), www.adobe.com/devnet/livecycle/policyserver/articles/pdrl.pdf
2. Backes, M., Pfitzmann, B., Schunter, M.: A toolkit for managing enterprise privacy policies. In: Snekkenes, E., Gollmann, D. (eds.) ESORICS 2003. LNCS, vol. 2808, pp. 162–180. Springer, Heidelberg (2003)
3. Barth, A., Datta, A., Mitchell, J.C., Nissenbaum, H.: Privacy and contextual integrity: Framework and applications. In: Proc. of the 2006 IEEE Symposium on Security and Privacy, pp. 184–198. IEEE Computer Society Press, Los Alamitos (2006)
4. Bettini, C., Jajodia, S., Wang, X.S., Wijesekera, D.: Provisions and obligations in policy rule management. Journal of Network and System Management 11(3), 351–372 (2003)
5. Chong, C.N., Corin, R.J., Doumen, J.M., Etalle, S., Hartel, P.H., Law, Y.W., Tokmakoff, A.: Licensescript: A logical language for digital rights management. Annals of telecommunications special issue on Network and Information systems security 61(3-4), 284–331 (2006)
6. Cooper, B., Montague, P.: Translation of rights expressions. In: Proc. the 4th Australasian Information Security Workshop, pp. 137–144 (2005)
7. Delgado, J., Gallego, I., Llorente, S., Garcá, R.: IPROnto: An Ontology for Digital Rights Management. In: Proc. Jurix 2003: The Sixteenth Annual Conference on Legal Knowledge and Information Systems, pp. 111–120 (2003)
8. Delgado, J., Prados, J., Rodriguez, E.: A new Approach for Interoperability between ODRL and MPEG-21 REL. In: Proc. 2nd Intl. ODRL Workshop (2005)
9. García, R., Gil, R., Gallego, I., Delgado, J.: Formalising ODRL Semantics using Web Ontologies. In: Proc. 2nd Intl. ODRL Workshop, pp. 1–10 (2005)
10. Geer, D.: Digital Rights Technology Sparks Interoperability Concerns. IEEE Computer 37, 20–22 (2004)

11. Gunter, C.A., Weeks, S.T., Wright, A.K.: Models and languages for digital rights. In: Proc. 34th Annual Hawaii Intl. Conference on System Sciences (2001)
12. Halpern, J., Weissman, V.: A Formal Foundation for XrML. In: Proc. 17th IEEE Computer Security Foundations Workshop, pp. 251–265. IEEE Computer Society Press, Los Alamitos (2004)
13. Hilty, M., Pretschner, A., Akeret, F.: Anforderungen für verteilte Nutzungskontrolle. Technical report, Siemens Schweiz AG (November 2005)
14. Hilty, M., Pretschner, A., Basin, D., Schaefer, C., Walter, T.: Monitors for usage control. In: Proc. Joint iTrust and PST Conferences on Privacy, Trust Management and Security (2007)
15. Hilty, M., Pretschner, A., Walter, T., Schaefer, C.: A system model and an obligation lanugage for distributed usage control. Technical Report I-ST-20, DoCoMo Euro-Labs (2006)
16. Hilty, M., Pretschner, A., Walter, T., Schaefer, C.: Usage control requirements in mobile and ubiquitous computing applications. In: Proc. International Conference on Systems and Networks Communication, p. 27 (2006)
17. Holzer, M., Katzenbeisser, S., Schallhart, C.: Towards a Formal Semantics for ODRL. In: Proc. 1st International workshop on ODRL, pp. 137–148 (2004)
18. Koenen, R.H., Lacy, J., MacKay, M., Mitchell, S.: The long march to interoperable digital rights management. Proceedings of the IEEE 92(6), 883–897 (2004)
19. Marlin Developer Community: The Role of Octopus in Marlin (2006), http://www.marlin-community.com/images/wp/RoleofOctopusinMarlin.pdf
20. Microsoft Corporation: Technical overview of windows rights management services for windows server 2003 (April 2005), available at http://www.microsoft.com/windowsserver2003/techinfo/overview/rmenterprisewp.mspx
21. Open Mobile Alliance: DRM Architecture (March 2006), available at www.openmobilealliance.org/release_program/drm_v2_0.html
22. Open Mobile Alliance: DRM Rights Expression Language (March 2006), available at www.openmobilealliance.org/release_program/drm_v2_0.html
23. Park, J., Sandhu, R.: The UCON ABC Usage Control Model. ACM Transactions on Information and Systems Security 7, 128–174 (2004)
24. Pnueli, A.: The temporal semantics of concurrent programs. In: Proc. International Sympoisum on Semantics of Concurrent Computation, pp. 1–20 (1979)
25. Pretschner, A., Hilty, M., Basin, D.: Distributed Usage Control. CACM (September 2006)
26. Pucella, R., Weissman, V.: A logic for reasoning about digital rights. In: Proc. 15th IEEE Computer Security Foundations Workshop, p. 282. IEEE Computer Society Press, Los Alamitos (2002)
27. Pucella, R., Weissman, V.: A Formal Foundation for ODRL. In: Proc. Workshop on Issues in the Theory of Security (2004)
28. Iannella, R. (ed.): Open Digital Rights Language - Version 1.1 (August 2002), odrl.net/1.1/ODRL-11.pdf
29. Sistla, A.P., Clarke, E.M.: The complexity of propositional linear temporal logics. Journal of the ACM 32(3), 733–749 (1985)
30. W3C: The Platform for Privacy Preferences 1.1 (P3P1.1) Specification (2005)
31. Wang, X., Lao, G., DeMartini, T., Reddy, H., Nguyen, M., Valenzuela, E.: XrML – eXtensible rights Markup Language. In: ACM workshop on XML security, pp. 71–79. ACM Press, New York (2002)
32. Zhang, X., Park, J., Parisi-Presicce, F., Sandhu, R.: A logical specification for usage control. In: Proc. 9th ACM symposium on access control models and technologies, pp. 1–10. ACM Press, New York (2004)

Countering Statistical Disclosure with Receiver-Bound Cover Traffic

Nayantara Mallesh and Matthew Wright

Department of Computer Science and Engineering,
The University of Texas at Arlington
{nayantara.mallesh,mwright}@uta.edu
http://isec.uta.edu

Abstract. Anonymous communications provides an important privacy service by keeping passive eavesdroppers from linking communicating parties. However, using long-term statistical analysis of traffic sent to and from such a system, it is possible to link senders with their receivers. Cover traffic is an effective, but somewhat limited, counter strategy against this attack. Earlier work in this area proposes that privacy-sensitive users generate and send cover traffic to the system. However, users are not online all the time and cannot be expected to send consistent levels of cover traffic, drastically reducing the impact of cover traffic. We propose that the mix generate cover traffic that mimics the sending patterns of users in the system. This *receiver-bound cover* helps to make up for users that aren't there, confusing the attacker. We show through simulation how this makes it difficult for an attacker to discern cover from real traffic and perform attacks based on statistical analysis. Our results show that receiver-bound cover substantially increases the time required for these attacks to succeed. When our approach is used in combination with user-generated cover traffic, the attack takes a very long time to succeed.

Keywords: privacy-enhancing technologies, cover traffic, anonymity.

1 Introduction

Anonymity systems are fundamentally challenging to build on top of the existing Internet architecture. The simplest and most secure approaches require all participants to send messages at the same rates, e.g. one message per given time interval. Users without a message to send must send fake messages, known as *cover traffic* or *dummies*, to ensure anonymity for themselves as well as for others. This provides no allowance for the realities of node failure, network partition, and simple user unwillingness to provide so many messages. Additionally, the costs of these messages can cause the system to not scale well with the number of users. In anonymity, this is a substantial matter for security, as the greater the number of users, the larger the crowd into which one can blend [1].

Existing implementations based on the mixes paradigm introduced by Chaum [2] remove this unrealistic requirement for constant participation, but

J. Biskup and J. Lopez (Eds.): ESORICS 2007, LNCS 4734, pp. 547–562, 2007.
© Springer-Verlag Berlin Heidelberg 2007

at a cost to their security. The changing group of users can be observed, along with outgoing messages, leading to powerful *intersection attacks*. In these attacks, differences in the membership of the set of users are matched with the differences in the message-sending behavior, leading to links between users and their receivers. Effectively, the attacker can observe information leaks over time.

The *statistical disclosure attack* is a particularly effective form of intersection, in which the attacker isolates his attack against a single user, which we will call Alice. The statistics used in this attack are the frequencies with which each recipient gets a message from the system. By taking differences between the frequencies observed when Alice is active and those observed when she is not active, the attacker can estimate Alice's contribution to the recipient set. This attack has been studied previously and is well-understood [3,4,5].

In this work, we explore defenses against intersection attacks such as statistical disclosure. In particular, we study the relative effectiveness of different defenses, and we present the first in-depth study of the idea of sending cover traffic to recipients that are outside of the system. To date, the possible defenses against intersection attacks have been limited to two basic techniques: the user sending more cover traffic into the network and increasing random delays for messages in the system. We explore the idea of how the presence and cover traffic of other users surprisingly fails to provide any help to the user. We also demonstrate that, with some additional cost, the system can significantly improve its defense against intersection attacks by sending dummies to recipients outside of the system. As this may not be appreciated by all recipients, we discuss ways in which this technique could be made practical.

In the next section, we describe our model and the statistical disclosure attack in more detail. We then motivate the two types of cover traffic that we are studying and analyze their effects in Section 3. Section 4 presents our simulation model and results. Discussion and analysis of the feasibility and costs of the cover traffic methods is presented in Section 6. We discuss related work in Section 7 and then conclude.

2   Statistical Disclosure

The *Statistical Disclosure Attack (SDA)* described by Danezis [4] is a long-term intersection attack against mix-based systems. SDA is an extension of the *disclosure attack* introduced by Kesdogan [3]. In this section, we first explain the network model used, then describe statistical disclosure attacks. We discuss why cover traffic delays statistical disclosure and how it can be used to counter this attack.

2.1   Model

Let us assume that there are N senders that wish to communicate with a set of R recipients using a mix network. We will generally set $R = N$ for simplicity, but the relationship between senders and receivers is many-to-many. The mix network may consist of a single mix or a network of connected mixes. The attacker is a global adversary who can observe all links from senders to the mix and all links from the mix to recipients. The target of the adversary is the sender Alice and the adversary's aim is to expose the set of recipients with whom Alice communicates.

In each round, b senders, sometimes including Alice, send messages to a set of recipients via the mix. The attacker observes a number of rounds, including rounds with and without Alice's participation, and tries to identify Alice's recipients. The attacker can observe only the incoming and outgoing links from the mix and cannot observe activity inside the mix network. This assumption is for the simplicity of the model, as there are many configurations for a mix network, but also because the statistical disclosure attack is effective without observations of activity in the network. We abstract away the mix-system details and refer to a single mix or a cascade of mixes as a *mix*.

2.2   Statistical Disclosure

Danezis' SDA is a probability-based approach to the disclosure attack and is a practical way to expose Alice's set of recipients [4]. The attacker makes observations in a number of rounds in which Alice participates and in each round records the recipient set in an observation vector $\overrightarrow{o}$. Each element of $\overrightarrow{o}$ contains the probability that the corresponding recipient has received a message from Alice in that round. The attacker models the behavior of senders other than Alice, known as the *background*, by recording their activity when Alice does not participate. Vector $\overrightarrow{u}$ captures the background model, in which a given element of $\overrightarrow{u}$ is the probability with which background senders send to the corresponding recipient. The attacker records $\overrightarrow{o}$ values over a large number of observations and takes the mean of $\overrightarrow{o}$ as $\overline{O}$. The mean of the background traffic observations is obtained and stored in $\overline{U}$. Alice's likely set of recipients can be determined by solving the below equation for vector $\overrightarrow{v}$:

$$\overline{O} = \frac{\overline{m}.\overrightarrow{v} + (\overline{n} - \overline{m})\overrightarrow{u}}{\overline{n}}$$

Here $\overline{m}$ is the average number of messages sent by Alice in each round and $\overline{n}$ is the average total number of messages sent by all senders, including Alice, in each round. The vector $\overrightarrow{v}$ denotes the sending behavior of Alice. Each element of $\overrightarrow{v}$ is the probability that Alice sends a message to the corresponding recipient in some round. An element of $\overrightarrow{v}$ will have a value of 0 for a recipient who is not in Alice's recipient set and will have a value greater than 0 and less than 1 for a recipient who belongs to Alice's recipient set. $\overrightarrow{v}$ is obtained from the above equation by substituting $\overline{U}$, the mean of background traffic, and $\overline{O}$, the mean of attacker observations in each round. The indices with the highest values in $\overrightarrow{v}$ correspond to the most likely recipients of Alice.

Mathewson and Dingledine extend SDA to pool mixes [5]. Their work relaxes some of the assumptions made in the original work [4]. A pool mix, as described in [6], operates by dispersing incoming messages from a given round across a number of later rounds. In each round, the mix chooses a set of messages with uniform probability and sends them to their respective recipients. When Alice sends dummy messages along with real messages, it becomes more difficult for the attacker to successfully perform statistical analysis. Dummy messages increase the average number of messages from the sender per round, as seen by the attacker, which substantially affects the results of statistical analysis. The attacker needs more observations to compensate for the presence of dummies and hence it takes a significantly longer time for the attacker to correctly identify Alice's set of recipients.

We model the relationships between senders and receivers as a scale-free network, in which the distribution of node degrees follows a power law relationship [7]. This means that most senders communicate with a few well-known recipients in addition to other less-known recipients. The well-known recipients hence communicate with many senders and thus receive more messages during their communication lifetime. Background senders tend to send more messages to their more well-known recipients rather than to the lesser-known ones. Alice, however, sends messages equally to all of her recipients.

In reality, most senders are not online all of the time. It is difficult for many users to consistently send cover traffic, as it requires them to be online all the time, without fail. This problem is potentially alleviated when the mix carries the onus of sending cover traffic. In the rest of this paper, we use the model of Mathewson and Dingledine to study the effectiveness of padding generated by the users and by the mix.

3   Cover Traffic

Cover traffic consists of dummy messages that are inserted into the network along with real user messages. Dummy messages have long been recognized as a useful tool to increase anonymity provided by mix-based systems. In the context of our model, cover traffic can be classified into three types based on where it is generated. *user cover* is cover traffic generated by Alice herself and *background cover* is cover traffic generated by other senders connecting to the mix. On the other hand, *receiver-bound cover (RB)* is generated by the mix and sent to message recipients.

Mathewson et.al. have shown that user cover helps delay statistical analysis [5]. When Alice generates cover traffic with a geometric distribution, she can significantly delay SDA. A more effective approach is for Alice to send a threshold number of messages in every round. If the number of real messages is less than the threshold, then Alice inserts dummy messages to compensate for the shortage. Both of these approaches become more effective as the mix exhibits higher delay variability, since the number of possibilities that the attacker must consider increases. Even if the sender is online 100% of the time, however, sender-originated dummy packets alone are not enough to protect against statistical analysis.

3.1   Background Cover Traffic

Background cover is created when many mix users generate dummies along with their real messages. Cover traffic from users other than Alice could be seen as providing cover for Alice's messages. Note that the users have a strong incentive to provide these dummies, as it helps to protect their own privacy. As we show in Section 5, this can be very effective in confusing a naive attacker. However, a slightly more sophisticated attacker can account for background cover and reduce its effectiveness.

We now describe how the naive attacker proceeds in the presence of background cover traffic. The attacker uses the Equation 2.2 to find $\overrightarrow{v}$ which contains an estimate of Alice's recipients. In each round, the attacker observes a number of messages entering and exiting the mix. He estimates the number of (i) Alice messages exiting the mix, n_{Alice} and (ii) the number of background messages exiting the mix per round, $n_{Background}$. These estimates are calculated from the mix's delay policy and on the number of messages seen entering the mix from Alice and from the other users. The attacker records the set of recipients who receive messages in each round in $\overrightarrow{r}$, which contains an element for every recipient in the system. $\overrightarrow{r}[i]$ contains the number of messages received by the ith recipient in a particular round. $\overline{O}$ is updated each round as follows:

$$\overline{O}[i] = \frac{\overrightarrow{r}[i] * n_{Alice}}{n_{Alice} + n_{Background}}$$

When background dummies are sent, the attacker sees more messages entering the mix. The dummies get dropped inside the mix and do not exit the mix along with real messages. The attacker, however, expects the messages to exit the mix and wrongly estimates the value of $n_{Background}$. As a result the calculation of $\overline{O}$ is upset, thereby affecting the number of rounds to correctly identify Alice's recipients.

To counter background cover, the attacker can discount away a percentage of incoming messages that he knows are dummies. We assume that the background user's policies for sending dummies are known to the attacker. This can be reasonable in many systems, as only the aggregate behavior is needed. Such policies may be observed by subtracting the number of real output messages from the number of input messages over a period of time in which Alice is not active. We show in Section 5 that background dummies do not help against this informed attacker, and that Alice cannot rely on help from her fellow users.

3.2   Receiver-Bound Cover Traffic

Receiver-bound (RB) cover consists of dummy messages generated by the mix. The dummies are inserted into outgoing user traffic in every round. The mix chooses the recipients of cover traffic uniformly and randomly from the list of recipients. $\overline{O}[i]$ contains the probability that a message received by the ith recipient has originated at Alice. The attacker updates elements in $\overline{O}$ in every round according to Equation 3.1. When RB dummies are present, elements in $\overline{O}$ are wrongly updated for messages that were in fact never sent by any sender. This upsets the attackers' statistical calculations. In order for the attack to be successful, the number of rounds the attacker must observe increases significantly. We discuss the practical issues with this approach in Section 6.

4   Simulation

Using the basic sender-mix-receiver model described in Section 2, we simulated the process of sending messages and the corresponding SDA. We first discuss the three main elements of the simulation design, which are the attacker algorithm, the generation of real traffic, and our metrics for attacker success. We then describe how we generate cover traffic.

4.1   Simulator Design

We built our simulations around the core simulator used by Mathewson and Dingledine, and we refer the reader to that paper for further detail [5].

Attacker Algorithm. The attacker algorithm is based on the statistical analysis approach *Attacking pool mixes and mix networks* described in [5]. Beyond this, we assume that the attacker makes reasonable adjustments to the algorithm in response to changes in the system, such as adjustments to background dummies described in Section 3.

Real Message Generation. Major elements in the simulated generation of real messages include:

- Background Traffic: To ensure comparability with previous empirical work, the number of messages sent by the background follows a normal distribution with mean 125 and standard deviation of 12.5. Additionally, we consider a more active set of users, with means of 1700 and 9000 messages per round. The senders follow a scale-free model in sending to recipients. We first created a scale-free network and then created a weighted recipient distribution for background senders. The weighted distribution allows background senders to send more messages to popular recipients. A uniform recipient distribution is created for Alice, which allows Alice to send uniformly to all of her recipients.
- Alice's Traffic: Alice has a recipient set of 32 recipients. In each round she sends messages to recipients chosen with uniform probability from this set. Alice generates real messages according to a geometric distribution with a distribution parameter of 0.6, which means that she sends about 1.5 real messages per round.
- Mix Behavior: In each round, the pool mix receives messages from a number of senders. Alice may or may not participate in a given round. At the end of each round, the mix chooses outgoing messages from the pool with equal probability. P_{delay} is the probability that a message in the mix pool remains in the pool until it is sent out in a later round. The mix applies P_{delay} to each message in the pool and decides if the message will exit the mix in the current round or not [6]. For our simulations we varied P_{delay} from 0.1 to 0.9. For simulations where P_{delay} does not vary, we set $P_{delay} = 0.1$.

Measuring Attacker Success. For most of our experiments, we measure the number of rounds that the attacker takes to correctly identify ten of Alice's recipients. This is a deviation from prior work, which chose to determine when the attacker correctly identified all 32 of her recipients. The latter is, in our opinion, an unnecessarily high bar for the attacker to meet. In particular, we discovered that finding the final recipient was a particularly challenging task that took many additional rounds of communication in most experiments. Worse, the variance for obtaining this final recipient is quite high, as it may depend on just a few messages that are sent with low probability.

We propose the lower threshold of ten recipients, although arbitrary, as a point at which the attacker has identified a substantial fraction of Alice's recipients. At this point, the attacker can correctly identify not only the popular members of Alice's recipient set, but also several of the less popular members as well. The attacker may not have the full profile that he seeks, but some of Alice's privacy has been lost, as the attacker has some picture of Alice's communication patterns. Since the attack could take many rounds, a partial picture may be all that the attacker could attain in a reasonable time frame.

It should be noted that we stop all runs after one million rounds. This could equate to almost one hundred and fifteen years, at one hour per round, or nearly two years at one minute per round. If the attacker cannot identify 10 of Alice's recipients in this time, the attack is taking very long. Even if the attacker is that patient, and Alice is that consistent, we focus our attention on stopping the attacker from defeating the system in a faster time frame. When we have strong methods for doing that, longer term attacks can be considered.

4.2   Cover Traffic Scenarios

The simulations in [5] focus mainly on the effects of user cover traffic. In this study, we describe the effects of RB cover and background cover. We use three scenarios to evaluate the effect of cover traffic on statistical analysis.

Alice and Background Cover Traffic. We first study how dummy messages sent by users other than Alice affects statistical analysis. We set $N = 2^{16}$ be the number of senders. Each of the $N - 1$ other senders apart from Alice, called background senders, generate 0 or more dummy messages in every round. Senders choose the number of dummies according to a geometric distribution with a parameter varying from 0.1 to 0.9. This means each sender sends between 0.11 to 9 dummy messages per round on average.

Alice also generates a number of dummy messages in each round that she participates. Like other senders, Alice follows a geometric distribution to select the number of dummies to send per round. Alice's dummy parameter, P_{dummy}, is varied from 0.1 to 0.9. In simulations where Alice's dummy traffic does not vary, we set P_{dummy} to 0.6, which is about 1.5 messages/round. The geometric distribution parameters for Alice dummies and background dummies are independent of each other. Cover traffic generated by senders is sent to the mix like real traffic. The mix can recognize real messages from dummies and drops all dummies that it receives. Hence, dummies sent from the users are dropped inside the mix network and are not propagated to any receivers.

Receiver-bound Cover Traffic. We also evaluate how RB cover traffic originating at the mix impacts statistical analysis. At the end of each round, the
mix selects a subset of messages in its pool and sends them to their respective
recipients. In addition to the real messages, the mix adds a number of dummy
messages to the outbound stream. The recipients for the dummy messages are
chosen uniformly at random from the set of recipients. For our simulations we
used the following dummy generation policy at the mix:

Receiver-bound Cover Policy. We ran simulations with the number of dummy
messages per round at 100%, 200%, and 300% additional traffic. In all cases, the
mix observes the number of real messages in each round and sends between one
to three dummy messages for each real message, according to the amount of RB
cover traffic desired. Fractional amounts are possible by sending according to a
uniform distribution. We use these fixed values for simplicity; in reality, the mix
must choose a random number of RB dummies per round based on a function
of the number of real messages exiting the mix in that round.

The recipient of each dummy message is chosen uniformly at random from the
set of recipients. This is somewhat unrealistic, as the mixes may not know the
full set, but a reasonable approximation can be constructed by using previously
observed recipients and a selection of recipient addresses from the general population. Dummy messages travel from the mix to the recipient and are observed as
part of the outgoing traffic by the passive attacker. However, since the attacker
cannot distinguish dummy messages from real messages, dummies are included
in the attackers analysis. Dummy messages reach the destination nodes and are
dropped by the recipient.

Alice and Receiver-bound Cover. In this scenario, Alice sends cover traffic
to the mix along with her real messages. These messages are dropped inside the
mix. The mix in turn generates dummy messages independent of Alice's dummy
messages. The mix dummies are sent out with real outbound user messages.

5   Results

In this section we present the results of our simulations. Please note the use of
logarithmic scales in our graphs.

5.1   Degree of Disclosure

It is easier for an attacker to obtain a subset of Alice's recipients than to find all
of Alice's recipients. We ran simulations to evaluate how different cover traffic
approaches affect the attackers ability to expose a number of Alice's recipients.
The graph in Figure 1 shows that as the attacker tries to expose more number of
recipients, the amount of observation rounds significantly increases. In comparison, Figure 2 shows that with more active background senders, the effectiveness
of cover traffic is more pronounced. When RB cover is used, the number of rounds
sharply increase when more than 70% of her recipients are exposed. When only

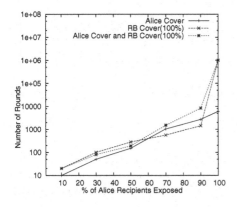
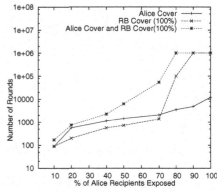

Fig. 1. Median rounds to identify a subset of Alice's recipients. Background (**BG**) volume = 125 messages/round. Mix delay probability P_{delay}=0.5.

Fig. 2. Median rounds to identify a subset of Alice's recipients. Background (**BG**) volume = 1700 messages/round. Mix delay probability P_{delay}=0.5.

Alice sends dummies, the rise in number of rounds is more modest when compared to when RB cover is also used. In our remaining experiments, we fix the number of recipients to be exposed at 30% which we simplify to 10 recipients.

5.2   Effect of Background Senders

The graph in Figure 3 illustrates the effect of background dummy messages on the number of rounds needed to correctly identify 10 of Alice's recipients. Alice generates dummies according to a geometric distribution. Alice's dummy distribution parameter varies from 0.1 to 0.9 as seen along the x-axis. The effect of background traffic volume (BG) is clearly visible in this graph. When $BG = 125$, the effect of background and Alice dummy messages is very low. In the case when $BG = 1700$, cover traffic has a greater impact. As Alice's dummy volume increases, the number of rounds needed to identify Alice's recipients increases. Further, we see that when the background senders also send cover traffic, it becomes increasingly difficult for the attacker to successfully identify Alice's recipients. When the background senders generate cover traffic at 10% of real traffic and Alice increases her dummy distribution parameter to 0.9, it takes more than one million rounds to correctly identify ten of Alice's recipients.

Attacker Adjustment. The attacker can counter the effect of background cover by estimating the number of dummies that the background sends per round. The attacker can observe the number of senders sending per round and has knowledge of their dummy policy. Once the estimate is obtained, the attacker simply has to subtract the number of estimated dummies from the number of observed background messages and continue as if there were no dummies. Figure 3 shows how attacker adjustment can completely negate the effect of background cover, even if background senders use 50% or 100% dummies.

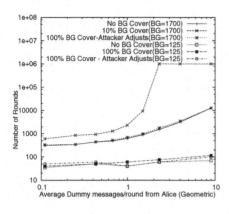 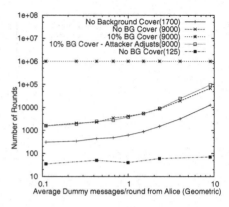

Fig. 3. Effect of Background Cover and Attacker Adjustment. Median rounds to guess 10 recipients.

Fig. 4. Effect of increase in Background Volume. Median rounds to guess 10 recipients.

The estimation of total background dummies per round is simple if all senders use the same dummy volume parameter. If senders use arbitrary dummy volume parameters, selected independently or even randomly varied over time, it becomes more difficult for the attacker to estimate the background dummy volume. The attacker could attempt to subtract the average system output from the average system input, as this provides an average of the sum of the background dummies plus Alice's dummies. This suggests another benefit of RB cover traffic, as the attacker would have greater difficulty in measuring the background cover traffic if the number of real messages is hidden in the system output as well. To gain this benefit, a dynamic amount of background cover traffic is required, rather than the fixed percentage of real traffic that we have studied in this paper.

Larger Number of Participants. Figure 4 shows that as the number of participants in the mix increases, the anonymity of individual participants correspondingly increases. In this simulation we increased the volume of background traffic from a normal distribution with mean 1700 to a normal distribution with mean 9000 messages per round. As observed in the graph, the time for the attacker to expose the same number of recipients more than doubles when participants send messages more frequently.

5.3   Effect of Receiver-Bound Cover

Figures 5 and 6 show the effect of RB cover traffic. The mix generates RB dummies equal to the number of real messages per round. We also studied whether the presence or absence of cover traffic from Alice would affect the number of rounds needed to identify Alice's recipients. As Figure 6 shows, cover traffic from Alice alone does not have a significant impact on number of rounds. When Alice sends dummies in the presence of RB cover the effects are more pronounced. Compared with Figure 5, we see the extent to which increasing the number of background

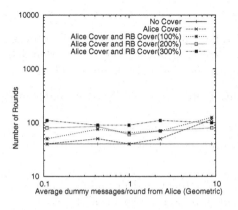

Fig. 5. Effect of RB cover traffic. Median rounds to guess 10 recipients. Background **(BG)** volume = 125 messages/round.

Fig. 6. Effect of RB cover traffic. Median rounds to guess 10 recipients. Background **(BG)** volume = 1700 messages/round.

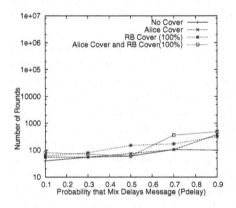

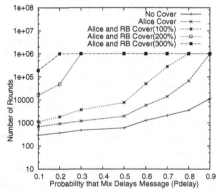

Fig. 7. Effect of increased delay distribution in the mix. Median rounds to guess 10 recipients. Background **(BG)** volume = 125 messages/round.

Fig. 8. Effect of increased delay distribution in the mix. Median rounds to guess 10 recipients. Background **(BG)** volume = 1700 messages/round.

messages helps improve the effectiveness of RB cover. When $BG = 125$, RB cover up to 300% does not significantly degrade the attack.

Figures 7 and 8 shows how the increase in delay distribution at the mix makes the attack harder. As before, there is greater benefit in increasing P_{delay} is when the background senders are more active. When the mix exhibits a delay probability higher than 0.5, the number of rounds increases more rapidly. When RB cover is increased to 200% and P_{delay} is more than 0.3, the attack takes more than one million rounds.

6   Discussion

In Section 5, we show how RB cover traffic can be used to successfully delay statistical analysis. We now touch upon the implementation aspects that RB cover should exhibit in real-world networks. There are three main considerations:

- Cover traffic must resemble real traffic in order for it to effectively anonymize user traffic.
- Receivers must tolerate the presense of dummy messages.
- The costs of the cover traffic should not be too high for the mixes or the receivers.

We study these both in the context of high-latency and low-latency mixes, as intersection attacks apply to both types of system. The two forms of cover traffic that we can use are encrypted and unencrypted, each with different advantages and applications.

6.1   Encrypted Dummies

Making cover traffic that looks like real traffic is challenging. Content, timing, and receiver selection must all appear to be the same as users' messages. Realistic content is relatively easy to generate if it is encrypted. For high-latency message delivery, such as anonymous email, we can craft packets that appear to be encrypted using PGP [8] or S-Mime [9] but with random payload bytes (in Radix-64). The receiver could attempt to decrypt the random payload and discard the email when it doesn't decrypt properly. There is some cost to the receiver in this case, although email clients could automate this process and remove most of the cost that the receiver actually notices.

One problem with only sending dummies designed to appear encrypted is that, if some of the real messages are not encrypted, the attacker can discount the presence of those encrypted messages. The attacker takes an estimate d' of the number of RB dummies (say, d), based on knowledge of the mixes' distribution of sending those dummies. If the total number of messages is n, and the number of unencrypted real messages is u, which are both measurable, then the chance that any packet with a random payload is a real message is estimated as $p'_{real} = (n - u - d')/(n - u)$. p'_{real} becomes a discounting factor on the additions to vector $\vec{o}$ in each round. The impact of this depends on the ratio of encrypted real messages to total real messages. If the ratio is high, we may be able to increase the number of dummies to compensate. If the ratio is low, i.e. there are few real encrypted messages, the attacker can discount much of the cover traffic.

6.2   Unencrypted Dummies

As real traffic may also be unencrypted, we propose the use of unencrypted dummies for some applications. There are many applications where users often do not use encryption, including email. In such a case, the mix has to generate cover traffic that carefully replicates real traffic. Messages with randomly-generated payloads would be useless since they can be easily differentiated from real traffic.

For email, messages must be constructed that look like real messages. Messages could be replayed, but the attacker could detect this. The techniques of email spammers could be employed fruitfully here, as copying real text passages, randomization, and receiver customization could all be used to avoid detection by automated systems. Further, the word choice can be designed to match non-spam emails perfectly, as the emails do not need to sell anything. This negates many of the standard Bayesian filtering methods for detecting spam [10,11,12]. While attackers could use humans to determine which messages are real, and which are dummies, this would be expensive and might require knowledge about the receiver.

A useful tool to help generate realistic dummies is the behavior of real users. In email, this could mean keeping a record of messages sent to each receiver, and then using this record to help generate new messages with appropriate key words.

6.3   Making Receiver-Bound Dummies Acceptable

Another critical issue in the use of RB cover traffic is their acceptance by the set of receivers. We have implicitly added some costs to receivers for the privacy of the senders, which may be classified as spam and cause the system to get unwanted negative attention. There are a number of issues and possible solutions which we touch on briefly here.

One way to cast to the problem is to note that RB cover traffic increases the anonymity of the senders connecting to the receivers. It is in the interest of anonymity for these users, so a receiver should allow anonymity networks to send cover traffic to it. Receivers who don't wish to help provide anonymous communications can block messages from the system. Some recipients block connections coming from anonymity systems like Tor [13] exit nodes. We could publish a 'White List' of servers that allow connections from the anonymity systems, so users can connect to those services via systems like Mixminion [14].

Another way to see the issue is in the light of spam. Today we see that a large percentage of network traffic consists of spam messages [15]. Receivers have developed a number of effective ways to drop or ignore spam messages. RB cover traffic would be a tiny addition to the millions of unwanted messages that flood the network. Further, these unwanted messages help enhance sender and receiver anonymity. Reciever-bound cover would be a small price to pay for the greater benefit of anonymity that it provides to network users. In some cases, especially in Web-browsing, the extra traffic could generally go unnoticed.

Anonymity systems have become popular over the past few years and the number of users participating these systems is continuing to grow. Currently, however, these users remain a small part of the global Internet community. The volume of traffic exiting anonymity systems is low as compared to non-anonymous traffic in the network. RB cover traffic generated to anonymize this fraction of Internet traffic would hardly burden the massive network resources that are in place.

7 Related Work

We are not the first to propose sending cover traffic to receivers. Berthold et. al have users send pre-generated dummy messages to the recipient when the sender is offline [16]. Mathewson and Dingledine suggest, and then dismiss, this approach in a footnote of their work on statistical disclosure [5]. They cite problems with the user sending to all receivers, which we avoid by having the mix generate the cover traffic. Shmatikov and Wang propose cover traffic sent to receivers to prevent active and passive timing analysis attacks in low-latency mix networks [17]. In their approach, senders generate the dummies in advance and send them to the mix, which later sends them when cover traffic is needed. The authors point out that dummy packets sent on the link between the mix and recipient can be easily recognized and dropped by the recipient. Mix-generated cover traffic is also useful in protecting reverse paths from malicious clients that use the Overlier-Syverson attack. The results from Section 5 of our work indicate that this approach can also help prevent intersection attacks.

System for anonymous peer-to-peer services, such as GNUnet [18], Freenet [19], and APFS [20], include receivers in the system by their nature. Sending cover traffic to receivers would be very reasonable in such systems. P5 is an anonymity system that provides sender, receiver, and sender-receiver anonymity[21]. P5 creates a hierarchy of broadcast channels with each level providing a different level of tradeoff between anonymity and communication performance. In P5, noise (dummy) messages are added to prevent statistical correlation of sources and sinks of a communication stream. Real messages and noise messages move from the source to the sink hop by hop across different nodes. Intermediate nodes cannot distinguish real packets from dummy packets and treat all transiting packets similarly. Furthermore, intermediate nodes are also sources and insert dummy packets into outgoing streams. Dummies are dropped at the final destination. By using these channels, each sender effectively creates a form of receiver-bound cover traffic, as each message is sent to a group of receivers. While this multicast approach would be one way to do receiver-bound cover traffic in mix-based anonymity systems, it would only work in non-encrypted communications.

8 Conclusions and Future Work

Anonymous communications remain challenging in the face of determined and powerful attackers. No matter how secure the process of mixing becomes, inconsistent usage patterns can give the attacker enough information to link users with their communication partners over time. Prior work had developed the notion of statistical disclosure as a powerful form of this attack. In this work, we explored defenses against this attack in greater depth. We found that the cover traffic of other users is surprisingly ineffective in protecting Alice, our user of interest; techniques to hide the amount of real traffic could help. Alice's own cover traffic has a limited effect on its own, or in combination with greater delays in the mix system. We proposed receiver-bound cover traffic and showed that it can have a substantial benefit to the user. We then discussed in detail the implications of using such an approach; we believe that it is feasible, and that the improvement in privacy could well be worth the costs.

Much work remains before receiver-bound cover traffic could be put into place. First, we need to have a deeper study of the use of unencrypted receiver-bound dummies. It is unclear whether it is a pure arms race between defense and attack, or whether one side has a clear advantage. We suggest that the attacker would find that deep content analysis does not scale well, while creating realistic automated messages is a well-understood problem from spam email generation.

Acknowledgements

This work is supported in part by a grant from the National Science Foundation under award CNS-0549998. We are grateful to Nick Mathewson for his statistical disclosure simulation code and to Thomas Heydt-Benjamin and Banessa Defend for useful discussions. We thank the reviewers for their detailed comments and suggestions which greatly helped to improve the clarity of this work.

References

1. Acquisti, A., Dingledine, R., Syverson, P.: On the economics of anonymity. In: Wright, R.N. (ed.) FC 2003. LNCS, vol. 2742, Springer, Heidelberg (2003)
2. Chaum, D.: Untraceable Electronic Mail, Return Addresses, and Digital Pseudonyms. Communications of the ACM 24(2), 84–88 (1981)
3. Kesdogan, D., Agarwal, D., Penz, S.: Limits of anonymity in open environments. In: Petitcolas, F.A.P. (ed.) IH 2002. LNCS, vol. 2578, Springer, Heidelberg (2003)
4. Danezis, G.: Statistical disclosure attacks: Traffic confirmation in open environments. In: Proc. Security and Privacy in the Age of Uncertainty (SEC) (May 2003)
5. Mathewson, N., Dingledine, R.: Practical traffic analysis: Extending and resisting statistical disclosure. In: Martin, D., Serjantov, A. (eds.) PET 2004. LNCS, vol. 3424, Springer, Heidelberg (2005)
6. Díaz, C., Serjantov, A.: Generalising mixes. In: Dingledine, R. (ed.) PET 2003. LNCS, vol. 2760, Springer, Heidelberg (2003)
7. Barabási, A.L., Albert, R.: Emergence of scaling in random networks. Science 286, 509–512 (1999)
8. Zimmermann, P.R.: The official PGP user's guide. MIT Press, Cambridge, MA, USA (1995)
9. Dusse, S., Hoffman, P., Ramsdell, B., Lundblade, L., Repka, L.: S/mime version 2 message specification (1998)
10. Graham, P.: A plan for spam (August 2002), available at http://www.paulgraham.com/spam.html
11. Meyer, T., Whateley, B.: Spambayes: Effective open-source, bayesian based, email classification. In: Proc. Conference on Email and Anti-Spam (CEAS) (July 2004)
12. Androutsopoulos, I., Koutsias, J., Chandrinos, K., Paliouras, G., Spyropoulos, C.: An evaluation of naive bayesian anti-spam filtering. In: Proc. Workshop on Machine Learning in the New Information Age (May 2000)

13. Dingledine, R., Mathewson, P.S.N.: Tor: The next-generation onion router. In: Proc. 13th USENIX Security Symposium (August 2004)
14. Danezis, G., Dingledine, R., Mathewson, N.: Mixminion: Design of a type III anonymous remailer protocol. In: Proc. 2003 IEEE Symposium on Security and Privacy, IEEE Computer Society Press, Los Alamitos (May 2003)
15. Weinstein, L.: Spam wars. Communications of the ACM 46(8), 136 (2003)
16. Berthold, O., Langos, H.: Dummy traffic against long-term intersection attacks. In: Dingledine, R., Syverson, P.F. (eds.) PET 2002. LNCS, vol. 2482, Springer, Heidelberg (2003)
17. Shmatikov, V., Wang, M.-H.: Timing analysis in low-latency mix networks: attacks and defenses. In: Gollmann, D., Meier, J., Sabelfeld, A. (eds.) ESORICS 2006. LNCS, vol. 4189, pp. 18–33. Springer, Heidelberg (2006)
18. Bennett, K., Grothoff, C., Horozov, T., Patrascu, I., Stef, T.: Gnunet – a truly anonymous networking infrastructure. In: Dingledine, R., Syverson, P.F. (eds.) PET 2002. LNCS, vol. 2482, Springer, Heidelberg (2003)
19. Clarke, I., Sandberg, O., Wiley, B., Hong, T.W.: Freenet: A distributed anonymous information storage and retrieval system. In: Federrath, H. (ed.) Designing Privacy Enhancing Technologies. LNCS, vol. 2009, pp. 46–66. Springer, Heidelberg (2001)
20. Scarlatta, V., Levine, B., Shields, C.: Responder anonymity and anonymous peer-to-peer file sharing. In: Proc. IEEE Intl. Conference on Network Protocols (ICNP), IEEE Computer Society Press, Los Alamitos (November 2001)
21. Sherwood, R., Bhattacharjee, B., Srinivasan, A.: P5: A protocol for scalable anonymous communication. In: Proc. 2002 IEEE Sym. on Security and Privacy, IEEE Computer Society Press, Los Alamitos (May 2002)

Renewable Traitor Tracing: A Trace-Revoke-Trace System For Anonymous Attack

Hongxia Jin and Jeffery Lotspiech

IBM Almaden Research Center
San Jose, CA, 95120
{jin,lotspiech}@us.ibm.com

Abstract. In this paper we design renewable traitor tracing scheme for anonymous attack. When pirated copies of some copyrighted content or content decrypting key are found, a traitor tracing scheme could identify at least one of the real users (traitors) who participate in the construction of the pirated content/key. When traitors are identified, the renewable scheme can revoke and exclude the decryption keys used by the traitors during piracy. Moreover, the revocation information included in the newly released content needs not only to disallow traitors to playback the new content, but also provide new tracing information for continuous tracing. This trace-revoke-trace system is the first such system for anonymous attack. It poses new challenges over the trace-revoke system that has extensively studied in the literatures for the pirate decoder attack. We hope the technologies described in this paper can shed new insights on future directions in this area for academia research.

Keywords: Content protection, traitor tracing, broadcast encryption, anti-piracy.

1 Introduction

This paper is concerned with the protection of copyrighted materials. There are many business scenarios that content needs to be distributed through broadcast channels. Examples of these business models include pay-TV systems (Cable companies) or movie rental companies like Netflix, and massively distributing prerecorded and recordable media. A broadcast encryption and traitor tracing scheme can be used to protect the content copyright and make sure the content can only be recovered by a privileged group of users. Since broadcast content is usually large, hybrid encryption system can be used to keep asymptotically optimal transmission rate (i.e., the ratio between cipher text size and plaintext size). More concretely, each device is assigned a set of unique secret keys (called device keys) but the broadcaster selects another random key (called media key) to indirectly encrypt the content. Distributed together with the content is a structure called Media Key Block (MKB) where the media key is encrypted by valid device keys again and again. Only those enabled devices can decrypt the

J. Biskup and J. Lopez (Eds.): ESORICS 2007, LNCS 4734, pp. 563–577, 2007.
© Springer-Verlag Berlin Heidelberg 2007

MKB and obtain the correct media key to decrypt the content. The disabled devices, with their device keys revoked, cannot decrypt the MKB correctly to access the content. Traitor tracing schemes are used to identify who have involved in the pirate attack when the disclosed pirate evidence is recovered.

There are three major pirate attacks in the above content protection system. The forensic evidences are different for different pirate attacks, which correspond to different types of traitor tracing system.

1. Pirates disclose secret device keys by building a clone pirate decoder.
2. Pirates disclose content encrypting key (media key): pirates stay anonymous.
3. Pirates disclose decrypted content: pirates stay anonymous.

The first type of pirate attack has been studied extensively. It is called "pirate decoder attack". Attackers hack legitimate players, extract secret device keys from the players and build a pirate decoder that will decrypt and extract the plaintext content. The pirates could widely redistribute the pirate decoders so that anyone can extract the clear content for themselves. For example, pirate attackers broke the CSS (Content Scrambling System), built and widely distributed DeCSS, a pirate program for decrypting encrypted DVD content. In order to find out which device keys are in the decoder, the tracing scheme interacts with the pirate decoder using carefully crafted cipher text (we call it "forensic MKB") and observes the decoder's outcome. Most existing broadcast encryption and traitor tracing schemes [2,3,4,5,6,7,8,9,10,11,12] targeted on this type of "pirate decoder attack". Some of these schemes are combinatorial [4,5,2], some are algebraic [6,9,11,12].

In this paper we are concerned with a different attack, namely, anonymous attack. In anonymous attack, instead of distributing a pirate decoder, attackers redistribute the actual content encrypting key or the decrypted content. Keep in mind when using hybrid encryption the content encrypting key and the clear content is same for every user/player and cannot be used to identify traitors. To defend against these types of anonymous attacks, one needs different versions of the content and decryption keys (media key) for different users.

Unfortunately in most one-to-many content distribution channels, like massively distributing DVDs, it is generally infeasible to prepare and send individualized (e.g., watermarked) movie discs to each user. On the other hand, it is also infeasible, usually for security reasons, to customize each copy at the receiving end[1]. A feasible technical approach is to choose certain points in the movie and create different variations for each of those points. Each variation is differently encrypted. The movie is thus augmented by all the variations. Each user receives the same bulk-encrypted movie. However, each user can only decrypt one of the variations at each point. In other words, each recipient would follow a different path through the variations during playback time. It effectively creates multiple versions of a movie. Over time, when recovering enough pirate movies, it may be possible to detect the players in a copyright attack by examining the

---

[1] Unauthorized copies generally imply a break the correct operation of the client. How can a broken client be expected to correctly generate the customizing marks?

variations recovered in the unauthorized copies of the movies. We together with [15,16,17,18,19] use this model to defend against anonymous attack. It is interesting to notice that all schemes for this attack are combinatorial. Traitor tracing schemes can be public-key based or secret symmetric key based. Combinatorial systems are typically designed for secret key setting.

AACS [1], *Advanced Access Content System*, was founded in July 2004 by eight companies, Disney, IBM, Intel, Matsushita, Microsoft, Sony, Toshiba, and Warner Brothers. It develops content protection technology for the next generation of high-definition DVD optical discs. Compared to the previous DVD CSS system, which could not revoke users because it is a shared-key scheme, AACS adopts a broadcast encryption scheme shown in [2]. The pirate attack this scheme was concerned with is the pirate decoder attack. The mechanism is designed to exclude clones pirate devices, such as the infamous "DeCSS" application used for copying "protected" DVD Video disks. It utilizes hybrid encryption and media key block (MKB). Once the attackers have been detected, they are excluded from newly released content because the new media key blocks in the new content exclude the keys known to the attackers. The detection of the traitors is performed by the traitor tracing approach in the scheme [2] when a pirate decoder is found. This responds to the first pirate attack mentioned above.

However, the AACS founders do not believe that it is sufficient to only respond to pirate decoder attack. AACS found it desirable to be able to respond to the anonymous attacks discussed above. To have a practical useful system, AACS is concerned with problems arise during the lifetime of a traitor tracing system. Basically AACS demands a traitor tracing system for anonymous attack that not only traces traitors, but also revokes traitors and can continue tracing traitors throughout its lifetime. Unfortunately existing schemes [16,17,15] for anonymous attack focus on the first part of a "trace-revoke-trace" system. They assume the detected traitor can be disconnected from the system in some way and the tracing can simply be repeated. The multiple needs from AACS on a practical tracing system are therefore still unsatisfied. AACS needs a complete trace-revoke-trace system for anonymous attack. That is the focus on this paper.

1.1 Main Results

The main contribution of this paper is that we provided a complete and practical trace-revoke-trace system to meet AACS' demand to defend against anonymous attack. The technologies we will describe in this paper have been adopted by this new industry content protection standard to protect the next generation of high-definition optical DVDs.

We build our trace-revoke-trace system on top of an existing tracing scheme [20] for anonymous attack. The first part "trace" of our trace-revoke-trace system uses the key assignment described in [20]. On top of that, we go on adding revocation capability similar to the design of Media Key Block in a broadcast encryption system. The traitor tracing keys serve the role of the device keys in a broadcast encryption system, and the actual content encrypting keys in our traitor tracing scheme serve the role of the media key in a broadcast encryption system. Of course, there are multiple versions of content encrypting key in our scheme while there is only one media key in a normal broadcast encryption system. Unfortunately, the above combined scheme cannot support multi-time continued tracing. It is possible that the license agency does not gain any useful information to continue detecting the unexposed traitors. We identified this new challenge and improved our scheme to support multi-time tracing.

Adding renewability and continued traceability was a crucial enabling factor for this first time adoption for large scale commercialization of a tracing traitor technology for anonymous attack. We hope the experience we gained when developing this complete system can shed new insights on future research directions on some problems that we believe have been overlooked by research community so far. We will discuss a little bit on these issues in the concluding Section 7.

In rest of the paper, we will describe our trace-revoke-trace system in three continuous sections. Section 3 is for the first part "trace" in the trace-revoke-trace system. We will summarize the existing tracing scheme shown in [20]. Section 4 is for the second "revoke" part of our trace-revoke-trace system. We will show how to add renewability into the scheme. Section 5 is for the third part of our trace-revoke-trace system, there we will show the challenges to provide continued traceability and show our solution to support multi-time tracing. We analyze the revocation capability and continued traceability in Section 6. We conclude in Section 7 with future work.

2   Pirate Model

AACS founders find it acceptable to makes the following marking assumption on the pirate model. Given two variants v_1 and v_2 of a segment, the pirate can only use v_1 or v_2, not any other valid variant v_i. The exact reason that has made AACS to accept this model is outside the scope of this paper. Indeed, this so-called marking assumption is often made by other traitor tracing schemes shown in the literatures. Also, in a key attack, the first model says it is impossible to calculate a valid random cryptographic key from combining two other valid random keys–which is obviously true.

3   First Part: Trace

In this section we show the restrictions on designing a practical traitor tracing system for AACS, and show how AACS can use the scheme shown in [20] as its first part.

In the AACS context, each movie is divided into multiple segments, among which n segments are chosen to have differently marked variations. Each of these n segments has q possible variations. Each playing device receives the same disc with all the small variations at chosen points in the content. However, each device plays back the movie through a different path, which effectively creates a different movie version. Each version of the content contains one variation for each segment. Each version can be denoted as an n-tuple or *codeword* $(x_0, x_1, \ldots, x_{n-1})$, where $0 \leq x_i \leq q - 1$ for each $0 \leq i \leq n - 1$.

As one can imagine, the variations take extra space on the disc. A practical traitor tracing scheme on a prerecorded optical movie disc should take no more than 10% of the space on the disc to store the variations. For a normal 2-hour movie, it corresponds to 8 additional minutes (480 seconds) of video. This puts practical restriction on the number of variations one can put into a movie. The market for such discs is huge, involving literally a billion playing devices or more. This means a tracing scheme needs to be able to accommodate large number of devices.

Unfortunately these requirements are inherently conflicting. Let us show some intuition on the conflicts between these parameters. Take a look at a code $[n, k, d]$, where n is the length of the codewords, k is the source symbol size and d is the Hamming distance of the code, namely, the minimum number of symbols by which any two codewords differ. q is the number of variations. Mathematically these parameters are connected to each other. The number of codewords is q^k, and Hamming distance has the property that $d <= n - k + 1$. q is also related to n, for example, for a "maximal difference separable" (MDS) code, $n <= q$. We know the number of variations q decides the extra bandwidth needed for distributing content. Without variations, $q = 1$. The extra bandwidth needed for the content is $(q - 1) * length\_of\_each\_variation * n$. The Hamming distance d decides its traceability. To defend against a collusion attack, intuitively we would like the variant assignment to be as far apart as possible. In other words, the larger the Hamming distance is, the better traceability of the scheme. On the other hand, to accommodate a large number of devices, e.g. billions, intuitively either q or k or both have to be relatively big. Unfortunately a big q means big bandwidth overhead and a big k means smaller Hamming distance and thus weaker traceability. It is inherently difficult to defend against collusions.

In order to meet these practical requirements, AACS uses the key assignment scheme shown in [20]. The basic idea there is to use two-level assignment and concatenate them. For each movie, there is an "inner code" used to assign the different variations at the chosen points of the movie; it effectively creates different movie versions. For example, 16 variations are created at each of the 15 points in the movie, its "inner code" generates 256 versions for each movie out of all the possible 16^{15} combinations. Any two of the 256 versions are guaranteed to differ at 14 points out of the entire 15 points in the movie. For a sequence of movies, there is an "outer code" used to assign movie versions to different players. For example, each player is assigned one of the 256 versions for each movie in a sequence of 255 movies. By concatenating the two levels of codes, the scheme managed to avoid having a big number of variations at any chosen point but can still accommodate the billions of devices we anticipate. The inner code and outer code assignments can be random or systematic. For example, both inner and outer codes can use Reed-Solomon codes. Suppose each variations takes 2-second clip, the extra video needed in this example is 450 seconds, within the 10% constraint placed by the studios. This example can accommodate more than 4 billion devices. In fact, there does not exist a single level MDS code that can satisfy all the practical requirements. The two-level concatenated code is essential to meet the practical requirements for AACS.

During playback time, each device needs to decrypt exactly one variation for each segment. Using the above parameters, a device needs to know $255 * 15$ variation encrypting keys. 255 corresponds to the outer code length for the 255 movies in the sequence, 15 corresponds to the inner code length. However, by adding a level of indirection, each device only stores 255 movie version keys corresponding to the 255 movies in the sequence. For each movie, the device can use its movie version key to unlock a table on the DVD disc that contains the actual variation encrypting keys for that movie. In other words, the variation encrypting keys which are assigned using "inner code" are embedded on the DVD disc. These movie version keys which are assigned using "outer side" are burned into the devices during manufacture time. Those outer code keys are called "sequence keys" in AACS.

The sequence keys for AACS are assigned from a large matrix. Each column corresponds to a movie. The number of columns corresponds to the number of movies considered in the sequence. The rows for each column correspond to multiple versions of the sequence keys for that movie. For example, if the variations inside the movie segments create 256 versions for each movie and we consider 255 movies in a sequence, then the matrix is 255 by 256. Each device is assigned a set of 255 keys, exactly one key from each column, corresponding to the 255 movies in the sequence. The key for each column has 256 versions. Many players will receive any given sequence key, but no two players will receive exactly the same set of 255 keys. Again, these sequence keys are placed in the players at manufacturing time. Figure 1 is an example of the matrix organization of the keys.

Based on the pirate model we mentioned in Section 2, the attackers can collude and construct the pirate copy of the content/key based on the available versions to them. When the license agency recovers pirated movies/keys, it tries to match the recovered movies/keys with the versions assigned to the devices to detect traitors. This detection algorithm must handle the collusion attack when attackers collude in the piracy. It is possible to use the typical highest-score approach as shown in [20,16]. AACS chose to use a more efficient detection algorithm. However, the actual detection algorithm is out of the scope of this paper.

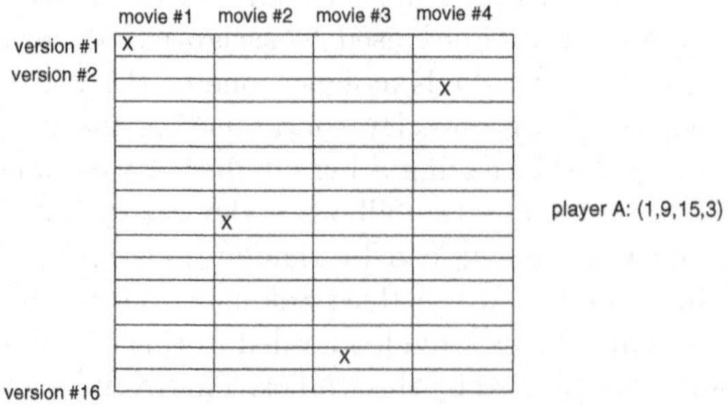

Fig. 1. Key assignment from a matrix

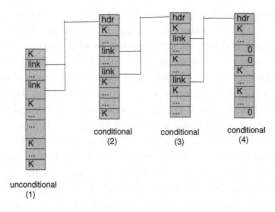

Fig. 2. Sample SKB

4 Second Part: Revocation

A traitor tracing scheme is defined to be finding at least a traitor if though there may exist a coalition. Indeed, all traitor tracing schemes [15,16,17,20] for anonymous attack stop when they detect a traitor. They assume this traitor can be disconnected in some way. If there still is piracy, the same scheme just needs to be repeated.

In reality, how does one disconnect a traitor technically? It is by rendering the compromised keys no longer usable for future content. In other words, a traitor tracing system must also be able to revoke compromised keys to be actually useful in real world.

Of course, many devices might share a single compromised key. Therefore, revocation of a single key is impossible. On the other hand, revocation of a unique set of keys is very possible; in fact, that is precisely what the Sequence Key Block (SKB) achieves.

The fundamental principle is that no two devices have many keys in common, so even if the system has been heavily attacked and a significant fraction of the Sequence Keys is compromised, all innocent devices will have many columns in which they have uncompromised keys. The purpose of the Sequence Key Block is to give all innocent devices a column they can use to calculate the correct answer, while at the same time preventing compromised devices (who have compromised keys in all columns) from getting to the same correct answer.

In an SKB there are actually many correct answers, one for each variation in the content. For the purpose of explanation, however, it is helpful to imagine that a single SKB is producing a single answer. We will call that answer the output key.

As shown in Figure 2, the SKB begins with a first column, called the unconditional column. By column, we mean a column of Sequence Keys in the matrix will be used to encrypt. (To be precise, the key used to encrypt is derived from the Sequence Key, not the Sequence Key itself.) The first column will have an encryption of the output key (denoted K in the figure) in every uncompromised Sequence Keys cell. Devices that do not have compromised keys in that column immediately decrypt the output key. Devices, both innocent and otherwise, that do have compromised keys instead decrypt a key called a link key that allows them to process a further column in the SKB. To process the further column they need both the link key and their Sequence Key in that column. Thus the subsequent columns are called conditional columns because they can only be processed by the device if it were given the necessary link key in a previous column.

The subsequent additional conditional columns are produced the same way as the first column: They will have an encryption of the output key in every uncompromised Sequence Keys cell. Devices with a compromised key will get a further link key to another column instead of the output key. However, after some number of columns depending on the actual number of compromised keys, the AACS licensing agency will know that only compromised devices would be getting the link key; all innocent devices would have found the output key in this column or in a previous column. At this point, rather than encrypting a link key, the agency encrypts a 0, and the SKB is complete. All innocent devices will have decrypted the output key, and all compromised devices have ended up decrypting 0.

How do the devices know they have a link key versus the output key? The short answer is they do not, at least not at first. Each conditional column has a header of known data (for example, "DEADBEEF16") encrypted in the link key for that column. The device decrypts the header with the key it currently has. If the header decrypts correctly, the device knows it has a link key and processes the column. If it does not decrypt correctly, the device knows it has either the output key or a link key for a different column. When the device reaches the end of the SKB without decrypting 0, it knows it must have an output key. Note that this device logic allows the licensing agency to send different populations of devices to different columns by having more than one link key output from a single column. For example, in the figure, column (1) links to both column (2) and column (5). This flexibility can help against certain types of attacks.

The preceding description is the basics of an AACS SKB and described in a simplified version. In an actual AACS SKB there is not a single output key, but multiple output keys called Variant Data D_v.

The SKB is generated by the AACS license agency and allows all compliant devices, each using their set of secret Sequence Keys to calculate the Variant Data, D_v, which in turn allows them to indirectly decrypt a table that contains the actual movie variation encrypting keys for the playback path of the movie assigned to that device. If a set of Sequence Keys is compromised in a way that threatens the integrity of the system, an updated SKB can be released that causes a device with one or more compromised sets of Sequence Keys to calculate invalid Variant Data. In this way, the compromised Sequence Keys are revoked by the new SKB. In fact, if a device correctly processes an SKB using Sequence Keys that are revoked by that SKB, the resulting final D_v will have the special value 00000000000000000016. This special value will never be an SKBs correct final D_v value, and can therefore always be taken as an indication that the devices Sequence Keys are revoked. Device behavior in this situation is implementation defined. As an example, a device could exhibit a special diagnostic code, as information to a service technician. If at any point, a device calculates a D_v value of zero, it should discontinue processing of the SKB and may conclude that it has been revoked.

5 Third Part: Trace Again After Revocation

The above solution provides a key management scheme that not only can trace traitors but also can revoke compromised keys. A real world traitor tracing system must be able to trace again after revocation. Although none of the existing traitor tracing system for anonymous attack even provides revocation capability, there are quite some trace-revoke systems out there for pirate decoder attack. Unfortunately there is big difference when coming to design a trace-and-revoke system for clone decoder attack and anonymous attack. In this section, we shall describe the new challenge and our solution for that.

5.1 Another Type of Collusion Attack: Combine Revoked Keys with Non-revoked Keys in Future Attacks

For pirate decoder attack, the license agency has the clone box in the testing lab. The tracing agency carefully produces some testing messages (called forensic Media Key Blocks) and feeds into the box in order to trace keys contained in the clone box. The real production MKB and the forensic MKB are two different things. Forensic MKBs are for tracing purpose only, they are not necessary production MKBs. On the other hand, real production MKB used in a broadcast encryption scheme, like [2], only needs to contain the revocation information and disable the detected compromised keys. It itself doesnt have to be able to trace. However, for anonymous attack, it demands the same SKB containing the revocation information in the newly broadcasted content to not only revoke the compromised keys but also enable continued tracing of new traitors. It poses new challenges to our design.

This is best understood by example. The bulk of a movie is encrypted by the media key, which in turn is calculated by each device using its set of device keys. At the point of variations in the movie, the media key alone does not suffice, the device must also use the variant key it has at that point. In a clone decoder attack, all that is needed is to exclude the clone's compromised device keys. The clone can no longer play the movie. In an anonymous attack, it is necessary but not sufficient to exclude the attacker's device keys; the attacker's variant keys must also be made unusable. If not, if the attackers are able to obtain a new set of device keys, they simply combine them with the previously-used variant keys and give the tracing agency no new information. This tactic is useless against the clone decoder attack because the tracing agency already has the clone in the lab.

The challenge here is to make sure the newly released SKB can continue to provide tracing information to the license agency to enable continued tracing.

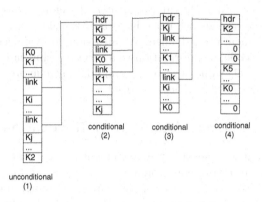

Fig. 3. It is possible that the new SKB will not provide new tracing information for continued tracing

As we know, each column in a SKB contains an encryption of the output key in every uncompromised sequence key's cell. More precisely, in every uncompromised sequence key's cell in each column, it contains an encryption of one of the variant data $D_{vi}(0 \leq i < k), k$ is the number of different variant data in the system. Notice the same set of variant data are encrypted in each column, although they are distributed differently in different columns. For a particular variant data D_{vi}, it can be obtained from any column in the SKB. An uncompromised device will process SKB and obtain a correct variant data from the first column in SKB that it has a non-revoked key. However, when attackers collude and the system still has undetected attackers at large. The attacker can mix-and-match their revoked keys and non-revoked keys when processing SKB. In turn they have multiple ways to process SKB and get a valid variant data to play back the content. They can choose in which column they want to use a non-revoked key to get a valid variant data. It does not have to be in the first column. Moreover, different keys need to be used in different columns to obtain the same variant D_{vi}. When the license agency observes a pirate copy corresponding to a particular variant data D_{vi}, since it can be obtained from any column, the license agency has no way to know which key has been used in obtaining that variant data. The entire path that the undetected traitors goes through to process SKB can even look like from an innocent device or from a path that was never assigned to any device, thus untraceable.

The figure 3 illustrates the issue discussed here. Keep in mind that the output key has multiple valid versions. If the attackers combine the revoked keys with the keys that have not been detected, it is not always possible to know from which column the SKB processing ends to get a valid key.

To force the undetected traitors to reveal the keys they use when processing SKB, we must make sure each column gets different variations so that when recovering a key/variation, the scheme knows from which column it comes from. Only by observing that, the tracing scheme can continue tracing. Unfortunately that means the q variations have to be distributed among the columns contained

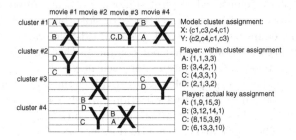

Fig. 4. Key assignment using "slots"

in the SKB. Each column only effectively gets q/c variations where c is the number of columns in the SKB. It is clear that traceability degrades when the effective q decreases. When the number of columns c becomes big enough, the traceability degrades to so low that it basically becomes untraceable. The scheme is overwhelmed and broken in that case. As a result, that puts a limit on the revocation capability of the scheme.

5.2 Improved Solution

In order to improve the above scheme and lift the limit on revocation capability, we have designed a two phase defense. In order to use this defense, the scheme assigns the sequence keys as shown in Figure 4 instead of Figure 1.

Basically we used a new concept called "slot". Now the rows in the key matrix are grouped into clusters. A slot is defined to be an assignment of row clusters, one cluster for each column. At any given column, two slots are either identical or completely disjoint. Slots can be assigned to individual manufacturers/models and the keys within the clusters are assigned to the devices made by the manufacturer/model. In effect, the outer code that is used to assign sequence keys to devices is now itself a two-level code. The first level codes assign clusters to the manufacturer/models X and Y and the second level codes assign keys to players A,B within model X, and players C, D within model Y. Model X gets the slot $(1,3,4,1)$, which means it is assigned cluster #1 for movie #1, cluster #3 for movie #2, and etc. Note that the second level code is the assignment inside the cluster. For example, player A gets *(1,1,3,3)* within the clusters assigned to model X, which makes its actual key assignment be $(1, 9, 15, 3)$ from the key matrix.

In AACS context, we anticipate about 4000 manufacturers/models. We divide all the rows in each column to have 64 clusters. Using Reed-Solomon code, $q = 64$, it takes $k = 2$ to accommodate 64^2 slots. Suppose we have $4K$ keys in each column, there will be 64 keys in each cluster. Again using Reed-Solomon code, $q = 64$, it takes $k = 3$ to accommodate 64^3 devices within each slot. The assignment can totally accommodate 64^5 devices. Each slot can be assigned to one manufacturer/model, A big manufacturer would, of course, overflow a single slot. He would just have more than one slot.

In the two-phase defense, when pirated movies/keys are found, the first SKB's would determine the slot used in the attack (or slots, but that is unlikely). Since the slot is assigned from the first level by using Reed-Solomon code $q = 64$, $k = 2$, there are only 64 variations needed per column in this case. Recall the "inner code" generates totally 256 variations for each movie. One can use 4 columns in the SKB and there is no problem with dividing the 256 variations across 4 columns. Each column would get 64 variations, which is all we need per column. By Reed-Solomon code's property, it takes only two ($k = 2$) movies to uniquely detect the slot. The above attack scenario does not work here.

Once the licensing agency detects the slot, it can produce new SKB's that are only trying to detect the device within the slot. In the SKB, all other slots in the column(s) would go to a single variation that we would expect would never be recovered. We would use all the remaining variations within the single slot. Again, the above attack scenario is not much a problem, because we can get up to 4 columns and still have unique keys for each variation. As long as we only need 4 columns in SKB, the above attack cannot work.

However, it still puts a limit on how many devices the scheme can revoke before it is overwhelmed. A single slot can be overwhelmed if it gets a lot of attacks. For example, if there are just 32 devices revoked from a single manufacturer, then 50% of the keys in the slot are compromised, and the SKB takes about 18 columns to winnow out that manufacturer's innocent devices. The 18 columns means the above attack can cause a problem, even with the two-phase approach. Because of this, a larger number of keys per column is preferred, for example, $16K$ keys/column would be a better number. These keys are still grouped by 64 clusters for slot purposes. Each slot can have 256 keys instead of 64 keys. Then we would be back down to 6 columns. Of course, anything more than 4 columns introduces the above attack problem, but it is still manageable.

6   Revocation Capability and Traceability

More formally, the revocation capability is calculated by the following formula. Suppose the number of rows in the matrix is m, p is the acceptable maximum probability for an innocent device to be revoked when revoking the actual guilty devices. r is the number of guilty devices to be revoked in SKB. c is the number of columns in SKB. The system still survives when the following holds.

$$(1 - (1 - 1/m)^r)^c < p \tag{1}$$

This formula can be used to determine how many columns c needed in a SKB when the licensing agency wants to revoke r devices. Due to the above attack scenario, there is a limit on the number of columns. We can also easily see that, the limit on the number of columns c in SKB induces a limit on the number of revoking devices that the system can survive. For example, suppose sequence keys are assigned from a matrix of 4096 by 256, there are 4096 rows.

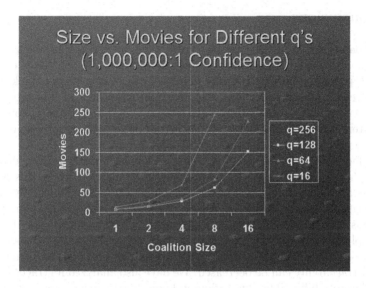

Fig. 5. Traceability with different q

We divide rows into 64 clusters for slot assignment. Suppose the acceptable rate for revoking innocent devices is $1/1,000,000$. Suppose there can be at most 18 columns in SKB. In the case of random hacking where we assume the attackers are distributed randomly from any slot and there is no evil manufacturers, Substituting $m = 4096$ gives us that maximum number of guilty devices that the system can revoke but still get useful tracing information for continued tracing. In the case of evil manufacturers or most hacking occurs in one slot, breaking one slot breaks the entire system. In the above example, there are 64 cluster in a $4096X256$ matrix, there are 64 rows in each cluster for slot assignment. Substituting $m = 64$ gives us that the system can maximally survive up to 32 revoked devices within a slot.

We have performed preliminary simulation on how many columns the scheme needs in its SKB in terms of the number of devices that needs to be revoked. It confirms the above formula 1.

The traceability is measured by the number of movies it takes to recover in order to detect traitors in a coalition of T traitors. Of course the traceability depends on the actual detection algorithm used when a series of pirated movies are recovered. We didnt show the actual traitor detection algorithm in this paper since it is out of the scope of this paper. However, we have used the same detection algorithm on different q to show the impact of deceased q on traceability. The traceability result is shown in graph 5. It includes both the two-phase solution and the basic single-phase scheme. There is different traceability in the life of the system depending on how many devices are currently being revoked in the SKB. The more devices revoked, the more columns it needs in SKB, the smaller the effective q is, the worse traceability.

7   Conclusions

In this paper, we study the problem of traitor tracing for anonymous attack where the legitimate users (traitors) illegally redistributing the clear content or the decryption keys on the Internet. This is a different type of attack with the pirate decoder attack which has been extensively studied in literature. In this paper we designed a complete trace-revoke-trace system for anonymous attack. Our system has been adopted by the new industry content protection standard AACS to protect the next generation DVDs.

Existing schemes for anonymous attack only focus on detecting a traitor. They assume the detected traitor can be disconnected in some way. In this paper we designed a system that can actually disable the detected traitor by revoking the identified compromised keys. We also studied the continued tracing problem which has been overlooked by existing schemes. They assumed that the tracing can simply be repeated for new traitors and the traceability will be same as before. We showed why this is not always possible to perform multi-time tracing and how traceability can be decreased. We have also analyzed its traceability and revocation capability. The revocation and continued tracing capability is one of the enabling factor for its adoption to be the first large scale commercialization of tracing traitor technology for anonymous attack.

We hope our work described in this paper sheds new insights on future directions in this area. So far, revocation is considered inside a broadcast encryption system, and tracing is considered inside a traitor tracing system. Broadcast encryption and traitor tracing have been viewed as two orthogonal problems. However, our experience working on a solution for real world has taught us that a traitor tracing scheme without revocation capability is practically useless in real world. Revocation should be considered together with tracing.

In fact, this is also true in the case of pirate decoder attack. Even though pirate decoder attack has been studied very extensively in literatures, they did not realize that tracing must be accompanied by revocation in order to be useful. Furthermore it is not always easy to add revocation on top of tracing if revocation is an afterthought. For example, for the very recent traitor tracing scheme [8] appeared in Eurocrypto 2006, if one needs to revoke a detected hacking device i, one would also have to revoke devices $i + 1...N$. Of course this is unacceptable.

Furthermore, a traitor tracing system must provide multi-time continued traceability in order to be useful. It is not as easy as simply repeating the same tracing. Again this issue can arise for pirate decoder attack too [11]. For example, after a pirate decoder of certain type is brought to the testing lab and rendered unusable, if there are undetected traitors in a coalition out there, the attackers can build a new clone decoder combining the previously revoked keys with untraced keys. This may or may not put difficulty on providing continued traceability. We believe this issue needs to be further studied in the future.

In the future, we will also continue to improve our revocation capability as well as traceability, not only theoretically, but also by taking into considerations of other features existing in a real system.

References

1. Pre-recorded Video Book: v0.91, ch. 4, http://www.aacsla.com/specifications
2. Naor, D., Naor, M., Lotspiech, J.: Revocation and Tracing Schemes for Stateless Receivers. In: Kilian, J. (ed.) CRYPTO 2001. LNCS, vol. 2139, pp. 41–62. Springer, Heidelberg (2001)
3. Fiat, A., Naor, M.: Broadcast Encryption. In: Stinson, D.R. (ed.) CRYPTO 1993. LNCS, vol. 773, pp. 480–491. Springer, Heidelberg (1994)
4. Chor, B., Fiat, A., Naor, M.: Tracing traitors. In: Desmedt, Y.G. (ed.) CRYPTO 1994. LNCS, vol. 839, pp. 480–491. Springer, Heidelberg (1994)
5. Chor, B., Fiat, A., Naor, M., Pinkas, B.: Tracing traitors. IEEE Transactions on Information Theory 46, 893–910 (2000)
6. Naor, M., Pinkas, B.: Efficient Trace and Revoke Schemes. In: Frankel, Y. (ed.) FC 2000. LNCS, vol. 1962, pp. 1–20. Springer, Heidelberg (2001)
7. Boneh, D., Gentry, C., Waters, B.: Collusion Resistant Broadcast Encryption With Short Ciphertexts and Private Keys. In: Shoup, V. (ed.) CRYPTO 2005. LNCS, vol. 3621, pp. 258–275. Springer, Heidelberg (2005)
8. Boneh, D., Sahai, A., Waters, B.: Fully Collusion Resistant Traitor Tracing With Short Ciphertexts and Private Keys. In: Vaudenay, S. (ed.) EUROCRYPT 2006. LNCS, vol. 4004, pp. 573–592. Springer, Heidelberg (2006)
9. Boneh, D., Franklin, M.: An efficient public key traitor tracing scheme. In: Wiener, M.J. (ed.) CRYPTO 1999. LNCS, vol. 1666, pp. 338–353. Springer, Heidelberg (1999)
10. Boneh, D., Waters, B.: A collusion resistant broadcast, trace and revoke system. ACM Communication and Computer Security (2006)
11. Kurosawa, K., Desmedt, Y.: Optimum traitor tracing and asymmetric schemes. In: Nyberg, K. (ed.) EUROCRYPT 1998. LNCS, vol. 1403, pp. 145–157. Springer, Heidelberg (1998)
12. Chabanne, H., Phan, D.H., Pointcheval, D.: Public traceability in traitor tracing schemes. In: Cramer, R.J.F. (ed.) EUROCRYPT 2005. LNCS, vol. 3494, pp. 542–558. Springer, Heidelberg (2005)
13. Stinson, D.R., Wei, R.: Key preassigned traceability schemes for broadcast encryption. In: Tavares, S., Meijer, H. (eds.) SAC 1998. LNCS, vol. 1556, Springer, Heidelberg (1999)
14. Gafni, E., Staddon, J., Yin, Y.L.: Efficient methods for integrating traceability and broadcast encryption. In: Wiener, M.J. (ed.) CRYPTO 1999. LNCS, vol. 1666, pp. 537–554. Springer, Heidelberg (1999)
15. Fiat, A., Tassa, T.: Dynamic traitor tracing. In: Wiener, M.J. (ed.) CRYPTO 1999. LNCS, vol. 1666, pp. 354–371. Springer, Heidelberg (1999)
16. Safani-Naini, R., Wang, Y.: Sequential Traitor tracing. IEEE Transactions on Information Theory 49 (2003)
17. van Trungand, T., Martirosyan, S.: On a class of Traceability Codes. Design, code and cryptography 31, 125–132 (2004)
18. Staddon, J.N., Stinson, D.R., Wei, R.: Combinatorial properties of frameproof and traceability codes. IEEE Transactions on Information Theory 47, 1042–1049 (2001)
19. Stinson, D.R., Wei, R.: Combinatorial properties and constructions of traceability schemes and frameproof codes. SIAM Journal on Discrete Mathematics 11, 41–53 (1998)
20. Jin, H., Lotspiech, J., Nusser, S.: Traitor tracing for prerecorded and recordable media. In: ACM DRM workshop, ACM Press, New York (October 2004)
21. Tardos, G.: Optimal Probabilistic fingerprint codes. In: Proceedings of the Theory of Computing, San Diego, CA, pp. 116–125 (June 9-11, 2003)

Modular Access Control Via Strategic Rewriting

Daniel J. Dougherty[1], Claude Kirchner[2], Hélène Kirchner[2],
and Anderson Santana de Oliveira[2]

[1] Worcester Polytechnic Institute
[2] INRIA & LORIA[*]

Abstract. Security policies, in particular access control, are fundamental elements of computer security. We address the problem of authoring and analyzing policies in a modular way using techniques developed in the field of term rewriting, focusing especially on the use of rewriting strategies. Term rewriting supports a formalization of access control with a clear declarative semantics based on equational logic and an operational semantics guided by strategies. Well-established term rewriting techniques allow us to check properties of policies such as the absence of conflicts and the property of always returning a decision. A rich language for expressing rewriting strategies is used to define a theory of modular construction of policies, in which we can better understand the preservation of properties of policies under composition. The robustness of the approach is illustrated on the composition operators of XACML.

1 Introduction

Access control is at the heart of computer security. It has grown beyond mediating operating-system interactions between users and files and now plays a central role in web-based systems, privacy policies, and business rules. Accompanying these expanded applications of access control, our conception of the mechanism of authorization now goes beyond the classical model [28] of access-control matrices, and we view access control decisions as the embodiment of a set of rules. We call such a set of rules an access-control *policy*. Although monitoring and enforcement mechanisms are important aspects of the study of access control, the size and complexity of the systems being treated mean that the policies themselves are interesting software artifacts in their own right. They are sensitive to complex conditions on the policy environment, which represents the data that a program respecting the policy manipulates, such as attributes of subjects and resources and relations among these. They are not easy to get right.

In light of these considerations, it is now typical in large or complex systems to disentangle policy from application code. Policies are written in domain-specific, typically declarative languages, such as the industrial standard XACML [34], and reasoning about the correctness of policies is a subtle matter. It is common wisdom that a key to designing, reasoning about, and maintaining a large system is modularity, with corresponding attention to the mechanisms by which the models in a system interact.

---

[*] LORIA: UMR 7503 CNRS-INPL-INRIA-Nancy2-UHP; Nancy, France.

J. Biskup and J. Lopez (Eds.): ESORICS 2007, LNCS 4734, pp. 578–593, 2007.

In this paper, we are interested in the question of building access-control policies in a modular fashion, and taking some initial steps towards a theory of how parts of a policy interact.

We propose *term rewriting* [6, 2] as a formalism for representing access control policies. Rewriting is a well-established paradigm whose applications include theoretical foundations for functional programming languages and theorem provers. It is flexible and expressive enough to capture a wide range of policy frameworks arising in practice and indeed it is a universal model of computation. It has a clean declarative semantics, based on equational logic. There is an active research community supporting efficient implementations and tools for reasoning about properties such as termination and confluence of rewrite systems. One can view rewrite systems as an intermediate language for policies; our thesis in this paper is that some of the more interesting aspects of reasoning about policies are profitably viewed in this context.

Indeed, rewriting is not a single formalism but rather a family of variations on a robust paradigm of directed equality. It is easy to see that simple term rewriting can capture policies such as Unix file-permissions rules, the richer setting of conditional rewriting is as rich as the language of Datalog explored by several authors (notably in trust-management research), and—as sketched below—core XACML policies can be captured by rewriting under strategy.

To give a flavor of how term rewriting can capture policy rules, we may consider the following rules, adapted from the XACML specification [34]: - A person, identified by his or her social security number, may read any record for which he or she is the designated patient:

$$req(patient(x), read, record(x)) \rightarrow permit.$$

Here *patient* names the function from patient numbers to patients as Subjects and *record* is a function from patient numbers to health records as Resources, while *read* is a constant symbol, of sort Actions.

The variable x is implicitly universally quantified, so that the rewriting above captures the generality of the access rule; and the repetition of the variable as a parameter has the effect of enforcing the binding between the patient and his record.

- An administrator shall not be permitted to write to medical elements of a patient record:

$$req(admin(x), write, record(y)) \rightarrow deny.$$

Here *any* administrator, named perhaps by his employee number, is denied write access to *any* health record: note the use of distinct variables in the rule. Also note the use of explicit *deny* as a decision. It is crucially important to modularity of policies that *deny* is not treated as the negation of *permit*: this will be further illustrated in the body of the paper.

- It is straightforward to capture certain notions of authorization hierarchy. For example, to say that subject s_2 inherits from subject s_1 all access rights involving resource r, it suffices to have the following rule in a policy:

$$req(s_1, x, r) \rightarrow req(s_2, x, r)$$

Here x is a variable ranging over actions. Note that this rule is a refinement of the type of inheritance typically incorporated into a Role-based Access Control Model (in which one role may inherit all privileges from another, uniformly across all actions and resources).

In a large organization, there are many classes of "Subjects" with different needs for access to an immense variety of "Resources". For example, in a hospital there are rules governing the access of patients to their health records, their financial records, and the like, while at the same time, there are rules for employee access to these same records as well as to resources quite different from health records. Meanwhile, other entities such as insurance carriers are subject to yet another set of rules for access to these data and more. The different constituencies (patients, staff, insurers) are almost certainly going to have somewhat different —even competing— requirements on their use of the data and place different emphases on the security goals (confidentiality, availability, integrity) of policies. It is natural to imagine that the sets of rules describing these various modes of access should not be authored and maintained in a single monolithic policy. In this setting, *the theory of composition* of policies becomes crucially important.

As a very simple example, imagine that rules for patient data access and rules for staff data access are composed in separate policy documents, $\wp_p$ and $\wp_s$ respectively. What should we say about the decision of $\wp_p$ in the context of a request by an administrator to write a health record? Assuming $\wp_p$ will not explicitly compute a decision (permit or deny) upon such a request, we must uniformly assume a *default* decision, perhaps default-deny, for all requests not handled directly. But this immediately leads to the conclusion that composing policies is something more subtle than taking their union. Consider by contrast a request by an administrator to read the next-of-kin information for a patient. A default-deny by $\wp_p$ for this request would mean that when $\wp_p$ was combined with $\wp_s$, which may explicitly compute a *permit* for this request, the resulting logical theory, taken in a naive sense, would be contradictory.

So at the very least, one must make a distinction between a policy decision which is computed in a "direct" way from the policy rules, and one taken as a default. The situation is even more interesting if two modules of a policy compute contradictory decisions: if the policy is to be coherent in practice there must be a principled way to combine the modules, a mechanism that lends itself to clean design and supports analysis and verification. The combination method we explore in this paper is that of *rewriting strategies*.

The remaining sections of this paper are organized as follows: we recall in Section 2 the main notions on rewrite rules and strategies used in this paper. In Section 3 we give the definition, suitable properties and examples of an access control policies expressed in the rewrite-based framework. We formalize policy composition in Section 4, its suitable properties, and we illustrate our approach on the composition operators of XACML. We discuss related and further works in Section 5.

2 Background

Basic definitions on term rewriting can be found in [6, 2]. Let us recall those which are used in the following. A many-sorted signature $(\mathcal{S}, \mathcal{F})$, or $\mathcal{F}$ for short, is a set of sorts $\mathcal{S}$ and a set of function symbols $\mathcal{F}$. Each $f \in \mathcal{F}$ has a profile $f : S_1 \times \ldots \times S_n \to S$,

where $S_1, \ldots S_n, S \in \mathcal{S}$, and is associated to a natural number by the arity function
(ar : $\mathcal{F} \to \mathbb{N}$). When $ar(f) = 0$, the function symbol f is called a constant.

$\mathcal{T}(\mathcal{F}, \mathcal{X})$ is the set of well-sorted terms built from a given finite set $\mathcal{F}$ of function
symbols and a denumerable set $\mathcal{X}$ of variables. The set of variables occurring in a term t
is denoted by $\mathcal{V}ar(t)$. If $\mathcal{V}ar(t)$ is empty, t is called a *ground term* and $\mathcal{T}(\mathcal{F})$ is the set
of ground terms. For $f \in \mathcal{F}$, $f(\mathcal{T}(\mathcal{F}), \ldots, \mathcal{T}(\mathcal{F}))$ denotes the set of ground terms with
f as top symbol.

A *substitution* σ is an assignment from $\mathcal{X}$ to $\mathcal{T}(\mathcal{F}, \mathcal{X})$, with a finite domain $\{x_1, \ldots, x_k\}$ and written $\sigma = \{x_1 \mapsto t_1, \ldots, x_k \mapsto t_k\}$.

A rewrite rule is an ordered pair of terms, denoted as $l \to r$, $l, r \in \mathcal{T}(\mathcal{F}, \mathcal{X})$, where l is
not a variable and $\mathcal{V}ar(r) \subseteq \mathcal{V}ar(l)$ such that l and r belong to a same sort. The terms
l and r are respectively called the left-hand side and the right-hand side of the rule. A
rewrite system R on $\mathcal{T}(\mathcal{F}, \mathcal{X})$ is a (finite or infinite) set of rewrite rules. Rules can be
labeled to easily distinguish among them. A rewrite rule $l \to r$ is a *collapsing rule* if r is
a variable. It is a *duplicating rule* if there exists a variable that has more occurrences in
r than in l. A function symbol which is not the top symbol of any rule in R is called a
constructor. Other symbols are called *defined functions*.

Given a rewrite system R, a term t rewrites to a term t', which is denoted $t \to_R t'$
if there exists a rewrite rule $l \to r$ of R, a position ω in t, a substitution σ, satisfying
$t_{|\omega} = \sigma(l)$, such that $t' = t[\sigma(r)]_\omega$.

A rewriting derivation of the rewrite system R is any sequence of rewriting steps
$t_1 \to_R t_2 \to_R \ldots$. The *source* of such a derivation is t_1. When the derivation is finite, its
last term is called its *target*. R induces a derivability relation $\xrightarrow{*}_R$ on terms: $t \xrightarrow{*}_R t'$
if there exists a rewriting derivation from t to t'. If the derivation contains at least one
step, it is denoted by $\xrightarrow{+}_R$. A rewrite system is terminating (or strongly normalizing)
if all rewriting derivations are finite. A term t is R-normalized (or in R-*normal form*)
when the empty derivation is the only one with source t; a derivation is *normalizing*
when its target is R-normalized. A rewrite system R is *weakly terminating* if every
term t is the source of a normalizing derivation. It is confluent if for all terms t, u, v,
$t \xrightarrow{*}_R u$ and $t \xrightarrow{*}_R v$ implies $u \xrightarrow{*}_R s$ and $v \xrightarrow{*}_R s$, for some s. When it is clear
from the context, we may omit the index R.

The notion of strategy used in this paper is fundamental in rewriting, and we give
here a general presentation of the main ideas. We adopt a general definition, slightly
different from the one used in [6]: a *rewrite strategy* ζ for the rewrite system R is a
subset of the set of all derivations of R. The *application of a strategy* ζ on a term t
is denoted $[\zeta](t)$ and defined as the set of all targets t' of the derivations of source t
in ζ. We denote $[\zeta](t)_\downarrow$ its subset that contains only the targets in normal form. The
domain of a strategy is the set of terms that are source of a derivation in ζ. When no
derivation in ζ has source t, we say that the strategy application on t fails. The result of
the application of a failing strategy on a term t is the empty set.

In this paper, we will consider only strategies that are stable by concatenation (i.e.
$t \xrightarrow{*}_R t' \in \zeta$ and $t' \xrightarrow{*}_R t'' \in \zeta$ implies $t \xrightarrow{*}_R t' \xrightarrow{*}_R t'' \in \zeta$). A strategy could
be described by enumerating all its elements or more suitably by a *strategy language*.
From elementary strategies expressions directly issued from a rewrite system R, more
elaborated strategies expressions are built like in ELAN [24], Stratego [39], Tom [3, 33]

or more recently MAUDE [30]. The semantics of such a language is naturally described in the rewriting calculus [9, 10]. We describe below the main elements of the strategy language of interest in this paper.

Given a rewrite system R over $\mathcal{T}(\mathcal{F}, \mathcal{X})$, rewrite rules in R are elementary or atomic strategies. For instance, if a and b are constants, the application of the rewrite rule $a{\rightarrow}b$ to the term a is denoted $[a{\rightarrow}b](a)$ and evaluates to $\{b\}$.

A strategy expression ζ may take arguments $\zeta_1, \ldots, \zeta_n$, and the resulting expression is expressed functionally: $\zeta(\zeta_1, \ldots, \zeta_n)$. Notice that this is consistent with the notation $\zeta(R)$ as soon as the definition of ζ does not depend on its arguments order. When it is clear from the context, we identify the strategy expression and the strategy (i.e. the set of derivations it represents). In a consistent way, the application of a strategy expression to a term is defined as the application of the strategy it represents.

A simple strategy is the sequential application of two rules. It is described by the concatenation operator "seq". For instance $[\text{seq}(l_1{\rightarrow}r_1, l_2{\rightarrow}r_2)](t)$ denotes $[l_2{\rightarrow}r_2]([l_1{\rightarrow}r_1](t))$. This strategy operator extends naturally to multiple arguments:

$$[\text{seq}(\zeta_1, \ldots, \zeta_n)](t) = [\zeta_n]([\zeta_{n-1}](\ldots [\zeta_1](t)))$$

Identity and failure are strategies easy to understand:

$$[\text{id}](t) = \{t\} \qquad [\text{fail}](t) = \emptyset$$

The strategy computing all derivations obtained by application of a rewrite system R is called universal; it takes as argument the set of rules under consideration:

$$[\text{universal}(R)](t) = \{t' \mid t \xrightarrow{*}_R t'\}$$

For instance, we have:

$$\begin{aligned}
[\text{universal}(a{\rightarrow}a)](a) &= \{a\} \\
[\text{universal}(f(x){\rightarrow}f(f(x)))](f(a)) &= \{f(a), f(f(a)), f(f(f(a))), \ldots\}
\end{aligned}$$

One can successively try to apply several strategies using the choice operator: its first argument is applied if it does not fail, otherwise the second one is applied (and may fail too).

$$\begin{aligned}
[\text{choice}(\zeta_1, \zeta_2)](t) &= [\zeta_1](t) \quad \text{if } [\zeta_1](t) \neq \emptyset \\
[\text{choice}(\zeta_1, \zeta_2)](t) &= [\zeta_2](t) \quad \text{if } [\zeta_1](t) = \emptyset
\end{aligned}$$

Clearly choice is associative and therefore its syntax is extended to be applicable to a list of strategies:

$$\text{choice}(\zeta_1, \zeta_2, \ldots, \zeta_n) = \text{choice}(\zeta_1, \text{choice}(\zeta_2, \ldots, \zeta_n))$$

Other strategies allow controlling the application of rules over sub-terms of a term. The strategy one must succeed on at least one of the sub-terms of a term. On the other hand, all application must succeed on each sub-term, otherwise, the result is failure:

$$\begin{aligned}
[\text{one}(\zeta)](f(t_1, \ldots, t_n)) &= f(t_1, \ldots, [\zeta](t_i), \ldots, t_n), \text{ if } [\zeta](t_i) \neq \emptyset \\
[\text{all}(\zeta)](f(t_1, \ldots, t_n)) &= f([\zeta](t_1), \ldots, [\zeta](t_n)), \text{ if } \forall i \in \{1, \ldots, n\}, [\zeta](t_i) \neq \emptyset
\end{aligned}$$

Using the above set of operators, we can define recursive ones which iterate the application of a strategy to a term, for example:

$$\mathtt{try}(\zeta) = \mathtt{choice}(\zeta, \mathtt{id}) \qquad \mathtt{repeat}(\zeta) = \mathtt{try}(\mathtt{seq}(\zeta, \mathtt{repeat}(\zeta)))$$

It is worth noticing that $\mathtt{try}$ and $\mathtt{repeat}$ never fail. Other high-level strategies implement term traversal and normalization on terms and are well-known in the rewrite system literature:

$$
\begin{aligned}
\mathtt{topDown}(\zeta) &= \mathtt{seq}(\zeta, \mathtt{all}(\mathtt{topDown}(\zeta))) \\
\mathtt{bottomUp}(\zeta) &= \mathtt{seq}(\mathtt{all}(\mathtt{bottomUp}(\zeta)), \zeta) \\
\mathtt{OnceTopDown}(\zeta) &= \mathtt{choice}(\zeta, \mathtt{one}(\mathtt{OnceTopDown}(\zeta))) \\
\mathtt{OnceBottomUp}(\zeta) &= \mathtt{choice}(\mathtt{one}(\mathtt{OnceBottomUp}(\zeta)), \zeta) \\
\mathtt{innermost}(\zeta) &= \mathtt{repeat}(\mathtt{onceBottomUp}(\zeta)) \\
\mathtt{outermost}(\zeta) &= \mathtt{repeat}(\mathtt{onceTopDown}(\zeta))
\end{aligned}
$$

Example 1. Some examples of strategy application are:

$$
\begin{aligned}
[\mathtt{universal}(a{\to}b, a{\to}c)](a) &= \{a, b, c\} \\
[\mathtt{choice}(a{\to}b, a{\to}c)](a) &= \{b\} \\
[\mathtt{choice}(a{\to}c, a{\to}b)](b) &= \emptyset \\
[\mathtt{try}(b{\to}c)](a) &= \{a\} \\
[\mathtt{repeat}(\mathtt{choice}(b{\to}c, a{\to}b))](a) &= \{c\}
\end{aligned}
$$

3   Rewrite-Based Policies

Recent developments in access control are aimed to express various constraints on the environment where policies run, in order to capture real world requirements from policy authors, such as time, location, and any other condition involving attributes of principals and objects.

In this context, it is important to embark expressive computational power in the definition of policies. As the notion of rule is quite natural in the context of policy specifications, we propose here a quite general definition of access control.

In our model, rewrite rules transform input terms representing access requests into access decision terms. In order to take the raw computational power of term rewriting and to enhance the agility of the policy specification language, we use strategies to explicitly control the rule application. We define rewrite-based policies as follows, where Q stands for queries (or requests) and D for decisions.

Definition 1 (Security Policy). *An access control security policy, $\wp$, is a 5-tuple $(\mathcal{F}, D, R, Q, \zeta)$ such that:*

1. *$\mathcal{F}$ is a signature;*
2. *D is a non-empty set of closed terms: $D \subseteq \mathcal{T}(\mathcal{F})$;*
3. *R is a set of rewrite rules over $\mathcal{T}(\mathcal{F}, \mathcal{X})$;*
4. *Q is a set of terms from $\mathcal{T}(\mathcal{F})$: $Q \subseteq \mathcal{T}(\mathcal{F})$;*
5. *ζ is a rewrite strategy for R.*

Let us explain the main design choices made in this definition.

- First we consider that the policy specification and its environment are described as terms built over the signature $\mathcal{F}$. The set of possible decisions to be taken by the policy is denoted by D. Indeed, D is often a set of constants and the two main constants in D are usually *permit* and *deny*. But since it is crucial to model also policies that do not directly take decision, it can be useful to have a constant *not applicable* that simply expresses the fact that the current policy in the current context cannot decide about the access. Moreover, the result returned by a policy could be more elaborated than just a constant and can be in general a term containing further information like the time and duration the access is granted. What is significant is not treating the failure to derive a permission as a denial. In contrast to [20] for example, in which this later design is followed, we can treat explicitly decisions such as *deny* and *not applicable*. This is a crucial advantage for merging rules, since in purely logic-based works, there is no way to handle in the theory what happens when a policy which derives *deny* for a request q is merged with another which then derives *permit* explicitly, for the same q.
- The rewrite system R describes the behavior of the policy as well as some necessary computations which explain how its environment evolves. The role of the strategy is to point derivations of R whose interest is to produce decisions.
- The requests are a subset of terms. They typically express questions of the form: should a certain entity be granted access to a resource given the current configuration of the policy environment.
- The last component is the strategy which allows one to finely specify the evaluation order of the policy rules.

One of the main nice consequences of this approach, in addition to its expressivity, which we illustrate on the examples below, is that it allows us to take advantage of all the results obtained by the rewriting community since the last thirty years. Amongst such results, we investigate in this section confluence, termination and sufficient completeness.

Example 2. This example is taken from the NetFilter how-to [1]. Suppose an Internet user wants to set his firewall to block any traffic coming from the exterior to the local network. Since the interface associated to Internet connections is usually ppp0, a simple method is to reject all new packets coming from this source. In order to demonstrate the fact that it might be convenient for a policy to contain rules beyond those which *directly* compute decisions, we also give some additional rules which allow two different local computers to share the same external IP address: for each outgoing packet whose origin is a local machine, its head is rewritten to a single address.

- Let the policy signature be:

$$
\begin{array}{lll}
pckt & : & Address \times Address \times State \rightarrow Packet \\
filter & : & Packet \rightarrow Decision \\
new, established & : & \rightarrow State \\
drop, accept & : & \rightarrow Decision \\
eth0, ppp0 & : & \rightarrow Address
\end{array}
$$

---
[1] http://www.netfilter.org

- The set of of constant symbols representing decisions is $D = \{accept, drop\}$
- Consider R as the following rules, where src, dst : $Address$, and s : $State$ are variables:

$$filter(pckt(src, dst, established)) \rightarrow accept$$
$$filter(pckt(eth0, dst, new)) \rightarrow accept$$
$$filter(pckt(ppp0, dst, new)) \rightarrow drop$$
$$pckt(10.1.1.1, ppp0, s) \rightarrow pckt(123.123.1.1, ppp0, s)$$
$$pckt(10.1.1.2, ppp0, s) \rightarrow pckt(123.123.1.1, ppp0, s)$$

- The set Q contains ground terms with top symbol $filter$.
- A possible strategy for this policy, among others that guarantee a normalization process, is $\zeta = \texttt{innermost}(R)$.

This defines a security policy as all conditions of Definition 1 are satisfied.

Example 3. As already suggested in the introduction, we can model a policy for a clinical system (this example is adapted from the **XACML** specification [34], and first presented in the rewrite-based formalism in [12]).

- The policy signature $\mathcal{F}$ contains the following symbols:

$accs$	:	$Request \times Condition$	$\rightarrow Decision$
req	:	$Subject \times Action \times Object$	$\rightarrow Request$
$read, write$	:		$\rightarrow Action$
$permit, deny, na$	:		$\rightarrow Decision$
$patient, phy$	:	$Number$	$\rightarrow Subject$
$admin, per$	:	$Number$	$\rightarrow Subject$
$record$	:	$Number$	$\rightarrow Object$
$guard$	:	$Subject \times Subject$	$\rightarrow Condition,$
$respPhy$	:	$Subject \times Subject$	$\rightarrow Condition$
$urgency$	:		$\rightarrow Condition$

- The set of decisions is $D = \{permit, deny, na\}$.
- R is the following set of rules, where variables are x, y : $Number$; r : $Object$; c : $Condition$:

$$accs(req(patient(x), read, record(x)), c) \rightarrow permit$$
$$accs(req(per(x), read, record(y)), guard(per(x), patient(y)))) \rightarrow permit$$
$$accs(req(phy(x), read, record(y)), respPhy(phy(x), patient(y))) \rightarrow permit$$
$$accs(req(phy(x), write, record(y)), respPhy(phy(x), patient(y))) \rightarrow permit$$
$$accs(req(admin(x), read, r), c) \rightarrow deny$$
$$accs(req(admin(x), write, r), c) \rightarrow deny.$$

In the order of appearance, these rules state that: a patient can read his own record, the guardian of a person can read the record for that person, the responsible physician of a patient can read or write data for his record, the last two rules deny any access of administrators to records.

- The set of requests Q is the set of all terms of the form $accs(\mathcal{T}(\mathcal{F}), \mathcal{T}(\mathcal{F}))$.

– One can adopt the strategy $\zeta = \texttt{choice}(R, accs(q, c) \rightarrow na)$, which introduces a default rule for this policy, where $q : Request$. The terms in Q which are not reduced by the rules from R will be rewritten into na. The example presented here is a security policy according to Definition 1.

The policy illustrated in this example has some desirable properties; for example the evaluation of a request is guaranteed to return a unique result, as will be demonstrated shortly.

A security policy is consistent if it computes at most one access decision:

Definition 2 (Consistency). *A security policy* $\wp = (\mathcal{F}, D, R, Q, \zeta)$ *is consistent if for every query* $q \in Q$, ζ *applied to* q *returns at most one result:* $\forall q \in Q$, *the cardinality of* $[\zeta](q) \cap D$ *is less than or equal to 1.*

This means that for every query evaluation, a deterministic result is computed by the application of ζ on the terms of Q. In the case where the strategy leads to a derivation that does not terminate on q, the cardinality of $[\zeta](q)$ is 0, the policy is still considered as consistent.

Example 4. Consider the following policy:

$$\wp_1 = (\ \mathcal{F}_1 \ = \ \{g : Decision \times Decision \rightarrow Decision, permit, deny : Decision\},$$
$$D_1 \ = \ \{permit, deny\},$$
$$R_1 \ = \ \{g(x, y) \rightarrow x, \ g(x, y) \rightarrow y\},$$
$$Q_1 \ = \ g(\mathcal{T}(\mathcal{F}), \mathcal{T}(\mathcal{F})),$$
$$\zeta_1 \ = \ \texttt{universal}(R))$$

Then $\wp_1$ is a security policy under the conditions expressed in Definition 1, but it clearly fails to be consistent, since $[\zeta](g(permit, deny)) = \{permit, deny\}$.

Since we assume strategies to be closed by concatenation, confluence under strategy can be simply expressed:

Definition 3 (Confluence under strategy). *A rewrite system* R *is confluent under a strategy* ζ *when* $\forall u, v_1, v_2 \in \mathcal{T}(\mathcal{F}, \mathcal{X})$ *such that* $\{v_1, v_2\} \subseteq [\zeta](u)$ *then* $[\zeta](v_1) \cap [\zeta](v_2) \neq \emptyset$.

If we consider the $\texttt{universal}$ strategy, the above definition reduces to the usual one of confluence. Therefore:

Proposition 1. *The policy* $(\mathcal{F}, D, R, Q, \texttt{universal})$ *is consistent as soon as* R *is confluent on* $\mathcal{T}(\mathcal{F}, \mathcal{X})$.

A second fundamental property is termination:

Definition 4 (Termination). *A security policy* $\wp = (\mathcal{F}, D, R, Q, \zeta)$ *is terminating if for every* $q \in Q$, *all derivations of source* q *in* ζ *are finite.*

A fundamental property is that terminating and confluent term-rewriting systems evaluate any term to an unique normal form.

Example 5. The policy from Example 3 is terminating and confluent, which can be easily checked by analyzing the rules in R. This guarantees that the evaluation of any request will return a unique decision.

Example 6. Consider the policy:

$$\wp_2 = (\ \begin{array}{rl} \mathcal{F}_2 & = \ \{a : Decision, permit : Decision, deny : Decision\}, \\ D_2 & = \ \{permit, deny\}, \\ R_2 & = \ \{a{\rightarrow}a, a{\rightarrow}deny\}, \\ Q_2 & = \ \{a\}, \\ \zeta_2 & = \ \texttt{universal}(R)) \end{array}$$

$\wp_2$ is a security policy. In contrast to the previous example, this policy is consistent (since the corresponding rewrite relation is confluent), but it is not terminating.

Some simple sufficient conditions allows us to apply termination results from rewrite theory:

Proposition 2. *A policy* $(\mathcal{F}, D, R, Q, \zeta)$ *terminates provided that all derivations in* ζ *are finite or if* R *is strongly terminating (i.e. all derivations in* $\texttt{universal}(R)$ *are finite).*

To ensure strong termination, classical quite powerful termination tools can be used like recursive path orderings [13] or dependency pairs [1]. Termination allows one to localize confluence check following Newmann's lemma and this can be made operational via the completion algorithm [25]. Therefore we inherit sufficient conditions for confluence and termination of policies using the universal strategy. Since in general we may use the finer notion of termination and confluence under strategies, this opens new research questions to establish sufficient conditions also for rich strategies.

Another expected property of a policy strategy is that it is able to evaluate every incoming request into at least one decision, following its strategy. This is expressed through the decision completeness property:

Definition 5 (Decision Completeness). *A security policy* $\wp = (\mathcal{F}, D, R, Q, \zeta)$ *is decision complete if* $\forall q \in Q$, $[\zeta](q) \neq \emptyset$ *and* $[\zeta](q)_{\downarrow} \subseteq D$.

This definition is close to the definition of sufficient completeness of a rewrite system, which states that every ground term evaluates to a term exclusively built with constructors and possibly variables [11, 23]. Several algorithms have been developed to check sufficient completeness or to complete a set of patterns to ensure this property [8].

Proposition 3. *A policy* $(\mathcal{F}, D, R, \mathcal{T}(\mathcal{F}), \texttt{universal}(\mathcal{R}))$ *is decision complete provided that* D *is the set of terms built from constructors only and that* R *is terminating and sufficiently complete.*

An alternative set of conditions ensuring completeness is that R is weakly terminating and that an innermost strategy is used, as shown in [17].

4 Policy Composition

Let us now focus on the problem of *combining* policies in a modular way, relying on the long history of research in combining rewrite systems. This combination consists in taking the union of signatures and rules of the two policy components, choosing the sets of requests and decisions, and building a strategy for the combination of the two strategies in each component of the composition. However, combining naively access-control policies can result in inconsistent or non-terminating policies and we show how syntactic conditions and strategies may help to keep these suitable properties for the composition of two policies. Based on the example of XACML policy combiners, we explore the idea of a rich combination language for policies based on rewriting strategies.

Definition 6 (Policy Composition). *A composition of the two policies* $\wp_i = (\mathcal{F}_i, D_i, R_i, Q_i, \zeta_i)$ $(i = 1, 2)$ *is any policy* $\wp = (\mathcal{F}, D, R, Q, \zeta)$, *where:*

1. $\mathcal{F}_1 \cup \mathcal{F}_2 \subseteq \mathcal{F}$;
2. $D_1 \cup D_2 \subseteq D \subseteq \mathcal{T}(\mathcal{F})$;
3. $R_1 \cup R_2 \subseteq R$;
4. $Q_1 \cup Q_2 \subseteq Q \subseteq \mathcal{T}(\mathcal{F})$;
5. ζ *is a rewrite strategy for* R.

Observe that when combining policies it may be convenient to introduce symbols not occurring in the original policies. The set of requests for the combined policy contains terms of the form determined by its sub-policies, but may also contain any additional well-formed closed terms that can be constructed from the combined policy signature. For example, suppose that $\mathcal{F}_1 = \{0, f\}$, $Q_1 = f(\mathcal{T}(\mathcal{F}_1))$ and $\mathcal{F}_2 = \{g\}$, $Q_2 = g(\mathcal{T}(\mathcal{F}_2))$, then a valid request would be $g(f(0))$.

The combination strategy is in charge of defining how the composed policy rewrites request terms. It may or not be built in a modular way by composing ζ_1 and ζ_2. It often can be expressed as a functional composition of component strategies.

Example 7. Based on the policy from Example 3, let us show how we can extend it with additional rules. Consider the access control rules R' below:

$$auth(req(phy(x), write, r), urgency) \rightarrow permit$$
$$auth(q, c) \qquad\qquad\qquad\qquad \rightarrow na$$

A strategy $\zeta' = \mathtt{choice}(R', R, auth(q, c) \rightarrow na)$ extends the previous policy by enforcing the rule for urgency cases first, and at the same time does not interfere with the decisions generated by the previous set of rules. In the case rule application fails for any of these cases, the combined policy delivers the *not-applicable* decision. This is a direct consequence of the semantics of the $\mathtt{choice}$ strategy.

The next example illustrates that much care must be taken in composing two policies.

Example 8. Consider the policies $\wp_1$, from Example 4, and the policy $\wp_3$ below.

$$\wp_3 = (\ \mathcal{F}_3 = \{\ f : Decision \times Decision \times Decision \rightarrow Decision,$$
$$permit : Decision, deny : Decision\}$$
$$D_3 = \{permit, deny\}$$
$$R_3 = \{f(permit, deny, x) \rightarrow f(x, x, x),$$
$$f(deny, permit, x) \rightarrow f(x, x, x),$$
$$f(x, x, x) \rightarrow x\},$$
$$Q_3 = f(\mathcal{T}(\mathcal{F}_2), \mathcal{T}(\mathcal{F}_2), \mathcal{T}(\mathcal{F}_2)),$$
$$\zeta_3 = \mathtt{universal}(R_2)\ )$$

The composition $\wp$ of $\wp_1$ and $\wp_2$ can be defined in a straightforward way as $\wp =:$

$$(\mathcal{F} = \mathcal{F}_1 \cup \mathcal{F}_3, D = D_1 = D_3, R = R_1 \cup R_3, Q = \mathcal{T}(\mathcal{F}_1 \cup \mathcal{F}_3), \zeta = \texttt{universal}(R))$$

These two policies are clearly terminating and share only symbols *permit* and *deny*. It is therefore quite intuitive to believe that their composition will be also terminating. But this is false since the following request has an infinite derivation:
$f(g(permit, deny), g(permit.deny), g(permit, deny)) {\rightarrow} f(permit, g(permit, deny),$
$g(permit, deny)) {\rightarrow} f(permit, deny, g(permit, deny)) {\rightarrow} f(g(permit, deny),$
$g(permit.deny), g(permit, deny)) \ldots$

A property of rewrite systems is said to be *modular* if it is preserved under composition of systems. Many modularity results for confluence and termination of rewrite systems have been produced and the interested reader can refer for instance to [35] for a survey. Confluence and termination are in general not modular properties for rewrite systems. In the context of rewrite systems on disjoint signatures, confluence is modular, while termination is not [37]. However, adding syntactic conditions on rewrite rules or on the existence of a simplification ordering, allows getting positive results. Relying on the results of the rewrite system community [38, 36, 31, 18, 26], we can state the following useful results about composition of security policies.

Proposition 4. *Let us consider two policies* $\wp_i = (\mathcal{F}_i, D_i, R_i, Q_i, \texttt{universal}(R_i))$ *($i = 1, 2$) such that* $\mathcal{F}_1$ *and* $\mathcal{F}_2$ *are disjoint and their composition* $\wp = (\mathcal{F}_1 \cup \mathcal{F}_2, D_1 \cup D_2, R_1 \cup R_2, \mathcal{T}(\mathcal{F}_1 \cup \mathcal{F}_2), \texttt{universal}(R))$. *If* $\wp_1$ *and* $\wp_2$ *are consistent, then* $\wp$ *is consistent. If* $\wp_1$ *and* $\wp_2$ *are terminating, then so is* $\wp$, *provided:*

1. *neither* R_1 *nor* R_2 *contain collapsing rules, or*
2. *neither* R_1 *nor* R_2 *contain duplicating rules, or*
3. R_1 *or* R_2 *contains neither collapsing rules nor duplicating rules, or*
4. *termination of* R_1 *and of* R_2 *are proved by a simplification ordering.*

Relaxing the disjointness assumption of signatures in the previous results led to consider constructor-sharing systems [27], composable systems [32] or hierarchical combinations of rewrite systems generalizing the previous ones by allowing a certain sharing of defined symbols [14].

The interest of rewriting strategies appears again in their composition. For instance, in contrast to termination, innermost termination has a nice modular behavior, for disjoint unions, constructor-sharing systems, composable systems and for certain hierarchical combinations. We can take advantage of such results about innermost termination [19] to state the following result:

Proposition 5. *Let us consider two policies* $\wp_i = (\mathcal{F}_i, D_i, R_i, Q_i, \texttt{innermost}(R_i))$ *($i = 1, 2$) such that* $\mathcal{F}_1$ *and* $\mathcal{F}_2$ *are disjoint or share only constructors, and* $\wp$ *be their composition* $(\mathcal{F}_1 \cup \mathcal{F}_2, D_1 \cup D_2, R_1 \cup R_2, \mathcal{T}(\mathcal{F}_1 \cup \mathcal{F}_2), \texttt{innermost}(R_1 \cup R_2))$. *Then* $\wp$ *is terminating as soon as* $\wp_1$ *and* $\wp_2$ *are.*

Example 9. Let us consider again the policies $\wp_1$, from Example 4 and $\wp_3$, from Example 8, but now with different strategies $\zeta_1' = \texttt{innermost}(R_1)$ and $\zeta_3' = \texttt{innermost}(R_3)$. Their combination $\wp = (\mathcal{F}_1 \cup \mathcal{F}_3, D, R_1 \cup R_3, \mathcal{T}(\mathcal{F}_1 \cup \mathcal{F}_3), \texttt{innermost}(R))$ is terminating according to Proposition 5.

Semantics of XACML Policy Combiners. In this paragraph, we show that the rewriting approach can capture the behavior of the access-control language XACML. Using rewriting and strategies it is easy to simulate the basic evaluation of XACML, computing *permit* or *deny* on a given request via a single policy. We do not present the translation from XACML to rewrite systems here due to the lack of space; details can be found in [15]. Instead, we show how the XACML policy *combiners* can be captured. The main combiners are listed below.

- *permit-overrides*: whenever *one* of the policies answers to a request with a *granting* decision, the final authorization for the composed policy will be granted. The policy will generate a *denial* only in the case at least one of the sub-policies denies the request, and all others return *not-applicable*.
- *deny-overrides*: this combiner has a similar semantics to *permit-overrides*, with the difference that denials take precedence.
- *first-applicable*: the decision produced by the combined policy corresponds to the authorization determined by the first sub-policy that does not fail, and whose decision is different from *not-applicable*.

To simulate *permit-overrides*, consider the following set of rules R_{po}.

$$
\begin{aligned}
po(permit, y) &\rightarrow permit \\
po(x, permit) &\rightarrow permit \\
po(deny, na) &\rightarrow deny \\
po(na, deny) &\rightarrow deny \\
po(na, na) &\rightarrow na
\end{aligned}
$$

We add an additional rule, R_{wrap}, whose purpose is to wrap any incoming request with the *po* function:

$$q(x) \rightarrow po(q(x), q(x))$$

In order to encode the *permit-overrides* combiner over two sub-policies, we can write the following strategy:

$$[\zeta_{po}](q) = \texttt{seq}([R_{wrap}](q), \texttt{onceBottomUp}(\zeta_1), \texttt{onceBottomUp}(\zeta_2), R_{po})$$

It means that the global policy intercepts requests before they are evaluated by the sub-policies. This builds a new term (of the form $po(t, t)$), containing two subterms, which will be separately evaluated in a bottom-up fashion by the component sub-policy strategies ζ_1 and ζ_2, then the reductions with R_{po} occur in the top position of the wrapped term, generating a final decision.

Therefore, given two policies $\wp_i = (\mathcal{F}_i, \{permit, deny, na\}, R_i, Q_i, \zeta_i)(i = 1, 2)$ the *permit-overrides* combiner is defined as

1. $\mathcal{F} = \mathcal{F}_1 \cup \mathcal{F}_2 \cup$
   $\{po : Decision \times Decision \rightarrow Decision, q : Request \rightarrow Decision\}$;
2. $D = \{permit, deny, na\}$;
3. $R = R_1 \cup R_2 \cup R_{po} \cup R_{wrap}$;
4. $Q = \{q(t) \mid t \in Q_1 \cup Q_2\}$;
5. $\zeta = \zeta_{po}$.

Clearly, *deny-overrides* can be simulated in an analogous way. In order to simulate the *first-applicable* combining algorithm, we need only to construct the strategy that schedules the rules in the order they appear in the policy file.

5 Related and Further Work

There are numerous proposals for languages in which to express access-control policies, many of them "logic-based". References [16, 20, 21, 22] represent a small sample of those.

With respect to policy composition, a number of works have a close relationship with the formalization introduced here. Bonatti et al. [7] address the composition problem through an algebra of composition operators that is able to define policy templates, among other operations; Wijesekera and Jajodia [40] take a similar approach. The operator definitions can be adapted to several languages and situations, since their definition is orthogonal to the underlying authorization language. On the other hand, we have shown how to deliver fine-grained control over the rule interaction of sub-policies.

Another alternative for composing access control policies is implemented by the Polymer system [5], which proposes rather classical operators on policies (conjunction, precedence, etc), and that allows reusing the policy objects, modifying them by executing additional actions, in order to specialize or enforce the policy.

A completely different approach to composition is taken by Lee et al in [29], based on the non-monotonic properties of defeasible logics. Here a single operator is proposed, which takes into account a precedence relation among the policies. We advocate that this kind of composition can also be achieved using rewriting strategies, which can readily define priorities on the rules.

Future work. We are using the Tom system to prototype and study the behavior of rewrite-based policies. Tom can also support the compilation process of our access control policies into JAVA classes, through the formal island framework [4]. The concepts presented in this paper provide a formal basis for reasoning about policies. This opens the way to the application of automated analysis tools to proving properties of policies.

References

[1] Arts, T., Giesl, J.: Termination of term rewriting using dependency pairs. Theoretical Computer Science 236, 133–178 (2000)
[2] Baader, F., Nipkow, T.: Term Rewriting and all That. Cambridge University Press, Cambridge (1998)
[3] Balland, E., Brauner, P., Kopetz, R., Moreau, P.-E., Reilles, A.: Tom Manual. LORIA, Nancy (France), version 2.4 edn. (October 2006)
[4] Balland, E., Kirchner, C., Moreau, P.-E.: Formal islands. In: Johnson, M., Vene, V. (eds.) AMAST 2006. LNCS, vol. 4019, pp. 51–65. Springer, Heidelberg (2006)
[5] Bauer, L., Ligatti, J., Walker, D.: Composing security policies with polymer. In: Sarkar, V., Hall, M.W. (eds.) PLDI, pp. 305–314. ACM Press, New York (2005)
[6] Bezem, M., Klop, J.W., de Vrijer, R. (eds.): Term Rewriting Systems. Cambridge University Press, Cambridge (2002)

[7] Bonatti, P.A., di Vimercati, S.D.C., Samarati, P.: An algebra for composing access control policies. ACM Trans. Inf. Syst. Secur. 5(1), 1–35 (2002)

[8] Bouhoula, A.: Spike: a system for sufficient completeness and parameterized inductive proofs. In: Bundy, A. (ed.) Automated Deduction - CADE-12. LNCS, vol. 814, pp. 836–840. Springer, Heidelberg (1994)

[9] Cirstea, H., Kirchner, C.: The rewriting calculus — Part I and II. Logic Journal of the Interest Group in Pure and Applied Logics 9, 427–498 (2001)

[10] Cirstea, H., Kirchner, C., Liquori, L., Wack, B.: Rewrite strategies in the rewriting calculus. In: Gramlich, B., Lucas, S. (eds.) Electronic Notes in Theoretical Computer Science, vol. 86, Elsevier, Amsterdam (2003)

[11] Comon, H.: Sufficient completeness, term rewriting systems and "anti-unification. In: Siekmann, J.H. (ed.) 8th International Conference on Automated Deduction. LNCS, vol. 230, pp. 128–140. Springer, Heidelberg (1986)

[12] de Oliveira, A.S.: Rewriting-based access control policies. In: Fernandez, M., Kirchner, C. (eds.) SecRet'06. Proceedings of the 1st International Workshop on Security and Rewriting Techniques (June 2006)

[13] Dershowitz, N.: Termination of rewriting. Journal of Symbolic Computation 3(1 & 2), 69–116 (1987)

[14] Dershowitz, N.: Hierarchical termination. In: Lindenstrauss, N., Dershowitz, N. (eds.) Conditional and Typed Rewriting Systems. LNCS, vol. 968, pp. 89–105. Springer, Heidelberg (1995)

[15] Dougherty, D.J.: Core XACML and term-rewriting systems. Technical Report WPI-CS-TR-07-07, Worcester Polytechnic Institute (2007)

[16] Dougherty, D.J., Fisler, K., Krishnamurthi, S.: Specifying and reasoning about dynamic access-control policies. In: Furbach, U., Shankar, N. (eds.) IJCAR 2006. LNCS (LNAI), vol. 4130, pp. 632–646. Springer, Heidelberg (2006)

[17] Gnaedig, I., Kirchner, H.: Computing constructor forms with non terminating rewrite programs. In: Bossi, A., Maher, M.J. (eds.) PPDP, pp. 121–132. ACM Press, New York (2006)

[18] Gramlich, B.: Generalized sufficient conditions for modular termination of rewriting. In: Kirchner, H., Levi, G. (eds.) Algebraic and Logic Programming. LNCS, vol. 632, pp. 53–68. Springer, Heidelberg (1992)

[19] Gramlich, B.: On proving termination by innermost termination. In: Ganzinger, H. (ed.) Rewriting Techniques and Applications. LNCS, vol. 1103, pp. 93–107. Springer, Heidelberg (1996)

[20] Halpern, J.Y., Weissman, V.: Using first-order logic to reason about policies. In: CSFW, pp. 187–201. IEEE Computer Society Press, Los Alamitos (2003)

[21] Jajodia, S., Samarati, P., Sapino, M.L., Subrahmanian, V.S.: Flexible support for multiple access control policies. ACM Trans. Database Syst. 26(2), 214–260 (2001)

[22] Kalam, A., Baida, R., Balbiani, P., Benferhat, S., Cuppens, F., Deswarte, Y., Miege, A., Saurel, C., Trouessin, G.: Organization based access control. In: Policies for Distributed Systems and Networks, 2003. Proceedings. POLICY 2003. IEEE 4th International Workshop, pp. 120–131. IEEE Computer Society Press, Los Alamitos (2003)

[23] Kapur, D., Narendran, P., Rosenkrantz, D.J., Zhang, H.: Sufficient-completeness, ground-reducibility and their complexity. Acta Inf. 28(4), 311–350 (1991)

[24] Kirchner, C., Kirchner, H., Vittek, M.: Designing clp using computational systems. In: Hentenryck, P.V., Saraswat, S. (eds.) Principles and Practice of Constraint Programming, ch. 8, pp. 133–160. MIT press, Cambridge (1995)

[25] Knuth, D.E., Bendix, P.B.: Simple word problems in universal algebras. In: Leech, J. (ed.) Computational Problems in Abstract Algebra, pp. 263–297. Pergamon Press, Oxford (1970)

[26] Kurihara, M., Ohuchi, A.: Modularity of simple termination of term rewriting systems. Journal of IPS Japan 31(5), 633–642 (1990)

[27] Kurihara, M., Ohuchi, A.: Modularity of simple termination of term rewriting systems with shared constructors. Theor. Comput. Sci. 103(2), 273–282 (1992)

[28] Lampson, B.: Protection. ACM Operating Systems Review. Vol 8, 18–24 (1974)

[29] Lee, A.J., Boyer, J.P., Olson, L., Gunter, C.A.: Defeasible security policy composition for web services. In: Winslett, M., Gordon, A.D., Sands, D. (eds.) FMSE, pp. 45–54. ACM Press, New York (2006)

[30] Martí-Oliet, N., Meseguer, J., Verdejo, A.: Towards a strategy language for maude. Electr. Notes Theor. Comput. Sci. 117, 417–441 (2005)

[31] Middeldorp, A.: A sufficient condition for the termination of the direct sum of term rewriting systems. In: Proceedings 4th IEEE Symposium on Logic in Computer Science, Pacific Grove, pp. 396–401. IEEE Computer Society Press, Los Alamitos (1989)

[32] Middeldorp, A., Toyama, Y.: Completeness of combinations of constructor systems. In: Proceedings 4th Conference on Rewriting Techniques and Applications, Como (Italy) (1991) (also Report CS-R9058, CWI (1990))

[33] Moreau, P.-E., Ringeissen, C., Vittek, M.: A pattern matching compiler for multiple target languages. In: Hedin, G. (ed.) CC 2003 and ETAPS 2003. LNCS, vol. 2622, pp. 61–76. Springer, Heidelberg (2003)

[34] Moses, T.: eXtensible Access Control Markup Language (XACML) version 2.0. Technical report, OASIS (2005)

[35] Ohlebusch, E.: Advanced Topics in Term Rewriting. Springer, Heidelberg (2002)

[36] Rusinowitch, M.: On termination of the direct sum of term rewriting systems. Information Processing Letters 26(2), 65–70 (1987)

[37] Toyama, Y.: Counterexamples to termination for the direct sum of term rewriting systems. Technical report, NTT Electrical Communications Laboratories Japan (1987)

[38] Toyama, Y.: On the Church-Rosser property for the direct sum of term rewritig systens. Journal of the ACM 34(1), 128–143 (1987)

[39] Visser, E.: Stratego: A language for program transformation based on rewriting strategies. System description of Stratego 0.5. In: Middeldorp, A. (ed.) RTA 2001. LNCS, vol. 2051, pp. 357–361. Springer, Heidelberg (2001)

[40] Wijesekera, D., Jajodia, S.: A propositional policy algebra for access control. ACM Trans. Inf. Syst. Secur. 6(2), 286–325 (2003)

On the Automated Correction of Security Protocols Susceptible to a Replay Attack*

Juan C. Lopez P.[1], Raúl Monroy[1], and Dieter Hutter[2]

[1] Computer Science Department
Tecnológico de Monterrey, Campus Estado de México
Carretera al lago de Guadalupe, Km 3.5, Atizapán, 52926, Mexico
{juan.pimentel,raulm}@itesm.mx
[2] DFKI, Stuhlsatzenhausweg 3, D-66123 Saarbrücken, Germany
hutter@dfki.de

Abstract. Although there exist informal design guidelines and formal development support, security protocol development is time-consuming because design is error-prone. In this paper, we introduce SHRIMP, a mechanism that aims to speed up the development cycle by adding automated aid for protocol diagnosis and repair. SHRIMP relies on existing verification tools both to analyse an intermediate protocol and to compute attacks if the protocol is flawed. Then it analyses such attacks to pinpoint the source of the failure and synthesises appropriate patches, using Abadi and Needham's principles for protocol design. We have translated some of these principles into formal requirements on (sets of) protocol steps. For each requirement, there is a collection of rules that transform a set of protocol steps violating the requirement into a set conforming it. We have successfully tested our mechanism on 36 faulty protocols, getting a repair rate of 90%.

1 Introduction

Although there exists formal development support, as well as informal design guidelines, a lot of protocols, whether recent or not, are faulty. Further aid for protocol development is thus required. In this paper, we introduce SHRIMP, a Smart metHod for Repairing IMperfect security Protocols. SHRIMP aims at speeding up the formal software development cycle, bridging the gap between design and analysis by means of diagnosis and repair. It offers benefits to practising security engineers, including getting a better insight into a protocol flaw and enabling incremental protocol design. These features are all of interest because nowadays protocols are more complicated than just 3—5 steps (e.g. the SET protocol) and their various parts are intertwined, making it hard for a human to cope with all the subtle dependencies.

---

* This paper has largely benefited from numerous discussions with Alan Bundy and Graham Steel. It is based on research Monroy conducted while on sabbatical leave at Edinburgh University and DFKI, Saarbrücken. Monroy's stay in Germany was funded by DAAD A/06/32941 and CONACyT J110.382/06.

J. Biskup and J. Lopez (Eds.): ESORICS 2007, LNCS 4734, pp. 594–609, 2007.

SHRIMP relies on existing state-of-the-art tools both to analyse an (intermediate) protocol and, if the protocol is flawed, to find one or more of protocol runs violating a given security requirement, called an *attack*. It then analyses the protocol and the attack[1] to pinpoint the faulty steps of the protocol and synthesises appropriate changes to fix them. This yields an improved version of the protocol that should be analysed and potentially patched again until no further flaws can be detected.

To identify and patch a protocol flaw, we have translated some of the informal principles for the design of security protocols of Abadi and Needham [1] into formal requirements on sets of protocol steps. For each requirement, there is a collection of rules that transform a set of protocol steps violating the requirement into a set conforming it. The correction of security protocols incorporates the use of several of these rules. However, the patches are not independent and the application of a rule requires preconditions to be applicable and should guarantee postconditions once it has been applied. As a general framework to organise the application of such rules, we have adopted the proof planning methodology [4], developed to automate inductive theorem proving.

We have hitherto focused on automatically fixing protocols subject to a replay attack,[2] since many known faulty protocols fail to resist it.[3] This paper introduces two patching methods which, together with a generalisation of that presented in [10], almost deal with the full class of replay attacks proposed by Syverson [14] (the only exception being the type flaw subclass.[4]) We have successfully tested SHRIMP on 36 protocols, 21 out of which were borrowed from the Clark and Jacob library, obtaining a repair rate of 90%. Since our approach to protocol repair requires an attack to reason about, to analyse a protocol and to get an attack whenever it was faulty, we used AVISPA, http://www.avispa-project.org/. So throughout this paper we shall refer to AVISPA's hierarchy of authentication.

The rest of this paper is organised as follows: §2 describes the types of flaws we want to automatically patch and describes the theoretical framework underlying our approach to protocol repair. SHRIMP is presented in §3. We recapitulate the experimental results found throughout our investigation in §4 and discuss related work in §5. Conclusions and indications for further work appear in §6.

2 Fixing Faulty Security Protocols

2.1 Abadi and Needham's Principles

Abadi and Needham postulated 11 principles for the prudent design of security protocols [1] after noticing common features amongst protocols they found hard

---

[1] Our experiments show that it is not necessary to explicitly consider the property the protocol fails to satisfy; this might be attributable to that such a property is already implicit in the attack.

[2] A *replay attack* is a form of attack where a data transmission is repeated or delayed.

[3] Most of the attacks reported in the Clark-Jacob library [7] are of type replay.

[4] A *type flaw attack* is an attack where a participant confuses a (field of a) message containing data of one type with a message data of another.

to analyse. We use some of these principles to diagnose the cause of an attack. In particular, SHRIMP takes care of replay attacks where the message being reused is a cypher-text, dealing with the following protocol flaws:

1. Two or more different cypher-texts of the same protocol cannot be distinguished from one another. This flaw violates principle 10, *recognising messages and encodings*, which prescribes being careful about the format of a message: principals should be able to associate which step or which run a message corresponds to, regardless of whatever protocol they are running;
2. The originator/recipients of a cypher-text in one message of the protocol cannot be distinguished. This flaw violates principle 3, *agent naming*, which prescribes that the agent names relevant for a message should all be derivable either from the format of a message or from its content; and
3. Two or more different runs of the same protocol cannot be distinguished from one another. Upon reception, a participant cannot separate which run the message belongs to. This flaw violates principle 10, since the message cannot be bound to a particular run of the protocol. It also violates principles 6—8, since the protocol does not guarantee association or temporal succession.

2.2   Strand Spaces

In order to reason about non-trivial messages and their intended role in a protocol, SHRIMP uses a formalisation of individual message notations. Most this formalisation has already been developed for protocol verification (e.g. strand spaces [15] or Paulson's logic [12]). SHRIMP's constructs might be accommodated within any logic. Here we choose strand spaces, because the method for fixing a protocol without a proper message encoding can be theoretically justified using authentication tests [9]. In the sequel, we assume knowledge of strands spaces, though notation and authentication tests are recalled below.

Messages, ranged over by $M_1, M_2, \ldots$, are also called terms. The set of terms, A, is freely generated from two disjoint sets, the set of texts (T) and the set of keys (K), by means of concatenation, $M_1; M_2$, and encryption, $\{M\}_K$ ($K \in \mathsf{K}$). T contains nonces, $N_a, N_b, \ldots$, timestamps, $T_a, T_b, \ldots$, agent names, $A, B, \ldots$, and tags, $\ell_a, \ell_b, \ldots$. There are two functions, one maps principals, $A, B, \ldots$, to their public keys, $K_a^+, K_b^+, \ldots$, and the other a pair of principals, $\langle A, B \rangle$, to their symmetric shared key, K_{ab}. K comes with an inverse operator mapping each member of a key pair for an asymmetric cryptosystem to the other, $(K_a^+)^{-1} = K_a^-$, and each symmetric key to itself, $(K_{ab})^{-1} = K_{ab}$. Let Safe denote the set of keys that are safe and Safe_a denote the set of keys known by a regular, non-compromised agent A.

The subterm relation, $\sqsubseteq$, is the least relation such that $M \sqsubseteq M$, $M \sqsubseteq \{M_1\}_K$ if $M \sqsubseteq M_1$, and $M \sqsubseteq M_1; M_2$ if $M \sqsubseteq M_1$ or $M \sqsubseteq M_2$. Notice that, for any $K \in \mathsf{K}$, $K \sqsubseteq \{M\}_K$ only if $K \sqsubseteq M$. A message is atomic if it is not an encrypted term or a concatenated one. A message M_0 is a component of M if $M_0 \sqsubseteq M$, M_0 is not a concatenated term, and for every $M_1 \neq M_0$ such that $M_0 \sqsubseteq M_1 \sqsubseteq M$ implies that M_1 is a concatenated term.

A *strand* is a sequence of nodes, each denotes a communicating event, where transmission (respectively reception) of a term M is denoted as $+M$ (respectively $-M$). So a node is either positive or negative. Let s be a strand and let $\langle s, i \rangle$ and $\langle s, i+1 \rangle$ denote the i-th and the $i+1$-th nodes of s. Then $\langle s, i \rangle \Rightarrow \langle s, i+1 \rangle$. $\Rightarrow^+$ and $\Rightarrow^*$ are used to respectively denote the transitive and the transitive-reflexive closure of $\Rightarrow$. $n \rightarrow n'$ denotes inter-strand communication; it requires the nodes to be complementary one another, in terms of polarity, $\mathsf{sign}(n) = + \neq \mathsf{sign}(n')$, and matching, in terms of the message being exchanged, $\mathsf{msg}(n) = \mathsf{msg}(n')$. A *strand space* Σ is a set of strands, where $\Rightarrow$ and $\rightarrow$ impose a graph structure on the nodes of Σ. Each strand represents a protocol run from the local perspective of a participant. If the participant is honest, the strand, as well as the strand nodes, is said to be regular and penetrator otherwise. A term M *originates* at a node n if $\mathsf{sign}(n) = +$; $M \sqsubseteq \mathsf{msg}(n)$; and $M \not\sqsubseteq \mathsf{msg}(n')$, for every $n' \Rightarrow^+ n$. M is said to be *uniquely originating* if it originates on only one node in the strand space. unique_s is the set of terms uniquely generated at strand s.

A finite, acyclic graph, $\mathcal{B} = \langle \mathcal{N}, (\rightarrow \cup \Rightarrow) \rangle$, is a *bundle* if for every $n_2 \in \mathcal{N}$, i) if $\mathsf{sign}(n_2) = -$, then there is a unique $n_1 \in \mathcal{N}$ with $n_1 \rightarrow n_2$; and ii) if $n_1 \Rightarrow n_2$ then $n_1 \in \mathcal{N}$ and $n_1 = \langle s, i \rangle$ and $n_2 = \langle s, i+1 \rangle$. Let $\mathcal{B}$ be a bundle, then $\prec_\mathcal{B}$ and $\preceq_\mathcal{B}$ denote respectively the transitive and the transitive-reflexive closure of $(\rightarrow \cup \Rightarrow)$.

For brevity, protocols will be specified by a sequence of steps, each of the form $q.\ A \rightarrow B : M$, meaning that, at step q, agent A sends message M to agent B, which B receives. Similarly, an attack will be given as a sequence of steps, each affixed with their session: $s : q.\ A \rightarrow B$ stands for the q-th step of the s-th run of a protocol. We find it convenient to respectively use S and Spy to refer to the server and the penetrator. So $A \rightarrow \mathsf{Spy}(B) : M$ and $\mathsf{Spy}(A) \rightarrow B$ respectively denote interception of M and impersonation of A. We will use K_a as an abbreviation for K_{as}.

Suppose that A is a participant in a protocol. Suppose that at node n_0 A creates a new term N, builds $M = \{\!|M'|\!\}_K$, such that $N \sqsubseteq M$ and M is a component of $\mathsf{msg}(n_0)$, and then transmits $\mathsf{msg}(n_0)$. Suppose that N is uniquely generated, that M is not a subterm of a component of any regular node in the protocol and that the decryption key is safe, $K^{-1} \in \mathsf{Safe}$. If N is later received, at node n_1, outside the form $\{\!|M'|\!\}_K$, then only a honest participant, not the penetrator, must have been responsible for N to have gone out of this form. The edge $n_0 \Rightarrow^+ n_1$ is an *outgoing test for N in M*. If, instead, N is sent possibly in clear and it later is received in encrypted form $\{\!|\ldots; N; \ldots|\!\}_{K'}$, where $K' \in \mathsf{safe}$, then only a honest participant, not the penetrator, must have been responsible for N to have entered to this form. The edge $n_0 \Rightarrow^+ n_1$ is an *incoming test for N in $\{\!|\ldots; N; \ldots|\!\}_{K'}$*.

2.3   Shrimp's Meta-logic

SHRIMP analyses the encoding of a message to determine when a cypher-text may be used to arm a replay and how it should be changed to prevent a replay. In the following we introduce a notion of similarity of messages and how messages can be modified to break a given similarity. Let $\square$ be a special symbol that is not an atomic message and S be a set of keys. The *pattern* [2] p of a message M visible wrt. S is given by:

$$p_S(M) = \{p_S(M)\}_K \text{ if } M = \{M\}_K \wedge K^{-1} \in S \quad p_S(M) = M \text{ if } M \text{ is atomic}$$
$$p_S(M) = p_S(M_1, S); p_S(M_2) \text{ if } M = M_1; M_2 \quad\quad p_S(M) = \square \text{ otherwise}$$

Definition 1 (Similarity). *Two messages M and M' are similar wrt. S, written $M \sim_S M'$, iff there is a bijective replacement α on patterns (with $\square\alpha = \square$), mapping symbols from M to M', such that $p_S(M)\alpha = p_{S\alpha}(M')$ holds.*

Definition 2 (Visible Content). *The visible content $ct_S(M)$ of a message M wrt. a set of keys S is given by:*

$$ct_S(M) = \{M\} \quad \text{if } M \text{ is atomic} \quad\quad ct_S(M_1; M_2) = ct_S(M_1) \cup ct_S(M_2)$$
$$ct_S(\{M\}_K) = ct_S(M) \quad \text{if } K^{-1} \in S \quad\quad ct_S(M) = \emptyset \quad \text{if } K^{-1} \notin S$$

Two messages M and M' are equivalent under rearrangement, $M \equiv M'$ for short, iff $ct_S(M) = ct_S(M')$ for all sets of keys S.

SHRIMP also includes symbols that allow us to compute the name of the agents involved in the exchange of a message and to reason about the name of the agents that can be inferred from the encoding of a message. Given a bundle $\mathcal{B}$, A is the *originator* (respectively *recipient*) of a term M, $A \triangleright_\mathcal{B} M$, (respectively $A \triangleleft_\mathcal{B} M$) iff there is a positive (respectively negative) node n in a strand played by A of $\mathcal{B}$ such that M originates at n (respectively $M \in ct_S(\mathsf{msg}(n))$, S being the keys known to A.)

Definition 3 (Correspondents). *Let $\mathcal{B}$ be a bundle. The participants involved in the exchange of M in $\mathcal{B}$, called the* correspondents *of M, Partners($[M]$)$_\mathcal{B}$, is given by $\{A : A \triangleright_\mathcal{B} M \vee A \triangleleft_\mathcal{B} M\}$.*

Definition 4. *The names of the agents that can be (safely) deduced from the encoding of a message is given by:*

$$\text{Agents}(\{M\}_K) = \{A\} \cup \text{Agents}(M) \quad\quad \text{if } K = K_a^+ \vee K = K_a^-$$
$$\text{Agents}(\{M\}_{K_{ab}}) = \text{Agents}(M)$$
$$\text{Agents}(M_1; M_2) = \text{Agents}(M_1) \cup \text{Agents}(M_2)$$
$$\text{Agents}(M) = \{M\} \quad\quad\quad \text{if } M \text{ is a name}$$
$$\text{Agents}(M) = \{\,\} \quad\quad\quad\quad \text{otherwise}$$

Notice that we do not infer names from symmetric encryption, because the flow of the message cannot be determined.

SHRIMP finds bugs in protocols by analysing a bundle containing a penetrator strand. Often this analysis suggests a change in the structure of a message and in that case SHRIMP identifies the node originating such message considering a bundle denoting an intended protocol run. With this, we compute the changes to be done in one such a regular bundle, which we then propagate to the protocol description. The following definitions aim at a meta-theory to allow for tracing the consequences of changing all the nodes in the set of strands depending on changes to a particular node.

Let $Pos(M)$ be the set of all positions π in M. Elements in Pos are sequences and $\cdot$ denotes sequence concatenation. Two positions π, π' are independent if there is no π'' that either $\pi = \pi' \cdot \pi''$ or $\pi' = \pi \cdot \pi''$ holds. $M_{|\pi}$ is the submessage of M at position π and $M[\pi \leftarrow M']$ is the message obtained by replacing $M_{|\pi}$ in M by M'.

Definition 5 (Explicit Replacement). *A set* $\zeta = \{(\pi_1, M_1), \ldots, (\pi_n, M_n)\}$ *is an* explicit replacement *iff for all* $1 \leq i \leq n : \pi_i \in$ Pos *and* M_i *are messages and for all* $i \neq j$: π_i *and* π_j *are independent.* $\mathcal{ER}$ *denotes the set of all explicit replacements.*

$\zeta = \{(\pi_1, M_1), \ldots, (\pi_n, M_n)\} \in \mathcal{ER}$ *is an* explicit replacement for a message M *iff* $\pi_i \in Pos(M)$ *for all* $1 \leq i \leq n$. *The application of* ζ *on a message* M *is given by* $\zeta(M) = M[\pi_1 \leftarrow M_1, \ldots, \pi_n \leftarrow M_n]$.

Changing a message that is sent from A to B changes the knowledge of B and thus its abilities to construct consecutive messages. If B should forward an encrypted messages coming from A and this latter message is changed in the protocol, then we also have to change the message forwarded by B. Hence we need a mapping between an old encrypted (sub-)message and the corresponding new message:

Definition 6 (P-Assignment). *A position* π *of a message* M *is* protected *wrt. a set of keys* S *iff* $M_{|\pi}$ *has the form* $\{|M'|\}_K$ *and* $K^{-1} \notin S$. *A protected position is* minimal *iff all smaller positions are not protected wrt.* S. $Prot_S(M)$ *denotes the set of all submessages of* M *at minimal protected positions of* M *wrt.* S.

Two messages M *and* M' *are* p-assigned *wrt.* S *iff for each* $\{|N|\}_K \in Prot_S(M)$ *there is a unique message* N' *with* $\{|N'|\}_K \in Prot_S(M')$. *The* p-assignment $\Delta_{M,M',S}$ *of* M *and* M' *is the set of pairs* $(\{|N|\}_K, \{|N'|\}_K)$ *of corresponding terms at minimal protected positions of* M *and* M'.

In many cases, a protocol change will simply enrich the messages exchanged by the principals with additional information. We capture this property as follows:

Definition 7 (Monotonicity). *Let* M, M' *be messages and let* $A_0 \subseteq A$. $M \leq_{A_0} M'$ *iff* $ct_S(M) \subseteq ct_S(M')$ *and* $ct_S(M') \subseteq ct_S(M) \cup ct_S(A_0)$ *for all* $S \subseteq K$.

An explicit replacement ζ *is* monotone *for* M *wrt.* A_0 *iff* $M \leq_{A_0} \zeta(M)$ *holds.* ζ *is strongly* monotone *iff for all* $S \subseteq K$ *and all* $(\{|N|\}_K, \{|N'|\}_K) \in \Delta_{M,M',S}$: $N \leq_{A_0} N'$ *holds.*

Definition 8 (Collision Freeness). *Let* S *be a set of keys,* M *a message and let* $A_0 \subseteq A$ *be a set of messages.* M *is* collision free *to* A_0 *iff* $\forall M' \in ct_S(M). \forall M'' \in A_0. (M' \not\prec_S M'')$.

Given a set of keys S, a set $\Delta_{M,M',S} = \{(M_1, N_1), \ldots (M_n, N_n)\}$ denotes also a term replacement function which maps messages to messages. Given a message

N, we obtain $\Delta_{M,M',S}(N)$ by replacing each occurrence of M_i in a minimal protected position of N by N_i.

Definition 9 (Admissibility). *An explicit replacement ζ for M is admissible for M wrt. a set of keys S iff M and $\zeta(M)$ are p-assigned. Let ζ be admissible for M then $\Delta_{M,\zeta(M),S}$ is the corresponding term replacement function of ζ wrt. M and S.*

Given a term replacement function Δ, a set of keys S and a node n with $M = \mathsf{msg}(n)$ then $\Delta^{n,S} = \{(\pi_1, \Delta(M_{|\pi_1})), \ldots, (\pi_n, \Delta(M_{|\pi_n}))\}$ with $\{\pi_1, \ldots \pi_n\}$ being all minimal protected positions π of M wrt. S with $\Delta(M_{|\pi}) \neq M_{|\pi}$.

Definition 10 (Representativeness). *A bundle $\mathcal{B} = \langle \mathcal{N}_\mathcal{B}, (\to_\mathcal{B} \cup \Rightarrow_\mathcal{B}) \rangle$ over a protocol is representative iff it is regular and for every node $\langle s, i \rangle \in \mathcal{B}$ and $s = r\alpha_s$ the replacement application operator α_s is injective and $r\alpha \subseteq \mathcal{N}_\mathcal{B}$.*

Definition 11 (Adaption). *Let $\mathcal{B} = \langle \mathcal{N}_\mathcal{B}, (\to_\mathcal{B} \cup \Rightarrow_\mathcal{B}) \rangle$ be a representive bundle over a protocol. The adaption ζ of $\mathcal{B}$ for an explicit replacement ζ_0 in a positive node $n_0 \in \mathcal{N}_\mathcal{B}$ maps each node of the bundle to an explicit replacement and is defined as follows:*

$$\zeta[n] = \emptyset \quad \text{if } n \preceq_\mathcal{B} n_0 \text{ and } n \neq n_0 \qquad \zeta[n] = \zeta_0 \quad \text{if } n = n_0$$
$$\zeta[n] = \zeta[n'] \text{ if } n' \to n \qquad \qquad \zeta[n] = \Delta^{n,S} \text{ if } n_0 \prec_\mathcal{B} n \text{ and } n \text{ is positive}$$

where $\Delta = \bigcup_{n' \in N} \Delta_{\mathsf{msg}(n'),\zeta[n'](\mathsf{msg}(n')),S}$ with N being the set of all negative nodes n' with $n' \Rightarrow n$ and S is the set of keys known by the principal playing the role associated with the strand where n lies, at the moment of sending $\mathsf{msg}(n)$. ζ is admissible on $\mathcal{B}$ iff, for all $n \in \mathcal{B}$, $\zeta[n]$ is admissible on $\mathsf{msg}(n)$.

Given a representative bundle and an injective function α_s mapping a strand s of the protocol to nodes of the bundle we can easily use the adaption of these nodes in order to change the strand s itself by applying $\zeta[\langle s, i \rangle]\alpha_s^{-1}$ to each node $\langle s, i \rangle$ of s. Given an adaption ζ on a representative bundle for P we write $\zeta(P)$ to denote the protocol that resuls after the application of $\zeta[\langle s, i \rangle]\alpha_s^{-1}$.

Using this procedure, SHRIMP is able to modify a protocol description, starting from the node originating the message that suggested the enhancement to all the successor nodes where the changes endure. This yields a path, we call a *change enduring path*. A change enduring path is guaranteed to be finite and acyclic both because bundles are also finite and acyclic and because changes are propagated considering only inter-strand transitions.

Proposition 1 (Monotonicity of Bundles). *Let $\mathcal{B} = \langle \mathcal{N}_\mathcal{B}, (\to_\mathcal{B} \cup \Rightarrow_\mathcal{B}) \rangle$ be a representive bundle over a protocol and ζ be an adaption for an explicit replacement ζ_0 in a positive node $n_0 \in \mathcal{N}_\mathcal{B}$. If ζ_0 is strongly monotone for $\mathsf{msg}(n_0)$ wrt. a set of messages A_0 then $\zeta[n]$ is strongly monotone for $\mathsf{msg}(n)$ wrt. A_0 for all $n \in \mathcal{N}_\mathcal{B}$.*

Proof (Outline). The proof is done by induction on the length of $\prec_\mathcal{B}$. As one base case we assume $n \prec_\mathcal{B} n_0$. Thus $\zeta[n] = \emptyset$ and the proposition holds trivially.

As another base case consider $n_0 = n$ then again the proposition holds trivially due to the given assumptions on ζ_0. Suppose n is negative and $\exists n'. \, n' \rightarrow n$. As an induction hypothesis we assume that $\zeta[n']$ is strongly monotone for $\mathsf{msg}(n')$ and S wrt. A. Since $\mathsf{msg}(n') = \mathsf{msg}(n)$ we conclude that $\zeta[n] = \zeta[n']$ is strongly monotone for $\mathsf{msg}(n)$ and S wrt. A. Now suppose n is positive and different from n_0. As an induction hypothesis we assume that $\zeta[n']$ is strongly monotone for all negative nodes n' with $n' \Rightarrow^+ n$. Thus, $N \leq_{\mathsf{A}_0} N'$ for all $(\{\!|N|\!\}_K, \{\!|N'|\!\}_K) \in \Delta_{\mathsf{msg}(n'),\zeta[n'](\mathsf{msg}(n')),S}$ and arbitrary $S \in \mathsf{K}$. Hence, $N \leq_{\mathsf{A}_0} N'$ for all $(\{\!|N|\!\}_K, \{\!|N'|\!\}_K) \in \Delta$ holds and $\zeta[n] = \Delta^{n,S}$ is strongly monotone wrt. A_0. $\square$

2.4 Patch Planning Faulty Security Protocols

A *patch method* is a 5-tuple (name, input, preconditions, patch, effect). The first component is the *name* of the method. The second component is the *input*, which is often the description of a faulty protocol P, a bundle $\mathcal{B}_A$ describing the attack, and a representative bundle $\mathcal{B}_R$ describing the intended run of the protocol. The third component is the *preconditions*, a formula written in a meta-logic that the input objects must satisfy. SHRIMP uses these preconditions to predict whether the associated patch will make the protocol no longer susceptible to the attack. The fourth component is the *patch*, a procedure specifying how to mend the input protocol. Finally, the fifth component is the *effects*, a formula specifying required properties of the newer version of the protocol.

Methods can be compound by invoking other methods using *methodicals* (functions that link methods together to control search). A *compound method* is a 4-tuple (name, input, preconditions, method). It involves the name of the compound method, the input, the preconditions, and then the method build from methodicals, mostly in our case *orelse_meth*. *orelse_meth* $meth_1$ $meth_2$ tries $meth_1$ and if that fails tries $meth_2$.

3 Fixing Faulty Protocols Subject to a Replay Attack

The chief method of SHRIMP is the *replay* compound method, see Fig. 1. It invokes three sub-methods: *message_encoding*, *agent_naming* and *session_binding*. The order in which methods are attempted is important as it imposes a hierarchy in terms of the complexity of implementing the patch. *message_encoding* is more viable because when modifying a protocol message it may not introduce additional components. *agent_naming* is more viable than *session_binding* because it only modifies protocol messages. By contrast, *session_binding* involves the insertion of protocol steps.

3.1 Patching Protocols Violating Principle 10

The *message_encoding* method, see Fig. 2, repairs a faulty protocol that portrays two or more cypher-texts that are different one another but have similar structure and so violates principle 10. The adversary may exploit this vulnerability by

---

Name: *replay*
Input: $P \in \Sigma, \mathcal{B}_A, \mathcal{B}_R$
Preconditions:

    % Spy reuses cypher-text $\{\!|M|\!\}_K$:

    $\exists i, j, k, M, K.$

      $\langle s_r, i \rangle \preceq_B \langle s_p, j \rangle \prec_B \langle s_q, k \rangle \wedge \{\!|M|\!\}_K \sqsubseteq \mathsf{msg}(\langle s_r, i \rangle) \wedge \{\!|M|\!\}_K \sqsubseteq \mathsf{msg}(\langle s_p, j \rangle)$

    % s_p is the penetrator while s_q the principal being deceived

    $\wedge \langle s_r, i \rangle$ and $\langle s_q, k \rangle$ are regular but $\langle s_p, j \rangle$ is not

    $\wedge \mathsf{sign}(\langle s_r, i \rangle) = + = \mathsf{sign}(\langle s_p, j \rangle)$ but $\mathsf{sign}(\langle s_q, k \rangle) = -$

Method:

    orelse_meth message_encoding$(P, \mathcal{B}_A, \mathcal{B}_R, M, K, \langle s_q, k \rangle)$

    orelse_meth agent_naming$(P, \mathcal{B}_A, \mathcal{B}_R, M, K, \langle s_q, k \rangle)$

        session_binding$(P, \mathcal{B}_A, \mathcal{B}_R, M, K, \langle s_q, k \rangle)$

Fig. 1. The *replay* compound method

making one cypher-text play the role of the other. An example faulty protocol with this vulnerability is Wide-Mouth Frog (WMF): (part of) the initiator's first message can be reused to mimic the result of another request the server has acted upon. AVISPA proves WMF fails to guarantee weak authentication of B to A, yielding:

WMF		Attack
1. $A \to S : A; \{\!|B; T_a; K_{ab}|\!\}_{K_a}$	1:1.	$A \to \mathsf{Spy}(S) : A; \{\!|B; T_a; K_{ab}|\!\}_{K_a}$
2. $S \to B : \{\!|A; T_a + d; K_{ab}|\!\}_{K_b}$	2:2. $\mathsf{Spy}(S) \to A$	$: \{\!|B; T_a; K_{ab}|\!\}_{K_a}$

To remove the protocol flaw, it suffices to break this similarity. When input WMF and the attack above, *message_encoding* successfully repairs it returning:[5]

$$1. A \to S : A; \{\!|\boxed{T_a; B}; K_{ab}|\!\}_{K_a} \qquad 2. S \to B : \{\!|A; T_a + d; K_{ab}|\!\}_{K_b} \qquad (1)$$

Proposition 2. *Let ζ be the adaption of the representive bundle $\mathcal{B}_R$ as given in Fig. 2. and $P' = \zeta(P)$ be the corresponding revised protocol. Then $\zeta(\{\!|M|\!\}_K)$ cannot be used to arm a message encoding replay attack on P'.*

Proof (outline). $\zeta(\{\!|M|\!\}_K)$ is not similar to any other component. Then, only the execution of a specific step in P' may cause $\zeta(\{\!|M|\!\}_K)$ to appear on the traffic, if ever. If P satisfies security property ϕ then so will P', because extra elements in $\zeta(\{\!|M|\!\}_K)$, if any, are all innocuous tags. □

3.2 Patching Protocols Violating Principles 6—10

The *session_binding* method deals with faulty protocols that contain a message which cannot be associated with a particular protocol run. An attack exploiting this flaw, called *replay protection*, causes an agent to consider that another is

---

[5] Protocol changes are enclosed within a solid box to ease reference.

Name: *message_encoding*
Input: $P \in \Sigma$, $\mathcal{B}_A$, $\mathcal{B}_R$, $n \in \mathcal{B}_A \cap \mathcal{B}_R$, $\pi \in Pos(\mathrm{msg}(n))$
    `% n lies on strand of deceived agent where` $\mathrm{msg}(n)_{|\pi} = \{\!|M|\!\}_K$ `is the`
    `% message used to elaborate replay`
Preconditions:
    `% different cypher-texts cannot be distinguished:`
    Let $S = \mathsf{Safe}_r$
        $\exists n' \in \mathcal{B}_A, \exists M', K'.$
        $(\{\!|M'|\!\}_{K'} \in \mathrm{msg}(n') \wedge \{\!|M'|\!\}_{K'} \sim_S \{\!|M|\!\}_K \wedge \{\!|M'|\!\}_{K'} \neq \{\!|M|\!\}_K)$
Patch:
    `% Break similarity of` $\{\!|M|\!\}_K$:
    select M'' such that $M \leq_{\mathsf{A}_0} M''$, A_0 is a minimal set of tags, and
    $\{\!|M''|\!\}_K$ is collision free with $L = \{\{\!|M'|\!\}_{K'} : \{\!|M'|\!\}_{K'} \sqsubseteq \mathrm{msg}(n), n \in \mathcal{B}_R\}$
    With $\zeta_0 = \{(\pi, \{\!|M''|\!\}_K)\}$ and ζ be the adaption of $\mathcal{B}$ for ζ_0 in n
    let $P' = \zeta(P)$.

Fig. 2. The *message_encoding* method

trying to set up a simultaneous session, when he is not [11]. Two example protocols subject to this type of attack, because none satisfies *strong authentication* of B to A, are (1) and the Denning-Sacco Shared Key (DSSK) protocol. The DSSK protocol and the attack that AVISPA finds are as follows:

DSSK		Attack
1. $A \rightarrow S : A; B$	1:1.	$A \rightarrow S : A; B$
2. $S \rightarrow A : \{\!|B; K_{ab}; T_s;$	1:2.	$S \rightarrow A : \{\!|B; K_{ab}; T_s;$
$\quad\{\!|B; K_{ab}; A; T_s|\!\}_{K_b}|\!\}_{K_a}$		$\quad\{\!|B; K_{ab}; A; T_s|\!\}_{K_b}|\!\}_{K_a}$
3. $A \rightarrow B : \{\!|B; K_{ab}; A; T_s|\!\}_{K_b}$	1:3.	$A \rightarrow B : \{\!|B; K_{ab}; A; T_s|\!\}_{K_b}$
	2:3.	$\mathsf{Spy}(A) \rightarrow B : \{\!|B; K_{ab}; A; T_s|\!\}_{K_b}$

Notice that both the DSSK and the WMF protocol prescribe the responder, B, to react upon an *unsolicited test* [9].

SHRIMP is equipped with a repair method that introduces a nonce-flow requirement to fix this flaw [1,13,11,9] (c.f. principle 7.) This requirement is realised by transforming the unsolicited test into an authentication one. Let $A \xrightarrow{\;\overline{M}\;} B$ denote the step at which the replay is realised and let $A \xrightarrow{M_1} B \xrightarrow{M_2} C$ abbreviate two consecutive protocol steps: $q. A \rightarrow B : M_1$ and $q + 1. B \rightarrow C : M_2$. Then, the nonce-flow requirement is introduced via the following transformation rules, called nonce_flow and tried to be applied in the order of appearance:

$$A \xrightarrow{M_1} B \xrightarrow{\;\overline{M_2}\;} C \rightsquigarrow A \xrightarrow{M_1} \boxed{C} \xrightarrow{M_1 \; ; \; \{\!|C; N_c; h(M_1)|\!\}_{K_b^+}} B \xrightarrow{M_2 \; ; \; \{\!|C; N_c; h(M_2)|\!\}_{K_b^-}} C$$

$$B \xrightarrow{\;\overline{M_1}\;} C \rightsquigarrow B \xrightarrow{M_1} C \xrightarrow{\{\!|C; N_c; h(M_1)|\!\}_{K_b^+}} \boxed{B} \xrightarrow{\{\!|C; N_c|\!\}_{K_b^-}} \boxed{C}$$

where $h(M)$ denotes a one-way, collision-resistant hash function, which is used to tie each test component to the current run. Notice that if $A = C$ then the first two steps of the right-hand side of the first rule merge. Also notice that if $A \xrightarrow{M} B \rightsquigarrow A \xrightarrow{M'} \boxed{C} \xrightarrow{M''} B$, the strands ought to be modified as follows: i) for A and B, $\exists n_a \in s_a, n_b \in s_b.\ \mathsf{msg}(n_a) = \mathsf{msg}(n_b) = M$, so we shall have $\mathsf{msg}(n_a) = M'$ and $\mathsf{msg}(n_b) = M''$; and ii) for C, two nodes, n_{c_1} and n_{c_2}, are inserted such that $\mathsf{msg}(n_{c_1}) = M'$ and $\mathsf{msg}(n_{c_2}) = M''$ with $\mathsf{sign}(n_{c_1}) = -\ \neq \mathsf{sign}(n_{c_2})$. The rule identifies where these nodes are to be inserted: c.f. C's participation, previous to the attack. Any other transformation is handled similarly.

We now introduce two refinements to this transformation. First, notice that applying nonce_flow without considering the structure of M_1 or M_2 may add unnecessary components. We shrink the message $M_1; \{\!|C; N_c; h(M_1)|\!\}_{K_b^+}$ (respectively $M_2; \{\!|C; N_c; h(M_2)|\!\}_{K_b^-}$) as follows:

$$\mathrm{shrnk}(M, M') = \mathrm{shrnk}_0(M, M') \qquad \text{if } \mathrm{shrnk}_0(M, M') \neq M$$
$$\mathrm{shrnk}(M, M') = M; M' \qquad \text{otherwise}$$

where

$$\mathrm{shrnk}_0(A, M) = A \qquad \text{if } A \text{ is atomic}$$
$$\mathrm{shrnk}_0(M_1; M_2, M') = \mathrm{shrnk}_0(M_1, M'); \mathrm{shrnk}_0(M_2, M')$$
$$\mathrm{shrnk}_0(\{\!|M|\!\}_K, \{\!|C; N_c; M'|\!\}_K) = \{\!|C; N_c; M|\!\}_K$$
$$\mathrm{shrnk}_0(\{\!|M|\!\}_{K_c^-}, \{\!|C; N_c; M'|\!\}_{K_b^+}) = \{\!|\mathrm{shrnk}_0(M, \{\!|C; N_c; h(M)|\!\}_{K_b^+})|\!\}_{K_c^-}$$
$$\mathrm{shrnk}_0(\{\!|M|\!\}_{K_c^+}, \{\!|C; N_c; M'|\!\}_{K_b^-}) = \{\!|\mathrm{shrnk}_0(M, \{\!|C; N_c; h(M)|\!\}_{K_b^-})|\!\}_{K_c^+}$$

where we assume that C originates the message $M_1; \{\!|C; N_c; h(M_1)|\!\}_{K_b^+}$ (respectively $M_2; \{\!|C; N_c; h(M_2)|\!\}_{K_b^-}$), the challenger, and B is the recipient, the champion. Second, notice that applying nonce_flow when the server is involved in the replay may yield a clumsy protocol. This is because the protocol would involve too many server participations and provide guarantees to the server rather than to the participants. We get around this situation by applying a very specific patching strategy, due to Lowe [11], which consists of making the participants handshake. The handshake messages are cyphered using the session key, similar to a key confirmation step. nonce_flow is thus attempted only if the following rules, called handshake, are *not* applicable:

$$\mathsf{S} \xrightarrow{\overline{M(K)}} X_i \rightsquigarrow \mathsf{S} \xrightarrow{M(K)\boxed{;\,T}} X_i \xrightarrow{\{\!|X_i; X_j; N_j|\!\}_K} X_j \xrightarrow{\{\!|X_j; N_j|\!\}_K} X_i$$

$$X_k \xrightarrow{\overline{M'}} \mathsf{S} \xrightarrow{M(K)} X_i \rightsquigarrow X_k \xrightarrow{M'} \mathsf{S} \xrightarrow{M(K)\boxed{;\,T}} X_i \xrightarrow{\{\!|X_i; X_j; N_j|\!\}_K} X_j \xrightarrow{\{\!|X_j; N_j|\!\}_K} X_i$$

where $T = \{\!|T'; h(M(K))|\!\}_{K_i}$ and where the last two steps of the protocol structure on the right-hand side are applied for all $j \neq i$ and so are actually rounds of messages. Notice that for handshake to be applicable the message M should carry a session key. This patching strategy is known to be susceptible to a known-key

Name: *session_binding*
Input: $P \in \Sigma, \mathcal{B}, \mathcal{B}_R, M, K, n = \langle s, k \rangle$
Preconditions:

% The deceived participant, associated to strand s,
% receives an *unsolicited test*:
$\forall n_0 \in \mathcal{B}$ if $n_0 \prec_\mathcal{B} n$ then $\forall M' \sqsubseteq \mathsf{msg}(n_0). (M' \not\sqsubseteq M \vee M' \notin \mathsf{unique}_s)$

Method:

% Introduce nonce-flow requirement, transforming unsolicited test
% into an authentication one:
orelse_meth handshake nonce_flow

Fig. 3. The *session_binding* method

attack,[6] but the insertion of the timestamp, T', makes it very difficult for an adversary to timely realise the replay.

Two consecutive applications of *session_binding*, Fig. 3, on input DSSK yield:

1. $A \to B : A; B$
2. $B \to S : A; B; \{\!|N_b; A|\!\}_{K_b}$
3. $S \to A : \{\!|B; K_{ab}; \boxed{T_s}; \{\!|\boxed{N_b}; B; K_{ab}; A; \boxed{T_s}|\!\}_{K_b}|\!\}_{K_a}$
4. $A \to B : \{\!|\boxed{N_b}; B; K_{ab}; A; \boxed{T_s}|\!\}_{K_b}; \{\!|A; B; Na|\!\}_{K_{ab}}$
5. $B \to A : \boxed{\{\!|B; Na|\!\}_{K_{ab}}}$

Step 2., together with N_b, is inserted in the first application, preventing a replay protection attack on B, while the handshake à la Lowe is inserted in the second one, preventing a replay protection attack on S.

Proposition 3. *Let P' be the revised version of the protocol and let N be the nonce introduced by an application of* nonce_flow *on the replay of M. If $N \in$* unique$_s$ *then M cannot be used to elaborate a replay.*

Proof (outline). Take the first rule, so $M = \boxed{M_2}$ Let $node_a^+(M')$ (respectively $node_a^-(M')$) denote the positive (respectively negative) node of strand A at which message M' is sent (respectively received), then if K_b^- is safe:

$$node_c^+(M_1 \boxed{; \{\!|C; N_c; h(M_1)|\!\}_{K_b^+}}) \Rightarrow^+ node_c^-(M_2 \boxed{; \{\!|C; N_c; h(M_2)|\!\}_{K_b^-}})$$

is an outgoing test for N_c in $\{\!|C; N_c, h(M_1)|\!\}_{K_b^+}$. Then by proposition 19 of [9] only a regular participant must have been responsible for N to exit the cyphertext $\{\!|C; N_c; h(M_1)|\!\}_{K_b^+}$ and then enter to $\{\!|C; N_c; h(M_2)|\!\}_{K_b^-}$. Any occurrence of M_i ($i = 1, 2$) is thus tied via $h(M_i)$ to a unique test and so the result follows. The proof for the other rule is similar. $\square$

---

[6] A *known-key attack* is an attack whereby, once getting knowledge of a session key, the adversary is able, if passive, to compromise keys of other sessions or, if active, to impersonate one of the (honest) protocol parties.

3.3   Patching Protocols Violating Principle 3

In this section, we generalise the method introduced in [10], designed to fix a faulty protocol containing a message without proper naming. Our generalisation consists of introducing the names of the correspondents of the reused message, rather than the names of the initiator or the responder in the protocol.

When input the NSPK protocol, *agent_naming*, Fig. 4, will add the name of the agent originating message 2, B in this case, arriving at Lowe's fix:

$$1.\ A \to B : \{\!|N_a, A|\!\}_{K_b^+} \quad 2.\ B \to A : \{\!|\boxed{B}, N_a, N_b|\!\}_{K_a^+} \quad 3.\ A \to B : \{\!|N_b|\!\}_{K_b^+}$$

Name: *agent_naming*
Input: $P, \mathcal{B}_A, \mathcal{B}_R, n \in \mathcal{B}_A \cap \mathcal{B}_R$ with $\mathsf{msg}(n)_{|\pi} = \{\!|M|\!\}_K$
Preconditions:

$$\bigvee_{A \in \mathrm{Partners}(\{\!|M|\!\}_K)} A \notin \mathrm{Agents}(\{\!|M|\!\}_K)$$

Patch:

Select M'' such that:
$M \leq_I M''$ with $I = \mathrm{Partners}(\{\!|M|\!\}_K]) \setminus \mathrm{Agents}(\{\!|M|\!\}_K)$
$\{\!|M''|\!\}_K$ is collision free with $\{\{\!|M'|\!\}_{K'} : \{\!|M'|\!\}_{K'} \sqsubseteq \mathsf{msg}(n), n \in \mathcal{B}_R\}$ wrt. Safe_r
With $\zeta_0 = \{(\pi, \{\!|M''|\!\}_K)\}$ and ζ be the adaption of $\mathcal{B}$ for ζ_0 in n, let $P' = \zeta(P)$.

Effects:

$\mathrm{Partners}([\zeta(\{\!|M|\!\}_K)]) = \mathrm{Agents}(\zeta(\{\!|M|\!\}_K))$

Fig. 4. The *agent_naming* method

Proposition 4. *Let P' and $\zeta(\{\!|M|\!\}_K)$ be the revised protocol and cypher-text. Then, $\zeta(\{\!|M|\!\}_K)$ may not be used to arm a naming replay attack.*

Proof (outline). Let $P(R, \vec{x})$ denote the set of strands of role R in P instantiated with parameters $\vec{x}$. Effects guarantee that $\forall R \in \mathrm{Partners}([\zeta(\{\!|M|\!\}_K)]).P'(R, \vec{x}) \subseteq P(R, \vec{x})$, because the parameters *agree* at least on the associated names of the correspondents of $\zeta(\{\!|M|\!\}_K)$. It follows that the cypher-text cannot be used to arm a naming replay.   □

4   Results

Table 1 summarises our results. We considered 36 experiments, of which 20 involve protocols borrowed from the Clark-Jacob library;[7] 4 are variants of some of these protocols (annotated with ⋆); and 12 are protocols output by SHRIMP, a next-generation of an input protocol. Next-generation protocols are shown in a separate row within the associated entry.

---

[7] The Clark-Jacob library comprehends 50 protocols, 26 out of which are known to be faulty. So our validation test set contains all but 6 of these security protocols. The faulty protocols that were left out are not susceptible to a replay attack.

Each row displays the result of testing a protocol against a (hierarchical) collection of properties: secrecy, s, weak authentication of the initiator, wa_i (respectively responder, wa_r) and strong authentication of the initiator, sa_i (respectively responder sa_r), where $wa_i < sa_i$ (respectively $wa_r < sa_r$.) The table separates the verification results for the original protocol, *before*, and the mended protocol, *after*, as output by SHRIMP. The field value that exists at the intersection between a protocol P and a property ϕ might be either T, meaning P satisfies ϕ, F, meaning P does not satisfy ϕ, or X, meaning this property was not tested (be-

Table 1. Experimental results

Protocol	before					M	after				
	s	wa_i	sa_i	wa_r	sa_r		s	wa_i	sa_i	wa_r	sa_r
ASRPC	T	T	T	T	F	B$_1$	T	T	T	T	T
BAN ASRPC	T	F	X	X	X	N	T	T	T	T	T
CCITTX.509(1)	T	F	X	X	X	N	T	T	X	X	X
	T	T	F	X	X	B$_1$	T	T	T	T	T
CCITTX.509(3)	T	F	X	T	T	N	T	T	T	T	T
DSSK	T	T	F	X	X	B$_1$	T	T	T	T	X
	T	T	T	T	F	B$_1$	T	T	T	T	T
NSSK	T	T	X	T	F	B$_1$	T	T	X	T	T
	T	T	F†	T	T	B$_2$	T	T	T	T	T
DSPK	T	F	X	X	X	N	T	T	X	X	X
	T	T	F	X	X	B$_2$	T	T	T	X	X
Kao Chow A. v1	T	T	F†	T	T	B$_2$	T	T	T	T	T
KSL	T	F	X	X	X	E	T	T	T	T	T
NSPK	F	X	X	T	T	N	T	T	T	T	T
BAN OR	T	F	X	X	X	N	T	T	X	X	X
Splice/AS	T	X	X	F	X	N	T	T	X	T	X
	T	T	F	T	X	B$_2$	T	T	T	T	T
CJ Splice	T	F	X	T	T	B$_2$	T	T	T	T	T
HC Splice	T	X	X	F	X	N	T	T	X	X	X
WMF	T	F	X	X	X	E	T	T	X	X	X
	T	T	F	X	X	B$_2$	T	T	T	T	T
WMF++ ⋆	T	T	F	X	X	B$_2$	T	T	T	T	T
ASRPC prune ⋆	T	F	X	X	X	N	T	T	X	X	X
	T	T	X	F	X	N	T	T	X	T	X
	T	T	X	T	F	B$_1$	T	T	X	T	T
	T	T	F	T	T	B$_1$	T	T	T	T	T
WLM	T	F	X	X	X	B$_2$	T	T	T	T	T
BAN Yahalom	T	T	T	F	X	E	T	T	T	T	T
A. DH ⋆	T	X	X	F	X	N	T	T	X	X	X
	T	X	X	T	F	B$_1$	T	X	X	T	T
2steps SK ⋆	T	X	X	F	X	N	T	X	X	T	X
	T	X	X	T	F	B$_1$	T	T	X	T	X
	T	T	F	T	T	B$_1$	T	T	T	T	T

cause P was not expected to satisfy it.) Column M specifies the method that was applied to modify each faulty protocol: message (E)ncoding, agent (N)aming or session (B)inding. For the latter method, B$_1$ refers to rule nonce_flow and B$_2$ to rules handshake. In all our experiments, the application of a patch method yielded a revised protocol able to satisfy the security property that the original one did not. Whenever applicable, each mended protocol was then further requested to satisfy the remaining, stronger properties in the hierarchy, thus explaining why some entries have several runs. Note that in the discovery of some attacks we had to specify the possibility of losing a session key (annotated with †.)

SHRIMP is thus able to identify a flaw and a successful candidate patch in 33 faulty protocols out of 36. Of these experiments, it applied 12 times *agent_naming*, 4 times *message_encoding*, 9 times rules nonce_flow and 8 times handshake. The protocols SHRIMP fails to fix, namely: Neumann-Stubblebine, Otway-Rees and Woo-Lam Pi, are all susceptible to the type flaw subclass of replay attack. It would be misleading to dismiss message encoding on account of the few protocols it patched. This is because while applying the other methods we use it to ensure the patch did not incur in an infringement of principle 10.

We have recently made SHRIMP try to patch the IKEv2-DS protocol, which is part of AVISPA's library and an abstraction of IKEv2. We found that if we abstract out the equational issues inherent to the AVISPA attack, SHRIMP successfully identifies a violation to a good practice for protocol design: the omission of principal names. While the revised protocol is up to satisfy strong authentication on the session key, this patch may be subject to a criticism because IKEv2 was deliberately designed so that no principal should mention the name of its corresponding one. We then deleted *agent_naming* and re-ran our experiment; this time SHRIMP applied handshake suggesting a protocol similar to IKEv2-DSx, which also is part of AVISPA's library and attack-free.

5   Comparison to Related Work

R. Choo [6] has also looked at the problem of automated protocol repair. His development framework applies a model checker to perform state-space analysis on an (indistinguishableness-based) model of a protocol, encoded using asynchronous product automata. If the protocol is faulty, Choo's approach automatically repairs it. A fair comparison between Choo's approach and ours cannot be conducted mainly because so far there is not an archival publication of [6].

When considering an automatic protocol repair mechanism like ours, one wonders whether there is an upper bound as to the information that every message should include to avoid a replay. If there is one, we could simply ensure that every message conforms it previous to any verification attempt. Carlsen [5] has looked into this upper bound. He suggested that to avoid replays every message should include five pieces of information: protocol-id, session-id, step-id, message subcomponent-id and primitive type of data items. In a similar vein, Aura [3] suggested one should also use several cryptalgorithms in one protocol and hash any authentication message and any session key. Protocol designers, however, find including all these elements cumbersome. By comparison, SHRIMP only inserts selected pieces of information considering the attack at hand but may add steps to the protocol if necessary to fulfil a stronger security property.

Complementary to ours is the work of Perrig and Song [13], who have developed a system, called APG, for the synthesis of security protocols. The synthesis process, though automated, is generate and test: APG generates (extends) a protocol step by step, taking into account the security requirements, and then discards those protocols that do not satisfy them. APG is limited to generate only 3-party protocols (two principals and one server). As a reduction technique, it uses an impersonation attack and so rules out protocols that (trivially) fail to provide authenticity. The main problem to this tool is the combinatorial explosion (the search space is of the order 10^{12} according to the authors).

6   Conclusions and Further Work

In this paper, we have presented SHRIMP, a method for automatically repairing faulty security protocols. SHRIMP consists of a collection of patch planning methods. Each patch method is designed to transform a set of protocol steps violating a design principle into one conforming it, while ruling out the possibility of violating other principles. We have carried out a large number of experiments to validate SHRIMP, finding that it successfully deals with the class of replay attacks, except for the subclass type flaw. Ongoing research thus is concerned with extending SHRIMP to cope with this type of attack. Ongoing research also is concerned with extending SHRIMP to account for more cryptographic primitives, including the equational properties thereof, and a greater variety of protocols. Patch methods are independent of the global security requirements required from the security protocol under investigation and the local change of one or two protocol steps may cause flaws in combination with other protocol steps which have been not considered at that point. Therefore, ongoing research involves considering global rules that may change a protocol depending on these global requirements to be achieved, controlling the local patch process.

References

1. Abadi, M., Needham, R.: Prudent engineering practice for cryptographic protocols. IEEE Transactions on Software Engineering 22(1), 6–15 (1996)
2. Abadi, M., Rogaway, P.: Reconciling two views of cryptography (the computational soundness of formal encryption). Journal of Cryptology 15(2), 103–127 (2002)
3. Aura, T.: Strategies against replay attacks. In: CSFW'97. Proceedings of the 10th IEEE Computer Security Foundations Workshop, pp. 59–69. IEEE Computer Society Press, Los Alamitos (1997)
4. Bundy, A.: The use of explicit plans to guide inductive proofs. In: Lusk, E.R., Overbeek, R. (eds.) 9th International Conference on Automated Deduction. LNCS, vol. 310, pp. 111–120. Springer, Heidelberg (1988)
5. Carlsen, U.: Cryptographic protocols flaws. In: Computer Security Foundations Workshop, CSFW'94. Proceedings of the 7th IEEE Computer Security Foundations Workshop, pp. 192–200. IEEE Computer Society, Los Alamitos (1994)
6. Raymond Choo, K.-K.: An integrative framework to protocol analysis and repair: Indistinguishability-based model + planning + model checker. In: Proceedings of Five-minute Talks at CSFW'06. Computer Security Foundations Workshop (2006)
7. Clark, J., Jacob, J.: A survey of authentication protocol literature: v1.0. Technical report, Department of Computer Science, University of York (November 1997)
8. Proceedings of the 7th IEEE Computer Security Foundations Workshop. In: CSFW'94. IEEE Computer Society (1994)
9. Guttman, J.-D., Thayer, F.-J.: Authentication tests and the structure of bundles. Theoretical Computer Science 283(2), 333–380 (2002)
10. López-Pimentel, J.C., Monroy, R., Hutter, D.: A method for patching interleaving-replay attacks in faulty security protocols. Electronic Notes in Theoretical Computer Science 174, 117–130 (2007)
11. Lowe, G.: A family of attacks upon authentication protocols. Technical Report 1997/5, Department of Mathematics and Computer Science, University of Leicester (1997)
12. Paulson, L.C.: The inductive approach to verifying cryptographic protocols. Journal in Computer Security 6(1-2), 85–128 (1998)
13. Perrig, A., Song, D.: Looking for diamonds in the desert — extending automatic protocol generation to three-party authentication and key agreement protocols. In: Proceedings of the 13th CSFW'00, pp. 64–76. IEEE Computer Society Press, Los Alamitos (2000)
14. Syverson, P.: A taxonomy of replay attacks. In: Computer Security Foundations Workshop, CSFW'94. Proceedings of the 7th IEEE Computer Security Foundations Workshop, pp. 187–191. IEEE Computer Society, Los Alamitos (1994)
15. Thayer Fabrega, F.J., Herzog, J.C., Guttman, J.D.: Strand spaces: Why is a security protocol correct? In: Proceedings Symposium on Security and Privacy, pp. 160–171. IEEE Computer Society Press, Los Alamitos (1998)

Adaptive Soundness of Static Equivalence[*]

Steve Kremer and Laurent Mazaré

LSV, ENS Cachan & CNRS & INRIA Futurs
{kremer,mazare}@lsv.ens-cachan.fr

Abstract. We define a framework to reason about implementations of equational theories in the presence of an adaptive adversary. We particularly focus on soundess of static equivalence. We illustrate our framework on several equational theories: symmetric encryption, XOR, modular exponentiation and also joint theories of encryption and modular exponentiation. This last example relies on a combination result for reusing proofs for the separate theories. Finally, we define a model for symbolic analysis of dynamic group key exchange protocols, and show its computational soundness.

1 Introduction

It is well-known that even simple security protocols are extremely error-prone. This is mainly due to the fact that they are executed in a hostile environment, *e.g.*, the Internet. The need for rigorous proofs was recognized very early and two distinct, competing approaches have been developed. The symbolic approach considers an abstract model, where messages and cryptographic primitives are modeled by a term algebra. The adversary manipulates terms according to a pre-defined set of rules, typically an inference system. The computational approach considers a more detailed execution model. Protocol messages are modeled as bitstrings and cryptographic primitives are polynomial-time algorithms. The adversary is an arbitrary probabilistic polynomial-time Turing machine. Security of a protocol is measured as the adversary's success probability.

Proofs in the symbolic model can be (partially) automated, but it is not clear whether this abstract model captures all possible attacks. Proofs in the computational model provide stronger security guarantees but are generally harder and difficult to automate. A recent trend tries to get the best of both worlds: an abstract model with strong computational guarantees. In their seminal paper, Abadi and Rogaway [4] have shown a first such *soundness result* for symmetric encryption in the presence of a passive attacker.

Recently, Baudet *et al.* [9] presented a general framework for reasoning about sound implementations of equational theories. Instead of a fixed set of cryptographic primitives, they allow a specification by the means of an equational theory. The formal indistinguishability relation they consider is static equivalence, a well-established security notion coming from cryptographic pi calculi [3] whose verification can often be automated [2,10]. Studying soundness of equational theories is motivated by the numerous recent works on extending the classical Dolev-Yao result with equations which are intended to capture algebraic properties of cryptographic primitives (see [17] for a

---

[*] Work partly supported by ARA SSIA Formacrypt and ARTIST2 Network of Excellence.

J. Biskup and J. Lopez (Eds.): ESORICS 2007, LNCS 4734, pp. 610–625, 2007.

survey). Showing a soundness result for an equational theory proves that indeed "enough" equations have been considered in the symbolic model.

In this paper we consider the question of soundness of static equivalence in the presence of an *adaptive adversary*, rather than a purely passive one. This extends the work by Baudet *et al.* in a similar way as the work of Micciancio and Panjwani [24] extended the work of Abadi and Rogaway [4]. An adaptive adversary is allowed to choose the messages whose implementation he will be given. The choice of the messages can hence depend on previously observed distributions. We illustrate the usefullness of such a model on dynamic group key exchange protocols.

More precisely the contributions of our paper are as follows. We define the notion of adaptive soundness of static equivalence in a general framework. The definition is parameterized by the equational theory and the concrete algebra implementing the symbolic model. Our notion is strictly stronger than the purely passive soundness from [9]. We also develop a combination based proof technique: it allows us to reuse soundness results of two disjoint abstract signatures and conclude soundness of the joint signature. While the conditions under which such a combination works are of course restrictive they nevertheless match cases of practical interest. We give adaptive soundness results for several theories: symmetric encryption provided that the encryption scheme respects a length-concealing IND-CPA security notion (this is similar to the main result in [24]), exclusive or (XOR), modular exponentiation in an Abelian group provided that the *Decisional Diffie-Hellman* (DDH) assumption is verified. Finally, we use our combination technique to derive adaptive soundness for the joint theory of encryption and modular exponentiation. We believe these are the first adaptive soundness results for modular exponentiation. Their importance is motivated by real-life protocols such as SSL/TLS that rely on Diffie-Hellman key exchange and thus use modular exponentiation.

To illustrate the usefulness of adaptive adversaries we define a symbolic model for dynamic group key exchange (DKE) protocols. A DKE protocol is a suite of protocols which allows three actions: exchange of an initial key between a group of users, joining and leaving the group. A typical example of DKE is the AKE1 protocol [12]. In our symbolic model we assume static corruption, as it was the case in [24], and allow the adversary to schedule these subprotocol and decide which users initially exchange the key, join, respectively leave the group. We use our adaptive soundness result to show that this symbolic model is sound with respect to a corresponding computational model.

Related work. As discussed above this paper generalizes both work by Baudet *et al.* [9] and Micciancio and Panjwani [24]. Abadi *et al.* [1] also use the framework of [9] to show soundness of an equational theory useful for reasoning about offline guessing attacks modeled in terms of static equivalence. In [8], Bana *et al.* argue that the notion of static equivalence is too coarse and not sound for many interesting equational theories. As an example they show that the DDH assumption is not sufficient to imply soundness of static equivalence. They introduce a general notion of *formal indistinguishability relation*. In this paper we prefer to stick to static equivalence which has the advantage of being a well-established, tool-supported equivalence relation. We address the problems highlighted in [8] by proving soundness for a restricted set of *well-formed* frames (in the same vein Abadi and Rogaway used restrictions to forbid key cycles). Regarding the theory of XOR, Backes and Pfitzmann [6] have shown an impossibility result in the reactive simulatability framework with active attackers and a soundness result for passive attackers. Note that we use the same model as [9] and restrict ourselves to the XOR of pure random values and not arbitrary payloads. While this is a restriction, it may nevertheless be useful for computing keys as the XOR of two random values when combining XOR and encryption. Concerning modular exponentiation, a soundness result in the style of Abadi and Rogaway [4] has recently been shown in [13]. However using the same proof technique for the adaptive case seems difficult as the security model of [13] is tightly linked to the passive adversary model: challenges cannot be chosen adaptively by the adversary.

There have also been numerous works considering an active adversary using approaches. Without being exhaustive this work includes reactive simulatability providing universally composable results in [7,15], soundness results (but not universal composability) for an automated tool are presented in [18], cryptographically sound type systems [23], a *Protocol Composition Logic* in [19] and an automatic tool that aims at directly generating cryptographic proofs via sequences of games in [11]. However these works stick to classical cryptographic primitives: digital signatures, symmetric and asymmetric encryption. We are not aware of any general results for equational theories in the active case. Considering an active adversary is technically more involved although incomparable to an adaptive adversary. The case of a both active and adaptive adversary is a challenging problem and a topic of active research.

Because of lack of space, proofs are omitted. They are available in [22].

2   Abstract and Computational Algebras

We introduce our model, which is the same up to some minor changes as in [9].

2.1   Abstract Algebras

Our abstract models—called *abstract algebras*—consist of term algebras defined over a many-sorted first-order signature and equipped with equational theories.

Specifically, a *signature* $(\mathcal{S}, \mathcal{F})$ is made of a set of *sorts* $\mathcal{S} = \{s, s_1 \ldots\}$ and a set of *symbols* $\mathcal{F} = \{f, f_1 \ldots\}$ together with arities of the form $\mathrm{ar}(f) = s_1 \times \ldots \times s_k \to s$, $k \geq 0$. Symbols that take $k = 0$ arguments are called *constants*; their arity is simply written s. We fix a set of *names* $\mathcal{N} = \{a, b \ldots\}$ and a set of *variables* $\mathcal{X} = \{x, y \ldots\}$. Names and variables are given with sorts and an infinite number of names and variables are available for each sort. The set of *terms of sort s* is defined inductively by

$$
\begin{aligned}
t ::= & & \text{term of sort } s \\
& \mid\ x & \text{variable } x \text{ of sort s} \\
& \mid\ a & \text{name } a \text{ of sort s} \\
& \mid\ f(t_1, \ldots, t_k) & \text{application of symbol } f \in \mathcal{F}
\end{aligned}
$$

where for the last case, we further require that t_i is of sort s_i and $\mathrm{ar}(f) = s_1 \times \ldots \times s_k \to s$. We also allow subsorts: if s_2 is a subsort of s_1 we allow a term of sort s_2 whenever a term of sort s_1 is expected. We write $sort(t)$ for the sort of term t. We define $root(t)$ to be f if $t = f(t_1, \ldots, t_n)$ and t otherwise, *i.e.* if t is either a name or a variable. We write var(t) and names(t) for the set of variables and names occurring in t, respectively. A term t is *ground* or *closed* if var(t) = $\emptyset$.

Substitutions are written $\sigma = \{x_1 \mapsto t_1, \ldots, x_n \mapsto t_n\}$ with domain dom(σ) = $\{x_1, \ldots, x_n\}$. We only consider *well-sorted, cycle-free* substitutions. Such a σ is *closed* if all of the t_i are closed. We let var(σ) = $\bigcup_i$ var(t_i), names(σ) = $\bigcup_i$ names(t_i), and extend the notations var(.) and names(.) to tuples and sets of terms and substitutions in the obvious way. The application of a substitution σ to a term t is written $\sigma(t) = t\sigma$ and is defined in the usual way. As usual the set of positions $pos(t)$ of a term t is defined inductively as $pos(c) = pos(a) = pos(x) = \{\epsilon\}$ where ar(c) = s and $pos(f(t_1, \ldots, t_n)) = \{\epsilon\} \cup \bigcup_{1 \leq i \leq n} i \cdot pos(t_i)$. If p is a position of t then expression $t|_p$ denotes the subterm of t at the position p, *i.e.*, $t|_\epsilon = t$ and $f(t_1, \ldots, t_n)|_{i \cdot p} = t_i|_p$.

Symbols in $\mathcal{F}$ are intended to model cryptographic primitives, whereas names in $\mathcal{N}$ are used to model secrets, *e.g.*, keys. The abstract semantics of symbols is described by an equational theory E, *i.e*, an equivalence relation (also written $=_E$) which is stable by application of contexts and substitutions of variables. For instance, symmetric encryption can be modeled by the classical theory $E_{\mathsf{enc}} = \{\mathrm{dec}(\mathrm{enc}(x, y), y) = x\}$.

2.2 Deducibility and Static Equivalence

We use frames [3,2] to represent sequences of messages observed by an attacker. Formally, a *frame* is an expression $\varphi = \nu\tilde{a}.\{x_1 = t_1, \ldots, x_n = t_n\}$ where $\tilde{a}$ is a set of *bound (or restricted) names*, and for each i, t_i is a closed term of the same sort as x_i. For simplicity, we only consider frames $\varphi = \nu\tilde{a}.\{x_1 = t_1, \ldots, x_n = t_n\}$ which restrict every name in use, *i.e.*, $\tilde{a} = $ names($t_1, \ldots, t_n$). A name a may still be disclosed explicitly by adding a mapping $x_a = a$ to the frame. Thus we assimilate such frames φ to their *underlying substitutions* $\sigma = \{x_1 \mapsto t_1, \ldots, x_n \mapsto t_n\}$ also denoted $\{x_i \mapsto t_i\}_{1 \leq i \leq n}$.

Definition 1 (Deducibility). *A (closed) term t is* deducible *from a frame φ in an equational theory E, written $\varphi \vdash_E t$, iff there exists a term M such that* var(M) $\subseteq$ dom(φ), names(M) $\cap$ names(φ) = $\emptyset$, *and $M\varphi =_E t$.*

For simplicity we only consider deducibility problems $\varphi \vdash_E t$ such that names(t) $\subseteq$ names(φ). For instance, let $\varphi_1 = \{x_1 \mapsto \mathrm{enc}(k_1, k_2), x_2 \mapsto \mathrm{enc}(k_4, k_3), x_3 \mapsto k_3\}$: under the the theory E_{enc} name k_4 is deducible from φ_1 since $\mathrm{dec}(x_2, x_3)\varphi_1 =_{E_{\mathsf{enc}}} k_4$ but neither are k_1 nor k_2. As also argued in [2] deducibility is not always sufficient to account for the knowledge of an attacker. For instance, it lacks partial information on secrets. That is why another classical notion in formal methods is *static equivalence*.

Definition 2 (Static equivalence). *Two frames φ_1 and φ_2 are* statically equivalent *in a theory E, written $\varphi_1 \approx_E \varphi_2$, iff* dom($\varphi_1$) = dom($\varphi_2$), *and for all terms M and N such that* var(M, N) $\subseteq$ dom(φ_1) *and* names(M, N) $\cap$ names(φ_1, φ_2) = $\emptyset$, *$M\varphi_1 =_E N\varphi_1$ is equivalent to $M\varphi_2 =_E N\varphi_2$.*

For instance, let 0 and 1 be two constants (which are known by the attacker). Then $\{x \mapsto \mathrm{enc}(0, k)\} \approx_{E_{\mathsf{enc}}} \{x \mapsto \mathrm{enc}(1, k)\}$. However $\varphi = \{x \mapsto \mathrm{enc}(0, k), y \mapsto k\}$ and $\varphi' = \{x \mapsto \mathrm{enc}(1, k), y \mapsto k\}$ are not statically equivalent for E_{enc}: let $M = \mathrm{dec}(x, y)$ and $N = 0$. M and N use only variables defined by φ and φ' and do not use any names. Moreover $M\varphi =_{E_{\mathsf{enc}}} N\varphi$ but $M\varphi \neq_{E_{\mathsf{enc}}} N\varphi$. The test $M \overset{?}{=} N$ distinguishes φ from φ'.

2.3   Concrete Semantics

We now give terms and frames a concrete semantics, parameterized by an implementation of the primitives. Provided a set of sorts $\mathcal{S}$ and a set of symbols $\mathcal{F}$ as above, a $(\mathcal{S}, \mathcal{F})$-*computational algebra* A consists of

- a non-empty set of bit-strings $[\![s]\!]_A \subseteq \{0,1\}^*$ for each sort $s \in \mathcal{S}$; moreover, if s_2 is a subsort of s_1 we require that $[\![s_2]\!]_A \subseteq [\![s_1]\!]_A$;
- a computable function $[\![f]\!]_A : [\![s_1]\!]_A \times \ldots \times [\![s_k]\!]_A \to [\![s]\!]_A$ for each $f \in \mathcal{F}$ with $\mathrm{ar}(f) = s_1 \times \ldots \times s_k \to s$;
- an effective procedure to draw random elements from $[\![s]\!]_A$, denoted $x \xleftarrow{R} [\![s]\!]_A$.

Assume a fixed $(\mathcal{S}, \mathcal{F})$-computational algebra A. We associate to each frame $\varphi = \{x_1 \mapsto t_1, \ldots, x_n \mapsto t_n\}$ a distribution $\psi = [\![\varphi]\!]_A$, of which the drawings $\widehat{\psi} \xleftarrow{R} \psi$ are computed as follows:

1. for each name a of sort s appearing in $t_1, \ldots, t_n$, draw a value $\widehat{a} \xleftarrow{R} [\![s]\!]_A$;
2. for each x_i ($1 \leq i \leq n$) of sort s_i, compute $\widehat{t_i} \in [\![s_i]\!]_A$ recursively on the structure of terms: $\widehat{f(t'_1, \ldots, t'_m)} = [\![f]\!]_A(\widehat{t'_1}, \ldots, \widehat{t'_m})$;
3. return the value $\widehat{\psi} = \{x_1 \mapsto \widehat{t_1}, \ldots, x_n \mapsto \widehat{t_n}\}$.

Such values $\phi = \{x_1 = e_1, \ldots, x_n = e_n\}$ with $e_i \in [\![s_i]\!]_A$ are called *concrete frames*. We extend the notation $[\![.]\!]_A$ to (tuples of) closed terms in the obvious way. We also generalize the notation to terms with variables, by specifying the concrete values for all of them: $[\![.]\!]_{A, \{x_1 = e_1, \ldots, x_n = e_n\}}$.

In the rest of the paper we focus on asymptotic notions of cryptographic security and consider families of computational algebra (A_η) indexed by a complexity parameter $\eta \geq 0$. (This parameter η might be thought of as the size of keys and other secret values.) The *concrete semantics* of a frame φ is a family of distributions over concrete frames $([\![\varphi]\!]_{A_\eta})$. We only consider families of computational algebras (A_η) such that each required operation on algebras is feasible by a (uniform, probabilistic) polynomial-time algorithm in the complexity parameter η. This ensures that the concrete semantics of terms and frames is efficiently computable (in the same sense).

Families of distributions (*ensembles*) over concrete frames benefit from the usual notion of cryptographic indistinguishability. Intuitively, two families of distributions (ψ_η) and (ψ'_η) are *indistinguishable*, written $(\psi_\eta) \approx (\psi'_\eta)$, if and only if no probabilistic polynomial-time adversary $\mathcal{A}$ can guess whether he is given a sample from ψ_η or ψ'_η with probability significantly greater than $\frac{1}{2}$. Formally, we ask the *advantage* of $\mathcal{A}$,

$$\mathrm{Adv}_{\mathcal{A}}^{\mathrm{IND}}(\psi_\eta, \psi'_\eta) = \left| \mathbb{P}[\widehat{\psi} \xleftarrow{R} \psi_\eta \ : \ \mathcal{A}(\widehat{\psi}) = 1] - \mathbb{P}[\widehat{\psi} \xleftarrow{R} \psi'_\eta \ : \ \mathcal{A}(\widehat{\psi}) = 1] \right|$$

to be a *negligible* function of η, that is, to remain eventually smaller than any η^{-n} ($n > 0$) for sufficiently large η. By convention, the adversaries are given access implicitly to as many fresh random coins as needed, as well as the complexity parameter η.

3   Adaptive Soundness

In this section, we recall the original notion of soundness for static equivalence which considers a passive adversary [9] and then extend it to an adaptive adversary. We show relations between the classical soundness and our new adaptive soundness and also provide a combination result which allows us, under some hypotheses, to prove adaptive soundness of computational algebras (A_η) from adaptive soundness of parts of (A_η).

3.1   Soundness Definitions

Definition 3 ($\approx_E$-soundness). *Let E be an equational theory. A family of computational algebras (A_η) is $\approx_E$-sound iff for every frames φ_1, φ_2 with the same domain, $\varphi_1 \approx_E \varphi_2$ implies that $(\llbracket \varphi_1 \rrbracket_{A_\eta}) \approx (\llbracket \varphi_2 \rrbracket_{A_\eta})$,*

Similarly, Baudet *et al.* [9] define soundness for $=_E$ and $\vdash_E$. We here concentrate on soundness of static equivalence. As shown in [9], for many theories soundness of static equivalence implies all of the other notions. Baudet *et al.* also introduce a strong notion of soundness that holds without restriction on the computational power of adversaries.

Definition 4 (Unconditional $\approx_E$-soundness). *Let E be an equational theory. A family of computational algebras (A_η) is unconditionally $\approx_E$-sound iff for every frames φ_1, φ_2 with the same domain, $\varphi_1 \approx_E \varphi_2$ implies $(\llbracket \varphi_1 \rrbracket_{A_\eta}) = (\llbracket \varphi_2 \rrbracket_{A_\eta})$.*

Unconditional soundness stipulates that for any pairs of equivalent frames, the related distributions are equal. Hence even an adversary which is not polynomially bounded cannot distinguish these two distributions.

3.2   Adaptive Security

We extend soundness of static equivalence to the adaptive setting from [24] where the adversary observes the computational value of a sequence of adaptively chosen terms.

The adaptive setting is formalized through the following cryptographic game. Let (A_η) be a family of computational algebras and $\mathcal{A}$ be an adversary. $\mathcal{A}$ has access to a left-right evaluation oracle $\mathcal{O}_{LR}$ which given a pair of symbolic terms (t_0, t_1) outputs either the implementation of t_0 or of t_1. This oracle depends on a selection bit b and uses a local store to record values generated for the different names (these values are used when processing further queries). With a slight abuse of notation, we omit this store and write: $\mathcal{O}^b_{LR, A_\eta}(t_0, t_1) = \llbracket t_b \rrbracket_{A_\eta}$. Adversary $\mathcal{A}$ plays an indistinguishability game with the objective of finding the value of b. Formally the advantage of $\mathcal{A}$ is defined by:

$$\mathrm{Adv}^{\mathsf{ADPT}}_{\mathcal{A}, A_\eta}(\eta) = \left| \mathbb{P}\left[\mathcal{A}^{\mathcal{O}^1_{LR, A_\eta}} = 1 \right] - \mathbb{P}\left[\mathcal{A}^{\mathcal{O}^0_{LR, A_\eta}} = 1 \right] \right|$$

Without further restrictions on the queries of the adversary, having a non-negligible advantage is easy in most cases. For example the adversary could submit a pair $(0, 1)$ to his oracle. We therefore require the adversary to be *legal*.

Definition 5 (Adaptive soundness). *An adversary $\mathcal{A}$ is legal if for any sequence of queries $(t_0^i, t_1^i)_{1 \leq i \leq n}$ made by $\mathcal{A}$ to its left-right oracle, queries are statically equivalent: $\{x_1 \mapsto t_0^1, \dots, x_n \mapsto t_0^n\} \approx_E \{x_1 \mapsto t_1^1, \dots, x_n \mapsto t_1^n\}$. A family of computational algebras (A_η) is*

- $\approx_E$-ad-sound *iff* $\mathrm{Adv}_{\mathcal{A},A_\eta}^{\mathsf{ADPT}}(\eta)$ *is negligible for any probabilistic polynomial-time legal adversary* $\mathcal{A}$.
- unconditionally $\approx_E$-ad-sound *iff* $\mathrm{Adv}_{\mathcal{A},A_\eta}^{\mathsf{ADPT}}(\eta)$ *is 0 for any legal adversary* $\mathcal{A}$.

Adaptive soundness implies the original soundness notion for static equivalence.

Interestingly, for unconditional soundness, the adaptive and non-adaptive case coincide.

Proposition 2. *Let* (A_η) *be a family of computational algebras.* A_η *is unconditionally* $\approx_E$*-ad-sound iff* A_η *is unconditionally* $\approx_E$*-sound.*

3.3   Combination Result

Our objective here is to provide a combination result of the form: let Σ_1 and Σ_2 be two signatures that do not share any symbol. If A_η^1 is $\approx_{E_1}$-ad-sound and A_η^2 is $\approx_{E_2}$-ad-sound, then the combination of A_η^1 and A_η^2 denoted $A_\eta^1 \times A_\eta^2$ is $\approx_{E_1 \cup E_2}$-ad-sound. However this is false in general. Therefore, we provide restrictions under which combination is possible: we consider disjoint signatures as well as layered signatures.

Definition 6 (Disjoint signatures). *Let* $\Sigma_1 = (\mathcal{S}_1, \mathcal{F}_1)$ *and* $\Sigma_2 = (\mathcal{S}_2, \mathcal{F}_2)$ *be two signatures. We say that* Σ_1 *and* Σ_2 *are disjoint iff* $\mathcal{F}_1 \cap \mathcal{F}_2 = \emptyset$ *and* $\mathcal{S}_1 \cap \mathcal{S}_2 = \emptyset$.

We denote by $\Sigma_1 \cup \Sigma_2 = (\mathcal{S}_1 \cup \mathcal{S}_2, \mathcal{F}_1 \cup \mathcal{F}_2)$ the union of the signature Σ_1 with Σ_2.

Definition 7 (Signature combination, layered signatures). *Let* $\Sigma_1 = (\mathcal{S}_1, \mathcal{F}_1)$ *and* $\Sigma_2 = (\mathcal{S}_2, \mathcal{F}_2)$ *be two disjoint signatures. A subsort relation* S *is a signature combination for* Σ_1 *and* Σ_2 *if* $\mathsf{S} \subseteq \mathcal{S}_2 \times \mathcal{S}_1$. *Then* $\Sigma = \Sigma_1 \cup \Sigma_2$ *is a* $(\Sigma_1, \Sigma_2)_\mathsf{S}$-*layered signature.*

Intuitively, if a signature is layered then a constructor of $\mathcal{F}_1$ never occurs under a constructor of $\mathcal{F}_2$ and S defines which sorts of Σ_2 can be used as subsort of Σ_1. Given a $(\Sigma_1, \Sigma_2)_\mathsf{S}$-layered signature Σ and a term t over Σ we define the set of Σ_1 positions of t, $pos_{\Sigma_1}(t) = \{p \mid p \in pos(t), sort(t|_p) \in \mathcal{S}_1\}$ and the set of Σ_2 minimal positions of t, $pos_{\Sigma_2}^\star(t) = \{p \mid p \in pos(t), sort(t|_p) \in \mathcal{S}_2, p = p' \cdot i \Rightarrow sort(t|_{p'}) \notin \mathcal{S}_2\}$.

As an example consider a theory with symmetric encryption and a pseudo-random generator. Signature Σ_1 contains a sort Data and two symbols enc and dec, both of arity $\mathrm{Data} \times \mathrm{Data} \rightarrow \mathrm{Data}$. Signature Σ_2 contains one sort Rand and a symbol prg (a pseudo-random generator) of arity $\mathrm{Rand} \rightarrow \mathrm{Rand}$. The signature combination S contains a single element $(\mathrm{Rand}, \mathrm{Data})$: elements of sort Rand can be used as keys or as plaintext. Σ_1 and Σ_2 are disjoint, and $\Sigma = \Sigma_1 \cup \Sigma_2$ is $(\Sigma_1, \Sigma_2)_\mathsf{S}$-layered. Given the term $t = \mathrm{enc}(\mathrm{enc}(\mathrm{prg}(r), k), \mathrm{prg}(\mathrm{prg}(r')))$ where $k \in \mathrm{Data}$ and $r, r' \in \mathrm{Rand}$, t is indeed a valid term of Σ. However, the term $t' = \mathrm{prg}(\mathrm{enc}(r, k))$ is not a term of Σ as it is not well sorted. We have that $pos_{\Sigma_1}(t) = \{\epsilon, 1, 12\}$ and $pos_{\Sigma_2}^\star = \{11, 2\}$.

Definition 8 (Hybrid functions). *Let* Σ_1, Σ_2 *be two disjoint signatures and* S *a signature combination such that* $\Sigma = \Sigma_1 \cup \Sigma_2$ *is* $(\Sigma_1, \Sigma_2)_\mathsf{S}$-*layered. Let* E_1, E_2 *be equational theories over* Σ_1 *and* Σ_2 *respectively. A* (E_1, E_2)-*hybrid function for a set* F *of pairs of frames is a function* σ *from lists of terms over* Σ *to terms over* Σ *such that:*

- *for any frame φ occurring in F, $\varphi \approx_{E_1} \sigma(\varphi)$ where we naturally extended σ over frames by $\sigma(\{x_1 \mapsto t_1, \ldots, x_n \mapsto t_n\}) = \{x_1 \mapsto \sigma([t_1]), \ldots, x_n \mapsto \sigma([t_1 \ldots t_n])\}$;*
- *for any $(\varphi, \varphi') \in F$, if $\varphi \approx_{E_1 \cup E_2} \varphi'$ then let $\varphi = \{x_1 \mapsto t_1, \ldots, x_n \mapsto t_n\}$ and $\varphi' = \{x_1 \mapsto u_1, \ldots, x_n \mapsto u_n\}$. We have that for all i in $[1, n]$,*
  - *$pos_{\Sigma_1}(\sigma([t_1 \ldots t_i])) = pos_{\Sigma_1}(\sigma([u_1 \ldots u_i])) = P$ and for any $p \in P$*

$$root(\sigma([t_1 \ldots t_i])|_p) = root(\sigma([u_1 \ldots u_i])|_p)$$

  - *$pos^\star_{\Sigma_2}(\sigma([t_1 \ldots t_i])) = pos^\star_{\Sigma_2}(\sigma([u_1 \ldots u_i])) = Q$ and we have that*

$$\{x_q \mapsto \sigma([t_1 \ldots t_i])|_q\}_{q \in Q} \approx_{E_2} \{x_q \mapsto \sigma([u_1 \ldots u_i])|_q\}_{q \in Q}$$

Moreover σ has to be computable in polynomial time (in its input).

Adaptive soundness may not hold on all frames, but only on a subset of well-formed frames, *e.g.*, when considering encryption one typically discards all frames that contain key cycles. Therefore we say that an abstract algebra A_η is $\approx_E$-*ad-sound for a set F of pair of frames* if the advantage $\mathrm{Adv}^{\mathsf{ADPT}}_{\mathcal{A}, A_\eta}(\eta)$ of any polynomial-time legal adversary $\mathcal{A}$, whose sequence of queries $(t_0^i, t_1^i)_i$ verifies that the pair $(\{x_i \mapsto t_0^i\}_i, \{x_i \mapsto t_1^i\}_i)$ is in F, is negligible. We typically show soundness for the set of all pairs of "well-formed" frames (the notion of well-formed frames depends on the particular equational theory).

Proposition 3 (Combination). *Let Σ_1 and Σ_2 be two disjoint signatures and S be a signature combination for Σ_1 and Σ_2. Let E_1 and E_2 be equational theories over Σ_1 and Σ_2 respectively. We consider a family of computational algebras (A_η^1) for Σ_1 and another family (A_η^2) for Σ_2 respecting S, i.e. $(s_2, s_1) \in S$ implies that $[\![s_2]\!]_{A_\eta^2} \subseteq [\![s_1]\!]_{A_\eta^1}$.*
  Let F be a set of pair of frames over $\Sigma_1 \cup \Sigma_2$ and σ be a (E_1, E_2)-hybrid function for F. If $A_\eta^1 \times A_\eta^2$ is $\approx_{E_1}$-ad-sound for $G = \{(\varphi, \sigma(\varphi)) \mid \varphi$ occurs in $F\}$ and A_η^2 is $\approx_{E_2}$-ad-sound for frames on Σ_2, then $A_\eta^1 \times A_\eta^2$ is $\approx_{E_1 \cup E_2}$-ad-sound for F.

The idea of the proof is that if an adversary $\mathcal{A}$ against $E_1 \cup E_2$-ad-soundness queries his oracle with a pair of frames (φ, φ') in F then it is possible to build an adversary $\mathcal{B}_1$ against E_1-ad-soundness who submits $(\varphi, \sigma(\varphi))$ to his oracle, an adversary $\mathcal{B}_2$ against E_2-ad-soundness who submits $(\sigma(\varphi), \sigma(\varphi'))$ and an adversary $\mathcal{B}_3$ against E_1-ad-soundness who submits $(\sigma(\varphi'), \varphi')$ such that the advantages of $\mathcal{A}$, $\mathcal{B}_1$, $\mathcal{B}_2$ and $\mathcal{B}_3$ are related. This combination result will be useful in Section 4 when combining encryption with modular exponentiation.

4 Adaptively Sound Theories

We now present adaptive soundness results for several equational theories. We consider probabilistic symmetric encryption and try to be as close as possible to the models from [4] and from [24]. We assume that the implementation of the symmetric encryption scheme is semantically secure [21] and use a relevant formal theory.

Symbolic model. Our symbolic model consists of the set of sorts $\mathcal{S} = \{\text{Data}\}$, an infinite number of names for sort Data called keys and the function symbols:

$$\begin{aligned}
\text{enc}, \text{dec} &: \text{Data} \times \text{Data} \rightarrow \text{Data} & \text{samekey} &: \text{Data} \times \text{Data} \rightarrow \text{Data} \\
\text{pair} &: \text{Data} \times \text{Data} \rightarrow \text{Data} & \text{tenc}, \text{tpair} &: \text{Data} \rightarrow \text{Data} \\
\pi_l, \pi_r &: \text{Data} \rightarrow \text{Data} & 0, 1 &: \text{Data}
\end{aligned}$$

We consider the equational theory E_{sym} generated by:

$$\begin{aligned}
\text{dec}(\text{enc}(x, y), y) &= x & \pi_l(\text{pair}(x, y)) &= x \\
\pi_r(\text{pair}(x, y)) &= y & \text{samekey}(\text{enc}(x, y), \text{enc}(z, y)) &= 1 \\
\text{tenc}(\text{enc}(x, y)) &= 1 & \text{tpair}(\text{pair}(x, y)) &= 1
\end{aligned}$$

Intuitively, the function symbols tenc, tpair are type testers. The meaning of the remaining symbols should be clear. As usual $\text{enc}(t, k)$ is also written $\{t\}_k$ and $\text{pair}(t, t')$ is also written (t, t'). A name k is used at a key position in a term t if there exists a sub-term $\text{enc}(t', k)$ of t. Else k is used at a plaintext position.

Well-formed frames and adversaries. The importance of key cycles was already described in [4]. In general IND-CPA is not sufficient to prove any soundness result in the presence of key cycles. Thus, as in numerous previous work, we forbid the formal terms to contain such cycles. Let $\prec$ be a total order among keys. A *frame φ is acyclic for* $\prec$ if for any subterm $\{t\}_k$ of φ, if k' occurs in t then $k' \prec k$. (Another possibility to handle key cycles is to consider stronger computational requirements like Key Dependent Message – KDM – security as done in [5].) Moreover as noted in [24], selective decommitment [20] can be a problem. The classical solution to this problem is to require keys to be sent *before* being used to encrypt a message or they must never appear as a plaintext. A *frame $\varphi = \{x_1 \mapsto t_1, \ldots, x_n \mapsto t_n\}$ is well-formed for* $\prec$ if

- φ is acyclic for $\prec$;
- the terms t_i only use symbols enc, pair, 0 and 1, and only names are used at key positions;
- if k is used as plaintext in t_i, then k cannot be used at a key position in t_j for $j < i$.

An *adversary is well-formed for* $\prec$ if the sequence of queries $(t_0^i, t_1^i)_{1 \le i \le n}$ that he makes to his oracle yields two well-formed frames $\{x_1 \mapsto t_0^1, \ldots, x_n \mapsto t_0^n\}$ and $\{x_1 \mapsto t_1^1, \ldots, x_n \mapsto t_1^n\}$ for $\prec$.

Concrete model. A symmetric encryption scheme $\mathcal{SE}$ is defined by three algorithms $\mathcal{KG}$, $\mathcal{E}$ and $\mathcal{D}$. The key generation algorithm takes as input the security parameter η and outputs a key k. The encryption algorithm $\mathcal{E}$ is randomized. It takes as input a bit-string s, a key k and returns the encryption of s using k. The decryption algorithm $\mathcal{D}$ takes as input a bit-string c (a ciphertext), a key k and outputs the corresponding plaintext. Given $k \leftarrow \mathcal{KG}(\eta)$, for any bit-string s, if $c \leftarrow \mathcal{E}(k, s)$ then $\mathcal{D}(c) = s$.

The family of computational algebras (A_η) giving the concrete semantics depends on a symmetric encryption scheme $\mathcal{SE} = (\mathcal{KG}, \mathcal{E}, \mathcal{D})$. The concrete domain $[\![\text{Data}]\!]_{A_\eta}$ contains all the possible bit-strings and is equipped with the distribution induced by $\mathcal{KG}$. Interpretation for constants 0 and 1 are respectively bit-strings 0^η and 1^η. The enc and dec function are respectively interpreted using algorithm $\mathcal{E}$ and $\mathcal{D}$. We assume the existence in the concrete model of a concatenation operation which is used to interpret the pair symbol. The corresponding left and right projections implement π_l and π_r. Finally, as we are only interested in well-formed frames, we do not provide any computational interpretation for tenc, tpair and samekey.

Semantic security. In this paper we use schemes that satisfy length-concealing semantic security. The definition that we recall below uses a left-right encryption oracle $LR_{S\mathcal{E}}^b$. This oracle first generates a key k using $\mathcal{KG}$. Then it answers queries of the form (bs_0, bs_1), where bs_0 and bs_1 are bit-strings. The oracle returns ciphertext $\mathcal{E}(bs_b, k)$. The goal of the adversary $\mathcal{A}$ is to guess the value of bit b. His advantage is defined as:

$$\text{Adv}_{S\mathcal{E},\mathcal{A}}^{cpa}(\eta) = \left| \mathbb{P}\left[\mathcal{A}^{LR_{S\mathcal{E}}^1} = 1\right] - \mathbb{P}\left[\mathcal{A}^{LR_{S\mathcal{E}}^0} = 1\right] \right|$$

Encryption scheme $S\mathcal{E}$ is IND-CPA secure if the advantage of any adversary $\mathcal{A}$ is negligible in η. The difference with standard semantic security is that we require the scheme to hide the length of the plaintext (and therefore we do not restrict bs_0 and bs_1 to have equal length). By abuse of notation we call the resulting scheme also IND-CPA secure.

Proposition 4. *Let $\prec$ be a total order among keys. In the remainder of this proposition we only consider well-formed adversaries for $\prec$. Let (A_η) be a family of computational algebras based on a symmetric encryption scheme $S\mathcal{E}$. (A_η) is $\approx_{E_{\text{sym}}}$-ad-sound if $S\mathcal{E}$ is IND-CPA but the converse is false.*

4.1 Exclusive OR

We study the adaptive soundness problem for the usual theory and implementation of the Exclusive Or (XOR) in the same model as given in [9]. The symbolic model $\Sigma_\oplus$ consists of a single sort $\text{Data}_\oplus$, an infinite number of names, the infix symbol $\oplus$: $\text{Data}_\oplus \times \text{Data}_\oplus \rightarrow \text{Data}_\oplus$ and two constants $0_\oplus, 1_\oplus$: $\text{Data}_\oplus$. Terms are equipped with the equational theory $E_\oplus$ generated by:

$$(x \oplus y) \oplus z = x \oplus (y \oplus z) \qquad x \oplus y = y \oplus x \qquad x \oplus x = 0_\oplus \qquad x \oplus 0_\oplus = x$$

As an implementation, we define the computational algebras A_η: the concrete domain $[\![\text{Data}_\oplus]\!]_{A_\eta}$ is $\{0,1\}^\eta$ equipped with the uniform distribution; $\oplus$ is interpreted by the usual XOR function over $\{0,1\}^\eta$, $[\![0_\oplus]\!]_{A_\eta} = 0^\eta$, $[\![1_\oplus]\!]_{A_\eta} = 1^\eta$. This implementation of XOR enjoys unconditional adaptive soundness with respect to $\approx_{E_\oplus}$.

Proposition 5. *The usual implementation for $E_\oplus$ is unconditionally $\approx_{E_\oplus}$-ad-sound.*

The result follows directly from unconditionally $\approx_{E_\oplus}$-soundness shown in [9] and Proposition 2.

4.2 Modular Exponentiation

As a third application, we study soundness of modular exponentiation. The underlying cryptographic assumption is hardness of the *Decisional Diffie-Hellman* (DDH) problem: given g^x and g^y, it is difficult for any feasible computation to distinguish between

g^{xy} and g^r, when x, y and r are selected at random. The original Diffie-Hellman protocol has been used as a building block for several key agreement protocols that are widely used in practice (e.g. SSL/TLS and Kerberos V5) as well as for group key exchange protocols such as AKE1 [12] or the Burmester-Desmedt protocol [14].

Symbolic model. The symbolic model consists of sorts G (group elements) and R (ring elements), an infinite number of names for R (but no name for sort G) and the symbols:

$$\begin{array}{llll}
\exp : R \to G & \text{exponentiation} & +, \cdot : R \times R \to R & \text{add, mult} \\
* : G \times G \to G & \text{mult in } \mathbb{G} & - : R \to R & \text{inverse} \\
& 0_R, 1_R : R & \text{constants} &
\end{array}$$

We consider the equational theory E_{DH} generated by:

$$\begin{array}{lll}
x + y = y + x & x \cdot y = y \cdot x & (x + y) + z = x + (y + z) \\
x \cdot (y + z) = x \cdot y + x \cdot z & (x \cdot y) \cdot z = x \cdot (y \cdot z) & x + (-x) = 0_R \\
0_R + x = x & 1_R \cdot x = x & \exp(x) * \exp(y) = \exp(x + y)
\end{array}$$

There exists a direct correspondence between terms of sort R and the set of polynomials $\mathbb{Z}[\mathcal{N}_R]$ where $\mathcal{N}_R$ is the set of names of sort R. An integer i simply corresponds to $\underbrace{1_R + \ldots + 1_R}_{i \ times}$ if $i > 0$, to $-\underbrace{(1_R + \ldots + 1_R)}_{i \ times}$ if $i < 0$ and to 0_R if $i = 0$. We also write x^n for $\underbrace{x \cdot \ldots \cdot x}_{n \ times}$.

We put two restrictions on formal terms: products have to be *power-free*, i.e., x^n is forbidden for $n > 1$, and products must not contain more than l elements for some fixed bound l, i.e. $x_1 \cdot \ldots \cdot x_n$ is forbidden for $n > l$. Both restrictions come from the DDH assumption and seem difficult to avoid [13]. Furthermore we are only interested in frames using terms of sort G. Any frame containing only terms of sort G can be rewritten as $\{x_1 \mapsto \exp(p_1), \ldots, x_n \mapsto \exp(p_n)\}$ by orienting the last equation form left to right. For such frames there is an immediate characterization of static equivalence. Two frames are statically equivalent if they satisfy the same linear equations.

Proposition 6. *We have that* $\{x_1 \mapsto \exp(p_1), \ldots, x_n \mapsto \exp(p_n)\} \approx_{E_{\mathsf{DH}}} \{x_1 \mapsto \exp(q_1), \ldots, x_n \mapsto \exp(q_n)\}$ *iff for any sequence of integer* $a_0, a_1, \ldots a_n$ *we have* $a_0 + \sum_{i=1}^{n} a_i p_i = 0 \Leftrightarrow a_0 + \sum_{i=1}^{n} a_i q_i = 0$

This characterization can be used to decide static equivalence efficiently.

Concrete model. An Instance Generator IG is a polynomial-time (in η) algorithm that outputs a cyclic group $\mathbb{G}$ (defined by a generator g, an order q and a polynomial-time multiplication algorithm) of prime order q. The family of computational algebras (A_η) depends on an instance generator IG which generates a cyclic group $\mathbb{G}$ of generator g and of order q: the concrete domain $[\![R]\!]_{A_\eta}$ is $\mathbb{Z}_q$ with the uniform distribution. Symbols $+$ and $\cdot$ are the classical addition and multiplication over $\mathbb{Z}_q$, $\exp$ is interpreted as modular exponentiation of g. Constants 0_R and 1_R are interpreted by integers 0 and 1 of $\mathbb{Z}_q$. The domain $[\![G]\!]_{A_\eta}$ contains all bit-string representations of elements of $\mathbb{G}$.

A family of computational algebras satisfies the DDH assumption if its instance generator satisfies the assumption: for every probabilistic polynomial-time adversary $\mathcal{A}$, his

advantage $\text{Adv}^{\text{DDH}}_{IG,\mathcal{A}}(\eta) = |\mathbb{P}\left[(g,q) \leftarrow IG(\eta) \ : \ a,b \leftarrow \mathbb{Z}_q \ : \ \mathcal{A}(g^a, g^b, g^{ab}) = 1\right] -$
$\mathbb{P}\left[(g,q) \leftarrow IG(\eta) \ : \ a,b,c \leftarrow \mathbb{Z}_q \ : \ \mathcal{A}(g^a, g^b, g^c) = 1\right]|$ is negligible in η. In the remainder, we generally suppose that for any η there is a unique group given by IG. We show that the DDH assumption is necessary and sufficient to prove adaptive soundness.

Proposition 7. *A family of computational algebras* (A_η) *is* $\approx_{E_{\text{DH}}}$*-sound iff* (A_η) *is* $\approx_{E_{\text{DH}}}$*-ad-sound iff* (A_η) *satisfies the* DDH *assumption.*

The proof of this result uses an adaptive variant of DDH called 3DH: it generalizes several previously used variants of DDH. The main difficulty in this proof consists in relating DDH and 3DH. Note that while adaptive soundness and (classical) soundness are not equivalent for symmetric encryption, they coincide in this case.

4.3   Combining Encryption with Exponentiation

We illustrate our combination result (Proposition 3) by establishing a joint soundness result for symmetric encryption and modular exponentiation.

Symbolic model. We consider an equational theory E containing both E_{DH} and E_{sym}. Let Σ_1 be the signature for symmetric encryption and Σ_2 be the signature for modular exponentiation, then signature $\Sigma = \Sigma_1 \cup \Sigma_2$ is $(\Sigma_1, \Sigma_2)_{\text{S}}$-layered where S contains only one element (G, Data).

Well-formed frames. Let $\prec$ be a total order between keys and exponentiations. A frame φ (on Σ) is well-formed for $\prec$ if:

- φ does not contain any dec, tenc, tpair, π_l, π_r or $*$ symbol, only names and exponentiations are used at key position.
- For any subterm $\exp(p)$ of φ used at a key position, p is linearly independent of other polynomials p' such that $\exp(p')$ is a subterm of φ.
- For any subterm $\{t\}_{t'}$ of φ, if t'' is a subterm of t which is a name of sort Data or an exponentiation then $t'' \prec t'$.

Concrete model. The concrete model is given by the models for symmetric encryption and modular exponentiation. We need to reflect that exponentiations can be used as symmetric keys. The family of computational algebras (A_η) giving the concrete semantics is parameterized by a symmetric encryption scheme $\mathcal{SE}$ and an instance generator IG. We require that the key generation algorithm of $\mathcal{SE}$ randomly samples an element of $IG(\eta)$. Giving an IND-CPA encryption scheme $\mathcal{SE}'$, it is possible to build another IND-CPA scheme $\mathcal{SE}$ which indeed uses such a key generation algorithm. This is achieved by using a *key extractor* algorithm Kex [16]. This algorithm (usually a universal hash function used with the entropy smoothing theorem) transforms group elements into valid keys for $\mathcal{SE}'$. The new encryption and decryption algorithms of $\mathcal{SE}$ apply the Kex algorithm to the group element which is used as key. This produces a symmetric key which can be used with the encryption and decryption algorithms of $\mathcal{SE}'$.

The family of computational algebras (A_η) implementing encryption with exponentiation is said *EE-secure* if the encryption scheme $\mathcal{SE}$ is secure against IND-CPA and uses a key generation algorithm as described above and IG satisfies the DDH assumption. Soundness is proven by applying Proposition 3.

Proposition 8. *Let $\prec$ be a total order between keys and exponentiations. An EE-secure family of computational algebras (A_η) is $\approx_E$-ad-sound for well-formed frames for $\prec$.*

A similar result is given for symmetric encryption and XOR in the full version [22].

5 Analysis of Dynamic Group Key Exchange

Micciancio and Panjwani exemplified their adaptive soundness result from [24] on multicast protocols. We propose another application: *dynamic group key exchange protocols* (DKE) such as the AKE1 protocol [12]. To keep the symbolic security notion as simple as possible we define security for protocols using only modular exponentiation: we consider a subtheory E of E_{DH} (Section 4.2) without $+$, $-$, 1_R and 0_R symbols and the related equations. However our definitions and soundness results can be adapted to other equational theories (e.g. symmetric encryption joint with modular exponentiation).

5.1 Dynamic Group Protocols

We take a simple model for DKE in the adaptive setting. A DKE protocol is described by four operations which specify the protocol. We suppose that this specification is given by four polynomial-time algorithms $(\mathcal{S}, \mathcal{J}, \mathcal{L}, \mathcal{K})$:

- $\mathcal{S}$ initializes a new group. The algorithm takes as an input a list of users and outputs the internal state s_0 of the protocol as well as a list of formal terms which model the messages that have been exchanged during the setup phase.
- $\mathcal{J}$ and $\mathcal{L}$ take as input the state of the protocol s and a list of users U_1 to U_n (to be respectively added to or suppressed from the group) and output the updated state of the protocol s' as well as a list of formal terms representing message exchanges.
- $\mathcal{K}$ takes as input the state of the group s and outputs a formal term representing the shared key of the group.

The internal state of the protocol can be thought of as the internal state of the four algorithms that describe the protocol.

We partition the set of names of sort R according to the users: n_i^j, $j \in \mathbb{N}$, are the nonces generated by user U_i. We require that the formal term output by $\mathcal{K}$ only uses nonces for users that are currently in the group.

5.2 Security in the Symbolic Model

In our symbolic setting, the security property is expressed as reachability in a transition system. We represent the states of this transition system as a triple $\langle L, C, T \rangle$ where

- L is the list of users that are currently in the group;
- C is the set of corrupted users;
- T is the list of formal terms sent during the protocol execution.

We suppose that the internal state of the protocol can be recovered from the state $\langle L, C, T \rangle$ and tend to assimilate these two notions of state. We now describe the possible transitions. For convenience, we use set notations for manipulating lists.

1. $\langle \emptyset, C, \emptyset \rangle \xrightarrow{c(U)} \langle \emptyset, C \cup \{U\}, \emptyset \rangle$: corruption of user U.

2. $\langle \emptyset, C, \emptyset \rangle \xrightarrow{s(\mathcal{U})} \langle \mathcal{U}, C, T \rangle$: setup of the group given by the list of users $\mathcal{U}$, *i.e.*, $\langle \mathcal{U}, C, T \rangle$ is computed by $\mathcal{S}(\langle \emptyset, C, \emptyset \rangle, \mathcal{U})$.

3. $\langle L, C, T \rangle \xrightarrow{j(\mathcal{U})} \langle L \cup \mathcal{U}, C, T \rangle \cup T'$: join of users in the list $\mathcal{U}$, *i.e.*, $\langle L \cup \mathcal{U}, C, T \cup T' \rangle$ is computed by $\mathcal{J}(\langle L, C, T \rangle, \mathcal{U})$.

4. $\langle L, C, T \rangle \xrightarrow{l(\mathcal{U})} \langle L \setminus \mathcal{U}, C, T \cup T' \rangle$: exclusion of the users in the list $\mathcal{U}$, *i.e.*, $\langle L \setminus \mathcal{U}, C, T \cup T' \rangle$ is computed by $\mathcal{L}(\langle L, C, T \rangle, \mathcal{U})$.

To simplify things up, we consider a static corruption model, *i.e.*, corruption transitions only occur at the beginning of the protocol. Then a setup transition is taken followed by leave and join transitions. A DKE protocol is secure if it is impossible for an adversary to get any bit of information on the group key when no corrupted users are in the group.

Definition 9. *We define a DKE protocol to be* symbolically secure *if for any state* $\langle L, C, T = \{t_1, ..., t_n\} \rangle$ *reachable from* $\langle \emptyset, \emptyset, \emptyset \rangle$ *and such that* $C \cap L = \emptyset$ *we have*

$$\{x_1 \mapsto t'_1, ..., x_n \mapsto t'_n, y \mapsto \mathcal{K}(\langle L, C, T \rangle)\} \approx_E \{x_1 \mapsto t'_1, ..., x_n \mapsto t'_n, y \mapsto \exp(r)\}$$

where r is a fresh nonce, $N = \{n_i^j \mid U_i \in C\}$ and t'_i is as t_i but nonces from N have been removed, i.e. if $t = \exp(m_1 \cdot \ldots \cdot m_\ell)$ then $t' = \exp(m'_1 \cdot \ldots \cdot m'_{\ell'})$ where $\{m'_1, \ldots, m'_{\ell'}\} = \{m_1, \ldots, m_\ell\} \setminus N$.

5.3 Security in the Concrete Model

We use a simplified version of the security model from [12]: some oracles in [12] are not useful anymore in the adaptive setting. Let $(\mathcal{S}, \mathcal{J}, \mathcal{L}, \mathcal{K})$ be a DKE and (A_η) a family of computational algebras. Adversary $\mathcal{A}$ interacts with the group via the following five oracles which store the current state s of the group and use a challenge bit b.

- Setup$(U_1, ..., U_n)$: initializes the group using $\mathcal{S}(U_1, ..., U_n)$ which produces the new state s and a list of formal terms t_1 to t_m. $\mathcal{A}$ is given $[\![t_i]\!]_{A_\eta}$ for any i in $[1, m]$.
- Join$(U_1, ..., U_n)$: users U_1 to U_n join the group. $\mathcal{J}(s, U_1, ..., U_n)$ is executed and outputs state s and a list of terms t_1 to t_m. $\mathcal{A}$ is given $[\![t_i]\!]_{A_\eta}$ for any i in $[1, m]$.
- Leave$(U_1, ..., U_n)$: users U_1 to U_n leave the group. $\mathcal{L}(s, U_1, ..., U_n)$ is executed and outputs state s and a list of terms t_1 to t_m. $\mathcal{A}$ is given $[\![t_i]\!]_{A_\eta}$ for any i in $[1, m]$.
- Corrupt(U): $\mathcal{A}$ corrupts user U; all nonces generated by U are given to $\mathcal{A}$. As $\mathcal{A}$ works in polynomial time, a polynomial number of values is sufficient.
- Test: $\mathcal{A}$ either receives the key of the group (output by $\mathcal{K}(s)$) if $b = 1$ or a random key if $b = 0$. This oracle can only be queried once.

As we consider a static corruption model, queries to the Corrupt oracle have to be done before all further queries. Then the Setup oracle is called and after that the adversary interleaves queries to the Join and Leave oracles. The adversary makes a final call to the Test oracle. Let $\mathcal{O}_b$ denote the oracles with challenge bit b. The advantage of an adversary $\mathcal{A}$ is given by: $\text{Adv}_{\mathcal{A},A_\eta}^{(\mathcal{S},\mathcal{J},\mathcal{L},\mathcal{K})}(\eta) = \mathbb{P}\left[\mathcal{A}^{\mathcal{O}_1} = 1\right] - \mathbb{P}\left[\mathcal{A}^{\mathcal{O}_0} = 1\right]$. A DKE is *secure in the concrete model* if the advantage of any adversary is negligible in η.

5.4 Soundness Result

Our symbolic model for DKE is computationally sound: if a DKE algorithm is secure in the symbolic model, then it is secure in the computational model, provided that static equivalence is adaptively sound (remember that we consider only modular exponentiation hence static equivalence is adaptively sound under DDH).

Proposition 9. *Let* (A_η) *be a family of computational algebras and* $\Pi = (\mathcal{S}, \mathcal{J}, \mathcal{L}, \mathcal{K})$ *be a DKE. If* (A_η) *is* $\approx_E$*-ad-sound and* Π *is secure in the symbolic model, then* Π *is secure in the concrete model.*

References

1. Abadi, M., Baudet, M., Warinschi, B.: Guessing attacks and the computational soundness of static equivalence. In: Aceto, L., Ingólfsdóttir, A. (eds.) FOSSACS 2006 and ETAPS 2006. LNCS, vol. 3921, pp. 398–412. Springer, Heidelberg (2006)
2. Abadi, M., Cortier, V.: Deciding knowledge in security protocols under equational theories. In: Díaz, J., Karhumäki, J., Lepistö, A., Sannella, D. (eds.) ICALP 2004. LNCS, vol. 3142, pp. 46–58. Springer, Heidelberg (2004)
3. Abadi, M., Fournet, C.: Mobile values, new names, and secure communications. In: Proc. 28th Annual ACM Symposium on Principles of Programming Languages (POPL'01), pp. 104–115. ACM Press, New York (2001)
4. Abadi, M., Rogaway, P.: Reconciling two views of cryptography (the computational soundness of formal encryption). In: Watanabe, O., Hagiya, M., Ito, T., van Leeuwen, J., Mosses, P.D. (eds.) TCS 2000. LNCS, vol. 1872, Springer, Heidelberg (2000)
5. Adão, P., Bana, G., Herzog, J., Scedrov, A.: Soundness of formal encryption in the presence of key-cycles. In: di Vimercati, S.d.C., Syverson, P.F., Gollmann, D. (eds.) ESORICS 2005. LNCS, vol. 3679, pp. 374–396. Springer, Heidelberg (2005)
6. Backes, M., Pfitzmann, B.: Limits of the cryptographic realization of Dolev-Yao-style XOR. In: di Vimercati, S.d.C., Syverson, P.F., Gollmann, D. (eds.) ESORICS 2005. LNCS, vol. 3679, pp. 336–354. Springer, Heidelberg (2005)
7. Backes, M., Pfitzmann, B., Waidner, M.: A composable cryptographic library with nested operations. In: Proc. 10th ACM Conference on Computer and Communications Security (CCS'03), pp. 220–230. ACM Press, New York (2003)
8. Bana, G., Mohassel, P., Stegers, T.: The computational soundness of formal indistinguishability and static equivalence. In: ASIAN'06. Proc. 11th Asian Computing Science Conference, 2006. LNCS, Springer, Heidelberg (to appear)
9. Baudet, M., Cortier, V., Kremer, S.: Computationally sound implementations of equational theories against passive adversaries. In: Caires, L., Italiano, G.F., Monteiro, L., Palamidessi, C., Yung, M. (eds.) ICALP 2005. LNCS, vol. 3580, pp. 652–663. Springer, Heidelberg (2005)
10. Blanchet, B.: Automatic proof of strong secrecy for security protocols. In: Proc. 25th IEEE Symposium on Security and Privacy (SSP'04), pp. 86–100. IEEE Computer Society Press, Los Alamitos (2004)

11. Blanchet, B.: A computationally sound mechanized prover for security protocols. In: Proc. 27th IEEE Symposium on Security and Privacy (SSP'06), pp. 140–154. IEEE Computer Society Press, Los Alamitos (2006)

12. Bresson, E., Chevassut, O., Pointcheval, D.: Provably authenticated group Diffie-Hellman key exchange – the dynamic case. In: Boyd, C. (ed.) ASIACRYPT 2001. LNCS, vol. 2248, pp. 290–309. Springer, Heidelberg (2001)

13. Bresson, E., Lakhnech, Y., Mazaré, L., Warinschi, B.: A generalization of DDH with applications to protocol analysis and computational soundness. In: Menezes, A.J. (ed.) CRYPTO 2007. LNCS, vol. 4622, pp. 482–499. Springer, Heidelberg (2007)

14. Burmester, M., Desmedt, Y.: A secure and efficient conference key distribution system (extended abstract). In: De Santis, A. (ed.) EUROCRYPT 1994. LNCS, vol. 950, pp. 275–286. Springer, Heidelberg (1995)

15. Canetti, R., Herzog, J.: Universally composable symbolic analysis of mutual authentication and key-exchange protocols (extended abstract). In: Halevi, S., Rabin, T. (eds.) TCC 2006. LNCS, vol. 3876, pp. 380–403. Springer, Heidelberg (2006)

16. Chevassut, O., Fouque, P.-A., Gaudry, P., Pointcheval, D.: Key derivation and randomness extraction. Technical Report 2005/061, Cryptology ePrint Archive (2005)

17. Cortier, V., Delaune, S., Lafourcade, P.: A Survey of Algebraic Properties Used in Cryptographic Protocols. Journal of Computer Security, 2005 (to appear)

18. Cortier, V., Warinschi, B.: Computationally sound, automated proofs for security protocols. In: Sagiv, M. (ed.) ESOP 2005. LNCS, vol. 3444, pp. 157–171. Springer, Heidelberg (2005)

19. Datta, A., Derek, A., Mitchell, J.C., Shmatikov, V., Turuani, M.: Probabilistic Polynomial-time Semantics for a Protocol Security Logic. In: Caires, L., Italiano, G.F., Monteiro, L., Palamidessi, C., Yung, M. (eds.) ICALP 2005. LNCS, vol. 3580, pp. 16–29. Springer, Heidelberg (2005)

20. Dwork, C., Naor, M., Reingold, O., Stockmeyer, L.J.: Magic functions. J. ACM 50(6), 852–921 (2003)

21. Goldwasser, S., Micali, S.: Probabilistic encryption & how to play mental poker keeping secret all partial information. In: Proc. 14th Annual ACM Symposium on Theory of Computing (STOC'82), ACM Press, New York (1982)

22. Kremer, S., Mazaré, L.: Adaptive soundness of static equivalence. Research Report LSV-07-09, Laboratoire Spécification et Vérification, ENS Cachan, France, 27 pages (February 2007)

23. Laud, P.: A composable cryptographic library with nested operations. In: Proc. 12th ACM Conference on Computer and Communications Security (CCS'05), pp. 26–35. ACM Press, New York (2005)

24. Micciancio, D., Panjwani, S.: Adaptive security of symbolic encryption. In: Kilian, J. (ed.) TCC 2005. LNCS, vol. 3378, pp. 169–187. Springer, Heidelberg (2005)

Author Index

Lecture Notes in Computer Science

Sublibrary 4: Security and Cryptology

Vol. 4083: S. Fischer-Hübner, S. Furnell, C. Lambrinoudakis (Eds.), Trust and Privacy in Digital Business. XIII, 243 pages. 2006.

Vol. 4064: R. Büschkes, P. Laskov (Eds.), Detection of Intrusions and Malware & Vulnerability Assessment. X, 195 pages. 2006.

Vol. 4058: L.M. Batten, R. Safavi-Naini (Eds.), Information Security and Privacy. XII, 446 pages. 2006.

Vol. 4047: M. Robshaw (Ed.), Fast Software Encryption. XI, 434 pages. 2006.

Vol. 4043: A.S. Atzeni, A. Lioy (Eds.), Public Key Infrastructure. XI, 261 pages. 2006.

Vol. 4004: S. Vaudenay (Ed.), Advances in Cryptology - EUROCRYPT 2006. XIV, 613 pages. 2006.

Vol. 3995: G. Müller (Ed.), Emerging Trends in Information and Communication Security. XX, 524 pages. 2006.

Vol. 3989: J. Zhou, M. Yung, F. Bao (Eds.), Applied Cryptography and Network Security. XIV, 488 pages. 2006.

Vol. 3969: Ø. Ytrehus (Ed.), Coding and Cryptography. XI, 443 pages. 2006.

Vol. 3958: M. Yung, Y. Dodis, A. Kiayias, T.G. Malkin (Eds.), Public Key Cryptography - PKC 2006. XIV, 543 pages. 2006.

Vol. 3957: B. Christianson, B. Crispo, J.A. Malcolm, M. Roe (Eds.), Security Protocols. IX, 325 pages. 2006.

Vol. 3956: G. Barthe, B. Grégoire, M. Huisman, J.-L. Lanet (Eds.), Construction and Analysis of Safe, Secure, and Interoperable Smart Devices. IX, 175 pages. 2006.

Vol. 3935: D.H. Won, S. Kim (Eds.), Information Security and Cryptology - ICISC 2005. XIV, 458 pages. 2006.

Vol. 3934: J.A. Clark, R.F. Paige, F.A.C. Polack, P.J. Brooke (Eds.), Security in Pervasive Computing. X, 243 pages. 2006.

Vol. 3928: J. Domingo-Ferrer, J. Posegga, D. Schreckling (Eds.), Smart Card Research and Advanced Applications. XI, 359 pages. 2006.

Vol. 3919: R. Safavi-Naini, M. Yung (Eds.), Digital Rights Management. XI, 357 pages. 2006.

Vol. 3903: K. Chen, R. Deng, X. Lai, J. Zhou (Eds.), Information Security Practice and Experience. XIV, 392 pages. 2006.

Vol. 3897: B. Preneel, S. Tavares (Eds.), Selected Areas in Cryptography. XI, 371 pages. 2006.

Vol. 3876: S. Halevi, T. Rabin (Eds.), Theory of Cryptography. XI, 617 pages. 2006.

Vol. 3866: T. Dimitrakos, F. Martinelli, P.Y A Ryan, S. Schneider (Eds.), Formal Aspects in Security and Trust. X, 259 pages. 2006.

Vol. 3860: D. Pointcheval (Ed.), Topics in Cryptology – CT-RSA 2006. XI, 365 pages. 2006.

Vol. 3858: A. Valdes, D. Zamboni (Eds.), Recent Advances in Intrusion Detection. X, 351 pages. 2006.

Vol. 3856: G. Danezis, D. Martin (Eds.), Privacy Enhancing Technologies. VIII, 273 pages. 2006.

Vol. 3786: J.-S. Song, T. Kwon, M. Yung (Eds.), Information Security Applications. XI, 378 pages. 2006.

Vol. 3108: H. Wang, J. Pieprzyk, V. Varadharajan (Eds.), Information Security and Privacy. XII, 494 pages. 2004.

Vol. 2951: M. Naor (Ed.), Theory of Cryptography. XI, 523 pages. 2004.

Vol. 2742: R.N. Wright (Ed.), Financial Cryptography. VIII, 321 pages. 2003.